The Blackwell Encyclopedia of Sociology

Volume VIII

Q–SE

Edited by

George Ritzer

Blackwell Publishing

BLACKWELL PUBLISHING
350 Main Street, Malden, MA 02148-5020, USA
9600 Garsington Road, Oxford OX4 2DQ, UK
550 Swanston Street, Carlton, Victoria 3053, Australia

First published 2007 by Blackwell Publishing Ltd

1 2007

Library of Congress Cataloging-in-Publication Data

Blackwell encyclopedia of sociology, the / edited by George Ritzer.
p. cm.
Includes bibliographical references and index.
ISBN 1-4051-2433-4 (hardback : alk. paper) 1. Sociology—Encyclopedias. I. Ritzer, George.

HM425.B53 2007
301.03—dc22

2006004167

ISBN-13: 978-1-4051-2433-1 (hardback : alk. paper)

A catalogue record for this title is available from the British Library.

Set in 9.5/11pt Ehrhardt
by Spi Publisher Services, Pondicherry, India
Printed in Singapore
by COS Printers Pte Ltd

The publisher's policy is to use permanent paper from mills that operate a sustainable forestry policy, and which has been manufactured from pulp processed using acid-free and elementary chlorine-free practices. Furthermore, the publisher ensures that the text paper and cover board used have met acceptable environmental accreditation standards.

For further information on
Blackwell Publishing, visit our website:
www.blackwellpublishing.com

Contents

Q

qualitative computing

César A. Cisneros-Puebla

Qualitative computing refers to the ensemble of technology and methodology for qualitative data analysis. Its development is rooted in qualitative sociology and the tradition of symbolic interactionism and is embedded in the evolution of computers. It goes beyond simple data management, incorporating features such as criticism of traditional approaches to data analysis, searching for new logical strategies for theory building, and innovative ways to visually represent multiple realities. Some criteria to differentially assess the software programs, among others, are ease of integration of all research process stages, type of data, process of searching units of analysis to read and review, memo-writing managers, categorization and code book access, analysis inventory and assessment, capability to export and import quantitative data, and options to merge data from different projects.

At the beginning of the 1980s, researchers from the US, Australia, and Europe developed prototypes of different computer programs to work with qualitative data, called CAQDAS since 1989, which stands for Computer-Assisted Qualitative Data Analysis. Similar to computational sociology, it seeks to deal with data complexity but its aim is not to model an "artificial society" as the former does. Qualitatively driven strategies of handling digital data provide a relational and dynamic model for conceptually mapping all research project components. Qualitative data are analyzed in inductive, iterative, and recursive traditions. Therefore, qualitative computing is composed of epistemological assertions of using computational devices to study language and meanings; methodological claims about using Boolean tools and algorithms to create new data; and ontological arguments on the computer's role in interpretive inquiry. There is no more debate about the implications of "computer-aided methods" in qualitative analysis because qualitative social scientists know using software is not synonymous with incontestable research design, methodological rigor, validity, or objectivity.

Qualitative computing is very often recognized as a computerized tool for grounded theory. Beyond applying the constant comparative method linked to this qualitative approach, there is increasing interest in understanding analytical induction strategies to theory building, and the related cognitive process of abduction. As a consequence of this concern, there have been some attempts to apply artificial intelligence tools and machine learning strategies. Qualitative computing also has features useful in conducting ethnographies, narrative research, phenomenological inquiry, and case studies. Data mining, knowledge representation, and knowledge discovery databases are also related areas of computational investigation. The emerging interest on hypermedia ethnography, visual narratives, fuzzy logic and natural language, large-scale video projects and hypertextual analysis is moving qualitative computing in new directions in advanced technological sophistication, which demands more creativity and researchers' imagination.

Qualitative computing is basically associated with the analysis of text, images, video, and audio. A seminal book on this field is Tesch's *Qualitative Research: Analysis Types and Software Tools* (1990), but Weitzman and Miles's *Computer Programs for Qualitative Data Analysis: A Software Sourcebook* (1995) is also important despite its now outdated format. As in other fields applying digital technology, any book attempting only to describe computational applications easily becomes useless as a result of the constant updating of programs. Of historical interest are the special issues prepared by David Heise for *Sociological Methods and Research* (titled "Microcomputers in Social Research," 1981) and by Conrad and Reinharz for *Qualitative Sociology* (titled "Computers and Qualitative Data," 1984). Another special issue by Mangabeira for *Current Sociology* (1996) portrays the worldwide diffusion of CAQDAS.

If the social sciences' "quantitative revolution" in the 1970s was associated with a technological transformation in the means of querying and handling numbers and statistical analysis, the increasing advance of qualitative computing in the ensuing "post-positivist" period has represented a kind of quiet revolution common to diverse social disciplines in the means of querying and handling words and qualitative data analysis as a consequence of the digital avalanche. A relevant impact on doing hybrid or mixed methods is noticeable in research design as a result of the application of qualitative computing strategies. In depicting the processes of qualitative data analysis by means of relationships among codes, categories, subcodes, textual, video, or audio files and memos, some metaphorical concepts have been built, hence there are analytical approaches from hierarchical trees, semantic networks, or case-based thinking. The promise and perils of the new frontiers in qualitative computing remain on the limits of researcher–computer integration given that such technological devices have superior abilities for processing patterns, although humans remain superior at interpreting meaning in patterns. Technology is a medium to transform traditional ways of inquiry and is a powerful tool to enhance our creative and qualitative thinking.

Even though qualitative computing has influenced fields and subfields of social and behavioral sciences such as psychology, education, nursing, public health, sociology, women's studies, anthropology, communication and market research, among others, its total integration into curricula and schooling practices is incomplete, just as qualitative methods are in the current state of the art over the world. The future of qualitative computing is connected to the deepest and most thoughtful analysis of the mathematical basis of qualitative inquiry and is related to the soft sociology legacy and reflection about soft data analysis. Computing with words appears as a discipline in the neighborhood of qualitative computing, although in its present stage there is no large collaboration in progress; some skepticism is around, just as in the case of using artificial intelligence to improve some features of particular software programs.

SEE ALSO: Analytic Induction; Computational Sociology; Computer-Aided/Mediated Analysis; Grounded Theory; Methods, Mixed; Validity, Qualitative

REFERENCES AND SUGGESTED READINGS

Burgess, R. G. (1995) *Studies in Qualitative Methodology: Computing and Qualitative Research*, Vol. 5. JAI Press, London.

Creswell, J. W. & Maietta, R. C. (2002) Qualitative Research. In: Miller, D. C. & Salkind, N. J. (Eds.), *Handbook of Design and Social Measurement*. Sage, Thousand Oaks, CA, pp. 143–97.

Fielding, N. G. & Lee, R. M. (1992) *Using Computers in Qualitative Research*. Sage, London.

Fisher, M. (1997) *Qualitative Computing: Using Software for Qualitative Data Analysis*. Ashgate, Aldershot.

Kelle, U. (1995) *Computer-Aided Qualitative Data Analysis: Theory, Methods, and Practice*. Sage, London.

Richards, L. (2002) Qualitative Computing: A Methods Revolution? *International Journal of Social Research Methodology* 5(3): 263–76.

Zadeh, L. A. & Kacprzyk, J. (1999) *Computing with Words in Information/Intelligent Systems I*. Physica-Verlag, Heidelberg.

quantitative methods

Julie Lamb

Quantitative methods are those that involve numerical data resulting in statistical analysis. The quantitative approach relies on the stance that an overall view of society (or the gathering of social facts) is preferable to in-depth information provided by a few individuals. In other words, data on social facts can be collected from a sample of individuals and applied to the societal level. This idea of generalization from a sample to the population of interest is of key importance in any quantitative method – data collected must be shown to be able to represent the population under study.

Data for use in quantitative methods have to be collected in an objective manner, usually taking the form of a survey interview or postal questionnaire which is highly structured to be sure to collect the same information from each individual. Using these data collection techniques, one ends up with a large collection of individual variables which can be coded into categories before being analyzed. In this manner, data collected can be tested for reliability (if the same instrument was used again by a different person would it give the same results?), validity (how true is the data to the real population?), and representativeness (how does the information apply to the population under study?) using statistical techniques. The measurement of variables in social research (social measurement) is of key importance to data quality and is a topic in its own right.

Statistics enable us to see a very large amount of information in a summary format, making it easier to understand. Statistics also make it possible to see the world in a structured way outside of the individual level so that theories and policies can be made in a reliable way on account of facts gathered to represent the whole population rather than individuals. One example of this are the labor force statistics gathered on a continuous basis from a sample of the population in the UK (other countries also routinely collect labor force information). These data are then analyzed using statistical methods to produce, for example, numbers of unemployed people in the country, which go on to inform policy decisions and sociological theories.

Quantitative methods do not have to involve a large element of mathematical reasoning. Descriptive statistics can be used as a basic way of backing up an idea or showing the basis for new research. For example, if one is interested in studying unemployment, statistics describing the basic situation at the time of the research can be used to show why the subject is of importance. This can be done from looking at materials already produced, such as reports on the labor market situation without any math involvement. It is when one is creating and testing theories that statistical techniques involving formulas can be used to test hypotheses.

"Doing" quantitative methods can be broken down into three stages: defining the research problem, data collection, and data analysis. Choosing a method of research is largely determined by the research topic and the researcher's own view on the world. Some research problems will be much better suited to quantitative methods than others; for example, it would be extremely difficult to gain a representative sample of homeless people. A survey of students' views of the university beer provision would be more feasible as there are already established lists of students attending the university which could be used for sampling.

Quantitative data collection is usually carried out using a survey method – a structured questionnaire or interview with predetermined response categories. Carrying out such surveys and sampling techniques can be extremely cost prohibitive, both in terms of money and time. Secondary analysis using the quantitative techniques outlined here of existing survey data is a cost and time effective strategy for researchers wishing to use quantitative methods. Data archives exist in many countries where data from existing large-scale surveys can be downloaded and reanalyzed by individual researchers.

Once data have been gathered and coded, statistical techniques can be used to analyze the variables. This is usually carried out using a software package such as SPSS or STATA. These packages allow basic and advanced statistical manipulation of data. Basic quantitative analysis of variables involves describing the data using frequencies (e.g., 35 percent of the sample were unemployed and of these 67 percent were male). These are descriptive statistics. The mean, median, and mode can also be used here. The standard deviation and tests of significance are used to describe the reliability and validity of the data. If the result of the analysis is significant above a certain threshold, then the findings of the research are not due to chance and the hypothesis can be seen to be proven.

Quantitative methods can go much further than this basic level. Why are people unemployed? How do they differ from others in the sample? Do they have a longstanding illness? Answering these questions can be achieved by using techniques of regression. Regression analysis can show whether there is a relationship between a dependent variable (unemployment) and one or more independent variables (health), and how strong (or weak) that relationship is. In this way we may see that if health is poor then the risk of unemployment rises or falls by X percent.

This is a gross summary of an extremely large field. More details of these techniques and how to perform them can be found in the suggested readings.

SEE ALSO: Descriptive Statistics; Statistical Significance Testing; Statistics; Survey Research; Variables; Variables, Dependent; Variables, Independent

REFERENCES AND SUGGESTED READINGS

Black, T. R (1999) *Doing Quantitative Research in the Social Sciences: An Integrated Approach to Research Design, Measurement and Statistics.* Sage, London

Bryman, A. & Cramer, D. (1997) *Quantitative Data Analysis with SPSS for Windows: A Guide for Social Scientists.* Routledge, London.

Council of European Social Survey Data Archives. Online. www.cessda.org.

Mcneil, P. & Chapman, S. (2005) *Research Methods*, 3rd edn. Sage, London.

Seale, C. (2004) *Researching Society and Culture*, 2nd edn. Sage, London.

queer theory

Chet Meeks

Queer theory is an interdisciplinary approach to the study of sexuality. Queer theory's insights derive from multiple sources: feminist scholarship, gay and lesbian studies, cultural studies, social constructionism, deconstructionist and poststructuralist social theory. In general, queer theory takes account of the cultural products (e.g., knowledges, films, television shows), social practices (e.g., dating and marriage), and institutions (e.g., the state) which together bestow on heterosexuality a sacred status and make it into a compulsory requirement. The origins of queer theory are themselves ambiguous; while as an academic movement queer theory is typically associated with the 1990s, its earliest articulations can be traced to the 1970s in the work of Michel Foucault (1978) and the 1980s in the work of scholars like Teresa de Lauretis (1987) and Gloria Anzaldúa (1987). As forerunners of queer theory, these scholars interrogated the way in which western social orders deploy rigid standards of gender and sexual intelligibility as a method of social regulation.

Many scholars commonly associated with queer theory have been trained in disciplines such as philosophy (Judith Butler) and English (Michael Warner), but the basic impulse of queer theory has a substantial history in social science disciplines. Before there was a distinct area of study called queer theory, sociologists criticized the conventional notion that society is divided between individuals who are, by birth, either heterosexual or homosexual, and that such a division is a constant feature of all societies across time and space (see, e.g., Weeks 1977). Contrary to this notion, social scientists have argued that "homosexuality" and "heterosexuality" are socially constructed. A social constructionist approach to sexuality argues that we must distinguish between "behaviors" and "identities." While homosexual or heterosexual behavior might be a constant throughout history and in different cultural settings, it is only in a specific historical and cultural context that something like homosexual behavior comes to be culturally codified as deviant and pathological, and where such a codification is used to ensure widespread social conformity to a heterosexual norm (MacIntosh 1968; Sagarin 1971). As well, it is only under specific social conditions that something like same-sex desire becomes the focal point of personal fulfillment, community building, and politics (D'Emilio 1983).

Queer theory shares the basic impulse of the social constructionist project – to illustrate the social underpinnings of homosexual and heterosexual difference, and to critique the idea that heterosexuality and homosexuality correspond to opposite natures. Queer theory, though, also criticizes two specific problems with the social constructionist approach. First, social constructionist approaches, while they recognize that sexual identities are social in origin and not natural or culturally universal, nevertheless often assume that once sexual identities *are* established, they exist as relatively stable empirical facts, and as valid ways of representing populations of people. Gay identity, though social in origin, and limited to a distinct time period and culture, is thought, once established, to refer fairly unproblematically to a delimited minority group. Queer theorists have argued that, although it is at times necessary and useful to refer to gays and lesbians using such an analytical lens, we must also attend to the ways differences among gays and lesbians complicate the representative and empirical validity of homosexual identity. The place of gay identity in one's life can vary dramatically, for example, depending on one's race.

Second, social constructionists, in viewing homosexual and heterosexual identities as stable, help to solidify the notion that heterosexual and homosexual worlds are separate and distinct. Heterosexuality is thought to correspond to a specific set of cultural meanings (family, romantic love, marriage, virtue), whereas homosexuality is thought to correspond to an alternative, even if positive, set of meanings (communal values, the positive affirmation of sexual pleasure, etc.). Queer theorists have argued that rather than being thought of as culturally separate, as referring to distinct worlds, communities, and meaning systems, heterosexuality and homosexuality are part of the same unstable system of cultural and linguistic signification. "Heterosexuality" and "homosexuality" do not refer to anything empirical, but rather, as signs in a language system, they refer to and derive their meaning from each other. Heterosexuality, in order to be articulated in any meaningful way, must make reference to homosexuality while also repudiating it. Consider the way heterosexual rituals such as the wedding ceremony work. During the "I now pronounce you" moment at a heterosexual wedding, homosexuality represents the unspoken, invisible, yet ever-present Other which makes such a pronouncement possible (Butler 1997). The wedding, as a cultural ceremony, betrays the usual claim that heterosexuality is natural; it illustrates, on the contrary, that heterosexuality has to be continually enacted and performed. That heterosexuality can only derive its cultural intelligibility from the invocation and repudiation of homosexuality in this way means that both heterosexuality and homosexuality are inherently unstable.

Queer theory is also closely related to queer politics. Gay and lesbian minority politics focuses on gaining expanded rights and positive recognition for gays and lesbians. The underlying claim of gay and lesbian minority politics is normalizing: gays and lesbians are normal and homosexuality represents a positive, morally equivalent counterpart to heterosexuality; homosexuals are no different than other American minorities. Queer politics, emerging in the 1990s in America out of groups like AIDS Coalition to Unleash Power (Act-Up), moved away from a normalizing, minority-based politics and focused instead on the way a hetero-sexual/homosexual binary operates to make heterosexuality superior, and to exclude more ambiguous and queer forms of sexual difference that threaten both heterosexual and homosexual intelligibility (see Berlant & Freeman 1993). Queer politics is anti-normalizing in that it contests not only the social dominance of heterosexuality, but also the mainstream of the gay and lesbian community, which makes a certain version of gay minority identity (white, middle class, usually male) into a representation of gay "normality." Gays and lesbians of color, transgender people, bisexuals, intersex peoples, gay people with AIDS, and working-class gays and lesbians argue that this identity excludes their experiences and political priorities. Sexual justice, from this point of view, cannot be achieved simply by arguing that gays and lesbians are "normal," because this sort of political rhetoric only solidifies the outsider status of queer, different others. Queer politics is critical of the minority logic of gay identity because it is exclusionary and reproductive of the "regime of normality" that is inherent in the western compulsion to classify, evaluate, and regulate desires, pleasures, and bodies.

In recent years, two developments have begun to change the shape of queer theory. First, in addition to theorizing heterosexual dominance, some scholars have begun to extend queer theory's critical insights to new areas of social analysis and political struggle. The social subjugation of homosexuality is taken to be part of a broader system of power, control, and discipline which privileges and makes normal some types of bodies while marking other bodies as other – as deviant, abnormal, unattractive, or disabled. New endeavors in the arena of disability studies, for example, bear the mark of queer theory. As a recent volume of *Gay and Lesbian Quarterly* (McRuer & Wilkerson 2003) makes clear, the challenge today is not so much theorizing the social machinery responsible for the subordination of homosexuals, but rather theorizing the possible coalitions between gays and lesbians and a wider variety of subjugated bodies. What sort of common politics could be forged between queers, people with HIV/AIDS, the uninsured, women, the elderly and the young, and third world victims of the first world pharmaceutical industries? All of these individuals, one could argue, occupy bodies that have been classified and then acted upon as weaker, less abled or disabled, less powerful or less attractive by a disciplinary order that makes hegemonic masculinity, strength, and virility into the most socially desirable mode of embodiment.

Second, some have argued that queer theory has been, perhaps, too overreaching in its critique of identity (see, e.g., Kirsch 2000; Green 2002). The tendency in queer theory has been, in a way, to dismiss identities due to their minoritizing, exclusionary, and normalizing consequences. Many queer theorists reduce identity to a "signifier" in a language-sign system, and in doing so, contribute to the erasure of homosexual actors and limit our understanding of the way that identities come to be embedded in institutions, social roles, and daily practices. Homosexuality is more than the effect of a linguistic or textual system; it is an identity that informs the practices of individuals in their daily lives, practices that vary depending on the contingencies of different institutional settings and the complexities of other social roles. "Queer" identity is often more present in theory than in actual politics, and can be written about in ways that pay little attention to concrete institutional dynamics and lived experience. The second trend in queer theory, then, has been to move away from a metatheoretical critique of identity and toward empirically rich and concrete analyses of lived sexualities (e.g., Seidman 2002).

The future of queer theory and politics will likely consist of continued attempts to think beyond the limits of a gay and lesbian minority model of sexuality and politics, beyond the analytical foci of social constructionist approaches, and to theorize the potential coalitions with others struggling against a variegated range of bodily and sexual norms. Alongside such work, future scholarship will likely consist of an endeavor to be more concrete, empirical, and sociological about the contribution of the social to the sexual, and about the way sexual identities come to be embedded in social institutions and roles. If the major contributors to queer theory in the 1990s were mostly literary scholars and philosophers, the future of queer theory – at least a large portion of it – belongs to sociology.

SEE ALSO: Body and Cultural Sociology; Body and Sexuality; Compulsory Heterosexuality; Constructionism; Foucault, Michel; Gay and Lesbian Movement; Heterosexual Imaginary; Homophobia and Heterosexism; Patriarchy; Plastic Sexuality; Poststructuralism; Sexual Identities; Sexual Politics

REFERENCES AND SUGGESTED READINGS

Anzaldúa, G. (1987) *Borderlands/La Frontera*. Aunt Lute Book Company, San Francisco.

Berlant, L. & Freeman, E. (1993) Queer Nationality. In: Warner, M. (Ed.), *Fear of a Queer Planet*. University of Minnesota Press, Minneapolis, pp. 193–229.

Butler, J. (1997) Critically Queer. In: Phelan, S. (Ed.), *Playing With Fire*. Routledge, New York, pp. 11–30.

De Lauretis, T. (1987) *Technologies of Gender*. Indiana University Press, Bloomington.

D'Emilio, J. (1983) *Sexual Politics, Sexual Communities*. University of Chicago Press, Chicago.

Foucault, M. (1978) *The History of Sexuality*, Vol. 1. Vintage, New York.

Green, I. (2002) Gay But Not Queer: Toward a Post-Queer Study of Sexuality. *Theory and Society* 31: 521–45.

Kirsch, M. (2000) *Queer Theory and Social Change*. Routledge, New York.

MacIntosh, M. (1968) The Homosexual Role. *Social Problems* 16: 182–92.

McRuer, R. & Wilkerson, A. (Eds.) (2003) Desiring Disability: Queer Theory Meets Disability Studies. *Gay and Lesbian Quarterly* 9(1–2).

Sagarin, E. (1971) Sex Research and Sociology: Retrospective and Prospective. In: Henslin, J. (Ed.), *Studies in the Sociology of Sex*. Appleton-Century-Crofts, New York.

Seidman, S. (2002) *Beyond the Closet*. Routledge, New York.

Weeks, J. (1977) *Coming Out!!* Quartet, London.

R

race

Mikaila Mariel Lemonik Arthur

To sociologists, race is a system of stratification based on physical differences ("phenotypes") that are seen as essential and permanent. These differences may be real or they may be imagined. Though individuals can and do come to identify in racial terms, race is most important as a system of categorization which is externally imposed. The fact that race is imposed externally is the major difference between it and the concept of ethnicity.

HISTORY OF RACE AS AN IDEA

While people have always found ways to stratify and differentiate in-groups from out-groups, the concept of race emerged relatively recently in human history. Many historians of race believe that the concept of race emerged with modernity and was in particular the consequence of two major developments in European society: first, the development of a capitalist ethos which blamed those who did not progress for their own fate; and second, the British experience of colonizing (and "othering") the Irish, which lay the ground for future experiences in colonization and racial hierarchies (Smedley 1999). Other analysts point to the important role of Christian religious thought in developing conceptions of race. In particular, these analysts point to the Myth of Ham, a biblical tale which tells how Noah's son Ham and his descendants were condemned to servitude because Ham "looked upon the nakedness of" his father (McKee Evans 1980). This story was used by some Christian religious authorities to justify the enslavement of black Africans, since they were seen as the racial descendants of Ham.

With the arrival of the Enlightenment and rational-scientific thought, people turned to scientific methods to seek an understanding of racial differences and to justify their conceptions of racial hierarchies. One of the first scientific projects for racial scholars was the development of comprehensive taxonomies of racial difference. First attempted by Carl Linnaeus in 1758, many European men of science followed behind with classification schemes which specified the number and variety of human races, ranging from a low of 3 (African, European, and Mongolian) to a high of over 30. It was not uncommon for racial taxonomists to divide Europeans, for example, into 4 racial groups: Nordic or northern, Alpine or central, Mediterranean or southern, and Slavic or eastern. These taxonomies were generally based on ideas of the physical, but also included some attributes which we would not today think of as biologically based, such as clothing and cultural behavior.

As the modern scientific method developed, scientists who studied human variation came to believe that it was not sufficient to label races based on classifiers' superstitions or beliefs. Instead, they pushed for the development of scientific techniques and experiments that were carefully designed to measure the degree of racial difference and inferiority. The earliest techniques, called craniometry, involved measuring skull capacity and other dimensions of the head. However, by the late 1800s most of these techniques had been discredited or were in doubt. After the IQ test was invented in 1905, it was used to demonstrate racial difference and inferiority. IQ tests were successful at producing results that lined up with people's expectations about race and intelligence.

While most contemporary social and biological scientists do not believe that there is any biological or genetic evidence for racial difference, some geneticists have turned to the field of population genetics to look for patterns of genetic expression among supposed racial groups. These geneticists believe that the differences they find may be useful in medical and forensic applications. However, new evidence about the degree of mixing between people from different continents over time casts doubt on this conclusion. In fact, some researchers have suggested that as many as 80 percent or more of American blacks may have some white ancestors in their family tree.

INTERNATIONAL CONTEXT

The contemporary image of racial difference varies across national and cultural contexts. In particular, the conception of the dividing lines between racial groups is not the same everywhere. For instance, in the US, race has traditionally been perceived through the lens of the "one-drop rule," meaning that anyone with any demonstrable degree of black ancestry (even so little as one 32nd of one's ancestry, and even when the individual appears phenotypically white) is seen as black. This racial ideology is related to a history in the US of cultural and legal barriers against miscegenation, or marital and sexual relationships across the color line. Though the increase in multiracial marriages and births has caused this "rule" to decline in force somewhat, as recently as 1985 the Louisiana Court of Appeals declared that Susie Guillory Phipps could not have her race on her birth certificate changed from black (or "colored") to white because she could not "prove" that fewer than one 32nd of her ancestors were black.

Not all nations and societies stick to such a rigid system of racial classification. For instance, in many Caribbean and Latin American societies there are gradations of race between black and white. Individuals' own places on these scales can vary according to class, education, and skin color, not just ancestry. In many of these countries, miscegenation was not considered to be an especially big problem. In fact, in Brazil, interracial unions were considered to contribute to a "unique Brazilian mixture" of racial backgrounds (Lesser 1999). It is important to remember, however, that mixing between races and a less rigid color line do not mean that race is any less important in regulating the life chances of individuals (Twine 1998).

Another variation in the conception of racial difference can be found in South Africa during the time of Apartheid. South Africa's racial order was, like that of the US, predicated upon restricting the mixing of races. However, instead of declaring all of those of mixed racial backgrounds to simply be black, in South Africa a new racial category called "colored" was created to take in those who were considered to be neither black nor white (Dubow 1995).

CONSEQUENCES

Though as noted above race is not a biological reality, as W. I. Thomas said, "if people define a situation as real, it is real in its consequences." Race continues to play an important role in individuals' daily lives. According to the American Sociological Association's 2003 statement on race, the effects that it has can be classified into three major categories: sorting people into categories on the basis of which they choose appropriate family members and friends; stratifying people in terms of their access to resources; and organizing people into groups through which they seek to challenge or maintain the racial status quo.

People often take race into account when choosing whom to count as potential family members or friends. Until 1967, when the Supreme Court declared them unconstitutional in *Loving* v. *Virginia*, laws in some US states prevented miscegenation, or interracial marriage. Though interracial marriage is now legal and occurs with some frequency, it remains rare between blacks and whites. Similarly, when individuals or couples choose to adopt, they continue to choose children who are phenotypically similar to them. In fact, until 1978, the National Association of Black Social Workers defended the practice of refusing to place black children with white parents.

Friendships and other social interactions also continue to divide along racial lines. In large part this has to do with the continuing presence of residential and educational segregation. While it has not been legal to engage in *de jure* ince the *Brown* v. *Board of Education* decision in 1954 or in *de jure* residential segregation since the passage of the Fair Housing Act in 1968, schools and neighborhoods remain segregated. Schools remain segregated first and foremost because most children are assigned to public schools based on where they live. Residential segregation is more complicated. One important factor in residential segregation is the wealth disparity between blacks and whites, as discussed below. In addition, real estate brokers and mortgage lenders continue to engage in racial steering, redlining, and other discriminatory practices so as to maintain the racial "stability" of particular neighborhoods. Finally, because of both stereotypes about blacks and the reality of falling property values in neighborhoods undergoing a transition in their racial makeup, whites continue to be likely to move away as black families move in ("white flight").

Race continues to play a significant role in dictating individuals' life chances in terms of financial, education, and general well-being. Most striking is the wealth gap between blacks and whites. The 2000 US Census data show that white families on average own almost 11 times the assets of black families. Though the disparity in income is not as significant (since income is earned by an individual, while wealth is compounded across generations), black men still earn only three quarters of what white men earn, while black women earn almost 90 percent of what white women do. Black families are also more likely than white families to live in poverty or experience unemployment.

While the picture in terms of education is more hopeful, racial disparities have not been erased. Blacks graduate from high school and start college in numbers nearly comparable to whites'. However, the gap between blacks and whites on the SATs remains at about 200 points, limiting the access of black students to the most selective colleges. And blacks remain significantly less likely than whites to graduate from college or graduate school.

There continue to be racial disparities in other areas of life as well, such as in terms of health and imprisonment. For instance, blacks continue to live fewer years than whites, have higher infant mortality rates, and have less access to good health care. Blacks are also more likely than whites to be arrested and imprisoned.

Because racial disparities have such significant affects on individuals' lives and are so important in sorting people into groups, many social movements have formed around racial interests. Movements like the US Civil Rights Movement and the anti-Apartheid movement in South Africa were formed to create change in the racial status quo. Other social movements, such as the American Indian Movement, La Raza Unida, and Black Power, have been formed to promote solidarity among and advance the perceived interests of members of particular racial groups.

Similarly, majority group members have organized on racial lines to defend the racial status quo. These organizing activities are not limited to far-right groups or extreme nationalists like the Ku Klux Klan or neo-Nazis. There are also much more mainstream groups who attack affirmative action, welfare, immigration, and other social practices and policies based on the effects that these have on the privileges that whites are accustomed to exercising in society.

Organizing around race is not limited to the social movement sphere. In fact, much of conventional politics is affected by the organization of race in society. Perhaps most importantly in the American case, voting districts have often been drawn in ways that disperse or concentrate voters of a particular racial group in an attempt to alter the electoral outcomes in that region ("racial gerrymandering"). Similarly, political candidates can target racial groups through their campaign in an attempt to influence voting blocs to support them.

SEE ALSO: Discrimination; Ethnicity; Eugenics; Health and Race; Interracial Unions; *Minzoku*; Race (Racism); Race and Crime; Race and the Criminal Justice System; Race and Ethnic Politics; Race and Schools; Race/Ethnicity and Friendship; Racial Hierarchy; Racism, Structural and Institutional; Racist Movements; Scientific Racism; Slavery; Stratification, Race/Ethnicity and

REFERENCES AND SUGGESTED READINGS

American Sociological Association (2003) *The Importance of Collecting Data and Doing Research on Race.* American Sociological Association, Washington, DC.

Bonilla-Silva, E. (2003) *Racism without Racists: Color-Blind Racism and the Persistence of Racial Inequality in the United States.* Rowman & Littlefield, New York.
Dubow, S. (1995) *Scientific Racism in Modern South Africa.* Cambridge University Press, Cambridge.
Gilroy, P. (2000) *Against Race: Imaging Political Culture Beyond the Color Line.* Belknap, Cambridge, MA.
Gould, S. J. (1996) *The Mismeasure of Man*, 2nd edn. W. W. Norton, New York.
Lesser, J. (1999) *Negotiating National Identity: Immigrants, Minorities, and the Struggle for Ethnicity in Brazil.* Duke University Press, Durham, NC.
McKee Evans, W. (1980) From the Land of Canaan to the Land of Guinea: The Strange Odyssey of the Sons of Ham. *American Historical Review* 85: 15–43.
Oliver, M. L. & Shapiro, T. M. (1995) *Black Wealth/White Wealth: A New Perspective on Racial Inequality.* Routledge, New York.
Smedley, A. (1999) *Race in North America*, 2nd edn. Westview Press, Boulder.
Twine, F. W. (1998) *Racism in a Racial Democracy.* Rutgers University Press, New Brunswick, NJ.
Winant, H. (2002) *The World is a Ghetto.* Basic Books, New York.

race and crime

Roland Chilton and Ruth Triplett

The importance of race in the production of criminal conduct has been an issue in American criminology for decades. The fact that minority groups, particularly African Americans, are disproportionately involved as offenders in the criminal justice system in the US is not in dispute. However, there is little agreement among criminologists on what this means. Some argue that the relationship between race and crime is largely the result of the conduct of African American men and boys. Others argue that the relationship between race and crime suggested by official statistics is the result of discrimination in the various systems of justice in the US.

Official arrest, incarceration, and public health data all point to a disproportionate involvement of black people, especially black men and boys, in predatory crime in the US. In 2003, the FBI's Uniform Crime Reports (UCR) indicated that blacks accounted for 37 percent of all arrests for violent crimes though blacks account for only about 13 percent of the population. Black men are also overrepresented as victims. US public health statistics consistently show homicide is a leading cause of death for black males (Anderson 1999). In addition, the FBI's Supplementary Homicide Reports suggest that black offenders are responsible for most homicides involving black victims. Black males have been over-represented in both victimization and offender figures for over 35 years.

The over-representation of minorities as both offenders and victims is found in victimization surveys as well. National crime victimization surveys published by the Bureau of Justice Statistics from 1973 through 2003 have consistently shown higher victimization rates for black respondents. While the information on offenders in the victimization surveys is limited to assault, rape, and robbery, it generally suggests higher black than white or other rates of offending. Hindelang (1978) found that victimization data were generally consistent with data on arrestees and that "most of the racial disproportionality in arrest data is shown by victimization survey data to be attributable to greater involvement of blacks in rape, robbery, and assault."

National Crime Victimization Survey (NCVS) and UCR data for 1996 to 2002 provide less support for this statement than do the numbers for 1974 that were used by Hindelang. The NCVS average percentage of robbery offenders described as black for this 7-year period was 46. In the UCR data, about 55 percent of those arrested for robbery during this period were black. For rape, the NCVS figure is 23 and the UCR figure is 37. Even taking into account the absence of reports of commercial robberies in the victimization data and the failure of many victims to recall and report victimizations by family members and friends, the NCVS percentages suggest the possibility of "over arrest" of black people for these offenses.

Early self-report studies suggested little difference in the number of black youths reporting involvement in criminal conduct in comparison with the number of white youths reporting such conduct. However, many of the early self-report studies focused on social class rather than race, with one important study dropping all black respondents because of a belief that the black respondents lacked the verbal skills needed to complete the surveys.

In addition, early self-report studies generally captured trivial offending rather than the serious predatory crimes captured by official data. However, in a review of later self-report studies, Hindelang et al. (1981) found that while there was little difference by race in the proportion of youths who reported having committed trivial offenses, race differences were found for serious offenses and in the *rate* of offending. These later self-report studies found that black youths were more likely to report having committed serious offenses and reported doing so at a higher rate.

In general, then, most official data and many independent studies suggest that black Americans, especially black men, are over-represented as both offenders and victims. But it would be misleading to present a discussion of race and crime without noting that it has become almost traditional when discussing murder rates to say that the high homicide offending rates for black males are a function of social class. Some recent studies provide support for this position. For example, Parker and McCall (1999), using race-specific independent variables for about 100 US cities, concluded that economic deprivation affects the intraracial homicide rates for whites and blacks. In a study of the impact of poverty and deprivation on black murder rates, Ousey (1999) reported black murder arrest rates that were five times as high as white murder arrest rates. Although he found that measures of poverty and deprivation had an impact on both black and white murder arrest rates, the effects of these variables were stronger for whites than for blacks.

Explanations for these differences have ranged from biological to sociological. At least one recent theory has attempted to explain the rates in purely biological terms. Although anthropologists have abandoned the notion of distinctive racial categories, Rushton (2000) suggested that the lower IQs, higher testosterone levels, and smaller cranial capacities of black people explained their high rates of criminality. This kind of biological explanation is clearly a racial theory of crime because the conduct being explained is attributed to what are called racial differences. Wilson and Herrnstein (1985) came close to presenting a racial explanation for differences in crime rates by race in their focus on intelligence as a "constitutional" cause of crime and in their subsequent conclusion: "The one factor that both seems closely associated with offending and appears disproportionately among blacks is a low intelligence score."

Today, however, most people trying to explain the differences in black and white arrest and incarceration rates focus on social, cultural, economic, or political factors. For these theorists, patterns of homicide rates by race suggest that the rates are primarily linked to exclusion and segregation – economic, racial, and ethnic – but especially to the separation and isolation of large segments of urban populations based on income and assets. This view is supported in part by a number of city-level analyses, such as Peterson and Krivo's (1993) analysis of homicide victimization rates for 125 US cities, which found that black homicide victimizations were linked to racial segregation.

One recent explanation which takes an Afrocentric approach focuses on the historical role of slavery in the US as a cause of high black crime rates. King (1997) argues that much of the violence today must be seen as an indirect result of enslavement and violence directed against African slaves combined with the impact of a violently discriminatory system of justice. He sees the net effect of this history accompanied by limited opportunity and mass media images that undermine appropriate value systems as the cause of high rates of violent conduct by black male teenagers and adults.

Other theorists focus more specifically on the cultural impact of isolation, while still others focus on the social structure. Ousey (1999) suggests that extensive and long-term disadvantage may have produced cultural and normative adaptations that have produced this gap in the rates. Anderson (1999) argues there exists a "code of the streets" in largely poor, inner-city black neighborhoods. The code is a set of informal rules for interpersonal behavior that describe when violence is acceptable. He argues that the code is a cultural adaptation that developed from alienation from mainstream society and the belief that the police and the criminal justice system cannot protect them from others.

Recently, Sampson and Wilson (1990) paid careful attention to both cultural and structural effects of segregation by race and class. They note the existence of neighborhoods highly segregated by race, class, and level of family disruption, isolated from mainstream culture. They argued neighborhood characteristics were the result of policies of racial segregation, structural economic transformation, black male joblessness, class-linked out-migration, and housing discrimination and suggested that the result of the segregation and isolation was structural and cultural disorganization.

Not every criminologist believes that the differences by race found in official data are the result of real differences in behavior. These criminologists tend to argue that the numbers reflect the racial bias of those operating the system of justice. Historically, racial bias in some state systems of justice was clear and obvious. The law itself was biased. Examples include the use of the legal system to take American Indian lands, the creation and use of opium laws in response to Asian immigration, and the use of Jim Crow laws to disadvantage African Americans. Many scholars see the sharply higher punishment for the possession of crack cocaine in comparison with the punishment for possession of cocaine in its powder form as a recent example of discriminatory law. Although it would be hard to show discriminatory intent, the impact of this legislation has been hardest on poor, inner-city, African Americans.

Although official definitions of crime are legislative, crime is also defined by administrative policies and enforcement practices. The police, for example, have wide discretion in decisions to arrest. Given the history of race relations in the US, it would be surprising to find that race does not play a role in some decisions to arrest. In a review of race and police discretion, Walker et al. (2000) found a number of explanations for the disproportionate arrest of black Americans, only one of which was that they commit more crime. They found research suggesting that situational factors, especially the type of crime committed and the attitude of the suspect, played an important role in decisions to arrest. They also found reports suggesting that African Americans commit more serious crimes and are more likely to have a disrespectful attitude toward the police, both of which are factors found to shape the arrest decision. Other studies in their review suggested that African Americans are often arrested on less stringent evidence than whites.

Reviews of court studies prior to the 1960s for sentencing disparity by race since suggest the evidence is inconsistent. Today, researchers in this area examine context, asking "When does race matter?" In their review of this literature, Walker et al. (2000) suggest there is evidence that race matters when the crime is less serious, when the victim is white and the accused is not, and when the accused is unemployed. In a recent example of researchers examining the context in which race matters, Steen et al. (2005) found that it is important to examine the factors that may indicate dangerousness and blameworthiness among felony drug offenders. They found that both black and white offenders who fit the criteria for "most threatening" were likely to be incarcerated. However, whites who fit the "less threatening" criteria were less likely to be incarcerated than African Americans who fit the same description. Their research suggests both a need to examine context and that most incidents of bias are found among less serious cases.

The ways and extent in which race is linked to specific criminal conduct remain unresolved issues in criminology. There is a strong indication that the relationship is different for serious and minor offenses and for predatory and nonpredatory offenses. Young black males may be "over arrested" for minor offenses and offenses involving drug possession or sale. And a disproportionate number of young black males may be involved in murders, rapes, robberies, and other forms of predatory crime. However, in the light of the sad history of race relations in the US it is hard to identify the reasons for the differences in any of these arrest and offending rates. Nevertheless, careful and sustained studies of questions about the linkages of race and crime are long overdue. As in many areas of criminology, there is no shortage of theory, assertion, and speculation. But there is a serious shortage of well-focused, dependable research on the relationship of race and crime.

SEE ALSO: Class and Crime; Crime; Measuring Crime; Race; Race and the Criminal Justice System; Race (Racism)

REFERENCES AND SUGGESTED READINGS

Anderson, E. (1999) *Code of the Street.* W. W. Norton, New York.

Hindelang, M. J. (1978) Race and Involvement in Common Law Personal Crimes. *American Sociological Review* 43 (1): 93–109.
Hindelang, M. J., Hirschi, T., & Weis, J. G. (1981) *Measuring Delinquency*. Sage, Thousand Oaks, CA.
King, A. E. O (1997) Understanding Violence among Young African Americans: An Afrocentric Perspective. *Journal of Black Studies* 28: 79–96.
Mann, C. (1993) *Unequal Justice: A Question of Color*. Indiana University Press, Bloomington.
Ousey, G. C. (1999) Homicide, Structural Factors, and the Racial Invariance Assumption. *Criminology* 37: 405–26.
Parker, K. F. & McCall, P. L. (1999) Structural Conditions and Racial Homicide Patterns: A Look at the Multiple Disadvantages in Urban Areas. *Criminology* 37: 447–77.
Peterson, R. D. & Krivo, L. J. (1993) Racial Segregation and Black Urban Homicide. *Social Forces* 71: 1001–26.
Reiman, J. (2001) *The Rich Get Richer and the Poor Get Prison*. Allyn & Bacon, Boston.
Rushton, J. P. (2000) *Race, Evolution, and Behavior: A Life History Perspective*, 3rd edn. Charles Darwin Research Institute, Port Huron, MI.
Sampson, R. J. (1987) Urban Black Violence: The Effect of Male Joblessness and Family Disruption. *American Journal of Sociology* 93: 348–82.
Sampson, R. J. & Wilson, W. J. (1990) A Theory of Race, Crime and Urban Inequality. In: Hagan, J. & Peterson, R. (Eds.), *Crime and Inequality*. Stanford University Press, Stanford.
Steen, S., Engen, R. L., & Gainey, R. R. (2005) Images of Danger and Culpability: Racial Stereotyping, Case Processing, and Criminal Sentencing. *Criminology* 43: 435–68.
Walker, S., Spohn, C., & DeLone, M. (2000) *The Color of Justice: Race, Ethnicity, and Crime in America*, 2nd edn. Wadsworth Thomson, Belmont, CA.
Wilson, J. Q. & Herrnstein, R. (1985) *Crime and Human Nature*. Simon & Schuster, New York.

race and the criminal justice system

Laurie Samuel

The criminal justice system is a system of social control designed to regulate the behavior of citizens. Through the creation and enforcement of the law, it defines what behavior is and is not acceptable. The criminal justice system is made up of several components, which include the police, courts, corrections, probation, and parole. Lawmakers guide the movements of these units and define those behaviors considered criminal. The process begins, however, with the police, who detect lawbreakers and arrest them. The process then moves to prosecution where arrestees are formally charged. Once a charge has been determined, arrestees may or may not go to court for a formal trial. In those cases where there is not a formal trial, offenders may admit guilt. Once guilt is established, the offender is either sentenced to a period of incarceration or may be given a sentence of probation, community service, or ordered to pay restitution to his or her victim(s). These less serious forms of punishment are usually reserved for first-time non-serious offenses and sometimes for juveniles. Though mechanisms exist for the structuring of discretion, the existence of discretion means that at each stage in the processing of individuals through the criminal justice system, the possibility for disparity in treatment exists. For example, decisions by the police on lawbreakers are sometimes based on personal biases and stereotypes. Researchers have long been interested in the factors that shape discretion. Race is a critical part of the discussion of factors that shape discretion as many of the decisions made by police, prosecutors, and judges are based on this factor.

Race is a socially constructed term designed to categorize groups of people based on certain physical qualities. The problem with the existence of varying socially constructed racial categories is that they are often accompanied by stereotypes. When one thinks of the color white, for example, one thinks about goodness and purity. On the other hand, the color black is often associated with things that are dark, predatory, and negative. Due to the enormous power of the media, these stereotypes are foremost in our minds and often taken as facts. Crime, then, is often linked with blacks and other minorities. Any discussion of race within the criminal justice system must acknowledge these biases.

The criminal justice system is responsible for detecting criminals and meting out punishment when crimes are committed. The term "justice," however, can be somewhat misleading as it implies a sense of fairness. When the system is applied unevenly, it negates the justice it claims to protect. Thus the same system that is supposed to restore order manifests itself as a dysfunctional entity needing reform. Over the last 20 years notable criminologists such as Coramae Richey Mann, Jeffery Reiman, and Michael Tonry have analyzed the historical relationship between race and the criminal justice system. They have found, for example, that throughout time blacks are routinely arrested, convicted, and incarcerated at rates far higher than their representative numbers in the general population. At no other time has this been more pronounced than with the enacting of stringent drug policies in the 1980s, often referred to as the "war on drugs." Aimed at reducing drug use, these policies imposed mandatory minimums for the possession of certain drugs. These guidelines, however, impose stiffer penalties for the possession of crack cocaine than for powder cocaine. Whether this was a purposeful move on the part of lawmakers to incarcerate a large number of the black community is debated, but the fact remains that crack cocaine is most likely sold by blacks and powder cocaine by whites. Furthermore, the visibility of black drug dealers who sold their product out in the open streets of disorganized neighborhoods made it very easy for them to be detected and arrested. White users and dealers, on the other hand, usually come from middle-class neighborhoods and therefore their behaviors are confined indoors.

Not only have these drug laws contributed to the increasing arrest rates of minorities, but also, unlike their white counterparts, minorities often lack the financial resources to secure superior legal representation and must therefore settle for a court-appointed public defender. Public defenders normally have large caseloads, leaving them little time to devote adequate attention these cases often need. Given these disadvantages, minorities are more likely to be denied bail and detained. Today, black men are being arrested, convicted, and sentenced at rates far greater than their white counterparts (Reiman 2001). The result has been a "warehousing" of minorities.

The discriminatory treatment of minorities is only part of the story, however. It is not only that minorities are treated more harshly, but also that the crimes of the majority are often ignored. In his well-known book *The Rich Get Richer and the Poor Get Prison*, Jeffrey Reiman (2001) provides a convincing and compelling argument that criminal justice officials overemphasize street crime, although many of the actions and behaviors of the ruling class cause far more widespread damage and impact. Corporate and white-collar crime, the crimes most likely to be committed by the ruling class, cause overwhelming financial and human cost to society. For example, white-collar crime has been estimated to cost the United States approximately $388 billion a year. However, one rarely hears about the fraud, death, and environmental destruction caused by large corporations. It is through the combined processes of the criminal justice system, which overemphasize the street crimes of minorities and ignore the white-collar crimes of the ruling class, that myths about race and crime are promulgated in society.

The issue of the differential treatment of minorities by the criminal justice system has become all the more important because of recent evidence regarding the level of crime relative to the use of imprisonment. Recently, criminologists have demonstrated that crime rates (particularly violent crime) have been steadily declining over the last few years (Tonry 1995; Reiman 2001), yet formal interventions (i.e., punishment) are increasing. For example, in 1993 the rate of violent crime was 747.1 per 100,000 and the rate of imprisonment was 359 per 100,000. In 2001, the violent crime rate dropped to 504.5 but the rate of imprisonment rose to 470. Punishment is not increasing equally for everyone, however. Whites represented 60 percent of violent crime arrests in 2001 whereas blacks accounted for approximately 37 percent. When violent crime arrests are compared to incarceration rates, blacks are clearly disproportionately imprisoned. Whites were incarcerated at a rate of 138 per 100,000 in comparison to 703 per 100,000 for blacks.

Over the years, politicians have created law and order platforms rooted in the menacing figure of crime. This get-tough approach plays on citizens' fear of crime and racial minorities have been typecast in the role of the criminal. Skin color is a paramount issue within the criminal justice system. For example, at every criminal justice system stage from arrest through incarceration, "blacks are present in numbers greatly out of proportion to their presence in the general population" (Tonry 1995: 49). Even with the decline in crime rates, blacks are "seven times more likely" to be incarcerated than whites (Tonry 1995). There is an overemphasis on blacks as perpetrators of violent crime in the criminal justice literature. African Americans and other minorities thus are stereotyped as violent, which excludes other groups from the discussion.

It has been argued that the study of race and the criminal justice system suffers from faulty, slanted research designs and poor operationalization. Much of the literature uses official records, which include arrest and incarceration rates, to measure crime. Official records may paint a false picture, often revealing more about police and criminal justice system practices than criminal behavior. For example, they do not tell us about people who are committing crimes but are not getting caught. The aggressive nature of police toward minorities contributes to overstating their involvement in crime. Therefore, other techniques such as self-reports (interviews and questionnaires) should be used to fill in the blanks left by official records.

Researchers in this area are interested in documenting not only the existence of discriminatory treatment but its effect as well. They argue convincingly that the effect of discrimination by the criminal justice system goes beyond the effect on the individual. According to Hagan and Coleman (2001), war on drugs crime policies from the 1980s aimed at controlling the crack epidemic have negatively impacted the inner-city black community. The war on drugs has caused an alarming rate of imprisonment among young black males and has had dramatic and devastating effects on the African American family. In addition to racism, discrimination, and lack of opportunity, these policies have worsened an already desperate and bleak situation. The criminal act should be put in context of the cultural and structural factors affecting the offender and the response to the offender as criminal is "a reflection of something larger and deeper" (Radosh 2002: 300). This approach has alienated, ostracized, and further pushed minorities to the bottom of the barrel and has made it exceedingly more difficult for them to claw their way back to a status that often still is inferior to the dominant class.

In 1904, African American sociologist W. E. B. Du Bois declared that "Negroes came to look upon courts as instruments of injustice and oppression and upon those convicted in them as martyrs and victims." Although these words were penned over 100 years ago, they are just as meaningful in the twenty-first century as the criminal justice system is a site of racism and oppression for racial minorities. Inequalities are now subtler, but disparities still exist. The criminal justice system was created to establish law and order and to ensure the proper functioning of society. Over time, however, it has become a system of power that serves the interest of the dominant class. While crime rates are decreasing across the nation, rates of incarceration for blacks and other racial minorities are increasing. It is vital that practitioners, scholars, and politicians alike further address the nexus between race and the criminal justice system and devise alternatives that ensure equity, fairness, and survival.

SEE ALSO: Class and Crime; Criminal Justice System; Criminology; Race; Race and Crime; Race/Racism

REFERENCES AND SUGGESTED READINGS

Barlow, M. & Barlow, D. (1995) Confronting Ideologies of Race and Crime in the Classroom: The Power of History. *Journal of Criminal Justice Education* 6: 105–22.

Bureau of Justice Statistics (2000) *Incarcerated Parents and their Children.* US Department of Justice, Bureau of Justice Statistics, Washington, DC.

Bureau of Justice Statistics (2002) *Sourcebook of Criminal Justice Statistics, 2002.* US Department of Justice, Bureau of Justice Statistics, Washington, DC.

Cernkovich, S., Giordano, P., & Rudolph, J. (2000) Race, Crime, and the American Dream. *Journal of Research in Crime and Delinquency* 37: 131–70.

Chilton, R. & Galvin, J. (1985) Race, Crime, and Criminal Justice. *Crime and Delinquency* 31: 3–14.

Griffith, T. & Verdun-Jones, S. (1994) *Canadian Criminal Justice.* Harcourt Brace, Toronto.

Hagan, J. & Coleman, J. (2001) Returning Captives of the American War on Drugs: Issues of Community and Family Reentry. *Crime and Delinquency* 47: 352–67.

Moyer, I. (2001) *Criminological Theories: Traditional and Nontraditional Voices and Themes.* Sage, Thousand Oaks, CA.
Radosh, P. (2002) Reflections on Women's Crime and Mothers in Prison: A Peacemaking Approach. *Crime and Delinquency* 48: 300–15.
Reiman, J. (2001) *The Rich Get Richer and the Poor Get Prison.* Allyn & Bacon, Boston.
Robinson, M. (2000) The Construction and Reinforcement of Myths of Race and Crime. *Journal of Contemporary Criminal Justice* 6: 133–56.
Samuel, L. & Nicholson, T. (2001) Racial Profiling and Civilian Review Boards: A Commentary. *Journal of Intergroup Relations* 18: 33–41.
Sutherland, E. (1947) Principles of Criminology. In: Akers, R. L. (Ed.), *Criminological Theories*, 3rd edn. Roxbury, Los Angeles.
Tonry, M. (1995) *Malign Neglect.* Oxford University Press, New York.
Young, V. & Greene, H. (1995) Pedagogical Reconstruction: Incorporating African American Perspectives in the Curriculum. *Journal of Criminal Justice Education* 6: 85–104.

race and ethnic consciousness

Steven J. Gold

Race and ethnic consciousness refers to the awareness of membership in a racial or ethnic group by both group members and the larger society in which they reside. The concept embodies both popular *and* social scientific understandings of classification and membership. Popular perceptions often attribute race and ethnicity to biological origins. In contrast, social scientists insist that these categories are the consequence of a social construction process. Despite the social basis of race and ethnicity, social scientists acknowledge that they are real in their consequences. Race and ethnicity shape social stratification, underlie individual and group identities, determine patterns of social conflict, and condition life chances. In fact, so important is the notion of consciousness to the comprehension of race that eminent scholar George Fredrickson defines race as "*consciousness* of status and identity based on ancestry and color" (1988: 3; emphasis added).

Fredrickson traces the concern with race and ethnic consciousness to the 1970s debate between neo-Marxists and Weberians on the origins of American racism. Prior to that time, racism was interpreted in light of psychological constructs including ignorance, prejudice, and the projection of hostility onto low-status groups. Rejecting the causal importance of these factors, Marxist scholars like Eugene Genovese emphasized the economic benefits acquired by slave owners in exploiting African-origin people. They contended that anti-black ideologies were determined by the relations of production, and reflected the class consciousness of slave owners who imposed these outlooks on non-slave-owning white workers. While admitting the importance of class in racial inequality, Fredrickson and colleagues countered Marxist contentions about the economic basis of racism by reviving a polemic first made in the 1940s by W. E. B. Du Bois. They cited the many ways that poor whites, who had little economic interest in exploiting the labor of African Americans, were nevertheless passionate white supremacists. Race and ethnicity were meaningful determinants of social differentiation in their own right. Paraphrasing Marx, Fredrickson utilized the term *race consciousness* as an alternative to class-based identities in shaping identification and solidarity.

Research by Van Ausdale and Feagin reveals the primacy of race consciousness in constructing identity by demonstrating that children as young as 3 years are well aware of racial and ethnic classification and deploy invidious distinctions based upon their comprehension thereof.

Much sociological knowledge about the nature and functioning of race and ethnic relations is rooted in the analysis of the highly structured situation of the American South prior to the Civil Rights Movement. However, recent research conducted within the highly diverse, multicultural, and globalized contemporary social environments, wherein migrants account for a significant fraction of the local population and explicitly racist statements are taboo, yields a much more intricate and varied array of racial and ethnic situations than in an earlier time. While race and ethnic consciousness remains a powerful force in such contexts, its codification is much more complex. As Winant,

Bonilla-Silva, and others argue in their theories of racialization, racism has multiple bases, impacts groups in different ways, and changes according to time, place, class, and gender (Bonilla-Silva 2001: 41).

Migration has the potential to radically transform the prisms and boundaries through which race consciousness is formulated. Accordingly, systems of racial and ethnic classification and consciousness defy general principles and must be studied at the local level. For example, a growing literature on African-origin immigrants in North America shows that despite the pervasive, phenotypically based ideology of racism that exists in the US, dark-skinned newcomers often reject the US system of racial classification and use language, social practices, and selective patterns of social interaction to exempt themselves from it.

In a large body of research on the children of immigrants in California and Florida, Portes and Rumbaut found that the more assimilated immigrant youth are, the less likely they are to call themselves American and the more likely they are to identify with their country of origin. As such, their self-proclaimed foreignness is "made in the USA" (Portes & Rumbaut 2001: 188). In contrast, the children of immigrants in the United Kingdom downplay national identities and instead emphasize their parents' religion, preferring to be classified as Hindus, Muslims, or Sikhs in their interactions with the native British, even if they do not practice their faiths any more assiduously than most British people practice Christianity (Banton 1997: 121).

In multi-ethnic societies, groups come to be seen, and to see themselves, as members of broadly inclusive pan-ethnic categories that were unknown in the country of origin. People who had thought of themselves as members of families, regions, religious groups, or nationalities learn to identify with labels such as Asians, Latinos, or Ukes (short for Ukrainians, this term denotes various Eastern European groups in Ontario) in the host society. Such categories can be influenced by language, class position, neighborhood, popular music taste, gender ideologies, and patterns of consumption.

Despite the merging of groups with common regional origins or phenotype into a single category, awareness of difference remains. The greatest rivalries sometimes occur among populations that the larger society believes to be members of the same race or ethnicity. In New York City, West Indians report conflicts with Haitians and African Americans, while South Americans collide with Dominicans and Puerto Ricans (Kasinitz et al. 2004).

In his study of white identity in black-majority Detroit, John Hartigan found that working-class whites attribute the declining quality of life in their neighborhoods not to African Americans – as popular stereotypes about urban whites might suggest – but rather to the racialized category of "hillbillies," relative newcomers who entered the Motor City from Appalachia in search of industrial jobs. Finally, some groups with a strong minority identity, such as Jews from the former Soviet Union, who arrive in the US and Canada are surprised to find themselves regarded as members of the white majority, albeit with a foreign accent.

Sociologists Jennifer Lee and Frank Bean have explored the changing nature of the color line in the US as the country incorporates a growing mixed-race population and numerous immigrants who are neither black nor white. The authors review theories and data that suggest that increasing racial and ethnic diversity will make American society either less concerned with such distinctions (yielding a color-blind society) or will result in a shift of the color line. Citing low rates of residential segregation and high rates of intermarriage between Asians and Latinos and native whites, as compared to lower rates of black–white interaction, the authors conclude that a new color line that sets off blacks from all others may be coming into existence, leaving African Americans in disadvantaged positions that are not qualitatively different from those perpetuated by the traditional black–white divide.

Since the 1960s, social scientists have increasingly understood race and ethnic consciousness as the basis for the evaluation of group status and the concomitant formation of collective action. Herbert Blumer's theory of race relations as a sense of group position contended that this feeling was critical to the relations between the dominant and the subordinate groups in society. It provided the dominant group with its perceptions, values, sensitivities, and emotions (Blumer 1999 [1958]: 101). More recent scholarship sees group position as applying to subordinate as well as dominant groups.

Theorists concerned with ethnic mobilization, ethnic economies, and social capital assert that shared notions of ethnic and racial membership underlie forms of trust, political and economic cooperation, and mobilization. In their pivotal work on social capital, Portes and colleagues identify mutual racial or ethnic consciousness as fostering the achievement of common goals. Among these are raising investment capital, encouraging academic achievement, fostering political activism, and stimulating self-help philanthropy. At the same time, however, they remind us that social capital can have a downside, such that members of an ethnic or racial group will sometimes disdain assimilation, achievement, and upward mobility as violating group norms. Those engaging in sanctioned behaviors will be seen as disloyal and barred from accessing group-based resources.

Race and ethnic consciousness is strongest in societies where populations are clearly divided and scarce and valued resources are unequally distributed on the basis of highly visible racial or ethnic characteristics. Often, the process is initiated as an elite group – such as white slave owners in the antebellum South – unites to dominate a minority population – Africans – using state power to legitimate the social and economic structures that underlie inequality. This, in turn, heightens the consciousness of the oppressed group, leading to conflict.

From the 1960s until the 1990s, several states undertook policies to reduce race and ethnic consciousness and, hopefully, dampen the associated resentment and conflict. This frequently involved the engagement of two-pronged policies that encouraged assimilation and minimized racial, ethnic, and gender differences in the distribution of jobs, education, and other social goods, while simultaneously fostering group consciousness through affirmative action and the implementation of multicultural programs that advanced the maintenance of language, identity, political incorporation, and religious practice. Michael Banton (1997: 65) offers an interpretation of this apparent paradox, asserting that individual goal-seeking reduces group consciousness and promotes assimilation, but certain goals (like public goods) can be attained only by collective action.

However, following the downfall of the Soviet Union in 1990, which resulted in the obsolescence of state socialism (a major alternative to ethnic and racial bases of identity), the outbreak of terrible ethnic conflicts in the Balkan region, and the events of September 11, 2001 a decade later, many states became much more cynical about their ability to manage the negative manifestations of race and ethnic consciousness through tolerance and moderate state support. Instead, majoritarian movements from the US and the Netherlands to Zimbabwe and Iran asserted that major social conflicts are best resolved by privileging an idealized version of these states' cultural, religious, racial, and national roots, while restricting immigration and making few concessions on behalf of the cultural dispositions of religious, ethnic, and racial minorities.

In her provocatively titled book *World on Fire* (2003), legal scholar Amy Chua argued that, at least for the short term, the correlates of western modernization – the expansion of free markets plus democratization – will amplify rather than reduce ethnic conflict. This happens because under economic liberalization, the enhanced affluence of ethnically distinct minorities contrasts dramatically with the dire circumstances typically encountered by the local majority. As a result, entrepreneurial "outsiders" including South Asians in Fiji, Chinese in Malaysia, Jewish "oligarchs" in Russia, and whites in Zimbabwe and Bolivia have been subject to the vengeance of impoverished but politically empowered majorities. Consciousness of the differences between haves and have-nots activates retribution and may provoke the exit of highly visible targets.

Given the multiform nature of ethnic and racial identities in a globalized world marked by economic transformations, transnational ties, border-crossing social and religious movements, and increasing access to communication and travel, it appears likely that forms of ethnic and race consciousness will continue to be both complex and volatile social forces in the coming years.

SEE ALSO: Balkanization; Boundaries (Racial/Ethnic); Color Line; Conflict (Racial/Ethnic); Double Consciousness; Transnationalism

REFERENCES AND SUGGESTED READINGS

Banton, M. (1997) *Ethnic and Racial Consciousness*, 2nd edn. Longman, London and New York.

Blumer, H. (1999 [1958]) Race Relations as a Sense of Group Position. In: Gallagher C. A. (Ed.), *Rethinking the Color Line: Readings in Race and Ethnicity*. Mayfield, Mountain View, CA, pp. 99–105.

Bonilla-Silva, E. (2001) *White Supremacy and Racism in the Post-Civil Rights Era*. Lynne Rienner, Boulder, CO.

Chua, A. (2003) *World on Fire: How Exporting Free Market Democracy Breeds Ethnic Hatred and Global Instability*. Doubleday, New York.

Fredrickson, G. (1988) *The Arrogance of Race: Historical Perspectives on Slavery, Racism, and Social Inequality*. Wesleyan University Press, Middletown, CT.

Hartigan, J., Jr. (1999) *Racial Situations: Class Predicaments of Whiteness in Detroit*. Princeton University Press, Princeton.

Kasinitz, P., Mollenkopf, J. H., & Waters, M. C. (Eds.) (2004) *Becoming New Yorkers: Ethnographies of the New Second Generation*. Russell Sage Foundation, New York.

Lee, J. & Bean, F. (2004) America's Changing Color Lines: Immigration, Race/Ethnicity, and Multiracial Identification. *Annual Review of Sociology* 30: 221–42.

Light, I. & Gold, S. J. (2000) *Ethnic Economies*. Academic Press, San Diego.

Portes, A. & Rumbaut, R. G. (2001) *Legacies: The Story of the Immigrant Second Generation*. University of California Press, Berkeley.

Van Ausdale, D. & Feagin, J. E. (2001) *The First R: How Children Learn Race and Racism*. Rowman & Littlefield, Lanham, MD.

Waters, M. C. (1999) *Black Identities: West Indian Immigrant Dreams and American Realities*. Harvard University Press, Cambridge, MA.

Winant, H. (2001) *The World is a Ghetto: Race and Democracy Since World War II*. Basic Books, New York.

race and ethnic etiquette

Charles Jarmon

Forms of etiquette exist in nearly every society where different racial and ethnic groups are separated by extreme differences in economic wealth, political power, or social status. They are most developed in caste or caste-like societies, in which the lower-status racial or ethnic groups are enslaved or belong to economically exploited or subjugated groups. In these situations the patterns of etiquette regulate interpersonal relations between the higher and lower-status groups, functioning as codes of behavior designed to maintain the status quo (or a state of harmony within it) within which the more privileged groups benefit. Sociologists and other social scientists have studied the emergence, practice, and impact of these codes on population groups in countries around the world, including the US, India, Brazil, South Africa, Spain, Germany, Australia, and the countries of the circum-Caribbean (Dubois 1899; Reuter 1927; Park 1928; Doyle 1937; Myrdal 1944; Cox 1948; Frazier 1957; Sowell 1983; Bell 1992; Marable 2005). In any given society, the unique complexity and changes in the codes must be understood in terms of its own history and the currents of broad social and cultural change affecting it both from within and without.

Blacks have lived in the US for nearly 400 years, and for most of this period were enslaved. When freed after the Civil War the approximately half million freemen were unprepared educationally and economically to compete in a society still inclined to continue their subjection. The majority remained in the South, living in small towns or on farms as tenants along the rural black belt. They were forcefully united, to use a term from van den Berghe (1967), into an "exploitative symbiosis." Others migrated to the ghettos of Northern cities. This is the historical context from which broad patterns of racial and ethnic etiquette developed. This relationship appeared to have been more important after slavery, reflecting a state in which blacks had to struggle against economic dependency and subservience. Because it fostered mutually restricted associations on personal and professional levels between blacks and whites, the racial etiquette prevented free communication between the groups and so created an illusionary world within which both claimed to understand one another, despite their different interests and expectations within the status quo. Thus, sometimes, when protests over adverse circumstances disrupted the peaceful environment in the community, leading white citizens would often express their amazement. For many of them, blacks on their own would naturally not feel offended by not having the privilege to vote, to sit on local councils, to be able to run for political office, to be treated equally in social intercourse and in places of public accommodation, or to have their stories told in the local newspaper in a dignified manner. Outside the exceptional personal relationships, some of which are well documented in the literature, etiquette prevented discussion of such matters.

Whatever friendliness blacks possessed towards whites, and vice versa, was constrained by deeply institutionalized codes. Again, exceptions existed. Certain relations were taboo (e.g, dating and marriage) and these taboos were enshrined in ideology and protected by custom and law. This is clearly evident in their development in the Southern slave states as well as in the apartheid system of South Africa, which in many instances began on egalitarian terms between Native Americans and Europeans in the former, and between Africans and Europeans in the latter. The doctrine of racial supremacy provided the white slave owners in the US with a rationalization for enslaving Africans, after the experiment failed with Native Americans. In post-Reconstruction America, it provided a basis for perpetuating a legal system of discrimination against the freed African Americans.

Major court decisions before and after the period of slavery established in law the antidemocratic practices that inveighed against the humanity of the slave and ex-slave. The role played by custom, as a basis for regulating and controlling black–white relations, centered on how the two groups got along together under the circumstances of both situations – slavery and legal and *de facto* segregation – in that they were often forced, out of economic necessity, to live and work in close physical proximity, but socially isolated one from the other. Just as the formal legal decisions were established to repress blacks and to keep them submissive, the patterns of etiquette emerged as an informal system to keep them in their place; they were embodied in the rituals and ceremonials of everyday life and reflected the accommodation between blacks and whites.

If one had grown up in a Southern city during the 1940s and 1950s, one would have witnessed the patterns of etiquette practiced in enforced segregated churches, schools, workplaces, homes, and on buses and trains; the proscriptions against personal relationships and sexual unions and marriage; the submissive and deferential manners of contact in public places; and in the injustice rendered by the legal system. The institution of the patterns of etiquette fundamentally derived from the strategies of the ruling class of whites to maintain the economic and political dependency of blacks, and they were prepared to invoke the force of the law or to resort to extra-legal means to punish violators.

The patterns of deference symbolized in much of the behavior of blacks towards whites depended on the nature of the relation involved. For example, black males interacted deferentially with white males and avoided close personal contact with white women (this latter patterned behavior is denoted in the 1955 case in Mississippi involving the murder of Emmett Till, who allegedly whistled at a white woman); white males avoided working under black male supervisors, but would pursue personal relations with black women; and black and white children played together until the age of puberty, but avoided one another as adults. Black communities, however, developed ways of mitigating such experiences, one of which was by developing parallel social systems apart from those established by whites. These were found in black churches, schools, lodges, dance halls, music, art, literature, and humor. However, this does not represent the totality of the reaction of blacks to the codes supporting slavery and discrimination. Many rebelled in slavery by escaping with the Underground Railroad and emigrating to the North as far as Canada, with many joining the abolitionist movement against the system of slavery; others refused to remain in the country and escaped to Haiti; and many died in failed insurrections protesting against the dehumanizing system. Much of the scholarly literature on the subject of etiquette has generally focused narrowly on the psychological trauma, or on adaptive ways to prevent it, through examining the various forms of accommodation by blacks in subservient positions in the black–white relationship (Johnson 1943; Aikiss 1944; Frazier 1957; Grier & Cobbs 1968). There are notable exceptions to this approach (Morris 1986; Scott 1997). The popular media tended to highlight stereotypes depicting the acceptance by blacks of their position in the system. Neither has devoted sufficient attention to their protests and struggles against living under such debasing conditions.

In the US today the traditional patterns of etiquette are breaking down in the wake of enormous changes, including the urbanization of blacks; the *Brown vs. Board of Education* desegregation case; the Civil Rights and Black Power movements; the social reorganization of workplaces, where many blacks perform similar work as whites and interact with them as peers; and in other public places, where, through daily association, different attitudes and perceptions have helped to redefine black–white relationships. The new generation of African Americans has not learned the old patterns of deferential behavior and the younger generation of whites do not expect it. We are observing similar patterns of change associated with recent protest movements in such countries as Brazil and France. In the broadest sense, this suggests that the traditional patterns of etiquette, as means of social control, have lost social and political legitimacy. Sociologists must develop new conceptual approaches to explain a different set of circumstances in racial and ethnic relations.

SEE ALSO: Accommodation; Immigration; Race and Ethnic Consciousness; Race and Ethnic Politics; Racial Hierarchy; Segregation; Slavery

REFERENCES AND SUGGESTED READINGS

Aikiss, T. (1944) Changing Patterns of Religious Thought Among Negroes. *Social Forces* 23(1): 212–15.

Bell, D. (1992) *Race, Racism and the American Law*. Little, Brown, Boston.

Cox, O. C. (1948) *Caste, Class, and Race*. Monthly Review Press, New York.

Doyle, B. W. (1937) *The Etiquette of Race Relations in the South: A Study of Social Control*. Kennikat Press, Port Washington, NY.

DuBois, W. E. B. (1899) *The Philadelphia Negro: A Social Study*. Ginn, Philadelphia.

Frazier, E. F. (1957) *Race and Culture Contacts in the Modern World*. Knopf, New York.

Grier, W. & Cobbs, P. (1968) *Black Rage*. Bantam Books, New York.

Johnson, C. S. (1943) *Patterns of Negro Segregation*. Harper & Brothers, New York.

Marable, M. (2005) The Promise of Brown: Desegregation, Affirmative Action and the Struggle for Racial Equality. *Negro Educational Review* 56: 33–41.

Morris, A. (1986) *The Origins of the Civil Rights Movement: Black Communities Organizing for Change*. Free Press, New York.

Myrdal, G. (1944) *An American Dilemma: The Negro Problem and Modern Democracy*. Pantheon, New York.

Park, R. E. (1928) The Basis of Race Prejudices. *Annals of the American Academy of Political and Social Science* 140: 11–20.

Reuter, E. B. (1927) *The American Race Problem*. Crowell, New York.

Scott, D. M. (1997) *Contempt and Pity*. University of North Carolina Press, Chapel Hill.

Sowell, T. (1983) *The Economics and Politics of Race*. Quill, New York.

van den Berghe, P. L. (1967) *Race and Racism: A Comparative Perspective*. John Wiley, New York.

race and ethnic politics

Mario L. Small

The sociology of race and ethnic politics examines the impact of political factors on the status of racial and ethnic minorities, and the impact of ethnicity and race on politics and public policy. The field has investigated political movements, voting rights, immigration laws, internal migration patterns, the judicial system, citizenship, and, recently, ethnic identity.

Throughout American history the struggle over the political rights of racial and ethnic minorities has been intertwined with the nation's economic and demographic growth, and neither can be understood without the other. Through the nineteenth century, legal slavery guaranteed the US a large, unpaid labor force that established the country's economic superiority. In the nineteenth, twentieth, and twenty-first centuries this economic strength has been sustained by large waves of low-skilled immigrants accepting very low wages for hard labor, from building railroads and canals, to fitting pipes and erecting steel and concrete buildings, to gardening, caring for children of middle-class families, cleaning toilets in hotels and office buildings, and washing dishes and delivering meals in restaurants. As the country has shifted from an agricultural, to a manufacturing, to a service economy, the labor of ethnic minorities has been central at every turn. Many of the political conflicts of the nation have emerged as these ethnic and racial minorities demand equal protection under the law and equal political participation.

NINETEENTH-CENTURY FOUNDATIONS

After the Emancipation Proclamation of 1863 the presence of free African Americans threatened the political and economic superiority of white Southerners. The end of Reconstruction brought the beginning of the Jim Crow era, as disgruntled white Southerners sought to retain the separation between blacks and whites. State legislatures throughout the South enacted laws requiring racial segregation in public facilities such as restaurants, theaters, and buses. Legal and illegal methods were employed to keep blacks from voting, such as the poll tax and the imposition of literacy requirements for a population that had been legally denied education for centuries. This era also saw the emergence of the Ku Klux Klan, a clandestine political white supremacist group that, through public lynching, fire-bombing, cross-burning, and death threats, terrorized the black population. The result was a widespread disenfranchisement of African Americans.

During this period the rest of the country was in the midst of a major industrial expansion, spurred by technological innovation and fed by the western expansion. Immigrants from Asia and Europe flocked to the country for work in the railroads and other industries and to search for higher incomes. Soon, anti-Chinese sentiment throughout the country, and especially in California, grew to the point of motivating legislative action. The Chinese Exclusion Act of 1882 suspended immigration of Chinese laborers for 10 years, and later, in 1904, suspended it indefinitely. This was the first major law to restrict immigration on a large scale. It also targeted a single ethnic group, not only restricting immigration but also establishing ineligibility for naturalization.

By the turn of the century it was clear to sociologist and essayist W. E. B. Du Bois (2003) that "the problem of the twentieth century" would be "the problem of the color line." Du Bois was referring to conflicts between people of all ethnic backgrounds, whom he saw in a persisting conflict over political and economic rights as the country faced unprecedented levels of racial and ethnic diversity. These conflicts inevitably involved questions of immigration and citizenship, which were often inextricably linked with questions of race.

By the 1920s the racial anxieties of the country were codified into law. The Immigration Act of 1924 restricted immigration based on national quotas aimed explicitly at maintaining a racial balance tilted toward whites of Western European heritage. The Act restricted the number of immigrants each year, favored immigrants from Western Europe, limited the number of immigrants from Eastern and Southern Europe and from Africa, and barred immigrants from Asia. Germany, for example, had a quota of more than 50,000 immigrants a year; Greece, 100 immigrants; the entire African continent (excluding Egypt), 100.

While Du Bois's predictions about interracial political conflict had proven increasingly accurate, his greatest concern as a sociological researcher was the status of African Americans. His theory about the conditions of African Americans was both a framework for understanding the present and a prescription for improving their future. For Du Bois, political disenfranchisement of blacks and their economic deprivation went hand in hand. Blacks who were segregated were unable to use the political system to secure the resources required for their education and economic development. In this, he famously disagreed with Booker T. Washington, former slave turned educator, who believed that the best way for blacks in the South to overcome poverty and destitution was to ignore the question of racial segregation and focus on self-education and building their own institutions from the ground up. Du Bois argued that resisting segregation and fighting for their political rights were indispensable; for him, economic development without political incorporation was impossible.

THE TWENTIETH CENTURY

The combination of the South's dwindling sharecropping economy, segregation, institutional discrimination, and political disenfranchisement prompted many African Americans to begin to look north for greater opportunities. The industrial expansion of Northern cities began to look extremely attractive to a population that had always been concentrated in the South. This was especially true given that factories, now significantly deprived of low-wage immigrant labor, clamored for laborers. The first half of the twentieth century saw the Great Migration of blacks to the industrial centers of the Northeast and Midwest, to cities such as Chicago, New York, Detroit, Philadelphia, and St. Louis. This decades-long migration produced high concentrations of African Americans in the inner cities of the North.

It also laid the foundation for the most significant moment in race and ethnic politics in the US of the twentieth century, the Civil Rights Movement. This movement was the largest and most sustained civil rights collective mobilization in the nation's history, aimed at eliminating legal segregation and enforcing the constitutional rights that guaranteed equal political participation. The movement took many forms, including collective protest in the form of sit-ins, boycotts, lawsuits, and non-violent civil disobedience, which often resulted in violent repression by the state.

Several key events marked the successes of the movement. Racial segregation had been upheld by the Supreme Court in *Plessy* v. *Ferguson* (1896), which held that "separate but equal" facilities for members of different races were constitutionally acceptable. After a series of challenges by lawyers from the National Association for the Advancement of Colored People, the Supreme Court in *Brown* v. *Board of Education* (1954) ruled that separate educational facilities were inherently unequal. Segregation suffered an additional blow with the passing of the Civil Rights Act of 1964, which outlawed discrimination in hotels, restaurants, theaters, and other public accommodations, or segregation on the basis of race, color, religion, or national origin. Finally, the Voting Rights Act of 1965 enforced the guarantees of the 15th Amendment that no person shall be denied a vote because of race or color, outlawing Jim Crow disenfranchisement tactics such as literacy requirements for voting.

That year also saw the passage of a law that radically altered the nation's approach to immigration. The Immigration Act of 1965 eliminated the quota system in place since the 1920s, such that the main factor in determining selection for admission was occupation. In addition, a central clause in the Act gave preference to those who had family in the US. This clause precipitated the large wave of immigration of Latin Americans, Asians, West Indians, and others, which continues today.

RACE, CLASS, AND POLITICS

The 1960s were pivotal. According to Wilson (1987), the Civil Rights Movement and Affirmative Action policies had succeeded in opening opportunities for African Americans during the 1970s and 1980s. The most resourceful African Americans were able to attend better educational institutions, work at better jobs, earn higher salaries, and move to the suburbs. In effect, the Civil Rights Movement contributed to the creation of a large African American middle class.

However, this growth also left a concentration of poor, low-skilled blacks in segregated inner cities. Many of the African Americans who first migrated to the Northern cities had found work in manufacturing industries, such as car companies. By mid-century, the large employers in the manufacturing sector had started to move to the suburbs in search of cheaper land and greater profits. The cities had begun major shifts from manufacturing-based economies to service-based ones, developing high concentrations of low-skilled blacks unable to find work. Limited occupational opportunities, increasing crime and incarceration, and financially strapped school systems reliant on a weaker tax base only worsened the prospects for this group. Wilson called this group the underclass.

Scholars debated the relative significance of race and class extensively. Wilson argued that economic factors, demographic shifts, and the political success of the Civil Rights Movement led to the creation of an underclass. However,

Massey and Denton (1993) argued that this theory, based on the political economy, ignored the impact of persistent racial discrimination and residential segregation. They argued that by focusing on class, Wilson had ignored the persisting significance of race. Discrimination by lenders, steering practices by real estate agents, legal covenants restricting home sales to minorities, and poor enforcement of antidiscrimination legislation made it difficult for blacks to find homes in neighborhoods with good schools and low crime rates. In fact, they argued, despite the important political gains of the Civil Rights Movement, segregation has persisted over the last half of the twentieth century.

Despite their disagreements, theorists of both political economy and residential segregation agreed that without intervention the problems of the underclass were likely to perpetuate themselves. So did lawmakers. The last decades of the twentieth century saw determined efforts by both conservatives and liberals to address inner-city poverty, and especially to reform the welfare system. Though these arguments were about public policy and the status of the poor, they were couched in explicitly political and racial terms, as images such as the "welfare queen" were used to discredit the welfare system. Conservatives tended to argue that the inner-city poor remained in this condition due to a weakened value system and absence of work ethic, or because the welfare system discouraged work. Liberals tended to argue that racial discrimination and poor labor-market prospects were at fault. This debate culminated in the Personal Responsibility and Work Opportunity Act (PRWORA) of 1996, which toughened eligibility requirements. Women with children seeking government or welfare aid faced time limits and work requirements in order to receive assistance.

PRWORA, riding the most recent wave of anti-immigrant sentiment, also denied public assistance to legal immigrants, who were now in a position of paying taxes to support government benefits for which they were not eligible. Later laws allowed limited assistance to immigrants who had entered the country before 1996. Anti-immigrant sentiment persisted through the end of the twentieth century. In California, voters in 1994 approved Proposition 187, which denied education and medical attention to undocumented immigrants, though the measure was later deemed unconstitutional.

This period also brought about the rapid growth of identity politics and a heightened discourse around immigrants, ethnic minorities, and national identity. On college campuses this was evident in the proliferation and growth of ethnic studies programs, modeled on the black studies programs started in the 1960s. Debates over the definition of an American, and over the identity of immigrants, and their children, have been ubiquitous in the media, books, theater, and the arts. Individuals increasingly claim more than one racial identity, and the 2000 Census for the first time allowed respondents to mark more than one race. In addition, immigrants increasingly live a transnational existence, sending large remittances to their home countries and participating in home country politics. Countries, in turn, have increasingly allowed immigrants to claim more than one nationality, such that many may vote in the US and in their home countries.

IDENTITY POLITICS WORLDWIDE

Throughout the world the interaction of race, economics, and politics has become intertwined with the problems of immigration and citizenship, as ethnic identity continues to shape political struggles. In some countries, particularly in Western Europe, rapid immigration from Africa and the Middle East has produced reactionary opposition in the receiving countries and organized mobilization for political and citizenship rights among immigrants. Recently in France, after a small incident in which two immigrant youths died electrocuted in a subway station after being chased by the police, the country experienced the most serious and extended period of civil unrest since the 1960s. The unrest was concentrated in the poor suburbs of the city among politically disenfranchised, primarily immigrant youths with high unemployment rates. In other countries the colonial legacy of placing traditionally distinct and opposing ethnic groups under a single rule has resulted in violent, long-lasting strife as former colonies became nation-states. In Rwanda, the genocide of 800,000 Tutsis in the mid-1990s can be traced directly to the efforts by majority Hutus to wrest control from Tutsis of the resources of the new nation-state after its independence from Belgium in the 1950s. Many of the continuing political struggles have been both ethnic and religious, as fundamentalist religious movements, particularly among conservative Christians and Muslims, enter the political fray in increasingly organized fashion, whether through the media, through grassroots political organizations, or, in extreme cases, through violent attacks. Despite the heterogeneity of these ethnic political conflicts, rarely can they be understood independently of the large and small-scale economic issues surrounding them, whether it is the supply of labor, the control of natural resources, or individuals' yearning for stable employment at home or abroad.

SEE ALSO: Identity Politics/Relational Politics; Immigration; Race; Race and Ethnic Consciousness; Race and Ethnic Etiquette; Race (Racism); Social Problems, Politics of

REFERENCES AND SUGGESTED READINGS

Alba, R. & Nee, V. (2003) *Remaking the American Mainstream: Assimilation and Contemporary Immigration.* Harvard University Press, Cambridge, MA.

Du Bois, W. E. B. (2003 [1903]) *The Souls of Black Folk.* Random House, New York.

Lieberson, S. (1980) *A Piece of the Pie: Blacks and White Immigrants Since 1880.* University of California Press, Berkeley.

McAdam, D. (1982) *Political Process and the Development of Black Insurgency, 1930–1970.* University of Chicago Press, Chicago.

Massey, D. & Denton, N. (1993) *American Apartheid: Segregation and the Making of the Underclass.* Harvard University Press, Cambridge, MA.

Portes, A. & Rumbaut, R. (1996) *Immigrant America: A Portrait.* University of California Press, Los Angeles.

Steinberg, S. (1981) *The Ethnic Myth: Race, Ethnicity and Class in America.* Simon & Schuster, New York.

Wilson, W. J. (1987) *The Truly Disadvantaged: The Inner City, the Underclass, and Public Policy.* University of Chicago Press, Chicago.

race (racism)

Pierre L. van den Berghe

The term "racism" widely entered the social science vocabulary in the 1930s, as part of the Boasian reaction against the social Darwinism of the late nineteenth and early twentieth centuries. Ruth Benedict, a student of Franz Boas, was one of the prominent early users. By the 1950s and 1960s, a broad consensus developed as to what racism meant, namely, an attitude or theory that some human groups, socially defined by biological descent and physical appearance, were superior or inferior to other groups in physical, intellectual, cultural, or moral properties. It was clearly understood that "races" were socially defined, differently in different societies, but according to physical phenotypes, such as skin color, facial features, or hair texture.

Racism, so defined, was differentiated from ethnocentrism, also a belief or theory of inequality between human groups, but where that inequality was ascribed to some aspect of culture, such as moral values, religion, language, or "level of civilization." Ethnocentrism, i.e., a preference for one's own cultural group, was held to be universal, but not so racism. The latter was generally ascribed to European expansion, imperialism, colonialism, and chattel slavery in the nineteenth century, and associated with Fascism and Nazism in the twentieth century.

During this earlier social science consensus, racism was also clearly kept analytically distinct from discrimination, segregation, and other features of systematic inequality between ascribed groups. Racism was defined as an attitude, a prejudice, a theory, in short, an ideational system held in individual human minds. Discrimination, segregation, ostracism, and so on, were treated as forms of behavior which included or excluded certain groups, and which were frequently, but not necessarily, associated with the racist beliefs of their practitioners. One could be an unprejudiced discriminator, or, conversely, a prejudiced non-discriminator. Behavior was held to be a function not only of beliefs, but also of sanctions. Unprejudiced discriminators could be found in racial caste societies, like apartheid South Africa. Conversely, where discrimination is punished, prejudiced individuals often refrain from discriminatory behavior.

This state of conceptual clarity did not last long. It gradually disintegrated under repeated attacks, mostly from the left, starting in the 1970s, and continuously escalating until the present. In a first stage, the distinction between race and ethnicity was increasingly confounded. Since race was socially, not biologically, defined, and since ethnicity was often based on a theory of common descent, the distinction between the two was held to be spurious. Explicitly or implicitly, authors began to use the two terms interchangeably, to the detriment of analytical rigor. Often, race was defined away as ethnicity, but, conversely, ethnocentrism was frequently denounced as racism. The term "racism" was increasingly used as an invective of ever widening scope.

On a second front, the distinction between belief and behavior, between prejudice and discrimination, came under growing assault. The key moment here was the rapid acceptance of the concept of "institutional racism," hailed by many as a great analytic advance, when, in fact, the only advance was in an ideological agenda. Institutional racism referred to the structural inequalities between racial and/or ethnic groups, in short, to the consequences of behavioral discrimination. These were said to be independent of individual attitudes, indeed, to have a self-perpetuating institutional life of their own. Attitudes were asserted to be irrelevant to the existence of institutional racism.

In brief, the double distinction between race and ethnicity, and between attitudes and behavior, was now defunct, so that almost any statistical difference between any two ascribed groups could now be termed "racism." Intention did not matter. (By analogy, any structural difference between men and women was now labeled "sexism.") The stage was now set for the transformation of racism from a relatively precise analytical concept to an elastic term of opprobrium applied to almost anything one disapproved of. Lucid analysis of complex multicultural and/or multiracial societies all too often yielded to ideologically inspired mush.

The ultimate extension of the concept of racism occurred during the last 10 or 15 years. Explicit refusal to take race into account, and profession of an ideology and practice of "race-blindness," are now often held to be a novel and subtle form of racism. If you say race matters, you are, by definition, a racist. If, however, you say race does not matter, you are a racist as well, because race really does matter. Thus, for instance, opposition to race-based "affirmative action," on the ground that it uses a racial criterion to produce racial discrimination, now qualifies as neoracism. Racism and anti-racism are neatly equated. The latter is merely a cryptic form of the former.

What are we to make of all this sociologically constructed confusion? Underlying the evolution of the concept of racism is a deeply contradictory "liberal" ideology. On the one hand, statistical differences between ascriptive groups based on race or ethnicity are declared illegitimate, or, at least, suspect, and therefore subject to remedial action, including policies based on the very criteria which constitute the foundation of the differences. One seeks to abolish or reduce differences by reinforcing and entrenching the criteria of group membership that underlie these differences. On the other hand, liberal ideology in multicultural and/or multiracial societies extols and celebrates "diversity." On the face of it, it would seem that one can not simultaneously eradicate differences between ascribed groups and extol them. At best, one can try to destigmatize existing differences and reduce their adverse consequences.

That said, social science theory and ideology – the two, by the way, are often hard to distinguish – must face two stubbornly persistent realities.

First, whenever two or more ethnic and/or racial groups have formed a common society (by conquest, slavery, or voluntary immigration), the result has, with few exceptions, been some degree of hierarchy and social differentiation between groups. Some groups are more powerful or affluent; groups tend to aggregate spatially; and an ethnic division of labor often sets in. Try to imagine a US society, for instance, where diamond cutters, taxi drivers, and basketball players would each have a proportional representation of Jews, Sikhs, and African Americans.

The elusive search for proportional group representation in every aspect of education, employment, residential distribution, and so on, often brings massive state intervention. The latter is not only doomed to failure in most cases, but frequently boomerangs. Such attempts have often consolidated group distinctions and exacerbated conflicts. This is not to say that ethnic or racial hierarchies are immutable. They can be rapidly overturned by revolution, for instance. But the proportional representation society is a utopia.

Second, one of the greatest human universals is that most people show a strong preference for others who are like themselves, and that the main fault lines of these preferences have largely followed the social boundaries of race and ethnicity. Indeed, these fault lines have been formed by these preferences. Whenever a phenomenon is universal in our species, it begs for an explanation that is not purely based on social constructionism.

Sociobiology has provided an answer for the universality of preference for one's "own kind," and for resistance to sharing scarce resources with unrelated others. Evolution by natural selection has predisposed us (as well as countless other species) to favor others to the extent that we are biologically related. By doing so, we have maximized our "inclusive fitness," i.e., the representation of our genome in successive generations. We are predisposed to favor kin over non-kin, and close kin over distant kin. Ethnic or racial groups are simply extensions of kinship. Ethnocentrism and racism are nepotism writ large.

Almost all cultures have normatively *reinforced this genetic predisposition.* They have regarded familism, nepotism, and ethnocentrism as normal, expected behavior, even if a few cultures have sought to control and limit them. Any culture that seeks to counteract nepotism faces an uphill battle. Perhaps the best social policy would be one that accepts the reality of nepotism, ethnocentrism, and racism, but seeks to contain them as preference for one's own kind, and to prevent their extension into hatred of others. *The latter does not follow from the former.*

Any sociology that claims to be a science of human behavior cannot continue to ignore the biological bases of that behavior, and explain it purely in social constructionist terms. Of course, we constantly construct and reconstruct our social reality, but not in a biological vacuum. Genes and culture complexly interact to produce behavior and social structure.

SEE ALSO: Boundaries (Racial/Ethnic); Conflict (Racial/Ethnic); Discrimination; Ethnic Groups; Ethnic and Racial Division of Labor; Ethnicity; Ethnocentrism; Race; Race and the Criminal Justice System; Race/Ethnicity, Health, and Mortality; Racial Hierarchy

REFERENCES AND SUGGESTED READINGS

Benedict, R. (1943) *Race, Science, and Politics.* Viking, New York.

Horowitz, D. L. (1985) *Ethnic Groups in Conflict.* University of California Press, Berkeley.

Mason, P. (1971) *Patterns of Dominance.* Oxford University Press, Oxford.

Rex, J. & Mason, D. (Eds.) (1986) *Theories of Race and Ethnic Relations.* Cambridge University Press, Cambridge.

Van den Berghe, P. L. (1967) *Race and Racism.* Wiley, New York.

Van den Berghe, P. L. (1981) *The Ethnic Phenomenon.* Elsevier, New York.

race and schools

Thomas F. Pettigrew

Race and schools become a social issue when educational opportunities are differentially available to members of diverse racial groups within a society. Educational discrimination has a variety of effects that often lead to interracial conflict. Since education is a major means of social mobility, discrimination in this domain forces the less-favored racial groups to occupy lower-status jobs and receive less income. Such results form a vital component in a wider system of racial oppression, as in South Africa during apartheid and the state-mandated segregation in the American South.

Racially segregated schools are the hallmark of racial discrimination in education. As under South Africa's apartheid and the South's segregation, separate schools allow for vastly fewer resources to be provided for the oppressed race. Indeed, racially separate schools are so central to systems of racial oppression that they are tenaciously maintained in the face of efforts to end them. The protracted and only partially successful efforts to end segregated schools in the US provides a striking illustration.

Public schools did not emerge in the American South until late in the nineteenth century, and these early schools were for whites only. Black schools came later after formal Southern state laws for racial segregation had been sanctioned in 1896 by the US Supreme Court in *Plessy* v. *Ferguson.* Homer Plessy, who had one black great-grandparent, had been arrested for riding in a rail car reserved for whites under a new Louisiana law. He sued and claimed the law unconstitutional. The High Court rejected his plea. Only Justice John Harlan, a former slaveholder, dissented with his famous assertion that "our Constitution is color-blind." While it involved railroad seating, this decision was promptly translated by the white South into separate schools as well. Although *Plessy* established the formula of "separate but equal," Southern schools became very separate and unequal.

It took 58 years before the High Court would overturn *Plessy.* By 1950, in two graduate education cases, the meaning of "equal" went beyond mere parity in brick-and-mortar terms to include such intangibles as faculty reputation and general prestige. The decisions prepared the ground for *Brown* v. *Board of Education* four years later to hold separate facilities to be inherently unequal. But implementing this unpopular decision in the hostile Southern US proved difficult.

Critical to the acceptance of mandated social change that runs counter to dominant public opinion is the perception of inevitability. The responses of the white South to the varying firmness of the High Court's rulings illustrate the point. With an uncompromising, nine-to-nothing decision in *Brown,* the Court in 1954 generated a strong sense of inevitability even in the Deep South. But in 1955 the Supreme Court retreated in its implementation order to a vague "all deliberate speed" formula (*Brown II*). This formula returned the enforcement of desegregation back to Southern federal district courts without guidelines. Only when this weak order undermined the sense of inevitability did Southern politicians become uniformly defiant and pro-segregationist organizations gain momentum. The opposition now believed *Brown* could be effectively opposed. *Brown II* is not solely responsible for the violent opposition that followed. But its vagueness contributed to the resistance by eroding the strong sense of inevitability that had prevailed.

Consequently, the region's school desegregation did not take hold until the federal courts lost patience between 1968 and 1973 (Orfield 1978; Orfield & Eaton 1996). This brief period saw court orders achieve sweeping gains – especially in the recalcitrant South, but also in the cities of the North and West. By the 1970s the South had more racial desegregation in its public schools than any other region. But this process ended abruptly in 1974 when the Supreme Court reversed direction. In *Milliken* v. *Bradley* the Court by five to four struck down a metropolitan solution ordered by a district court to remedy the intense racial segregation of Detroit's public schools. What makes this decision so regressive is that such remedies are the *only* means available to desegregate the public schools of many of the nation's largest cities (Orfield & Eaton 1996; Pettigrew 1981). Moreover, between-district segregation is now by far the major component today in metropolitan school segregation (Clotfelter 2004). Decisions of the High Court from 1974 into the twenty-first century continued this trend, and allowed racial segregation of the public schools to return not only in the South but also throughout much of the US.

In short, *Brown* was largely reversed without the High Court ever stating that it was overturning the famous decision. By 2000, black children were more likely to be attending majority-black schools than at any time since the 1960s; 70 percent went to predominantly black schools and 37 percent to schools with 90 percent or more black students. The greatest retrogression during the 1990s occurred in the South, the region that had previously witnessed the greatest gains (Orfield 2001). And Latino school children became more educationally segregated from white children than African American children (Orfield & Eaton 1996).

Supporting this retreat from desegregated schools, the sociologist James Coleman claimed in a highly publicized speech that urban interracial schools were impossible to achieve because desegregation causes massive "white flight." It led, he claimed, to whites fleeing to the suburbs and leaving minority concentrations in central city cores. This research had serious weaknesses and its policy recommendations ignored metropolitan solutions (Pettigrew 1981).

The white flight thesis is actually far more complex than Coleman claimed (Pettigrew & Green 1976). Some whites did move from large cities when school desegregation began. However, this movement was neither universal nor permanently damaging. Some cities without any school desegregation also experienced widespread white suburbanization. Other cities experienced little such movement at the time of desegregation. And where so-called white flight to the suburbs did occur, it constituted a "hastening up" process; within a few years the loss was what would have been expected without desegregation (Farley et al. 1980).

But does school desegregation improve the life chances and choices of African Americans? From the 1970s to the 1990s, black high school completion rates rose sharply. While less than half finished high school at mid-century, by 2000 the figure approached that of white Americans. During these same years, the mean difference between black and white achievement test scores steadily narrowed. White scores were improving, but blacks who entered school during the late 1960s revealed especially strong gains – when extensive school desegregation began. But these positive trends stalled and were even reversed by the late 1990s once the federal courts allowed resegregation. Yet these trends are only suggestive, since other factors were also influential – notably, rising black incomes and such effective national educational programs as Headstart.

More to the point, did school desegregation expand opportunities for African Americans in the long term? An array of sociological studies tracked the products of desegregated schools in later life to find answers (Pettigrew 2004). With social class controlled, black children from desegregated schools, when compared with black children from segregated schools, are more likely later (1) to attend and finish majority-white colleges; (2) to work with white co-workers and have better jobs; (3) to live in interracial neighborhoods; (4) to have somewhat higher incomes; and (5) to have more white friends and contacts and more positive attitudes toward whites. Similarly, white products of desegregation have more positive attitudes toward blacks than comparable whites from segregated schools. In short, desegregated education prepares black and white Americans for an interracial world.

These positive lifetime effects of desegregation do not primarily reflect test score gains. More important is the fact that desegregation enables African Americans to break through the monopoly that white Americans have traditionally had on informational flows and institutional access. Sociologists have identified several interrelated processes underlying this phenomenon (Pettigrew 2004). These processes mirror the harsh fact that life chances in America flow through white-dominated institutions.

Desegregation involves interracial contact. Intergroup contact is one of social psychology's best established theories. A comprehensive meta-analysis found that 95 percent of 714 independent samples with 250,000 subjects show that intergroup contact reduces prejudice (Pettigrew & Tropp 2006).

Desegregation teaches interracial interaction skills. Given the nation's racist past, neither black nor white Americans are skilled in interracial interaction. The products of desegregated schools have the opportunity to learn these skills. Their anxiety about such interaction is reduced. This is highly useful for both blacks and whites, for it contributes to their willingness to enter biracial environments and their acceptance in these situations.

Desegregation erodes avoidance learning (Pettigrew 1964). After facing discriminatory treatment, some black Americans learn to avoid whites. But this reaction has negative consequences. It closes off for ghetto dwellers the better opportunities that exist in the wider society. And, like all avoidance learning, it keeps one from knowing when the situation has changed. Desegregated schooling overcomes such avoidance.

Desegregated blacks gain access to formally all-white social networks. Information about colleges and jobs flows largely through formally all-white networks. This process does not require personal friendships. Weak interpersonal ties are the most informative, because close friends are likely to possess the same information (Granovetter 1983). Interracial schools allow black students to gain access to these networks.

Thus, although not popularly recognized, the racial desegregation of American's public schools has led to positive outcomes. But the resegregation of the nation's schools in the twenty-first century threatens to retard and even reverse these beneficial processes.

While America's racial scene has many unique features, social research in other nations suggests that similar intergroup processes operate in schools throughout the world. Additional research is needed, but the separation of groups in schools and other societal institutions, whether the groups are racial or not, appears to have comparably negative effects. In addition to thwarting beneficial intergroup contact, intergroup separation triggers a series of interlocking processes that make group conflict more likely. Negative stereotypes not only persist but are magnified, distrust accumulates, and misperceptions and awkwardness typify the limited intergroup interaction that does take place. The powerful majority comes in time to believe that segregated housing, low-skilled jobs, and constrained educational opportunities are justified, even "appropriate," for the minority.

Intergroup schools have proven to be one of the needed antidotes for combating these negative processes – from Northern Ireland to the Republic of South Africa.

SEE ALSO: *Brown* v. *Board of Education*; Education; Education Inequality; Massive Resistance; School Segregation, Desegregation

REFERENCES AND SUGGESTED READINGS

Clotfelter, C. T. (2004) *After Brown: The Rise and Retreat of School Desegregation.* Princeton University Press, Princeton.

Farley, R., Richards, T., & Werdock, C. (1980) School Desegregation and White Flight: An Investigation of Competing Models and their Discrepant Findings. *Sociology of Education* 53: 123–39.

Granovetter, M. S. (1983) The Strength of Weak Ties: A Network Theory Revisited. *Sociological Theory* 1: 201–33.

Orfield, G. (1978) *Must We Bus? Segregated Schools and National Policy.* Brookings Institution, Washington, DC.

Orfield, G. (2001) *Schools More Separate: Consequences of a Decade of Resegregation.* Harvard University Civil Rights Project, Cambridge, MA.

Orfield, G. & Eaton, S. E. (1996) *Dismantling Desegregation: The Quiet Reversal of Brown v. Board of Education.* New Press, New York.

Pettigrew, T. F. (1964) *Profile of the Negro American.* Van Nostrand, Princeton.

Pettigrew, T. F. (1981) The Case for Metropolitan Approaches to Public School Desegregation. In: Yarmolinsky, A., Liebman, L., & Schelling, C. S. (Eds.), *Race and Schooling in the City.* Harvard University Press, Cambridge, MA, pp. 163–81.

Pettigrew, T. F. (2004) Justice Deferred: A Half Century after *Brown v. Board of Education. American Psychologist* 59(6): 521–9.

Pettigrew, T. F. & Green, R. L. (1976) School Desegregation in Large Cities: A Critique of the Coleman "White Flight" Thesis. *Harvard Educational Review* 46: 1–53.

Pettigrew, T. F. & Tropp, L. (2006) A Meta-Analytic Test of Intergroup Contact Theory. *Journal of Personality and Social Psychology.*

race/ethnicity and friendship

Will Tyson

Race and ethnicity are important factors in friendship formation. People tend to form friendships with others who live near them and who occupy similar social positions, belong to the same organizations, and are like themselves in terms of attitudes, values, and behaviors. Race and ethnicity are often cues of these similarities; therefore, race and ethnicity structure friendship formation (McPherson et al. 2001). People are likely to associate with others of their own race if the racial composition of the populations and distribution of members of a race throughout substructures of the population provide opportunities for same-race friendships to form.

Researchers have found evidence that race and ethnicity influence various types of relationships, ranging from marriage to workplace relationships to friendships to mere discussion networks (McPherson et al. 2001). These studies show that interracial relationships occur less often than would be expected given the available opportunities for them. Structures such as families, workplaces, organizations, and neighborhoods bring people together as kin, co-workers, members, and neighbors, but they do not ensure the formation of strong ties or close friendships (Feld & Carter 1998).

A recent Brown University study finds that interracial friendships are no more common in the United States than they are in post-apartheid South Africa, probably because elements of apartheid are found in America. Massey and Denton (1993) coined the term "American apartheid" to describe the unique residential hypersegregation of blacks across large metropolitan areas in the United States. Scholars have referred to residential segregation as the "structural linchpin" of race relations in America (Bobo & Zubrinsky 1996). People of different races generally do not live close to each other, so interracial interaction and interracial friendships are not as common as they might be otherwise.

Lack of proximity contributes to social distance between people of different races. Zipf (1949) asserts that people are willing to expend little effort toward establishing ties outside their local area. People with low interracial contact in their local area are more likely to be attracted to those they perceive to be similar to themselves, probably through racial cues. Growing up in predominantly white neighborhoods can teach blacks and other minorities to forgo racial cues and choose friends based on similarity to themselves on more attitudinal dimensions (Korgen 2002: 73). Interracial contact within neighborhoods is often a result of racial preferences. Blacks prefer to live in mixed neighborhoods, but few whites accept living in a neighborhood that is more than 20 percent black (Massey & Denton 1993). In fact, whites generally do not want to live near blacks, even when controlling for socioeconomic status (Steinhorn 2000).

Those who form interracial friendships may face social sanctions from same-race friends. Blacks with a white close friend overwhelmingly report disapproval from black friends, family, or acquaintances. Whites with a black close friend report generally positive reaction to their interracial friendships, but these reactions seem to imply that black–white friendships are a novelty and provide false evidence of harmony between blacks and whites in America (Korgen 2002).

Black–white racial tension in America has led to the current research emphasis on black–white friendships, but interracial tension between white, black, Latino, and Asian people in society is an emerging area of scholarship to complement research on black–white conflict. Classic research by Bogardus (1959) and consequent follow-up studies continue to suggest that the social distance between whites and blacks is greater than the distance between whites and people of other ethnicities. When given an option, whites prefer to associate with Latinos and Asians instead of with blacks (Bobo & Zubrinsky 1996). A Latino or Asian person with a third grade education is more likely to live among whites than a black person with a doctoral degree. With higher intermarriage rates with whites compared to blacks, native-born Latinos and Asians are assimilating while blacks have not been able to integrate fully (Steinhorn 2000). Blacks often face social pressures to end interracial friendships with white peers, but black peers typically accept friendships with Asians and Latinos (Korgen 2002).

Few social arenas promote social interactions between people of diverse racial and ethnic backgrounds, so a great deal of research on multi-ethnic interracial friendship takes place in educational contexts, specifically in colleges and universities. Fifty years of desegregation in American education since *Brown* v. *Board of Education* has provided researchers with social settings in which to study how diverse people interact and form friendships. Multicultural universities emphasize the importance of diversity in bringing people together to encourage positive interracial contact. Administrators believe that positive contact in cooperative environments leads to positive attitudes and positive interracial relationships. Critics of increasing diversity claim that it leads to conflict, while its proponents claim that the university plays an invaluable role in promoting interracial friendships among students who bring their own individual friendship experiences and expectations to the college setting.

Research shows that interracial interaction in an egalitarian setting such as a university can both promote and discourage interracial friendship. Administrators seek to increase racial and ethnic diversity in hopes that positive interactions among young people of similar age, intelligence, and academic background in residential, social, classroom, extracurricular, and co-curricular settings will lead to interracial friendship. Critics of affirmative action and other policies that seek to increase diversity often emphasize self-segregation among college students as evidence of negative consequences of multicultural universities. Minority students may feel marginalized in their campus surroundings and seek out friendships with other students of their own race (Tyson 2002). The term "self-segregation" implies that minority students segregate themselves from their white classmates despite sufficient opportunities for contact and friendship formation with white students around campus. Critics of affirmative action and other programs that promote diversity often do not recognize that white students also fail to take advantage of opportunities to form friendships with minority students.

Current and past research suggests that people will form friendships with others with similar behaviors and characteristics. Future research should continue to explore interaction among people of different races and ethnicities in situations in which friendship development is possible. This research should examine the similarities among these people across multiple dimensions such as proximity, psychological characteristics, background, and experiences and how these similarities contribute to friendship formation despite racial and ethnic differences.

SEE ALSO: *Brown* v. *Board of Education*; Cultural Diversity and Aging: Ethnicity, Minorities, and Subcultures; Friendship, Social Inequality, and Social Change; Friendship: Structure and Context; Gender, Friendship and; Race and Schools; School Segregation, Desegregation

REFERENCES AND SUGGESTED READINGS

Bobo, L. & Zubrinsky, C. (1996) Attitudes on Residential Integration: Perceived Status Differences, Mere In-Group Preference, or Racial Prejudice? *Social Forces* 74(3): 883–900.

Bogardus, E. S. (1959) *Social Distance.* Antioch, Yellow Springs, OH.

Feld, S. L. & Carter, W. C. (1998) When Desegregation Reduces Interracial Contact: A Class Size Paradox for Weak Ties. *American Journal of Sociology* 103(5): 1165–86.

Granovetter, M. (1973) The Strength of Weak Ties. *American Journal of Sociology* 78: 1360–80.

Korgen, K. O. (2002) *Crossing the Racial Divide: Close Friendships Between Black and White Americans.* Praeger, Westport, CT.

McPherson, M., Smith-Lovin, L., & Cook, J. M. (2001) Birds of a Feather: Homophily in Social Networks. *Annual Review of Sociology* 27: 415–44.

Massey, D. S. & Denton, N. A. (1993) *American Apartheid: Segregation and the Making of the Underclass.* Harvard University Press, Cambridge, MA.

Steinhorn, L. (2000) Martin Luther King's Half-Won Battle. *Ace Magazine.*

Tyson, W. (2002) Understanding the Margins: Marginality and Social Segregation in Predominantly White Universities. In: Moore, R. (Ed.), *The Quality and Quantity of Contact: African Americans and Whites on College Campuses*, pp. 307–22.

Zipf, G. K. (1949) *Human Behavior and the Principle of Least Effort.* Addison-Wesley, Menlo Park, CA.

race/ethnicity, health, and mortality

Parker Frisbie and Robert A. Hummer

Few issues are of greater importance for a society than the health of its members. And, based on the US Department of Health and Human Services Healthy People 2000 and 2010 reports, few issues are of greater concern than race/ethnic differentials in health and mortality in the United States. Any discussion of this topic places us squarely at a crucial interface of sociology (especially social demography) and social epidemiology. Although health (or morbidity) and mortality clearly are biological phenomena, one point of general agreement across these disciplines is that race/ethnicity is properly conceived as a sociocultural construct, not a genetic one. That is, we assume that if all race/ethnic compositional differences could be controlled, race/ethnic disparities in health and mortality would vanish – or at least be greatly reduced. A useful definition of an ethnic group is "a collectivity within a larger society having real or putative common ancestry, memories of a shared historical past, and a cultural focus on one or more symbolic elements defined as the epitome of peoplehood" (Schermerhorn 1970: 12). It is from this vantage point that the American Sociological Association (ASA) has endorsed and encouraged the continuation of research on race disparities across a wide range of topics (ASA 2003, as cited by Takeuchi & Williams 2003).

The current race categories (self-reported) most often found in US data are white, black (or African American), Asian, Pacific Islander, and American Indian/Alaska Native. More specific identifiers may be reported. For example, Asians may identify as Chinese, Japanese, Filipino, etc., and Pacific Islander individuals may identify as Hawaiian, Samoan, etc. Although the small size of many of the subgroups often makes it necessary to collapse data into a broader category, finer-grained distinctions are useful because of the well-documented heterogeneity within the larger categories. Hispanic identity is treated separately, so that the "race" categories become non-Hispanic white, non-Hispanic black, and so on, and Hispanics (or their component subgroups) are treated as one of a larger set of "race/ethnic" categories. Data may be retrieved and reported for certain Hispanic subpopulations (e.g., Mexican, Puerto Rican, Cuban). Definitional matters have become even more complex since the Office of Management and Budget began to allow respondents to identify with more than one racial category.

INTELLECTUAL CONTENT AND ANALYTIC DIMENSIONS

The health of groups that are disadvantaged socially, economically, and/or politically is often compared to non-Hispanic whites, which means a comparison of minority groups with the majority. This body of work becomes closely linked with social stratification in that group-specific disadvantages and advantages are described and then attempts are made to understand the factors that explain them. A voluminous literature throughout the twentieth century compared the health and mortality of the black and white populations (or, in the earlier, more limited data, whites and non-whites). With few exceptions, this research reported excess mortality and poor levels of health among blacks in comparison to whites. More recently, research on Hispanic groups, particularly the Mexican-origin population (i.e., both Mexican immigrants and US-born Mexican Americans), has been greatly expanded, and increasing attention is being paid to Asian and Pacific Islanders (APIs) and American Indians. In general, morbidity and mortality rates are highest for blacks. Puerto Ricans and American Indians also have poorer overall health and higher mortality rates than do non-Hispanic whites. The same is true for Pacific Islanders, including Hawaiians. The health and mortality profiles of most Hispanic groups are similar to those of non-Hispanic whites, while most, but not all, Asian groups have superior health and higher life expectancies compared to all other race/ethnic populations.

Differential access to socioeconomic (SES) resources has been found to be critical in helping to explain health and mortality differences between race/ethnic groups, although in most cases residual differences between groups remain even after SES factors are taken into account. Further, certain Hispanic groups, particularly Mexican Americans, were found to have overall mortality rates similar to those of the non-Hispanic white majority. This near parity has been termed an "epidemiologic paradox" due to the disadvantaged risk profiles of the former populations (Markides & Coreil 1986). A number of other risk factors, including disparities in access to preventive and curative care, stress produced by discrimination, behavioral differences, nativity, and religiosity have also been linked to the health and mortality differences between the majority and race/ethnic minorities and continue to be a major focus of theory and research.

The study of race/ethnic variation in health and mortality encompasses a broad spectrum of health and mortality outcomes, beginning with the analysis of race/ethnic patterns of fetal loss all the way through investigations of disability and mortality among the oldest old. Throughout the life course, the topics of investigation vary depending on the outcomes most relevant by age group. During infancy, research often revolves around differential birth outcomes (i.e., birth weight and gestational age), as well as age- and cause-specific infant mortality. Throughout childhood (when mortality rates are at their lowest), research typically analyzes health and development outcomes such as differential levels of asthma, childhood obesity, exercise patterns, and even academic outcomes across groups. During adolescence and young adulthood, the focus often shifts to health and sexual behavior patterns, as well as the accidental and violent causes of death that characterize this age group and that have been shown to be higher among most minority groups in comparison to non-Hispanic whites. Studies during adulthood are often geared toward patterns of chronic disease, the development of disabilities, and premature mortality. Finally, older adult studies typically focus on active life expectancy, disability, and cause-specific mortality.

As with much empirically based research in sociology, investigations of these topics have become more and more complex over time with the development of sophisticated individual-level surveys, record linkage across surveys, and heightened computing power. Much early work dealt with aggregate units of analyses (e.g., county rates), but with the advent of richer vital statistics data sets and specialized surveys, micro-level comparisons of race/ethnic variation in health and mortality moved to center stage. Currently, considerable emphasis is being placed on multilevel research in which the effects of both individual risk factors and contextual (e.g., neighborhood) variables on race/ethnic disparities are explored. Changing patterns across time is another major analytic dimension – one that has been given impetus by the increasing diversity of the US population as immigrants come to constitute an increasing share of the total US population.

CURRENT SUBSTANTIVE EMPHASES

Perhaps the most prominent conceptual model for health inequalities among race/ethnic groups is based on the premise that social inequities give rise to disparities in health and mortality. Specifically, the ability of individuals to reduce the risk of disease and death "is shaped by resources of knowledge, money, power, prestige, and beneficial social connections" (Link & Phelan 2002: 730).

Research has begun to focus on the implications of dramatic advances in the treatment and prevention of disease guided by the proposition that, as improvements in health care and technology lead to overall diminution of the risk of morbidity and mortality, relative disparities between race/ethnic populations will tend to widen. For example, while the overall levels of infant mortality have dropped, the relative gap between white and black infants (as indicated by the black–white rate ratio) has grown over the past two decades. This perspective follows directly from the fundamental social causes paradigm, as some substantial portion of this growing black–white inequality appears to have resulted from the greater survival benefits that accrued to white infants in the case of two of the five leading causes of infant death: respiratory distress syndrome (RDS) and sudden infant death syndrome (SIDS) after the introduction of perinatal care innovations designed to reduce risk of infant death from these conditions (Frisbie et al. 2004).

It has long been known that the health and mortality outcomes of immigrants and of infants born to immigrant mothers from virtually every country of origin tend to be more favorable than those of their US-born co-ethnics (e.g., Hummer et al. 1999) – even though immigrants are typically disadvantaged with respect to access to the formal health care system and often in terms of SES. The most frequently offered explanations for the superior health and survivorship of immigrants include positive selection of migration for the most robust individuals and cultural buffering. Some authors have suggested that the paradox is a data artifact (as described below). In any event, the health and mortality advantages of immigrants appear to erode as individuals spend a longer period of time in the United States, a finding consistent with the notion of "negative acculturation," although the relative lack of access by immigrants to the formal health care system represents a plausible alternative explanation.

While a number of social factors are associated with race/ethnic disparities in morbidity and mortality, a central question continues to be: what are the mechanisms through which race/ethnicity is related to health and mortality outcomes? As an example, consider the effects of SES. Compared to their more affluent counterparts, persons of low income will often lack the resources to access high-quality medical care, healthier residential environments, and occupations that involve a low risk of illness and injury. Even so, race/ethnic disparities in health and mortality often persist even after rigorous controls for individual-level measures of socioeconomic status. One potentially fruitful avenue involves the study of differential accumulation of stress for race/ethnic populations created by discrimination and residential segregation.

METHODOLOGICAL ISSUES

One set of methodological challenges revolves around the identification and measurement of race/ethnicity itself. Issues such as changing race/ethnic identities over time by individuals (e.g., as in the case of the growing number of individuals in the US who have identified as Native Americans since the 1960s), inconsistent reporting of race/ethnicity for individuals depending upon who reports the information, and the growth of multiple-race/ethnic reporting make even seemingly simple descriptions of race/ethnic patterns of health and mortality a major methodological challenge.

Studies in which immigrant characteristics are featured face the problem of a rapidly changing race/ethnic composition and increasing group diversity of the US population that is associated with a series of changes in immigration law since 1965. Circular migration between the US and other nations, particularly Mexico, poses a related methodological difficulty. To illustrate, longitudinal studies of mortality in the US often "statistically follow" individuals who were interviewed in sample surveys through matches to identifying information on death certificates. If sampled individuals leave the country, they become "statistically immortal" because their deaths will never be recorded in the US vital statistics. Some recent investigations of this issue report that Mexican immigrant adult mortality in the US is probably underestimated. However, even the most careful adjustments show favorable Mexican immigrant mortality patterns in light of their disadvantaged social and economic status (Elo et al. 2004).

Differential reporting, as well as misreporting, of health on social surveys by race/ethnicity can also create analytical difficulties. There remains concern about the extent to which the often used respondent reports of health reflect clinical reality, but a number of evaluative studies indicate that self-reported health is closely related to both morbidity and mortality.

Analysts that hypothesize socioeconomic-based differences to be the root of many race/ethnic health and mortality disparities regularly adjust for available measures of SES, such as education and income. However, such conventional measures, while helpful, are limited in that they fail to tap into many other dimensions of SES, such as wealth, quality of education, and access to health insurance.

FUTURE DIRECTIONS

Fruitful future directions for research in this substantive area include at least the following. Additional research is needed that sheds light on the mechanisms through which social attributes and characteristics "get into the body" and lead to higher risks of morbidity and mortality. Some important findings have emerged regarding the effects of stress associated with race/ethnic disparities in SES and quality of life, but a greater degree of collaboration between social science and public health/medical researchers should be encouraged. In sum, both the "social" and "medical" models seem clearly necessary, but neither alone is sufficient.

A fair degree of progress has been made through multilevel (or contextual) research in which the effects of both micro- and macro-level variables on race/ethnic differences in health and mortality are explored, but considerable expansion of this research agenda is needed. This will require more data sets constructed specifically with multilevel analyses in mind.

Additional studies are needed regarding the explanation for the superior health and survival of immigrant members of most race/ethnic groups. Those who embrace "negative assimilation" as an explanation must confront the fact that, while we have some useful measures of cultural attachment (e.g., continuing to use language of place of origin), there is a virtual absence of measures of cultural content. To illustrate, the culture of Hispanics is not the same as that of Asians, which, in turn, is not the same as that of European immigrants. The most likely explanation may well be positive selection of migration, but demonstration of the validity of this interpretation would seem to depend on development of data sets that capture important characteristics of immigrants at both origin and destination – as has been accomplished by Landale and associates in the study of Puerto Ricans (Landale et al. 2000).

The importance of panel surveys and the leverage that such data sets provide for inferring causality are well known. Perhaps less obvious is the importance of temporal effects that occur over the life course and intergenerationally. For example, morbidity and mortality risk in adulthood may be affected both directly and indirectly by birth outcomes and later child well-being. Policies designed to enhance child health can be expected to have beneficial effects in adulthood (Hayward & Gorman 2004: 87).

Finally, a greatly expanded research agenda is needed that explores the relationship between advances in health care and a widening gap between race/ethnic groups. It is ironic and unacceptable that relative (and in some instances, absolute) race/ethnic disparities in health and mortality have followed in the wake of overall advances in health care. Thus, race/ethnic health and mortality differentials remain a pressing cause of concern.

SEE ALSO: Health and Race; Infant, Child, and Maternal Health and Mortality; Social Epidemiology; Socioeconomic Status, Health, and Mortality; Stratification, Race/Ethnicity and

REFERENCES AND SUGGESTED READINGS

Elo, I. T., Turra, C. M., Kestenbaum, B., & Ferguson, B. R. (2004) Mortality among Elderly Hispanics in the United States: Past Evidence and New Results. *Demography* 41: 109–28.

Frisbie, W. P., Song, S. E., Powers, D. A., & Street, J. A. (2004) Increasing Racial Disparity in Infant Mortality: Respiratory Distress Syndrome and Other Causes. *Demography* 41: 773–800.

Hayward, M. D. & Gorman, B. K. (2004) The Long Arm of Childhood: The Influence of Early-Life Social Conditions on Men's Mortality. *Demography* 41: 87–107.

Hummer, R. A., Biegler, M., de Turk, P. B., Forbes, D., Frisbie, W. P., Hong, Y., & Pullum, S. G. (1999) Race/Ethnicity, Nativity, and Infant Mortality in the United States. *Social Forces* 77: 1083–118.

Landale, N. S., Oropesa, R. S., & Gorman, B. K. (2000) Migration and Infant Death: Assimilation or Selective Migration among Puerto Ricans? *American Sociological Review* 65: 888–909.

Link, B. G. & Phelan, J. (2002) McKeown and the Idea that Social Conditions Are Fundamental Causes of Disease. *American Journal of Public Health* 92: 730–2.

Markides, K. S. & Coreil, J. (1986) The Health of Hispanics in the Southwestern United States: An Epidemiologic Paradox. *Public Health Reports* 101: 253–65.

Schermerhorn, R. A. (1970) *Comparative Ethnic Relations: A Framework for Theory and Research.* Random House, New York.

Scribner, R. (1996) Editorial. Paradox as Paradigm: The Health Outcomes of Mexican Americans. *American Journal of Public Health* 86: 303–5.

Takeuchi, D. T. & Williams, D. R. (2003) Race, Ethnicity, and Mental Health: Introduction to the Special Issue. *Journal of Health and Social Behavior* 44: 233–6.

racial hierarchy

Miri Song

Racial hierarchies are systems of stratification premised upon the belief that some racial groups are either superior or inferior to other racial groups. A racial hierarchy in which white Europeans were deemed innately superior to all other "races" in virtually every respect was crucial for imperialist expansion in all parts of the world, as well as for the creation and practice of slavery. Without the stated belief that white people are superior – intellectually, spiritually, artistically – than non-white people, it would not have been possible to subordinate and dehumanize conquered peoples.

Sidanius and Pratto (1999) argue that the means by which group-based hierarchies, including racial and ethnic hierarchies, are established and maintained, are similar across social systems. Nevertheless, there is no one definition or indicator of racial hierarchy (or inequality) which is used consistently in different countries.

Systems of ethnic and racial stratification have differed historically, not only in terms of the groups involved, but also the complexity and the magnitude of the distinctions made between them. Racial hierarchies in societies with a relatively high degree of intermarriage, such as in Brazil or other countries in Latin America, can be subtle or denied to exist altogether. By comparison, the workings of formal institutionalized systems of racial stratification, as existed in South Africa prior to 1990, or under slavery and Jim Crow in the US, were clear cut and transparent. In the former South Africa (though this is only the most paradigmatic and contemporary historical example of racial hierarchy), Africans were deemed inferior to both "coloreds" and whites, and they lived in segregated townships as lesser beings. In all aspects of their lives – economically, politically, and socially – whites were indisputably at the top, Africans at the bottom, and the "colored" population comprised a formal intermediate category.

In the US today, there appears to be a fairly widespread view, both among many academics and the wider public, that white Americans are at the top of a racial hierarchy, African Americans at the bottom (with sporadic reference to Native Americans as an equally oppressed group), and groups such as Asian Americans and Latinos somewhere in between (Bashi & McDaniel 1997). Many analysts in the US believe that the historical legacy of slavery is fundamental in explaining the relatively disadvantaged status of many African Americans today. Feagin (2000) argues that white Americans have simply expended much less time and energy in exploiting and oppressing other groups such as Asian Americans and Latino Americans. In addition to arguments about their distinctive historical treatment and experiences, African Americans have fared badly according to various socioeconomic indicators, such as educational attainment, housing, and income. In the US, black families earn about 60 percent of what white families earn and survive on roughly 12 percent of the wealth of average white families. As individuals, their life spans are 6–7 years shorter than whites. Both in the past and in the present, African Americans have often been the victims of horrific racial attacks.

Most conceptions of racial disadvantage and oppression in the US have to date relied upon a rather unitary (i.e., anti-black) understanding of racism and racial disadvantage – though there is now significant research into the class differentiation of African Americans. In recent years, a growing number of studies have begun to investigate the specific racialized experiences of other minority groups. For example, social psychologists researching the effects of racism have begun to question whether models of racial identity based on the experiences of African Americans (the group most studied regarding the effects of racial prejudice in the US) are adequate to understand the racial and ethnic identities of other groups, such as Latino and Asian Americans.

Although forms of both overt and covert discrimination and prejudice are still all too prevalent in the US and Europe, many countries are no longer characterized by rigid sociopolitical constraints, but rather by a gradual modification of the social and economic parameters dividing white and non-white peoples. While there is considerable agreement about the persistence of white power, privilege, and racism, the question of which groups do and do not constitute disadvantaged ethnic minority groups is now more contested than ever. Among other factors, significant demographic changes, such as intermarriage, as well as diverse flows of immigration, are unsettling longstanding understandings of hierarchy in many western contemporary societies.

The ways in which debates about racial inequality get framed in the first place depend a great deal upon the specifics of each national context, with their distinctive histories of colonization and settlement, the specific mix of various minority and majority populations, discourses about racial inequality and minority experience, and state policies concerning "integration" or multiculturalism. Particular racial paradigms are associated with specific national contexts and cultures.

In Britain, unlike the US, most research has (until recently) stressed the *commonality* of experience of ethnic minorities in relation to the white majority, suggesting a common disadvantaged status in relation to the housing and labor markets, racial abuse, and certain forms of social exclusion and marginalization. This may be because, in Britain, many South Asians and African Caribbeans have shared in common the history of British colonialism in the Indian subcontinent, the Caribbean, Africa, and South Asia and came to Britain in the post-war period to work in predominantly unskilled or semi-skilled jobs as disadvantaged minorities.

Turning to France, Silverman and Yuval-Davis (1999) note that Jews and Arabs have long been central to theorizations of racism in France, and this model has tended to eclipse the black/white paradigm more commonly found in Britain and the US. Furthermore, the political culture in France militates against the specification of ethnic difference and origins, based upon the orthodoxy that, in France, one does not question a single and indivisible republican citizenship.

In contrast to the US situation (in which a predominantly anti-black conception of racism is employed), it is much more common in Britain for analysts to identify a variety of racisms which are flourishing in contemporary Europe, such as anti-Jewish, anti-Muslim, anti-Turk, anti-African, and anti-Gypsy racism (Cohen 1996). While many British analysts acknowledge that each of these racisms has its own specific history and characteristic features, the implication of such a wide-ranging list of racisms, discussed together, is that they are equivalent and comparable.

While some analysts (especially in North America) believe that the concept of a top-down racial hierarchy should be retained, pointing to significant differences in the life chances and well-being of disparate racial groups, others argue that this concept is simply divisive, contributing to assertions about a "hierarchy of oppression" (Hickman 1998). Rather than argue that some minority groups are more racially oppressed or disadvantaged than others, British analysts such as Mary Hickman and Phil Cohen argue for a complex and pluralistic cartography of racism which would recognize anti-Semitism and anti-Romany racism alongside the racism experienced by African Caribbeans and South Asians.

Why do claims about racial hierarchy still matter today? Because a great deal is at stake. Groups which successfully claim an oppressed status can gain both moral and material capital. Belief in the existence of a top-down hierarchy can also shape group relations, public policy formation, and political alliances. The question of whether some groups are worse off than others is highly pertinent at a time when there is growing recognition of multiple forms of racisms and racial oppression.

The concept of racial hierarchy is suggestive of a "big picture" of how disparate groups fare. In both the US and Britain, analysts' references to a wide range of indicators of disadvantage and privilege can make it difficult to assess the *overall* positions and experiences of groups in relation to each other. One of the key difficulties encountered in scholarship about racial hierarchies is the fact that analysts privilege certain indicators of racial disadvantage or well-being over others in making claims about the positions of groups in a top-down hierarchy. The identification of specific criteria means that we privilege certain social indicators as fundamental, while rendering other markers, problems, and people relatively invisible to public concern and public policy.

Thus there is a lack of consensus in discussions about the criteria one applies in constructions of racial hierarchy, as well as the *methodological* difficulties of measuring and comparing different forms of racial oppression across disparate groups. In comparison with racial prejudice (e.g., in various public places), how relevant are factors such as a group's average family income, the nature of their representation in the popular media, or their participation in politics, for the overall assessment of how a group fares? There are many and different (though in many ways related) dimensions of a group's status and experience. While it is possible that some groups are consistently disadvantaged across a whole range of indicators, it is also possible that a group may fare badly according to some indicators, but may be relatively privileged according to others.

Differential levels of material resources possessed by various ethnic minority groups (including different subgroups of "Asians" and "blacks") surely make a difference to these groups' overall sense of well-being and social status. But in recognizing the centrality of material resources, we must not overlook other areas of social experience which truly give meaning to the idea of "belonging" and social inclusion in the wider society (Song 2003). Nor do material resources guarantee a group's ability to participate fully in society. For instance, the Chinese in Britain have virtually no public presence in the arts or popular culture of Britain, and there is hardly any Chinese participation in political parties in Britain. In this sense, while they are "successful" according to some socioeconomic measures, the Chinese are very much at the margins of British society.

Thus, taking a broader view of social inclusion and exclusion complicates the neat, top-down picture one might derive from reliance on socioeconomic indicators alone. The issue of which criteria or indicators are used in claims about the existence of a racial hierarchy is also complicated by the fact that distinctive yet simultaneous hierarchies can occur along various dimensions of experience, whether these be based upon race, class, or gender locations.

Unfortunately, claims about the ordering of groups on a top-down hierarchy can encourage politically divisive comparisons between groups. Amid the scramble for scarce group resources, and against a backdrop in which disparate groups may know very little about each other, there can be little room for empathy. Members of disparate minority groups may believe that they are more disadvantaged than others, and these competing beliefs can contribute to interethnic tensions.

Given the difficulties that can arise in assertions about racial hierarchies, should we simply jettison this concept in scholarship about "race" and racial inequalities? Most analysts, especially those in the US, would say no – though they point to the need to qualify and refine this concept. We need to remember that the ethnic and racial landscapes of many multiethnic western societies are undergoing vast and significant change. We are certainly moving towards societies in which the meanings of "race" and ethnicity, the assertions of ethnic and racial difference and experience, and the manifestations of inequality are increasingly complex and varied.

The state, and its national political leaders, also play key roles in the adjudication of conflicts and competing claims among racialized minority groups. In the US, despite the prevalence of an official multiculturalist discourse which suggests an unproblematic ethnic and racial diversity, major demographic changes have brought blacks, Latinos, and Asian Americans into direct conflict (Kim 2004). According to Claire Kim, through their espousal of multiculturalist discourse, political leaders in the US have actually discouraged Americans from addressing these intergroup tensions. In the course of discussing the notion of racial hierarchy (as a counter-narrative to official multiculturalist discourse), Kim argues instead for the notion of "racial positionality" – a concept which allows for the recognition of disparate forms of racial disadvantage, as well as the reality of interethnic tensions.

As stated earlier, a key difficulty in arguments about racial hierarchies is that, given the numerous indicators of well-being and disadvantage which can be used (and their potentially complex combination in relation to specific groups), it can be difficult to summarize groups' overall experiences along a monolithic, top-down hierarchy. Therefore, in addition to applying the concept of racial positionality, more delimited hierarchies which position groups on the basis of specific indicators of well-being or disadvantage (such as poverty or entrance into higher education) are a useful way forward.

SEE ALSO: Apartheid and Nelson Mandela; Boundaries (Racial/Ethnic); Caste: Inequalities Past and Present; Endogamy; Multiculturalism; Race; Race (Racism); Racism, Structural and Institutional; Racist Movements

REFERENCES AND SUGGESTED READINGS

Bashi, V. & McDaniel, A. (1997) A Theory of Immigration and Racial Stratification. *Journal of Black Studies* 27(5): 668–82.

Cohen, P. (1996) A Message from the Other Shore. *Patterns of Prejudice* 30(1): 15–22.

Feagin, J. (2000) *Racist America*. Routledge, New York.

Hickman, M. (1998) Reconstructing Deconstructing "Race": British Discourses about the Irish in Britain. *Ethnic and Racial Studies* 21(2): 288–307.

Kim, C. J. (2004) Imagining Race and Nation in Multiculturalist America. *Ethnic and Racial Studies* 27(6): 987–1005.

Sidanius, J. & Pratto, F. (1999) *Social Dominance.* Cambridge University Press, Cambridge.
Silverman, M. & Yuval-Davis, N. (1999) Jews, Arabs and the Theorization of Racism in Britain and France. In: Brah, A., Hickman, M., & Mac an Ghaill, M. (Eds), *Thinking Identities*, Macmillan, Basingstoke, pp. 25–48.
Song, M. (2003) *Choosing Ethnic Identity.* Polity Press, Cambridge.

racialized gender

April L. Few

Racialized gender is a sociological concept that refers to the critical analysis of the simultaneous effects of race and gender processes on individuals, families, and communities. This concept recognizes that women do not negotiate race and gender similarly. For instance, white women's oppression has been linked with their privilege as white people, but they have not escaped the bonds of sexism. Black women's and First Nation women's oppression has been linked to the struggle of self-definition, agency, and collective empowerment. Latina and Asian women's oppression has been linked more to sexism emerging from immigration and multigenerational experiences. Historical, social, and geographic context influence the expression, interpretation, and performance of gender relations over the life span of an individual. Multiracial feminists and ethnic scholars have written extensively about racialized gender particularly as it relates to social constructions of family and sexuality.

Racialized gender concerns the study of the influence of socialization practices on the individual. Social environments such as the family, communities, and institutions provide the frame in which experience is interpreted and communicated and the self (e.g., identity) is defined in relation to difference. Social environments impose or limit culturally appropriate cues, scripts, behaviors, and outcomes for individuals through hierarchical raced, gendered, and classed systems of privilege and domination. The development of gender and racial identities is an important milestone, as an individual's self-identity perception has been shown to be instrumental in overriding the effects of harmful, external, stereotyped messages. The family is the primary site for the racial socialization of children and socialization of gender identity. For this reason, scholars have focused on the extent to which ethnic families have performed traditional gender norms (as defined by the majority discourses) and used those norms to organize family responsibilities and to socialize children.

The sociohistorical frameworks of race, ethnicity, gender, class, and sexual orientation are embedded in how the sexuality of ethnic women has been created, reproduced, and disseminated for public consumption. Racialized gender can be observed in the study of sexual images and scripts and body image as it relates to perception of beauty. Multiracial feminists and womanists have identified various sexual scripts and the distinctive identity processes women negotiate due to historical and economic circumstances. For instance, sexual stereotypes for black women in the US have been "transformed" from one context, American slavery, to the current subcontext of Hip Hop. Black feminists and womanists have traced how the Jezebel, Mammy, Welfare Mother, Tragic Mulatto, and Matriarch stereotypes have "evolved" into more sexually explicit images and scripts such as the Diva, Gold Digger, Freak, Dyke, Gangster Bitch, Sister Savior, Earth Mother, and Baby Mama (Collins 1991; Stephens & Phillips 2003). A close examination of these stereotypes reveals racialized and sexualized colonial tropes of African primitivism and hypersexuality. Theracist imagery and expectations embedded in these narrowly defined stereotypes of black female sexuality have been constructed deliberately to constrict black women's ability to replace or eliminate negative images of black womanhood.

The concept of racialized gender is also found in comparative research concerning physical attractiveness and body image. Physical attractiveness stereotypes have been found to be the dominant component of gender stereotypes, consistently implicating other components of gender stereotypes. For instance, scholars have observed that white women seem to have a uniform notion of what "beauty" should be, and their conception of beauty tended to match the culturally popular images of women in the mainstream media. Black women, however, have been found less likely to hold uniform notions of beauty, and far more likely to describe beauty in terms of personality traits rather than physical ones. Parker et al. (1995) conducted a study of African American, Asian American, Mexican American, and white female high school students. They found that white adolescents' conceptions of beauty were much more rigid, fixed, and uniform than those of African Americans, who were much more flexible and fluid in their notions of beauty. The African American girls' perceptions of beauty focused on personality traits and a personal sense of style, rather than a certain "look." Poran (2002) argued that beauty must be reconceptualized as a race experience in order to understand and explore fully the diverse experiences women have in relation to, and within, cultures. She believed that images that convey beauty may hold different meanings for different women. In her study, she found that white women seemed to respond to cultural standards of beauty on the basis of what was attractive to western, white men. Black women initially reported that there was a white-defined standard, but then reported Afrocentric characteristics as a beauty standard to pursue. Latina women seemed to have a less straightforward, more complex response to dominant imagery.

There is a need to conduct more empirical research that examines racialized gender. For example, more research is needed to determine how institutions transmit and define "appropriate" gender relations. Second, more research is needed to analyze how class diversity and mobility among different ethnic groups influences the expression, reproduction, or termination of specific gender ideologies and behaviors.

SEE ALSO: Black Feminist Thought; Multiracial Feminism; Intersectionality; Race; Womanism

REFERENCES AND SUGGESTED READINGS

Anzaldua, G. (1990) *Haciendo caras / Making Face, Making Soul: Creative and Critical Perspectives by Women of Color.* Aunt Lute Press, San Francisco.

Collins, P. H. (1991) *Black Feminist Thought: Knowledge, Consciousness and the Politics of Empowerment*, 2nd edn. Routledge, New York.

Frankenberg, R. (1993) *White Women, Race Matters: The Social Construction of Whiteness.* University of Minnesota Press, Minneapolis.

hooks, b. (1992) *Black Looks: Race and Representations.* Between the Lines Press, Toronto.

Lu, L. (1997) Critical Visions: The Representation and Resistance of Asian Women. In: Shah, S. (Ed.), *Dragon Ladies: Asian American Feminists Breathe Fire.* South End Press, Boston, pp. 17–28.

Parker, S., Nichter, M., Nichter, N., Vuckovic, N., Sims, C., & Ritenbaugh, C. (1995) Body Image and Weight Concerns Among African American and White Adolescent Females: Differences That Make A Difference. *Human Organization* 54: 103–14.

Poran, M. A. (2002) Denying Diversity: Perceptions of Beauty and Social Comparison Processes Among Latina, Black, and White Women. *Sex Roles: A Journal of Research* (July): 1–10.

Stephens, D. & Phillips, L. (2003) Freaks, Gold Diggers, Divas, and Dykes: The Sociohistorical Development of African American Female Adolescent Scripts. *Sexuality and Culture* 7: 3–49.

Wing, A. K. (Ed.) (1997) *Critical Race Feminism: A Reader.* New York University Press, New York.

racism, structural and institutional

Mikaila Mariel Lemonik Arthur

When most people think about racism, they think about the concept of individual prejudice – in other words, negative thoughts or stereotypes about a particular racial group. However, racism can also be embedded in the institutions and structures of social life. This type of racism can be called structural or institutional racism (hereafter, institutional racism) and it is significant in creating and maintaining the disparate outcomes that characterize the landscape of racial inequality.

The term institutional racism was first used by Carmichael and Hamilton in 1967 with the intent of differentiating individual racist acts from what we can describe as policies or practices that are built into the structures of various social institutions and which continue to operate even without the active support and maintenance of individuals. Institutional racism has probably been with us for as long as human societies have been formally or legally divided into races. There are two main types of institutional racism. The first, which can be called "direct," occurs when policies are consciously designed to have discriminatory effects. These policies can be maintained through the legal system (such as in the case of apartheid in South Africa or Jim Crow in the US) or through conscious institutional practice (such as redlining in residential real estate or underfunding urban public schools). The second type, "indirect" institutional racism, includes practices that have disparate racial impacts even without any intent to discriminate (such as with network hiring in workplaces).

Institutional racism continues to affect many areas of life, in particular education, housing, economic life, imprisonment, and health care. Indirect institutional racism also continues to affect the lives of people of color, and because it is unconscious, those who maintain institutional structures and policies may not be aware of its existence unless it is challenged by activists or lawsuits. For instance, the Rockefeller drug laws in New York State, enacted in 1973, include very heavy penalties for those selling or possessing narcotics. These laws were enacted with the intent of protecting communities from the scourge of drug sales, but have led instead to disparate imprisonment of young black men. This is because though individuals of all races use drugs at similar rates, young black men are disproportionately likely to use the particular drugs targeted by the Rockefeller drug laws.

Institutional racism affects people of color in many aspects of their lives. Sociologists and other researchers continue to seek empirical evidence of institutional racism as they study such questions as the black–white test score gap and its effects on college admissions. However, it is much harder for researchers to find evidence of institutional racism than of individual discrimination. This is because it is possible for a set of guidelines to disadvantage a particular racial group while being consistently and fairly applied to all individuals. One of the most powerful tools used to uncover evidence of institutional racism is the audit study method, where testers are matched on all characteristics except for race and sent to apply for jobs or housing. These studies present powerful evidence of the continued effects of institutional racism. For instance, Pager (2003) showed that white men with prison records and black men without prison records who are matched on other characteristics such as education and prior work experience are about equally likely to be hired for entry-level jobs. Similar research has shown that black applicants for home loans or rental apartments are much less likely to be approved, and that people searching for residential real estate are likely to be steered to neighborhoods which match their skin color.

While civil rights legislation banning discrimination both in the public sphere (voting and *de jure* segregation) and the private sphere (universities and housing developments) was passed in the 1960s with the aim of outlawing direct institutional racism, lawsuits are of limited utility when it comes to enforcing such legislation in the absence of concrete evidence of harm to specific individuals (Crenshaw 1995). Another limitation of strategies designed to combat institutional racism is that they may be coopted. For instance, affirmative action was designed as a program to combat institutional racism in education and employment. Lawsuits targeting affirmative action programs, such as *Gratz* v. *Bollinger* and *Grutter* v. *Bollinger*, have suggested instead that affirmative action policies themselves are direct institutional racism, since they supposedly provide an advantage to particular racial groups. However, as Justice O'Connor pointed out in her majority opinion in *Grutter* v. *Bollinger*, institutional racism still limits the access of students of color to selective higher education institutions. Though these difficulties make it hard to find ways to combat institutional racism, analysts suggest that becoming conscious of its existence is the first step. Brown et al. (2003) then suggest that the best steps to take include setting up a formal regulatory apparatus to challenge institutional racism when it exists and to develop policies to deal with the "legacy of disaccumulation" in communities of color.

SEE ALSO: Apartheid and Nelson Mandela; *Brown v. Board of Education*; Health and Race; Occupational Segregation; Race and Crime; Race and the Criminal Justice System; Race and Schools; Redlining; Residential Segregation; School Segregation, Desegregation

REFERENCES AND SUGGESTED READINGS

Better, S. J. (2002) *Institutional Racism: A Primer on Theory and Strategies for Social Change*. Burnham, Chicago.

Bobo, L. D. (2001) Racial Attitudes and Relations at the Close of the Twentieth Century. In: Smelser, N. J., Wilson, W. J., & Mitchell, F. (Eds.), *America Becoming: Racial Trends and their Consequences*, Vol. 2. National Academy Press, Washington, DC, pp. 264–301.

Brown, M. K. et al. (2003) *Whitewashing Race: The Myth of a Color-Blind Society*. University of California Press, Berkeley.

Carmichael, S. & Hamliton, C. (1967) *Black Power: The Politics of Liberation in America*.

Crenshaw, K. (Ed.) (1995) *Critical Race Theory: The Key Writings that Formed the Movement*. New Press, New York.

Law, I., Phillips, D., & Turney, L. (Eds.) (2004) *Institutional Racism in Higher Education*. Trentham, Stoke-on-Trent.

Lieu, T. A. & Hacker, A. (1992) *Two Nations: Black and White: Separate, Hostile, Unequal*. Scribners, New York.

Omi, M. & Winant, H. (1994) *Racial Formation in the United States*. Routledge, New York.

Pager, D. (2003) The Mark of a Criminal Record. *American Journal of Sociology* 108: 937–75.

racist movements

Kathleen M. Blee

Racist movements are organized, collective efforts to create, preserve, or extend racial hierarchies of power and privilege. Such movements explicitly espouse the ideologies of white supremacism and/or anti-Semitism (anti-Judaism or hatred of Muslims or Arabs) that were consolidated in the western world in the eighteenth and nineteenth centuries. Manifestations of intergroup antagonism in earlier times, even conflicts that cross what later would be regarded as racial lines, generally are not considered racial movements because these are not based in modern ideas of race as an essential, biological, polarized, and unchanging attribute of social groups. Denoting as racist only social movements that take place in western societies is a common practice in sociological research, as most scholars regard white supremacism and anti-Semitism as the legacy of ideologies by which European colonists sought to exonerate their brutal conquests and occupations. However, this restriction has been challenged by studies that use the concept racist (or racial) movements to describe subnational intergroup antagonisms in a number of non-western societies, including China, India, Indonesia, and Russia.

Racist movements take a variety of forms over time and in different places. Some arise in response to political opportunities for asserting enhanced racial superiority; others as countermovements organized to oppose perceived gains by other racial groups. Some recruit sizable proportions of the population, thereby accruing significant influence over state policy or even the ability to elect candidates to political office. Such large racist movements often are linked, overtly or covertly, to right-wing political parties, nationalist efforts, or fascist groups. In other contexts, racist movements are small and politically marginal. These tend to shun mainstream politics, relying instead on violence or terrorist tactics to achieve racist goals.

Racist movements also vary in their ideologies and agendas. Some favor the creation or preservation of racially homogeneous societies, generally through exclusion, expulsion, or extermination of those they regard as racially different. Others promote racial supremacy or separatism within heterogeneous societies. Although movements that promote racial superiority or separatism such as black nationalism or black separatism in the US are sometimes referred to as racist, scholars generally reserve this term for collective efforts that promote white or Aryan dominance because these seek to bolster established racial systems of subordination and superordination. White supremacist, Nazi and neo-Nazi, white power skinhead, Aryan supremacist, and white/Aryan separatist movements are types of modern racist movements.

The ideologies of racist movements typically are quite complex. All have a core belief in racial supremacism or racial separatism, but this may coexist with philosophies that seem quite antithetical, such as environmentalism, women's rights, atheism, or anti-colonialism. The ability to embrace beliefs from widely differing ideologies and social contexts while retaining racism as a central agenda is described as the "scavenger" aspect of modern racism. Racist movements are generally adept at recruiting members by presenting racial solutions to a wide range of non-racial social concerns, including anxieties about crime, the quality of children's education, the global economy, or national pride. Such ideological flexibility is why some racist movements with very extreme racial views manage to attract a wide base of adherents.

Until the late twentieth century, racist movements tended to be fervently nationalistic. Racist leaders identified the interests of whites or Aryans as what was best for the nation as a whole and advocated national purges of other races. In the twenty-first century, a number of racist movements have rejected narrow nationalist appeals in favor of global racist politics, what some term a movement of "pan-Aryanism." The waning of nationalism in these racist movements is due to a variety of factors. Opportunities to spread the influence of racist movements through transnational venues such as the Internet have proven attractive. Also compelling is the global circulation of racist mercenary soldiers and terrorists, as well as a global trade in armaments and other contraband that presents the possibility for enhanced funding of racist movements. Equally important has been the declining support for national governments by racist movements. Many racist movements in the US, Canada, and Europe embrace extreme anti-Jewish philosophies, often based on variants of Christian Identity, a racist philosophy that regards Jews as the powerful and literal descendants of the devil. These movements describe western governments as under the control of a Jewish elite, or, in racist terminology, as "Zionist Occupied Governments (ZOG)" and thus as obstacles to racist agendas.

The penchant for secrecy about strategies and future plans that is characteristic of virtually all modern racist movements makes it difficult to predict their future course, but it is likely that they will be small and very violent. In the aftermath of the atrocities of World War II, particularly the extermination of millions of European Jews through deliberate policies of racial supremacy, overt racist appeals became less legitimate in many parts of the western world, making explicitly racist mass movements less likely. Also, racial hierarchies of privilege and subordination were sufficiently institutionalized in much of the West in the post-war period that there was little impetus for mass racist mobilization to challenge existing arrangements. Racist movements that mobilized in the latter half of the twentieth and early twenty-first centuries thus tended to be small groupings of white power advocates, neo-Nazis, and Aryan supremacists. Except where they allied with political parties in some European and Southern African nations, these movements have had little direct impact on the policies of the nations in which they are located. Instead, some of the most influential racist movements have turned to strategies of violence and terrorism, seeking to disrupt the social order and provoke social chaos, a strategy they describe as instigating an apocalyptic "race war" to eradicate Jews and non-whites.

WHY DO RACIAL MOVEMENTS ARISE?

Theories of why racist movements begin and how they attract adherents generally use frustration–reaction or intergroup competition frameworks. Frustration–reaction theory is based in older scholarly understandings of racist movements as collective and irrational expressions of anger by members of one racial group toward members of another. According to this theory, racist movements might accurately target groups that are responsible for their perceived problems, but, more often, they displace anger from the antagonist to a more vulnerable group that serves as a scapegoat and target of collective aggression. The case of Nazism in Germany – especially before the Nazi seizure of state power – often is used as an example of how racist movements emerge as a response to collective frustration. The Nazis, in this formulation, took advantage of the discontent evoked by economic turmoil and the national humiliation of Germany in World War I to build a popular movement. Jews, Roma (Gypsies), and others became scapegoats for collective anger over Germany's national distress. When the Nazi movement took control of the German state, such sentiments made it possible to unleash a "final solution" of racial extermination, with catastrophic consequences.

A competing and later theory regards racist movements as the product of antagonisms that stem from competition between racial groups for social, economic, cultural, or territorial advantages. Competition theory has been used to explain the rise and fall of such racist movements as the Ku Klux Klan (KKK), a series of largely unconnected white supremacist movements that have appeared and collapsed in the US from the 1870s to the present. The first KKK emerged in the Reconstruction-era South. This Klan was a small, loosely organized grouping of rural white men who used terror to bolster Southern white male privileges and combat what they feared to be the growing strength of African Americans and Northern politicians after the Civil War. This Klan collapsed in the 1870s in the wake of federal sanctions and, perhaps more importantly, because whites perceived political or economic competition from African Americans to have waned as the result of racist legislation and renewed white control of the Southern economy. In the mid-1910s, a new Klan emerged in the South, but this KKK movement grew strongest in the cities of the Midwest, East Coast, and West Coast. Competition theory explains the shift in the Klan's base as the result of changes in patterns of interracial rivalry. White Protestants in Northern and coastal states turned to the Klan when they felt threatened by large numbers of Catholic and Jewish immigrants and the migration of African Americans from the South. The second Klan thus used economic boycotts and electoral politics to curb competition and maintain the privileges of white native-born Protestants. After the collapse of the second Klan in the late 1920s, subsequent eruptions of the KKK were small and concentrated in the South, emerging largely in response to racial integration of schools.

Competition and, less commonly, frustration–reaction theories are widely used in the study of racial movements, but there are problems with each theory. Frustration–reaction theory has been criticized for reducing social phenomena to individual psychological states, making it difficult to account for the varying appeal of racist movements in times or places in which people are likely to experience similar levels of anger or distress. Moreover, research on racist movements, even German Nazism, finds that factors other than intergroup hostility are significant in mobilizing people toward racist collective action, and that racist activists are no less logical or rational than others in a similar social context. Frustration–reaction theory also can be circular, using the presence of racist movements as evidence of antecedent collective anxiety. Competition theory is generally more robust for explaining racist movement. This theory suggests that racist movements emerge as the result of economic and political competition among racial groups. The spike in racist movements and racial violence in late twentieth-century Europe that accompanied the influx of migrants from former colonies in Northern Africa and South Asia is an example, as is the racist backlash that occurred with post-communist economic and political uncertainty in Russia and Eastern Europe. However, counterexamples suggest that competition theory might not be universally applicable. The largest racist movements in the twentieth-century US occurred in the 1910s–1920s, 1950s–1960s, and 1980s, times of relative economic prosperity for many whites in which racial competition for jobs and social benefits was relatively low; in contrast, the serious economic depression of the 1930s, with its severe competition for jobs and economic benefits, witnessed comparatively fewer racist movements.

DATA AND METHODOLOGIES

Racist movements pose complicated problems for researchers. Most evident is the danger of studying groups in which violence is common and directed not only at those perceived to be enemies of the movement, but also at allies, even members. Researchers may find it difficult to avoid becoming a target of a violence that tends to suffuse organized racism. Moreover, since racist groups generally seek to avoid public scrutiny and are particularly concerned about infiltration by government authorities, researchers face danger if they are perceived as disseminating negative information about racist groups or as potential government informants.

Another problem for the study of racist movements is that these tend to operate illegally or on the margins of legality. Except in the rare cases where racist movements operate in the political mainstream, visible racist activists also face sanction from family, friends, and employers. Most racist movements thus operate in ways that are difficult for anyone – including authorities and researchers – to trace, creating few documents and attempting to obfuscate the identities, intentions, and activities of their members.

Concerns about researcher safety and the inaccessibility of racist groups have had a pronounced effect on the methodologies used in racist movement studies, especially by shaping the techniques of data collection. Much research on racist movements is based on information made publicly available by racist groups, such as group propaganda, evidence from rallies and protests, and interviews with racist spokespersons. These have proven useful in detailing changes over time in the ideological direction of racist groups and their ability to mobilize adherents for public events. However, the validity of such data is questionable since these reflect what racist leaders deem useful to be disseminated and reveal little about how racist groups actually operate. Such important questions as how racist movements are funded, what alliances exist among racist groups, and how organized racists formulate strategies cannot be addressed with information garnered from racist movements themselves. Moreover, such data tend to overemphasize the importance of self-designated leaders, making it difficult to understand the composition and activities of their overall memberships, which increasingly are composed of substantial numbers, even majorities, of women and teenagers who are almost never regarded internally as leaders or spokespersons for racist groups.

A second source of data on racist movements is government intelligence and information from private anti-racist monitoring agencies such as Searchlight (England) or the Southern Poverty Law Center (US). These agencies collect and disseminate information from the public events of racist groups, as well as information acquired through arrests and criminal and civil prosecutions of racist members and groups, and from infiltrators or defectors from the racist movement. Such data have been used effectively to analyze the strategic and tactical operations of racist movements across the world. Yet the validity of such information too can be questionable since it is often collected to meet the needs or enhance the political advantages of monitoring agencies rather than for purposes of social scientific research.

A third and much less common source of data on racist movements is ethnographic observation of the inner workings of racist groups or interviews with their members. To get access to accurate information while protecting the safety of a researcher requires lengthy and delicate negotiation with racist activists, so these data have only been collected on a small number of racist groups, limited geographical areas, and subsets of racist activists such as women or teenaged white power skinheads. Conclusions derived from analyses of these data may have limited generalizability.

GAPS IN RACIST MOVEMENT RESEARCH

There are large gaps in what is known about racist movements. The difficulty of collecting valid data on secretive and dangerous groups, as well as widespread scholarly aversion to studying loathsome social movements, has resulted in a paucity of research on racist social movements relative to social movements that advocate progressive social change. There is a need for additional research on four important aspects of racist movements.

First, there is virtually no data on global circulation of ideas, strategies, resources, or members of racist movements. It is unclear whether or how racist movements in various parts of the world have coordinated their efforts, or even how the notion of pan-Aryan unity has been received across different racist movements.

Second, scholars do not fully understand how and why people are attracted to racist ideas and movements. The theory that adherence to racist groups is a product of individual pathologies or irrational emotions is clearly inadequate, but a clearer understanding of the mechanisms and motivations of racist movement recruitment has not been formulated.

Third, there is only fragmentary evidence about the range of outcomes that are associated with different types of racist movements. It is unclear, for example, whether the adoption of Christian Identity precepts is likely to precipitate strategies of terrorist violence. It is also unknown whether small, secretive racist groups will prove to be more durable than larger racist movements.

Finally, the connections between racist movements and the social contexts in which they emerge and are sustained needs additional study. It is not enough to assert that racist societies provide the social environment in which racist movements can develop, as there is considerable variation in the extent to which this occurs. Rather, researchers need to explore the mechanisms that link the extreme ideologies of racist movements with the normative and institutionalized racist practices of their societies.

SEE ALSO: Anti-Semitism (Social Change); Conflict (Racial/Ethnic); Ethnic, Racial, and Nationalist Movements; Race; Race and Ethnic Politics; Race (Racism); Racial Hierarchy; Scapegoating; Separatism; Social Movements; Terrorism

REFERENCES AND SUGGESTED READINGS

Barkun, M. (1997) *Religion and the Racist Right: The Origins of the Christian Identity Movement.* University of North Carolina Press, Chapel Hill, NC.

Bennett, D. H. (1988) *The Party of Fear: From Nativist Movements to the New Right in American History.* University of North Carolina Press, Chapel Hill, NC.

Blee, K. M. (1991) *Women of the Klan: Racism and Gender in the 1920s.* University of California Press, Berkeley.

Blee, K. M. (2002) *Inside Organized Racism: Women in the Hate Movement.* University of California Press, Berkeley.

Brustein, W. (1996) *The Logic of Evil: The Social Origins of the Nazi Party, 1925–1933.* Yale University Press, New Haven.

Cunningham, D. (2004) *There's Something Happening Here: The New Left, the Klan, and FBI Counterintelligence.* University of California Press, Berkeley.

Dobratz, B. & Shanks-Meile, S. (1997) *"White Power, White Pride!": The White Separatist Movement in the United States.* Twayne, Boston.

Ezekiel, R. (1995) *The Racist Mind: Portraits of Neo-Nazis and Klansmen.* Viking, New York.

Fredrickson, G. M. (1981) *White Supremacy: A Comparative Study in American and South African History.* Oxford University Press, New York.

Fredrickson, G. M. (2002) *Racism: A Short History.* Princeton University Press, Princeton.

Futrell, R. & Simi, P. (2004) Free Spaces, Collective Identity, and the Persistence of US White Power Activism. *Social Problems* 51(1): 16–42.

Kaplan, J. & Bjørgo, T. (Eds.) (1998) *Nation and Race: The Developing Euro-American Racist Subculture.* Northeastern University Press, Boston.

MacLean, N. (1994) *Behind the Mask of Chivalry: The Making of the Second Ku Klux Klan.* Oxford University Press, New York.

Olzak, S. (1992) *The Dynamics of Ethnic Competition and Conflict.* Stanford University Press, Stanford.

Twine, F. (1998) *Racism in a Racial Democracy: The Maintenance of White Supremacy in Brazil.* Rutgers University Press, New Brunswick, NJ.

Radcliffe-Brown, Alfred R. (1881–1955)

Bernd Weiler

Alfred Reginald Radcliffe-Brown and Bronislaw Malinowski (1884–1942) are generally considered to be the "founding fathers" of British social anthropology. Born into a poor family in Sparkbrook, Birmingham, Radcliffe-Brown attended King Edward's School and worked in a library in Birmingham before being awarded a scholarship for Trinity College, Cambridge, in 1902. At Cambridge Radcliffe-Brown, whose interest in the social sciences was allegedly stimulated by his acquaintance with H. Ellis and P. Kropotkin, took his undergraduate work in Mental and Moral Science. Toward the end of his formal education he turned to anthropology, studying with, among others, W. H. R. Rivers, A. C. Haddon, and C. S. Myers, all veterans of the famous Torres Straits Expedition (cf. Kuper 1989: 36–49; Stocking 1996: 306). In 1906, after one year of preparation, Radcliffe-Brown went to do fieldwork among the Andaman Islanders, who in the evolutionist framework were supposed to be among the "lowest" peoples on earth. Upon his return in 1908, Radcliffe-Brown became a fellow at Trinity College and, as he wrote in a letter to M. Mauss in 1912, found himself "in complete agreement with the view of sociology put forward in the *Année sociologique*" as well as being "the first person to expound ... [Durkheim's] views in England." Between 1910 and 1912 he conducted further ethnographic research in Western Australia. After World War I Radcliffe-Brown, whose ethnography on *The Andaman Islanders* (1922) appeared in the same year as Malinowski's work on the Trobrianders, led a nomadic academic existence, teaching anthropology at Cape Town, Sydney, Chicago, Yenching, Oxford, São Paulo, London, Manchester, Alexandria, and Grahamstown, South Africa. From the late 1930s, when Malinowski left for the United States and Radcliffe-Brown returned to England, to the early 1950s, Radcliffe-Brown's (structural) functionalism dominated British social anthropology. Social scientists influenced by Radcliffe-Brown's teaching in and outside Great Britain include (the early) E. E. Evans-Pritchard, M. Fortes, S. F. Nadel, M. Gluckman, I. Schapera, A. P. Elkin, M. N. Srinivas, F. Eggan, R. Redfield, S. Tax, and W. L. Warner.

As a theorist Radcliffe-Brown, together with Malinowski, is generally credited for having led the "synchronic and nomothetic revolution" in anthropology, thereby discarding at the same time the theories of social evolutionism and diffusionism. Radcliffe-Brown defined social anthropology as the comparative sociology of "primitive societies." He concurred with F. Boas and his school that the schemes of social evolutionism had often been highly speculative based upon flimsy facts and that anthropology had to employ thorough methods of observation and data collection. In contrast to the Boasians, however, who sought to reconstruct the history of a particular culture or culture area, he argued that the objective of anthropology was to find social laws. The discovery of these laws required generalizing about a particular society's "social structure," which was amenable to direct observation, and to bring to light its "structural form," its recurrent patterns of relationships. In a second step of generalization, one was to compare the "structural forms" of different societies. Radcliffe-Brown hoped that this comparative analysis would eventually yield social laws akin to those that had already been found in the natural sciences (Barnard 2001: 70–9).

Radcliffe-Brown's theoretical work is commonly subsumed under the heading of functionalism or structural functionalism. Rejecting the idea that societies are mere agglomerates of fortuitous elements and relying upon the "organic analogy," Radcliffe-Brown emphasized the fact that all communities had to have a certain level of interconnectedness and unity in order to survive. In contrast to Malinowski, who argued that culture was "functional" to the extent that it satisfied individual biopsychological needs, Radcliffe-Brown followed the sociological approach of Spencer and Durkheim and defined the function of a recurrent activity, for example a funeral ceremony, as "the part it plays in the social life as a whole" (Radcliffe-Brown 1952: 180). Denouncing the search for origins as futile, Radcliffe-Brown argued that in order to understand a typical activity or an institution, it was not necessary to know its history and how it had developed over time but to know how it contributed to the continuity of the structure in the present. Despite the later critique of Radcliffe-Brown's work, especially of his anti-historical bias, his disregard of social change, his "oversocialized conception of man," his all-too-harmonious depiction of society, the colonialist ideology implicit in functionalism, and the vagueness of his central concept of "structural continuity," his ideas were formative not only for modern kinship studies and for political and legal anthropology, but also for subsequent functionalist and structuralist theory building in anthropology and sociology. In histories of anthropology, Malinowski is often portrayed as the "culture hero" of fieldwork, whereas Radcliffe-Brown is seen as the first truly scientific theorist of British social anthropology whose enduring legacy lies in his emphasis on comparative and generalizing analyses.

SEE ALSO: Anthropology, Cultural and Social: Early History; Culture; Durkheim, Émile; Function; Functionalism/Neofunctionalism; Malinowski, Bronislaw K.; Parsons, Talcott

REFERENCES AND SUGGESTED READINGS

Barnard, A. (2001) *History and Theory in Anthropology*. Cambridge University Press, Cambridge.

Fortes, M. (Ed.) (1949) *Social Structure: Studies Presented to A. R. Radcliffe-Brown.* Clarendon Press, Oxford.
Kuper, A. (Ed.) (1977) *The Social Anthropology of Radcliffe-Brown.* Routledge & Kegan Paul, London.
Kuper, A. (1989) *Anthropology and Anthropologists: The Modern British School.* Routledge, London.
Langham, I. (1981) *The Building of British Social Anthropology: W. H. R. Rivers and his Cambridge Disciples in the Development of Kinship Studies, 1898–1931.* D. Reidel, Dordrecht.
Radcliffe-Brown, A. R. (1923) The Methods of Ethnology and Social Anthropology. *South African Journal of Science* 20: 124–47.
Radcliffe-Brown, A. R. (1952) *Structure and Function in Primitive Society: Essays and Addresses.* Free Press, Glencoe, IL.
Radcliffe-Brown, A. R. (1957) *A Natural Science of Society.* Free Press, Glencoe, IL.
Radcliffe-Brown, A. R. (1958) *Method in Social Anthropology: Selected Essays by A. R. Radcliffe-Brown.* Ed. M. N. Srinivas. University of Chicago Press, Chicago.
Stocking, G. W. (1984) Radcliffe-Brown and British Social Anthropology. In: Stocking, G. W. (Ed.), *Functionalism Historicized: Essays on British Social Anthropology.* University of Wisconsin Press, Madison, WI.
Stocking, G. W. (1996) *After Tylor: British Social Anthropology, 1888–1951.* Athlone Press, London.

radical feminism

Eve Shapiro

Radical feminism arose in the US, Canada, and Britain out of young women's experiences within the civil rights, New Left, and anti-war movements of the 1960s. Drawing on de Beauvoir's concept of "sex-class" from *The Second Sex* (1952), radical feminism – emerging from what was known in the late 1960s as the women's liberation movement – developed an analysis of women's inequality at the social structural level and was a revolutionary (as opposed to reformist) movement that called for fundamental institutional and cultural changes in society. There were three key beliefs guiding radical feminist analysis and activism. First and foremost, radical feminism argued that gender was the primary oppression all women face in society. Second, it asserted that women were, either essentially or due to social construction, fundamentally different from men. Third, it held that social institutions and norms rely on women's subordination, and consequently are constructed to maintain and perpetuate gender inequality in all aspects of life, including around deeply personal facets like sexuality and reproduction.

Radical feminism was distinct from the surge in liberal feminist activism committed to fostering change within existing institutions that also emerged in the late 1960s. As Sara Evans documented in *Personal Politics* (1980), during the 1960s women gained experience as activists and were simultaneously faced with sexism within progressive movements. Out of these experiences women formed radical feminist groups such as the Chicago Women's Liberation Union, the London Women's Liberation Workshop, and the Redstockings, seemingly overnight in 1967 and 1968. Within a year there were hundreds of radical feminist groups across the US, Canada, and Britain that combined personal education, public protests, and cultural development. Radical feminism was the most dominant force in the development of feminist activism and scholarship through the mid-1970s and has continued to influence offshoots including cultural feminism and lesbian feminism, and academia in the form of women's studies.

A REVOLUTIONARY MOVEMENT

In her article "The Women's Rights Movement in the US: A New View" (1968), Shulamith Firestone argued that the women's liberation movement has historically been a revolutionary movement. Firestone retold the story of first wave feminist activism as a radical movement, drew historical connections to anti-racist and anti-capitalist movements, and asserted that the emerging feminist movement was the continuation of this legacy. It was this belief that equality demanded a drastic transformation of social institutions that made radical feminism revolutionary.

Radical feminists theorized that sex-class (women as a distinct class unto themselves) was a social phenomenon maintained through violence and social sanctions, and advocated women's autonomy from men in all aspects of society. Out of this ideology developed critiques of all social institutions, including language, science, capitalism, family, violence, sexuality, and law. These radical critiques examined how institutions maintained inequality and oppressed women. For example, Susan Griffin and Susan Brownmiller both argued that rape was not about sex but about the enforcement of patriarchal control and misogyny. Activists such as Ti Grace Atkinson argued that patriarchal oppression pervaded all aspects of women's personal and public life and that the only path toward equality was a fundamental restructuring of all social institutions.

PERSONAL IS POLITICAL

One of the most important concepts to come out of radical feminism was the idea that the "personal is political." What radical feminists meant by this was that women's intimate experiences of oppression (e.g., within the family) were not isolated experiences, but rather products of institutional inequality. Out of the analysis that oppression affected all facets of life came a number of social-movement tactics.

Consciousness-raising (CR) groups – small gatherings where women shared their experiences of sexism and developed a collective feminist critique – were a fundamental part of radical feminist organizing. Originating with the New York Radical Women, CR groups quickly became a staple of radical feminism. They were aimed at helping women understand their own experiences through the lens of radical feminist ideology and politicizing them around gender oppression in the process. It was through these groups that issues such as rape, abortion, and sexuality (both heterosexuality and homosexuality) became politicized issues for feminist movements.

Radical feminism also created new movement structures and organizational forms. In an effort to eradicate what were viewed as patriarchal power relations, radical feminist groups developed non-hierarchical, consensus-based structures and processes. Radical feminist organizations often developed numerous subcommittees to address the many arenas of social change women's liberation groups saw as central. The Chicago Women's Liberation Union, for example, had more than 20 working groups, including daycare, an abortion referral service, a prison project, a graphics collective, and a newspaper. Radical feminism utilized a number of new social-movement tactics, including "zaps," or action-oriented protests, guerrilla theater, and the creation of alternative institutions such as women-run health care centers, music labels, and mechanics shops.

DEMANDING STRUCTURAL CHANGE

One of the first radical feminist protests was held at the opening of Congress in January 1968. The "Jeanette Rankin Brigade," named after the first woman elected to Congress and led by Rankin herself, brought 5,000 women affiliated with women's peace groups to demonstrate against the Vietnam War. At this protest the New York Radical Women staged a guerrilla theater piece titled "Burial of Traditional Womanhood," and it was at this protest that the phrase "sisterhood is powerful" was first used.

A much more highly publicized protest was held a few months later on the Atlantic City boardwalk during the Miss America Beauty Contest. Joining forces with members of the New York chapter of the National Organization for Women, a liberal-feminist organization, radical feminist groups disrupted the Miss America pageant and demonstrated on the boardwalk. Drawing on radical feminist ideology, the street theater performed on the boardwalk drew connections between capitalism, patriarchy, mass media, and beauty myths and catapulted the burgeoning women's liberation movement into the public spotlight. It was out of this protest that the myth of "bra burning" arose, even though no bras were burned. A similar protest was staged in Britain in 1970 at the Miss World competition in London. Radical feminist protesters interrupted the competition shouting "We're not beautiful, we're not ugly, we're angry" and throwing tomatoes and flour bombs at the emcee Bob Hope.

While radical feminist activism was decentralized with no national leadership or organization as part of empowering all women to be feminist activists and leaders, groups did work together. In 1971 British women's liberation groups held a conference at Ruskin College in Oxford to discuss movement goals and strategies. In the US on August 26, 1970 radical feminist groups across the country participated in "strike for equality" marches to commemorate the 50th anniversary of women's suffrage. Reflecting the exponential growth of feminist movements between 1967 and 1970, 50,000 women marched in New York City, 3,000 in Chicago, 2,000 in Boston, and countless others in cities and towns across the country.

Some of the most significant legacies of radical feminist organizing are the service organizations that grew out of women's liberation groups. Domestic violence shelters were founded in the early 1970s, as were rape crisis centers, feminist bookstores, and women's studies programs. Canadian radical feminists worked through the Women's Legal Education and Action Fund to argue and win a Canadian Supreme Court obscenity case. Echoing the radical feminist analysis that "pornography is the theory, rape is the practice," the 1992 Butler decision ruled that the potential harm pornography could inflict on women was more significant, legally, than freedom of expression. US scholar Andrea Dworkin and lawyer Catherine MacKinnon, who worked to introduce antipornography legislation in the US, influenced this legal approach to institutional change.

"GAY–STRAIGHT SPLIT" AND CULTURAL FEMINISM

As Nancy Whittier explored in *Feminist Generations*, an in-depth study of the radical feminist community in Columbus, Ohio, by the end of the 1970s, differences between radical and liberal feminisms became less clear as liberal groups radicalized and radical feminism moved toward self-help and service organizations. Similarly, Suzanne Staggenborg documented how radical feminist organizations became more centralized and hierarchical in structure over time. Radical feminists criticized this shift toward what came to be called cultural feminism as a diversion from revolutionary change. But as Taylor and Rupp argued in "Women's Culture and Lesbian Feminist Activism: A Reconsideration of Cultural Feminism" (1993), the development of women-focused institutions, community, and culture was a successful means of perpetuating feminist activism in an increasingly hostile environment.

As part of the development of cultural feminism, there was a split within radical feminist communities around sexuality. Sparked by homophobia within feminist movements, nascent lesbian-centered feminist theorizing such as Adrienne Rich's "Compulsory Heterosexuality and Lesbian Existence" (1983), and sexism within the gay liberation movement, lesbian-identified feminists developed a separate branch of feminism. Lesbian feminism extended radical feminist ideology and argued that gender and sexuality are inexorably linked and work dialectically to reinforce patriarchal power.

SCHOLARSHIP

Guided by radical feminist ideology, scholars such as Kate Millett and Anne Koedt created a body of feminist research that emerged in the 1970s and has continued to the present. Early anthologies documented the emergence and ideological development of feminist movements. This early scholarship focused on reclaiming contemporary and canonic theories from a woman-centered viewpoint. For example, drawing on and elaborating Marx's concept of historical materialism, Shulamith Firestone developed a theory of women's oppression and the primacy of sexism in the *Dialectics of Sex* (1970). Other authors focused on substantiating claims about the structural norms that maintain gender inequality. Gayle Rubin's 1975 article, "The Traffic in Women: Notes on the Political Economy of Sex," asserted that kinship and marriage norms functioned to trade women as property in the service of men's social relationships. Similarly, Mary Daly argued in *Gyn/Ecology: The Metaethics of Radical Feminism* (1978) that language itself was patriarchal and that women needed to create new words to replace oppressive language. Much of this research supported the radical feminist belief in fundamental differences between men and women. For example,

Carol Gilligan's controversial book *In a Different Voice* (1981) argued that women make different moral judgments than men, and radical feminists used this to support arguments that women were, indeed, morally superior.

Other feminist scholars documented feminist activism and elaborated ideological tenets. Books such as *The Politics of Women's Liberation: A Case Study of an Emerging Social Movement and Its Relation to the Policy Process* (1975), by Jo Freeman, and Alice Echols's groundbreaking *Daring to Be Bad: Radical Feminism in America, 1967–1975* (1989), helped bridge feminist academic research and activism. More recently, scholars like Belinda Robnett and Verta Taylor have examined radical feminist movements in more detail from a social movement's perspective. Benita Roth argues in *Separate Roads to Feminism: Black, Chicana, and White Feminist Movements in America's Second Wave* (2004) that while earlier case studies have erased or dismissed the involvement of black and Chicana women in radical feminism and other second wave movements, significant numbers of women of color participated in feminist movements.

CRITIQUES

The central critique of radical feminism, which emerged alongside organizing and scholarship, was that theorizing women as a sex-class obscured differences between women, especially in terms of race, class, and nation. In *Black Feminist Thought: Knowledge, Consciousness, and the Politics of Empowerment* (1990) Patricia Hill-Collins described the interrelationships of oppression as a "matrix of domination" and argued that radical feminism marginalized women of color and poor women and perpetuated classism and racism in the process. This marginalization happened within activism, scholarship, and theorizing. In one of the first and most important anthologies by women-of-color feminists, *This Bridge Called My Back* (Moraga & Anzaldua 1981), women of color wrote about the intersections of race, class, gender and nation, feminist movements, and marginalization. Over time, more specific anthologies about Chicana, Asian/Pacific Islander, and black women also appeared, such as *Homegirls: A Black Feminist Anthology* (1983), edited by Barbara Smith.

The second significant critique of radical feminism has been the focus on identity and women's difference. Post-modern and queer theorists such as Judith Butler and Elizabeth Grosz have asserted that radical feminist ideology essentialized differences between men and women, and in so doing reinforced and reified gender roles and indeed gender itself. Transgender activists have developed similar critiques of radical feminism and argued that attributing traits to essentialist notions of womanhood and manhood reinforces the naturalization of both gender and sex.

Regardless of these critiques radical feminist theorizing has continued to influence feminist activism and scholarship. The institutional legacies, in the form of rape crisis centers, women's studies programs, and community political organizations, continue to thrive, and radical feminist ideology continues to shape contemporary feminist movements.

SEE ALSO: Black Feminist Thought; Cultural Feminism; Essentialism and Constructionalism; Feminism; Feminism, First, Second, and Third Waves; Feminist Activism in Latin America; Lesbian Feminism; Matrix of Domination; Personal is Political; Pornography and Erotica; Social Movements; Socialist Feminism; Women's Movements

REFERENCES AND SUGGESTED READINGS

Crow, B. (Ed.) (2000) *Radical Feminism: A Documentary Reader.* New York University Press, New York.

Howe, F. (Ed.) (2000) *The Politics of Women's Studies: Testimony from Thirty Founding Mothers.* Feminist Press, New York.

Marx Ferree, M. & Hess, B. (1994) *Controversy and Coalition: The New Feminist Movement.* G. K. Hall, Boston.

Moraga, C. & Anzaldua, G. (Eds.) (1981) *This Bridge Called My Back: Writings by Radical Women of Color.* Kitchen Table Press, New York.

Rudy, K. (2001) Radical Feminism, Lesbian Separatism, and Queer Theory. *Feminist Studies* (Spring).

Taylor, V., Wittier, N., & Pelak, C. F. (2000) The Women's Movement: Persistence through Transformation. In: *Feminist Frontiers V.* McGraw-Hill, New York.

radio

Tim Crook

Human social life depends upon the constant development and varied uses of modes of communication. Social existence also relies on shared and contested understandings of the world. This necessitates the systematic study of communication and culture, and of their mediation through a variety of channels. The sociology of radio concentrates on the role of the radio medium in this process. Radio is now embedded in a complex intermedia world. It is not a medium that has been substantially substituted by the subsequent development of alternative modes of communication. But the changing nature of communications technology has led to a change in style of content and social function of radio in human communities.

In most societies radio enjoyed a paradigmatic status in the electronic arena prior to the establishment of television. During this time radio content contained a significant amount of speech programming. Following the assertion of television as the dominant form of electronic entertainment and information, radio formats became dominated by music programming. In the post-industrial age speech and cultural affairs programming now tends to be underwritten by public/state broadcasting institutions.

The sociological approach investigates the regional, national, and global order in which the radio cultural and communications industries have played an increasingly central role, and the way radio media forms and practices participate in social and political organization and creative expression. It concentrates on understanding the role of radio in contributing to symbolic structures in human interaction, and the specific tasks involved in addressing their changing role in contemporary societies.

The sociology of radio is an interdisciplinary and multidisciplinary process that draws from the arts, humanities, and social sciences. As such, it involves the mapping and testing of concepts and theories in a cartographic intellectual arena marked by many locations of academic contestation. Both quantitative and qualitative methods of inquiry have been employed. In simple terms, the subject oscillates between qualitative analysis of radio texts, a discourse on the relationship with social, cultural, political, and economic contexts, and social scientific measurements of quantifiable data so that there is an inductive background to deductive assertions.

The sociology of radio is an academic process that is central to the modern subject of media or communication studies. Indeed, it could be argued that an intellectual sociological investigation of radio was a key starting point for studying the nature of human communication in society in the twentieth century.

Qualitative textual analysis borrows from "rhetoric" (the study of oral and written communication), an academic discipline stretching back to the time of ancient Greece and Rome. It was a key subject in the Middle Ages and during the European Renaissance and Enlightenment. The sociology of radio is also influenced by the development of academic disciplines over the last three centuries that interrogated concepts such as public opinion, mass audience, propaganda, information war, and communications media. The paradigmatic age of radio stimulated academics to see the links between radio broadcast content and oral and written communications of social, political, and aesthetic discourse. The study of the electronic medium of radio appeared to stimulate a much more complex interdisciplinary analysis of media and linked sociology with psychology, anthropology, and other subjects.

T. H. Pear of Manchester University appears to have undertaken the first serious academic investigation of the social psychological impact of radio. In research conducted between 1927 and 1931 he focused on the relationship between voice and personality. His methodology would be considered crude by contemporary standards, but it was qualitative and quantitative and conducted in accordance with the prevailing notions of scientific and laboratory discipline. He even had the cooperation of the BBC in broadcasting special performances so that listeners could fill out questionnaires distributed by the BBC's listings magazine, *Radio Times.* He wanted to explore the process of listening to radio drama on the BBC. He approached the project by exploring radio drama from the listener's end, the psychological problems of listening to radio drama, imagining the unseen through experiments connected with radio drama, a discourse on the issue of radio and talking films, and whether radio broadcasting and listening had any role in the construction of the radio personality. He published his research in *Voice and Personality* in 1931.

In the US, Hadley Cantril and Gordon W. Allport followed up Pear's work in Britain. Again, they concentrated on the social psychology of radio. However, they extended the inquiry with wider sociological concerns. As a result they contextualized radio listening not only from the point of view of radio as a psychological novelty, but also to include issues such as the influence of radio upon mental and social life, the nature of the American radio industry, its institutions, the process of "fashioning the listener's attitudes and opinions," censorship, propaganda, the sponsorship and content of programs, and listeners' tastes and habits. They also conducted experiments concerning voice and personality, sex differences in radio voices, the differences between human speaker and electronic speaker reception, listening versus reading, and whether there were effective conditions for broadcasting. Their approach was practical as well as abstract. They wanted to assess the sociological implications of broadcasting technique, entertainment, advertising, education, and the argument that radio could extend the social environment. This research was published in *The Psychology of Radio* in 1935.

In Britain, Hilda Matheson published a book called *Broadcasting* in the Home University Library of Modern Knowledge series in 1933 that appears to be one of the first sociological discourses on radio's role in twentieth-century society. Matheson had been head of talks at the BBC, had commissioned the development of an independent news section, and had background expertise on the role of propaganda as a result of her career in the Security Service (MI5) during World War I. Matheson analyzed the role of radio historically and its social context from the point of view of living speech, public opinion, literature and drama, music, entertainment, education, and its relationship with the state. Her approach was logical and pioneering: "When we talk of the effects of broadcasting, we usually think in the first instance of the effects upon the body of actual listeners – upon their tastes in music, their general interests, and their social habits. It is obvious, however, that the ripples in the pond reach much further than this." Despite her modest avowal that the text was a mere "brief sketch of broadcasting," Matheson had set out a sociological agenda with an appreciation of the cultural and aesthetic role of radio broadcasting.

One of Matheson's colleagues at the BBC, Charles A. Siepmann, emigrated to the US and took up the sociological baton of analysis with the polemical *Radio's Second Chance* in 1946 and the more academic *Radio, Television and Society* published in 1950. Siepmann declared that his primary purpose was to outline "the history of a cultural revolution and to show what has been discovered by research concerning the effects of radio and television upon our tastes, opinions, and values. The second purpose is to deal with broadcasting as a reflection of our time and to throw light upon the problems of free speech, propaganda, public education, our relations with the rest of the world, and upon the concept of democracy itself" (Siepmann 1950: v). Siepmann widened Matheson's international analysis between UK and US broadcasting and he divided his study between systems and institutions of broadcasting and the social implications of radio in terms of propaganda and public opinion, freedom of speech in theory and practice, radio and education, and world listening. His engagement with television was somewhat peripheral, as by 1950 it was still a somewhat inchoate medium, though expanding exponentially in its social and cultural role in American and British societies.

Among the more influential thinkers who have linked sociological approaches with other disciplines are Harold Innis (1894–1952), associated with the "bias of communications"; Marshall McLuhan (1911–80), who wrote about the concept of the "global village"; and Jürgen Habermas, the German post-Frankfurt School sociologist who has highlighted the role of the public sphere as a social zone for the discourse of ideas and expression of a public view. Each of them lived during the so-called Golden Age of radio when it was the dominant electronic medium of communication. All three touched on, though did not prioritize, the social role of radio in their writing.

Radio has been both an origin and a bridge for distinctive genres and forms of storytelling across the timeline of human communities. Thus, the television serial was derived from the radio serial, which was derived from the serialized novel published in magazines during the nineteenth century. The use of speech balloons in twentieth-century cartoons and comic books was present in Renaissance religious art. The newspaper strip cartoons were both based on and inspired radio serials as an established popular genre of entertainment and comedy.

Moral panics and condemnation of new media forms have followed the popularity of charismatic public poetry in the age of Plato, plays performed in the seventeenth and eighteenth centuries, published romances, "penny dreadfuls," the "yellow press," and "muck-raking" pamphleteers in the nineteenth century. In the early days of radio there were fears that transmitters could change the weather, make women pregnant, host the souls of the deceased, and induce insanity. States were quick to ration, control, and censor radio broadcasting and reception and there were debates, as was the case with film, television and the Internet, that radio broadcasting could be a causal factor in generating social delinquency, sociopathy, and sexual deviance.

The groundbreaking social science research project into the link between radio broadcasting and social action, perhaps the first mass media moral panic inquiry, was conducted by Hadley Cantril with the assistance of Hazel Gaudet and Herta Herzog between 1938 and 1940. They investigated, quantitatively and qualitatively, the impact of the Halloween broadcast by Orson Welles's CBS Mercury Theatre of the Air in October 1938. The radio broadcast of the dramatization of H. G. Wells's *War of the Worlds* appeared to have been a causal factor in widespread panic and anxiety. Thousands of listeners were unable to distinguish its fictional content from the reality of a news broadcast. The *War of the Worlds* study stemmed from the setting up of the Office of Radio Research with Paul F. Lazersfeld as director, and Frank Stanton and Hadley Cantril as associate directors. The Rockefeller Foundation made the office's first grant to Princeton University in 1937. The *War of the Worlds* study was funded by a special grant from the General Education Board. The field HQ of the research office had been based in New York City, and when it was felt that the project should be relocated to a more local university, it transferred to Columbia University in the spring of 1940. The Office of Radio Research became the most significant center for sociological analysis of radio as a mass medium in the history of the subject and its record of research output is unrivalled. It had the opportunity of investigating radio during its primacy as a mass medium and so historically it is the laboratory control phase without the competition from television that emerged after World War II. Furthermore, the studies centered on the largest and most complex and powerful capitalist society. The research also occurred during a period of extraordinary social human catastrophe. Lazersfeld and his wife Herzog and many of the researchers associated with the office were German/Austrian Jewish exiles. It is likely their background of Nazi persecution heavily influenced their intellectual and cultural approach. Their study and analysis of US society was dominated by a Marxist critical framework.

The office's first significant publication was *Radio and the Printed Page* in 1940. The premise of the study was that in less than 20 years radio had just about reached the goal toward which print had been working for 500 years: to extend its audience to include the whole population. The researchers wished to pose these questions: Will radio displace reading? Is the average man as much affected, moved to action, by what he hears as by what he reads? And most important of all, who listens to what? The office based its findings on thousands of detailed interviews held with radio listeners of every type all over the US. The study focused on the conflict of radio and the press and its economic, educational, sociological, and political implications.

Radio Research 1941 published a rich range of sociological analysis. Rudolf Arnheim and Martha Collins Bayne investigated foreign-language broadcasts over local American stations, Duncan MacDougald, Jr. analyzed the role of radio and the popular music industry, Theodor Adorno studied "The Radio Symphony – an experiment in theory," Edward A. Suchman turned his attention to the study of the creation of new music listeners by the radio, and

Frederick J. Meine concentrated on radio and the press among young people. Meine focused on answering three questions: Where do young people get most of their news? What are the factors which influence news consumption? What are the factors which influence knowledge of the news?

William S. Robinson's work on radio and the farmer constituted a complex sociological study. He started with the phenomenon of radio and the rural individual, ways of studying individual effects, interest in national and international affairs, radio as an educational instrument, and the effect of radio and migration from the farm. He extended his study to investigate the issue of controlling rural opinion and action via radio, some social effects of radio in terms of unorganized social intercourse, organized social intercourse, deliberateness of decisions and the social effects of radio, and radio and church attendance.

Rudolf Arnheim had published a qualitative discussion of radio aesthetics in *Radio* published in 1935. His writing was primarily poetic and philosophical and progressed from discussion of issues such as the imagery of the ear and the world of sound, to practical production techniques of direction and distance, spatial resonance, sequence and juxtaposition, and the necessity of radio-film. He did touch on sociological questions when analyzing "In Praise of Blindness: Emancipation from the Body," the relationship between author and producer, the art of speaking to everybody, wireless and the nations, and the psychology of the listener.

By 1941 Theodor Adorno had completed a masterful qualitative study of the phenomenon of neo-fascist charismatic US radio broadcasters such as Father Charles Coughlan. Adorno focused on the broadcaster called Martin Luther Thomas. *The Psychological Technique of Martin Luther Thomas's Radio Addresses* was not published until 1976 in German and 2000 in English. His study represents a seminal textual analysis of the cultural technique and sociology of using radio to propagandize the listener into social action. Adorno concentrated on the personal element in self-characterization of the agitator, Thomas's broadcasting method, the religious dimension of broadcasting and reception, and Thomas's engagement with ideological bait.

Radio Research 1942–43 marked a significant expansion of the center's sociological work on radio in the US. Herta Herzog and Rudolf Arnheim investigated the textual content and reception of daytime serials that constituted the primary form in the talk broadcasting of the time. Charles A. Siepmann began an important study on the role of radio in wartime. This involved looking into the relation between government and industry, the dissemination of information, and the use of radio in furthering understanding.

The head of radio audience research at the BBC, Robert J. E. Silvey, made a contribution on studying radio listening in Britain. Ernst Kris, Hans Herma, and Howard White presented a substantial analysis of German radio propaganda. Radio in operation was represented by studies in program profiling and the industry's use of a system called the Program Analyzer. John Gray Peatman explored radio and popular music. Progress in listener research was represented by Boyd R. McCandless's study on why people did not listen or stopped listening to radio. Alfred Udow and Rena Ross investigated the role of bias in radio broadcasting and Ernest Dichter presented a paper on the psychology of radio commercials.

The Office of Radio Research became a division of an expanded Bureau of Applied Social Research at Columbia University and radio's role in the 1940 presidential election was represented in the substantial quantitative and qualitative project *The People's Choice* (Lazarsfeld et al. 1944). Chapter 14, "The Radio and the Printed Page," investigated the concentration of exposure to radio compared to print publication during the election, and whether radio had a key role in decisions taken by voters. Quantitative analysis indicated people highly exposed to one medium of communication also tend to be highly exposed to other media, there are relatively few who are highly exposed to one medium and little exposed to the other, and people highly exposed at one time also tend to be highly exposed at another time of the campaign. The study sought to pose the question: Which is more influential: radio or newspaper?

The People Look at Radio (1946) and *Radio Listening in America* (1948) involved collaboration between nationwide surveys conducted by the National Opinion Research Center at the universities of Denver and Chicago and analysis by the Bureau of Applied Social Research at Columbia University. Both these studies investigated the listener's attitude to radio broadcasting, including the content and process of advertising. The research was critical and complex in its conclusions. Lazersfeld reported in 1946 that "for different groups of the population radio has quite different functions: group tastes and their expectations vary much more than the ordinary listener, and very often the individual broadcaster is aware" (Lazersfeld & Field 1946: viii). *Radio Listening in America* extended the analysis and confirmed that tastes in radio content differed widely in terms of social and economic status, education, age, sex, and urban or rural existence. Persons in upper-income groups, for example, tended to favor serious music and radio forums more often than did people lower on the economic scale. Far more men than women regularly listened to news broadcasts. City dwellers preferred classical music, whereas rural residents were partial to plaintive western music.

Sociological examination of radio became subsumed into a wider communications approach with television becoming paradigmatic from the early 1950s. The key landmarks in the social history of broadcasting are the five-volume series *The History of Broadcasting in the United Kingdom* by Asa Briggs and the three-volume series *A History of Broadcasting in the United States* by Erik Barnauw. Paddy Scannell and the late David Cardiff began an elegantly written *A Social History of British Broadcasting.* However, this project did not progress to subsequent volumes and it is understandable that Briggs and Barnauw transferred their focus to the social history of television in later volumes.

In recent years there has been a promising development in "radio studies" which is primarily grounded in the disciplines of sociology and cultural studies. The *Journal of Radio Studies* (US) and *Radio Journal: International Studies in Broadcast and Audio Media* (UK) provide an opportunity for peer-reviewed papers. Goldsmiths College, University of London offers a defined postgraduate course in "Radio Studies: A Cultural Enquiry," and there is evidence of increased interest in continuing significant research into both the textual form and contextual social topography of radio broadcasting.

SEE ALSO: Adorno, Theodor W.; Mass Media and Socialization; Media; Media and the Public Sphere; Moral Panics; Public Broadcasting; Public Opinion

REFERENCES AND SUGGESTED READINGS

Adorno, T. (2000) *The Psychological Technique of Martin Luther Thomas's Radio Addresses.* Stanford University Press, Stanford.

Arnheim, R. (1935) *Radio.* Faber & Faber, London.

Barnauw, E. (1966–90) *A History of Broadcasting in the United States*, 3 vols. Oxford University Press, Oxford.

Briggs, A. (1961–95) *The History of Broadcasting in the United Kingdom*, 5 vols. Oxford University Press, Oxford.

Cantril, H. & Allport, G. W. (1935) *The Psychology of Radio.* Harper & Brothers, New York.

Cantril, H., Gaudet, H., & Herzog, H. (1940) *The Invasion From Mars: A Study in the Psychology of Panic with the Complete Script of the Famous Orson Welles Broadcast.* Princeton University Press, Princeton.

Lazersfeld, P. F. (1940) *Radio and the Printed Page.* Duell, Sloan, & Pearce, New York.

Lazersfeld, P. F. & Field, H. (1946) *The People Look at Radio.* University of North Carolina Press, Chapel Hill.

Lazersfeld, P. F. & Kendell, P. L. (1948) *Radio Listening in America: The People Look at Radio – Again.* Prentice-Hall, New York.

Lazersfeld, P. F. & Stanton, F. N. (1941) *Radio Research 1941.* Duell, Sloan, & Pearce, New York.

Lazersfeld, P. F. & Stanton, F. N. (1944) *Radio Research 1942–1943.* Duell, Sloan, & Pearce, New York.

Lazersfeld, P. F., Berelson, B., & Gaudet, H. (1944) *The People's Choice: How the Voter Makes Up His Mind in a Presidential Campaign.* Duell, Sloan, & Pearce, New York.

Pear, T. H. (1931) *Voice and Personality.* Chapman & Hall, London.

Scannell, P. & Cardiff, D. (1991) *A Social History of British Broadcasting*, Vol. 1: *1922–1939.* Blackwell, Oxford.

Siepmann, C. A. (1946) *Radio's Second Chance.* Little, Brown, Boston.

Siepmann, C. A. (1950) *Radio, Television and Society.* Oxford University Press, New York.

Sterling, C. H. (2004) *The Museum of Broadcast Communications Encyclopedia of Radio*, 3 Vols. Fitzroy Dearborn, New York.

random sample

Roger E. Kirk

A census, which is a survey of every unit in a population, is rarely used to gather information in the social sciences because it is often costly, time consuming, or impracticable. Instead, researchers gather the information from a sample that is assumed to be representative of the population. Such a sample can be obtained by using a *simple random sampling procedure*. The procedure selects a sample of size n without replacement from a finite population of size $N < n$ such that each of the $N![n!(N - n)!]$ possible samples is equally likely to be selected. The resulting sample is called a *simple random sample*. Simple random sampling is a type of *probability sampling*. Probability sampling procedures have three common characteristics: (1) the units that compose the population and the units that are excluded from the population are explicitly defined; (2) every potential sample of a given size that could be drawn from the population can be enumerated; and (3) the probability of selecting any potential sample can be specified. In the case of simple random sampling, each sample has the same probability of being selected and the probability of selecting a particular sample is $1/\{N![n!(N - n)!]\}$. Non-probability sampling procedures do not satisfy one or more of the three characteristics. A familiar example of a non-probability sampling procedure is *volunteer sampling*. As the name suggests, people volunteer to be in the sample. Television viewers, for example, are frequently encouraged to express their opinion about an issue of the day by calling a 900 number. Those viewers who choose to call the number are a non-random sample. Such callers typically have stronger opinions about the issue than non-callers.

Simple random sampling has two interrelated advantages over non-random sampling. First, randomness avoids bias, that is, a systematic or long-run misrepresentation of the population. Second, randomness enables researchers to apply the laws of probability in determining the likely error of sample statistics. A particular random sample rarely yields an estimate of the population characteristic that equals the population characteristic. However, the expected value of the sample estimate over an indefinitely large number of samples will equal the population characteristic. Furthermore, for any random sample, it is possible to estimate the magnitude of the error associated with the estimate.

Four other sampling procedures also are used to obtain a probability sample: systematic random sampling, stratified random sampling, cluster sampling, and multistage sampling. A *systematic random sampling procedure* is one that (1) selects a unit randomly from the first $k = N/n$ units in a list of the population and (2) selects every kth unit in the list after the initial selection. A *stratified random sampling procedure* divides the population into separate groups, called strata, and then selects a simple random sample from each stratum. The sampling is called *proportional* if the proportions of the sample chosen in the various strata are the same as those existing in the population. The sampling is disproportional if the sampled proportions differ from the population proportions. A *cluster sampling procedure* divides the population into a large number of groups, called clusters. A number of clusters are selected randomly to represent the population, and then all units within the selected clusters are included in the sample. The procedure differs from stratified random sampling in that all units within the selected clusters are included. A *multistage sampling procedure* is similar to cluster sampling, but has at least two stages. For example, in the first stage, a random sample of clusters is chosen. In the second stage, units are randomly chosen from the selected clusters.

One of the earliest serious efforts to apply statistical theory to random sampling procedures was made by A. L. Bowley (1913). It remained for J. Neyman to solidify the role of statistical theory in random sampling procedures. In a landmark paper published in 1934, Neyman emphasized, among other things, the importance of random rather than purposive selection of units and extended stratified simple random sampling to the sampling of clusters.

A simple random sample can be obtained in a variety of ways once a list of the units in the population has been made. The list is called the *sampling frame*. To obtain a sample that contains half the units in the sampling frame, a researcher can flip a fair coin. If the coin toss yields, say, a head, the unit is in the sample. Alternatively, a researcher can record the name or identifying code for each unit in the sampling frame on a slip of paper. The slips of paper are placed in a container and thoroughly shuffled. The first n slips drawn without bias from the container compose the sample. The most common method of obtaining a simple random sample uses random numbers. Tables of random numbers can be found in most statistics textbooks. Computer packages such as SAS, SPSS, and MINITAB and many hand calculators have routines that produce numbers that in every observable way appear to be random. Tables of random numbers contain a sequence of random digits whose terms are chosen so that each digit is equally likely to be 0, 1, . . ., 9 and the choices at any two different places in the sequence are independent. For convenience, the digits in a random number table are often grouped with two digits, four digits, and so on in each group. To use a table to select a simple random sample of size, say, $n = 20$ from a population of size $N = 895$, assign the numbers 001, 002, . . ., 895 to the units in the sampling frame. Select a starting point in the table by dropping a pointed object on the table. Choose three-digit numbers beginning at the starting point until 20 distinct numbers between 001 and 895 are obtained. The sample consists of the units corresponding to the 20 numbers selected. This procedure is called *sampling without replacement* because once a number has been selected, the number is ignored if it is encountered again.

SEE ALSO: Chance and Probability; Convenience Sample; Experimental Methods; Statistical Significance Testing

REFERENCES AND SUGGESTED READINGS

Bowley, A. L. (1913) Working-Class Households in Reading. *Journal of the Royal Statistical Society* 76: 672–701.

Neyman, J. (1934) On the Two Different Aspects of Representative Method: The Method of Stratified Sampling and the Method of Purposive Selection. *Journal of the Royal Statistical Society* 97: 558–625.

Scheaffer, R. L., Mendenhall III, W., & Ott, L. O. (1996) *Elementary Survey Sampling*, 5th edn. Duxbury, North Scituate, MA.

Schutt, R. (2004) *Investigating the Social World: The Process and Practice of Research*, 4th edn. Sage, Thousand Oaks, CA.

rape culture

Joyce E. Williams

Rape culture is a concept of unknown origin and of uncertain definition; yet it has made its way into everyday vocabulary and is assumed to be commonly understood. The award-winning documentary film *Rape Culture* made by Margaret Lazarus in 1975 takes credit for first defining the concept. The film's narration relies heavily on jargon such as "rapism" and "phallocentric society" and is more illustrative than definitive in dealing with rape as depicted in movies, music, and other forms of entertainment. Authors of the popular *Transforming a Rape Culture* define the phenomenon as "a complex of beliefs that encourages male sexual aggression and supports violence against women . . . a society where violence is seen as sexy and sexuality as violent" (Buchwald et al. 1993: v). An earlier definition was offered by Herman (1984), who characterized the US as a rape culture because the image of heterosexual sex is based on a model of aggressive male and passive female. At the other end of the continuum of definitions are efforts to define a rape culture empirically, such as are found in the work of Baron and Straus (1989) and Ellis (1989). Some empirical works on rape theorize its emanation from a subculture of violence, for example societies with high homicide rates also tend to have high rape rates (Amir 1971; Baron & Straus 1989). Other researchers have stressed that social settings such as created by some male gangs or fraternities produce rape-prone subcultures (Boswell & Spade 1996; Sanday 1996). Clearly, rape is more common and acceptable in some environments than in others. However, the concept of rape culture inextricably connects rape with the cultural fabric of the *whole* of society.

All indications are that the term rape culture emerged simultaneously from a number of sources in the 1970s as a part of the anti-rape crusade of the women's movement. The concept of a rape culture is socially constructed as a result of feminist consciousness-raising over the past three decades. This makes the phenomenon no less real but suggests that the activities and public rhetoric of the anti-rape feminists raised public awareness to the point that a large segment of society, and certainly the media, intuitively know what is meant by rape culture. Social scientists, however, still struggle to define the term and most resort to dealing with it operationally or as a cluster of characteristics or variables. The linkage of rape and culture is an interesting one if dissected grammatically. Rape, a noun or verb transitive, is used as an adjective modifying culture, suggesting a deliberate inseparability: all of rape is linked to culture and all of culture is permeated by rape. To link the two words has the intended effect of linking learned behavior and attitudes (culture) in a causal way to non-consensual sex (rape). Use of the word rape as descriptive of culture suggests a pattern of behavior created, organized, and transmitted from generation to generation as part of the expectations associated with being male and being female. Rape culture is not an either/or phenomenon but exists in varying degrees, from the institutionalization of rape to its perfunctory punishment as crime. In the most strident form of rape culture, women are the property of men who deny them respect and the right to control their own bodies (Brownmiller 1975).

Although the concept of a rape culture is somewhat murky in meaning, its popularization helped to shift the causal paradigm of rape from psychology to sociology and, cross-culturally, to anthropology. Until the 1970s, rape was viewed not as a social problem but as the act of predator against victim, and the "sick rapist" was the most facile explanation. A cultural or societal explanation of rape moved causation from a micro to a macro level. The underlying assumption is clear: rape is not just the problem of individual rape victims who were accosted by sex-crazed rapists. Rape is a socially and culturally produced problem and it must be addressed at the societal level. A rape culture is a product of behaviors and attitudes as well as of the institutions supporting those behaviors and attitudes. While the United States is not the only society to have a rape problem, rape is not a universal problem (Mead 1963 [1935]; McConahay & McConahay 1977; Sanday 1981a), nor is the term rape culture or even rape a meaningful concept cross-culturally.

Feminists theorize a direct cause and effect between women's empowerment and rape – societies where women are empowered politically and economically will be characterized by low incidence of rape and the opposite will be true in societies where women lack empowerment. Most feminists contend that rape culture is generated and maintained by a social structure of gender inequality: political, economic, and social. Such a structure allows and enables men, as arbiters of power, to exploit and abuse women – consciously and unconsciously. By contrast, a society where women are strong or equal to men in positions in government and in the financial world, and have been for some time, is a society where women are less likely to be exploited in pornography or by demeaning stereotypes and where rapes against women are infrequent.

Gender equality is more complex than can be represented by drawing a direct inverse relationship between the status of women and rape, as evident in the fact that rape rates sometimes go up even as the status of women improves (Baron & Straus 1989). At least two other variables may intervene: the status of women vis-à-vis men and the temporal dynamics of male–female gender roles. First, the status of women is meaningful only in relation to that of men. For example, it is not how much women earn but how much they earn in comparison with males, and the same is true of the number of women in positions of decision-making power, or of their legal/statutory equality. Second, it is essential to look at the dynamics of the status of women vis-à-vis men and to know how these dynamics have changed over time or if they are currently in a state of change. It is in the latter case that rape rates will often increase even as the status of women is improving – that is, things will get worse before they get better. There are two explanations for this phenomenon. According to the "backlash theory," as the status of women begins to change, it represents a disruption of traditional male authority and female subordination and men become more aggressive toward women in an attempt to retain their control, and in the short term rape rates will increase (Baron & Straus 1989; Austin & Young 2000). As Sanday (1981b: 163) put it, "when the cup of life that defines the male world is broken, men organize to protect their traditional rights," but she goes on to cite examples of women doing the same thing when their traditions are threatened. An alternative but related explanation is that as women become more equal, their social and work-related activities and movements are less restrictive and they become more vulnerable to a male population whose roles and attitudes have not changed to keep pace with new female sex roles. The activities of the "liberated female" may simply make her more accessible or signify to a traditional male that she is "asking to be raped." Cross-culturally, McConahay and McConahay (1977) found a significant positive correlation between sex-role rigidity and violence (including rape).

Rape is historically a product of women's lower status and at the same time works as a mechanism to keep women unequal (Sanday 1981a; Baron & Straus 1989). This circularity is no doubt the reason that empirical data fail to show a consistent inverse relationship between rape and women's equality. The concept of a rape culture also represents something of a contradiction in the culture and social organization of the United States: rape is culturally produced and maintained by a culture that then makes it illegal. On the one hand, rape is encouraged if not condoned by popular representations of sexuality and of socially scripted male–female behaviors. On the other hand, rape is a culpable crime although its handling by police and the judiciary is selective and leaves much to be desired (Williams & Holmes 1981). Rape and other forms of sexual assault are legally defined by a governmental entity as (in the case of the US) one of the 50 states. Due in large measure to the success of the anti-rape movement, many states have replaced rape laws with more gender-neutral and inclusive sexual assault laws. While there are many variations, in general these laws prohibit sexual penetration when it is carried out by force or without consent of the victim (male or female). The exception is statutory rape, where age rather than consent is the determining factor. The old rape laws defined unwanted and forced sex as between a man and a woman and also included a spousal exemption, which meant that a man could not (by legal definition) rape his wife. Feminists lobbied for and succeeded in changing these laws on the basis of their being designed more to protect women as the property of men than women for their own worth.

A rape culture is characterized by a high frequency of rape and other forms of violence against women, the full extent of which is unknown. Incidents of rape are the lowest when measured by police reports, about 65 per 100,000 females in 2002 (Uniform Crime Reports 2002). A victimization survey, based on a 2002 sample of households, recorded 80 rape victims per 100,000 population over age 12, with just over half of the self-reported victims having reported the offense to the police (Rennison & Rand 2003). Other research studies among samples or populations of women put self-reports of rape or some form of sexual abuse over a lifetime as still higher (Russell 1984; Koss 1992). Cross-cultural and international statistics on the incidence of rape are also available, although comparisons are difficult because of varying definitions and methods of reporting. Using any of these reports, however, the US, compared with other industrialized nations, is characterized by a high incidence of rape and sexual assault (Mayhew & van Dijk 1997; Austin and Young 2000).

A rape culture is characterized by female moral and social responsibility. Women are socialized to assume responsibility for controlling the "naturally aggressive" behavior of men in interpersonal relations and by restricting their own movements and behavior. Failure to meet this responsibility leads to victim-blaming of women who are raped if they are deemed of questionable reputation or engaged in activities such as hitchhiking or drinking alone in a bar (Williams & Holmes 1981). This element of a rape culture links the perception of women as the moral guardians of society with a kind of supermacho syndrome, or what Baron and Straus (1989) termed "hypermasculinity." Both females and males are socialized to believe that men are by nature sexual predators. Sexual limits and restraints are to be set by the female because men will "do what men do." When coupled with the all too common myth that women like the aggressive approach from males and even need such aggression to overcome their inhibitions about sex, the outcome is often women who feel violated and men who are surprised when accused of rape. In the same context, males who hold traditional gender roles frequently see females who violate these roles by the way they dress or behave or the kind of work they do as "asking to be raped" (Malamuth 1981).

A rape culture is a culture of fear for women, one in which girls at a very early age internalize fear and a sense of restriction simply because they are female. As Brownmiller (1975: 15) put it, rape serves as "a conscious process of intimidation by which all men keep all women in a state of fear." Before they have a name for it, girls are socialized to know that something terrible could happen to them. Gordon and Riger (1989) label this as women's "special fear" that limits mobility and, in general, restricts the way they lead their lives. To grow up female in the United States and in some other countries is to internalize a fear unknown to males – knowledge that you can be raped. There is also the knowledge, constituting a part of the fear, that if you are raped you will be subjected to character scrutiny and perhaps blame from others and from the criminal justice system that should be your advocate (Williams & Holmes 1981). This is not to say that men cannot be and are not raped, but they are not socialized to expect it whereas women are. For women rape is part of the "natural environment" (Gordon & Riger 1989). Women are taught to protect themselves against unknown sexual predators by avoiding provocative dress, "unlady-like" behaviors and activities, and even association with the "wrong" people, or being in the wrong place at the wrong time. If males fear for their safety, it is not (except perhaps in prison) because of sexual predators.

A rape culture is one in which the media defines and depicts women as secondary and subordinate to males. These negative images range from the most pernicious form of pornography to seemingly innocuous "dumb blond" stereotypes. Research about the influence of the media on rape has focused largely on pornography and, to a lesser extent, on violence in general (Baron & Straus 1989). Perhaps equally important are the more socially acceptable entertainment venues such as magazines, movies, television, and videos that fail to distinguish between the passion of love, the passion of sex, and the passion of power in rape. Even television and radio commercials, music, and print advertisements still perpetrate stereotypes that women are, at best, weak and, at worst, manipulative. They are portrayed as unable to make decisions, as in need of direction, and as using sex appeal to exploit males. Such images make their way into the popular subconscious and continue to keep women vulnerable and rapeable. Baron and Straus (1989) established a linkage between the circulation of non-violent pornographic materials and state-by-state rape rates. However, they rejected a direct cause-and-effect relationship in favor of pornography's indirect effect on rape in that it is symbolic of a macho or hypermasculinity culture. On the other hand, feminists such as Brownmiller (1975) link pornography to denigration of women and to the Freudian myth of a woman's rape fantasy that many men choose to believe.

A rape culture includes a spillover impact from other forms of violence – illegitimate and legitimate or institutional. Some researchers report a positive association between homicide rates and rape rates (Amir 1971; Austin & Young 2000). Sanday's (1981a) cross-cultural research found that where violence is a way of life, it frequently achieves sexual expression. One example of institutionalized violence is war. Whether preemptive or defensive, war is historically and inevitably linked with rape. Brownmiller (1975) documented this linkage from the crusades through the Vietnam conflict. Rape is a "hallmark of success in battle," a method of retaliation or reprisal against the enemy. Another example of the spillover effect of institutional violence is that of slavery, where rape of black slave women by their white masters and other males associated with the master was routine, and even expected. In fact, slave masters sometimes offered young black girls to their guests or business associates as a favor or part of the household hospitality (Brownmiller 1975).

The major criticism of the concept of rape culture and of the feminist and social learning theories from which it draws is its monolithic implication that ultimately all women are victimized by all men (Ellis 1989). In reality, of course, all men are only potentially rapists. All women are not victims of rape or sexual assault in a physical sense. Symbolically, however, freedom for women will come only when rape is no longer a common element of the culture in which we live. Women will be free of their "special fear," and the need for labels such as rape culture will disappear when females and males are equally empowered, when a woman's safety is no longer her responsibility alone, and when masculinity is not equated with aggression and passivity with femininity. The concept of rape culture will lose its rhetorical usefulness when violence is a last resort rather than the preferred method of problem solving, when the media find female exploitation no longer profitable, and when rape as a criminal incident and as a personal tragedy becomes rare or unknown. In Sanday's (1981a) research of 95 tribal societies, almost half were categorized as "rape free," that is, rape was rare or unknown. Such societies are characterized by sexual equality, gender role complementarities, and an absence of interpersonal violence. Sanday used Minangkabau, a matriarchal tribal society in Indonesia, as her prototype, although in later research (1996) she expressed concern that Minangkabau was losing its rape-free culture to modernization. Nonviolent, egalitarian, and rape-free societies may exist in the present largely as an ideal type. It is, however, an ideal type that represents a goal for the obliteration of rape culture.

SEE ALSO: Consciousness Raising; Culture, Gender and; Gender Oppression; Gendered Aspects of War and International Violence; Inequality/Stratification, Gender; Male Rape; Pornography and Erotica; Rape/Sexual Assault as Crime; Sexual Harassment; Sexual Violence and Rape; Sexualities and Culture Wars; Sexuality; Socialization, Gender

REFERENCES AND SUGGESTED READINGS

Amir, M. (1971) *Patterns in Forcible Rape*. University of Chicago Press, Chicago.

Austin, R. L. & Young, S. K. (2000) A Cross-National Examination of the Relationship Between Gender Equality and Official Rape Rates. *International Journal of Offender Therapy and Comparative Criminology* 44(2): 204–21.

Baron, L. & Straus, M. A. (1989) *Four Theories of Rape in American Society*. Yale University Press, New Haven.

Boswell, A. A. & Spade, J. Z. (1996) Fraternities and Collegiate Rape Culture. *Gender and Society* 10(2): 133–47.

Brownmiller, S. (1975) *Against Our Will: Men, Women, and Rape*. Fawcett Columbine, New York.

Buchwald, E., Fletcher, P., & Roth, M. (1993) *Transforming a Rape Culture*. Milkweed Editions, Minneapolis.

Ellis, L. (1989) *Theories of Rape*. Hemisphere, New York.

Gordon, M. T. & Riger, S. (1989) *The Female Fear*. Free Press, New York.

Herman, D. (1984) The Rape Culture. In: Freeman, J. (Ed.), *Women: A Feminist Perspective*, 3rd edn. Mayfield, Palo Alto, CA, pp. 20–38.

Koss, M. (1992) The Underdetection of Rape: Methodological Choices Influence Incidence Estimates. *Journal of Social Issues* 48(1): 61–75.

McConahay, S. A. & McConahay, J. B. (1977) Sexual Permissiveness, Sex-Role Rigidity, and Violence Across Cultures. *Journal of Social Issues* 33: 134–43.

Malamuth, N. M. (1981) Rape Proclivity Among Males. *Journal of Social Issues* 37: 138–57.

Mayhew, P. & van Dijk, J. J. M. (1997) *Criminal Victimization in Eleven Industrialized Countries*. Ministry of Justice, The Hague.

Mead, M. (1963 [1935]) *Sex and Temperament in Three Primitive Societies*. Morrow Quill, New York.

Rennison, C. M. & Rand, M. R. (2003) *Criminal Victimization, 2002*. US Department of Justice, Washington, DC.

Russell, D. E. H. (1984) *Sexual Exploitation*. Sage, Beverly Hills, CA.

Sanday, P. R. (1981a) The Socio-Cultural Context of Rape: A Cross-Cultural Study. *Journal of Social Issues* 37(4): 5–27.

Sanday, P. R. (1981b) *Female Power and Male Dominance*. Cambridge University Press, New York.

Sanday, P. R. (1996) Rape-Prone Versus Rape-Free Campus Cultures. *Violence Against Women* 2: 191–208.

Williams, J. E. & Holmes, K. A. (1981) *The Second Assault: Rape and Public Attitudes*. Greenwood Press, Westport, CT.

rape/sexual assault as crime

Dawn Beichner

Prior to the mid-1970s, the crime of rape was defined by most state statutes in terms of the British Common Law and involved the "carnal knowledge of a female, not his wife, forcibly and against her will" (Bienen 1983: 140). Legislative reforms, designed primarily to reduce rape case attrition, redefined the crime of rape in sex-neutral language and replaced the single offense of rape with a series of calibrated sexual offenses and commensurate penalties (Largen 1987). Definitional changes resulted in an expansive category of sexual offenses, relabeled in such terms as "sexual battery," "sexual assault," or "criminal sexual conduct" (Bienen 1983).

Although there are jurisdictional variations in criminal statutes, the crime of rape is typically categorized as a first degree sexual assault or battery. *Rape* refers to completed or attempted sexual intercourse with another person by the use of forcible compulsion. The concept of *forcible compulsion* may refer to physical force or psychological coercion. The act of forced sexual intercourse may involve vaginal, anal, or oral penetration by the offender, using either his/her body or an inanimate object. This crime may involve heterosexual or homosexual intercourse, as well as male or female victims.

Second and third degree sexual assaults incorporate a wide range of completed or attempted sexual victimizations that are distinct from the crime of rape. These assaults include unwanted sexual contact with another person and may or may not involve the use of force on the part of the perpetrator. Some behaviors that are common in these categories are inappropriate fondling or grabbing; however, these crimes may also involve the perpetrator's lewd or lascivious behavior or speech while in the presence of the victim.

Regardless of statutory classification, sexual victimizations are among the most highly underreported crimes. Thus, given that victims may be unwilling to report their victimizations to strangers – police officers and researchers alike – determining the actual rates of sexual victimizations is highly problematic (Belknap 2001). Although there is no way to determine the exact number of sexual victimizations that are not reported to researchers, the most recent National Crime Victimization Survey data suggests that nearly half (46 percent) of all victimizations are not reported to police (Bureau of Justice Statistics 2003).

The issues surrounding underreporting notwithstanding, there are two primary sources for data on sexual victimizations in the United States: the National Crime Victimization Survey (NCVS) and the Uniform Crime Reports (UCR). Whereas the NCVS is a collection of information from US households for all victims – male and female – age 12 and older for sexual victimizations reported and not reported to the police, the UCR provides data on all completed and attempted forcible rapes and sexual assaults against female victims that have been reported to the police. The NCVS data suggest that there were an estimated 247,730 completed and attempted rapes and sexual assaults in 2002, resulting in a sexual victimization rate of 1.1 per 1,000 persons age 12 or older (BJS 2003). Comparable data from the UCR indicate that 95,136 sexual victimizations against female victims were reported to police in 2002, yielding a rate of 64.8 forcible rapes per 100,000 females (Federal Bureau of Investigations 2003).

A number of noteworthy trends emerge in the NCVS data related to disparities in sexual victimizations based upon victim sex, race, and age. Females are victimized at much higher rates than males; the rate of female victimization is 1.8 per 1,000, compared to the male rate of .3 per 1,000, respectively (BJS 2003). A second trend that emerges in comparisons of female and male victimizations is that females are more likely to be assaulted by non-strangers than their male counterparts; sexual crimes against females are generally committed by friends/acquaintances (40 percent), intimate partners (20 percent), or other relatives (7 percent). With respect to victim race, the NCVS data indicate that blacks are more likely to be victimized than whites; the black victimization rate (2.5 per 1,000) is significantly higher than that for whites (.8 per 1,000). Similarly, there are important differences in victimization rates related to age; victims aged 16–19 years have the highest victimization rate (58.2 per 1,000), compared to other categories (i.e., 12–15 years – 44.4; 20–24 years – 47.4; 25–34 years – 26.3; 35–49 years – 18.1; 50–64 years – 10.7; and 65 years or older at 3.4 victimizations per 1,000).

A number of scholars, in a variety of social and natural science disciplines, have attempted to explain what compels perpetrators to commit sexual victimizations. Generally, rape and sexual assault theories may be partitioned into three main categories: evolutionary/biobehavioral, feminist/sociocultural, and integrative. *Evolutionary or biobehavioral* explanations of sexual assault are derived from the core principles of biology, and more specifically, the process of natural selection (Jones 1999). Basically, evolutionary theorists consider rape as an aggressive copulatory tactic in response to natural selection pressures for males (Ellis 1989: 15). *Feminist or sociocultural* perspectives, on the other hand, posit that sexual gratification is not considered the prime motive for action; rather, sexual assault is seen as the use of sexuality to establish or maintain dominance and control of women by men (Ellis 1989: 11). Major proponents of this perspective acknowledge gender differentials in power and emphasize the role of socialization and culture in perpetuating sexual assault, asserting that sexual violence is learned and reinforced by societal themes which posit the male role as dominant over the female (Stock 1991: 68). *Integrative theories* of sexual assault posit explanations that encompass components of both evolutionary/biobehavioral and feminist/sociocultural theories, usually emphasizing one perspective over another.

SEE ALSO: Male Rape; Measuring Crime; Rape Culture; Sexual Violence and Rape

REFERENCES AND SUGGESTED READINGS

Belknap, J. (2001) *The Invisible Woman: Gender, Crime, and Justice*, 2nd edn. Wadsworth, Belmont, CA.

Bienen, L. (1983) Rape Reform Legislation in the United States: A Look at Some Practical Effects. *Victimology* 8: 139–51.

Bureau of Justice Statistics (BJS) (2003) *National Crime Victimization Survey: Criminal Victimization, 2002.* US Department of Justice, Washington, DC.

Ellis, L. (1989) *Theories of Rape: Inquiries into the Causes of Sexual Aggression.* Hemisphere, New York.

Jones, O. (1999) Sex, Culture, and the Biology of Rape: Toward Explanation and Prevention. *California Law Review* 87(4): 827–942.

Largen, M. A. (1987) Rape-Law Reform: An Analysis. In: Burgess, A. (Ed.), *Rape and Sexual Assault.* Garland, New York, pp. 271–92.

Stock, W. (1991) Feminist Explanations: Male Power, Hostility, and Sexual Coercion. In: Grauerholz, E. & Koralewski, M. (Eds.), *Sexual Coercion: A Sourcebook on its Nature, Causes, and Prevention.* Lexington Books, Lexington, pp. 61–74.

United States Federal Bureau of Investigation (2003) *Uniform Crime Reports for the United States, 2002.* US Government Printing Office, Washington, DC.

rapport

C. Richard King

Rapport is best understood as a set of practices and problems in qualitative research describing how simultaneously to get along with one's informants and get information from them. Specifically, it refers to the establishment of good relationships between interviewers or ethnographers and their research subjects. Rapport covers a range of moral and methodological concerns at the heart of the social inquiry, including empathy, immersion, participation, friendship, honesty, collaboration, trust, exploitation, negotiation, and loyalty.

Rapport should not be read as a synonym for friendship, though researchers may become friends with those with whom they work and play. Certainly a means to deeper understanding, it is not, however, an instrumental circuit under the control of the researcher, but something informants, in part, must give (up). And while terribly desirable, even ideal, it is not an end, but a beginning. At root, rapport is a social relationship, an achieved outcome and continuous process emerging from human interaction. It describes a context or connection that makes people feel comfortable enough to open up, be themselves, and share unknown aspects of their lives. In this light, ethnographers and interviewers often conceive of rapport as an ineffable bond, the trust and intimacy they share with their informants. Ideally, this bond binds the two together, granting researchers the capacity to capture the humanness of the other and render it in emphathetic, if not internal, terms, while creating a safe space in which informants may set aside pretension and confide hidden truths and unappreciated experiences. Far from selfless, then, rapport remains a pathway to information and the foundation for interpretation. Qualitative researchers regularly talk about establishing rapport as a means to gain access, a way to get into a community, and subsequently get better, truer, more authentic accounts from informants.

Rapport demands reciprocity, risk, and responsibilities. Qualitative research, rather than an extraction of information or one-way transfer of data, hinges on sharing and collaboration, human interactions and meaningful, if always unequal, exchanges of knowledge and affect. In this context, rapport emerges when scholars and subjects give of themselves, committing one to another. Informants contribute stories, experiences, commentary, and connections with others, while interviewers and ethnographers affirm, validate, and give voice. Rapport demands, moreover, that both researchers and their informants take risks. To create safe spaces, they must make themselves vulnerable, opening themselves, reaching beyond expected boundaries, and exposing parts of themselves often kept hidden. Finally, rapport takes shape and persists only in contexts in which participants remain accountable to one another, at once honest and forthcoming. The notion of commitment acts (Feldman et al. 2003) captures each of these elements. In the field or the interview session, a researcher must join, ally, or commit to her informants. These might be small gestures such as hanging out and completing mundane tasks unexpectedly. These might be grander endeavors, for instance refusing to cooperate with the police. Or these might be more long term, as when a black urban community over time comes to welcome a white ethnographer because she lives with them in poverty. Big and small, spontaneous, unspectacular, and daring, such displays and deeds make real and material a researcher's commitment to his subjects, binding one to the other and ultimately contributing to the establishment and maintenance of rapport.

As a consequence of intersubjective and instrumental elements, rapport has long presented qualitative researchers with a series of dilemmas. These might be productively grouped together under the headings of distance, difference, and deceit.

Many scholars have struggled with how close to get to their informants. Researchers have long been warned about the dangers of going native – that is, of losing the detachment essential for balanced and penetrating insights. They once struggled with how to immerse themselves in a community while remaining objective and how to be intimate and alive in the field without threatening their subsequent analyses. For a time, perhaps for many still, rapport has encouraged scholars to get close, to get along, and to get information, but not confuse these processes with relationships that might alter or distort their findings. Hence, rapport mediates the troubling tensions some locate at the heart of qualitative inquiry.

At the same time, the ideal of rapport has forced researchers to reflect upon the promise and limitations of difference for social inquiry. Specifically, they have argued over whether alterity or identity is more important for the cultivation of rapport.

Until quite recently, difference between scholar and subject was preferred in qualitative research. Not only was it held that encountering the unfamiliar would foster enhanced objectivity, and hence more reliable findings, but it was also posited by many that the gap between self and other could actually facilitate the establishment of rapport, unfettered by conventional assumptions and social arrangements. Perhaps most importantly, uniting these arguments was the belief that strangeness fostered greater insight because informants will reveal more to an interested and empathetic outsider. As a black informant told Rhodes (1994) during her work in Britain: "I wouldn't have had a talk like this with another black person. I can discuss these sorts of things more easily with you. With a black person, you would just take it for granted." Nevertheless, critics have countered that being an outsider can limit access and empathy, making intimacy and analysis more challenging, unless or until scholar and subject find a common ground of experience or circumstance, often through acts of commitment.

In the wake of struggles for racial, sexual, and gender equality and reflective of a broader postmodern trend in social inquiry, researchers increasingly have championed the importance of similarity and identity to the establishment of rapport. This perspective asserts that if scholars and subjects share one or more cultural attributes or social locations, such as gender, sexual identity, race, or spirituality, it will be easier for them to build an open, honest, and empathetic relationship. Researchers can more easily enter into and gain acceptance in such contexts, while also understanding their informants and making them more comfortable. Consequently, they have an advantaged position that enhances their access and understanding. Critiques of the matching of scholar and subject on the basis of race, gender, and other socially ascribed features have highlighted a number of weaknesses with this position. First, it assumes that trust is established through rather superficial qualities, such as skin color or language, when in fact the connections between researchers and informants is much more complex and processual. Second, it essentializes experience and identity, suggesting, for instance, that women will bond with women because they are women, when in fact issues of class, education, age, sexuality, or race might individually or collectively work to make it harder for specific women to trust a female interview or ethnographer. Third, and worse, for many researchers striving to establish rapport from the inside, there are greater expectations and in turn heightened pressure on them to act in accordance with local norms. Perhaps what the personal struggles and professional debates about difference and identity reveal most fundamentally about rapport is that there is no secret formula or sure way to achieve it. Instead, as the concern over getting inside and being inside illustrates, establishing trust, fostering openness, and gaining access always emerge out of the expectations, interactions, and interpretations of researchers and their informants.

Even if one can find comfortable ways to negotiate questions of difference and distance, rapport poses a third, arguably more vexing, problem: to what extent does the cultivation of trust and the maintenance of productive connections with informants mandate that researchers deceive them? Scholars routinely hide aspects of themselves from the people whom they study. Keeping one's sexual identity, religious values, or political views hidden can be crucial as researchers seek to secure access and intimacy. Such lies of omission make it possible for their informants to talk openly and honestly, and if they were told it is likely that the kind and quality of research conduct would suffer. Less frequently, but not uncommonly, researchers have opted to lie about their objectives, background, and everyday lives to foster trust, honesty, and openness. While such falsehoods may be productive, granting scholars access to individuals and information, they unsettle the ethical compact at the core of social inquiry.

In many respects, rapport posits that it is desirable for researchers to bond with those they study, cultivating compassionate understandings of their beliefs and behaviors. Indeed, rapport remains productive as long as ethnographers approach the people they study empathetically, sharing political and social commitments, no less than interpersonal attachments. Once researchers begin to think critically, to study up, to disagree with, or even dislike the people they study, rapport begins to lose its luster. The emotive and intellectual bonds facilitating trust, collaboration, and identification at the core of rapport become uneasy when one focuses on relationships of domination and dehumanization or studies those who participate in or benefit from hurting other informants in a social field. Researchers have rightly asked how they can and should approach repugnant others. Several alternatives have been suggested as a means to get beyond the limitations of rapport. Some have insisted that critique replace compassion at the heart of social inquiry, making rapport less attractive or feasible, while encouraging novel points of departure and forms of engagement (Springwood & King 2001). Others have proposed that scholars confront their subjects, forcing them to engage individuals they belittle, demonize, or harm (Wieviorka 1993).

Undoubtedly, rapport will continue to anchor qualitative inquiry, even as technological innovations, such as the Internet, and novel questions encourage sociologists to rethink it. Indeed, rapport will continue to matter to scholars and subjects precisely because it mediates moral and methodological concerns, as well as the tensions between intersubjectivity and interpretation, central to qualitative research and the social worlds it struggles to comprehend.

SEE ALSO: Ethics, Fieldwork; Ethics, Research; Ethnography; Interviewing, Structured, Unstructured, and Postmodern; Key Informant; Naturalistic Inquiry; Objectivity; Observation, Participant and Non-Participant

REFERENCES AND SUGGESTED READINGS

Duncombe, J. & Jessop, J. (2002) Doing Rapport: And the Ethics of "Faking Friendship." In: Birch, M., Jessop, J., & Miller, T. (Eds.), *Ethics in Qualitative Research*. Sage, London, pp. 107–22.

Feldman, M. S., Bell, J., & Berger, M. T. (2003) *Gaining Access: A Practical and Theoretical Guide for Qualitative Researchers*. Alta Mira Press, Walnut Creek, CA.

Gordon, D. (1987) Getting Close by Staying Distant: Fieldwork with Proselytizing Groups. *Qualitative Sociology* 10: 267–87.

Rhodes, P. J. (1994) Race-of-Interviewer Effects: A Brief Commentary. *Sociology: The Journal of the British Sociological Association* 28(2): 547–58.

Springwood, C. F. & King, C. R. (Eds.) (2001) Coming to Terms: Reinventing Rapport in Critical Ethnography. Special Issue of *Qualitative Inquiry* 7(4).

Wieviorka, M. (1993) *The Making of Terrorism*. University of Chicago Press, Chicago.

Wong, L. M. (1998) The Ethics of Rapport: Institutional Safeguards, Resistance, and Betrayal. *Qualitative Inquiry* 4(2): 178–99.

ratings

Geoff Lealand

Ratings is a term with wide currency, used in activities as diverse as judgments about standards of hotel accommodation to judgments of the economic health of corporations or nations (such as the Standard & Poor's Financial Strength Ratings). In contemporary media, however, the term ratings has more specific meanings, especially in respect of television, radio, and film, but there is also considerable ambiguity and confusion in its use and application.

Movie ratings, placed on films by regulatory bodies or industry self-regulation, are widely used across the globe to determine parameters for admission or guidance about content. They do not measure audiences (as in the box office), but guide or control Motion Picture Association of America (MPAA) and the national audiences according to their eligibility to see sexual, violent, or language content. In the United States, for example, the movie-rating system, jointly administered by the Association of Theater Owners, assigns movie ratings ranging from G (General Audience) to NC-17 (No Children 17 and Under).

Such American ratings cannot be legally enforced; they are strictly voluntary and carry no force of law. Nevertheless, it can be argued that they have acquired quasi-legal status in that they provide movie theaters with a premise to restrict admission. In other countries, they have clearer legal power. In the United Kingdom, for example, the ratings provided for films by the British Board of Film Classification (BBFC) can be enforced by local authorities, and there have been cases where local councils have attempted to contest BBFC ratings. BBFC ratings for videos are legally binding. In Singapore, all films to be distributed and exhibited are subject to ratings imposed by the government-controlled Media Development Authority (MDA), with no intermediary rating between PG (Parental Guidance) and NC16 (No Children Below 16).

The different application of movie ratings across the world means that in countries where there is significant government control of the circulation and exhibition of film, ratings are equivalent to direct censorship; in other cases, they are formal or informal guidelines. It can be argued, however, that even when ratings are not legally enforceable, they are still instrumental in encouraging industry self-censorship in film production and distribution. The imperatives of obtaining a box office-friendly MPAA rating can determine funding decisions, shape film content and marketing, and define the eventual audience. Shaping a film project to receive a G rating, for example, will mean that least objectionable content will be privileged, plot and narrative will follow an established and safe formula, and marketing is shaped to match the film to a broad, cross-generational audience of adults and children.

Conversely, a film with an NC-17 MPAA rating is regarded as box office poison as it effectively excludes the highly prized teenage market. Producers and distributors put great effort into avoiding such a rating. In 1999, for example, Paramount Pictures, as the distributor of the animated feature *South Park: Bigger, Longer, and Uncut*, successfully appealed the original NC-17 rating, in favor of a more box office-friendly R rating.

Because, in the United States, movie ratings operate as a system of classification rather than as formal censorship, there is a long-established and continuing tension between social norms and artistic and/or commercial freedoms. In July 2004, for example, a study conducted by the Harvard School of Public Health pointed to a decade-long "ratings creep," which had "allowed more violent and sexually explicit content into films, suggesting that movie raters have grown more lenient in their standards" (Waxman 2004). Other commentators have argued that the presence of such content merely reflects broader social changes or attitudinal shifts.

Newer media technologies such as the Internet and electronic gaming have embraced ratings. The Entertainment Software Rating Board (ESRB) has designed games ratings information for video and computer game content, which provide ratings symbols (recommended age appropriateness) and content descriptors (indicating elements in a game which may trigger a particular rating). Rating symbols range from EC-Early Childhood to AO-Adults Only, and content descriptors describe content such as Alcohol Reference and Sexual Violence (www.esrb.org). A World Wide Web consortium (W3C) determines standards for rating systems and rating information through the Platform for Internet Ratings (PICS), to counter the problem of minors accessing adult content on the Internet (msdn.microsoft.com/workshop/security/rating/ratings.asp).

Radio ratings, gathered through annual or half-yearly surveys of radio markets, are instrumental in constructing league tables which set advertising rates. In television, ratings have two major applications. The January 2000 compulsory insertion of the content-blocking V-chip in all new TV sets sold in the United States enables a TV Parental Guidelines system modeled after the MPAA rating system. Programs are encoded by broadcasters and are detected by the V-chip. Championed as a government response to a perceived problem (television violence), this technological fix appears to be little used and largely ineffectual.

Television ratings provide the primary source audience measurement, assigning value to audience demographics (factors such as age, gender, economic class, and area). Such measurement is carried out by global, specialist research companies, with Nielsen Media Research (owned by the Dutch conglomerate VNU) dominating the North American market. Given the imperatives of contemporary television ("delivering audiences to advertisers" in respect of commercial television; justifying broadcasting fees or sponsorship in respect of public service or non-commercial television), reliable audience measurement is critical. Peoplemeters (electronic diaries) are placed in a representative sample of television-viewing homes. The cumulative, self-reported viewing of these homes constitutes the official television audience, determining popularity of programming and channels as well as commodifying the television audience. There have been challenges from academic critics (Ang 1991; Lull 1998) who argue, for example, that observed behavior often contradicts the claims of ratings measurement. There have been industry criticisms of measurement distortions, viewer exhaustion (or "button burnout"), and the difficulties of measuring viewing in an increasingly fragmented and diversified media environment. Nevertheless, ratings continue to prevail, for they provide a continuous and viable means of providing tidy measurement, packaging, and institutional control of audiences.

SEE ALSO: Audiences; Film; Mass Media and Socialization; Media; Media Monopoly; Media Network(s) and; Media Regulation of; Public Broadcasting; Public Opinion; Radio; Television

REFERENCES AND SUGGESTED READINGS

Ang, I. (1991) *Desperately Seeking the Audience*. Routledge, London.

Lull, J. (1998) The Audience as Nuisance. *Critical Studies in Mass Communication* 5(3): 239–42.

Waxman, S. (2004) Study Finds Film Ratings Are Getting More Lenient. Online. www.nytimes.com/2004/07/14/movies/14MOVI.html?ex=1098417600&en=5bfcd9f55adb4891&ei=5070&oref=regi. Accessed 25 October, 2004.

rational choice theories

Brent Simpson

Rational choice theories explain social behavior via the aggregated actions of *rational* or *purposive* actors. The actors are rational in the sense that, given a set of values and beliefs, they calculate the relative costs and benefits of alternative actions and, from these calculations, make a choice that maximizes their expected utility. Rational choice models assume that the range of alternatives open to actors is constrained by the environment or by institutions within which they make their decisions. In their purest form, these theories also assume that actors possess complete information about their values and the various courses of action through which they can pursue them. Actors collect, organize, and analyze this information prior to making a decision. Thus, rational choice theories are means–end theories. That is, they describe the means or rational calculus through which actors go about obtaining their desired ends, or values.

Rational choice theory received its first formal treatment in economics, where it has long been the dominant paradigm. More recently, rational choice theory has become one of the dominant approaches in political science and has made a number of inroads into psychology and sociology.

RATIONAL CHOICE SOCIOLOGY AND LEVELS OF EXPLANATION

The introduction of rational choice into sociology has generated a fair amount of controversy, and debates about the place of rational choice approaches in sociology are ongoing. The position sociologists take in these debates is determined in part by whether they subscribe to *methodological individualism* or *methodological holism*. For methodological holists and the majority of methodological individualists, the objective of sociology is to explain macro-level social systems. (Other methodological individualists seek to explain the workings of micro-level social systems.) The two disagree on whether these social systems can be explained solely with other social systems (the holist position), or whether the theorist must "come down" to the micro level to explain the effects of one social system on another with reference to individual actors that comprise these systems (the individualist position).

All rational choice sociologists subscribe to some form of methodological individualism. The methodological individualist position holds that a theory must begin by stating how a social system (e.g., law or religion) affects the options available to individuals and how this (limited) range of options, in turn, affects individuals' decisions. The theory must then build back up to the macro level by describing how individuals' choices "aggregate" to impact a second system-level variable (e.g., economic development).

Much of the individualism/holism debate – and, by extension, the debate surrounding rational choice theory – is set against the backdrop of sociologists' attempts to clearly distinguish the discipline from other social sciences, especially economics and psychology. Advocates of methodological individualism and rational choice theory claim that obscured in these debates is that most ostensibly holist approaches actually incorporate individual-level assumptions (Heckathorn 1997). Because these micro assumptions are left implicit, however, the theories only give the appearance of being holist. From this point of view, these explanations could be made more precise (and the individualist–holist debate resolved) if holists simply stated their individual-level assumptions more explicitly.

While all rational choice theorists subscribe to some form of methodological individualism, not all methodological individualists are rational choice theorists. That is, some maintain that sociology needs a model of the actor, but oppose models based on rational choice principles. Others claim that rational choice theory is currently the most explicitly stated model of the actor, thus making it the best choice for a scientific sociology. These scholars often point to the success of rational choice theory in other social sciences as evidence that it should be adopted by sociology. While proponents of this position may concede that there remain important problems with the application of rational choice models, they maintain that the model simply needs refining.

There are important overlaps between the issues that lead some scholars to view rational choice theory as in need of a tune-up and those who view it in need of a complete overhaul. Some of these problems concern the *means* assumed in the rational choice approach (the rationality component), while other problems have to do with the *ends* typically assumed in applications of rational choice theory, i.e., that individuals are motivated by self-interest. Broadly speaking, research on the means assumptions is most closely associated with the work of psychologists and decision theorists. Sociologists have contributed much more to debates and research on the ends assumed in rational choice explanations.

MEANS

One of the main criticisms of rational choice theory (from all corners of social science) is the extensive cognitive and computational demand it places on actors. Decision scientists have shown that rather than judiciously gathering data about all possible courses of action, as rational choice theory assumes, humans greatly simplify their social worlds. For instance, instead of calculating the implications of all possible courses of actions, we generally consider a much smaller range of possible actions than are actually available to us, or simply act out of habit. When we do collect information about alternatives, we do not organize and process that information according to the dictates of rational choice theory. Instead, the organization and processing of information is subject to systematic cognitive biases. For instance, we often exaggerate the likelihood of events consistent with our beliefs and downplay inconsistent information. Similarly, we generally assign higher subjective probabilities to desirable outcomes than is warranted by a prudent assessment of the facts. That is, wishful thinking often short-circuits rational deliberation.

Decision scientists have directed attention to developing more realistic models of decision-making. *Bounded rationality* models recognize that humans are only capable of gathering, organizing, and processing a finite amount of information, and that much of this activity is subject to cognitive biases. Thus, these models replace the complex calculations assumed in traditional (unbounded) rational choice models with heuristics or rules of thumb.

One of the best-known bounded rationality approaches is Simon's (1982) *satisficing* model. In contrast to the maximizing principle assumed to guide decision-making in unbounded rationality approaches, the satisficing model assumes that an individual sets an aspiration level and then surveys various courses of action one by one. Once the individual happens upon a course of action that meets or exceeds the aspiration level, she stops surveying and selects that course of action.

Various learning and reinforcement models are also included under the bounded rationality rubric. These models eschew the optimization assumption of rational choice models in favor of reinforcement principles. Thus, these models assume that actors repeat choices that were rewarded in the past and avoid those that were punished. Like other bounded rationality approaches, learning models have been successfully applied to phenomena that do not readily lend themselves to traditional rational choice explanations. For instance, it is difficult to explain why a rational actor would shoulder the costs entailed in casting a vote in a large national election when the likelihood that the vote would be the deciding one is not significantly different from zero. Yet many do vote in these elections. Satoshi Kanazawa has used a learning model to explain voter turnout. The model assumes first that a citizen perceives a link between her decision (to vote or abstain) and the outcome (the preferred candidate wins or loses). That is, these outcomes are experienced as *reinforcers* or *punishers*. Thus, whether a person votes in a given election depends on whether the person voted in the previous election, and whether the person's preferred candidate was elected. Under specified conditions, this learning model is a good predictor of voter turnout patterns.

Successful applications notwithstanding, there are problems with bounded rationality models. For example, while there is little doubt that learning models more accurately reflect recurrent decisions than unbounded rationality approaches, they are generally silent about decisions made in novel situations. This is because actors have no past actions from which to make choices in new situations. Similarly, some contend that bounded rationality models are often left underspecified. For example, to make predictions, the satisficing model must specify the point at which the actor will satisfice (the actor's aspiration level) and exactly how the actor selects among alternatives to consider. But many contend that the specification of these parameters depends on the type of decision being made, and is context specific. Thus, a common criticism is that the increased realism of bounded rationality models is too often accompanied by a decrease in precision.

Some rational choice proponents argue that it does not matter whether the rationality assumptions closely match human behavior. The most important issue to these scholars is predictive power. If the rational choice model generates more precise predictions across a wider range of situations than alternative approaches, rational choice is the preferred theory. More generally, those taking this position contend that actual behavior need not coincide with rational choice axioms, so long as it results in outcomes similar to those that would obtain if it did.

Summing up, behavioral decision theorists have made much progress toward understanding the nuances of human decision-making, and how it differs from the assumptions of rational choice theory. The question for many is whether these understandings can be developed into models with the level of specification and generality of unbounded rationality approaches.

ENDS

At least since Weber, sociologists have been interested in the study of values. Although an explicit focus on values waned when functionalism fell out of favor, sociology has recently witnessed renewed interest. This can be attributed in part to debates about the place of rational choice theory in sociology.

Rational choice theory is officially silent on what actors value. In practice, however, rational choice theorists almost always assume actors are motivated by self-interest, narrowly defined to include only material wealth (and, less commonly, power and prestige). In fact, the assumption that actors seek to maximize their wealth and nothing else is so common in rational choice approaches that many mistakenly believe narrow self-interest to be axiomatic, rather than a "default" auxiliary assumption.

Some justify the assumption that actors pursue only material wealth by noting that wealth can be exchanged for valued immanent goods. When it can, these scholars contend, rational choice theory can safely use wealth as a proxy for these other ends. Others justify the typical value assumption on the grounds that it works well when predicting macro-level outcomes. For instance, Hechter (1994) notes that while there is generally variation in what actors value in a specific situation, this (micro-level) variation cancels out when decisions are aggregated to predict systemic outcomes. If so, under certain conditions, the typical value assumption may be sufficient for predicting aggregate outcomes.

Although some lines of research in rational choice sociology have fared well by employing the typical value assumption, many see a need to develop more realistic models of values. But the introduction of values into rational choice theory faces two hurdles, one measurement-related and the other theory-related.

Measuring values. At first glance, measuring values seems straightforward: simply ask people what they value. But such surveys pose a number of problems. First, people often conceal their true values in order to give off particular impressions to researchers or to others. Additionally, research shows that people may not always know what they value. Because of these problems, some researchers have focused on developing inferential approaches to ascertaining values.

One inferential approach, the *revealed preference method*, asks respondents to choose between pairs of goods. Assuming values are stable (which is not always the case), these revealed preferences can then be used in conjunction with the means assumptions of rational choice theory to predict outcomes in future choice scenarios. While such inferential methods are an improvement over survey measures of values, they can be much more expensive. Furthermore, inferential methods may sometimes be subject to some of the same problems as survey measures. For example, a respondent may make choices that are not consistent with his or her value-sets in order to make a good impression.

Explaining values. Sociologists generally trace values to some combination of natural selection, ecological conditions, and a person's memberships in various groups and social categories. These various sources are assumed to create a hierarchy of values. At the base, natural selection generates values essential to reproduction and survival (e.g., securing food and shelter). While evolutionary logic typically leads us to expect common values, other evolutionary theorizing leads us to expect, for example, sex differences in values. For example, Kanazawa (2001) has argued that males value wealth, power, and prestige more than females, tracing this difference to the different reproductive strategies males and females have evolved to pursue. He notes a rare point of agreement between evolutionary logic and feminist sociologists' critiques of rational choice theory – that the "typical value assumption" in rational choice sociology is more applicable to males than females.

At the next level, ecological conditions are expected to generate societal differences in values. As societies respond to unique historical and environmental conditions, sets of values are likely to emerge that are relatively similar within and different between societies. For example, sociologists have pointed to trust differences between Japanese and Americans. On average, Americans place a higher value than Japanese on trusting strangers, while Japanese prefer to stick to lower-risk, long-term relations. Toshio Yamagishi and his associates have traced these different values to societal differences in social networks and group organization.

Finally, at the highest (and most personal) level are those values that result from a person's membership in a unique set of groups and social categories. As suggested by Georg Simmel, because every person is affiliated with a unique set of groups, each can be expected to subscribe to a unique set of values. From this perspective, ceteris paribus, the fewer overlapping group (or category) memberships two persons share, the more distinct value-sets will be.

While persons undoubtedly select group affiliations based on existing values, sociologists have demonstrated how groups and categories influence the values to which people subscribe. For example, Melvin Kohn and his colleagues showed that the different occupational roles of working-class versus middle-class persons tend to generate different value systems. Compared to the middle class, working-class persons tend to place greater weight on values such as neatness and obedience. Middle-class persons, on the other hand, tend to place greater weight than members of the working class on values such as happiness and curiosity. Moreover, Kohn showed that these different values get passed down from one generation to the next. The effect of these values, once transmitted, can be to channel offspring into occupations similar to their parents.

Research by Frank et al. (1993) demonstrates how social categories such as college major can influence values. Specifically, they found that economics majors seem to satisfy the typical value assumption (i.e., place greater weight on self-interest) better than non-economics majors. They traced this difference to economics majors' continual exposure to rational choice theory and its typical value assumption. These results, like Kohn's, have important implications for how institutions and organizations pass on certain values.

An important question for rational choice sociology is how to synthesize such disparate findings from values research into a formal, coherent model of values. Only a few efforts have been directed toward this end. For instance, Lindenberg's (1992) *social production function theory* distinguishes universal goals (physical and social well-being) and the instrumental goals that humans pursue to achieve these ultimate ends. For example, actors may pursue status and affection as means to social well-being. At a higher level, the theory specifies alternative routes to each instrumental goal.

The alternative routes (or higher-order goals) through which a given individual can pursue instrumental and ultimate goals are determined in large part by the groups and institutions to which she belongs. For instance, Kohn's research shows us that those in working-class occupational roles adopt values instrumental to success in working-class jobs and, ultimately, to their physical and social well-being. Members of the middle class, on the other hand, adopt values more conducive to success in their occupations.

Social production function theory and related approaches give us a picture of humans as rational agents who pursue various (socially sanctioned) routes to ultimate and instrumental ends in a cost-effective (optimizing) manner. While such models are certainly a step in the right direction, much work remains in effectively integrating theory and research on individual differences into a formal model of values.

APPLICATIONS

As noted earlier, much rational choice sociology has focused on explicitly theorizing multiple levels of analysis. This is especially evident in two lines of sociological work that have strong roots in rational choice theory, network exchange theories (Willer 1999) and social dilemmas research (Kollock 1998). Thus, these two areas are offered as illustrations of rational choice sociology.

Network exchange theories predict interpersonal power from actors' locations in exchange networks. Exchange networks are special cases of social networks in which ties represent exchange opportunities. It is these differential exchange opportunities that generate power differences. A key insight of network exchange approaches is that power differences are not simply a function of the number of potential exchange partners a person has. Rather, exchange networks have important distal properties, such that an individual's power may be determined not only by her number of partners, but also by her partners' partners, her partners' partners' partners, and so on. While network exchange theories give special attention to these structural-level variables, they also incorporate micro-level assumptions about individual preferences and bargaining strategies.

The network exchange approach provides a clear illustration of multilevel theorizing for the following reasons. First, it demonstrates the important role of structural constraints on individual choices, thus clearly linking down from the macro to micro level. Second, it accounts for individual preferences and bargaining processes that occur at the micro level. Finally, it explains how bargaining and negotiations at the micro level aggregate back up to the macro level to generate power differences. In so doing, it provides a guide for explicitly modeling both structural and individual levels of analyses (Markovsky 1987).

Rational choice theory also has had a major impact on sociological research on social dilemmas. Social dilemmas are situations that pose conflicts between individual and collective interests. Several features of rational choice theory make it a useful theoretical tool for analyzing such problems. First, rational choice theory explicitly focuses on actors' interests. In so doing, it commits the analyst to a careful distinction between the interests of individuals and the interests of the groups to which they belong. By extension, rational choice theory's focus on the aggregation of individual choices makes clear how the rational pursuit of individual interests can lead to disastrous outcomes at the system level. Well-known examples of how individually rational outcomes produce collective disasters include overfishing and nuclear armament buildups. Because social dilemmas pose such important social problems, and because rational choice theory is well equipped to model such situations, many rational choice theorists consider the study of social dilemmas and how actors solve them the central task of sociology.

THE FUTURE OF RATIONAL CHOICE SOCIOLOGY

While rational choice theory has made important inroads into a number of areas of sociology, its status in the discipline as a whole remains uncertain. One indicator of sociologists' disparate views on the status of rational choice theory is its treatment in introductory texts. There, statements on rational choice theory and its place in sociology run the gamut: some texts contain no mention of rational choice theory in any of its variants (Macionis's *Sociology*); others mention rational choice approaches to specific topics but omit the general rational choice approach (Lindsey & Beach's *Sociology*); others maintain that rational choice theory is the unifying theory in sociology (Stark's *Sociology*).

In short, there is currently very little agreement about the status of rational choice theory in sociology, and about what it should be. Heckathorn (1997) suggests that the reluctance of many sociologist to embrace rational choice theory is paradoxical because the approach differs very little from traditional mainstream sociology. To the extent that there is a difference, he suggests, it is that rational choice theory makes explicit what much of sociology leaves implicit: a model of the individual.

Others praise the precision of rational choice theory for a different reason. They suggest sociologists should view rational choice principles not as accurate reflections of reality, but as explicit baselines against which to measure more realistic alternatives. This position is illustrated by research described earlier that refines the means and ends typically assumed in rational choice models. More generally, it is doubtful whether so much progress could have been made on departures from rationality if social scientists did not have an explicit model of rationality. Similarly, the ubiquitous simplifying assumption that humans are wealth-maximizers has provided a convenient baseline against which to measure the conditions under which human behavior is guided (however rationally) by a broader range of values. If present trends continue, we can expect psychologists and decision theorists to work on further refinements to the means component of rational choice models while sociologists will proceed with developing richer models of the ends to which boundedly rational actors aspire.

SEE ALSO: Exchange Network Theory; Game Theory; Mathematical Sociology; Metatheory; Micro–Macro Links; Power-Dependence Theory; Rational Choice Theory: A Crime-Related Perspective; Rational Choice Theory (and Economic Sociology); Social Exchange Theory; Structure and Agency; Theory

REFERENCES AND SUGGESTED READINGS

Coleman, J. S. (1990) *Foundations of Social Theory.* Harvard University Press, Cambridge, MA.

Frank, R. H., Gilovich, T., & Regan, D. T. (1993) Does Studying Economics Inhibit Cooperation? *Journal of Economic Perspectives* 7: 159–71.

Hechter, M. (1994) The Role of Values in Rational Choice Theory. *Rationality and Society* 6: 318–33.

Heckathorn, D. D. (1997) The Paradoxical Relationship between Sociology and Rational Choice. *American Sociologist* 28: 6–15.

Kanazawa, S. (2001) De Gustibus *Est* Disputandum. *Social Forces* 79: 1131–63.

Kollock, P. (1998) Social Dilemmas: The Anatomy of Cooperation. *Annual Review of Sociology* 24: 183–214.

Lindenberg, S. (1992) The Method of Decreasing Abstraction. In: Coleman, J. S. & Fararo, T. J. (Eds.), *Rational Choice Theory: Advocacy and Critique.* Sage, Newbury Park, pp. 3–20.

Markovsky, B. (1987) Toward Multilevel Sociological Theories: Simulations of Actor and Network Effects. *Sociological Theory* 5: 101–17.

Simon, H. (1982) *Models of Bounded Rationality.* MIT Press, Cambridge, MA.

Willer, D. (Ed.) (1999) *Network Exchange Theory.* Praeger, Westport, CT.

rational choice theory: a crime-related perspective

Jeffrey A. Bouffard and Kelly Wolf

As an explanation of crime, the rational choice perspective in essence argues that would-be offenders consider the potential costs and benefits before deciding whether to engage in crime. To be accurate, there is not a single, well-defined rational choice theory, but rather a series of models that attempt to explain criminal events and/or criminality. The rational choice perspective in criminology has evolved largely from two previous and complementary explanations of human behavior. One of these is the classical school of thought characterized by the Enlightenment scholars Cesare Beccaria (1764) and Jeremy Bentham (1789). These early philosophers proposed that individuals would refrain from offending out of fear of the potential punishment that would result from such behavior (this is also the conceptual basis for the deterrence perspective in criminology). The rational choice perspective on crime also has more recent roots in a second explanation of human behavior, specifically, the attempts of economists to explain consumer purchasing decisions based on a consideration of the perceived potential utility of a product.

Both perceptual deterrence (focused on the perceived rather than objective likelihood and severity of punishment) and the rational choice perspective share several assumptions about human nature. Specifically, both agree that individuals have "free will," they are hedonistic and utilitarian, and they will be dissuaded from offending by a consideration of potential costs. Unlike the deterrence perspective, however, rational choice includes a specific focus on the rewards of crime. Thus, while deterrence considers only potential sanctions, rational choice draws attention to the weighing of costs and benefits within the offending decision. Because of their shared assumptions, some have suggested that rational choice is simply an expansion of the deterrence perspective, while others see rational choice's focus on benefits as a substantial divergence from deterrence.

Rational choice explanations of crime also have more recent roots in the field of economics. During the 1960s and 1970s, economists became interested in expanding their work on decision-making to include a consideration of criminal behavior. The most noted proponent of this view of rational choice in criminology is Gary Becker, who proposed a "subjective expected utility" model of rational choice. This "economic" approach to offender decision-making assumes that individuals strive to maximize their gains (i.e., utility) from crime while minimizing their costs and other efforts/risks. It also proposes that would-be offenders engage in relatively complex deliberations involving their perception of the certainty (likelihood) and severity (utility or value) of the costs and benefits of crime. This approach also attempted to assign monetary values to all relevant costs and benefits of crime, comparing the dollar values of these consequences in modeling the offender decision-making process.

Overall, the rational choice perspective on crime conceives of would-be offenders as more or less rationally weighing the expected costs and benefits of criminal conduct before acting. The rational choice perspective has also assumed that individuals were at least minimally rational and able, for the most part, to make these types of calculations. Most models of decision-making from this perspective, however, seem to acknowledge that individuals possess "bounded rationality." That is, individuals are not "purely" rational, but rather only seek generally to maximize their gains, even though their behavior may not appear overtly "rational" to others. The bounds on the extent of this rationality are imposed by factors such as the availability of information on potential consequences, the individuals' cognitive abilities, time pressures on the decision itself, and other factors that have an impact on the ability to adequately consider various consequences.

TWO RATIONAL CHOICE MODELS

Most of the research and theorizing to date has focused on one of two main rational choice models of criminal decision-making. The subjective expected utility (SEU) model proposed by Becker (1968) suggests that crime will be more likely if the individual's perceived expected utility (expressed in monetary terms) for criminal behavior is greater than the expected utility of some legal alternative. This model is often represented mathematically with the following formula:

$$EU = pU(Y - f) + (1 - p)U(Y)$$

where EU represents the expected utility from the behavior; p = the probability of punishment (the certainty of the costs); Y = the anticipated benefits of the behavior; f = the anticipated punishment; and U = the "utility" (the severity) of costs or benefits.

Other criminologists have taken issue with the complex mathematical nature of the SEU model for several reasons, including the deliberative approach to decision-making it implies. According to Cornish and Clarke (1987), would-be offenders are unlikely to go through such a deliberative, calculating mental process when making a decision. Instead, they propose a more "informal" model of rational choice in which offenders evaluate costs and benefits in a manner described as "rudimentary" and "cursory" (Cornish & Clarke, 1987: 935). This model of decision-making is based on "decision diagrams" in which various individual (e.g., temperament, past experience) and situational factors (e.g., needs, available alternatives) influence the evaluation of potential courses of action.

This informal rational choice model, originally developed to aid thinking about situational crime prevention, is also presented as an explanation of both criminality and criminal events.

In fact, proponents of this informal rational choice model suggest it can explain several components of criminality, including the decisions to become involved in crime, to continue such involvement, and eventually to desist from crime. The informal model is also used to explain several aspects of the criminal event decision, including the choice of particular crime targets, offense types, and offense methods. In addition, the informal model takes into consideration the impact of several other individual and situational factors that may impact the offending decision itself. Supporters of this model point out that this type of flexibility is needed because the content of offending decisions is crime and individual specific, and that inclusion of these influences on decision-making allows rational choice to explain multiple types of crimes, including those more "expressive" crimes which may appear irrational and even unplanned to others. They also point out that these crime types are not well explained by economic versions of rational choice.

RATIONAL CHOICE RESEARCH

Most criminological research on rational choice has examined the effect of various costs and benefits on offending decisions, commonly using one of three methodologies. First, ethnographic approaches have been employed that involve interviewing known offenders about their past decision-making processes. This line of research has discovered various facts about offender decision-making, for instance, that residential burglars attend to such factors as the ease of entry to a house when considering where to commit their crimes. Second, some longitudinal studies have examined self-reported offending and related that offending to perceptions of costs and benefits assessed at another time period. Finally, a large amount of research has used either simple hypothetical offending questions (e.g., how likely is it that you would commit a burglary?) or more detailed hypothetical scenarios depicting brief, fictional stories about potential offending situations to elicit intentions to offend and relate those intentions to the perception of various consequences. The detailed hypothetical scenario design has been relatively commonly employed, at least partly because it avoids the issues of incorrect temporal ordering that plague some longitudinal studies while providing more consistent context for the would-be offender's decision than the simple hypothetical offense question design, thus minimizing measurement error. Research using all three of these design types has generally found support for the rational choice contention that the perception of various costs and benefits impacts the decision to offend.

The potential costs of criminal conduct commonly proposed by rational choice authors as relevant to criminal decision-making include, among other things, the possibility and severity of formal legal sanctions, lost legitimate opportunities forsaken by criminal behavior (like the loss of a job or being removed from school), and various informal costs, such as social censure, loss of the esteem and emotional support of loved ones, and any potential loss of self-respect. The benefits which have typically been considered by rational choice researchers are somewhat more limited but include such considerations as perceived material or financial gains, acceptance by peers or any enhancement of respect that may accrue from others as a result of engaging in criminal behavior, and even an individual's emotional state such as feelings of excitement, pride, or satisfaction from committing a crime. Several studies have looked at feelings of anticipation, excitement, thrill, and arousal state as benefits of crime. Jack Katz (1988), in particular, has written about the "sneaky thrills" that some individuals may perceive as benefits of crime, engaging in the behavior simply for the "thrill" of getting away with something deviant rather than for material gain.

CRITICISMS AND FUTURE DIRECTIONS

Some critics have suggested that rational choice theories have essentially added nothing new to the field of criminology, as other theories, such as social learning and social control theories, already suggest that individuals are responsive to the consequences of crime (e.g., censure from family or friends). However, proponents of rational choice theories argue that the perspective offers several advantages over other theories, including that it calls needed attention to the issue of "choice" in crime, it focuses attention on the decision-making process itself, it attempts to explain several crime decision points, and anticipates that many other factors may have an impact on the offending decision. The rational choice perspective also recognizes that crime is not a unitary concept and that explanations of crime must take into account the offense-specific and individualized nature of offending decisions.

Finally, despite its advantages, some authors have recently criticized the hypothetical scenario design commonly used to test rational choice propositions because researchers using this design present a potentially limited set of researcher-derived consequences to participants. Bouffard (2002) proposes that individuals be allowed to develop their own consequences in response to hypothetical offending scenarios, so that researchers can more accurately determine the full range of individually relevant and crime-specific consequences that influence offending decisions.

Additional challenges to those testing the rational choice perspective remain. For example, research is needed to examine the factors that may contribute to "bounded rationality," in addition to emotional states and substance abuse, which have been examined to date. In addition, research using the hypothetical scenario design has typically used student samples and has not yet demonstrated that what is known about decision-making generalizes to actual offenders.

SEE ALSO: Beccaria, Cesare; Criminology; Decision-Making; Deterrence Theory; Deviance, Theories of; Rational Choice Theories; Routine Activity Theory; Theory

REFERENCES AND SUGGESTED READINGS

Bachman, R., Paternoster, R., & Ward, S. (1992) The Rationality of Sexual Offending: Testing a Deterrence/Rational Choice Conception of Sexual Assault. *Law and Society Review* 26: 343–72.

Beccaria, C. (1764) *On Crimes and Punishments.* Hackett, Indianapolis.

Becker, G. (1968) Crime and Punishment: An Economic Approach. *Journal of Political Economy* 76(2): 169–217.

Bentham, J. (1789) *An Introduction to the Principles of Morals and Legislation.* Clarendon Press, Oxford.

Bouffard, J. A. (2002) Influence of Emotion on Rational Decision Making in Sexual Aggression. *Journal of Criminal Justice* 30: 121–34.

Clarke, R. & Cornish, D. (1985) Modeling Offenders' Decisions: A Framework for Policy and Research. In: Tonry, M. & Morris, N. (Eds.), *Crime and Justice*, Vol. 6. University of Chicago Press, Chicago.

Cornish, D. & Clarke, R. (1987) Understanding Crime Displacement. *Criminology* 25: 933–47.

Grasmick, H. G. & Bursick, R. J., Jr. (1990) Conscience, Significant Others, and Rational Choice: Extending the Deterrence Model. *Law and Society Review* 24: 837–61.

Katz, J. (1988) *Seductions of Crime.* Basic Books, New York.

Klepper, S. & Nagin, D. (1989) The Deterrent Effect of Perceived Certainty and Severity of Punishment Revisited. *Criminology* 27: 721–46.

Nagin, D. & Paternoster, R. (1993) Enduring Individual Differences and Rational Choice Theories of Crime. *Law and Society Review* 27: 201–30.

Paternoster, R. & Simpson, S. (1996) Sanction Threats and Appeals to Morality: Testing a Rational Choice Model of Corporate Crime. *Law and Society Review* 30: 549–84.

rational choice theory (and economic sociology)

Thomas J. Fararo

Two major themes are part of the tradition of sociological analysis as it relates to economics. One theme concerns the sociology of economic phenomena, while the other concerns the relationship between economic theory and sociological theory. The first theme is the central focus of economic sociology, and the second has been a central focus of sociological theory in its phases of development. The two themes are closely connected. In recent decades, economists have endeavored to apply their theoretical approach to a wide variety of social phenomena very much in the domain of sociological research, such as religion and the family. Such "economic imperialism" has been met with some controversy and with opposition that includes a kind of reverse invasion, in which economic sociologists delve into the details of economic phenomena traditionally within the purview of the discipline of economics, e.g., the behavior of markets. In this mutual invasion of territories, economic sociologists criticize economic theory for postulating a "hyperrationality" on the parts of actors that is unreal and therefore misleading in its derived consequences even in regard to economic phenomena. Thus economic sociology itself is a major domain in which the controversial interplay of the disciplines occurs.

In the classical phase of sociological thought, both Pareto and Weber migrated from economics to sociology. Both were trained in and produced contributions to economics before they each arrived at the conclusion that the approach of economic theory was too narrow to contain their aspiration to develop a more generalized analysis of society. Each accepted the idea that a sociological approach required a foundation in what we can call, following Parsons (1949 [1937]), "the action frame of reference," including the idea that human action is purposive and involves normative elements. But each theorist moved beyond the idealized rational action of economic theory. As Parsons later put it, the task was to provide an analysis of the residual category of non-rational action. Pareto invoked sentiments that motivate behavior that is then rationalized after the fact. Weber set out a very useful roster of four types of action, only one of which corresponds to the postulated action of economic actors in neoclassical economic theory. First, he distinguished between two types of rational action: instrumental rational action, as in consumer or producer choices, and ultimate-value rational action, in which an actor's choice results from some inner sense of duty that must be undertaken regardless of the costs. In addition, Weber noted the empirical significance of two other types of action: traditional (or habitual) action and affectual (or emotional) action. He was not unaware that the instrumental rational type could play an important baseline role in social analysis, but cautioned that the other types could not be neglected in sociology.

When Parsons elucidated these and other shifts from the "utilitarian" type of theory in which he embedded the economics that Pareto and Weber had transcended in their respective theoretical approaches, he went on to define "the rational unit-act" as a *special case* of a more general concept of the unit-act, a basic unit of action as a process in which actors attempt to realize their ends in situations that include constraints. In his later writings, as well, Parsons treated economically rational action as a mode of action that he characterized as "institutionally motivated," i.e., as linked to social roles in a social structure defined in normative cultural terms. This differs from the logically more primitive desire to optimize gratification that already occurs in infancy but that is channeled through social processes into various forms – such as those of Weber's typology. Similarly, firms and customers are not fundamental entities of social theory but rather types of collectivities and roles that are characteristic of a modern economy with its particular historically emergent institutions. So economic theory, as it had developed in the last few centuries, was a scope-restricted branch of the general theory of action, both in regard to its rationality postulate and in regard to its assumptions about the social environment of economic action.

In short, it is fair to say that for most contemporary sociologists, "rational choice theory" is the theory of instrumental rational action (Weber) employing a rational unit-act special case of action (Parsons) that excludes non-rational sentiments (Pareto).

Parsons also combined his general action framework with functional analysis based upon systems thinking. The culmination of this approach was a study in the integration of sociological and economic theory (Parsons & Smelser 1956) that formed one phase of the development of economic sociology. The key theme in the book is that economic theory is a special case of the theory of action, with the economy as a special type of social system.

However, later theorists such as Coleman (1986) argued that in taking the path of functional analysis, Parsons had not really followed up on the logic of generalizing economic theory. The basis for Coleman's critique is that microeconomics, the home base of rational choice theory, is actually a *micro–macro* theory. Its aim is not a detailed and accurate analysis of individual choices. Rather, its goal is to explain the behavior of market phenomena, especially the price system that allocates goods and services in modern societies. Rational choice is a postulated property of the individual or collective actors at the micro level of households and firms whose aggregated behavior leads to the market outcomes. The theory in microeconomics consists of logical derivations of the macro-level outcomes from postulates about acting units, idealized as instrumental rational actors. Parsons's theory, whatever its merits, did not proceed in this manner and therefore failed to truly explain the macro-level phenomena of concern in sociology on the basis of a presumed generalized action theory. While Parsons was appreciative of the role of mathematics in science, he did not attempt to emulate the mathematical methods of economic theory in its representation of mechanisms that enable the micro–macro linkage to be explicitly made.

In contrast to Parsons, some more recent sociologists have adopted a mode of theorizing that is inspired by rational choice theory. Lindenberg (1992) has defined and defended a methodological strategy of gradual movement from initial simplicity to more complex models that extend the realism and scope of the simpler starting models, employing actor models of the type employed in economic theory. This extension of scope aspect of sociological rational choice theory, along with the methodological features of idealization and approximation in the construction of theoretical models, are key aspects of rational choice theory as employed in economic sociology and more widely within contemporary social science. In this type of theoretical strategy, the key problem shifts from the nature of the act to the nature of the mechanism that combines the numerous acts into the eventual social outcome. Perhaps in some cases it is simply a surface feature of social life, as in elections in which votes are counted by some authorized agency. But in other cases, social interactions and social relationships among the actors mediate the outcome, e.g., as in a social exchange process of vote trading among legislators.

More or less explicitly, Coleman (1990) has followed the strategy outlined by Lindenberg. Purposive action is the key assumption and rational choice is the idealized form of it for the sake of analytical tractability. For instance, purposive action is represented as based upon a maximization of expected utility. This is part of Coleman's effort to employ the mathematical approach that Parsons bypassed. For instance, what is called general equilibrium theory in economics is a mathematical theory of a system of interdependent markets in terms of the simultaneous determination of prices on all markets. Coleman employs the theory as a generalized exchange model for use in sociology. This effort can be reconstructed as having two phases. The first phase simply employs the same mathematical theory used in economics but with a more generalized vocabulary, e.g., *actors* instead of firms and households and *resources* instead of commodities. Two types of relations link actors and resources: *control* (generalizing ownership) and *interests* (as parameters of the utility function). In the second phase, the formal apparatus is scope-extended by including representations of such features of real exchange systems as barriers to trade and social relations among actors.

Subsequently, in an overview of rational choice theory in relation to economic sociology, Coleman (1994) argues for the superiority of the theory in comparison with other sociological perspectives on grounds of its explanatory strategy of methodological individualism, its principle of optimization at the actor level, and its explicit and refined concepts dealing with macro-level outcomes such as social equilibria. Referring mainly to his own work, he adds to features inherited from neoclassical economics some further developments of the ideas in a social direction, including the concept of social capital and the analysis of conflicts over rights in the formation of constitutions, and he goes on to discuss some applications of the theory in economic sociology. One of these applications is the theory of the design of economic organizations with sensitivity to emergent informal social systems that may act to support or to counter the objectives of the design. Other applications include the use of the concept of social capital to explain how immigrants build and expand specialized niches of economic activity and the analysis of collective behavior in the economy, such as panics, "bubbles," and crashes, by reference to the same type of mechanism – concatenation of rational choices – that explains other market phenomena.

Nevertheless, most economic sociologists are not committed to the application of rational choice theory. Rather, the tendency is to view rational choice theory as based upon a defective vision of society insofar as it presupposes a set of independent actors, each with a given utility function. Where do these utility functions come from? How independent are the choices? What economic culture is presupposed? These sorts of questions about the transport of the economic method into sociology express a deep skepticism about the use of rational choice theory as a foundation for research in economic sociology. If actors are socially located in positions in social structures, the very meaning of social structure as pertaining to social relationships suggests research to investigate the *connections* among actors as significant features of the explanatory task of economic sociology. For instance, in a certain production market, firms may be closely studying each other's behavior for clues as to volume and quality of production they should plan upon in order to survive and prosper in the market, as in the treatment of markets as social structures in the sense of network analysis (White 2002). To be sure, at least to some degree – although never with complete information – acting units may make rational choices, but the patterning of relationships among the firms is part of the explanation of the choices.

In response, the advocates of rational choice models as parts of an overall explanatory micro–macro theoretical strategy would point out that their approach involves not just a micro–macro link, but also a macro–micro link. The latter "locates" actors in situations within a given macrosocial context, providing a basis for postulating their relative control and interests in various resources as well as institutional constraints on their action. Thus, they would argue that the focus on social networks and other forms of social structural relationships between actors is not excluded by the sociological rational choice approach; on the contrary, it is very much a part of the overall explanatory strategy. Contributions that aim to reconcile rational choice theory and structural analysis in sociology as a whole, and in economic sociology in particular, are on the agenda of research in this area.

It should be noted that sociologists who adopt the rational choice theoretical strategy are not exclusively or even mainly concerned with economic phenomena, and this is one aspect of the cross-purposes that may account for the current situation. Theorists such as Hechter (1987) are interested in the general problem of social order as understood within a tradition that goes back to Thomas Hobbes with his Leviathan solution in the form of a central authority as a necessary condition for order. In this context, rational choice theorists in sociology have emphasized an important obstacle to the translation of social values into social order, namely, the free-rider problem, and proposed mechanisms that overcome the problem.

SEE ALSO: Coleman, James; Economy (Sociological Approach); Micro-Macro Links; Parsons, Talcott; Rational Choice Theories

REFERENCES AND SUGGESTED READINGS

Coleman, J. S. (1986) Social Theory, Social Research, and a Theory of Action. *American Journal of Sociology* 91(6): 1309–35.

Coleman, J. S. (1990) *Foundations of Social Theory.* Harvard University Press, Cambridge, MA.

Coleman, J. S. (1994) A Rational Choice Perspective on Economic Sociology. In: Smelser, N. J. & Swedberg, R. (Eds.), *The Handbook of Economic Sociology.* Russell Sage Foundation and Princeton University Press, Princeton, ch. 7.

Hechter, M. (1987) *Principles of Group Solidarity.* University of California Press, Berkeley.

Lindenberg, S. (1992) The Method of Decreasing Abstraction. In: Coleman, J. S. & Fararo, T. J. (Eds.), *Rational Choice Theory: Advocacy and Critique.* Sage, Newbury Park, CA, ch. 1.

Parsons, T. (1949 [1937]) *The Structure of Social Action.* Free Press, New York.

Parsons, T. & Smelser, N. J. (1956) *Economy and Society: A Study in the Integration of Economic and Social Theory.* Free Press, New York.

White, H. (2002) *Markets from Networks.* Princeton University Press, Princeton.

rational legal authority

Dirk Bunzel

According to German sociologist Max Weber, rational legal authority represents a form of legitimate domination, with domination being the "probability that certain commands (or all commands) from a given source will be obeyed by a given group of persons" (Weber 1947: 324). While this probability implies a certain interest on the part of those obeying in the effects of their compliance, such interest can be diverse, and individuals may act upon calculated self-interest, habituation, affection, or idealistic orientations. For domination to endure, however, it depends on the belief in the legitimacy of the command and its source. Accordingly, Weber distinguishes three types of legitimate domination. Charismatic authority rests upon a belief in the extraordinary, sacred, and/or exemplary qualities of the person commanding, while traditional authority calls for submission to those who are privileged to rule by historical convention. In contrast, rational legal authority differs in its unique combination of impersonality, formality, and everyday profaneness (*Alltäglichkeit*). It rests upon "a belief in the 'legality' of patterns of normative rules and the right of those elevated to authority under such rules to issue commands (legal authority)" (Weber 1947: 328).

Significantly, Weber conceptualized legitimate domination ideal-typically, thus producing a theoretical idealization that simplifies or accentuates those aspects of social evidence he deemed significant, regardless of their concrete empirical correspondence. Existing modes of authority will therefore most likely constitute hybrids, with one of the three forms of domination prevailing. It is precisely its status as an ideal type, however, that allowed Weber to place rational legal authority at the center of his theory of capitalist development and occidental rationalization.

Historically, rational legal authority unfolded from the medieval monasteries and evolved along with capitalist production, the administration of growing populations within defined territories, and reformist religious movements in late Renaissance Europe. Inspired by these developments, a new mode of governance emerged that was founded on general and formal systems of rules and regulations and on a systematic conduct of life. At the societal level, such governance derived from the implementation of positive rational law (*Satzungsrecht*) and rational administration within a bureaucratic state apparatus. The impersonal rule of formal and universally applied law – a law that was systematically created (*gesatzt*) by professionally trained jurists – replaced arbitrary rule and privileges and thus established the equality of contractual parties as a legal basis of capitalist market economies. Simultaneously, administrative rights and duties were delegated to public officials. These would neither inherit nor own their hierarchically regimented offices, would comply with formal rules and regulations, would produce and act upon written documents, and would be recruited according to expertise. In so doing, they would put an end to the personal, arbitrary, and more haphazard conduct of patriarchical or patrimonial rule and would constitute a more efficient form of administration: bureaucracy. Hence, rational jurisdiction combined with governmental bureaucracy would render the modern state into an archetype of rational legal authority. At an individual level, the *vita communitas* practiced in medieval monasteries instigated a systematic conduct of life that would culminate in the doctrines of Calvinism, which commanded thrift, duty of work, and inner-worldly asceticism. This methodical approach to life generated both the entrepreneurial attitude of early capitalists and the work ethic demanded of free laborers. Consequently, economic, political, and ethico-religious elements formed an "elective affinity" to bring about a rationalization of production, government, and life-conduct that was unique in its occidental roots and that has since become imperialist in tendency.

The innate ambivalence of the principles that constitute rational legal authority provoke ambiguous and, occasionally, conflicting consequences. In Weber's conceptualization, rational legal administration is most effective and efficient the more it operates along the lines of formal rationality, thus excluding any substantive values and eradicating personal emotions, sentiments, or ideals. While such impersonal procedure promotes impartiality and equality, it may also advance rigidity and aloofness. Similarly, the loyalty shown toward rules and regulations discourages developing personal integrity and responsibility as opposed to reliance on an external framework of rules – a fact that tends to provoke rampant formalization and dependence on written evidence, thus compromising efficiency. Formalization, in turn, supports routinization and homogenization. While the latter promote calculability and predictability, they are also notoriously prone to rigidity. Finally, the coalescence of impersonality, adherence to rules and procedure, and formalization subjects virtually all spheres of life to an anonymous but stringent order of formal rationality. However, this process of rationalization has looted modern society of its magic, amazement, and intimacy.

Not surprisingly, then, rational legal authority and its archetypical materialization, occidental bureaucracy, have stimulated much debate. Most commonly, they have been charged with ethical poverty and with provoking irrational consequences. Weber himself was well aware of potential dangers, and in a rather dystopian vision he predicted that ongoing rationalization would create an "iron cage" of obedience (*Hörigkeit*) to imprison the modern individual. Others went even further, identifying overexposure to instrumental rationality, the blind following of rules, and the disregard for substantive values such as empathy or compassion as producing a "bureaucratic personality" that – inspired by a perverse sense of duty and obedience – was capable of partaking within the greatest crimes against humanity. Finally, the very efficiency Weber ascribed to bureaucratic administration has been questioned in the wake of recent neoliberal campaigns that prescribe private ownership and markets as antidotes to "red tape" and inflexibility. Against such criticism, other authors have pointed out that privatization and marketization have not increased efficiency but, instead, have created a politicization of civil service and a prioritization of measurable short-term gains at the expense of integrity, loyalty, and fairness. Refuting the moral absolutism and romanticism of the critics, they stress the significance of bureaucratic administration for the development of democracy, long-term sustainability, and social equality.

While state bureaucracies and hierarchical organizations may have given way to informational networks and embryonic industries, while sovereign subjects may experience a "corrosion of character," and while the diversity and contingency of "life orders" are increasing, rational legal authority has changed its face, but it has not withered away. Rationalization of production, consumption, and life pursuit is still prevalent, as cathedrals of consumption, supranational institutions, and lateral careers demonstrate. In fact, where rational legal structures have retreated – be it in international disputes, in ethnic and religious affairs, or in industrial relations – brute power or even violence seems to prevail. Perhaps McDonaldization rather than bureaucratization is the dominant form these days; yet still, our saturated selves rely upon "civilization" within somewhat more "fancy" iron cages.

SEE ALSO: Bureaucratic Personality; Charisma; Civilizations; Consumption, Cathedrals of; Elective Affinity; Ideal Type; Legitimacy; McDonaldization; Neoliberalism; Weber, Max

REFERENCES AND SUGGESTED READINGS

Bauman, Z. (1989) *Modernity and the Holocaust*. Polity Press, Cambridge.

Bendix, R. (1960) *Max Weber: An Intellectual Portrait*. Methuen, London.

Bendix, R. & Roth, G. (1971) *Scholarship and Partisanship*. University of California Press, Los Angeles.

Clegg, S. R. (1975) *Power, Rule, and Domination*. Routledge & Kegan Paul, London.

Clegg, S. R. (1989) *Frameworks of Power*. Sage, London.

Du Gay, P. (2000) *In Praise of Bureaucracy: Weber, Organization, Ethics*. Sage, London.

Gergen, K. J. (1991) *The Saturated Self: Dilemmas of Identity in Contemporary Life*. Basic Books, New York.

Löwith, K. (1993) *Max Weber and Karl Marx*. Routledge, London.

Mommsen, W. (1974) *The Age of Bureaucracy: Perspectives on the Political Sociology of Max Weber*. Blackwell, Oxford.

Ritzer, G. (1999) *Enchanting a Disenchanted World: Revolutionalizing the Means of Consumption*. Pine Forge Press, Thousand Oaks, CA.

Ritzer, G. (2004) *The McDonaldization of Society: Revised New Century Edition*. Pine Forge Press, Thousand Oaks, CA.

Schluchter, W. (1996) *Die unversöhnte Moderne*. Suhrkamp, Frankfurt am Main.

Schluchter, W. (1998) *Die Entstehung des modernen Rationalismus: eine Analyse von Max Webers Entwicklungsgeschichte des Okzidents*. Suhrkamp, Frankfurt am Main.

Sennett, R. (1998) *The Corrosion of Character: The Personal Consequences of Work in the New Capitalism*. W. W. Norton, New York.

Weber, M. (1947) *The Theory of Social and Economic Organization*. Ed. A. M. Henderson & T. Parsons. Oxford University Press, New York.

Weber, M. (1968) *Economy and Society: An Outline of Interpretive Sociology*. Ed. G. Roth & C. Wittich. Bedminster Press, New York.

Weber, M. (1972) *Wirtschaft und Gesellschaft: Grundriß der verstehenden Soziologie*, 5th edn. Revised by J.Winckelmann J. B. C. Mohr (Paul Siebeck), Tübingen.

Weber, M. (1988 [1920]) *Gesammelte Aufsätze zur Religionssoziologie*. J. B. C. Mohr (Paul Siebeck), Tübingen.

rationalization

Zeynep Atalay

It is likely that the concept of rationalization is most often linked with the work of Sigmund Freud on psychological defense mechanisms. However, while such usage is not unknown in sociology, the concept is most often associated with the work of Max Weber and his followers. For Weber, rationalization occurred only, at least to its fullest extent, in the modern West. Other parts of the world, for example India and China, failed to rationalize to any great extent because of barriers there such as basic idea systems and structures that were antithetical to rationalization. On the other hand, there was a series of factors in the West that expedited the development of rationalization in that region of the world. The best known of these factors is the role that the Protestant ethic played in the rise of rational capitalism, but Weber made it clear that this ethic was but one of many distinctive characteristics in the West that made rationalization possible. Furthermore, the rise of capitalistic society was only one of many manifestations of rationalization that also included the rise of the bureaucracy as an organizational form, and of the modern state, corporation, military, university, and church. While Weber saw all of these, and more, as undergoing a process of rationalization, he was careful to avoid a general model of rationalization and to outline the ways in which each of them rationalized.

Weber's thinking on rationalization is based on his analysis of the basic types of rationality, only one of which – formal rationality – emerged in the modern West. In Weber's terms, *practical* rationality involves the utilization of pragmatic, calculating, and means-ends strategies in order to pursue mundane ends and overcome the obstacles to their pursuit that exist in everyday life. *Theoretical* rationality refers to the employment of abstract ideas and conceptual schemes to describe, elucidate, and comprehend empirical reality. *Substantive* rationality is involved in decision-making that is subject to the values and ethical norms of the particular society. *Formal* rationality, which became ubiquitous in the modern West, involves decision-making in accordance with a set of universal rules, laws, and regulations. It is only in the West that formal rationality emerged and became predominant. And it is that type of rationality that lies at the base of the rationalization process.

Rationalization constitutes the centerpiece of Weber's general sociology, as well as his sociologies of religion, law, bureaucracy (rationality also lies at the heart of his methodology for the social sciences), the city, and so on. Everyday life is rationalized, and while that brings with it great advantages such as increased efficiency, it also leads to a variety of negative consequences such as disenchantment and alienation. Most generally, Weber feared the development of an "iron cage" of rationalization that would increasingly enslave people and from which it would be increasingly difficult to escape.

In the domain of authority systems, rationalization involved the replacement of traditional and charismatic authority by rational-legal authority in which rulers' legitimacy stems from achieving their position on the basis of following a series of legally prescribed steps such as an election. In the religious realm, the process involved, among other things, the professionalization of the clergy and the production of a systematic body of religious knowledge. Law also involved professionalization, this time of lawyers, and it was transformed from a system dominated by the traditions of common law into a systematized, generalized, and codified set of universally valid legal principles.

Bureaucracy plays a key role in Weber's sociology and can be seen as the paradigm of the rationalization process. The bureaucracy is an organizational form that is rationally designed to perform complex tasks in the most efficient way possible. The critical features of bureaucracy, according to Weber, are specialization of work, hierarchy of offices, technical competence in decision-making process, rationally enacted rules and regulations, the impersonal character of the administrative staff, and the recording of any decision-making in writing in a filing system. The task-oriented character of the western bureaucratic organization promotes efficiency. Specifically, it limits the unpredictable and partial nature of personal decision-making and levels social and economic differences by offering an impersonal and impartial mechanism for decision-making.

Although Weber saw the ideal-typical bureaucracy as an efficient system, he did not fail to note the substantial irrationalities that are inherent in it. Weber was unmistakably conscious of bureaucracy's dehumanizing and alienating potential, as reflected in his view that formal organizations reduce the human being to "a small cog in a ceaselessly moving mechanism" (1978: 988). Bureaucracy, which is all but indissoluble once it is established, applies the same set of abstract rules to individual cases and limits the autonomy of the individual. Therefore, the domination of bureaucracy is likely to result in injustices given the fact that the particularity of cases is not taken into consideration in rendering decisions. Another of the irrationalities associated with the bureaucracy is that while it is supposed to operate efficiently, the fact is that it often suffers from inefficiencies and, as a result, often fails to accomplish the tasks that it exists to perform. Finally, of course, the bureaucracy can represent a clear case of the kind of "iron cage" Weber feared and that was described brilliantly in the novels of Franz Kafka, especially *The Trial* and *The Castle*.

Overall, Weber offered a world-historical theory of rationalization in which he attempted to account for why that process emerged in the West and not elsewhere, as well as for its great advantages and numerous disadvantages in comparison to less or non-rationalized systems.

Weber's German colleague Georg Simmel also theorized about rationalization, although it has a far more limited role in the latter's work. In *The Philosophy of Money*, Simmel (1978 [1907]) sets out to deal with money as an abstract and universal system that provides a fundamental model of the rationalization process. Money, as the symbol of abstract social relations, exemplifies the declining significance of the individual (and subjective culture) in the face of the expansion of objective culture, which is associated with intellectual rationality, mathematical calculability, abstraction, objectivity, anonymity, and leveling. Furthermore, the impersonal nature of exchange relationships, which are facilitated by the monetary system, imposes a progressively more rationalized system on individuals. As is true in Weber's work on rationalization, Simmel emphasizes the importance of quantitative over qualitative factors, as well as growing intellectuality, in the modern rationalized world.

Also of note is Karl Mannheim's thinking on rationalization. Mannheim borrows heavily from Weber (and Simmel), and develops a similar view about the rationalization of society. Resembling formal rationality in his work is the concept of functional rationality, which he sees as growing increasingly ubiquitous and coercive over people. Instead of substantive rationality, Mannheim deals with substantial rationality, which fundamentally involves people's ability to think intelligently. He sees the latter as being undermined by the former. Mannheim develops a rich set of ideas about rationalization, as well as an elaborate and useful set of concepts to deal with it. For example, he sees an increasing trend toward self-rationalization and self-observation in which people are seen as better able to control themselves rationally rather than being controlled by functionally rational systems.

Inspired by the work on the rationalization of the modern western society, especially that of Weber, critical theorists associated with the Frankfurt School criticized the consequences of the growth of rationality, or instrumental reason, for modern society. In response to early Marxian theorists who accorded the economy centrality in their analysis of the modern world, neo-Marxists of the Frankfurt School were committed to the analysis of culture, especially cultural repression and the decline of individual autonomy in modern society. In this perspective, the repression produced by rationality replaces economic exploitation as the dominant social problem. As elaborated by Adorno and Horkheimer, the rationality of capitalism is consolidated through the decline of individualism, and that has made it more difficult to achieve the goals of the Enlightenment. Marcuse (1964), in *One-Dimensional Man*, inspired in part by Weber's rationalization theory, focused on the relationship between technology and rationalization. Marcuse contended that formally rational structures have replaced more substantially rational structures and that capitalist society has become one-dimensional, in the sense that it is dominated by organized forces that restrict opposition, choice, and critique. Although there appears to be democracy, liberty, and freedom, society prevents radical change since it is able to absorb criticism and opposition, and to render these criticisms futile.

Habermas agrees with Weber that the development of modern society is driven by an underlying logic of rationalization. However, he maintains that this has a dual quality. In his view, Weber fails to distinguish between instrumental and communicative rationality, which corresponds to different patterns of development in modern society: technological and moral progress, respectively. Rejecting the pessimism of Weber, Adorno, and Horkheimer, Habermas argues that the concept of the "iron cage" gives too much weight to the importance of instrumental rationality in modern society. Rather, in his view, the development of both instrumental and communicative rationality can produce not only unprecedented technical achievements, but also the kind of humanity that can utilize those advancements to better itself rather than being enslaved by them.

The concept of rationalization has profoundly affected the direction of social theory, perhaps most notably theories of state formation, governmentality, organization, politics, and technology. The concept has also triggered debates regarding the central issues of the contemporary world such as the culture of consumption. Ritzer's McDonaldization thesis, in particular, illustrates the continuing importance of the Weberian notion of rationalization as it extends it into many new domains, especially consumption, popular culture, and everyday life.

SEE ALSO: Bureaucracy and Public Sector Governmentality; Critical Theory/Frankfurt School; McDonaldization; Mannheim, Karl; Marcuse, Herbert; Modernity; Rational Legal Authority; Simmel, Georg; Weber, Max

REFERENCES AND SUGGESTED READINGS

Adorno, T. & Horkheimer, M. (1979) *Dialectic of Enlightenment*. Verso, London.

Habermas, J. (1971) *Toward a Rational Society*. Heinemann, London.

Habermas, J. (1981) *The Theory of Communicative Action*. Beacon Press, London.

Horkheimer, M. (1974) *Critique of Instrumental Reason*. Seabury Press, New York.

Mannheim, K. (1940 [1935]) *Man and Society in an Age of Reconstruction*. Harcourt, Brace, & World, New York.

Marcuse, H. (1964) *One-Dimensional Man: The Ideology of Industrial Society*. Sphere Books, London.

Ritzer, G. (2004) *The McDonaldization of Society: Revised New Century Edition*. Pine Forge Press, Thousand Oaks, CA.

Simmel, G. (1978 [1907]) *The Philosophy of Money*. Ed. and Trans. T. Bottomore & D. Frisby. Routledge & Kegan Paul, London.

Weber, M. (1958) *The Protestant Ethic and the Spirit of Capitalism*. Scribner, New York.

Weber, M. (1978) *Economy and Society*, 3 vols. Bedminster Press, Totowa, NJ.

Ratzenhofer, Gustav (1842–1904)

Bernd Weiler

Besides Ludwig Gumplowicz, the Viennese-born Gustav Ratzenhofer is the best-known representative of the so-called Austrian Struggle or Conflict School. After only a few years of formal schooling and an apprenticeship as clockmaker (his father's business), Ratzenhofer entered the Austrian Army in 1859. In a highly successful military career he rose to the position of a lieutenant field marshal and, a few years before his retirement, was also appointed president of the military supreme court in Vienna. During his time in the army Ratzenhofer acquired a first-hand knowledge of the national struggles which were increasingly besetting the Austro-Hungarian Empire. His political worldview was marked by a tension between the commitment to the liberal ideals of the revolution of

1848 and the conviction that a strong, centralized state was needed to counteract the centrifugal forces in the Habsburg monarchy. Before Ratzenhofer turned to sociology he had written numerous treatises on military history and strategy (e.g., Ratzenhofer 1881) and had also provided an in-depth analysis of the peculiar political nature of the Habsburg monarchy (Renehr 1877–8). In 1893 he published his first explicitly sociological work, the three-volume *Wesen und Zweck der Politik*, followed shortly thereafter by *Die sociologische Erkenntnis* (1898) and by the posthumous work *Soziologie: Positive Lehre von den menschlichen Wechselbeziehungen* (1907), which contains a number of anti-Semitic and racist remarks. Ratzenhofer was mainly self-taught and remained on the margins of Viennese academia throughout his life. One of his few scientific allies in Austria was his fellow-countryman Ludwig Gumplowicz, who assumed the role of a mentor and made his name known in the international sociological community. Ratzenhofer died in 1904 on his return trip from the St. Louis Congress of Arts and Sciences where he had presented a sociological paper.

The major intellectual influences on Ratzenhofer were the French Enlightenment, with its emphasis on the universal and inevitable progress of humanity, British empiricism, and the writings of cultural historians such as H. T. Buckle (Oberhuber 2002). Above all, Ratzenhofer was heir to the time-honored tradition most famously associated with Heraclitus that "war is the father of all and king of all." Like many of his contemporaries, Ratzenhofer was impressed by the success of the natural sciences and emphasized that human history was not beyond or above, but part of, nature. Sociology's prime task was to uncover the universal laws governing social life (Ratzenhofer 1904). In his late writings Ratzenhofer refined this idea of the unity of nature and history and of the iron regularity of social phenomena into a grand systematic, monistic worldview with metaphysical overtones. Even though he clung to the idea that society was a natural product evolving out of necessity, he still shared the Comtean sociocratic optimism that an understanding of the laws could be used for society's reorganization.

At the core of Ratzenhofer's sociology lies the idea that from the very beginning social life had been inherently antagonistic, "absolute hostility" marking the starting point. In a highly conjectural scheme of social evolution he sketched the various stages through which society had developed, paying (like Gumplowicz) particular attention to the formation of the state through conquest. At each stage the antagonistic character of social life assumed a peculiar form. In contrast to Gumplowicz, with whom he shared many key ideas, the units of analysis in Ratzenhofer's conflict theory were not the concrete, empirically given groups competing against each other but the diverging "interests" that the sociologist had to abstract from real life. Society was the battlefield of "interests," understood as social forces manifested in groups. Of particular importance were the "general interest," the "kinship interest," the "national interest," the "creedal interest," the "pecuniary interest," the "class interest," the "rank interest," and the "corporate interest" (Ratzenhofer 1967: 161–85; Small 1905: 252). By introducing the category of "interest" Ratzenhofer, unlike Gumplowicz, was able to argue that within an empirically given group there could be more than one "interest" at work, allowing for more intragroup dynamics, that individuals could partake in more than one group, and that not all potential social forces were always necessarily manifested in the competing real groups. Ratzenhofer's ideas exerted a great influence on the early American sociologists A. W. Small, L. F. Ward, E. A. Ross, and F. H. Giddings, and especially on the American political scientist and so-called founder of pluralism, A. F. Bentley (1967).

SEE ALSO: Comte, Auguste; Conflict (Racial/Ethnic); Conflict Theory; Gumplowicz, Ludwig; Pluralism, American; Pluralism, British; Positivism; Small, Albion W.

REFERENCES AND SUGGESTED READINGS

Bentley, A. F. (1926) Simmel, Durkheim, and Ratzenhofer. *American Journal of Sociology* 32: 250–6.

Bentley, A. F. (1967 [1908]) *The Process of Government*. Ed. P. H. Odegard. Belknap Press of Harvard University Press, Cambridge, MA.

Gumplowicz, L. (1894) Review of *Wesen und Zweck der Politik*. *Annals of the American Academy of Political and Social Science* 5(1): 128–36.

Gumplowicz, L. (1908) Review of *Soziologie. Positive Lehre von den menschlichen Wechselbeziehungen. American Journal of Sociology* 14: 101–11.
Oberhuber, F. (2002) Das Problem des Politischen in der Habsburgermonarchie: Ideengeschichtliche Studien zu Gustav Ratzenhofer, 1842–1904. Unpublished PhD thesis, University of Vienna.
Ratzenhofer, G. (1881) *Die Staatswehr: Wissenschaftliche Untersuchungen der öffentlichen Wehrangelegenheiten.* Cotta'sche Buchhandlung, Stuttgart.
Ratzenhofer, G. (1898) *Die sociologische Erkenntnis: Positive Philosophie des socialen Lebens.* Brockhaus, Leipzig.
Ratzenhofer, G. (1904) The Problems of Sociology. *American Journal of Sociology* 10: 177–88.
Ratzenhofer, G. (1907) *Soziologie: Positive Lehre von den menschlichen Wechselbeziehungen.* Brockhaus, Leipzig.
Ratzenhofer, G. (1967 [1893]) *Wesen und Zweck der Politik: Als Teil der Soziologie und Grundlage der* Staatswissenschaften, 3 vols. Scientia Verlag, Aalen.
Renehr, G. [Ratzenhofer, G.] (1877–8) *Im Donaureich.* Karl Bellmann, Prag.
Schmid, R. (1948) Gustav Ratzenhofer: Sociological Positivism and the Theory of Social Contacts. In: Barnes, H. E. (Ed.), *An Introduction to the History of Sociology.* University of Chicago Press, Chicago, pp. 374–84.
Small, A. W. (1905) *General Sociology: An Exposition of the Main Development in Sociological Theory from Spencer to Ratzenhofer.* University of Chicago Press, Chicago.

Rawls, John (1921–2002)

Mark R. Rank

John Rawls is generally considered the most significant moral philosopher of the twentieth century. His work has had a profound influence upon political philosophy, as well as political science, sociology, economics, social work, theology, and law. For much of his career he was a faculty member in Harvard's department of philosophy.

Rawls's major work was his 1971 book entitled *A Theory of Justice.* In it he details the basic components of a just or fair society. He begins with what he refers to as the original position. Imagine, Rawls states, that "no one knows his place in society, his class position or social status, nor does anyone know his fortune in the distribution of natural assets and abilities, his intelligence, strength, and the like" (p. 12). Behind such a veil of ignorance, Rawls asks, what would be an acceptable social contract for most people? He argues that individuals in this original position would invariably choose two fundamental principles.

The first is that each of us would want to be guaranteed access to the most basic liberties. These would include "political liberty (the right to vote and to be eligible for public office) together with freedom of speech and assembly; liberty of conscience and freedom of thought; freedom of the person along with the right to hold (personal) property; and freedom from arbitrary arrest and seizure as defined by the concept of the rule of law" (p. 61). Consequently, all citizens, no matter where they fall in society, should be entitled to these rights.

The second principle chosen would be to allow social and economic inequalities to exist, but only under two conditions: (1) "if they result in compensating benefits for everyone, and in particular for the least advantaged members of society" (pp. 14–15); and (2) that offices and positions in society are open to all. The reason that inequalities would be tolerated in the first place is because such inequalities often provide incentives to greater production, which can benefit all citizens. According to Rawls, a just society therefore does not necessitate that the distribution of income or wealth has be equal, but rather that an unequal distribution is to everyone's advantage, particularly those at the lower end of the income distribution. For example, from a Rawlsian perspective, a just society would be one that provides a strong social safety net to protect the economically vulnerable, with the funding for such programs coming through a redistribution of some of the gains earned by those at the middle and upper ends of the income gradient.

These two principles, referred to as the "liberty principle" and the "difference principle," form the core of Rawls's conception of "justice as fairness." In his later work, Rawls elaborated and extended the ideas laid out in *A Theory of Justice.* In particular, his 1993 book *Political Liberalism* dealt with addressing how the liberty and difference principles can exist and be applicable within democratic societies, given the wide variety of ideological and religious viewpoints within such societies. He argued in *Political Liberalism* and in his final book, *Justice as Fairness: A Restatement*, that his principles of justice should be understood as a political guideline rather than as a moral doctrine. Consequently, the plurality of religious, philosophical, and moral viewpoints within democracies can successfully coexist under a political interpretation of justice as fairness.

SEE ALSO: Civil Society; Distributive Justice; Nozick, Robert; Social Justice, Theories of; Social Policy, Welfare State; Welfare State, Retrenchment of

REFERENCES AND SUGGESTED READINGS

Rawls, J. (1971) *A Theory of Justice*. Harvard University Press, Cambridge, MA.

Rawls, J. (1993) *Political Liberalism*. Columbia University Press, New York.

Rawls, J. (1999) *The Law of Peoples; with "The Idea of Public Reason Revisited."* Harvard University Press, Cambridge, MA.

Rawls, J. (2001) *Justice as Fairness: A Restatement*. Harvard University Press, Cambridge, MA.

realism and relativism: truth and objectivity

Andrew Tudor

Although the doctrine of relativism has a lengthy pedigree in philosophy – conventionally traced to the 5th-century BC sophist Protagoras and his "man is the measure of all things" – it was only in the twentieth century that its full force was unleashed. The "linguistic turn," the "cultural turn," and the "postmodern turn" all brought with them profoundly relativistic claims. Late twentieth-century thought sought to relativize aesthetics, ethics, and even that last bastion of Enlightenment certainty, natural science. But relativism takes many forms, and relativists do not speak with one voice. This is especially apparent where conceptions of science are concerned, for a very wide variety of relativistic arguments have been marshaled against the conviction that science provides privileged access to the independent, objective, external reality of nature. These range from the various perspectival relativisms that increasingly undermined philosophy of science orthodoxy from within, right through to the far-reaching social constructionist relativism of the sociology of scientific knowledge and the so-called science wars to which it gave rise.

It was apparent from the Greeks onward that relativistic claims all too often led to paradoxes, regresses, and to problems of self-reference. These can take various forms, although the general pattern can be typified by this simple variant of the well-known truth paradox. Consider the statement "all truth is relative to cultural context." In what sense can this statement be true? If it is an absolute truth, as the "all" suggests, then it is its own refutation. But if its truth is (only) relative to cultural context, then there may be cultural contexts in which it is thought false and is, therefore, true. Much energy has been expended over the centuries in dealing with the consequences of such circularity, and while this has been entertaining enough, it has not served to undermine the appeal of relativistic claims. Nor should it, of course, since few serious relativistic positions on matters of truth and knowledge deal in these kinds of absolutes. They tend to recognize, rather, that how we know the world is dependent on both the nature of that real world itself and the conceptual systems through which we seek to understand it. Since Kant, it has been impossible not to recognize the constitutive character of concepts in forming our knowledge. But to what degree are they constitutive? And if they are strongly so, how – if we should and if we could – are we to stop the perspectival regress from theory to meta-theory to meta-meta-theory, and so on? For Kant, of course, the resolution lay with the a priori transcendental categories – the preconditions for all thought. But if we cannot make that transcendental move, how then are we to conceptualize the relation between the terms in which (we think) we know and the real world about which we presume to know, but only from within the terms, languages, and perspectives available to us?

The relativistic issues that arise here – those of alethic, epistemic, and even ontological relativism – are central to radically changing views of science in the modern period. But to assess the impact of these ideas requires some attempt at classification. What is it that is relativized? And relative to what? Such questions have often been the starting point for those concerned to impose order on the somewhat inchoate world of relativistic thinking. Only equipped with, at least, rudimentary answers to such deceptively simple questions is it possible to begin to assess the impact of relativistic thinking on our understanding of science. To commence, then, with the most general, post-Kantian classification of the "what" that is relativized, we may distinguish between cognitive, aesthetic, and ethical relativism. Although questions of aesthetic relativism may not be irrelevant to science (at least some scientists are given to speaking of theoretical models in aesthetic terms – the double helix was "pretty," as Watson famously described it), and although ethical issues clearly cannot be dismissed, it is primarily the family of cognitive relativisms that are of most interest in relation to science. Here we find variously far-reaching relativistic accounts of knowledge, truth, objectivity, and the constitution of "reality" offered from a range of relativizing perspectives. Let us consider four such clusters: limited theory-based conceptual relativism; radical language-based conceptual relativism; cultural and "worldview" relativism; social constructionist relativism.

In the domain of conceptual relativism, the most straightforward, and least problematic for those seeking to defend science from relativistic doubt, are the conventionalist arguments which arose from within the logical positivist tradition. Here, the major relativistic frame was "theory," and the initial questions raised were most notably those of "theory-laden" observation and the consequent necessity for methodological conventions to prevent perspectival regress. As the mid-twentieth century "received view" in philosophy of science moved away from the apparent certainties of the distinction between observation and theory languages – at least in part because of the difficulties of drawing that distinction systematically – it increasingly embraced conventionalist solutions to its conceptual problems. Thus, for example, Popperian falsificationism openly recognized that decisions about the falsificatory significance of experimental results irreducibly involved methodological conventions, even though Popper sought to draw a critical-rational line beyond which at least some "conventionalist stratagems" were scientifically unacceptable.

However, the space opened up by this need to incorporate conventionalist decision making was to prove something of a black hole into which more radical relativistic arguments were drawn. Once science's thoroughgoing reliance on its conceptual schemes was admitted, it became increasingly difficult to prevent the slide toward the more powerful conceptual relativisms. Thus, for example, Quine, having famously rejected the familiar halt to that slide offered by the analytic/synthetic distinction, and having also argued that contradictory evidence could always be dealt with by making adjustments to some other part of the conceptual system, then further extended his thesis in terms of the indeterminancy of translation. Taken together, these arguments appear to lead toward relativistic conclusions, and Quine's image of knowledge as a "web of belief" which relates to experience only "at the edges" lends force to that interpretation. In a much-quoted passage, Quine (1960: 24–5) himself denies that we must therefore "settle for a relativistic doctrine of truth," claiming instead that "within our total evolving doctrine, we can judge truth as earnestly and absolutely as can be; subject to correction, but that goes without saying." That may be so, but as the qualification "within" suggests, Quine is clearly espousing a radical conceptual relativism which is consonant with his view of science as "self-conscious common sense."

Although Quine's conceptual relativism is primarily language based, it is not a great leap from his "web of belief" to the more overtly culture and "worldview" based relativisms. The best known of such approaches to science, of course, is that of Thomas Kuhn in his influential 1962 study, *The Structure of Scientific Revolutions*. At the heart of Kuhn's analysis lies the "paradigm," a concept which – whatever Kuhn's original intentions – has subsequently come to refer to the body of presuppositions, concepts, methods, and acculturated practices which make up "normal science" at any given moment. The paradigm defines the fundamental terms within which scientists operate – their culture – and all scientific knowledge is in that sense relative to the paradigm. Change, when it comes, is revolutionary change: the entire paradigm shifts when anomalies are perceived to be too important to be ignored and when there is a changing balance of power relations within the scientific community. Paradigms are therefore "incommensurable" in as much as there exists no independent position from which knowledge claims within one paradigm can be assessed in relation to those within another. Much debate has followed on this issue, not least with Feyerabend, but it seems clear that, as far as Kuhn is concerned, lack of direct translation between paradigms does not necessarily mean that they are entirely incomparable. Any attempt to compare them will entail what has been called "Kuhn-loss" but, just as we can achieve some level of translation between cultures, so there will still be areas of meaningful overlap between the theories generated within different paradigms.

However one assesses the strength of Kuhn's own relativism – and commentators do not agree on this – there is no question but that *The Structure of Scientific Revolutions* significantly helped to open up the study of science to more socially and culturally oriented empirical analysis. Prior to the 1960s sociological research into science had ring-fenced scientific knowledge itself. However, where Kuhn had led, later sociologists of science were more than willing to follow, a development accelerated by growing interest in social constructionist perspectives within sociology. From this context emerged the sociology of scientific knowledge (or SSK as it likes to refer to itself), the so-called strong program in the sociology of knowledge and, in their wake, what became known as the science wars. The strong program aimed to examine the social and cultural grounds for knowledge claims, and is most briefly characterized by its four basic principles as advanced by Bloor (1976). It was to provide causal explanations; to be impartial in explaining both successful and failed knowledge claims; to be symmetrical in using the same kinds of causal explanations for both true and false beliefs; and to be reflexive in as much as it could be applied to sociology itself. Quite how relativist is this perspective (and, indeed, SSK more generally) is open to some debate. From the point of view of a hard-line scientific realist, the strong program is an affront to rationality and to demonstrable scientific achievements in comprehending and manipulating the real world. "No one is a social constructionist at 30,000 feet," as Richard Dawkins vividly, albeit misleadingly, claimed in a typically vitriolic contribution to the science wars. But many proponents of SSK (including the founders of the strong program) profess at least some degree of realism in their views of science, even if the excessive rhetoric of the "debate" on this issue has too often forced the various parties into untenable positions. It is a measure of how foolish the science wars became that the mildly entertaining Sokal hoax (Sokal had a parody article published in the journal *Social Text*, apparently drawing on relativistic and constructionist approaches to science) has been paraded as somehow undermining relativist and constructionist *arguments*. Whatever failings may be exhibited by the editorial policies and methods of a journal can hardly count as clinching arguments for or against any intellectual case.

What the Sokal hoax and its aftermath did demonstrate, however, is the antagonistic confusion that has been characteristic of the guerrilla warfare between naïve relativist and naïve realist positions. Boudon (2004) has suggested that relativism more generally is in the process of becoming the new "secular religion," a development of which he does not approve. Whether that characterization turns out to be accurate remains to be seen, but, in any case, in the science wars we have already seen its fundamentalists at work on both sides.

SEE ALSO: Kuhn, Thomas and Scientific Paradigms; Objectivity; Science, Social Construction of; Scientific Knowledge, Sociology of; Scientific Revolution; Strong Program

REFERENCES AND SUGGESTED READINGS

Baghramian, M. (2004) *Relativism*. Routledge, New York.

Barnes, B., Bloor, D., & Henry, J. (1996) *Scientific Knowledge: A Sociological Analysis*. University of Chicago Press, Chicago.

Bhaskar, R. (1975) *A Realist Theory of Science.* Leeds Books, Leeds.
Bloor, D. (1976) *Knowledge and Social Imagery.* Routledge, London.
Boudon, R. (2004) *The Poverty of Relativism.* Bardwell Press, Oxford.
Feyerabend, P. F. (1975) *Against Method.* New Left Books, London.
Feyerabend, P. F. (1987) *Farewell to Reason.* Verso, London.
Harré, R. & Krausz, M. (1996) *Varieties of Relativism.* Blackwell, Oxford.
Kuhn, T. (1962) *The Structure of Scientific Revolutions.* University of Chicago Press, Chicago.
Quine, W. V. O. (1960) *Word and Object.* MIT Press, Cambridge, MA.
Quine, W. V. O. (1963) Two Dogmas of Empiricism. In: *From a Logical Point of View.* Harper & Row, New York.

reception studies

Sonia Livingstone

Reception studies derives primarily from the application of literary theories of textual interpretation to the everyday activities of mass media audiences. Drawing on ideas from the interpretation of the literary texts of high culture, reception studies argues that media texts must also be interpreted, made sense of, worked on by their audiences. Reception studies began in the 1980s in reaction to the predominant conception of audiences as passive and – in tandem – of media texts as moving wallpaper occasioning little or no effort of interpretive activity. For, ever since the advent of mass media over a century ago, the major theories of the audience have been strongly influenced both by sociological theories of ideology and hegemony and by social psychological theories of media effects and attitudinal or behavioral change. The result has been an image of the audience as homogeneous, vulnerable, and easily manipulated in the face of a powerful and all-pervasive mass media. Reception studies has sought to critique each element of this image, proposing instead that audiences are active, heterogeneous, resourceful, motivated, and even resistant in their responses to mass media texts. Since its inception, reception studies has mapped out a theoretical and empirical program of research on the "active audience" for mass media, establishing an influential strand of audience research, together with a series of innovations in both theory and methodology (Livingstone 1998).

Most importantly, in media and communication research emphasis shifted from the structuralist analysis of meanings "in" the text to an analysis of the process of reading a text, where the meanings which are activated on reading depend on the interaction between text and reader. Reception theorists (from both the American reader-response and European reception-aesthetic traditions) argue that an implied or model reader (i.e., an ideal decoding strategy, inscribed in the conventions of medium, genre, or address) is encoded into the text. This "model reader" is an implicit set of assumptions detectable within the structure of a text which render the meaning of the text fundamentally open or unstable, depending on the actual interpretive contribution of "real readers." This in turn depends on what Eco (1979) termed the "textual competencies" required to decode the text. However, as the empirical reception context may not meet this specification of the ideal reader presumed in the construction of the text, and, moreover, it may provide alternative interpretive resources, reception studies became an empirical project focused on audiences, linking their interpretive activities to both text and context.

In retrospect, the success of reception studies in challenging and changing dominant theories of audiences merits a more complex explanation than simply the extension of a theory from high to popular culture, although this innovation gave reception studies its conceptual starting point. But the literary approach is not primarily an empirical one, and what was striking about the early reception studies was the enthusiasm with which researchers began conducting empirical projects on audience's reception of mass media (mainly television) texts, rather, that this was the response of social science to a new idea, it being strongly felt that one could no longer simply assume that audiences would automatically interpret media texts as either their producers or their critics blithely supposed. Hence, the ways in which audiences interpreted media texts was recognized as an empirical question, one that demanded the combined analysis of media texts with media audiences (e.g., see readings in Brooker & Jermyn 2003). This in turn required the development of new methods of research – not just looking for measures of impact or effect, but rather seeking to uncover the interpretive processes of diverse audience members in particular cultural and social contexts, and so methods such as focus group interviewing, discourse analysis of audience talk, and ethnographic observation have become particularly prominent.

Within social science approaches to media audience, several distinct strands of research seized on the potential of literary approaches to interpretation, resulting in what is variously termed "reception studies," "audience reception studies," or work on the "active audience." These include, perhaps most importantly, the cultural studies interest in the production and reproduction of mass-produced meanings, centering on the twin analysis of encoding and decoding of media texts, with decoding taking place in specific yet influential social contexts of everyday life (Morley 1992). But the uses and gratifications perspective, which asked not what media do to audiences but what audiences do with media, also found resonances in reception studies, as did the social cognitive and social constructivist approaches in social psychology, concerned with the micro-analysis of people's interpretive processes. Two approaches gave a more politicized welcome to reception studies – one, critical mass communications research, was interested in the possibilities of audience critique and resistance to dominant ideological messages; the other, feminist media studies, was concerned to challenge the typically gendered image of the passive audience as housewife by revaluating audiences in more active and critical terms.

In integrating these different strands, reception studies has taken a range of approaches over recent years, while developing further as researchers respond to new empirical challenges, particularly those posed by different cultural contexts (resulting in a comparative, cross-national program of research for reception studies), and by new forms of "audiencing" (Fiske 1992) resulting from changing texts and technologies (e.g., public participation in talk shows, reality shows, and media events; audiences as fans joining in and acting out, rather than simply watching, the text; engagement with emerging or hypertext genres online or across multiple media). In so changing, reception studies has both gained in strength and encountered some problems. One problem has been the temptation to overclaim audiences' abilities to resist or rework the text so as to avoid the dominant message. Also problematic has been the ethnographic turn evident across much of the social sciences, for reception studies has expanded the focus on the reception context to the point where audiences' interpretive engagement with the text itself has become more marginalized; thus reception studies merges with audience studies more generally, and the specific strength of reception studies which stressed the empirical reception of specific textual features, conventions, genres, or codes receives less weight in current studies of audiences.

Nonetheless, the key arguments of reception studies have now become paradigmatic in sociological studies of mass media, namely: (1) that audiences must interpret what they see even to construct the message as meaningful and orderly, however routine this interpretation may be; (2) that audiences will diverge in their interpretations, generating different understandings from the same text; and (3) that the experience of viewing stands at the interface between the media (and their interpretations) and the rest of viewers' lives, blurring into the everyday so that watching television is no longer to be denigrated or neglected as an automatic, passive, standardized phenomenon.

SEE ALSO: Audiences; Critical Theory/Frankfurt School; Cultural Resistance; Encoding/Decoding; Fans and Fan Culture; Popular Culture Forms

REFERENCES AND SUGGESTED READINGS

Abercrombie, N. (1996) *Television and Society*. Polity Press, Cambridge.

Brooker, W. & Jermyn, D. (2003) *The Audience Studies Reader*. Routledge, London.

Eco, U. (1979) *The Role of the Reader: Explorations in the Semiotics of Texts*. Indiana University Press, Bloomington.

Fiske, J. (1992) Audiencing: A Cultural Studies Approach to Watching Television. *Poetics* 21: 345–59.
Livingstone, S. (1998) *Making Sense of Television: The Psychology of Audience Interpretation*, 2nd edn. Routledge, London.
Morley, D. (1992) *Television, Audiences, and Cultural Studies*. Routledge, London.

recidivism

Paula Smith

Recidivism refers to reoffending, or the repetition of criminal acts by a convicted offender. The term is derived from the French word *récidiver*, and based on the Latin word *recidivus*, back," to denote a relapse into prior criminal habits. Recidivism is an important consideration for modern penologists as a large proportion of incarcerated offenders in most countries are classified as recidivists. Studies in several countries across North America and Europe, for example, indicate that between one-half and two-thirds of inmates have served previous sentences (Bonta et al. 1992; Farrington 1992). According to Langan and Levin (2002), a recidivism rate as high as 70 percent has been reported within three years of release for inmates in the United States. Research also indicates that recidivists tend to have lengthier criminal histories, and the recidivism rate appears to be highest for those convicted of property offenses (Bonta et al. 1992; Langan & Levin 2002). Women are much less likely to recidivate than men (Bonta et al. 1992).

The measurement of recidivism is plagued by a number of conceptual and methodological issues that affect how statistics are interpreted. Recidivism is most often defined as an official record of reoffending behavior (e.g., rearrest, reconviction, reincarceration, technical violation of parole or probation condition, readmission to secure hospital, etc.). Official records are impacted by a number of factors, however, and inconsistencies in the interpretation of results have culminated in much misunderstanding and controversy. Several commentators (see Skogan 1977; Bartol 2005) have noted that official records tend to underestimate the incidence of criminal offenses as many crimes are unreported, or undetected, by law enforcement agencies. As an alternative, self-report studies (e.g., respondents are asked what offenses they have committed and how often) as well as national and regional victimization studies have been used to estimate recidivism rates. Moreover, recidivism rates also depend on how and when reoffending is measured. At the most basic level, certain measures of recidivism (e.g., reconviction, reincarceration) provide a more conservative estimate of reoffending in comparison with others (e.g., rearrest, technical violation of parole or probation condition). To illustrate, not all individuals who are rearrested are reconvicted, and not all individuals who are reconvicted are reincarcerated. Thus a measure of recidivism based on reconvictions would give a more conservative estimate than a measure based on rearrest. In addition, the severity of new convictions may or may not reflect the severity of the offenses actually committed (e.g., consider the effects of plea-bargaining). Other methodological issues that limit the comparative value of statistics on recidivism include differing post-release follow-up periods (i.e., lengthier follow-up periods generally produce higher estimates of recidivism than shorter periods), varying data sources (e.g., official records versus self-report data), unrepresentative or small samples, regional disparities in legal and procedural codes, as well as the discretionary decision-making practices of law enforcement agencies. All estimates of recidivism should be interpreted in light of how and when reoffending was measured.

A variety of statistical methods are used to calculate recidivism rates. Two of the most common are: (1) the *frozen time method*, or the calculation of the cumulative percentage of offenders who have recidivated after a specified follow-up period; and (2) *survival rate analysis*, or the estimation of the probability and rate of recidivism (i.e., time to reconviction) for different cohorts of offenders (Lievore 2004).

Reducing recidivism is, arguably, the primary goal of correctional agencies that aim to rehabilitate offenders. As such, recidivism is often the criterion of interest in assessing future risk, and in evaluating the effectiveness of correctional interventions. Several meta-analyses have identified numerous causal or functional variables as robust predictors of recidivism. These variables are referred to as *risk factors* and are subdivided into two categories: (1) *static*, or immutable, risk factors (e.g., age, gender, criminal history); and (2) *dynamic*, or malleable, risk factors (e.g., pro-criminal associates, substance abuse). Research indicates that high-risk offenders (i.e., those with an increased likelihood for recidivism) can be reliably distinguished from low-risk offenders through actuarial assessments of both static and dynamic risk factors. Furthermore, dynamic risk factors are prime treatment targets given their amenability to change, and the likelihood of future criminality is substantially reduced when such offender characteristics are altered. Several meta-analyses (e.g., Gendreau et al. 2000) have identified the following dynamic risk factors as the most robust predictors of recidivism: (1) pro-criminal attitudes, values, beliefs, and cognitive-emotional states; (2) pro-criminal associates; (3) personality and temperamental factors, including weak self-control, impulsivity, and adventurous pleasure-seeking; (4) problematic circumstances in the domains of marital/family relationships, education, employment, and leisure/recreation; and (5) substance abuse. Meta-analyses have also demonstrated that other attributes once regarded as important treatment targets (e.g., low self-esteem, personal distress, depression, and anxiety) are relatively weak predictors of recidivism (Gendreau et al. 2000).

SEE ALSO: Crime; Criminal Justice System; Criminology; Criminology: Research Methods; Deviant Careers; Measuring Crime

REFERENCES AND SUGGESTED READINGS

Andrews, D. A. (2003) *The Psychology of Criminal Conduct*, 3rd edn. Anderson, Cincinnati.

Bartol, C. R. (2005) *Criminal Behavior: A Psychosocial Approach*, 7th edn. Prentice-Hall, Upper Saddle River, NJ.

Bonta, J., Lipinski, S., & Martin, M. (1992) *Characteristics of Federal Inmates Who Recidivate.* Statistics Canada, Ottawa.

Farrington, D. P. (1992) Criminal Career Research in the United Kingdom. *British Journal of Criminology* 32: 521–36.

Gendreau, P., Little, T., & Goggin, C. (2000) A Meta-Analysis of the Predictors of Adult Recidivism: What Works? *Criminology* 34: 575–607.

Langan, P. A. & Levin, D. J. (2002) *Recidivism of Prisoners Released in 1994.* Bureau of Justice Statistics, US Department of Justice, NCJ 193427, Washington, DC.

Lievore, D. (2004) *Recidivism of Sexual Assault Offenders: Rates, Risk Factors, and Treatment Efficacy.* Australian Institute of Criminology.

Skogan, W. G. (1977) Dimensions of the Dark Figure of Unreported Crime. *Crime and Delinquency* 23: 41–50.

recognition

James J. Chriss

One of the more notable trends in the human sciences of late is a growing concern with reflection, reflexivity, and reflexive or reflective practice (Sandywell 1996). Wilhelm Dilthey is most directly linked to the concept of reflexivity as it has developed in hermeneutics, phenomenology, existentialism, and other interpretive theories in sociology. Dilthey's thought is located within the line of German idealism beginning with Kant and especially Hegel, the latter of whom is famous for the dialectical method. Hegel had attempted to overcome the dualism of subject/object by conceptualizing Spirit (*Geist*, or mind) as a triadic structure composed of *subjective Spirit* (thesis, or Spirit *in* itself, i.e., the pure subjectivity of the individual); *objective Spirit* (antithesis, or Spirit *for* itself, the subject projecting onto the outer world itself, for itself); and *absolute Spirit* (synthesis, or Spirit *in and for* itself, whereby Spirit returns to itself) (Tolman 2001: 184).

From Mead and later as codified by Blumer, the symbolic interactionist perspective posits reflexivity as an essential human capacity, one that is vitally important to the development of the self and the sustenance of everyday social interaction. Consistent with this position, Vaughan and Sjoberg (1986) argue that the capacity for social reflectivity is the most essential characteristic of our humanity. The human ability to reflect on ourselves and our social location and situation gives us all, potentially, the power to shape social reality even as we are being shaped by it. This is in essence our humanness: the ability, through a mindful and reflective consciousness, to transcend particular settings.

Vaughan and Sjoberg value subjectivity as a moral good and suggest conversely that oppressive social conditions which treat persons as objects reduce them to subhuman or nonhuman status. It is interesting to note, however, that from another theoretical perspective, under specifiable conditions it is actually necessary to render persons as objects *before* they can become subjects. This, of course, refers to the Hegelian dialectic. It seems here we have a fundamental contradiction between the hermeneutic approach, which suggests that self and self-consciousness arise only under liberative social conditions in which reflexivity is assured, and the Hegelian or dialectic approach, which suggests that the self and subjectivity arise just as readily out of oppressive conditions whereby, for a period of time at least, selves are treated as objects. On its face, this contradiction or disagreement is traceable to the split between Kant and Hegel over transcendental reason, or the ultimate grounding of understanding and interpretation.

For Kant, the universality of judgments acts as the transcendental ground of reason. In making this move, Kant limited knowing to the objects of possible experience, shared collectively, and declared that noumenon, the thing-in-itself, behind appearances was unknowable. Hegel's main objection to this line of thinking is that by separating the appearance from the thing-in-itself, Kant was in effect imbuing reason with too much power. In essence, reason has no limit, because it is reason and reason alone that is able to discern the presumed distinction between appearances and things-in-themselves. But what makes a limit a limit always includes knowledge of what is on both sides of it. As Gadamer (2000: 343) explains, "It is the dialectic of the limit to exist only by being superseded." Like the dialectic of master–bondsman, subjectivity arises out of the limits imposed by objectification; it does not emerge necessarily in and for itself. Kant's separation between appearance and the thing-in-itself makes transcendental reason the arbiter of reality. But rather than absolute reason, self-consciousness for Hegel arises only out of the difficult battle to be recognized by the other.

This issue of recognition has come to the fore especially within political and social theory over the conceptualization of social justice or the "good life" more generally. Indeed, over the years across modern western society and increasingly among the so-called developing and less-developed nations, social movements have arisen based upon group demands for recognition of the unique identity or cultural attributes such groups are claiming for themselves. Further, these demands for recognition are grounded in the claim that the dominant culture and major social institutions of society (especially the polity and economy) have systematically ignored and injured members of these groups through their failure to provide mechanisms for assuring members' full participation in society.

Charles Taylor (1994: 25) argues that groups that perceive that they are being misrecognized or not recognized at all are suffering real damage insofar as persons in the wider society are routinely mirroring back to members of these groups confining, demeaning, or contemptible images of themselves. This distorted image of the self leads to a host of problems in the living conditions and life chances of members of misrecognized or unrecognized groups. For example, feminists claim that patriarchal societies operate in such a way as to socialize women into internalizing a depreciatory image of themselves. Likewise, for centuries whites have projected a negative image onto blacks, and these powerful cultural scripts and practices have made it virtually impossible for blacks to resist adopting a deleterious self-image.

With the rise of the modern welfare state, citizens' demands go beyond those based on economic hardship or political injustice. Now, above and beyond claims being made on the basis of "citizen" or "worker," within constitutional welfare states persons are making identity- or recognition-related claims on the basis of gender, race, ethnicity, age, disability, sexual orientation, marital status, and so forth. This progression in the change of western polities could be interpreted as a slow but inexorable move toward incorporating greater reflexivity into law and policy. Many things "taken for granted" in earlier times are being looked at in different ways and are subject to reflective critique or appraisal pertaining to the treatment of persons, objects, other living entities, and the environments within which they are situated. Examples include "green politics," the animal rights movement, and economic reparations to African Americans for American slavery.

The idea that the development of the welfare state, as well as more recent claims for recognition by a growing number of persons and groups, is spurred on by a growth in reflexivity and heightened awareness about the plight of the other, is made explicit in John Rawls's (1971) theory of justice. Through the process of reflective equilibrium, that is, by reflecting on their own situation and placing themselves in the shoes of the less fortunate in society, persons come to an understanding of the justness or goodness of welfare as institutionalized and enacted within government policy.

We must be cautious, however, in equating too easily the notions of rightness or goodness on the one hand, and justice on the other. As Nancy Fraser (2001: 22) points out, questions of distributive justice and rights are typically aligned with Kantian *Moralitat* (morality), while questions of recognition and "the good" are aligned with Hegelian *Sittlichkeit* (ethics). Norms of justice are thought to be universally binding, thus consistent with Kant's categorical imperative, while claims for recognition of difference involve qualitative assessments of the relative worth of various cultural practices which cannot be universalized, thereby maintaining consistency with Hegel's dialectic. Fraser attempts to bring these two divergent impulses together in a more comprehensive theory of justice that incorporates both redistribution and recognition. Specifically, she suggests that recognition ought to be treated as a question of *social status*. Here, what is required is not recognition of group-specific identity – which tends to cause difficulty insofar as such claims of identity get entangled in ethical considerations of the various claims made by various groups – but rather the status of group members as full participants in social life. Hence, misrecognition or non-recognition is no longer seen as distorting group identity, but rather is seen as causing the social subordination of group members to the extent that they do not enjoy full participation in ongoing group relations, as peers alongside those not similarly misrecognized. Fraser's (2001: 24) "status model" aims, then, to overcome subordination "by establishing the misrecognized party as a full member of society, capable of participating on a par with other members."

From the perspective of the status model, misrecognition arises wherever social structures or cultural norms or practices distort interaction so as to impede parity of participation. In many ways this is similar to the position of Vaughan and Sjoberg (1986). To reiterate, Vaughan and Sjoberg assert that the right to human status is fundamental, and that to achieve human status social conditions must be present that facilitate social reflectivity. Lacking such social conditions, persons would be cut off from self-actualization or their own subjectivity, in essence being treated merely as subhuman "objects" within the social system.

There is seemingly good evidence of a growth in claims for recognition among various groups in society, and these recognition claims go beyond the more longstanding strategy of seeking economic reparations for the historical harm done to these groups (whether because of slavery, colonialism, internment, racism, classism, heterosexism, sexism, and so forth). The ongoing waves of juridification culminating in the modern welfare state and beyond, as outlined by Habermas (1987), seem to point to an opening up of reflexive awareness on the part of legislators and citizens about past and current mistreatment of certain groups and persons. With regard to recognition claims per se, the recognition or acknowledgment of this mistreatment amounts to a new view that persons deserve respect and should be assured full participation in society as fellow human beings (Honneth 2001; Walby 2001).

Even as we move seemingly toward a "one world order" under globalization, there is evidence of powerful countermovements – resembling something like a new tribalism – as more and more groups are making claims of collective identity based upon any number of attributes or statuses, for example, gender, religious affiliation, sexual orientation, citizenship status, ethnicity, and so forth (Gamson 1995: 2; Bendle 2002: 8). There appears to be a proliferation of social movements in which members seek recognition for identities that are disvalued or overlooked by legislators and/or the general public. This is the essence of current political and sociological concern with recognition, reflexivity, and identity (Douzinas 2002).

SEE ALSO: Existential Sociology; Hegel, G. W. F.; Human Rights; Identity Politics/Relational Politics; Phenomenology; Reflexivity; Social Justice, Theories of; Social Movements

REFERENCES AND SUGGESTED READINGS

Bendle, M. F. (2002) The Crisis of "Identity" in High Modernity. *British Journal of Sociology* 53 (1): 1–18.

Douzinas, C. (2002) Identity, Recognition, Rights, or What Can Hegel Teach Us About Human Rights? *Journal of Law and Society* 29(3): 379–405.

Fraser, N. (2001) Recognition Without Ethics? *Theory, Culture, and Society* 18(2–3): 21–42.

Gadamer, H. (2000) *Truth and Method*, 2nd rev. edn. Trans. J. Weinsheimer & D. G. Marshall. Continuum, New York.

Gamson, W. A. (1995) Hiroshima, the Holocaust, and the Politics of Exclusion. *American Sociological Review* 60: 1–20.

Habermas, J. (1987) *Theory of Communicative Action*, Vol. 2. Trans. T. McCarthy. Beacon Press, Boston.

Honneth, A. (2001) Recognition or Redistribution? Changing Perspectives on the Moral Order of Society. *Theory, Culture, and Society* 18(2–3): 43–55.

Rawls, J. (1971) *A Theory of Justice*. Harvard University Press, Cambridge, MA.

Sandywell, B. (1996) *Reflexivity and the Crisis of Western Reason*. Vol. 1 of his *Logological Investigations*. Routledge, London.

Taylor, C. (1994) The Politics of Recognition. In: Gutmann, A. (Ed.), *Multiculturalism*. Princeton University Press, Princeton, pp. 25–73.

Tolman, C. W. (2001) Philosophical Doubts About Psychology as a Natural Science. In: Green, C. D., Shore, M., & Teo, T. (Eds.), *The Transformation of Psychology: Influences of 19th-Century Philosophy, Technology, and Natural Science*. American Psychological Association, Washington, DC, pp. 175–93.

Vaughan, T. R. & Sjoberg, G. (1986) Human Rights Theory and the Classical Sociological Tradition. In: Wardell, M. L. & Turner, S. P. (Eds.), *Sociological Theory in Transition*. Allen & Unwin, London, pp. 127–41.

Walby, S. (2001) From Community to Coalition: The Politics of Recognition as the Handmaiden of the Politics of Equality in an Era of Globalization. *Theory, Culture, and Society* 18(2–3): 113–35.

reconstructive analyses

Phil Carspecken III

Reconstructive analysis refers to a specific method of analyzing qualitative data based primarily on principles from universal pragmatics and critical theory, but employing adapted insights from hermeneutics and structuralism as well. It is used to study meaning and symbolically structured forms of experience at many different substantive levels: from analysis of singular meaningful actions to the analysis of themes and discourses that distinguish an entire culture or subculture. It is a non-empiricist, interpretive method because its object of inquiry – meaning – is not objective in nature. Participants' intuitive knowledge is first grasped tacitly by the researcher through some combination of maeutic interviewing, participant observation, and/or stimulated recall. Analysis then proceeds based on hermeneutically guided understandings of the tacit knowledge routinely employed by participants, in order to reconstruct (put into explicit discourse) what was formerly implicit. The standard by which to determine successful or unsuccessful reconstructions resides in the intuitive knowledge of one's subjects, who should recognize the researcher's formulations as being accurate.

The historical roots of reconstructive analysis can be traced to Habermas's use of the expression "reconstructive sciences" during the 1970s for distinguishing a methodology that had already been in use within subfields of linguistics, logic, analytic philosophy, and developmental psychology (Habermas 1976, 1979, 1982). Inferences used to move from data to research findings are neither deductive nor inductive in these sciences, but rather use a process called "explicitation" by Brandom (1994). The term "explicitation" is roughly synonymous with "reconstruction," though the former refers to everyday processes of making implicit understandings explicit while the later emphasizes the more theoretically guided efforts of a researcher. The researcher learns the underlying "structures" (generative rules, interpretive schemes, cognitive or moral schemes, logical relations) intuitively and implicitly in the way her subjects understand them through a process resembling the "hermeneutic circle," though theoretically informed by a concept of "cultural typifications" (Carspecken 1996, 1999), and then moves the implicit understandings into explicit, reconstructed formulations with the help of universal pragmatics, structuralist semantics, and empirical-contingent pragmatics.

The reconstructive sciences identified by Habermas differ from "reconstructive analysis" partly because of the effort of the former to seek out universal structures, rules, and normative orders. Reconstructive analysis makes use of universals in the pragmatics of communication to do research on particular and contingent structures of meaning, though nothing in principle bars reconstructive analysis from making contributions to the quest for structures universal to human communication. The universal structures of pragmatics include the internal relation of criticizable validity claims to meaning and the division of validity claims into objective, subjective, and normative categories – each of which is intrinsic to all meaningful acts (Habermas 1976, 1979, 1982). Reconstructive analysis makes use of this pragmatic theory of validity in the development of the concept of a pragmatic meaning horizon (Carspecken 1996, 1999), which includes a validity horizon, an identity claim, and an empirical-contingent pragmatic shell as structures of every meaningful act. For meaningful acts that employ language, a level of semantic structure is also part of the pragmatic meaning horizon. The researcher uses this theory of meaningful action to build from analyses of micro-level actions to cultural themes, discourses, and other macro and meso-level sociological phenomena. Results of such analysis can then be further analyzed with the use of systems theory to examine the relation between macro and meso-level cultural themes and non-cultural features of society such as economic systems, formal-legal organizational structures, and political orders and laws.

The theory of meaning central to universal pragmatics and reconstructive analysis alike takes implicit, pragmatic structures to be fundamental, with semantics and empirical-contingent pragmatic structures having a secondary status, reducible to pragmatics. This means that the reconstruction of meaning is most closely achieved through the explication of validity horizons. All representations of meaning semantically, symbolically, artistically, and so on never reach a full one-on-one correspondence with the meanings represented. In other words, all representations of meaning resulting from reconstructive methodology will implicate additional implicit and holistic understandings to make any sense. Though these also may be reconstructed this results in an unending chain of representations and meta-representations, each still dependent on an implicit horizon of understandings to make sense. The precision of reconstructive analysis can be continuously refined in this way without an end ever being possible to reach. The implicit understandings chronic to meaning are intersubjectively constructed and ultimately rooted in expectations of how others will understand an act and act next themselves. Such expectations are within culturally normed boundaries. This has consequences for reconstructive analysis that are explained below.

MEANING, CONTEXT, SETTING, AND CULTURAL TYPIFICATION

Reconstructive analysis employs a model of meaningful action that includes a number of key elements. People interact meaningfully through a process of taking the position (with or without much awareness) of other subjects in the situation. Meaning is therefore constituted intersubjectively. Other subject positions have an assumed status enabled through cultural typifications and a normative infrastructure referred to as the interactive setting. This means that position-taking need not be (and often is not) accurate. The researcher will have an interest in attaining both accuracy in taking the positions of others in an interaction and in grasping and then articulating the typification and setting infrastructures that her participants use to position-take with each other. The first goal of the researcher, then, is to position-take as her subjects do.

Meaningful acts are therefore always contextually dependent, in that they build features of cultural typifications and specific normative infrastructures into their constitution. A meaningful act is understood in this approach to deliver a holistic meaning that is analytically divisible into many various components. Components are distinguished along a temporal dimension pertaining to the assumptions made by actors regarding shared understandings about actions just gone by as well actions likely to come next. This pertains to interactive syntax in relation to the setting infrastructure.

A paradigmatic dimension also distinguishes components of meaning with the major divisions pertaining to a culturally contingent pragmatic structure through which the act is delivered, a semantic level of structure, an existential identity claim, and a validity horizon. The concept of "structure" here refers to many levels of implication between categories and rules having a variety of inference relations between them (similarity and contrast relations, metaphor, analogy, homology, binary, hierarchy, material implication). These are instantiated as claims by the meaningful act. Thus, structures can vary from act to act because they are reproduced or slightly altered by ongoing action.

MEANING FIELDS

Actors in everyday life do not understand each other simply and straightforwardly, but rather understand a bounded field of possible meanings with every act. The researcher learns to understand fields of meaning as the subjects do, and the boundaries of such fields. Thus, the concept of meaning field is another tool key to reconstructive analysis. Meaning fields are implicit to understanding and cannot be exhaustively formulated, but central themes of interpretation can be articulated so as to specify the boundaries of possible meaning. Central interpretations within a single field will display a conjunctive/disjunctive structure and are formulated with "OR," "AND," and "AND/OR" connectives between them.

VALIDITY HORIZON

Because meaning ultimately depends upon implicit, pragmatic understandings, there is no way to represent it directly and completely. Hence the most direct way to reconstruct meaning is to specify the horizon of criticizable validity claims constituting it. This is because the validity claims constituting a meaningful act pertain directly to the implicit intersubjective assumptions used by actors to try to make themselves understood and to respond to each other. Reconstructing the validity claims results in what is called the validity horizon in reconstructive analysis. A validity horizon is the most precise articulation of meaning, but because it is a semanticization of something that is at root pragmatic and implicit, it is a fallible interpretation and must be supported by the responses of one's subjects to it.

A validity horizon articulates claims along two dimensions: a dimension of discrete distinctions between Habermas's three fundamental validity claims plus a category for identity claims, and a dimension of continuous distinction from foregrounded portions of meaning to backgrounded portions. The "identity claim" is added to Habermas's three validity claims. Identity claims are chronic to all acts though often not foregrounded, and they consist of claims to being a certain type of person and not other types of persons, given a cultural repertoire of possible identities (which itself will have reconstructable structure). In general, the foreground of the validity horizon consists of the validity claims emphasized by the actor, while the mid-regions and backgrounds of validity horizons are assumptions that must be understood for the foreground to make sense. Mid and back regions of the horizon are often not within the full awareness of actors, but can be drawn out with maeutic techniques.

SEMANTICS

One can examine semantic structures unique to a culture or discourse by focusing on key lexical items and the structures of implication necessary to understand these items as one's subjects do. Lexical structures have terms that implicate each other in various ways: through homologies, oppositions, relations of similarity, analogies, hierarchies, and metaphors. Reconstructing both the terms and the relations of implication between them is necessary. Semantic structures are ultimately understood to deliver meaning through delivering validity horizons.

CULTURALLY CONTINGENT PRAGMATICS

Meaningful acts also employ culturally contingent pragmatics, which include such things as (giving a list at diverse levels here): roles, intonations, gestures, facial expressions, pacing, power relations between actors, interactive infrastructures pertaining to the sequencing of acts, and many other things. Pragmatic features of meaningful action also implicate structures. For example, the contribution of something like intonation to meaning depends upon implicitly understood differences and similarities with other intonation patterns. Pragmatic structure is claimed with each act and involves relations of exclusion, complementarity, and contrast to characterize them. There are even pragmatic metaphors and allusions. But pragmatic structures are all implicit and para-linguistic, in contrast with semantic structures. Once again, the bottom line for an analysis of meaning, in this case with a focus on pragmatic structures distinguishing a discourse, culture, or subculture, is the validity horizon.

USES

Mastery of the validity horizon method of analysis is used for many purposes, including the reconstruction of general cultural themes, ideologies, discourses, small-group cultures, and dyadic normative infrastructures. It is a method helpful in analyzing culture at many diverse levels and in many diverse contexts. Findings then allow for further analysis of the relation between the cultural forms revealed and non-cultural features of social life.

Because reconstructive analysis emphasizes the criticizable validity claims of everyday life, it is an appropriate method for critical inquiries. Validity claims typical to one's participants can be examined and critiqued in their own terms because validity claims always include, necessarily, certain claims to universality (Habermas 1982) and bear a relation to the existential identity claims of actors which put validity claims of all types in relation to ontological needs for valid social identities, self-actualization, autonomy, and freedom (Carspecken 1996, 1999).

SEE ALSO: Critical Theory/Frankfurt School; Hermeneutics; Structuralism; System Theories

REFERENCES AND SUGGESTED READINGS

Brandom, R. (1994) *Making it Explicit: Reasoning, Representing, and Discursive Commitment.* Harvard University Press, Cambridge, MA.

Carspecken, P. F. (1996) *Critical Ethnography in Educational Research: A Theoretical and Practical Guide.* Routledge, New York.

Carspecken, P. F. (1999) *Four Scenes for Posing the Question of Meaning, and Other Explorations in Critical Philosophy and Critical Methodology.* Peter Lang, New York.

Habermas, J. (1976) Was heisst Universalpragmatik? In: Apel, K.-O. (Ed.), *Sprachpragmatik und Philosophie.* Suhrkamp Verlag, Frankfurt am Main.

Habermas, J. (1979) What is Universal Pragmatics? In: McCarthy, T. (Ed.), *Communication, Evolution, Society.* Beacon Press, Boston.

Habermas, J. (1982) *The Theory of Communicative Action.* Vol. 1: *Reason and the Rationalization of Society.* Beacon Press, Boston.

redlining

Rachel Dwyer

Redlining is a form of discrimination in credit markets where banks and financial institutions identify entire neighborhoods as too "high-risk" for financial investment in both residential and commercial property. Financial institutions "redline" neighborhoods for a number of reasons including the physical characteristics of the housing stock and undesirable location, but most important has been the presence of minority, especially black, residents. Racial redlining occurs not only because of the correlation of race with indicators of financial risk, but also because investors interpret the racial category itself to signal risk apart from the quality and prosperity of the neighborhood on other measures. In short, redlining is a critical form of community disinvestment that occurs when resources (e.g., home mortgages, insurance, home improvement loans) are made unavailable to residents because of the high proportion of ethnic or racial minorities living in their neighborhood, regardless of objective socioeconomic characteristics (e.g., wealth, income, age of housing).

Social historians argue that while discrimination against minority neighborhoods occurred throughout US history, redlining became standard practice in the 1930s. The collapse of the housing market during the Depression and the development of new financial instruments led to increased concern with assessing neighborhood risk. Jackson (1985) found that government agencies were crucial in the institutionalization of redlining during this period. A New Deal agency created to halt widespread foreclosures by giving loans, the Home Owners Loan Corporation (HOLC), developed detailed "Residential Security" maps that categorized neighborhoods by risk and interpreted any minority presence to increase hazards for investment, placing all black neighborhoods into the highest risk category. HOLC coded the highest risk category red on the maps, originating the term redlining. While the HOLC maps represent some of the most striking evidence of redlining in the 1930s, Hillier (2003) argues that the practice predated the maps, and many other housing market actors were actively creating their own rating systems and maps at the same time (both in dialogue with HOLC and separate from it), including the financial services industry, which used them to decide where not to invest, and the Federal Housing Administration (FHA), which used them to decide where not to insure investments.

Neighborhood risk assessments profoundly influenced the post-war housing boom. In fact, the well-documented suburban bias of the FHA derived in some measure from the agency's judgment that almost any central city neighborhood – even if inhabited by whites – could potentially become minority and thus was higher risk than suburban areas ("protected" by restrictive covenants and other forms of racial discrimination). The disadvantages of US cities in the post-war political economy can thus be interpreted to be in part a form of redlining on a large scale.

Routine use of redlining by both industry and government persisted until the 1960s and 1970s, with devastating consequences for cities and minority neighborhoods. Starved of commercial and residential capital, the physical stock in redlined neighborhoods declined and urban areas were disinvested. Redlining thus created the conditions it supposedly merely identified, degrading the financial health and quality of properties in minority neighborhoods regardless of their starting position. Redlining not only resulted from racial segregation, it also worsened it by blocking wealth accumulation among minority households, contributing to persistent poverty by foreclosing job creation, and making integration against the financial interests of white households.

Civil rights activism in the 1960s and 1970s resulted in laws that made redlining illegal, including the Equal Credit Opportunity Act in 1974. These laws (combined with community action to ensure their enforcement) increased access to credit and investment in some minority neighborhoods in the 1980s and 1990s (Immergluck 2004). Study and monitoring of redlining were facilitated by the passage of the Home Mortgage Disclosure Act (HMDA) in 1975, which required annual reports from lenders, producing an invaluable source of data for researchers.

Despite progress made since the civil rights legislation, there remains substantial disparity in the level of investment in minority compared to white neighborhoods. Yet there is debate over the degree to which the credit disadvantage of minority neighborhoods is due to ongoing racial redlining, or whether instead it is simply the result of the correlation of race with reasonable, objective measures of risk used by financial institutions (Goering & Wienk 1996). In an exhaustive review of this literature and analysis of the methodological issues raised, Ross and Yinger (2002) conclude that both individual mortgage discrimination and racial redlining did still occur in the 1990s, even if financial institutions were not as blatant in their methods as in earlier decades.

Others have challenged the terms of the debate over whether the assessment of risk in neighborhoods involves racial discrimination. First, scholars point out that even if minority neighborhoods receive less investment as a result of poor performance on objective measures of risk and not overt racial discrimination, policies of risk assessment are discriminatory in their *consequences*. This "disparate impact" cannot be ignored, not least because it is in large part the legacy of past redlining that makes many neighborhoods higher risk on objective measures.

Second, an even more ambitious critique draws on economic and organizational sociology to question the very conception of "objective" risk used within financial services companies. Stuart (2003) argues that risk assessment cannot be interpreted solely as an objective matter, determined through rational analysis. Instead, he argues that risk is socially constructed within particular organizational structures with particular histories and imperatives. In the taken-for-granted practices of institutions and industry conventions, policies perpetuate racial discrimination and redlining even when not explicitly framed in racial terms. Stuart demonstrates that because they subscribe to a fundamentally flawed (and outdated) theory of economic organization, regulations and studies that define racialized policies only as the most overt differential treatment miss the many more subtle ways that real estate practices are racially discriminatory (see Gotham 2002 for a related argument).

Another important area of recent scholarship is study of alternative and new forms of redlining in financial services. Squires (2003a) has detailed the prevalence of "insurance redlining," where properties in minority neighborhoods are denied insurance, a prerequisite for obtaining a mortgage. Predatory lending is also increasingly interpreted to be a form of redlining where minority neighborhoods are targeted for investment, but on highly unfavorable terms that drain resources from communities perhaps even more effectively than denial of credit (Squires 2003b). Changes in the financial services industry and its regulatory framework made predatory lending much more prevalent in the 1990s, and other changes (including the rise of electronic banking and automated underwriting, industry consolidation, and the proliferation of lending instruments) may significantly impact the incidence of redlining in ways social science has only begun to explore.

Analysis of redlining has become increasingly difficult, however. Because of changes in the industry since the passage of the reporting legislation, HMDA collects fewer data from a smaller percentage of lenders than in the past (Holloway & Wyly 2002). In addition, whole segments of industry like property insurance have never been required to report. Thus, just as the institutional terrain has become more complex, the data have become less reliable.

Even with the data difficulties, social science must keep pace with the industry and push for better government data collection as well as seek new sources of data on the financial services market. It is important that redlining continues to be studied, against the tendency in the literature to focus more on individual discrimination than on the geographical dimensions of credit inequality. Despite some progress toward integration, the profound link between race and space in US metropolitan areas will persist into the foreseeable future, including in the historical legacy and continuing incidence of redlining.

SEE ALSO: Blockbusting; Hypersegregation; Inequality and the City; Invasion-Succession; Restrictive Covenants; Steering, Racial Real Estate; Urban Renewal and Redevelopment

REFERENCES AND SUGGESTED READINGS

Goering, J. & Wienk, R. (Eds.) (1996) *Mortgage Lending, Racial Discrimination, and Federal Policy.* Urban Institute Press, Washington, DC.

Gotham, K. F. (2002) *Race, Real Estate, and Uneven Development: The Kansas City Experience, 1900–2000.* State University of New York Press, Albany.

Hillier, A. E. (2003) Redlining and the Home Owners' Loan Corporation. *Journal of Urban History* 29(4): 394–420.

Holloway, S. R. & Wyly, E. K. (2002) Empirical Destabilization of Racial Categories: Implications for Civil Rights Enforcement in Mortgage Lending. *Review of Black Political Economy* 30(1): 57–89.

Immergluck, D. (2004) *Credit to the Community: Community Reinvestment and Fair Lending Policy in the United States.* M. E. Sharp, Armonk, NY.

Jackson, K. T. (1985) *Crabgrass Frontier: The Suburbanization of the United States.* Oxford University Press, Oxford.

Ross, S. & Yinger, J. (2002) *The Color of Credit: Mortgage Discrimination, Research Methodology, and Fair Lending Enforcement.* MIT Press, Cambridge, MA.

Squires, G. D. (2003a) Racial Profiling, Insurance Style: Insurance Redlining and the Uneven Development of Metropolitan Areas. *Journal of Urban Affairs* 25(4): 391–410.

Squires, G. D. (2003b) The New Redlining: Predatory Lending in an Age of Financial Service Modernization. *Sage Race Relations Abstracts* 28(3): 5–18.

Stuart, G. (2003) *Discriminating Risk: The US Mortgage Lending Industry in the Twentieth Century.* Cornell University Press, Ithaca, NY.

reference groups

Kristine J. Ajrouch

The term reference group denotes a cluster of social psychological concepts pertaining to the relationship between individual identities, social norms, and social control. Reference groups may constitute a group into which individuals are members, as well as those groups to which one does not belong. The utility of the term lies in its ability to provide an explanation as to how social groups influence individual values, attitudes, and behavior.

Muzafer Sherif articulated early applications of reference group theory in the 1940s. At the time, understanding of human behavior focused on subjective interpretations and classic behaviorism regarding the relationship between the individual and his or her environment. Sherif instead started moving away from subjective interpretations by introducing the concept of "frames of reference" to highlight the significance of the individual actively striving to gain acceptance into a group. Sherif's work challenged prevalent thinking; his contribution included emphasis on relationships between people, underscoring group dynamics for understanding individuals. One important aspect of Sherif's thinking for reference group theory is the notion that reference groups do not automatically constitute membership groups. The link between individual identities and reference groups is determined by the context within which individuals interact with groups. Perhaps his most significant contribution is that Sherif presented a way to understand social group influence on the individual as well as to discern those situations when such influence does not shape the individual.

Reference groups have also been useful in understanding the development of identity boundaries, particularly concerning ethnicity and adaptation among children of immigrants. Many scholars interested in second-generation immigration highlight the tensions that exist between the ideals of two conflicting reference groups, that of the immigrant culture and that of dominant American society. The values and behaviors of each reference group provide powerful socializing forces on the children of immigrants. Thus, inquiries into identity development often seek to determine to what extent each group serves as an audience in front of whom the second generation acts to achieve acceptance. For instance, in a recent study focusing on adolescent children of Lebanese immigrants living in an ethnic community, Ajrouch discovered the usage of two terms representing reference groups – boater and white. A boater is the term second-generation adolescents ascribe to immigrants. It signifies that the immigrant has not yet acquired the "American" cultural habits with which the adolescents identify, including fluent, unbroken English and clothing that reflects current American fashion trends. A white represents members of dominant American society, and has both positive and negative aspects. The positive dimensions include access to education and privilege. The negative dimensions include a lackadaisical attitude and no sense of obligation, commitment, or responsibility. As adolescents describe themselves, defining their identity, they reference these groups to designate who they are not, and portray themselves as somewhere in between. Attitudes about who one is stem from comparison with those one would like to emulate as well as comparison with those with whom one does not want to associate.

The use of reference groups has had enormous impact on the development and use of measures in the social sciences. Self-report measures of social, psychological, and biological phenomena including attitudes, behaviors, and physical well-being invariably are influenced within a context, by social comparison. For example, inequalities in society may be as much a product of subjective interpretation involving an individual comparing his or her situation to a group or category as they are a consequence of objective, observable differences. The reference group concept has furthermore served to highlight the potential confounding effects of group comparison research, especially concerning cross-cultural studies. Building off the awareness that most people's self-understanding results from how people compare themselves with others around them, and in particular others similar to them, the suggestion emerges that different groups have diverse standards by which evaluations are made. Moreover, shifting evaluations may occur depending on the context. Thus, analyses that seek to compare mean scores from different cultures (who invariably have different referents) risk the threat of misleading results.

The areas in the social sciences to which the concept reference group applies have expanded over the years, demonstrating its utility for understanding a variety of social phenomena. Initially developed as a theoretical concept by which to illuminate the effect of social context on human attitudes and behavior, the term has recently shown its value as a means by which to explain social processes ranging from identity development to methodological fallacies. The application of the reference group concept will continue to illuminate the ways by which context influences the individual.

SEE ALSO: Generalized Other; Group Processes, Interaction Order; Interpersonal Relationships; Looking-Glass Self; Role; Role-Taking; Social Control; Social Psychology

REFERENCES AND SUGGESTED READINGS

Ajrouch, K. J. (2000) Place, Age, and Culture: Community Living and Ethnic Identity among Lebanese American Adolescents. *Small Group Research* 31(4): 447–69.

Heine, S. J., Lehman, D. R., Kaiping, P., & Greenholz, J. (2002) What's Wrong with Cross-Cultural Comparisons of Subjective Likert Scales? The Reference-Group Effect. *Journal of Personality and Social Psychology* 82(6): 903–18.

Merton, R. & Rossi, A. (1950) Contributions to the Theory of Reference Group Behavior. In: Merton, R. & Lazersfeld, P. (Eds.), *Studies in the Scope of and Method of "The American Soldier."* Free Press, New York, pp. 40–105.

Sherif, M. (1936) *The Psychology of Social Norms.* Harper, New York.

Sherif, M. & Sherif, C. W. (1964) *Reference Groups: Exploration into Conformity and Deviation of Adolescents.* Harper, New York.

Yngwe, M. A., Fritzell, J., Lundberg, O., Diderichsen, F., & Burstrom, B. (2003) Exploring Relative Deprivation: Is Social Comparison a Mechanism in the Relations Between Income and Health? *Social Science and Medicine* 57: 1463–73.

reflexive modernization

Jens Zinn

Ulrich Beck introduced the term reflexive modernity (also called second modernity) by explicitly demarcating himself from postmodern approaches which would imply that current developments go beyond modernity (Beck et al. 2003).

He first outlined his argument in *Risk Society* (published in German in 1986 and in English in 1992) and later developed it further. The central thesis is that modernity has transformed itself by the radicalized application of the core concepts of modern industrialized society (also called first modernity or simple modernity). Central principles (e.g., the distinction between nature and culture or science and politics), as well as basic institutions (e.g., the gender division of labor, the traditional family, the normal model of the life course), have been transformed into a new modernity.

Since "reflexive" often causes misunderstandings Beck has repeatedly emphasized that it does not mean that people in today's society are more self-conscious than in the past. It indicates rather a heightened awareness that mastery of nature, technique, the social, and so on is impossible.

Originally, Beck (1992) developed the concept of reflexive modernization referring to the occurrence of a risk society and growing institutional individualization. New risks would occur as unexpected side effects of industrialization that take place in nature (e.g., climate change, depleted ozone layer) and as technical catastrophes (e.g., accidents in Bhopal, Chernobyl, *Challenger*). They would erode the belief in the managability of nature by science and thereby politicize risk decisions. Additionally, individualization processes would release people from traditional institutions, which at the same time erode and became supplanted by secondary institutions (e.g., the labor market, the welfare state, mass media). Individualization demands individual decisions where routines and traditions prevailed before.

Reflexive modernization resonates in the discourse on social change in Britain. Beck et al. (1994) critically discussed social change in modernity. While Lash emphasized the cultural aspects of these changes ("risk culture"), Giddens prefers the expression "institutional reflexivity" and emphasizes growing individual self-awareness and self-responsibility, which lead to more political considerations regarding a "Third Way" in politics. Beck developed his theoretical considerations in the direction of a general theory and tried to specify the changes more empirically. He broadened the concept of social change from "risk" and "individualization" to a general change of central institutions and principles of first modernity into a reflexive modernity.

The multiplication of boundaries (or attempts to draw boundaries) is introduced as a central criterion to identify the change from first to reflexive modernity (Beck et al. 2003). For example, instead of one identity linked to a specific cultural background there is the possibility of several identities referring to different (often contradictory) backgrounds without the necessity to decide for one or the other. The result is in many respects a change from a so-called either-or society to a this-as-well-as-that world. Boundaries between nature and culture, life and death, knowledge and superstition, us and others, expert and laymen, for example, become blurred.

Although many of Beck's observations are acknowledged, the theory itself is still contested. It is criticized as often being too general to explain concrete behavior. It is faulted for a lack of empirical evidence and whether it can be empirically tested at all.

SEE ALSO: Individualism; Modernity; Risk, Risk Society, Risk Behavior, and Social Problems; Uncertainty

REFERENCES AND SUGGESTED READINGS

Beck, U. (1986) *Risikogesellschaft: auf dem Weg in eine andere Moderne*. Suhrkamp, Frankfurt am Main.

Beck, U. (1992) *Risk Society: Towards a New Modernity*. Sage, Newbury Park, CA.

Beck, U., Giddens, A., & Lash, S. (1994) *Reflexive Modernization: Politics, Tradition and Aesthetics in the Modern Social Order*. Stanford University Press, Stanford.

Beck, U., Bonß, W., & Lau, C. (2003) The Theory of Reflexive Modernization: Problematic, Hypotheses and Research Programme. *Theory, Culture and Society* 20(2): 1–33.

reflexivity

Mats Alvesson

Reflexivity can be broadly defined to mean an understanding of the knowledge-making enterprise, including a consideration of the subjective, institutional, social, and political processes whereby research is conducted and knowledge is produced. The researcher is part of the social world that is studied and this calls for exploration and self-examination. A reflexive researcher "intentionally or self-consciously shares (whether in agreement or disagreement) with her or his audiences the underlying assumptions that occasion a set of questions" (Robertson 2002: 786).

The recent interest in reflexivity has been linked to the influence of postmodernism and poststructuralism whose insights have drawn attention to the problematic nature of research, the dubious position of the researcher, the crisis of representation, and the constructive nature of language, as well as an admission of the fact that there is no "one best way" of conducting either theoretical or empirical work. Reflexivity is about dealing with "a sense of uncertainty and crisis as increasingly complex questions are raised concerning the status, validity, basis and authority of knowledge claims" (Mauthner & Doucet 2003: 417).

Leading philosophers of science and intellectuals have struggled with issues similar to those brought forward by the "reflexive turn" for a long time. The work of Kuhn (1970) has been vital in raising questions around the limits of scientific rationality and progress. Popper (1969: 95) cast doubt on the objectivity of the single researcher, whom he described as "often very biased, favouring his pet ideas in a one-sided and partisan manner." Popper declared his faith "upon a critical tradition which, despite resistance, often makes it possible to criticize a dominant dogma." Much work on reflexivity expresses similar interests, but tends to be skeptical of Popper's belief in the community of scholars jointly producing scientific objectivity. Instead, this work typically takes ideas of constructionism and the linguistic turn(s) seriously, and rejects or downplays the possibility or ideal of objectivity.

Postmodern thinking, critical studies, feminism, and interpretive and other qualitative work more generally all cast doubt on the idea that "competent observers" can "with objectivity, clarity, and precision report on their own observations of the social world." They also challenge the belief "in a real subject" who is "able to report on his or her experiences" (Denzin & Lincoln 1994: 11–12), and typically go much further than writers such as Popper by problematizing the pillars of the scientific project. Informed by the linguistic turn, such researchers have increasingly stressed the ambiguous, unstable, and context-dependent character of language; noted the dependence of observers and data on interpretation and theory; and argued that interpretation-free, theory-neutral facts do not exist but, rather, that data and facts are constructions that result from interpretation.

VARIETIES OF REFLEXIVITY

There are reasons to draw attention to the varieties of reflexivity: rather than talking about reflexivity, we should perhaps refer to reflexiv*ities*. Most texts emphasizing reflexivity seem to propose one – possibly "The" – form of reflexivity as different authors favor a particular approach. For some, it is the researcher-self and the personal experiences of the research process: "reflexive ethnographies primarily focus on a culture or subculture, authors use their own experiences in the culture reflexively to bend back on self and look more deeply at self–other interactions" (Ellis & Bochner 2000: 741). For others, it concerns the cognitive aspects around construction processes in research (Glasersfeld 1991). For still others, reflexivity revolves around language, inviting the investigator "into the fuller realm of shared languages. The reflexive attempt is thus relational, emphasizing the expansion of the languages of understanding" (Gergen & Gergen 1991: 79). Other versions of reflexivity revolve around the research text and authorship (Richardson 1994), theoretical perspectives and vocabularies and what they accomplish (Rorty 1989), or the empirical subjects "out there" and how their voices are being (mis-)represented (Fine et al. 2000).

For some authors, reflexivity is intimately connected to the broad intellectual stream of postmodernism and/or radical social constructionism. This may imply a broader set of considerations, for example, postmodernism is frequently associated with the indecidabilities of meaning, fragmented selves, power/knowledge connections, the problematic nature of master narratives, and problems of representation, providing an ambitious set of themes for reflexive work. Again, for others, reflexivity means the breaking of the logic associated with a particular stream – reflexivity involves confronting dataistic, interpretive, critical, and postmodern lines of reasoning and challenging the truths and emphasis following from each of these (Alvesson & Sköldberg 2000).

The spectrum for reflexivities is probably endless. Five major versions – these can be referred to as positions or practices – indicate the most common ones and are described below.

Destabilization. This form of reflexivity is inspired by the work of Derrida and Foucault and emphasizes the "negative" or "dangerous" aspects of knowledge claims.

In different ways, Foucault and Derrida encouraged the exploration of the shortcomings and limitations of claims to knowledge, creating rather than revealing the truth. The production of knowledge, particularly positive versions that try to establish "the truth," leads to a certain, in a sense, arbitrary version of the social world, with associated power effects, that neither reveals nor distorts the truth but, rather, creates it. All knowledge projects are thus dangerous, insofar as any version of truth carries with it a particular configuration of political privileges and should therefore be closely interrogated. The means to do so lie with postmodern theoretical and epistemological assumptions that see social reality as ambiguous, fragmented, and contested, and temporarily held in place through the operations of certain discourses (Rosenau 1992). Accordingly, reflexive researchers try to undermine the idea that research is ultimately a progressive path toward universal "truths." Reflexivity means keeping a skeptical eye on how the phenomenon under study is being ordered by the researcher's use of discourse – or the discourse's use of the researcher.

Combining alternative perspectives. Instead of treating epistemological positions as manifestations of metaphysical principles, as some people taking the paradigm idea seriously tend to do, using the paradigms reflexively involves seeking out anomalies among them "in a way that is mindful of the historically and politically situated quality of our reasoning. By becoming more practically reflexive about the conditions of theorizing, we move away from an external and seemingly authoritative form of analysis and towards an immanent, self-consciously situated form of critique" (Willmott 1993: 708). Accordingly, researchers use tensions among different perspectives to expose different assumptions and open up new ways of thinking.

Rorty (1989) warns about being convinced of the superiority of a final vocabulary, and suggests what he refers to as an ironic way of reasoning – where the researcher is highly aware that the vocabulary in use is not the only one possible or not necessarily the superior one. The reflexive researcher can draw upon a set of alternative perspectives – transcending a strictly paradigm-bound position – to draw attention to the limitations in using a single frame of reference and, in so doing, provide new insights about limitations as well as possibilities in the use of a specific perspective or sort out which is "best." It is the *accumulation* of these perspectives that amounts to reflexivity, not the adoption of one to undermine another. In this regard, reflexive practice is more a matter of bricolage, where different perspectives help to understand otherwise "incomplete" research.

Voicing and representation in fieldwork. Rather than just going out there to find out what is going on – and go through the seemingly linear route of planning the study, collecting data, and then analyzing data – the precarious, messy, political, subjective, and basically non-rational process of fieldwork is viewed as calling for reflexivity. Struggles to speak authentically about the "Other" call for careful consideration of what is happening here and what the researcher is doing in relationship to the Other (and vice versa). A focus on the researcher-as-subject recognizes that the researcher is part of the research project, a subject just like any other that is constructed in and through the research project: we do not simply "*bring* the self to the field" so much as "*create* the self in the field" (Reinharz 1997: 3). As a result, it is incumbent on the researchers to present the details of their particular experiences and interests – to declare the authorial personality and to acknowledge their participation. Another element is that, being reflexive, researchers tend to divulge the steps they have taken in order to present their work as respectable research – to confess their sins by way of extensive personal disclosure.

Narration and representation in textwork. A key theme for many "reflexivists" is a change of emphasis in research from fieldwork to textwork. Over time, the researcher has become less of a neutral, objective social scientist who reports faithfully and accurately on the activities of research subjects, and instead has taken on a more "modest, unassuming style" while struggling "to piece together something reasonably coherent out of displays of initial disorder, doubt and difficulty" (Van Maanen 1988: 75). The resulting crisis of representation weakens researchers' voices and, especially, their claims to report reliably on the experiences of research subjects. In short, "writing up the results" is viewed as an extremely difficult and contested enterprise. This calls for reflexivity.

One key theme here concerns the self-critical questioning of how the researcher-authors convince, how literary tropes, seductive narratives, and rhetorical devices are used to show how, by hiding behind the cloak of science, researchers take steps to produce authoritative accounts.

Another theme relates to how to produce "better" representations or narratives, by being more creative and experimental in writing. Reflexivity is here associated with how various literary techniques are employed to open up space for the Other in research accounts through the self-conscious use of writing techniques by using fiction, drama, narrative, and metaphor (e.g., Richardson 1994). As a result, an array of practices such as reflexive ethnographies, literary autoethnographies, narratives of the self, first-person accounts, and lived experience have been employed. These devices have been used in particular in feminist work.

Sociopolitical contingencies. Another version of reflexivity views the problematic relationship between the knowledge-creating process and the produced knowledge in terms of the sociopolitical context of research. It is thus not the individual researcher – as a subject ordering the world, using a particular perspective or theoretical vocabulary, doing fieldwork or textwork – nor the relationship between researcher and research subject but the societal context that imprints the researcher as well as the research outcome. Relativism is not necessarily a matter of researcher subjectivity, but can be seen as the outcome of a social and highly intersubjective theoretical, methodological, or cultural position (Bernstein 1983).

Social processes shape knowledge through control embedded in the research process, meaning that the researcher can construct "knowledge" only in the context of a particular research community and society. The norms and conventions of the research field, the struggle for position and resources, the adaptation to the criteria of prestigious journals and publishers are all seen as elements shaping research and calling for reflexive scrutiny (Hardy et al. 2001). Such is also the case with societal cultures and traditions, with fashions and other macro elements exercising a directive force on research. One can here see how the reflexive project is not an outcome of progression and added insights in social science, but is associated with the trendiness of postmodernism and the linguistic turn, which are perhaps contingent upon the developments of capitalism into a system less concerned with the production of "substance" than with the free flow of signifiers and images around marketing and consumptions. Reflexivity as a theme, then, can be understood in the context of career options and moves associated with new fashions in social science as well as with broader societal trends toward deobjectivization, providing space for a reflexive turn.

CRITIQUE OF REFLEXIVITY

Some commentators believe that reflexivity may encourage narcissism and self-indulgence. Critics worry about excessive reflexivity turning the self "into a fieldsite" (Robertson 2002: 786), and making the text and author-maneuvers the key issue at the expense of the research subjects. Reflexivity may become a dead end rather than a route to more thoughtful and interesting social studies. As such it may fulfill more ceremonial purposes of legitimation – similar to the methods section in academic papers where quantitative and qualitative research is disciplined by neopositivist templates and (mis)represented as highly rational, linear, coherent, controlled, and based on a clear (but fundamentally misleading) division between framework, researcher, and data. There are other risks and costs associated with practicing reflexivity – it takes time, brain power, and text space, and perhaps leads away from conventional theoretical and/or empirical work.

Whether reflexivity encourages more thoughtful and realistically assessed and framed research or leads to ceremonial exercises, whether it makes researchers more sensitive and creative in theory, field, text, and political work or takes attention, energy, and time away from what has traditionally been seen as the core activities in research will, of course, vary. Possible outcomes and tradeoffs between ideals are among the worthy themes of acts of reflexivity.

SEE ALSO: Autoethnography; Constructionism; Journaling, Reflexive; Knowledge; Knowledge, Sociology of; Methods; Poststructuralism

REFERENCES AND SUGGESTED READINGS

Alvesson, M. & Sköldberg, K. (2000) *Reflexive Methodology: New Vistas for Qualitative Research.* Sage, London.

Bernstein, R. (1983) *Beyond Objectivism and Relativism*. Blackwell, Oxford.
Denzin, N. & Lincoln, Y. (1994) Introduction: Entering the Field of Qualitative Research. In: Denzin, N. & Lincoln, Y. (Eds.), *Handbook of Qualitative Research*, 1st edn. Sage, Thousand Oaks, CA, pp. 1–17.
Ellis, C. & Bochner, A. (2000) Autoethnography, Personal Narrative, Reflexivity: Researcher as Subject. In: Denzin, N. & Lincoln, Y. (Eds.), *Handbook of Qualitative Research*, 2nd edn. Sage, Thousand Oaks, CA, pp. 769–802.
Fine, M., Weis, L., Weseen, S., & Wong, L. (2000) For Whom? Qualitative Research, Representations, and Social Responsibilities. In: Denzin, N. & Lincoln, Y. (Eds.), *Handbook of Qualitative Research*, 2nd edn. Sage, Thousand Oaks, CA, pp. 107–32.
Gergen, K. & Gergen, M. (1991) Toward Reflexive Methodologies. In: Steier, F. (Ed.), *Research and Reflexitivity*. Sage, London.
Glasersfeld, E. von (1991) Knowing Without Metaphysics: Aspects of the Radical Constructivist Position. In: Steier, F. (Ed.), *Research and Reflexitivity*. Sage, London, pp. 12–29.
Hardy, C., Phillips, N., & Clegg, S. (2001) Reflexivity in Social Studies: A Study of the Production of the Research Subject. *Human Relations* 54: 3–32.
Kuhn, T. S. (1970) *The Structure of Scientific Revolution*. University of Chicago Press, Chicago.
Mauthner, N. & Doucet, A. (2003) Reflexive Accounts and Accounts of Reflexivity in Qualitative Data Analysis. *Sociology* 37: 413–31.
Popper, K. (1969) On the Logic of the Social Sciences. In: Adorno, T. W. et al., *The Positivist Dispute in German Sociology*. Heinemann, London.
Reinharz, S. (1997) Who Am I? The Need for a Variety of Selves in Fieldwork. In: Hertz, R. (Ed.), *Reflexivity and Voice*. Sage, Thousand Oaks, CA, pp. 3–20.
Richardson, L. (1994) Writing: A Method of Inquiry. In: Denzin, N. & Lincoln, Y. (Eds.), *Handbook of Qualitative Research*, 1st edn. Sage, Thousand Oaks, CA, pp. 516–29.
Robertson, J. (2002) Reflexivity Redux: A Pithy Polemic on Positionality. *Anthropological Quarterly* 75(4): 785–93.
Rorty, R. (1989) *Contingency, Irony, and Solidarity*. Cambridge University Press, Cambridge.
Rosenau, P. M. (1992) *Post-Modernism and the Social Sciences: Insights, Inroads, and Intrusions*. Princeton University Press, Princeton.
Van Maanen, J. (1988) *Tales of the Field: On Writing Ethnography*. University of Chicago Press, Chicago.
Willmott, H. (1993) Breaking the Paradigm Mentality. *Organization Studies* 145: 681–719.

refugee movements

Courtland Robinson

Refugee movements are defined as the involuntary migration of people across international borders as a result of generalized conflict and disorder, or of more particularized threats of persecution and physical insecurity. The concept of "refugee" generally is treated as one category within a broader typology of forced migration, which includes involuntary movements both within and across international borders and encompasses other categories such as internally displaced persons, development-displaced persons, and trafficked and smuggled persons.

While, in common usage, refugee may refer to people fleeing their homes due to any number of threatening situations, the prevailing international legal definition of refugee, endorsed by 145 member states of the United Nations General Assembly, is an individual who, "owing to a well-founded fear of being persecuted for reasons of race, religion, nationality, membership of a particular social group or political opinion, is outside the country of his nationality and is unable or, owing to such fear, is unwilling to avail himself of the protection of that country." In 1969, the Organization for African Unity adopted the UN definition but added that a refugee is also a person who has fled his or her country "owing to external aggression, occupation, foreign domination or events seriously disturbing public order."

Related to the definition of a refugee as a person crossing an international border to escape persecution or conflict is that of the asylum seeker, an individual who has a claim to be a refugee. Whether that claim is real or fraudulent, and whether it is accepted, rejected, or ignored by a state authority, it is the claim to refugee status, and the protection thus entailed, that distinguishes the asylum seeker from other categories of migrants.

In 2003, the number of refugees was estimated at 11.9 million people, the majority of whom were from the Middle East (4.4 million), Africa (3.2 million), and South and Central Asia (1.9 million). Of these, about half are female and about 45 percent are under the age of 17. More than 80 percent of refugees are from developing countries and more than two-thirds have sought refuge in developing countries. More than 7 million have been living in camps and settlements, "warehoused" for at least 10 years or more.

Asylum seekers, who numbered 600,000 in 2003, are primarily from developing countries though they principally are seeking asylum in Europe and North America. While most refugees and asylum seekers find themselves in limbo for extended periods, some manage to find a more durable solution in the form of permanent resettlement or voluntary repatriation. In 2003, however, only 54,000 refugees were offered permanent resettlement in another country. A much larger number – at least 925,000 in 2003 – voluntarily returned home, although more than 50,000 were forcibly repatriated.

In describing his "kinetic model" of displacement, which borrowed the "push" and "pull" factors of traditional migration models and adapted them to refugee movements, Egon Kunz (1973) said that he used the term kinetics rather than the more general term dynamics because refugee movements lacked inner direction but were instead propelled, like billiard balls, by external forces and frictions. More recent conceptualizations of refugee movements, and forced migration in general, largely reject the notion that refugees are like billiard balls and, instead, emphasize that their paths reflect complex patterns of volition and choices made in the face of often poor information and worse odds.

While theories and concepts of migration previously described types of movements in dichotomous terms – push versus pull, "distress" versus "livelihood," voluntary versus involuntary – more recent approaches promote the idea of a continuum, proactive at one end and reactive at the other end, between which varying degrees of choice and coercion are involved.

Even the distinction between international and internal migration, one involving movement between nation-states and the other within a state, has been blurred in two ways with respect to concepts of forced migration in general, and "refugeehood" in particular. The first is that growing attention is being paid to populations who are internally displaced by conflict, disasters, and development projects. In 1998, the UN Commission on Human Rights agreed to define internally displaced persons (IDPs) as "persons or groups of persons who have been forced or obliged to flee or to leave their homes or places of habitual residence in particular as a result of or in order to avoid the effects of armed conflict, situations of generalized violence, violations of human rights, or natural or human-made disasters and who have not crossed an internationally-recognized State border." It further noted that the right to protection from arbitrary displacement extended to those displaced by development projects. The number of people internally displaced by armed conflict, generalized violence, and human rights abuse has been estimated at more than 23 million in 2003. Development projects displaced an estimated 10 million people per year in the 1990s.

The distinction between refugees and internally displaced persons, for some, is not of conceptual significance, however much it matters from a legal or policy perspective. Whether a person is displaced internally or externally may be of issue to a state, but in terms of the experience of those displaced, the commonalities outweigh the differences. For others, crossing an international border in flight from conflict, persecution, and insecurity is a definitive event, compounding the physical vulnerability of displacement from home and familiar surroundings with displacement into a foreign jurisdiction within which the refugee has no rights and protections as a citizen.

Several definitions of refugee attempt to bridge this gap between internal and external displacement. Matthew Gibney (2004) defines refugees as people who need a new state of residence because returning home or staying where they are would subject them to persecution or physical insecurity. Emma Haddad (2004) suggests that the main criterion for refugee status is the breakdown in the state–citizen relationship, while crossing an international border should not be a defining factor.

There is another way in which national borders have become increasingly blurred. Decolonization in the 1960s and 1970s led to "imperial" diasporas – the Portuguese from Africa, the French from Algeria and Indochina, and the Dutch from Southeast Asia – and to the movement of non-European peoples, including Indians and Chinese, originally imported as "colonial auxiliaries" or "middleman minorities." Waves of labor migration, as well as refugee populations and internally displaced persons, have experienced repeated expulsions and migrations to the point where they have come to form transnational communities, defined by Stephen Castles (2003) as groups based in two or more countries that engage in recurrent, enduring, and significant cross-border activities, which may be economic, political, social, or cultural in character.

The formation of transnational communities or networks has been spurred by the forces of globalization, which seek to open borders for the movement of goods and a regulated flow of labor migration while closing borders to irregular and unwanted migration flows. The demand for labor in the North, coupled with restrictive entry policies, has stimulated new forms of organization in the "migration industry," which rely on transnational companies, communities, and networks to move people by whatever routes prove most efficient. The development of trafficking and smuggling networks has given rise to a $6 billion industry moving an estimated 4 million people per year, the majority of whom are women and children.

The definition of the term "refugee" will always be shaped by those who use it. The perspective of governments will emphasize a narrower, legalistic definition in value of security at the borders and state sovereignty within them. The perspective of institutions like the United Nations will emphasize a definition that recognizes state sovereignty while valuing protection for persecuted individuals. Academics will value a definition that is at least adequate to the task of distinguishing who is a refugee from who is not, in such a way as to promote better understanding of the phenomenon.

How would refugees define themselves? The answer may be nearly as varied as the millions of people who, depending on the circumstances, might call themselves or be called refugees. The plurality of experiences and the evolving forms and dynamics of displacement make the pursuit of a comprehensive approach or a unitary definition ever more elusive.

Richard Black (2001) notes that the study of refugees and other forced migrant populations is always intimately connected with policy developments. This practical orientation can be a strength, by focusing on humanitarian consequences and avoiding overly abstract theorizing, but it can also be a weakness, leading to research that is ahistorical, reactive, and narrow. New, more holistic approaches to the study of refugee movements seek to build interdisciplinary and comparative understandings of such topics as the political economy, gender dimensions, and causes of refugee movements, as well as the dynamics of mobility and of settlement.

SEE ALSO: Diaspora; Disasters; Migration, Ethnic Conflicts, and Racism; Migration: Internal; Migration: International; Migration: Undocumented/Illegal; Refugees; Traffic in Women; Transnational Movements

REFERENCES AND SUGGESTED READINGS

Black, R. (2001) Fifty Years of Refugee Studies: From Theory to Policy. *International Migration Review* 35(1): 57–78.

Castles, S. (2003) Towards a Sociology of Forced Migration and Social Transformation. *Sociology* 37(1): 13–34.

Gibney, M. J. (2004) *The Ethics and Politics of Asylum.* Cambridge University Press, Cambridge.

Haddad, E. (2004) Who Is (Not) a Refugee? European University Institute Working Paper SPS No. 2004/6, Florence.

Kunz, E. (1973) The Refugee in Flight: Kinetic Models and Forms of Displacement. *International Migration Review* 7(2): 125–46.

Robinson, W. C. (1998) *Terms of Refuge: The Indochinese Exodus and the International Response.* Zed Books, London.

Shacknove, A. (1985) Who Is a Refugee? *Ethics* 95(2): 274–84.

United Nations (1999) *Guiding Principles on Internal Displacement.* Office for the Coordination of Humanitarian Affairs, New York.

United Nations High Commissioner for Refugees (1988) *Collection of International Instruments Concerning Refugees.* UNHCR, Geneva.

Van Hear, N. (1998) *New Diasporas: The Mass Exodus, Dispersal, and Regrouping of Migrant Communities.* University of Washington Press, Seattle.

refugees

Steve Loyal

In international law "refugee" refers to individuals who are residing outside of their country of origin and who are unable or unwilling to return because of a well-founded fear of persecution on account of race, religion, nationality, membership of a particular social group or political opinion.

The term derives from the Latin *refugere* – to flee – and is believed to have first been applied to the Huguenots who fled France in the seventeenth century. Its modern legal usage follows the UN General Assembly's establishment of the United Nations High Commission on Refugees (UNHCR) in 1950. Within a system of nation-states with fixed borders, and a burgeoning Cold War rivalry, the UNHCR's principal aim was to guarantee and provide international protection and assistance to individuals who had become displaced by World War II. By becoming signatories to the 1951 UN Convention, nation-states agreed to grant special protection on an international basis to citizens of a state that could not guarantee their human rights and physical security. This remit for protection was later extended beyond Europe to encompass refugees from all over the world, as the problem of displaced people became more global, with the signing of the 1967 Bellagio Protocol. There are currently 137 states that are signatories to both the 1951 Convention and Bellagio Protocol.

The Convention defines a refugee as any person who, "owing to a well-founded fear of being persecuted for reasons of race, religion, nationality, membership of a particular social group or political opinion, is outside the country of his nationality and is unable or, owing to such fear, is unwilling to avail himself of the protection of that country; or who, not having a nationality and being outside the country of his former habitual residence . . . is unable or, owing to such fear, is unwilling to return to it."

There are, however, a number of conceptual distinctions within refugee discourse. People who are forced from their homes for reasons outlined in the 1951 UN definition of a refugee, but who remain within the borders of their own country, are known as internally displaced persons (IDPs), of which the UN estimates the number to be 25 million. By contrast, those who seek refugee status outside of their own state of origin must make an application to the country where they arrive and are referred to as asylum seekers. Hence, an asylum seeker is a person who is seeking asylum on the basis of his or her claim to be a refugee. Refugee status may be granted to asylum seekers following a formal legal procedure in which the host country decides whether to grant refugee status or otherwise. Although those who are not accepted as refugees may be deported, in some cases they may be given leave to remain on humanitarian grounds. If, however, the applicant is successful in gaining refugee status, he or she is granted certain rights that are often similar to the citizenship rights of indigenous nationals. These include freedom of movement, the right of refoulement, which outlaws the forcible return to the country of origin from which persons have sought refugee status, and basic social and economic rights. Refugees are in turn expected to obey the laws and regulations of the host country. This in turn raises questions concerning their assimilation or integration within the host nation.

The 1970s witnessed both a shift from the post-war inter-European migration and a rise in the number of asylum seekers and refugees from Asia, Africa, Latin America, and the Caribbean. According to the UNHCR, the number of refugees has grown considerably over the last 20 years. In 1984 it is estimated that there existed 10.7 million refugees. This figure almost doubled to 20.6 million by the end of 2002, reaching a peak in 1994, with 27.4 million refugees. The causes of this increase in numbers are diverse. Coinciding with increasing restrictions on labor migration and a global recession in the 1970s were improved travel and communication, which facilitated migration generally. However, more specific factors included the instability of developing or third world states following decolonization, and a rise in civilians fleeing civil wars or ethnonational, tribal, and religious violence. Thus the breakup of the Soviet Union and the former Yugoslavia engendered protracted ethnic conflicts, the latter producing over 2 million refugees, with over 400,000 going to Europe. However, the single largest ethnic group remains the 2.7 million

Palestinians, who are not designated as refugees but fall under the United Nations Relief and Works (UNRWA) agency.

Although some governments have remained tolerant of refugees and their plight, the majority, especially within Europe, have reacted to the increase in numbers of asylum seekers and refugees by enacting a series of restrictive policies and practices aimed at their deterrence. Such measures have often been reinforced, if not engendered, by negative media portrayals of refugees as "bogus" and as responsible for increasing unemployment, housing/health crises, or rising crime levels. This, in turn, as part of a vicious cycle, has fueled xenophobic public opinion. The restrictive measures of states have included the tightening of border surveillance and narrower definitions of refugee status – often placing the burden of proof on the asylum seeker. Together with the disappearance of borders within Europe, allowing the free movement of various Europeans citizens, the enactment of stricter coordinated policy to prevent the entry of non-EU nationals – such as that effected by the Schengen Agreement (1995) – has been referred to as part of an attempt to create "Fortress Europe." However, despite these actions, migration continues to occur to Europe.

The rising numbers of asylum seekers and refugees, as a specific type of migration, has also raised problems concerning how to conceptualize processes of migration. In contrast to the dominant rational choice theories of migration, which postulate individuals rationally weighing the costs and benefits of leaving one area for another in order to maximize their utility, refugee movement is often conceptualized as "forced" or "impelled." Discussions concerning refugees refer to involuntary migrations that distinguish between the forced movements of refugees and the free movements of economic migrants. They also look to the political sphere rather than to economic forces as explanatory factors. Such conceptualizations raise questions concerning agency and structure, as well as the very accounting practices that determine what is "chosen" or "forced."

SEE ALSO: Assimilation; Boundaries (Racial/Ethnic); Diaspora; Immigration; Migration, Ethnic Conflicts, and Racism; Refugee Movements; Transnationalism

REFERENCES AND SUGGESTED READINGS

Castles, S. (2003) Towards a Sociology of Forced Migration and Social Transformation. *Sociology* 37(1): 13–34.

Joly, D. & Cohen, R. (1990) *Reluctant Hosts: Europe and its Refugees.* Avebury, Aldershot.

Sassen, S. (2000) *Guests and Aliens.* New Press, New York.

United Nations High Commission on Refugees (2003) *Global Report 2003.* United Nations, New York.

Zolberg, A., Suhrke, A., & Aguayo, S. (1992) *Escape from Violence: Conflict and Refugee Crisis in the Developing World.* Oxford University Press, Oxford.

regression and regression analysis

Stephen E. Brown

Regression is a statistical technique for writing an equation to predict the values of a dependent (y) variable from values associated with one or more independent (x) variables. An important caveat, however, is that predictive success does not imply causality, as prediction is only one of the criteria for establishing causality. The most rudimentary regression form is ordinary least squares (OLS) linear regression. In addition to estimating the association with the independent variable(s), such an equation also incorporates a constant (alpha), or value of y when x is equal to 0, and an error or disturbance term (epsilon) comprised of variation in y not accounted for by the remainder of the equation. The better the fit of the equation, the more variation in y is explained, as reflected in the value of R squared. As the explained variance of the equation increases, ability to predict values of y associated with any particular values of x (or sets of x in multiple regression) is enhanced. That is, as the explained variance in y increases, the prediction error of the equation is reduced until an equation that explains all variance in y (R squared = 1.0) would perfectly predict y for any set of x values and have an error term of 0. Conversely, as prediction error of the equation increases, explained variance declines until the prediction of the equation offers no improvement over the mean of y as the best predictor of values of y for any level of x. A regression or slope coefficient (beta) is calculated for each x variable and represents the predicted change in y values for each unit change in the value of x. This coefficient may be positive or negative and is multiplied by the level of x for which y is being predicted. The greater the absolute value of the regression coefficient, the steeper the angle of the line (right angle for positive; left angle for negative) that best describes the relationship between x and y. Thus the generalized form of the regression equation is as follows:

$$Y = \text{alpha} + \text{beta}(X) + \text{epsilon}$$

In multiple regression the equation is extended to incorporate additional x variables.

Regression is closely wedded to correlation, but is more useful to the analyst because the correlation coefficient is limited to the statistical significance and strength of the relationship, while the regression coefficient facilitates prediction. Both coefficients are typically examined in conjunction with one another, however, and cannot be understood in isolation from the other. Unfortunately, neither establishes causal direction which is required for drawing causal inferences. The coefficients are bivariate when one dependent variable is regressed on one independent variable. The immense value of regression in analyzing social data, however, lies in the multivariate relationship that entails one dependent variable that the equation defines as a function of two or more independent variables. Such a multiple regression equation allows scrutinizing social factors by estimating coefficients that simultaneously control for the effects of all other independent variables entered in the equation. This serves as a tool for identifying spurious relationships and allows the researcher to sort out the relative association of the independent variables. Moreover, all of this can be accomplished with modest sample sizes.

There are several forms of regression, each resting on certain assumptions that are reasonably met in some research scenarios, but not in others. The OLS regression model is appropriate for analyzing data comprised of one continuous and normally distributed dependent and one or more continuous independent variables, as well as resting on several other assumptions. It is considered a quite robust technique, meaning that it is such a powerful statistical model that the various assumptions can be relaxed to a considerable degree without appreciably distorting estimates of the coefficients. It is widely accepted, for example, that categorical variables may be included as independent variables through dummy coding schemes (1 = member of the category, 0 = not a member of the category). The OLS regression model also assumes linear relationships between the independent and dependent variables. Similarly, the assumption of a linear relationship between the independent and dependent variables is often addressed by undertaking transformations of the independent variables to fit the data to a straight line.

Not only is regression a very useful statistical technique in its own right, it is also at the center of a family of statistics referred to as the general linear model. These techniques all explain variation in the dependent variable as a function of the distribution of values at different levels or categories of the independent or predictor variables. Thus principles of regression are important to fully comprehend simpler techniques such as analysis of variance and correlation. In addition, multiple regression lies at the foundation of most contemporary advanced statistical techniques such as logistic and probit regression models that accommodate binary dependent variables, survival models that assess time to an outcome, and poisson models to study nonnormally distributed rare events and a variety of other specific scenarios.

SEE ALSO: ANOVA (Analysis of Variance); Correlation; General Linear Model; Statistics; Variables

REFERENCES AND SUGGESTED READINGS

Allison, P. D. (1999) *Multiple Regression: A Primer.* Pine Forge Press, Thousand Oaks, CA.

Keith, T. Z. (2006) *Multiple Regression and Beyond.* Allyn & Bacon, Boston.

Hoffman, J. P. (2004) *Generalized Linear Models: An Applied Approach.* Allyn & Bacon, Boston.

regulation theory

Bob Jessop

Regulation theory is a distinctive paradigm in critical political economy. It originated in Europe and North America in the 1970s in response to the emerging crisis of the post-war economy and it has since been applied to many other periods and contexts. Its name derives from its French originators, who describe it as *la théorie de régulation* or *l'approche en termes de régulation.* Similar ideas were also developed by other schools. The core concern of all such work is the contradictory and conflictual dynamics of contemporary capitalism considered in terms of its extra-economic as well as economic dimensions. In highlighting the extra-economic aspects of accumulation, regulation theorists draw on, and provide links to, other social sciences. Regulation theory was influential in economic, urban, and regional sociology in the 1980s and 1990s. This was partly because of its Marxist roots and partly because of its general heuristic power in organizing research on a wide range of sociological themes.

Regulation theory has many intellectual precursors. Nonetheless, as it is conventionally understood in economics and also became influential in sociology, this approach was developed in the mid-1970s by a few French heterodox economists whose work is collectively identified as the Parisian School (Aglietta 1979; Lipietz 1987; Boyer 1990). Two less well known and relatively minor French regulation schools date from the 1960s and 1970s and analogous approaches, based on different theoretical starting points, emerged elsewhere (Jessop & Sum 2006). Thus, regulation theory is not so much a single, unified paradigm as a broad research program in economics with major implications for other social sciences. Its several schools examine the role of extra-economic as well as economic factors in securing, albeit for limited periods and in specific economic spaces, what they regard as an inherently improbable and crisis-prone process of capital accumulation. Overall, while well aware of the invisible hand of market forces in this regard, regulation theorists also explore how extra-economic factors embed profit-oriented, market-mediated capitalist production in the wider society and help to tame, displace, and defer its contradictions and class conflicts. This process is associated with alternating periods of relatively stable expansion and crisis-induced restructuring, rescaling, and reregulation. For, precisely because capitalism's contradictions and conflicts can never be fully mastered, crises will provoke a trial-and-error search process to find new ways of regularizing capitalist expansion.

Starting from real social relations in specific historical periods rather than from the abstract, transhistorical, rational economic man (*homo economicus*) favored in orthodox economics, different regulation schools share four goals: (1) describe the historically specific institutions and practices of capitalism; (2) explain the various crisis tendencies of modern capitalism and likely sources of crisis resolution; (3) analyze different periods of capitalism and compare their respective accumulation regimes and modes of regulation; and (4) examine the social embedding and social regularization of economic institutions and conduct through their articulation with extra-economic factors and forces.

The dominant Parisian School introduced four key concepts to analyze different forms of capitalism. First, an *industrial paradigm* is a model that guides the development of the technical and social division of labor (e.g., mass production, flexible specialization). Second, an *accumulation regime* is a specific pattern of production and consumption that can be reproduced over a long period. For example, Fordism, which derives its name from Henry Ford, who is generally acknowledged as the pioneer of the moving assembly line and high wages, is based on a virtuous circle of mass production and mass consumption. Third, a *mode of regulation* is an ensemble of norms, institutions, organizational forms, social networks, and patterns of conduct that can stabilize an accumulation regime. Parisian theorists generally analyze it in terms of five dimensions: (a) the wage relation includes topics such as labor markets, individual and collective bargaining, welfare rights, and lifestyles; (b) the enterprise form includes corporate organization, the main source of profits, forms of competition, interfirm linkages, and links to banking capital; (c) the dominant form of money, the banking and credit system, the allocation of money capital to production; (d) the state, considered in terms of the institutionalized compromise between capital and labor, forms of state intervention; and (e) international regimes, including the regulation of trade, investment, and monetary flows and the political arrangements that link national economies, nation-states, and the world system. Fourth, when an industrial paradigm, accumulation regime, and mode of regulation reinforce each other enough to promote continued expansion, the resulting complex is analyzed as a *model of development.*

Regulation theory originated to explain a chronic economic crisis in advanced capitalism that emerged in the 1970s. This was unexpected because it followed "30 glorious years" of post-war economic expansion when policies based on an institutionalized compromise between big labor, big business, and big government seemed to have abolished savage economic crises, to have routinized class struggle, and to have moderated ideological antagonisms. Regulation theorists described this system as Fordist and offered various explanations for its crisis. For example, it was attributed to the exhaustion of the growth potential of mass production, to satiated demand for mass consumer durables, to a tax and expenditure crisis of the post-war state, and to growing levels of internationalization, which allegedly undermined the scope and effectiveness of national economic and political regulation. Depending on how the main cause(s) of this crisis were identified, regulation theorists proposed different solutions. These included *neo-Fordism* based on intensification of the Fordist labor process; *flexible accumulation* based on increased flexibility using flexible equipment; and an initially ill-specified *post-Fordism* marked by a new industrial paradigm, accumulation regime, and mode of regulation. This implied the need for changes not only in economic organization but also in extra-economic institutions and behavior, including education and training, the science and innovation system, lifestyles, spatial organization, and state forms and functions. Some early work had assumed a quasi-automatic transition from a crisis-ridden Fordism to an effective post-Fordist accumulation regime and mode of regulation. Later work explored the difficulties involved in the search for solutions to the crisis within the existing Fordist model and/or for alternative models of post-Fordism and also described the obstacles to consolidating post-Fordist accumulation regimes and modes of regulation. More recently, it seems agreed that post-Fordism has, as its positive content, a globalizing knowledge-based economy that is being realized on many different scales of economic, political, and sociocultural organization.

Regulationist analyses of Fordism and its crisis appealed to many critical social scientists in the 1980s and 1990s. They used regulation theory to explore the social as well as economic dimensions of the Fordist labor process, new forms of class conflict, stages and varieties of capitalism, new social movements, the distinctive economic geography of Fordism, urban forms and urban crises, and changes in the state. The loss of taken-for-grantedness of the national economy and the national state associated with the Fordist period has allegedly led to three interrelated changes in economic policy: (1) a shift from the primacy of national states in determining economic and social policy to a multi-scalar approach based on multiple supranational, national, regional, and local political actors; (2) a shift in the primary mechanisms to coordinate the economic and extra-economic conditions for capital accumulation from the typical post-war bifurcation of market and state to new forms of network-based forms of policy coordination that cross-cut previous "private-public" boundaries and that involve "key" economic players from local and regional as well as national and, increasingly, international economies; and (3) a shift from policies concerned with full employment and social welfare to a stress on full employability and personal responsibility. All three changes are reflected at local or regional level in the development of "entrepreneurial" cities and regions.

Regulationists also argue that the crisis of Fordism leads to spatial restructuring (Amin 1995; Lauria 1997). They assume continuing mutual adaptation between accumulation regimes and urban development. For example, Fordist cities were marked by (1) single-storey production facilities, which are well-suited to mass production and depend on cheap fuel and road transport; (2) low-density (sub)urbanization based on mass private and public transport – enabling the normalization of nuclear family households, which consume many consumer durables, buy bigger ticket items on credit, and depend on automobility; (3) municipal reformism and urban planning designed to promote the role of cities as centers of consumption as well as production; and (4) regional policy concerned to secure even economic development based on spreading mass production industries and their growth dynamic. Unsurprisingly, then, the crisis of Fordism also had a big impact on cities. This is said to include growing fiscal problems that made it harder to sustain the infrastructure needed for Fordism; the hollowing out of cities through a flight to the suburbs; a new spatial division of labor with low-cost jobs moving abroad or to more peripheral regions; and increasing social problems due to deindustrialization, rising inner-city unemployment, and racial tensions. It is claimed that the Fordist economic and political regime has failed and, if cities and regions are to escape the effects of this failure, they must modify economic strategies, economic institutions, modes of governance, and state forms. These must be redesigned to prioritize "wealth creation" in the face of international, interregional, and intraregional competition because continued growth is necessary for social redistribution and welfare.

One response to these problems is the rise of entrepreneurial cities and public-private partnerships to replace the Fordist pattern of municipal socialism and managerialism. "Entrepreneurial cities" actively promote the competitiveness of their respective economic spaces in the face of intensified international, inter- and intraregional competition. This may involve little more than a defensive, deregulatory "race-to-the-bottom," but it can also involve offensive, supply-side intervention to upgrade a wide range of extra-economic as well as economic conditions considered essential for cutting-edge competitiveness. One effect of these varied policies is that, in contrast to Fordism, post-Fordist policies tend to promote uneven development and growing polarization between prosperous and crisis-ridden cities. Los Angeles was once regarded as the archetypal post-Fordist city on the basis of its supposedly post-industrial economic profile, spatial organization, social heterogeneity, and patterns of social exclusion (Scott & Soja 1994). But other types of post-Fordist city have also been explored (Brenner 2004). In any case, there are major continuities between Fordist and post-Fordist cities, thanks to the impact of the built environment, automobility, and single-family households.

Regulation theory remains a progressive research program (for Parisian work, see Boyer & Saillard 2002). Some early critical historical and econometric work challenged the validity of the initial analyses of Fordism and its crisis and criticized the whole approach on this basis. Mainstream social scientists criticize its one-sided concern with the economic logic of capital accumulation and neglect of other dimensions of social life. Conversely, fundamentalist left-wing critics have claimed that regulation theory implies that capitalism is inevitable (because crises are always eventually overcome) and thereby supports reformism rather than acknowledging the need for the overthrow of capitalism. Regulationists have responded to these and other lines of criticism by refining their concepts, developing new analyses, and reasserting the contradictory nature of capitalism (Boyer 2004; Jessop & Sum 2006).

SEE ALSO: Capitalism; Consumption, Mass Consumption, and Consumer Culture; Economy (Sociological Approach); Enterprise; Information Technology; Labor Markets; Labor Process; Mass Production; Post-Industrial Society; Urban Political Economy

REFERENCES AND SUGGESTED READINGS

Aglietta, M. (1979) *A Theory of Capitalist Regulation: The US Experience*. New Left Books, London.

Amin, A. (Ed.) (1995) *Post-Fordism*. Blackwell, Oxford.

Boyer, R. (1990) *The Régulation Approach: A Critical Introduction*. Columbia University Press, New York.

Boyer, R. (2004) *Une Théorie du capitalisme est-elle possible?* Odile Jacob, Paris.

Boyer, R. & Saillard, Y. (Eds.) (2002) *Regulation Theory: State of the Art*. Routledge, London.

Brenner, N. (2004) *New State Spaces: Urban Restructuring and State Rescaling in Western Europe*. Oxford University Press, Oxford.

Jessop, B. & Sum, N.-L. (2006) *The Regulation Approach and Beyond: Putting Capitalist Economies in their Place*. Edward Elgar, Cheltenham.

Lauria, M. (Ed.) (1997) *Reconstructing Urban Regime Theory: Regulating Urban Politics in a Global Economy*. Sage, London.
Lipietz, A. (1987) *Mirages and Miracles: The Crises of Global Fordism*. Verso, London.
Scott, A. J. & Soja, E. (Eds.) (1994) *The City: Los Angeles and Urban Theory at the End of the Twentieth Century*. University of California Press, Los Angeles.

Reich, Wilhelm (1897–1957)

Ken Plummer

Wilhelm Reich was a controversial theorist of the early and mid-twentieth century who attempted to wed the ideas of Freud and Marx through a radical theory of the "sexual revolution" (a term he coined in the 1920s). His Marxism led him to the Communist Party in Austria, and to being a member of the Psychoanalytic Society. These organizations were at mutual odds, and Reich was soon expelled from both.

Reich's theoretical work combined a social theory of sex economy – an economy which may hinder, gratify, regulate, or promote sexuality – a theory of characterology, and an account of both personal and social change due to orgasmic liberation. He provided a critique of the contemporary society, which he saw as creating a fascist, authoritarian character, machine-like and subservient to the existing social order. For Reich, political analysis was equated with sexual liberation.

At the core of his hydraulic theory, Reich argued that it was "sexual energy which governs the structure of human feeling and thinking ... it is the life energy *per se*. Its suppression means disturbance of fundamental life functions" (1969 [1935]: xxv). From the working of the libido, Reich stressed the development of character-analysis. His most famous (notorious) theory stressed the existence of the orgone, a pale blue liquid that needed regular discharge through sexual relations. For societies and individuals to function well, all individuals should have regular orgasms. His ideas spiraled out of control, and eventually took off into wild fancy. For instance, Reich produced a famous box, something like an original, old-fashioned wooden telephone box lined with metal, that could capture orgasms: the orgone energy accumulator. This could improve "orgiastic potency" and mental health. Despite these eccentric views, much of Reich's work is seen as providing a useful, critical, and synthesizing social theory.

Reich analyzed *The Mass Psychology of Fascism* (1931) through a consideration of Polish field anthropologist Bronislaw Malinowski's *Sexual Life of Savages* (1930) (indeed, Reich and Malinowski became friends). Malinowksi's fieldwork had suggested the existence of societies that were largely matriarchal, where adolescents were allowed to be sexually free. Sexual pleasure was encouraged. By contrast, Reich suggested that much of history had been dominated by sex-repressive, patriarchal societies. Societies had moved from sex-affirming (with a matriarchal, natural, genital love life and little social hierarchy) to sex-negating (predominantly patriarchal with a compulsory marital bond and strong social division).

In a sex-repressive society (which Reich saw as widespread), a character armor was formed that was characterized by rigidity and control, represented in physical muscular rigidity which needed breaking down. The family and socialization were themselves a "conveyor belt" of "authoritarian personalities." In *The Invasion of Compulsory Sex-Morality*, Reich outlines armoring through marriage, childhood subservience, the creation of the mass individual, and the lack of rebellion, backed by every reactionary institution. As he says: "All this, taken together, means the ideological anchoring of the existing, authoritarian system in the character structure of the mass individual, thus serving the suppression of life" (1971 [1932]: 165). The character armor revealed itself in muscular tensions and gestures; through the wider therapy of "vegetotherapy," the orgasm reflex could break out.

For Reich, adult neuroses could be found via compulsive, monogamous, bourgeois marriage. Humans were naturally polygamous. When there was polygamy, concerns such as rape, sadism, prostitution, pedophilia, and sadomasochism would be replaced by true orgiastic potency.

Reich was born in 1897 in Dobrzynica, Galacia, part of the Austro-Hungarian Empire. Much of his life was lived in the shadows of psychoanalysis and Marxism. He published *The Function of the Orgasm* in 1927, moved to Berlin in 1930, and subsequently fled from Germany in the 1930s, living briefly in Denmark, Norway, and Scandinavia before settling in the US in 1939. Here, some of his more extreme ideas came to fruition and led him to be seen in his last years as variously a genius, criminal, madman, and eccentric. He died in 1957 at Lewisburg Penitentiary, serving a sentence for the distribution of orgone accumulators in violation of the US Food and Drug Administration.

Parts of Reich's theory can be found in the works of philosophers such as Marcuse, Fromm, and Adorno (the Frankfurt School), who saw how repression may well lead to a restrictive and authoritarian society. In the 1960s, for a short while, Reich was a guru of both the student and countercultural movements on account of his advocacy of the need for full orgasmic sex for good functioning and for the slogan Make Love Not War. He features in the writing of Alan Ginsberg, Jack Kerouac, and William Burroughs; is mocked somewhat by Woody Allen with his "orgasmotron" in the film *Sleepers*; and had a serious film made about his life and work, Makavejev's *W: Mysteries of the Organism* (1968).

SEE ALSO: Adorno, Theodor W.; Critical Theory/Frankfurt School; Freud, Sigmund; Marx, Karl; Repressive Hypothesis; Sexuality; Sexuality Research: History

REFERENCES AND SUGGESTED READINGS

Corrington, R. (2003) *Wilhelm Reich: Psychoanalyst and Radical Naturalist.* Farrar, Straus, & Giroux, New York.

Ollendorf, I. (1969) *Wilhelm Reich: A Personal Biography.* St. Martin's Press, New York.

Reich, W. (1969 [1935]) *The Sexual Revolution*, 4th edn. Farrar, Straus, & Giroux, New York.

Reich, W. (1961) *Selected Writings: An Introduction to Orgonomy.* Farrar, Straus, & Giroux, New York.

Reich, W. (1971 [1932]) *The Invasion of Compulsory Sex-Morality.* Farrar, Straus, & Giroux, New York.

Rycroft, C. (1971) *Reich.* Viking, New York.

Sharaf, M. (1994) *Fury on Earth: A Biography of Wilhelm Reich.* Da Capo, New York.

reification

Rob Beamish

In general, reification refers to the act (or its result) of attributing to analytic or abstract concepts a material reality. Through reification people regard human relations, actions, and ideas as independent of themselves, sometimes governing them. People frequently reify the abstraction "society" into an entity and give "it" the power to act. Society does not act – people do. Reification is an error of attribution; it is corrected by eliminating the hypostatization of abstractions into things or agents.

For phenomenologists, reification is a potential outcome of the social construction of reality. To enter the lifeworld, human expression and subjective intention are externalized through "objectivation" where they become part of a socially constructed reality. Language is the common vehicle, although objectivation occurs through various symbolic forms.

Reification occurs when people understand objectivations as if they were non-human or suprahuman things and act "*as if* they were something other than human products – such as facts of nature, results of cosmic laws, or manifestations of divine will." Reification indicates we have forgotten our "own authorship of the human world" (Berger & Luckmann 1966: 89). A reified world is a dehumanized one.

In Marxist sociology, reification is conceptualized differently. Reification is created by the "fetishism of commodities" where "the social character of labor appears as the objective (*gegenständliche*) character of the products themselves." To the producers, "the social relationships of their private labors appear as what they are, not as the immediate social relations of people in their labors but as thingly (*sachliche*) relations of people and the social relations of things" (Marx 1922: 39). The producers' own social movements "possess for them the form of a movement of things (*Sachen*) under the control of which they stand rather than the producers controlling it" (p. 41).

Here, reification – *Verdinglichung* (*ver-* connoting a process; *dinglich* "thingly" – thus "thingification") – is a real social process whereby the social relations among producers do become "thingly." Their social relations really are those of commodities (and their value). Human characteristics matter little; one's "properties" as the bearer of commodities, especially labor power, do. This thing-like relation of commodity production dominates the workers actually engaged in production.

Reification links to Marx's early concern with alienation, where the products and production process under private property are separated from and stand against their human producers. It is a real social process that must be overturned to put social production under the control of its immediate producers.

Lukács (1971) argued that reification created false consciousness, thwarting a spontaneous, workers' class consciousness, supporting Lenin's argument for a revolutionary, vanguard party. Other Marxists, like Gramsci and Korsch, argued that workers would, amid the contradictions of commodity production, break through reified, commodity fetishism and force social change.

SEE ALSO: Alienation; Commodities, Commodity Fetishism, and Commodification; Marx, Karl; Phenomenology

REFERENCES AND SUGGESTED READINGS

Berger, P. & Luckmann, T. (1966) *The Social Construction of Reality.* Doubleday, Garden City, NY.

Lukács, G. (1971 [1923]) *History and Class Consciousness.* Trans. R. Livingstone. MIT Press, Cambridge, MA.

Marx, K. (1922 [1890]) *Das Kapital,* 4th edn., Vol. 1. Otto Meissner, Hamburg.

relational cohesion theory

Omar Lizardo

Relational cohesion theory was designed to explain when and how people involved in exchange relations become committed to their relationship. This extensive research program was developed by Edward Lawler, Jeongkoo Yoon, and Shane Thye and has become one of the most cumulative research programs in sociological social psychology (Lawler & Yoon 1993, 1996, 1998; Lawler et al. 2000). The theory predicts that dyads embedded in equal power relations within exchange networks are more likely to engage in repeated exchange relations than dyads embedded in more unequal power arrangements. These frequent successful exchange episodes are, in turn, predicted to lead to a higher frequency of experience of positive emotions. When individuals attempt to ascertain the source of positive and negative feelings, relational cohesion theory predicts that these positive feelings are interpreted as a product of the relationship by way of an attribution process. This serves to make the relationship a cognitively salient object ("setting it off" as distinct from other alternative relations) and to imbue it with positive affect. Thus the relationship becomes an independent object of emotional attachment for the individual, which helps create perceptions of their relation as a cohesive unit. This perceived *relational cohesion* is thought to result in a host of behavioral outcomes associated with relational *commitment*, such as staying in the relationship even when alternatives of equal value become available, starting new ventures with the current partner, and expressing positive regard for the partner in the form of unilateral gift-giving.

Relational cohesion theory began (Lawler & Yoon 1993, 1996) as an attempt to establish the conditions under which repeated exchange within dyads would lead to higher (or lower) rates of commitment. The initial insight of the theory at this stage consisted of the connection between the relative power differential within dyads and the probability of successful completion of exchange opportunities, which, in turn, led to more instances of commitment (answering the *when* question). Lawler and Yoon theorized that if agreements are more likely to occur when partners are more open to making concessions and when they are not subject to terms of agreement that they consider unfair, then equal power dyads should be able to complete more exchange opportunities than dyads in which one partner has an overwhelming power differential in relation to the other. Following Emerson

(1981), the theory conceptualizes and operationalizes power in terms of power–dependence theory: A is more powerful than B if A is less dependent on B than B is on A. Dependence is a function of the number of alternative exchange opportunities made available to A and B in the exogenously given network of connections between all of the actors and the distribution of resources throughout the network. Thus, A is more powerful than B if (1) she has a larger number of alternative exchange partners or (2) given an equal number of partners, A's partners are able to offer more valuable resources than B can offer. In this theory, power is conceptualized in structural terms, as a potential *capability* (i.e., the capacity to exclude a given number of potential partners from an exchange in a negatively connected network) inherent in the network, and is distinct from specific instances of *power use* (i.e., the actual act of exclusion). Thus one position may have a lot of power but display very few instances of power use. Equal power is more likely to lead to commitment due to the higher likelihood of completion of successful exchange. Exchanges between equal power dyads are less likely to exhibit concessions and more likely to feature satisfactory terms than unequal power exchanges.

STRUCTURAL COHESION

While initially (1993) using a simple equal power/unequal power distinction to predict frequency of exchange and relational commitment, Lawler and Yoon (1996, 1998; Lawler et al. 2000) later generalized this classification by introducing the concept of *structural cohesion.* In contrast to relational cohesion, structural cohesion is defined as the structural potential for instrumental cooperation in an exchange relation. Instrumental cooperation exists in an exchange relation when each actor is more likely to benefit from achieving agreement in that relation than by resorting to one of her alternatives. Lawler and Yoon further differentiate between the total power inherent in a dyad (the *sum* of the power of actor A and actor B) and the relative power of the dyad (the *ratio* of the power of actor A over that of actor B). In Lawler and Yoon's formulation, structural cohesion is a positive (curvilinear) function of the total power of the dyad and a negative function of the relative power of one actor over the other. Thus, maximum structural cohesion should exist on equal power dyads with high total power. Lawler and Yoon (1996) reason that agreement is easier to reach when power inequality is low (one actor is prevented from taking advantage of the other, which results in refusals to reach agreement) and total power is high (which results in greater expected benefits for both parties). Further repeated mutual agreement increases actors' mutual dependence.

Commitment in relational cohesion theory is defined as the attachment that the individual feels to a collective entity, such as a relationship, a group, or an organization. Attachment in this sense can involve a wide variety of interests, from purely instrumental interests (when the actor is interested in an inflow of valued material resources that the relationship makes possible) to emotional and normatively mediated attachment. When the actor is committed to the collective due to the perceived costs of leaving the relationship, she is said to be instrumentally committed. When the actor remains in the relationship largely due to an emotional attachment, she is said to be affectively committed to it. Finally, when the actor remains in the relationship because such membership is normatively sanctioned and perceived by the actor as an obligation that she must fulfill, she is said to be normatively committed to the collective. Relational cohesion theory highlights the role of emotional commitment as an explanatory mechanism that sheds light on why actors are likely to stay in certain frequently activated exchange relations. The theory highlights a process whereby a relationship initially based on purely instrumental motives and commitments comes to acquire expressive value and is transformed into one founded, at least partially, on emotional and cathectic sources of commitment. A common behavioral indicator of commitment is based on Kanter's concept of "stay behavior" or forgoing forming new partnerships even when these become available. More recent empirical tests of the theory have come to highlight other more expressive indicators of commitment (i.e., gift-giving).

In order to tackle the *how* question, relational cohesion theory posits an affective mechanism: the completion of a joint task (such as an exchange agreement) is seen as a mutual accomplishment which makes the participants feel good, by giving them an "emotional buzz." Frequent successful interactions result in a consistently generated stream of mild and shortlived positive emotions. These positive emotions unleash an attribution process, which culminates in the relationship being considered the source of the positive emotions. Lawler and Yoon (1993, 1996, 1998) draw on a psychological model of emotions known as the circumplex model. The circumplex model distinguishes between two principal dimensions of emotional experience: pleasure and arousal. Arousal can be positive or negative, while pleasure can be present or absent. Lawler and Yoon treat interest/excitement as a positive form of arousal that is distinct from pleasure. Interest/excitement is a motivational state of curiosity and fascination; it is equivalent to feeling energized, while pleasure is closer to feeling satisfied. Interest/excitement is based on expectation of future rewards, while pleasure/satisfaction is a product of rewards received. Experimental evidence has shown that pleasure/satisfaction is a more consistent product of exchange frequency and predictor of relational cohesion than interest/excitement. Lawler and Yoon see these two emotions as representative of different attitudes to social exchange, one backwards looking and focused on rewards already obtained (pleasure) and the other forward looking and focused on anticipated accomplishments (interest). They theorize (1996) that it is a possibility that pleasure is more strongly connected to routine, less complex joint tasks, while interest is a more consistent product of complex, non-routine exchange contexts.

Relational cohesion theory is built on an impressive empirical record, which has repeatedly confirmed its basic premises. Laboratory studies have shown that structural cohesion leads to higher frequency of exchange, and that the effect of exchange frequency on relational commitment is primarily mediated by positive emotions and the effect of the latter on the perceived cohesiveness of the relationship by the participants. Empirical tests of the theory have also uncovered new findings, such as a possible alternative pathway toward commitment by way of the reduction of uncertainty (the traditional explanation of commitment in exchange theory), and a small residual direct effect of frequency of exchange on commitment that does not operate through the affective pathway (interpreted as an operant conditioning effect). A recent refinement and empirical assessment of the theory (Lawler 2001) showed that indeed two alternative pathways toward commitment do appear to exist, but the uncertainty reduction path toward commitment *does not* operate by inducing greater relational cohesion, and does not affect the more expressive forms of commitment behavior. Further, positive emotions lead to higher levels of cohesion which result in more commitment even after the effect of predictability (as a measure of uncertainty reduction) has been held constant. However, predictability of the relationship does have a direct effect on the most risky indices of commitment (such as engaging in a new joint venture with a high probability of defection on the parts of other participants), indicating that predictability might have a basis in trust. Thus, there appears to exist a *dual process* which leads to different forms of commitment: a trust-based cognitive process that goes from frequency to predictability to willingness to engage in risky new ventures, and an emotion/cohesion-based process that produces stay behaviors and expressive forms of commitment behavior.

Relational cohesion theory goes beyond the standard view in exchange theory that commitment is a direct effect of uncertainty reduction processes (Emerson 1981). In the traditional view, actors are motivated to search for stability and predictability in exchange relations, since exchange contexts are characterized by the basic trust dilemma where actors cannot be sure of the motives of their exchange partners, and thus leave themselves open for potential malfeasance on the part of their partners at every exchange opportunity. To this largely cognitive non-emotional account of the process of commitment, relational cohesion theory adds an emotional component (Lawler & Thye 1999): the completion of successful exchanges, beyond serving to reduce uncertainty, is an independent source of positive emotions which come to be attributed to the exchange relation itself. Thus, from the actor's point of view, the exchange relation comes to be an independent source of emotional gratification, and thus becomes a valued object in itself.

The theory has its classical roots in the work of George Homans, and in the power–dependence exchange theory of Richard Emerson (1981). From Homans, relational cohesion theory draws its key insight connecting rates of interaction and positive sentiments. From Emerson, the theory takes its specific form as an *affect theory of social exchange* (Lawler 2001), which conceives of the network of exchange opportunities (the initial setup determining who can exchange with whom) as the primary exogenous factor which brings certain pairs of actors to interact more frequently than others. The theory draws on another wing of the classical tradition, the social constructionist work of Berger and Luckmann on the conditions that produce "incipient institutionalization." In relational cohesion theory, the process that results in the relationship acquiring an objective standing from the individual's viewpoint is analogous to the process of institutionalization from repetitive behavioral patterns outlined in Berger and Luckmann. Finally, the connection between affect and the process through which social relationships come to acquire an objective, constraining force on the individual harks back to Durkheim's pioneering connection between joint ritual activity, emotional arousal ("collective effervescence"), and the emergence of the group as an overarching, independent social reality. This connection between affect, arousal, and emotional energy is also present in Collins's neo-Durkheimian theory of interaction rituals, which see these repeated sets of affect-producing interactions as the microfoundation of larger social orders.

The theory has a host of implications and explanatory utility in terms of accounting for real-world phenomena. The most obvious application of the theory is to the explanation of the stickiness of transactions in real-world markets, which, in contrast to the neoclassical image of disconnected actors that come together for one-shot transactions and which have equal probabilities of interaction with any exchange partner, show instead that exchange transactions tend to increase the probability of future transactions, and that actors become involved in exchange relations and come to regard them in terms that go beyond the purely instrumental benefits that they bring in. Further, the theory can also be used to explain when and how people become attached (and disengaged) from real groups, organizations, and networks (Lawler 2001), thus forming the basis for a general theory of group commitment and affective attachment to collectivities.

SEE ALSO: Emerson, Richard M.; Homans, George; Power-Dependence Theory; Social Exchange Theory; Social Psychology

REFERENCES AND SUGGESTED READINGS

Emerson, R. M. (1981) Social Exchange Theory. In: Rosenberg, M. & Turner, R. H. (Eds.), *Social Psychology Sociological Perspectives.* Basic Books, New York, pp. 30–65.

Lawler, E. J. (2001) An Affect Theory of Social Exchange. *American Journal of Sociology* 107: 321–52.

Lawler, E. J. & Thye, S. R. (1999) Bringing Emotions into Social Exchange Theory. *Annual Review of Sociology* 25: 217–44.

Lawler, E. J. & Yoon, J. (1993) Power and the Emergence of Commitment Behavior in Negotiated Exchange. *American Sociological Review* 58: 465–81.

Lawler, E. J. & Yoon, J. (1996) Commitment in Exchange Relations: Test of a Theory of Relational Cohesion. *American Sociological Review* 61: 89–108.

Lawler, E. J. & Yoon, J. (1998) Network Structure and Emotion in Exchange Relations. *American Sociological Review* 63: 871–94.

Lawler, E. J., Thye, S. R., & Yoon, J. (2000) Emotion and Group Cohesion in Productive Exchange. *American Journal of Sociology* 106: 616–57.

reliability

Robin K. Henson

Reliability refers, at a general level, to *consistency* of measurement. Consistency can be conceptualized somewhat differently for different forms of reliability estimation, but in all cases reliability is focused on whether a measurement yields consistent results.

Such consistency is critical to research practice, where variables must be operationalized and measured in some fashion. For example, the measurement of socioeconomic status can be operationalized as average family income, whether a child receives a reduced lunch rate at school, education level of parent, or by other variables. Regardless of the way in which the variable is defined, however, it must be measured with consistency within the research study such that the scores obtained reflect dependable characterizations of the units of observation (e.g., people, families) on the variable of interest. In the example above, if a head of household does not know his or her average family income, he or she might simply guess at an estimate. Conversely, another head of household in the same study may give an accurate average family income. In such a case, the variable is not being consistently measured across the units of observation.

There are three dominant measurement theories that can be used to conceptualize reliability of scores: *classical test theory*, *generalizability theory*, and *item response theory*. In research practice, however, it is much more common for researchers to employ the classical test theory framework than the other two methods, at least in part due to ease of use and historical precedence (Hogan et al. 2000).

In classical test theory, sometimes called *true score theory*, a score is perfectly reliable only when the obtained score is measured without error. A practical ramification of this idea is that variables in the social sciences are seldom, if ever, measured without error. The assessment of socioecomonic status, as noted above, can have inconsistency (i.e., error) in how family income is reported. Researchers investigating parenting self-efficacy must wrestle with how to measure this construct, with full knowledge that their measurement will not be perfect.

Theoretically, however, there is a reliable measure of both of these variables, and therefore, the true score is a function of the obtained score and some degree of error, as indicated by

$$X_T = X_O + \text{error}$$

where X_T is the theoretical true score and X_O is the obtained score from a given measurement. Of course, within a given study, only the obtained score is available, and the true score is not directly known.

An observation's true score can be thought of as the theoretical average obtained from an infinite number of independent assessments of the same person with the same assessment (Allen & Yen 1979). Therefore, for any measurement occasion that is less than perfect, an obtained set of scores will contain variance that is true score variance (measuring the trait of interest) and variance that is due to error (factors inhibiting trait measurement, e.g., randomness in responses due to fatigue). These two variances (σ^2) yield the total score variance of the observed scores, such that

$$\sigma^2_{\text{OBSERVED}} = \sigma^2_{\text{TRUE}} + \sigma^2_{\text{ERROR}}$$

In classical test theory, non-systematic errors (e.g., fatigue effects, random guessing) lower the reliability estimate because they increase the amount of variance in the observed scores that is due to factors other than trait measurement. However, systematic errors (e.g., consistent fatigue effect across the sample such that similar errors are made) are not considered measurement error and can increase the reliability estimate because of their systematic nature.

In this framework, then, reliability (r_{XX}) can be conceptualized as the ratio between the true score variance and the observed score variance:

$$r_{XX} = \sigma^2_{\text{TRUE}}/\sigma^2_{\text{OBSERVED}}$$

If all of the variance in the observed scores is due to true score differences, then the reliability would be perfect (1.00). Unreliability is introduced to the degree that the observed score differences are due to factors (i.e., error) other than true differences.

In generalizability or G theory, analysis of variance methodology is employed to partition the variance of the observed scores into more than just two portions. The primary advantage of G theory lies with its ability to determine more specific sources of measurement error and the interaction between sources of measurement error. Once these sources of error are determined, then the researcher has a better idea on the degree of error in his or her data, and the potential reasons for that error. This is much different than the classical test theory perspective, where error is not simultaneously differentiated as originating from different sources (e.g., error due to test items, error due to time of measurement).

In item response theory (IRT), focus is not on the true scores or what constitutes the variance of the observed scores, but rather on the latent trait of interest. That is, it is the unobserved trait that theoretically causes the responses of a given person on a given test, and therefore the estimation of this latent trait is more central to the concept of reliability than the observed or even the true score.

IRT has significant advantages over classical test theory through its advancement of item and test information functions as a replacement of classical concepts of reliability. These information functions speak to reliability of measurement based on the ability of an item or test to discriminate among test-takers along various levels of the latent trait of interest. In general, greater levels of information on the functions indicate greater precision of measurement, and by extension, greater reliability.

Generalizability theory and item response theory notwithstanding, reliability continues to be most often conceptualized using the classical theory, and there are several ways to estimate reliability in this framework, including test-retest, alternate-forms, internal consistency, and interrater reliability. Each of these methods attempts to separately account for measurement error due to different sources. It should be noted, however, that this is not the same as the ability of G theory to account for multiple sources of measurement error (and their interactions) simultaneously.

Test-retest reliability assesses the consistency of measurement across time, or stability. This estimate is obtained by giving the same sample of subjects the same measure, with the two assessments separated by some period of time. The amount of time that is needed between the measurement occasions depends on many factors, and it can vary from as little as a week to as long as multiple years. Most often a few weeks is the time interval used. The test-retest coefficient is obtained by simply correlating the two sets of scores using a correlation coefficient such as Pearson *r*. If the measurements are consistent across time, then this correlation should be strong and positive. The degree it is not is the degree of measurement error due to time of assessment.

To estimate *alternate-forms reliability*, two different assessments which presumably assess the same trait of interest are given to the same group of subjects. The resulting scores are then correlated to determine the degree of equivalence between the alternate forms.

Internal consistency reliability is the most common form of reliability estimate, and it can be computed based on a single administration of a measure to a single group of subjects. There are various formulas for its estimation, but the most frequently employed of these is Cronbach's alpha (α). Internal consistency assesses the degree that a test's individual items are consistent within themselves and therefore are an appropriate sampling of items from the domain of all possible items that could be used in the assessment. Because of this focus, Cronbach's alpha tends to increase (greater reliability) when (1) the items responses are highly correlated, (2) the total score variance is large, and (3) there are a large number of items on the test. An alpha coefficient of 1.00 would indicate perfect reliability due to item sampling, and a coefficient of 0 would indicate a lack of reliability.

Interrater reliability addresses whether multiple judges can rate subjects consistently between themselves. Again, there are multiple ways to compute interrater reliability, ranging from the simple correlation between raters' scores to more complex statistics such as *Cohen's kappa* or the *intraclass correlation* (ICC). The ICC can also be employed for other reliability situations.

Regardless of the method of estimation or the measurement theory used, reliability is best considered as a function of obtained scores rather than as a function of the test itself. This is because the same test, when administered to different samples, can yield reliability estimates that vary. To some degree IRT overcomes this sample dependence by placing focus on the latent trait of interest and the item information functions. However, even with IRT, it is the obtained scores on items that are assessed for reliable information, not the test itself.

The meta-analytic approach of *reliability generalization* (RG) makes this point explicit and also has great value for evaluating how reliability can change from sample to sample. Originally developed by Vacha-Haase (1998), RG explores how reliability can change from study to study and attempts to determine whether certain study or sample features can predict this variation. Reliability generalization studies have also served to highlight the great frequency with which research authors fail to report reliability estimates for their obtained scores, which represents a noteworthy flaw to a research study (Vacha-Haase et al. 2002). Instead, many authors rely on reliability estimates from prior studies or the test manual (a process called *reliability induction*), which unfortunately may not be applicable to the current data. In sum, reliability is a critical element to any research study, and therefore its estimation is central to the research outcomes of interest.

SEE ALSO: Correlation; Descriptive Statistics; Effect Sizes; General Linear Model; Reliability Generalization; Validity, Qualitative; Validity, Quantitative

REFERENCES AND SUGGESTED READINGS

Allen, M. J. & Yen, W. M. (1979) *Introduction to Measurement Theory*. Brooks/Cole, Monterey, CA.

Henson, R. K. (2001) Understanding Internal Consistency Reliability Estimates: A Conceptual Primer on Coefficient Alpha. *Measurement and Evaluation in Counseling and Development* 34: 177–89.

Hogan, T. P., Benjamin, A., & Brezinski, K. L. (2000) Reliability Methods: A Note on the Frequency of Use of Various Types. *Educational and Psychological Measurement* 60: 523–31.

Huck, S. W. (2004) *Reading Statistics and Research*, 4th edn. Allyn & Bacon, Boston.

Nunnally, J. C. & Bernstein, I. H. (1994) *Psychometric Theory*, 3rd edn. McGraw-Hill, New York.

Shavelson, R. & Webb, N. (1991) *Generalizability Theory: A Primer*. Sage, Newbury Park, CA.

Thompson, B. (Ed.) (2003) *Score Reliability: Contemporary Thinking on Reliability Issues*. Sage, Thousand Oaks, CA.

Vacha-Haase, T. (1998) Reliability Generalization: Exploring Variance in Measurement Error Affecting Score Reliability Across Studies. *Educational and Psychological Measurement* 58: 6–20.

Vacha-Haase, T., Henson, R. K., & Caruso, J. (2002) Reliability Generalization: Moving Toward Improved Understanding and Use of Score Reliability. *Educational and Psychological Measurement* 62: 562–9.

reliability generalization

Tammi Vacha-Haase

Reliability generalization (RG) is a measurement meta-analytic method proposed by Vacha-Haase (1998) characterizing score reliability across multiple administrations of a measure as well as identification of study features predictive of measurement error variation. RG identifies (1) the typical score reliability for a given measure, (2) the variability in score reliabilities across administrations of a given measure, and (3) which features of the measurement protocol do and do not explain or predict these variations in score reliability. Reliability generalization is similar to the theoretical concepts of validity generalization. Meta-analysis of validity coefficients were the precursors to validity generalization, which began in the late 1970s to test whether the validity of scores for a given measure or set of related measures was generalizable. Meta-analysis was the testing of the hypotheses of "situation-specific validity."

In validity generalization inquiries, studies are used as the unit of analysis, and means, standard deviations, and other descriptive statistics are computed for the validity coefficients across studies. The validity coefficients across studies may also be used as the dependent variables in regression or other analyses. In these analyses the features of the studies (e.g., sample sizes, types of samples, ages of participants) that best predict the variations in the obtained validity coefficients are investigated. The same premises and methods utilized in validity generalization studies can be applied to explore score reliability – that is, reliability generalization.

Unfortunately, it is all too common to read about "the reliability of the test" or hear statements such as "the test is reliable" (Thompson 2003). Such statements contribute to the confusion and misunderstanding of reliability. Many have written about the confusion, attempting to clarify that scores, not tests, are reliable. For example, Pedhazur and Schmelkin (1991: 82) write: "Statements about the reliability of a measure are . . . inappropriate and potentially misleading." Thompson (1992: 436) summarizes: "This is not just an issue of sloppy speaking – the problem is that sometimes we unconsciously come to think what we say or what we hear, so that sloppy speaking does sometimes lead to a more pernicious outcome, sloppy thinking and sloppy practice." Thus, RG is based on the suggestion that scores, not tests, are reliable or unreliable. In addition, RG assumes that the reliability of scores on the same instrument will change from study to study, and characteristics of participants and other study features will influence reliability coefficients. This is in contrast to the classic test theory (Lord & Novick 1968) that stated increases in observed score variance result in increases in score reliability, and the assumption that the error variance remains constant in the two populations or, equivalently, that changes in observed score variance are caused solely by changes in true score variance. RG studies address this issue directly as attempts are made to explain variation in the scale-dependent error variance in addition to, or instead of, attempting to explain variation in the scale-free reliability coefficient.

Thus, reliability refers to the results obtained with an evaluation instrument and not to the instrument itself, as an instrument itself is neither reliable nor unreliable. The same instrument can produce scores which are reliable and other scores which are unreliable, as reliability is dictated by scores on a test for a particular group of examinees at a specific time. As an example, use the Beck Anxiety Inventory (BAI). This instrument lists 21 symptoms of anxiety, including descriptors such as feeling hot, unable to relax, dizzy, and face flushed. Individuals rate how much they have been bothered by each symptom during the past week by checking a 4-point likert scale, from "not at all" to "severely." In research study 1 and 2 the dependent variable is anxiety, as measured by the BAI. In the first study, all participants, who are all currently being treated at an inpatient facility for anxiety, complete the BAI. All scores were 3s or 4s; reliability analyses of these scores indicate the alpha coefficient is 0.6961. In a second study, participants are from an outpatient clinic; some are being treated for anxiety, others are not. The BAI scores vary, with some participants indicating a high degree of anxiety, others moderate, and still others reporting little or no symptoms of anxiety. The alpha coefficient for this group of participants is 0.9975.

This example illustrates – using the same instrument – that there were very different reliability coefficients. In this particular example, the instrument, number of participants, and even type of study were similar. What changed was the population or setting of the participants – and even that was only changed from an inpatient to an outpatient setting. That is, the participants themselves will have an influence on the score quality. "The same measure, when administered to more heterogeneous or more homogeneous sets of subjects, will yield scores with differing reliability" (Thompson 1994: 839).

This example also illustrates that a large total score variance led to high alpha coefficients. The more heterogeneous the group (outpatients in this example), when compared to a more homogeneous group (inpatients being treated for anxiety in this example), led to a higher alpha coefficient (0.9975 versus 0.6961). This has implications for individual studies, as reliability of the data actually being analyzed directly impacts results and interpretation. The practical effects of low score reliability may include underestimated effect sizes and less power to find statistical significance.

RG studies have been conducted in which the standard error of measurement (the square root of the error score variance) was employed as a primary dependent variable (Yin & Fan 2000). Alternatively, Shields and Caruso (2003) presented a new methodology in which the true and error variance in each sample were partitioned prior to analysis. Then the study and sample characteristics are allowed to have their effect on score reliability through their differential relationships with true and error variance. Thus it can be determined not only which study and sample characteristics affect score reliability, but also to what extent they do so by affecting the amount of true score variance, or the amount of error variance, or both.

Since the original article (Vacha-Haase 1998), more than 30 RG studies have been published. Scores on instruments such as the Meyer's Briggs Type Indicator, Coopersmith Self-Esteem Inventory, Career Decision-Making Self-Efficacy Scale, Revised Children's Manifest Anxiety Scale, Alcohol Use Disorders Identification Test, and MMPI, as well as concepts such as teacher self-efficacy and the "Big Five Factors" of personality, have been explored.

Future directions include the continuing use of RG methodology to explore score reliability of a multitude of instruments and constructs. This opens the door for the potential for completing meta-meta-analyses (i.e., the meta-analysis of RG studies), as described by Vacha-Haase et al. (2002).

SEE ALSO: Reliability; Validity, Qualitative

REFERENCES AND SUGGESTED READINGS

Lord, F. M. & Novick, M. R. (1968) *Statistical Theories of Mental Test Scores.* Addison-Wesley, Reading, MA.

Pedhazur, E. J. & Schmelkin, L. P. (1991) *Measurement, Design, and Analysis: An Integrated Approach.* Lawrence Erlbaum, Hillsdale, NJ.

Shields, A. L. & Caruso, J. C. (2003) Reliability Generalization of the Alcohol Use Disorders Identification Test. *Educational and Psychological Measurement* 63: 404–13.

Thompson, B. (1992) Two and One-Half Decades of Leadership in Measurement and Evaluation. *Journal of Counseling and Development* 70: 434–48.

Thompson, B. (1994) Guidelines for Authors. *Educational and Psychological Measurement* 54: 837–47.

Thompson, B. (Ed.) (2003) *Score Reliability: Contemporary Thinking on Reliability Issues.* Sage, Newbury Park, CA.

Vacha-Haase, T. (1998) Reliability Generalization: Exploring Variance in Measurement Error Affecting Score Reliability Across Studies. *Educational and Psychological Measurement* 58: 6–20.

Vacha-Haase, T., Henson, R. K., & Caruso, J. (2002) Reliability Generalization: Moving Toward Improved Understanding and Use of Score Reliability. *Educational and Psychological Measurement* 62: 562–9.

Yin, P. & Fan, X. (2000) Assessing the Reliability of Beck Depression Inventory Scores: Reliability Generalization Across Studies. *Educational and Psychological Measurement* 60: 201–23.

religion

Roberto Cipriani

The concept of religion is based on an idea of reality which goes back to the beginnings of humankind and provides an explanation for the existence of itself as well as the world surrounding it. Since the beginning of history, the idea of religion has manifested itself in diverse forms, across human societies. These forms, which constitute bodies of knowledge, beliefs, and social institutions, form an ordered, operative system. In Durkheimian terms, a religion gradually emerges as the members of a particular tribe or society build a system of beliefs and rites that bind them.

From barely conceived ideas, beliefs and practice proceed toward more elaborate systems (there are many "sacred" scriptures or oral traditions that are accepted, orthodox, and acknowledged), and, from informal interpersonal relationships, toward collective events (ceremonies which are more or less fixed at ritual level where it is possible to experiment and to reinforce the agreement between individuals, cognitive attitudes, and subsequent behaviors).

It would be misleading, however, to begin with just one definition of religion as it would be far too recent with respect to the birth of religions in general, and those which are considered historically organized (dating back many millennia before the beginning of the Common Era). However, the main reference is Marcus Tullius Cicero, who lived in the first century BCE. In his *De Natura Deorum* (*The Nature of Gods*) (2, 72), the concept of religion was linked to the Latin verb *relegere*, to reread, read over, to read repeatedly; to consider something with diligence; to check constantly what is important for the correct veneration of the gods.

The ancient Romans carried out their rituals with great precision and accuracy and their gestures and rites were consolidated in tradition. It could be said that their rituals had great respect for the law, and orthopraxis, to create a bond of loyalty with the past and not because of any predisposition of the soul. It is for this reason that religion was seen as a necessary response and reaction to unfavorable signs from the gods. Substantially, it was necessary to ingratiate oneself with the gods by carrying out the right actions that would win their favor. Not surprisingly, the art of divining was well developed and its practice was used to obtain the necessary information to understand which way the gods were oriented with respect to an individual or to a particular action.

Another variant, again of Latin origin, of the meaning of the term religion goes back to the original interpretation of the word *religare*, that is, to tie, attach, unite, or conjoin. This meaning suggests a relationship, a bond, but also an obligation, a commitment, or a submission. Evident in this relationship is the position of superiority assumed by the divinity, who functions as the obliger with regard to the human subject, who is consequently the obliged. Additionally, one of the strongest bonds between people and gods is created when making a pledge, that is, when a person makes a promise to a divinity upon the realization of a wish. If, then, after the pledge has been made the wish comes to fruition, the obligation toward the divinity is then fulfilled and the connection between the person and divinity is canceled out (although there will be further occasions where the pact can be renewed). The real effect though is a continued association: when a pledge is respected, there is concrete evidence of the human demonstrating faith, that is, loyalty and hope.

As mentioned, the etymology of the term religion can be traced to the Latin *religare* and has been attributed to the Christian writer Lactantius, who lived in the fourth century CE. According to this African writer, the bond between humans and God exists because humans recognize their creator and therefore obey, follow, and express *pietas*, that is, a sense of duty, devotion, and respect which is then duly returned by God in the form of justice, clemency, and divine benevolence. The central problem nevertheless persists, and it is that of fine-tuning a sociological definition of religion, one that is metaconfessional, universalistic, scientific, and whose results in theoretical and empirical research in the field of the social sciences of religion are precise. In this sense, and in order to maintain a scientific non-judgmental attitude, it appears useful to opt for an approach that is not instrumental (in Habermas's terms). Therefore, it is useful to begin from some of the empirical data which embody the various contemporary religions.

THE PRINCIPAL CHARACTERISTICS OF RELIGIONS

In the so-called primitive religions, the religious relationship is essentially manifested between humans and nature, and consists of forms of pantheism (which means that divine presence is found in every part of the human environment). God is seen to be operating in every facet of reality. A different approach can be seen in the modern form of Hinduism, which, with its Vedas tradition, has its beginnings probably in the third millennium BCE, if not earlier, and has developed a more universalistic outlook compared with its past form. There have been tendencies toward embracing all believers in God, irrespective of their faith.

With *Mahatma* (the great spirit) Mohandas Gandhi (1869–1948), violence, solidarity, and tolerance became paths toward truth and ethical and political commitment. Central to the concept of Hinduism is faith in Brahman, the supreme being who is also seen as Vishnu, and Shiva, who make up the sacred Trimurti. Brahman is one and all. In every individual there exists the divine and eternal breath, *ātman*, and the *karman*, which administers retribution for all acts committed, and deals with the cycle of life and rebirth. In order to free oneself from the vicissitudes of reincarnation, one is to practice self-denial, meditate, or be so devout as to embrace the essence of oneness between the infiniteness present in each being, *ātman*, and the absolute which is Brahman, the only truth, beginning and end of everything.

In Judaism (originating in the nineteenth century BCE), the core trait is community afflatus. Its main reference is the Torah, passed on from generation to generation and which makes up part of the Pentateuch (the five books relating the teachings of God to Moses). Judaism places emphasis above all on one's actions and relies on the alliance with God.

Buddhism (whose beginnings date back to the sixth century BCE) is surrounded by a controversy as to whether it is a religion or whether it should be considered merely as a philosophy. In reality, there are many elements which lead one to consider it a form of religion like any other. Initially Buddhism stemmed from Hinduism and the writings of the Indo-Aryan "holy sciences," unlike the Vedas. There was no system of sacrifice nor any concept of a personal God. Later developments in Buddhism led to the beginnings of monastic experiences, the search for perfection, the universalism of the *bodhisattva* (that is, "one whose essence is *bodhi*, enlightenment"), to principles of wisdom and compassion for human suffering, as well as a variety of kinds of worship and devotion, together with the pain of existence, detachment from earthly illusions, and the attainment of illumination. For Buddhism nothing is permanent, not even joy or suffering, so that even a moment of joy will only intensify the state of illusion of well-being. Buddhism denies the principles of Hinduism: both Brahman as god and *ātman* as individual reality. The ultimate objective is to eliminate that which causes pain by creating an awareness of both the transience of reality and the frailty of the human condition. Only by detaching oneself completely can there be freedom from suffering and the cycle of birth–death–rebirth. Morality, meditation, and wisdom are the only roads to control strength of mind along the *eightfold paths* of right faith, right purpose, right speech, right conduct, right means of livelihood, right effort, right mindfulness, and right meditation. This is the way of attaining *nirvana*, a state of being which is beyond good and evil.

Confucianism, which also had its beginnings in the sixth century BCE, involves more of an earthly quest based on human relationships. According to Confucius, divineness was present in the background: the search for God was through humans and their virtues; searching for the answers to the questions regarding the meaning of life, fate, and the question of good and evil. In fact, in Confucianism, human nature is essentially good, so, to maintain this state, one need only keep one's passions at bay.

In Taoism (whose beginnings date back to the sixth century BCE) the main principle is the *dao* (as with the Buddhist *nirvana*, it goes beyond the notions of good and evil). It is immanent in the universe and in humans and so it is evidence of the identity between absolute and relative. Taoism, a people's religion, was distinct from Confucianism as the latter was practiced by the elite of the Chinese government. Complementing the *dao* are the concepts of *yin* and *yang*: female and male, darkness and light, passive and active, potentiality and action, within and without. The world is born in five stages which combine with *yin* and *yang*: wood, fire, earth, metal, and water.

In Shintoism (whose beginnings go as far back as the sixth century BCE when the term *shinto* was adopted) there is a combination of thought, rites, and institutions which operate at a local level, within villages, as well as at a national level, within a sovereign state, represented by the emperor of Japan. The origins of Shintoism lie within the primordial dualism between male and female represented by the figures of Izanagi and Izanami, who create a number of other beings thus making this a polytheistic religion with a plurality of gods. There is no real difference between God, humans, and nature. The differences between them are barely perceptible. Shintoism is founded on a variety of doctrines, ceremonial practices, places of worship, and hierarchies of priests. Gods (*kami*) are present in mythology (legends dealing with divinities) and appear very powerful and mysterious. The popular *kunitsukami*, earth spirits, are veritable tutelary deities and enjoy greater familiarity and closeness with people. Shintoism also boasts a great number of rituals within the community of its followers.

In Christianity, which was born more than 2,000 years ago, there is one God in three persons: Father, Son, and Holy Spirit. Christ, the Son of God, came to earth, became human, and died on the cross to redeem humankind from original sin, inherited by each human being, according to Christian theology. Over the centuries there have been schisms and separations, and different Christian churches have arisen: Catholic, Orthodox, and Protestant.

In Islam (founded by Mohammed, who died in 632 CE) religion is conceived as *dīn*, an Arabic term (though Persian in origin) meaning "custom" but also "tribunal." Islam embodies a sense of faith (*iman*), customary practices (*islām*), and behavior (*aklāq* or *ihsān*). Also fundamental to Islam are the notions of testimony, prayer, fasting during *Ramadan* (the sacred month of Islam), contributing to the social taxation system (*zakāt*) and the pilgrimage to Mecca (*hadjj*).

In the so-called new religious movements (both in the West and the East), which, in reality, are based on practices and beliefs rooted in a variety of ancient religions, there is a tendency toward the esoteric, toward looking internally (with a certain amount of secrecy). These emphasize the individual needs of followers but without having to deny a universalistic outlook, one expressed through pacifism. There are, of course, movements of a different nature modeled on magic, therapy, and mysticism.

SOCIOLOGICAL THEORIES OF RELIGION

According to Durkheim, "a religion is a unified system of beliefs and practices relative to sacred things, that is to say, things set apart and forbidden – beliefs and practices which unite into one single moral community, called a church, all those who adhere to them" (Durkheim 1995 [1912]: 44).

In paragraph 1, chapter 5 of Weber's *Economy and Society* (1978 [1922]) the author assures his readers that he will provide a definition of religion but fails to do so because it would merely describe a "peculiar form of behavior within a community." In his writings on the sociology of religions, however, he refers to the "economic ethos of world religions" and describes "systems for regulating human existence" capable of "grouping around themselves a large number of faithful."

The difficulty Weber experienced in defining religion is common to many other authors, who prefer to avoid any involvement that might be evaluative or might risk bias toward a particular view regarding the essence of religion (with reference to Christianity, this was an issue already subject to strong debate between Feuerbach and Marx). The problem consists primarily in finding agreement on the specific contents of religion and these cannot be, from a sociological point of view, those established by the religions themselves given that they are, in their view, the standard and thus come into conflict with the others. Nor can the contents be those defined by sociologists given that any such definitions are necessarily expressed on the basis of their own theoretical and methodological stances. In both cases such a defining operation would seem unnecessary. This debate stems from the actual sphere of study of the discipline itself: some prefer to talk about the sociology of religion and others about the sociology of religions. The latter opt for the expression in the plural in order to avoid their scientific approach being limited to a single religious confession. But, on the other hand, if one talks about religion in the singular, meaning every religious manifestation and not merely that which is historically dominant in a given geographical context, the use of the expression sociology of religion aims to comprise all those religions which are empirically recognizable in the field of sociological research.

If anything, the most significant and discriminating point is another: whether to take into consideration every experience bearing similarities to those traditionally conceived as religion, that is, recognized as classic religions (including Buddhism, notwithstanding the reservations put forward by some scholars regarding its more philosophical rather than religious characteristics). The issue is important given that the consequences that depend on it are also of importance, that is, whether or not to classify as religion those movements whose religious nature is somewhat more metaphoric than substantial. This, however, does not mean having to search for the essence of religion; rather, it implies picking out those minimal elements which make a social phenomenon a religious fact based on its content, motivations, and customs.

Within contemporary societies there exist metaphorical forms of religion which, especially by way of their reference to values, seem to substitute traditional religious systems: these could, in fact, be defined as "religions of values." We are led to believe that they can replace historical religions. Thomas Luckmann (1967) shares the same view and his *The Invisible Religion* is based on the new "modern religious themes" of individual autonomy, the mobility ethos, self-realization, self-expression, sexuality, familism, and private life. This series of reference values recalls in some measure the Weberian concept of the "polytheism of values" where variety and sacredness of values are the result of ethical individualism.

Once the way has been opened to include new expressions of religion in the category of what is considered a religion, the number of possible alternatives increases but these all depend very much on the diverse sociological theories of religion. In this context it is important to define as secular religions those ways of experiencing politics, economy, art, science, and so on, as if they were a religion with their respective beliefs, relevant rites, and specific structures. Therefore, a funeral intended to be non-religious will actually follow and reiterate those patterns and procedures of a service in a religious temple; when a political appointment is made, the ceremony takes on the characteristics of a religious liturgy; a street protest has the semblance of an open-air religious assembly; and even the opening of new company headquarters has its propitiatory inauguration ceremony.

In order not to confuse and overlap religions, metaphoric religions, secular religion, and other para-religious forms, it seems correct to establish some common references, which point out the differences in such a way as to also recognize the affinities. Lambert (1991) rightly made the distinction between a substantive definition and a functional definition of religion where the former refers to the contents of a religion (according to Durkheim, for example, these relate to its beliefs and rituals), and the latter emphasizes the role and the function of religion in society (as is the case for Luhmann, who considers religion useful in facing life's uncertainties). However, within the substantive definitions, the functional aspect is not completely absent and, moreover, elements pertaining to the content of the functional definition cannot be completely expunged. All things considered, the substantive and functionalist perspectives tend to converge in the practical aspects of social life. A careful reading of Durkheim reveals functional aspects of religion while in Luhmann (and even Luckmann) it is possible to find substantive elements of religion. All in all, the belief in God, acts of devotion, the eschatological attitudes (relative to the final destiny for humanity and the universe), and the meaning of life are recurring themes within the religious experience, but none of these represents just one condition without which (*conditio sine qua non*) there can be a religious fact.

In other words, neither the *substantive-content related* nor the *functional-finalistic* represent the efficient cause (that is, the single determinant which directly and actively produces the effect) and/or the exclusive criterion necessary to recognize the religious feature of a sociological phenomenon. Here is where Aristotle made the clear distinction between material cause (the material of which something is made), formal cause (that by which matter is formed), efficient cause (that which produces a certain outcome), and final cause (the end of the process of development by which something becomes what it is). The Aristotelic schema provides an answer to the need to both adapt and contemplate, that is, to include aspects of substance and scope both formal and content based.

Classical sociology of religion has opted for more of a substantive stance on religion, whereas modern sociology of religion has broadened its horizons to embrace a functional stance to the extent that it has lost sight of the reference point needed to identify the usual indicators of religious phenomena. Perhaps a less dichotomous solution, one which maintains the contents and does not exclude the objectives, might be considered more adequate for an approach to the research of religion and religions.

From their tasks, sociologists correctly should strive to: identify the religious actuality from within other aspects of social structures; distinguish possible varieties pointing out any connections or divergences; discover any formulations which share consensus as to what is definable as religion; and always bear in mind what is real and not be influenced by ideological and/or personal presuppositions.

Simmel (1997), in the beginnings of the twentieth century, defined the boundaries between the kind of religion which is founded on history and organized as a product of culture, and religiousness seen as an openness to being religious, experienced by the individual as an internal human experience and necessary requisite for a union with God. Equally similar, however affine, is the position put forth, almost coevally, by William James in his reflections on *Varieties of Religious Experience: A Study in Human Understanding* (1902), in which he outlines a fundamental distinction between institutional religion and personal religion. The first is characterized as being ritualistic, well established, corporative, exterior, regulative, theological, organized, and ecclesiastic; the second, however, is oriented more toward interiority, the conscience, sentiment, the non-ritual, individuality, experience, the human dimension, mysticism, a direct rapport between souls, between humans and their creator, and lastly, communion from within and dialogue with the divine power.

It is debated whether it is worthwhile proceeding with an empirical analysis of religion when starting with a specific definition of religion in mind, or whether it is better to arrive at postulating a definition only upon completion of the research. Actually, it is the same problem of having to choose between an approach which presupposes the existence of a preformulated theory with respect to field research and an option which allows the researcher to come up with elements useful in the construction of a theory only after having collected the data. Perhaps the most effective solution is that which sees an initial conceptualization of the theme in question in order to be guided (but avoiding any constraints), and which ought to "sensitize" (in the way proposed by Herbert Blumer). It might be preferable, then, to opt for definitions which are not too rigid, which are open and possibilistic with regard to the outcomes of any empirical work.

If behind a religion there is a history dating back centuries, if not millennia, it would be difficult to deny its status. Such a religion would be acknowledged and accepted to the point of there not being any hesitation to accredit it sociologically. Consequently, in the case of phenomena that clearly belong to a historically rooted religious context, their nature as a religion is therefore accepted beyond any doubt. Even those marginal, dissenting, and minor forms of the great religions of the contemporary world are to be counted as religious forms in their own right.

The problem becomes more complex when qualifying as religious or not those manifestations with no historical precedent and which diverge significantly from the more accredited and accepted religious systems. Obviously, no judgment of a theological or confessional nature can impede these being considered as religious if they exhibit aspects which are commonly accepted as particular to a religion.

Even so, as Émile Poulat sustains (in *Le Grand Atlas des Religions*, 1992), "being able to say what is or what is not religious is not an academic problem: it is a question of politics, a continually renewed social debate, and one which produces countless answers and is divided into two extremes: the theocratic regime and the atheist regime." Undoubtedly, defining that which is religious also assumes a political nature, though this does not solve the basic scientific problem of whether or not to at least produce broad boundaries of the *proprium* of religion. Such boundaries cannot have an absolute or definitive meaning forever. In fact, religion is part of culture and therefore changes with it and the context in which it develops.

THE SOCIOLOGICAL CONCEPT OF RELIGION

A first criterion for defining religion is derived largely from a metaphysical, meta-empirical reference, which recognizes from within something (a divine form or superior being with divine characteristics which cannot be subjected to rational or scientific proof) the origin and control of the fate of humankind. Such a criterion, as it stands, is not sufficient as there can be attitudes and behaviors which present themselves as religions though they are not inspired by a God and which find from within nature strength and ubiquitous and creative power equal to that of the divine. Furthermore, even without presupposing the presence of a God, one's existence can be lived in a religious and metaphysical manner by a commitment to oneself, to others in a spirit of profound alterity, and a commitment to the problems of humanity.

A second criterion could be constituted by beliefs and convictions, irrespective of how deep they might be, based largely on spiritual and not material content. A third criterion sees the significant contribution of rituals deeply inspired by faith, and surrender to a divinity or, at any rate, a supernatural being. In a fourth criterion it is possible to contemplate behavioral norms as dictated by a charismatic leader and by its followers and/or on the basis of a series of written texts and the observance of commandments. As a fifth criterion there are the various actions which denote subscribing to defined religious views professed in a clear manner. The personal effort in observing the major principles of a faith, in identifying the coherent religious orientation which should be lived out, more or less, as a basic point of reference and as an ethical principle: this is the sixth criterion.

Religion can be expressed on a level of emotions and feelings. This seventh criterion was widely developed in, and is the fruit of, recent research, both theoretical and empirical, and recalls specifically the new religious tendencies, the so-called new religious movements, which are based on the peculiar emphasis of a subject's aspect. In some cases, as with the eighth criterion, there is a reverential attitude with respect to the divinity and generally that which is sacred. The ninth, a qualifying criterion, is one where even principles, dogmas, and official teachings represent a significant corpus which cannot be disregarded. A tenth criterion is based on the observance of norms and rules considered fundamental and demanding much attention, so much so that oaths are made with respect to these rules.

As can easily be concluded from this simple list of criteria, it is in no way possible to disregard – in the abstract – specific cultural situations. The idea of *religare*, that is, of maintaining a link, is about obligation toward laws, traditions, praxis, but also toward belonging, content of faith, and confessional orientation. At the same time, it can mean belief in God but also rendering service to God.

There still remains a principle for which none of the above criteria completely satisfies the requisites for recognizing something in terms of religion. Otherwise stated, for a group, organization, or movement, it is not necessary to have a precise concept of God, nor to take part in any rites, nor observe dogmas of faith, and not even to respect ethical norms.

The sociolinguistic weight of the term religion should not be forgotten: it originates from the defined framework of the Latin language but it can be applied indiscriminately to every kind of ethnicity. The relationship with the divine, the holy, is undoubtedly a widely accepted notion and has the intent of attributing the characteristics of religion to a specific social phenomenon. It should be noted that its origins are also a limitation: its beginnings and its christianocentric disposition have ideological repercussions which privilege the existence of God, the belief in an immortal soul, and the existence of a universal ethic – prime indicators of a religious fact. If adding to the natural, almost spontaneous characteristics of a religion the preponderant weight of a supernatural religion revealed by God, any scientific activity would be hindered and forced to stop before prerequisites that are loaded with mystery, filled with unfathomable, divine will, and which cannot be subjected to.any attempt at corroboration through information gathered in fieldwork.

If talking of natural religion as the result of an action of human reason, it belongs more to the realm of theology than that of sociology, even if Hume (fundamentally a deist) is credited with extracting religion from the control of religious institutions, favoring a less conditioned approach.

Unlike the philosophy of religion, the sociology of religion does not attempt to seek out the essence of religion, it does not question whether a spirit exists or not, nor does it assess the justness of any religious aspirations; it simply records its effects in a social context. Moreover, this does not imply that sociology need espouse the idea of necessary atheism, nor that a direct and operational involvement of a religiously militant nature is desirable. It can also be said to be true for any forced choice which is agnostic, indifferent, areligious, as if it were the unavoidable condition necessary to carry out scientific research on religious phenomena. However, any other option would give rise to atheistic religion which is not at all mandatory for scientific research inasmuch as it would lead to the idea of a slide of the unknowability of the divine absolute toward the unknowability of a religious fact purely because it is linked to the divine. Schleiermacher sustained, philosophically, the feasibility of a religion without a God.

But it was another philosopher, Henri-Louis Bergson, who, in his work *Two Sources of Morals and Religion* (1932), favored a distinction between static religion and dynamic religion. The former was considered a reduced historical version of the view regarding the survival instinct humans opt for in order to solve the problem of death by inventing divine figures, with a human likeness, and which serve as tutelary deities. The latter, on the other hand, was regarded as not being the work of humans but of God, where humans enter the realm of God in a mysterious way, and allow themselves to be led by their God toward forms of institution and dogma. The characteristics of static religion are more human, earthly, and natural, whereas those of dynamic religion are more metaphysical, superterrestrial, and divine. Bergson is far from the idea of humankind's concerns about the numinous. For him, humans are directed toward a God who is far more than human inasmuch as it is a mysterious superior being, majestic, irascible, *tremendum* (frightening), and *fascinans* (enchanting).

Indeed, little do these philosophical perspectives influence sociological thought, which tends not to subscribe to a transcendental explanation, does not question objective truth, and excludes itself from any salvific implication of religious activity. That which truly interests sociology is the socioreligious activity humans are involved in within their community and society. Needless to say, a sociological definition of religion cannot be restricted or limiting. It does, however, open itself to every possible aspect within the variety of phenomena that can be identified empirically. It is because of this that it is deeply interconnected with many other forms of social experience, ranging from family to economic life, from political choices to moral choices, from ideology to the meaning of symbols, and from art to technology.

The starting point, hence, is that a sociological definition of religion should be an observation which brings about a necessarily comparative approach between similar religious systems in different societies. This is possible by perhaps identifying connotations which corroborate the idea of a natural religion that is more human than divine in its origins, divided and channeled into different eras and into different societies. In the second half of the nineteenth century, Max Müller pointed out, and not by chance, that the Indo-European roots of religion go back as far as the Vedas traditions, and date back even further than the beginnings of Hinduism. He emphasized how the personification of gods was the result of the human tendency to anthropomorphize every phenomenon. Tylor (1871) followed the same line of thinking, stating that the religions of the so-called primitive peoples created the roots for every expression of religion that followed, which moved toward animism, then polytheism, and finally monotheism.

Monotheism, in its contemporary forms, bases itself on unicity and the truth of a single God. It offers an opportunity to so-called rational choice (or the "new paradigm," tied to Peter Berger's idea of the religious market), applied to the economic model in order to prove that the "one true God" theory works convincingly in the context of the religious market. This happens because it is privileged by the "exclusive exchange relationship" accompanied by a kind of lifetime guarantee. Hence, the only true God is to be seen as a successful product also because it is a common affair related to groups. But such a point of view necessarily presupposes a supernatural dimension, and this, inevitably, is not applicable to all religions in their manifestations.

In addition, the one, true, convincing explanation would exclude other evidence: religion is able to explain but it also mystifies; it creates peace but also conflict; it consoles and strikes fear; it is governed by an elite few but practiced largely by the masses (this is the point from which the continual contrast between official and popular religion stems). This is not to mention the continuing dialectic between religion and culture, which shapes the attitudes and behavior of social actors.

After all, the two prevailing perspectives are those which compare religion to a relationship between human subjects and a divine being or, contrarily, which insist that the religious dimension is an "earthly" social construct created by social actors in response to needs which are by no means metaphysical but totally human.

From magic to pre-animism, from animism to totemism, from fetishism to polytheism, and from mythology to monotheism, the religious processes are many, overlapping, and not necessarily linear or evolutionary, but in general they produce beliefs, rites, symbols, and institutions. The formations which come as a result appear so distinct from one another that every sociologist of religion attempts to give a personal definition of the contents and forms of religion. The result, however, is almost always incomplete, vague, or circumscribed. Therefore a sociological definition of religion is, at most, applicable to a limited context and to a short time frame.

From Kant's social morality to the conception of the universe as seen by Hegel, to the emotions referred to by Schleiermacher, and to the search for security analyzed by Fromm, religion nevertheless constitutes a desire in one way directed to the divine, and yet in another it is addressed to humankind and sometimes toward both. For this reason, one of the most convincing definitions appears to be Geertz's (1973), which explains religion as a system of symbols that provide humankind with an ongoing, realistic, and factual justification through concepts pertaining to a general order of existence. This final attempt at a definition put forth by Geertz seems to end the diatribe between substantive and functional definitions and that between restrictive and more open perspectives.

Peter Beyer (2001) also searched for a solution by proposing an ideal-typical typology (and therefore not empirically verifiable) organized into three meanings: analytical, theological, and popular/official. He rightly observed that the formation and development of some religions (such as Christianity, Judaism, Islam, Sikhism, Buddhism, and Hinduism) are clearer and more noticeable than others (such as Taoism, Shintoism, and Confucianism), although they all share an unquestionable social concreteness. The analytical approach strives to discover similar institutions and attributes in the various religions even when they belong to different periods in history. This approach therefore attempts to identify universal elements in all societies but cannot exclude the fact that there are other forms of religion which do not have such aspects in common. On the other hand, the theological approach, which concerns a universal ontological truth, postulates something which in itself escapes empirical observation in that it deals with a metaphysical reality, but this does not hinder the existence of different kinds of knowledge and forms of communication. Finally, it appears to be quite similar to the religious model within the popular/official views of religion, given these views are not characterized by universality but by what the members of a religious movement or religious organization ask to be considered as religion. In other terms, it deals with a specific form of religion which has its own distinctive institutional traits as well as a series of human experiences. It is no coincidence, then, that religion is a personal affair, which is practiced in groups, but often it is done so independently compared to organized religious manifestations (as proved by pilgrimages or large gatherings, communal liturgies, or local or domestic religiousness).

The different degrees of religiousness, that is, the amount of fervor and commitment in a religion, depend on historical and personal factors which, sociologically, are not easily identifiable and interpretable, for the following reasons: the vast extent of possible religious manifestations; sociocultural influences; economic, political, and ideological relationships; and emotional, sentimental, and psychological interaction. This web of interferences and relationships does not allow for an aprioristic definition of religion, but nevertheless – as Assad (1993) notes – "there cannot be a universal definition of religion, not only because its constituent elements and relationships are historically specific, but because that definition is itself the historical product of discursive processes."

On the other hand, Talcott Parsons has seen a number of answers in religion: an answer to humanity's desires (in the sense of salvation versus suffering), to the need for values (in the sense of justice versus injustice), to the affirmation of ideas (truth versus fallacy).

One of the most accredited Chinese scholars of religion, Lü (1998), is of a very different opinion, stating that "religion is a kind of social consciousness regarding superhuman and supernatural forces, and its consequent believing and worshipping behaviors toward such forces; it is the normalized and institutionalized social-cultural system that synthesizes this consciousness and the behaviors." Lü's definition, coming from a non-western sociocultural framework, is worthy of particular attention also "for its scientific nature and liberating effect" in an environment, such as China's, which until fairly recently did not favor the development of scientific study of religion (Yang 2004).

Not so easy is that sphere which includes religions and para-religions or quasi-religions, those which include therapies, systems for healing the body, diets, martial arts, methods of self-help, sports, and many more phenomena which describe themselves as religious and which may share some of the characteristics typical of a religion. A distinction can be made between para-religion and quasi-religion. Para-religion possesses some religious features and thus resembles a religion (without giving itself that definition). A quasi-religion only barely manifests any affinity with religion. The real problem is not whether to establish what share of religion is present in these phenomenologies, but to ascertain whether any relationships have been established with the entire belief system (including religious beliefs) that each individual controls and manifests.

The variability of religion does not allow for steel cages, peremptory definitions, or inescapable criteria: "far from being a fixed or unitary phenomenon, religion is a social construct that varies in meaning across time and place" (Beckford 2003). A formulation such as "a patterning of social relationships around a belief in supernatural powers, creating ethical considerations" (Gustafson & Swatos 1990: 10) might be considered efficient: it is synthetic and allows for a great number of scholars from every cultural and intellectual background to share its content. In this case as well, it is also obviously necessary to avoid unfounded empirical absolutes. Intrinsic to this definition is the suggestion not to confuse religion with faith (an individual issue) or morals. In addition, the supernatural is distinct from the transcendent in that the former may possess a characteristic which could be also immanent (in nature, for instance, as strength or as entity), whereas the latter refers to a God. Indeed, religion has a characteristic indicative of action. It possesses its own conceptual vocabulary common to all those who belong; it furthermore involves subjective experiences which may or may not be extensive or intense. It is clear that no firm, dogmatic definition can be given to religion because of the extreme variability of its manifestations. These can be evaluated and interpreted taking into account the definition of a situation as given by the social actors. In short, a possible operative definition should be "grounded," that is, based on data. A possible starting point for such a definition may even make use of a "sensitizing" (Blumer) characteristic in order to approach the actor's point of view.

The procedure with which a definition of religion is constructed begins with the collection of empirical data, some indicative concepts are put forth, and then strategies for research are established. Accordingly, it would be preferable to have the individual express its orientation. By so doing, both pure descriptivism and theoretical prospectivism can be avoided. And so the researcher operates within the framework arranged contemporarily by the social actors, who create their religion, hence their experiences of religion, and by the sociologist, who constructs her analytical points of view in order to make her observations of religion and religions. There is, in effect, a return of the social actor to the field of religion. The actor is no longer governed by confessional concepts or concepts that may be irrelevant to the object of scientific research. Both concepts are destined generally to cancel out the social individual's point of view. Also, in order to avoid any impediments and misinterpretations, it is useful for the sociologist of religion to declare explicitly not only personal religious tendencies, but also basic values, choices of behavior, and underlying attitudes.

Within many sociological definitions of religion there is a significant amount of overinterpretation, that is, interpretation that disregards the facts. On the other hand, self-definition given by social actors is not the only possible point of reference in that it should be compared with other definitions put forward by other subjects and within different contexts and with different emphases. The task of the sociologist, then, is to scientifically coordinate and recompose the different concepts observed.

To this it is possible to add as a fundamental premise the careful and thorough study of practice, and the value influences which guide it. The most difficult question to solve concerns the distinction (if any) between belief and experience. Nevertheless, it should be taken into account that there are ways of interpreting religion without referring to either: belief without experience and experience without belief, or as Davie (1990) put it, "believing without belonging," or contrarily, "belonging or experiencing without believing."

At this point it should be clear that sociological analysis of religion does not aim to confirm the plausibility of what is metaphysical, transcendent, or supernatural, but rather how men and women of the contemporary world live their personal and social experience of religion. According to his scientific solution, Beckford (2003) suggests experimenting with a socioconstructionist approach to religion, thus tending to analyze "the ways in which human beings express what they regard as religious ideas and sentiments in social and cultural forms," independent of whether or not religion is a socioanthropological need to be gratified in order to solve existential problems (according to Luhmann's indetermination reduction, or Berger and Luckmann's social construction of meaning). Hence, definitions of religion which appeal to common sense would be of little use; indeed, it would be more effective to observe the processes of the social construction of religion as they happen. If not, any attempts to define what religion is would be destined to fail because they would find no adequate scientific consensus. Nonetheless, typological attempts should be made, with the intent of at least being indicative, sensitizing, and creating awareness. After all, the field is not entirely empty, much has already been sown, while some areas left fallow, it has yielded good fruit, and, with the fertility of cumulative knowledge, research can then begin with an essential point of reference in mind. So, for religion, the following approaches to research can be considered, either separately or combined with other approaches, according to the logic dictated by the individual's experience and chosen method of analysis.

First, religion is composed of interpersonal experiences with other humans and/or with one or more divinities. Such relations are made up principally of convictions (beliefs), sentiments (emotions), principles (values), and practice (rituals, i.e., cultural acts and also actions, whether they occur daily or on specific occasions), all of which are more or less coherently interconnected. The subject's freedom to be unpredictable produces unexpected events as well as one-off conjunctions. In the meantime, however, the traditions of historically recognized religions continue to reaffirm their most significant features through notions, precepts, ceremonies, and according to the circumstances of the time and their environment. What does not pertain to sociological research are the questions of whether or not God exists, the immortality of the soul, the cycle of reincarnation, rewarded or sanctioned behavior, life beyond death, or divine revelation to humanity, but each of these elements can be used as a qualifier for whatever religion and can therefore be part of a defining framework (accurately contextualized) although not subject to empirical proof. It goes without saying that none of the religions appears to be a religion par excellence, thus removing any doubt from the use of the wording sociology of religion rather than sociology of religions.

Second, religion is expressed as a connection with the divinity, which gives humans unity, in the universal sense, by means of devotion toward a God, and the respect due to it. Moreover, the object of such veneration becomes sacred, something significantly different, untouchable, and superior; and great care is taken to observe with deference and reverence every correct rule and praxis according to preestablished precepts.

Third, religion is the manifestation of profound belief; it is professing one's faith; it is not necessarily critical, compared with those concepts of life which have a feature that is cogent and paradigmatic, and accepted almost unconditionally. Faith is expressed indeed by entrusting the values one considers fundamental and unfaltering, and these preside over almost all decisions, however small.

Fourth, religion is fervor, dedication, ongoing practice, devout behavior, and piety; it is religiousness outwardly expressed through recollection, repentance, meditation, reflection, and silence.

These distinctive features of religion are simply a dialogic and open path to be used as a guide for theoretical and empirical research, and not further tokens to add to the great cemetery of definitions of religion.

SEE ALSO: Animism; Asceticism; Atheism; Belief; Buddhism; Catholicism; Charisma; Christianity; Church; Civil Religion; Confucianism; Fundamentalism; Globalization, Religion and; Hinduism; Islam; Jehovah's Witnesses; Judaism; Laicism; Magic; Millenarianism; New Religious Movements; Orthodoxy; Pietism; Popular Religiosity; Primitive Religion; Protestantism; Religion, Sociology of; Religions, African; Religious Cults; Rite/Ritual; Sacred; Sacred, Eclipse of the; Scientology; Sect; Secularization; Shintoism; Taoism; Televangelism; Theology; Totemism

REFERENCES AND SUGGESTED READINGS

Assad, T. (1993) *Genealogies of Religion: Discipline and Reasons of Power in Christianity and Islam.* Johns Hopkins University Press, Baltimore.

Beckford, J. A. (2003) *Social Theory and Religion.* Cambridge University Press, Cambridge.

Berger, P. L. (1969) *The Social Reality of Religion.* Faber & Faber, London. Originally published as *The Sacred Canopy: Elements of a Sociological Theory of Religion.* Doubleday, Garden City, NY, 1967.

Beyer, P. (2001) Contemporary Social Theory as it Applies to the Understanding of Religion in

Cross-Cultural Perspective. In: Fenn, R. K. (Ed.), *The Blackwell Companion to Sociology of Religion.* Blackwell, Oxford, pp. 418–31.

Casanova, J. (1994) *Public Religions in the Modern World.* University of Chicago Press, Chicago.

Cipriani, R. (2000) *Sociology of Religion: An Historical Introduction.* Aldine de Gruyter, New York.

Davie, G. (1990) Believing Without Belonging: Is This the Future of Religion in Britain? *Social Compass* 37(4): 455–69.

Dortier, J.-F. & Testot, L. (Eds.) (2005) *La Religion: Unité et diversité* (*Religion: Unity and Diversity*). Presses Universitaires de France, Paris.

Durkheim, É. (1995 [1912]) *The Elementary Forms of Religious Life: The Totemic System in Australia.* Trans. K. E. Fields. Free Press, New York.

Fenn, R. K. (Ed.) (2001) *The Blackwell Companion to Sociology of Religion.* Blackwell, Oxford.

Geertz, C. (1973) *The Interpretation of Cultures.* Basic Books, New York.

Gustafson, P. M. & Swatos, W. H., Jr. (1990) Max Weber and Comparative Religions. In: Swatos, W. H., Jr. (Ed.), *Time, Place, and Circumstance.* Greenwood Press, New York.

Hervieu-Léger, D. (1993) *La Religion pour mémoire (Religion as Memory).* Cerf, Paris.

Hervieu-Léger, D. (1999) Religion. In: Akoun, A. & Ansart, P. (Eds.), *Dictionnaire de sociologie* (*Dictionary of Sociology*). Le Robert/Seuil, Paris, pp. 447–9.

Lambert, Y. (1991) La "Tour de Babel" des Définitions de la Religion (The "Babel Tower" of Definitions of Religion). *Social Compass* 38(1): 73–85.

Lambert, Y., Michelat, G., & Piette, A. (1977) *Le Religieux des sociologues: Trajectoires personnelles et débats scientifiques* (*The Religious of Sociologists: Personal Trajectories and Scientific Debates*). L'Harmattan, Paris and Montréal.

Lü, D. (1998) Zongjiao shi shenme? – Zongjiao de benzhi, jiben yaosu, jiqi luoji jiegou (What is Religion? – The Essence, Elements, and Logical Structure of Religion). In: Cao, Z. (Ed.), *1996 Zongguo zongjiao yanjiu nianjian* (*Annual of Religious Research, 1996*). China Social Sciences Press, Beijing.

Luckmann, T. (1963, 1967) *The Invisible Religion: The Transformation of Symbols in Industrial Society.* Macmillan, New York and London.

Luhmann, N. (1977) *Funktion der Religion* (*Function of Religion*). Suhrkamp, Frankfurt.

O' Toole, R. (1984) *Religion: Classical Sociological Approaches.* McGraw-Hill Ryerson, Toronto.

Roberts, R. H. (2002) *Religion, Theology, and the Human Sciences.* Cambridge University Press, Cambridge.

Simmel, G. (1997) *Essays on Religion.* Ed. H. G. Helle. Yale University Press, New Haven.

Stark, R. & Bainbridge, W. S. (1987) *A Theory of Religion.* Peter Lang, Bern and New York.

Swatos, W. H., Jr. (Ed.) (1998) *Encyclopedia of Religion and Society.* AltaMira Press, Walnut Creek, London, and New Delhi.

Towler, R. (1974) *Homo Religiosus: Sociological Problems in the Study of Religion.* Constable, London.

Turner, B. S. (1991) *Religion and Social Theory.* Heinemann, London.

Tylor, E. E. (1871) *Primitive Culture: Researches into the Development of Mythology, Philosophy, Religion, Art, and Custom.* Murray, London.

Wallis, R. (1984) *The Elementary Forms of New Religious Life.* Routledge & Kegan Paul, London.

Weber, M. (1978 [1922]) *Economy and Society: An Outline of Interpretive Sociology,* 2 vols. Ed. G. Roth & C. Wittich. University of California Press, Berkeley.

Willaime, J.-P. (1995) *Sociologie des religions* (*Sociology of Religions*). Presses Universitaires de France, Paris.

Wuthnow, R. (1978) *Experimentation in American Religion.* University of California Press, Berkeley.

Yang, F. (2004) Between Secularist Ideology and Desecularizing Reality: The Birth and Growth of Religious Research in Communist China. *Sociology of Religion* 65(2): 101–19.

religion, sociology of

Michele Dillon

The sociology of religion is a core component of the discipline, having a critical place in the classical theorizing of Max Weber and Émile Durkheim and comprising one of the more researched areas of interest among contemporary sociologists (for an introduction to sociological theory and religion, see Cipriani 2000). The sociology of religion is concerned with the multiplicity of ways in which religion is part of human society and thus it focuses on its institutional, cultural, and individual expression across varying social, geographical, and historical contexts. A common typology is to differentiate between substantive and functional approaches to studying religion. The former is concerned with the symbolic contents or meanings contained within a religious worldview and the latter with religion's purposes or functions in society. Following Weber's (1958) analysis of the doctrinal tenets of the Calvinist ethic, substantive approaches focus on delineating particular religious beliefs, defined in terms of concerns about transcendence and other-worldly salvation, and how these beliefs are understood and give meaning to everyday life.

Functionalist definitions, by contrast, give attention to the social implications of religious belief and behavior. Following Durkheim's (1976) analysis of how religious affiliation and commitment serve purposes of social integration and belonging, there is a long tradition in sociology of not paying too much attention to the doctrinal content of belief and its associated meanings, but to how such beliefs impact other aspects of social life ranging from national identity to political, health, and sexual behavior. Unlike for Weber, the content of religion is seen in substantially broader terms and this too follows from Durkheim's definition of what constitutes "sacred things": any things so defined by society or by particular communities, whether they be Episcopalians, Buddhists, pagans, yoga practitioners, or fans of a particular sports team. Clearly, how broadly or narrowly one defines religion matters to the sorts of theoretical questions and research projects sociologists of religion deem relevant.

In practice, however, drawing too sharp a line between substantive and functional definitions of religion runs the risk of missing out on the multifaceted ways in which religion seeps through everyday life. As indeed Weber elaborated, Calvinists' beliefs were instrumental – or functional – to the development of capitalism, and as intimated by Durkheim (in *Suicide*), the content of doctrinal tradition differentiated levels of social integration; although Catholicism and Protestantism were equally opposed to suicide, Catholics were less likely than Protestants to commit suicide, a fact that Durkheim traced to the greater emphasis on social ties emanating from Catholic doctrine as reflected in its structures (e.g., the mediating sacramental role of the priest).

INTELLECTUAL AND SOCIAL CONTEXT

The directions taken by the sociology of religion reflect both the intellectual context in which the discipline of sociology itself emerged, as well as differences in the national contexts in which sociologists have studied religion. Because sociology grew out of the Enlightenment it took on many of its philosophical assumptions and values. Most specifically, although the Founding Fathers rejected Enlightenment thinkers' emphasis on man as the primary unit of society in favor of a perspective that emphasized the individual's relationality to other people as well as to history and social processes (e.g., capitalism) and institutions, they embraced the Enlightenment values of rationality and scientific method. One consequence of the Enlightenment – and of sociology's scientism – was that it regarded religion as crystallizing the nonrational elements in society and thus delegitimated it as a domain of knowledge and of experience. This had two important and interrelated consequences for the study of religion. One, it led to an elitist and dismissive attitude toward the relevance of religion, a view that regarded religion as the vestige of pre-Enlightenment times: a coercive, anti-democratic, and hierarchical force that fostered inequality and unenlightened ways of being.

Second, it nurtured the view that even if religion persists as an individual or social phenomenon, it is not a domain of knowledge that is accessible to scientific investigation. Sociology was not alone in cultivating this view; while some cultural anthropologists paid attention to religion as part of their interest in primitive or traditional societies, psychology essentially ignored the place of religious belief in child and adult development, personality, and psychological functioning. In essence, the thesis of religion's inaccessibility to scientific investigation argues that because the existence of God cannot be ascertained, therefore it is of little use for social scientists to dabble in the study of anything pertaining to religion and that those who do so must surely have a regressive ideological or dogmatic bias. Clearly, this is a remarkably blinkered view of both social science and of religion. While it is generally a good thing for a social scientist, as indeed for the ordinary citizen, to bring a "hermeneutic of suspicion" to what counts as knowledge, expertise, or common sense in society, this hermeneutic should not be directed a priori toward sociologists studying religion as opposed to some other topic.

Religious belief is about belief in a transcendent presence that cannot be verified, but the essence of a lot of the phenomena that sociologists study is equally invisible. Longstanding scholarly debates about how social class can be reliably measured, or how micro–macro linkages should be assessed, point to the complexity of the sociological task as a whole. The sociology of religion is not interested in speculating about or studying the existence of God. It is concerned, rather, with how individuals, social institutions, and cultures construe God or the sacred (following Weber), how these ideas penetrate public culture and individual lives, and with the implications of these interpretations for individual, institutional, and societal processes. Thus, similar to their peers who specialize in other areas of the discipline, sociologists of religion develop conceptually and methodologically valid indicators that they use to investigate theoretically informed questions about religion's meaning and place in society. Standardized indicators include finely differentiated measures of religious affiliation and beliefs, frequency of church attendance, private prayer and religious reading, the self-perceived importance of religion in an individual's life, and personal images of God. A reliable and fairly comprehensive selection of questions is asked in the General Social Survey (GSS), an annual cumulative survey conducted since 1972 by the National Opinion Research Center at the University of Chicago; other useful resources are survey data gathered by the International Social Survey Program (archived at the Zentralarchiv, University of Cologne) and by the Gallup and Pew polling organizations.

At a broad level of generality, the research undertaken by sociologists of religion has been shaped by the societal contexts of the researchers. Specifically, there is a discernible difference in the kinds of overarching questions that have informed European in contrast to American sociology of religion. Reflecting their very different national histories as well as the Enlightenment concern with church–state alliances, European researchers have paid a lot of attention to examining the intricacies of church–state institutional relations and how these impact national cultures and laws and public policies. In the American context, by contrast, with its very different history – religious pluralism and its associated emphases on religious freedom and voluntarism – much attention has been given to investigating the institutional and cultural dynamics of denominationalism, a defining characteristic of American society (e.g., Herberg 1955).

Another way in which the influence of social context is apparent is in the greater tendency of Europeans to apply a critical neo-Marxist perspective in their analyses of religion (a concern, for example, with the hegemony of the church in society), whereas American scholars reflecting on a very different societal context (of denominationalism and ethnic and religious pluralism) and more strongly influenced by Parsonian functionalism than neo-Marxism, discuss the culturally unifying possibilities and implications of a civil religion – how a nation's founding values and ideals are sacralized in political and public discourse (e.g., Bellah 1967). In sum, scholarly work in the sociology of religion, as is true of all knowledge, is contingent on the particular social and historical context in which it is conducted and the attendant prioritization of research topics and questions is related to the realities of the sociologists' social and institutional environment (e.g., Davie 2003).

SECULARIZATION AND RATIONAL CHOICE THEORY

A dominant theme in the sociology of religion and vigorously engaged by scholars on both sides of the Atlantic is secularization. The term is conceptualized differently by various scholars (for an extensive review, see Tschannen 1991), but for the most part refers to the constellation of historical and social processes that allegedly bring about the declining significance of religious belief and authority across private and public life. The secularization thesis has its roots in the writings of both Weber and Durkheim. Weber predicted that the increased rationalization of society – bureaucratization, scientific and technical progress, and the expanding pervasiveness of instrumental reason in all domains of everyday life – would substantively attenuate the scope of religion, both through the specialization of institutional spheres (of family, economy, law, politics) and as a result of disenchantment in the face of competing rationalized value spheres (e.g., science). Durkheim, although a strong proponent of the centrality of the sacred to society, nonetheless predicted that the integrative functions performed by church religion in traditional societies would increasingly in modern societies be displaced by the emergence of differentiated professional and scientific membership communities.

The secularization thesis, especially its Weberian understanding, was highly influential in the paradigm of social change articulated by Talcott Parsons and subsequently by modernization theorists in the 1960s who theorized religion's loss of institutional and cultural authority. Most notably, in Peter Berger's (1967) language, religion would lose plausibility and its power as an integrative sacred canopy, or as argued by Thomas Luckmann (1967), become socially invisible. The modernization-secularization thesis was widely accepted by western sociologists and though there were some exceptions (e.g., Greeley 1972; Martin 1978), many assumed a priori that religion had lost its significance in modern societies despite the ongoing empirical evidence that secularization was not as all-encompassing as theorized by its proponents. Various societal factors (e.g., the increased public visibility of religious social movements, such as the Moral Majority in the United States, Solidarity in Poland, and the religious roots of the Iranian Revolution), intradisciplinary theoretical challenges to modernization theory, and greater scholarly attentiveness to the critical importance of nonrational sources of meaning and authority in everyday life (including religion, emotion, and tradition), converged in the late 1970s and has resulted in a more complex and nuanced sociological assessment of secularization.

Contributing to this paradigm reassessment, the application of rational choice theory to religion has resulted in an intense debate about the ways in which competitive religious environments (religious economies) produce religious vitality and church growth (e.g., Finke & Stark 2005). This approach rejects the assumptions of secularization theory as being more appropriate for the historically monopolized religious markets found in Europe, but at odds with the American context of religious pluralism (cf. Warner 1993). In view of the cumulative body of empirical knowledge that exists on religion, secularization should be understood in terms of a balance between extensive empirical evidence in favor of the continuing sociological significance of religion in the public domain and in individual lives, and the coexistence of these trends with equally valid empirical evidence indicating selectivity in, and reflexivity toward, the acceptance of religion's theological, moral, and political authority. Both sets of trends must necessarily be interpreted with a cautious and differentiated understanding of the nature and place of religion in earlier historical eras and across diverse social contexts, and with greater attentiveness to how the contextual meanings of religion and of religious belief, affiliation, and commitment change over time (Gorski 2003; Hout & Fischer 2002).

CONTEMPORARY RESEARCH

Much of the contemporary research on religion documents the complexity and multidimensionality of religion as it is lived out across diverse contexts (see the contributions to Dillon 2003). Many studies document trends in the continuing significance of religious beliefs and practices, especially in the US (e.g., Greeley & Hout 1999), but also in Europe (e.g., Davie 2000), where the institutional presence of churches is weaker (with the exception of Ireland) than in the United States. It is also apparent that the symbolic vestiges of religion matter even in countries where various indicators would suggest a comparatively greater deinstitutionalization of religion (e.g., Quebec, Italy). Many individuals still value the presence of church rituals in marking significant life transitions (e.g., marriage, death), and participate in pilgrimages and other forms of religious tourism and consumption (e.g., the popularity of Christian rock music and religious theme books and movies), while not necessarily adhering to a denominational identity or to any specific doctrinal teachings.

The cultural hold of religion is also documented in research on the increased prominence of global religious movements (e.g., Pentecostalism, Islam), the continuing attraction of participation in (socially marginalized) New Religious Movements, the increased political legitimacy of faith-based social movements, the significant impact of religion on individual voting behavior independent of other social factors (e.g., ethnicity, social class), and in shaping public policy debates. In many western countries, religiously derived values frame the prioritization of activism on particular issues (e.g., abortion, gay rights, stem cell research) and how they are debated in the public sphere. In some countries, debate centers on the extent to which religious heritage should be formally acknowledged (e.g., the recent European Union debate about its new constitution) and given visibility in institutional settings (e.g., the debate in France about the wearing of Islamic veils and other religious icons in schools).

Much research engages diverse theoretical questions in sociology to address the complexity of religious identity and particular attention has been given to investigating the multifaceted role played by religion in mediating the assimilation patterns of transnational immigrants (Ebaugh & Chafetz 2000). Relatedly, a lot of current research focuses on congregations (local churches/parishes) and the varying impact of this core social unit in building social networks, mediating political activism, and enriching the everyday lives of members (e.g., Ammerman 2005; Chaves 2004). There is also a rapidly expanding body of research documenting the relations between religious behavior and various aspects of social and psychosocial functioning, including social support and physical and mental health (e.g., Ellison & Levin 1998). This research tends to show that there is an overall positive relation between religion and health and social functioning, though the precise mechanisms involved and their life course patterns are still relatively underdeveloped areas of inquiry.

One of the newer areas of study is the attempt to understand the nature of deinstitutionalized religious practices, customarily referred to as spiritual seeking (e.g., Roof 1999; Wuthnow 1998). While there is concern among some sociologists that spiritual seeking may undercut individuals' commitment to others (long a staple of church involvement), longitudinal studies spanning life course and cultural changes suggest that traditional religious participation and newer spiritual practices provide individuals with different but equally positive ways of carving socially engaged lives (Dillon & Wink 2006).

The overarching methodological challenge in studying religion involves the ongoing monitoring of the validity of existing measures of religious behavior across all levels of analysis (individual, institutional, and societal). In view of the dynamic interplay between religion and society, and the way that changing sociohistorical and cultural contexts impact how religion is construed and practiced, it is important to have conceptually and empirically sound measures that can apprehend the presence and significance of the full range and multidimensionality of public and private religious activity that may characterize a given context. This approach should be sufficiently sociological so that it enables attention to the substantive content of religious-spiritual belief, as well as to the mechanisms of how different aspects of religion impact social outcomes (e.g., voting, health, concern for others, violence), while also being sensitive to the comparative geographical and historical breadth necessary to evaluating secularization/religious vitality theses.

At the same time, however, the theoretical challenge is to move beyond the lens clamped on scholarly inquiry by the intellectual legacy of the secularization frame. In this regard it would be fruitful if systematic meta-theoretical analyses could result in theoretical generalizations that would point to the micro-macro social conditions and contexts in which different types of religious behavior and social outcomes could be identified. More broadly, contemporary sociological theorists (with the exception of Pierre Bourdieu) give little attention to the continuing significance or complexity of religion. Consequently, a challenge for sociologists of religion is to show persuasively that an understanding of a society's religious practices must necessarily be part of any theory that seeks to have relevant explanatory power in today's global, multicultural, risk society.

SEE ALSO: Culture; Denomination; Durkheim, Émile; Identity: The Management of Meaning; Identity: Social Psychological Aspects; Knowledge, Sociology of; Modernization; Religion; Ritual; Secularization; Social Movements; Structural Functional Theory; Weber, Max

REFERENCES AND SUGGESTED READINGS

Ammerman, N. (2005) *Pillars of Faith: American Congregations and their Partners.* University of California Press, Berkeley.

Bellah, R. (1967) Civil Religion in America. *Daedalus* 96: 1–21.

Berger, P. (1967) *The Sacred Canopy.* Anchor Books, Garden City, NY.

Chaves, M. (2004) *Congregations in America.* Harvard University Press, Cambridge, MA.

Cipriani, R. (2000) *Sociology of Religion: An Historical Introduction.* Aldine de Gruyter, New York.

Davie, G. (2000) *Religion in Modern Europe.* Oxford University Press, Oxford.

Davie, G. (2003) In: Dillon, M. (Ed.), *Handbook of the Sociology of Religion.* Cambridge University Press, New York, pp. 61–75.

Dillon, M. (Ed.) (2003) *Handbook of the Sociology of Religion.* Cambridge University Press, New York.

Dillon, M. & Wink, P. (2006) *Lived Religion Through Sixty Years of Life Course and Cultural Change.* Forthcoming.

Durkheim, É. (1976 [1912]) *The Elementary Forms of the Religious Life.* Oxford University Press, Oxford.

Ebaugh, H. R. & Chafetz, J. (2000) *Religion and the New Immigrants.* AltaMira Press, Walnut Creek, CA.

Ellison, C. & Levin, R. (1998) The Religion–Health Connection. *Health Education and Behavior* 25: 700–20.

Finke, R. & Stark, R. (2005) *The Churching of America.* Rutgers University Press, New Brunswick, NJ.

Gorski, P. (2003) *Historicizing the Secularization Debate.* In: Dillon, M. (Ed.) *Handbook of the Sociology of Religion.* Cambridge University Press, New York.

Greeley, A. (1972) *Unsecular Man.* Schocken Books, London.

Greeley, A. & Hout, M. (1999) Americans' Increasing Belief in Life After Death. *American Sociological Review* 64: 813–35.

Herberg, W. (1955) *Protestant–Catholic–Jew.* Doubleday, Garden City, NY.

Hout, M. & Fischer, C. (2002) Why More Americans Have No Religious Preference: Politics and Generations. *American Sociological Review* 67: 165–90.

Luckmann, T. (1967) *The Invisible Religion.* Macmillan, New York.

Martin, D. (1978) *A General Theory of Secularization.* Blackwell, Oxford.

Roof, W. C. (1999) *Spiritual Marketplace: Baby Boomers and the Remaking of American Religion.* Princeton University Press, Princeton.

Tschannen, O. (1991) The Secularization Paradigm: A Systematization. *Journal for the Scientific Study of Religion* 30: 395–415.

Warner, R. S. (1993) Work in Progress Toward a New Paradigm for the Sociological Study of Religion. *American Journal of Sociology* 98: 1044–93.

Weber, M. (1958 [1904–5]) *The Protestant Ethic and the Spirit of Capitalism.* Scribners, New York.

Wuthnow, R. (1998) *After Heaven.* University of California Press, Berkeley.

religions, African

Bernardo Bernardi

African religions are based on oral cultures. They represent the old tradition surviving within a context deeply influenced by monotheistic religions, mainly Christianity and Islam, not only through their various denominations but also by supporting the attack of modern secularism.

To propose a definition of religion with reference to the oral African cultures is no easy matter. Within those cultures, religion does not exist as a distinct domain. Indeed, it is part and parcel of normal culture, i.e., the mode of life implying both the ideological perception of the world and a practical kind of social organization. In such situations, religion possesses a denomination of its own, but it may be only conceived as that particular aspect of any culture including beliefs and rituals. In such a perspective, it would be possible to describe religion as that part of culture, or of social life, connected with beliefs and rituals.

Field research, in direct contact with the people, is the only method that can afford the possibility of obtaining reliable information on the theoretical ideas and the actual practices of the local people. As is known, such a method implies a fluent knowledge of the local languages and dialects so as allow for an intense observation of people's behavior and personal participation in their mode of life. Cosmological ideas are fundamental, but in order to acquire a proper knowledge of their content, patience and time are required so as to gain the confidence and trust of local people. Every informant is to be trusted, but in order to gain an acceptable degree of reliability, several other informants are to be approached in order to compare the information received. Field research is considered to be the initiation into the anthropological profession. In other words, it demands a previous theoretical apprenticeship and subsequent practical experience in the field. Such a method is required for every aspect of human culture, but when religion is the matter of research a deeper attention is certainly required, since it involves not merely external ritual practices but intimate and personal involvement as well.

The idea of a divinity, i.e., of some being above nature upon whom life and death are thought to depend, constitutes a common element of religious belief. However, there is no homogeneity in this kind of belief. Normally it is conceived in terms of each mode of livelihood. In order to describe the variety of such a concept, the term *theism* will be used in its ethnological sense. According to this view, it is possible to distinguish a sylvester theism, a pastoral theism, and an agrarian theism.

Sylvester theism. This may be better explained by reference to the Bambuti Pygmies of the Ituri forest, who have been studied by Paul Schbesta and Colin Turnbull. The forest is also symbolically conceived by the Bambuti in its global entirety as their protector. If anything goes wrong, if a child is sick or game is scarce, or whether any other malaise occurs, it is a sign that the forest has been offended and is displeased, and therefore the forest must be placated. The *molimo* ritual is then performed in the silence of night, by playing a bamboo flute, normally kept in running water.

Pastoral theism. Shepherds are nomads who, following their herds, take an interest in observing the sky. Not only do they consider the sky as the abode of God, but they identify it with God himself; they even do so with regard to certain atmospheric phenomena. Thus, for the Oromo of Southern Ethiopia, *waq*, the sky, is also *Waq*, God. For the Masai of Kenya and Tanzania, *en kai*, the rain, is also God, *En Kai.* For them, clouds are regarded as a manifestation of God. Thus, black clouds, heavy with rain, a blessing for the pastures, are a symbol of God's bounty; white clouds, which do not produce rain, are regarded as a sign of God's anger; thunder and lightning are interpreted as a sign of some of God's displeasure.

Pastoral people practice collective kinds of rituals. They gather together, when they need to pray, asking for God's blessing for their children and their cattle as well as for their pastures. The headman or the oldest elder takes the lead. Whilst everyone else in the congregation takes a crouching position, the headman stands up and he leads the prayers, to which the entire assembly responds in one voice, in a mystic atmosphere, *En Kai ai*, my God.

Agrarian theism. Agriculture is the main trait of the Bantu peoples. The Bantu are primarily distinguished as a linguistic family; while they are organized in a variety of social and political systems, they all practice agriculture as their form of livelihood. From the religious point of view, their idea of God is strongly related to creation.

However, it is commonly believed that, after completing creation, God somehow retired, ceasing to take an interest in creatures. As a consequence, he has been defined as a *Deus otiosus*. God's names are normally connected to the idea of creation: *Mungu*, *Mulungu*, *Mumbi*, *Nzambi*, and so forth. Théophile Obenga, a Congolese scholar, has defined Mulungu as an Engineer God.

The idea of *Deus otiosus* is related to the preponderant cult of the ancestors. Ancestors are normally defined as *the living dead*, because they take an interest in their descendants. Every kind of malaise is attributed to their influence, and therefore ancestors are most frequently prayed to. But the main reason that may offend the ancestor is anger or even hatred among relatives and their descendants. How may the latter expect the ancestors' protection if the latter are offended by their behavior? Casting out anger is a necessary presupposition before invoking the ancestors' aid. Notwithstanding the extension of the ancestors' cult, too much emphasis, perhaps, has been given to the idea of God's otioseness. There are times, in fact, especially during severe social crises, when the ancestors are prayed to join with their descendants in prayers to God, for the situation is such that only God's help will be effective.

In the face of mounting secularism, the question "why religion?" is to the point. The first answer that comes to mind recalls the fact that every religion is essentially therapeutic. Peace of mind is the deepest effect of proper religious practice. But the curing of the body may also be important. If properly conceived and properly practiced, religion may produce an equilibrium of forces, or in case of disease it may give support and even acceptance of a state of suffering. Finally, religion may be a source of inspiration for every aspect of human life. Personal education may be inspired by religion, public life might be sustained by religious inspiration. It is true that, in the past, religious wars for centuries stressed different states' relations. Even today the effects of religious fundamentalism, a phenomenon entirely opposed to religious ideals, are felt.

SEE ALSO: Belief; Civil Religion; Globalization, Religion and; Religion; Religion, Sociology of; Rite/Ritual; Ritual; Secularization

REFERENCES AND SUGGESTED READINGS

Clarke, P. B. & Byrne, P. A. (1993) *Religion Defined and Explained*. Macmillan, Basingstoke.
Douglas, M. (1966) *Purity and Danger*. Routledge & Kegan Paul, London.
Durkheim, É. (1915) *The Elementary Forms of the Religious Life*. George Allen & Unwin, London.
Evans-Pritchard, E. E. (1965) *Theories of Primitive Religion*. Clarendon Press, Oxford.
Weber, M. (1965) *The Sociology of Religion*. Methuen, London.

religious cults

Giuseppe Giordan

The cult is intended to be the concrete form through which man expresses his veneration for a superhuman entity or force whom he believes superior and deems worthy of honor and devotion. With this term, one usually makes a reference to the relationship of dependence and adoration between man and the divine, be it a personal entity, a force of nature, or an ancestor's spirit. The cult therefore is placed in the center of every religion and carries across the ritual behaviors, which are usually presided over by a special individual believed to be particularly competent for the job: he can be a priest, a wizard, a shaman, or even a member of the group who is believed to be in possession of special gifts.

It is interesting to note, especially for the consequences within the fields of the social sciences in general and of sociology in particular, that the term *cult* shares the same Latin root as the term *culture*: the recognition of man's dependence upon the divine, which he expresses in acts of adoration, supplication, and thanksgiving, forms, develops, and is an expression of different social and cultural contexts. It is precisely the different cultures that create and give meaning to the various ways of structuring the time and space of the cult, hence establishing which cult actions are most appropriate, which times are most opportune to celebrate the feasts, and which significant places to erect temples. The expression of the cult therefore depends upon the conception of man and the deity typical of each social and cultural system; the mutual dependence and penetration of a cult and culture not only allows for mutation of the cult in correspondence of the different historical moments, but also highlights how the expressive forms of a given culture, both at a semantic and symbolic level, give the essential frame of reference to elaborate the cult's actions. In this way a circular process is created, on one hand linking the cult to the expressive forms of a concrete social and cultural context, and on the other underlining how the different forms of a cult influence the development of the social and political life of society.

The semantic passage from religious cult to religious cults testifies to just such a deep bond between religion and the evolution of a social and cultural context in which it is inserted. The expression religious cults tries to describe certain aspects of contemporary beliefs, characterized by the relative loss of influence of traditional religious institutions, which according to Michel (1994) lose the monopoly of meaning, and by the progressive liberty of the subject in building his own itineraries of meaning in a syncretic manner, according to the logic of the *bricolage*.

THE CULT IN THE SOCIAL SCIENCES

The notion of cult has always been at the center of scientific studies of religion, both in an anthropologic and ethnographic setting, as even within sociology its use has often been the source of disputes, especially regarding its relationship, and at times its opposition, to the concept of rites. For some exponents of the historical cultural school, such as Robert Will and Sigmund Olaf Plytt Mowinckel, the cult represents the clearest manifestation of the religious experience, and as opposed to the magical experience that results in rites: if religion manifests man's acceptance of a radical dependence on the divine, magic is man's attempt to control and dominate superhuman forces. Gerardus Van der Leeuw, from a phenomenological point of view, goes beyond the opposition cult-religion and rite-magic, introducing an equilibrium, represented by the cult, between the human dimension and that of the divine. With Adolf Jensen the superimposition and the identification of the two terms can be seen: the cult and the rite coincide in ritual actions, which are defined as the renovation of a myth of foundation through the experience of being taken by the primordial strength that gives the basis of existence to human culture.

For Durkheim (1965), the cult represented the traditions and the social conditions of a community: the subject of the cult is always the community, and therefore not the individual who finds in the cult the concrete manifestation of his aspirations and religious intentions. Durkheim defines the cult as a system of rites, and differentiates it from the latter because, on top of being a collective experience, it is systematic and stable, while the rite can be individualistic and sporadic, not bound to periodic events of life, such as birth, marriage, or death. According to Durkheim, the peculiarity of religious phenomena resides, other than in their explicit or implicit obligatory aspect, in relation to particular representations that make reference to the sacred, which are nothing more than an allegory of society itself: it is the social world that reproduces the actual symbols, imposing them upon the individual conscience through actions of the cult, which unify the strength of religious beliefs, especially reviving social structures, strengthening the social bond between its members.

The notion of the cult, in anthropology as much as in ethnology and sociology, is strictly connected to the concept of symbol and of belief. According to the intellectualism of E. B. Tylor, magical and religious beliefs are theories which, introducing explanations based on supernatural elements, overcome the limits of empirical explanations offered by observation and common sense. From this perspective, religious beliefs are the intellectual activities that do not differ from man's other intellectual activities within the sciences; if there is a difference, this consists not in the content, but in the attitude towards the theories: while the scientist is open to criticism in the matters of scientific theories, since he is conscious of the possibility of alternative theories, the religious person is instead closed to every type of criticism, because every questioning of the established beliefs is perceived as an error, as a risk of chaos and of sin. The cult is therefore reduced, according to an intellectualistic approach, to a simple instrumental activity without proper value.

In Durkheim's symbolistic approach, religious belief and the cult are not simply theoretic constructions of natural and abstract reason that remain the same through time, then becoming modified only from the quantity and quality of data made available to it: for this school of thought, the general idea and the religious idea in particular are social facts that have social motivations, and therefore are historically determined. Therefore, religious beliefs and the actions of the cult receive their strength and legitimation from their social function: they are constructed by society itself because they are socially shared. Religious beliefs are ultimately a symbol of society, and the power of such symbolic acts that become tangible in the cult is the strength of the society itself, which shares and imposes them on successive generations.

Weber's (1963) contribution goes beyond Durkheim's symbolistic approach, too rigidly sociocentric, to give space, together with social meaning of religious beliefs and of the cult, even for individual interpretation of the subject, who for its own nature is hard to codify and cannot be reduced in an exclusive way to the logic of a functioning society. According to Weber, religious phenomena even have origins in the attempt, on the part of man, to give meaning to life's tragic events, such as illness, pain, and death. Therefore, the cult and its creed also have the function of controlling and rendering bearable the anxiety that arises in suffering and unexplainable occurrences.

The two attitudes, of Durkeim and Weber, far from being contradictory, show two useful perspectives on interpreting religious beliefs and the cult: these are the fruit of a dynamic that reciprocally integrates both collective and individual meanings. Religion therefore cannot be reduced to an exclusively obligatory and coercive dimension. According to Valeri (1996), it is above all a system of communication, a place where individual interpretations and social structure meet, and it is exactly this communicative role of religion that finds substance mainly in the practices of the cult. The cult can also be thought of in terms of communication between men, the social structure, and the sacred entity. Only within the cult can the relationship between men and the gods become a true relationship, restrained by rules and by most juridical norms, resulting in transformations that are verifiable either on the material or spiritual level. In order to exist the gods need man's continual participation in the cult, so much so that without the cult the gods become insignificant and die. On the other hand, if they are the objects of the cult, the gods are capable of rewarding those who worship them with devotion. Prayer, sacrifice, divination, possession – all make up a complex circulation of messages that constitute a complex communicative structure, which, in the specific space of Jewish and Christian traditions, is the liturgy.

ELEMENTS OF THE CULT

The history of religions, and in particular ethnology and phenomenology, have revealed the multiple forms of the cult where the diverse religious experiences become tangible, highlighting both specific characteristics and common aspects. The religious man, to whichever culture he may belong, chooses precise places and times to enter in relationship with the divine world as well as people and objects that seem particularly suitable for expressing his religiousness with; he separates them from the daily aspects and from the profanity of life to give them a symbolic value, which is fully expressed in cult and ritual forms.

Both time and space, meaning the feasts and the temples, as well as the people who preside over the cult, become symbolically transfigured once they enter into the religious sphere: such change depends on the fundamental distinction between the sacred and the profane. Durkheim and the French sociology school are credited with the definition of religion based on the division/opposition between the sacred and the profane. Such a dichotomy goes beyond to prove the characteristic absoluteness of the sacred and its complete independence from other types of phenomena, thus reintroducing the distinction between the individual and society. The sacred is in fact a collective representation that classifies and orders the material world not based on natural elements, but on social and cultural conventions. Starting exactly from this dichotomy leads to understanding the various aspects that constitute the cult: temples, feasts, prayers, ministers of the cult, and the rites.

The temple is a privileged place, even if it is not exclusive, where the divine manifests itself; it is a sacred space, separated from profane space, where the cult celebrates. These special areas or religious structures are separate from ordinary space with barriers which can be physical, ritual, or psychological. Sacred enclosures – synagogues, mosques, churches, temples – manifest a discontinuation of space. The same distinction between the sacred and the profane structures time as well, creating the feasts. The religious interpretation of time that is expressed in cultural forms moreover determines the direction and attitude of the believers regarding the meaning of existence. Time can be conceived in a linear way, as a succession of equal instants, or it can be conceived as a progression. Some religions believe time to be circular and therefore static, while other religions perceive it as a degenerative process. The emphasis in the distinction between relativity of historical time and absoluteness of eternal time also differentiates the religious concept of time from the nonreligious one. The social distinction between sacred and profane defines the role and functions of the people who can get in contact with the sacred universe. Ministers, according to Weber's indications, are only one of the sacred figures that are appointed for a magical-sacred function; specialists legitimized to perform the acts of cult and with a mediating role between gods and men. The role of ministers, however, is not enclosed inside the religious sphere but, as Douglas (1986) observed, also has a noteworthy relevance in the public scene, since it operates as guarantor of stability in social institutions.

FROM CULT TO CULTS

In recent years it is possible to record a shift from the term cult to cults. Such grammatical passage from singular to plural is the sign of how, in the last few decades, the religious dimension is changing deeply and, at times, in a contradictory manner. On one hand, the secularization process, which many thought to be inevitable and irreversible, was supposed to bring forth a progressive irrelevance of religion. On the other hand, the dynamicity of certain religious movements calls for a return of the sacred, although in a very different way if compared with traditional society. The various characteristics of traditional cult, as synthetically described in the previous paragraphs, are creatively reinterpreted and often liberally reinvented.

Weber's renowned thesis, which speaks of society's disenchantment followed by its reenchantment with religion, is utilized by various authors, such as Peter L. Berger and Niklas Luhmann. For them, religion in contemporary society, far from disappearing, has instead taken on new roles and is fulfilling new functions. It is an evolution which leads the faithful not to refer exclusively to traditional religions, to their coded and immutable heritage of beliefs and symbols, but to undertake a quest founded on the individual's freedom of choice. This transition is defined by Thomas Luckmann in terms of moving from religion to religiousness, while other authors such as Wuthnow (1998), Roof (1999), and Flory and Miller (2000) prefer to use the dichotomy of religion–spirituality. Such a transition of legitimation of religious beliefs from the institution to the individual brings with it changes even on an organizational level. Traditional churches are overcome by small groups, whose variety mirrors the extreme diversity which characterizes religious phenomena in the contemporary era, putting together apocalyptic tensions with mysticism and spiritualism, or occultism with theosophy and new age.

As Terrin (2001) has observed, starting from World War II, and with a particular acceleration at the beginning of the 1960s, there is a progressive process of religious destructuralization, which led the great traditional religions to lessen their hold over the symbolic boundaries of their belief systems and in the end to the birth of new religions. Such increased circulation of religious symbols, outside their traditional contexts, created a market – a very differentiated market of requests and offers of religious goods. In this context, on the one hand, new figures of religious entrepreneurs arise, such as founders of new cults, spiritual gurus, charismatic leaders, and television evangelists. On the other hand, a new kind of follower was born, who, freed from the control of traditional institutions, constructs his own system of belief, according to the syncretistic logic of *bricolage*.

The new forms of religiousness that have developed in the western world in the last few decades, among which even new cults are found, give evidence of a deep coherence with the typical features of postmodernity. Individualism and pragmatism become the backbone, which guides the way one believes and belongs to a group. This brings forth a great variety in the kinds of adhesion, a personalization of beliefs which are chosen according to their efficacy, an acceptance of belonging to several groups which answer to the need of authenticity, and to the predominance of experience above the objective truth that one is obliged to believe. Immediate needs, arising from perceptions of one's emotions, together with a pluralist and tolerant vision of beliefs, are the testing field for today's various religious options, be they traditional or modern.

The term cults, which usually has a marked negative connotation, is utilized in sociology to designate some of the new religious movements, which embody the characteristics described above. For Robert Wallis, cults are distinguished from other religious organizations by their epistemological orientation and by their more or less difficult relationship with the social contexts in which they are found. While traditional churches and sects ascribe to themselves the exclusive truth of their beliefs, cults are characterized by an epistemological individualism, which is perfectly in tune with the tolerant pluralism of postmodernity. Hence, followers can exercise freedom of conscience in adhering to (or not) the moral and doctrinal contents, and they consider such freedom as legitimate even for the followers of other religious movements. Both cults and sects find themselves in a controversial tension with society, but while sects demand an exclusive faithfulness and exercise a certain amount of control over their members, cults do not request such exclusiveness, and their tension with their surroundings can be seen mainly as alternative therapeutic practices.

Even Stark and Bainbridge (1985) have distinguished between sects and cults on the basis of the fact that the social organization of the latter is very weak and in some cases completely absent. Further, while sects are born from opposition to, and a break with, the traditional church, cults do not have origins in this contraposition. And, from the beginning, cults are independent of any reference or bond with the ecclesiastic world. This total freedom and independence from any reference to the traditional religious organization even raised doubts about whether cults could be considered proper religious communities. Stark and Bainbridge describe some cults that never organized according to any model of a formal group. One such example is the "audience cult," whose members are connected to each other and with the spiritual guide through the media alone.

Reference to the concept of religious cults within the sociology of religion, however, has not yet found a consensus which would allow an appropriate and agreed upon use. It describes phenomena ranging from forms of paganism to druidism, from Wicca to a variety of movements which put together psychosomatic therapeutic practices with techniques that enhance personal potential. As Pace (2001) has noted, all these movements of renewal and religious revival, sometimes labeled as cults and at other times as new religious movements, strongly solicit the traditional institutions of beliefs, which no longer seem to be able to control the continuity and coherence of their belief systems. It will be the task of the social sciences to find the conceptual instruments able to describe both theoretically and empirically the new situation of contemporary beliefs and, therefore, to offer a more refined and precise definition of the concept of religious cults.

SEE ALSO: Charismatic Movement; Consumption, Religion and; Cults: Social Psychological Aspects; Emotions and Social Movements; Fundamentalism; New Age; New Religious Movements; Popular Religiosity; Primitive Religion; Religion; Rite/Ritual; Ritual; Sacred; Sacrifice; Science and Religion; Symbolic Interaction; Televangelism

REFERENCES AND SUGGESTED READINGS

Barker, E. (1989) *New Religious Movements: A Practical Introduction.* HMSO, London.

Brown, P. (1981) *The Cult of the Saints.* University of Chicago Press, Chicago.

Cipriani, R. (1977) Per una definizione dell'ambito della sociologia della religione: da Durkheim a Yinger. *Sociologia* 11(2–3): 141–50.

Douglas, M. (1986) *How Institutions Think.* Syracuse University Press, New York.

Durkheim, É. (1965) *The Elementary Forms of the Religious Life.* Free Press, New York.

Flory, R. W. & Miller, D. E. (Eds.) (2000) *GenX Religion.* Routledge, New York.

Introvigne, M. (1989) *Le nuove religioni.* Sugar Co, Milan.

Michel, P. (1994) *Politique et religion. La grande mutation.* Albin Michel, Paris.

Pace, E. (2001) Rinnovamenti-Revivalismi. In: Lenoir, F. & Tardan-Masquelier, Y. (Eds.), *La religione*, Vol. 6. UTET, Turin, pp. 445–60.

Robbins, T. (1988) *Cults, Converts and Charisma: The Sociology of New Religious Movements.* Sage, London.

Roof, W. C. (1999) *Spiritual Marketplace: Baby Boomers and the Remaking of American Religion.* Princeton University Press, Princeton.

Stark, R. & Bainbridge, W. S. (1985) *The Future of Religion: Secularization, Revival, and Cult Formation.* University of California Press, Berkeley.

Terrin, A. N. (2001) *Antropologia e orizzonti del sacro. Culture e religioni.* Cittadella, Assisi.

Valeri, V. (1996) Credenze e culti. In: *Enciclopedia delle Scienze Sociali*, Vol. 2. Istituto della Enciclopedia Italiana, Rome, pp. 565–75.

Weber, M. (1963) *The Sociology of Religion.* Beacon Press, Boston.

Weber, M. (1968) *Economy and Society: An Outline of Interpretative Sociology.* Bedminster Press, New York.

Wilson, B. R. (1990) *The Social Dimensions of Sectarianism: Sects and New Religious Movements in Contemporary Society.* Oxford University Press, Oxford.
Wuthnow, R. (1998) *After Heaven: Spirituality in America since the 1950s.* University of California Press, Berkeley.

reparations

Rutledge M. Dennis

Reparations refer to the actions of an aggrieved nation, group, or individual to seek redresses and compensations for the loss of land, money, works of art, jewelry, or other valuable objects, due to the actions of a country, group, or another individual. The claim of those seeking redresses or reparations is that their property was knowingly and willfully stolen and they now seek a just payment for their loss. In the United States the major demands for reparations have been made by Native Americans that they be compensated for the loss of land given them by treaties, but subsequently taken by whites. As a result of the many broken treaties, there are now dozens of claims against the federal government by Native Americans relating to many square miles of land now a part of the urban corridor in the Northeast and New England.

In modern Europe, the first major reparation demand occurred after the defeat of Germany in World War I. As punishment for initiating the war, Germany was forced to compensate the countries devastated by German militarism. This was reparation, which many believe, in its harshness, resulted in Germany's economic collapse, which contributed, partially or totally, to the rise of Hitler and Nazism. During the early stages of World War II, before he entered the "final solution" phase, Hitler launched a national program to deny Jews employment in major institutions and organizations, and seized their land, artworks, jewelry, money and bank accounts, stocks, and other tangible properties. Many of these items and properties were placed in vaults, presented to museums and art galleries, and tagged as possessions of the German government. In some cases the items were sold to other individuals, kept as family heirlooms, smuggled out of Germany, and sold to museums and art galleries abroad. As the Holocaust became a major Jewish cultural reference point beginning in the 1970s, lawyers were hired to reclaim stolen property, and claims were made against governments and state institutions which sanctioned the theft by knowingly possessing property known to belong to those victimized by the Nazis. The German government has paid billions of dollars in reparations both to German Jews whose lands were confiscated and to the Israeli government.

World War II also precipitated reparation claims by many Japanese Americans against the American government for the confiscation of property after many were placed in internment camps in Oregon, Montana, Washington, and Oklahoma. Though many Japanese Americans were opposed to suing the government for fear of resurrecting latent anti-Japanese feelings among the American population, a small group decided to pursue the claims, and in 1983 a nine-member Commission on Wartime Relocation and Internment awarded the claimants $1.5 billion, of which $20,000 would be given to each internment survivor.

A more contemporary, and even more controversial, reparation issue centers on the desire of a few black American organizations to seek reparation from the United States government for the enslavement of the black population from the early founding of the nation until its demise with the defeat of the South during the American Civil War. Unlike the Native American claim of land stolen or the Jewish claim of reparations for stolen houses, land, artwork, bank accounts, money, and so on, at the heart of the slavery reparation claim is the demand for just compensation for the free labor that contributed greatly to the birth of America's surging worldwide economic power throughout the eighteenth and nineteenth centuries. Moreover, the reality of having been kept in bondage for generations, and later having been "freed" without land or money, placed the black American population in a greatly disadvantaged position vis-à-vis other individuals and groups in the society. The thrust of the slavery reparations claims does not focus only on claims against the American government. There are also claims against banks, insurance companies, stock companies, and other private corporations which profited from the slave trade.

Given the fact that the overwhelming proportion of black Americans can trace their ancestry from slavery, it would not be difficult to make the claim for such a connection. Any serious discussion of the issue must confront the moral question of the relative difference between the theft of land and other tangible property against the theft of one's body and person. There is a point at which property and bodily theft coincide with both Native Americans and Jews: for the former, the theft of land and the forceful imprisonment of Indian "bodies" on federally sanctioned reservations; for Jews, it was both in the theft of tangible property and ghettoization and later imprisonment in concentration camps.

Lacking property as slaves, black Americans had only their imprisoned bodies as objects of commodity in the exchange-reparation formula. But the claim cannot be ignored which views the human body as an object in itself, in a way an object more important than land and other tangible properties. Hence, if the body is required to perform free labor, there should be ways of arriving at monetary solutions, for free labor resulted in the production of cotton, rice, tobacco, and other products that were crucial to the economy of the South and the entire nation. Like many Japanese Americans who opposed the Japanese American claim against the US government for compensation for their internment, many black Americans are divided on the issue of reparation. Many, associating it with compensation given European Jews and Native Americans, believe the demand for reparation is just. Others view it as a non-issue, a futile effort in light of the overwhelming opposition of white Americans to any idea of reparation. In fact, many white Americans view the idea of reparation as closely linked to the idea of affirmative action, which they oppose.

SEE ALSO: Affirmative Action; Ethnic Groups; Ghetto; Holocaust; Marginality; Slavery

REFERENCES AND SUGGESTED READINGS

Aguirre, A., Jr. & Turner, J. (2001) *American Ethnicity*. McGraw-Hill, Boston.

Cruse, H. (1987) *Plural But Equal*. William Morrow, New York.

Hilberg, R. (1967) *The Destruction of European Jews*. Quadrangle Books, Chicago.

Johnson, P. (1983) *Modern Times: The World from the Twenties to the Eighties*. Harper & Row, New York.

Kessler, L. (1993) *Stubborn Twig*. Random House, New York.

Kuper, L. (1981) *Genocide*. Yale University Press, New Haven.

McKissick, F. (1969) *Three-Fifths of a Man*. Macmillan, London.

Schuchter, A. (1970) *Reparations*. J. B. Lippincott, Philadelphia.

replicability analyses

Bruce Thompson

Researchers have traditionally but erroneously presumed that statistical significance tests evaluate the replicability of results (Thompson 1996, 2006). But p values evaluate the probability of the sample, assuming the null hypothesis perfectly describes the population, and *not* the probability of the population. Therefore, p values do not bear upon questions of replicability. As Cohen (1994) noted, the statistical significance test "does not tell us what we want to know, and we so much want to know what we want to know that, out of desperation, we nevertheless believe that it does!"

Because isolating relationships that replicate under stated conditions is the ultimate objective of social science research, methods that *do* evaluate result replicability become fundamentally important. Thompson (1996) suggested that result replicability evaluation methods can be grouped into two classes: "external" and "internal" methods. *External* replicability analyses involve true replication via data collection with an independent sample. External replication is the ultimate, best method for evaluating result replicability. However, researchers may not have the luxury of external replication of every study they conduct. *Internal* replicability evaluation methods attempt to approximate real replication studies in various ways. "Internal" evidence for replicability is never as good as an actual replication, but certainly is better than incorrectly presuming that statistical significance evaluates result replicability. Three internal replicability analyses have been identified: cross-validation, the jackknife, and the bootstrap (Thompson 1994). These combine the study participants in hand in different ways to determine whether results are stable across sample variations. Thus, the methods address the extent to which the idiosyncracies of individuals impact results. Individual differences are what make generalization in social science so much more challenging than generalization in the physical sciences, where personality does not impact results.

Cross-validation involves randomly splitting the sample into two groups, and then separately repeating the analyses (e.g., regression, analysis of variance) in both groups. If the resulting weights (e.g., regression beta weights) and effect sizes (e.g., R^2) are both identical, the results replicate perfectly. However, if the weights are not identical, replicability must then be empirically investigated by applying the group A weights to the group B data, and the group B weights to the group A data, and quantifying the shrinkage in estimated effect sizes. Thompson (1989, 2006) provides a primer on these methods. Cross-validation methods are applicable for all parametric methods, because all these methods (e.g., analysis of variance, analysis of covariance, regression, descriptive discriminant analysis) are correlational (Thompson 2000). However, it must be emphasized that the sampling splitting is the basis for evaluating replicability, and *not* the basis for result interpretation. The analysis for the total sample is most stable and therefore is always the focus of interpretation.

Jackknife methods require that the analysis is conducted using all participants. And the analysis is then repeated when k participants at a time (usually $k = 1$) are omitted from the analysis. Then some additional computations are performed to test for result stability. The jackknife is particularly useful for identifying outliers.

Bootstrap methods create repeated resamples (usually several thousand) in each of which the analysis is repeated. In each resample, exactly n participants are randomly drawn *with replacement* from the original sample, where n is the sample size in the original sample. Thus, participant Kelly's data might all be drawn three times in the first resample, not at all in resample two, and once in resample number three. Then parameter estimates (e.g., R^2, beta weights, factor pattern coefficients) are averaged. The standard deviation of the estimates of a given parameter is an empirically estimated standard error for a given parameter. Replicability is suggested when these standard errors are small.

Diaconis and Efron (1983) provide a very readable, non-technical explanation of the bootstrap. The bootstrap can be applied with both univariate and multivariate analyses. However, when multivariate bootstrap analyses are conducted, solutions in each resample must be rotated to best fit position with a target solution, so that resamples results can be compared apples-to-apples (Thompson 1988).

The three internal replicability analyses have different advantages and disadvantages. Only cross-validation can be implemented without specialized software. Cross-validation is conceptually simple, but different and even contradictory replicability results may emerge for the same data because numerous different random splits are possible for a given data set.

Both the jackknife and the bootstrap are computer-intensive methods. Because both are complex and require specialized software, many researchers conducting these analyses will select the bootstrap because it is elegant and combines the participants in so many different ways to evaluate replicability. Software is widely available for implementing the bootstrap on modern personal computers in a matter of minutes.

SEE ALSO: Effect Sizes; General Linear Model; Methods, Bootstrap; Statistical Significance Testing

REFERENCES AND SUGGESTED READINGS

Cohen, J. (1994). The Earth is Round ($p < .05$). *American Psychologist* 49: 997–1003.

Diaconis, P. & Efron, B. (1983) Computer-Intensive Methods in Statistics. *Scientific American* 248(5): 116–30.

Thompson, B. (1988) Program FACSTRAP: A Program that Computes Bootstrap Estimates of Factor Structure. *Educational and Psychological Measurement* 48: 681–6.

Thompson, B. (1989) Statistical Significance, Result Importance, and Result Generalizability: Three Noteworthy But Somewhat Different Issues. *Measurement and Evaluation in Counseling and Development* 22: 2–5.

Thompson, B. (1994) The Pivotal Role of Replication in Psychological Research: Empirically Evaluating the Replicability of Sample Results. *Journal of Personality* 62: 157–76.

Thompson, B. (1996) AERA Editorial Policies Regarding Statistical Significance Testing: Three Suggested Reforms. *Educational Researcher* 25(2): 26–30.

Thompson, B. (2000) Canonical Correlation Analysis. In: Grimm, L. & Yarnold, P. (Eds.), *Reading and Understanding More Multivariate Statistics*. American Psychological Association, Washington, DC, pp. 285–316.

Thompson, B. (2006) *Foundations of Behavioral Statistics: An Insight-Based Approach*. Guilford Press, New York.

representation

Rex Butler

Although popularly associated with postmodernism, the idea that the world is a representation goes back to the origins of western thought. In Plato's allegory of the cave, it is said that we cannot see the truth but only a reflection of it. In Descartes's hypothesis of the Evil Demon, it is argued that all we know is merely an illusion produced by another, alien intelligence. And after Descartes there are a variety of philosophical Idealisms, in which it is claimed that the world comes about only as an effect of our will or that the world exists only insofar as it is perceived. In postmodernism, however, these essentially metaphysical speculations are seen to be socially embodied through such mass media as the movies, television, advertising, and the Internet. Thus, a film like the Wachowski Brothers' *The Matrix* is understood at once as a revival of the old Platonic fantasy and a powerful metaphor for our contemporary society of the spectacle. Indeed, in the now-celebrated catchphrase of the film, uttered by the leader of the resistance, Morpheus, to the newcomer, Neo, "Welcome to the desert of the real," the filmmakers even acknowledge the prominent postmodern theorist Jean Baudrillard and his theory of simulation, which is often taken for an argument that the world has become its own representation.

However, as revealed by his own repeated distancing of himself from the film, Baudrillard is not simply to be identified with the condition he analyzes. If he does perceive a world in which all is – or soon will be – representation, his fundamental question is how to think something real outside of this, or how to think this at all. (The same might be said of Jacques Derrida's notorious and much-quoted aphorism, "There is nothing outside of the text." Here, too, Derrida's real concern might be understood precisely as the attempt to think that "nothing" outside of the text.) In other words, to generalize and to make a connection between Baudrillard and Derrida and others, we might say that what defines postmodernism is the attempt to think critically about this mass-mediated world in which all is representation. How to take a distance on it – the traditional aim of criticism – when the analyst necessarily participates in the same regime of representation as what they analyze, when they can only employ representation against representation? We seek to answer these questions here through an examination of three writers whose work is extremely influential upon philosophically derived accounts of sociology: Jean Baudrillard, Slavoj Žižek, and Fredric Jameson.

Let us begin with Jameson, who for a long time – against its progressive disappearance from the academic scene – has attempted to put forward a Marxist analysis of culture and society. In such early works as *Marxism and Form* (1971) and *The Political Unconscious* (1981) he dealt essentially with problems of literary criticism, as much as anything wishing to make that tradition of cultural critique that comes out of Marx and Engels available to American readers. But in such essays as "Postmodernism and Consumer Society" (1983), eventually expanded to book length as *Postmodernism, or, The Cultural Logic of Late Capitalism* (1991), he sought to apply those arguments originally developed in the context of literature to society as a whole, or what he called "totality." Coming out of the long problematic within Marxist thought of the relationship of the base (the economic) to the superstructure (the social or cultural), it is in these writings that Jameson first spoke of the various elements that make up contemporary society – in a description that would become extraordinarily influential – as reversible, commutable, exchangeable. That is to say, the problem Jameson is grappling with in these later writings is that there is no "finally determining instance" of the economic, no underlying truth of society, but only a series of free-floating, seemingly independent elements that on closer inspection each turn into the other, as in a Möbius strip. As he writes in *Postmodernism*: "So it would also seem in the postmodernist debate, and the depoliticized bureaucratic society to which it belongs, where all seemingly cultural positions turn out to be symbolic forms of political moralizing, except for the single overtly political note, which suggests a slippage from politics back into culture again" (Jameson 1991: 64; see also 152). Everything in this sense is representation, or to use the German word Jameson often takes up, *Darstellung*; although it would be, as Jameson admits, not the re-presentation of any original, but rather the endless deferral or displacement of any original.

It is this conception of society as a series of linkages and encodings, of translations between the most apparently disparate fields, that licenses some of Jameson's more spectacular readings of well-known cultural objects: in the essay "Modernism and its Repressed" he reads the French New Novel in terms of European colonialism; in the last chapter of *Marxism and Form* he reads 1950s sci-fi as a fantasy of unalienated labor; in "Historicism and *The Shining*" he reads Stanley Kubrick's *The Shining* as treating class in Jazz Age America. The crucial thing to remember in each instance here is that, if it is always in fact a reading of a cultural phenomenon in terms of an underlying social or economic force, absolutely implicit in Jameson's argument – and the question, finally, is whether this applies just to our postmodernist societies or it is true of all societies – is the possibility of this going the other way. However, to understand this properly – and Jameson is very clear on this – this is not merely to say that we can also read the economic in terms of the cultural, but that we can only grasp the economic in the first place because of the cultural (and vice versa). It is this Jameson calls the *figural*: the fact that any part of society can only be comprehended by means of its comparison with another. In what looks at first sight like an overturning of the Marxist model of base and superstructure, we would say that no particular category comes first, but only the very relationship between them. In a sense, all the previously constituted fields that are understood to make up society henceforth become metaphors, representations of one another, but without some literal or original that is being metaphorized or represented.

However, to give the argument a final twist, we would say that, if the economic is reduced to merely another in a series of equivalents, it is also what they all have in common. That social force Jameson is trying to put his finger on – postmodernism as capitalism – is both what induces this endless series of exchanges between disparate areas and can be seen only in the momentary connections formed between them. This is again Jameson's rejection of any kind of a homology between preconstituted areas, which inevitably proceeds for him along the lines of biblical typology (and hence also his distaste for allegory and its modern equivalent for him, structuralism). As he argues in *Marxism and Form*: "The task of a dialectical criticism is not indeed to relate these two dimensions: they are already related ... Rather, such criticism is called upon to articulate the work and its content in such a way that this relationship stands revealed, and is more visible" (Jameson 1971: 406). In other words, it is in these connections themselves and not in what is connected that Jameson believes he can capture the assimilative power of capital, show the process of value being formed and not value as product. (And the value of Jameson's own work lies in the relationships he makes between different fields, which allow us to see them as though for the first time – say, Robbe-Grillet's novel *Jealousy* and European colonialism, Kubrick's *The Shining* and American history – beyond any notion of speaking their truth or "reading off" these cultural products against any underlying instance.)

It is again this process of representation that is to be seen in the chapter "How Did Marx Invent the Symptom?" of Žižek's *The Sublime Object of Ideology* (1989). In this chapter, as its title indicates, a parallel is drawn between the analysis of the dream by Freud and the analysis of the commodity by Marx. In both – hence the possibility of a certain Freudo-Marxism – there is observed a kind of "symptom," something that is constitutively repressed in order to allow the formation of a system of meaning or representation. That is, with regard to psychoanalysis, Žižek stresses that in Freud's dream analysis it is not at all a matter of seeing some original latent thought that is then expressed in a manifest content. This would be exactly that deciphering of dream symbolism in terms of preexisting symbols or archetypes that Freud objected to (like that biblical typology Jameson similarly rejects). Rather, what must be thought is the very passage from the latent to the manifest, the refiguring of words and symbols that gives to an often perfectly innocent thought the particular form of the dream. It is this translation itself – which at once is on the surface and deeper than even the most latent thought – that *is* the unconscious. And the same goes for Marx's analysis of the commodity form, where it is not a matter of the labor force being exploited insofar as it is not adequately compensated, but of economic exchange producing a certain surplus-value, which is the exploitation of labor. It is not some objective value of labor that is subsequently commodified; it is the commodity form itself that retrospectively gives rise to the value of labor in the form of its economic exploitation. As Žižek insists, what must above all be analyzed is not the "secret behind the form but the secret of this form itself" (Žižek 1989: 15). In other words, the "symptom" here, as in the dream, is not some reality that precedes translation or exchange, but is the enigma of exchange itself: what must be excluded from it insofar as everything is to be given a value, a "value" that cannot be accounted for insofar as labor is to be given a value. Or, as Žižek will elsewhere write, what is at stake is the "foreclosing" of the impossible origin of such an all-encompassing system of signification or value, in which everything – as in the symbols of psychoanalysis or the commodity in capitalism – is differentially defined by everything else (Žižek 1991b: 197–8). What is at stake is precisely the unrepresentable origins of a system in which all is representation.

We see something like this in Žižek's well-known pop-cultural analyses (e.g., his reading of Alfred Hitchcock's *The Birds* in *Looking Awry* or Stephen Spielberg's *Jaws* in *Enjoy Your Symptom!*). In both, Žižek begins by canvassing a number of different interpretations of the films: with regard to *The Birds*, the idea that the birds represent either the fundamental disorder of the cosmos, an imbalance in nature or unspoken family tensions; with regard to *Jaws*, the idea that the shark represents either repressed sexuality, unbridled capitalism, or the threat of the third world against America. That is, in a manner akin to cultural studies analyses, the films are read as bringing out certain tensions and tendencies within contemporary society. But Žižek does not leave it at this, for this apparent state of society can only be seen through these films. Or, to put it the other way around, we undoubtedly have the feeling that in most cultural studies analyses the author already has a certain image of society and simply seeks to illustrate it by means of a film. In fact, in each case here what Žižek wants to do – just as with his analysis of the genesis of value in Marx – is show how this circle of representation actually begins. Ultimately, he suggests, such cultural objects as the birds of *The Birds* and the shark of *Jaws* exert their power – this is the exact meaning of the fetish that he is trying to develop – by hiding through their sheer physical presence the vicious circle implied in the generation of value, by their ability to create the illusion that these various readings really do start with something, that there is something that precedes representation (Žižek 1991b: 106; Žižek 1992: 134). In a sense, even though everything is representation – or, to use Lacan's expression, symbolic – what Žižek is trying to do by means of these examples is think how this synchronic system of representation, in which each term is defined by its relationship with all others, first comes about.

And for all of his obvious differences from Jameson and Žižek, we see the same thing in Baudrillard. Baudrillard is, of course, well known for his critique of Marxism and the idea of any stable referent behind representation, but in fact he still remains profoundly "Marxist" and, for all of his seeming to do away with reference in his theory of simulation, this is only to mistake the situation he analyzes for his own critical position (the error he condemns in the makers of *The Matrix*, who fail in attributing to him both the idea that there is no outside to simulation, that there is only the illusory world of the Matrix, and the idea that there is some simple outside to simulation, the counter-world of the insurgents led by Morpheus). Indeed, there is a certain "outside" to representation in Baudrillard, which we might call the "Real," but it is the very form of illusion itself. In the same way as we saw with Jameson and Žižek, it is the fact that all is illusion, that everything can be seen in terms of something else, that necessarily implies some point outside of this, which is at once its origin (the impossibility of explaining how this system of representation began in its own terms) and its end (the possibility of us being able to think the fact that all is representation).

Let us take, for example, the opening chapters of Baudrillard's *The Transparency of Evil* (1993), entitled "Transaesthetics," "Transsexuality," and "Transeconomics." Baudrillard's idea here, as with Jameson's similar idea of transcoding – although, in truth, it is Jameson's "Postmodernism and Consumer Society" that is indebted to Baudrillard – is that none of these areas (not even economics) is any more fundamental than the others, that none can be grasped outside of its relationship with the others. Rather, each is only already those others: economics is aestheticized; aesthetics is only to be seen today in the form of economic speculation, etc. And yet, for all of this loss of external standards – and this is the kind of "limit" Baudrillard plays on throughout his work – there is still something at stake in pointing this out. There is a certain critical power brought about in remarking upon this equivalence or exchangeability between hitherto disparate areas; it is a kind of perpetual collapse and not a simple equivalence between them that Baudrillard speaks of. In other words, as with Jameson and Žižek, it is the exchange between things and not what is exchanged that is the real subject of Baudrillard's work, an economy that his own criticism necessarily participates in. It is representation or more precisely re-presentation that is at once the problem to be analyzed and the possible solution to this problem, in an ambiguity that, as Derrida points out, goes all the way back to Plato. And this is to say that postmodernism is not at all a new period, a sudden fall into the world of representation (and certainly none of the thinkers discussed here make this mistake); the same paradox of representation stretches all the way back to the origins of western philosophy. If anything, we would say that the originality of postmodernism lies precisely in this realization – and that henceforth all thought or critique is bound by this double limit: that it is necessary to think the limits of representation within representation itself; that it is not a matter of thinking what is outside of representation, but of thinking what is outside of it to ensure that nothing is outside it.

SEE ALSO: Deconstruction; Marxism and Sociology; Mass Culture and Mass Society; Postmodern Social Theory; Postmodernism

REFERENCES AND SUGGESTED READINGS

Baudrillard, J. (1993) *The Transparency of Evil: Essays on Extreme Phenomena*. Verso, London.

Derrida, J. (1981) Plato's Pharmacy. In: *Dissemination*. University of Chicago Press, Chicago.

Jameson, F. (1971) *Marxism and Form: Twentieth-Century Dialectical Theories of Literature*. Princeton University Press, Princeton.

Jameson, F. (1981) *The Political Unconscious: Narrative as a Socially Symbolic Act*. Methuen, London.

Jameson, F. (1991) *Postmodernism, or, The Cultural Logic of Late Capitalism*. Duke University Press, Durham, NC

Žižek, S. (1989) *The Sublime Object of Ideology*. Verso, London.

Žižek, S. (1991a) *For They Know Not What They Do: Enjoyment as a Political Act*. Verso, London

Žižek, S. (1991b) *Looking Awry: An Introduction to Jacques Lacan through Popular Culture*. MIT Press, Cambridge, MA.

Žižek, S. (1992) *Enjoy Your Symptom! Jacques Lacan in Hollywood and Out*. Routledge, New York.

repressive hypothesis

Christian Klesse

The publication of Michel Foucault's first volume of the *The History of Sexuality* thoroughly transformed theoretical thinking around sexuality. A range of Foucault's longstanding concerns around power, knowledge, discourse, truth, and subjectivity culminate in this text about the genealogy of sexuality in Christian western societies. With this book, Foucault attempted to write the history of sexuality "from the viewpoint of the history of discourses." In Foucault's work, the concept of discourse is intrinsically interwoven with what he perceived to be distinctively modern forms of power. The insistence that modern power is *productive* rather than simply *repressive* is one of the central assets of his novel theory of power. Premodern forms of power were based on the idea of *power-sovereignty* or *power-law*. They were derived from monarchical techniques of government and drew upon the binary ruler/ruled. From within this paradigm, power is conceived as *negative*. It works through measures such as censorship, prohibition, prevention, exclusion, or spectacular forms of punishment. In contradistinction, power as a modality of discourse is *positive* in that it is productive of social relationships, forms of knowledge, and modes of subjectivity. Moreover, it is more difficult to pin it down clearly or to identify its origin in any particular agent, institution, or social space. Foucault describes discursive power as having a dispersed, contradictory, and all-pervasive character.

Foucault (1990) applies this understanding of power to the subject of sexuality in order to challenge what he calls the repressive hypothesis. By questioning the dominant historical narrative of sexual repression, he undermines commonsense views about the interrelationship between power and sexuality. Whereas in the traditional understanding, power is exerted to repress, silence, censor, or erase sexuality, Foucault starts to conceive of sexuality as being an immediate effect of power. From this point of view, the most significant strategies of power in modern societies are not the exclusion of sexuality from discourse, but its regulation through the production of public discourses on sexuality. Foucault identifies an institutional incitement to speak about sex at the heart of western culture (s). It is in the multiplication of discourses on sexuality and the assumption that sex would reveal the truth of our innermost selves that the power–sexuality relation is realized. Thus, Foucault speaks of "confessional power" to designate this "putting into discourse" of sex in the Catholic tradition of confession or the secular discourse of psychoanalysis.

With his insistence that power is productive of sexuality rather than repressive, Foucault attacks the basic assumptions of sexual liberationism that had a strong hold in the New Left, the counter-culture, and the feminist and lesbian and gay social movements throughout the 1960s and 1970s. Foucault suggests that it would be naïve to assume that it is possible to revolutionize society by fighting off sexual restrictions and freeing our repressed natural sexual selves. Discussing the repressive hypothesis, he occasionally refers to the "Reichians" in order to characterize the discourse that he wishes to challenge. The German psychoanalyst and communist Wilhelm Reich emphasized the instrumentality of sexual repression through state, churches, and authoritarian family structures for class domination in capitalistic societies. As a theorist and activist, Reich was a core figure in organizing the so-called *Sexpol* movement, a working-class (youth) movement for class struggle and sexual liberation in the late 1920s and early 1930s. *Sexpol* had a short history. It was allowed to work within the ranks of the GCP only until 1932, when Reich was excluded from the party and some of his controversial publications were banned. The ideas of Reich gained an enormous popularity in the revival of sexual liberationism in the 1960s and 1970s, when the Freudo-Marxist theories of Herbert Marcuse were widely endorsed in progressive social-movement contexts.

Like other historians of sexuality, Foucault emphasizes the enormous relevance of medico-psychiatric discourses for shaping modern thoughts on human sexuality throughout the eighteenth and nineteenth centuries (Weeks 1990). The notion of sexuality was produced in this period through an engagement of early sexologists with sexual deviance or "perversion." What was previously seen as a sin or temporary aberration in Christian canonical law became reinterpreted as a matter of character or mental pathology. In sexological discourse the sexual norm was carefully defined in a process of increasing specification of sexually perverted types. This provides the backdrop to Foucault's famous thesis of the "invention of homosexuality." The "homosexual," according to Foucault, came into existence as a form of being through the self-affirmative appropriation of these sexological knowledges in a kind of "reverse discourse." Sexuality, consequently, presents (nothing more than) a discursive formation, a power/knowledge configuration, or an apparatus in the service of power.

Foucault coined the term bio-power to conceive of the strategies of modern nation-states to regulate human life through expert techniques. He describes the working of bio-power on two levels: the "anatomo-politics of the body" (i.e., disciplinary power governing sexual identities and acts) and the "bio-politics of the population" (the regulation and control of the life of the population, through statistics, eugenics, demographics, etc.). In light of the concept of bio-power, sexuality can be understood as a "technology of government." Since Foucault ascribes a wide range of meanings to the concept of government, he also applies it to phenomena not directly linked to political and bureaucratic processes. In its most generalized meaning, government designates the "conduct of conduct." This definition does not only refer to the conduct of others, but also the regulation of our own conduct in the "relation to ourselves." At this point, Foucault's writing on sexuality conjoins with his critical work on subjectivity.

While Foucault's work on sexuality chimes in well with the historicizing and anti-essentialist arguments advanced within social constructionist scholarship, it also points beyond it. His method of critical genealogy opens up a set of new and different questions aiming to explore the (historical) context of the emergence of certain social and sexual phenomena. In that he conceives of the sexual subject as an effect of discourse and power his work further contains an anti-identitarian element that has fueled the deconstructive endeavor of recent queer theorizing (Halperin 1995).

The pathbreaking influence of Foucault's thought notwithstanding, a range of criticisms has been leveled against his work on sexuality. Although being primarily concerned with the complexity of power, he failed to address the centrality of gender and race to the bio-politics he studied. Some have further complained that his thesis of the ubiquity of power would not be helpful to theorize agency or resistance and that his claim that "there is no relation of power without resistance" would at best be tautological. Foucault tried to address the latter issue in his work on ethics in volumes 2 and 3 of *The History of Sexuality*. Here he claims that the imperative within classical Greek ethics to "take care of yourself" would bear the potential for a non-prohibitive ethics based on the "techniques of self-stylization" or an "aesthetics of existence." Foucault labels these practices alternately "practices of freedom" or the "government of self." It is an issue of contention in how far this work stands in an unbridgeable tension with his earlier claims. A high degree of ambivalence certainly remains.

SEE ALSO: Discourse; Essentialism and Constructionism; Foucault, Michel; Homosexuality; Poststructuralism; Queer Theory; Reich, Wilhelm; Sexual Identities; Sexuality Research: History

REFERENCES AND SUGGESTED READINGS

Bland, L. & Doan, L. (Eds.) (1998) *Sexology Uncensored: The Documents of Sexual Science*. Polity Press, Cambridge.

Burchell, G., Gordon, C., & Miller, P. (Eds.) (1991) *The Foucault Effect: Studies in Governmental Rationality*. Harvester Wheatsheaf, London.

Faubion, J. D. (Ed.) (1997) *Michel Foucault: Power*. New Press, New York.

Foucault, M. (1980) *Power/Knowledge*. Pantheon, New York.

Foucault, M. (1985) *The History of Sexuality*, Vol. 2: *The Use of Pleasure*. Penguin, London.

Foucault, M. (1986) *The History of Sexuality*, Vol. 3: *The Care of the Self*. Penguin, London.

Foucault, M. (1990) *The History of Sexuality*, Vol. 1: *An Introduction*. Penguin, London.

Halperin, D. (1995) *Saint Foucault: Towards a Gay Historiography*. Oxford University Press, Oxford.

Lotringer, S. (Ed.) (1996) *Foucault Live: Interviews, 1961–1984 (Michel Foucault)*. Semiotext(e), New York.

McNay, L. (1994) *Foucault and Feminism*. Polity Press, Cambridge.

Marcuse, H. (1968) *One Dimensional Man: The Ideology of Industrial Society*. Sphere Books, London.

Marcuse, H. (1972) *Eros and Civilisation*. Abacus, London.

Probyn, E. (1996) *Outside Belongings*. Routledge, London.

Reich, W. (1972) *Sex-Pol: Essays, 1929–1934*. Random House, New York.

Stein, E. (Ed.) (1992) *Forms of Desire: Sexual Orientation and the Social Constructionist Controversy.* Routledge, London.
Weeks, J. (1990) *Coming-Out: Homosexual Politics in Britain from the Nineteenth Century to the Present*, 2nd edn. Quartet, London.

republicanism

Peter Murphy

Republicanism presents an idealized version of a republic. This is a state where no single person (such as a monarch) rules. Usually, this means a written or unwritten constitutional order that distributes the power of the state among different persons and offices, and then organizes those persons and offices into a functional whole. Republics ideally combine the power of the one, the few, and the many with the aim of minimizing personal rule. Republicanism seeks to replace the unchecked personal authority of an arbitrary or despotic ruler with the carefully balanced impersonal authority of a city-state or federal-legal system.

The term republic is Roman. The Roman Republic began its history when the city-state expelled its kings. Kingship was equated with despotism, and republicanism signified opposition to tyranny. In order to rule without a king, Rome instituted a set of balances of power between executive office-holders, classes, and councils (the Senate, the People) in the state. Council-type rule depended on public debate about common matters. It replaced rule by fiat or diktat. The concept of a balance of powers prefigured the modern idea of a constitutional separation of powers.

The ancient Greek city-states did much the same things as Rome, beginning around the same time in the eighth century BCE. The Greeks, though, invented the idea of federalism, unfamiliar to the Romans. The Greek idea of a federation of states became the basis for the great modern republic, the US. The Greeks theorized extensively about their innovations – notably in Plato's *Republic* and Aristotle's *Politics*. These theories had their roots in pre-Socratic ideas of the equilibrium and proportionality of powers – the key idea of any republic. The great Roman statesman Cicero later synthesized these theories in his *Republic*, a canonical text for republicanism for 2,000 years.

The Roman Empire and Christianity eclipsed ancient republicanism, though republican ideas like the rule of law survived for centuries in late antique administration and urbanism and in Christian natural law. Republican ideas reappeared with the rebirth of Italian city-states by the twelfth century – notably Florence and Venice. These cities were based on forms of collective rule. The Florentines Leonardo Bruni and Machiavelli produced important theories of the Italian city republic, in part stimulated by their reading of ancient sources.

The Dutch revolted against Spain in the seventeenth century, and created a republic based on a federation of seven provinces. Although this period produced some brilliant thinkers (Grotius and Spinoza), no great treatise on republicanism was written, though key ideas – of the freedom of the seas and of states based on the natural rights of life and liberties of movement and property – were added to the republican corpus. The Dutch pioneered liberal republicanism.

When the American colonies rebelled against the English Crown, American thinkers ransacked history for models of republics. They were intimately familiar with Sparta, Athens, Rome, Venice, and the Dutch Republic. They also drew on Commonwealth ideas (James Harrington, Henry Neville) and Whig ideas (Shaftesbury, Burke) circulating in England. Whig and Commonwealth ideas were para-republican – models of regal republics in which the Crown was a limited element in a constitutional state. In the thought of the Americans Thomas Jefferson and James Madison, multiple threads of historic republicanism coalesced into a new model that combined familiar features (opposition to despotism, rejection of monarchy, constitutional balance, free speech, rule of law) with startlingly new elements, including a written constitution enforced by an independent court and an ambition to build a republic on a massive scale.

Republicanism originally was the worldview of individual city-states. The Greeks experimented with federations of cities. The Dutch developed the idea as a federation of provinces. The Americans were more adventurous still: they thought of their union of states as an "empire of liberty" that regularly enlarged itself by adding new states and by making treaties and alliances with other states. The greatest treatise produced on the American republic was Hannah Arendt's *On Revolution* (1973).

In the modern age, many countries toppled their monarchies and replaced them with elected or unelected presidents and called themselves republics. But these republics bore little resemblance to the models of historical republicanism whose practical expression was limited to the US and Whig Commonwealths like Australia.

SEE ALSO: Democracy; Empire; Federalism; Sovereignty; State

REFERENCES AND SUGGESTED READINGS

Arendt, H. (1973) *On Revolution*. Penguin, London.
Cicero, M. T. (1998) *The Republic and The Laws*. Trans. N. Rudd. Oxford University Press, New York.
Murphy, P. (2001) *Civic Justice*. Humanity Books, Amherst, NY.
Pocock, J. G. A. (1975) *The Machiavellian Moment*. Princeton University Press, Princeton.
Rahe, P. A. (1994) *Republics Ancient and Modern*, vols. 1–3. University of North Carolina Press, Chapel Hill.

reputation

Gary Alan Fine

Reputation, as a social scientific concept, refers to the existence of a socially recognized persona: an organizing principle by which actions of a person (or group, organization, or collectivity) are linked into a common assessment. On one level a reputation constitutes a moral gestalt that is linked to a person – an organizing principle for person perception. However, reputations are more than this social psychological claim: they are collective representations, enacted in relationships. In this, the opinion that one individual might form of another often differs from a shared, established image. Reputations are embedded within social relations, and, as a consequence, reputation is connected to forms of communication, tied to a community.

Social identification and reputation operates in several domains: personal, mass-mediated, organizational, and historical. While reputations often begin within circles of personal intimates, they spread outward. First, people create and share the reputations of those who exist within their social circle – friends and consorts. Personal reputations are of immediate consequence, because the actions of those in our social world have the potential to shape our lives and interaction outcomes. People are concerned with the repute in which they are held because of the options that reputations open and close, and because reputations permit us to evaluate our selves in particular ways: those identities that we are given channel those identities that we can select. Further, these public reputations directly affect how we come to see ourselves: a reason we attempt to shape our behavior when with those whose opinions matter to us (Vinitzky-Seroussi 1998). People engage in forms of self-presentation and impression management to modify their images in the eyes of others. As a result, "status" has been a central concept of sociology from Max Weber on, whether personal standing or group position.

Second, the media help to determine who we should know and care about. In addition to individuals who are famous by virtue of their formal institutional roles (e.g., political leaders), this space is populated by "celebrities": figures that by virtue of their prominence in the central institutions of society are deemed worthy of shared attention (Gamson 1994). Even if we recognize the thinness of our knowledge, the celebrity of these figures connects us to each other and provides an unthreatening space to converse about vital social matters. We feel that we know these celebrities (O. J. Simpson, for instance) and can speculate on their motives. The discussion of the sexual appetites of former President Clinton, and whether he suffers from a "sexual addiction," is part of this personalizing of "great men," as is the debate over whether these intimacies matter as to his performance of affairs of state. This discussion results from media choices, an enlarged emphasis that is a function of what Daniel Boorstin (1961) has labeled the "graphic revolution," referring to the increased visual displays of public figures, emphasizing their immediacy.

Public figures are legitimate topics of conversation among audiences who have never met them, but who consider them "known." Their reputations are used in interactional transactions among strangers: strangers to them and often strangers to each other. We have the right to judge these figures, even though we are not familiar with them personally. This is a form of "parasocial interaction" (Caughey 1984).

Not only do individuals have reputations, but so also do organizations. Organizations develop reputations that influence their effectiveness (Fombrun 1996). Even if not always known to the wider public, CEOs characterize their companies in the business community. What we know of Apple, Disney, General Motors, and Time-Warner parallels in important ways what we know of persons. The dramatic growth of the public relations profession since the 1920s testifies to the need for reputation specialists to shape organizational images. Ratings of professional schools or consumer product evaluations are part of this process.

Finally, history, constituting narratives of linked biographies, serves as a more formal and sedimented version of reputation work. Citizens learn of the reputations of others through institutionally sanctioned knowledge. History represents "settled" cultural discourse about the past, determined by experts as important for people to be culturally literate. This knowledge is acquired through the social institutions of the school and the media. Reputational history provides lessons necessary for citizenship. Historical knowledge is not merely a technical skill, but a moral aptitude, necessary for public involvement. History is narratives as taught; collective memory is how such narratives are recalled. When reputations are too hotly contested by rivalrous parties, schools and other institutions simply ignore the battles or attempt to pacify them, creating non-controversial versions of the American Civil War, segregation, or treatment of American Indians.

In one sense, a person without reputational knowledge could function well in social domains; yet, this individual would not really "belong" to the polity. Whether or not people choose to embrace the consensual moral evaluation of great figures, as revolutionaries and progressives often refrain from doing, they should at least be aware of what they are rejecting.

Reputations attempt to teach how citizens should think about those issues that confront them. People share memory by virtue of what they have been taught about others, and by what these others are supposed to "mean." As sociologist Charles Horton Cooley (1966 [1918]: 342) asserted, "Fame may or may not represent what men were, but it always represents what humanity needs for them to have been."

The analysis of reputations is closely linked to the examination of collective memory or social mnemonics (Olick & Robbins 1998; Fine 2001), and builds on cognitive sociology, social movements research, and the sociology of knowledge. Major figures in this tradition include Charles Horton Cooley, Maurice Halbwachs, Karl Mannheim, and more recently Barry Schwartz, Kurt and Gladys Lang, and Pierre Nora. As research questions become more sophisticated, other linkages will be explored with political science, psychology, organizational studies, as well as extended historical and comparative analyses.

SEE ALSO: Celebrity and Celetoid; Celebrity Culture; Collective Identity; Collective Memory; Halbwachs, Maurice; Political Leadership; Politics and Media; Status

REFERENCES AND SUGGESTED READINGS

Boorstin, D. (1961) *The Image, or What Happened to the American Dream*. Atheneum, New York.

Caughey, J. (1984) *Imaginary Social Worlds*. University of Nebraska Press, Lincoln.

Cooley, C. H. (1966 [1918]) *Social Process*. Southern Illinois University Press, Carbondale.

Fine, G. A. (2001) *Difficult Reputations: Collective Memories of the Evil, Inept, and Controversial*. University of Chicago Press, Chicago.

Fombrun, C. J. (1996) *Reputation: Realizing Value from the Corporate Image*. Harvard Business School Press, Cambridge, MA.

Gamson, J. (1994) *Claims to Fame: Celebrity in Contemporary America*. University of California Press, Berkeley.

Olick, J. K. & Robbins, J. (1998) Social Memory Studies: From "Collective Memory" to the

Historical Sociology of Mnemonic Practices. *Annual Review of Sociology* 24: 105–40.
Vinitzky-Seroussi, V. (1998) *After Pomp and Circumstance: High School Reunion as an Autobiographical Occasion.* University of Chicago Press, Chicago.

residential segregation

John Iceland

Residential segregation refers to the differential distribution of groups across space, and is usually thought of in terms of the degree to which various groups reside in different neighborhoods. People are residentially segregated across a number of dimensions, including age, socioeconomic status, and (the focus here) race and ethnicity. It is commonly thought that differences in residential patterns across racial and ethnic groups reflect social distance.

Residential segregation, particularly when resulting from discrimination, has negative consequences for minority group members. Residential segregation limits residential choice, constrains economic and educational opportunities by limiting people's access to good schools and jobs, serves to concentrate poverty in disadvantaged neighborhoods, and contributes to social exclusion and alienation. Residential segregation also affects the nature and quality of intergroup relations in society: segregation reduces contact between groups and both causes and reflects polarization across communities.

HISTORICAL TREATMENT OF RESIDENTIAL SEGREGATION ISSUES

The residential patterns of minority groups in the US have been the object of study for many decades. W. E. B. DuBois, for example, documented the residential patterns of blacks in Philadelphia's seventh ward in his 1899 book, *The Philadelphia Negro*. Another example is Louis Wirth's *The Ghetto* (1928), which compared the similarities between the Jewish ghettos in Europe and those in New York and Chicago. Taeuber and Taeuber (1965) note that new immigrants to the US in the nineteenth and early twentieth centuries were by-and-large poor and poorly educated. They often lived in ethnic enclaves in low-rent districts. As the immigrants and their children accumulated financial resources and knowledge of opportunities, many left ethnic enclaves, often to be replaced by new immigrants.

This process of residential assimilation, however, did not apply to the large waves of black migrants from the South to the North in the early and mid-twentieth century. African Americans faced a range of social, economic, and residential barriers that were higher than those that immigrants faced. In the South, segregation was enforced by whites with the Jim Crow system. In the North, segregation developed because of white-dominated real estate practices and because of the violence directed toward blacks who entered formerly white neighborhoods.

With the decline in immigration in the 1920s and 1930s, studies on segregation in the decades after World War II tended to focus on the segregation of blacks from whites. Studies such as Taeuber and Taeuber's (1965) volume on *Negroes in Cities* provided an impressive and thorough examination of general patterns of black–white segregation and the role of social and economic factors in producing these patterns. Throughout the first six decades of the twentieth century, segregation between blacks and whites in metropolitan areas actually increased, largely due to continued racial polarization and white suburbanization over the period.

Massey and Denton (1993), among others, built upon this tradition, and discussed the extreme levels of racial stratification in American metropolitan areas, and described how racism and discrimination perpetuated high levels of segregation. *American Apartheid* focused on black–white segregation, though other work by Massey and Denton examined the segregation of other groups from whites as well.

With the rapid growth of the Hispanic and Asian populations in the US since the 1960s, in response to changes in immigration policy, there has been growing attention paid to the residential segregation of these groups in American society. It is likely that future research on racial and ethnic residential segregation will increasingly focus on the residential patterns of multiple groups.

RECENT PATTERNS AND TRENDS IN SEGREGATION

While Taeuber and Taeuber (1965) and others described how black–white segregation increased through the early and middle part of the twentieth century, trends in subsequent decades have been characterized by moderate declines in such segregation. A 2002 Census Bureau report (Iceland et al. 2002) examined the residential segregation of various groups across all US metropolitan areas using a variety of measures and found that declines in African American segregation over the 1980 to 2000 period occurred across all dimensions of segregation. Despite these declines, residential segregation was still higher for African Americans than for the other groups. Hispanics were generally the next most highly segregated, followed by Asians and Pacific Islanders, and finally American Indians and Alaska Natives. Asians and Pacific Islanders, as well as Hispanics, tended to experience increases in segregation over the period, though results varied by measure used. Increases were generally larger for Asians and Pacific Islanders than for Hispanics.

Residential segregation tended to be higher in larger metropolitan areas and in those with large minority populations. While the Census Bureau report thoroughly documented various basic patterns and trends in residential segregation, it did not discuss the factors causing these trends.

INTERNATIONAL RESEARCH

Residential segregation has been receiving greater attention in countries around the globe, in large part due to continued high levels of international migration (and improvements in data, methods, and computational resources for studying segregation). Europe and Canada, for example, have been experiencing growth in their minority populations, and this has been accompanied by concerns about the assimilation (social, economic, and residential) of these groups in society. Thus, we are likely to see a growing body of research on residential segregation in a comparative international perspective in the coming years (e.g., White et al. 2003).

CAUSES OF RACIAL AND ETHNIC RESIDENTIAL SEGREGATION

Two broad theoretical perspectives have been used to explain patterns and trends in residential segregation in the US: spatial assimilation and place stratification. According to the spatial assimilation model, which is often used to explain settlement patterns of immigrants or migrants, newcomers settle in fairly homogeneous racial/ethnic enclaves within a given metropolitan area. This may be due to migrants feeling more comfortable with and welcomed by fellow co-ethnics and the fact that minority members may simply not be able to afford to live in the same neighborhoods as more affluent whites. According to this model, individuals eventually convert socioeconomic gains over time into better housing, and this leads to higher levels of integration with whites.

In contrast to the spatial assimilation model, the place stratification perspective holds that a group's residential patterns and integration into society depend on the group's position in the social hierarchy. The dominant group (non-Hispanic whites) is at the top of the hierarchy, and other groups follow in some order, depending on prejudices and preferences of society at large. Negative stereotypes, for example, reduce openness to integration with certain groups, and blacks tend to be perceived in the most unfavorable terms.

Thus, many have argued that the spatial assimilation model simply does not hold for all groups, especially blacks, in part because prejudices lead not only to avoidance of particular groups but also to racial discrimination. Discriminatory practices include racial steering by real estate agents, unfair mortgage lending patterns, and even in some cases physical attacks when moving into white neighborhoods.

Both theoretical perspectives have received some support from past research. For example, Iceland (2004a) has found that higher socioeconomic status blacks, Hispanics, and Asians are less segregated from non-Hispanic whites than their lower socioeconomic status counterparts. Immigrants also have higher levels of segregation than the native-born of a particular race group. Nevertheless, findings also indicate that race still plays a large role in determining residential patterns, especially for African Americans.

METHODOLOGICAL ISSUES

Residential segregation has been studied extensively with a variety of measures. The main methodological issues involved in analyzing racial and ethnic segregation revolve around the definition of racial and ethnic categories, geographic boundaries, and segregation measures.

Race and Ethnicity

The way in which racial and ethnic groups have been defined has changed over time. Residential segregation indexes generally rely on official government definitions, given that the data needed to calculate indexes come from the decennial census. In 1790, the first decennial census of the population, information was collected about whites and blacks only. Over time, data on other groups were collected, often reflecting changing social views of race. In the 2000 census there were five race categories: White, Black, American Indian and Alaska Native, Asian, and Native Hawaiian or other Pacific Islander. Individuals could also identify with more than one race, in contrast to previous censuses. Hispanic origin was gathered in a separate question.

In practice, the minority groups most studied today are African Americans, Hispanics, and Asians. Examining the segregation of the American Indian population, and particularly trends over time, is challenging due to the relatively small population of this group, as well as changing patterns of self-identification among American Indians.

Geographic Areas

Residential segregation typically describes the distribution of different groups across smaller areal units within larger areas. Thus, to measure residential segregation, one has to define both the appropriate larger area and its component parts. The most common larger geographic unit chosen is the metropolitan area, which is a reasonable approximation of a housing market. They generally contain at least 50,000 people, and in 2000 there were 331 of them in the US. The smaller unit chosen is typically the census tract, which was originally designed to represent neighborhoods. Tracts typically have between 1,500 and 8,000 people, with an average size of about 4,000. Using smaller component units, such as census-defined blocks, tends to yield higher segregation scores, as smaller units tend to be racially more homogeneous than larger ones.

Segregation Measures

The two most common measures of segregation are the dissimilarity and isolation indexes. The dissimilarity index is a measure of evenness, and it ranges from 0 (complete integration) to 1 (complete segregation). It describes the proportion of a group's population that would have to change residence for each neighborhood to have the same race-ethnic distribution as the metropolitan area overall. The isolation index is a measure of exposure, and also ranges from 0 to 1, with 1 indicating the highest level of isolation. It basically indicates the probability that a typical minority group member would come into contact with another minority group member in a metropolitan area.

Many other segregation measures have been developed and used by researchers. In 1988, Massey and Denton compiled 20 existing measures and identified five dimensions of residential segregation: evenness, exposure, concentration, centralization, and clustering. *Evenness* describes the differential distribution of subgroups of the population. *Exposure* measures potential contact between groups. *Concentration* refers to the relative amount of physical space occupied by a minority subgroup. *Centralization* indicates the degree to which a group is located near the center of an urban area. *Clustering* measures the degree to which minority group members live in contiguous areas. A more thorough discussion of these dimensions and various issues related to measuring segregation can be found in Massey and Denton (1988) and Iceland et al. (2002).

Finally, other measures of segregation are continually being developed, such as *multigroup* measures that allow researchers to consider multiple racial and ethnic groups, geographic levels (e.g., metropolitan area or regions), or dimensions (race, class, age) simultaneously. It is likely that these measures will become more popular in the coming years.

SEE ALSO: Chicago School; Ethnic Enclaves; Hypersegregation; Inequality and the City; Invasion-Succession; Migration: Internal; Redlining; Restrictive Covenants; Steering, Racial Real Estate; Urban Ecology

REFERENCES AND SUGGESTED READINGS

Charles, C. Z. (2003) Dynamics of Racial Residential Segregation. *Annual Review of Sociology* 29(1): 167–207.

DuBois, W. E. B. (1967 [1899]) *The Philadelphia Negro: A Social Study*. Schocken, New York.

Farley, R. (1991) Residential Segregation of Social and Economic Groups among Blacks, 1970–80. In: Jencks, C. & Peterson, P. E. (Eds.), *The Urban Underclass*. Brookings Institution, Washington, DC.

Iceland, J. (2004a) Trends in Racial and Ethnic Residential Segregation: 1980–2000. National Fair Housing Conference Research and Policy Forum, Washington, DC.

Iceland, J. (2004b) Beyond Black and White: Residential Segregation in Multiethnic America. *Social Science Research* 33, 2 (June): 248–71.

Iceland, J., Weinberg, D. H. & Steinmetz, E. (2002) *Racial and Ethnic Residential Segregation in the United States: 1980–2000*. US Census Bureau, Census Special Report, CENSR-3. US Government Printing Office, Washington, DC.

Massey, D. S. & Denton, N. A. (1988) The Dimensions of Residential Segregation. *Social Forces* 67: 281–315.

Massey, D. S. & Denton, N. A. (1993) *American Apartheid: Segregation and the Making of the Underclass*. Harvard University Press, Cambridge, MA.

Taeuber, K. E. & Taeuber, A. F. (1965) *Negroes in Cities: Residential Segregation and Neighborhood Change*. Aldine, Chicago.

White, M. J., Fong, E., & Cai, Q. (2003) The Segregation of Asian-Origin Groups in the United States and Canada. *Social Science Research* 32, 1 (March): 148–67.

Wirth, L. (1928) *The Ghetto*. University of Chicago Press, Chicago.

resocialization

Linda Morrison

Resocialization is a process of identity transformation in which people are called upon to learn new roles, while unlearning some aspects of their old ones. The need to learn new roles may result from voluntary or involuntary changes in status. When the role requirements of the new status conflict with an individual's earlier or primary socialization, the process of resocialization may be necessary. This process often requires an unlearning of internalized norms, values, beliefs, and practices, to be replaced by a new set which is considered appropriate to the new role.

Resocialization most often occurs when an individual is called upon to adopt a new specialized status, often in adulthood. Thus it is sometimes referred to as adult socialization. Examples include joining the military or a religious order; training to become a doctor, lawyer, or police officer; becoming a prisoner; or being hospitalized for mental illness. In each case, a person is required to take on a new identity as a professionalized or institutionalized self, and must adopt new ways of relating to both self and others. Behaviors and values that were considered normal in ordinary society are seen as deviant and undesirable in the new situation and must be unlearned. In addition, many of the new behaviors and values are considered deviant on "the outside." For these reasons, the person's previously socialized self becomes an obstacle to achieving the new identity and status. In order to make this transition, role and identity transformations are required.

In the classic formulation, the resocialization process occurs within the context of "total institutions." Goffman (1961) describes the features of these special environments (e.g., prisons and mental hospitals), in which a person is removed from the ordinary everyday world and resocialized in a social context which encompasses all or most of an individual's daily life. In this controlled environment, individuals are stripped of their social identities through "mortification processes" and socialized into new relationships with their peer group and a complex hierarchy of ranking and power.

Ordinary social practices are no longer valid. People are ridiculed and punished for acting like their normal selves, and are rewarded for adopting new behaviors and attitudes that are appropriate to the new social setting.

Within total institutions, various forms of mortification practices and degradation rituals operate to break down accustomed realities and weaken the boundaries of existing identities. The inmates or initiates may be stripped, shaved, punished, and humiliated; subjected to painful, stressful, and disorienting events; given new clothing, tools, and responsibilities; and assigned new identities or labels based on membership in a particular group within a strictly hierarchical structure. New practices and values are introduced and enforced in an environment of extensive surveillance and social control. The norms, values, and behaviors of the institutional setting are most successfully reinforced by keeping the incarcerated individuals totally separate from their ordinary environment (the outside) and retraining them into the distinct new role system of the inside. As with childhood socialization, resocialization of an individual occurs in relationship to the status and roles of others. Through relating to these others, in an ongoing process of rewards and punishments, the inmate or trainee will learn the responses and behaviors required by the new social environment, internalizing its acceptable norms, values and beliefs.

Goffman's ideal type of resocialization in a total institution can be used to understand the process occurring in other, less total institutional settings. Settings can vary in relation to their voluntariness, their purpose and goals, their degree of separation from the outside world, the active or passive role of the individual in the process, the level of surveillance and control, and the permanent or temporary nature of involvement. Resocialization in the interest of professional training such as a medical school or police academy, while it involves degradation and subordination of initiates, also holds the promise of an enhanced future status when training for membership is complete. A person in training is socialized into new responses to people and their bodies, to sickness, to crime, to danger, to death. The challenges and humiliations of socialization into a professional identity are difficult but carry substantial rewards. Upon completion, the person will carry a new identity and will be differently socialized.

Individuals experiencing drug rehabilitation programs, imprisonment, and psychiatric treatment may not experience actual transformation of identity, but may resist and maintain their core identity, especially when contact with the outside is maintained or eventual return is promised. Active reconstruction of the self in certain contexts may be contrasted with a more passive or receptive condition. The amount of personal initiative, privacy, and choice can also be seen to vary according to setting and individual. Brainwashing of cult members or prisoners of war could be seen as the extreme case of resocialization and loss of the original self in transformation to the new status and role.

In a non-voluntary therapeutic environment, the individual may gain permission to leave the facility only when his or her identity has been sufficiently transformed by being there. This includes rehabilitative treatment for substance abuse, as well as psychiatric treatment. The person who enters the facility is defined as deficient; denial of this definitional reality is proof of continued deficiency. Through the mortification, deculturation, and rebuilding process described by Goffman (1961), the therapeutic milieu is designed to shape inmates into a new status/role combination, including incorporation of a prescribed set of preferred norms and values. When their behaviors and beliefs are deemed acceptably transformed, including display of sufficient respect for the rules and the status hierarchy, then release may be secured. The new social role of reformed addict, or psychiatric patient, will define their status upon release back into society. In such circumstances, it is possible to maintain one's core identity to varying degrees, and undergo a process of change in combination with a newly reconstructed presentation of self in order to meet the requirements of the program and gain release to the outside. This is a form of resocialization, learning new roles, without a true transformation of identity.

In a training environment, the new identity is acquired through modeling the behaviors of those who are superior in status, though subservient and submissive behaviors must be maintained for an appropriate length of time.

After showing adequate preparation at appropriate intervals, the deserving initiate will go through a status enhancement ritual to reach the next level, and corresponding changes in role behaviors will be learned, always in relation to others in higher, lower, or peer status positions. In turn, the individuals moving through this pathway assist in shaping the behaviors of others entering the statuses below them. Eventually, the graduation or credentialing ritual will reward the long period of degradation, subservience, and obedience to authority with a full status transformation, and ultimately an identity transformation as well. To become a doctor rather than a medical student, an officer rather than a cadet, or a priest rather than a seminarian, is to transform one's identity in relation to others as well as to the self. To fully enter the new status and associated roles, a person must experience the self in a new way and relate to "ordinary" persons (their own former status) differently, as well as to others in related statuses. One's core identity has been transformed and enhanced, or transformed and degraded.

For individuals in environments designed to treat or punish, the basic value of the self is diminished as a result of entering the status of prisoner, patient, or addict. As noted above, the goal of the institution is to transform the deviant self, participation is less voluntary, and the object is to produce conformity or reduce deviance. Once resocialization occurs, when return to society is gained, the individual still carries a stigmatized identity on re-entry: that of ex-mental patient, ex-con, or ex-addict. Ritual reincorporation into the community is rarely attained, and the new position is seldom celebrated. This is an important distinction between forms of and outcomes of resocialization.

Clearly, the purpose of resocialization helps to determine its nature. Whether a suspension of previous identity or a transformation to a new identity is achieved, or something in between, will depend on multiple factors. Oversimplification of the resocialization process leads to a misunderstanding of its complexity, and of the complexity of human beings in relation to themselves and to one another.

Identity construction involves individual and contextual factors of agency, resistance, and choice; awareness of these factors in the context of resocialization allows a more nuanced understanding of the process.

SEE ALSO: Goffman, Erving; Identity Theory; Organizations as Total Institutions; Self; Socialization; Socialization, Adult; Status

REFERENCES AND SUGGESTED READINGS

Fox, R. (1988) The Autopsy: Its Place in the Attitude-Learning of Second-Year Medical Students. In: Fox, R., *Essays in Medical Sociology: Journeys into the Field.* Transaction Books, New Brunswick, NJ, pp. 51–77.

Goffman, E. (1961) *Asylums: Essays on the Social Situations of Mental Patients and Other Inmates.* Doubleday, New York.

Harris, R. (1973) *The Police Academy: An Inside View.* Wiley, New York.

McCorkel, J. (1998) Going to the Crackhouse: Critical Space as a Form of Resistance in Total Institutions and Everyday Life. *Symbolic Interaction* 21 (3): 227–52.

Merton, R., Reader, G., & Kendall, P. (Eds.) (1957) *The Student-Physician: Introductory Studies in the Sociology of Medical Education.* Harvard University Press, Cambridge, MA.

Schmid, T. & Jones, R. (1991) Suspended Identity: Identity Transformation in a Maximum Security Prison. *Symbolic Interaction* 14 (4): 415–32.

Van Maanen, J. (1973) Observations on the Making of Policemen. *Human Organization* 32 (4): 407–18.

resource mobilization theory

Bob Edwards

A renaissance of social movement research occurred in both North America and Europe during the 1970s as a then younger generation of scholars sought to understand the emergence, significance, and effects of the social movements of the 1960s (see Jenkins 1983; McAdam et al. 1988; Dalton et al. 1990). On neither side of the Atlantic did the received academic wisdom of the 1950s and 1960s view social movements in a favorable light. In the US, the most hospitable theories treated social movements as temporary disequilibria soon to be reintegrated into smoothly functioning social systems. In Europe, "new social movements" theory formed around the core problematic of explaining the origins, identity, and cultural significance of newly emerging social change constituencies (Melucci 1980). By contrast, resource mobilization theory tended to take the existence of such constituencies for granted in order to explain how they mobilized effectively to pursue desired social change. Both resource mobilization and new social movement theories are variants within the broader conflict paradigm in sociological theory. Resource mobilization predominated in the rapidly growing sociological subfield of social movement research (Gamson 1968, 1975; Oberschall 1973; Freeman 1975; McCarthy & Zald 1977; Tilly 1978; McAdam 1982; Morris 1984; Zald & McCarthy 1987; Staggenborg 1988; Tarrow 1994).

The organizational-entrepreneurial branch of resource mobilization theory (RMT) reoriented social movement analysis by taking the analytical insights of organizational sociology and extending them by analogy to social movements. More recent exemplars of this perspective include Minkoff's (1995) analysis of women's and race/ethnic organizations, Smith et al. (1997) on transnational social movement organizations, Andrews's (2005) study of the impact of the Civil Rights Movement, and a special issue of *Mobilization* edited by Caniglia and Carmin (2005). From this perspective a social movement is a set of preferences for social change within a population. Individuals who share those social change preferences are called *adherents*, while those who contribute resources of various kinds to help the movement mobilize are *constituents*. Those who watch from the sidelines are *bystanders*. A key analytical issue for RMT is understanding how social movements turn bystanders into adherents and subsequently adherents into constituents, and ultimately mobilize constituents to active participation. Such tasks of mobilization are undertaken most often by *social movement organizations* (SMOs).

In their classic formulation, McCarthy and Zald identified a trend in US social movements toward the increasing significance of large, formally organized SMOs deploying professional staff to pursue the broad social change goals of their constituents. Early RMT was closely associated with the trend toward professionalization and debates over its impact were a focus of much research (Staggenborg 1988; Andrews & Edwards 2004). Yet, while many SMOs are quite large with professional staffs and substantial resources, most are small, less formally organized groups operating at the local level (Edwards & Foley 2003). At a minimum, an SMO is a named group that undertakes actions to further the social change goals of the social movement.

All SMOs pursuing the goals of the movement comprise a *social movement industry* (SMI). SMIs vary in size, and the capacity of a movement to engage in collective action is influenced greatly by type, amount, and distribution of resources within its SMI. RMT expects that the greater the mobilization capacity of an SMI, the greater its potential for achieving some of its social change goals. The broader *social movement sector* (SMS) is composed of all SMIs and their component SMOs. In leaning on organizational sociology to reorient the study of social movements, RMT holds that SMIs and SMOs differ from governmental and market sector organizations because of watershed differences in goals, their structural location in civil society, and in the varied resources and power they wield. Nevertheless, the SMS has grown dramatically over the last 30 years and has contributed to the increasing social change potential attributed to "civil society" worldwide.

Early formulations of RMT focused on broad patterns of resource availability and paid disproportionate attention to the mobilization of material resources from external sources. By contrast, recent RMT analysts emphasize more explicitly the uneven distribution of resources in a society, and seek to understand how individual and collective actors endeavor to alter that distribution in order to direct resources to social movements. In other words, RMT is becoming more explicitly a partial theory of overcoming resource inequality. Thus, questions of general resource "availability" have shifted toward questions of specific means of resource access.

Two longstanding debates about resource access center around whether social movements obtain their support primarily from internal or external sources and the closely related question about the extent to which external supporters constrain movement goals and activities. Recent developments in RMT seek to reframe this debate in several ways. Research has made it clear that social movements and individual SMOs generally obtain their resources from a combination of internal and external sources. All but the very smallest SMOs gain access to resources by multiple means. Four mechanisms of resource access are particularly important: self-production; aggregation from constituents; appropriation/cooptation; and patronage (see Edwards & McCarthy 2004).

Self-production. A fundamental mechanism by which social movements gain access to resources is to produce those resources themselves through the agency of existing organizations, activists, and participants. Movements produce social organizational resources when they launch SMOs, develop networks, and form issue coalitions. They produce human resources by socializing their children into the ways and values of the movement, or by training participants and developing leaders. Movements like those for civil and human rights have produced out of their struggle a moral authority that is a powerful resource. Social movements also produce items with movement-symbolic significance like T-shirts, coffee mugs, posters, art, and even cakes and cookies for bake sales which can be sold to raise money or used directly to promote the movement.

Aggregation. Resource aggregation refers to the ways a movement or specific SMO converts resources held by dispersed individuals into collective resources that can be allocated by movement actors. Social movements aggregate privately held resources from beneficiary and conscience constituents in order to pursue collective goals. Monetary or human resources are aggregated by soliciting donations from broadly dispersed individuals in order to fund group activities, or recruiting volunteers to help with an activity. Yet, social movements also aggregate other types of resources as well. For example, moral resources held by others can be aggregated by compiling and publicizing lists of individuals and organizations that endorse group goals and actions, as is common in the global justice movement currently.

Cooptation/appropriation. Social movements often utilize relationships they have with existing organizations and groups to access resources previously produced or aggregated by those other organizations. Resource cooptation generally carries the tacit understanding that the resources will be used in mutually agreeable ways. In the US context, churches and church-related organizations have probably produced resources most often coopted by social movements from buildings, members and staff, social networks, rituals and discourses or moral authority.

Patronage. Social movements also gain access to resources through patronage. Patronage refers to the provision of resources to an SMO by an individual or organization that often specializes in patronage. Foundation grants, private donations, or government contracts are common in financial patronage. In monetary patronage relationships patrons external to the movement or SMO provide a substantial amount of financial support and usually exert a degree of control over how their money can be used. Patrons may even attempt to influence an SMO's policy decisions and day-to-day operations. Human resources can be acquired through patronage relationships as when one SMO loans staff to another for a set period of time, as is common in issue campaigns or coalitions.

Despite the obvious centrality of resources to RMT, analysts were slow to develop a clear conceptualization of resources. Analysis and often heated debate focused on a narrow range of material and human resources. Yet, resources important to social movement mobilization are more varied. In recent years RMT analysts have benefited from broader developments in social science and made considerable gains in specifying and differentiating between different types of resources. Five distinct types of resources will be discussed below: moral, cultural, social organizational, human, and material (see Edwards & McCarthy 2004).

Moral resources. Moral resources include legitimacy, integrity, solidary support, sympathetic support, and celebrity. Of these, legitimacy has received the most theoretical attention, and celebrity perhaps the least. Collective actors who most closely mimic institutionally legitimated or "mainstream" expectations gain advantages over groups that fit those expectations poorly. Similarly, celebrity endorsements of an issue campaign can increase media coverage, generate public attention, and open doors to policymakers and resource providers alike. Moral resources tend to originate outside of a social movement or SMO and are generally bestowed by an external source known to possess them, as in a celebrity lending his or her fame, the receipt of awards like the Nobel Peace Prize by a prominent activist, or the certification by an external credentialing body like the Internal Revenue Service. Nevertheless, some movements succeed in the difficult task of creating moral resources, as was clearly the case with the US Southern Civil Rights Movement or more recently the international human rights movement. Because moral resources can often be retracted, they are both less accessible and more proprietary than cultural resources.

Cultural resources. Cultural resources are artifacts and cultural products such as conceptual tools and specialized knowledge that have become widely, though not necessarily universally, known. These include tacit knowledge about how to accomplish specific tasks like enacting a protest event, holding a news conference, running a meeting, forming an organization, initiating a festival, or surfing the web. This category includes tactical repertoires, organizational templates, and technical or strategic know-how required to either mobilize, produce events, or access additional other resources. Specific cultural resources are widely available in a given society, but neither evenly distributed nor universally available. In other words, not every member of a society or social group possesses specific competencies or knowledge that could be valuable to a social movement or SMO. This points to a key difference between cultural and moral resources. Cultural resources are more widely accessible and available for use independent of favorable judgments from those outside a movement or SMO. Cultural resources include movement- or issue-relevant productions like music, literature, magazine/newspapers, or film/videos. Such cultural products facilitate the recruitment and socialization of new adherents and help movements maintain their readiness and capacity for collective action.

Social organizational resources. There are three general forms of social organizational resources: infrastructures, social networks, and organizations, each varying in its degree of organizational formality. Infrastructures are the social organizational equivalent of public goods like postal service, roads, or the Internet that facilitate the smooth functioning of everyday life. Infrastructures are non-proprietary social resources. By contrast, access to social networks and especially groups and formal organizations can be limited by insiders. Thus, access to resources embedded in them can be hoarded by insiders and denied to outsiders. Such differential access only intensifies existing inequalities among groups in their ability to utilize crucial resources of other kinds. This resource category includes both resources intentionally produced by social movements to further their aims, like SMOs, and those produced by others for non-movement purposes but coopted by social movements, like churches, schools, service organizations, occupational groups, or more broadly civil society. The ease of SMO access to resources produced by others for non-movement purposes will vary depending on the perceived compatibility of the groups involved.

Human resources. Human resources are both more tangible and easier to appreciate than the three resource types discussed so far. This category includes resources like labor, experience, skills, expertise, and leadership. Human resources are characteristics of individuals rather than of social organizational structures or culture more generally. Individuals typically have control over the use of their labor and human resources and make them accessible to social movements or SMOs through participation. Yet, not all participants offer the same mix of capabilities. SMOs often require expertise of varying kinds and having access to lawyers, web designers, dynamic speakers, organizers, or outside experts when the need arises can be vitally important. Yet, the use value of expertise often depends on the situation. For example, a prominent scientist may have little more to offer than a high school intern if an environmental group needs to restore its web page after a crash. Similarly, a celebrated musician participating in a blockade contributes no additional human resource to the blockade, yet, from the standpoint of the moral resources contributed by the celebrity's presence, the evaluation would be much different.

Material resources. The category of material resources combines what economists would call financial and physical capital including monetary resources, property, office space, equipment, and supplies. The importance of monetary resources for social movements should not be underestimated. No matter how many other resources a movement mobilizes, it will incur costs and someone has to pay the bills. Material resources have received the most analytic attention because they are generally more tangible, more proprietary, and in the case of money more fungible than other resource types. In other words, money can be converted into other types of resources while the opposite is less often the case.

Combining the four means of access with the five types of resources discussed above specifies 20 specific exchange relationships through which social movements or SMOs acquire the resources they use to pursue their social change goals. The RMT perspective encourages analysts to consider the range of exchange relationships through which specific SMOs, coalitions, issue campaigns, or event organizers mobilize resources. By contrast, the long debate among social movement analysts over the extent to which acquiring resources from external sources constrains the actions of SMOs has been cast very narrowly. From the RMT perspective sketched here, that debate focused almost exclusively on a single exchange relationship – monetary patronage. Yet, the typical SMO, much less SMI, simultaneously manages numerous exchange relationships. Each exchange relationship that makes resources accessible also carries a set of expectations and obligations between the parties, giving each relationship varying potential for social control. For example, the exchange relationship involved in an SMO aggregating small donations from a dispersed list of external conscience constituents will not constrain the group's actions as much as if they received the same amount of money through the monetary patronage of a single large donor, everything else being equal.

SEE ALSO: Collective Action; Collective Identity; New Social Movement Theory; Oligarchy and Organization; Political Opportunities; Political Process Theory; Social Change; Social Movement Organizations; Social Movements; Social Movements, Networks and; Social Movements, Relative Deprivation and

REFERENCES AND SUGGESTED READINGS

Andrews, K. T. (2005) *Freedom is a Constant Struggle.* University of Chicago Press, Chicago.

Andrews, K. T. & Edwards, B. (2004) Advocacy Organizations in the US Political Process. *Annual Review of Sociology* 30: 479–506.

Caniglia, B. S. & Carmin, J. (Eds.) (2005) Special Focus Issue on Social Movement Organizations. *Mobilization* 10(2): 201–308.

Dalton, R., Kuechler, M., & Burklin, W. (1990) The Challenge of New Movements. In: Dalton, R. & Kuechler, M. (Eds.), *Challenging the Political Order: New Social Movements in Western Democracies.* Oxford University Press, New York, pp. 3–20.

Edwards, B. & Foley, M. W. (2003) Social Movement Organizations Beyond the Beltway: Understanding the Diversity of One Social Movement Industry. *Mobilization* 8(1): 85–107.

Edwards, B. & McCarthy, J. D. (2004) Resources and Social Movement Mobilization. In: Snow, D. A., Soule, S. A., & Kriesi, H. (Eds.), *The Blackwell Companion to Social Movements.* Blackwell, Malden, MA, pp. 116–52.

Freeman, J. (1975) *The Politics of Women's Liberation.* David McKay, New York.

Gamson, W. A. (1968) *Power and Discontent.* Dorsey Press, Homewood, IL.

Gamson, W. A. (1975) *The Strategy of Social Protest.* Dorsey Press, Homewood, IL.

Jenkins, J. C. (1983) Resource Mobilization Theory and the Study of Social Movements. *Annual Review of Sociology* 9: 248–67.

McAdam, D. (1982) *Political Process and the Development of Black Insurgency, 1890–1970.* University of Chicago Press, Chicago.

McAdam, D., McCarthy, J. D., & Zald, M. N. (1988) Social Movements. In: Smelser, N. (Ed.), *Handbook of Sociology.* Sage, Beverley Hills, pp. 695–737.

McCarthy, J. D. & Zald, M. N. (1977) Resource Mobilization and Social Movements: A Partial Theory. *American Journal of Sociology* 82: 1212–41.

Melucci, A. (1980) The New Social Movements: A Theoretical Approach. *Social Science Information* 19: 199–226.

Minkoff, D. (1995) *Organizing for Equality: The Evolution of Women's and Race-Ethnic Organizations in America, 1955–1985.* Rutgers University Press, New Brunswick, NJ.

Morris, A. (1984) *The Origins of the Civil Rights Movement: Black Communities Organizing for Change.* Free Press, New York.

Oberschall, A. (1973) *Social Conflict and Social Movements.* Prentice-Hall, Englewood Cliffs, NJ.

Smith, J., Chattfield, C., & Pagnucco, R. (Eds.) (1997) *Transnational Social Movements and Global Politics: Solidarity Beyond the State*. Syracuse University Press, Syracuse, NY.
Snow, D. A. & Benford, R. (1988) Ideology, Frame Resonance, and Participant Mobilization. *International Social Movement Research* 1: 197–217.
Staggenborg, S. (1988) The Consequences of Professionalization and Formalization in the Pro-Choice Movement. *American Sociological Review* 53: 585–606.
Staggenborg, S. (1991) *The Pro-Choice Movement*. Oxford University Press, New York.
Tarrow, S. (1994) *Power in Movement*. Cambridge University Press, Cambridge.
Tilly, C. (1978) *From Mobilization to Revolution*. Addison-Wesley, Reading, MA.
Zald, M. N. & McCarthy, J. D. (1987) *Social Movements in an Organizational Society*. Transaction, New Brunswick, NJ.
Zald, M. N. & McCarthy, J. D. (2002) The Resource Mobilization Research Program: Progress, Challenge, and Transformation. In: Berger, J. & Zelditch, M. (Eds.), *New Directions in Contemporary Social Theory*. Rowman & Littlefield, Lanham, MD, pp. 147–71.

restrictive covenants

Jerome Krase

Restrictive covenants are deed restrictions on particular kinds of real estate. For example, they may restrict use of land in a subdivision to residential purposes only and define the maximum and minimum square footage of homes to be built. They might also place restrictions regarding construction of other buildings on the property, as well as control activities that take place within its boundaries, such as rentals. Real estate professionals argue that such legal restrictions give a development a more standard appearance and when enforced, protect property values. Racially restrictive covenants were legally enforceable contractual agreements between property owners and neighborhood associations that prohibited the sale, occupancy, or lease of property and land to certain ethnic and racial groups. While now unenforceable by the courts, racially restrictive covenants had been one of the primary ways by which access to housing had been blocked for racial and ethnic minorities.

During the long history of housing discrimination in the US there have been many ways by which access has been blocked for racial and religious minorities. In the past the major pillars of segregated neighborhoods such as racially restrictive covenants were *de jure* or legal. Since Fair Housing in 1968 even the publication of a real estate ad that indicates preferences, limitations, or other discrimination based on race, color, religion, sex, handicap, familial status, or national origin has been illegal. That is not to say that *de facto* segregation and discrimination no longer exists. "Gentlemen's agreements," informal networks, and other voluntary agreements between realtors and homeowners, and among owners themselves, make it possible for housing discrimination to continue. *De jure* discrimination which is not overtly racial or ethnic for example may also continue in the form of zoning, and in residential developments which are limited to specific incomes, ages, and family status. In this way builders and developers can also perpetuate *de facto* class and racial segregation through the use of non-racial restrictive covenants.

Prior to the turn of the twentieth century, legal restrictions on the transfer of and sale of property to people of color were usually contained in individual deed restrictions. After 1910 the use of restrictive covenants became more widespread through the promotional efforts of large "community builders," local real estate boards and national real estate associations, especially the National Association of Real Estate Boards created in 1908. During the 1910s and 1920s, state courts upheld and enforced these racially restrictive covenants and argued that they did not violate the due process rights of non-white citizens. Ironically, racial discrimination in housing was also supported by liberal reformers who equated black neighborhoods with crime and other social pathologies. Therefore, it was agreed that the presence of non-white residents would decrease property values. Racially restrictive covenants were the primary mechanism used by the emerging real estate industry to create and maintain racially segregated neighborhoods in response to the Great Migration of rural Southern blacks to the urban North as well as the 1917 *Buchanan* v. *Warley* US Supreme Court ruling that made racial zoning ordinances unenforceable.

By 1920 it was unethical for real estate firms and land developers *not* to restrict certain ethnic groups, especially blacks, to specific areas of the city through the use of racially restrictive covenants. These stigmatizing ideas further contributed to the "racialization of urban space" by linking race and culturally specific behavior to place of residence in the city. It could be argued that the rise of the modern real estate industry was crucial in the creation of segregated neighborhoods beyond the South through the use and enforcement of racially restrictive covenants. Other significant groups who were victims of racially restrictive covenants were Asians, Jews, and Latinos. It was estimated that until 1948 racially restrictive covenants were in place in more than half the new subdivisions built in the US. As a result, these discriminatory practices influenced the shape of entire subdivisions and metropolitan areas.

Another powerful example of institutionalized racism was the Federal Housing Administration, established in 1934, which instructed in its manual that blacks were adverse influences on property values and therefore homes should not be federally insured unless there is a racially restrictive covenant. Although the agency removed the racially explicit language in the 1950s, it found expression by private insurers, as well as in codes of ethics for realtors, until the 1970s.

In 1948 the Supreme Court held that restrictive covenants were illegal, and more importantly, that government could not help enforce them (*Shelley* v. *Kraemer*). Shelley, an African American family, argued that racially restrictive covenants in deeds violated their constitutional rights. Specifically, the petitioner contended that the racially restrictive covenant violated the Equal Protection Clause of the Fourteenth Amendment and the court ruled in its favor. However, it is important to note that the Supreme Court did not specifically renounce racially restrictive covenants. It held that the covenants alone did not violate constitutional rights. Rather, the judicial enforcement of racially restrictive covenants violated the petitioner's rights because it was an action of the state. This decision helped other challenges as courts throughout the nation cited Shelley in racially restrictive covenant cases, so that today they are no longer legal.

SEE ALSO: Blockbusting; Hypersegregation; Redlining; Residential Segregation; Social Exclusion; Uneven Development; Urban Policy

REFERENCES AND SUGGESTED READINGS

Gotham, K. F. (2000) Urban Space, Restrictive Covenants and the Origins of Racial Residential Segregation in a US City, 1900–50. *International Journal of Urban and Regional Research* 24, 3 (September): 616–33.
Hobson, L. (1947) *Gentleman's Agreement.* Simon & Schuster, New York.
Krase, J. (1982) *Self and Community in the City.* University Press of America, Lanham, MD.
Massey, D. S. & Denton, N. A. (1993) *American Apartheid: Segregation and the Making of the Underclass.* Harvard University Press, Cambridge, MA.
Osofsky, G. (1963) *Harlem: The Making of a Ghetto.* Harper Torchbooks, New York.
Plotkin, W. (1999) Deeds of Mistrust: Racial Restrictive Covenants in Chicago, 1900–1953. PhD Dissertation, University of Illinois at Chicago.
Weaver, R. (1948) *The Negro Ghetto.* Harcourt, Brace, New York.

retirement

Angela M. O'Rand

Retirement has traditionally been defined as an age-related and permanent transition from an income status based on employment to one based on transfers and assets at the end of the work career. The relationship of retirement to age has been defined more by state and market institutions that have provided age-based incentives to exit the labor force than by the physical aging process itself. These institutions developed since the late nineteenth century to replace income from earnings with pensions and to support access to health care systems through public and private insurance systems, although they vary across countries in their eligibility criteria and share of public funding support. However, all countries now confront major fiscal challenges associated with population aging, economic restructuring at a global level, and changing family and household arrangements that are motivating the reorganization of income- and health-support policies. As such, the institution of retirement is changing.

RETIREMENT IN US HISTORY

The major demographic trend over the twentieth century associated with these institutions in the US was the decline in labor force participation of the elderly, and especially of elderly men (Costa 1998). Early in the twentieth century, ill health and unemployment were factors in this decline. However, the spread of pensions across the public and private sectors contributed increasingly to older men's labor force exits. The passage of the Social Security Act in 1935 established 65 as the age of eligibility for worker retirement. Thirty years later, age 65 was the most common age of retirement. This legislation also accelerated the spread of private pensions whose benefit calculations – based on age, years of service, and salary levels – became strong inducements for pension-covered workers to remain with their employers until eligibility for their private pensions or for both Social Security and their pensions. However, these private pensions were available in only the most advantaged labor markets, including manufacturing, communications and transportation, and financial and professional sectors. Service and trade sectors offered far less pension coverage.

By the 1960s two contrasting patterns associated with retirement emerged. The first was the "discovery" of poverty among the elderly; one in three elderly persons fell below the poverty line. Medicare, an array of community-level programs under the rubric of the Administration on Aging, and early reduced-benefit retirement at age 62 were implemented over the years following this discovery to respond directly to the needs of this subgroup. The Supplementary Security Income program was also enacted in 1972 to add a final safety net for the poorest retirees without eligibility for normal worker Social Security benefits.

Since the implementation of these programs, lower-income groups comprised largely of minorities and women have tended to retire earlier (at age 62). Longitudinal studies of their retirement experiences have revealed that the disadvantages among these groups accumulate after retirement, placing them at higher risks of poverty and institutionalization in old age (Haveman et al. 2003). Moreover, a significant portion of this group moves onto Social Security retirement benefits from disability rolls and from years of under-employment and unemployment (Flippen & Tienda 2000). Current trends related to escalating medical costs and out-of-pocket expenses among the elderly have added to the deteriorating life conditions of these elderly groups.

The other pattern that was observable by the late 1960s was the emergence of a "pension elite": a subgroup of retirees who benefited by the spread of generous pensions, some of which were linked to retiree health insurance. After 30 years of tenure with the same employer, pension-covered workers began to retire earlier than the age of Social Security eligibility. Higher pension wealth coupled with access to early Social Security spawned the trend towards "early retirement," which persisted among men until the 1990s. Figure 1 displays the trend towards acceptance of early (and reduced) worker benefits among men and women between 1970 and 2000. In 1970 a very small portion of retired men's benefits were being distributed at aged 62 (about 19 percent). This portion more than doubled by 1985, then rose slowly and finally reversed by 2000. Women have had higher rates of early retirement than men, historically. However, their pattern somewhat parallels men's: the trend in women's early retirement rates peaked in 1985 and has fallen since.

What happened between the 1980s and 1990s to slow (and perhaps reverse) these trends? First, structural changes that altered the relationship between employers and workers steadily accumulated over this period. Long-term employment relationships, once the hallmark of industrial and related sectors, were abandoned and replaced by outsourcing, offshore labor markets, and contingent arrangements as global market competition and economic restructuring increased (Levy 1998). This shift was especially evident in new forms of pensions that were offered to replace the traditional defined benefit plans. The new plans moved the responsibility for pension saving to workers, whose tax sheltered contributions were allocated to a mix of stock, bond, real estate, and related holdings

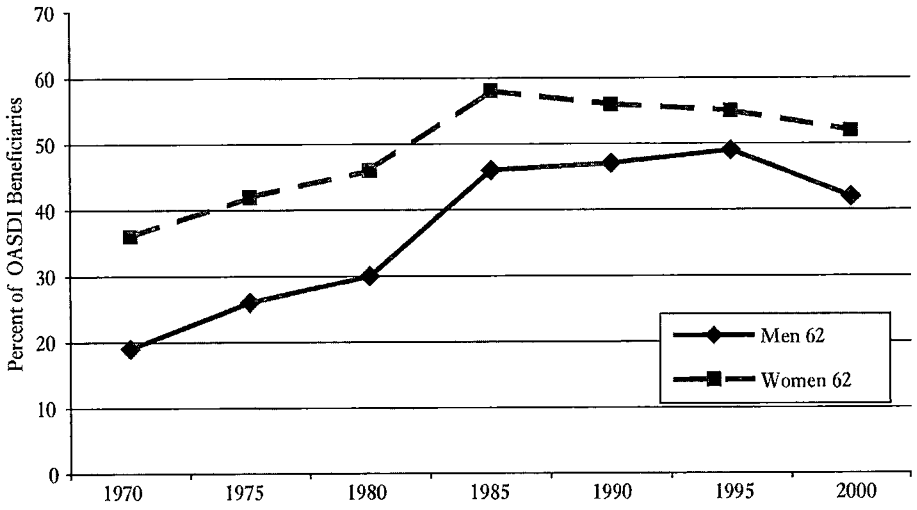

Figure 1 Percent Social Security distributions to early retired worker benefits by gender between 1970 and 2000.
Source: Social Security Administration (2004) *Annual Statistical Supplement to the Social Security Bulletin*, Table 6.B5.

selected and managed by workers themselves. Pensions can no longer be expected to provide predictable lifetime benefits easily calculated from pre-retirement earnings, years of service, and age. Rather, the pensions that now predominate in the workplace are account balances accumulated through workers' voluntary contributions and affected by their risk preferences for investing these accounts. The stock market bubble of the 1990s influenced workers' behaviors, leading them to exit work at the peak of the boom and to delay their retirements when the bust occurred (Gustman & Steinmeier 2002). Moreover, some scholars argue that this structural change will be pivotal in extending the trend away from earlier retirement among the baby boom cohorts born between 1946 and 1964 (Hughes and O'Rand 2004).

Second, demographic changes have amplified the impact of structural change. Chief among these changes are the extension of life expectancy, women's increased labor force participation over the life span, and changing family and living arrangements across age groups. Life expectancy in the US has increased more than 60 percent over the twentieth century, from 47 years in 1900 to 77 years in 2000. A significant trend underlying these aggregate figures is the more rapid growth of those aged 85 and older, termed the "oldest old" and comprised primarily of single women (Himes 2001). Consequently, the number of years between early and normal retirement and average life expectancy are increasing and rapidly feeding concerns about the future fiscal health of pension and health insurance systems to support growing dependency.

Accompanying these life expectancy projections are increases in the heterogeneity and inequality of the older population. Ethnic, class, and gender differences stratify the older population to be among the most unequal in advanced industrial societies. Married couples persist as the most advantaged in income and benefit receipt, while single individuals (especially divorced and widowed women) are at high risk of poverty, in part as a result of their more limited earnings histories and in part as a result of pension policies that privilege traditional marriage and penalize nontraditional living arrangements. The demographic diversity of the baby boom cohorts in these regards (i.e., higher levels of income inequality, higher rates of divorce, and greater ethnic heterogeneity than earlier cohorts) have combined with structural changes in the workplace and reforms of the

Social Security Act to alter future patterns of retirement in ways that will increase the variability in retirement timing with such diverse patterns as the delay of final labor force exits or the combination of retirement with continued labor force participation (Hughes & O'Rand 2004).

CROSS-NATIONAL PATTERNS

Other advanced industrial societies have preceded the US in both population aging and early retirement. Fertility rates decreased in Europe earlier than in the US. In addition, efforts to control the age composition of the labor force to make more room for younger workers encouraged early retirement in European countries (Kohli et al. 1991). These trends in Europe are challenging their more publicly based pension and health insurance systems (Esping-Andersen 1999). At the same time, less advanced countries are also facing population aging and are being forced to confront the challenges of population aging and global restructuring in the development of their policies.

Most advanced countries have been proposing and/or implementing changes in their policies in order to discourage early retirement behaviors. Figure 2 compares the differences between average life expectancy and statutory early retirement ages for workers in six countries as of 2002. The disparities between life expectancy and the earliest pensionable age of men and women varied slightly from country to country. The gender differences in life expectancy were generally consistent, but gender-specific versus gender-neutral policies related to retirement timing varied. In the case of the US, age 62 is the earliest pensionable age for all workers and 65 the normal age – at least until the baby boom cohorts begin to retire; then full benefits will be extended to age 66 for the early boomer cohorts and continue to shift upward to age 67 for the later boomers and younger cohorts. In addition, the levels of early benefits at age 62 will be cut for these groups to discourage early retirement further.

Other countries are shifting their gender-related policies and also changing tax and benefit schedules. The United Kingdom and Germany have adopted gender-neutral policies since 2002, to be implemented over the future, that raise statutory retirement for all to age 65 with no earlier option for future cohorts. Austria and Japan have retained early retirement options, but made full retirement the same for women and men at age 65. And Sweden, which has been among the most socially democratic

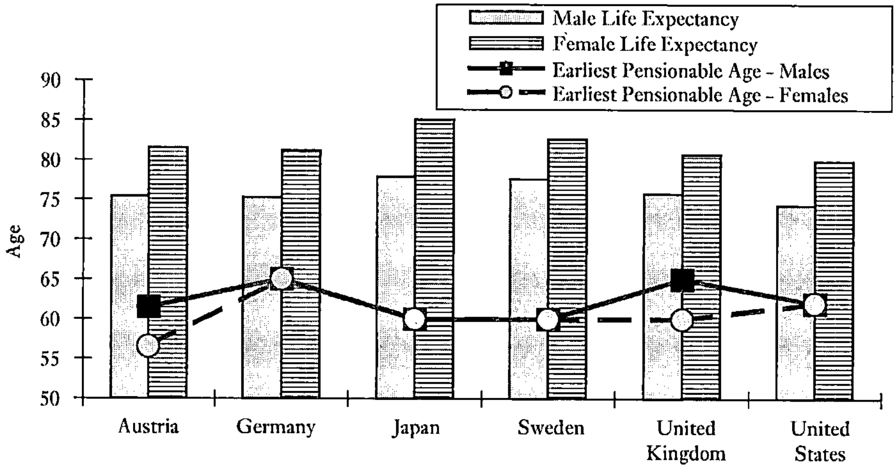

Figure 2 Comparison of early retirement age to life expectancy by gender across six countries.
Sources: Life expectancy data from the Population and Statistics Divisions of the UN Secretariat (unstats.un.org/unsd/demographic/socials/health.htm). Pension data from Social Security Administration (2002).

welfare systems, has shifted towards policies to discourage early retirement by linking benefits to individual contribution levels, while still retaining gender-neutral early and late age thresholds (Social Security Administration 2002).

In short, retirement policy is on the table throughout the world (Social Security Administration 2002). Some developing countries (like Spain and China) have moved to gender-neutral policies, while others (like Brazil) have not. Key concerns of these countries are centered on economic development and the inclusion of larger proportions of their populations in the formal economy. But above and beyond economic development issues, the demographic pressures of population aging and the changing roles of women in the marketplace are relevant to the development of retirement policies.

SEE ALSO: Aging, Demography of; Aging and Social Policy; Aging and Work Performance; Gender, Aging and; Retirement Communities

REFERENCES AND SUGGESTED READINGS

Costa, D. (1998) *The Evolution of Retirement: An American Economic History 1880–1990.* University of Chicago Press, Chicago.

Esping-Andersen, G. (1999) *The Social Foundations of Post-Industrial Economies.* Oxford University Press, Oxford.

Flippen, C. & Tienda, M. (2000) Pathways to Retirement: Patterns of Labor Force Participation and Labor Market Exit among the Pre-Retired Population by Race, Hispanic Origin, and Sex. *Journals of Gerontology-Psychological and Social Sciences* 55B: S14–S27.

Gustman, A. & Steinmeier, T. L. (2002) Retirement and the Stock Market Bubble. *NBER Working Paper 9494.* National Bureau of Economic Research, Cambridge, MA.

Haveman, R., Holden, K., Wilson, K., & Wolfe, B. (2003) Social Security, Age of Retirement and Economic Well-Being. *Demography* 40: 369–94.

Himes, C. (2001) Elderly Americans. *Population Bulletin* 56 (December). Population Reference Bureau, Washington, DC.

Hughes, M. E. & O'Rand, A. M. (2004) *The Lives and Times of the Baby Boom.* Census 2000 Bulletin. Russell Sage/Population Reference Bureau, New York/Washington, DC.

Kohli, M., Rein, M., Guillemard, A. M., & van Gusteren, H. (Eds.) (1991) *Time for Retirement.* Cambridge University Press, Cambridge.

Levy, F. (1998) *The New Dollars and Dreams: American Incomes and Economic Change.* Russell Sage, New York.

Social Security Administration (2002) *Social Security Programs Throughout the World.* Washington, DC. Online. www.ssa.gov/policy/docs/progdesc/ssptw/index.html.

retirement communities

Gordon Streib

Retirement communities are residential areas designated by federal law requiring, for the purpose of excluding younger residents, that at least 80 percent of their occupied dwelling units must have at least one person of 55 years of age or older living there, and that the communities must publish and follow policies and procedures that demonstrate an intent to be 55 and older housing. This legal definition does not describe the wide range of communities housing older persons. There are two major kinds of retirement communities: (1) Planned Leisure-Oriented Retirement Communities, and (2) Continuing Care Retirement Communities (CCRCs). A third type is called Naturally Occurring Retirement Communities. These do not need to meet the precise legal requirements, but their age-dense populations qualify them as a type of retirement community. In addition, public housing projects primarily restricted to low-income older persons are mostly for retirees, although some projects permit younger disabled persons to live there.

Demographic and political-economic social forces have shaped the context for retirement communities. The gradual increase in life expectancy in the US and the related increase in the older population has provided the base for specialized housing of many varieties. The political-economic factors are complex and provide basic economic security for many older persons. The economic fundamentals include public programs, notably Social Security and Medicare, public and private pension plans, plus savings and a high amount of home ownership. The latter is important for those older persons who move permanently to a retirement community and also for seasonal residents ("Snow Birds") who have a second home in the Sunbelt.

The major components of the retirement housing industry involve available land and real estate developers who recognize there is a market for specialized housing for older persons. The high amount of occupational and residential mobility experienced by many Americans makes them amenable to both seasonal and permanent moves to warmer climates.

Retirement communities are labeled correctly because the overwhelming majority of residents have left the labor force. The possibility of an early retirement made possible by Social Security has undoubtedly added to the interest in retirement community living. The exploration of residing in a new setting leads many older persons to consider the services and amenities provided by developers for this new "leisure class."

The retirement community industry has grown and changed over the past half century. After World War II mobile home parks and modest homes (both for rent and for purchase) developed for the growing cohort of retirees. Over time these early communities have provided very economical housing for the lower end of the retirement community market. In recent years the kind of housing, the amenities, the services, and the ambience have become more upscale. Some older communities have now become economically stratified. In the older growing communities, like the Sun Cities, neighborhood stratification can be easily identified by the type of housing, lot size, and adjacent leisure facilities. However, it must be noted that in these larger communities there is a broad array of programs and activities that involve residents with a wide range of income. Some communities are income differentiated, but that is not always the case in large, older, class-integrated communities.

CCRCs are a burgeoning aspect of the industry involving both profit and not-for-profit sponsorship. The CCRCs developed from the concept of life care or continuum of care that provides a full range of services to meet changing needs as older persons become functionally impaired. A CCRC usually has three levels of living: independent housing, assisted living, and 24-hour nursing care. The leadership for CCRCs emerged primarily from the not-for-profit sector as some religiously affiliated homes adapted services to changing needs. Providing housing and care for members, clergy, and their widows has a long history in different religious traditions. The typical CCRC today is controlled by a complex set of federal and state regulations to protect residents who usually must pay a sizable up-front fee in addition to monthly service charges.

Another growing segment of the industry is retirement communities of various kinds that are now being built in or near major metropolitan areas. These communities may be either leisure oriented or CCRCs and often serve higher income persons who choose to remain in the area where they have lived in order to continue contact with family, kin, and friends, and also to enjoy the cultural, social, and recreational opportunities that are available in metropolitan areas.

CCRCs affiliated with universities are also a growing part of the market. Signed agreements spell out the reciprocal arrangements in which schools and colleges (e.g., nursing, physical education, music) have staff and students working at or studying the living environment of the CCRC. The residents have opportunities to attend programs, lectures, musical events, galleries, or sports events at the affiliated university.

Retirement communities may be located in terms of theory and research in the fields of sociology and gerontology. The proliferation of specialties in these fields and the complexities of modern society result in a diffused agenda. There is an opportunity for integration of theoretical approaches and research methods. As one surveys sociology and gerontology, one notes different models, paradigms, and perspectives. Various qualitative and quantitative methods are adapted and employed, but most research has been descriptive.

A theoretical grounding for studying age-dense communities based on Durkheim's concept of social integration, as well as the later concept of age segregation derived from the racial integration-segregation arguments, was developed by social gerontologists. Although some earlier writers viewed the age segregation inherent in retirement communities in a negative light, Rosow (1967) and Osgood (1982) provided theoretical and empirical support for their socially integrating capacities.

A useful orientation to age-dense housing in general and specifically to retirement communities is the work of Charles Lindblom (1977): "In all the political systems of the world much of politics is economic, and most economics is political" (p. 8). This orientation has been adapted to studying the linkages of retirement communities to local, state, and national political and market structures. Political economic embeddedness provides the context for retirement communities with attention to the specifics of locality, and research has shown that retirement communities generally have a positive economic impact on the surrounding area.

Another theoretical orientation is socio-historical or evolutionary. Although retirement communities are of recent historical vintage in the US, there are older evolutionary developments in some European countries. Great Britain and the Scandinavian countries have evolved unique retirement communities that are contextually congruent with their cultures and climates. Social democracies have been adaptable and more systematic in meeting the housing needs of older persons than the market-driven US.

Suzanne Keller (2003: 215) concludes her 30-year study of a planned community reflecting on "the territorial community as an anchor of human existence." Her research is based on a nuanced adaptation of community (*Gemeinschaft*) and society (*Gesellschaft*) originated by Ferdinand Tönnies. The concepts are analytically distinct, but in real life they interact, and the boundaries must be determined empirically in retirement communities.

Much research has shown that the residents of retirement communities are overwhelmingly satisfied with their choice of this living environment. Research on conflict in retirement communities, however, indicates that a few residents view participation in community conflict as a form of "recreation." Conflict is socially constructed by a few individuals and some groups. Most of the residents stay out of community disagreements or stay on the margins. Unless their economic interests or basic style of life are threatened, or a major change is involved, the residents generally will attempt to avoid situations resulting in conflict. Residents generally are sensitive and concerned that they not give offense. Conflict with administration is minimized if the management is perceived as benign. Democratic procedures are valued, but decision-making is usually left in the hands of management.

A considerable literature on retirement communities has concentrated on the internal structure and activities that take place. There are persons who practice an active lifestyle and they are a visible minority who are highlighted for marketing goals. A less visible majority practices a more sheltered and passive lifestyle, with television and reading occupying their time. CCRCs provide some transportation services for their residents, but most retirement communities expect that residents will drive a car. When physical limitations make driving difficult, the loss of independence is felt keenly, although caring neighbors may offer help. Travel to places outside the community to shop or visit family and friends provides an occasional break for many.

Activities are an important, opportunistic way to create new acquaintances and friendships. Some relationships could be described as friendship with social distance. Participation in the life of the community is a way to avoid being marginalized. Personality and sociability skills are important factors in participating and making new friends. Widows, widowers, singles, and newcomers may live on the margin unless they exercise some initiative. The aging in place of the populations evolves slowly into a decline in community participation and the activists are challenged to find new leadership and participants for programs.

Theoretical ideas derived from sociology of consumption could provide future research directions for students of retirement communities. Older persons deciding to move are making decisions that go beyond buying a home because the structure and functions of retirement communities are different from the typical housing subdivision. The prospective residents are concerned not only with costs, quality, and location, but also with lifestyle, services, amenities, safety, and community spirit. Some of these aspects may be involved in the purchase or renting of a home by younger persons, but the potential retirement community residents are asking new questions related to community involvement from an older person's perspective.

Rational choice may enter the consumer's decision-making in different ways because the final choice is not a housing move related to employment, and the time pressures are less stringent. The prospective retiree often personally visits many communities for several years before deciding on his or her choice. Family relationships, finances, legacies, and health status are involved in intricate ways. Moving to a CCRC considerably reduces dependency on children, kin, or friends. However, rational choice theory does not explain why so many older persons do not choose to move to a retirement community. Only about 5 percent finally move. Economic considerations are only part of the answer, for ageism may be more important. Some older persons are repelled by the idea of living in an age-dense community. How a person defines his or her personal aging requires research in terms of consumer theory.

The future direction of retirement communities in terms of theory, research, and methodology lies in part in the adaptation of perspectives outlined above. However, the future sociology of retirement communities will also be strongly influenced by the realities of the political-economic context and on how incoming cohorts (e.g., baby boomers) individually and collectively make decisions about home ownership, financial security, migration patterns, and residential preferences. The Golden Age of Retirement their parents experienced will probably be an uncertain template for their decision-making.

SEE ALSO: Aging, Demography of; Friendship During the Later Years; Retirement

REFERENCES AND SUGGESTED READINGS

Bultena, G. L. & Wood, V. (1969) The American Retirement Community: Bane or Blessing? *Journal of Gerontology* 24: 209–17.

Folts, W. E. & Yeatts, D. E. (Eds.) (1994) *Housing and the Aging Population: Options for the New Century*. Garland Publishing, New York.

Golant, S. M. (1992) *Housing America's Elderly: Many Possibilities/Few Choices*. Sage, Newbury Park, CA.

Hunt, M. E., Feldt, A. G., Marans, R. W., et al. (1984) *Retirement Communities: An American Original*. Haworth Press, New York.

Keller, S. (2003) *Community: Pursuing the Dream, Living the Reality*. Princeton University Press, Princeton.

La Greca, A. J., Streib, G. F., & Folts, W. E. (1985) Retirement Communities and their Life Stages. *Journal of Gerontology* 40: 211–18.

Lindblom, C. E. (1977) *Politics and Markets: The World's Political-Economic Systems*. Basic Books, New York.

Osgood, N. J. (1982) *Senior Settlers: Social Integration in Retirement Communities*. Praeger, New York.

Rosow, I. (1967) *Social Integration of the Aged*. Free Press, New York.

Streib, G. F. (1990) Retirement Communities: Linkages to the Locality, State and Nation. *Journal of Applied Gerontology* 9: 405–19.

Streib, G. F. (Ed.) (2002) Special Issue: Retirement Communities. *Research on Aging* 24 (1): 3–164.

Streib, G. F., Folts, W. E., & La Greca, A. J. (1985) Autonomy, Power and Decision-Making in Thirty-Six Retirement Communities. *Gerontologist* 25: 403–9.

revolutions

John Foran

Ever since the French Revolution of 1789, revolutions have helped define the modern age. Though rare events, they have been associated with the emergence of, and transitions to, democracy, capitalism, and socialism. They are significant as often inspiring, human-directed attempts to refashion the world for the better; they have also typically fallen far short of the goals of their makers. Their complexity has challenged scholars and revolutionaries alike – just as consequences have been unforeseen and outcomes uncontrollable by actors, prediction has proven next to impossible for scholars, and even the more modest goal of explanation has opened up extensive debates about the causes, makers, and outcomes of revolutions.

Currently, the study of revolutions has flowered into ever more ambitious theoretical syntheses, comparative studies, and new topics, including the roles played by emotions, culture, race/ethnicity, gender, and social class. As the world enters further into the twenty-first century and the era of globalization, the issue of the continued relevance of revolutions, and the possibility that they are changing in nature, will challenge the sociological imaginations of some of the best students of social change, as well as pose crucial tasks for the practical application of strategies of radical social change among activists seeking solutions to some of the world's most acute social problems.

DEFINITIONS AND METHODS OF STUDY

Among many definitions of *social revolutions*, or the great revolutions of history, Theda Skocpol's remains the most widely cited and in many ways is still unsurpassed: "Social revolutions are rapid, basic transformations of a society's state and class structures; and they are accompanied and in part carried through by class-based revolts from below" (1979: 4). This definition stresses the conjuncture of deep political and socioeconomic change with the mass participation of social forces. It has the virtue of leaving violence – a commonsense element of revolutionary change – to the side, allowing us to consider non-violent paths to revolution, as in Chile 1970, Iran 1979, Eastern Europe 1989, and in Chiapas since 1994. It does not specify how much social change qualifies an event as a social revolution, nor how rapidly the process must occur, which means that scholars will argue over whether particular cases merit inclusion.

We can also use this definition to distinguish the more thorough-going social revolutions of France 1789, Mexico 1910, Russia 1917, China 1949, Cuba 1958, and Iran 1979 from *political revolutions*, where the holders of state power change through mass participation but without deep social transformation, such as the "People's Power" movement that toppled Ferdinand Marcos in the Philippines in 1986, the fall of dictators like Mobutu in Zaire in 1996 and Duvalier in Haiti in 1986, the collapse of the Manchu dynasty in China in 1911, and the end of apartheid in South Africa in 1994. Mass participation by revolutionaries that fails to change either government or social structure is classified as a *failed* or *attempted revolution*; examples include El Salvador, Guatemala, and Peru in the 1980s, or China's Tiananmen Square uprising in 1989. When power is seized by the army or an elite movement and then turned somewhat surprisingly in the direction of radical social transformation, we speak of a *revolution from above*, such as those of the 1868–73 Meiji Restoration in Japan, Atatürk in 1920s and 1930s Turkey, Nasser in 1952 Egypt, or the revolutionary armed forces of Peru between 1968 and 1975.

Two other sets of cases also qualify as social revolutions: one set consists of the *anti-colonial* revolutionary movements that achieved relatively deep social change in Algeria in the 1950s, Angola, Mozambique, and Zimbabwe in the 1970s, and Vietnam's long struggle for independence from 1945 to 1975. The main difference of these cases when compared with the classical social revolutions is the overthrow not of an internal regime but of a colonial power – France, Portugal, England, or (indirectly in Vietnam) the United States. Many such movements of national liberation do not, however, result in the degree of social transformation that would earn them the title of social revolution, as in most of Africa after World War II, or in India in 1947. A final set of cases might be termed *reversed revolutions*, instances of social revolution where revolutionaries achieved power and embarked on a process of social transformation but could not hold onto that power more than a few years, usually falling to a combination of external intervention and its internal right-wing and military allies, as with Iran from 1951 to 1953, Guatemala 1944–54, and Chile's elected socialist government from 1970 to 1973, or Nicaragua's Sandinistas who governed from 1979 to 1991 when they lost elections, and Grenada's New Jewel Movement which overthrew the dictator Eric Gairy in 1979 but self-destructed in a power struggle that opened the door to US invasion in 1983.

These typologies are important for distinguishing different phenomena that can be grouped under the general rubric of revolutions. For most sociologists of revolution, the focus has been on the set of fewer than 20 instances of social revolution, whether these be classical, anti-colonial, or reversed revolutions. It is noteworthy that with the exceptions of France, Russia, and Eastern Europe, all the rest have occurred in the third world regions of Latin America, Africa, Asia, and the Middle East, with the most in any one region coming from

Latin America. The reasons for this will be explored below.

The methods of studying such complex phenomena are diverse: we have many fine archival-based histories, some excellent ethnographic-based work, and a few notable quantitative studies (Paige 1975; Goldstone 1991), but leaving aside single case studies, the vast majority of sociological work on revolutions has been comparative-historical in nature, with sets of cases ranging from two or three to several dozen, and sources ranging from archival and other primary documents to the secondary scholarship of historians and social scientists. The most common methodologies for comparing cases have been John Stuart Mill's methods of agreement and difference, brought into the study of revolutions by Skocpol (1979), and more recently Boolean or qualitative-comparative analysis, as developed by Charles Ragin (1987) and first used by Timothy Wickham-Crowley (1992), which is suitable for studies involving more than a half-dozen cases. Some studies combine these methods with each other, and with such approaches as regional/ecological analysis, demography, content analysis, or interviewing. A younger generation of scholars is doing more intensive fieldwork, inspired by new theories of agency, culture, and race, class, and gender.

A BRIEF HISTORY OF THEORIZING ABOUT THE CAUSES OF REVOLUTIONS

Given the multiple possible determinants of these rare, large-scale events, it should come as no surprise that theories about their causes have been offered by successive generations of historians and social scientists, and that there has never been general agreement among them. The French Revolution put this question on the agenda, and one of its first and most insightful interpreters was Alexis de Tocqueville, writing 70 years later, who noted the importance of the state and elites, village autonomy, and ideology in bringing about the revolution, arguing that the moment of greatest danger for an autocratic regime was when it started granting reforms, for this only encouraged people to demand more: "For it is not always when things are going from bad to worse that revolutions break out. On the contrary, it oftener happens that when a people which has put up with an oppressive rule over a long period without protest suddenly finds the government relaxing its pressure, it takes up arms against it" (Tocqueville 1955 [1856]: 176).

Another influential theorist of the French Revolution was Karl Marx, who stressed the role played by class struggles as structured by the mode of production (the unequal social relations that arise from a particular labor process) found in societies undergoing economic transition. For Marx, the key to understanding revolution was the tensions generated by vast economic transformations, resolved only when exploited social classes organized to take possession of political power. Thus the French Revolution as well as the earlier English Civil War (1640–88) were considered products of the rise of capitalist economic forms in the midst of feudal societies, and their success spelled the end of feudalism and led to the consolidation of capitalism in the two countries.

The Marxian idea of a socialist revolution was first enacted in Russia in 1917, and that experience gave powerful impetus to one of its organizers, Leon Trotsky, to offer his own theory of its causes. Trotsky lays emphasis on what he calls the peculiarities of Russia's development to explain the paradox of why a largely peasant society was the first to have a working-class revolution, making use of a concept called "combined and uneven development," that is, the uneasy mixture of older and more recent forms of social organization, such as the vestiges of feudalism and the emergence of large-scale factory production, respectively. He also identifies elements which would become popular much later in the works of Skocpol and other theorists who lay great emphasis on the state: "In the historic conditions which formed Russia, her economy, her classes, her State, in the action upon her of other states, we ought to be able to find the premises [or causes] both of the February revolution and of the October revolution which replaced it" (1959 [1930]: xii). In another memorable line, he anticipates the latest wave of interest in human agency, warning: "Let us not forget that revolutions are accomplished through people, though they be nameless" (1959 [1930]: 249).

Scholarly theorizing in a formal sense took wing in the 1920s and 1930s when comparative historians such as L. P. Edwards (*The Natural*

History of Revolutions, 1927), Crane Brinton (*The Anatomy of Revolution*, 1938), and G. S. Pettee (*The Process of Revolution*, 1938) searched for common patterns among such major revolutions as the French, American, English, and Russian cases. They developed a "natural history" of revolutions to describe their course, emphasizing a sequence of events that started when intellectuals cease supporting the regime, forcing the state to undertake reforms in the face of a crisis it cannot resolve, thus opening a space for a revolutionary coalition to come to power, which in its turn fragments as first moderate reformers are overturned by radicals who often take extreme measures to implement their program, and who in their turn yield power to military leaders before more moderate pragmatic leaders once more return to power.

More descriptive than explanatory, the natural history school led subsequent social scientists in the 1960s to develop models derived from the then dominant paradigm in US sociology of Parsonian structural functionalism, and its relative, modernization theory. The aim of Ted Robert Gurr (*Why Men Rebel*, 1970) and James Davies (1962) was to develop theories of political violence based on aggregate psychological states, notably relative deprivation, a thesis that echoes Tocqueville in arguing that regimes were most vulnerable when a period of growing prosperity raises people's expectations for improvements in their lives, but leads instead to revolt when these expectations are not met. As structural functionalists, Neil Smelser (*Theory of Collective Behavior*, 1962) and Chalmers Johnson (*Revolutionary Change*, 1966) looked for imbalances in the political, economic, or cultural subsystems (arrangements) of a society which disoriented people and made them more prone to embrace radical ideologies. While critics have found these theories wanting because of the difficulty of measuring such aggregate psychological states or the pitfalls of tautological reasoning in knowing whether structural subsystems are in disequilibria, the value of these approaches lies in their attention to human agency and culture.

This was definitely not the emphasis of a new generation of theorists in the 1970s and after led by Theda Skocpol, probably the single most influential scholar of revolutions, who insisted that "Revolutions are not made; they come" (1979: 17). She argued that revolutions should be studied in terms of the relations between nations, between the state and the economy, and between social classes, and applied this structural perspective to the French, Russian, and Chinese revolutions, where a common pattern emerged: political crises arose when the state could not meet external military or economic challenges because of a limited agricultural base. In France, foreign wars led to fiscal crisis and efforts to tax nobles led to elite revolts; peasants then took advantage of the crisis and were able to mobilize due to communal solidarity structures. In Russia, collapse in World War I led to state crisis; in China the Japanese invasion and World War II created an opportunity.

Charles Tilly (*From Mobilization to Revolution*, 1978) took the renewed interest in the political causes of revolution in another direction by advancing a "resource mobilization" perspective that draws attention to the organizational and other resources available to contending groups (states, elites, challengers). More recently, he and collaborators Doug McAdam and Sidney Tarrow have elaborated a political process theory stressing the role of such factors as broad socioeconomic processes, expanded political opportunities, and "cognitive liberation frames," the ideas that motivate people into action (McAdam et al. 1996).

Skocpol's emphasis on the state has been extended by Jeff Goodwin (2000), who finds that repressive dictatorships and colonial regimes were most vulnerable to revolutionary challenge across the third world after World War II, a model he extends to the Eastern European revolutions of 1989. Jack Goldstone (1991) used a state-centered approach, combined with a demographic analysis of blocked opportunities for marginal elites, to explain why states broke down in early modern Europe and Asia. Tim Wickham-Crowley (1992) also followed in Skocpol's footsteps with a structuralist theory of Latin American revolutions looking at the repressive state-type he terms "mafiacracies," the ability of guerrillas to attract peasant support, and the absence of intervention from outside to prevent revolutions from coming to power in Cuba and Nicaragua.

As critiques of state-centered structuralism's one-sided approach to revolutions emerged in the 1990s, a renewed interest in culture, agency, and ideas came to the fore, in the work of Eric Selbin (1999) and others who insisted that structural factors could not by themselves bring revolutions to power in the absence of broad coalitions of motivated actors. A new and growing group of theorists, sometimes referred to as the "fourth generation" of scholars of revolution, has attempted to integrate structure and agency, and the political, economic, and cultural dimensions of causality, in a variety of multicausal models of revolution that draw on the insights of many of the theorists who preceded them. An early exemplar is John Walton (1984), whose study of failed revolutions in the Philippines, Colombia, and Kenya takes into account uneven economic development, the role of the state, cultural nationalism, and an economic downturn. Farideh Farhi's (1990) study of Iran and Nicaragua combined Skocpol's emphasis on the state and social structure with a Gramscian analysis of ideology. In a comparative study that covers Eastern Europe, China, Vietnam, Cuba, Nicaragua, Iran, and South Africa, James DeFronzo proposes a model of five factors, including mass frustration, dissident elites, "unifying motivations," a crisis of the state, and "a permissive or tolerant world context" (1991: 10). Misagh Parsa's (2000) study of Iran, Nicaragua, and the Philippines integrates economic factors (particularly the degree of state intervention in the economy) with the ideology of state challengers and the political vulnerabilities of repressive regimes. John Foran's (2005) study of three dozen third world revolutions synthesizes the effects of dependent development, the vulnerabilities of both repressive, exclusionary states and truly open democratic polities which may permit the left to come to power through elections (as in Chile in 1970), political cultures of opposition, an economic downturn, and a world-systemic opening, referring to the disruption of supportive ties between the regime and first world powers.

The consuming question, then, of what particular combination of causes is most likely to explain revolutionary success and failure has produced a number of suggestive answers, but is still not settled. What we do know is that a balance must be sought between structure and agency, internal and external factors, and the proper weight and roles of economic, political, and cultural causes must be addressed. This seems a fitting challenge for those who wish to contribute to the theorizing sketched in above.

THE ISSUE OF ACTORS

A second set of debates revolves around the question of who, precisely, makes revolutions, and why. Until recently, the answer has usually been couched in terms of social class, with some stressing a single key class: classically, for Marx, industrial workers; more recent candidates have been peasants (Wolf 1969), or even, to some degree, elites. Others have seen this in terms of peasants or workers providing the mass base of revolutions plus dissident intellectuals, including students, playing leadership roles. Much recent work has identified the significance of broad coalitions of actors, since it requires the collaboration of many social forces to overthrow an absolutist monarchy, an entrenched dictator, or a colonial occupier, or to elect a radical government where the system is open enough to permit this (among others, see Parsa 2000). John Foran (2005 and in earlier work) has spoken of this kind of tactical alliance of lower-, middle-, and even upper-class elements as a multiclass populist coalition, since it pits actors drawn from all social classes, representing "the people," and each contributing its own part to the making of a revolution, against the government and its dwindling set of supporters. This kind of alliance has been prominent in all the great revolutions of the twentieth century, although the degree to which a given percentage of the population has participated actively has varied across cases.

Recent work on the roles of women and diverse ethnic and racial groups in the making of revolution has forced consideration of what we might call the "race/class/gender" dimensions of such populist alliances. Karen Kampwirth (2002) and Julie Shayne (2004) have done much to sensitize us to the crucial and complex ways in which revolutions have been shaped by the contributions of women. Kampwirth's study of Latin American cases accounts for the increasing mobilization of women through an astute synthesis of personal factors such as birth order for daughters, family traditions of resistance, access to school, and age cohort with such cultural developments as the rise of liberation theology, and structural causes including male work migration and land concentration. Shayne's work on a similar set of cases has given us the concept of women as "gendered revolutionary bridges" who use the advantages of their closeness to the population and relatively less threatening appearances for bringing "ordinary" people into the ranks of revolution in a variety of capacities crucial for success in protracted guerrilla and civil wars. Such roles can be instrumental (male revolutionaries making use of women's unique abilities for their own purposes) or strategic (women deploying their femininity consciously in the cause of revolution), and they may result in feminist outcomes where women organize around their own issues either during or after the revolution.

Race has been studied far less, yet it too is now coming into clearer focus as a significant factor in the rise and fall of revolutions. The historical record shows people of color at the forefront of some of the great revolutions, such as the Haitian Revolution around 1800, in complex, more tenuous alliances with whiter revolutionaries as in the Mexican or Cuban cases, and in mixed roles in such revolutions as Nicaragua's, where the Sandinistas possessed significant indigenous support in certain cities on the Pacific coast but alienated the English-speaking Afro-Nicaraguan communities of the Atlantic coast (see Foran et al. 1997 and McAuley 1997 for consideration of these cases). The growing weight of indigenous revolutionaries has been marked across Latin America since the 1980s, and in the twenty-first century it has become preponderant in the various struggles in Bolivia, Ecuador, and most dramatically in the Zapatista insurgency in Chiapas, which has centered demands for indigenous rights and autonomy.

This raises the question of why people, often at great personal risk, choose to become involved in revolutions that shatter the fabric of their everyday routines. Perhaps the most common view is that "misery breeds revolt" – that poverty and oppression and exploitation lead people to participate in revolution. While this may well be true in some cases, and is possibly at the root of virtually all revolutions to some degree, it has to be pointed out that given societies produce different reactions to situations of poverty and oppression. Sometimes people do not feel that revolt is possible, sometimes they protest in more private ways, or only in their local areas. If poverty alone caused revolutions, we would see more revolutions than we have in the third world. While the existence of exploitation may be necessary to impel many groups into revolutions, it does not seem to be sufficient by itself. This "why" question has been addressed by scholars whose interests lie in the intersection of culture and agency. Eric Selbin (1997) has laid stress upon collective memories – the stories, folk tales, songs, plays, myths, and symbols that circulate in societies about past or present resistance to oppression – as indispensable to the making of revolutions, indeed, turning Skocpol's aphorism on its head: revolutions do not come, they are made by people. Jean-Pierre Reed and John Foran (2002) have developed the concept of "political cultures of opposition" to suggest the connections among people's lived and shared experiences of political and economic oppression, the collective memories identified by Selbin, revolutionary ideologies such as socialism and liberation theology, and the networks that draw these together. Sometimes a single powerful political culture is forged, as with Sandinismo in the Nicaraguan Revolution; at other times, diverse political cultures appeal to different strata in society as in the Iranian Revolution, where several strands of Islam and secular political cultures brought particular groups to the demonstrations that toppled the shah. Emotions are now being recognized as further factors that compel people to participate in revolutions. All of this work has strengthened what we know about who makes revolutions, and why, opening the way for future scholars to bring fresh energy to this question.

THE OUTCOMES OF REVOLUTIONS

With all of the attention that has been lavished on the causes of revolutions, it is surprising indeed that relatively little systematic theorizing or comparative study has been done on their outcomes. A few pointers and leads may be advanced here, with much work ahead for others.

In assessing the positive side of revolutionary outcomes, Theda Skocpol has noted that the great revolutions of France, Russia, and China succeeded in terms of creating stronger, more centralized states capable of competing economically with their main rivals than had the pre-revolutionary monarchies in each case. Many of the twentieth century's third world revolutions have delivered a degree of material improvement in people's lives, at least for a time, as in Chile and Nicaragua.

Cuba in particular, the longest-lived revolutionary society on the planet, has registered some impressive gains that are remarkable and unprecedented in the history of revolutions: unemployment was virtually wiped out; income distribution became the fairest in Latin America; high-quality medical care and education through the university level were afforded the population at no cost. Cubans came to consume more food on the average than citizens anywhere in Latin America except Argentina; infant mortality fell to 6.2 per thousand, compared with 126.9 in Haiti, and was lower than the 18.1 per thousand among African Americans in the US. After 1958, life expectancy rose from 57 years to over 77 years.

But considered from the viewpoint of meeting the expectations they have unleashed about human liberation, the outcomes of revolutions to date have generally been disappointing in nature. The Russian Revolution achieved heavy industrialization and the creation of a military that proved capable of contributing massively to the defeat of Nazi Germany in World War II, but devolved into the murderous excesses of Stalin and ultimately the sclerosis of the communist state, which fell to a popular reform movement in 1989–91. The 1949 Chinese Revolution raised the living standards and dignity of the peasant majority tremendously, but went through many changes of political and economic direction under Mao, leading to much persecution before the Communist Party moved away from socialism altogether in the 1980s while retaining its own unquestioned power. In Cuba, Fidel Castro held onto power unchallenged for almost 50 years, during which many basic freedoms – of the press, of expression, of religion, of sexual orientation, and of party and trade union organization – were rigorously controlled by the state. Other revolutions, more promising in terms of a potential for democratically directed change, have ended in foreign intervention: Nicaragua, Chile, and a host of others. For Val Moghadam (1997), all modern revolutions have featured either a patriarchal outcome for women which returns them to traditional family roles, as in France and Iran, or, in the case of the socialist revolutions, fallen short of real emancipation for women. The same mixed results have been experienced by people of color and ethnic minorities across many revolutions. Looking at the overall record, one might ask whether there is some kind of inevitable tradeoff between economic gains and political rights after a revolution, with virtually no case having been able to deliver both.

What might explain these disappointing, or at best, highly mixed outcomes? Two key ideas may be suggested: the pressure put on revolutionary societies by powerful external enemies (in most cases in Latin America and the Middle East, the United States has opposed and tried, with some notable successes, to reverse revolutions), compounding and compounded by the fragmentation of the broad coalitions that are required to bring about revolutions. Such coalitions, so effective in opposing the military power of the state, have typically broken into competing factions after taking power themselves. This is logical, given the differing interests and political cultures that the diverse social groups involved may possess. This process narrows the scope for democratic participation, as one faction typically gains the upper hand, often with much bloodshed, as in Iran. When foreign intervention or wars follow the seizure of power, this further concentrates authority in the state and military and is used to justify curtailment of social and political justice. This in turn makes economic improvements harder to realize, already difficult in the poorer, dependent societies where most revolutions have occurred (these arguments are found in Foran & Goodwin 1993).

THE FUTURE OF REVOLUTIONS

All of these topics will likely be explored by the next generation of scholars, as they continue the search for a grand synthesis of economics, politics, and culture, get deeper into the race/class/gender stories of revolutionary actors, and attempt to understand outcomes with more sophistication. The study of revolutions offers great scope for the development of ideas and theories about all of these matters, touching on some of the most fundamental and seemingly intractable problems of understanding how societies are structured and how they change.

A final dimension to this discussion must be the future of revolutions themselves. The end of the Cold War, the inexorable rise of globalization, and the crushing turning points of September 11, 2001 and the 2003 US invasion of Iraq all raise questions about where revolutions are heading. The Cold War removed the hand of the Soviet Union from the revolutionary equation, with mixed consequences: the USSR could no longer subsidize the Cuban Revolution or provide aid and cover to would-be socialist revolutionaries, but its fall also freed a space for creative new political cultures drawing on more democratic and non-violent means of change to emerge, and it removed one of the main explicit justifications of US intervention against revolutions in the third world.

Globalization followed quickly on the heels of the end of the Cold War, and it, too, has deeply impacted world politics in economic, political, and cultural terms. It increasingly appears that the neoliberal capitalist globalization favored by both transnational corporations and institutions like the World Trade Organization, the International Monetary Fund, and the World Bank creates new forms of dependency, inequality, and poverty that may fuel national revolutions. A new global movement for change – the global justice movement – has also arisen to bring together activists from across the globe into "a movement of movements" encompassing demands for deep economic reform, the expansion of political and human rights, gender and racial justice, and efforts to mitigate the looming perils of global climate change and the coming shortages of fossil fuels. The rise of the Internet and other communications technologies has both aided this movement and at the same time given new tools for governments' efforts to contain them. The global justice movement's diversity, size, and decentralization present similar opportunities and challenges, raising the possibility of global forms of revolution on the one hand, and on the other presenting daunting problems of organizing its many constituent parts into an effective vehicle for deep social change. The World Social Forum gatherings held in Brazil and India from the year 2001 on have provided spaces for sharing experiences and working toward a common set of goals and strategies. The potential of this movement to counter the juggernaut of capitalist globalization remains unclear, and offers a vital research agenda for those interested in the future of revolutions.

A more localized revolutionary movement that has been shaped by the end of the Cold War and driven in part by the impact of neoliberal globalization is that of the Zapatistas. Since 1994, this movement has attempted to achieve indigenous rights in Chiapas and elsewhere in Mexico, to expand popular participation throughout the country, and to reject the prevailing national and global models of capitalist development in favor of new forms of community and economy that have inspired activists well beyond Mexico. These goals have been explicitly framed in terms of *not* taking state power in any direct sense, either through elections or armed struggle, but rather opening up spaces throughout society for democratic discussion of, and work toward, their goals. The end of the 70-year reign of the ironically named Party of the Institutionalized Revolution in 2000 was due in part to the Zapatistas' principled critiques. What the movement can ultimately achieve will only become more apparent as time passes; meanwhile, there are rich lessons to be learned by scholars from the Zapatista experiment.

After the terrorist attacks on the World Trade Center in New York and the Pentagon in Washington on September 11, 2001, the attempt of the US Bush administration to create a new type of global war against Islamic terrorism also altered the picture for the future. Upsetting the smooth operation of globalization from above by its militarized approach to foreign policy in Iraq has made for a more unstable US and global economy and increased the risks of terrorist attacks on the West, with uncertain implications for the revolutions of the future, which scholars must assess.

There may well continue to be national revolutions since the conditions that fuel and enable them do not seem to be disappearing. These may take democratic routes to power through elections, especially in Latin America, where radical reformers came to power in Brazil, Venezuela, and Uruguay in the first years of the twenty-first century. Whether such peaceful strategies can bring about deep and lasting social change on a national basis given the constraints posed by globalization remains to be seen. The Zapatistas in Chiapas offer a non-violent, non-electoral path to deep social transformation and a less authoritarian, more inclusive approach to building coalitions to confront social powers. As in Iraq and Palestine, there will also continue to be both armed and peaceful resistance to foreign occupations. The global justice movement holds out the possibility of a new form of world revolution across borders that may bring the old revolutionary dream of social justice closer to reality. Revolutions – in whatever form – are likely to be with us to the end of human time, and present ever hopeful possibilities for humanly directed social change as well as rich opportunities for scholarly understanding of the processes of this type of change.

SEE ALSO: Collective Action; Culture, Social Movements and; Emotions and Social Movements; Global Justice as a Social Movement; Political Opportunities; Political Process Theory; Resource Mobilization Theory; Revolutions, Sociology of; Social Change; Social Movements; Social Movements, Non-Violent; Social Movements, Political Consequences of; Social Movements, Relative Deprivation and; Transnational Movements

REFERENCES AND SUGGESTED READINGS

Davies, J. C. (1962) Toward a Theory of Revolution. *American Sociological Review* 27: 5–19.

DeFronzo, J. (1991) *Revolutions and Revolutionary Movements.* Westview Press, Boulder, CO.

Farhi, F. (1990) *States and Urban-Based Revolutions: Iran and Nicaragua.* University of Illinois Press, Urbana and Chicago.

Foran, J. (2005) *Taking Power: On the Origins of Third World Revolutions.* Cambridge University Press, Cambridge.

Foran, J. & Goodwin, J. (1993) Revolutionary Outcomes in Iran and Nicaragua: Coalition Fragmentation, War, and the Limits of Social Transformation. *Theory and Society* 22(2): 209–47.

Foran, J., Klouzal, L., & Rivera [now Reed], J.-P. (1997) Who Makes Revolutions? Class, Gender, and Race in the Mexican, Cuban, and Nicaraguan Revolutions. *Research in Social Movements, Conflicts and Change* 20: 1–60.

Goldstone, J. A. (1991) *Revolution and Rebellion in the Early Modern World.* University of California Press, Berkeley.

Goodwin, J. (2000) *No Other Way Out: States and Revolutionary Movements, 1945–1991.* Cambridge University Press, Cambridge.

Kampwirth, K. (2002) *Women and Guerrilla Movements: Nicaragua, El Salvador, Chiapas, Cuba.* Pennsylvania University Press, University Park.

McAdam, D., Tarrow, S., & Tilly, C. (1996) To Map Contentious Politics. *Mobilization* 1(1): 17–34.

McAuley, C. (1997) Race and the American Revolutions. In: Foran, J. (Ed.), *Theorizing Revolutions.* Routledge, New York, pp. 168–202.

Moghadam, V. M. (1997) Gender and Revolutions. In: Foran, J. (Ed.), *Theorizing Revolutions.* Routledge, New York, pp. 137–67.

Paige, J. M. (1975) *Agrarian Revolution: Social Movements and Export Agriculture in the Underdeveloped World.* Free Press, New York.

Parsa, M. (2000) *States, Ideologies, and Social Revolutions: A Comparative Analysis of Iran, Nicaragua, and the Philippines.* Cambridge University Press, Cambridge.

Ragin, C. C. (1987) *The Comparative Method: Moving Beyond Qualitative and Quantitative Strategies.* University of California Press, Berkeley.

Reed, J.-P. & Foran, J. (2002) Political Cultures of Opposition: Exploring Idioms, Ideologies, and Revolutionary Agency in the Case of Nicaragua. *Critical Sociology* 28(3): 335–70.

Selbin, E. (1997) Bringing Agency Back In. In: Foran, J. (Ed.), *Theorizing Revolutions.* Routledge, New York, pp. 123–36.

Selbin, E. (1999) *Modern Latin American Social Revolutions*, 2nd edn. Westview Press, Boulder, CO.

Shayne, J. D. (2004) *The Revolution Question: Feminisms in El Salvador, Chile, and Cuba.* Rutgers University Press, New Brunswick, NJ.

Skocpol, T. (1979) *States and Social Revolutions: A Comparative Analysis of France, Russia, and China.* Cambridge University Press, Cambridge.

Tocqueville, A. de (1955 [1856]) *The Old Regime and the French Revolution.* Trans. S. Gilbert. Doubleday, Garden City, NY.

Trotsky, L. (1959 [1930]) *The Russian Revolution: The Overthrow of Tzarism and the Triumph of the Soviets.* Selected and Ed. F. W. Dupree. Doubleday, Garden City, NY.

Walton, J. (1984) *Reluctant Rebels: Comparative Studies of Revolution and Underdevelopment.* Columbia University Press, New York.

Wickham-Crowley, T. P. (1992) *Guerrillas and Revolution in Latin America: A Comparative Study of*

Insurgents and Regimes Since 1956. Princeton University Press, Princeton.
Wolf, E. R. (1969) *Peasant Wars of the Twentieth Century*. Harper Colophon, New York.

revolutions, sociology of

John Lie and Nicholas Hoover Wilson

What distinguishes revolution from riot or rebellion, collective action or collective violence, or *coups d'état* or just plain old regime change? Historical records are replete with instances of sudden, violent, extra-constitutional, and consequential regime change. However, the modern concept of revolution is the product of the French Revolution of 1789–94. The events that came to be known as the Revolution denoted and dominated modern politics. Henceforth, revolution referred to a sudden, violent political change that leads to consequential extra-political transformation. The French Revolution generated a new class of political actors – revolutionaries – and a new political ideology – the possibility and desirability of intentional, mass uprising to achieve sudden, extra-constitutional political change. In the modern political imagination, revolution came to denote the possibility of a better – indeed, utopian – future through the seizure of state power and the construction of a new revolutionary order.

Before the French Revolution, the concept of revolution was used in a radically different way. Though today we may speak of the Roman Revolution or the English Revolution, contemporary observers employed other categories. Thus, the English Revolution was usually called the Great Rebellion, while what we would call restoration was called the Great – and later the Glorious – Revolution (the first such event to be called revolution by contemporaries). When the "world turned upside down" in seventeenth-century England, rebelling or revolting referred to the fall of the powers that be (Hill 1972). Overturning the overthrow was then the revolution. True to the Latin etymological root of *revolutio*, revolution referred to circling back to the status quo ante. The older vocabularies of betrayal, treason, and rebellion were replaced by revolution only *after* the French Revolution.

After the late eighteenth century, however, revolution became inextricably intertwined with the events of late eighteenth-century France. Concurrently, revolution became a modular keyword to describe rapid, qualitative, significant, and positive change. Thus, all manners of radical, progressive change became known as revolution. The War of Independence, for example, became the American Revolution. The industrial revolution, along with the French Revolution, was said to define the nineteenth century. Popular and scholarly discourses employed the language of revolution, whether the scientific revolution or the military revolution, the democratic revolution or the information revolution.

The "echoes of the Marseillaise" reverberated for two centuries after 1789, and defined and sometimes dominated the nature and discourse of modern politics (Hobsbawm 1990). The self-conscious revolutionaries sought to replicate the Revolution in their own countries, overthrowing the old regime in favor of the new order. Almost immediately after 1789, the 1791 "revolution" in Haiti augured many later instances of anti-colonial movements and revolutions. Yet by far the most consequential event was the second, "October" revolution in Russia in 1917. The Bolshevik Revolution colored radical politics in the twentieth century. The vanguard party, often identified as socialist or communist and allied with the Soviet Union, became the dominant technique and imaginary of the revolutionaries. Indeed, the French Revolution in particular and revolution *tout court* came to be seen retrospectively from a Marxist-Bolshevik perspective (Furet 1986).

Given the significance of the Bolshevik Revolution, Karl Marx – or, more accurately, Marxist theory through Lenin's lens – established the broad parameters of understanding and explaining the causes, courses, and consequences of revolution. In terms of cause, the dominant mode of explanation stressed the role of social classes. Hence, the French Revolution was said to be caused by the rise of the bourgeoisie. Moore's (1966) classic study, for example, analyzes the class relations between the existing ruling class, the bourgeoisie, and the peasantry. While Marx expected socialist revolutions to emerge in capitalist societies, Moore's study stressed the revolutionary outcome in "backward" societies. Certainly, the twentieth-century revolutions belied the Marxist-Leninist expectation and occurred largely in agrarian societies (Wolf 1969). In terms of consequences, revolution was believed to be progressive, pointing to a socialist or a communist future. Counter-revolution, in turn, referred to those defending the capitalist present that was soon to be moribund.

The geopolitics and the ideological conflicts of the Cold War inflected the scholarly and popular understanding of revolution. Modernization theory sought to counter Marxist explanation by employing functional analysis. Yet functional analysis was often tautological (e.g., revolution happens because the existing regime was not working). In retrospect, however, both Marxist and modernization theorists held highly normative and politicized understandings of revolution. The Marxist-Leninist view regarded the Bolshevik Revolution as the paradigmatic revolution: a conscious vanguard party inspires mass mobilization, seizes state power, and creates a revolutionary (socialist) future. Concrete analyses would have cast doubt on the certitudes, but any sudden, qualitative political change came to be called a revolution, whether agrarian-based revolts, such as Mexico in 1910, or urban, religious-based upheavals, such as Iran in 1979. In fact, very few cases – if any – fitted the Marxist-Leninist imaginary of the revolution (and certainly not the French Revolution). Revolution turned out to be a nominal term without much substantive content. Dunn (1989) trenchantly exposed the wide diversity of phenomena that are usually classed unproblematically as revolutions. In this regard, consider that the Nazi seizure of power was almost never regarded as an instance of revolution when in fact the regime was revolutionary in almost every way: a vanguard party, mass mobilization, the seizure of state power, and the construction of a revolutionary order.

The political palatability of actually existing revolutions faded with the recognition of the politically authoritarian and economically destructive nature of the Soviet Union and other revolutionary societies. By the very late twentieth century, scholars questioned the desirability and even the very possibility of revolution. In a sense, they echoed the first sustained analysis, Edmund Burke's *Reflections on the Revolution in France* (2001). That is, scholars stressed its human costs, both during and after the upheaval, and questioned whether it denoted anything more than a *coup d'état*. Skocpol's (1979) influential study followed Tocqueville's (2004) pioneering analysis in stressing that revolution is not "made" but "come" because of the corrosion of the state apparatus. Her attention to state power and geopolitics also pointed to the significance of military struggle, which is in fact crucial to any successful revolutionary upheaval (Chorley 1943). Revolution, after all, is a form of civil or internal war. Moreover, the survival of a revolutionary regime depends profoundly on geopolitics. US intervention, for example, accounted in large part for the failure of Latin American "revolutions" beginning with Guatemala in 1944 and Bolivia in 1952 (Grandin 2004).

In the early twenty-first century the very study of revolution has become unpopular. In part the earlier consensus on the necessity or the desirability of revolution has withered away, reflecting the perceived failures of the actually existing revolutions. In part the very focus on regime transformation and the state apparatuses seems outmoded. Certainly, few political groups today are committed to a violent seizure of state power to create a revolutionary future. The "echoes of the Marseillaise" have softened to the point of silence. The very dominance and diffusion of the terminology has obfuscated the description and explanation of concrete political transformations. Not surprisingly, then, no one has yet to predict the coming of revolution because we encounter an order of distinct entities and events about which our theories remain impotent.

SEE ALSO: Collective Action; Marx, Karl; Political Sociology; Revolutions; Tocqueville, Alexis de; Violence

REFERENCES AND SUGGESTED READINGS

Burke, E. (2001 [1792]) *Reflections on the Revolution in France.* Stanford University Press, Stanford.

Chorley, K. (1943) *Armies and the Art of Revolution.* Faber & Faber, London.

Dunn, J. (1989) *Modern Revolutions*, 2nd edn. Cambridge University Press, Cambridge.

Furet, F. (1986) *Marx et la révolution française*. Flammarion, Paris.
Grandin, G. (2004) *The Last Colonial Massacre*. University of Chicago Press, Chicago.
Hill, C. (1972) *The World Turned Upside Down*. Penguin, London.
Hobsbawm, E. (1990) *Echoes of the Marseillaise*. Rutgers University Press, New Brunswick, NJ.
Moore, B. (1966) *Social Origins of Dictatorship and Democracy*. Beacon Press, Boston.
Skocpol, T. (1979) *States and Social Revolutions*. Cambridge University Press, Cambridge.
Tocqueville, A. de (2004 [1856]) *L'Ancien régime et la révolution française*. In: *Oeuvres*, Vol. 3. Gallimard, Paris, pp. 41–451.
Wolf, E. R. (1969) *Peasant Wars of the Twentieth Century*. Harper & Row, New York.

Riesman, David (1909–2002)

Craig D. Lair

David Riesman was not a formally trained sociologist. Nevertheless, his 1950 book *The Lonely Crowd: A Study of the Changing American Character*, written in collaboration with Nathan Glazer and Reuel Denney, has earned a unique distinction in American sociology: excluding textbooks and "classical" works, it is the only book by an American sociologist to sell over a million copies (Gans 1997). This means that the all-time bestselling work in American sociology was written by someone who never earned a degree in this discipline.

Riesman was born in Philadelphia and studied biochemistry at Harvard as an undergraduate. Later, he attended Harvard Law School, where he received his law degree in 1934. After graduating from law school Riesman both taught and practiced law. For a time, he served as a clerk to Supreme Court Justice Louis Brandeis. During World War II Riesman took an executive position in the private sector, working at the Sperry Gyroscope Company. It was not until 1946 that Riesman took an academic post in the social sciences, first as a visiting lecturer, then, three years later, as a full professor, at the University of Chicago. In 1958 he would return to Harvard as a faculty member, where he would stay until the end of his career.

However, it was during his early years at Chicago, and in collaboration with Glazer and Denney, that he wrote what was to become his most famous work: *The Lonely Crowd*. The subject of this work is a historical exploration of what Riesman et al. call "social character," or that part of an individual's personality that is shared in common with other members of a social group. This common element of personality is the result of individuals living in similar social and material environments and also a means by which a society generates a degree of conformity from its members. As such, Riesman et al. use the terms "social character" and "mode of conformity" interchangeably.

Riesman et al. argue that there have been three distinct social character types that have existed over time. These character types are: tradition-directed, inner-directed, and other-directed. The shifts between these social character types were linked by Riesman et al. to demographic changes that roughly correspond to a three-stage demographic transition: tradition-directed societies are in a state of "high growth potential"; inner-directed societies are in a state of "transitional population growth"; and other-directed societies are seen to be in a stage of "incipient population decline." However, Riesman et al. note that the linking of population factors to changes in social character is "shorthand" for many other social, technological, institutional, and informational changes that took place at the same time as these demographic shifts, such as industrialization, the birth and expansion of capitalism, urbanism, rationalization, and the growth and expansion of various media.

The historically first social character type identified by Riesman et al. is the tradition-directed personality. This character type is formed in "family- and clan-oriented" societies where much of life is socially institutionalized, stabilized, and lived in accordance with collective mandates and rules. Accordingly, levels of individuation and innovation in tradition-directed societies are low, as the motivation for individual thought and action are rooted, not in individual motivations, but rather in the collective practices and norms that have been transmitted over the ages. This conception of the tradition-directed personality is similar to Durkheim's conception of mechanical solidarity and Tönnies's conception of *Gemeinschaft* s the collective that flows through and guides individuals throughout their lives.

Riesman et al. see the tradition-directed monopoly upon personality being broken by the emergence of the inner-directed character, who began to surface in the social, political, and economic upheavals of the seventeenth century, particularly the Industrial Revolution and the Protestant Reformation. This social character has a very different mode of orientation than that of his or her traditional counterpart. For the tradition-directed person, most features of life were socially regulated. Riesman et al. argue that this personality type was not flexible enough to cope with the expanding populations and production systems of this time that led to an increase in both social and geographical mobility, and new forms of work. It was in response to an expanding social environment that the inner-directed person emerged.

The inner-directed person's source of direction comes from general yet forceful goals that are instilled early in the child by parents which he or she comes to internalize (e.g., goals such as to be a good person, to be successful or productive, to do God's work). While not as encompassing and detailed as the social dictates found in tradition-directed societies, these internalized goals are still powerful enough to give inner-directed people guidance throughout their lives, even if they are in new, different, or changing social environments. That is, once instilled, inner-directed people are not directed by what is outside them, but rather, they are guided by their inner convictions. As such, Riesman et al. conceive of these early implanted goals as a kind of "psychological gyroscope" that gives individuals clear direction wherever they may be. Riesman et al. offer Weber's description of the Protestant work ethic as being emblematic of this personality type, with its emphasis on morality and industriousness despite the surrounding environment.

However, as population growth steadies, as work moves from a more entrepreneurial mode to a more bureaucratic one, and as material scarcity fades in the face of abundance, Riesman et al. see a new mode of orientation coming into being. If the tradition-directed character was anchored to the past and custom, and if the inner-directed person followed the directions set in his or her internal gyroscope, then the other-directed personality, which Riesman et al. see developing in the "new middle class" of bureaucratic and salaried employees, is controlled and corralled by the thoughts and evaluations of others that he or she picks up on his or her "radar." That is, the prime mode of orientation for other-directed persons is to live in harmony with others. In this regard, the other-directed personality is very much a socialized one, in that their overriding goal is to please those around them. However, this socialization lacks the stability found in tradition-directed societies, being more akin to changes in fashion than to time-honored customs. Moreover, this personality is more flexible and open than either the tradition- or inner-directed person, as each other-directed person looks to others for cues of how they should act in certain situations. Indeed, "others" are the central problematic for other-directed people.

Ironically, though, Riesman et al. see the other-directed person as a lonely personality who tries to overcome loneliness by flocking into groups. However, the authors argue that "they no more assuage their loneliness in a crowd of peers than one can assuage one's thirst by drinking sea water" because what they try to escape to is exactly what they need to escape from: others. What individuals really need in order to quench their thirst is not to be surrounded by more people, but rather something which transcends others' thoughts and evaluations altogether: autonomy.

Riesman et al. see three possible modes of adaptation open to the individual in response to the prevalent mode of conformity at the time. People can either be adjusted (i.e., live in proper accordance with their social character type), anomic (i.e., be either under- or overly-adjusted to the prevalent mode of conformity), or they can live a life of autonomy. Autonomy for the authors is seen as the ability of an individual to decide whether or not to live in accordance with a social character without, in the process, slipping into an anomic state. The key to autonomy is self-consciousness and as other-directed persons are more self-conscious than the inner-directed, just as the latter are more self-conscious than the tradition-directed, Riesman et al. see the increased self-consciousness of the other-directed as opening the door to the possibility of living an autonomous life. In part this self-consciousness is tied to changes in the material environment: as scarcity is overcome via increased production, more attention can be devoted to developing one's self. However, Riesman et al. see the most promising space for this development not in terms of work or "species being" as classical Marxism would argue, but instead in terms of consumption and leisure. As such, it is the abundance of modern society that allows for individuals to be exposed to a greater diversity of goods and lifestyles, while also offering them more free time to enjoy these things that allow for a greater sense of self-consciousness to be formed. Riesman would later modify these ideas by noting that work was a more important sphere of life than he gave it credit for in *The Lonely Crowd* and that the levels of production needed to satisfy a consumer-style autonomy were formed in an "era of innocent optimism" (Riesman 1998) that could not be sustained into the future.

Nevertheless, Riesman et al.'s cry for autonomy struck a chord in the time of the "organization man" and other forms of conformism. In this regard, *The Lonely Crowd* is often lumped together with other critiques of "mass" society (e.g., the work of Fromm and Mills). While undoubtedly critical of aspects of other-directedness, Riesman et al. did not see the emergence of this character type as a wholly negative development. In fact, one positive development to come out of an other-directed attitude was a greater tolerance for, and sensitivity to, others and their concerns. This made the possibility of living an autonomous life even greater than in the past. However, Riesman also took great pains to point out that inner-direction was not a universally good character type whose passing we should mourn and whose reemergence we should strive for (for example, the inner-directed person could be intolerant of others and too single-minded in nature), nor should inner-direction be equated with autonomy, as some who misread this work did. In the end, it was autonomy and the ability to live a self-directed life that these authors pinned their hopes on, even if this was a "utopian" thought.

The Lonely Crowd was later supplemented by *Faces in the Crowd: Individual Studies in Character and Politics* (1952), which presented transcripts of some 20 interviews that were used, in part, to make the case of *The Lonely Crowd*, and also some of the individual essays put forward in *Individualism Reconsidered* (1954). Later in his career, however, Riesman was to modify, sometimes greatly, some of the claims made in *The Lonely Crowd*, calling some of them "wrong," claiming others to be based on an "ethnocentric" perspective, and saying that others were based on notions of American "exceptionalism." In particular, he abandoned the linkage made between character types and demographic shifts (Riesman noted this was an issue of concern even before the book was originally published) and even questioned the adequacy of the tradition-directed and other-directed character types. Riesman was also dismayed at how the ideas he put forward were to his mind misappropriated in radical calls for social change while he himself advocated a more reformist approach.

While undoubtedly his most popular work, *The Lonely Crowd* and related works were far from his only interests. In 1953 Riesman published *Thorstein Veblen: A Critical Interpretation*, a psychological biography of this thinker, and in 1976 he published *Adam Smith's Sociological Economics*, which argues, as the name implies, for a more sociological reading of Smith's economics. In 1964 Riesman published *Abundance for What? and Other Essays*, a collection of works ranging from Veblen and de Tocqueville, to suburbanization and the Cold War, and essays which reformulate and revise some aspects of what was said in *The Lonely Crowd.* In 1967 Riesman and his wife Evelyn Thompson Riesman published a book on Japan: *Japan: Modernization, Politics, and Culture.* Riesman also founded and edited the antinuclear journal *The Correspondent*, which sought to be a forum through which intellectuals could influence government policy on this and other issues. However, much of Riesman's later career was focused on higher education, particularly how academic institutions were becoming standardized, how intellectual diversity was being squeezed out, and how some disadvantaged groups were being excluded from the meritocratic promises of the educational system. Riesman's works on education include *Constraint and Variety in American Education* (1956), *The Academic Revolution* (1968; co-authored with Christopher Jencks), *The Perpetual Dream: Reform and Experiment in the American College* (1978; co-authored with Gerald Grant), and *Education and Politics at Harvard* (1975; co-authored with Seymour Martin Lipset), as well as a contributed field report to Lazarsfeld and Thielens's *The Academic Mind* (1958).

There have also been two volumes of critical commentary on Riesman's work. One is Seymour Martin Lipset and Leo Lowenthal's edited book *Culture and Social Character: The Work of David Riesman Reviewed* (1961). The other is an edited volume by Herbert Gans, Nathan Glazer, Joseph Gusfield, and Christopher Jencks entitled *On the Making of Americans: Essays in Honor of David Riesman* (1979).

Though Riesman was never formally trained in sociology, his influence on the discipline is beyond question. His thoughts captured the imagination of a generation and continue to influence sociological discussions to this day (see Wolfe 2001: 72).

SEE ALSO: Demographic Transition Theory; Fromm, Erich; Mass Culture and Mass Society; Social Change; Solidarity, Mechanical and Organic

REFERENCES AND SUGGESTED READINGS

Gans, H. (1997) Best-Sellers by Sociologists: An Exploratory Study. *Contemporary Sociology* 26(2): 131–5.

Horowitz, I. L. (2002) Reflections on Riesman. *American Sociologist* 33(2): 118–22.

Riesman, D. (1980) Egocentrism: Is the American Character Changing? *Encounter* 55: 19–28.

Riesman, D. (1992) Comments on "Dennis Wrong: 'The Lonely Crowd' Revisited." *Sociological Forum* 7(2): 391–3.

Riesman, D. (1998) Innocence of The Lonely Crowd. *Society* 35(2): 339–43.

Wolfe, A. (2001) Moral Freedom: The Search for Virtue in a World of Choice. W. W. Norton, New York.

Wrong, D. (1992) "The Lonely Crowd" Revisited. *Sociological Forum* 7(2): 381–9.

Riot Grrrls

Pamela Aronson

Riot Grrrls are participants in a social movement focused on a radical female youth culture. The movement was originally formed as a reaction to a male-dominated punk rock music scene. With mostly male performers, girls often felt that the issues that concerned them were not reflected in their music. Before Riot Grrrl, girls who listened to this type of music were commonly perceived as connected to punk rock culture through their boyfriends rather than their own interests. The Riot Grrrl movement originated as punk rock feminism, which had two main goals: demarginalizing women in punk rock and providing a critique of patriarchy. Later in its history, the Riot Grrrl movement expanded to include participation in other cultural and political outlets. Ideas spread through the Internet and zines, which are inexpensive newsletters with individual reflection, and political and feminist commentary. Riot Grrrls themselves produced the zines and they were shared with other girls to raise awareness about feminist issues and help create a network of activists. Many women active in Riot Grrrl situate their activism within the "third wave" feminist movement.

Riot Grrrl was founded in 1991 in Olympia, Washington, when a group of girls set out to expand girls' and young women's involvement in predominantly white, male punk rock. The International Pop Underground Festival, organized by K Records in Olympia, designated the first night as Girls' Night with the goal of demarginalizing the role of women in punk rock. In 1992 a Riot Grrrl convention took place in Washington, DC. Bands such as Bikini Kill, Bratmobile, and Heavens to Betsy provided a critique of patriarchy, as well as role models for young women to get involved in the production of their own music. Zines such as *Girl Germs* and *Jigsaw* provided girls with an alternative perspective, and helped create a network of Riot Grrrls in diverse locations. Riot Grrrl chapters began across the country, and, later, in other countries like Britain. There have been a number of Riot Grrrl conventions, where girls and young women meet to perform music, exchange zines, and attend workshops on topics such as sexual assault, abuse, self-defense, and eating disorders. Eventually, the mainstream media began to report on Riot Grrrl, although engagement with the mainstream press has been controversial within the movement.

The Riot Grrrl philosophy is pro-girl and separatist, as it seeks to establish a distinct female youth culture apart from boys and adults. Riot Grrrls express themselves angrily and frankly, as they reclaim the power of girlhood with "an added growl to replace the perceived passivity of 'girl'" (Rosenberg & Garofalo 1998: 809). As a girl active in the movement put it, it is "loud, aggressive, and in your face" (p. 837). This social movement emphasizes empowerment, the "do it yourself" philosophy of punk rock, and anger at mainstream and patriarchal culture. In fact, Riot Grrrls frequently reclaim derogatory terms used to describe women to call attention to the objectification of women. As they seek a "Revolution girl-style now," they make visible through their music and zines often unspoken topics like rape and abuse. Their cultural productions also serve to create a network of girls who have felt isolated from others who share similar beliefs.

Riot Grrrl culture is also an explicitly youth culture that rejects the concerns of adult women. Reacting to the second wave feminist movement of the late 1960s and 1970s, Riot Grrrl seeks to provide a critique of patriarchy based on the concerns of girls. For example, while the second wave feminist movement was concerned with opening up workplace opportunities and equal rights, these issues are not viewed as central for many Riot Grrrls, who are too young to feel the effects of workplace discrimination. Instead, the Riot Grrrl movement works to make cultural and personal changes, such as seeing their own concerns reflected in their music and raising awareness about issues like sexual assault and incest. Riot Grrrl is often viewed as a white, middle to upper middle-class movement, which may result from the largely white punk rock audience from which it emerged.

Riot Grrrl represents an important space for girls and young women to develop and voice their own experiences, as well as to articulate an alternative feminist vision. Riot Grrrl meetings and conventions are frequently compared to the consciousness-raising groups of the second-wave women's movement, where women could connect with each other and become aware of the ways that personal concerns are actually political issues. Those who are involved stress the importance of community and the development of mutual emotional support.

In 1993 Riot Grrrls began a press blackout, in which they refused to talk or be photographed by the popular media. The blackout followed what many considered to be a trivialization of their community in outlets such as the *New York Times* and *Newsweek*. The blackout was motivated by a concern that the mainstream media would continue to commodify and misrepresent Riot Grrrl culture.

Several writers pinpoint the heyday of the Riot Grrrl movement as occurring in the 1990s. Since Riot Grrrl was never a movement with membership lists, others have argued that the decline of the movement is largely an interpretation by the media.

SEE ALSO: Consciousness Raising; Consumption, Girls' Culture and; Feminism; Feminism, First, Second, and Third Waves; Gender, Social Movements and; Personal is Political; Radical Feminism

REFERENCES AND SUGGESTED READINGS

Heywood, L. & Drake, J. (1997) *Third Wave Agenda: Being Feminist, Doing Feminism.* University of Minnesota Press, Minneapolis.

Kearney, M. C. (1998) "Don't Need You": Rethinking Identity Politics and Separatism from a Grrrl Perspective. In: Epstein, J. S. (Ed.), *Youth Culture: Identity in a Postmodern World.* Blackwell, Oxford, pp. 148–88.

Rosenberg, J. & Garofalo, G. (1998) Riot Grrrl: Revolutions from Within. *Signs* 23 (3): 809–41.

Schippers, M. (2002) *Rockin' Out of the Box: Gender Maneuvering in Alternative Hard Rock.* Rutgers University Press, New Brunswick, NJ.

riots

Daniel J. Myers

A riot is an unruly collective act of violence that is temporary, discontinuous from everyday routines, and results in damage to persons or property of either the participants or targets of the collective actor. Although most social scientists have an intuitive sense of what constitutes a riot, the edges of the definition are fuzzy and it can be difficult to determine whether or not some events are actually riots. For example, it is agreed that a riot is a collective act. That is, more than one individual must be involved and at least minimally coordinate action in order for a riot to occur. Two people acting together, however, would not constitute a riot, even though it is a collective act of violence. Thus, the lower limit for participation, damage, and duration to define a riot is difficult to establish and has led many sociologists to analyze events more ambiguously referred to as civil disorders or collective violence. For most, however, unless there are at least 30–50 people involved, the events last more than a few moments, and there is action that could result in property damage or injury requiring medical attention, a riot has not occurred.

Even those events that consensus would label as riots are a diverse lot. The American sociologist's vision of rioting is heavily influenced by the race-related urban riots that occurred in the 1960s, including the infamous Watts 1965, Newark 1967, Detroit 1967, and Washington, DC 1968 riots. These riots were typically ignited by a confrontation between police and African American citizens and, although injuries occurred, the activity in the riots was dominated by attacks on property and looting. Injuries most typically resulted from attempts by police and military officials to prevent damage and contain or extinguish the riot. These kinds of riots have been echoed in other urban environments over the years, including riots in Britain in the early 1980s, in Los Angeles following the Rodney King verdict, in Cincinnati, Ohio following accusations of police brutality, and most recently in the Parisian suburbs of France, as immigrants from North Africa took to the streets and burned thousands of cars in protest of perceived police brutality and poverty.

While these kinds of events are important, there are many other kinds of collective events that have been treated as riots, including food riots, machine breaking raids, murderous ethnic purges, lynching, brawls at sporting events, and even victory celebrations. Horowitz (2001), for example, documents what he calls "deadly ethnic riots," which are collective lethal attacks of one ethnic group on another and include events ranging across the globe from Hindu attacks on Muslims in India, anti-Catholic violence in Northern Ireland, and attacks on Ibo citizens in Nigeria. In practice, these different types of riots are not completely distinct. Rather, riots are complex events in which different kinds of people with different motivations participate in a variety of ways in the larger riot. For example, the celebration riots that followed the string of National Basketball Association Championships in Chicago and later in Los Angeles took on many of the characteristics of the urban street riots of the 1960s.

Concern with riots, and crowd behavior more generally, has a long history in sociology, reaching back to the founding moments of the discipline when thinkers such as Gustave Le Bon and Sigmund Freud produced a view of crowds as unanimous, crazed, criminal, anonymous masses whose constituent individuals had ceded control of themselves to the mob and/or a hypnotically suggestive leader. Although subsequently debunked in sociological scholarship, this view of the crowd and of rioters lives on in the popular mind, in journalistic accounts of riots, and even in introductory textbooks. Empirical research on crowds, however, indicates that riot participants are certainly not of unanimous mind and in fact their participation and behaviors reveal diverse motivations, actions, and experiences of the event. Furthermore, individuals in crowds are not anonymous, as they typically attend the event in small groups made up of friends and family members. These small groups remain intact throughout the event, move through the larger crowd together, and are the fundamental unit in which decisions about what to do are made. Nor do individuals in crowds become hypnotized by the situation or cede control of themselves to crazed irrationality. In fact, even when engaging in some of the most extreme and heinous atrocities (such as genocidal purges), riot participants retain an extraordinary level of rationality, going to great lengths, for example, to ensure they are killing the right kind of person (Horowitz 2001). Rioters, for example, may stop rioting to actually interrogate those suspected of being on the wrong side. Horowitz relates one such instance in which Sinhalese rioters in Sri Lanka questioned a man once, held him as a prisoner while they proceeded to kill other Tamils, later questioned him further, and eventually (mistakenly, since he was a Tamil) released him.

Because of this unfortunate history of thinking about riots and crowds, care must be taken when using the riot label – not just because it is not always clear if an event is a riot, but also because the term has inherently pejorative connotations. For some, the riot label invokes images of mob psychology, hooliganism, opportunism, and criminality and thereby immediately marginalizes the participants. Rather than being seen as political actors with a legitimate protest agenda, rioters are viewed as dangerous criminals that must be controlled. The riot label, therefore, reflects the views of social control agents and the act of labeling is itself inherently political. Once the riot label has been applied, it leads authorities and observers to focus on controlling rioters with heavy-handed repressive tactics rather than attending to the social conditions and political concerns that underlie the unrest. As a result, some scholars prefer to refer to these events as rebellion or revolt. Others disagree, believing that most incidents labeled riots fall short of the kind of politically revolutionary agenda necessary to be a rebellion.

RIOT PARTICIPANTS

Based on historical thinking about rioting and crowds, scholars also developed expectations about what kinds of persons would be more likely to participate in a riot. Criminals, socially marginalized, isolated, unemployed, and uneducated were all stereotypes portrayed in earlier writing on riots. As has been the case with mob psychology notions more generally, these ideas have been proven false by empirical research. When the characteristics of riot participants have been compared to those of non-participants (particularly to those living in geographic proximity to riots), few differences have been detected (Mason & Murtagh 1985). Even though, for example, unemployment in a city predicts rioting, the unemployed are not disproportionately represented among the actual rioters: their rates of participation are virtually identical to those who are employed. Nor do rioters tend to be more psychologically frustrated with their circumstances or feel more deprived than non-participants. Thus, rioters do not fit the image of marginalized societal refuse held by early crowd theorists.

What can be said about rioters? First, as with most violence, the participants are considerably more likely to be men than women. Second, rioters tend to be younger than the average person living in the area where a riot occurs, although rioting is clearly not just an activity of the young. More important, however, is simple biographical availability, which in part accounts for the presence of the young at riots. Those who happen to be spatially close to a riot are more likely to join in. Those who are not at work, watching children, or attending classes are more likely to be able to break free from their routines and become part of the crowd. There is, for example, a clear daily pattern of riot activity that peaks after usual work hours and then dies down when people have to return to their jobs and schools (McPhail 1994). Third, rioters tend to have higher senses of personal efficacy than those who do not participate. They are more likely than those who stay at home to believe that their actions matter and will make some kind of a difference (Snow & Oliver 1995).

ECONOMIC HARDSHIP AND RIOTING

Sociological research and theorizing about riots has focused on the causes of rioting. What conditions contribute to its emergence? Many factors have been posited as important contributors to, or preconditions for, rioting. Economic factors such as unemployment and poverty have been cast as both absolute and relative deprivation conditions that produce what is essentially a violent protest about these conditions. This theoretical argument seemed more than plausible and the emergence of so much rioting in poor, urban areas disproportionately involving racial and ethnic minorities buoyed the notion. The research, however, has been less than definitive. Research attempting to explain the variation among cities in riot frequency and riot severity based on relative and absolute deprivation measures as well as other indicators of social and economic well-being has been hard pressed to find any consistent relationship supporting the basic theoretical notions (Spilerman 1970, 1976). Related concepts, such as the pressure that rapid changes in population place on the provision of social services and the notion that poor political representation prevents the opportunity to redress grievances through conventional means, have not fared any better.

More recently, competition theory has been used somewhat more successfully to predict rioting. Here, analysts propose that battles over economic (and to a lesser degree, residential) turf escalate into collective violence as one group attempts to improve its position or maintain relative advantage over another advancing group. After all this research though, economic factors, however they may have been cast, still remain a fairly weak predictor of rioting. Economic hardship is too ubiquitous and rioting is too rare for economic conditions to produce rioting directly. Thus, economic conditions may be seen as providing fertile ground for rioting and other collective violence, but are not, by themselves, a sufficient explanation for the emergence of violence.

SOCIAL CONTROL AGENTS

The role of state authorities, especially local police, in producing, escalating, and quelling riots has been a major topic of research, not only because interaction between police and citizens so often seems to ignite rioting, but also because state authorities have a responsibility to maintain order and therefore are expected to wield repressive forces to bring riots under control, to return the social environment to a state of calm, and to protect the persons and property that might be targeted by rioters.

These two dynamics have produced different hypotheses about the roles of police in riots. On one hand, if confrontations with citizens and heavy-handed policing tactics provide the sparks that set off riots, then increases in police presence ought to increase rioting. Likewise, if police engage rioters with escalated engagement as they attempt to quell the riot, they may inflame rather than extinguish the riots. On the other hand, repression can actually stop or slow rioting, and although police intervention can lead to more discontent and grievances, police presence, especially if early and formidable, can prevent or reduce rioting by raising the anticipated costs of participation.

The quantitative empirical evidence on the role of policing has been inconsistent. Some scholars have found that larger police forces are related to more and more severe riots, while others have found no relationship or just the opposite. Qualitative and historical studies, however, have demonstrated that it is not just the strength of the police in terms of number and firepower that matters, but rather, it is how they wield their power and what kinds of relationships exist between the police and the community that matter most. Those communities that have a history of antagonism between the police and some segment of the citizenry seem much more likely to erupt after a publicized instance of heavy-handed police behavior.

DIFFUSION, MASS MEDIA, AND EFFECTIVENESS

The mass media are another key player in understanding the origins and trajectory of rioting, particularly as rioting spreads and becomes a wave of unrest rather than a single or a few isolated events. When the National Advisory Commission on Civil Disorders published its report on the US riots of the summer of 1967, it put substantial responsibility for the spread of riots on the mass media and how it handled reports of the riots, as had the McCone Commission's report on the Watts riot of 1965. Since then, scholars and politicians have routinely criticized mass media for their conduct during and after riots. The mass media contribute to riots in two mains ways. First, they can fan the flames of a riot while it is happening by live broadcasts of the action on the streets. These reports immediately draw the attention of potential participants, who can be drawn out into the street and increase the size of the crowd, the complexity of the situation, and the chances for further inflammatory confrontations as police try to control the situation. The pressure for immediacy can also contribute to inaccurate and inflammatory reporting as reporters rely on hearsay and rumors as they quickly attempt to piece together the story. Second, media reports of riots spread information about riots and their outcomes and seem to suggest rioting as a behavioral tactic to potential actors in other locations. Thus, in modern times, mass media distribution has become the key network structure that provides a conduit for the diffusion of collective violence.

Rather than the mindless imitation posited by early crowd theorists, however, modern takes on the diffusion of collective violence are inherently rationalist. These approaches to diffusion understand the imitation process as involving transmission of information about the actions of rioters, the reactions by social control agents, and the outcomes of the riot to other potential rioters in other locations. The potential rioters then evaluate the outcomes of the prior act and then, individually and collectively, make decisions about whether they will be likely to adopt the behavior, should the opportunity arise. When an opportunity does arise, such as when a crowd gathers around to observe an arrest, rioting is then more likely to develop.

Because media distribution areas and the cultural salience of actors are both geographically concentrated, information flows that could inform further rioting are geographically concentrated as well. In addition, the salience of past events wanes quickly as the riots become old news, and thus the chances of imitations are concentrated in brief periods, thereby inducing short-lived bursts of action or mini-waves of rioting reflected in the relatively jagged pattern of rioting most often observed in riot waves.

The rationalist logic requires that riots are observed and evaluated positively so that the evaluation would lead to imitation. A negative appraisal would presumably dissuade diffusion. Contrary to what might be expected by an outsider viewing the sometimes devastating effects of riots on neighborhoods and businesses, surveys conducted by social scientists after urban riots in the 1960s repeatedly demonstrated that many African Americans viewed the riots positively. Even in the very neighborhoods where the riots caused the most damage, the residents often believed that the riots were necessary to call attention to the problems of the area and would ultimately do more good than harm (Feagin & Hahn 1973). Many of those who participated in the riots and later testified before congressional committee expressed a sense of pride and efficacy for both their own actions and of others they observed (US Senate 1967–70). Likewise, in 2005, many French Muslims often expressed supportive attitudes toward the actions of rioters, believing that these destructive protests were finally calling attention to the problems of a population that had been systematically neglected by French policymakers. These positive evaluations of rioting are consistent with and lend support to rationalist, diffusion-based explanations for the spread of rioting.

Whether riots actually do produce positive outcomes is an open question. There is little doubt that riots draw attention to the community in which they occur and invite speculation about the causes of the riots and what might be done to correct them. Government commissions are formed and legislative bodies investigate and sometimes introduce policy and allocate resources to address the posited problems. Because riots seem to appear in relatively impoverished areas, for example, policy interventions have been targeted toward improving the economic conditions in these areas. The Model Cities program in the late 1960s was one key federal program that was developed at least in part as a response to the riots of the era (Gale 1996). Thus, riots can produce attention to problems in a community as rioters often seem to expect. Whether this attention and the resulting programs ultimately have any positive effect is a different question and one that has been harder to demonstrate. Often, the programs are underfunded or dismantled before any effect has been felt. Furthermore, the long-term effects on the economies of riot-stricken areas are difficult to overcome – some areas never seem to recover from the devastation (Collins & Margo 2004).

SEE ALSO: Collective Action; Crowd Behavior; Protest, Diffusion of; Urban Poverty

REFERENCES AND SUGGESTED READINGS

Collins, W. & Margo, R. A. (2004) The Labor Market Effects of the 1960s Riots. In: Gale, W. &

Pack, J. (Eds.), *Brookings–Wharton Papers on Urban Affairs*. Brookings Institution, Washington, DC.
Feagin, J. R. & Hahn, H. (1973) *Ghetto Revolts: The Politics of Violence in American Cities*. Macmillan, New York.
Gale, D. (1996) *Understanding Urban Unrest: From Reverend King to Rodney King*. Sage, Thousand Oaks, CA.
Horowitz, D. (2001) *The Deadly Ethnic Riot*. University of California Press, Berkeley.
Le Bon, G. (1952 [1896]) *The Crowd: A Study of the Popular Mind*. Ernest Benn, London.
McPhail, C. (1991) *The Myth of the Madding Crowd*. De Gruyter, New York.
McPhail, C. (1994) Presidential Address – The Dark Side of Purpose: Individual and Collective Violence in Riots. *Sociological Quarterly* 35: 1–32.
Mason, D. T. & Murtagh, J. A. (1985) Who Riots? An Empirical Examination of the "New Urban Black" versus the Social Marginality Hypotheses. *Political Behavior* 7: 352–73.
Myers, D. J. (1997) Racial Rioting in the 1960s: An Event History Analysis of Local Conditions. *American Sociological Review* 62: 94–112.
Myers, D. J. (2000) The Diffusion of Collective Violence: Infectiousness, Susceptibility, and Mass Media Networks. *American Journal of Sociology* 106(1): 173–208.
Myers, D. J. & Caniglia, B. S. (2004) All the Rioting That's Fit to Print: Selection Effects in National Newspaper Coverage of Civil Disorders, 1968–1969. *American Sociological Review* 69(4): 519–43.
National Advisory, Commission on Civil, Disorders (1968) *Report of the National Advisory Commission on Civil Disorders*. Bantam Books, New York.
Olzak, S. & Shanahan, S. (1996) Deprivation Race Riots: An Extension of Spilerman's Analysis. *Social Forces* 74(3): 931–61.
Snow, D. A. & Oliver, P. E. (1995) Social Movements and Collective Behavior: Social Psychological Dimensions and Considerations. In: Cook, K., Fine, G., & House, J. (Eds.), *Sociological Perspectives on Social Psychology*. Allyn & Bacon, Boston.
Spilerman, S. (1970) The Causes of Racial Disturbances: A Comparison of Alternative Explanations. *American Sociological Review* 35(4): 627–49.
Spilerman, S. (1976) Structural Characteristics of Cities and the Severity of Racial Disorders. *American Sociological Review* 41: 771–93.
US Senate, Government Operations Committee (1967–70) *Riots, Civil and Criminal Disorders: Hearings before the Permanent Subcommittee on Investigations of the Committee on Government Operations*. Government Printing Office, Washington, DC.

risk, risk society, risk behavior, and social problems

Alfons Bora

Modern society is undergoing a deep-rooted structural change. This change concerns both the internal relations between all parts of society and external relations with nature. During the nineteenth century, the industrial and technological revolution shook up the structures of a society that had been shaped traditionally by crafts and agriculture. In the same dramatic way, the "second modernity" or "risk society," as Ulrich Beck (1992) calls the period at the end of the second millennium, transforms the nucleus of the industrial society. New technologies confront society with problems that are connected to the term "risk" (Perrow 1987). This is not so much because the quantitative amount of dangerous situations has increased – this amount might have been relatively higher in earlier societies. However, what has significantly changed is the fact that social actors and institutions are being made accountable for those dangers. The new quality of the risk society consists of socially generated risks – or, at least, of the increase in assigning dangers to social behavior. Socially caused dangers will regularly produce more social conflict than inevitable natural disasters. In this sense, science and technology contain risks for each individual, for social groups, for contemporary society as a whole, and for future generations. The examples for this diagnosis are numerous. One may think of nuclear energy, IT technologies, biotechnology, or nanotechnologies, for instance. All these technological innovations are embedded in rapid social change, entailing growing individualization, patchwork-biographies, significant changes in employment structures and occupational situation, and an accelerating transformation of many established institutions of the welfare state. They make clear that the issue of "risk" is a central category in societal self-observation and self-description.

RISK AND INFORMATION THEORY

Generally, the risk of a certain event ($R_{(E)}$) is defined as the probability of a dangerous event ($p_{(E)}$) multiplied by the amount of the expected damage (D) connected to this event: $R_{(E)} = p_{(E)} \times D$. We can call this concept of risk an information-theoretical concept. Insurance companies usually work with this approach. Law courts and administrations make use of it when deciding cases. In this conception, risk is a question of complete or incomplete knowledge. Risk management, in this perspective, has the task of dealing with an information problem, namely, the problem of acquiring as much information as possible about probability and damage. Therefore, in the information-theoretical perspective, risk management is mainly information management, trying to shift an imaginary border between knowledge and non-knowledge. In the best case, this shift will dissolve non-knowledge.

The information-theoretical approach has historical roots. The idea of risk was born in the emerging seafaring and long distance trade, where shipowners and traders tried to secure their investments by the first insurances calculating probability and estimated damage. Until today, this connection with information is constitutive for the understanding of risk. It also has coined risk research from its early stages (Knight 1921). In addition, newer risk theories are influenced by information theory (Elster 1993).

However, the information-theoretical concept brings with it certain problems. One critical issue in many cases is the quantification of possible benefits and damages. What if they are qualitatively different? It is often impossible to compare both sides on the same scale. Often there is no clear indicator for the estimation of the damage. This holds true for "catastrophic" damage, as for instance in the case of a nuclear catastrophe. Therefore, many situations in technological decision-making, as well as in everyday life, make it difficult to establish a uniform risk measure. The socially contested cases are often those in which, owing to a lack of empirical experience, an exact calculation of probabilities is not feasible. Last but not least, commercial calculations in many cases lie across the risk perceptions of individual actors and of the political public. In summary, the information-theoretical risk concept can be said to be closely related to a concept of knowledge that is rather static and which treats the relation between knowledge and non-knowledge as a zero-sum-game. Complementary to this approach, it can therefore be argued from a sociological point of view that new knowledge in every case instantly creates new non-knowledge. It is, for epistemological reasons, impossible to eliminate non-knowledge. Risk theory can try to take profit from this insight.

RISK AND DECISION THEORY

Risk research has turned its attention toward all forms of social knowledge and non-knowledge. From this sociological perspective, the distinction between specific and unspecific non-knowledge (Japp 1997) is of great importance. Specific non-knowledge describes the case in which an actor explicitly knows that she lacks knowledge in a certain aspect. Specific non-knowledge, therefore, is a reason to start an inquiry and to try to produce new knowledge. It is the characteristic condition of scientific research: we try to expand our knowledge in an area where we still do not have (enough) knowledge. From the point of view of risk research, positively knowing about the existence of our non-knowledge is decisive. This form of specific non-knowledge has to be sharply distinguished from any kind of unspecific non-knowledge. Unspecific non-knowledge describes a case of categorical ignorance, a case in which an actor cannot know that she lacks knowledge in a certain aspect. Unspecific non-knowledge transcends the barriers of our epistemic capacities in a given moment.

Social forces produce all kinds of damage, danger, and catastrophe. The causes for risk, therefore, are social, and not primarily natural. Under such a condition, the question of causation and accountability gains increasing importance. Consequently, the distinction between the social roles of decision-maker and those affected by the decision come increasingly to the center of interest. Accordingly, a growing amount of social protest can be expected from those who are (even potentially) affected by decisions. Insofar as events are understood as consequences of social decisions and not as effects of natural processes, the category of decision becomes relevant for the analysis and understanding of risk. For these reasons, decision theory becomes relevant for a sociological analysis of risk.

The central characteristic of a risk decision consists of a situation arising from the need to select between different options, which may all entail negative consequences for third parties and therefore will provoke the issue of responsibility (Luhmann 1991). The risk of decision-making expresses a specific form of what Luhmann calls "temporal coupling" (*Zeitbindung*). A decision becomes risky insofar as three aspects are intertwined. These are (1) the knowledge that non-decision is impossible; even inactivity contains a decision; (2) the knowledge that unspecific knowledge is unavoidable; this knowledge makes us aware that consequences will appear later that are epistemologically unknown when the decision is taken, and that they will bear negative effects for others; and (3) the knowledge that future consequences will be attributed to the decision and to the decision-maker's responsibility. In the co-occurrence of these three aspects, some fundamental dilemmas become apparent. Firstly, we observe the control dilemma that Collingridge (1980) mentioned. The term indicates that at a time when it is still possible to control a new technology, our technological knowledge goes far beyond the knowledge about social factors and consequences. The social effects of a given technology are not visible at the moment of the decision. However, when they are detected, the technology is often very deeply embedded in the social practice, so that it is usually almost impossible to control it. This dilemma clearly points to the temporal structure of decision-making. At the same time it leads to a second dilemma, what we call the risk dilemma, which consists of the constitutive connection between the pressure to decide and the impossibility of holding the necessary knowledge. This aspect of uncertainty entails a paradoxical moment, which Clausen and Dombrowsky (1984) called the warning paradox. According to this paradox, warning against possible dangers does not help to decide risky cases. The reason is that we can learn whether the warning was reasonable only if we fail to heed it. If we follow the warning, we will never know whether it was well founded or not.

RISK AS A SOCIAL PROBLEM

The notion of risk, as formulated in the decision theory of risk, is sharply distinguished from the notion of danger. Whether an event will be perceived as risk or as danger mainly depends on the question of whether it can be attributed to the decision in the social dimension. Risk – in contrast to a natural disaster, for instance – is caused by social decisions, and is therefore related to the decision-making actor or institution. Danger, on the other hand, relates to those who are affected by the consequences of the decision. This differentiation not only helps to describe the historical trend from danger to risk, it also indicates a change in social attitude toward the future. A greater number of far-reaching consequences have to be taken into consideration. Very distant futures are relevant to our contemporary decisions. The effects of acting as well as of not acting are equally complex and uncertain. Modern societies are fundamentally characterized by the difference between decision-makers and those affected by their decisions. Every individual may occupy either side of this distinction in various social contexts.

Looking at those affected by a decision and threatened by the danger of a negative consequence, we can see that this side of risk decisions is related to social inequalities. These inequalities can be conceived under the terms inclusion and exclusion. The distinction between inclusion and exclusion describes a very general form of social inequality (Stichweh 2000). This inequality can be realized in different gradual forms and modalities. Social regions of exclusion, which may be highly integrated internally but are characterized by strong differentiation from all central political and legal institutions, usually show a dramatic potential for social dangers. Absence of health care, low levels of education, high rates of criminal victimization, as well as a high level of environmental damage and poor nutrition, are significant indicators for social exclusion. It is in this area that social movements find cause to protest, pointing out the dangers for the excluded that stem from social decisions taken elsewhere. Social communication about risk becomes politicized under these conditions.

RISK THEORIES IN THE SOCIAL SCIENCES

Scientific concern with risk theory reaches from medical epidemiology via mathematics and economic theory to the legal and social sciences. Within the realm of the social sciences, three groups of risk theory can be distinguished.

Psychology and cognition theory. Approaches from psychology and cognition theory refer to the difficulties resulting from the dilemma of risk decision. Given that in a fundamental sense we never have sufficient information to make an ex-ante assessment of risks, the question rises as to how decision-making actors (individuals as well as organizations) empirically arrive at their decision (Jungermann & Slovic 1993). Psychological risk analysis is interested in analyzing individual and collective attitudes to risk behavior and risk management under given situational conditions. In this respect, it has produced numerous valuable insights into the mechanisms of risk behavior (see, e.g., Jungermann & Slovic 1993). It shows that risks which are undertaken voluntarily are viewed as much more acceptable than those which are not voluntarily assumed. Moreover, the acceptance of a given risk depends on the amount of perceived control over the risk and/or over the source of the risk. Risks from new technologies will usually be estimated as much higher than those from older or "well-known" technologies. The fairer the possible consequences seem to be, the lower the risk of a decision will be judged. Risk acceptance in particular depends on the perceived reversibility of the decision.

Cultural theory. Whilst the cognitive approaches are mainly concerned with individual perceptions, cultural theory looks at social groups as the decisive factor. This approach understands risk as a collective social construct (in the sense of an interpretive pattern, or *Deutungsmuster*). The particular form of this construct depends on the properties of the social group in which it occurs. Cultural theory categorizes social groups along two main dimensions, namely, "group" and "grid" (Douglas & Wildavsky 1982; Thompson 1999). Group stands for the external boundaries of a social collective and describes the extent of the group's differentiation from its social environment. Grid refers to the social distinctions within the group that regulate its internal behavior. By cross-tabulation of these two dimensions, four types of social groups (cultures) can be found, each with a specific concept of risk:

1. Hierarchical culture has high values in both dimensions. It is characterized by high differentiation against the external world and by high internal integration. In this culture, risks are treated as manageable.
2. Individualistic market culture bears low grid and low group values. It attributes risks to the sphere of individual action frames and generally accepts them as calculable issues.
3. Egalitarian culture (sometimes also called "sectarian" culture) has low grid and high group values. Usually it is highly risk aversive and very sensitive to every kind of danger.
4. Fatalist culture is characterized by high grid and low group values. Risks are conceived as imposed by others. They provoke passive reactions rather than active avoidance or risk management.

Based on these differentiations, cultural theory analyzes social categorizations of risk. It explains these categories from the structures of the different risk cultures (for an overview see Thompson 1999). In contrast to psychological theories, cultural theory allows an understanding of risk as a social (i.e., socially constructed) phenomenon and thus as a social problem.

Systems theory. The new (or autopoietic) sociological systems theory also looks at risk as a social phenomenon. It describes the characteristic features of risky decisions (Luhmann 1991; Japp 2000). Risk is the result of a tension between temporal and issue dimensions. In modern society, the increasing use of risk as a category of social observation and interpretation indicates a change in the relation of society and its environment:

1. Risk communications show that dangers increasingly are attributed to decisions. This holds true even for phenomena that until recently had been understood as inevitable natural disasters, such as flooding, for example.
2. The future increasingly becomes a relevant dimension with respect to the legitimation

of decisions, and is no longer seen as constitutively incalculable. The issue of risk assessment becomes pervasive for all social systems.

3 Social differentiation between decision-makers and those affected by the consequences of decisions helps to explain why social movements mobilize protest through risk communication and why they politicize decisions with respect to risk.
4 At the same time, social systems tend to externalize risks and to shift responsibility for risky decisions to other functional systems. This process can be observed, for instance, in the relation between politics, law, and economy (Luhmann 1991).

These three types of social risk theory refer to decision-making processes in different aspects. They are distinguished from each other by their central term of reference – individual behavior, rational calculus, group identity, social systems. Thus, they differ from each other with respect to their level of generalization. It is doubtful whether approaches related to individuals and groups can cover the general (sociological) aspects of risk decisions. Nevertheless, they offer highly developed tools for the description of particular strategies in decision-making. Systems theory, in contrast, focuses on the general sociological problems of risk decisions.

RISK PERCEPTION, TRUST, AND EXPERTISE

Individual assessment of risk depends on a large number of factors, such as the opportunity for control. Besides the individual perspective, public opinion about risk and risk regulation is of great importance for the understanding of modern society. Public opinion, as numerous studies show, is far from being averse to modern technology in general. This holds true for all countries and regions (Durant et al. 1998; Hampel & Renn 1999; Gaskell & Bauer 2001). With regard to certain issues, such as different applications of biotechnology (e.g., plant biotechnology, human stem cells, to mention two prominent examples), public opinion is ambivalent. However, what is more relevant than the attitude toward the technological issue at stake is the fact that public opinion does not depend on the level of information about a particular technology. A common hypothesis contending that more information and enlightenment would raise acceptance (the so-called "deficit hypothesis") must be considered inadequate from a sociological point of view. On the contrary, a higher level of education probably leads to a more critical attitude toward risk and technology, as other studies report (Levidow & Marris 2001). Obviously, public opinion is strongly influenced by very general patterns of interpretation and often by a generalized suspicion toward misapplications of any kind. The options for regulating risk and technology that modern society provides for are usually estimated as too low or insufficient (Durant et al. 1998; Hampel & Renn 1999). A significant number of people think that the possibility of controlling and regulating risk through the law and legal institutions is inadequate. More than 80 percent say that existing laws are not applied and that surveillance is not strong enough. As a result, political and legal instruments of regulation can be said to be one – if not *the* – factor for explaining public opinion toward risk: risk perception is a question of trust in institutions. The role of the mass media in this process is important, but not as decisive as might be supposed (Durant et al. 1998; Hampel & Renn 1999). At the European level, for instance, no significant correlation could be observed between media coverage and public perception (Durant et al. 1998).

Historically, the first answer to the perceived weakness of regulatory means has been expertise (control by knowledge, in Max Weber's formulation). The assumption is that the relevant knowledge for the control of risks can best be produced by scientific expertise. Law and politics have made use of this model from the very beginning of regulatory activities in technology and risk. However, as debates over the last few decades have shown, the expert model is burdened with some serious difficulties. Experts are, for epistemological reasons, not able to eliminate risk. Their status is embedded in what has been called "mode 2" of knowledge production (Gibbons et al. 1994). Mode 2 means that the process of knowledge is not linear but undirected, more like a large reservoir to which many different institutions have an input. Expertise is often contested and uncertain. Society itself becomes a large laboratory, in which "real-world experiments" are conducted (Groß et al. 2003). On the other hand, on the basic level of cognition, there is no way out from expertise, because it is only scientific knowledge that aims to deal with our questions about truth and reliable information. No delegitimization of expertise could destroy its basic function for society. One may even speak of an increasing importance of expertise in politics and law (Weingart 1999, 2001).

The crisis of expertise mentioned above has led to an increase in participatory decision-making. Participation is usually understood as a form of dialogical process shaping technology and managing possible risks. It can be observed in areas where research, regulation, and public opinion overlap. In most political contexts, participation is a relevant tool for decision-making. It is conceptually based on a critique of expertise and on a discourse of "democratizing expertise" (Liberatore & Funtowicz 2003). Participatory procedures, according to a common hypothesis, are more likely to evoke the motivation to engage in decision-making, to broaden the basis of knowledge and values involved, to initiate learning processes, to produce new possibilities for conflict resolution, to realize common interests, and to increase acceptance and legitimacy of a decision (Durant 1999; Fischer 1999; Joss & Bellucci 2002). The term "participatory procedure" describes instruments and methods aimed at the inclusion of laypersons and/or stakeholders. Scientific expertise is a relevant feature in participatory procedures, but is usually embedded in concepts of deliberation among laypersons and stakeholders. This combination results from the fact that the function of such procedures is to integrate the issue dimension (e.g., information, facts, truth) and the social dimension (e.g., acceptance, trust, legitimacy, values, preferences). With respect to risk decisions, such procedures represent an important mechanism of risk externalization. The broad inclusion of those people potentially affected by a decision may help to absorb protest. Someone who has participated in the decision-making process will find it difficult to blame decision-makers for any negative effects.

In addition to the possible advantages of participation, its weaknesses should be considered. Participatory procedures will not develop sufficient commitment from all parties unless they lead to a real win-win solution. Participants' loyalty to their organizational background may even force them to leave the procedure if serious conflicts arise. The functional differentiation of society may create insurmountable barriers to communication. Furthermore, these procedures often provoke questions such as their political representativity, imbalance of power, or lack of political mandate for those involved. One cause of such problems may be seen in their lack of embeddedness in the institutions of representative democracy. Participation, therefore, is a means to cope with risk decisions and their problems. At the same time, it creates new problems.

The regulation of risks challenges science and practice in modern society. The concept of decision theory sheds light on the fact that every regulatory approach entails new consequences, which can be found in the realm of unspecific non-knowledge. They consequently provoke effects that cannot be known in advance and that will raise serious problems of risk and danger, thereby leading to social protest and conflict. The value of this theoretical approach for political, legal, and scientific practice could lie in its ability to reduce expectations about social capacities for eliminating risk from social life to a realistic amount.

SEE ALSO: Autopoiesis; Benefit and Victimized Zones; Expertise, "Scientification," and the Authority of Science; Luhmann, Niklas; Reflexive Modernization; Science and the Measurement of Risk; Science and the Precautionary Principle; Science and Public Participation: The Democratization of Science; Technological Determinism; Technological Innovation; Trust

REFERENCES AND SUGGESTED READINGS

Abels, G. & Bora, A. (2004) Demokratische Technikbewertung. MS. Bielefeld.

Beck, U. (1992) *Risk Society: Towards a New Modernity*. Sage, London.

Bora, A. (Ed.) (1999a) *Rechtliches Risikomanagement. Form, Funktion und Leistungsfähigkeit des Rechts in der Risikogesellschaft*. Duncker & Humblot, Berlin.

Bora, A. (1999b) *Differenzierung und Inklusion. Partizipatorische Öffentlichkeit im Rechtssystem moderner Gesellschaften.* Nomos, Baden-Baden.
Clausen, L. & Dombrowsky, W. R. (1984) Warnpraxis und Warnlogik. *Zeitschrift für Soziologie* 13 (4): 293–307.
Collingridge, D. (1980) *The Social Control of Technology.* Frances Pinter, London.
Daele, W. van den (1993) Zwanzig Jahre politische Kritik an den Experten. Wissenschaftliche Expertise in der Regulierung technischer Risiken; die aktuelle Erfahrung. In: Huber, J. & Thurn, G. (Eds.), *Wissenschaftsmilieus: Wissenschaftskontroversen und soziokulturelle Konflikte.* Edition Sigma, Berlin, 173–94.
Douglas, M. & Wildavsky, A. (1982) *Risk and Culture.* University of California Press, Berkeley.
Durant, J. (1999) Participatory Technology Assessment and the Democratic Model of the Public Understanding of Science. *Science and Public Policy* 26(5): 313–19.
Durant, J., Bauer, M. W., & Gaskell, G. (Eds.) (1998) *Biotechnology in the Public Sphere.* Science Museum, London.
Elster, J. (Ed.) (1993) *Deliberative Democracy.* Cambridge, Cambridge University Press.
Fischer, F. (1999) Technological Deliberation in a Democratic Society: The Case for Participatory Inquiry. *Science and Public Policy* 26(5): 294–302.
Gaskell, G. & Bauer, M. W. (Eds.) (2001) *Biotechnology, 1996–2000: The Years of Controversy.* Science Museum, London.
Gibbons, M., Limoges, C., Nowotny, H., Schwartzman, S., Scott, P., & Trow, M. (1994) *The New Production of Knowledge: The Dynamics of Science and Research in Contemporary Societies.* Sage, Thousand Oaks, CA.
Groß, M., Hoffmann-Riem, H., & Krohn, W. (2003) Realexperimente: Robustheit und Dynamik ökologischer Gestaltungen in der Wissensgesellschaft. *Soziale Welt* 54: 241–58.
Hampel, J. & Renn, O. (Eds.) (1999) *Gentechnik in der Öffentlichkeit. Wahrnehmung und Bewertung einer umstrittenen Technologie.* Campus, Frankfurt and New York.
Japp, K. P. (1997) Zur Beobachtung von Nichtwissen. *Soziale Systeme* H.2: 289–312.
Japp, K. P. (2000) Risiko. MS. Bielefeld.
Joss, S. & Bellucci, S. (Eds.) (2002) *Participatory Technology Assessment.* European Perspectives, London.
Jungermann, H. & Slovic, P. (1993) Charakteristika individueller Risikowahrnehmung. In: Bayerische Rück (Ed.), *Risiko ist ein Konstrukt: Wahrnehmungen zur Risikowahrnehmung.* Knesebeck u. Schuler, Munich, pp. 89–107.
Kaplan, S. & Garrik, B. J. (1993) Die quantitative Bestimmung von Risiko. In: Bechmann, G. (Ed.), *Risiko und Gesellschaft. Grundlagen und Ergebnisse interdisziplinärer Risikoforschung,* 2nd edn. Westdeutscher Verlag, Opladen, pp. 91–124.
Knight, F. H. (1921) *Risk, Uncertainty, and Profit.* Houghton Mifflin, Boston.
Levidow, L. & Marris, C. (2001) Science and Governance in Europe: Lessons from the Case of Agricultural Biotechnology. *Science and Public Policy* 28(5): 345–60.
Liberatore, A. & Funtowicz, S. (2003) "Democratizing" Expertise, "Expertizing" Democracy: What Does This Mean and Why Bother? *Science and Public Policy* 1 (June): 146–50.
Luhmann, N. (1991) *Soziologie des Risikos.* De Gruyter, Berlin and New York.
Perrow, C. (1987) *Normale Katastrophen: die unvermeidbaren Risiken der Grosstechnik.* Foreword by K. Traube. Campus, Frankfurt am Main.
Stichweh, R. (2000) Zur Theorie der politischen Inklusion. In: Holz, K. (Ed.) *Staatsbürgerschaft: soziale Differenzierung und politische Inklusion.* Westdeutscher Verlag, Opladen, pp. 159–70.
Thompson, M. (Ed.) (1999) *Cultural Theory as Political Science.* Routledge, London.
Weingart, P. (1999) Scientific Expertise and Political Accountability: Paradoxes of Science in Politics. *Science and Public Policy* 26(3): 151–61.
Weingart, P. (2001) *Die Stunde der Wahrheit? Zum Verhältnis der Wissenschaft zu Politik, Wirtschaft und den Medien in der Wissensgesellschaft.* Velbrück, Weilerswist.

rite of passage

Rodanthi Tzanelli

The term rite of passage was first used in anthropology to encapsulate rituals that symbolize the transition of an individual or a group from one status to another, or to denote the passage of calendrical time, but soon it was embraced in other disciplines. The concept was developed by the Durkheimian anthropologist Arnold Van Gennep in *Les Rites de passage* (1909), in which he explored the nature of ceremonies that mark personal or collective changes of identity (childbirth, puberty, marriage, motherhood, and death), as well as collective celebrations of seasonal change (Easter, harvest). Van Gennep identified three phases in these rites: (1) separation, when the individual or the group is distanced from their former identities; (2) liminality, the phase in between two conditions (the one from which the individual/group departs and the one which they will enter); and (3) reaggregation (or incorporation), the final stage in which the individual/group is readmitted to society as bearer of new status. Because rites of passage belong to sacred time (not the profane of everyday life), their performance is formalized. The initiate(s) are placed in a symbolically subordinate position vis-à-vis those who have been initiated (elders, married, mothers) and have to go through elaborate "trials" (isolation, humiliation, fasting) before they are accepted back into the community.

The flexibility of Van Gennep's theory led to its implementation and use in a vast array of contexts in different human sciences (anthropology, sociology, history). Van Gennep influenced two of the most important twentieth-century symbolic anthropologists, Victor Turner and Mary Douglas. In *The Ritual Process: Structure and Anti-Structure* (1966), Turner illustrated the significance of liminality as a dangerous phase for the initiate(s) and the whole community, which both challenges and sustains social order. This idea reappeared in Mary Douglas's *Purity and Danger: An Analysis of the Concepts of Pollution and Taboo* (1966) in a more structuralist fashion. Douglas regarded liminality as a point that negotiates two opposing structural situations: her analysis of "dirt" as a moral sign that enables societies to establish boundaries between social categories (e.g., clean and unclean, good and evil, dangerous and safe) echoes Van Gennep's tripartite schema of the rite of passage.

One of the problems highlighted about the concept is its inherent vagueness, because it invites social scientists to construct almost every transitional stage as a rite of passage. Van Gennep also stressed that not all rites of passage retain their tripartite structure: one phase may be ritualistically exaggerated at the expense of the other two (e.g., baptism as incorporation into society). Again, this led to confusion concerning the classification of transitional rituals as rites of separation, liminality, or incorporation (e.g., marriage can be all three). The concept of liminality, however, found extensive use in sociology, especially in tourism and leisure studies. Unfortunately, its association with ambiguity, indeterminacy, and displacement also invited its abuse by "cultural theorists" who are often not informed of its origins.

SEE ALSO: Consumption, Tourism and; Durkheim, Émile; Rite/Ritual; Structuralism

REFERENCES AND SUGGESTED READINGS

Bell, C. (1995) *Ritual Theory, Ritual Practice*. Oxford University Press, New York.

Diver, T. F. (1998) *Understanding the Transformative Power of Ritual*. Westview Press, Boulder, CO.

Douglas, M. (1966) *Purity and Danger: An Analysis of the Concepts of Pollution and Taboo*. Routledge & Kegan Paul, London.

Eliade, M. (1994) *Rites and Symbols of Initiation: The Mysteries of Birth and Rebirth*. Spring, Putnam, CO.

Turner, V. (1966) *The Ritual Process: Structure and Anti-Structure*. Cornell University Press, Ithaca, NY.

Turner, V. (1975) *Dramas, Fields, and Metaphors: Symbolic Action in Human Society*. Cornell University Press, Ithaca, NY.

Van Gennep, A. (1960 [1909]) *The Rites of Passage*. University of Chicago Press, Chicago.

rite/ritual

Aldo Natale Terrin

The field of ritual studies has expanded dramatically over the past 20 years. Rituals are analyzed in anthropology, sociology of religion, religious studies, and theology, and also in the study of literature, philosophy, theater, political science, and education, especially from the perspective of performance theory (Schechner 1977). Many disciplines have taken different theoretical approaches to this broad and complex topic, and thus a great variety of definitions have been proposed, no single one of which is adequate. For present purposes ritual will be defined as a formal and symbolic behavior that leads to the creation or recreation of an emotion in order to obtain or maintain a correct balance between persons and the world.

"Formal and symbolic behavior" speaks of the particular behavior included in ritual. Certain acts, gestures, utterances, and so on seem to be of a particular kind that sets them off from acts performed in other contexts and situations. This intuitive demarcation from other behaviors is the first step in any consideration of ritual. Analyses of ritual should begin by describing what is distinctive about it, rather than what makes it similar to other forms of social interaction. Symbolic behavior is generated from the word "ritual" itself, which derives from the Indo-European root *ri* – like "rhyme," "rhythm," and "river" – and signifies something like an ordered flow, governed by rules, repetitions, and conventions. As rule-governed behavior, ritual is collective, repetitive, and stylized. It normally follows a pattern established on earlier occasions or by tradition and has since become "holy," having been instituted by the ancestors or ordered by a deity. Ritual is also formal in the sense that it distances participants from their spontaneous selves and their private motives. Formal gestures are fewer in number than informal ones and are more prescribed and impersonal. During the practice of ritual, participants observe rules, conforming themselves to what is prescribed for them. Bloch (1989) argues these formalized ways of behavior and communication normally have to be considered as a complex of primitive behavioral modes, like dance, song, and formulaic speech. These stylized behaviors tend also to be closely connected with traditional forms of social hierarchy and authority. In other words, using standardized forms of speech in which vocabulary, syntax, and intonation are reduced to a minimum, ritual reinforces power and the status quo. The most highly formalized of such behavior is perhaps religious ritual.

It is very difficult to discuss the sense of the symbolic in ritual. Ritual is particularly symbolic when it evokes a foundational myth. For instance, Turner's (1967) *mudyi* tree and Rappaport's (1999) *rumbim* each bring together in ritual multiple significations, ranging from the physiological to the ideological and the cosmic. The contemplation of representations in which ideological significations are emotionally present in association with the physiological constitutes an attempt to integrate and unify the whole of reality. This is capable of arousing great emotion.

The repetition, the invariance, and the formalization of ritual – producing rhyme, rhythm, *phoné*, and music – allow a new interpretation of ritual as having an unconscious force from which an ancient emotion can emerge. Ritual's strong link with the physiology of the body is important here. Ritual behavior is in fact a performance in which the value of the body is manifested through a multifaceted sensory experience. Like any other performance, ritual communicates on multiple sensory levels, involving imagery, dramatic sounds, and tactile, olfactory, and gustatory stimulation. All the communicative codes are involved. In this sense ritual is constructed in order to prioritize the body and to valorize knowledge through the performance of the body.

Why should ritual action accord primacy to bodily techniques in this way? We know in the first place that bodily movements can do more than words can say. It is through the ritual itself that one understands this, both phylogenetically and ontogenetically. Thinking and communicating through the body precede and to a great extent always remain beyond speech. In this sense we can understand ritual as not opposed to rationality, but as inhabiting another level of rationality, constructed not by semantic truths, but established by experiential and expressive truths and emotional constructs. Indeed, the practical understanding and deep knowledge demanded by ritual operate best without concepts (e.g., through the gestures and emotions of the body and in the body). For instance, we understand the language of facial expressions, postures, gestures, and involuntary bodily changes first and best, just as a child understands the facial expression of its mother long before it understands verbal language (Vygotsky 1962). And this type of knowledge is in any case the deepest knowledge. Another example stems from the common experience we have when our familiar environment is disrupted: we feel suddenly uprooted, we lose our footing, we collapse, we fall. This experience is not solely metaphorical. Rather, the shock and disorientation occur in the body and the mind, and refer to a basic physiological and ontological structure – to our "being-in-the-world" (Binswanger 1963). In the same manner, in dance and music we may obtain the best knowledge of ourselves and we may recognize ourselves, for instance, as members of a community: we become emotionally a common body.

From this perspective, we arrive at the most important expression of the proposed definition of ritual: "behavior that leads to the creation or recreation of an emotion." Above all, ritual must be seen in its relationship with the "emotional body." Such emotion probably derives from the hypothalamus and the amygdala, the most ancient part of the brain. Newberg and D'Aquili (2000) reviewed a number of studies that apparently established links between sustained attention associated with the practice of ritual or meditation and electroencephalography (EEG) theta waves above the prefrontal cortex. The two authors confirmed these data and enlarged them using single-photon emission computed tomography (SPECT). Results demonstrated significantly increased blood flow to the inferior frontal and dorsolateral prefrontal cortical regions when subjects were engaged in intense meditation or ritual.

The definition of ritual suggested here is therefore partly dependent upon this result. The expression "correct balance between persons and the world" is the most interpretive part of the definition and provides the *sine qua non* for social life and survival. This interpretation is very broad in content and therefore not in contrast with other definitions, but it is also very narrow in the sense of a physiological and emotional experience. By stressing this fundamental data of ritual it is possible to surmount all the difficulties associated for instance with the so-called "meaninglessness" of ritual (Staal 1975), which is the negative outcome of previous studies made by ritologists and anthropologists, who asked which type of functionality, communication, and expressivity were included in ritual.

In Durkheim, for instance, we find both a passive and an active notion of the relationship between religion and society: while religion is a system of ideas with which individuals represent to themselves the society of which they are members, rituals really strengthen the bonds between individuals and society. But is this reciprocity between society and religion all we can say by means of the concept of function? And is the concept of symbolic function sufficiently clear? We have gone from social functions and instrumental/non-instrumental theories of ritual, to communication theories based on the idea that ritual is a particular form of social action with its own modalities of communicative and meta-communicative framing; from expressive-performative theories for which ritual is symbolic drama, to those based on the simple semiotic value of rite. In this perspective ritual is regulated only by formal rules and is comparable to syntactic or musical structures. This would mean that ritual actually is not a language, but something "like" a language. In this sense the inner structure of ritual is not a structure based upon meanings, but constructed only on a complex of signs. Ritual, says Staal (1975), is like a bird song.

The most recent theories are no less important and problematic. "Cognitivist" theories of ritual that turn to the psychological aspects of the representation of action ask whether the religious meaning of ritual can be reformulated in terms of the connections established by participants between representation of the ritual sequence and other types of religious assumptions. Meanwhile, "ecological" theories, for instance, examine the new space-time relationship in which ritual appears as the ground for anthropological spatial direction and bodily division. The construction of time in ritual is important because ritual provides grounds for the creation and recurrence of time as well as space. Further, such ecological theories posit an essential adaptive function of rite as a type of "sanctification" of the environment in connection with the ecosystem. Burkert (1996) suggests that "through manifold forms as functions of ritual behavior and cultural interpretations, religion can still be seen to inhabit the deep values of the landscape of life." What should be stressed here is that religion – through ritual – not only relates to the social sciences, but also connects with the ecosystem, with naturalism, and with life and biology itself.

All these contributions can be understood in a renewed epistemological context if we suppose that in the beginning religion was not a matter of reflection and consciousness, but one of simple biological and physiological *arousal* of human nature in front of the varieties of events and situations. If we consider the links between ritual and the autonomous nervous system, it is clear that by means of (especially) repetition and formalization the system is driven unconsciously to maintain or recreate a very particular "primitive emotion." Rite stirs up an emotion that does not really reach consciousness and self-awareness, but reaches deeper, into the most ancient and original point of consciousness, leading to an emotional balance, a *habit* that is not an emotion derived from a situation or routine. This is also the way to understand the "serious" or non-empirical aspect of ritual.

In other words, language and consciousness are functions that are too developed for the subcortical structure of the brain. Ritual belongs to the primitive structure of humanity, dominated not by language but by physiological emotion. In this sense Langer (1969) was right to think about the "presemantic" and "preverbal" dimension of ritual. She suggested that rite belonged to a prelinguistic world and carried out a dramatic emotional logic.

Can an emotion exorcise the fear of death? Using the definition of ritual advanced here, it is easier to see the "synthetic" value of ritual and to write a new history of ritual in which it is possible to stress without contradiction its connections with social, religious, functional, biological, adaptive, and ecosystemic dimensions. This multimodality is explained by the fact that ritual arouses a deep, primitive emotion in which all is convergent.

SEE ALSO: Emotion: Cultural Aspects; Myth; Performance Ethnography; Ritual; Sacrifice; Society and Biology

REFERENCES AND SUGGESTED READINGS

Binswanger, L. (1963) *Being-in-the-World: Selected Papers.* Basic Books, New York.

Bloch, M. (1989) *The Past and the Present: The Collected Papers of Maurice Bloch.* Billings, Worcester.

Burkert, W. (1996) *The Creation of the Sacred: Tracks of Biology in Early Religions.* Harvard University Press, Cambridge, MA.

Langer, S. (1969) *Philosophy in a New Key: A Study in the Symbolism of Reason, Rite, and Art.* Harvard University Press, Cambridge, MA.

Newberg, A. B. & D' Aquili, E. G. (2000) The Neuropsychology of Religious and Spiritual Experience. In: Andresen, J. & Forman, R. K. C. (Eds.), *Cognitive Models and Spiritual Maps: Interdisciplinary Explorations of Religious Experiences.* Imprint Academic, Thorverton, pp. 251–66.

Rappaport, R. (1999) *Ritual and Religion in the Making of Humanity.* Cambridge University Press, Cambridge.

Schechner, R. (1977) *Essays on Performance Theory.* Drama Books Specialists, New York.

Staal, F. (1975) The Meaninglessness of Ritual. *Numen* 26: 2–22.

Turner, V. W. (1967) *The Ritual Process: Structure and Anti-Structure.* Cornell University Press, Ithaca, NY.

Vygotsky, L. S. (1962) *Thought and Language.* John Wiley, New York.

ritual

Philip Smith

Ritual involves conventionalized and stylized human actions. These are often organized with reference to overarching cultural codes, have a communicative intent, and generate powerful emotional responses among participants. Historically marginalized as a concern for anthropologists, since the cultural turn became institutionalized in social theory in the 1980s the concept of ritual has become more and more central to the sociological enterprise. The core debates revolve around the following themes: (1) whether priority should be given to analyzing rites (embodied actions, doing) or beliefs (cosmologies and symbols, thinking); (2) how a model conceived in functionalism can be adapted to include understandings of power and domination; (3) whether we should understand ritual in collectivistic or more microsociological ways.

The canonical text for the study of ritual in social science is Durkheim's *Elementary Forms of Religious Life.* Here, Durkheim drew upon ethnographic material about Aboriginal Australia to argue that societies needed periodically to renew social bonds and solidaristic ties. Tribal gatherings involving ritual activity – the corroboree – performed this function. They involved the manipulation and invocation of symbols, totems, and supernatural forces; coordinated bodily motions and expressive actions, feasting and sexual activity, the enactment of myths and legends. The result was a heightened emotional sensibility and sense of excitement that Durkheim called *collective effervescence.* Durkheim emphasized the interplay of such socially integrative rites with underlying systems of belief and classification that marked out the sacred from the profane. He understood religion as this complex of cultural codes and ritual actions, and society as being founded upon this religious core. The history of ritual theory in sociology can be broadly understood as the story of elaborations upon, challenges to, and creative readings of *The Elementary Forms.*

Although he drew his material from what he thought of as a "primitive" society, Durkheim explicitly intended his insights on the characteristics and social functions of ritual to have universal relevance. Yet sociologists were slow on the uptake. When Marcel Mauss, Durkheim's nephew, wrote about *The Gift* in the 1920s, he gave more attention to theorizing exchange relationships and economic life than the ritual qualities of gift giving. In the 1930s France Bataille and the College de Sociologie were seemingly more interested in elaborating the qualities of the sacred and the ways this could be immanently experienced without the mediation of collective social activity. For this reason W. Lloyd Warner's application of the ritual model to "advanced" societies in his study of American small-town life marks an important intervention. Although rather simplistic in retrospect, his analysis of America's Memorial Day ceremonies as a "cult of the dead" attempted to validate Durkheim's broader thesis. Likewise the attempt by Edward Shils and Michael Young to interpret the 1952 coronation of Queen Elizabeth II as a ritual of national communion stands out from this period. Subsequent work in the 1960s by Robert Bellah on civil religion, Edward Shils on center and periphery, and Mary Douglas on purity and pollution saw the leading Durkheimians focus once more on classifications and cosmologies rather than ritual activity. In Durkheim's own terms, scholars were looking at beliefs rather than rites, even if they bought into the general proposition that society had a quasi-religious foundation. The most important exception was the work of Victor Turner. Although Turner rarely cites Durkheim, his theorizing of the solidaristic, egalitarian, and creative social relations he called *communitas* owes a clear debt to the strand of *The Elementary Forms* concerned with ritual practices.

The period extending through the 1970s and 1980s saw the consensual normative functionalism of Durkheim and Talcott Parsons come under attack. New visions of ritual as an instrumental strategy fell into place. These directly or indirectly challenged what was seen as a cognitive and integrative bias in Durkheim's thinking, arguing instead for ritual as a form of political practice. In a seminal article, Steven Lukes (1975) argued that we needed to understand rituals as events with sponsors and as attempts at domination. David Kertzer agreed, suggesting that rituals were a medium of contestation and mobilization that could work even in the absence of an overarching consensus or set of shared beliefs. Pierre Bourdieu's analysis of gift exchange, unlike the work of Mauss, put strategy and reflexive calculation center stage. Scholars like Stuart Hall in the emergent area of cultural studies spoke of youth subcultures as "rituals of resistance" characterized by stylized critique of the dominant social order. Michel Foucault spoke of the "spectacle of the scaffold" and the ways this reproduced systems of power.

A second front against the Durkheimian mainstream emerged out of Erving Goffman's work on face-to-face interaction. This microsociological approach drew as much from Arnold van Gennep's (1960) early study of the "rite of passage" as from *The Elementary Forms.* Van Gennep had argued that ritual interventions were ways in which societies conferred legitimate and recognizable identities on subjects, especially at times of status transition. What Goffman (1967) called *interaction rituals* were everyday encounters between people in which appropriate displays of deference and demeanor were expected. These offered mutual confirmation of the value of the self, of social status, and of role expectations, thus providing a sense of ontological security and allowing interactions to be successfully accomplished by more or less reflexive social agents. The work of Randall Collins combined this line of thinking on ritual with that of conflict sociology, asserting that collective identities and solidarities are built from the bottom up through *interaction ritual chains*. These not only generate pro-social emotions, such as enthusiasm and esprit de corps, but also play a role in the formation of stratification hierarchies and exclusionary cliques.

The contemporary sociology of ritual continues to debate these themes, often through reinterpretations of *The Elementary Forms* itself (see Alexander & Smith 2004). Some focus on what Durkheim had to say about the sacred and profane, and see rituals as the enactment of deeply held beliefs. Others see this as idealism, point to the weak, incoherent, and inchoate nature of many belief systems, and suggest that rituals are really all about embodied and practical actions. Some look to the solidaristic, universalist, and egalitarian outcomes of rituals and others to their uses as a tool for domination; some focus on ritual and ritualization as an emergent property of action and others on ritual as the social fact that constrains and motivates action in the first place. Such underlying controversies are being played out currently in a number of established and emergent empirical domains where the concept seems to pay dividends: studies of political scandals, controversies and contests; investigations of play, sport, tourism, and pilgrimage; accounts of collective memory and commemoration; the literature on bodies, emotions, and everyday interactions; research on revolutions, protests, and collective mobilization; discussions of punishment, regulation, and control; and last but not least, of course, in the sociology of religion itself.

SEE ALSO: Durkheim, Émile; Goffman, Erving; Religion; Religion, Sociology of

REFERENCES AND SUGGESTED READINGS

Alexander, J. & Smith, P. (Eds.) (2004) *The Cambridge Companion to Durkheim*. Cambridge University Press, Cambridge.

Durkheim, É. (1968 [1912]) *The Elementary Forms of Religious Life*. Allen & Unwin, London.

Goffman, E. (1967) *Interaction Ritual*. Aldine, Chicago.

Lukes, S. (1975) Political Ritual and Social Integration. *British Journal of Sociology* 9 (2): 289–308.

van Gennep, A. (1960 [1908]) *The Rites of Passage*. Routledge & Kegan Paul, London.

Rizal, José (1861–96)

Syed Farid Alatas

José Rizal, Filipino thinker and activist, may be considered the first systematic social thinker in Southeast Asia. While the bulk of his writings were not in the social sciences, it is possible to extract a sociological theory from his works. This would be a theory that explains the nature and conditions of Filipino colonial society, and the requirements for emancipation.

José Protasio Rizal y Alonso was born in Calamba, Laguna, the Philippines, on June 19, 1861, to a wealthy family. His father ran a sugar plantation on land leased from the Dominican Order, while his mother was a highly educated woman. Rizal was educated at home till he was 11 years of age, after which he attended the best schools in Manila. He went on to study at the Ateneo de Manila University and then the University of Santo Thomas. He was known to be a well-rounded student, having studied medicine and the humanities simultaneously. In addition to being a qualified ophthalmic doctor, Rizal was also a writer, poet, ethnologist, sculptor, cartoonist, fencer, sharpshooter, and linguist (Coates 1978: 1905–6). In 1882 Rizal left for Spain where he continued his studies in medicine and the humanities at the Universidad Central in Madrid. At the same time, he became familiar with liberal movements and modern constitutions and began to draw lessons for the analysis of Spanish rule in the Philippines. Within a few years, Rizal's activities with a group of Filipino students in Madrid led to his being acknowledged as the leader of the Philippine reform movement (Coates 1978: 1906).

His first novel, *Noli Me Tangere* (*Touch Me Not*), was published in Berlin in 1887, the year that Rizal returned to the Philippines. The novel was a reflection of exploitative conditions under Spanish colonial rule and enraged the Spanish friars. Fearing for his safety, Rizal left the Philippines for Japan, the United States, and Britain in 1888. At the same time in Spain, the nationalist movement started a fortnightly newspaper, *La Solidaridad*, to which Rizal contributed. His second novel, *El Filibusterismo* (*The Revolution*), was published in 1891 in Ghent, Belgium, and thematized the possibilities and consequences of revolution. As Rizal's political ideas became known to the authorities, he and his family suffered many hardships. His parents were dispossessed of their home and the male members deported to the island of Mondoro (Coates 1978: 1908). Rizal himself was finally exiled to Dapitan, Mindanao, from 1892 to 1896, implicated in the revolution of 1896, tried for sedition, and executed by firing squad on December 30, 1896, at the age of 35. Although he lived such a short time, his productivity remains unsurpassed by anyone in Southeast Asia, perhaps even Asia. He wrote several poems and essays, three novels, and conducted studies in early Philippine history, Tagalog grammar, and even entomology. Rizal's achievements were all the more remarkable when it is realized that great obstacles were put in the way of the educational and intellectual advancement of the Filipinos during the colonial period.

Rizal lived in colonial Filipino society and was deeply affected by the colonial exploitation of the Filipinos. The early Filipino nationalists were priests who pressed for reforms. For example, an 1826 royal decree required that parishes previously in the hands of Filipino priests be gradually returned to Spanish friars. Several Filipino priests worked for the revocation of this anti-Filipino decree. Their political activities led to the execution of three Filipino priests, Mariano Gomez, José Burgos, and Jacinto Zamora in 1872. Rizal dedicated his *El Filibusterismo* to them.

Rizal also lived at a time when there was little critique of the state of knowledge on the Philippines among Spanish colonial and Filipino scholars. Rizal was well acquainted with the world of Orientalist scholarship in Europe (Mojares 2002: 54). Rizal himself took an interest in this, as can be seen in his annotated reedition of Antonio de Morga's *Sucesos de las Islas Filipinas*, which first appeared in 1609. Prior to producing this work, Morga served eight years in the Philippines as Lieutenant Governor General and Captain General as well as a justice of the Supreme Court of Manila (Audiencia Real de Manila) (Morga 1991 [1890]: xxxv). Rizal believed that Spanish colonization had virtually wiped out the precolonial past from the memory of Filipinos and presented the reedition in order to correct what he saw as false reports and slanderous statements to be found in most Spanish works on the Philippines ("To the Filipinos," in Morga 1962 [1890]: vii). This includes the destruction of pre-Spanish records such as artifacts that would have thrown light on the nature of precolonial society (Zaide 1993: 5). Rizal found Morga's work an apt choice as it was, according to Ocampo (1998: 192), the only civil history of the Philippines written during the Spanish colonial period, other works being mainly ecclesiastical histories. The problem with ecclesiastical histories, apart from the falsifications and slander, was that they "abound in stories of devils, miracles, apparitions, etc., these forming the bulk of the voluminous histories of the Philippines" (Morga 1962 [1890]: 291 n4). For Rizal, therefore, existing histories of the Philippines were false and biased as well as unscientific and irrational. Rizal's interests were thus to reform Filipino society in both sociopolitical and intellectual terms.

If we were to construct a sociological theory from Rizal's works, this would be a theory of colonial society, one that explains the nature and conditions of colonial society and the meaning and requirements for emancipation. The outline of Rizal's perspective is as follows. A corrupt Spanish colonial government and its officials oppress and exploit the Filipinos. Rizal's novels, political writings, and letters provide examples such as the confiscation of lands, appropriation of farmers' labor, high taxes, forced labor without payment, and so on (Rizal 1963a). Rizal's *Noli Me Tangere* is a diagnosis of the problems of Filipino society. This novel is a socially descriptive text in which the various characters represent the social malaise and wrongs of his time (Majul 1999: 3). Rizal was tireless in pointing out the hypocrisies of the Spaniards. He was critical of the "boasted ministers of God [the friars] and *propagators of light* (!) [who] have not sowed nor do they sow Christian morals, they have not taught religion, but rituals and superstitions" (Rizal 1963b: 38).

Rizal noted that the Spaniards blamed the backwardness of the Filipinos on their indolence. The Spaniards charged that the Filipinos had little love for work. Rizal, however, made a number of important points in what was the first sociological treatment of the topic (Alatas

1977: 98). First of all, Rizal noted that the "miseries of a people without freedom should not be imputed to the people but to their rulers" (Rizal 1963b: 31). Secondly, that the Filipinos are an inherently lazy people was not true. Rizal admits that there was some indolence but does not attribute it to backwardness. Rather, it was the backwardness and disorder of Filipino colonial society that caused indolence. Prior to the colonial period, Filipinos were not indolent. They controlled trade routes and were involved in agriculture, mining, manufacturing, and so on. But when their destiny was taken away from them, they became indolent. Rizal's approach to the problem is interesting in that he made a distinction between being "indolent" as a reaction to climate, for example, and indolence in terms of the absence of love for work or the avoidance of work. The second kind of indolence was a result of the social and historical experience of the Filipinos under Spanish rule. Rizal examined historical accounts by Europeans from centuries earlier which showed Filipinos to be industrious. Therefore, indolence must have social causes and these were to be found in the nature of colonial rule (Rizal 1963c).

The backwardness of colonial society is not due to any inherent defects of the Filipino people but to the backwardness of the church. Emancipation could only come from enlightenment. Spanish colonial rule was exploitative because of the backwardness of the church in that the church was against enlightenment, the supremacy of reason. The European Enlightenment was good for Filipinos, while the church was against it because it established reason as authority, not God or the church. Thinkers such as Marx, Weber, and Durkheim were products of the Enlightenment but recognized that reason had gone wrong. Modernity, which was a creation of reason, was unreasonable because it was alienating, anomic, and ultimately irrational. It is interesting to note that Rizal, who was also writing in the nineteenth century, had a different attitude to the Enlightenment and to reason (Bonoan & Raul 1994). His writings do not show disappointment with reason and he was not dissatisfied with modernity in the way that Marx, Weber, and Durkheim were. This is probably because for Rizal the Philippines was not modern enough and was kept backward by the anti-rational church.

This results in the emergence of the *filibustero*, the "dangerous patriot who should be hanged soon," that is, a revolutionary. Revolution, in other words breakaway from Spanish rule and church, is inevitable and the only means of emancipation. Rizal's *El Filibusterismo* is a prescription for revolution. His *Noli Me Tangere* of 1887 gives the impression of Rizal merely being in favor of breaking the friars' civil power. This can be seen from the characters in the novel. The villains were the Franciscan *padres*. But the civil and military power exercised by the Spanish Captain General, a colonial officer, is rational and progressive. Elias, a noble, patriotic, and selfless Filipino, dies in the novel, while the egoist Ibarra survives. The sequel, *El Filibusterismo*, implies a shift in Rizal's thinking. The villains are the Dominican priests as well as the Captain General, who turns out to be a mercenary. The revolution fails, reflecting Rizal's assessment of the readiness and preparedness of the Filipinos for revolution. He saw those who would lead a revolution as working out of self-interest rather than on behalf of a national community (Majul 1999: 19). Rizal was reluctant to join a revolution that was doomed to failure due to lack of preparation, the egoism of the so-called revolutionaries, and the lack of a cohesive front. Nevertheless, his very actions and writings were revolutionary and he was executed for treason against Spain.

While a serious assessment of Rizal's studies of Filipino history and colonial society would reveal the extent to which his claims were true or exaggerated, it is important to note the contra-Eurocentric significance of his works. This suggests a redefining of classical social theory, recognizing that another context of the rise of sociological theory is the historical fact of European political and cultural domination from the fifteenth century onwards, and colonization. Looking at colonized peoples as part of the process of the rise of modernity would lead to a consideration of the ideas of the contemporaries of Marx, Weber, and Durkheim in colonized areas as classical social theorists.

SEE ALSO: Colonialism (Neocolonialism); Decolonization; Eurocentrism

REFERENCES AND SUGGESTED READINGS

Alatas, S. H. (1977) *The Myth of the Lazy Native: A Study of the Image of the Malays, Filipinos, and Javanese from the 16th to the 20th Century and its Function in the Ideology of Colonial Capitalism.* Frank Cass, London.

Bonoan, S. J. & Raul, J. (1994) *The Rizal–Pastells Correspondence.* Ateneo de Manila Press, Quezon City.

Coates, A. (1978) Phoenix in December. In: *Filipino Heritage: The Making of a Nation. The Spanish Colonial Period (Late 19th Century): The Awakening.* Lahing Pilipino Publishing, Manila, pp. 1905–12.

Majul, C. A. (1999) Rizal in the 21st Century: The Relevance of His Ideas and Texts. *Public Policy* 3 (1): 1–21.

Mojares, R. B. (2002) *Waiting for Mariang Makiling: Essays in Philippine Cultural History.* Ateneo de Manila Press, Manila.

Morga, A. de (1962 [1890]) *Historical Events of the Philippine Islands by Dr. Antonio de Morga, Published in Mexico in 1609, recently brought to light and annotated by José Rizal, preceded by a prologue by Dr. Ferdinand Blumentritt.* Centenary edition. Writings of José Rizal Volume 6. National Historical Institute, Manila.

Morga, A. de (1991 [1890]) *Sucesos de las Islas Filipinas por el Doctor Antonio de Morga, obra publicada en Méjico el año de 1609, nuevamente sacada a luz y anotada por José Rizal y precedida de un prólogo del Prof. Fernando Blumentritt.* Centenary edition. Writings of José Rizal Volume 6. José Rizal Centenary Commission, National Historical Institute, Manila.

Ocampo, A. R. (1998) Rizal's Morga and Views of Philippine History. *Philippine Studies* 46: 184–214.

Rizal, J. (1963a) Filipino Farmers. In: *Political and Historical Writings.* National Historical Institute, Manila, pp. 19–22.

Rizal, J. (1963b) The Truth for All. In: *Political and Historical Writings.* National Historical Institute, Manila, pp. 31–8.

Rizal, J. (1963c) The Indolence of the Filipino. In: *Political and Historical Writings.* National Historical Institute, Manila, pp. 111–39.

Rizal, J. (1989) Mi Último Adiós (My Last Farewell). In: *Dr. José Rizal's Mi Último Adiós in Foreign and Local Translations,* Vol. 1. National Historical Institute, Manila.

Zaide, S. (1993) Historiography in the Spanish Period. In: *Philippine Encyclopedia of the Social Sciences.* Philippine Social Science Council, Quezon City, pp. 4–19.

robbery

Scott H. Decker

Robbery is the use or threat of force to take another's property and ranks among the most serious crime problems in the US. Robbery is one of the four crimes of violence (murder, rape, robbery, and aggravated assault) and is the second most prevalent of the four. Robbery is also a central component of the fear of crime, magnifying its impact particularly for women, the elderly, and suburban residents. As Conklin (1972: 4) has observed: "Although the public certainly fears murder and rape, it is probably fear of robbery . . . which keeps people off the street, makes them avoid strangers, and leads them to lock their doors."

Data reported to the police indicate that victims and offenders in most robberies are strangers. Robbery is a crime committed disproportionately by drug users, is more likely than other violent offenses to involve black offenders, and seldom nets large sums of money. Robbery rates are highest in urban areas. Many inner-city neighborhoods experience high rates of robbery. Robbery poses a serious risk of injury or death. One in three robbery victims sustains at least minor injuries during the offense (Reaves 1993), and more than 10 percent of all homicides occur in the context of a robbery (Cook 1991).

The findings from interviews with armed robbers underscore the versatility of offending patterns among robbers, their high levels of victimization, and the role of lifestyle pressures among this group of offenders.

Jacobs (2000) conducted research among drug robbers (offenders who robbed drug dealers) in St. Louis, Missouri, a city with high levels of violence. Jacobs notes that while robbery is the "purest" of offenses with regard to motive and intent (cash), robbers engage in a variety of other offenses. The robbers interviewed by Jacobs were involved in both legal and illegal activities that involved them in a variety of contingencies that they could not escape. These individuals also had very high rates of victimization.

Wright and Decker (1997) studied 85 active armed robbers in St. Louis, Missouri, conducting interviews and "ride-alongs" with these individuals. This group of armed robbers committed a large number of diverse offenses, including burglary, drug sales, auto theft, and assault. Wright and Decker found that offenders engaged in minor forms of offending, would be victimized, and would then retaliate by engaging in a robbery. This pattern increased their level of offending, both in terms of frequency and seriousness. Not many of these offenders reported their victimization to the police. Lacking legal recourse, many offenders take the law into their own hands, circumventing legal means, and thereby increasing the odds of engaging in additional crime.

The research with armed robbers found a strong link between their lifestyle and their patterns of lawbreaking. This research has examined the separate steps in robberies: motivation, target selection, and confrontation, documenting their key components.

Most armed robbers report in interviews that the primary goal of their offense was a pressing need for cash. However, the majority of robbers report that the proceeds of their crimes did not go to pay for necessities. Rather, most indicate that they used the cash to initiate or sustain various forms of illicit street action (e.g., drinking, drug-taking, gambling). Other robbers indicated that they committed robberies to ease financial burdens that were largely of their own making, such as gambling debts or other personal obligations.

Target selection among street robbers seldom matches the rational, well-planned target selection process that might be imagined. Two key factors seem to be most important: the availability of good hiding places and getaway avenues. The primary goal in selecting potential victims is to select someone who appears to be carrying a good deal of cash. Often this means someone involved in criminal activities, such as a drug dealer, a customer of prostitutes, or gamblers. As Jacobs (2000) found, drug dealers can be particularly attractive targets for robbery. Other robbers may search for potential victims in environments where there is plenty of cash, such as areas around check-cashing places, entertainment or restaurant districts, or automatic teller machines.

Robbery of commercial establishments takes a somewhat different form requiring considerably more planning and expertise. Only a small proportion of the offenders in Wright and Decker's sample targeted commercial establishments. Most of these offenders targeted small local businesses such as liquor stores, taverns, or pawn shops. They claimed that they liked robbing commercial targets because they could count on the ready availability of a reasonable amount of cash – something that could not be taken for granted with many street robberies. Few of the commercial robbers could be classified as sophisticated, high-level, or "professional" criminals.

The confrontation between perpetrators and victims is the final step in the robbery process. This stage of a robbery is likely to be the briefest, often taking no more than a few seconds. While robbers generally may prefer not to inflict harm, the ability to convince potential victims that they are willing to do so is an important part of being successful as a robber. Another key element of the confrontation between robber and victim is to frighten victims into compliance. This is done most effectively when a convincing illusion of impending death can be conveyed.

SEE ALSO: Crime; Index Crime; Insecurity and Fear of Crime; Property Crime; Urban Crime and Violence; Violent Crime

REFERENCES AND SUGGESTED READINGS

Conklin, J. (1972) *Robbery*. J. B. Lippincott, Philadelphia.

Cook, P. (1991) Robbery in the United States: Analysis of Recent Trends and Patterns. In: Weiner, N., Zahn, M., & Sagi, R. (Eds.), *Violence: Patterns, Causes, Public Policy*. Harcourt, Brace, & Jovanovich, New York, pp. 85–98.

Federal Bureau of Investigation (1995) *Crime in the United States 1994*. Government Printing Office, Washington, DC.

Jacobs, B. A. (2000) *Robbing Drug Dealers: Violence Beyond the Law*. Aldine, New York.

Reaves, B. (1993) *Using NIBRS Data to Analyze Violent Crime*. Bureau of Justice Statistics Technical Report, US Department of Justice.

Wilson, J. Q. & Boland, B. (1976) Crime. In: Gorham, W. & Glazer, N. (Eds.), *The Urban Predicament*. Urban Institute, Washington, DC, pp. 179–230.

Wright, R. T. & Decker, S. H. (1997) *Robbers on Robbery: Stick-Up and Street Culture*. Northeastern University Press, Boston.

Robert E. Park, Ernest W. Burgess, and urban social research

Barbara Ballis Lal

The style of social research associated with the Chicago School of American sociology owes much to the determination of Robert E. Park and his younger colleague, Ernest Burgess, to understand city life. (Park was a faculty member in the department of sociology/anthropology at the University of Chicago between 1913 and 1934. Burgess was a faculty member in the department between 1916 and 1952. In 1929 sociology and anthropology became separate departments.) Other scholars who aided them in this endeavor included W. I. Thomas, Louis Wirth, Everett Hughes, Clifford Shaw, Donald Cressey, Frederick Thrasher, St. Clair Drake, and Horace Cayton. Economic growth, industrialization, population increase, immigration, and rural–urban migration, including the large-scale movement of African Americans from the South, contributed to the emergence of Chicago as a city in which diversity of occupation was complemented by differences having to do with race, ethnicity (whether or not foreign-born), religion, and language. Chicago, and cities like it, differed profoundly from the rural towns that had hitherto shaped American social life and politics. What, asked Park in an essay published in 1926, is to be the basis of a "moral order" which supposes communication and obligation between individuals and groups, in an urban environment characterized by "physical propinquity" and "social isolation"? The monographs *The Crowd and the Public* (1904), *Old World Traits Transplanted*, in the most part the work of W. I. Thomas but with authorship attributed to Park and H. A. Miller (1921), and *The Immigrant Press and Its Control* (1922), along with numerous essays, reflect his concerns.

Park and Burgess enjoined faculty and graduate students to view the city of Chicago as "a social laboratory." With this in mind, investigations proliferated of the ongoing group life of hobos, gangs, the Jews of Maxwell Street, criminals, denizens of the gold coast and the slum, taxi-hall dancers, the preachers in Bronzeville, and participants and onlookers involved in the 1919 race riot in Chicago. Each of these small-scale studies was a contribution to a larger "mosaic" representing the urban context of which each was a part. Both Park and Burgess edited collections of essays suggesting future lines of research in cities (Park 1967; Burgess 1926).

Urban ethnography and the analysis of "human documents" such as newspapers, life histories, letters, and court records combined theory and empirical data. These strategies of research, although preferred, especially in the period before 1927, existed alongside of quantitative procedures based upon surveys and mapping the changing distributions of demographic and occupational statistics, land use, real estate values, vice, juvenile delinquency, and other phenomena of interest to social scientists investigating city life. Urban ethnography, that is to say, social research in a "natural setting," directed sociologists to document and interpret the nature of social life in cities as lived experience in a specific locality. The "narrative, case study approach" insisted that the subjective point of view of the actor and the collective representations made possible by language and local narratives be collected in an effort to find out what gives meaning and purpose to the life of those groups that sociologists study. The examination of "culture as process" (Matthews 1989) animated studies such as *The Ghetto* (1928), *The Gang* (1927), *The Gold Coast and the Slum* (1929), and *The Jack-Roller* (1930), *Taxi-Dance Hall* (1932), and *Black Metropolis* (1945). Later sociological monographs continue to reflect the development of the tradition of urban ethnography originating at Chicago. Current emphasis on fieldwork as "a way of knowing" as well as "immersion" in the ongoing activities of a group (Emerson 2001) complements rather than diminishes Park's injunction that sociologists study urban life and culture in much the same spirit as anthropologists study unfamiliar people in premodern settings.

Urban sociology at Chicago also developed the perspective of human ecology as a way of approaching city life. Human ecology charts the changing spatial distribution of groups, institutions, and activities, as well as examining the distribution of a population in an occupational order. Spatial and occupational distributions result from competition among individuals and groups for both living space and an economic niche. Competition in turn results in "symbiosis," defined by Park as "the living together of distinct and dissimilar species, especially when the relationship is mutually beneficial." Symbiosis is a condition in which there is cooperation sufficient to maintain a common economy, but lacking sufficient consensus to sustain collective action. Competition is a type of "non-social" interaction because there is neither communication nor the reciprocal adjustment of activity in pursuit of a common goal.

Ecological processes such as competition, "succession, and "dominance" describe observable, aggregate properties of a group. Ecological explanations are not concerned with the actor's point of view.

Human ecology made use of maps and graphic representations based on the collection of numerical data. Burgess's influential essay "The Growth of the City: An Introduction to a Research Project" (1967) displayed the physical growth and expansion of the city as a dynamic process in which a central business district "invaded" encircling zones of transition, workingmen's homes, residential areas, and commuter suburbs. Burgess pointed out that the processes and rate of expansion of cities "may be studied not only in the physical growth and business development, but also in the consequent changes in the social organization and in personality types." He further depicted zones of the city in terms of "natural areas" which are differentiated from one another on the basis of social organization and disorganization as indicated by the occupations and mobility of residents, type of housing, land values, and the rates of crime, vice, poverty, and homelessness. Burgess's model of the growth of cities was an "ideal construction" which he thought would capture the nature of urban growth generally.

Park never confused sociology, whose objective is to study culture and communication, with human ecology. Human "society" as opposed to plant and animal "communities" exists on two levels: the "biotic" and the "cultural." These levels can be presented analytically as a "spatial pattern" and a "moral order" (Park 1952b). Human ecology deals with the "biotic" (e.g., the biological and the geographical) aspects of group life, while sociology investigates "culture" and the subjectively motivated activities of "persons." Human ecology is of interest because social relations are so often reflected in spatial patterns and because "social distances" are frequently expressed as physical distances. As Park's student Louis Wirth (1945) pointed out, human ecology "is not a substitute for, but a supplement to, other frames of reference and methods of social investigation." The "cultural order" is imposed upon and modifies the "ecological order."

Park, Burgess, Wirth, and other colleagues at Chicago thought that the problematic features of urban life were amenable to social reform at the local level. In this spirit these scholars participated in local political activities and joined civic organizations. They were confident that increased communication between educated urbanites informed by expert knowledge could be directed towards ameliorating social problems such as ethnic conflict, race discrimination and race riots, juvenile delinquency, vice, labor strikes, unfair employment practices, and political corruption.

SEE ALSO: Chicago School: Ecology; Ethnic Groups; Ethnography; Life History; Observation, Participant and Non-Participant; Park, Robert E. and Burgess, Ernest W.; Race; Race (Racism); Social Control; Symbolic Interaction; Urban; Urbanization

REFERENCES AND SUGGESTED READINGS

Burgess, E. W. (Ed.) (1926) *The Urban Community*. University of Chicago Press, Chicago.

Burgess, E. W. (1967 [1925]) The Growth of the City: An Introduction to a Research Project. In: Park, R. E., Burgess, E. W., & McKenzie, R., *The City*. University of Chicago Press, Chicago.

Cressy, P. G. (1932) *The Taxi-Dance Hall*. University of Chicago Press, Chicago.

Drake, S. C. & Cayton, H. R. (1945) *Black Metropolis: Negro Life in a Northern City*, 2 vols. Harcourt, Brace, New York.

Emerson, R. (2001) Introduction: The Development of Ethnographic Field Research. In: *Contemporary Field Research*, 2nd edn. Waveland Press, Prospect Heights, IL, pp. 1–26.

Matthews, F. H. (1989) Social Scientists and the Culture Concept, 1930–1950: The Conflict Between the Processual and Structural Approaches. *Sociological Theory* 7: 87–101.
Park, R. E. (1952a [1915]) The City: Suggestions for the Investigation of Human Behavior in the Urban Environment. In: Hughes, E. C. et al. (Eds.), *Collected Writings of Robert E. Park*, Vol. 2: Human Communities, the City, Human Ecology. Free Press, Glencoe, IL, pp. 13–51.
Park, R. E. (1952b [1926]) The Urban Community as a Spatial Pattern and a Moral Order. In: Hughes, E. C. et al. (Eds.), *Collected Writings of Robert E. Park*, Vol. 2: Human Communities, the City, Human Ecology. Free Press, Glencoe, IL, pp. 165–77.
Park, R. E. (1952c [1929]) The City as a Social Laboratory. In: Hughes, E. C. et al. (Eds.), *Collected Writings of Robert E. Park*, Vol. 2: Human Communities, the City, Human Ecology. Free Press, Glencoe, IL, pp. 73–87.
Park, R. E. (1970 [1922]) *The Immigrant Press and Its Control.* Greenwood Press, Westport.
Park, R. E. (1972 [1904]) The Crowd and the Public. In: Elsner, H. Jr. (Ed.), *The Crowd and the Public and Other Essays.* University of Chicago Press, Chicago.
Park, R. E. & Miller, H. A. (1969 [1921]) *Old World Traits Transplanted.* Arno Press and the New York Times, New York.
Park, R. E., Burgess, E. W., & McKenzie, R. (1967 [1925]) *The City.* University of Chicago Press, Chicago.
Shaw, C. (1930) *The Jack-Roller: A Delinquent Boy's Own Story.* University of Chicago Press, Chicago.
Wirth, L. (1928) *The Ghetto.* University of Chicago Press, Chicago.
Wirth, L. (1945) Human Ecology. *American Journal of Sociology* (May): 483–8.
Zorbaugh, H. W. (1929) *The Gold Coast and the Slum.* University of Chicago Press, Chicago.

role

David D. Franks

Social role is a critical analytical tool for sociology and social psychology because it provides the nexus between social structure and individual behavior. The term role is a metaphor that comes from the theater and Shakespeare's famous statement about people playing roles with entrances and exits throughout their lives. Social structures consist of roles or performance parts that provide vehicles for the organization of selves and social relations. People have many different sides, and different roles can produce very different behaviors from the same person. In the past century, role theory has evolved from a framework wherein "causation" flows down from preexisting roles shaping individual behavior, to a theory wherein "causation" also flows upward from social interaction to establishing a constant recreation of structure.

STRUCTURAL APPROACHES

The macro-level notion of role was first presented by Park and further developed by the anthropologist Ralph Linton, and adopted by the mid-century functionalists. In structural formulations a person occupies a social position. A position is a person's placement on a larger organizational map. The position has a status and one plays a behavioral role attached to the position. A status is a ranking on a continuum of invidious distinctions in social regard, importance, and privilege. Linton used status as synonymous with position and role, blurring these three meanings. Linton explained role "as the dynamic aspect of status that puts the rights and duties that constitute the status into effect." Roles usually involve a number of supporting roles referred to as *role-sets.*

Role strain and role conflict illustrate two fruitful elaborations of structural role analysis. Since selves play many roles, contradictions within and between role expectations can present challenges to self-formation. Persons feel *role strain* when a role important to their identity demands contradictory identities. For example, some professors feel a strain between the demands of teaching and publishing. *Role conflict* occurs when pressures arise *between* the demands of several roles, such as those of career and family (see Hochschild's *Commercialization of Intimate Life*, 2003). Here again, the degree to which both roles are important to the individual will determine the amount of stress felt. Insofar as adolescents care equally about what their parents and peers think of them, they are vulnerable to role conflict. Balance between determinism and agency is maintained by considering the coping abilities of the person.

INTERACTIONAL APPROACHES

A very different micro-level meaning of role comes to us from the pragmatist philosopher G. H. Mead. His conception of *role-taking* stems from the insight of the Scottish philosophers that humans have the reflexive capacity to see themselves as others see them. Role-taking involves imagining the other's responses to one's behavior and using this anticipation to guide one's line of conduct. Here role refers not to a theatrical part but to the *perspective* people will have towards the actor's emerging talk and gestures. This is very different from "taking on" a preexistent societal role and passively enacting its prescriptions.

Mead's formulation of role-taking still remains the only thoroughly social theory available of the flexible and voluntary *self-control* of behavior. In this perspective self-control is also social control because the anticipated response of the other shapes the way actors manage their own oncoming behavior. It is thoroughly social because a preexistent pool of *shared* meanings must exist if actors are to respond to their oncoming behavior as would the other. Thus, role-taking is decidedly more tentative and flexible than Linton's script-like conception of role-playing (i.e., playing out role expectations). Depending on others' overt reactions, one can change one's tone or original intention in the middle of a sentence.

Structural roles can be *played* with only minimal role-taking. The teacher telling a high school class that a fact is an "empirically verifiable statement about phenomena in terms of a conceptual scheme" is surely playing the role of teacher in contrast to role-taking. Role-taking is thus episodic, and sociologists have inquired into those social situations that trigger role-taking and those that make it relatively unnecessary (Thomas et al. 1972).

Frequently, one must role-take with whole groups rather than individuals. A speaker may need to decide what Republicans would be interested in hearing in contrast to Democrats, or what freshman students can be expected to understand rather than seniors. This is referred to as taking the role of the "generalized other." As Mills (1939) originally argued, this process allows for impersonalized, objective reflection. When people attempt to write in clear logical sequences, or to carefully follow rules of due process, they are taking the role of the generalized other. Mead associated the generalized other with taking the role of one's community. However, as communities become broader and more complicated, unified responses become problematic, as does self-formation.

OTHER CONTRIBUTIONS TO INTERACTIONAL APPROACHES

Znaniecki and Lopata rejected the "confused and static image" of Linton's approach, especially his assumptions about the direction of causation where "social role is somehow a consequence of its status." According to Znaniecki and Lopata, the Lintonian model confused status with position and failed to see that the meaning of a given role could only be determined by specifying its part in the larger social placement system. She also stressed what Turner (1962) had referred to as "self-other" roles (i.e., roles that are only meaningful in relation to other reciprocal roles). One actor's duty is the other actor's right.

Rather than taking roles as reified "givens," Gross and Stone suggested that roles arise out of the need for actors to be poised and readied for *relevant* interactions. Relevancy and readiness is achieved by establishing identities – placing each other on the social map in regard to the situation at hand. What is relevant in one self-other role is irrelevant in another. Gross and Stone "speak of role as consensual attitudes mobilized by announced and ratified identities." Following Mead, attitudes are seen as incipient acts and meaningful discourse requires incorporating each other's incipient activities into one's emerging actions. When announcements and ratifications go awry embarrassment ensues, role performances suffer, and interactions break down. This offers another important explanation of how causation flows upward from social interaction to maintain and recreate role expectations and structure.

RALPH TURNER'S RECONCILIATION BETWEEN STRUCTURAL AND INTERACTIONAL APPROACHES

R. Turner's (1962) critical contribution to role theory offers a reconciliation of the partisan structural and interactional views of social roles. Currently, leading theorists such as Ritzer (1992) and J. Turner (2002) have stressed the importance of integrating the macro and micro levels in sociology. "Role analysis" is an important part of such integration.

For many functionalists, the motivation for role behavior consisted of three elements: the actor *conforms* to the *expectations* of others in order to gain their *approval.* While this simplification may be true in many cases, it is hardly adequate to explain the whole range of role behaviors. Therefore, R. Turner replaces *conformity* with "the efficient accomplishment of an objective." For example, a person may conform to another's linguistic style, but only as a deliberate means to enhance communication. *Expectations* are broadened to "a preparedness to interpret behavior as consistent with the role." The teacher lecturing a class from underneath the table is presumed to be making some academic point to be explained later in the lecture. The president who misnames his staff in public is seen as "being preoccupied with more important matters." Finally, rather than seeking *approval* per se, we are more usually "confirming an identity," as with the delinquent who is trying to demonstrate what a "bad actor" he or she is by being as offensive as possible.

For R.Turner, a role is a loosely shared mental set or gestalt. The actor's task is to act in a way that can be plausibly interpreted as congruent with the role. The audience's contribution is a willingness to interpret behavior as congruent with the role. As the ethnomethodologists have shown, actors will go to extremes in order to explain away inconsistencies in roles, thus rendering others' behavior intelligible.

In regard to transcending the overconformist implications of the old role theory, Turner has made it possible for a normal person to act in a way contrary to social expectations and simultaneously be effective socially. The role-playing scheme in functionalism placed such novel behavior outside of normality because conformity and the approval motive formed the exclusive explanation for routine social behavior.

ROLE-MAKING

R. Turner's broader and more "agentive" analysis allows him to talk about role-*making* as well as role-playing, wherein two people interpret each other's behavior within the loose framework of very general roles, and make their own unique relationships within that role. This allows more room for creativity, spontaneity, and authenticity in role behavior. Formal situations limit role-making, but it is fostered in everyday informal situations. Role-making stresses the importance of the other person's anticipated response rather than merely playing out a self-sufficient script that is independent of the other persons involved in the role. In replacing *expectations* with "preparedness to interpret behavior as consistent with the role," much depends on the ability to "take each other's meanings." This puts a premium on role-taking because the confirmation of one's identity is contingent on others. Role-taking is thus at the heart of R. Turner's analysis of role-making.

OTHER USES OF ROLE THEORY

Baker and Faulkner focus on roles as resources strategically used to gain access to other beneficial roles. Stryker (1980), McCall and Simmons (1978) and Peter Burke have emphasized the human tendency to identify more strongly with roles congruent with important self-conceptions and to show "role distance" in roles contradicting these self-conceptions. This "role identity" framework articulates in detail the close connection between roles and self. The self-conception is comprised of the differential emotional attachments to the various roles played. Generally, performance is better when role and self-concept are congruent.

CURRENT ASSESSMENT

The broader contribution of Ralph Turner's movement from oversimplified, fixed scripts to self-other processes is that he avoids the old parochial split between micro- and macro-level thinking. Currently, the aim of role analysis is simultaneously to handle the reality of constraints in social structure as well as the more "processual" character of the production of action by individuals engaged in self-other roles. Scheff warns that macrostructural concepts are certainly necessary, but to the extent that they are not related point by point to micro processes, they become reifications hovering detached from empirical grounding in the activities of real people. The history of role theory shows consistent movement toward demonstrating how micro- and macro-levels are inseparably implicated in each other.

Among those most dedicated to moving role analysis towards an empirically testable theory are Stryker (1980), R. Turner (1962), and J. Turner (1989). They have consistently contributed to isolating "if/then" statements of general tendencies in role behavior into a more tightly integrated whole.

SEE ALSO: Gender Ideology and Gender Role Ideology; Generalized Other; Interaction Order; Interpersonal Relationships; Mead, George Herbert; Reference Groups; Role-Taking; Role Theory; Self; Status

REFERENCES AND SUGGESTED READINGS

McCall, G. & Simmons, J. (1978) *Identities and Interactions.* Basic Books, New York.

Mead, G. H. (1934) *Mind, Self and Society.* University of Chicago Press, Chicago.

Mills, C. W. (1939) Language, Logic, and Culture. *American Sociological Review* 4: 670–913.

Ritzer, G. (1992) *Contemporary Sociological Theory.* McGraw-Hill, New York.

Stryker, S. (1980) *Symbolic Interaction: A Structural Version.* University of California Press, Menlo Park.

Thomas, D., Franks, D., & Calonico, J. (1972) Role-Taking and Power in Social Psychology. *American Sociological Review* 7: 605–14.

Turner, J. (1989) *The Structure of Sociological Theory,* 6th edn. Wadsworth, Belmont, CA.

Turner, J. (2002) *Face to Face Interaction: Toward a Sociological Theory of Interpersonal Behavior.* Stanford University Press, Stanford.

Turner, R. (1962) Role-Taking: Process Verses Conformity. In: Rose, A. (Ed.), *Human Behavior and Social Processes.* Houghton Mifflin, Boston, pp. 20–40.

role-taking

Steven P. Dandaneau

Role-taking refers to social interaction in which people adopt and act out a particular social role. If, adapting Shakespeare, society is a stage, then people may be thought of as social actors performing roles, each the other's fellow player. Rendered more clinically, and following Ralph H. Turner, role-taking is a process of anticipating and viewing behavior as motivated by an imputed social role. From the child playing at being "a mother" to the adult playing at being "a police officer," role-taking is a ubiquitous feature of social life. This initial definition belies, however, considerable theoretical and, even more so, empirical complexity.

The original impetus to conceive role-taking as an elementary feature of social life is found in the pragmatist social psychology of George Herbert Mead. In Mead's view, society is best understood not as any sort of organic or mechanical object but as an open-ended symbolic universe created and recreated through ongoing, emergent, and ultimately indeterminate symbolic interaction. This constantly (even though usually subtly) changing symbolic universe mediates all major facets of human experience, as in the title of his most famous collection of lectures, *Mind, Self, and Society* (1934).

For Mead, the process of "taking the role of the other" is, however, no simple process. From one perspective, Mead theorizes the growing complexity of role-taking as roughly corresponding to stages in the development of perceived "Otherness." In the "play stage," the initial and most rudimentary, the roles that are taken, so to speak, are simple, derived typically from proximate experience, and discrete. Children who play at being "a mother," for example, at first typically model their own mother's expected and routine behavior. Whether or not this "mother" bore the child, is a woman, or contributed genetic material to the children's biological origin are equally beside the point. The child's general notion of a symbolically defined mothering role is initially derived from imitation of a specific instance of mothering, and is only later expanded, conceptually abstracted, and complicated on the basis of additional social experience.

The "game" stage follows. In game, the roles taken are multiple and related systematically by rules. Mead employs the example of "ball nine," or baseball, to illustrate this stage of role-taking competence. If a batter strikes the ball to the short-stop and all the short-stop's fellow defenders, from the third baseman to the right fielder, join her in charging the ball, evidence would be had of a team not yet having mastered role-taking at the game level of interactional skill. People who have witnessed children clumped together around a soccer ball as it makes its way up and down a pitch have observed an exactly similar phenomenon. If, however, the same batted ball leads the short-stop to charge the ball and the first baseman to retreat to her own bag in anticipation of a successful catch-and-throw from the short-stop, or if a soccer team's players space themselves across a pitch in order better to deploy a strategy to maintain possession of the ball, and only ultimately direct it toward the opponent's goal, then there is evidence of these teammates taking one another's roles as though toward themselves and, thus, of the game stage of role-taking.

Implied in the above is an expansive view of role-taking, which is typical of Mead and of great significance to sociology. Indeed, Mead's final stage of role-taking, the so-called generalized other stage, implies that humans can and must come to see their actions as more than simply behavior aligned with the rule-governed actions of others as these same others present themselves through narrowly defined roles. Taking the role of the generalized other means taking the attitude of some abstract community toward oneself. The boundaries of community are conceptually indeterminate. Even though he never traveled from his hometown of Königsberg, Immanuel Kant imagined life on other planets and, not incidentally, conceived a universal humanity. Whereas in game, then, one might say to oneself, "if I were the short-stop who was mindful of the rules and game situation, I would respond to the ball being struck in that direction by. . .," today's social actors who take the role of the generalized other would typically need to position themselves in a symbolic universe that is ever more integrated and independent on a planetary scale and therefore requiring each actor to relate her action and attitudes to those of her fellow six-plus billion earthlings. "If I were a slave on a coca plantation in Côte d'Ivoire, how would I view Tiger Woods's notable success at the annual golf tournament in Dubai?" In this view, critically discussed by Walter Coutu as a psychological rather than a sociological phenomenon, role-taking is but a narrow version of attitude-taking, but from attitude-taking worlds are won and lost.

Mead is the first but far from the last influential social theorist to place role-taking at the center of their social view. Mid-century luminaries as divergent as Talcott Parsons, on the one hand, and Hans H. Gerth and C. Wright Mills, on the other, also regarded role-taking as elemental to a general theory seeking to trace the linkages between social institutions and individuals. In *The Social System* (1951), Parsons construes roles as component parts of group structure, where groups are then incorporated schematically into the functionally differentiated institutional subsystems of the social system itself. Parsons conceptually divides role from "status," the latter defined as a social location or position and the former a set of actions generally prescribed for those who occupy a particular position. He also elaborates on such basic sociological concepts as role differentiation, role expectations, and role conflict. Even though Parsons's exposition is decidedly weighted in the direction of stressing the objective, constraining properties of the social role, his sociology is necessarily drawn to role-taking as a means for explaining socialization in particular, and societal reproduction generally.

In *Character and Social Structure* (1953), Gerth and Mills use the concept of "role" as the chief mediating concept between character structure and social structure. As these authors stress, roles are inherently interpersonal. Role-taking always occurs in relation to the expectations of others and with respect to shared understandings of given social situations. And more than does Parsons, Gerth and Mills are wont to stress the constructed nature of roles, that is, that actors possess the power not only to enact roles but also to alter them by their actions, recast them altogether, or, as Ralph H. Turner also emphasized with his notion of role-*making*, create new roles out of whole cloth. This attention to agency is also reflected in Gerth and Mills's relatively historical approach to role-taking. Whereas Parsons's social system is typically understood *in abstracto* and in stasis, Gerth and Mills are interested in the relationship between an open-ended role-taking and an equally open-ended history-making.

The enigmatic "dramaturgical" sociology of Erving Goffman provides a third and, to some extent, synthetic mid-century approach to role-taking in sociology. In Goffman's view, people do not play roles so much as roles play people. That is, for Goffman, there is no moral substratum providing a transcendent basis for humanity lying beyond role-playing itself. We are what we make ourselves to be on the stage of life and no more (and no less). To rid sociology of its humanistic metaphysics, Goffman attended scrupulously to such phenomena as that highlighted by the title of his first and perhaps most famous book, *The Presentation of Self in Everyday Life* (1956). Thus, Goffman no less than Parsons is interested in carefully mapping a detailed, complex social world of roles, stages, and scripts, but he is also, as with Gerth and Mills, keenly attentive to the creativity and critical historical significance of social actors.

One superb if perhaps also ironic contemporary application of Goffman's approach to sociology is found in Bogdan and Taylor's (1989) study of "the social construction of humanness," a process they studied with respect to people who are severely disabled. Bogdan and Taylor's focus is not disabled persons per se but those who interact with them, such as family members and medical personnel. When these people act toward persons who are disabled in ways that attribute thinking, highlight individuality and reciprocity, and incorporate the disabled person as a player in the life of the larger group, they are, for Bogdan and Taylor, actively creating humanness. These efforts are often necessitated because, as Goffman (1964) himself had shown, persons with disabilities are typically the victims of "stigma" or "spoiled identity," which, by definition, is dehumanizing. Bogdan and Taylor's is a critical social psychology that presents empirical evidence of ongoing efforts to challenge the prevailing yet harmful stigmatization of the disabled role, and as such demonstrates the duality of roles as both constructed and constraining.

Another important contemporary application of role-taking theory is given in Arlie Russell Hochschild's *The Managed Heart* (1983). Hochschild studies what she terms "the commercialization of human feelings" through a close-up examination of flight attendants and, to a lesser extent, bill collectors. Would-be flight attendants and, in a converse way, bill collectors are required to engage in workplace role-playing that drains them of their emotional energy, whether in politely providing face-to-face service for airline passengers or in aggressively creating alarm among debtors interacted with via telephone. Hochschild's study stimulated considerable research on role-taking with respect to human emotions, the construction of gender, and the distinctive characteristics of workplace alienation in post-industrial economies.

As Clifford Geertz once observed, social science often "blurs genres" by using borrowed metaphors such as text, game, and drama. Role-taking is a prominent example of the last. While the concept of role has been subjected to sustained criticism for over 50 years, including especially by feminist scholars (see Connell 1987, but also Komarovsky 1992), it is perhaps more the case that it has been so criticized due to its elemental standing among sociology's most basic concepts than for essential reasons deriving from inherent limitations or necessarily adverse consequences that follow from its use. It is, after all, a concept, and a heavily metaphorical one at that. As such, its value to sociology is very much dependent on its use and abuse by practicing sociologists and their readers. Criticism aside, then, the concept of role-taking has the advantage of emphasizing the interactional nature of social order and, equally as well, disorder, and of linking contemporary sociology in the postmodern world to its not so distant origins in what C. Wright Mills called the classical tradition of sociology. The critical empirical question remains as to whether or not role-taking is an everyday occurrence in societies the world over. Evidence seems to suggest that it is; that children are, as Mead put it, wont to "play at something," even if that something might involve a hand-held video game that offers up a cyber-stage on which fictional characters carry out fictional interactions, replicating the old-fashioned world of face-to-face human interaction such as one still occasionally finds in a game of ball nine.

SEE ALSO: Dramaturgy; Game Stage; Generalized Other; Goffman, Erving; Interaction; Komarovsky, Mirra; Mead, George Herbert; Mills, C. Wright; Parsons, Talcott; Play Stage; Role; Role Theory

REFERENCES AND SUGGESTED READINGS

Bogdan, R. & Taylor, S. J. (1989) Relationships with Severely Disabled People: The Social Construction of Humanness. *Social Problems* 36(2): 135–48.

Castells, M. (1997) *The Power of Identity*. Blackwell, Oxford.

Connell, R. W. (1987) *Gender and Power*. Stanford University Press, Stanford.

Cook, G. A. (1993) *George Herbert Mead: The Making of a Social Pragmatist*. University of Illinois Press, Urbana.

Coutu, W. (1951) Role-Playing vs. Role-Taking: An Appeal for Clarification. *American Sociological Review* 16(2): 180–7.

Gerth, H. H. & Mills, C. W. (1953) *Character and Social Structure: The Psychology of Social Institutions*. Harcourt, Brace & World, New York.

Goffman, E. (1956) *The Presentation of Self in Everyday Life*. Penguin, London.

Goffman, E. (1964) *Stigma: Notes on the Management of Spoiled Identity*. Prentice-Hall, Englewood Cliffs, NJ.

Hochschild, A. R. (1983) *The Managed Heart: Commercialization of Human Feeling*. University of California Press, Berkeley.

Ibanez, T. & Iniguez, L. (Eds.) (1997) *Critical Social Psychology*. Sage, London.

Kim, K.-K. (2003) *Order and Agency in Modernity: Talcott Parsons, Erving Goffman, and Harold Garfinkel*. SUNY Press, Albany, NY.

Komarovsky, M. (1992) The Concept of Social Role Revisited. *Gender and Society* 6(2): 301–13.

Lemert, C. & Branaman, A. (Eds.) (1997) *The Goffman Reader*. Blackwell, Oxford.

Mead, G. H. (1934) *Mind, Self, and Society: From the Standpoint of a Social Behaviorist*. University of Chicago Press, Chicago.

Parsons, T. (1951) *The Social System*. Free Press, New York.

Platt, G. & Gordon, C. (Eds.) (1994) *Self, Collective Behavior, and Society: Essays Honoring the Contributions of Ralph H. Turner*. JAI Press, Greenwich, CT.

Turner, J. (1988) *A Theory of Social Interaction*. Stanford University Press, Stanford.

Turner, R. H. (1956) Role-Taking, Role Standpoint, and Reference-Group Behavior. *American Journal of Sociology* 61(4): 316–28.

Turner, R. H. (1962) Role-Taking: Process Versus Conformity. In: Rose, A. M. (Ed.), *Human Behavior and Social Process: An Interactionist Approach*. Houghton Mifflin, Boston, pp. 20–40.

role theory

Michelle J. Hindin

Role theory is designed to explain how individuals who occupy particular social positions are expected to behave and how they expect others to behave. Role theory is based on the observation that people behave predictably and that an individual's behavior is context-specific, based on their social position and situation. Role theory is often described using the metaphor of the theater.

There has been substantial debate over the meaning of the key concept in role theory: that of role. A role can be defined as a social position, behavior associated with a social position, or a typical behavior. Some theorists have suggested that roles are expectations about how an individual ought to behave, while others consider how individuals actually behave in a given social position. Others have suggested that a role is a characteristic behavior or expected behavior, a part to be played, or a script for social conduct. Although the word role (or roll) has existed in European languages for centuries, as a sociological concept the term has only been around since the 1920s and 1930s. It became more prominent in sociological discourse through the theoretical works of Mead, Moreno, and Linton.

Two of Mead's concepts – the mind and the self – are the precursors to role theory. The mind emerges through communication with others during childhood. Children develop the capacity to extrapolate from communications with others and eventually learn how and when to respond to others. Mead's concept of the self includes three stages of development. In the initial stage, infants interact or "play" with others and eventually are able to empathize with or take on the role of others. In the second stage, referred to as the "game," the child becomes sophisticated enough to play multiple roles, first consecutively then playing several roles at once.

The child must be able to understand and anticipate the behaviors of other people, and then cast herself into their roles in order to play her own role. Once the child is able to understand and internalize the roles of multiple others, the child is able to interact with groups or the society. In this third stage, Mead refers to the ability to take on the role of the "generalized other." Individuals take on the values, norms, and beliefs of a group or society. Moreno used a dramaturgical approach of role-playing to learn how taking on different roles is related to changing behaviors. Linton also contributed to the concept of a role by making the distinction between a status or position and a role. Linton considered a status as a collection of rights and duties, while a role is the dynamic aspect of a status.

In summary, theorists have used the term role to connote characteristic behaviors, social parts to be played, or social conduct, depending on the theorist's definition. While some agreement exists that the basic concerns of role theory are with characteristic behaviors, parts to be played, and scripts for behavior, theorists differ on whether roles are norms, beliefs, or preferences. Because the term is used in everyday language, imprecision in the sociological definition has led to misinterpretations of role theory itself and some disagreement concerning key aspects of role theory (e.g., whether expectations about behaviors associated with social positions are based on norms, beliefs, or preferences).

TYPES OF ROLE THEORY

Depending on the general perspective of the theoretical tradition, there is a range of "types" of role theory. For example, there is a more functional perspective of role theory, which can be contrasted with the more micro-level approach of the symbolic interactionist tradition. The type of role theory will dictate how closely related individuals' actions are to the society, as well as how empirically testable a particular role theory perspective may be.

Functional role theory emerged out of Linton's perspective on roles, as well as functionalism as described by Parsons. Under functional role theory, roles are considered to be prescriptive and based on a shared understanding of expectations. These roles are learned and individuals are expected to conform to roles and sanction others who deviate from their roles. One of the key aspects of functional role theory is that the social system is considered stable. Individuals within this perspective learn roles which are normative expectations that dictate appropriate behavior. With the general decline of functionalism starting in the mid-1970s, the functional role theory perspective has faded in importance. As with functionalism in general, functional role theory is limited by the fact that social positions and roles are not necessarily clearly delineated or fixed and that most social systems are not stable.

Symbolic interactionist role theory is based on Mead's development of the mind and self. Roles are learned through social interaction, and unlike functional role theorists, symbolic interactionist role theorists suggest that norms are developed through social interaction and are therefore less prescriptive. This perspective on role theory is the one most closely linked with the theater and the writings of Simmel and Goffman's "looking-glass self." Theorists coming to role theory from the symbolic interactionist tradition consider how roles are played out and how this playing out of roles impacts on both the actor and others. There is often little attention to actors' expectations for other persons or to structural constraints on expectations and roles. For this type of role theory, the research tends primarily to be ethnographic and of limited generalizability.

Structural role theory is the perspective most related to the dramaturgical tradition. Structural role theory considers roles as parts played by actors in scripts written by society. The social structure or script is relatively fixed, much like in the functionalist perspective. Society is described as a system of functional substructures and actors learn their roles through repeated interactions. Individuals generally interact in groups delineated by people with shared goals and who are therefore willing to cooperate. Despite shared goals, not everyone has the same role within a group. It is unclear from this type of role theory how social change is accomplished and what happens to actors who choose not to conform to the groups' shared goals.

Organizational role theory is concerned with the role of formal organizations and how individuals interact with these organizations. Roles are associated with social positions and come from normative expectations generated by the organization. An individual's roles are based both on normative expectations from a given social position as well as from informal groups within the organization. This perspective on role theory allows for role conflict and role strain. Organizational role theory has often been used for business applications, as well as among psychologists and sociologists interested in organizational theory. This perspective has been used to do empirical analyses more often than some of the other perspectives.

Cognitive role theory has most often been applied by social psychologists. This perspective focuses on the relationship between the individual, role expectations, and behaviors. It is one of the perspectives that has generated more empirical research. There are several subfields of cognitive role theory. The first looks at role playing along the lines of the work of Moreno. A second subfield considers the roles of leaders and followers within groups. A third branch considers the relationship between an individual's beliefs about behavior and the beliefs of others. A final branch emerged out of Mead's work on role-taking. This perspective, with its emphasis on individual behavior and roles, minimizes the importance of social positions and social structures.

KEY CONCEPTS

Consensus is used by role theorists to denote agreement among expectations that are held by various people. Underlying consensus or "dissensus" is the question of under what conditions are the individual and others likely to agree or disagree about role definitions. Consensus is most likely to occur when individuals have been socialized in a similar way or when individuals have experience in similar types of interactions. Social psychologists view negotiation as a key way to overcome disagreements about role definitions.

Role strain refers to the difficulty of meeting the normative expectations of the roles that an individual either chooses or is pressured to play. Role strain or role pressure may arise when there is a conflict in the demands of roles, when an individual does not agree with the assessment of others concerning his or her performance in roles, or from accepting roles that are beyond an individual's capacity. An individual may have limited power to negotiate away from accepting roles that cause strain because he or she is constrained by the societal norms, or because the individual has limited social status relegating him or her to having a poorer hand for negotiation. Role strain is often described as a conflict within a role. For example, in the role of a professor, strain may be caused by the demands of teaching a course well and the demands of submitting research grants. Within role strain there are two commonly used subtypes: role overload and role conflict.

Role conflict occurs when people experience contradictory or incompatible expectations based on the roles they occupy. For example, parents may experience role conflict when an employer requires overtime hours while their young children need their attention. This is a conflict across two or more roles rather than within a role. Another type of role conflict occurs when there is a mismatch of expectations, poor communication of the demands of the role, or conflicting demands within a role. For example, the principal of a school may need to cut after-school activities due to limited funding for such programs and the demands of the school board. However, cutting after-school programs would be harmful for the students and parents. The concept of role conflict may bridge the experiences of individuals in particular roles with the societal or cultural expectations for those roles. The concept of role conflict is generally attributed to the functionalist perspective on role theory.

Role overload occurs when an individual is unable to perform all of his or her expected roles. For example, a woman who occupies the roles of a full-time employee, mother, and daughter may feel she has too many roles and therefore does not have the time, energy, or resources to perform all of them to the satisfaction of others or the society. An area of growing empirical research considers whether the benefits of multiple roles outweigh the stress caused by them.

SEE ALSO: Goffman, Erving; Mead, George Herbert; Simmel, Georg; Role; Role-Taking; Social Psychology

REFERENCES AND SUGGESTED READINGS

Adler, P. & Adler, P. A. (1980) Symbolic Interactionism. In: Douglas, J. D. et al. (Eds.), *Introduction to the Sociologies of Everyday Life*. Allyn & Bacon, Boston.

Biddle, B. J. (1986) Recent Developments in Role-Theory. *Annual Review of Sociology* 12: 67–92.

Collins, R. (1994) *Four Sociological Traditions*. Oxford University Press, New York.

Heiss, J. (1990) Social Roles. In: Rosenberg, M. & Turner, R. H. (Eds.), *Social Psychology: Sociological Perspectives*. Transaction Publishers, New Brunswick, NJ.

Stryker, S. (2001) Traditional Symbolic Interactionism, Role Theory and Structural Symbolic Interactionism: The Road to Identity Theory. In: Turner, J. H. (Ed.), *Handbook of Sociological Theory*. Kluwer Academic/Plenum Publishers, New York.

Thomas, E. J. & Biddle, B. J. (1966) The Nature and History of Role Theory. In: Biddle, B. J. & Thomas, E. J. (Eds.), *Role Theory: Concepts and Research*. John Wiley & Sons, New York.

Turner, J. H. (1986) Early Interactionism and Phenomenology. In: *The Structure of Sociological Theory*, 4th edn. Dorsey Press, Chicago.

Turner, R. H. (2001) Role Theory. In: Turner, J. H. (Ed.), *Handbook of Sociological Theory*. Kluwer Academic/Plenum Publishers, New York.

Rosenberg, Morris (1922–92)

Elena Fazio and Kim Nguyen

An American social psychologist, Morris (Manny) Rosenberg was a leading scholar in the study of the self-concept and a significant contributor to the intellectual and scientific advancement of the broader discipline of sociological social psychology. Over the course of his long and prolific career, Manny advanced sociological inquiry theoretically, methodologically, and substantively by critically addressing a host of social psychological issues; pioneering methodological practices with the use of large-scale samples and codifying the logic of survey data analysis; and carrying out an impressive range of research efforts. While his scholarly interests spanned a wide spectrum of sociological concerns, including political ideology and behavior, occupations and values, class stratification, social distance, and mass communication, it would ultimately be his intellectual engagement with self-concept research – particularly the dimension of self-esteem – for which he would become best known.

Rosenberg received his masters and doctoral degrees from Columbia University where he studied under the guidance of C. Wright Mills, Paul Lazarsfeld, and Robert K. Merton – eminent sociologists whose careful attention to theoretical and methodological issues would later influence his own work. After graduating in 1953, Rosenberg spent the early part of his career teaching at Cornell and Columbia universities before moving on to the Laboratory of Socio-Environmental Studies at the National Institute of Mental Health, first as chief of the Section on Social Studies in Therapeutic Settings and subsequently as chief of the Section on Social Structure. During this period – which would span nearly two decades – Rosenberg also held visiting professorships at various universities, including Stanford University and the London School of Economics and Political Science. In 1975 he went on to become professor of sociology at the University of Maryland, where he stayed until his death in 1992.

Over his lifetime Rosenberg also authored or edited numerous books, including *The Language of Social Research* (1955) with Lazarsfeld, *Occupations and Values* (1957), *Society and the Adolescent Self-Image* (1965), *The Logic of Survey Analysis* (1968), *Conceiving the Self* (1979), and *Social Psychology: Sociological Perspectives* (1981), co-edited with Ralph Turner. Rosenberg's characteristic imprint is evident throughout these endeavors, with their rigorous wedding of theory and research, application of suitable methodology, and incorporation of interdisciplinary research.

Of particular importance was his research and writing on the self and self-processes. Through these efforts, Rosenberg became a leading figure in reviving scholarly interest in the self-concept that had been lying fairly dormant for the larger part of a half-century. Despite the fact that Cooley had laid out the conceptual groundwork for the sociological study of the self-concept as early as 1902, sociological publication on the self-concept did not emerge until the mid-1950s. Scholarship on the self has since flourished as an area of sociological inquiry and Rosenberg's work on the self-concept remains at the forefront of social psychological research, serving to explain the importance of self-esteem, and more generally, the importance of research on the self-concept in the theoretical and empirical work of the discipline.

In his groundbreaking book *Society and the Adolescent Self-Image*, Rosenberg undertook the first large-scale systematic study of the self-concept. Employing a sample of over 5,000 adolescents, he examined the influence of social structure, culture, context, and interpersonal relations on shaping self-esteem and how self-esteem affects social behavior. Defined as a positive or negative attitude toward oneself – an overall evaluation of one's self-worth – self-esteem was viewed as an important determinant of well-being but one that had received little sociological attention until that time.

For the study, Rosenberg developed a 10-item global self-esteem scale. Today, the Rosenberg Self-Esteem Scale remains the most widely used self-esteem measure in social science research. Its popularity, Rosenberg suspected, was attributed in part to the conciseness of the research instrument and, consequently, its easy adoption by interested investigators. While retaining the reliability and validity of comparable but more elaborate measures previously developed by psychologists, Rosenberg's self-esteem scale was constructed with an economy and conceptual appropriateness amenable to social survey research. His accomplishment helped bridge the gap between the disciplines of sociology and psychology and renewed research on the self and self-processes.

In a later classic of the self-concept literature, *Conceiving the Self*, Rosenberg expanded the theoretical framework for thinking about the self-concept that has remained central to the study of self within sociology as well as related disciplines. Conceptualizing the self as "the totality of the individual's thoughts and feeling having reference to himself as object" (1979: 7), Rosenberg set forth a detailed cartography of the self-concept, mapping out its motives and structure (forms, content, dimensions, boundaries) and delineating four fundamental principles underlying the process of self-concept formation – reflected appraisals, social comparison, self-attribution, and psychological centrality.

Drawing on three survey data sets, Rosenberg identified the conditions under which these self-processes operate and analyzed how larger social forces, such as social structural position and institutional context – through their bearing on self-formation processes – exercised their influence on the self and are in turn shaped by it. A central theme throughout Rosenberg's analyses is this idea that the self-concept is not merely a social product but also a social force.

With respect to the larger discipline, Rosenberg co-edited with Ralph Turner an authoritative reference on the field, *Social Psychology: Sociological Perspectives*. Commissioned by the Social Psychology Section of the American Sociological Association (ASA), the book was an official effort to offer a sociological perspective on an emerging discipline in need of theoretical and empirical synthesis. At the same time, the volume was notable for its attention to interdisciplinary work, especially its attempt to unite contributions from psychology. For this undertaking, Rosenberg and Turner organized a broad and diverse set of topics around five parts – theoretical orientation, socialization, social interaction, society and social behavior, and society and personality – with each capturing various styles and approaches to the subject area from outstanding authorities in the field. The handbook has since become a landmark collection in social psychology.

Beyond these contributions, Manny's scholarship touched upon other areas as well, although these interests have received relatively less attention, such as his inquiries into other aspects of the self such as mattering, his reflection on the relationship between reflexivity and emotions, and his turn toward a more symbolic interactionist position at the end of his life, apparent in his last book, *The Unread Mind* (1992).

A dedicated sociological social psychologist, Manny's enduring contributions to sociology rest with his innovative study of methodology, values, and self and self-processes. These achievements – particularly his conceptualization of the self-concept and his extensive work on one component of the self-concept, self-esteem – stand as permanent legacies to the field. His theoretical, methodological, and substantive efforts, furthermore, have left behind a remarkable body of work that has influenced generations of subsequent scholars within and outside the discipline in their intellectual pursuits. Inquiries about Rosenberg's self-esteem scale regularly flow into the Foundation that bears his name. Questions and correspondence about research based on his self-esteem measure come from scholars in child and adolescent health research, sociology, occupational therapy, nursing, social work, psychology, and beyond. The sheer volume of research produced outside the field of sociology, based on his work, is a true testament to Rosenberg's broad-reaching ideas and his emphasis on interdisciplinary scholarship.

SEE ALSO: Cooley, Charles Horton; Merton, Robert K.; Mills, C. Wright; Self; Self-Concept; Self-Esteem, Theories of; Social Psychology

REFERENCES AND SUGGESTED READINGS

Gecas, V. (1990) Morris Rosenberg: 1989 Cooley-Mead Award Recipient. *Social Psychology Quarterly* 53: 1–2.

Lazarsfeld, P. F. & Rosenberg, M. (Eds.) (1955) *The Language of Social Research: A Reader in the Methodology of Social Research.* Free Press, Glencoe, IL.

Rosenberg, M. (1957) *Occupations and Values.* Free Press, Glencoe, IL.

Rosenberg, M. (1965) *Society and the Adolescent Self-Image.* Princeton University Press, Princeton.

Rosenberg, M. (1968) *The Logic of Survey Analysis.* Basic Books, New York.

Rosenberg, M. (1979) *Conceiving the Self.* Krieger, Malabar, FL.

Rosenberg, M. (1992) *The Unread Mind: Unraveling the Mystery of Madness.* Lexington, New York.

Rosenberg, M. & Turner, R. (Eds.) (1981) *Social Psychology: Sociological Perspectives.* Basic Books, New York.

Rosenfeld, Rachel (1948–2002)

Stephanie Moller

Rachel Rosenfeld established herself as a leading figure in sociology through groundbreaking research on the diversity of occupational mobility patterns. Rosenfeld's interest in diversity emerged during her youth when she witnessed the effects of institutionalized school segregation in Little Rock, Arkansas. Her interests expanded during her undergraduate studies at Carleton College and graduate studies at the University of Wisconsin at Madison, where she learned more about the women's movement and gender scholarship (during the late 1960s and early 1970s).

Rosenfeld began studying sociology during a period of social change and unrest; a period when diversity and difference influenced public discourse. Yet, only a small segment of the sociological community had embraced such an orientation to diversity. Indeed, among mobility scholars, substantial research focused on intergenerational mobility among white men, with little attention to variations based on race, ethnicity, or gender. To the extent that researchers had examined women's mobility, they only examined the link between fathers' and daughters' occupations. Thus, Rosenfeld was poised to profoundly influence the discipline through her interest in difference and her exceptional understanding of quantitative methods.

In 1976, under the advisement of her esteemed mentor Aage Sørensen, Rosenfeld earned her PhD in sociology, with a concentration in economics and statistics. She began her career as an assistant professor at McGill University. During her first three years at McGill, she published research on women's career and mobility patterns in the top sociology journals, including the *American Sociological Review*, *Social Forces*, *Social Science Research*, and *Demography*. This marked the beginning of a productive and influential career. Rosenfeld's research illuminated the diversity of mobility patterns by showing that mothers' employment patterns are important determinants of women's intergenerational mobility

(Rosenfeld 1978); that occupational sex segregation impacts women's mobility and wages (Wolf & Rosenfeld 1978; Rosenfeld 1983); and that mobility patterns vary by gender and race (Rosenfeld 1980).

Early in her career, Rosenfeld left academia to work for the National Opinion Research Center (1978–81), where she conducted research on farm women (Rosenfeld 1985). After this brief divergence, Rosenfeld returned to the academy as an Assistant Professor of Sociology at the University of North Carolina at Chapel Hill, where she continued her research on careers and mobility. Later in her career, Rosenfeld broadened her influence to the cross-national literature through collaborative research on comparative income inequality and job-shifting patterns (Rosenfeld & Kalleberg 1990; Trappe & Rosenfeld 1998).

In addition to her outstanding research, Rosenfeld influenced the discipline through exceptional mentoring of future scholars that culminated in numerous mentoring awards. These awards included the Sociologists for Women in Society Award for Outstanding Mentoring in 1992 and the first Graduate Student Association Award for Excellence in Mentoring at the University of North Carolina's Department of Sociology in 1998. These awards acknowledged Rosenfeld's efforts to embrace the differences among her students and colleagues. In essence, Rosenfeld's mentoring style reflected the goals of her research: to uncover difference and diversity.

At the time of her death, Rachel Rosenfeld was a distinguished professor and the chair of the Sociology Department at the University of North Carolina at Chapel Hill and recent president of the Southern Sociological Society. Rosenfeld's presidential address to the society in 2002 was published in *Social Forces* (Rosenfeld 2002). This address allowed her an uncanny opportunity to discuss her life, her research, and the state of gender scholarship. Rosenfeld's legacy is lasting because she demonstrated how sociological processes work differently for different groups in society. Her research helped pioneer a burgeoning subfield in sociology, entitled *race, gender, and class.*

SEE ALSO: Difference; Doing Gender; Inequality/Stratification, Gender; Intergenerational Mobility: Core Model of Social Fluidity; Occupational Mobility; Occupational Segregation; Stratification, Gender and

REFERENCES AND SUGGESTED READINGS

Rosenfeld, R. A. (1978) Women's Intergenerational Occupational Mobility. *American Sociological Review* 43: 36–46.

Rosenfeld, R. A. (1980) Race and Sex Differences in Career Dynamics. *American Sociological Review* 45: 583–609.

Rosenfeld, R. A. (1983) Sex Segregation and Sectors: An Analysis of Gender Differences in Returns from Employer Changes. *American Sociological Review* 48: 637–55.

Rosenfeld, R. A. (1985) *Farm Women: Work, Farm, and Family in the United States.* University of North Carolina Press, Chapel Hill.

Rosenfeld, R. A. (2002) What Do We Learn about Difference from the Scholarship on Gender? *Social Forces* 81: 1–24.

Rosenfeld, R. A. & Kalleberg, A. L. (1990) A Cross-National Comparison of the Gender Gap in Income. *American Journal of Sociology* 96: 69–106.

Trappe, H. & Rosenfeld, R. A. (1998) Comparison of Job-Shifting Patterns in the Former East Germany and the Former West Germany. *European Sociological Review* 14: 343–68.

Wolf, W. C. & Rosenfeld, R. (1978) Sex Structure of Occupations and Job Mobility. *Social Forces* 56: 823–44.

routine activity theory

Sharon Chamard

Routine activity theory is a theoretical approach that explains the components of a criminal incident. It breaks down a crime into three basic elements: (1) a likely offender, (2) a suitable target, and (3) the absence of a capable guardian. It is only when these three elements converge in time and space that a crime occurs. Despite this focus on the crime event, routine activities is considered a macro-level theory, as it concerns how broad changes in society lead to alterations in community life that create new opportunities for crime.

Routine activities is one of a constellation of theoretical approaches generally referred to as environmental criminology. These approaches include rational choice, crime pattern theory, situational crime prevention, and explanations for victimization that focus on lifestyles. Routine activities draws upon the work of early human ecologists such as Amos Hawley and members of the Chicago School (such as Parks and Burgess) who looked at the relationship between humans and the environment.

Unlike many theories attempting to explain criminal behavior, routine activities does not spend much time trying to explain why offenders do what they do in terms of motivation or preexisting factors that predispose a person to break the law. The assumption is that there is a large group of persons who have the potential, or the likelihood, to be offenders, and crime only occurs when the likely offender comes into contact with a good target and there is no capable guardian around to prevent the interaction. Routine activities is thus a theory of crime, not a theory of criminality.

A suitable target can be a person or an item. What makes a target attractive or desirable to likely offenders depends on four things included in the VIVA acronym: value, inertia, visibility, access. More valuable items are typically more attractive to thieves because they can be converted to more cash than can less valuable objects. The idea of value applies to persons as well. Certain people may be targeted because they have a characteristic that is appealing to the offender. Rapists tend to prefer younger women. Armed robbers victimize those who would be expected to have money or other valuables. Inertia refers to how easily an item can be carried away. Small, light items are ideal theft targets, while heavy objects generally have a low risk of theft, unless they have wheels. If the target is visible, it will more easily capture the eye of a potential thief, hence the good advice to keep valuables in your trunk and close your curtains at night. Items that are accessible are more suitable as targets than those that are locked up or in an area that cannot be easily entered.

Routine activities differs from many approaches to explaining crime because it mentions the absence of something as a contributing factor to crime events. When guardians are not present, there is nothing to protect the target from the predations of the likely offender. Crime can be the result. It is explicit in routine activities that a capable guardian is seldom a police officer. Rather, a capable guardian is most probably a property owner, friend, family member, employer, or passer-by.

Like other theoretical approaches with a connection to the Chicago School and environmental criminology, routine activities emphasizes the importance of temporal and spatial factors. It recognizes that crime cannot be explained solely in terms of characteristics of offenders, but that environmental factors are as, or more, important. It is intuitively obvious that patterns of criminal behavior vary from place to place – your car is much more likely to be stolen or broken into if it is parked in a public parking lot than in your residential garage – and across different time periods. Why an area might be safe during the day but dangerous at night has a lot to do with who is using the space at particular times. During traditional business hours, a downtown park might be filled with lunching office workers, food vendors, and elderly people feeding pigeons and so on. While there may be plenty of suitable targets, there are also many capable guardians. The same park at night might be populated with drunks staggering home from the taverns, youth hanging out, and a few straggling commuters. There may be fewer targets compared to the day when the park is bustling with activity, but capable guardians are in short supply.

The routine activities approach was developed by Lawrence Cohen and Marcus Felson, and was proposed in a 1979 article in the prominent journal *American Sociological Review*. Cohen and Felson (1979) attempted to explain the paradox of dramatic increases in crime from 1960 to 1975, while during that same 15-year period the social factors that supposedly cause crime had changed for the better: in urban areas there were reductions in poverty and unemployment, and increases in income and average education level. The traditional criminological theories seemed of little use to account for the increases in violent crime or property crime.

Cohen and Felson, then, looked at how crime rates might be related to broader social and technological patterns. They observed that the *routine activities* of people had changed.

Routine activities refer to "recurrent and prevalent activities" that people do to meet their needs. These activities can occur at home or away from home, and include going to work or school, shopping, socializing, and playing. Cohen and Felson argued that during the 1960s, more women entered the workforce or post-secondary education, and there were more households comprising one person. People also traveled out-of-town more. These changes pointed to what Cohen and Felson termed a "dispersion of activities away from households."

As more people's routine activities took them away from their homes, there was less guardianship of those homes, and hence more burglary. As mothers moved into the workplace, there was less supervision of children and teenagers. This did two things: it increased their risk of victimization (because no adults were around to protect them) and also increased the chances they would become involved in criminal activity.

In addition to changes in daily life on the home front, the movement of women into the workplace and college created more targets for opportunistic offenders in public life. Commuting places people and their property, especially their vehicles, at high risk for victimization, relative to staying at home. People coming together in schools and in work settings likewise create new criminal opportunities.

Beyond these demographic changes, routine activities also considers technological changes with respect to crime rates. Positing that aspects of a physical item are strongly related to its "attractiveness" to motivated offenders, Cohen and Felson (1979) found that the supply and characteristics of "durable goods" (such as television sets and cars) were strongly associated with levels of property crime. Over the years 1960 to 1970 there was a dramatic increase in the number of motor vehicles and electronic household appliances sold, and hence an increase in the number of potential targets. These targets also became more *suitable* because they became lighter and, in many cases, smaller. During this period, products with relatively high "values-per-pound" (e.g., home entertainment items) and those that have low inertia, meaning they are easily transportable (e.g., motor vehicles and bicycles), comprised a large and hugely disproportionate majority of stolen items.

Also during the 1960s the amount of goods sold increased, even as the number per person of business establishments selling durable goods remained fairly constant. Businesses themselves were busier, but a smaller proportion of the workforce was employed as salespeople, so there were fewer employees to keep an eye on customers. This, coupled with changes in retailing practice that made shopping a largely self-service activity, contributed to an increase in shoplifting.

A significant change in the routine activities approach was the explicit addition of concepts from Travis Hirschi's control theory. Felson (1986) summarized the four components of control theory – attachment, commitment, involvement, and belief – with one word: handle. Society controls people, argued Felson, by making them fear the consequences of bad behavior (their future will be jeopardized or they will damage their relationships with friends and family) and placing practical limitations on behavioral options by encouraging involvement in conventional activities and by manipulating belief systems to make people feel guilty when they are bad. The social bond we have to others is the "handle" that can be used to informally control our behavior. The "intimate handler" became a fourth element of the routine activities approach. This element is closely linked to the offender, as the handler is someone who knows the potential offender well enough to act as a curb on criminal behavior.

A more recent incorporation into routine activities is the "place manager." First suggested by John Eck (see Felson 1995), this is someone who controls or monitors places. Examples are doormen, receptionists, janitors, security guards, and building superintendents. With this addition and that of the intimate handler, the original conception of routine activities (a likely offender and suitable target converging in time and space in the absence of a capable guardian) can be thought of in terms of two triplets. The likely offender is supervised by the intimate handler, the suitable target is protected by the capable guardian, and the time and space where the convergence occurs is monitored by the place manager (Felson 1995).

Criticism has been leveled at routine activities (and other theories of crime as well) for their apparent neglect of the "root causes" of crime, such as poor parenting, poverty, blocked opportunities, and the like. In addition, opponents argue that these theories fail to take into account differences in disposition, as it is assumed that motivation is irrelevant. The latter point is specifically addressed by Felson (1986). He notes that while "some people are inclined to break laws . . . others are inclined to protect their own person and property [and] others are inclined to keep their children out of trouble" (p. 120). The routine activities approach is not concerned with why some people are likely to be motivated offenders while others are more prone to be capable guardians or intimate handlers. This is not to say the approach assumes that we are all equally disposed to be offenders, just that the differences in levels of motivation are not a focus.

The routine activities approach is used in studies of victimization patterns. The observation that victims and offenders often have similar characteristics has led to use of the routine activities approach and related lifestyle theories to explain violence. Richard Felson (1997), for example, found that routine activities associated with having an active "night life" were a good predictor of involvement in violence as an actor, witness, or victim. Some research on shoplifting refers to aspects of the theory that concern target suitability and attractiveness. Other researchers have used the routine activities approach to account for differences in burglary rates, particularly repeat victimization. Routine activities only partially explains the difference, perhaps because it only addresses initial target selection (because of target attractiveness and guardianship factors) and does not account for why offenders chose the same target repeatedly (Tseloni et al. 2004).

SEE ALSO: Environmental Criminology; Rational Choice Theory: A Crime-Related Perspective; Social Control; Victimization

REFERENCES AND SUGGESTED READINGS

Cohen, L. & Felson, M. (1979) Social Change and Crime Rate Trends: A Routine Activity Approach. *American Sociological Review* 44: 588–608.

Felson, M. (1986) Linking Criminal Choices, Routine Activities, Informal Control, and Criminal Outcomes. In: Cornish, D. B. & Clarke, R. V. (Eds.), *The Reasoning Criminal: Rational Choice Perspectives on Offending*. Springer-Verlag, New York, pp. 119–28.

Felson, M. (1995) Those Who Discourage Crime. In: Clarke, R. V. (Ed.), *Crime and Place*. Crime Prevention Studies, Vol. 4. Criminal Justice Press, Monsey, NY.

Felson, R. (1997) Routine Activities and Involvement in Violence as an Actor, Witness, or Target. *Violence and Victims* 12: 209–21.

Tseloni, A., Wittebrood, K., & Farrell, G. (2004) Burglary Victimization in England and Wales, the United States, and the Netherlands. *British Journal of Criminology* 44: 66–91.

ruling relations

Marjorie L. DeVault

The term ruling relations is associated with the feminist thought of Dorothy E. Smith, who came to prominence in the academic movement that arose from women's activism in the 1960s and 1970s. Her work takes up the project of locating lived experiences of oppression within the social contexts that produce those experiences. Ruling relations identifies the institutional complexes (emerging from the development and elaboration of capitalist economies) that coordinate the everyday work of administration and the lives of those subject to administrative regimes.

Smith wrote in the early days of feminist scholarship and explains that she drew insights from her location as a single mother and the awareness that she and her children were seen, institutionally, as a "defective" family (Smith 1987; Griffith & Smith 2005). She began to write about women's "bifurcated consciousness" in the mid-1970s (Smith 1974) and produced an extended account of her approach in *The Everyday World as Problematic* (1987). Drawing from Marx a materialist mode of analysis and the analytic of "social relations," she noted that developments since Marx's time have produced an expansive "ruling apparatus" encompassing not only state and economy, but also academic, professional, and bureaucratic knowledge and associated practices. The categories and concepts of these institutional complexes textualize lived experience, so that people's circumstances can be "worked up" to fit administrative and managerial schemata (that is, they come to be seen and treated as "mentally ill," for example, or as "defective" in relation to the "ideological code" of a "Standard North American Family") (Smith 1999).

Smith sketches an experience and knowledge associated with single motherhood in her early writing: the experience of sole responsibility for children and the capacity to shift from an embodied consciousness tied to caring work to an abstracted professional outlook tied to the conceptual frames of administration. She indicates, however, that her aim is not to identify a determinate womanly "experience" with specific content, but rather to direct thought to actual sites of everyday living as "points of entry" for empirical inquiry, with the experiences of single mothers providing one example. Smith's formulation of ruling relations is also meant to direct attention to actual practices; it is not only a heuristic device, but is also meant to refer to the complex web of discourse and practice that constitutes an expansive, historically specific formation of power that arose with the development of corporate capitalism in developed nations and which supports its operation. In later writings, Smith discussed the historical emergence and trajectory of "the ruling relations" (Smith 1999) and those who have adopted her "institutional ethnography" approach pursue inquiries that locate embodied and particular experiences within the institutional complexes identified with those relations (Campbell & Gregor 2002; Smith 2005).

SEE ALSO: Bifurcated Consciousness, Line of Fault; Consciousness Raising; Feminism and Science, Feminist Epistemology; Feminist Methodology; Feminist Standpoint Theory; Matrix of Domination

REFERENCES AND SUGGESTED READINGS

Campbell, M. & Gregor, F. (2002) *Mapping Social Relations: A Primer in Doing Institutional Ethnography.* Garamond, Aurora, ON.

Griffith, A. I. & Smith, D. E. (2005) *Mothering for Schooling.* Routledge Falmer, New York.

Smith, D. E. (1974) Women's Perspective as a Radical Critique of Sociology. *Sociological Inquiry* 44: 7–13.

Smith, D. E. (1987) *The Everyday World as Problematic: A Feminist Sociology.* Northeastern University Press, Boston.

Smith, D. E. (1990) *Texts, Facts, and Femininity: Exploring the Relations of Ruling.* Routledge, New York.

Smith, D. E. (1999) *Writing the Social: Critique, Theory, and Investigations.* University of Toronto Press, Toronto.

Smith, D. E. (2005) *Institutional Ethnography: A Sociology for People.* Alta Mira Press, Lanham, MD.

rural aging

B. Jan McCulloch

Rural aging is an area of scholarship focusing on issues affecting quality of life for older persons living in areas of low population density. Rural versus urban (or metropolitan versus nonmetropolitan) conceptualizations are rooted in characteristics of folk or traditional societies versus contemporary or urban societies. Elders living in rural areas are portrayed as valuing independence and self-sufficiency, having strong family and religious ties, mistrusting "outsiders," and giving and receiving help through informal networks of families and neighbors (Shenk 1998; Lawrence & McCulloch 2001).

Rural areas have significant proportions of elders (14.4 percent compared with 11.5 percent in urban areas). In addition, three trends suggest that this proportion will increase in the future: (1) the overall US population is aging; (2) young adults are migrating from rural areas in search of better economic opportunities; and (3) some rural areas, especially those with recreational amenities and planned retirement communities, are relocation destinations for retirees (Longino & Haas 1993).

Rural aging envelops the study of aging within a contextual focus. Increasingly, the diversity found within rural areas is recognized. The experience of aging is also quite different in the more populated rural areas of the East – rural Appalachia or the Mississippi Delta, for example – as compared to that in the West where specific areas remain quite isolated, with some having as few as six persons per square mile (Coward & Krout 1998).

Inherent in the majority of research addressing rural aging has been the comparison of rural elders with their urban counterparts. Topics consistently of interest include health, informal social support, formal support services and issues focusing on barriers to health and service delivery, and persistent poverty. When social structural measures are assessed, rural elders are portrayed as being disadvantaged – they have poorer health, more chronic health conditions, fewer formal social services, greater difficulty assessing existing health and social services, higher rates of poverty, and more limited lifelong opportunities to accrue financial resources for later life. They also live in small communities that have limited economic bases and suffer from the political and economic biases toward urban areas.

Perhaps the most disconcerting result of over five decades of research focusing on rural aging is that researchers have continued to investigate the same topics for a long period of time. Early comparisons with urban older adults outlined the poorer income, health status, and social life of rural elders, and the disadvantage they faced in having access to public transportation and health care (Youmans 1967, 1977). Later Youmans (1977) addressed the "triple jeopardy" of rural elders who "have extremely small incomes, inadequate transportation, a restricted social life, and poor physical and mental health." More recently, Coward and Krout (1998) introduced their edited volume on this topic with similar comments including individual as well as community-level disadvantages. It is encouraging that recently researchers have recognized the complexity of identifying rural issues; the variation in the experiences of rural older adults must be acknowledged if progress is to be made concerning the historic and persistent identification of disadvantages for persons aging in these areas.

The most longlasting and dominant methodological issue relating to "rural aging" is the definition of this concept (Friedland 2002). Historically, residence has been operationalized as a dichotomy (i.e., rural versus urban). Several scholars have noted that this approach is too simple. The need to address the complexity of rural aging, however, has led to a number of different proposed conceptualizations – a result that, while improving operationalization, makes comparisons across studies difficult. For example, at least three definitions of "rural" are provided by the federal government (Dibartolo & McCrone 2003). In addition, Halfacree (1993) promotes a three-part rural definition including an overall assessment of "rural" across descriptive, sociocultural, and locality characteristics. Continued attention is needed to bring consistency to the ways in which rural is operationalized.

Also needed is the application of theoretical approaches that link the micro processes related to individual aging with the macro structures that affect the probability of "a good old age" within the context of residence, including aging in rural areas. Success will require a consistent definition of residence that will capture the diversity of what a rural context is. This work is particularly relevant if policies are to be developed that adequately address the persistent disadvantages that examinations of rural aging confirm – disadvantages in personal health status and income as well as more limited access to health care and formal social services.

SEE ALSO: Aging and the Life Course, Theories of; Aging, Mental Health, and Well-Being; Aging, Sociology of; Elderly Poor; Health, Neighborhood Disadvantage; Life Course Perspective; Older Adults, Economic Well-Being of; Rural Sociology; Socioeconomic Status, Health, and Mortality; Urban–Rural Population Movements

REFERENCES AND SUGGESTED READINGS

Coward, R. T. & Krout, J. A. (Eds.) (1998) *Aging in Rural Settings: Life Circumstances and Distinctive Features*. Springer, New York.

Dibartolo, M. C. & McCrone, S. (2003) Recruitment of Rural Community-Dwelling Older Adults: Barriers, Challenges, and Strategies. *Aging and Mental Health* 7: 75–82.

Friedland, W. H. (2002) Agriculture and Rurality: Beginning of the "Final Separation"? *Rural Sociology* 67: 350–72.

Halfacree, K. (1993) Locality and Social Representaton: Space, Discourse, and Alternative Definitions of the Rural. *Journal of Rural Studies* 9: 23–37.

Lawrence, S. S. & McCulloch, B. J. (2001) Rural Mental Health and Elders: Historical Inequities. *Journal of Applied Gerontology* 20: 144–69.

Longino, C. F., Jr. & Haas, W. H. (1993) Migration and the Rural Elderly. In: Bull, C. N. (Eds.), *Aging in Rural America*. Sage, Newbury Park, CA, pp. 17–29.

Shenk, D. (1998) *Someone to Lend a Helping Hand: Women Growing Old in Rural America*. Gordon & Breach, Amsterdam.

Youmans, E. G. (1967) *Older Rural Americans*. University of Kentucky Press, Lexington.

Youmans, E. G. (1977) The Rural Aged. *Annals of the American Academy of Political and Social Science* 429: 81–90.

rural sociology

William W. Falk and Thomas A. Lyson

Like nearly all major concepts in sociology, *rural* sociology has come to mean a variety of things and like all things social, there is a historical context for understanding what rural sociology is. Intellectually, rural sociology grew out of the same historical era and ferment as sociology more broadly, but whereas the discipline from whence it sprang was rooted heavily in liberal arts colleges, rural sociology – in America – was heavily indebted institutionally to the rise of the land grant university. This was a uniquely American initiative, deeding land to states specifically for establishing universities that consciously sought to link teaching, research, and service – in this latter case, in the form of another institution, the Cooperative Extension Service. The federal legislation which began this was the Morrill Act of 1862. This was a time when racial segregation still ruled the land. Ironically, in the South, all of the original land grant universities were black, but white universities quickly became the dominant ones in all states, including the Southern ones. The Morrill Act of 1890 provided the enabling legislation for a system of historically black colleges and universities, virtually all of which were Southern (for a wonderful source on rural sociology's history, see this web page: www.ag.ohiostate.edu).

In the late 1800s and on into the early 1900s, it was also true that America was still a decidedly "rural" place, with most Americans living in the countryside and working directly or indirectly in production agriculture. Many land grant universities recognized this with "A&M" (Agricultural and Mechanical) as part of their name and legacy. While some states established an "Ag" school as the comprehensive university, others established a companion university more oriented toward traditional liberal arts; examples abound – the University of Texas and Texas A&M; the University of Virginia and Virginia Polytechnic Institute and State University; the University of Oklahoma and Oklahoma State University; the University of Idaho and Idaho State University; the University of Washington and Washington State University; the University of Mississippi and Mississippi State University, and so on. Interestingly, some historic "ag" schools can hardly be identified by their names (e.g., Rutgers, Clemson, Auburn, and Purdue). In time, all states had land grant universities and many (but not all) had departments of rural sociology.

Rural sociology's foci historically and contemporarily have followed closely what is generally meant by "rural." This is a term written and debated about by rural sociologists (Bealer 1966; Falk & Pinhey 1978; Miller & Luloff 1981). In general, the term was thought to have three meanings. First, "rural" often was a short-hand for areas with relatively low population density; this placed it in sharp contrast with "urban" areas notable for their high population density. The population emphasis was also true in US census categories, where people were sorted by such residential distinctions as farming, open land; small town, less than 2,500 total population; population 2,500–25,000 (or sometimes 50,000); and so on up to and including large cities. In time, this kind of categorization changed to be called non-metropolitan and metropolitan (among other schemes). Regardless, the overriding issues were (1) the population density and (2) where people lived. A second way of characterizing rural areas was by occupation. This usually meant giving great emphasis to farming both as activity and as industry. Rural areas not only had more of this activity, but as one consequence they had comparatively less of many other occupations and industries which were more likely to be found in urban areas. This was especially true at the turn of the twentieth century, when millions of Americans migrated from rural areas to urban ones to work in the emerging "industrial" America. A third way of thinking about rural areas was one based on values; in this case, "tradition" was paramount, often thought of in sharp contrast to urban areas. Where urban areas were heterogeneous (in all ways), sophisticated, hip, progressive, and modern, rural areas were homogeneous, unsophisticated, unhip, unprogressive, and traditional. Early sociologists, including Redfield and Tönnies, among others, captured this difference with terms such as "folk" and "urban" or *Gemeinschaft* and *Gesellschaft*. While this is primarily a stereotype, there is no question that in many people's minds (according to public opinion data) this sense of contrast still holds. Indeed, in American politics, "red" states and "blue" states follow somewhat this same distinction.

The first department of rural sociology was established in 1915 at Cornell (Larson & Zimmerman 2003: 13). Subsequently, many state universities developed similar programs, often merged with other programs, usually agricultural economics. Rural sociology, because it was so much smaller than the larger discipline, has always had a more limited intellectual vision as well as a much greater emphasis on application. This is easily understood when considering its place in the "mission"-oriented land grant university and, again, given its size. For example, while the American Sociological Association had about 14,000 members in 2005, the Rural Sociological Society had about 1,000.

Despite its size, rural sociology has had considerable impact. This is partly because its work has been more narrowly focused – on issues such as population, community, family, stratification, development, and more recently the environment. For much of its history, rural sociology research often responded to a sense of local need and as a result had considerable application; this was facilitated by many rural sociologists having appointments funded in part by the Cooperative Extension Service. Many early rural sociologists were former or currently practicing ministers, something that helps to explain rural sociology's historical penchant for being relevant to any given era's social issues and problems. As with all sociologists, their "sociological imaginations" were grounded in the eras in which they were living.

Again because of its size, the full range of sociological "theories" has never been found in rural sociology. For much of the twentieth century, rural sociology was nearly monotheoretical with its use of structural functionalism (Falk & Zhao 1989). It flirted some with more Marxist ideas but, in part, because so much of its institutional base was in state-funded land grant universities (again, with mission-driven principles and usually supported by federally funded research dollars), Marx – no matter his prominence in the sociological pantheon – was cited and employed rarely by rural sociologists (for a notable exception, see the "political economy" approach of Friedland et al. 1991). More broadly adopted were the apolitical principles of social psychology, often coupled methodologically with social surveys.

Rural sociology has always been heavily empirical and data-driven. Indeed, to say that it was often atheoretical would be accurate (thus making it much like demography, a prominent style of scholarship in rural sociology throughout its history). In the early years, rural sociologists did considerable fieldwork and helped to pioneer social surveys (for a good overview, see Bertrand 1958). And some of the early rural sociologists (e.g., Dwight Sanderson, Charles Loomis, and William Sewell) were elected as president of both the Rural Sociological Society and the American Sociological Association. Rural sociologists also did a series of "community" studies and while the study of community faded from much of mainstream sociology for nearly a generation (essentially the 1970s and 1980s), it was always a staple of rural sociology (see especially Luloff & Krannich 2002). Indeed, one of rural sociology's best departments – Penn State's – was famous in part for training community scholars.

Coming out of World War II, rural sociology entered a period of both institutional and organizational growth. States and federal funding for rural sociological research, along with funding for the social sciences in general, grew throughout the 1950s and 1960s. Substantively, rural sociologists continued to study rural institutions such as the family, religion, education, and governance. The units of analysis were generally communities, regions, and states. These studies were undertaken as the US farm sector saw the number of producers fall from nearly 6 million at the end of the war to just over 2 million by 1980. Rural to urban migration and non-agricultural economic development strategies attracted the attention of the rural sociological community in the post-war years.

During this same period the federal government began to pour resources into area studies and international development programs. The imperatives of the Cold War meant that the US needed to know as much as possible about the lives of the people living in the third world to combat the spread of communism and ensure that western models of economic development prevailed. Universities like Cornell, Wisconsin, and Michigan State became centers of international rural sociology scholarship. Many rural sociologists changed their research foci from domestic to international topics and cadres of rural sociology graduate students, often fresh out of the Peace Corps, were recruited to expand scholarship and build intellectual capacity on the international front. At the same time, rural sociology programs saw an influx of graduate students from the developing world.

Organizationally, after World War II, virtually all states had either a department of rural sociology ensconced in their land grant universities or a strong rural sociology unit nested in their departments of sociology. Many universities awarded PhDs in rural sociology and jobs were plentiful in the land grant system, in government, and in an expanding network of non-governmental organizations.

During the 1970s the organizational fabric of rural sociology came under scrutiny as states began to withdraw support from higher education in general and agricultural programs in particular. Funds for international development work stagnated. To be sure, the changes affecting rural sociology varied from state to state, often depending on the economic viability of agriculture in the state. States with strong constituents of family farmers and/or large rural populations maintained economically viable colleges of agriculture and usually strong rural sociology programs. States in which agriculture diminished in economic importance and in which rural interests waned experienced a downsizing of programs and staff. Rural sociology programs that developed expertise in international development in the previous decades were more likely to be maintained. At the same time, paralleling work in the larger discipline, some scholars engaged in sociology of rural sociology inquiries, spurred on, in part, by a famous Rural Sociological Society presidential address in which James Copp (1972) asked about the discipline's "relevance." Not long after, studies had been done on rural sociology theory (Gilbert 1982), methods (Stokes & Miller 1985), paradigms (Picou et al. 1978), and future (Friedland 1982).

In the 1980s the field of rural sociology experienced a resurgence of sorts, in part to accommodate scholarship in the area of the environment. Many of the key debates in what has become the subfield of environmental sociology were inspired by work undertaken by rural sociologists (Field & Burch 1988; Buttel 1996). And while environmental sociology has entered the mainstream of sociology, rural sociology still maintains both organizational capacity and scholarly depth in this area. Also during the 1980s, rural sociology rediscovered rural poverty; in fact a task force was formed to pursue this topic which led to both academic and policy-related work and activity (Summers et al. 1993).

As the twentieth century ended and the twenty-first began, the sociology of agriculture and food systems emerged as a burgeoning area of scholarship and outreach in many rural sociology programs around the country (Lyson 2004). Partly in response to the globalization of the food system and partly in response to the economic decline of rural areas, rural sociologists have begun looking at local agricultural and food systems as engines of economic and community development. The agriculture and food foci has also developed an ancillary health component, which links agriculture, food, nutrition, and health.

Unlike conventional or mainstream sociology, rural sociology has always been more driven by the needs and concerns of a client base. In the early years of the discipline the client base was the farm sector and rural communities. Today, rural sociologists are responding to broader constituencies, ones concerned about environmental problems, food safety, and health. However, rural sociology's longstanding focus on rural people and communities has remained a staple, and it is easy to find rural sociologists working on topics related to these things, especially population, family, social capital, and various forms of inequality, including some of the dominant variables found in many sociological analyses – race, class, and gender (for a notable essay on gender and rural sociology, see Tickamyer 1996).

In the contemporary era, rural sociology has struggled to keep its competitive advantage – both broadly (in sociology) and narrowly (in ag schools). Much of the funding for ag-school rural sociology projects has been based on what are called formula funds. These are federal funds based on a state's rural population, provided from the US Department of Agriculture to the Agricultural Experiment Station (always housed with colleges of agriculture on land grant university campuses). Since the rural population has become smaller and smaller over the years, so, too, have these funds. Rural sociologists, almost always the smallest cadre of scholars in colleges of agriculture (where they have usually been housed), have seen their proportion of the research pie shrink along with other recipients of these funds. But since rural sociology programs were small to begin with, many have been merged with other departments or been eliminated altogether. It is notable and increasingly normative for rural sociologists to seek outside funding to support their work, a kind of entrepreneurial activity which may help to secure their longevity in the years ahead.

While much of what has been said thus far applies primarily to the American experience, some of the general intellectual emphases of the discipline are also found overseas. There, agriculture and all things related to it – farming as both activity and industry, farm families, social change in all its manifestations related to the changing importance of agriculture, and the impact on natural resources and the environment – have been dominant. This has been especially true among scholars examining less developed societies, where modernity (and all things related to it) has received considerable attention. Indeed, this is one part of rural sociology – in and out of the US – where more Marxian informed theoretical views are likely to be found. It is also true, however, that while an emphasis on agriculture, food systems, and related issues has received considerable attention, nearly anything related to population studies and demography has long been a staple of rural sociology as done overseas.

As rural sociology enters the twenty-first century, especially in the US, its research funds and, importantly, undergraduate students have continued to decline. Consequently, it is likely to see its autonomy diminished along with its sense of itself as a coherent organizational and institutional discipline. Some programs may remain essentially intact as traditional rural sociology departments (e.g., Wisconsin, Penn State) and award PhDs in rural sociology. Other programs will reorganize themselves into speciality niches that emphasize some key aspect of rural sociology (e.g., development sociology at Cornell; community and leadership development at the University of Kentucky). In some cases, rural sociology will be folded into "hybrid" departments (e.g., human and community resource development at Ohio State) or either remain with or become part of the usually much larger departments of agricultural economics (e.g., Auburn, Louisiana State University, Texas A&M University). In most cases, it is likely that rural sociology programs will maintain their status as subunits or cognate areas in larger programs (e.g., Michigan State University, Iowa State University). This parallels what one usually finds overseas, where rural "sociologists" are often trained in fields other than sociology; what unites them is not the name of their academic departments but their substantive focus on rural issues which in some cases, especially in Great Britain, may be called more inclusively "rural studies."

When considering the discipline's future, we are certain about one thing: by whatever name, there will be scholars whose work will focus on rural people and places, and this will remain true both in the US (where nearly one quarter of the population lives in rural areas) and abroad.

SEE ALSO: Community; Environment and Urbanization; Globalization; Rural Aging; Tradition; Urban–Rural Population Movements

REFERENCES AND SUGGESTED READINGS

Bealer, R. C. (1966) A Discussion of Leo F. Schnore, "The Rural–Urban Variable: An Urbanite's Perspective." *Rural Sociology* 31: 144–8.

Bertrand, A. S. (Ed.) (1958) *Rural Sociology: An Analysis of Contemporary Rural Life*. McGraw-Hill, New York.

Buttel, F. (1996) Environmental and Resource Sociology: Theoretical Issues and Opportunities for Synthesis. *Rural Sociology* 61: 56–66.

Copp, J. H. (1972) Rural Sociology and Rural Development. *Rural Sociology* 37: 515–33.

Falk, W. W. & Pinhey, T. A. (1978) Making Sense of the Concept "Rural" and Doing Rural Sociology: An Interpretative Perspective. *Rural Sociology* 43: 547–58.

Falk, W. W. and Zhao, S. (1989) Paradigms, Theories and Methods in Contemporary Rural Sociology: A Partial Replication and Extension. *Rural Sociology* 54: 587–600.

Field, D. R. and Burch, W. R., Jr. (1988) *Rural Sociology and the Environment*. Greenwood Press, Westport.

Friedland, W. H. (1982) The End of Rural Society and the Future of Rural Sociology. *Rural Sociology* 47: 580–608.

Friedland, W. H., Busch, L., Buttel, F. H., & Rudy, A. (Eds.) (1991) *Towards a New Political Economy of Agriculture*. Westview Press, Boulder.

Gilbert, J. (1982) Rural Theory: The Grounding of Rural Sociology. *Rural Sociology* 47: 609–33.

Larson, O. F. & Zimmerman, J. N. (2003) *Sociology in Government: The Galpin-Taylor Years in the US Department of Agriculture, 1919–1953*. Pennsylvania State University Press, University Park.

Luloff, A. E. & Krannich, R. S. (2002) *Persistence and Change in Rural Communities: A Fifty-Year Follow-Up to Six Classic Studies*. CABI Publishing, Okon.

Lyson, T. A. (2004) *Civic Agriculture: Reconnecting Farm, Food and Family*. Tufts University Press, Medford, MA.

Miller, M. K. & Luloff, A. E. (1981) Who is Rural? A Typological Approach to the Examination of Rurality. *Rural Sociology* 46: 608–25.

Picou, J. S., Wells, R. H., & Nyberg, K. L. (1978) Paradigms, Theories and Methods in Contemporary Sociology. *Rural Sociology* 43: 559–83.

Stokes, C. S. & Miller, M. K. (1985) A Methodological Review of Fifty Years of Research in Rural Sociology. *Rural Sociology* 50: 539–60.

Summers, G. F. et al. (Eds.) (1993) *Persistent Poverty in Rural America*. Westview Press, Boulder, Co.

Tickamyer, A. R. (1996) Sex, Lies and Statistics: Can Rural Sociology Survive Restructuring? (Or) What is Right with Rural Sociology and How Can We Fix It? *Rural Sociology* 61: 5–24.

Rustbelt

John M. Hagedorn

The Rustbelt historically refers to the Great Lakes and Northeastern regions of the US that had been hardest hit in the 1970s by the decline in manufacturing. The term uses as metaphor the "rusting" of the physical plants of factories to represent the economic and social decay of the older industrial cities and their attendant social problems.

A Rustbelt city is one that experiences population loss, rising crime rates, loss of union jobs (particularly in manufacturing), white flight to the suburbs, and a generally declining urban environment. Cities like Gary, Indiana, Detroit, Michigan, and Milwaukee, Wisconsin saw a steady stream of manufacturing jobs leave to lower-wage regions of the country, Mexico, and overseas. Massive but abandoned factories rusted away and scarred the landscape of once vibrant cities.

The Rustbelt was contrasted in the 1970s to the rise of the "Sunbelt," or cities in the South and Southwest characterized by high rates of immigration, low wages, retirement communities, and new defense, oil, and high-tech industries. The Sunbelt also corresponded with the rise to power of the Republican Party in the 1980s, as electoral votes shifted to the South and Southwest states, adding political to economic advantage.

Theoretically, the term Rustbelt is associated with some of the major trends of thought in urban sociology. While popular thinking saw the rusting of the industrial centers and the rapid growth of the Southwest as a natural process, some social scientists disagreed. Perry and Watkins (1977) posited the Rustbelt–Sunbelt dyad as one outcome of uneven capitalist development. Rejecting "convergence" theories that saw such processes as an inevitable consequence of the "invisible hand," these urban political economists attributed the decline of the Rustbelt to conscious decisions by political and economic actors.

The crisis of the Rustbelt was seen as a crisis of the state, and particularly its redistributive policies. Sunbelt cities were dominated by private capital while the Rustbelt poor were dependent on public works or welfare. As the political spectrum swung to the right during the Reagan years, budget cuts further undermined the income and well-being of workers, the unemployed, and the "underclass" in Rustbelt cities. Investment in aerospace and other defense industries and later the information economy enriched the Sunbelt as the Rustbelt declined.

Wilson (1987) looked more closely at the social consequences of the deindustrialization for the "truly disadvantaged" or black urban poor. In the 1970s and 1980s, Chicago was a prime example of a Rustbelt city with a corresponding growth in African American concentrated poverty. Chicago also saw sharp population losses, increases in rates of single-parent families, high unemployment, a persistent violent gang problem, and an overall decay in African American social institutions.

While Wilson (1978) had earlier pointed to the "declining significance of race," the Rustbelt led to work disappearing precisely in those cities, like Chicago, that African Americans had concentrated on in order to get high-wage manufacturing jobs. Thus the "spatial mismatch" of jobs and workers made Rustbelt cities' African American population the "truly disadvantaged." No other ethnic group, Wilson and Sampson (1995), Massey (1990), and others pointed out, suffered from such high rates of concentrated poverty.

In recent years, the Rustbelt concept has diffused internationally. For example, China describes its northeastern provinces of Heilongjiang, Jilin, and Liaoning as its Rustbelt. Saskia Sassen, Manuel Castells, and other urban sociologists have subsumed the Rustbelt concept into explanations of various processes of globalization and the new economy. In Sassen's terms, some cities and regions are "valorized" in the global era, while others are marginalized. The strength of former industrial cities like Manchester, Mumbai, or Detroit turns into a disadvantage as cities seek to become major players in the information economy.

Some US cities appear to have rebounded from Rustbelt to information city status. Pittsburgh, for example, has shed its dependence on steel to become a center of software and finance. Boston's maze of universities and electronics industries provided it with an entrée into the new economy as it shed its textile and other light industry past.

Other cities failed to find a niche in the information era, and have stagnated. Detroit saw its auto industry relocate and has continued to experience major population loss, including nearly all of its white residents. Gary's steel mills lie darkened in a row on the banks of Lake Michigan, interrupted only by the bright lights of Harrah's gambling casino. Rustbelt cities have looked to gambling, tourism, and entertainment venues to try to provide jobs and keep their more affluent population from leaving. When old factories are not torn down, some are refurbished as shopping malls. Rustbelt cities today continue to lose population and have high rates of urban violence.

The term Rustbelt is used less in the twenty-first century, as cities look to define themselves more in terms of the new economy than to be held captive to nineteenth- and twentieth-century labels. Research, like the reputation of cities, has moved from looking at the nature of urban transitions from the industrial era, to the challenges of confronting the inequalities of the new global order.

SEE ALSO: Global/World Cities; Sunbelt

REFERENCES AND SUGGESTED READINGS

Castells, M. (1989) *The Information City: Information Technology, Economic Restructuring, and the Urban-Regional Process.* Blackwell, Oxford.

Massey, D. S. (1990) American Apartheid: Segregation and the Making of the Underclass. *American Journal of Sociology* 96: 329–57.

Perry, D. C. & Watkins, A. J. (Eds.) (1977) *The Rise of the Sunbelt Cities*, Vol. 14. Sage, Beverly Hills, CA.

Sassen, S. (1991) *The Global City: New York, London, Tokyo*. Princeton University Press, Princeton, NJ.
Wilson, W. J. (1978) *The Declining Significance of Race*. University of Chicago Press, Chicago.
Wilson, W. J. (1987) *The Truly Disadvantaged*. University of Chicago Press, Chicago.
Wilson, W. J. (1996) *When Work Disappears: The World of the New Urban Poor*. Alfred A. Knopf, New York.
Wilson, W. J. & Sampson, R. J. (1995) Toward a Theory of Race, Crime, and Urban Inequality. In: Hagan, J. & Peterson, R. D. (Eds.), *Crime and Inequality*. Stanford University Press, Stanford.

S

Sacks, Harvey (1935–75)

Martin M. Jacobsen

Harvey Sacks was a sociologist who developed the methodological subdiscipline called conversation analysis. It conceptualized conversation as a means of social action rather than as an indicator of cognitive or psychological intent. Conversation analysis examines the surface structure and sequencing of linguistic exchanges as social acts rather than as indications of a speaker's intent, as is the case with speech act theory, pragmatics, or sociolinguistics. Sacks's focus on the surface structure of language use as an end in itself places him alongside such modern thinkers as Harold Garfinkel and Noam Chomsky.

Sacks's interest in conversation grew from his experience in legal studies. After earning an LLB (Yale Law School) in 1955, Sacks turned his attention to developing analytical approaches toward the analysis of conversation as a behavior that accomplishes social ends. Most of this early work emerged while a graduate student at MIT and the University of California system, where he earned a PhD in sociology (UC-Berkley, 1966) and rose through the ranks to full professor at UC-Irvine in 1974, one year before his death in an automobile accident.

Sacks occupies an important position in the interdisciplinary field of discourse analysis. He is contemporary with the generation of scholars who, after adapting sociological, anthropological, and philosophical methods to analyze linguistic behavior as a social phenomenon, became interested in language itself. Sacks's publications (whether submitted by him before his death or by his intellectual heirs after it) focus primarily on methodology, and both his publications and his collected lectures privilege real-world data as opposed to the created or literary examples of many of his contemporaries. By concentrating on the act of conversation as a thing in itself, Sacks took a radical step away from the mainstream view of sociology as mass psychology. His preference for examining the work done with language rather than using language as a way to examine the mentality of the speaker placed him as firmly in the discipline of linguistics as it did in the discipline of sociology.

SEE ALSO: Conversation Analysis; Discourse; Emic/Etic; Ethnography; Facework; Frame; Goffman, Erving; Interaction; Intersubjectivity; Intertextuality; Language; Lifeworld; Orality; Reference Groups; Semiotics; Stratification, Distinction and; Symbolic Interaction

REFERENCES AND SUGGESTED READINGS

Sacks, H. (1963) Sociological Description. *Berkeley Journal of Sociology* 8: 1–16.

Sacks, H. (1972) An Initial Investigation of the Usability of Conversational Data for Doing Sociology. In: Sudnow, D. (Ed.), *Studies in Social Interaction*. Free Press, New York, pp. 31–74.

Sacks, H. (1992). *Lectures on Conversation*, 2 Vols. Ed. G. Jefferson. Blackwell, Oxford.

Sacks, H., Schegloff, E. A., & Jefferson, G. (1974) A Simplest Systematics for the Organization of Turn-Taking for Conversation. *Language* 50: 696–735.

Schegloff, E. A., Jefferson, G., & Sacks, H. (1977) The Preference for Self-Correction in the Organization of Repair in Conversation. *Language* 53(2): 361–82.

Silverman, D. (1998) *Harvey Sacks: Social Science and Conversation Analysis*. Oxford University Press, Oxford.

sacred

Stephen Hunt

The Latin word *sacer*, from which the term sacred is derived, denotes a distinction between what is and what is not pertaining to the gods. In not a dissimilar fashion, the Hebrew root of *k-d-sh*, which is usually translated as "Holy," is based on the idea of separation of the consecrated and desecrated in relation to the divine. Whatever the specific expression of the sacred, however, there is a fairly universal cultural division where the sacred constitutes phenomena which are set apart, revered, and distinguished from all other phenomena that constitute the profane or the mundane. However, in Hinduism there has long existed the belief that the sacred and the unclean both belong to a single linguistic category. Thus, the Hindu notion of pollution suggests that the sacred and the non-sacred need not be absolute opposites; they can be relative categories; what is clean in relation to one thing may be unclean in relation to another, and vice versa.

The interest of sociologists in the social significance of the sacred is largely derived from the concerns of the subdiscipline of the sociology of religion. However, considerable disagreement exists as to the precise social origins of that which is designated sacred. Hence, an understanding of the sacred is frequently intimately bound up with broad definitions of religion itself, the categorization of certain social activities as religious, and particular sociological approaches to the subject. Such concerns have subsequently ensured that sociological perceptions of what constitutes the sacred as a social manifestation are subject to constant change and have led to a divergence of thought as to its nature.

The exploration of the cultural perception of the sacred is by no means limited to the discipline of sociology. Psychoanalytical theory and anthropology have also brought their own unique reductions and these have not infrequently informed past sociological speculations. In terms of psychoanalytical accounts, the sacred is discussed in Freud's theory of totemism and is central to his famous analysis of religion in *Totem and Taboo* (1938). For Freud, the link between totemism and the sacred is evident in certain aspects of the development of religion which have left their traces in historical myth and legend. In Freud's account the Oedipus myth symbolizes a son's desire to possess his mother and murder his father. Freud interpreted sacred animal sacrifices in "savage" tribes as partly a reenactment of the original parricide and partly an expiation of it and where the totemic animal is the symbolic substitute for the father or the dominate male. However, in more civilized communities where in the totemic feast the totem animal is slaughtered and eaten, Freud believed that sacrifice loses its sacredness and becomes an offering to the gods rather than a representation of the gods.

In anthropological terms, Robertson Smith (1889) identified the principal difference between primitive taboo and rules of the sacred as the difference between friendly and unfriendly deities. The separation of sacred and consecrated things and persons from profane ones, which is an integral part of the religious cult, is basically the same as the separation which is inspired by fear of malevolent spirits. Separation is the essential idea in both contexts, only the motive is different, since friendly gods are also to be feared on occasion. Robertson Smith maintained that distinguishing between the holy and the unclean marks a real advance above savagery. In this way he produces a criterion for classifying religions as "advanced" or "primitive." If primitive, then rules of sacredness and rules of uncleanliness are indistinguishable; if advanced, then rules of uncleanliness disappear from religion.

While early anthropological accounts of the nature of the sacred have informed sociological theorizing, it was in turn heavily influenced by the work of Durkheim. In the opening chapter to *The Elementary Forms of the Religious Life* (1915) Durkheim summarized and rejected earlier definitions of religion. He dismissed Tylor's (1903) "substantive" definition of religion, namely "belief in spiritual beings." This definition was bound up with Tylor's account of the origins of religion in a system of thought which he referred to as "animism" – the belief that all things, organic and inorganic, contain a soul or a spirit which infuses them with their particular sacred nature and characteristics. Durkheim insisted that this emphasis was erroneous since it ignored practices, the real essence of religion, which are more important than beliefs. Durkheim likewise dismissed Marett's (1914) conjecture that the essence of religion is the experience of a mysterious, sacred occult power or force that was associated with deep and ambivalent emotions of awe, fear, and respect of natural phenomena which predated conceptualizations of spirits, deities, and the like.

Durkheim then proceeded to adopt two criteria which he assumed would be found to coincide: the communal organization for the community cult and the separation of the sacred from the profane. For Durkheim, the sacred was the object of worship. The rules of separation between religion and the secular are the distinguishing marks of the sacred, the polar opposite to the profane. The sacred, according to Durkheim, is frequently projected as abstract religious entities, but these are merely collective ideas and expressions of collective morality. Moreover, the sacred needs to be continuingly enforced by prohibitions. The sacred must always be treated as contagious because relations with it are bound to be expressed by rituals of separation and demarcation and by beliefs in the danger of crossing forbidden boundaries.

Durkheim's advanced his own "functional" definition of religion which amounted to a distinction between the sacred and profane, so that religion was "a unified system of beliefs and practices relative to sacred things, that is to say, things set apart and forbidden – beliefs and practices which unite them into one single moral community called a church of all those who adhere to them" (Durkheim 1915: 47). Thus, beliefs and practices in relation to the sacred are the defining factors of all religions.

Durkheim's deductionist approach gave way to an examination of what he perceived as the most simple and primitive religion, that of the Australian aborigine, which he believed would provide insights into the origins of religion that are predominantly social in cause. Durkheim described the clan organization of aboriginal society and the association between each clan and a sacred totem animal or plant species. These totems are represented by stylistic images drawn on stones or wooden objects called *churingas* which, since they bear the representation of the sacred totem, are also sacred. In aboriginal collectives *churingas* are surrounded by taboo and treated with the utmost respect. These totemic symbols, Durkheim insisted, are emblems of the clan in much the same way as a flag of a country. The *churingas* are the most sacred objects in aborigine ritual – the outward and visible form of the totemic principle or god.

Durkheim argued that by sacred things we should not understand simply those things which are called gods or spirits – a rock a tree, a river, a pebble, a building – which are frequently held as sacred, as displaying inherent sacred qualities. The totem is the emblem of the clan, but more than what the *churingas* represents. The *churingas* are at once the symbol of the sacred and society, for the sacred and society are one. Thus, through worship of god or the totem, human beings worship society – the real object of religious veneration. It is a relationship of inferiority and dependency. Durkheim argued that it is easier for human beings to visualize and direct feelings of awe towards a symbol than such a complex thing as a clan. This is what gives the totem, hence society, its sacred quality.

Durkheim also explored how human beings partake of the sacred. At one level social members express their faith in common values and beliefs. In the highly charged atmosphere of collective worship, the integration of society is strengthened. Members of society express, communicate, and acknowledge the moral bonds between them. At the same time, as members of clans with sacred totems and who believe themselves to be descended from such totems, they too are sacred. Through totemic representation to which they belong, they are in some sense of the same essence as the totemic species and consequently, sacred. In the same way, in the totemic system of ideas, since all things are related with one or another clan totem, natural phenomena such as rain, thunder, and clouds become sacred. As totemic clans partake of a universal principle they are part of an anonymous impersonal force which constitutes society as a whole greater than its parts and which has a sacred quality. This impersonal force has a particular mysterious quality related to the totem and the social consciousness and unity which it represents. This force may be understood by the Polynesian term *mana*, which has parallels among some North American Indian tribes with the notion of *orenda* and in ancient Persian, *maga*.

There are a number of problems frequently identified with Durkheim's definition of the sacred. Firstly, such a definition is derived from a western context that is not readily appropriate to the worldviews of a number of non-western societies, since it carries various culture-bound connotations. Thus, Durkheim's assertion that religion is related to the sacred and that this is a universal conception in human society has been disputed by anthropologists: Evans-Prichard (1937), for example, found that the distinction was not meaningful among the Azunde tribe he studied. The idea of the sacred, therefore, is one which exists in the mind of the observer and not necessarily of the believer or social agent. It might nonetheless be argued that the distinction remains a useful analytical conception by which sociologists can operationalize the study of religion. However, there remain difficulties with such a methodology even as an analytical distinction that focuses on the criteria by which the sacred is distinguished from the profane. Anthropologists point out that this is not useful in distinguishing a sacred from a profane sphere in at least some societies. While many cultures do have a category of things set apart and forbidden, these things are not always those that feature in religious belief and ritual and, on the other hand, things which do figure in religious belief and ritual may not be set apart and forbidden.

Durkheim also speaks of the sacred as commanding an attitude of respect. This does not, however, provide a consistent criterion because, in many religious systems, religious objects and entities do not necessarily receive reverence. Idols, and the gods and spirits they symbolize, may be punished if they do not produce the benefits they are called upon to bring. Such difficulties have led Goody to abandon the attempt to define religion in terms of the sacred. Goody (1961) maintains that it is far from legitimate for the observer to establish a definition of religious activity on a universal perception of the sacred world – no more than is the actor's division of the universe into a natural or supernatural sphere.

Despite such critiques of Durkheim's distinction between the sacred and profane, his work inspired important schools of anthropological thought. Radcliffe-Brown, for instance, saw the nature of the sacred as a communal cult. In his classic study *The Andaman Islanders* (1933) Radcliffe-Brown was heavily influenced by Durkheim in asserting that ritual provided a socially integrative force which compensated for a lack of unitary political structure. Ritual is a symbolic action regarding the sacred and essentially expressed social sentiments, although Radcliffe-Brown recognized that not all rituals are sacred rituals. Taboo rituals related to the sacred express, for example, the value of childbirth taboos among Andaman Islanders – emphasizing the value of marriage and maternity, alongside the danger to life in the birthing process.

There are aspects of Mary Douglas's work which also developed some of the themes of Durkheim's thesis, although she also departed significantly from a number of his basic tenets (Douglas 1966). Like Durkheim, Douglas identified the sacred and the impure as opposite poles, but noted that in some primitive cultures the sacred is a very general idea meaning little more than prohibition. In that sense the universe is divided between things and actions which are subject to restrictions and others which are not. Among such restrictions some are intended to protect the divine from profanations, and others to protect the profane from the dangerous intrusion of the divine. Sacred rules are thus merely rules hedging divinity off, and uncleanliness is the two-way danger of contact with the divine.

Douglas established the sacred as the polar opposite of uncleanliness, although what constitutes either she understood as socially defined and thus varied between cultures. For Douglas, religion often sacralized boundaries related to food, sexuality, dress, etc., as integral to caste systems, gender relations, or distinguishing communities. This is exemplified by a number of the rules of pollution in the "abominations" as outlined in the Judaic scriptures of the book of Leviticus, which are associated with ambiguities such as animals which part the hoof but are not cloven footed and the stipulation that those who touch them are likewise polluted (Leviticus 11).

A rarely observed perspective on Durkheim's work is that it also constituted a study in the sociology of knowledge. For Durkheim, the basic social concepts and categories of thought, time, space, and causation, in addition to the distinction between the sacred and the profane, are born in religion as a community enterprise. Through the shared beliefs and moral values which form the collective conscience, social order is made possible and the social and natural world understood and given meaning by those who comprise the "sacred" community. Durkheim proceeded to show how the totemic system was also a cosmological system and how such basic categories had origins within totemism and the clan structure.

A more stringent phenomenological approach to the sacred was offered by Peter Berger in a series of influential works written since the late 1960s (e.g., Berger 1967). In Berger's account religion is essentially derived from a subjective interpretation of reality from which meaning is given to the world (including the social world) and, indeed, the entire cosmos. Religion is thus one of the most important means by which human beings categorize and make sense of their existence. Such an enterprise is a collective one and, in constructing a universe of meaning, human beings perceive a "plausibility structure" of understanding which, in turn, feeds back to inform and sustain the social order. According to Berger, this plausibility structure constructs a "sacred canopy" which includes not just religious belief systems but also philosophical notions about how the world is and enforces everyday taken-for-granted knowledge. In doing so, the sacred canopy upholds the precariousness of human existence. Therefore, in most historical societies religion helped build, maintain, and legitimate a universe of meaning and provided ultimate answers to ultimate questions. This was achieved through beliefs in supernatural powers that created all things and further functioned to legitimate social institutions through a sacred and cosmic frame of reference. Since the sacred canopy is derived from a social base, that which is regarded as "true" and legitimate is only so in the minds of the human actors who have conceived it. Hence, through notions of the sacred, as an ultimate frame of reference, any given social order comes to see itself as the center of the world and the cosmos.

In a more recent account, in which he makes a contribution to the secularization debate, Demerath (1999) differentiates the concept of religion from that of the sacred. Demerath argues that the sociological study of religion has long labored under the constraint and misleading premise of concepts of religion, and has not sufficiently dwelt on the sacred. He thus argues that religion should be defined "substantively" and the sacred "functionally," thus resolving the longstanding tension in earlier definitions of both. Religion, according to Demerath, is a category of activity, and the sacred a statement of function. Demerath observes that religious activities do not always have sacred consequences. This is very often because religion frequently displays organized expressions and bureaucratic encumbrances. Nonetheless, the substantive definition of religion does suggest an orientation towards the supernatural world and "externally" imposed moral systems. By contrast, "the sacred" is a category of social phenomena which is not religious in conventional terms even though sacred phenomena may display some aspects of religion. Demerath therefore sees "folk," "implicit," "quasi," and "para" religions as part of the "sociology of the sacred," conceptions which hitherto had the disadvantage of using a conventional image of religion with unfortunate consequences, one of which has been to narrow the search for the sacred to include those things which are religious in character. There are sacred entities and symbols which have a compelling power without necessarily being religious. Since any social activity has potentially sacred functions there may be a large inventory of any society's cultural stock which constitutes the sacred.

SEE ALSO: Durkheim Émile; Primitive Religion; Religion; Religion, Sociology of; Sacred, Eclipse of the; Sacred/Profane

REFERENCES AND SUGGESTED READINGS

Berger, P. (1967) *The Sacred Canopy: Elements of a Sociological Theory of Religion.* Doubleday, New York.

Demerath, N. (1999) The Varieties of Sacred Experience: Finding the Sacred in a Secular Grove. Presidential Address, Society for the Scientific Study of Religion, November 6, Boston.

Douglas, M. (1966) *Purity and Danger: An Analysis of Concepts of Pollution and Taboo.* Routledge & Kegan Paul, London.
Durkheim, E. (1915) *The Elementary Forms of the Religious Life.* Allen & Unwin, London.
Evans-Prichard, E. E. (1937) *Witchcraft, Oracles and Magic Among the Azunde.* Clarendon Press, Oxford.
Freud, S. (1938) *Totem and Taboo.* Penguin, London.
Goody, J. (1961) Religion and Ritual: The Definitional Problem. *British Journal of Sociology* 12: 142–64.
Marett, R. R. (1914) *The Threshold of Religion.* Methuen, London.
Radcliffe-Brown, R. (1933 [1922]) *The Andaman Islanders.* Cambridge University Press, Cambridge.
Robertson Smith, W. (1889) *The Religion of the Semites.* Edinburgh, A. & C. Black.
Tylor, E. (1903 [1871]) *Primitive Culture.* Murray, London.

sacred, eclipse of the

Sabino Acquaviva

The thesis of the eclipse of the sacred, which is built on psychological experience of the sacred and measures of its decline, moves in a different space than many other theories of secularization that – according to the scholars who defend the eclipse – give less importance to the problem of the level of experience and therefore to the presence of the sacred and instead concentrate on cultural and structural analysis. The theory of the eclipse proceeds from the definition of the sacred as experience (which nearly all individuals have). Sacred experience exists when an aspect of the real is recognized as "radically other" compared to natural reality. In different cultures and societies there are different hierophanies of sacred experience. This experience, lived as individual psychological reality and as the central nucleus of religiousness and religion, is considered to be the center around which religiously significant social acts and facts orbit.

The sacred, which is present (a quantifiable presence) in various ways ranging from individual psychology to social life, is in decline if there is a progressive retreat from the forms of the sacred in individual and social experience. This approach has been challenged by the claim that an invisible religion exists that transcends the practical data on religious practice and the religious value of social events and so the eclipse of the sacred then is merely an apparent phenomenon. This approach attempts to refute the most widely accepted theories of secularization by claiming that we cannot ignore (or must adequately take into consideration) individual experience of the sacred as an expression of the biological and psychological characteristics of men and women.

The basic theoretical hypothesis of the theory rests on the fact there is a strict relation between religious experience (or the sacred) and human needs. Analysis of the system of needs and the ways in which they are sublimated when they are unsatisfied is thus fundamental to the theory: the genetically based need of amortality, the need to love and to be loved (by considering God or the gods as both objects and subjects of love it is possible to satisfy the genetic and psychological need to love and to be loved), the need to know (the so-called exploratory instinct), and the need to give meaning. The lack of satisfaction of these and other biopsychological needs stimulates the mechanisms of sublimation, including religious sublimation.

For those who espouse the theory of the eclipse of the sacred, conventional theories concerning the crisis of religion move predominantly within the analytical space of religious and cultural systems that lie behind the sublimations, which are then translated in a series of interpretations of the phenomenon that often contradict each other. For this reason a methodological turn is necessary.

In its first phase, the theory of the eclipse accounted for psychological components, but perhaps not adequately because of a lack of experimental data. Its initial formulation, developed in 1960–1, was exposed to criticism. After several years of debate in response to some of these critiques, a distinction between experience of the sacred and magical use of the sacred was introduced. However, further analysis (carried out within the psychology of religion) seems to validate the fundamental thesis of the theory of the eclipse of the sacred. This is especially true for Europe, but it is less so for other continents to the extent that they were shielded from the changes that are the expression of the consumer and technical scientific revolution. The situation changed during the 1970s and 1980s as great improvements in the experimental psychology of religion made it possible to verify the hypothesis. Experimental findings allowed it to be established that a vast area of religious experience exists outside the church, but also that – data in hand – the presence of religious experience is quite high among practitioners, is lower among non-practicing members of a religion, and is even lower among agnostics and atheists. In society today – especially in Europe and China – practitioners have decreased dramatically, and non-practitioners and agnostics have increased, and thus, generally, the presence of experience of the sacred has seriously declined. In conclusion, the supporters of the thesis of the eclipse of the sacred claim that it can be demonstrated that the crisis discussed in the early 1960s continues along the same trajectory.

The experimental methodology of the psychology of religion has made possible the measurement of the presence of religious experience and has led to a logical and methodological transformation in the formulation and the analysis of the problem. This methodology, according to many, is a sound analytical tool capable of verifying theories, data, and tendencies that otherwise would be difficult to understand and define, and it is able to confirm the (growing) size of the eclipse of the sacred. It is a pity the experimental application of the theory to Islamic religiousness is inadequate at present, even if some minor findings seem to make plausible the emergence of similar phenomena to that which has been found in Europe and other developed countries.

SEE ALSO: Atheism; Cults: Social Psychological Aspects; Materialism; Modernization; New Age; New Religious Movements; Religion, Sociology of; Religious Cults; Sacred; Sacred/Profane; Secularization; Spirituality, Religion, and Aging

REFERENCES AND SUGGESTED READINGS

Acquaviva, S. (1979 [1961]) *The Decline of the Sacred in Industrial Society*. Blackwell, Oxford.

Acquaviva, S. (1993) *Eros morte ed esperienza religiosa*. Laterza, Bari.

Acquaviva, S. (1999) L'esperienza religiosa alla soglia del terzo millennio. In: Acquaviva, S. & Scarsini, F. (Eds.), *Giovani sulle strade del Terzo millennio*. San Paolo, Turin.

Acquaviva, S. & Guizzardi, G. (1971) *Religione e irreligione nell'età postindustriale*. AVE, Rome.

Acquaviva, S. & Stella, R. (1989) *La fine di un'ideologia: la secolarizzazione*. Borla, Rome.

Cipriani, R. (2000) *Sociology of Religion: An Historical Introduction*. Aldine de Gruyter, New York.

D' Aquili, E. G. (2000) *Why God Won't Go Away: Brain Science and Biology*. Ballantine, New York.

D' Aquili, E. G. & Neuberg, B. A. (1999) *The Mystical Mind: Probing the Biology of Religious Experience*. Fortress Press, Philadelphia.

sacred/profane

William H. Swatos, Jr.

The significance of the sacred/profane distinction in sociology is to be most directly credited to Durkheim's *The Elementary Forms of the Religious Life* (1915), first published in France as *Les Formes élémentaires de la vie religieuse* in 1912. The distinction had an enormous direct effect in the sociology of religion, but also powerfully influenced the broader sociological theoretical paradigm of functionalism, since in the *Forms*, which was published at the culmination of a distinguished career, Durkheim saw religion as the bearer of the sacred and the sacred as maintaining social order or equilibrium. As *Forms* was the capstone work of Durkheim's career, "sacred" became the capstone of social structure. Hence, although the sacred/profane distinction is the device that Durkheim used to make his point, in fact *sacred* is the crucial concept within the distinction; that is, it is the concept of the sacred that makes the sacred/profane distinction theoretically powerful within functionalist sociology. Crucial to the widespread influence of Durkheim's specific paradigm was its integration into Talcott Parsons's *The Structure of Social Action* (1938), which became the foundational theory text for a generation of sociologists from the end of World War II until the mid-1960s – although when Parsons came to reformulate Durkheim in his own writings he substituted "supernatural" for sacred, something Durkheim consistently avoided because of its theological bias.

THE SACRED AND SOCIETY

The sacred/profane distinction lies at the heart of Durkheim's definition of religion in *Forms* (which was actually his second attempt at a definition, his first being generally unwieldy, and quickly discarded): "A religion is a unified system of beliefs and practices relative to sacred things, that is to say, things set apart and forbidden – beliefs and practices which unite into one single moral community called a Church, all who adhere to them" (Durkheim 1915: 47). The sacred thus involves *things set apart and forbidden.* Everything else is profane. As a result, "profane" is always easy to define: it is anything within a society (or social system/institution) that is not sacred. To come to this conclusion about the sacred and its role in establishing a "single moral community," Durkheim read anthropological works, specifically on the Australian aborigines and particularly the role of totems among clans or tribes of what were considered "primitive" peoples. This is the significance of the word *elementary* in the title of his book. He wanted to study what was generally considered in his day the simplest (or least complex) societies in existence anywhere in the world. Durkheim, like many other early sociologists, believed that by studying the maintenance of social organization among these peoples significant insights could be obtained about core processes that enabled societies to develop and maintain themselves – and, as a corollary, what changes in the transition to modernity might explain the emerging social problems of his day. Durkheim thus saw the sacred object as a symbol of society: in this totemic sense, "God" was really society. Religion was simultaneously a human social product, hence essentially false, and the producer of social order, hence powerfully true. "Education" was the process by which the symbolic realities contained within this "truth" were passed from generation to generation so that social structure could be maintained, hence function.

In the Parsonian synthesis that popularized and standardized Durkheim's definition for an especially formative generation of sociologists, the notion of "church" in the original Durkheimian formulation of the definition of religion was gradually secularized into "society" – that is, whereas Durkheim spoke quite specifically of a moral community "called a Church," later generations came to identify the moral community with society or in other cases with virtually any other ongoing social group. Rather tautologically, in fact, social scientists began to look for "the sacred" in all groupings and structures that one would not normally associate with religion – ranging as widely, for example, from the flag and related patriotic paraphernalia in the US, the tombs of Lenin and Stalin in the Soviet Union (where there were no formal state churches), to Babe Ruth's bat as sacred to baseball. This also led to some groups trying to create rituals and symbolic centers, as evidenced by various halls of fame or signs of identification – the flags of the Confederacy and Nazi Germany having particular significance at this writing. Regardless of the specific items or ceremonies of veneration, the underlying logic is the same: there must be some set-apart and forbidden object or objectifiable process both to create and maintain the structure and function of any social group.

This understanding of sacrality had a twofold effect on the study of both society and religion. On the one hand, it made religion an essential social institution: no religion, no society. On the other hand, it also said that while religion was good (functional), it was not true. That is, it reduced the end point of religion (the divine, in whatever name or form) to a social construction. One might almost say that at the level of society Durkheim served as religion's funeral director: embalming the corpse or providing an urn of ashes that sustained family unity as if the loved one were really there.

OUTCOMES AND CRITICISMS

The Janus-faced character of Durkheim's sacrality proposition led in at least two directions in the study of religion. The positive outcome was a significant corpus of work on political religion that flowed freely and broadly from an initial seminal essay by Parsons's former student Robert Bellah, "Civil Religion in America"

(1963). In this use, the concept refers to a "transcendent religion of the nation" and resonates well with the functionalism of both Durkheim and Parsons. Bellah's definition of American civil religion is that it is "an institutionalized collection of sacred beliefs about the American nation," which he sees symbolically expressed in America's founding documents and presidential inaugural addresses. It includes a belief in the existence of a transcendent being called "God," an idea that the American nation is subject to God's laws, and an assurance that God will guide and protect the US. Bellah sees these beliefs in the values of liberty, justice, charity, and personal virtue and concretized in, for example, the words *In God We Trust* on both national emblems and on the currency used in daily economic transactions. Although American civil religion shares much with the religion of Judeo-Christian denominations, Bellah claims that it is distinct from denominational religion. Crucial to Bellah's Durkheimian emphasis is the claim that civil religion is definitionally an "objective social fact."

Hence, although the civil religion thesis claims that civil religion exists *symbolically* in American culture, such symbols must be perceived and believed by people within the society if the symbols are to be said to have meaning. Several studies by Ronald Wimberley and others (1976) developed statements on civil religious beliefs and obtained responses on them from various public samples. Their findings show that people do affirm civil religious beliefs, although most would not know what the term "civil religion" means. These large surveys and factor analytic studies give credence to Bellah's conceptual argument that civil religion is a distinct cultural component within American society that is not captured either by American politics or by denominational religiosity. The result of both Bellah's initial conceptual foray and these empirical studies has not only established the validity and usefulness of the civil religion concept in understanding important cultural and social dynamics within American society, but also spawned comparative studies around the world – Crystal Lane's studies of the former Soviet Union being particularly significant.

Ironically, a move away from functionalism generally in sociology beginning in the late 1960s brought in its wake first secularization theory, and then a reaction against the Durkheimian (or Parsonian-Durkheimian) formulation as an adequate understanding of religion. The term *secularization* was coined quite apart from Durkheim by Max Weber, who used it as a way of conceptualizing the process by which the world was "robbed of gods." In many respects Weber would have seen Durkheim as part of that process, since Durkheim himself was influenced by an ongoing French tradition that looked toward a "religion of Humanity." Parsons, however, attempted an integration of Durkheim and Weber in the *Structure of Social Action*, hence secularization became integrated into a neo-Durkheimian framework. C. Wright Mills (1959: 32–3), one of Parsons's most trenchant early critics, critically summarizes Parsons's religious historiography: "Once the world was filled with the sacred – in thought, practice, and institutional form. After the Reformation and the Renaissance, the forces of modernization swept across the globe and secularization, a corollary historical process, loosened the dominance of the sacred. In due course, the sacred shall disappear altogether except, possibly, in the private realm." Although many social scientists had come to accept this analysis, which implies historical description, it is in fact based on almost no historical evidence. Rather than systematic studies of the past, it draws from commonsense generalizations about history related to systematic studies of the present. Put differently, the aborigines of 1900 were just as "contemporary" as the French of 1900.

Secularization theory hence led to antisecularization theory, which amounted to a rethinking of both religion and sacrality in the Durkheimian context. Runciman (1970: 98) has raised three specific issues regarding the Durkheimian approach, the most telling of which is that Durkheim's "explanation" of religious beliefs in a this-worldly terminus (society) does not actually "explain" them at all (except to explain them away): "Why, after all," Runciman asks, "is the worship of society any more readily explicable than the worship of gods?" Intimately connected with this "explanation," however, is Durkheim's search for the source of social solidarity, and behind this is his *presumption* of solidarity. The integrating power in society of religion is *not*, in fact, what Durkheim would call a "social fact," but a largely unsubstantiated social anthropological *belief* stemming from Durkheimian sources. This belief underlies the "religion" of secularization; that is, contemporary secularization theory is based on the view that religion is defined by religion's "function" of social integration or the maintenance of social solidarity. Not only is the notion of solidarity as definitive of society now suspect (Beyer 1989), but even if we do accept some concept of solidarity into our sociological arsenal, there is no reason to presume an integrated wholeness that certainly is now difficult to see, and may well have never existed. On the one hand, this may be evidenced by the observation that many so-called primitive societies do not, strictly speaking, have a linguistic equivalent for the word "religion" (our "way" or "culture" being both better translations), while people in advanced industrial societies increasingly express a preference for describing themselves as "spiritual" rather than religious. What is especially missing in this shift is the relative absence of Durkheim's hope that the "sacred" would become a "religion of humanity" (viz., morality), which is an increasingly rationalized and bureaucratized civilizational element associated with formal boards of ethical review, hence more a matter of the sociology of law and industrial/work relations than of religion and culture.

SEE ALSO: Asceticism; Durkheim, Émile; Ideal Type; Jehovah's Witnesses; Networks; Primitive Religion; Religion, Sociology of; Sacred; Sacred, Eclipse of the; Scientology; Weber, Max

REFERENCES AND SUGGESTED READINGS

Bellah, R. (1963) Civil Religion in America. *Dædalus* 96: 1–21.

Beyer, P. (1989) Globalization and Inclusion. In: Swatos, W. H., Jr. (Ed.), *Religious Politics in Global and Comparative Perspective*. Greenwood Press, New York, pp. 39–53.

Durkheim, E. (1915) *The Elementary Forms of the Religious Life*. Allen & Unwin, London.

Lane, C. (1981) *Rites of Rulers*. Cambridge University Press, Cambridge.

Mills, C. W. (1959) *The Sociological Imagination*. Oxford University Press, New York.

Runciman, W. G. (1970) *Sociology in Its Place*. Cambridge University Press, Cambridge.

Swatos, W. H., Jr. (1999) Revisiting the Sacred. *Implicit Religion* 2: 33–8.

Wimberley, R. C. (1976) Testing the Civil Religion Hypothesis. *Sociological Analysis* 37: 341–52.

Wimberly, R. C. et al. (1976) The Civil Religious Dimension. *Social Forces* 54: 890–900.

sacrifice

Simone Ghiaroni

Sacrifice is a ritual practice that includes the removal of goods (objects, vegetables, animals, human beings) from profane use or their destruction in relation to a supernatural sphere, but not necessarily with an offer or dedication. Sacrifices that involve the killing of a victim and the shedding of blood are called blood sacrifices.

The issue of the definition of sacrifice, a focal point in contemporary debate, went so far as to deny the empirical existence of a ritual identifiable as a sacrifice. Marcel Detienne (Detienne & Vernant 1986) criticized the concept, claiming that it was an arbitrary category built on elements drawn from the Christian tradition and adopted in order to lump different phenomena together. The study of sacrifice should therefore be based on a historical analysis of the rituals within their own contexts. Thus, for instance, Grecian sacrifice turns out to be nothing but a culinary practice; there does not exist any ritual designated as a sacrifice, but simply a meat-eating mode of a historically determined human group. In Detienne's view, the concept of sacrifice should be dropped because it is a "category of yesterday's thought" that has no interpretive or descriptive value. Detienne hit the mark when he recognized the Christian inheritance underlying many theories of sacrifice, but many scholars felt that the dissolution of the concept of sacrifice was an interpretive impoverishment. Seeking refuge in historical particularism is not the solution to the problem of definition: the concept of sacrifice still has a heuristic value and is an excellent instrument for interpreting some social facts. The solution consists rather in replacing a rigid, clear-cut definition with a more flexible, inclusive family of notions. The concept of sacrifice turns out to be a modern theoretical construction that is useful for analysis but has been devised artificially in order to interpret a category of phenomena interconnected by family resemblances (Valeri 1994). The noun "sacrifice" does not correspond, in the real world, to any unequivocally defined substance: it denotes a group of social facts among which it is possible to trace analogies based on some common criteria. As Ivan Strenski (2003) pointed out, the modern study of sacrifice cannot be founded on theological bases, identifying an ideal central concept that is essential in all types of sacrifice, for instance offer or abnegation: it is necessary to analyze the formal characteristics of the rites that can be interpreted as sacrifices. In this sense, Strenski recognizes the study of sacrifice by Durkheim's followers Hubert and Mauss (1964 [1899]) as a scientific attempt to achieve emancipation from an ethnocentric and Christian outlook.

Among the phenomena that are subsumed into the category "sacrifice," three main types can be distinguished: *firstfruit offer*, *gift-sacrifice*, and *communion*. Firstfruit offer consists in leaving to the supernatural sphere a part of the goods obtained from hunting or collecting, concentrating sacrality on that part and thus desacralizing the remaining part so it can be eaten by men and women without any danger. Gift-sacrifice consecrates and offers to the supernatural world a part of the goods produced by human labor. Communion sacrifice, finally, is the sacrifice rite that stresses the communal consumption of the sacrificial victim. From a formal point of view, a sacrifice rite comprises four main stages: the obtaining and preparation of the sacrificial object, its destruction or removal from the human sphere, renunciation, and consumption. Within the ritual, it is possible to isolate and analyze three types of relationships: between human beings and the superhuman world, between human beings and the victim, and among human beings. The combination and emphasizing of different stages and relationships, and of the kind of object that is sacrificed, determine the type of sacrifice.

Various theories of sacrifice have been produced within the analysis of religious practices. On the whole, they are aligned with distinct theoretical lines: some are based on utilitarian ideas; some emphasize emotional and religious aspects; some highlight the symbolic and communicative nature of the rite; some neglect the social and cultural aspects and stress the importance of attention to pure violence; and others underscore the ecological function of rituals. Moreover, in the history of theories there is a constant intertwining of themes such as the idea of reciprocality between the human world and the supernatural one; offer and gift; debt and credit between humankind and deity; self-sacrifice and abnegation; and, finally, the themes of the scapegoat, the symbolic replacement of the sacrifier with the victim, violence, consecration, and desacralization.

One of the first theories of sacrifice was proposed in 1871 by the evolutionist-anthropologist Edward B. Tylor in his work *Primitive Culture*. Tylor interpreted sacrifice on the basis of the utilitarian principle of *do ut des* ("I give that you may give"): "primitives," in his view, offer gifts to the extrahuman powers in order to gain their benevolence, in the same way as gifts are offered to high-ranking people. This practice was included in the general evolutionary scale: a *self-interested gift* aiming at a reward was followed, at a more "civilized" evolutionary stage, by a *free gift* that did not hope for a reward, and, finally, by *abnegation*, self-sacrifice, the highest expression of the moral evolution of humankind. Tylor did not seek an explanation of the mechanism of sacrifice, and failed to recognize the symbolic aspects of the offer, regarding it only as "material goods." Moreover, since he concentrated entirely on the ideal content of the rite, he did not account for the widespread custom of partly or totally eating the sacrificial victim. This was attempted by the Scottish scholar William Robertson Smith by supplying, in his *Lectures on the Religion of Semites* (1894), an early "sociological" explanation of sacrifice, based on the theory of totemism. In Smith's opinion, the function of the sacrificial rite was to reinforce the bonds within the totemic community through the sharing of a sacrificial meal. The latter was the only occasion in which it was possible to kill and eat the totemic animal, symbol of the community, regarded as the common ancestor. The commensals, by eating this animal, strengthened the social bonds among themselves and the ideal ones between them and the deity. Within the evolutionist area, another contribution was contained in James G. Frazer's monumental work *The Golden Bough* (*editio maior* published in the period 1911–15). In sacrifice, Frazer picked out the intertwining of two themes: that of the scapegoat and that of the ritual killing of the "divine king." Sacrifice is based on the analogy between the health of the king and that of his community: when the king's health begins to decline, he must be killed, in order to ensure the stability of the kingdom. All the evil, guilt, and sins of the subjects are conveyed into the sovereign's body and atoned for by the king's sacrifice. Moreover, Frazer, focusing on the sphere of agrarian sacrifices and beginning from the idea of the totemic relationship with the victim and of its sacred character, analyzed the "killing of the Corn-spirit." According to him, the gods are killed because they take on the role of scapegoat, sweeping away disease, death, and sin from the community, and are eaten in order to be assimilated. Frazer's theory does not add much to Smith's contribution, except for a Christian sense of atonement and purification of the human world through the sacrifice of the god.

Dissatisfied with these idealistic theories, in 1899, Durkheim's followers Henri Hubert and Marcel Mauss published their fundamental contribution to the study of sacrifice, entitled *Essai sur la nature et la fonction du sacrifice* (*Sacrifice: Its Nature and Function*), which decisively broke away from the evolutionist approach of the previous theories. They defined sacrifice as a religious act that – through the consecration of the victim – changes the state of the person who performs it and the sacrality state of certain objects involved in the ritual. This definition immediately reveals the difference between this theory and the previous ones: here sacrifice is no longer a mere oblation performed in the hope of a reward or with the purpose of reinforcing social relationships, but a process of consecration and transformation of the people who take part in the rite. Moreover, the victim takes on the role of a mediator between the sacred sphere and the profane one, and the entire sacrificial process is therefore interpreted as a process of communication between the sacred and the profane through an intermediary that is destroyed during the ceremony. The mediation and subsequent destruction of the mediator are made necessary by the dangerous, "untouchable" character of the sacred sphere in Durkheim's view: no human being can come into contact with any sacred entity without undergoing harmful consequences. As Valeri (1985: 64–5) remarks, the mediation does not logically make it necessary for the sacrificed commodity to be interpreted as an offering: the concept of sacrifice as communication is broader than that of sacrifice as a gift to the supernatural world. In addition, referring to Mauss's celebrated *Essai sur le don* (*The Gift*) (1990 [1923–4]), there is a much more complex vision of the meaning of an offer of goods. The gift must be interpreted in its social and symbolic dimension in "primitive" societies, that is, as a social fact consisting in the obligation to *give*, *receive*, and *requite*, and as if each gift metonymically implied a self-offering of the sacrifier. Within this theory, there appears a new conception of the sacrificial offer: in relation to this idea of gift and as a result of the fact that the victim becomes a mediator between the sacred and the profane, the sacrificial offer becomes a symbolic substitute of the sacrifier. Moreover, Hubert's and Mauss's study is the first one that undertakes a formal analysis of the "pattern of sacrifice," implements used, and ritual procedures. This attention to the technical and formal procedures leads the two sociologists to include the ritual stages of the sacrificial process in a parabola of sacrality. At the top of this parabola is the killing of the victim, preceded by a period of increasing consecration and followed by relative desacralization, important for enabling the human utilization of the victim's flesh and the reintroduction of the participants into the profane world. In a similar way, this interest in the material aspects leads to an analysis of the ritual space, outlining a pattern of concentric circles that correspond to different levels of sacrality, with the altar or sacrificial pole at the center. This study, finally, has the merit of stabilizing the terms that define the participants in the rite. According to this classification, the person who benefits from the sacrifice and undergoes its effects, and who usually supplies the victim, is called the *sacrifier*, while the officiant (sometimes a priest) who guides or materially carries out the sacrifice is called the *sacrificer*.

Besides Hubert's and Mauss's sociological reaction, there were other theories of sacrifice that aimed at removing from this concept the utilitarian ideas introduced by Tylor. Among them, the most significant were those of the philosopher Georges Gusdorf, the Protestant theologian Jan van Baal, and the scholar in phenomenology of religions Gerardus van der Leeuw. Gusdorf, in his book *L'Expérience humaine du sacrifice* (*The Human Experience of Sacrifice*), published in 1948, reversed the traditional perspective of *do ut des*, contending that the sacrificial offer was the recognition of an unrepayable preexisting debt toward the divine sphere: human beings, perpetually indebted to the gods who sustained their existence, were forced to give, without ever completely discharging their life debt. Van Baal, on the contrary, argued that the sacrificial gift was a disinterested expression of submission to the divine sphere, without any expectation of a reward: thus he included all sacrifices in the third stage outlined by Tylor, that of abnegation. The development of the Tylorian theme of *do ut des* by van der Leeuw, in his book of 1933 entitled *Phänomenologie der Religion* (*Religion in Essence and Manifestations*), advanced the idea that in sacrifice the gift always consisted in the offer of oneself, thus bringing something of the sacrifier in the sphere of the sacred. This took place in relation to the law of participation – detected in pre-logic thought by Lucien Lévy-Bruhl – whereby a person's possessions were an integral part of his or her personality, so any sacrificial offer was always an offer of oneself.

Referring to Hubert's and Mauss's idea of sacrifice as a rite that is significant in all its parts and not only in a special aspect such as the offer, gift, or communion, Alfred Loisy, in his *Essai historique sur le sacrifice* (*Historical Essay on Sacrifice*) of 1920, regarded sacrifice as an efficacious representation, a symbolic action that produced some effects on social reality. The rite is allegedly a representation of the result that the sacrifier wishes to achieve, performed by means of the manipulation of icons and symbols. The meaning of the sacrificial victim, therefore, does not consist in its value as a commodity for exchange or communion, but in the symbolic semantics it exhibits. In other words, it is not so much a gift as an icon that represents the extrahuman powers, the human beings, the sacrifier, and their interrelationships. This theoretical line was followed also by the British anthropologist Godfrey Lienhardt (1961), who argued that sacrifice controls and solves situations of conflict or uncertainty by manipulating the symbols involved in the ritual. In his opinion, these symbols, like the gods, are representations or reified images that reflect the experience of social life.

The social anthropologist Edward E. Evans-Pritchard (1956) proposed a criticism of the social and communal visions of sacrifice like those of Smith and of Hubert and Mauss, starting from a perspective of communication between the individual and the superhuman powers. Evans-Pritchard focused on personal and expiatory sacrifices. The need for expiation, in his view, depends on the danger resulting from the intervention of the spirits in the human world: this is a criticism of the totemic-origin theories that regard sacrifice as a union between the supernatural world and the human one. The function of the gift is to separate these two worlds through the symbolic replacement of the sacrifier with the victim, which is accepted by the extrahuman powers in the sacrifier's stead. In Evans-Pritchard's view, sacrifice always has an apotropaic (that wards off evil) and prophylactic function (that defends and protects), expressed through the polysemanticity of the sacrificial victim, which acts as a substitute of the sacrifier, a scapegoat and a mediator between the gods and humankind. Thus the sacrificial rite is celebrated in case of diseases or other negative events caused by an intervention of the gods due to a misdeed. Evans-Pritchard's vision, which emphasizes the concepts of guilt, sin, remorse, and purification, seems to be strongly influenced by Christian theology.

In the opinion of the Belgian anthropologist Luc de Heusch (1986), on the contrary, even the sacrifice of the Nuer, to which Evans-Pritchard refers, should not be understood in terms of individual guilt or expiation, but in terms of the restoration of cosmological order. De Heusch, as a matter of fact, maintains that a structured thought (similar to that outlined by Claude Lévi-Strauss about myths) underlies the various sacrificial systems. For this reason, any sacrifice must be deciphered on the basis of the symbolic and mythological structure it postulates, produces, and reproduces. As regards the African sacrificial systems, de Heusch attempts a structural reunification of them by making use of the notion of sacrificial debt and of reproduction of the cosmogonal myths from which humankind's life debt began.

The anthropologist Valerio Valeri (1985) advanced a theory of sacrifice that referred directly to the tradition that interpreted sacrifice as an efficacious symbolic action. In Valeri's view, sacrifice is a cognitive and communicative instrument that makes it possible – within the framework provided by the ritual context – for the sacrifier and the overall society to obtain information about their position in the social world. This position is defined by the contact with the supernatural sphere, regarded as a paradigmatic model of the ideal social order. Sacrifice, therefore, is allegedly a symbolic process having a dialectic nature: the subjective *self* of the sacrifier, through the sacrificial substitution, takes on the value of its antithesis, that is, of the extrahuman powers; thus, at the end of the rite, a synthesis is achieved that amounts to a *process of objectification of the subject in the social world*. Sacrifice as *dialectics of the subject* makes it possible to "tune in" the social properties of the subject to the ideal properties of the transcendent subject. The result of the sacrifice is thus the recovery of the sacrifier's awareness of his/her position in the social world. Moreover, Valeri (1994) maintains that in the sacrificial exchange, what must be highlighted is not the renunciation but the benefits and the symbolic or material enjoyment that issue from it.

Other theories regard the violence of the sacrificial killing as the central element of sacrifice. According to René Girard (1977), every sacrifice is a mechanism of expulsion of the violence inherent in social life. Mutual, widespread violence, introduced by a primeval "society-founding lynching" committed on an innocent victim, is allegedly concentrated on a single object, the victim of the sacrifice, which always appears as a scapegoat. In Girard's theory, the sacrificial violence does not mean anything more than itself: he inverts the theory of consecration by arguing that the victim is not killed because it is sacred, but is sacred precisely because it must be killed. The violence of the sacrifice must be kept distant from the level of consciousness, and, for this reason, the expelled violence is, at the same time, an unacknowledged violence. This theory assumes that the psychological datum can be attained transcending any cultural form; the latter is thus treated like a false motivation or hypocritical rationalization. The Hellenist Walter Burkert (1987), too, places violence at the center of his interpretation of sacrifice. He maintains that humankind's phylogenetic heritage, formed during the Paleolithic hunting and collecting period, involved the development of a violence between individuals that was expelled and transcended through hunting. When sedentary agriculture set in, the inherited violence was transferred to the killing of farmed animals in specific ritual settings that ensured the peaceable perpetuation of human society: this was the origin of sacrifices.

Besides these theories, there are others that emphasize the material aspect and ecological function of sacrifice. According to Marvin Harris (1977), the sacrifice of human beings or animals followed by the sharing of the victim's flesh is correlated with the availability of noble protein in the diet and with the examined population's technical and environmental possibility of breeding animals. In Roy Rappaport's (2000 [1968]) view, on the contrary, the sacrifice of a great number of pigs by a population of New Guinea took on a homeostatic function in the ecological balance between the population and the resources. Rappaport endeavored to evaluate the capability of that particular ecosystem to sustain the human population and a growing pig population, with reference to a periodic sacrificial feast during which the number of pigs was drastically cut down, bringing the ecological system back to a state of equilibrium.

Besides the interpretation of sacrifice as a ritual, it is possible to regard sacrifice as a special case within a broader system of practices pertaining to symbolic classification, manipulation, and consumption of living creatures (Douglas 1966; Lévi-Strauss 1968). In sacrifice, the symbolic correlations by which the natural and social world is regulated become evident: for instance, the relation between dietary prohibitions, the animal offered in the sacrifice, and the division of the victim's flesh, understood also as a practice that reproduces the social hierarchy. It is important, moreover, to highlight the relation between sacrifice and divination, not only as an examination of the body of the victim or of some of its parts, but also as a divinatory practice based on the observation of the progress of the rite (interpreting, for instance, the victim's movements). Finally, it is useful to draw attention to the question of the discontinuation or survival of the sacrificial themes. Blood sacrifice does not survive only in "exotic" religions, and the sacrificial themes – though subjected to transformation and abstraction – are still present in the great monotheistic religions, for instance in the Catholic sacrament of the Eucharist, which reintroduces the salvific death of a divine victim with an expiatory function.

SEE ALSO: Durkheim, Émile; Religion; Rite/Ritual; Ritual; Sacred; Sacred/Profane; Symbolic Classification

REFERENCES AND SUGGESTED READINGS

Bloch, M. (1992) *Prey into Hunter: The Politics of Religious Experience.* Cambridge University Press, Cambridge.

Burkert, W. (1987) *Homo Necans: Anthropology of Ancient Greek Sacrificial Ritual and Myth.* Trans. P. Bing. University of California Press, Berkeley.

Detienne, M. & Vernant, J.-P. (Eds.) (1986) *The Cuisine of Sacrifice Among the Greeks.* Trans. P. Wissing. University of Chicago Press, Chicago.

Douglas, M. (1966) *Purity and Danger: An Analysis of Concepts of Pollution and Taboo.* Routledge & Kegan Paul, London.

Durkheim, É. (1995 [1912]) *The Elementary Forms of Religious Life: The Totemic System in Australia.* Trans. K. E. Fields. Free Press, New York.

Evans-Pritchard, E. E. (1956) *Nuer Religion.* Oxford University Press, New York and Oxford.

Girard, R. (1977) *Violence and the Sacred.* Trans. P. Gregory. Johns Hopkins University Press, Baltimore.

Grottanelli, C. (1999) *Il sacrificio.* Laterza, Rome.

Harris, M. (1977) *Cannibals and Kings: The Origins of Culture.* Random House, New York.

Heusch, L. de (1986) *Sacrifice in Africa.* Manchester University Press, Manchester.

Hubert, H. & Mauss, M. (1964 [1899]) *Sacrifice: Its Nature and Function.* University of Chicago Press, Chicago.

Lévi-Strauss, C. (1968) *The Savage Mind.* University of Chicago Press, Chicago.

Lienhardt, G. (1961) *Divinity and Experience: The Religion of the Dinka.* Oxford, Clarendon Press.

Mauss, M. (1990 [1923–4]) *The Gift: The Form and Reason for Exchange in Archaic Societies.* Trans. W. D. Halls. Norton, New York.

Rappaport, R. (2000 [1968]) *Pigs for Ancestors: Ritual in the Ecology of New Guinea People.* Waveland Press, Long Grove.

Strenski, I. (2002) *Contesting Sacrifice: Religion, Nationalism, and Social Thought in France.* University of Chicago Press, Chicago.

Strenski, I. (2003) *Theology and the First Theory of Sacrifice.* Leiden, Brill.

Valeri, V. (1985) *Kingship and Sacrifice: Ritual and Society in Ancient Hawaii.* University of Chicago Press, Chicago.

Valeri, V. (1994) Wild Victims: Hunting as Sacrifice and Sacrifice as Hunting in Huaulu. *History of Religions* 34(2): 101–31.

sadomasochism

Gert Hekma

The word sadomasochism refers to sexual pleasure in physical or psychic pain or humiliation. The psychiatrist Richard von Krafft-Ebing coined the word in 1891. It stems from the names of the philosopher Marquis Donatien Alphonse François de Sade (1740–1814) and the novelist Leopold von Sacher-Masoch (1836–95). Both men were primarily masochists. Sociological research on sadomasochism, its practitioners and their subcultures, is rare. In the arts, the subject is abundantly available and both literary historians and philosophers have discussed it more than have social scientists. The life and work of the men who lent their names to this sexual variation have been the subject of many studies, especially the Marquis de Sade.

Although there can be little doubt that earlier generations erotically enjoyed violence, for example in the Roman arenas, at scaffolds, for martyrs depicted in Christian art, and with religious and medical flagellations, the specific articulation of feelings of sexual pleasure in pain goes back to the eighteenth century, when Jean-Jacques Rousseau and the Marquis de Sade expressed such emotions. In the *Psychopathia Sexualis* (1886) of Krafft-Ebing, the desire for giving and receiving real or imaginary pain is put on a scale. This psychiatrist found it normal when such pleasures were an addition to sexual play, but they became an abnormality when they were its central element. The prevention and therapy of "perverted" sexual identities was the work of psychiatrists. The Greek neologism "algolagnia" (pleasure in pain) was an alternative word, while later psychiatrists created new terms for the many specific forms of sadomasochism (whipping, bondage, hanging, slavery, military or police uniforms, use of excrement). Objects of this psychiatric interest welcomed the handbooks of sexology that offered the rare possibility of identification and excitement (Oosterhuis 2000). Nineteenth-century England had bordellos for the spanking of men who learned to enjoy this pleasure as boys at boarding school.

Oosterhuis (2000) explains the invention of the various perversions as a result of growing self-reflection and individualism and of the anonymity in the quickly expanding metropoles. Noyes (1998) has argued that s/m became visible in this liberal era at the end of the nineteenth century also because this sexual practice so completely contradicted liberal ideals of free will and self-determination. The issue of consent of the masochist partner remains an essential point of discussion in s/m circles, as his or her dependent position flatly contradicts modern ideas of erotic equality and free choice. The answer of the aficionados has been that the submissive partner consents beforehand with the choreography of the erotic scene and can stop its continuation with code words or signs. While many abhor the real or imaginary violence of s/m, few practitioners have dared to take pride in its transgressiveness, certainly not when it gets beyond liberal issues of consent. Notwithstanding restrictive sexual ideologies, modern sexual citizens continue to believe in a liberal ideology of free choice and erotic equality that feeds their unrealistic, romantic ideas of love and pleasure.

Specialized s/m subcultures developed first in Germany from 1900 and later in other places after World War II. Bordellos took a central place in this world. The sexual revolution saw a further rise in organizations and in representations of s/m in novels, movies, and porn. The subcultural imagery of leather and sex toys made a breakthrough in the 1980s in the punk scene and in the 1990s in fashion and music. Notwithstanding its cultural popularity, psychiatric handbooks such as the latest editions of the *Diagnostic and Statistical Manual of Mental Disorders* (DSM) continue to consider sadism and masochism to be psychic disturbances. Nowadays its best-known expression is the gay and straight leather scene, while the Internet has many sites and chat rooms for the manifold variations of s/m desire. Its followers see no reason why psychiatrists and psychologists declare them insane. Their fantasies are obvious examples of the social construction of sexual pleasure, as their contents always refer to concrete external stimuli such as soldiers, bikers, slavery, rape, child beating, and medical care, while unpleasant, cruel, and humiliating scenes are transformed into excitement. Sociologists have rarely taken up this fascinating topic of how the social has become so deeply embedded in the individual psyche.

The contemporary literature on sadomasochism takes most often a psychological stance, discussing its individual manifestations and issues of consent (Phillips 1998). Most surveys of its practitioners were made some time ago (Spengler 1979). The work of Gosselin and Wilson (1980) relates the great variety of sadomasochistic desires. These authors were sympathetic to this world while others took a negative stance. General surveys asked few questions on sadomasochism, but the data indicate that some 10 percent of the respondents admit having kinky fantasies. Historical studies focus on the nineteenth-century history of perversion and discuss the invention of sadomasochism or specialized kinky tastes (Noyes 1998; Oosterhuis 2000). Vandermeersch (2002) researched the path of flagellation from religious practice and medical therapy to sexual specialty. More sociological works studied kinky scenes and desires in relation to spaces (Rubin 1991). Most literature includes both personal and emancipatory perspectives or discussions on politics (Thompson 1991; Thompson 1994; Califia 1994).

Methodological issues are similar to those regarding other sexual variations. Additional problems concern the sometimes criminal and often pathological status of sadomasochism. Research may endanger the safety and privacy of respondents, while many practitioners feel ashamed, guilty, or insecure on their preferences. Most literature still stems from psychiatry and psychology and follows the dated ideas from the DSM. It means that researchers of kinky sex have to be particularly sensitive to the social discrimination that their subjects are facing.

As few studies have been done on sadomasochism, the terrain is open. Main issues will be the roots of these sexual preferences in their social context and their subcultural, historical, and spatial development. Sadomasochism is interesting for sociology because it mixes sexuality and violence and eroticizes social inequality, going against a trend that promotes non-violent and equal sexual relations. It shows as well through its many variations the specificity of sexual pleasures that sociologists in general neglect. The research on sexual scripts, stories, or narratives should take kinky variations as its topic because they are a concrete example of the connection between individual desires and social worlds. The social and historical backgrounds of s/m preferences and organizing are still hidden in the dark and offer interesting themes for further research in their connections to liberal politics, the rise of individualism and self-reflection, the belief in consent and equality, and the denial of violence in sexual relations.

SEE ALSO: Liberalism; Plastic Sexuality; Scripting Theories; Sexual Practices; Sexuality Research: History; Violence

REFERENCES AND SUGGESTED READINGS

Califia, P. (1994) *Public Sex: The Culture of Radical Sex.* Cleis Press, Pittsburgh.

Gosselin, C. & Wilson, G. (1980) *Sexual Variations: Fetishism, Sadomasochism and Transvestism.* Simon & Schuster, New York.

Noyes, J. K. (1998) *The Mastery of Submission: Inventions of Masochism.* Cornell University Press, Ithaca, NY.

Oosterhuis, H. (2000) *Stepchildren of Nature: Krafft-Ebing, Psychiatry, and the Making of Sexual Identity.* University of Chicago Press, Chicago.

Phillips, A. (1998) *A Defence of Masochism.* Faber & Faber, London.

Rubin, G. (1991) The Catacombs: A Temple of the Butthole. In: Thompson, M. (Ed.), *Leatherfolk: Radical Sex, People, Politics and Practice.* Alyson, Boston, 1991, pp. 119–41.

Spengler, A. (1979) *Sadomasochisten und ihre Subkulturen.* Campus, Frankfurt.

Squires, J. (Ed.) (1993) Perversity. Special issue of *New Formations* 19 (Spring).

Thompson, B. (1994) *Sadomasochism: Painful Perversion or Pleasurable Play?* Cassell, London.

Thompson, M. (Ed.) (1991) *Leatherfolk: Radical Sex, People, Politics and Practice.* Alyson, Boston.

Vandermeersch, P. (2002) *La Chair de la passion. Une histoire de foi: la flagellation.* Cerf, Paris.

Weinberg, T. & Levi Kamel, G. W. (Eds.) (1983) *S and M: Studies in Sadomasochism.* Prometheus, New York.

safer sex

Benjamin Shepard

Safer sex emerged as a strategy to prevent the spread of disease with the advent of the AIDS epidemic in the early 1980s. Richard Berkowitz and Michael Callen, two gay New Yorkers, first outlined the theory and application of safer sex in their 1983 tract, "How to Have Sex in an Epidemic." As an alternative to the confusing, all-or-nothing early approaches to HIV prevention, safer sex offered a practical strategy. People were going to have sex. As such, it was best to do it in a safe, mutually satisfying, caring manner. Berkowitz and Callen presented a harm-reduction approach now recognized around the world as a model that allows for both intimacy and protection.

The third key inventor of safer sex was Dr. Joseph Sonnabend, a gay-friendly doctor working in a Greenwich Village health clinic who treated Berkowitz, who was working as a hustler at the time. In the course of frequent appointments for antibiotics to battle VD, Berkowitz and Sonnabend developed a frank relationship. When Berkowitz developed a case of hepatitis, swollen lymph nodes, and a bump behind his ear that got in the way of his cruising, Sonnabend counseled him to stop "screwing around." It was not a welcome piece of advice for someone whose livelihood depended on sexual commerce. In 1982, as the health crisis mounted, Sonnabend engaged Berkowitz and another patient, the late Michael Callen, to write a call for gay men to protect themselves. "You must celebrate gay sex in your writing and give men support," Sonnabend counseled (Berkowitz 2003: 121). At first, Berkowitz and Callen borrowed from the "just say no" rhetoric of the early 1980s, but the response was negative.

One day Berkowitz received a knock on his door from one of his former clients, begging for services. Berkowitz pulled out two gloves to create a safe seal between himself and his client. This led to a eureka-like recognition. It dawned on Berkowitz that prohibition is more dangerous than acknowledgment, careful expression, and prevention. Before this, it had never occurred to Berkowitz, Callen, or Sonnabend that latex offered the necessary life-saving compromise. Berkowitz and Callen drew on the lessons of gay liberation to draft "How to Have Sex in an Epidemic." The result was a revolution allowing for personal and political protection, both for sex and for the movement that liberated it. With time, safer sex practices spread around the globe as a theoretical and practical approach to preventing the spread of HIV. Safer sex became the model for sex-positive discourses that rejected the politics of sexual shame, temperance, and prohibition.

For more than 20 years, safer sex has been a key element in debates about effective HIV prevention. Queer theorist and activist Douglas Crimp (1988) argues that gay people invented safe sex based on an implicit understanding that sexuality comes in many forms. Sex, after all, is not limited to penetration. For Crimp, the lessons of queer "promiscuity" can be understood in terms of multiple understandings of the possibility and multiplicity of pleasures. Thus, the gay public sexual cultures of previous decades resulted in a sort of "psychic preparation" and appetite for experimentation, which cultivated a culture which was capable of absorbing wide-ranging changes in sexual norms and practices.

Crimp's words suggest that safer sex can be understood as a cornerstone of a harm-reduction approach to sexuality. Harm reduction sets out to "meet people where they're at" instead of where others want them to be. Advocates of safer sex argued that messages that promote prohibition without offering alternatives push people into unnecessarily high-risk behavior. HIV prevention could be most effective through community-based approaches that built on personal connections.

The safer sex message is that practices – not places – cause HIV transmission. While prohibitionists sought to close down spaces where gay men congregate to have sex, safer sex advocates promoted these spaces as sites for education. Prevention activists and peer outreach workers could reach people where they were having sex and establish healthy community norms and grassroots models of peer-based HIV prevention and mutual protection. In 1997 Allan Bérubé argued: "These activities, sex outside the home, I call it – they need to be preserved and used to eroticize safer sex, and to take advantage of the fact that men are already congregating." As such, HIV prevention work should take place in tearooms, parks, bathhouses, theaters, bookstores, and other places where people meet for sex.

A decade after the invention of safer sex, reports suggested that many men who "knew better" continued to have unsafe sex. Walt Odets, a clinical psychologist who has a private practice working with gay men in Berkeley, California, reported that many men he saw reported that practicing safer sex for a lifetime was not sustainable. Odets contended that the standard "100 Percent Safe All the Time" AIDS prevention message was ill conceived and needed to be reconsidered. For Odets, unsafe sex had to be viewed as a response to ambiguous feelings in an environment saturated with death, crisis, guilt, and depression. Unlike advertising campaigns, Odets sought to embrace the complexities of queer sexuality. Prevention activists and therapists across the country called for new approaches to HIV prevention (Patton 1996). "HIV prevention requires taking into account the diversity of people's sex lives, that prevention should be grounded in people's desires and pleasures," Michael Warner argued (Smith 1998). The result was a wave of discussions in the late 1990s referred to as the Sex Panic debate or the Gay Men's Sex Wars.

Future research will need to contend with the problems of safer sex and explore alternative technologies, such as microbicides, which can serve as substitutes for latex. In the two decades since the birth of safer sex, new practices of safer sexual activity have emerged. These include community-based approaches such as "jack off" clubs, where men meet to have the safest type of safe sex – mutual masturbation – and more distant approaches such as telephone sex and cybersex. As Waskul (2003) elaborates: "In outercourse, images and/or words fully replace the corporal body as they are crafted among participants to represent the whole of sexual and erotic interactions between them." Thus, while corporal sexual pleasure takes place between bodies, Waskul concludes, "the pleasures of outercourse are encapsulated in dislocated and disembodied erotic communication where participants latently rearrange taken-for-granted relationships between bodies, selves, and situated social interactions" (p. 73).

SEE ALSO: AIDS, Sociology of; Oral Sex; Queer Theory; Sex Education; Sex Panics; Sexual Practices; Sexual Health

REFERENCES AND SUGGESTED READINGS

Berkowitz, R. (2003) *Stayin' Alive: The Invention of Safe Sex, A Personal History*. Westview Press/ Perseus Books, Cambridge, MA.

Berkowitz, R. & Callen, M. (2001 [1983]) How to Have Sex in an Epidemic. In: Bull, C. (Ed.), *Come Out Fighting: A Century of Essential Writing on Gay and Lesbian Liberation*. Thunder's Mouth Press, New York.

Crimp, D. (1988) How to Have Promiscuity in an Epidemic. In: Crimp, D. (Ed.), *AIDS: Cultural Analysis/Cultural Activism*. MIT Press, Cambridge, MA.

Odets, W. (1995) *In the Shadow of the Epidemic: Being Negative in the Age of AIDS*. Duke University Press, Durham, NC.

Patton, C. (1996). *Fatal Advice*. Duke University Press, Durham, NC.

Scarce, M. (1999) *Smearing the Queer: Medical Bias in the Health Care of Gay Men*. Harrington Park Press, Binghampton.

Smith, D. (1998) "Queer Theory" is Entering the Mainstream. *New York Times* (January 17): B9.

Warner, M. (1999) *The Trouble with Normal: Sex, Politics, and the Ethics of Queer Life*. Free Press, New York.

Waskul, D. (2003) *Self Games and Body Play: Personhood and Online Chat and Cybersex*. Peter Lang, New York.

Said, Edward W. (1935–2003)

Syed Farid Alatas

Edward W. Said was born to an Arab Christian family in Talbiyeh, Jerusalem when it was under British control, but spent most of his teenage years with his family in Egypt and Lebanon. The creation of the State of Israel in 1948 resulted in Said living in exile from Palestine for most of his life. He attended high school and college in the US, obtaining degrees at Princeton and Harvard and then beginning his career in English and Comparative Literature at Columbia University, where he became University Professor in 1992.

Said is best known as a literary critic as well as a political activist. His political activism for the Palestinian cause was provoked by Golda Meir's infamous statement in 1969 to the effect that Palestinians did not exist. This motivated Said to undertake "the slightly preposterous challenge of disproving her, of beginning to articulate a history of loss and dispossession that had to be extricated, minute by minute, word by word, inch by inch." Said's political interests are not to be distinguished from his literary concerns, which also dealt with the critique of received knowledge and the generation of alternative discourses. This is where Said's work is most relevant to sociology; that is, where it concerns the study of Orientalism as an ideology conditioned by colonial and imperial interests. Said's works most relevant in this regard are *Orientalism* (1978), *Covering Islam* (1981), *Culture and Imperialism* (1993), and *Representations of the Intellectuals* (1994). Said died in 2003 after battling leukemia for 12 years.

An important aspect of Said's background that greatly influenced his intellectual concerns and political activism was the formation of the State of Israel, the resulting displacement of masses of Palestinians, and the emergence of a discourse that distorted these realities. To a great extent this was simply a specific case of the more general phenomenon of colonization, decolonization, and the accompanying European and American discourses that attempted their respective constructions of the Arab and Muslim worlds. In any case, there was the problem of loss and dispossession and the need, as felt by Said, to resist such discourse.

Although Said's main field was literary criticism, he brought to it a sociological dimension by bringing in the context of colonialism and empire. In *Orientalism* Said argued that there was a lack of correspondence between what was said in Orientalism and the Orient itself and that Orientalism was a discourse that functioned to systematically manage and produce the Orient politically, sociologically, militarily, ideologically, scientifically, and imaginatively during the post-Enlightenment era. *Orientalism* seeks to expose this function. Herein lies the sociology of knowledge in Said's work. He studied Orientalism as a reflection of a "whole series of 'interests' which, by such means as scholarly discovery, philological reconstruction, psychological analysis, landscape and sociological description, ... not only creates but also maintains" (Said 1978: 12). In sociological terms, therefore, Said was interested in the critical study of the ideology of Orientalism and its connections with colonialism and imperialism. The problem of the objectivity of knowledge was raised in Said's critique of Orientalism, a theme not unknown in the sociology of knowledge. What Said did, however, was to give this theme its Islamic and Middle Eastern content. His analysis of media representations of Islam in the Middle East in *Covering Islam* was also along these lines, but of a more polemical nature. These interests also led Said to be interested in the role of intellectuals, another issue of sociological relevance. Thus, in *Culture and Imperialism*, the focus shifts to discourses that attempt to resist Orientalist ones. Said noted the presence of resistance discourse among Europeans as well; that is, those who wrote in sympathetic alliance with non-Europeans (Said 1993: 259). On the latter, Said discusses the work of intellectuals from the colonies or ex-colonies who used the ideas and techniques of western scholarship to critique western discourses. He discusses four texts as examples of such resistance discourse: C. L. R. James's *The Black Jacobins*, George Antonius's *The Arab Awakening*, Ranajit Guha's *A Rule of Property for Bengal*, and Syed Hussein Alatas's *The Myth of the Lazy Native*.

A project that Said did not have time to engage in but which he regarded as important was the undertaking of studies of contemporary alternatives to Orientalism, studying societies and cultures from non-repressive and non-manipulative perspectives (Said 1978: 24). In sociology, this has yet to be recognized as an important task as far as the future development of the discipline is concerned.

SEE ALSO: Captive Mind; Eurocentrism; Islam; Orientalism; Theory

REFERENCES AND SUGGESTED READINGS

Alatas, S. H. (1977) *The Myth of the Lazy Native: A Study of the Image of the Malays, Filipinos and Javanese from the Sixteenth to the Twentieth Century and Its Function in the Ideology of Colonial Capitalism.* Frank Cass, London.

Antonius, G. (1969 [1938]) *The Arab Awakening: The Story of the Arab National Movement.* Librairie du Liban, Beirut.

Guha, R. (1963) *A Rule of Property for Bengal: An Essay on the Idea of Permanent Settlement.* Mouton, The Hague.

James, C. L. R. (1963 [1938]) *The Black Jacobins: Toussaint L'Overture and the San Domingo Revolution.* Vintage, New York.

Said, E. W. (1978) *Orientalism.* Pantheon Books, New York.

Said, E. W. (1981) *Covering Islam.* Pantheon Books, New York.

Said, E. W. (1993) *Culture and Imperialism.* Vintage, London.

Said, E. W. (1994) *Representations of the Intellectuals.* Pantheon Books, New York.

Sainsaulieu, Renaud (1935–2002)

Norbert Alter and Dominique Martin

Renaud Sainsaulieu was born in Paris on November 4, 1935 and died there on July 26, 2002. After secondary studies in a Jesuit school, he went on to obtain advanced degrees in law and psychology from the Sorbonne. It was there that he committed himself to sociological studies and wrote his doctoral dissertation, with Michel Crozier as his adviser. Named Professor of Sociology at the Institut d'Études Politiques de Paris in 1975, he managed the Laboratory for the Sociology of Institutional Creation (LSCI). Renaud Sainsaulieu was also one of the main European promoters of sociology outside academia. He created a specific master's program for that purpose, as well as the Association Professionnelle des Sociologues d'Entreprise (APSE), a professional association for in-house sociologists. He also served as an active member and president of the Association Internationale des Sociologues de Langue Française (AISLF).

With *L'Identité au travail* (*Identity at Work*) (1977), Renaud Sainsaulieu revived the French school of the sociology of organizations by integrating into it an analysis of the cultural dimension of work; power does not directly define the rationality of actors, who act according to the representations, norms, and values that they carry with them. Furthermore, power is not divided equally in a company. Based on these two premises, social experiences are sufficiently differentiated that one can distinguish specific "actor logics." For the mass actor, in a large group of unskilled workers, relations are marked by fusion: power is inaccessible and the collective is valorized as a refuge and as a form of protection. On the other hand, if access to power is made possible through a professional or hierarchical status, negotiation of interpersonal relations is characterized by a rich affective and cognitive dimension, with the possibility, for the strategic actor, of coping with differences. The self-promoting actor, who privileges social advancement, carefully cultivates selected affinities with a few colleagues, to the detriment of groups, which are perceived as threatening. Finally, retreat is the stance of the actor for whom work is above all an economic necessity and the means to achieve other goals.

This cultural approach is also original because of the importance it gives to the idea of social change: "cultural apprenticeship" occurs and can subsequently recur in relation to changes in the division of labor. This apprenticeship is not, however, systematic: in certain cases the actors withdraw and resist because they do not have the resources to project themselves into a new frame of action.

The approach that Renaud Sainsaulieu developed under the term *sociologie de l'entreprise* (sociology of the company) extends these observations and opens new fields of investigation. This theoretical approach defines the company as an object of analysis and puts the concept of culture at the center. It does not limit its space of observation to the workshop or to specific professional groups or to relations of power, and thus privileges analysis of the relationship between the company and the global society, understood as the cultural, economic, and political environment of the firm's activity. The analysis of contingencies that is centered on the relationship of the company to these environments is complemented by two other types of analysis: strategic analysis, which studies informal relationships of power, and cultural analysis, which is concerned with what "cements" the identities by which the subjects cope with the trials of their daily working lives.

While the company is usually criticized in the sociology of labor as a place of domination, it is here understood as an "institution," as a place of integration and collective dynamics. The major management issue for companies is, according to Sainsaulieu, to put the "social at the heart of the economic," in order to provide them with an efficiency and meaning that conventional methods have failed to generate. This research approach is also "interventionist" in that sociology is conceived not only as a tool for analysis but also as a means of action. The goal of researchers is thus to participate in the functioning and transformation of companies by making their expertise available to the actors, and also by defining programs of action based on empirically and theoretically grounded diagnoses. The boundary-defying idea, formulated in terms of the "social development of the company," is that companies can move from a defensive and bureaucratic logic to a creative and democratic functioning through change and innovation, and that this evolution requires the mobilization of all the actors, whatever their importance, whether they are institutionalized or not.

SEE ALSO: Organization Theory; Organizational Contingencies; Organizations; Work, Sociology of

REFERENCES AND SUGGESTED READINGS

Sainsaulieu, R. (1972) *Les Relations de travail à l'usine*. Dunod, Paris.
Sainsaulieu, R. (1977) *L'Identité au travail*. Presses de la FNSP, Paris.

salary men

Tomoko Kurihara

In contemporary Japanese society the term salary men refers mainly to white-collar elites in multinational corporations (who represent approximately 20 percent of the total working population). As described in Beck and Beck's *A Change of a Lifetime* (1994) salary men constitute a managerial class that occupies the top stratum of the business community and is accorded high status in society. Its members have almost exclusively obtained degrees from Japan's most prestigious universities. However, in practice, a wider use of and flexible self-identification with the term is common. The term can therefore refer to both non-elite white-collar and occasionally blue-collar workers. Such flexible usage is made possible by Japan's industrial structure – the *keiretsu* system – which links large corporations to medium-sized and small subcontracting firms. The combination of English terms is used to signify, literally, a worker whose firm guarantees him a salaried income.

The reference to salary men as a category of workers in society arose in parallel with the concept of the nation-state, and industrialization and urbanization, which can be traced to the Meiji period in the late nineteenth century. In the twentieth century, salary men are most strongly associated with the post-war economic boom. This period in Japanese history is also associated with the emergence of the nuclear family (often headed by the salary man), a large new middle class (of which the salary man was a member) associated with a consumerist lifestyle, and the rise of corporatism or corporate-centered society. In this context, they came to signify the economic and social development of Japan.

Western sociological and anthropological writing on salaried workers developed in parallel to the growth and strength of the Japanese economy, which in the post-war period became a powerful player in the international market. Writers have explored notions of development (Dore 1987), the structure of the economy, the Japanese management system (such as the lifetime employment and seniority based wage and promotion system, *nenkōjyoretsu seido*), and the harmonious characteristic of interpersonal relationships within firms (Nakane 1970; Rohlen 1974; Clark 1979; Cole 1979). Contemporary scholars are critical of contributions made before the late 1970s (the early period) for applying a culturalist approach (i.e., the discredited *nihonjinron* perspective) to understanding Japanese working culture. Nonetheless, the detailed studies by early scholars of the meaning and significance of emic terms continue to serve as essential referents in much of contemporary literature, for any level of analysis – interactional, organizational, theoretical – on changes in contemporaneity and the critical development of theoretical perspective is impossible without reference to these native concepts. Mouer and Kawanishi (2005) provide a comprehensive guide to the history and future orientation of research into working life in Japan.

In the best-known study (albeit grounded in the *nihonjinron*) of Japanese society based on white-collar organizations, Nakane (1970) examines the internal structure of firms while suggesting a correlation to the functioning of society. The most significant relationships that constitute the core of the organization's structure are vertical relations, which are experienced between senior (*senpai*) and junior (*kōhai*) workers, and, horizontal relations, which are experienced between individuals of the same rank or horizontal stratum (*dōryō*). These relations bring a sense of cohesion and stability to the organization: this is important to a consensus-based society which values the ethos of collectivism. Ties between individuals within an organization are strong by nature of the fact that individuals belong to a particular group (or "frame"); because membership to a group is the essential basis of Japanese social structure; and also because contact between individuals lays stress on the emotions and morals of belonging to the group which breeds loyalty, dependency, and affection between individuals within vertical ties. It is in this sense that the operation of a strong consciousness of ranking order effectively exerts control over individual behavior and thought.

Salary men are known as corporate warriors (*kigyō senshi*), as their lifestyles (daily commutes, transfers to subsidiaries, and the ability to support non-working wives) is said to resemble the lifestyle of samurai warriors of the pre-Meiji (1868) class system (Vogel 1963; Ueno 1987). However, whereas the samurai ideology upholds qualities of courage, boldness, and capacity for individual action, the salary man is bound to the organization, unable to make independent choices (Plath 1964). For example, the culture of large corporations requires salary men to work long hours, at times doing overtime without pay, and reporting to work or being available for consultation on work-related emergencies during holiday time. However, salary men experienced benefits from the lifetime employment and seniority based wage and promotion system, such as financial stability and security, which was a return for the loyalty shown to the company. This in turn enabled the salary man to provide an identity for his family. Salary men, in essence, reflect a certain cultural ideal of masculinity, both at the level of corporate discourse and by individuals who uphold these moral values and work very hard (Morinaga 1995; Ueno 1995; Dasgupta 2000). These values are also expressed via specific physical and personal attributes typically exemplified by a sombre and conservative dress code, politeness and deference to senior workers, and sensitivity to social codes. Moreover, work for salary men does not end when they leave the office. Work continues, only it shifts to a different venue – bars, restaurants, or clubs – where socializing with co-workers and clients is obligatory for the salary man who wants to keep ahead of his game. An exchange of vital information about projects and people takes place in an informal atmosphere and deals might be sealed with clients (Allison 1994).

Furthermore, during the bubble economy, salary men became the vehicle by means of which economic and political tensions in international relations were articulated. This is due to the association between salary men and the ideals which foster notions of nationalism, as salary men come to embody the economic strategies and goals of the Japanese government and corporations for which they work. While the ideology behind salary men can be seen to support part of the national discourse that perpetuates the myth of Japanese uniqueness, conversely, the opposite holds true whereby militaristic and gendered connotations are often used to extend the general discourse of Orientalism about Japan. Particularly, in western media in the 1980s, parallels were drawn between an image of Japan's ruthless and savage wartime activities and the corporate infiltration of western markets to near-saturation while pursuing isolationist economic strategies, despite British and Dutch corporations having a similar high degree of foreign investment in the US. This parallels the general discourse of Orientalism directed against the non-West.

In the period of decelerating economic growth, an internal critique of Japan's characteristically hierarchical and male-dominated corporate culture became prominent. During the 1980s and 1990s Japanese companies faced two notable problems: a downturn in the economy which forced a strict reassessment of labor costs, and the aging of their personnel, corresponding to aging of the Japanese population as a whole. Personnel policy has been the main point of focus for revision in companies, whereby the lifetime employment system, and seniority wage and promotion systems, are being abolished or altered. Furthermore, the greater acceptability of transfers and job changes even among the managerial elite of large corporations has followed on from economic necessity and has been greeted with greater cultural acceptability.

Overall, however, the social and structural effects of restructuring have been negative as well as positive (Kurihara 2007). In the late 1990s and early 2000s the unemployment rate was high, as was the rate of unemployment accounted for by redundancies, which is a direct result of companies engaging in restructuring through job cuts. Under the lifetime employment system companies are bound by non-contractual agreement to provide jobs for life to their employees; therefore, companies have responded by creating redundancies either by encouraging older employees to retire early, or by asking volunteers to take early retirement or temporary leave. The greatest number of job losses are among middle-aged male workers, and also suicide rates and divorce rates are increasing. To aid this growing body of retrenched salary men, the government proposed to extend financial support to new small and medium-sized ventures because of the likelihood that these will soak up these individuals.

The changing economy also has had implications for new graduates. As a result of companies cutting back on recruitment in the late 1990s, a smaller proportion of new university graduates was able to find employment within the same year, as opposed to the early 1990s, during the tail-end of the economic bubble. As a flexible and relatively lower-cost response to the drop in levels of intake of new recruits, the larger and traditional companies have set up internship programs. Internship schemes provide university students summer work experience and help to develop creativity and inspiration among them, while creating a smoother flow in the transition between university and the workplace. The future trend points to small companies incorporating internship schemes into existing recruitment methods.

Alongside the structural changes in the economy, labor markets, and management practices which took place in the post-bubble period, cultural changes to the lifestyles of salary men have also been subject to much debate. The critique of corporate-centered society by Osawa (1994) best exemplifies the cultural side of the debate. One recognition in this has been the need for freedom among corporate men that will enable them to have a richer private life free from the constant demands of the corporation. The ethic guiding the conduct of the salary man – enforcing a strict division between private and public roles and insisting on sacrificing life at home – is generally seen to be outdated. The salary man, called a *kaisha ningen* (company person) who would be proud to be seen acting out his appropriate role, was a positive and desirable image for men during the rapid-growth period. But in the late 1990s and early 2000s the self-identification that is common among salary men is of a man of principle, committed to hard work, but equally to his family, which is called *mai hōmu shugi*. The term salary man has (in a loose sense) lost its former hard image of workaholics.

SEE ALSO: Enterprise Unions; Japanese-Style Management; *Shushin Koyo*

REFERENCES AND SUGGESTED READINGS

Allison, A. (1994) *Nightwork: Sexuality, Pleasure and Corporate Masculinity in a Tokyo Hostess Club.* University of Chicago Press, Chicago.

Clark, R. (1979) *The Japanese Company.* Yale University Press, Cambridge, MA.

Cole, R. E. (1979) *Work, Mobility, and Participation: A Comparative Study of American and Japanese Industry.* University of California Press, Berkeley.

Dasgupta, R. (2000) Performing Masculinities? The "Salaryman" at Work and Play. *Japanese Studies* 20(2): 189–200.

Dore, R. P. (1987) *Taking Japan Seriously: A Confucian Perspective on Leading Economic Issues.* Stanford University Press, Stanford.

Kurihara, T. (2007) *Japanese Corporate Transition in Time and Space.* Palgrave Macmillan, London.

Morinaga, E. (1995) The Oppression of a Corporate Centred Society: Amidst an "Insular Society" of the Corporation (*Kigyô chshin shakai no yokuatsu: kigyô to iu "shazen shakai" no nakade*). In: Inoue, T., Ueno, C., & Ehara, Y. (Eds.), *Feminism in Japan: Studies in Masculinity.* Iwanami Shoten, Tokyo, pp. 217–20.

Mouer, R. & Kawanishi, H. (2005) *A Sociology of Work in Japan.* Cambridge University Press, Cambridge.

Nakane, C. (1970) *Japanese Society.* Charles E. Tuttle, Tokyo.

Osawa, M. (1994) Bye-Bye Corporate Warriors: The Formation of a Corporate-Centered Society and Gender-Biased Social Policies in Japan. *Annals of the Institute of Social Science* 35: 157–94.

Plath, W. D. (1964) *The After Hours: Modern Japan and the Search for Enjoyment.* University of California Press, Berkeley.

Rohlen, T. P. (1974) *For Harmony and Strength: Japanese White-Collar Organization in Anthropological Perspective.* University of California Press, Berkeley.

Ueno, C. (1987) The Position of Japanese Women Reconsidered. *Current Anthropology* 28(4): S75–S84.

Ueno, C. (1995) Introduction. In: Inoue, T. et al. (Eds.), *The Oppression of a Corporate Centred Society: Amidst an "Insular Society" of the Corporation.* Iwanami Shoten, Tokyo, p. 216.

Vogel, E. F. (1963) *Japan's New Middle Class: The Salary Man and His Family in a Tokyo Suburb,* 2nd edn. University of California Press, Berkeley.

same-sex marriage/civil unions

Brian Heaphy

Same-sex marriage refers to a union by two people of the same sex that is legally sanctioned by the state, where identical rights and responsibilities are afforded same-sex and heterosexual married couples. The term "gay marriage" is popularly used to refer to same-sex partnerships or cohabiting relationships that are formally registered in some way as a "civil union" (variously known as civil partnerships, registered partnerships, and registered cohabitation), although the latter are in fact legally distinct from marriage. The term is also sometimes employed to talk about unregistered same-sex couple cohabitation or partnerships acknowledged through commitment ceremonies. Few states currently afford same-sex couples the opportunity to participate in marriage (those that do include Belgium, Spain, the Netherlands, and Canada, but see the following websites for detailed information on changing status in different countries: www.marriageequality.org; www.samesexmarriage.ca; www.stonewall.org.uk). Civil unions, civil partnerships, and registered cohabitation, which include some exemptions from the automatic rights and responsibilities afforded heterosexual married couples, are the most common forms of legal recognition. They offer some of the symbolic and material advantages associated with marriage, but with more limited legal status. At a global level, most same-sex partners must currently rely on "do-it-yourself" affirmation and commitment ceremonies, or seek religious blessings where available.

Same-sex marriage and civil unions have become high-profile political issues in many countries since the early 1990s. In Europe the number of states that have extended, or are planning to extend, legal recognition to lesbian and gay relationships through civil unions has increased steadily since the first civil partnership legislation was passed in Denmark in 1989. Elsewhere, Australia, Argentina, Brazil, New Zealand, South Africa, and other countries have either nationwide or regional legal facilities for the recognition of same-sex partnerships or cohabiting relationships. In the United States, the issue of same-sex marriage has been an especially contentious one. While some states have introduced legislation to recognize same-sex marriage or civil unions (e.g., Massachusetts, Connecticut, Vermont), other states have enacted constitutional amendments that explicitly forbid same-sex marriage, or have passed legislation that bars civil union-type recognition. This points to the strength of support and opposition that the issue of same-sex marriage can generate in the US and most other countries where the issue is debated. On the one hand, some constituencies see same-sex marriage and civil unions as an ultimate marker of social and political tolerance. On the other hand, some groups view the issue as indicative of the decline in religious and moral values in an increasingly secular world. Amongst conservative religious and social groups especially, same-sex marriage is often interpreted as an attack on the primacy and "naturalness" of the heterosexual married bond that is assumed to underpin a stable society.

Same-sex marriage and civil unions therefore touch on important sociological themes to do with sexuality, family life, and social change, and raise questions about social "rights" and responsibilities, sexual politics, and citizenship. The topic features highly in debates on the demise of the "traditional" family, the legitimacy of new family forms, and the blurring of the "public" and "private" in contemporary social contexts. Existing theory and research has focused on the social, cultural, and political forces that have brought the issue to the fore; the extent to which same-sex marriage represents full "sexual citizenship"; the meanings afforded partnership recognition by lesbians and gay men; and the implications of recognition for couples and their "blood" or "chosen" families (Weston 1991).

A number of social developments have influenced the current focus of lesbian and gay politics on same-sex marriage. AIDS, some theorists argue, was a catalyst in mobilizing a new lesbian and gay relational politics in the 1980s. This was initially focused on the recognition of same-sex partners' caring commitments, and protecting "rights" in relation to property and next-of-kin issues. Community responses to

AIDS facilitated the institution building and political confidence that made same-sex marriage seem like a realizable political objective. Since the 1980s new possibilities have opened up for lesbian and gay parenting (through self and assisted insemination, surrogacy, fostering, adoption, and so on) and a growing number of same-sex couples are choosing to parent. Same-sex marriage is seen as a crucial strategy for recognizing and protecting co-parenting commitments.

Another social development is the changing nature of heterosexual marriage itself. The separation of marriage from the needs of reproduction and women's increasing economic independence from men are transforming the meanings of heterosexual marriage. Some theorists cite statistics on divorce, cohabitation, single parenting, and solo living as an indication of the fragility of the institution of marriage. For others, these statistics are indicative of how processes of detraditionalization and individualization make marriage a "zombie" institution (Beck 2000). The recognition of same-sex marriage can therefore be interpreted as an attempt to reinvigorate or reinvent an ailing institution. A different perspective suggests that the changing role of welfare states can explain the political support that same-sex marriage has received from unexpected quarters. Some argue that as welfare states seek to shift social and care responsibilities back onto individuals and their families and communities, the recognition of same-sex marriage makes sense as it formalizes the responsibilities of lesbians and gay men for their partners and families.

The tendency is for sociological analyses of same-sex marriage to reflect broader political and social debate, and to be framed around dichotomies of accommodation and resistance. The core debate is the extent to which same-sex marriage represents a radical challenge to heteronormativity or a triumph of heterosexual norms. This is sometimes referred to as the "Sullivan versus Warner" debate. On the one hand, marriage is viewed as the legitimate aim of lesbian and gay politics, and as the most appropriate strategy for non-heterosexual citizenship (Sullivan). This position understands the marriage contract as symbolizing an emotional, financial, and psychological bond and highlights the economic and social advantages of marriage. Some analyses suggest that the legalizing of same-sex unions can reshape and modernize the institution of marriage in keeping with gender and sexual equality.

On the other hand, feminist, liberationist, and queer critics have argued that same-sex marriage represents the dominance of heterosexual values and undermines the distinctiveness of lesbian and gay cultures. This views the extension of marriage to same-sex couples as a form of social regulation, with profound normalizing implications for same-sex relationships and queer identities (Warner). The political desire for marriage, it is argued, is based on outmoded notions of commitment. Ultimately it may lead to normative constructions of socially responsible and irresponsible homosexuals, and to the imposition of rules which may stifle the creativity of same-sex partnerships. Feminist critics have further argued that the valorization of marriage as "full citizenship" for lesbians and gay men is a naïve political strategy. They point to the historical role of the institution of marriage in the reproduction of patriarchal structures and its grounding in gendered inequalities.

Some researchers have explored the dilemmas that marriage poses for lesbians and gay men. Opinions about the value of same-sex marriage range from enthusiasm to outright rejection, and many individuals and couples are ambivalent about the issue. Lesbian and gay research participants generally endorse the principle of equality with heterosexual relationships. They desire social validation, and feel that same-sex couples should be entitled to the legal benefits, rights, and responsibilities that are traditionally associated with marriage (such as medical decision-making, child support, inheritance, and so on). However, individuals' ambivalence is underscored where research suggests that while most lesbians and gay men feel that they *should* have the right to marry, only a small minority *would* marry given the opportunity. While lesbians and gay men appear keen to take up some of the entitlements and responsibilities traditionally associated with marriage, in comparing heterosexual marriage to their own relationships they often perceive the latter to offer greater opportunities for creativity and equality.

Some researchers suggest that lesbian and gay ambivalence about same-sex marriage is indicative of the legal and cultural privileging of the institution. This leaves individuals with "no choice" but to see it as a crucial marker of social inclusion and citizenship – irrespective of their personal or political reservations. Others have argued that this ambivalence is rooted in the tensions between the desire for validation and participation in the existing traditions that marriage represents, and the desire to retain choice and creativity in "doing" and affirming relationships. A number of studies suggest that the lack of institutional supports and cultural guidelines for same-sex relationships enables the development of distinctly creative partnerships and family practices. Studies also indicate that same-sex relationships tend to be underpinned by a friendship ethic that generally promotes a commitment to equality. Monogamy as the basis of commitment, and the primary significance of the couple, tend to be open to negotiation and are rarely assumed. This has led some theorists and researchers to argue that same-sex relationships are creative "life experiments." Such creativity is also noted in the research on commitment affirmation, where the playfulness of "do-it-yourself" traditions and rituals is highlighted. While elements of conformity are evident in how same-sex relationships are celebrated and ritualized, couples often challenge or go beyond traditional ways of doing things. Research has further illustrated how commitment ceremonies simultaneously indicate conformity to wider values and introduce "queering" messages at crucial points.

Same-sex marriage and civil unions are distinctly contemporary phenomena, and they offer fertile ground for theorizing and new research. Several dimensions and questions could be explored. Established themes that warrant further exploration in different national and local contexts include: the ways in which same-sex marriage challenges heterosexual norms or otherwise; the motivations for accepting or rejecting same-sex marriage at state, political, couple, and personal levels; and alternative strategies for recognizing and validating same-sex relationships and identities, such as the individualization of "rights" and responsibilities. Other areas for research open up as the availability and take-up of marriage and civil unions increase. These include the implications for supporting same-sex couple commitments; for a sense of connectedness to family and community traditions; and for a sense of couple and familial security. Research might also explore the implications (normalizing or otherwise) of legal and symbolic recognition for how couples structure and "do" their relationships. What, for example, are the implications for sexual exclusiveness and longevity? Studies could also examine the implications for non-heterosexual identities. Does recognition enhance a sense of individual security or otherwise? Are individuals judged (by themselves and others) on their capacities or willingness to marry? Finally, there is limited research on the breakup of same-sex relationships. What are the implications of legal recognition for this? What are the implications of "divorce" and deregistration?

These topics and questions require creative research strategies and methodologies, an area where sexualities research has particular strengths and weaknesses. One obstacle is the "hidden" nature of lesbian and gay populations. This often means that particular experiences (white, middle-class, and urban) are taken to represent *the* lesbian and gay experience. As the possibilities offered by same-sex marriage and civil partnerships are likely to have profound implications for lesbians and gay men, future research should attempt to capture a fuller range of voices, experience, and opinions than has previously been the case.

SEE ALSO: Cohabitation; Family Diversity; Gay and Lesbian Movement; Intimate Union Formation and Dissolution; Lesbian and Gay Families; Marriage

REFERENCES AND SUGGESTED READINGS

Adam, B. D. (2004) Care, Intimacy and Same-Sex Partnerships in the 21st Century. *Current Sociology* 52(2): 265–79.

Beck, U. (2000) Zombie Categories. In: Rutherford, J. (Ed.), *The Art of Life*. Lawrence & Wishart, London.

Clarke, V. & Finaly, S. (2004) "For Better or Worse?" Lesbian and Gay Marriage. *Feminism and Psychology* 14(1): 17–23.

Giddens, A. (1992) *The Transformation of Intimacy*. Polity Press, Cambridge.

Lewin, E. (2004) Anxiety at the Altar: Some Comments on Same-Sex Marriage from the United States. *Feminism and Psychology* 14(2): 323–6.

Lewin, E. (1999) *Recognizing Ourselves: Ceremonies of Lesbian and Gay Commitment.* Columbia University Press, New York.
Sullivan, A. (1996) *Virtually Normal.* Vintage Books, New York.
Sullivan, A. (Ed.) (1997) *Same-Sex Marriage: Pro and Con – A Reader.* Vintage Books, New York.
Warner, M. (2000) *The Trouble with Normal: Sex, Politics, and the Ethics of Queer Life.* Harvard University Press, Cambridge, MA.
Weeks, J., Heaphy, B., & Donovan, C. (1999) Partnership Rites: Commitment and Ritual in Non-Heterosexual Relationships. In: Seymour, J. & Bagguley, P. (Eds.), *Relating Intimacies: Power and Resistance.* Macmillan, London.
Weeks, J., Heaphy, B., & Donovan, C. (2001) *Same-Sex Intimacies: Families of Choice and Other Life Experiments.* Routledge, London.
Weston, K. (1991) *Families We Choose: Lesbians, Gays, Kinship.* Columbia University Press, New York.

sampling, qualitative (purposive)

Michael Quinn Patton

Perhaps nothing better captures the difference between quantitative and qualitative methods than the different logics that undergird sampling approaches. Qualitative inquiry typically focuses in depth on relatively small samples, even single cases (n = 1), selected *purposefully.* Quantitative methods typically depend on larger samples selected randomly. Not only are the techniques for sampling different, but also the very logic of each approach is unique because the purpose of each strategy is different.

The logic and power of random sampling derives from statistical probability theory. In contrast, the logic and power of *purposive sampling* lies in selecting *information-rich cases* for study in depth. Information-rich cases are those from which one can learn a great deal about issues of central importance to the purpose of the inquiry, thus the term *purposive* sampling (or alternatively, purposeful sampling). What would be "bias" in statistical sampling, and therefore a weakness, becomes intended focus in qualitative sampling, and therefore a strength. Studying information-rich cases yields insights and in-depth understanding rather than empirical generalizations. For example, if the purpose of a program evaluation is to increase the effectiveness of a program in reaching lower-socioeconomic groups, one may learn a great deal more by studying in depth a small number of carefully selected poor families than by gathering standardized information from a large, statistically representative sample of the whole program. Purposive sampling focuses on selecting information-rich cases whose study will illuminate the questions under study. There are several different strategies for purposefully selecting information-rich cases. The logic of each strategy serves a particular purpose.

Extreme or deviant case sampling involves selecting cases that are information-rich because they are unusual or special in some way, such as outstanding successes or notable failures. The highly influential study of high performing American companies published as *In Search of Excellence* (Peters & Waterman 1982) exemplifies the logic of purposeful, extreme group sampling. The sample of 62 companies was never intended to be representative of US industry as a whole, but rather was purposefully selected to focus on innovation and excellence. In the early days of AIDS research when HIV infections almost always resulted in death, a small number of cases of people infected with HIV who did not develop AIDS became crucial outlier cases that provided important insights into directions researchers should take in combating AIDS.

In program evaluation, the logic of extreme-case sampling is that lessons may be learned about unusual conditions or extreme outcomes that are relevant to improving more typical programs. Suppose that we are interested in studying a national program with hundreds of local sites. We know that many programs are operating reasonably well, that other programs verge on being disasters, and that most programs are doing "okay." We know this from knowledgeable sources who have made site visits to enough programs to have a basic idea about what the variation is. If one wanted to document precisely the natural variation among programs, a random sample would be appropriate, one of sufficient size to be representative and permit generalizations to the total population of programs. However, with limited resources and time, and with the priority being how to improve programs, an evaluator might learn more by intensively studying one or more examples of really poor programs and one or more examples of really excellent programs. The evaluation focus then becomes a question of understanding under what conditions programs get into trouble and under what conditions programs exemplify excellence. It is not even necessary to randomly sample poor programs or excellent programs. The researchers and intended users involved in the study think through *what cases they could learn the most from* and those are the cases that are selected for study.

Examples of other purposeful sampling strategies are briefly described below.

Maximum variation sampling involves purposefully picking a wide range of cases to get variation on dimensions of interest. Such a sample can document variations that have emerged in adapting to different conditions as well as identify important common patterns that cut across variations (cut through the noise of variation).

Homogenous sampling is used to bring focus to a sample, reduce variation, simplify analysis, and facilitate group interviewing (focus groups).

Typical case sampling is used to illustrate or highlight what is typical, normal, average, and give greater depth of understanding to the qualitative meaning of a statistical mean.

Critical case sampling refers to certain cases that can make a point quite dramatically or are, for some reason, particularly important in the scheme of things. A clue to the existence of a critical case is a statement to the effect that "if it happens there, it will happen anywhere," or, vice versa, "if it doesn't happen there, it won't happen anywhere." Another clue to the existence of a critical case is a key informant observation to the effect that "if that group is having problems, then we can be sure all the groups are having problems." Looking for the critical case is particularly important where resources may limit the inquiry to the study of only a single site. Under such conditions it makes strategic sense to pick the site that would yield the most information and have the greatest impact on the development of knowledge. While studying one or a few critical cases does not technically permit broad generalizations to all possible cases, *logical generalizations* can often be made from the weight of evidence produced in studying a single, critical case.

Physics provides a good example of such a critical case. In Galileo's study of gravity he wanted to find out if the weight of an object affected the rate of speed at which it would fall. Rather than randomly sampling objects of different weights in order to generalize to all objects in the world, he selected a critical case: the feather. If in a vacuum, as he demonstrated, a feather fell at the same rate as some heavier object (a coin), then he could logically generalize from this one critical comparison to all objects. His finding was both useful *and* credible because the feather was a convincing critical case.

Critical cases can be found in social science and evaluation research if one is creative in looking for them. Identification of critical cases depends on recognition of the key dimensions that make for a critical case.

For a full discussion of these and other purposive sampling strategies and the full range of qualitative methods and analytical approaches, see Denzin and Lincoln (2000) and Patton (2002).

SEE ALSO: Action Research; Evaluation; Methods, Case Study; Methods, Mixed; Paradigms

REFERENCES AND SUGGESTED READINGS

Denzin, N. & Lincoln, Y. (Eds.) (2000) *Handbook of Qualitative Research*, 2nd edn. Sage, Thousand Oaks, CA.

Lincoln, Y. & Guba, E. (1985) *Naturalistic Inquiry*. Sage, Beverly Hills, CA.

Patton, M. Q. (2002) *Qualitative Research and Evaluation Methods*, 3rd edn. Sage, Thousand Oaks, CA.

Peters, T. & Waterman, R. (1982) *In Search of Excellence*. Harper & Row, New York.

Stake, R. (1995) *The Art of Case Research*. Sage, Thousand Oaks, CA.

Sanskritization

Vineeta Sinha

It is crucial to make a distinction between the word Sanskritization and its conceptualization as a tool of sociological analysis. The word itself, having been derived from the root "Sanskrit," labeled the sacred language of Hindus and Hinduism, together with related terminology such as "Sanskritic," "Sanskritized," and "Sanskritizing," is already present in nineteenth- and twentieth-century European Indological literature. These terms are used variously, but predominantly describe either elite-based, Brahmanic, "Hindu" culture or note its influence on the diverse, non-Brahmanic, non-Hindu elements of Indian society. As a point of historical interest, it is notable that although the conceptualization of the term is rightly attributed to the late eminent Indian social anthropologist M. N. Srinivas, it (and associated descriptions) was already in use by sociologist, historian, and economist Benoy Kumar Sarkar in the 1930s and by linguist Suniti Kumar Chatterjee in 1950.

As formulated by Srinivas, the word Sanskritization sometimes connotes a perspective, a theory, a concept or a cluster of concepts, all relevant for theorizing social change in India and firmly embedded in an anthropological model of Indian society. The concept has had a checkered history, but is probably the single most important contribution to social science scholarship from India, and a good candidate for the title of a culturally specific and "indigenous" category of analysis. It is first named and appears in Srinivas's *Religion and Society Amongst the Coorgs of South India* (1952), but the germ of the idea was present in his earlier work on *Marriage and Family in Mysore* (1942). Already at this time, the concept was criticized by such Indian social science luminaries as Datta-Majumdar, Karve, and Raghavan (Bopegamage & Kulahalli 1971). Despite this early challenge, the term was welcomed by a section of Indian and western sociologists and anthropologists (Bailey 1957; Singer 1959; Gould 1961; Sahay 1962), and viewed as a concept that addressed the uniqueness and peculiarity of the Indian social structural situation. Yet, in the mid-1950s, Srinivas himself agreed that the term was "ugly," although it was nonetheless valuable in analyses of social change in India.

In his first book published in 1942, Srinivas had already observed a process that he would subsequently name and define in his 1952 book on the Coorgs. According to Srinivas's first definition, the process of Sanskritization referred to a low caste, over a few generations, rising in the community "to a higher position in the hierarchy by adopting vegetarianism and teetotalism, and by Sanskritizing its ritual and pantheon," by taking over not only the customs and rites, but also the beliefs of the Brahmin. Srinivas acknowledges here that the adoption of the Brahmanic way of life by a low caste, although forbidden theoretically, occurred regularly in practice.

In *Caste in Modern India* (1965), his argument is expanded to include the realm of values and ideas as well as ritual practices, "which have found frequent expression in the vast body of Sanskritic literature, sacred as well as secular" (p. 48). Finally, in *Social Change in Modern India* (1967), Srinivas provided an integrated definition of the term. Sanskritization "is a process by which a 'low' Hindu caste, or tribal or other group, changes its customs, ritual, ideology and way of life in the direction of a high caste" (p. 6). The term also carried notions of upward social mobility and prestige, a central feature of the process.

Srinivas acknowledged that this process is not to be viewed as a singular, monolithic whole but that empirically many models of Sanskritization could be identified, noting that regional variation is a crucial, determining factor. For example, he listed the Brahmanic, Kshatriya, Vaishya, and Sudra variants, the nature of caste hierarchy being determined by the dominant caste groups in question. He further acknowledged that the process may be occurring amongst tribal, non-Hindu groups as well, thus placing Sanskritization well outside the "Hindu" framework. In fact, he even holds open the possibility of "de-Sanskritization" amongst all these groups as a reverse process.

Srinivas's career as a social anthropologist and analyst committed to theorizing Indian social structure, through the impact of modernizing and westernizing forces, can be viewed as resting on his sustained intellectual engagement with the process of Sanskritization, which continued well into the 1990s. Thus, one observes an evolution in Srinivas's thinking about the concept, as he strived to refine, justify, and modify it in an effort to demonstrate its relevance as a meaningful instrument of investigation for Indian society. This makes it impossible to "define" the term Sanskritization briefly. It is more valuable to undertake a historical perspective to see its shifting nuances and constitutive elements within the context of Srinivas's own thinking.

Scholars have applied the concept of Sanskritization to a variety of diverse sociocultural, religious phenomena, in both Indian and diasporic settings, some with greater success than others. Despite objections, the concept has been embraced and applied by Indian and western social scientists alike, while remaining controversial. One prominent example of such application is the association of village deities with Sanskritic deities and the requisite elevation of folk ritual practices to a higher, Sanskritic, and more legitimate status. The term continues to be popular and is subject to a variety of usages and interpretations. The downside is that it is often somewhat loosely applied to a variety of substantive domains (Staal 1963), to the extent that it seems to have little conceptual rigor and coherence, for which Srinivas cannot be held responsible. But the point remains that one continues to see rather awkward applications of the term, in ways that Srinivas himself would have found problematic. One line of critique notes problems in expanding the term beyond a highly specific and localized analytical frame to a theory of grand, all-encompassing proportions, presented as relevant for making sense of social change and mobility in all of India. This claim to universal reference as an "all-India" category has been contested for failing to acknowledge regional variation across the Indian landscape. Another noted shortcoming is that the concept tends to gloss over, erase, or veil the many complexities, contradictions, and nuances of castes and their relations at the level of practice. In a self-critical stance Srinivas himself admitted, in later reflections on the concept he devised and popularized, that it was too broad and too loose conceptually in its original formulation, suggesting that it should be discarded if necessary.

Through these moments of reflection, which have culminated in a reworked concept, Srinivas avoids defining it substantively, that is, it is not delimited by content. Rather, it signifies a generic process by which lower-caste groups (or other subordinate groups) attempt to raise their status (ritual or otherwise) by imitating, emulating, or adopting the behavior and thinking of groups with higher status. The concept is inevitably rooted in Brahmanic tradition, the Sanskrit language, and Brahmins as guardians of the former, and carries an implicit statement about the superiority of Sanskritic tradition. Despite varied challenges to the concept, Srinivas continues to reaffirm its value, albeit in altered modes and suited to contemporary problems, reiterating the cohesive, integrating, and unifying role of Sanskritization in the plural context of sovereign, secular India. He writes in *The Cohesive Role of Sanskritization and Other Essays* (1989) that independent India's heterogeneous population can be unified, even while adhering to "what is valuable in Sanksrit thought and culture," and that to ensure this it would be "necessary for Hindus to accept the entire Indian tradition to which all sections of the population have contributed, and for the latter (i.e., non-Hindus) to regard the Sanskrit heritage as their own."

Such grounding brings into sharp focus several interrelated categories and dichotomies upon which the logic of Sanskritization rests, and which have structured social science analyses of Indian society well into the 1990s. Examples include the "Great" and "Little" traditions, the "folk–urban" divide, and "non-Sanskritic Hinduism" and "Sanskritic Hinduism." Several other observations in Srinivas's explication of Sanskritization are pertinent. To begin, the term carries explicitly religious overtones. Next, it selects Hinduism and caste as the twin structural pillars of Indian society. This rendering connects the term "Sanskritization" explicitly (perhaps unintentionally) to both Indological and Orientalist discourses which read India as defined by caste and Hinduism, and a classical, textual, Brahmanic and Sanskritic variety of Hindu religiosity. In this, one can see the role of Sanskritization and its inventor as perpetuating the image of India as distinct from the West, in being defined exclusively by caste principles and by Hindu religiosity – central in Orientalist imaginings of India – critiqued by postcolonial and postorientalist scholarship. In this context, the concept of Sanskritization has neither been historicized sufficiently nor received rigorous, intellectual attention, but instead continues to be accepted rather uncritically by its proponents. At least some of this has to do less with assessment of ideas and more with reservations against contesting and refuting one of the most eminent researchers India has produced, a man who is justifiably still considered an intellectual giant and an icon amongst Indian social scientists.

In recent years, a section of Indian social scientists has wondered about the continued relevance of the notion of Sanskritization. Despite being regularly contested since its formulation in the 1950s, it persists in analyses of Indian and Hindu domains, including amongst diasporic communities. It is a tribute to its potency, prestige, popularity, and malleability that in a 1996 volume on caste in India, edited by Srinivas, there are several pieces that return to the idea of Sanskritization, but now with a different meaning and intent. For instance, here one encounters the idea of Sanskritization as an "ideology," a word that Srinivas had used in his 1989 publication to refer to the spiritual ideas carried in Brahmanic ritual practices, but importantly without the tone of control, domination, hegemony, and oppression current in later renditions. This transformation occurs in the aftermath of decades of challenges to Brahmanical orthodoxy in India and the initiation of policy, legislative, and institutional measures that acknowledge, and thus attempt to ameliorate, the socioeconomic status of non-Brahmin castes therein. The practice, motivation, and consequences of "Sanskritization" are now confronted, particularly by the Dalit and non-Brahmin social movements launched and active in both northern and southern parts of India. Consequently, one has to ask if the concept of "Sanskritization" has been attentive to possible deleterious effects of the transformative process, or does it assume its effects to be desired, desirable, and beneficial, or is there silence on the subject?

The concept is further important in contemporary discussions amongst proponents of alternative discourses, especially in the realm of concept and theory construction. One strong critique of mainstream social science wisdom is the overwhelming reliance on "western" and "European" cultural experiences and traditions as the exclusive source and origin of concepts and categories of analysis, which are then presented as being of universal relevance. A suggested corrective is the search for "indigenous" concepts, from non-western traditions. Sanskritization has been popularly cited as an example of such a category, which is independently derived and thus autonomous. This is ironic, for as we have seen, as originally constructed the appeal of the concept was precisely its cultural boundedness and specificity as well as its capacity to explain a uniquely Indian situation, thus viewed as a particular, indigenous concept tied to Indian realities. The present quest for indigenous categories in alternative discourses is precisely the reverse, in seeking categories that may have a broader, generic, universal relevance beyond their context of origin. However, distance from the substantive dimensions (and Indian/Hindu grounding) of the concept allows one to consider the general viability of the notion, given that it refers to a process which potentially has universal implications. For instance, it might be possible to use the concept to understand the process of gentrification occurring amongst rural peasant communities in Eastern Europe, or the rise of the *nouveaux riches* in many parts of the world. It is a pity that, to date, there has been little attempt to abstract from this concept any universal validity or see it as relevant for comparative, cross-cultural analysis.

SEE ALSO: Folk Hinduism; Gentrification; Hinduism; Popular Religiosity; Religion; Religion, Sociology of; Sarkar, Benoy Kumar

REFERENCES AND SUGGESTED READINGS

Bailey, F. G. (1957) *Caste and the Economic Frontier*. Manchester University Press, Manchester.

Bopegamage, A. & Kulahalli, R. N. (1971) "Sanskritization" and Social Change in India. *Arch. Europ. Sociol.* 12: 123–32.

Charsley, S. (1998) Sanskritization: The Career of an Anthropological Theory. *Contributions to Indian Sociology* (n.s.) 32(2): 527–49.

Chatterjee, S. K. (1950) KIRATA-JANA-KIRTI: The Indo-Mongoloids, Their Contributions to the History and Culture of India. *Journal of the Royal Asiatic Society of Bengal* (3rd series) 16: 148.

Gould, H. A. (1961) Sanskritization and Westernization: A Dynamic View. *Economic Weekly* 13(25): 409–14.
Sahay, K. N. (1962) Trends of Sanskritization Among the Oraon. *Bulletin of the Bihar Tribal Research Institute* 4(2): 1–15.
Singer, M. (Ed.) (1959) *Traditional India: Structure and Change*. University of Texas Press, Austin.
Staal, J. F. (1963) Sanskrit and Sanskritization. *Journal of Asian Studies* 22: 261–75.

Saraswati, Pandita Ramabai (1858–1922)

Vineeta Sinha

Pandita Ramabai Saraswati was born in the forest of Gungamal in the Indian state of Maharashtra. Her father, Ananda Shastri Dongre, was a learned Brahmin and a social reformer, who at the age of 44 had taken a second wife, Lakshmibai, of 9 years, in keeping with the custom of child marriage at the time. Shastri educated his wife in Sanskrit, a highly unorthodox move for the times, as girls were denied formal education and learning of sacred Hindu texts, the exclusive right and privilege of males. His unorthodox beliefs and practices led to his ostracization from the community. Consequently, he led a rather nomadic and secluded life, delivering religious lectures and sermons to support his young family. It was in such a context that Ramabai was born, the youngest of six children, but of which only three ultimately survived. Her formative years were spent in this rather drifting and atypical setting. She received early education in the Hindu scriptures from her mother, learnt Sanskrit, and could recite the Puranas proficiently from a young age. She was not married off as a child, but remained unmarried beyond age 10 and continued her learning. After the death of her parents between 1874 and 1877, she sustained their lifestyle and traveled across India with her brother, giving lectures in Sanskrit and engaging religious experts on a variety of social and spiritual matters. At the end of her travels, she arrived in Calcutta and spent a significant part of her adult creative life in this city. It was here that she was honored by Brahmins of Calcutta with the title "Pandita," which translates as "eminent scholar and teacher," on the basis of her command and knowledge of sacred Hindu texts. She was also seen as a modern-day incarnation of Saraswati, the Hindu goddess of learning. The inclusion of these two titles produced the name by which she was to be subsequently remembered. In 1880, at the age of 22, Ramabai broke all conventions in marrying by choice a friend of her brother's, a man of a low caste and a non-Brahmin of Shudra background. She had a daughter, Manorama, in 1881, but lost her husband to cholera the following year. She led a full life, intellectually and spiritually, and died in 1922, but has left a legacy of works that warrant closer academic attention than has so far been forthcoming.

In 1883, she left for England with her 2-year-old daughter and enrolled at the Cheltenham Women's College to study the natural sciences, mathematics, and English. She had also decided to join the Episcopalian Church. She had raised part of the travel fare to England through the sale of her book, *Stri Dharma Neeti* (*Morals for Women*, 1882), in which she urged women to become self-reliant and take charge of their own lives. To support herself in a foreign land, she taught Sanskrit and Marathi to women missionaries who were planning to work in Maharashtra, India. In 1886 she sailed to the United States to attend the graduation of her cousin, Dr. Anandibai Joshi, who is considered the first Indian woman medical doctor. She wrote another book, *The High-Caste Hindu Woman* (1886), to pay for her travel expenses to the US. This was primarily to secure support for funding a school for child widows in India. Back from her travels in February 1889, Ramabai was at the forefront of educational reform for women and strived to provide institutional alternatives for abandoned women and widowed women/girls. In April 1889, "Sharada Sadan," the first home for widows in Maharashtra, was established in Bombay. But Ramabai's conversion to Christianity created much controversy, and unfortunately her social reform initiatives were received with suspicion, given her connection with missionaries and her own religious conversion, which was viewed as a rejection of her Hindu identity.

Ramabai was a woman ahead of her times, living in an age that was not ready to accept her radicalism and critique of society. She overtly confronted both patriarchy and British imperialism. She was a staunch nationalist and her opposition to British colonial presence was publicly articulated. She was distinctive amongst her contemporaries for her direct critique of patriarchy, its ideologies and institutions. She challenged long-held discriminatory social and cultural practices and their debilitating effect on girls, i.e., the institution of child marriage for girls, enforced widowhood, and restrictions on education of girls. Her rallying call encouraged women to be self-reliant, urging them to lead autonomous, self-reliant, and independent lives. In terms of concrete contributions, Ramabai was instrumental in establishing schools for girls, an act that was opposed by male and female reformers of her time. She also founded institutions that provided food and shelter to homeless widows and other needy women, to reduce their dependence on often hostile and non-supportive families. Being an exemplar, she encouraged women to participate in public life and take an interest in political issues, taking the lead herself in running large organizations and addressing public gatherings on issues of social and political relevance. Apart from her activism, Ramabai was a prolific writer, producing numerous books, pamphlets, brochures, and newspaper articles. Some prominent examples include the following: *Stri Dharma Neeti* (1882), *The High-Caste Hindu Woman* (1886), *The Peoples of the United States* (1889), and *My Testimony* (1907).

This profile reveals Ramabai as a complex and multidimensional personality. She has most often been described in the literature as a social reformer, educationalist, feminist, and activist. In making a case for viewing her as an independent social thinker, it is crucial to abstract her intellectual thought from her activism, which in her case sharply intersect. Ramabai's life shows an explicit and engaged social reformist tone and in particular a strong concern with the status of high-caste Hindu women of India, a cause to which she remained committed till the end of her life. Her primary concern was the status of women, in particular the status of high-caste Hindu women, whose lives she demonstrated and argued were most constrained by a highly rigid and patriarchal social arrangement. She was not thus speaking of the condition of all Hindu women in Indian society. Of all her publications, *The High-Caste Hindu Woman* (henceforth *hchw*) is probably the most successful and has made the most impact, even during her lifetime. It sold 10,000 copies and did much to promote and raise public consciousness about her mission and agenda, particularly outside India. Sociologically too, this book is salient. Scholars have argued that on the basis of this text, Ramabai should be considered the first sociologist of kinship and family in India (Shah 1977; Kosambi 1988). The book takes the reader through the various crucial moments in the life of high-caste Hindu women, from childhood to married life and widowhood, with a view to outlining their place and status in society. Using simple, direct language, Ramabai communicates the everyday life of a Hindu girl/woman and reflects on the consequences this carries for men, women, and society in general. Interestingly, the final chapter is entitled "How the Condition of Women Tells Upon Society," a theme that carries huge sociological significance. What is particularly striking here is Ramabai's insight that women's status and their societal treatment are an index of the broader structural ethos. She argues that a society cannot progress until it acknowledges the unjust and inhumane treatment doled out to the most vulnerable and oppressed members of society, including women. She also makes a powerful statement in the text about how the "degradation of women" affects not just women but also men, since their existence is mutually interdependent and shapes the future of that society. According to Kosambi (1988: 43), there is in her work a "causal connection between the condition of women and the state of the nation." A strong case has also been made to view her as a pioneering figure who directed scrutiny to the domain of kinship, family, and women's status in Hindu society, a call that has not been seriously pursued. For instance, in *hchw*, she questioned the ascription of women's roles exclusively through marriage and the institution of the family, and their confinement to the domestic domain. She encouraged women's move into the public domain, applauded their greater political participation, and worked to raise women's self-awareness about these issues. Scholars have identified a strongly feminist stance in such thinking, which challenged patriarchy and discrimination against women, calling for their emancipation and equal treatment.

Ramabai was quite a prominent public and international figure in her lifetime. Her intellectual output was focused and committed to particular social and political agendas. Her activism was daring and effective, and grounded in a body of social and political thought. She was not just an armchair critic, but strived to translate into concrete terms her condemnation of outdated and non-progressive practices vis-à-vis the treatment of Indian women, by initiating relevant structural changes. Additionally, as a result of her overseas travels, we also have access to Ramabai's reflections about the places she visited and the cultures and peoples she encountered, including her important critique of religion and Christianity. One such document is *The Peoples of the United States*, a text Kosambi describes as an "ethnography of American society," which carries Ramabai's account of its religious and political domains. Ramabai openly admires the anti-colonial ideology, liberal democratic principles, and feminist thinking she finds here. This is in stark contrast to her anti-British sentiments, negative appraisal of the style of governance, the rigid hierarchical ordering of society, and the ideology of colonialism in England (Kosambi 2003). This is an important text for a number of reasons. Substantively, it is comparative in looking at societal forms in England, the US, and India; it also carries her critique of, and resistance to, colonial subjugation and oppression. Historically, it stands out as a rare commentary by a colonized subject – a woman – on a "western" society in the nineteenth century. But it has also been noted that her positive assessment of American society is somewhat idealistic and polemical, and that she only reluctantly mentions its inherent problems, such as slavery, racism, and the non-political participation of women (Kosambi 2003).

According to the prominent historian A. B. Shah (1977), Ramabai was "the greatest woman produced by modern India and one of the greatest Indians in all history ... the one to lay the foundations for a movement for women's liberation in India." Despite this high acclaim, others have noted that Ramabai has "a surprisingly hazy presence in contemporary consciousness – if she is indeed a presence at all" (Tharu & Lalitha 1995: 243). Consulting numerous historical social science dictionaries and encyclopedias does not produce too many entries about her. Those that do include her merely notice that she worked for women's education and widow remarriage, but seldom mention her in an independent capacity as a social thinker or reformer. This neglect continues despite the fact that there is no dearth of contemporary knowledge and evidence of Ramabai's intellectual and activist contributions. Neither Ramabai nor her "work" (broadly defined to include her writings and activism) have to date received serious scholarly attention, either in the history of Indian social reformist discourse or as a social thinker, theorist, or sociologist in her own right. A variety of reasons for such neglect can be cited, ranging from androcentric social science scholarship to plain ignorance and apathy. We do have some good biographical accounts of her life, and a few stalwarts who plod on, producing the raw material (translations of Ramabai's writings) so necessary for other practitioners (educationalists and researchers alike) in the field to begin to direct intellectual and academic attention to this marginalized and forgotten figure for future generations.

SEE ALSO: Discourse; Eurocentrism; Feminist Pedagogy; Khaldun, Ibn; Rizal, José; Sarkar, Benoy Kumar; Theory

REFERENCES AND SUGGESTED READINGS

Fuller, M. L. B. (1939) *The Triumph of an Indian Widow: The Life of Pandita Ramabai*, 3rd edn. American Council of the Ramabai Mukti Mission, Havertown, PA.

Kosambi, M. (1988) Women, Emancipation, and Equality: Pandita Ramabai's Contribution to Women's Cause. *Economic and Political Weekly* 23(44): 38–49.

Kosambi, M. (2003) *Returning the American Gaze: Pandita Ramabai's The Peoples of the United States*. Permanent Black, New Delhi.

Macnicol, N. (1926) *Pandita Ramabai*, 3rd edn. Association Press for YMCA, Calcutta.

Sengupta, P. (1970) *Pandita Ramabai Saraswati*. Asia Publishing House, London.

Shah, A. B. (Ed.) (1977) *The Letters and Correspondence of Pandita Ramabai.* Maharashtra State Board for Literature and Culture, Bombay.
Tharu, S. & Lalitha, K. (Eds.) (1995) *Women Writing in India, 600 BC to the Present*, 2 vols. Oxford University Press, New Delhi.

Sarkar, Benoy Kumar (1887–1949)

Vineeta Sinha

Benoy Kumar Sarkar was born in the district of Malda in the then Indian part of Bengal. At the young age of 13, he distinguished himself by coming top of the entrance exam for Calcutta University. He was educated at the Presidency College in Calcutta, where in 1905 he topped the undergraduate cohort with a double honors degree in history and English, and completed a master's degree in 1906. Apart from his solid academic credentials, he was a prominent public figure and well regarded in Bengali academic and intellectual circles. Sarkar was committed to nationalist, socialist, and social service agendas, embedded in the patriotic stance of securing for India political freedom from British colonial rule. To this end, Sarkar was active in both the Swadeshi (self-rule) and the National Education movements in Bengal.

The years 1914 to 1925 saw Sarkar spending a considerable period of time outside India. He visited Egypt, England, Scotland, Ireland, the United States, Japan, China, Korea, Germany, Austria, and Italy. In these countries he was based in universities and research institutes and lectured to academics and other communities of intellectuals. He spent a significant period of time in Germany and Italy and was able to acquire linguistic competence in several European languages, such as French, German, and Italian, in addition to already having mastered English, Bengali, and Hindi, a truly impressive linguistic feat. He delivered lectures in German and Italian, and also published in these languages. He doubled up as an ambassador for India (and, more broadly speaking, Asia) and tried to facilitate greater understanding on both sides of the East–West divide. He returned to India in 1925 and was appointed lecturer at the Department of Economics at Calcutta University, where in 1947 he was promoted to professor and head of department. In 1949 he traveled to the US, a trip arranged by the Institute of International Education, New York and the Watamull Foundation, Los Angeles. During this trip, he lectured in various American universities (including Harvard) and research institutes and addressed business organizations and political centers on the subject of East–West relations, amongst other issues. This hectic tour took its toll on his health. In October 1949 he suffered chest pains, and died a month later at the Freedman's Hospital in Washington, DC (Mukhopadhyay 1979).

Sarkar was not an armchair intellectual, and his thinking was very much grounded in concrete issues facing Bengali society, India, and "Asia." He was an institution builder. His early interest in pedagogical issues saw him establishing schools and at least nine research institutes in Calcutta, including: the Bengali Institute of Sociology, Bengali Asia Academy, Bengali Dante Society, and Bengali Institute of American Culture. He trained and supervised the research of innumerable postgraduate students, emphasizing the importance of mastering knowledge from a "world perspective" in addition to the value of learning at least one European language other than English and the mother tongue. Sarkar was fully aware that institutional and infrastructural changes were necessary before any intellectual shifts could occur in the various social science disciplines. He was at the forefront of instituting curriculum and disciplinary reform in tertiary institutions, introducing changes with the intention of producing a generation of Indian social scientists with a global and cosmopolitan outlook, but also with a firm awareness of Indian problematics.

Sarkar's published writings are vast and his scholarship can only be described as encyclopedic. He was a prolific writer, with tremendous intellectual output, straddling a range of social science perspectives from economics to political philosophy, history, sociology, literature, demography, political science, and anthropology (Mukherjee 1953), which would make his work "interdisciplinary" in contemporary language. Sarkar published predominantly in English and

Bengali. He wrote 53 books in English (many of which were published in Europe and the US) and countless articles in leading Indian, American, and European journals and periodicals. Some examples of the latter include: the *Calcutta Review*, *Modern Review* (Calcutta), *Political Science Quarterly* (New York), *American Political Science Review*, *International Journal of Ethics*, *Indian Historical Quarterly*, and *Insurance and Finance Review*. It is impossible to name all his writings here, and only a selection of books in English is offered (see Bandyopadhyay 1984 for a comprehensive list): *The Positive Background of Hindu Sociology* (Books 1 and 2, 1914/1921), *Chinese Religion Through Hindu Eyes* (1916), *The Futurism of Young Asia* (1922), *The Sociology of Population* (1936), *Villages and Towns as Social Patterns* (1941), *Political Philosophies Since 1905* (Vols. 1 and 2, 1942), and *Dominion in World-Perspectives* (1949). He also translated several social science books by European authors into Bengali. It is notable that Sarkar's intellectual interests were not confined to an "Indian" problematic. His substantive focus was often on issues concerning "Asia" in addition to providing critique and analysis of social, economic, cultural, and political issues in European settings. In no sense did he see himself narrowly as an "Indian social scientist," qualified to speak exclusively to "local" concerns. He did not shy away from engaging ideas of prominent American and European social scientists of his time, critiquing and challenging their theorizing. Some examples include his critique of Oswald Spengler's "urban–rural" and "culture–civilization" dichotomies and Pitirim Sorokin's progress theories.

He was unorthodox and revolutionary in his thinking and challenged conventional mainstream wisdom about everything, often providing his own original theorizing on the subject. The term "Sarkarism" was coined by his peers to refer to his unique intellectual stance, but is invoked as a metaphor, a perspective, or an orientation. Here is a sampling from his vast intellectual contribution to social science thinking. While Sarkar's works are infused with a strong historical perspective, he was not a historical determinist. The concept of "creative disequilibrium" is an original contribution to ongoing debates about the source of historical change and societal human progress. While he acknowledged the role of history (and the past) in shaping the future, he also held open the possibility of forces independent of past events and processes, thereby highlighting the role of chance, accidents, unpredictable events, and uncertainties, and thus assumed a different position from Bankimchandra, Sorokin, Spengler, Marx, and Hegel. He avoided a stage theory of change and saw the "disequilibrium" (between the forces of "good" and "evil") as creative, in constructively moving humanity toward an improved, more perfect state, and as the basis for change. Unlike Bankimchandra's view, he held that "history-less groups and classes have often by sheer energism and self-determination succeeded in changing the face of the world" (Sarkar 1942: 112).

In *The Positive Background of Hindu Sociology*, Sarkar argues for the basic universalism of the human species, despite a recognition of "pluralities" at individual and national levels. This work is an early critique of Indological and Orientalist thinking, predating by decades Said's *Orientalism* (1979). As a theorist of modernity, he addressed the problematics of the Industrial Revolution, both for "Eur-America" and the "East" (including India and China) in the encounter with forces of industrialization and modernization, but for the latter within the context of colonialist and imperialist experiences. Sarkar refuted the assumption of fundamental and irreconcilable differences between Asia and Europe, a view that was pervasive in popular thinking, political and international relations discourses, and in much of social science scholarship of the time, both Indian and European. Through historical research, he demonstrated overwhelming similarities between India and Europe vis-à-vis scientific, material, and technological developments. In so doing, he challenged the definition of India as a predominantly mystical and spiritual society (and superior), in contrast to the "West," which was defined as material, scientific, and industrial. He thus provided an alternative and contrary reading of India, one that was at odds with current opinion, fortified through the works of Max Muller, Rudyard Kipling, Max Weber, Vivekananda, and Sri Aurobindo, to name a few. These premises were debunked as myths and rejected by Sarkar as offering an analytical frame for explaining India's "backwardness" and Europe's "progress." Sarkar located the reasons for India's underdevelopment elsewhere – in the domination, control, and hegemony of colonial experience(s) and their debilitating effects on material advancement.

While it is possible to abstract evidence of sociological and political thought from the huge corpus of Sarkar's writings, this task has yet to be undertaken systematically. In particular, Sarkar's political thought needs to be fleshed out, given that he was a pioneer in calling for an objective analysis of political institutions, values, and ideologies (Bandyopadhyay 1984), and highlighting the secular nature of politics. He was a nationalist, a liberal, and a firm believer in social democracy with a strong place for the individual and the state, in a culturally and politically plural social context. He was a staunch supporter of socialist and communist thought and was a firm advocate for the rights of the less privileged groups in society, such as the lower classes and lower castes of Hindus, Muslims, and tribals. In this context, Sarkar made an important contribution to the debates about such concepts as "culture," "intelligence," and "civilization." He argued that literacy and formal education were recent, modern phenomena, and that illiteracy could not be correlated with lack of intellect, morality, or culture. His socialism viewed the natural intelligence and practical experience of illiterate members of the community as "valuable intellectual assets" (Mukherjee 1995: 55). In a related vein, he challenged the patterns of social differentiation in Spengler's urban–rural dichotomy. He also rejected in this discourse the romanticized (non-political and soulful) image of the village community, and the more negative portrayal of the average city dweller. He writes: "The milk of human kindness does not flow more frequently in the interactions of the village 'community' than those in the town 'society'" (Sarkar 1941).

Despite such credentials and achievements, Sarkar's students and supporters note that he is a nonentity amongst contemporary social science students, even in India. In the historiography of the social sciences, knowledge about this talented social thinker is indeed dismal. What little information – biographical and intellectual – that does exist has been documented by a few of his colleagues, friends, and students (Dutt 1932, 1939; Dass 1939; Ghosal 1939; Chaudhury 1940; Mukherjee 1953, 1995; Mukhopadhyay 1979; Bandyopadhyay 1984). The most recent of this material can be dated to the 1980s, with little new secondary work on Sarkar coming in the following two decades. In his lifetime, Sarkar enjoyed tremendous public visibility (perhaps more outside India) and popularity, but his genius was probably unrecognized by his peers.

As a social scientist, Sarkar operated with a cosmopolitan, trans-Asian frame of reference and recognized unifying forces in the space labeled "Asia" despite the diversity and complexity within, more so than in the present, where a fragmented view of Asia prevails. Sarkar's pioneering status as a social thinker and a theorist of modernity, speaking at the turn of the twentieth century from a non-western locale but deeply and critically engaged with social science concepts, theories, issues, and problematics current in the "West" (where social science disciplines were institutionalized), marks his distinction. He is a perfect candidate (in alternative, counter-Eurocentric and counter-Orientalist discourses) for the title of a social thinker whose ideas and activities transgressed given boundaries, making his ideas modern, universal, and relevant.

SEE ALSO: Discourse; Eurocentrism; Khaldun, Ibn; Orientalism; Rizal, José; Saraswati, Pandita Ramabai; Sorokin, Pitirim A.; Theory

REFERENCES AND SUGGESTED READINGS

Bandyopadhyay, B. (1984) *The Political Ideas of Benoy Kumar Sarkar.* K. P. Bagchi, Calcutta.

Chaudhury, N. N. (1940) *Pragmatism and Pioneering in Benoy Sarkar's Sociology and Economics.* Chuckervertty, Chatterjee, Calcutta.

Dass, B. (Ed.) (1939) *The Social and Economic Ideas of Benoy Sarkar.* Chuckervertty, Chatterjee, Calcutta.

Dutt, S. C. (1932) *Fundamental Problems and Leading Ideas in the Works of Prof. Benoy Kumar Sarkar.* Calcutta.

Dutt, S. C. (1939) *Conflicting Tendencies in Indian Economic Thought: Sarkarism in Economics.* Chuckervertty, Chatterjee, Calcutta.

Ghosal, S. K. (1939) *Sarkarism: The Ideas and Ideals of Benoy Sarkar on Man and His Conquests.* Chuckervertty, Chatterjee, Calcutta.

Mukherjee, H. (1953) *Benoy Kumar Sarkar: A Study*. Shiksha-Tirtha Karyalaya, Calcutta.
Mukherjee, H. (1995) Social Thoughts of Benoy Kumar Sarkar. *Journal of Indian Anthropological Society* 30: 51–8.
Mukhopadhyay, A. K. (1979) Benoy Kumar Sarkar: The Theoretical Foundation of Indian Capitalism. In: Mukhopadhyay, A. K. (Ed.), *The Bengali Intellectual Tradition from Rammohun Ray to Dhirendranath Sen*. K. P. Bagchi, Calcutta, pp. 212–34.
Sarkar, B. K. (1941) *Villages and Towns as Social Patterns*. Calcutta.
Sarkar, B. K. (1942) *Political Philosophies Since 1905*, Vol. 1. Lahore.

Sartre, Jean-Paul (1905–80)

Eric Margolis

The introduction to Sartre's monumental *Critique of Dialectical Reason* (1960) was published in English as *Search for a Method* (1963). Sartre saw the social sciences as in deep crisis arising from a basic contradiction: "We are not only knowers, in the triumph of intellectual self-consciousness, we appear as the known" (Sartre 1963: 9). Sociologists also remarked upon the discipline's state of arrested development. For instance, at the time Sartre was writing, C. Wright Mills (1959) had characterized sociology as a split between an "abstracted empiricism" and "grand theory." This is a similar notion to the Sartrian criticism of sociology and Marxism as an unprincipled empiricism on one side and pure fixed knowledge on the other. *Search for a Method* is a critical comparison of Marxism and sociology by the existential philosopher who defined his goal as "revisionism," the ongoing process in any living philosophy which takes place in thought but is also part of the "movement of society" (Sartre 1963: 7). Sartre is critical of sociology for being "an idealistic static knowing, the sole function of which is to conceal history," and a "practical empiricism in the hands of the capitalists which supports human engineering" (pp. 67–8); and critical of Marxism for no longer knowing anything: "Its concepts are dictates; its goal is no longer to increase what it knows but to be itself constituted a priori as an absolute knowledge" (p. 28). Sartre castigated "lazy" Marxists who, "stand(ing) in their own light," transformed Marxism into determinism through the a priori application of Marx's theory (pp. 38–3), and the mechanical materialism of sociology that reduced persons-in-the-world to a system of objects linked by universal relations (see Sartre 1955: 200).

In keeping with existentialism's philosophy of free will, Sartre rejected all determinisms. In *Being and Nothingness* he had remarked: "The historian is himself historical ... he historicizes himself by illuminating 'history' in the light of his projects and of those of his society" (Sartre 1971: 643). Destroying the possibility of an objective "social physics," the statement opens the possibility for a social science based on praxis. Unifying theory and practice, asserting with Marx that people not prior conditions make history, Sartre sought to revise Marxism, which he saw as salvageable if it approached the social heuristically: "its principles and its prior knowledge appear as regulative in relation to its concrete research" (Sartre 1963: 26).

The praxis of "historical-structural anthropology" Sartre termed the progressive-regressive method. He borrowed LeFebvre's (1953) approach, which had three moments. First is the way Sartre conceived of sociology, a horizontal enterprise aimed at uncovering social structure in all its relations and functions (demographic, family, religion, etc.). Noting that at different times there have been other structures, the second, vertical, moment describes the history and genesis of social structures. The third moment calls for dialectical totalization – seeking to understand the "principle of the series." Sartre added the reservation that method itself must be subject to "modifications which its objects may impose on it – *in all the domains of anthropology*" (Sartre 1963: 52). This is because "the foundation of anthropology is man himself, not as the object of practical knowledge, but as a practical organism producing knowledge as a moment of praxis" (p. 179). Research is a "living relationship" in which "the sociologist and his 'object' form a couple, each of which is to be interpreted by the other; the relationship between them must be itself interpreted as a moment of history" (p. 72). Sartre argued that a structural-historical anthropology must "devise its concepts from the new experiences which it seeks to interpret": "the particular man in his social field, in his class, in an environment of collective objects, and of other particular men. It is the individual, alienated, reified, mystified, as he has been made to be by the division of labor and by exploitation, but struggling against alienation with the help of distorting instruments. And, despite everything, patiently gaining ground" (p. 133).

SEE ALSO: Dialectic; Dialectical Materialism; Existential Sociology; Lefebvre, Henri; Marx, Karl; Marxism and Sociology; Materialism; Paradigms; Praxis

REFERENCES AND SUGGESTED READINGS

LeFebvre, H. (1953) *Problème de sociologie rurale. La communauté paysanne et ses problèmes.* Cahiers Internationaux de Sociologie, Vol. 9. Seuil, Paris.

Mills, C. W. (1959) *The Sociological Imagination.* Oxford University Press, New York.

Sartre, J.-P. (1955 [1946]) Materialism and Revolution. In: *Literary and Philosophical Essays.* Trans. A. Michelson. Collier Books, New York, pp. 198–256.

Sartre, J.-P. (1963 [1960]) *Search for a Method.* Trans. H. E. Barnes. Alfred A. Knopf, New York.

Sartre, J.-P. (1968 [1960]) *Critique of Dialectical Reason.* Trans. A. Sheridan-Smith. New Left Books, London.

Sartre, J.-P. (1971 [1943]) *Being and Nothingness.* Trans. H. E. Barnes. Washington Square Press, New York.

Satanism

Massimo Introvigne

While organized Satanism includes quite small groups, social scientists have studied Satanism mostly as the subject matter of juvenile deviance and social panics. Satanism may be defined as the adoration of the figure known in the Bible as the Devil or Satan. Its first incarnation was in the circle operating at the Versailles court of Louis XIV (1638–1715) around Catherine La Voisin (ca. 1640–80) and the defrocked Catholic priest Father Guibourg (1603–83), who invented the so-called "Black Mass," a parody of the Roman Catholic Mass. La Voisin was burned at the stake in 1680 and Guibourg died in jail in 1683. Small rings imitating what they had read of the group were subsequently discovered in France, Italy, and Russia in the eighteenth and nineteenth centuries.

In the 1880s, reporter Jules Bois (1868–1943) and novelist Joris-Karl Huysmans (1848–1907) explored the French occult underworld, and in 1891 Huysmans published his bestselling novel on Satanism, *Là-bas* (Down There), which included one of the most famous literary descriptions of a Black Mass. Public opinion overreacted and sensational revelations of a worldwide Satanic conspiracy were offered to the French public by journalist Léo Taxil (1854–1907). Taxil, claiming to be an ex-Freemason converted to Catholicism, revealed that a Satanist organization called Palladism was behind Freemasonry and anti-clericalism. Eventually, in 1897, Taxil confessed that both his revelations and conversion to Catholicism had been a hoax conceived in order to convince the world just how gullible the anti-Masonic Catholics of his time actually were.

Although a body of literature inspired by the Taxil fraud continued to be published well into the twentieth century, anti-Satanism was largely discredited until British magus Aleister Crowley (1875–1947) shocked his contemporaries by styling himself "the Beast 666" and "the wickedest man in the world." Crowley made use of Satanic imagery and is still regarded by many as the founding father of contemporary Satanism. The British occultist, however, was a "magical atheist" who did not believe in the actual existence of Satan; and, although he has been influential on later Satanic movements, he cannot be regarded as a Satanist in the most technical sense of the term. On the other hand, it is true that Crowley enthusiasts, including movie director Kenneth Anger, were instrumental in creating the Church of Satan.

The latter's founder, Anton Szander LaVey (1930–97), joined a Crowleyan group in 1951, and through this milieu he came into contact with Anger. In 1961 they founded an organization known as the Magic Circle, which gradually evolved into the Church of Satan, founded on April 30, 1966. The Church of Satan did not literally believe in the existence of the Devil. It was more an idiosyncratic and militantly anti-Christian human potential movement, devoted to the exaltation of human beings who, having been freed from religious superstitions and the false Christian notion of sin, would eventually become able to enjoy life and flourish.

In 1968 LaVey met Michael Aquino, an officer and intelligence specialist in the US Army with an academic education, who gradually became the main organizer of the Church of Satan. During the early 1970s, however, a contrast developed between LaVey and Aquino, since the latter believed in the real, physical existence of a character known as Set or Satan, and became increasingly disillusioned with LaVey's "rationalist" Satanism. In 1975 Aquino left LaVey and went his separate way into the newly established Temple of Set, probably the largest international Satanist organization still active today.

Currently, after LaVey's death in 1997, the Church of Satan is largely a mail organization, and has generated several splinter groups, including the First Satanic Church led by LaVey's own daughter, Karla. The current combined active membership of all organized Satanism does not reach a thousand.

LaVey's notoriety certainly played a role in the early stages of the anti-Satanist campaign of the 1970s and 1980s. The McMartin case began in 1983, when the principals and a number of teachers of a respected California preschool were accused of operating an underground Satanic cult, which ritually abused and tortured children. Mental health professionals involved in the case were later accused of having "planted" the stories in the children's minds, based on their own theories about Satanism. The McMartin trial ended in 1990 with no convictions. It had an enormous media impact, however, and undoubtedly had something to do with the hundreds of subsequent similar accusations of Satanic ritual abuses in both day-care centers and in family settings. Although complete statistical data are lacking, it is possible that as many as 2,000 cases of Satanic ritual abuse of children were investigated in the decade 1983–92, with only a handful of convictions. Sociologists and other academics emerged as the most vocal critics of the theory of a secret Satanic network. In 1994 two official reports, one by the US National Center for the Prevention of Child Abuse and Neglect, and one by sociologist Jean S. La Fontaine on behalf of the UK government, concluded that stories of Satanic ritual abuse were largely figments of the accusers' imaginations. In subsequent years, the number of court cases involving allegations of Satanic ritual abuse sharply decreased.

The debate on the alleged Satanic ritual abuse of children should not be confused with discussions of adolescent Satanism. There is little doubt that there are gangs of teenagers performing some sort of homemade Satanic ritual (copied from comics, books, or movies), often also involving drugs. These teenagers are often guilty of minor crimes such as vandalism or animal sacrifice. In fewer than a dozen cases over the last two decades, more serious crimes appear to have been committed, including a handful of murders, some of them uncovered in northern Italy in 2004. In these cases, it is difficult to determine whether drugs, gang-related violence, or Satan worship are mostly responsible for crimes which do not appear to be related to organized Satanism.

SEE ALSO: Millenarianism; New Religious Movements; Religion, Sociology of; Religious Cults; Sect

REFERENCES AND SUGGESTED READINGS

Introvigne, M. (1997) *Enquête sur le satanisme. Satanistes et anti-satanistes du XVIIe siècle à nos jours* (Investigating Satanism: Satanists and Anti-Satanists from the 17th to the 20th Century). Dervy, Paris.

Richardson, J. T., Best, J., & Bromley, D. G. (Eds.) (1991) *The Satanism Scare.* Aldine de Gruyter, New York.

Victor, J. S. (1993) *Satanic Panic: The Creation of a Contemporary Legend.* Open Court, Chicago.

Saussure, Ferdinand de (1857–1913)

J. I. (Hans) Bakker

Ferdinand de Saussure is an important linguist and, along with C. S. Peirce, one of the two main contributors to semiotics (Sebeok 2001; Sanders

2004). His distinction between the signifier and the signified is central. The theory of signification, the idea that a sign is an entirely arbitrary verbal or written phonemic and phonetic device, is attributed to him. The word "cat" and the word "chat" are different only linguistically; the signified "object" remains the same (Koerner 1973). The standard view of Saussure is based on posthumous publication of his lecture notes (Saussure 1967, 1968, 1989 [1916]). Like work by Weber and Mead, the *Course in General Linguistics* (1916) is the product of other hands. Between 1906 and 1911, Saussure taught three courses on general linguistics. Student notes have now been published separately (Saussure 1993 [1910–11], 1996 [1907], 1997 [1908–9]). Bouissac (2005) argues that the standard view of Saussure is incorrect; he did not reach any definitive conclusions concerning general linguistics or semiology. Indeed, Saussure (2002) found many ideas in linguistics problematic epistemologically. He linked "signology" (*signologie*) to psychology. He poses epistemological questions, but there is debate concerning his answers. His emphasis on evolutionary change can be thought of as sophisticated neo-Darwinian theory (e.g., cognitive neuroscience). This makes it possible to think of an "algorithmic" version of semiotics (Bouissac 2005). Saussurean scholarship (*Cahiers Ferdinand de Saussure*) has questioned some of the poststructuralist critiques (e.g., Roland Barthes, Jacques Derrida) of Saussure's structuralist linguistics.

SEE ALSO: Barthes, Roland; Derrida, Jacques; Epistemology; Language; *Langue* and *Parole*; Semiotics; Signs; Sociolinguistics

REFERENCES AND SUGGESTED READINGS

Bouissac, P. (2005) Does Saussure Still Matter? *Semiotic Review of Books* 14(3): 1–19.

Harris, R. (2001) *Saussure and His Interpreters*. Edinburgh University Press, Edinburgh.

Koerner, E. F. K. (1973) *Ferdinand de Saussure: Origin and Development of His Linguistic Thought in Western Studies of Language*. Vieweg & Sohn, Braunschweig.

Sanders, C. (Ed.) (2004) *The Cambridge Companion to Saussure*. Cambridge University Press, Cambridge.

Saussure, F. de (1967, 1968, 1989 [1916]) *Ferdinand de Saussure. Cours de linguistique générale. Édition critique*, Vols. 1 and 2. Ed. R. Engler. Otto Harrassowitz, Wiesbaden.

Saussure, F. de (1983) *Course in General Linguistics*. Trans. R. Harris. Duckworth, London. (Translation based on Payot editions of 1916, 1922, 1931, 1949, and 1955.)

Saussure, F. de (1993 [1910–11]) *The Third Course of Lectures on General Linguistics from the Notebooks of Émile Constantin, 1910–11*. Ed. E. Komatsu. Trans. R. Harris. Pergamon, Oxford.

Saussure, F. de (1996 [1907]) *Saussure's First Course of Lectures on General Linguistics from the Notebooks of Albert Riedlinger, 1907*. Ed. E. Komatsu. Trans. G. Wolf. Pergamon, Oxford.

Saussure, F. de (1997 [1908–9]) *The Third Course of Lectures on General Linguistics from the Notebooks of Albert Riedlinger and Charles Patois*. Ed. E. Komatsu. Trans. G. Wolf. Pergamon, Oxford.

Saussure, F. de (2002) *Écrits de linguistique générale*. Ed. S. Bouquet & R. Engler. Gallimard, Paris.

Sebeok, T. A. (2001) *Signs: An Introduction to Semiotics*. University of Toronto Press, Toronto.

Starbobinski, J. (1979) *Words Upon Words: The Anagrams of Ferdinand de Saussure*. Trans. O. Emmet. Yale University Press, New Haven.

scapegoating

Evans Mandes

Scapegoating is the process of unjustly accusing or blaming an individual or a group for the actions of others not of their own doing. It is derived from the tendency to displace aggression toward a minority group. Typically, innocent individuals or groups receive the displaced aggression when others feel threatened by them. These targets of aggression are often perceived as "safe" targets because they are victimized and often powerless to fight back. They are frequently vilified, criticized, and rejected. In a non-pathological sense, scapegoating may also be perceived as the natural outgrowth of stereotypes associated with race, religion, sex, gender, and ethnicity. This point of view, sometimes referred to as the exaggeration hypothesis, is based upon perceptual contrasts or cognitive processing limitations. The group conflict model, however, sees scapegoating in more motivational terms, where exaggeration grows out of individual or group conflict. Scapegoating can also be seen as the outgrowth of prejudice, which develops either in the personal sense where some group is perceived as a threat to one's own interests, economically, socially, or as a group endeavor where conformity becomes an issue. In order to conform, one's group expects you to express and support the view of the collective group.

"Scapegoat" originates from the Hebrew practice of transferring ritualistically and symbolically the sins of individuals to goats. The chosen goat was driven into the desert by the Hebrew priests to atone for guilt, thus absolving individuals and groups from their individual or collective sins. The most horrific example of scapegoating in modern times was that of the Jews by the Nazis in World War II. Prior to the war, Germany had undergone a period of economic and political upheaval. The economic failures of the Weimar Republic after Germany's defeat in World War I produced a period of economic depression, unprecedented inflation, and social unrest. These conditions set the stage for Adolf Hitler and his followers to blame Germany's social and economic problems on the Jews, thus heightening to new levels the anti-Semitism already present in the country. One Nazi leader, explaining the need for the convenient scapegoating of the Jews, noted: "If the Jews did not exist, we would have invented them" (quoted by Koltz 1983).

Other researchers have used scapegoating as a descriptive term to explain racial tensions during periods of social and economic unrest. The negative correlation between the number of lynchings of blacks by Southerners and economic conditions in the South is often cited in the popular literature on race relations. These studies have led to the promulgation of the frustration-aggression hypothesis in social psychology. In this hypothesis, tensions associated with frustrated needs often are associated with violence and aggression.

Current research using scapegoating as an explanatory tool is varied and interdisciplinary. Psychoanalysis, for instance, views scapegoating in group therapy as an example of projective identification. The scapegoat is the source of hostility because she or he demonstrates traits that group members care to reject or wish to repress, deny, or otherwise remove from their conscious experiences. Bullying or victimization is seen in this context; the bullies tend to think others are attacking them. They tend to interpret relatively neutral interpersonal relations as attempts to dominate others aggressively. Their worldview is commonly seen in terms of polar opposites – winning or losing, domination or subservience, triumph or shame. Studies examining family values show similar results. Men who display aggression toward their families often misinterpret the behavior of family members. Neutral acts or words by family members are seen as deliberate attacks, again an amplification or exaggeration of events due to underlying pathology.

Risk behavior is another contemporary area of research by sociologists interested in drug behavior and risk denial. By studying the cannabis use of French adolescents, researchers have found that the cannabis users often scapegoat other "hard drug" users. They deny their own addictions, thereby challenging the "risky" label for them and convincing themselves of their ability to control their own addictions (Peretti-Watel 2003).

In social psychology, studies performed on the scapegoating mechanism tend to take a similar form. Using students as subjects, the paradigm introduces some element of failure. Failure is ensured either by employing extremely difficult tasks or by setting up unrealistic competitions among rival peer groups. Attitudes toward individual racial groups falsely associated with these failures or competitions were taken before or after the induced exposure to failure/competition. The data showed predictably lowered attitude scores after the subjects were frustrated by induced failure or competition. The researchers consider these results as evidence of scapegoating.

Most recently, research on scapegoating has examined attitudes toward family values and political attacks against the Muslim world. Both use scapegoating as descriptive mechanisms for understanding the human process. During recent campaigns, studies of the political rhetoric surrounding the issue of family values tend to identify the family as the absolute site for social change (Cloud 2001). In these studies minorities and economically disadvantaged Americans are scapegoated for social problems.

In a similar vein, attacks on the Muslim world are seen as attempts to heal the humiliation suffered by the United States due to the destruction of the World Trade Center and the Pentagon. The Muslim world is regarded in this analysis as the collective scapegoat of US frustration, which can be assuaged only through direct military action.

A history of the use of the term scapegoat can be found in Victor (2003).

SEE ALSO: Authoritarian Personality; Discrimination; Pogroms; Scientific Racism; Slurs (Racial/Ethnic)

REFERENCES AND SUGGESTED READINGS

Cloud, D. (2001) The Rhetoric of Family Values: Scapegoating, Utopia, and the Privatization of Social Responsibility. *Western Journal of Communication* 62: 387–419.

Koltz, C. (1983) Scapegoating. *Psychology Today* (December): 68–9.

Peretti-Watel, P. (2003) Neutralization Theory and the Denial of Risk: Some Evidence from Cannabis Use Among French Adolescents. *British Journal of Sociology* 54: 21–42.

Victor, G. (2003) Scapegoating: A Rite of Purification. *Journal of Psychohistory* 30: 271–88.

www.birchgrave.org/html/scapegoating.html/.

www.scapegoating.demon.co.uk (Scapegoat Society).

school choice

Scott Davies

School choice refers to the use of public funds that give parents more discretion in their children's education. It usually entails making available to parents a wider variety of educational options beyond a standard, local public school. Examples of choice initiatives include charter schools, home schooling, voucher programs, tax credits for private schools, and the formation of magnet schools. While many parents exercise a "hidden" form of school choice via their selection of residential location, choice programs stir most controversy when they entail privatization, that is, the redirecting of governing authority from a public body to parents and/or school staff.

In North America the impetus for choice needs to be understood in the context of the mass expansion of public education. The achievement of universal enrolments at elementary and then secondary levels over the twentieth century gave rise to large, bureaucratic schools. Known somewhat derisively as the "one best system" approach to education, large urban schools grew to be characterized by standardized offerings and a bureaucratic governing structure (Tyack 1974). While perhaps administratively efficient, such schools disenchanted many educators, students, and parents in the 1960s and 1970s. A variety of actors, including minority advocates and experimental pedagogues, portrayed mass public schools as dehumanizing, inequitable, and unresponsive to children's needs. In response, they initiated a flurry of educational alternatives, including "Free" and "Open" schools, often mandated to serve collective goals and notions of minority rights. Though most of these innovations were short-lived, they brought to the public system a more "progressive" curriculum, and a greater concern with educational equity.

A very different type of choice movement emerged in the early 1980s, marked by rationales of providing avenues for individual status-striving and for the benefits of school competition. Declaring public schools to be substandard, many policymakers began to seek initiatives to boost the quality of education. Some reasoned that if public schools faced competition for clients from new schools of choice, the quality of both would necessarily rise. Simultaneously, many middle-class parents acquired preferences for more intensive education, looking to prep their children for prized slots in higher education, or to provide them an experience tailored to their needs. Choice was seen as a solution to both of these concerns.

This type of choice resonates with policymakers who embrace a "market" approach to schooling. A resounding theme among these proponents is that markets can be an antidote to the "one best system." They see public bureaucracies as too slow to adapt to a world in which parent, student, and teacher preferences for pedagogy are increasingly specialized and varied. According to Chubb and Moe (1990), the most renowned market theorists, markets can free schools from the grip of central administration. Regular public funding arrangements, they argue, encourage schools to conform to legal conventions rather than provide effective service, and thus make public schools unresponsive to their clients. In contrast, many choice arrangements force schools to attract fee-paying parents in order to survive. This is said to make their educational decision-making more entrepreneurial and attuned to boosting student achievement. Markets are thus hailed by their advocates as the optimal medium for linking the preferences of parents to educators, and delivering a more personalized, customized education.

This theory of market-based choice has spawned one of the most polarized debates in contemporary education. The intensity of this controversy is rooted in enduring philosophical issues. Many defenders of public schools see choice initiatives as threatening the common school tradition, in which schools draw students from the immediate area and bind them into a vibrant local citizenry, creating the grounds for grassroots democracy (see Fuller 2000). Choice, some warn, can only further decay the populace's common experience and their participation in collective endeavors. Further, many fault the choice movement for equating the value of school with individualistic status-striving rather than collective goals, thereby further diluting the public spirit of education.

Beyond these philosophical disputes, sociologists commonly address empirical dimensions of choice, and in so doing have made some advances. Much of the choice literature in the early 1990s was highly polemical, due partly to the absence of adequate data and the novelty of most choice initiatives. The past decade, however, has produced a sprawling interdisciplinary literature, with an extensive stockpile of studies conducted by educationalists, sociologists, political scientists, and, increasingly, economists. This corpus of research has four major themes.

One theme examines how choice affects the sorting of students among schools. Advocates claim that choice can effectively reduce race and class segregation by allowing poor and minority families to escape substandard institutions. In contrast, critics claim that such policies will only "cream off" the best students from mediocre schools, resulting in a renewed form of segregation. Interestingly, research to date suggests that choice neither lessens nor worsens existing levels of segregation. While relatively few minority parents take advantage of choice initiatives, charter schools appear roughly to reflect the composition of their neighborhoods, since they are often bound to regulations that ensure minimal levels of diversity (Goldhaber 1999).

The second theme has received the greatest attention in the US: the impact of choice on performance outcomes, particularly standardized test scores. While students in private schools have higher aggregate scores than their public counterparts, private schools can select more affluent and motivated students. The core issue is therefore whether or not choice mechanisms boost student performance net of the composition of students. A body of research has emerged that attempts to sort out those effects. While there is little consensus, and while disputes usually entail statistical intricacies, there is not any clear data that choice indeed provides a net increase in test scores. Evidence suggests that parents of students in such schools report high levels of satisfaction, and that choice can allow schools to be responsive to the vagaries of parental demand. But such evidence has led some to conclude that public schools would perform similarly given the same resources and ability to select students (Witte 2000).

A third issue deals with organizational characteristics. A central claim by choice advocates is that market forces spark innovations in school pedagogy, curricula, and personnel. Yet research to date on this issue is mixed. American studies suggest that innovation among charter schools is limited (Lubienski 2003). Canadian research similarly suggests that new private schools are rarely innovative in their instruction and structure, though many form niches and specialized identities (Davies & Quirke 2005). One provisional conclusion is that market-style choice can trigger more specialized schools, but that such schools rarely deviate from the "fundamental grammar" of schooling that has been institutionalized over the past century.

A fourth issue involves whether the presence of market competition motivates local public schools to improve, presumably by threatening those schools with the risk of losing students to rivals. For instance, after making a series of bold statistical assumptions, Hoxby (2003) claims that public school test scores indeed climb when they face greater competition. Others acknowledge this broad finding, but attribute it to the greater resources available to public schools in areas with large private enrolments (Arum 1996).

Much of this research is embroiled in methodological disputes. A core issue among quantitative researchers is how to isolate differences in school performance that are attributable to student versus school characteristics. To better sort out these effects, many researchers use measures of achievement growth instead of cross-sectional data, but these longitudinal data are sometimes beset by attrition effects and by limited measures that fail to fully capture differences in motivation and academic preparedness among students. Qualitative researchers face the challenge of exploring emerging types of choice, such as home schooling, private tutoring, and the variety of charter schools. Such studies can potentially contribute to the choice literature by addressing holistic issues such as how parents and educators understand and experience choice, as well as its impact on less quantifiable outcomes like citizenship and community cohesion.

Choice movements will likely continue to thrive as long as competition for prized slots in post-secondary education continues, and as families continue to embrace "intensive parenting," a practice that values intimate educational experiences tailored to children's unique needs (Davies & Quirke 2005). It will probably thrive best where public education is not strong, creating niches for schools with small classes and/or special curricular themes, or in cities with atrophied public offerings. While public schools will continue to cater to the vast bulk of students, choice will be sought by those who are most advantaged, and sometimes by those who are most disadvantaged.

SEE ALSO: Schooling, Home; Schools, Charter; Schools, Magnet; Schools, Public

REFERENCES AND SUGGESTED READINGS

Arum, R. (1996) Do Private Schools Force Public Schools to Compete? *American Sociological Review* 61(1): 29–46.

Chubb, J. & Moe, T. (1990) *Politics, Markets and American Schools.* Brookings Institution, Washington, DC.

Davies, S. & Quirke, L. (2005) Providing for the Priceless Student: Ideologies of Choice in an Emerging Educational Market. *American Journal of Education* 111(4).

Fuller, B. (2000) Introduction. In: Fuller, B. (Ed.), *Inside Charter Schools.* Harvard University Press, Cambridge, MA, pp. 1–11.

Goldhaber, D. D. (1999) School Choice: An Examination of the Empirical Evidence on Achievement, Parental Decision-Making, and Equity. *Educational Researcher* 28(9): 16–25.

Hoxby, C. M. (2003) *The Economics of School Choice.* University of Chicago Press, Chicago.

Lubienski, C. (2003) Innovation in Education Markets: Theory and Evidence on the Impact of Competition and Choice in Charter Schools. *American Education Research Journal* 40(2): 395–443.

Tyack, D. (1974) *The One Best System: A History of American Urban Education.* Harvard University Press, Cambridge, MA.

Witte, J. F. (2000) *The Market Approach to Education: An Analysis of America's First Voucher Program.* Princeton University Press, Princeton.

school climate

Robert Crosnoe

School climate refers to the general tone of social relations in and around schools: how people in the school relate to each other, the culture that emerges among these people, the norms that they construct. Quite simply, it represents the general "feel" of the school. This aspect of school context taps the informal processes that occur within schools. Like the more formal processes (e.g., instruction, delivery of curricula), these informal processes affect a wide variety of student outcomes and are important ingredients in the general functioning of schools themselves.

More than other aspects of education, the theoretical and empirical research on school climate bridges multiple disciplines – sociology, psychology, education – and integrates qualitative and quantitative methods. The late James Coleman played a major role in this development. His pioneering study *The Adolescent Society* (1961) vividly captured the intense dynamics of peer cultures in a group of Midwestern high schools, depicting how the social climate of a school can undermine its formal educational mission. More recently, his formulation of the social capital framework drew explicitly on the positive aspects of school climate, such as supportive intergenerational networks between young and old that form in and around schools (Coleman 1990). These social aspects of schooling, he argued, could actually facilitate the educational mission of schools. This basic argument was also a major theme in the effective schools movement of the 1970s (Lightfoot 1982), which emphasized that the social psychological, interpersonal, and political aspects of school cultures and surrounding communities were the building blocks of successful teaching and learning.

The concept of school climate in general and Coleman's discussion of social capital in schools in particular have served as both foundation and foil to sociologists. Some have pursued a more thorough understanding of the linkage between the formal and informal processes of school or the role of the school as a context of human development, while others have objected to the lack of precision in social capital concepts, the apparent lack of amenability of the cultures that arise in schools to policy intervention, and the overgeneralizations of schools and students that arose from early studies in this field. Still, this back and forth has ultimately resulted in a rich body of empirical research on school climate, which can be broken down into three general areas: peer culture in the school, intergenerational relations in the school, and the school community.

First, schools, especially middle schools and high schools, serve as the most concrete, identifiable, bounded site of peer culture in the early life course. They group together – in a specific physical location under a common institutional identity – large numbers of young people for extended periods of most days in the majority of weeks in the year. At the same time, class enrollment patterns and curricular assignments further differentiate these larger groups of young people into smaller subsets characterized by sustained interaction. The work of Maureen Hallinan and her colleagues has demonstrated how, on both of these levels, schools affect the formation of friendships and the construction of peer networks (Kubitschek & Hallinan 1998). In effect, schools organize systems of social relations, which have their own distinct norms, values, and behavioral patterns. These diverse peer cultures, in aggregate, affect the general climate of the school. This peer dimension of school climate can range from positive (e.g., prosocial, academically focused) to negative (e.g., oppositional). The type of school-based peer climate to which students are exposed, in turn, influences their academic progress and general development. On a more macro level, this aspect of school climate can effect larger patterns of inequality.

Numerous ethnographies, such as *School Talk* (Eder et al. 1995), have illustrated how these cultural patterns constructed among young people in a school can make that school an incredibly difficult – or alternatively, supportive – place to be. The ability of schools to teach and transmit knowledge is intricately related to what goes on among students. Indeed, quantitative analyses have revealed that students' social psychological functioning is highly reactive to the general norms of the student body and its subgroups and that this social psychological functioning is a major factor in their academic functioning. Also related to these in-school cultures is the integration of diverse student populations and the magnitude of race and class inequality. Research has consistently shown that the ease with which school integration proceeds is, in part, a function of the cross-pollination of the peer networks of different racial populations (Moody 2001).

Second, schools are a primary point of contact between young and old, in that schools serve children and adolescents but are operated by adults. The degree to which teachers and other school personnel connect to students is a crucial element in school climate. Whether conflict or cordiality reigns is important to students' trajectories through their years in that school. The nature of the intergenerational climate in the school can be thought of according to different dimensions, including support, warmth, and mutual respect. Students tend to do better academically in schools with climates that encompass all three, but, importantly, they are also happier in these schools. In other words, positive intergenerational climates foster better mental health as well as better academic performance. Indeed, as seen in the research of Bryk et al. (1993), as well as others interested in school size and sector, the relative costs and benefits of attending a large or small school, a Catholic or public school, are often predicated on the type of intergenerational climates that characterize each. At the same time, Alexander and Entwisle's (1988) seminal research on the early school years has demonstrated the central role of student–teacher relations in race and class differences in academic achievement and learning, patterns that have been replicated on the high school level. Teachers and students are the two primary populations in schools, and so the distance between them helps to determine if a school climate is good, bad, or essentially inequitable.

Third, the climate of schools is a function of factors nominally outside the school as well as those that occur on school grounds. In short, the school is part of a larger community. On one level, this community refers to the actual neighborhoods surrounding the school. In its simplest form, the school is a building that rests in a certain area. That area is an ecology in which the school "lives and grows." Certainly, a wealth of evidence has demonstrated that the characteristics of the community in which the school is situated can affect what occurs in the school. Criminal activity and poverty in the surrounding area, for example, complicate the educational mission of schools – students have more trouble learning, and teachers teaching, when they are distracted, distressed, and frightened. The climate of education suffers in these areas, despite the best efforts of schools. The case for the significance of this aspect of school climate has emerged from both detailed ethnography, such as *Ain't No Making It* (McLeod 1995), and demographic analysis of neighborhood effects. On another level, the school community refers to the collection of families whose children attend the school; how closely connected students' parents are to the school and to the other families in the school matters. Parents are better able to manage and monitor their children's education – and stay involved in their children's lives in general – when they feel welcomed at school, when they feel support from other parents, when they have teachers or other parents to whom they can turn. Likewise, strong bonds between the adults who have ties to the school provide a dense protective cover around children as they grow and develop. Coleman was a leader in stressing the value of this aspect of school climate, but the field of inquiry around it has, in effect, taken on a life of its own. Certainly, the idea of the school community is one of the driving forces in contemporary school reform and educational policy. Children go to school, but, in schools with a positive climate, they do not leave their families behind when they do.

The centrality of school climate to both education and developmental research has increased considerably in recent decades. It is a true growth field in sociology and related disciplines. Interest in the climates of school and their significance continues to be spurred on by new theoretical perspectives, such as human ecology; by new educational philosophies, such as the ethos of caring advocated by educational researchers like Nel Noddings; improvements in data collection, such as Add Health's large in-school samples, which allow the creation of summary measures of the behaviors, beliefs, and adjustment of the student body; and, unfortunately, by public events, such as Columbine, that drive home the importance of making schools good places to be as well as centers of learning.

SEE ALSO: Cultural Capital in Schools; Friendship: Structure and Context; Networks; Parental Involvement in Education; Race/Ethnicity and Friendship; Schools, Common; Social Capital and Education

REFERENCES AND SUGGESTED READINGS

Alexander, K. & Entwisle, D. (1988) *Achievement in the First Two Years of School: Patterns and Processes.* University of Chicago Press, Chicago.

Bryk, A. S., Lee, V. E., & Holland, P. B. (1993) *Catholic Schools and the Common Good.* Harvard University Press, Cambridge, MA.

Coleman, J. (1961) *The Adolescent Society.* Free Press of Glencoe, New York.

Coleman, J. (1990) *Foundations of Social Theory.* Harvard University Press, Cambridge, MA.

Eder, D., Evans, C., & Parker, S. (1995) *School Talk: Gender and Adolescent Culture.* Rutgers University Press, New Brunswick, NJ.

Kubitschek, W. & Hallinan, M. (1998) Tracking and Students' Friendships. *Social Psychology Quarterly* 61: 1–15.
Lightfoot, S. L. (1982) *The Good High School: Portraits of Character and Culture.* Basic Books, New York.
McLeod, J. (1995) *Ain't No Making It.* Westview Press, Boulder.
Moody, J. (2001) Race, School Integration, and Friendship Segregation in America. *American Journal of Sociology* 107: 679–716.
Noddings, N. (1992) *The Challenge to Care in Schools: An Alternative Approach to Education.* Teacher's College, New York.

school discipline

Sandra Way

School discipline refers to a system of rules, monitoring, sanctions, and rewards implemented by school personnel with the intent of shaping student behavior. Commonly associated with teachers and principals imposing order in classrooms and corridors by exerting control and maintaining student compliance through supervision and punishment, school discipline also plays a role in educational and moral development. There is general agreement that discipline in school is necessary. The extent and nature of that discipline, however, is variable and, at times, controversial.

School discipline has two main goals: maintenance of order and socialization. First, discipline is associated with the need to maintain a safe environment conducive to learning. Misbehavior can distract from the educational function of the school, and particularly disruptive behavior, such as violence, harassment, and theft, victimizes teachers and students. Discipline is also a mechanism of socialization. In addition to teaching academic subjects, schools help inculcate the values that turn children into productive citizens. Discipline is a tool for teaching students socially appropriate behaviors and attitudes.

The most influential theoretical writings related to school discipline come from the sociologist Émile Durkheim, the progressive education scholar John Dewey, and the postmodern philosopher Michel Foucault. Durkheim and Dewey were particularly interested in how discipline, defined as restraint placed on human behavior, is related to how individuals internalize the principles that guide attitudes and behaviors. Both theorists viewed the school as an important location for childhood socialization. In contrast, Foucault's discussions on discipline focused primarily on prisons with only a cursory look at schools. His work is more important for how it has informed recent critical analyses of school discipline than for any concrete theory of schooling.

Durkheim and Dewey claimed that discipline, or behavioral restraint, is beneficial for both the individual and society. In *Moral Education* (1961 [1925]), Durkheim argued that discipline is an essential element of morality, while Dewey argued in *Democracy and Education* (1966 [1916]) that discipline is important for the development of individual character and social democracy. In both cases, the goal is the development of internal, or self, discipline. The two scholars diverge, however, on their views of school discipline, which instead of being *internally motivated* tends to be *externally imposed* upon children.

Durkheim recognized external discipline as an instrument of socialization and a means for inculcating moral authority; a respect for social rules. He believed that respect for school rules helps children develop self-control. He also approved of punishment as a mechanism for preserving disciplinary authority, although he questioned its usefulness as a deterrent. The role of the teacher is to inculcate the belief in the moral authority of social rules and to provide the external sanctioning needed to maintain it.

In contrast, Dewey was critical of teacher-directed discipline and acknowledged external discipline only as an instrument of control. He claimed that traditional authoritarian disciplinary practices worked against the socializing goal of the school by alienating students. Self-discipline develops from students' active engagement with the curriculum and task completion; teacher-imposed discipline subverts this process by serving to dull initiative. According to Dewey, the teacher should not impose ideas or habits on children but rather assist them in selecting and interacting with their environment.

On further analysis, the difference between the two positions narrows. Dewey acknowledged that some external discipline may be necessary to control chaotic environments and Durkheim suggested that excessive regulation can lead to resistance or extinguish initiative. From both perspectives, as internal discipline develops there should be less need for external discipline. For Durkheim, as individuals rely on an internalized respect for the authority of rules, or moral authority, they need less external pressure to behave in a moral manner. For Dewey, when students are engaged, active learners there is less disorder to control.

Foucault approached discipline through the lens of power. In *Discipline and Punish* (1977), he argued that discipline imposes a diffuse will on individuals with the aim of controlling individuals to efficient and productive ends. Disciplinary power relies on ubiquitous monitoring and the process of normalization, where individuals are controlled through constant comparisons with those who are "normal." In schools, examinations, grades, and rules serve normalizing functions. Foucault's approach also stimulates critical discussions about student resistance and how enactments of school discipline may help produce "troublemaker" identities. While Durkheim viewed the power of the social over the individual as moral, Foucault's aim was to uncover these power relations so that they could be recognized and questioned.

Regardless of whether the focus of discipline is order or socialization, student behavior is usually the measure of effectiveness. Disciplinary systems that lead to less misbehavior and more orderly environments are viewed as effective. In some cases, however, sociologists have gauged discipline by examining academic achievement, such as grades, test scores, or graduation rates.

Social scientists have found that discipline is generally most effective when schools establish and communicate clear expectations, consistently enforce rules, and provide rewards for compliance and punishments for violations. Children appear to respond better to fair disciplinary guidelines that are not overly strict or lenient and are enforced by authority figures perceived as legitimate. Parental reactions to school discipline can also influence its effectiveness. When parents are involved and supportive of the school, legitimacy is reinforced. When parents and communities are in disagreement with schools, however, policies and practices tend to be less effective.

Various political, cultural, and institutional forces have helped shape school discipline. Changing perceptions of children, challenges to institutional authority, and fear of violence and crime are three of the most important influences.

Historically, society has vested school personnel with in loco parentis authority. Teachers were expected to assume the parental duties and responsibilities, including discipline, on the absent parents' behalf. As society and in turn schooling bureaucratized, schools were transformed. The school became a custodial institution responsible for managing large numbers of children. As such, the control of student behavior became important for the smooth functioning of the organization. Instead of substitute parents, school personnel began acquiring more of their disciplinary authority from their professional position. Although more bureaucratized, school authority remained strong until the 1960s. At this time, a general climate of discontent with the established social order was developing and would give birth to student, civil rights, and feminist movements. These movements, along with changing public attitudes, expanded individual rights and social equality. Within this context, traditional school discipline came under scrutiny.

In the United States, the clearest blow to school-based authority came from a series of court decisions that limited discipline practices. One of the most important and best-known cases was the 1969 Supreme Court decision in *Tinker* v. *Des Moines Independent Community School District* in which Justice Fortas, writing for the majority opinion, states that students are persons under the US Constitution and do not "shed their constitutional rights to freedom of speech or expression at the schoolhouse gate." While this case was about freedom of speech, other rulings limited activities such as the ability to dictate student appearance and conduct locker searches. School guidelines and sanctions were only legitimate to the degree they could be shown to be directly relevant to the functioning of the school. Another influential US Supreme Court decision, *Goss* v. *Lopez,* established students' right to due process. The court concluded that because long suspensions and expulsions denied students access to public education, it was necessary to implement procedural safeguards. Consequently, students currently have the right to a disciplinary hearing before being expelled or suspended for longer than 10 days. The discretionary prerogative of the school to control student misbehavior had been curtailed.

Schools also faced challenges from outside the legal arena. Similar to other institutions, schools were accused of maintaining discriminatory policies and practices. Discipline systems in racial and ethnically integrated schools in particular became strained under racial and ethnic conflict. Critics pointed out that disciplinary actions were differentially applied to minority and lower socioeconomic students and argued that race- and class-based discrimination in education was reproducing social inequalities in the larger society. For example, neo-Marxist sociologists argued that working-class children were subject to more authoritarian discipline with the goal of producing a submissive, obedient, and disciplined workforce. Today, some children are still more likely to be disciplined than others; boys, children from lower socioeconomic families, racial or ethnic minorities, and low achievers are all more likely to be subject to authoritarian control and punishment.

Instead of directly challenging authoritarian discipline, some parents and educators established alternative models. Based on Dewey's educational theories, "free" schools were developed in the United States and Great Britain that minimized teacher direction and control. These schools purposefully deemphasized or attempted to eliminate hierarchical relations between students and teachers. Although a few of these schools have survived, in general the free school movement did not provide a widespread alternative to traditional school organization. More modest attempts at restructuring classroom discipline appear to have been more successful. Today, there are a variety of "classroom management" approaches available to educational practitioners.

In the United States, increasing crime rates and a shift to political conservatism in the 1980s corresponded with changing views on school discipline. In contrast to the anti-authoritarianism of the 1960s and 1970s, public sentiment began to favor stricter school discipline as "get-tough" approaches gained popularity not only in the United States but also in countries such as Britain, Canada, and Australia. Even in the late 1960s there was some indication of concern. Respondents in the US annual Gallup Poll of attitudes toward public schools have ranked lack of school discipline as a top problem since 1969. There is evidence of similar concern in many western countries where formal government inquiries have been made into the matter. In addition, discipline is increasingly being defined as a problem in Asian countries such as Japan.

Images of violence and disorder in chaotic urban schools and later school shootings in several US suburban schools reinforced this trend by spurring concern for teacher and student safety. Policy began to reflect these changes as governments passed tighter controls and schools implemented zero tolerance policies. Under zero tolerance policies, certain punishments are mandatory for designated offenses, leaving little flexibility for circumstance. Proponents of zero tolerance claim that these policies hold students accountable for inappropriate behaviors and serve to deter other students from similar behavior. Opponents of zero tolerance argue that these policies disproportionately affect poor and minority students, are overly harsh and unfair, and alienate students without any clear evidence that they effectively reduce misbehavior. While strict controls are generally targeted at serious misconduct, more mundane behaviors are also increasingly being restricted. Drawing on arguments that general "disorder" is at the root of more serious disorder and violence, some schools have implemented stricter codes of conduct and dress.

Stricter discipline and policies providing teachers with the explicit authority to remove students from their classrooms have not reinstated the teacher as the primary school disciplinarian. Teachers continue to have the most interactions with students in the classroom but much of the responsibility for formal sanctioning resides elsewhere. Teachers often send misbehaving students to the principal and larger or more disorderly schools designate an administrator to handle disciplinary issues. Mandatory punishments in zero tolerance policies take authority away from educators. In some schools, the punitive control of the justice system has replaced the authority of teacher and administrators as schools increasingly employ police officers, fences, security cameras, and metal detectors.

Although the meaning and purpose of school discipline are variable, in popular and political contexts "discipline" often refers to the sanctioning of children who disobey school rules. What is defined as misbehavior may be different from school to school and classroom to classroom and can range from chewing gum and talking in class to more serious criminal behaviors. Some regulations are codified into school or classroom rules but others may be unwritten and subject to interpretation. Similarly, while most schools have formal sanctions for rule violations, sanctions also occur informally and can be idiosyncratic. Because schooling in the United States is decentralized, disciplinary policy can vary significantly between states and school districts. Where schooling is more centralized, such as Europe, policies tend to be more consistent.

At the most mundane level, teachers and administrators frequently correct behavior by asking or demanding that students alter their behavior. Punishments for misbehavior may take many forms, including verbal reprimand, humiliation, the removal of privileges, lower grades, corporal punishment, and permanent or temporary discharge. At the primary school level, sanctions often include such actions as scolding, placement in "time out," or withholding play time. Some schools also apply corporal punishment in which school personnel strike misbehaving children with a hand or object such as a paddle or cane. At the secondary school level, school discipline tends to take a different form. Detention and suspension are common disciplinary measures for adolescents. Students in detention are required to spend additional time at school, usually before or after the official school day or on the weekend, studying or performing a task assigned by the teacher. In some schools, administrators may impose formal removal from the classroom by placing offenders on suspension for a designated amount of time. For in-school suspension, students spend time in a segregated room within the school. Out of school suspension requires that students stay home from school. Schools also sanction students by barring participation in extra-curricular activities such as athletic events, clubs, or field trips. For serious infractions, schools are increasingly referring the situation to law enforcement. Students may be expelled or transferred to an alternative educational institution.

Corporal punishment is the most controversial type of sanction. Reflective of discipline in the home, prior to the nineteenth century corporal punishment was common. Supported by the Christian ideology that to "spare the rod" was to "spoil the child," teachers were free, and often encouraged, to physically punish students. While there were limitations to the amount of force that could be used, physical force was common and severe according to today's standards. In the early 1800s, the United States witnessed successful efforts to limit corporal punishment and by the end of the nineteenth century some urban districts had banned its use. In the third quarter of the twentieth century, a concentrated challenge to corporal punishment resurfaced. Since then a little over half of all US states and several school districts have banned its use. Today, all industrialized countries, except Australia and the United States, as well as many developing countries have eliminated the official use of corporal punishment in schools. The current trend is toward restricting corporal punishment, with countries such as Canada, India, and South Africa only recently banning its use. Consistent with the "get tough" approach, some areas in the United States, however, have actually seen an increase in the use of corporal punishment.

Corporal punishment remains controversial. Opponents argue that corporal punishment should be eliminated on the grounds that it is inhumane and teaches children that the use of violence is acceptable. Proponents argue that corporal punishment is an effective tool for controlling misbehavior and teaching authority and self-control. While the empirical evidence is mixed, the majority of research suggests that physical punishment is ineffective. Some studies even suggest that corporal punishment may possibly lead in the long term to alienation and increases in antisocial behavior.

SEE ALSO: Dewey, John; Disciplinary Society; Durkheim, Émile; Foucault, Michel; Juvenile Delinquency; Parental Involvement in

Education; Race and Schools; School Climate; Social Control; Socialization; Urban Education

REFERENCES AND SUGGESTED READINGS

Arum, R. (2003) *Judging School Discipline: The Crisis of Moral Authority*. Harvard University Press, Cambridge, MA.

Bowditch, C. (1993) Getting Rid of Troublemakers: High School Disciplinary Procedures and the Production of Dropouts. *Social Problems* 40(4): 493–509.

Dewey, J. (1966 [1916]) *Democracy and Education: An Introduction to the Philosophy of Education*. Free Press, New York.

DiPrete, T., Muller, C. M., & Nora, S. (1981) *Discipline and Order in American High Schools*. National Center for Education Statistics, Government Printing Office, Washington, DC.

Durkheim, É. (1961 [1925]) *Moral Education: A Study in the Theory and Application of the Sociology of Education*. Trans. E. K. Wilson & H. Schnurer. Free Press, Glencoe, IL.

Ferguson, A. A. (2000) *Bad Boys: Public Schools in the Making of Black Masculinity*. University of Michigan Press, Ann Arbor.

Fields, B. A. (2000) School Discipline: Is There a Crisis in Our Schools? *Australian Journal of Social Issues* 35(1): 73–84.

Foucault, M. (1977) *Discipline and Punish: The Birth of the Prison*. Trans. A. Sheridan. Vintage, New York.

Gottfredson, D. C. (2001) *Schools and Delinquency*. Cambridge University Press, Cambridge.

Grant, G. (1988) *The World We Created at Hamilton High*. Harvard University Press, Cambridge, MA.

Hollingsworth, E. J., Lufler, H. S., Jr., & Clune, III, W. H. (1984) *School Discipline: Order and Autonomy*. Praeger, New York.

Hurn, C. J. (1993) Schools as Organizations: Problems of Order, Control, and Motivation. In: Hurn, C. J., *The Limits and Possibilities of Schooling: An Introduction to the Sociology of Education*. Allyn & Bacon, Boston, 225–63.

Lawrence, R. (1998) *School Crime and Juvenile Justice*. Oxford University Press, New York.

Metz, M. (1978) *Classrooms and Corridors: The Crisis of Authority in Desegregated Schools*. University of California Press, Berkeley.

Moles, O. C. (Ed.) (1990) *Student Discipline Strategies: Research and Practice*. SUNY Press, Albany, NY.

Noguera, P. A. (2003) Schools, Prisons, and Social Implications of Punishment: Rethinking Disciplinary Practices. *Theory into Practice* 42(4): 341–51.

school segregation, desegregation

Roslyn Arlin Mickelson

The United States has a long history of providing racially segregated and unequal public education to its children. Racially separate and unequal public education was not an accident; it was created by public laws and policies enacted and enforced by state governments and local school systems. After a series of Supreme Court decisions eliminated the formal legal foundation for segregation, it was recreated through racially discriminatory practices in federal housing policies, lending for home purchases, employment, wages, and school assignment practices.

Desegregation is the process that removes the formal and informal barriers preventing students from diverse racial and ethnic backgrounds from learning in the same classrooms and schools. Since the middle of the twentieth century, various desegregation policies have been widely used to remedy *de jure* (by law) and *de facto* (by practice) segregation. Among the policies employed were mandatory and voluntary busing, pairing of white and minority schools, using magnet programs to attract diverse students to segregated schools, redrawing of school attendance boundaries, and siting new schools in areas between minority and white neighborhoods. Desegregation also involved creating racially diverse faculty and staff, employing multicultural curricula, and nurturing diversity in extra and cocurricular activities. These processes ensure that, once in desegregated schools, all children have equitable opportunities to learn.

The still-unfinished process of school desegregation commenced with the landmark 1954 *Brown* v. *Board of Education* decision, in which the Supreme Court declared that "separate educational facilities are inherently unequal" and "a denial of the equal protection of the laws." The 50th anniversary of the Supreme Court's *Brown* decision offered the opportunity to reflect upon the meaning of the decision and to assess what has and has not been accomplished in its name.

The *Brown* decision was a sea change, overturning the essence of the infamous *Plessy* v.

Ferguson case, which had legitimized racially "separate but equal" public spheres. However, *Brown* only addressed public actions, not private behaviors. This tension between legal mandates for racial justice in education and private actions to preserve white educational privileges slowed effective school desegregation for decades. Arguably, the most enduring legacy of the *Brown* decision is not desegregated public schools – especially in light of nationwide trends toward resegregation and the continuing struggle for educational equity. Rather, *Brown* enshrined in US law the concept that all people are citizens of this nation and that state-enforced racial segregation is unconstitutional.

Southern schools remained segregated well into the 1960s and northern schools until the 1970s. Nevertheless, since the *Brown* decision, some regions of the United States were more successful in desegregating their schools than others. Southern and border states eventually experienced the greatest degree of desegregation. In some southern school systems the percentage of blacks attending extremely segregated minority schools dropped from 78 percent in the late 1960s to 25 percent at its lowest in the mid-1980s. Other regions of the country, where *de facto* segregation was the norm, also desegregated to a large degree. In the middle of the 1980s the national trend toward greater interracial contact in public schools stalled and began a slow reversal by the decade's end (Clotfelter 2004; Orfield & Eaton 1996).

There are a number of reasons that the significant strides toward desegregated public education began to reverse in the late 1980s. The convergence of white interests in economic growth through interracial tranquility with black interests in educational and occupational mobility that permitted desegregation in the first three quarters of the last century (Bell 1980) did not survive through the 1990s. Other reasons for resegregation trends include the lifting of federal court orders mandating desegregation, demographic shifts in the US population – especially the explosive growth in ethnic minority populations – and the suburbanization of US communities. As a result, school systems that were once relatively desegregated are now becoming resegregated. Much of current segregation is between districts – especially central cities and their metropolitan area suburbs – rather than among schools within a single district, as was historically the case. Some observers estimate that the levels of interracial contact in public schools will soon return to pre-*Brown* levels of racial isolation.

WITHIN-SCHOOL SEGREGATION

A nuanced discussion of desegregation must begin with the acknowledgment that segregation exists both between and within schools, a distinction often discussed in terms of first- and second-generation segregation (Wells & Crain 1994). First-generation segregation generally involves the racial composition of schools within a single district or between adjacent districts and has been the focus of national desegregation efforts since *Brown*. Second-generation segregation involves the racially correlated placement of students within schools typically brought about by ability grouping (in primary grades) and tracking (in secondary grades).

Some form of tracking or ability grouping is an organizational feature of most US public education (Oakes 2005), even though most school systems no longer have rigid tracks for vocational, college preparatory, or commercial courses of study (Lucas 1999). Black, Latino, and Native American students are disproportionately assigned to lower level classes, or tracks, compared to their comparably able white and Asian peers. Blacks, Latinos, and Native Americans are relatively absent from the accelerated tracks (Mickelson 2001; Oakes 2005). Racially stratified tracks create a discriminatory cycle of restricted educational opportunities for disadvantaged minorities. This cycle leads to diminished school achievement and, in turn, contributes to race and social class differences in school outcomes. Ability grouping and tracking often resegregate students even in school districts operating under court-mandated desegregation plans. In these ways, first- and second-generation segregations intersect in ways that often subvert the goals of desegregation.

DESEGREGATION EFFECTS

Effects of desegregation typically fall into two categories: long-term effects, which refer to adults' educational and occupational attainment trajectories that are influenced by their intergroup experiences during elementary and secondary school; and short-term effects, which refer to what happens to students' academic achievement and racial attitudes as a result of intergroup contact (Braddock & Eitle 2003; Wells & Crain 1994). The evidence showing that desegregation has a positive effect on minority students' long-term outcomes is well documented and rarely controversial: minorities who attended desegregated schools have greater educational and occupational attainment and are more likely to work and live in integrated environments than those who went to segregated schools. Both majority and minority adults who attended desegregated schools have lower levels of racial fears and antagonisms than those who attended racially isolated schools.

Most of the scholarly and policy debates concern the short-term effects of desegregation on achievement. Earlier research on short-term effects on achievement was equivocal. Some social scientists found that desegregated education modestly benefited minority students' academic outcomes (especially in language) without harming whites' achievement; other studies found no systematic effects. But most early empirical studies of desegregation suffered from limitations in their design and samples (Cook 1984). Another reason for the mixed results of earlier research on short-term desegregation effects was the high correlation between social class and race. Some researchers contended that desegregation could not address racial inequality in educational outcomes caused by social class differences among students (Rossell, Armor, & Walberg 2002). Other social scientists concluded that desegregation policies were essentially ineffective in raising minority achievement because the larger societal problems at the root of racially correlated school outcomes are left untouched by school desegregation (Bankston & Caldas 2002).

A growing body of newer research demonstrates desegregation's significant positive effects on the achievement of minority and majority students, even after controlling for social class differences among the groups. Recent analyses of large, representative samples permit researchers to control for family background and prior achievement when they examine the effects of desegregation on achievement. US military schools, for instance, are thoroughly desegregated, highly effective for all students, and have very small racial gaps in achievement compared to civilian schools. Black students' National Assessment of Educational Progress test scores in reading, science, and math rose during the years between the 1970s and the 1980s when desegregation was at its peak. Scores have not increased since the trend toward resegregation began in the 1990s (NCES 2001). Many social scientists attribute these gains in achievement to desegregation.

Whites and Asians benefit from desegregation as well. NAEP scores rapidly rose for whites and Asians between the 1970s and the 1980s, but the rise leveled off since desegregation peaked in the 1980s (NCES 2001). Using the 1990 National Educational Longitudinal Study, Brown (2004) found that high schools with enrollments that are almost entirely white do not necessarily produce the best academic outcomes for all students. Schools with a racial mix of 44–75 percent white and/or Asian American, and 25–54 percent black and/or Hispanic show the highest average academic achievement for all racial groups and the smallest gap between the races in test scores. Mickelson (2001) found whites as well as blacks in Charlotte, North Carolina benefited from attending racially integrated schools and classrooms. Borman and Dorn's (2004) analysis of Florida achievement data indicates students from all ethnic groups in integrated (compared to racially segregated) schools performed better on Florida's standardized tests. Muller and her colleagues (2004) used the Adolescent Health data set to examine opportunities to learn across ethnic groups in schools with varying levels of desegregation. They found greater opportunities to learn in integrated schools and that minorities performed better in them than in segregated schools.

The likely explanations for the positive effects of desegregated learning environments on student achievement point to greater human and material resources and more rigorous school climates. Desegregated schools are more likely than racially isolated minority schools to have highly qualified teachers instructing in their field of expertise, stable teacher and student populations, smaller class sizes, and modern equipment. In addition, students in desegregated schools are more likely to have peers who are motivated, and who value achievement, and encourage it among their classmates. Parental involvement is higher in desegregated schools. In desegregated schools, students have greater interracial contact in classrooms, in extracurricular activities, and in peer groups. Such diversity stimulates higher order thinking among all students (Gurin et al. 2002). Taken together, these factors create an academic climate with higher expectations and greater opportunities to learn for all students (Hallinan 1998).

Braddock and Eitle (2003) propose a logical and empirical connection between short-term and long-term effects of desegregation. Their conceptual framework links desegregation's short-term effects of enhanced achievement, socialization, and positive intergroup relationships and attitudes to its long-term effects of greater social inclusion and social mobility. Attending desegregated schools has a positive effect on minority students' interracial attitudes, aspirations, self-esteem, locus of control, standardized tests, grades, and class rank. These academic credentials and socialization experiences, in conjunction with broadened social networks, directly influence post-secondary educational and occupational attainment that, in turn, enhance minority adults' income, job status, and the diversity of the institutions in which they participate. These adults are then better able to facilitate their own children's educational success and social mobility.

THE FUTURE OF DESEGREGATION

Since the withdrawal of vigorous federal efforts in pursuit of desegregation and the disappearance of the political consensus supporting it, a number of school districts are pursuing student diversity using strategic school siting in integrated neighborhoods, or socioeconomic status and/or test performance diversity as criteria for pupil assignment. Their goal is to avoid creating schools with concentrations of low income and poor performing students. Because socioeconomic status and race are highly correlated, SES diversity generally results in racially desegregated schools as well. Socioeconomic status diversity is not merely a back door to racial desegregation; concentrating poor, low performing students in the same schools makes improving educational outcomes extremely difficult and very expensive.

The use of racial criteria to diversify public schools has not been eliminated by court rulings, just restricted. The 2003 University of Michigan Law School's affirmative action case, *Grutter* v. *Bollinger*, may provide an impetus for desegregating public K-12 schools. In *Grutter*, the majority of the Court held that because diversity in higher education is a compelling state interest, the law school may use race, among other criteria, in a narrowly tailored admission policy. In 2004, two post-*Grutter* appeals court decisions addressed voluntary public school desegregation plans with explicit race-conscious assignment strategies. A decision by the First Circuit Court of Appeals explicitly agreed that public schools have an educational rationale – that is, a compelling state interest – in promoting diversity. However, the Ninth Circuit Court of Appeals rejected a high school assignment plan that relied on this argument (Johnston 2004).

CONCLUSION

School desegregation was launched 50 years ago by a judicial decision of extraordinary simplicity and moral clarity (Clotfelter 2004). Yet once school systems actually began the process of dismantling racially segregated school systems, white parents seized opportunities to circumvent integration through practices such as tracking and school choice (then called freedom of choice plans). The willingness of school officials and other state actors to accommodate white parents seeking ways to retain their race privileges within public schools, and the weakening resolve among federal officials to carry out court mandates to desegregate, made it increasingly difficult to fully implement the policy during the last twenty years of the twentieth century.

During the second half of the twentieth century, *de jure* segregation was dismantled and for a period between the 1970s and the late 1980s *de facto* segregation was markedly reduced. The regions of the country that were once the most segregated became the most highly desegregated. At the time that the nation's public schools were the most racially balanced, achievement levels improved for all students and the racial gaps in academic achievement narrowed considerably. By the end of the 1980s, the nation's will to continue school desegregation faltered and public schools began a slow retreat from the policy of equality of educational opportunity through desegregation. As schools became resegregated, the earlier national trends toward greater minority achievement and smaller racial gaps in school outcomes began to plateau.

In light of the dismantling of much of the legal framework for desegregation and the recent trends toward resegregation, the future of desegregated public education is uncertain. Even some minority citizens who once supported desegregation have expressed doubts about the policy. They have grown weary of continuing political struggles and are disappointed by the results of the policy's implementation for their children's academic outcomes. Moreover, they have been wounded by the costs of desegregation to their communities' cohesion, cultural identity, and by the loss of minority educators' jobs.

Over time, these social forces have eroded the nation's capacity to fully realize the potential social and academic benefits from diverse public education, and ultimately have resulted in a retreat from desegregation as the keystone to equality of educational opportunity. Ironically, this erosion is occurring at a time that research increasingly indicates diverse learning environments are essential for preparing students to be citizens of a multi-ethnic, democratic society and successful workers in the globalizing economy.

SEE ALSO: *Brown* v. *Board of Education*; Educational Inequality; Race and Schools; Schools, Magnet; Schools, Public; Social Capital and Education; Tracking; Urban Education

REFERENCES AND RECOMMENDED READINGS

Bankston, C, L., III & Caldas, S. J. (2002) *A Troubled Dream: The Promise and Failure of School Desegregation in Louisiana.* Vanderbilt University Press, Nashville.

Bell, D. (1980) Brown and the Interest-Convergence Dilemma. *Harvard Educational Review* 93: 518–33.

Borman, K. M. & Dorn, S. (2004) A Half Century After Brown v. Board of Education: The Impact of Florida Education Policies on Student Outcomes and Equity. *American Educational Research Journal.*

Braddock, J. H., II, & Eitle, T. M. (2003) School Desegregation: Research, Policy, Practice, and Future Directions. In: Banks, J. A. & McGee, C. (Eds.), *Handbook of Research on Multicultural Education*, 2nd edn. Jossey-Bass, San Francisco, pp. 828–46.

Brown, S. (2004) High School Racial Composition: Balancing Excellence and Equity. Paper presented at the annual meeting of the American Sociological Association, 19 August, Chicago.

Clotfelter, C. T. (2004) *After Brown: The Rise and Retreat of School Desegregation.* Harvard University Press, Cambridge, MA.

Cook, T. (1984) *School Desegregation and Black Achievement.* US Department of Education, Washington, DC.

Gurin, P., Dey, E. L., Hurtado, S., and Gurin, G. (2002) Diversity and Higher Education: Theory and Impact on Educational Outcomes. *Harvard Educational Review* 72(3): 330–66.

Hallinan, M. T. (1998) Diversity Effects on Student Outcomes: Social Science Evidence. *Ohio State Law Journal* 59: 733–54.

Johnston, S. (2004) Hints in Ruling on How to Get Court OK for Use of Race. *Educate!* October 29: 1.

Lucas, S. R. (1999) *Tracking Inequality: Stratification and Mobility in American High Schools.* Teachers College Press, New York.

Mickelson, R. A. (2001) Subverting Swann: First- and Second-Generation Segregation in Charlotte, North Carolina. *American Educational Research Journal* 38(2): 215–52.

Muller, C., Franks, K., & Schiller, K. (2004) Race and Academic Achievement in Integrated High Schools: Opportunity and Stratification. Department of Sociology, University of Texas, Austin.

National Center for Educational Statistics (NCES) (2001) *Digest of Educational Statistics 2000.* NCES 2001-034. US Department of Education, Washington, DC.

Oakes, J. (2005) *Keeping Track*, 2nd edn. Yale University Press, New Haven.

Orfield, G. & Eaton, S. (1996) *Dismantling Desegregation: The Quiet Reversal of Brown v. Board of Education.* Free Press, New York.

Rossell, C., Armor, D. J., & Walberg, H. J. (Eds.) (2002) *School Desegregation in the 21st Century.* Praeger, Westport, CT.

Wells, A. S. & Crain, R. (1994) Perpetuation Theory and the Long-Term Effects of School Desegregation. *Review of Educational Research* 64: 531–55.

school transitions

Michelle L. Frisco

School transitions signify students' entries into new schools. They are important milestones that lead to both positive and negative events that affect young people's lives. There are two broad categories of school transitions: (1) normative school transitions (e.g., the transition into elementary school, from elementary to junior high school, from junior high to high school); (2) non-normative school transitions or school transfers.

This entry discusses the causes and consequences of school transitions. Schools are one of the primary social institutions in which young people spend time. Therefore, changes in school life can be particularly disrupting, both academically and socially.

NORMATIVE SCHOOL TRANSITIONS

The types, number, and levels of schools in a district vary markedly and are primarily determined by a district's physical size and the number of students that it serves. In rare instances in the US, a student remains in the same school from kindergarten through grade twelve, and some students only make one school transition. Most students today, though, experience two transitions – from elementary to junior high school and from junior high into high school.

Normative school transitions lead to many physical, social, and academic changes. Students begin attending school in a new location and building, which is usually much larger than their original school. In addition, peer relationships become more complicated, students become the youngest rather than the oldest students within the school's hierarchy, and the racial and ethnic composition of a school's students may change (French et al. 2000). Young people's interactions with school officials also change and often become more anonymous. Finally, the level and difficulty of coursework increases. Therefore, normative school transitions can be high-risk periods when students are vulnerable to negative academic and social consequences.

The educational consequences include declining academic achievement (Seidman et al. 1996; Reyes et al. 2000), lower school attendance (Seidman et al. 1996), and lower school engagement and attachment (Barber & Olsen 2004). In addition, the likelihood of school dropout and stop-out rises during the transition from junior high to high school (Roderick 1993).

Negative social consequences include lower levels of overall student functioning (Barber & Olsen 2004), decreased self-esteem (Reyes et al. 2000), and less rewarding and more impersonal interactions with school personnel (Barber & Olsen 2004).

There is some evidence that school transitions can be positive (or at least neutral). For instance, students who were "nerds," unpopular, or isolated can reinvent themselves (Kinney 1993).

A host of factors can influence how easy or difficult normative school transitions are for students. Gender, race and ethnicity, academic ability, school location, and students' ages all influence how well students make normative school transitions. In addition, teachers, peers, and parents can all provide valuable support to students as they make school transitions. This helps to minimize the negative consequences of normal school mobility.

SCHOOL TRANSFERS

School transfers are not a common event when compared to normative school transitions. This is one reason why researchers posit that transfers are more disruptive to students' academic and social lives than normative school transitions. Students usually experience this transition without peers and often also undergo other changes – such as a residential move or change in family structure – simultaneously. Transfers also result from school choice programs, which may or may not decrease the amount of isolation adolescents experience as they change school environments.

There is less sociological research on school transfers than on normative school transitions, most likely because transfers are often viewed as an unavoidable consequence of residential mobility or family structure change. Nonetheless, transferring has been associated with negative academic and social consequences, including behavioral problems, decreased mathematics test score gains, and an increased risk of school dropping out and stop-out (Astone & McLanahan 1994; Swanson & Schneider 1999). Transferring also changes the composition of students' friendship networks and may lead them to lower-status positions within these networks (South & Haynie 2004).

In recent decades, one specific type of school transfer has become its own area of study: school choice. It is a relatively new type of school mobility and there is great variability in school choice policies from school district to school district. There is also no clear answer as to whether school choice programs lead to positive or negative social and academic consequences for American students.

CONCLUSION

Sociologists who study education are beginning to understand school mobility. Nonetheless, we know far more about school transitions earlier as opposed to later in students' educational careers. Researchers must continue to investigate the causes and consequences (both negative and positive) of school mobility, the support systems that help students make these transitions, and the best ways to meet the educational needs of students who undergo abrupt changes in schooling experiences.

Greater investigation of school transfers is particularly needed. For instance, sociologists still only have limited knowledge about complex relationships and interactions between school mobility, residential mobility, and changing family structure. The effects of transfers that result from different forces (e.g., school choice versus a residential move) are also not well understood. Findings from these areas of inquiry will help policymakers develop programs that help students cope with changing school environments that disrupt their lives academically and socially.

SEE ALSO: Dropping Out of School; Family Structure and Child Outcomes; School Choice; Schools, Magnet; Transition from School to Work

REFERENCES AND SUGGESTED READINGS

Astone, N. & McLanahan, S. (1994) Family Structure, Residential Mobility, and School Dropout: A Research Note. *Demography* 31: 575–84.

Barber, B. K. & Olsen, J. A. (2004) Assessing the Transition to Middle and High School. *Journal of Adolescent Research* 19(1): 3–30.

French, S. E., Seidman, E., Allen, L., & Aber, J. L. (2000) Racial/Ethnic Identity, Congruence with the Social Context, and the Transition to High School. *Journal of Adolescent Research* 15: 587–602.

Kinney, D. A. (1993) From Nerds to Normals: The Recovery of Identity among Adolescents from Middle School to High School. *Sociology of Education* 66: 21–40.

Reyes, O., Gillock, K., Kobus, K., & Sanchez, B. (2000) Adolescents from Urban, Low-Income Status, and Predominantly Minority Backgrounds. *American Journal of Community Psychology* 28: 519–44.

Roderick, M. (1993) *The Path to Dropping Out: Evidence for Intervention.* Auburn House, Westport.

Seidman, E., Aber, J. L., Allen, L., & French, S. E. (1996) The Impact of the Transition to High School on the Self-System and Perceived Social Context of Poor Urban Youth. *American Journal of Community Psychology* 24: 489–515.

South, S. J. & Haynie, D. L. (2004) Friendship Networks of Mobile Adolescents. *Social Forces* 83: 315–50.

Swanson, C. & Schneider, B. (1999) Students on the Move: Residential and Educational Mobility in America's Schools. *Sociology of Education* 72: 54–67.

schooling and economic success

David B. Bills and James E. Rosenbaum

The empirical association between schooling and economic success is one of the most secure findings in the social sciences. With rare exceptions, across societies and historical periods those with more schooling or particular types of schooling have held significant material advantages over those with less schooling. While not perfect, the empirical associations between schooling and economic success are high, persistent, and according to many accounts, increasing. Schooling in many societies is now generally regarded as the key to both individual and collective social mobility.

Educational attainment is consistently associated with virtually every standard measure of socioeconomic success. For example, in the United States only a little more than three out of five individuals who have not completed high school are in the labor force. This number rises steadily as educational attainment rises, with nearly nine out of ten college graduates participating in the labor force. Similarly, as educational attainment goes up, unemployment rates unambiguously go down. This does not mean that providing high school dropouts with diplomas will suddenly provide adequate opportunities for them, but it does mean that when jobs are scarce, the least educated have the least access to them.

The relationship between education and socioeconomic success goes beyond whether or not people are working, to the types of work they do and the rewards associated with that work. Level of schooling is consistently and strongly related to occupational status, worker autonomy, earnings, employment stability, access to learning opportunities at work, and job benefits.

The good life afforded by schooling is not equally accessible to everyone. For example, at all levels of education, African Americans and Hispanics are more likely to be unemployed than are whites. The difference is especially great for African Americans. Further, women earn less than men at all levels of schooling.

Precisely why schooling is such a consistent predictor of economic success is less certain. Human capital theory (Becker 1964; Mincer 1989) maintains that schooling provides marketable skills and abilities relevant to job performance. This makes the more schooled more valuable to employers, thus raising their incomes and their opportunities for securing jobs. In this view, employers act rationally by selecting on educational credentials (although this need not be the only hiring criterion) because schooling has prepared the more educated to be better workers. Similarly, job seekers (in their prior role as students) act rationally by investing in their own human capital.

Credentialism offers a different vision of the association between education and work (Berg 1971; Collins 1979). This view holds that educational credentials are little more than arbitrary and exclusionary means of preserving socioeconomic advantage across generations and socioeconomic groups. Rather than indicating job skills, credentials are the ways in which gatekeepers restrict access to privileged positions. By using such putatively objective indicators of merit as educational credentials, elite classes can reproduce themselves in what appears to be a fair and equitable manner (Bourdieu & Passeron 1974).

Credentialism can refer to two very different processes that may or may not be directly related. For some, credentialism describes *credential inflation*. This position describes a system of job assignment in which employers demand more and more education for the same work. As evidence, analysts point to a rate of expansion in educational enrollments that is much more rapid than technologically induced growth in the demand for skills. Of course, economies can and do experience skill shortages and skill surpluses at the same time. Credential inflation may well operate in some sectors and not in others.

A second way to think about credentialism is as "sheepskin effects." These are usually defined as disproportionate increases in returns to schooling after the completion of a year that usually is associated with a degree (Park 1999: 238). In other words, people are economically rewarded simply for holding a given degree. (One could as easily say that they are economically penalized for not completing a degree.) The difference in earnings between, for example, someone with four years of postsecondary education but no degree and someone with the degree (the sheepskin) is in effect the "rent" one collects for being credentialed.

Other theories of the relationship between schooling and economic success lie closer to the human capital theory, while incorporating aspects of the skepticism of credentialist theory. These include theories of screening, signaling, and filtering (Bills 2003). While there are important differences between these theories, they are unified by the claim that the importance of schooling is not so much that it enhances ability but rather that it reveals it. Because employers cannot know which potential hires are most likely to be productive, they need to identify and gather trustworthy labor market information (Rosenbaum 2001). Educational credentials provide this information. More able job seekers can thus signal their market value by acquiring educational credentials, which in most societies have attained the status of legitimate indicators of the kinds of ability valued by employers.

Both analysts and policymakers show recurrent concern for *overeducation* (variously referred to as overqualification, surplus education, or educational mismatch, but rarely, strangely enough, overskilled). The idea behind overeducation is that some workers, usually considered to be a growing number, have more education than is "needed" for the jobs they hold (Halaby 1994). Determining the criteria for how much education is "needed" is far from self-evident, and there is no uniform definition about what counts as overeducation. Some see overeducation subjectively, as workers' own assessments of the adequacy of their educational backgrounds for the demands of the jobs they hold. Those who see their own credentials as significantly higher than those needed to either secure or perform a job are held to be overeducated. Others measure overeducation more in terms of the objective characteristics of jobs. One might, for example, compare the educational level of a given worker to the educational level of the typical worker in that occupation or to some "job-level requirements" of the occupation. In objective conceptualizations, workers who are significantly more highly educated than other workers in the same occupational category (regardless of their self-assessments) are considered to be overeducated.

The evidence on overeducation and its social, political, and economic consequences is less than definitive. Empirical findings differ quite substantially across societies, and different conceptualizations of overeducation often produce different results. Most analysts believe that overeducation is both fairly common (sometimes held to be nearly a third of the workforce) and increasing (Green et al. 1999). Others believe there may have been some decline in the incidence of overeducation (Groot & van den Brink 2000). Some data suggest that women are more likely to be overeducated, and men more likely to be undereducated. In general, the returns to overeducation (typically taken as "years of surplus schooling") are lower than the returns to "matched" schooling, but are positive nonetheless.

Theory and research on the relationships between schooling and economic success should continue to develop. The emergence of several integrated efforts to conduct cross-societal comparative studies of social stratification, the development of high-quality nationally representative data sets for an increasing number of countries, and solid methodological and conceptual apparatuses provide a solid foundation for further progress.

SEE ALSO: Capital: Economic, Cultural, and Social; Dual Labor Markets; Education and Economy; Educational and Occupational Attainment; Income Inequality and Income Mobility; Life Chances and Resources; Mobility, Intergenerational and Intragenerational; Transition from School to Work

REFERENCES AND SUGGESTED READINGS

Becker, G. S. (1964) *Human Capital.* National Bureau of Economic Research, New York.

Berg, I. (1971) *Education and Jobs: The Great Training Robbery.* Beacon, Boston.

Bills, D. B. (2003) Credentials, Signals, and Screens: Explaining the Relationship between Schooling and Job Assignment. *Review of Educational Research* 73: 441–69.

Bourdieu, P. & Passeron, J.-C. (1974) *Reproduction in Education, Society and Culture.* Sage, Beverly Hills, CA.

Collins, R. (1979) *The Credential Society: An Historical Sociology of Education and Stratification.* Academic Press, New York.

Green, F., McIntosh, S., & Vignoles, A. (1999) *"Overeducation" and Skills: Clarifying the Concepts.* Unpublished paper, Centre for Economic Performance, London.

Groot, W. & van den Brink, H. M. (2000) Overeducation in the Labor Market: A Meta-Analysis. *Economics of Education Review* 19: 149–58.

Halaby, C. N. (1994) Overeducation and Skill Mismatch. *Sociology of Education* 67: 47–59.

Mincer, J. (1989) Human capital and the Labor Market: A Review of Current Research. *Educational Researcher* 18 (4): 27–34.

Park, J. H. (1999) Estimation of Sheepskin Effects Using the Old and the New Measures of Educational Attainment in the Current Population Survey. *Economics Letters* 62: 237–40.

Rosenbaum, J. E. (2001) *Beyond College For All: Career Paths for the Forgotten Half.* Russell Sage Foundation, New York.

schooling, home

Mitchell L. Stevens

Home schooling, the practice of educating one's own children, has seen dramatic growth in the last three decades, and has transformed from a peculiarly American innovation to a truly global movement. An estimated 15,000 US children were home schooled in the late 1970s; by 2003 the number was over a million, and the practice had won adherents throughout the industrialized world (National Center for Education Statistics 2004; Stevens 2003). Parent-directed education was almost entirely eclipsed with the accomplishment of universal compulsory schooling in the early twentieth century. But as part of the "anti-Establishment" cultural ferment of the 1960s and 1970s home schooling reemerged as a social movement, championed by advocates across a wide ideological spectrum.

Even while all racial groups and socioeconomic levels are represented among them, home school families are disproportionately middle class, well educated, and white. The vast majority of home schooling work is conducted by mothers; most home school households are headed by married couples and supported by a sole, male breadwinner (National Center for Education Statistics 2001). Home schooling enables women with traditionalist conceptions of motherhood to incorporate some of the status of professional teaching into their full-time domesticity. This is part of why the practice is particularly appealing to conservative religious women (Stevens 2001).

What may at first appear as an individual, quixotic educational choice has from its beginnings been a collective one. Home school families have long cooperated with one another in order to lobby for the legality of the practice and to build often-elaborate home school communities. Home schooling is best understood as a social movement, one with a distinctive dual history. One branch began in the left-liberal alternative school movement of the 1960s, a cause which sought to radically democratize teacher–student relationships and give students greater discretion over their own educations. John Holt, long a prominent advocate of alternative schooling, began to promote home education (which he called "unschooling") in the 1970s. Before his death in 1985, Holt had successfully nurtured a national grassroots network of home school converts. Another branch comes out of the conservative Protestant day school tradition, specifically through the work of Raymond and Dorothy Moore, whose several books and national speaking tours advocating home education reached an audience of religious families already skeptical of public schools.

Despite these cultural differences the early home school advocates shared a conviction that each child has an essential, inviolable self, and that standardized methods of instruction are harmful to children's self-development. Both Holt and the Moores, for example, frequently invoked factory metaphors to derogate conventional schools and to contrast them with the educational customization home education makes possible. But to this shared conviction about children's essential individualism these leaders added rather different ideas: Holt conceived of children as essentially virtuous beings with innate abilities to educate themselves; the Moores tended to view children as essentially good but also sinful, and thus in need of discipline and direction from wiser adults. This mix of commonality and difference in early home school philosophy presaged subsequent organizational conflict between the two branches of the cause.

One of the first tasks of the fledgling movement was to secure the legality of home education nationwide. Spurred by a remarkably well-organized home school lobby, judicial and legislative activity throughout the 1980s rendered home education legal throughout the US by the end of the decade (Henderson 1993). The process of legalization was facilitated by the distinctive jurisdictional structure of American education. Because authority over schooling is largely in the hands of state and local governments in the US, activists were able to wage localized battles and win victories in piecemeal fashion.

While the two branches of the home school movement cooperated amicably through the 1980s, the differences in their organizational sensibilities split the cause in the subsequent decade. From their different cultural traditions home school advocates had inherited contradictory organizational ideas: some of them favored highly democratic, consensual organizational forms and were wary of excluding families from their associations on the basis of religion or educational philosophy; by contrast, conservative Protestants preferred hierarchical organizational forms and often were eager to define their associations as distinctively "Christian" in character and membership. Home schoolers' different ways of thinking about collective action ultimately divided the movement into two organizational worlds: one officially "diverse" and non-sectarian, the other officially "Christian."

This turbulent political history was largely hidden from public view by the movement's very success. By the mid-1990s home schooling had shed much of its countercultural stigma and had become an acceptable educational choice for families with a wide range of lifestyles. Interested parents could choose from an array of support and advocacy groups at the local and national levels, and shop in a vital sector of small businesses supplying varied curriculum materials to the growing home school market.

Because quantitative research on home schooled children's academic outcomes has been piecemeal, at present researchers lack the kind of systematic data that would enable them to say definitively if the practice confers a net advantage or disadvantage relative to conventional schooling. Nevertheless, the preponderance of available evidence indicates that the average home schooled child performs at least as well as her conventionally schooled peers on nationally normed standardized tests. While not all home schooled students are academic stars, research to date has yielded no cause for alarm regarding home schoolers' basic academic aptitudes and rates of school completion (Stevens 2001).

In both its history and its character, home schooling is an American invention. The jurisdictional boundary between parents and the state has always been especially blurry in the US, a cultural reality which made the basic logic of home schooling initially more palatable in this country than it might have been elsewhere.

Nevertheless, home education has diffused globally over the last two decades. The national homes of the movement's earliest adherents are telling: England, with its long tradition of private schooling; and Japan, where an extremely competitive, exam-driven education system has fostered novel means of educational advancement and exit. Home education is now practiced throughout the industrialized world, even in nations such as Germany, where it is technically illegal (Spiegler 2003), and we might predict that it will further flourish internationally as a neoliberal logic of citizens as discretionary consumers of state services continues its ascendancy (Stevens 2003).

The home school movement teaches three general sociological lessons. First, it reminds us of the inherent tensions at the boundary between family and school. Few would dispute that schools and families have very different functions, timetables, and emotional valences; often overlooked, however, are the problems that arise from the simple fact that these two institutions share the same children. Even while the personnel requirements for the two spheres are radically different, we tend to presume that people can easily transit from one to the other on a regular – indeed daily – basis. But at this formidable institutional intersection things are bound sometimes to go awry: parents will dispute the extent to which schools adequately honor the specialness of particular children; schools will be skeptical or dismissive of parent opinions; school and family priorities will conflict. Home education represents one, particularly radical response to the chronic contradictions between these very different spheres of social life. Evidence for this is the frequency with which parents explain their decision to home school their children by referencing obstacles and problems they experienced in public schools.

Second, the popularity of home education highlights the importance of individualism as a contemporary pedagogical ideal. Home schooling shares with other currently fashionable pedagogies (e.g., the Montessori and Reggio Emilia methods) the presumption that children are best served by highly customized instruction, and that standardized curricula are harmful to young people's self-development. These ideas neatly reverse the ideal of uniform curricula common among educational leaders a century ago (Tyack 1974). While it is difficult to trace the causes of such a cultural shift definitively, it seems reasonable to posit that one driver of the change was the growing fascination with self-actualization that characterized American culture in the 1960s and 1970s, and the simultaneous critiques of large bureaucratic institutions popular during this time (Bellah et al. 1985; Clecak 1983). Indeed, many early advocates of home education describe their effort as part of this broader cultural ferment (Stevens 2001). In any case, evidence from multiple studies suggests that the highly individualized instruction so valued by home schooling parents is becoming the presumed best practice in upper-middle-class households throughout North America (Lareau 2003; Davies et al. 2002).

Third, the emergence and endurance of home schooling is appropriately seen as part of the growing importance placed on parental choice in education generally. In the contemporary US, education is increasingly understood as a private good that families appropriately consume in the manner of their own discretion (Labaree 1997). A common corollary is the notion that educational services are best distributed through market mechanisms, which are thought to ideally match educational "products" with parents' and students' "preferences" (Chubb & Moe 1990). Within this market framework home schooling appears as but one of many potential options among which parents can choose as they see fit. The contrary idea that helped give rise to mass public schooling a century ago – namely, that education is a public good best distributed universally to all citizens – has become increasingly marginalized even while home education has moved toward the mainstream.

SEE ALSO: Childhood; Collective Action; Culture, Social Movements and; Motherhood; Neoliberalism; New Left; New Religious Movements; Parental Involvement in Education; School Choice

REFERENCES AND SUGGESTED READINGS

Bellah, R. N., Madsen, R., Sullivan, W. M., Swidler, A., & Tipton, S. M. (1985) *Habits of the Heart.* University of California Press, Berkeley.

Chubb, J. E. & Moe, T. M. (1990) *Politics, Markets, and America's Schools.* Brookings Institution, Washington, DC.

Clecak, P. (1983) *America's Quest for the Ideal Self.* Oxford University Press, New York.

Davies, S., Aurini, J., & Quirke, L. (2002) New Markets for Higher Education in Canada. *Education Canada* 42: 36–41.

Henderson, A. C. (1993) The Home Schooling Movement: Parents Take Control of Educating Their Children. *Annual Survey of American Law 1991*: 985–1009.

Labaree, D. F. (1997) *How to Succeed in School Without Really Learning.* Yale University Press, New Haven.

Lareau, A. (2003) *Unequal Childhoods.* University of California Press, Berkeley.

National Center for Education Statistics (2001) *Homeschooling in the United States: 1999* (NCES 2001–003). US Department of Education, Washington, DC.

National Center for Education Statistics (2004) *1.1 Million Homeschooled Students in the United States in 2003* (NCES 2004–115). US Department of Education, Washington, DC.

Spiegler, T. (2003) Home Education in Germany: An Overview of the Contemporary Situation. *Evaluation and Research in Education* 17(2&3): 179–90.

Stevens, M. L. (2001) *Kingdom of Children: Culture and Controversy in the Homeschooling Movement.* Princeton University Press, Princeton.

Stevens, M. L. (2003) The Normalization of Home Education in the United States. *Evaluation and Research in Education* 17(2&3): 90–100.

Tyack, D. B. (1974) *The One Best System.* Harvard University Press, Cambridge, MA.

schools, charter

Amy Stuart Wells

In 1991, Minnesota passed the first charter school law in the United States, allowing state funds to support schools that operate autonomously from the public educational system. The charter school idea caught on quickly, with

40 states and the District of Columbia passing charter school laws between 1991 and 2006. By fall 2005, there were approximately 3,600 charter schools enrolling about 1 million students across the country.

The basic premise of charter school reform is to allow educators, parents, and/or entrepreneurs to receive per-pupil funding to run schools that are exempt from many rules and regulations of the public system, including student assignment policies. Thus, charter schools not only have a great deal of autonomy in terms of their daily operations, they also have greater control over their enrollments than most public schools. They are schools of choice, enrolling students through an admissions process that often, but not always, involves a lottery. In exchange for this greater autonomy, charter schools are supposed to be held accountable for student outcomes. Each school's chartering agreement with one of various charter-granting institutions – a school district, a state board of education, a state charter school board, or a university – describes its educational philosophy and goals. If a charter school fails to achieve these goals, the charter-granting authority has the right to revoke the charter.

Beyond these similarities, each state charter school law is slightly different. Some laws are far more lenient than others in terms of the number of charters that can be granted or the number of charter school authorizing organizations. Furthermore, some states allow private schools to be converted into charter schools. Others allow charter schools to serve home schooling families or students who want to finish school via independent study. (These are known as non-classroom-based charter schools.) As a result of these differences in state laws, as well as demographic distinction in the K-12 populations, there is wide variation in the number of charter schools and their enrollments from one state to the next. For instance, in the 2005–6 school year, California claimed almost 600 charter schools serving about 200,000 students. In the same year, Mississippi had only one charter school serving 380 students.

In fact, charter school reform, as a national movement, is fairly lopsided, with only six states – Arizona, California, Florida, Michigan, Ohio, and Texas – housing nearly two-thirds of the charter schools and students (see Ziebarth et al. 2005). On the other end of the spectrum, 12 of the 40 states with charter school laws have fewer than 20 charter schools, accounting for only 3 percent of all the schools and less than 3 percent of all the students.

Thus, the popularity of charter schools is widespread but uneven, as different states and local officials embrace the reform to different degrees. This diversity across state and local lines also reflects the varied political roots of the charter school reform movement, as various supporters of charter schools jumped on the bandwagon for divergent reasons.

Charter school reform was born in the late 1980s and early 1990s, when there was growing frustration with many of the equity-based policies of the 1960s and 1970s, particularly with programs such as school desegregation, compensatory education, and bilingual education, which were seen as overregulated. Policymakers were bent on trying to improve the quality of the overall educational system via an emphasis on higher educational standards – i.e., "excellence" – as well as an infusion of choice and competition.

The argument was that a rising tide would lift all boats and that both standards-based accountability systems via systemic reform and a strong dose of market forces, namely competition and choice, would force all schools to respond to the needs of all students. All of this coincided with a growing demand for greater decentralization of educational governance and control. Charter school reform was in sync with all three of these efforts and is grounded in the ideology of each (see Wells et al. 2002).

CHARTER SCHOOL REFORM AFTER 15 YEARS: WHAT WE HAVE LEARNED

Despite charter school reform's political origins in both systemic reform and decentralization movements, in many ways it has been the free market advocates who have most directly shaped charter school policies. Given that 90 percent of the charter schools in the US exist in states with more deregulatory laws, much of the research on charter school reform conducted thus far provides insight into how effective the market model of school change is in the real world of schools and children. The results are not optimistic, especially in light of the many claims attached to charter school reform at the birth of the movement. Proponents claimed that charter schools would promote achievement through their more autonomous structure. They also expected that charter schools would have greater accountability for student outcomes and public dollars, because of the possibility of losing their charter as a consequence of poor performance. Finally, charter school advocates claimed that these schools would provide choice for families and competition for public schools, improving the educational marketplace. Below, the research to date on each of these claims is summarized.

Student Achievement

Efforts to summarize and synthesize studies conducted on charter schools and student achievement have produced inconclusive but fairly negative results. In studies of national data and studies of specific state assessments, there is no evidence that charter schools are consistently outperforming regular public schools; in some cases, they are doing worse.

In Levin's (2005) review of the research on charter schools and student achievement, he concludes that although charter school advocates and opponents each choose particular studies that favor their points of view, overall there is no reliable pattern of difference between charter and public schools.

Another comprehensive review of the literature on charter schools and student achievement by Carnoy et al. (2005) examined separately those studies that drew upon the National Assessment of Educational Progress (NAEP) test scores across states and those that examined charter schools within the context of particular states by drawing on state test data. The vast majority of state-level studies conclude that charter schools do not outperform public schools, even when charter schools have become well established. Carnoy et al. (2005) conclude that even when strong measures are used to control for selection bias, the effect on students of being in the charter schools appears to be negative.

Another review of literature on charter schools and student achievement by a more pro-charter reform researcher demonstrates that of 35 charter school achievement studies conducted since 2000, only 15 show positive results for charter schools (Hill 2005: 23). The 35 studies reviewed in this analysis include those conducted by politically conservative think tanks that are outspoken proponents of charter schools and vouchers.

Finally, a study conducted by the Rand Corporation (2003) found that in California, only the start-up charter schools – those that, on average, over-enroll white students – had slightly higher test scores than comparable public schools. Meanwhile, the charter schools that had been converted from regular public schools and enrolled a higher percentage of black and Latino students had test scores that were comparable to demographically similar public schools. And worse yet, the non-classroom-based charter schools – e.g., the online and independent study charter schools that enroll larger numbers of low-income and/or low-achieving students at a very low per-pupil cost – had lower test scores than public schools with similar enrollments (see Wells & Holme 2005).

Accountability

As evidence mounts that current charter school laws have done little to improve student achievement, additional research suggests that they are rarely held accountable for student achievement. The lack of serious academic accountability for charter schools was documented in a US Department of Education study, which found that more than half of the charter school authorizers surveyed said they had difficulty closing charter schools that were failing. In fact, only 12 percent of those surveyed said they had ever revoked a charter or denied a renewal of a charter. And in those instances when an authorizer enforced a formal sanction, it was almost always due to financial problems with the charter school and rarely because of enforcement of the academic accountability provisions of the charter school laws (Finnigan et al. 2004).

Charter school reform in Dayton, Ohio, provides an example of the lack of academic accountability within the movement. Dayton experienced a proliferation of charter schools, despite evidence that the existing charter schools – many of which were operated by the same management companies that were requesting the new charters – were performing at a lower level on state exams. A full 26 percent of students in Dayton are enrolled in charter schools, a much higher rate than in any other American city, but few of Dayton's charter schools perform better than its public schools (Dillon 2005).

In addition to the lack of academic accountability, there is also growing evidence that charter school reform opens the door for fraud and misappropriation of funds. In other words, public funding for these schools is deregulated to the degree that opportunists can make money at the public's expense. And while charter schools are more likely to be shut down because of fiscal as opposed to academic accountability issues, numerous examples of charter school closures suggest that it often takes a long time before fiscally questionable schools are closed (see Dillon 2004).

While solid research on charter school accountability – academic or fiscal – is lacking, there is no evidence that these publicly funded schools are being held *more* accountable than the regular public schools, especially in the states with the more deregulated charter school laws.

Choice and Competition

The claim that charter schools would provide students and parents with greater choice in education certainly speaks to the experiences of some of the students some of the time. Yet, research on charter school enrollments suggests that charter schools are more racially and socioeconomically segregated at the school level than the already highly segregated public schools. Further distinctions appear when researchers examine factors such as parent education and parental involvement.

Charter school proponents tout the fact that overall, when aggregated national data only are examined, charter schools serve a slightly higher percentage of students of color, if not more poor students. But more careful analyses of the data broken down by state, district, and surrounding communities demonstrate that charter schools disproportionately serve less disadvantaged students within their contexts. In other words, charter schools may well be located in low-income neighborhoods and enroll low-income students of color, but oftentimes we see that the students enrolled in charter schools are less poor, have more involved and/or better educated parents, and are less likely to be labeled special needs or English language learners than their peers in nearby public schools. These data suggest that within each state, charter schools create more stratification at the school level (Cobb & Glass 1999; Fuller et al. 2003; Carnoy et al. 2005).

Furthermore, there are major differences across states in terms of the demographics of charter schools. In some states – especially Illinois, Ohio, and Michigan – charter school reform is a mostly urban reform designed to serve predominantly low-income students of color. In other states, such as California, Arizona, and Colorado, it has appealed to a much wider range of people and communities, including many that are predominantly white and well-off (Wells et al. 2000). Those states in which charter school minority enrollment is lower by more than 5 percent from the district enrollments house more charter schools overall than the states in which minority enrollment in charter schools is greater on average than district demographics by at least 5 percent (Ziebarth et al. 2005).

Roy and Mishel (2005) compare charter school demographics to the nearest public schools and demonstrate that in several states with the largest charter school enrollments, including Arizona, California, and Florida, charter schools enroll higher percentages of white students than their nearby public schools. They also find that charter schools in these states enroll a much lower percentage of students eligible for free or reduced price lunch than their nearby public schools.

Even when the racial/ethnic makeup of charter schools is similar to other nearby public schools, the students enrolled in charter schools are often "advantaged" in other ways. For instance, minority students attending charter schools in states where minority enrollment in charter schools is higher than in public schools tend to be socioeconomically advantaged compared to minority students in public schools (Carnoy et al. 2005). Of course, an argument could be made that even if the students enrolled in charter schools are slightly less disadvantaged than those who attend nearby public schools, the mere fact that these public schools down the street operate within a competitive educational market means they will respond to the competition for students by improving. In reviewing this literature, Levin (2005) argues that the available results from a variety of charter school and voucher settings suggest only a modest competitive response by public schools at best.

Overall, there is little evidence that charter schools and the policies that create and support them have delivered on their promises of raising student achievement, making schools more accountable, or providing choices that the most disadvantaged students can take advantage of within a given community or context. Still, they remain a popular reform effort in great part because they are steeped in popular beliefs about the free market and competition. Researchers must continue to ask hard questions about whose interests are being served by this reform.

SEE ALSO: Education; Educational Attainment; Parental Involvement in Education; School Choice; Schools, Public

REFERENCES AND SUGGESTED READINGS

Asimov, N. (2002) Audit Blasts Charter School Oversight. *San Francisco Chronicle*, November 8.

Bifulco, R. & Ladd, H. F. (2004) *The Impacts of Charter Schools on Student Achievement: Evidence from North Carolina*. Terry Stanford Institute of Public Policy, Duke University, Durham, NC.

Borja, R. R. (2003) US Audit Raps Arizona's Use of Charter Aid. *Education Week* 23(14): 1, 25.

Carnoy, M., Jacobsen, R., Mishel, L., & Rothstein, R. (2005) *The Charter School Dust-Up: Examining the Evidence on Enrollment*. Economic Policy Institute and Teachers College Press, Washington, DC, and New York.

Chubb, J. E. & Moe, T. M. (1990) *Politics, Markets, and America's Schools*. Brookings Institution, Washington, DC.

Cobb, C. D. & Glass, G. V. (1999) Ethnic Segregation in Arizona Charter Schools. *Educational Policy Analysis Archives* 7(1). Online. epaa.asu.edu.

Dillon, S. (2004) Collapse of 60 Charter Schools Leaves Californians Scrambling. *New York Times*, September 17.

Dillon, S. (2005) Charter Schools Alter Map of Public Education in Dayton. *New York Times*, March 27.

Finnigan, K., Adelman, N., Anderson, L., Cotton, L., Donnelly, M. B., & Price, T. (2004) *Evaluation of the Public Charter School Program: Final Report*. Doc. No. 2004–08 US Department of Education, Washington, DC.

Friedman, M. (1962) *Capitalism and Freedom*. University of Chicago Press, Chicago.

Fuller, B., Gawlik, M., Gonzales, E. K., & Park, S. (2003) *Charter Schools and Inequity: National Disparities in Funding, Teacher Quality, and Student Support Journal*. Policy Analysis for California Education, Berkeley.

Hill, P. (2005) Assessing Achievement in Charter Schools. In: Lake, R. & Hill, P. (Eds.), *Hopes, Fears, and Reality: A Balanced Look at American Charter Schools in 2005*. National Charter School Research Project, University of Washington, Seattle, pp. 21–32.

Levin, H. M. (2005) Market Behavior and Charter Schools. Prepared for the Think Tank on Educational Entrepreneurship, Institute for the Study of Educational Entrepreneurship, UCLA, Los Angeles.

May, M. (2000) Oakland Charter School Cuts Costs, Seeks County Reprieve. *Chronicle Staff Writer*, January 10.

Pilcher, J. (2000) Some Students Return to CPS: Since Fall, Public School Exodus Has Slowed and Turned Around. *Cincinnati Enquirer*, April 6.

Rand Corporation (2003) How California Charter Schools Operate and Perform. Rand Education Brief. Online. www.rand.org/publications/RB/RB8022/RB8022.pdf.

Roy, J. & Mishel, L. (2005) *Advantage None: Reexamining Hoxby's Findings of Charter School Benefits*. Economic Policy Institute, Washington, DC.

Scott, J. & Holme, J. (2002) Public Schools, Private Resources: The Role of Social Networks in California Charter School Reform. In: Wells, A. S. (Ed.), *Where Charter School Policy Fails: The Problems of Accountability and Equity*. Teachers College Press, New York, pp. 102–28.

Wells, A. S. & Holme, J. J. (2005) Marketization in Education: Looking Back to Move Forward with a Stronger Critique. In: Bascia, N., Cumming, A., Datnow, A., Leithwood, K., & Livingston, D. (Eds.), *International Handbook of Educational Policy*. Springer, New York, pp. 19–52.

Wells, A. S., Holme, J. J., Lopez, A., & Cooper, C. W. (2000) Charter Schools and Racial and Social Class Segregation: Yet Another Sorting Machine? In: Kahlenberg, R. (Ed.), *A Notion At Risk: Preserving Education as an Engine for Social*

Mobility. Century Foundation Press, New York, pp. 169–222.
Wells, A. S., Vasedeva, A., Holme, J. J., & Cooper, C. W. (2002) The Politics of Accountability: California School Districts and Charter School Reform. In: Wells, A. S. (Ed.), *Where Charter School Policy Fails: The Problems of Accountability and Equity*. Teachers College Press, New York, pp. 29–53.
Ziebarth, T., Celio, M. B., Lake, R. J., & Rainey, L. (2005) The Charter Schools Landscape in 2005. In: Lake, R. & Hill, P. (Eds.), *Hopes, Fears, and Reality: A Balanced Look at American Charter Schools in 2005*. National Charter School Research Project, University of Washington, Seattle, pp. 1–20.

schools, common

Ann Owens

The rise of a common school system in nations around the world provides some evidence for a sociological theory of educational origins and expansion focused on socialization and social organization. While more functional arguments often point to the need for a well-trained workforce as the driving force in the rise of public education, a more sociological interpretation argues that modernizing countries, facing increased social differentiation, must transfer the socialization task from families to an institution like schools (Dreeben 1968). Another aspect of this argument is that with modernization, increased individualism also occurs, and a common school system is needed to promote national citizenship and induction into a general collectivity (Ramirez & Meyer 1980).

Current empirical evidence does not provide conclusive support for any one theory of why developing nations promote a free education system. However, in countries where this ideology of minimizing social differentiation and creating good citizens exists, this theory appears plausible. In France, for example, public education was first proposed by Enlightenment philosophers in the late 1700s in line with goals of universal citizenship and order (Alexander 2000). In the United States, common schools were established to provide a free, state-controlled education system for all citizens in line with the ideological goals of these theories. The creation of the common school system in the nineteenth century drew on the ideology of the developing republican government in that a republic depends on having a well-educated and morally trained populace to direct the decisions of the government and monitor its actions. A free, state-controlled education system would also alleviate political and social stratification based on education level by providing all citizens with equal opportunity to obtain a basic education, and therefore to exercise an equal vote in the new government and be competitive in the economy. Schooling became centrally controlled and organized and provided universal education.

THE NEED FOR COMMON SCHOOLS

The goal of socialization into one national collectivity was particularly salient for the US as it developed into an independent nation. In the US during the seventeenth and eighteenth centuries, education was the responsibility of parents and local communities. Demand for uniform, compulsory education grew from both pragmatic and ideological needs. First, citizens wanted a basic education to eliminate the disparate literacy levels between native colonists and British immigrants and between North and South; second, literacy was necessary to study the Bible, essential for salvation to Calvinists and Protestants; and finally, the growing economy in the colonies demanded the ability to read and do basic math for trading and planning purposes (Kaestle 1983). Availability and quality of schools, teachers, and curriculum were unregulated and unequal across towns and states, producing educational differences across regions. Low quality and limited availability of elementary schooling were reasons enough for the education system to be reformed; however, it was the political and ideological climate of the time that gave rise to the development of the common school system in the nineteenth century (Kaestle 1983; Tyack et al. 1987).

As the US government developed, political theorists began to see education as a key tool in maintaining the republican ideals on which the country was founded, with education acting as "the fourth branch of government" (Tyack et al. 1987). The republican system of government depended on an enlightened general populace that understood what was in their best interest. Additionally, citizens needed to be well informed to be able to prevent some of the corruption that the Americans saw and eschewed in the European governments. Therefore, common education would serve as a training ground for citizens: citizens could be taught basic literacy and numeracy skills, but also receive "moral training" consistent with Protestant ideals and be informed on political and economic issues (Kaestle 1983, 2000). Further, with a country as big as America, republican government would not work without a well-ordered population, and education was seen as a way to produce this orderly public. Common education would protect the government from having to act on an uninformed will, and also give the people power to protect themselves from a corrupt government. Education became a tool to distribute power more equitably among the populace.

In addition to maintaining republican goals, the common school system was seen as a way to reduce social and political stratification. At this time, the "haves" and "have-nots" were distinguished by their levels of literacy and education, as education was necessary to be successful in trading and business and also necessary to be considered an appropriate choice for government office. Because there was no free school system, only those with money were able to send their children to school, and this system of education resulted in social reproduction wherein power stayed in the upper class. There were marked disparities in education by gender, race, nativity, and region. Women were rarely educated, nor were blacks or Native Americans. Northern states, New England in particular, had developed a more widespread system of education since the region was organized around highly populated towns compared with the less densely populated South (Kaestle 1983). European immigrants had often attended better schools in their home countries than were available to native colonists. Common schools were seen as a way to allow all citizens to have an equal chance to be qualified to hold positions of power, and education began to be seen as a mechanism for social mobility.

THE CREATION OF A COMMON SCHOOL SYSTEM

The earliest attempts to establish a common school system were by individual states, with New York, Massachusetts, and Connecticut leading the way. These early attempts often resulted in states using taxes from land or land grants to partially fund schools, but tuition was still charged to cover remaining expenses. From the late 1700s through the 1830s, the types of schools supported by state funds were not uniform; for example, New York state money went toward supporting existing private schools rather than supporting free schools (Ravitch 2000). In states where state funds were not allocated for education, particularly in the South, schools continued to be funded entirely by tuition payments, doing little to alleviate knowledge stratification among the classes. Apprenticeship and charity church education programs also existed.

In the early nineteenth century, the population and economy of America were booming, and these social changes helped pave the way for educational reform. While the economy prospered, the rewards to individuals were unequal, with the more educated generally being more successful. Also, with the population boom, America was experiencing higher rates of crime, a more diverse population, and more crowded cities. While the ideology of common schools had existed for some time, education now began to be seen as a pragmatic solution for decreasing stratification and cultural conflicts and maintaining social order. Schools could be designed as "factories" that could teach moral discipline (an increasingly popular movement in the early nineteenth century) and arm American citizens with basic education so that everyone had an equal chance for upward mobility in the thriving economy (Tyack et al. 1987). Also wanting to protect citizens' power from the growing government, the public began to more vocally support the idea of a common school system, treating it as a necessity rather than rhetoric. The environment was ripe to implement reforms.

From the 1830s through the 1860s, reformers worked to pass legislation to establish a compulsory free schooling system. Two of the most prominent common schools reformers were

Henry Barnard and Horace Mann. In the late 1830s, each pushed through reforms in their respective state legislatures (Barnard in Connecticut, Mann in Massachusetts) similar to those being supported across the country and modeled after reforms in Europe. The basic demands of the common school supporters were that states should provide "free schooling, improved facilities, better classification, longer school years, better teacher training" (Kaestle 1983). Reformers also attempted to pull support from private schools by depicting them as non-republican institutions that reproduced social stratification, and states were encouraged to provide entirely free, high-quality schools to reduce the appeal of private schools.

While the South considerably lagged behind the North in initiating changes, most states had established common schools by 1860. More students were attending school, and for longer periods of time. Schools became more highly organized, with a system of high schools serving as an umbrella under which to organize district schools. The concept of teacher training was debated, and the earliest education schools were set up, although few teachers attended them (Kaestle 1983). At the urging of reformer John Philbrick, schools were organized under a principal who had 10 to 12 usually female teachers. Major changes occurred with respect to centralizing control. In the early nineteenth century, schools were under the control of local community governments, which many argued allowed for inconsistent teaching and facilities standards. During the 1840s and 1850s, schools in most states were reorganized into larger districts and became state controlled and supervised. The office of school superintendent was created at the state level and was often combined with the secretary of state position. Schools became an organization run by this state superintendent, and large cities began to create school boards with officials elected by the public to work with the school leaders (Tyack 1974).

The reformers had made progress, but a minority in the population did not support the creation of a common school system. One major dispute was over the centralized control of schools as an organization. Some citizens felt that centralized control was too bureaucratic and would turn schools into a "mindless machine" directed by the state superintendent (Tyack 1974). Also, a centralized school governing body could ignore local actors and regional and cultural differences (e.g., factory towns wanting more vocational education for their children), and individuals would not have a choice in how schools were run. However, supporters argued that centralized control would equalize school spending between rich and poor by providing free and regulated schools, and schools would also regulate discipline and offer all citizens the same basic curriculum. Political lines were drawn, with Democrats favoring local control of schooling and less government intervention and Whigs favoring state-controlled systems and a more uniform training for all. Individual ethnic and religious groups wanted to keep elements of their culture and teachings in the school curriculum, and they too opposed state-regulated schools and curricula. Eventually, the push for state-controlled schools succeeded largely because of the strength of the republican rhetoric regarding the need for equal education and thus an equal voice for all, and because of the appeal of free, high-quality schools open to everyone (Kaestle 1983).

The success of school reform required spending, and some citizens were reluctant to pay increased taxes. Some argued that common schooling supported by general taxation favored the rich. The working class resented having to pay the same taxes for schooling as people who could readily afford to send their children to private schools. These opponents of the free common schools argued that states should not require poor communities to support free schools if they were not able to. Additionally, those citizens who did not have children who were attending school resented having to pay education taxes. When higher taxation was proposed, poor communities rejected these proposals, while other communities felt compelled to support the ideals of common schools by paying what their superintendents required. Because of the economic boom in America, many states had sufficient funds to finance school initiatives, and increased taxation could be avoided. In states and communities that had fewer financial resources, ways to cut costs were proposed, including the hiring of female teachers, who, while not readily received or respected, were cheaper than male teachers. This early use of women as cheap labor, some argued, established a gender hierarchy in education and other institutions that remains today (Kaestle 1983). By the 1870s, reformers were for the most part able to assuage opponents of tax-supported schools by developing appropriate local tax formulas and by persuading the public that everyone benefited from a well-educated populace because of the social order it facilitated, and therefore everyone should pay.

By the 1860s, a common school system had been set up in America with public access to state-funded education under the control of state governments. Rural schools were still often heavily influenced by local taxpayers rather than state legislation, few teachers were properly trained, and disagreements over the curriculum and religion's place in it still persisted. However, the reformers had created a common school system based on ideology that still pervades the American educational system today. First, education for all is a republican ideal which allows everyone an equal chance; providing everyone with an equitable foundation will allow for social mobility for all racial, ethnic, and socioeconomic groups. Second, by centrally controlling education, equality and uniformity of instruction are guaranteed. This nascent common school system provided the foundation for the system of schooling that is in place today.

The origins of education systems vary across the world, and one factor in this variation is the ideological goals of each country. The economic system and degree of industrialization as well as the development of the nation-state also influenced the rise of education systems around the world, but in countries where increasing social differentiation was seen as a threat to stability and where democratic ideals needed to be taught to a mass citizenry, common schools arose in part to serve these needs.

SEE ALSO: Education; Educational Attainment; Schools, Public; Schools, Religious; Socialization

REFERENCES AND SUGGESTED READINGS

Alexander, R. (2000) *Culture and Pedagogy: International Comparisons in Primary Education.* Blackwell, Malden, MA.

Cubberley, E. (1922) *A Brief History of Education: A History of the Practice and Progress and Organization of Education.* Houghton Mifflin, New York.

Dreeben, R. (1968) *On What Is Learned in Schools.* Addison-Wesley, Reading, MA.

Kaestle, C. F. (1983) *Pillars of the Republic: Common Schools and American Society, 1780–1860.* Hill & Wang, New York.

Kaestle, C. F. (2000) Toward a Political Economy of Citizenship: Historical Perspectives on the Purpose of Common Schools. In: Mc Donnell, L. & Timpane, M. (Eds.), *The Democratic Purposes of Education.* Kansas University Press, Lawrence, pp. 47–73.

Ramirez, F. O. & Meyer, J. W. (1980) Comparative Education: The Social Construction of the Modern World System. *Annual Review of Sociology* 6: 369–99.

Ravitch, D. (2000) *The Great School Wars: A History of the New York City Public Schools.* Johns Hopkins University Press, Baltimore.

Tyack, D. B. (1974) *The One Best System: A History of American Urban Education.* Harvard University Press, Cambridge, MA.

Tyack, D., James, T., & Benavot, A. (1987) *Law and the Shaping of Public Education, 1785–1954.* University of Wisconsin Press, Madison.

schools, magnet

Amy G. Langenkamp

Magnet schools are public schools defined by three principal characteristics: a distinctive curriculum or instructional approach, enrollment of students from outside the designated neighborhood attendance zones, and desegregation as their explicit purpose. Magnet schools have been used for desegregation since the mid-1970s. However, the concept of magnet schools is based on district specialty schools which have been present since the 1900s. Currently, there are two major national studies of magnet schools.

Blank et al. (1983) conducted a study in 1973 which found a significant increase in magnet schools since being accepted as a voluntary strategy for desegregating schools, from 14 to 138 districts during the first five years. Second, Steel and Levine conducted a nationally representative study of 600 multischool districts in

1992 and found magnet programs offered in at least 230 public school districts, serving 1.2 million students mostly in districts with a court-ordered desegregation plan. Most magnet schools emphasize a particular subject area, and one-fifth offer a distinctive instructional approach. Magnet schools are not homogeneous. Instead, magnet programs are offered at the elementary, middle, and high school level and function as Programs-Within-Schools (PWS) or whole school magnets (Steel & Levine 1994). For simplicity, PWS and whole school magnets will be referred to interchangeably unless otherwise indicated.

HISTORY AND DEVELOPMENT OF MAGNET SCHOOLS

The concept of magnet schools comes from district-wide specialty schools such as the Bronx High School of Science in New York City. Magnet schools are also historically linked to school desegregation efforts. Court decisions of the civil rights era outlawed segregation in schooling and required school districts to produce racially mixed schools, such as the 1968 Supreme Court case of *Green* v. *Board of Education* in Virginia and *Swann* v. *Charlotte-Mecklenburg* in North Carolina (see Steel & Levine 1994 for a review). Faced with the challenge of integrating schools and whites' hesitancy to voluntarily transfer their children to majority minority schools, districts began forced busing. Violent protests and the exodus of many white families from the public and urban school system ensued (Meeks et al. 2000). Therefore, in 1975, magnet schools were allowed as a voluntary strategy for desegregation. Since that time, magnet schools' prevalence has grown enormously. In 1996, 85 percent of magnet schools were in court-ordered districts (Steel & Levine 1994).

However, the connection of magnet schools to desegregation is only the initial reason for their growth in the US educational system. The report *A Nation at Risk* (1983) spurned education reform for more high-quality and locally controlled public schools, the goal being to develop a stronger sense of community and increased parental involvement in their children's education (Steel & Levine 1994; Gamoran 1996). In addition, federal funding has facilitated the growth of magnet schools.

Desegregation efforts have been funded principally through two federal programs, the Emergency School Aid Act (ESAA) from 1975 to 1981 and the Magnet School Assistance Program (MSAP), which began funding the start of new magnet programs or adding to current magnet programs in the mid-1980s. Funding from MSAP is conditional on schools' mission of reducing minority isolation, eliminating minority isolation, or preventing minority enrollment from rising above the district levels (Steel & Levine 1994). Funding for staff development, curriculum planning, supplies, and outreach contributed to 80 percent of the $739 million spent between 1985 and 1991. Magnet programs are more extensive in districts that received MSAP funding; schools without funding have fewer outreach programs to recruit new students and provide limited transportation to students. MSAP funding affects the broader district as well. Districts without MSAP funding but with magnet programs can strip other public schools in that district of funding (Estes et al. 1990). For example, when compared to other public schools in the same district, magnet schools have additional staffing allowances, smaller classes, and more expenditure per pupil (Steel & Levine 1994).

PREVALENCE OF MAGNET SCHOOLS

Part of the difficulty in studying the effects of magnet schools, despite their increasing prevalence in urban school districts, is their heterogeneity. Typically, magnet schools have a distinctive curriculum, attract students from outside the neighborhood attendance zone, and have desegregation as their goal (Steel & Levine 1994). Fifty-eight percent of magnet schools are in elementary schools and 38 percent are PWS magnets. Whole school magnets are more common in elementary schools while PWS magnets are more common in middle and secondary schools. Among magnets, instructional approaches are broken down as follows: 37 percent have an emphasis in a specific subject area, 27 percent offer a particular instructional approach, 14 percent have career-vocational emphases, 12 percent are gifted and talented magnets, and 11 percent have specific arts programs.

Even with their increase in urban districts, all schools in Steel and Levine's study maintain waiting lists for student attendance. To attract students to their schools, a typical district uses a variety of outreach strategies such as recruiting students from surrounding schools. Approximately one-third of magnet schools are "dedicated" magnets, where there is no attendance zone and all students must choose to attend. The rest of the magnet schools have a neighborhood attendance zone and attract additional students from other attendance zones. Typically, those non-dedicated magnets are comprised of white students attending magnet schools in minority neighborhoods (Steel & Levine 1994). About one-third of magnet schools use program-specific selection criteria; this practice is most common at gifted and talented magnet schools. In addition, the use of selection criteria is more common at magnet high schools.

Much of the research on magnet schools has been concerned with desegregating urban schools. Within magnet schools, the racial balance of students has been shown to differ from their schools' racial composition. For example, 71 percent of the students in PWS magnets are minority but only 61 percent of the students in the magnet program are minority (Steel & Levine 1994). In addition, magnet enrollment in white districts is predominantly minority, while minority district enrollment is predominantly white. Overall, most magnet schools are in predominantly minority urban school districts. Given this, researchers have debated the validity of magnet schools as true indications of desegregation. In addition, low-income, special education, and limited English proficient students are underrepresented in magnet schools. Desegregation is a central theme for research on magnet schools: whether they contribute to desegregation efforts, if they increase educational quality in the district, and the types of magnets that are more or less successful in attaining these goals.

EMPIRICAL RESEARCH ON MAGNET SCHOOLS

Besides the two large reports referenced above, most empirical research on magnet schools consists of district and school case studies. Partly, this is because the goals of desegregation for magnet schools are largely dependent on the type of magnet programs and minority trends of enrollment in a particular school or district. Many researchers find that tailoring magnet schools to needs of communities is more responsive to students' needs and makes a greater impact.

Much research on magnet schools involves the definition and measurement of desegregation. Desegregation can be measured by the simple racial composition of schools, which is often called a reduction of minority isolation. This is a prevalent measure for regional magnet schools. On the other hand, PWS magnets could "reduce isolation" at the school level but still have classrooms with very little interracial exposure (Estes et al. 1990).

Although most magnet schools' mission is desegregation, they are still voluntary. This creates a challenge for school districts. While court-ordered magnet schools have been found to increase interracial exposure more effectively, these are also more likely to resegregate once the court directive period has ended (Rossell 1990). Researchers have hypothesized why this might occur; magnet schools can only attract white students into minority areas if the district puts additional funds and a special curriculum into that school, whereas minority parents have been found to transfer their children to white schools categorically.

Concerning their quality, magnet schools have been found to offer a high quality of education, with higher levels of student achievement in certain areas (Gamoran 1996) and more teacher/student satisfaction with the learning environment (Estes et al. 1990). Magnet schools also improve the quality of education in their district by creating models of parent/school communication as well as raising the bar for non-magnet schools to compete for students. At the same time, researchers conclude that magnet schools must be considered as separate entities from other public schools (Gamoran 1996). Minority students attending magnet schools are a selective group, with well-informed parents and often passing an entrance exam. White students attending magnets often have parents who are dedicated to interracial exposure for their children. In addition, magnet schools are typically better funded than other public schools.

Future research of magnet schools needs to be conducted, particularly research concerning the impact of magnet schools on long-term desegregation efforts. Currently, there is a heavy reliance on magnet schools for efforts of desegregation. In addition, magnet schools are most widespread in urban districts, more often attracting white students into high-quality magnet schools in the minority district than vice versa. This serves a relatively small percentage of students within the district (Estes et al. 1990; West 1994). To determine the impact of interracial exposure on the problem of minority isolation and the race/ethnic achievement gap, research should focus on two aspects of magnet schools: for whole school magnets, comparing magnet schools to other schools in the same district, and for PWS magnets, comparing student performance of magnet students and nonmagnet students. Research examining equity of access for parents and students to other public school choice policies is relevant for the study of magnet schools as well (see Coleman et al. 1993 for an example).

Many scholars agree that magnet schools are high-quality public schools with a targeted goal of reducing or eliminating minority isolation. They keep white students and students from higher socioeconomic groups in the public school system when they might otherwise opt for a private school. Perhaps most importantly, magnet schools use the goal of desegregation to enhance students' education through a diverse student body. Critique of magnet schools rarely focuses on their quality. Instead, researchers are concerned about magnet schools' ability to function as a broad-based solution of school desegregation. Future research on magnet schools is needed in areas such as the local context of successful magnet schools, magnet schools' ubiquity in reaching the goal of desegregated public schools, and the extent to which student learning is improved.

SEE ALSO: *Brown* v. *Board of Education*; Diversity; Race and Schools; School Choice; School Segregation, Desegregation; Schools, Public; Stratification, Race/Ethnicity and

REFERENCES AND SUGGESTED READINGS

Blank, R. K., Dentler, R. A., Baltzell, D. C., & Chabotar, K. (1983) *Survey of Magnet Schools: Analyzing a Model for Quality Integrated Education. Final Report of a National Study*. ED 236 304. James H. Lowry & Associates, Washington, DC.

Coleman, J. S., Schiller, K. S., & Schneider, B. (1993) Parent Choice and Inequality. In: Schneider, B. & Coleman, J. S. (Eds.), *Parents, their Children, and Schools*. Westview Press, Boulder, CO, pp. 147–82.

Estes, N., Levine, D. U., & Waldrip, D. R. (Eds.) (1990) *Schools of Choice: Leadership for the 21st Century*. Morgan, Austin, TX.

Gamoran, A. (1996) Student Achievement in Public Magnet, Public Comprehensive, and Private City High Schools. *Educational Evaluation and Policy Analysis* 18: 1–18.

Meeks, L. F., Meeks, W. A., & Warren, C. A. (2000) Racial Desegregation: Magnet Schools, Vouchers, Privatization, and Home Schooling. *Education and Urban Society* 33(1): 88–101.

Rossell, C. H. (1990) *The Carrot or the Stick for School Desegregation Policy: Magnet Schools or Forced Busing*. Temple University Press, Philadelphia.

Steel, L. & Levine, R. H. (1994) *Educational Innovation in Multiracial Contexts: The Growth of Magnet Schools in American Education*. US Department of Education, Washington, DC.

West, K. (1994) A Desegregation Tool That Backfired: Magnet Schools and Classroom Segregation. *Yale Law Journal* 103(8): 2567–92.

schools, professional

Elizabeth McGhee Hassrick

Professional schools play an important role in socialization and stratification processes in modern societies. The credential process for professions, in which a person trains to become a legitimate practitioner, is currently dominated by universities. Universities established certification programs during the late 1800s, successfully outcompeting the guild-based apprenticeships and mentorships of earlier centuries (Stevens 1983). Before World War II, most professional schools were located in elite private universities, accessible only to the wealthy, but enrollment in professional schools dramatically increased post-World War II, shifting participation from an elite arena to one more accessible across social class. Sociological researchers have explored the social and psychological effects of participation in professional schools (Becker et al. 1961; Hughes et al. 1973; Fox 1979), and sorting processes have been identified that influence the stratification of people from different classes, races, and genders as they seek to gain entrance and successfully complete professional school programs (Spaeth 1968; Spangler et al. 1978; Stolzenberg 1994; Schleef 2000). Much of the research about professional schools has been conducted within specific professions, in the service of practitioners. Cross-disciplinary studies investigating the connections among professional schools, professions, and larger social processes have been neglected.

PROFESSIONALS-IN-TRAINING

Sociological evaluation of professional school programs began when enrollment dramatically increased during the late 1950s and early 1960s. Research debates over the role of professional students brought social and psychological considerations to the forefront. The Columbia group (Merton et al. 1957) argued that professional students were practitioners-in-training, participating in social processes and curricular content that prepared them for their future careers as professionals, able to "live up to the expectations of the professional role, long after they have left the sustaining value-environment provided by the school" (p. 138). Such things as vague descriptions of expectations and clinical opportunities to observe physicians dealing with the inconsistencies of pharmaceutical outcomes and the experimental aspects of diagnosing provided medical students with exposure to the limits and uncertainties of their chosen profession (Fox 1979). The Chicago group (Becker et al. 1961) claimed that professional students gained mastery at being students, not professionals. Becker et al. focused their studies on the interactions students had with each other when faced with the day-to-day problem of being successful students. The conduct of the "boys in white" was significantly shaped by situational constraints placed on students by institutions that emphasized their role as temporary and interchangeable subordinates. Both approaches were focused on socializing processes that occurred during professional school training.

PROFESSIONAL SCHOOLS AND SORTING PROCESSES

Educational processes greatly influence the positions people occupy in a stratified society. Determining what part professional schools play in the stratification process requires attention to the stages of participation (entry, progress through, and placement after completion) as well as to the differentiation found within as well as between professions and their related schools.

Enrollment

Modern stratification research has revealed that parents play a significant role in high school and college enrollment, but what about graduate schools? Studies on the effect that parents have on graduate school enrollment have produced mixed findings, once types of graduate schools were disaggregated. Parents were found to have no effect on student enrollment into MBA programs (Stolzenberg 1994) and little effect on master's programs. However, a strong parent effect was found for first-professional and doctoral programs. The effect was indirect, related to student undergraduate institutions, academic performance, educational expectations, and career values. The academic achievement of students was determined as having a strong independent effect on enrollment in all kinds of professional studies. Students sometimes choose to enroll in a professional school, not to become a particular kind of professional but to maintain their lifestyle and social status. Schleef's (2000) study about law and business school choice found that students expressed ambiguity about a specific preference between law or business, and were most interested in being intellectually stimulated and maintaining their lifestyles and social status.

Achievement

Identifying the processes that influence achievement during professional school attendance has been a highly segregated project, implemented by each separate profession in the service of improving its own professional schools. Academic progress through law school has been shown to be affected by the concept of tokenism. When women were a small minority of the student body, factors such as role entrapment and social isolation had a negative effect on women's achievement (Spangler et al. 1978). More recent studies reveal a lessened effect on women enrolled in law schools after 1991, but a sustained negative effect on ethnic minorities (Clydesdale 2004) that diminishes achievements and increases academic differences between majority and minority groups. While research about law schools centers around issues of equity, business school critics struggle over the divide between research and practice. Recent business school critics complain of excessive "pure" research at the expense of messy multidisciplinary practice (Zell 2005). More research about achievement across different professions is needed.

Placement

Placement after completion of professional school has been associated with prestige. Graduates from elite graduate programs win jobs with higher professional prestige. Each kind of professional work commands different levels of intraprofessional prestige. For example, the surgeon commands more professional respect than the family doctor, or the tax lawyer as compared with the labor lawyer. Abbott (1981) attributes the intraprofessional status hierarchy to the amount of "pure" professional work that each role demands, meaning, for example, that a surgeon is able to exclude more non-medical tasks than the family doctor. In contrast, Heinz and Laumann (1982) assert that the status of different kinds of professional work is tied to the client base that pays for the work to be done. Corporate lawyers who negotiate complex legal contracts have high levels of intraprofessional prestige because their clients are wealthy. In both formulations, generalists command less prestige within professions as compared with specialists. Professional schools reflect task and prestige hierarchies differently across professions. For example, in medical school, students compete for the chance to receive extended specialized training, whereas in law school, students from elite programs win placement in firms that practice specialized work that is considered more prestigious (Heinz & Laumann 1982). Graduates from prestigious law schools are more likely to be employed by elite firms with corporate clients, whereas "local" school graduates are more likely to have solo practices or be employed by small firms that serve individuals.

Differentiation

The differentiation found between professions impacts the status, quality, and quantity of professional schools. The number and types of colleges and their related professional training programs have diversified post-World War II, and occupational categories have aligned themselves accordingly. Hughes et al. (1973) identified a task hierarchy where mundane and easily routinized tasks were relegated to various subprofessions, for example, lab technicians, dental assistants, and paralegals. These trades are most often learned in vocational and two-year community schools, whereas related professionals, such as dentists and lawyers, are trained in professional schools situated in four-year universities. The resources necessary to establish and sustain professional schools at four-year universities are related to the status and power of particular professions. Competition between occupations vying for secure professional standing has been understood both as a systemic process (Abbott 1988), where historically situated, interdependent professions combine, expand, change, and die, and as a market-driven process (Larson 1977), where professions seek to monopolize markets to retain power. Sociologists have also sought to identify the essential features of professions, citing specialized knowledge, shared standards of practice, and strong service ethics (Freidson 1994) as characteristics of well-established professions. Professions most aligned with the "ideal type" have the greatest amount of public support. Research about how struggles between professions impact professional schools has been neglected.

In conclusion, professional schools remain the final frontier in educational research across school types. Most often, professional schools are grouped as a subcategory in higher education, but the close connection they share with the professions and the important role that they play in socialization and stratification processes in modern societies merit closer examination and theory development across professions. Research conducted within each profession regarding professional school performance does not provide the kind of analysis that will reveal how professional schools impact social processes.

SEE ALSO: Colleges and Universities; Education, Adult; Educational Attainment; Expectations and Aspirations; Medical School Socialization; Schooling and Economic Success

REFERENCES AND SUGGESTED READINGS

Abbott, A. (1981) Status and Status Strain in the Professions. *American Journal of Sociology* 86: 819–35.

Abbott, A. (1988) *The System of Professions*. University of Chicago Press, Chicago.

Becker, H., Geer, B., Hughes, E., & Strauss, A. L. (1961) *Boys in White*. University of Chicago Press, Chicago.

Clydesdale, T. (2004) A Forked River Runs Through Law Schools: Toward Understanding Race, Gender, Age, and Related Gaps in Law School Performance and Bar Passage. *Journal of the American Bar Association* 29(4): 711–69.

Fox, R. (1979) *Essays in Medical Sociology*. Wiley, New York.

Freidson, E. (1994) *Professionalism Reborn: Theory, Prophesy, and Policy*. University of Chicago Press and Polity Press, Chicago and Cambridge.

Granfield, R. & Koehing, T. (1992) Learning Collective Eminence: Harvard Law School and the Social Production of Elite Lawyers. *Sociological Quarterly* 33: 503–20.

Heinz, J. P. & Laumann, E. O. (1982) *Chicago Lawyers: The Social Structure of the Bar*. Russell Sage Foundation and American Bar Foundation, New York.

Hughes, E., Gurin, A., Thorne, B., Williams, D., & De Baggis, A. M. (1973) *Education for the Professions of Medicine, Law, Theology, and Social Welfare*. Carnegie Foundation, New York.

Kerckhoff, A. C. (1995) Institutional Arrangements and Stratification Processes in Industrial Societies. *Annual Review of Sociology* 21: 323–47.

Larson, M. S. (1977) *The Rise of Professionalism: A Sociological Analysis*. University of California Press, Berkeley.

McGill, C. (2002) Producing Lawyers: The Effects of Institutional Hierarchies on the Social Structure of Law Schools. PhD. Duke University. AAT 3066066.

Merton, R. K. (1982) *Social Research and the Practicing Professions*. Abt Books, Cambridge, MA.

Merton, R. K., Reader, G. G., & Kendall, P. L. (Eds.) (1957) *The Student-Physician: Introductory Studies in the Sociology of Medical Education*. Harvard University Press, Cambridge, MA.

Schleef, D. (2000) "That's a Good Question!" Exploring Motivations for Law and Business School Choice. *Sociology of Education* 73: 155–74.

Spaeth, J. L. (1968) The Allocation of College Graduates to Graduate and Professional Schools. *Sociology of Education* 41: 342–9.

Spangler, E., Gordon, M. A., & Pipkin, R. M. (1978) Token Women: An Empirical Test of Kanter's Hypothesis. *American Journal of Sociology* 84: 160–70.

Stevens, R. (1983) *Law School: Legal Education in America from the 1850s to the 1980s*. University of North Carolina Press, Chapel Hill.

Stolzenberg, R. (1994) Educational Continuation by College Graduates. *American Journal of Sociology* 99: 1042–77.

Zell, D. (2005) Pressure for Relevancy at Top-Tiered Business Schools. *Journal of Management Inquiry* 14(3): 271–4.

schools, public

Ann Owens

For most nations, a free school system exists to provide all citizens with the basic skills needed to function successfully in society. Public schools teach basic literacy and numeracy skills and also socialize students into the incentive structure and power hierarchy of industry (Tyack 1974). From a functionalist perspective, many industrializing nations depended on workers with a basic education, requiring a universal system that could educate the workforce.

Industrialization also required more specialized workers, and highly organized public schools were necessary for advanced curricula and training. In addition to the pragmatic need for public education in maintaining an ordered society of viable workers, some nations' ideological goals also pervaded the creation and evolution of the education system. Public education is considered a tool for social mobility, a way for all children to obtain a common foundation for advancement, improvement, and success in society despite the background of their parents (Coleman & Hoffer 1987). Public schools teach a common curriculum and singular value system that allows students to effectively function in society and the economy. By equalizing the basic education all students receive, differences between community and family background characteristics can be minimized, alleviating stratification based on race/ethnicity or background resources. Education is also seen as fundamental investment in one's human capital (Becker 1993). Human capital is defined as investments one can make in oneself by pursuing training, knowledge accumulation, and health or medical care that will improve later well-being and outcomes. The public school system provides a strong and universally available foundation for training and education, which serves as human capital that improves later financial gains and success.

Public schools do not have the same origins in all nations, however. The functional argument that industrialized nations drove the creation of schooling because of their need for educated workers does not ring true in places like Scotland, Prussia, France, and Japan, where schooling systems were developed before industrialization in those countries (Ramirez & Meyer 1980). Perhaps because of international pressure from the global community, many developing countries have also offered free and compulsory education to students from all social backgrounds, such as systems in Hong Kong, Malaysia, and even such highly stratified places as South Africa (Buchmann & Hannum 2001). Other empirical evidence points to the importance of a strong nation-state in developing an education system; for example, the concurrent development of the education system and nation-state in France and Prussia, although this theory does not hold in places such as Britain and the US (Ramirez & Meyer 1980). While theories about the origins of a public education system have not converged around a singular conclusion, education is generally seen as a fundamental part of society, and its creation in various nations often coincides with the creation of other major institutions like government and the economy or in line with ideological goals of equality.

ORGANIZATIONAL CHANGES IN US PUBLIC SCHOOLS

Practical and ideological demands for free and compulsory schooling developed in the nineteenth century in many western countries. In the US, as in many European countries, societal changes of an economy increasingly dependent on industry and a booming population demanded an education system that could teach citizenship, social order, and standards for employment (Tyack 1974). Public education moved from being provided by families and churches to a highly organized, freely accessible system designed to prepare students for the modernizing world of work. In addition, a focus on social issues such as worker rights and equal wages also amplified the ideological debate on equal opportunity. Throughout the late nineteenth and twentieth centuries, movement toward free public education in the American school system was paralleled in other western countries, i.e., England (the Educational Act of 1870), France (the creation of the Republican schools), and Germany (whose eight-year program of free schooling precedes most other countries, as it was established in the eighteenth century). The organization of public schools in the United States was tightened compared with the earlier common schools. Public schools needed to be reorganized to serve an increasingly stratified society, create effective workers, and to ensure that social control was maintained. Despite efforts by common school organizers in the late 1800s, disparities in curriculum, resources, and teacher training existed in schools. Public schools were to give all citizens an equal base in education, and therefore standards needed to be more uniformly established.

The main changes in the US public school system in the first half of the twentieth century were with respect to control. Common schools were run by a superintendent and a large city school board. There was often conflict between the superintendent, viewed as a "professional" educator, and the members of the board, who were general citizens. The board and general public often saw the superintendent as a professional living off public tax money, and the superintendent saw a large, untrained, and meddling school board. In contrast to common school reformers, public school reformers argued for professionally controlled, more bureaucratically structured schools based on a science of education rather than community ideals. School boards were overhauled to be comprised of a small number of businessmen and professionals: schools were mimicking the organization of industry, where corporate board membership was entrusted only to the most highly qualified professionals. Schools now operated under a professionally trained superintendent, who, in conjunction with a professionally trained school board, advised and governed the school principal, who in turn oversaw teachers.

Aside from reorganization, progressive reformers were able to pass legislation mandating state standards for teachers with respect to training and hiring policy, thus increasing the professionalization of teaching as a profession, compulsory attendance, health and sanitation requirements, building standards, and regulated curricula like physical education (Tyack et al. 1987). Another change was the legal requirement of children to attend school, with parents eligible for punishment if their offspring were truant, emphasizing the organizational and socialization functions of public schools. Because of high costs for these reforms, new initiatives to supply federal aid to education were proposed in the late 1940s and early 1950s. Federal funding was often contested because of fears of centralization and disregard for local traditions or needs, and Catholic schools were outraged at the prospect of being cut out of funding, which would only serve public schools. To compromise, federal aid was offered to "federally impacted" communities whose schools were overcrowded because of an influx of federal workers; over the decades, increasing numbers of districts were able to qualify themselves as "federally impacted" to receive aid. However, the majority of funding still comes at the state and local level (Ravitch 1983).

CONTROVERSY AND REFORM IN US PUBLIC SCHOOLS

Several of the most controversial changes in public education have stemmed from the goals of social mobility and equal opportunity for all. The racial integration of schools is perhaps the most major and significant reform. In 1896, the *Plessy* v. *Ferguson* decision guaranteed "separate but equal" facilities for blacks and whites. However, equal education was rarely provided to blacks and whites in the first half of the twentieth century, when a dual school system existed wherein public funds, teacher training and pay, and facilities were far better for whites than blacks (Ravitch 1983). Along with the rising Civil Rights Movement and campaigns by the National Association for the Advancemet of Colored People (NAACP), the *Brown* v. *Board of Education* decision in 1954 resulted in the Supreme Court declaring that separate schooling on the basis of race was inherently unequal. This decision set the stage for the slow and often opposed process of school integration.

Despite the legal sanctions, school integration happened very slowly and was examined in the Equality of Educational Opportunity Report, which was commissioned by the Civil Rights Act of 1964, and led by James S. Coleman (1966). The Coleman Report concluded that few schools were actually significantly racially diverse, and that family background and social composition of the school were more important predictors of academic success than school resources. This controversial report resulted in the idea that racial integration was key to academic success, and integration programs were developed which often involved busing lower-resource or minority children to wealthier schools. This solution, however, led to further problems, with Coleman among others arguing that forced integration contributed to white flight, with white families leaving large urban districts that included lower-resource families to create all-white districts.

The equality of public schools has been examined again and again, on different bases. The establishment of Head Start preschool programs was influenced by research indicating that poor children were culturally or educationally "deficient" at the beginning of schooling.

Head Start was intended to be geared specifically toward the culture of impoverished children to give them not only academic preparation but also cultural skills to be competitive with middle-class children. Head Start was partially funded by the 1965 passage of the Title I program of the Elementary and Secondary Education Act, which was designed to "meet the special educational needs of educationally deprived children" (Ravitch 1983: 159).

The 2001 No Child Left Behind (NCLB) Act signified the movement in educational reform toward accountability and standards testing. This movement draws on the ideology of schooling as a tool for social mobility and the pragmatic goal of readying all children for viable employment. By pushing for more stringent evaluations and standards, reformers are attempting to ensure that the quality of instruction between schools becomes more uniform, arming children with equal foundations. Standards testing provides an opportunity to gather data about students and schools, opening performance in public schools to parents, educational reformers, and policymakers. By closely evaluating students and identifying substandard teachers, NCLB attempts to strongly couple federal guidelines to curriculum and teaching to results, with consequences for schools who fail to improve test scores (i.e., requiring supplemental free tutoring and eventual reconstitution of a school that continually does not meet standards). Reform efforts have been constant since the establishment of an organized school system, with mixed results. However, the intention of the US public school system remains unchanged today: to provide all citizens with access to a basic education necessary for employment and success in society, and to provide equal opportunity for future advancement to all.

GLOBAL PATTERNS IN PUBLIC SCHOOL SYSTEMS

Public schools (often called state (in England) or free schools abroad) in other countries are similar in that they are government funded and offer free education for some compulsory length of time; however, systems across the globe vary with respect to degree of centralization or decentralization of schooling and the existence of a national curriculum. France, for example, is considered to be highly centralized regarding curricula, but teaching methods are not strictly controlled (Alexander 2000). India is also fairly centralized, with policy changes and interventions occurring at the national level, although state and local governments influence some matters of expenditure and day-to-day functioning (Alexander 2000). In England, where the origins of the state school system occurred later than many other industrialized countries (not until the late nineteenth century), control of the public school system is in the hands of the central government, and schools and teachers have little autonomy (Alexander 2000). While national assessment standards, much like NCLB, are in place in England, the ideology of the English system does not reflect this centralization; since 2003, the focus has been on differences between children and serving individual needs, as outlined in the "Every Child Matters" green paper published by the Department for Education and Skills (2003). In contrast, Russia has moved toward a more decentralized system, focusing on an ideology of individualism and differentiation among students and developing a system (since the early 1990s) wherein the local government is responsible for financial, pedagogical, and professional development matters (Alexander 2000).

Most countries have established a national curriculum that is taught with little variation throughout districts. Language, mathematics, natural science, social science, the arts, and physical education are the subjects most often included in national curricula (Benavot et al. 1991). Regionally, there are some differences in the national curricula: for example, Latin American countries tend to spend less time on language instruction and more time on natural and social sciences, while countries in the Middle East or North Africa are more likely than other countries to include religious instruction in their national curricula (Benavot et al. 1991). Examining curricula globally, researchers have argued that stable patterns in curricula type can be seen across countries and over time, and that the rise and fall of certain curricula in different countries depend on the world political and historical climate at the time of their adoption, rather than economic, political, or social factors at the national level (Kamens et al. 1996), implying that public education systems are moving toward a convergence around curricular choices. Public school systems around the world have responded to different reform movements as the national ideology, centralization of government power, and economic system have demanded, but the goal of providing free basic education for all citizens has persisted.

SEE ALSO: *Brown* v. *Board of Education*; Coleman, James; Early Childhood; Education; Massive Resistance; School Segregation, Desegregation; Schools, Common; Schools, Religious

REFERENCES AND SUGGESTED READINGS

Alexander, R. (2000) *Culture and Pedagogy: International Comparisons in Primary Education*. Blackwell, Malden, MA.

Becker, G. S. (1993) *Human Capital: A Theoretical and Empirical Analysis with Special Reference to Education*, 3rd edn. University of Chicago Press, Chicago.

Benavot, A., Cha, Y., Kamens, D., Meyer, J., & Wong, S. (1991) Knowledge for the Masses: World Models and National Curricula, 1920–1986. *American Sociological Review* 56: 85–100.

Buchmann, C. & Hannum, E. (2001) Education and Stratification in Developing Countries: A Review of Theories and Research. *Annual Review of Sociology* 27: 77–102.

Coleman, J. S. et al. (1966) *Equality of Educational Opportunity*. Government Printing Office, Washington, DC.

Coleman, J. S. & Hoffer, T. (1987) *Public and Private High Schools: The Impact of Communities*. Basic Books, New York.

Kamens, D. H., Meyer, J. W., & Benavot, A. (1996) Worldwide Patterns in Academic Secondary Education Curricula. *Comparative Education Review* 40 (2): 116–238.

Ramirez, F. & Meyer, J. (1980) Comparative Education: The Social Construction of the Modern World System. *Annual Review of Sociology* 6: 369–99.

Ravitch, D. (1983) *The Troubled Crusade: American Education, 1945–1980*. Basic Books, New York.

Tyack, D. B. (1974) *The One Best System: A History of American Urban Education*. Harvard University Press, Cambridge, MA.

Tyack, D. B., James, T., & Benavot, A. (1987) *Law and the Shaping of Public Education, 1785–1954*. University of Wisconsin Press, Madison.

Weick, K. E. (1976) Educational Organizations as Loosely Coupled Systems. *Administrative Science Quarterly* 21: 1–19.

schools, religious

Jaap Dronkers

Religion and education have a long common history, dating back to prehistoric times. Religion and religious practices require structures for the preparation, initiation, and training of new members and of priests and teachers. For that reason, religious groups in premodern societies sooner or later took the responsibility of organizing the socialization of their new members and of their religious specialists. This does not mean that all education in premodern societies was organized by religious organizations. Non-religious authorities, including kings, lords, cities, and guilds, organized a part of the socialization of the new societal members (for instance, warrior schools, apprenticeships, and academies for the training of bureaucrats), but in most premodern societies the major part of education outside the family was organized by or on behalf of religious organizations. One can argue that most schools in premodern societies were religious schools. Education was organized and financed by religious organizations, the content of education was controlled by religious authorities, and, in most cases, teachers were incorporated into these religious organizations, e.g., as monks or members of rank. This was true not only for schools at a basic level, but also for higher levels of education.

The transition from premodern to modern societies in Europe and North America between the sixteenth and nineteenth centuries led in most societies to a struggle between the state and the established church over the organization, financing, and content of education. This struggle was inspired by growing skepticism regarding religious teaching during the Enlightenment, by the increasing need for knowledge and skills not related to the needs of the churches (growing technological sophistication, modern languages), and by the need of states, instead of a partly hostile church, to define the content of citizenship. It is important to note that this struggle between the state and the established churches took a different path in Anglo-Saxon countries than in continental European societies (Archer 1984). In those European societies that were influenced by the French Revolution (including the United States), a legal and often constitutional separation between church and state was introduced at some point. Depending on the conditions of this separation and on the political parties involved, public and religious schools were allowed and sometimes partly or fully funded by the state. Although de facto separation between church and state emerged during the nineteenth century in many Anglo-Saxon societies, with the exception of the United States, there was no constitutional separation between church and state in these societies. This made the distinction between public and private schools less clear. One consequence of the distinction between public and religious schools was the growing need of churches for the direct socialization of their new members, for which there had become less room in the public schools. Sunday schools, Qur'an schools, and the like emerged beginning in the nineteenth century in modern societies, but they were set up purely for religious socialization and no longer for the general education of their pupils. Although these institutions for religious socialization are often called schools, they should not be confused with religious schools, which are schools with mainly the same educational goals and programs as public schools, but which are organized and maintained by a private body that also has religious goals.

As a consequence of the struggle between the church and the state in many European societies, modern religious schools have different relations with the state. Within the educational systems of western industrial societies, schools can be roughly categorized on two dimensions. On the one hand, the issue is who makes decisions concerning the organization and curricula that schools provide; on the other hand, the source of funding for this education is key. In relation to the first issue, two types of religious schools have emerged in most western countries. As a result of the struggle between the state and the established church, states have taken on the responsibility of organizing education. Here lies the root of public education that is fully governed and financed by public agencies (Archer 1984). At the same time, religious schools have been established or maintained by the efforts of churches and other religious institutions. However, it is important to note that non-religious ideological and commercial organizations have also established private schools. Although schools of this type often still have to comply with government regulations to a certain extent, partly depending on the amount of financial support received from the government, the crucial decisions regarding the schools' affairs are made by private entities. Within this private sector, religious schools can again be classified as either government-dependent or government-independent by the extent to which they are subsidized by the state. Governmental subsidization of religious schools is secured by law in many countries, either in the constitution, as in The Netherlands and Germany, or in common law, as in France and Hungary. In many cases, this right results from claims of mostly religious groups to education based on the values and ideologies of the parents who are members of these groups and who are considered to be responsible for the way their children are raised. Alongside these religious government-dependent schools, there exist in a number of countries, including Italy and the United States, religious schools that do not receive any government support. These schools finance themselves by means of pupil fees, donations, private sponsoring, and the like. Again, the two dimensions – governance and financing – cannot be considered to be completely independent of each other. When the amount of governmental financial support of private schools becomes larger, these governments will also demand a higher degree of influence on the programs that the schools offer. However, even schools that are completely independent financially will generally not be entirely free to determine the contents of their programs and will have to comply with minimal requirements on quality and safety. Moreover, the social context will also place constraints on schools' freedom. For example, diplomas that meet generally accepted standards have become indispensable in modern societies.

Public and religious schools can be seen as the result of two different approaches to schooling. According to one point of view, schooling is an instrument of society as a whole (as represented by the central state) to prepare individuals for a life within society, independent of their social background, and in which religious convictions are considered to be a private matter. Public schools result from this point of view. The competing standpoint states that schools are an instrument not just of society but of parents and the social and cultural groups to which they belong. The aim of schooling according to this point of view is to offer young people an education that is in accordance with the religious way of life of their parents and their environment. Religious schools, more or less subsidized by the state, are the consequence of this approach (Coleman & Hoffer 1987; Godwin & Kemerer 2002).

Catholic schools are not the only examples of religious schools. Depending on the religious history and composition of a society, religious schools can also be Protestant, either related to a specific Protestant denomination (Lutheran, Evangelical, Baptist) or more general. The same holds for the de facto degree of orthodoxy of religious schools; it can be quite strong in some religious schools, while hardly existing in others. Religious schools are not only Christian. Depending on the history of a society, religious schools can also be Hindu, Islamic, Jewish, or other religions. "Parochial school" is therefore a misleading phrase, because it refers only to schools organized within the Catholic tradition. Despite the increasing irrelevance of church and religion in the everyday lives of most Europeans, religious schools have not dwindled. On the contrary, the religious school sector in societies with relatively religiously inactive populations is growing or is strongly overrepresented. This is true not only for societies that traditionally have had such schools, but also for those in which religious schools were abolished under communist regimes (Hungary, the new German Länder). One possible explanation is that the teachings of religious schools are generally more effective than those of public schools because religious schools, although they no longer strive for the religious socialization of students, still try to attain other non-cognitive goals, such as tolerance, social cooperation, and discipline, that are valued by unreligious parents. There also are other explanations for the rise of religious schools in the former communist societies, including distrust of the state as provider of collective goods like education, the lower effectiveness of public schools as a consequence of malfunctioning state bureaucracies, and a lower level of community building by parents and teachers around public schools than around religious schools.

Empirical evidence of the higher effectiveness of teaching in religious schools is increasing although not yet conclusive. Differences in school success and cognitive outcomes clearly exist between public and religious schools in modern societies on both sides of the Atlantic, but these differences are not very large and are not always found when comparing individual schools. However, these differences cannot be explained by the different social composition of the student populations or by other obvious social characteristics of pupils, parents, schools, or neighborhoods. Given the high level of state support for religious schools in European societies and the relatively low school fees, differences in school effectiveness of religious and non-religious public schools cannot be explained by large financial contributions from parents whose children attend religious schools. In various continental European countries the law forbids large financial contributions from parents as a condition for obtaining state grants. Spending levels are mostly equal across the public and the state-funded private school sectors because, in most cases, that is an essential element of the compromise between the state and the churches.

However, significant differences in non-cognitive achievements, often the main argument for the existence of state-funded religious schools, are hardly found in modern societies. There also exist a number of indications in multiple societies that children often attend religious schools for academic or social – not religious – reasons, whatever the policies of the schools. The two last points contradict the raison d'être of state-funded religious schools, because the right of parents to determine the moral and religious education of their children has always been more or less explicitly the basis of state recognition and funding of religious schools. The higher cognitive effectiveness of state-funded religious schools also contradicts the raison d'être of religious schools, which maintain throughout that they do not want to compete with state schools for better academic outcomes.

The best explanation of the higher cognitive effectiveness of religious schools involves the different school climates in public and religious schools. A school climate (or culture) specifies different patterns of behavior for teachers and students. These patterns, which form the basis of a school climate, indicate shared beliefs about what students should learn, the proper norms of instruction, and how students and teachers should relate to each other. They affect the effectiveness of teaching and learning within schools and may also affect teacher morale, which can also influence teaching effectiveness. The school climate argument shows some resemblance to Coleman and Hoffer's social capital explanation (Coleman et al. 1982; Coleman & Hoffer 1987). They distinguish between two types of communities as related to schools: functional communities and value communities. The members of functional communities constitute a structural system of social interaction; they encounter each other in different kinds of social situations and know each other personally. In contrast, value communities are communities in which members (parents and teachers) share values and expectations regarding education but which are not functional communities; outside the school, there is no structural interaction or social network between the members. According to Coleman and Hoffer, functional communities like religious schools can be beneficial to their members because of the social capital they offer. Because there is interaction between parents inside and outside the religious school, norms can be maintained that create a stable and positive school climate, improving the pupils' scholastic achievement.

SEE ALSO: Economy, Religion and; Educational Inequality; Religion; School Choice; School Climate; Social Capital and Education

REFERENCES AND SUGGESTED READINGS

Archer, M. S. (1984) *Social Origins of Educational Systems.* Sage, Beverly Hills.

Bryk, A. S., Lee, V. E., & Holland, P. B. (1993) *Catholic Schools and the Common Good.* Harvard University Press, Cambridge, MA.

Coleman, J. S. & Hoffer, T. B. (1987) *Public and Private High Schools: The Impact of Communities.* Basic Books, New York.

Coleman, J. S., Hoffer, T. B., & Kilgore, S. (1982) *High School Achievement: Public, Catholic, and Other Private Schools Compared.* Basic Books, New York.

Dronkers, J. (2004) Do Public and Religious Schools Really Differ? Assessing the European Evidence. In: Wolf, P. J. & Macedo, S. (Eds.), *Educating Citizens: International Perspectives on Civic Values and School Choice.* Brookings Institution Press, Washington, DC, pp. 287–312.

Godwin, R. K. & Kemerer, F. R. (2002) *School Choice Tradeoffs: Liberty, Equity, and Diversity.* University of Texas Press, Austin.

schools, single-sex

Cornelius Riordan

Single-sex schools refer to education at the elementary, secondary, or post-secondary level in which males or females attend school exclusively with members of their own sex. Alternatively, males and females may attend all classes separately even though they may be housed in the same facilities, a phenomenon referred to as a dual academy. A related though different phenomenon is single-sex classes, whereby schools that are otherwise coeducational provide separate classes for males and/or females in selected subjects.

Most people take coeducation for granted. Typically, their own schooling has been coeducational; often, they have little awareness of single-sex schools. Our political culture reinforces the taken-for-granted character of American coeducation. It implies that schools reflecting the variety of society exemplify what is best about democratic societies. Many people also take for granted that coeducation provides equality of educational opportunity for women. Like racial and ethnic minorities, women have long been excluded from the educational process. Thus, many people regard coeducation as a major milestone in the pursuit of gender equality. Single-sex education, by contrast, appears regressive.

Coeducation, however, began not because of any firm belief in its sound educational effect, but rather because of financial constraints (Riordan 1990). Historically, mixed sex schools were economically more efficient. In America, boys and girls have usually attended the same public schools. This practice originated with the "common" school. Of course, at one time throughout all society, only boys received an education. At other times, the only education for either boys or girls was single-sex schooling, either public or private. Even today, single-sex schooling remains the dominant form of school organization in many countries.

In most western, democratic countries, however, once mass and state-supported public education had been established, it was clearly the exception for boys and girls to attend separate schools. By the end of the nineteenth century, coeducation was all but universal in American elementary and secondary public schools (Tyack & Hansot, 1990; Riordan 1990). Recently, however, there has been a resurgence of interest in single-sex schools in western modern societies across the globe, both in the public and private sector (Riordan 2002).

EMPIRICAL RESEARCH ON SINGLE-SEX SCHOOLS

There are very few formal reviews of the relative effects of single-sex and coeducational schools or classrooms. Of course, all researchers have conducted their own literature reviews, but these are often incomplete. Moreover, research on single-sex classrooms is not systematic or rigorous since there are many varied forms of this type of structure.

There are two exhaustive reviews of research on single-sex schools. The first of these was conducted by Moore et al. (1992) for a US Department of Education report. This review concluded that the empirical evidence clearly supported the proposition that single-sex schools may produce positive outcomes, especially for young women. In the most recent and thorough review employing What Works Clearinghouse standards, Mael et al. (2005) concluded that the preponderance of studies supports the view that single-sex schooling has positive benefits for both sexes in terms of both academic short-term achievement and socioemotional development.

The academic and developmental consequences of attending single-sex versus coeducational schools are typically insignificant for middle-class or otherwise advantaged students (Riordan 1990). By contrast, the consequences appear to be significantly favorable for students who are historically or traditionally disadvantaged – minorities and/or low and working-class and/or at-risk students (Riordan 1990, 1994a; Salomone 2003). The major factor which conditions the strength of single-sex effects is social class, and since class and race are inextricably linked, the effects are also conditioned by race, and sometimes by gender.

Specifically, disadvantaged students in single-sex schools, compared to their counterparts in coeducational schools, have been shown to have higher achievement outcomes on standardized tests of mathematics, reading, science, and civics. They show higher levels of leadership behavior in school, do more homework, take a stronger course load, and have higher educational expectations. They also manifest higher levels of environmental control, more favorable attitudes towards school, and less sex role stereotyping. They acknowledge that their schools have higher levels of discipline and order and, not surprisingly, they have a less satisfactory social life than students in coeducational schools. In the long term, women who attended a girls' school continue to have higher test scores than women who attended coeducational schools (for an opposing conclusion, see Marsh 1989, 1991).

It is important to note, however, that single-sex school effects are fairly robust even when social class or race is not partitioned. In their Catholic school study, Lee and Bryk (1986, 1989) analyzed the data by statistically controlling for social class, race, and other background characteristics and applied the results to students generally (assuming that there were no differences in social class, race, or background variables). They found 65 of 74 separate dependent variable effects to be in favor of single-sex schools. Thirty of 74 effects obtained an effect size (ES) of .18 or higher favoring single-sex schools, equally distributed among boys and girls and the mean effect size was .13 favoring single-sex schools.

The results for students attending women's colleges parallel and substantiate the secondary school results. They manifest higher levels of environmental control, greater satisfaction with school (though not social life), and they achieve higher occupational success despite the fact that there is no difference in educational achievement when compared to women who attended a coeducational college (Miller-Bernal 2000; Riordan 1990, 1994b). This latter finding strongly suggests that their schooling has been of a higher quality since ultimately they have the same level of educational achievement as women attending coeducational schools. Amazingly, women who attend a women's college for even a single year and then transfer still obtain a significant gain in occupational success (Riordan 1994b).

These positive effects, however, are not universal. In a cross-national study of four countries (Belgium, New Zealand, Thailand, and Japan), Baker et al. (1995) have shown that single-sex schools do not have uniform and consistent effects. The effects appear to be limited to those national educational systems in which single-sex schools are relatively rare. They argued that the rarity of a school type may enhance single-sex effects under certain conditions. When single-sex schools are rare in a country, the pro-academic choice-making by parents and students will result in a more selective student body who will bring with them a heightened degree of academic demands. In turn, rare school types are better able to *supply* the quality of schooling *demanded* by these more selective students. Being less normative, these schools are likely to possess greater autonomy.

Despite this array of positive effects, it is important to note that the most common finding in the systematic review by Mael and his colleagues (2005) was null or mixed results. The mixed results reflect the fact that often the effects are for females but not for males, or for at-risk students but not for middle-class students. Furthermore, these significant effects for at-risk students are small in comparison with the much larger effects of socioeconomic status and type of curriculum in a given school. This basic social science finding that school effects are small has been shown to be true since first identified in the famous Coleman Report, and data persistently confirm this educational fact over the past four decades (for a full review of studies, see Riordan 2004).

It is important also to emphasize that white middle-class (or affluent) boys and girls do not suffer any loss by attending a single-sex school (they are not better off in coeducational schools). Moreover, there does exist the possibility that they do acquire small gains that are undetectable. This is consistent with the large number of null effects noted above. There are, in fact, very few studies reporting more favorable results of any sort for students attending coeducational schools (see Mael et al. 2005).

As with most studies of school effects, the problem of "selection bias" always lurks in the shadows. All researchers acknowledge that students attending each type of school vary in a number of ways, including socioeconomic status, previous academic achievement, family structure, etc. And everyone agrees that it is critical to statistically control (and thereby equate) these preexisting characteristics in order to sort out the effects of the school from the effect of the home. Some researchers believe that the appropriate strategy is to control or equate exhaustively. Others argue that this strategy might control on some of the very characteristics that drive the entire success of single-sex schools; namely, making a pro-academic choice (see below).

WHY ARE SINGLE-SEX SCHOOLS MORE EFFECTIVE THAN COEDUCATIONAL SCHOOLS?

There are at least a dozen theoretical rationales that provide support for the contention that single-sex schools are more effective academically and developmentally than mixed-sex schools, especially for minorities and at-risk students. Single-sex schools provide more successful same-sex teacher and student role models, more leadership opportunities, greater order and discipline, fewer social distractions to academic matters, and the choice of a single-sex school is a pro-academic choice. Students also gain advantages because of significant reductions in gender bias in both teaching and peer interaction, and via access to the entire curriculum. Single-sex schools allow greater sensitivity to gender differences in learning, maturation, and school readiness. They provide safety from sexual harassment and sexual predatory behavior and have been shown to aid in spiritual and moral development.

IMPLICATIONS

Single-sex schools are places where students go to learn; not to play, not to hassle teachers and other students, and not primarily to meet their friends and have fun. Aside from affluent middle-class communities, private and alternative schools, coeducational schools are not all about academics. This has been noted often with alarm by respected and distinguished investigators across a variety of disciplines using a variety of methodologies (Goodlad 1984; Steinberg et al. 1996).

Given their rarity in western culture, single-sex schools are likely to require pro-academic choice that is made by parents and students. This choice sets into motion a set of relationships among teachers, parents, and students that emphasize academic and de-emphasize youth culture values, which as suggested above dominate coeducational schools. Thus, single-sex schools provide a set of structural norms conducive to academic learning. This pro-academic single-sex school environment operates in concert and harmony with the choice-making process that is made by students who attend single-sex schools. In this regard, it is entirely different from a set of structures or programs that are put into place by educators. In single-sex schools, the academic environment is normative in a true sociological sense. It is a set of rules established by the subjective reality (definitions) of participants which takes on an objective reality as a set of social structural norms. This idea is similar to that proposed by Bryk et al. (1993) of a "voluntary community" for public school policy, which would resemble Catholic schools in every respect except for religion.

These academic definitions of school contradict the non-academic definitions that students will otherwise bring to school and which come to constitute a youth culture. In effect, single-sex schools mitigate the single largest obstacle which stands in the way of effective and equitable schooling, and it does this by using a fundamental sociological principle of how real social structures are created. Structures that are imposed and which contradict deeply cherished beliefs (regardless of how wrong headed and problematic they may be) will be rejected out of hand by any group with substantial power in numbers such as students in schools.

The challenge of effective and equitable schooling in the next century is to overcome the resistance and the recalcitrance of youth cultures in and out of the school. This is not a new problem and undoubtedly predates the modern school. But the intensity and the complexity of the problem is new, and it is the most important obstacle in schools today. Single-sex schools provide an avenue for students to make a pro-academic choice, thereby affirming their intrinsic agreement to work in the kind of environment that we identify as an effective and equitable school. Single-sex schools should not be expected to correct the gender equity problems that exist in society and in coeducational schools. Moreover, students do not automatically do better in single-sex schools. The important thing is the selection of a type of school that best suits each individual student.

SEE ALSO: Gender, Education and; School Choice; School Climate; School Discipline; Schools, Religious

REFERENCES AND SUGGESTED READINGS

Baker, D. P., Riordan, C., & Schaub, M. (1995) The Effects of Sex-Grouped Schooling on Achievement: The Role of National Context. *Comparative Education Review* 39: 468–81.

Bryk, A. S., Lee, V. E., & Holland. P. B. (1993) *Catholic Schools and the Common Good.* Harvard University Press, Cambridge, MA.

Goodlad, J. (1984) *A Place Called School.* McGraw Hill, New York.

Lee, V. E. & Bryk, A. S. (1986) Effects of Single-Sex Secondary Schools on Students' Achievement and Attitudes. *Journal of Educational Psychology* 78: 381–95.
Lee, V. E. & Bryk, A. S. (1989) Effects of Single-Sex Schools: Response to Marsh. *Journal of Educational Psychology* 81(4): 647–50.
Mael, F., Alonso, A., Gibson, D., Rogers, K., & Smith, M. (2005) Single-Sex Versus Coeducational Schooling: A Systematic Review. Prepared under contract to RMC Research Corporation for the United States Department of Education.
Marsh, H. W. (1989) Effects of Attending Single-Sex and Coeducational High Schools on Achievement, Attitudes, Behavior, and Sex Differences. *Journal of Educational Psychology* 81(1): 70–85.
Marsh, H. W. (1991) Public, Catholic Single-Sex, and Catholic Coeducational High Schools: Effects on Achievement, Affect, and Behaviors. *American Journal of Education* 11: 320–56.
Miller-Bernal, L. (2000) *Separate by Degree: Women Students' Experiences in Single and Coeducational Colleges.* Peter Lang, New York.
Moore, M., Piper, V., & Schaefer, E. (Mathematica Policy, Research, Inc) (1992) Single-Sex Schooling and Educational Effectiveness: A Research Overview. In *Single-Sex Schooling: Perspectives from Practice and Research, A Special Report from the Office of Educational Research and Improvement.* US Department of Education, Washington, DC.
Riordan, C. (1990) *Girls and Boys in School: Together or Separate?* Teachers College Press, New York.
Riordan, C. (1994a) Single Gender Schools: Outcomes for African and Hispanic Americans. *Research in Sociology of Education and Socialization* 10: 177–205.
Riordan, C. (1994b) The Value of Attending a Women's College. *Journal of Higher Education* 65(4): 486–510.
Riordan, C. (2002) What Do We Know About the Effects of Single-Sex Schools in the Private Sector? Implications for Public Schools. In: Datnow, A. & Hubbard, L. (Eds.), *Gender and Policy in Practice.* Routledge-Falmer, New York.
Riordan, C. (2004) *Equality and Achievement: An Introduction to the Sociology of Education.* Pearson Prentice-Hall, New York.
Salomone, R. (2003) *Same, Different, Equal: Rethinking Single-Sex Schooling.* Yale University Press, New Haven.
Steinberg, L. B., Brown, B., & Dornbusch, S. M. (1996) *Beyond the Classroom.* Simon & Schuster, New York.
Tyack, D. & Hansot, S. L. (1990) *Learning Together: A History of Coeducation in American Schools.* Yale University Press, New Haven.

Schumpeter, Joseph A. (1883–1950)

Yuichi Shionoya

Joseph Alois Schumpeter is generally acknowledged as one of the first-rank economists of the twentieth century, along with John Maynard Keynes. Schumpeter was born in Tešt', a small Moravian town in the Austro-Hungarian Empire. (The town, once called by the Germans Triesch, today belongs to the Czech Republic.) His father, a textile manufacturer, died when Schumpeter was 4 years old. Blessed with opportunities owing to his mother's remarriage to a high-ranking army officer, Schumpeter was able to enter the high society of the empire and was educated at the Theresianum in Vienna and at the University of Vienna.

Although Schumpeter's principal teachers were Eugen von Böhm-Bawerk and Friedrich von Wieser, the major figures of the Austrian School of Economics, he was not accepted among the Austrian School because he was critical of its essentialism and psychologism. In his early academic years, he taught at a number of provincial universities (Czernowitz, Graz, and Bonn), and for a short period after World War I he held the posts of finance minister under the Austrian socialist government and of president of a private bank in Vienna. In 1932 Schumpeter moved to Harvard University, and stayed there until his death in 1950.

His outstanding distinction was his broad erudition, his wide-ranging and large-scale work, combining economic theory with history and sociology, and his grand vision of synthesizing conflicting schools of thought. His intellectual background primarily consisted of neoclassical economics (represented by Léon Walras), Karl Marx, and the German historical economics (represented by Gustav von Schmoller). His central concern was the formulation of the evolution of the capitalist economic system. When he explained the nature of his theory of economic development, he referred to Walras and Marx, to whom he had been indebted. According to him, Walras provided "a pure logic of the interdependence between economic quantities," and Marx "a vision of economic evolution as a distinct process generated by the economic system itself." Schmoller taught him the method of approach to historical process in which all aspects of social life will change interdependently.

The wide-ranging work of Schumpeter can be interpreted as consisting of a system of substantive theory, i.e., (1) economic statics, (2) economic dynamics, and (3) economic sociology, and a system of metatheory, i.e., (4) the philosophy of science, (5) the history of science, and (6) the sociology of science, and is called a three-layered, two-structure approach to mind and society (Shionoya 1997). Substantive theory is addressed to society including economy, while metatheory is addressed to mind, knowledge, and theory including economics. The two systems are parallel in viewing the economy on the one hand and theory on the other from the viewpoint of, first, static structure, second, dynamic development, and third, their activities in a social context. They are linked together by the sociological dimension where economy and knowledge or mind and society are interrelated. The ambitious aim Schumpeter cherished throughout his academic life was a "comprehensive sociology," an approach to social phenomena as a whole, which is supposed to be a synthesis of interaction between every single area and all others in a society. Its core idea is the *Soziologisierung* (sociologizing) of all social sciences. What he actually accomplished was the interaction of two sociologies, economic sociology and the sociology of science. Economic sociology is an analysis of the economy institutionally embedded in a society, and the sociology of economic knowledge concerns economic views (or the *Zeitgeist*) as social phenomena. Schumpeter's two-structure approach was intended to replace Marx's social theory based on the economic interpretation of history concerning the relationship between the substructure and the superstructure of a society.

Schumpeter defined economic sociology as "a sort of generalized or typified or stylized economic history." Economic sociology is the concept of an institution that can generalize, typify, or stylize the complexities of economic history. In his view, the concept of institution is intended to achieve the synthesis of theory and history in that, while it is a means of generalizing historical events, it is limited due to its historical relativity and specificity. This is a compromise between the generality meant by theory and the individuality meant by history. He identified economic sociology as the fourth basic technique of economic analysis besides theory, statistics, and history.

His first book (Schumpeter 1908) covered the branches of economic statistics and the philosophy of science. While the book was a recapitulation of neoclassical economics on the line of the general equilibrium theory of Walras, it was essentially a methodological work that aimed to make a contribution to the solution of the *Methodenstreit* (debate on method) between theory and history in economics, or between Carl Menger and Gustav von Schmoller. Schumpeter ingeniously adapted the philosophy of science of Ernst Mach to economics and developed the methodology of instrumentalism.

Among his various accomplishments, his theory of economic development (Schumpeter 1926 [1912]) is best known. He defined economic development by reference to innovation (the cause of development), entrepreneurs (the carriers of development), and bank credit (the means of development). His concept of entrepreneur was a special case of the leader as the carrier of innovation in a wider area of social life. He also established an enduring reputation in his work on the history of economics (Schumpeter 1954). For him, the development of economy and society, on the one hand, and the development of thought and science, on the other, are two aspects of the same evolutionary process. Thus, economic dynamics and the history of science are the essential coordinates in the two-structure approach to mind and society.

The general idea of Schumpeter's economic sociology was first described in chapter 7 of the first edition of the development book. Although this chapter was eliminated in the second and subsequent editions, he kept the idea. Specifically, he developed a theory of social classes (Schumpeter 1927) that would serve as the crucial link between the concept of leadership in various areas of social life on the one hand, and the overall concept of civilization or the *Zeitgeist* on the other. In other words, social classes mediate the relationship between the economic and the non-economic areas, between the mind and society, or between economic sociology and the sociology of science. This idea, combined with the sociological investigation of the collapse of the tax state (Schumpeter 1918), was finally developed to *Capitalism, Socialism, and Democracy* (1942), in which he presented his famous thesis on the demise· of capitalism as the result of its success. For Schumpeter, this does not mean pessimism from the perspective of a society as a whole because a locus of innovation and social leadership would shift from economic pursuits to other areas.

The relevance of Schumpeter's idea of economic sociology is its impact on the growth of institutional economics and evolutionary economics after World War II with a focus on innovation in technology, industry, and institution.

SEE ALSO: Capitalism; Economic Development; Leadership; Technological Innovation

REFERENCES AND SUGGESTED READINGS

Schumpeter, J. A. (1908) *Das Wesen und der Hauptinhalt der theoretischen Nationalökonomie* (*The Nature and Substance of Theoretical Economics*). Duncker & Humblot, Leipzig.

Schumpeter, J. A. (1918) *Die Krise des Steuerstaates.* Leuschner & Lubensky, Graz and Leipzig. ("The Crisis of the Tax State." Trans. W. F. Stolper & R. A. Musgrave. *International Economic Papers*, No. 4, 1954.)

Schumpeter, J. A. (1926 [1912]) *Theorie der wirtschaftlichen Entwicklung*, 2nd edn. Duncker & Humblot, Leipzig. (*The Theory of Economic Development.* Trans. R. Opie. Harvard University Press, Cambridge, MA, 1934.)

Schumpeter, J. A. (1927) "Die sozialen Klassen in ethnish homogenen Milieu." *Archiv für Sozialwissenschaft und Sozialpolitik* 5: 1–67. (*Imperialism and Social Classes.* Trans. H. Norden. Augustus M. Kelly, New York, 1951.)

Schumpeter, J. A. (1950 [1942]) *Capitalism, Socialism, and Democracy*, 3rd edn. Harper & Brothers, New York.

Schumpeter, J. A. (1954) *History of Economic Analysis.* Oxford University Press, New York.

Shionoya, Y. (1997) *Schumpeter and the Idea of Social Science: A Metatheoretical Study.* Cambridge University Press, Cambridge.

Swedberg, R. (1991) *Schumpeter: A Biography.* Princeton University Press, Princeton.

Schütz, Alfred (1899–1959)

John R. Hall

Alfred Schütz was best known for his work on the sociological approach known as *phenomenology.* His first book provided a critique of Max Weber's interpretive sociology of meaningful action. He subsequently wrote a series of phenomenologically inspired essays as well as a second book, *Structures of the Lifeworld*, with Thomas Luckmann. Over the years of his life and beyond, Schütz influenced diverse sociologists. Social phenomenology remains an important stream of sociology and Schütz's insights and the analysis that he advanced have percolated through wider currents. The discipline as a whole has become more "phenomenological" as a result, most notably through the social constructionist approach and emphases on the concepts of lived action and embodiment.

Born in Vienna as the only child of well-to-do Austrian Jewish parents, Schütz completed his gymnasium education there in 1917, and immediately served for a year and a half in the Austro-Hungarian Imperial Army on the Italian front. He returned to Vienna in 1918, where he pursued studies in law, the social sciences, and economics at the University of Vienna. He received a doctorate in law in 1921, and participated, both as a student and after, in intellectual circles that included economist Ludwig von Mises and Frederick von Hayek. He married Ilse Heim in 1926. In 1927 Schütz was appointed executive officer for Reitler, the Vienna-based international banking firm. In the years to come, he would continue to support his family and intellectual pursuits with one or another high-level "day job" in banking.

Schütz's initial intellectual interests in Vienna included economic theories of marginal utility, musicology (he played piano), language, and jokes. His core analytic pursuits emerged from his effort to criticize and ground the interpretive sociology of Weber, whom Schütz had heard lecture in Vienna in 1918. In the mid-1920s this ambition led him to Henri Bergson's writings. By the latter 1920s Schütz concluded that Bergson's *Time and Free Will* would not prove an adequate point of departure for the philosophical theorization of social meaning, and he turned to the work of Edmund Husserl, whose analysis of the temporal flow of events as experienced in the mind itself became the basis of Schütz's critique of Weber. After this analysis was published in 1932 (later translated into English as *The Phenomenology of the Social World*), Schütz developed a close personal intellectual relationship with Husserl, visiting him occasionally in Freiburg up until Husserl's death in 1938.

In the shadow of Hitler's rise in Germany, other Jewish intellectuals emigrated from Austria beginning in the 1930s. Schütz himself was in Paris on business when the Nazi annexation of Austria took place on March 13, 1938. He worked to arrange the migration of his wife and children, and helped other Austrian intellectuals escape. On July 13, 1939, with war widely anticipated in France, Schütz and his family emigrated to New York. In the United States he aided other immigrants and worked with the US Bureau of Economic Warfare by providing economic analyses of Germany and Austria. He continued working with the Reitler firm in New York but, like a number of other European expatriates, began teaching on the Graduate Faculty of the New School for Social Research, where he became a full-time professor in 1956. His health began to decline within only a few years, and he died on May 29, 1959 with his second major book still only in outline and draft form. Three volumes of his *Collected Papers* on philosophical, epistemological, and sociological topics were published posthumously, as was *Structures of the Lifeworld* (1973), completed by Thomas Luckmann on the basis of Schütz's schema.

In the political upheavals of his times, Schütz played his role as a citizen, even a world citizen. He was resolutely apolitical in his own work, however, and his phenomenological sociology contains no significant consideration of power and authority. Yet social phenomenology clearly has utility for political analysis, as fruitful extensions of Schütz's analysis of the "well-informed citizen" have demonstrated. In the long term, Schütz's greatest legacy may be his critical analyses of modernity and its mediations of consciousness.

Schütz's central contributions to sociology are based on his development of a phenomenology of the social world. He came to this project through his engagement with Max Weber's methodology of *Verstehen*: analytically rigorous interpretive understanding of meaningful action. Schütz agreed with Weber that the human sciences both could and should employ *verstehende* analysis, since meaning is an intrinsic basis of action, and action is a core element constitutive of social phenomena. Weber used ideal types to describe meanings (e.g., innerworldly asceticism), social actions (e.g., rational action), and culturally inscribed patterns of social interaction (e.g., patrimonialism). Thus he could theoretically link action with broader social patterns and history – something that eluded numerous other theorists who either ignored meaning and action altogether, or analytically distinguished structure from action in ways that make meaning inaccessible.

Schütz praised Weber's achievements, but criticized his discussion of subjective meaning. For Schütz, Weber treated the problem of meaning from an *observer's* point of view without considering how meaning is constituted *subjectively*. Such a project would require an analysis of unfolding mental events of a social actor as a person – an Ego-consciousness. Initially, Schütz sought such an account in Henri Bergson's idea of duration as the flow of conscious experience. But Edmund Husserl had a more richly developed account of consciousness and temporality. His "transcendental phenomenological reduction" sets aside ("brackets") the *contents* of cognition (e.g., an idea, visual image, or words) to examine the *acts* of consciousness by which contents are mediated in the flow of inner time. Drawing on transcendental phenomenology, Schütz characterized subjective meaning by connecting it to the flow of mental experience in (1) the vivid present, (2) its sedimentation in memory (and recollection), and (3) its anticipation of the future. Meaning thereby becomes located in specific acts of consciousness – pleasure, pain, nostalgia, remorse, anticipatory excitement or anxiety, and so forth. Out of an array of such possibilities, Schütz emphasized meaning associated with the "in-order-to motive" that imaginatively anticipates the future completion of a project, and the "because motive" that an actor might deploy retrospectively to account for a given set of events. He demonstrated that the meanings a person gives to actions shift according to the actor's temporal relation to them; that is, meanings of actions are not always "the same," even for the actor herself. Weber's typologies of meaning and action represent observers' interpretations, whereas (various) subjective meanings themselves are situated within streams of unfolding individual consciousness.

Despite the power of transcendental phenomenology as the basis for understanding meaning, Schütz recognized its limitations as a basis for a phenomenology of the social world. Specifically, intersubjectivity – the social relation between an Ego and others in the vivid present – cannot be accounted for within the transcendental reduction, because the reduction deliberately brackets the content of any perceptions. The internal time consciousness that structures formations of meanings is a basic feature of the individual acting in the lifeworld, but the lifeworld – specific subjective meanings, other people, and cultural meanings – is only perceptible within a mundane "natural attitude" in which the individual does not doubt the "world-given-to-me-as-being-there," and interprets the world on the basis of built up social and cultural frameworks of meaning (Schütz 1967: 43).

Building from his critique of Weber, Schütz (esp. 1962–6, 1970; Schütz & Luckmann 1972) concentrated on developing a mundane or lifeworldly phenomenology of the social world that would describe its transhistorical and transcultural structures. The result is a formal description of Ego-consciousness, time, accents on reality, Others, intersubjectivity, meaning, horizons of life and death, and operations of meaningful action. These are described in terms of events of consciousness in relation to thematic issues that come to the fore, and motivational and interpretive structures of "relevance" that frame constructions of meaning.

Like Husserl, Schütz faced a basic difficulty: a transcendental phenomenological description must itself depend on socially based features of the lifeworld (e.g., language) available only within the natural attitude. Schütz came to terms with this dilemma by keying his phenomenology of the natural attitude to existential conditions of embodiment and historicity.

Critics of Schütz wonder whether his ego-based phenomenology has any adequate basis for moving from consciousness to society, especially as a phenomenon sui generis. However, intersubjectivity is central to his analysis, and his phenomenology describes the epistemological status not only of Schütz's own analyses but of actors' typifications and knowledge more widely. It thus accounts for the situated character of meaning construction both for people in general and for observers with particular analytic interests (e.g., in social and other sciences, history, and other "finite provinces of meaning") (Hall 1999: 16–19). In turn, Schütz's more descriptive phenomenological essays on the character of particular types of actors and forms of interaction (e.g., the man on the street, the stranger, making music) are important in their own right. They also serve as exemplars of applied phenomenology (Hall 1977), and participant-observation research demonstrates that Schütz's critique of Weber can be extended to specify relationships between Weberian typifications of social structure and alternative constitutions of the lifeworld described in Schützian terms (Hall 1978).

Like certain other twentieth-century social theorists (e.g., Vilfredo Pareto), Schütz has been underutilized relative to the power of his ideas. Nevertheless, his influence has been substantial, and the broad currents of sociology have moved in his direction. The major direct influences are telling. Schütz sought to engage the pragmatist interactionists. Talcott Parsons and Schütz engaged in a lively interaction, and Parsons's student, Harold Garfinkel, drew on core Schützian ideas in his *Studies in Ethnomethodology*, which examines the actor's situated methods of knowledge construction. John O'Neill (*Making Sense Together*, 1974) and Kurt Wolff (*Surrender and Catch*, 1976) also have built on everyday epistemology themes in Schütz's work. Peter Berger and Thomas Luckmann centrally invoked Schütz in their pathbreaking book, *The Social Construction of Reality*. Pierre Bourdieu used a phenomenologically centered analysis of situated meanings in *Outline of a Theory of Practice* (1977) to challenge atemporal and ahistorical features of structuralism in its semiotic and social anthropological dispensations. And critical theorist Jürgen Habermas's 1987 *Theory of Communicative Action, Volume 2* employed

Schütz's key concept of the lifeworld in describing the modern tendencies of rationalized systems to colonize and subordinate everyday social life by defining, circumscribing, and organizing its meaningful options.

More generally, after structural functionalism and systems theory reached their points of maximum influence in the 1960s, sociology has moved in a Schützian direction. Neither logical positivism nor a presuppositionless transcendental phenomenology holds up philosophically any more, and postfoundational social epistemologies, including the feminist epistemology of Dorothy Smith, as well as social studies of science, confront precisely the existential conditions of embodiment and knowledge that Schütz described. Although quantitative sociologists have rarely sought to accommodate social phenomenology in their research, a wide range of sociological theories – including those of a structuralist bent – now incorporate formulations about the social construction of reality. Explanatory and interpretive empirical work – both in historical sociology and using qualitative methods – also has become highly sensitive to the issue of multiple social realities and the play of situated meanings. Most generally, sociologists now typically want to specify mechanisms of social processes on the ground, rather than simply delineating abstract factors and their causal relationships to one another. All these developments are foreshadowed by the phenomenological sociology of Alfred Schütz. However, they do not yet consolidate a fully developed phenomenological analysis of society. Thus, Schütz's work remains an important resource in sociology, the full potential of which remains unrealized.

SEE ALSO: Everyday Life; Lifeworld; Phenomenology; Pragmatism; Symbolic Interaction; Weber, Max

REFERENCES AND SUGGESTED READINGS

Barber, M. (2002) Alfred Schütz. In: Zalta, E. N. (Ed.), *Stanford Encyclopedia of Philosophy*. www.plato.stanford.edu/archives/win2002/entries/schutz/>.

Hall, J. R. (1977) Alfred Schütz, His Critics, and Applied Phenomenology. *Cultural Hermeneutics* 4: 265–79.

Hall, J. R. (1978). *The Ways Out: Utopian Communal Groups in an Age of Babylon*. Routledge, London.

Hall, J. R. (1999) *Cultures of Inquiry: From Epistemology to Discourse in Sociohistorical Inquiry*. Cambridge University Press, Cambridge.

Kurrild-Klitgaard, P. (2003) The Viennese Connection: Alfred Schütz and the Austrian School. *Quarterly Journal of Austrian Economics* 6: 35–67.

Schütz, A. (1962, 1964, 1966) *Collected Papers, Vols. 1–3*. Martinus Nijhoff, The Hague.

Schütz, A. (1967 [1932]) *The Phenomenology of the Social World*. Northwestern University Press, Evanston, Il.

Schütz, A. (1970) *Structures of the Lifeworld*. Ed. T. R. Zaner. Yale University Press, New Haven.

Schütz, A. & Luckmann, T. (1973) *The Structures of the Lifeworld*. Northwestern University Press, Evanston, Il.

Wagner, H. (1983) *Alfred Schütz: An Intellectual Biography*. University of Chicago Press, Chicago.

science

Ian Varcoe

Sociological frameworks used in the study of science move between two epistemological extremes. First, it is held that nature is recorded by science provided that the latter is in a fit state as a social institution to do so. Second, it is held that science is a social construction and in this sense in principle no different than any other part of culture.

If one is convinced of the first proposition, one's interest will be directed towards: the "goal" of science; the institutional norms that regulate the activity of the community of scientists; competition; the reward structure of science operating through "recognition" (citation practices, Nobel prizes, peer review); and similar topics. If one is convinced of the second proposition, one will be interested not so much in the institution and community of science, but rather in scientific knowledge and the question of how scientists reach a point where it can be said to have been "made." One will be interested in the "negotiation" through which a stable order of scientific objects is arrived at. In this "negotiation" there is included writing practices and the empirical study of "talk" (or discourse).

The great American sociologist Robert K. Merton was certain that science had social underpinnings. It was not the product of timeless individual curiosity. In its modern form – as understood by historians of science – it had its roots in seventeenth-century European society. Twentieth-century experience showed that it could be affected by political ideology (the Nazis' "Aryan physics," the Bolsheviks' "bourgeois" versus "proletarian" science). In the West, however, science seemed to retain its "autonomy." While located within capitalist society it was insulated from it, to a certain extent, by a set of distinctive norms the upholding of which cemented the community of scientists, and functioned to allow the pursuit of reliable (or certified) knowledge to go on. Priority disputes demonstrated how important recognition was to scientists as their only reward. Scientists are expected to share their findings, to subject the claims of others to rigorous critical tests, to be disinterested, and to judge claims not by persons but by universal criteria. Merton's norms suffered from two basic criticisms: (1) empirically, the evidence for them actually working was thin; and (2) the suggestion was made that this was the "public face" of science, ritually evoked for public consumption and infinitely flexible as a rhetorical resource. Evidence showed that scientists were not open-minded universalists. They condemned unconventional "science" without testing it and hung on to cherished ideas in the face of apparently disconfirming evidence. To his enduring credit Merton was concerned with the distinctiveness of science. He founded the sociology of science and initiated a program of research carried out mainly by American followers.

A second research tradition grew up in opposition to the Mertonian, known generically as the sociology of scientific knowledge. This movement was catalyzed by Thomas Kuhn's *The Structure of Scientific Revolutions* (1962), which challenged the philosopher's picture of science as demarcated by *a* method and put in its place a historical one in which scientists placed their faith in a paradigm and proceeded to solve fairly routine "puzzles" within it until such times as crisis set in and a "revolution" ensued consisting of a mass change of allegiances. Following this encouragement to create a realistic – in Kuhn's case, a historical – rather than a philosophical account of "science," sociologists in Britain (based in Edinburgh University and other centers) issued manifestos declaring their intention to carry through Mannheim's sociology of knowledge to its logical conclusion, not exempting scientific beliefs from its injunction to study the social bases of all beliefs (Mannheim, however, had equivocated over science and mathematics). The aim should be to open what Merton and his followers had left as a "black box": why it was argued should sociological analysis halt at the threshold of scientists' beliefs as if these could not be socially influenced (because *the* scientific method applied to Nature was assumed to be fully responsible for them). The sociology of scientific knowledge was avowedly relativist in its approach to scientific knowledge. Two broad schools are identifiable.

The first to appear was the "interests" approach. Owing to "interpretive flexibility," replication is not a sure, decisive way to close down uncertainty about the "results" of experiments; and the closure which stabilizes "knowledge" is brought about by a range of social factors rather than something in the data: the struggle is to define the data (or the "phenomenon"). Numerous interview-based case studies "showed" this.

To critics of this approach the idea that social interests cause interpretive behavior represents a failure to carry the "interpretive" perspective through to its full logical conclusion, namely that there is *only* interpretation in scientific life and social life generally. Causal analysis has no place anywhere. This point of view, inspired by the ethnomethodology of Harold Garfinkel, was backed up by the offering of an alternative: the ethnographic study of the laboratory through usually prolonged participant observation to see how science is "made" from the messy materials to be found therein. A second alternative was the analysis of scientists' discourse to see the devices by which they sustain their sense of a reality "out there" and their own access to it, against their competitors. Both approaches call for a thoroughgoing reflexivity – more thoroughgoing than the interests approach, despite advocating it, practiced in reality. On this view, sociological analyses must be recognized as interpretations; they cannot be anything else.

These approaches came in the wake of the "strong program" in the sociology of science. It desired an approach that was symmetrical (as between "true" and "false" belief), causal, reflexive, and impartial. Arguably, interest-type studies fail in full reflexivity (by claiming to be authoritative) and are not based on the empirical testing of deductive theory, but rather on the *post hoc* interpretation of the interview data. Interview material is used to construct a "story" of what was "really going on" in disputes (i.e., such material is taken at face value as a faithful account rather than rhetoric and some of it is favored over the rest by the sociologist as being closer than other parts to "what really happened"). Ethnographic study has also been criticized for failing to meet its own requirements: (1) by drawing on theory and thus not truly letting the discourse "speak" as far as possible without interpretation; (2) by having no way of recognizing the basis of differential authority in science, the *effect* of which the approach brings out; and (3) through acknowledging the role of rhetoric, allowing implicitly causal forces while denying them programmatically. It was noted that "forces outside of the laboratory" were drawn on to provide tacit explanations and that full-blown discourse reductionism is as debilitating a dogma as the denial of language and social construction of reality, for here reality is collapsed into language.

To the discourse analyst the "interests" researcher can be seen applying empiricist *rhetoric* in claiming to provide a causal account of beliefs. Both approaches run into difficulties in that neither can in practice do entirely without reference to wider social realities beyond the research setting itself. The interests approach cannot examine these to a sufficiently high empirical standard (i.e., the rigorously high empirical standard it has set itself through the use of interviews and other forms of direct observation) and the ethnographic and discourse approaches find reference to these wider factors beyond the research setting simply unavoidable, although here again they cannot in practice be treated as the approach requires (i.e., as discourse). It might appear that both approaches, in being methodologically purist programmatically, are mirror reflections of the dogmatism about science that they reject, namely that it straightforwardly records nature. Strong antidotes to naturalism were needed at the start of sociological research, but these commitments – while directing the focus of research – failed to permit the handling in full of the complexity of the phenomenon of science as a social enterprise.

In the twentieth century, particularly following 1945, "scientific research and development" became increasingly organized on a large scale. It attracted financial support from the state and consumed a significant proportion of GDP in the developed societies of the world. The prewar debate over whether science should be planned was settled willy-nilly in terms of some form of planning following the Physicists' War, which showed the indispensability of scientific investment to state power. Research and development became an institutional complex formed of the universities, industrial laboratories, and government research establishments. With state funding attention came to focus on a policy for science and technology. The institutions of organized science and science policy became an object of study and the latter began to be assessed by rational criteria. Recently, a theme in this assessment has been "science and the public," the public understanding of science as a goal and a reality, and a "science for the people" with the regulation of science and technology came to the fore. Merton's liberal view of science's autonomy in democratic societies was not shared by J. D. Bernal, who between the two world wars argued that the benefits that science could bestow on humankind were not being realized. The direction of scientific research and the application of its results were being dictated by capitalism. A question raised by Bernal was whether a people's science would be a different science from the one existing under capitalism. Analysts of the "social function of science" have divided on this issue, with some like Bernal (who later drew back from it) adopting a relativist position. The philosopher Herbert Marcuse took this position. Freed from existing relations of domination, human society would generate a new kind of science, different from the existing one, geared to emancipation. The alternative view to this one is that scientific knowledge is effectively neutral knowledge of nature, but the direction research takes and the uses fostered of results are influenced by the social, political, and economic relations of capitalism. Profit and military needs dictate the use to which a basically neutral science is put. This view tends to share with Merton the belief that nature speaks through science (or to use a phrase of Norbert Elias's, that it is relatively more "object adequate" than say religion and magic; or as Ernst Gellner put it, science "works" in producing a powerful technology even though we cannot root it in a secure epistemology, ungrounded in society and history). It is critical of the sociology of scientific knowledge for its failure to connect its detailed case and ethnographic studies to the larger social structures in which science and technology have come to be embedded, and for its provisional relativist standpoint. The "interests" approach has so far mainly promised to establish connections between science and the wider society, while discourse analysts are engaged in a campaign to revolutionize sociology, making it an interpretive and reflexive discipline, so that it is difficult to see the categorical ground for any rapprochement. These, however, would find Marxist models, either of the use/abuse or "science as ideology" kind, empirically unsound, the tradition lacking a record of the scrupulous empirical inquiry needed to "read" science successfully in the locales where research is actually done. Micro versus macro and external versus internal analyses are divides that still tend to dog the social study of science.

Everyone in this field is agreed that science is a product in some form of social processes. "Science," however, is a contested terrain, academically and socially. Disciplinary boundaries are insecure and contestation takes place to define them. Social study of science today is an interdisciplinary area involving historians, philosophers, sociologists, and others, who often have indistinct, hybrid professional identities.

Science has become an arena of social contestation too, as the risk society thesis, postmodernism, and the sociology of expert knowledge have recently tended to confirm. Increasingly, experts confront other experts in the public domain where high-consequence risks are debated before an often apprehensive and sometimes skeptical public. The authority of science appears to be in crisis, while its involvement in the reproduction of everyday life appears to grow. Everyday life appears increasingly hazardous, at least to those in the developed world who face man-made risks in which science and technology are implicated as cause and proffered aids to solutions. The social constructivist approach in the sociology of science is playing and has played a role in the study of "risk" (e.g., environmental and latterly social issues arising from the new genetics, to which Marx-inspired sociology has also contributed).

Social movements such as the animal rights, environmental, and anti-capitalist ones are preoccupied with "science issues," as formerly were the peace and socialist movements mainly from the 1960s onwards. Feminism, seen as scholarship, moreover, has been intensely preoccupied recently with the study of science. Its divisions can usefully be drawn parallel – but only partly so – to those familiar in the social studies of science. Broadly, a liberal feminism is concerned with and about the under-representation of women in science and their position within a male-dominated profession. A second strand is devoted to examining representations of women in science, historically and in contemporary terms, with particular attention having been given recently to *in vitro* fertilization and embryo research (the so-called new reproductive technologies). A third approach mirroring in certain respects the sociology of scientific knowledge is epistemologically oriented. However, unlike the latter, it does make connections to the structural fact of gender relations and discrimination in the wider society, and it is not reflexive (applying its relativism consistently to itself). In this respect it resembles the idea of an emancipatory science yet to be born, found in places in the Marxian tradition.

This "standpoint feminism" raises the question of whether the science made by men is androcentric and oriented to domination of nature. It suggests that a feminine science would be likely to engage feeling, empathy, and listening as distinct from "cold," rational, detached observation. Such a science, it is suggested, subsumes its predecessor, completing knowledge in a higher synthesis. Against this view it is protested (1) that it may in fact be in the process of attempting to replace one gender-biased approach with another; and (2) related to this, that, inconsistently, it applies its relativism to "male science" but not to itself. The negotiation which is such a central part of the findings of sociology of scientific knowledge studies does not seem apparent in this approach. It may, it is suggested, be reifying the masculine and the feminine. There are other feminist approaches, however. These seek to avoid these alleged pitfalls (e.g., postmodern feminism). There are also less uncompromising, more meliorist assessments of what currently constructed science might have to offer women that is of benefit to them.

The arena in which science is practiced, studied, and fought over today is not likely to change from its current divided, complex character in the immediate future. The certainties of the Enlightenment have indeed collapsed. The faultlines that divide research traditions continue to define those traditions as somewhat separate. Parallel positions can be found between them, dividing them internally but establishing wider sympathies (e.g., between anti-relativist philosophers, Mertonians, and liberal feminists; between Marxists and standpoint feminists; and between postmodern feminists, ethnographers, discourse analysts, and postmodernists). Wider political commitments, which are themselves the distillation of political traditions, continue to affect attitudes towards science and the "social world." The question of the relation between them, and how it should be conceptualized, is still unresolved. As the boundary between research institute, university department, industrial laboratory, and defense establishment and the surrounding network of social relations – often extending globally – becomes ever more permeable, sociologists of science are forced to adopt ever more inventive methodologies. These transcend the entrenched positions of the past, pointing to a new flexibility, the beginnings of which are visible.

SEE ALSO: Epistemology; Feminism and Science, Feminist Epistemology; Science, Commercialization of; Science across Cultures; Science, Proof, and Law; Science, Social Construction of; Scientific Knowledge, Sociology of; Scientific Norms/Counternorms; Scientific Productivity

REFERENCES AND SUGGESTED READINGS

Bernal, J. D. (1964 [1939]) *The Social Function of Science*. MIT Press, Cambridge, MA.

Chalmers, A. (1982) *What Is This Thing Called Science?*, 2nd edn. Open University Press, Milton Keynes.

Collins, H. M. (1975) The Seven Sexes: A Study in the Sociology of a Phenomenon, or the Replication of Experiments in Physics. *Sociology* 9: 205–24.

David, M. (2005) *Science in Society*. Palgrave Macmillan, Basingstoke.

Elias, N. (1971) Sociology of Knowledge: New Perspectives. *Sociology* 5: 146–68, 355–70.

Gellner, E. (1988) *Plough, Sword and Book: The Structure of Human History*. Chicago University Press, Chicago.

Harding, S. (1986) *The Science Question in Feminism*. Open University Press, Milton Keynes.

Latour, B. & Woolgar, S. (1986) *Laboratory Life: The Construction of Scientific Facts*, 2nd edn. Sage, London.

Merton, R. K. (1957) *Social Theory and Social Structure*. Free Press, New York.

Mulkay, M. J. (1979) *Science and the Sociology of Knowledge*. George Allen & Unwin, London.

Polanyi, M. (1973) *Personal Knowledge*. Routledge & Kegan Paul, London.

Popper, K. R. (1969) *The Logic of Scientific Discovery*. Hutchinson, London.

Ravetz, J. R. (1971) *Scientific Knowledge and its Social Problems*. Clarendon Press, Oxford.

Rose, H. (1984) *Love, Power and Knowledge: Towards a Feminist Transformation of the Sciences*. Polity Press, Cambridge.

Woolgar, S. (1986) *Science: The Very Idea*. Tavistock, London.

science, commercialization of

Daniel Lee Kleinman

Neither science-based industry nor university involvement in commercially relevant science is a new phenomenon. In certain sectors, US firms employed scientists in the late nineteenth century, and examples of university–industry collaboration in the United States can be found in the early twentieth century. That said, the advent of the biotechnology industry in the late 1970s and 1980s prompted sustained policy and scholarly attention to the place of science in the economy.

The standard recent history of the commodification of science highlights several pieces of US legislation that analysts suggest altered the landscape in which science is undertaken. Most prominent among these is the Bayh-Dole Act of 1980. A central aim of this law was to encourage university–industry collaboration by permitting universities and small businesses to retain title to inventions produced with federal funding. Indeed, at the center of virtually all discussions of the commodification of science is the blurring boundary between academia and industry and the possibilities for transforming scientific research into marketable products.

Scholarly discussion of the commercialization of academic science can be divided into two waves. Early work focused on the threat to traditional academic norms of autonomy and openness posed by industry support for academic research and the array of university–industry relationships that flourished with the development of the biotechnology industry. Much of the early research was anecdotal and highlighted egregious cases of conflict of interest and industry pressure to keep academic research findings secret. During this period and subsequently, researchers have undertaken surveys in an effort to capture the extent to which traditional academic norms have been eroded by industry involvement in the university. This research has found academic scientists torn by conflicting pressures, but also shows that many factors besides connections to industry prompt scientists to restrict the flow of information (Blumenthal et al. 1986; Campbell et al. 2002).

If early research on the place of the academy in the knowledge economy focused on erosion of norms, the second wave has been more interested in understanding the social organization of the knowledge economy and the place of the university in it. Some such work explores networks of interdependence between industry and academic science (Powell 1998). Other scholarship suggests the emergence of a new mode of knowledge production in academia and industry that tends to be collaborative, non-hierarchical, interdisciplinary, and organized through work teams and networks (Gibbons et al. 1994). Still other work sees a movement toward what the proponents call "academic capitalism" in which those university fields, departments, and faculty members who are closer to the market have greater access to resources and status than those further from the market (Slaughter & Leslie 1997). Finally, theorists of "asymmetrical convergence" (Kleinman & Vallas 2001) contend that a process is underway in which the norms and practices characteristic of industry are increasingly, if unevenly, found in academia, while academic norms are in increasing and surprising ways found in science-based industry.

SEE ALSO: Economy, Networks and; Economy (Sociological Approach); Fordism/Post-Fordism; Knowledge; Knowledge Societies; Political Economy of Science; Science; Science and Public Participation: The Democratization of Science

REFERENCES AND SUGGESTED READINGS

Blumenthal, D., Gluck, M., Louis, K., Stoto, A., & Wise, D. (1986) University–Industry Research Relations in Biotechnology: Implications for the University. *Science* 232 (June 13): 1361–6.

Campbell, E. G., Clarridge, B. R., Gokhale, M., Birenbaum, L., Hilgartner, S., Holtzman, N. A., & Blumenthal, D. (2002) Data Withholding in Academic Genetics: Evidence from a National Survey. *Journal of the American Medical Association* 287(4): 473–80.

Gibbons, M., Limoges, C., Nowotny, H., Schwartzman, S., Scott, P., & Trow, M. (1994) *The New Production of Knowledge: The Dynamics of Science and Research in Contemporary Societies.* Sage, Thousand Oaks, CA.

Kleinman, D. L. & Vallas, S. P. (2001) Science, Capitalism, and the Rise of the Knowledge Worker: The Changing Structure of Knowledge Production in the United States. *Theory and Society* 30: 451–92.

Powell, W. W. (1998) Learning from Collaboration: Knowledge and Networks in the Biotechnology and Pharmaceutical Industries. *California Management Review* 40(1): 228–40.

Slaughter, S. & Leslie, L. L. (1997) *Academic Capitalism: Politics, Policies, and the Entrepreneurial University.* Johns Hopkins University Press, Baltimore.

science and culture

Daniel Breslau

Philosophers of the European Enlightenment defined science in opposition to culture or humanistic knowledge. Science was truth based on verifiable observation and certain logical procedures, and thus stood opposed to all traditional beliefs. Francis Bacon, who initiated the philosophical tradition of elaborating "demarcation principles" to distinguish science from non-science, differentiated science from all knowledge that is based on tradition and all humanistic knowledge, thus defining it in opposition to most of what we think of as pertaining to culture (Bacon 2001). Science was distinct from culture due to both its method, which followed transhistoric, universal rules, and its results.

The Enlightenment distinction between science and culture has been thoroughly eroded since the late twentieth century. It is one of the major transformations in western intellectual life that science and scientific knowledge are now legitimate objects of study for the human sciences.

While classical sociological writers provide some of the tools for the analysis of scientific knowledge, they observed the Enlightenment science/culture distinction, and only subjected the latter to sociological analysis. When supposedly scientific knowledge was subjected to a critical sociological gaze, as in the young Karl Marx's critique of political economy, the term *ideology* allowed him to distinguish the object of his criticism from science. Durkheim and Mauss argued that systems for classifying the natural world originate in social classifications, but maintained that scientific knowledge, through the use of pure logic, had become independent of its socially based origins.

Twentieth-century sociology of science refrained from sociological analysis of the content of scientific thought, taking as its task the description of the social conditions under which knowledge is liberated from social determinants. Joseph Ben-David's historical sociology of the role of the scientist examined the historical emergence and institutionalization of the scientist's role, which Ben-David assumed to be a necessary condition for supporting and motivating inquiry that would be interested solely in truth as such. After careful consideration of the possibility of social influences on the content of scientific knowledge, Ben-David concluded that such influences were marginal at best, and that therefore "the possibilities for either an interactional or institutional sociology of the conceptual and theoretical contents of science are extremely limited" (Ben-David 1971).

Robert Merton's functionalist analysis of science approached the same issues in a synchronic manner. Merton was interested in describing the particular features of the social subsystem of science that allowed for the continuous production of validated knowledge. Scientists internalize an ethos that enables them, or constrains them at pain of social sanction, to detach their scientific judgments from any personalistic social considerations (Merton 1973). Both Merton and Ben-David were therefore describing the social determinants of the freedom of science from social determination.

While the functionalist sociology of science is neglected today, it should be credited with transposing the question of the basis of scientific efficacy from the rules of method to the social conditions under which it is practiced. It retained much of the traditional demarcation of science from culture, but restated the demarcation criteria in social, rather than moral, psychological, or methodological terms.

In the mid-twentieth century a number of philosophical developments challenged the absolute divide between science and culture, suggesting that scientific knowledge is inseparable from a broader culture, which is specific to a social group and historical period. Wittgenstein's arguments about the insufficiency of formal rules and the impossibility of drawing a necessary course of action from them without reference to a specific "form of life" demonstrated that the formalism of mathematics and logic do not free science from its broader cultural horizons. Quine, like Wittgenstein treating science as composed of linguistic elements, insisted on the dependence of observation on theoretical assumptions, and of hypotheses on a fabric of often unstated, often conventional, assumptions. Others, such as Michael Polanyi and Thomas Kuhn, attacked the assumption that scientific knowledge is independent of a specific historical, and cultural, context. Polanyi emphasized personal judgment based on connoisseurship and tacit knowledge, while Kuhn emphasized the dependence of scientific work on shared traditions of scientific communities. Both argued that these cultural dimensions were not obstacles to scientific knowledge, but were indeed among its necessary conditions.

Licensed by the new philosophical understanding, a number of sociologists of science located at the University of Edinburgh in the late 1970s initiated a program of theoretical statements and case studies that aimed to extend the sociology of knowledge to science. David Bloor's *Knowledge and Social Imagery* (1991) is the best known of these works. It is ironic that Bloor's work has been classified among so-called postmodernist studies of science, since Bloor could not have been more explicit in his modernism, calling for a causal science of science. Bloor argued that the sociology of science harbored a contradiction, and a betrayal of a thoroughgoing social scientific treatment of science. Only false or rejected knowledge was assumed to have social causes and a sociological explanation, while validated knowledge was assumed to be caused only by the objects to which it refers. By subjecting only discarded knowledge, or error, to sociological analysis, and assuming that validated knowledge did not have social causes, the sociology of science was inconsistent, and engaged in explanations by final causes. Arguing that both rejected and validated knowledge should be explained in terms of the same kinds of causal antecedents, Bloor proposed a "strong program" for the sociology of science, also known as the sociology of scientific knowledge (SSK).

While the Edinburgh School did not elaborate a detailed sociological theory of scientific knowledge, the works of its adherents share what might be called a neo-Mannheimian or conflict sociology of knowledge. Following Mannheim's "perspectival" method, the Edinburgh studies of scientific controversies relate opposed positions on scientific questions to opposed positions in a social structure, with opposed interests. For instance, Shapin's (1979) study of the phrenology controversy in early nineteenth-century Edinburgh based its explanation on the opposed interests of the middle-class proponents of phrenology and its opponents among the traditional academic elites. Opposed views on the structure of the brain and the interpretation of variation in human skulls were related to opposed interests in cultural authority.

While members of the Edinburgh School and SSK built their sociology of scientific knowledge around the classical tradition of the sociology of knowledge, with sources in Durkheim, Marx, and Mannheim, others approached the question of science as the phenomenological question of the genesis of facts as such. While the SSK approach sought social explanations for given beliefs, these studies made the very existence of knowledge a problem for explanation. Also phenomenological in their methodology, researchers in what came to be called the laboratory studies approach sought to observe first-hand the work involved in stabilizing scientific facts. Studies by Lynch (1979), Latour and Woolgar (1979), and Knorr-Cetina (1981) treated facts, and indeed the existence of a taken-for-granted external reality, as tied to the instruments, procedures, and social arrangements of scientific work.

The most influential approach to emerge from this phenomenological tradition is that associated with Bruno Latour, Michel Callon, and John Law, and known as actor-network theory. It begins with the principle of generalized symmetry articulated by Callon, by which one should not make an a priori metaphysical divide between humans and all other entities, attributing agency only to the former. There is no prior basis to presume that the social world is real while the natural world is constructed, any more than the opposite. To attempt to explain scientific knowledge in terms of social factors is to commit prematurely to a social realism. What is real and what is relative should be an outcome of the processes we examine. Actor-network therefore allows for a proliferation of agents, which are all both constructed and constructing.

The objects of science, and indeed the world, are constructed through the linking of heterogeneous agencies in a network. All entities are located on a continuum from nebulous, poorly defined, controversial facts or artifacts to "black boxes," facts or artifacts that can be put to use without reference to the circumstances of their production. The difference between an incontrovertible fact and an uncertain claim is a function of the difference in the scope and strength of the network connections.

Actor-network theory was presented as a comprehensive challenge to social science. It contained a principled rejection of the social explanation of scientific knowledge and of any explanatory priority of the social. The actor-network theorists argued that there is no ground for an a priori distinction between the social and the natural, and the presumption that the social can be used to explain the natural (as described by science). A sociological reduction of science would impose the product of the researcher's own network on an object in which the social is itself an outcome. It rejects an a priori distinction between science and culture, but not by collapsing science into culture. Rather, culture and science both refer to the mutual construction of the world through the elaboration of networks.

North American interactionist traditions have yielded yet another variant of sociological study of the content of science. With some sources in the "social worlds" research of symbolic interactionists such as Howard Becker and Anselm Strauss, scientific knowledge is here regarded as part of the local world that scientists construct. Sociologists such as Adele Clarke and Joan Fujimura applied this perspective, as it had been applied to work in cultural, industrial, and professional organizations, to the work of scientists. The work of scientists is then viewed as a process of negotiating a social order and its boundaries.

Philosophical challenges to the universality of scientific knowledge also resonated with feminist studies. While women's marginalization in scientific fields had been a topic of historical and sociological study, feminist research now argued that a historically specific form of gender domination was in fact built into scientific knowledge, and into the official definition of scientific method. Evelyn Fox Keller (1985) examined the history of the British Royal Society, and argued that the scientific method pioneered by Francis Bacon and his followers was based on a definition of masculinity. Male attributes of rationality, objectivity, and affective detachment were elaborated into the qualities of a scientist, with the use of an explicitly gendered metaphor. The relationship of the scientist to nature was described in terms of the male conquest of female sexuality. With this thesis of the gendered origins of scientific method, was the argument that a method based on detachment was in fact unnecessary, and was used to suppress equally valid ways of knowing, based on aptitudes more likely to be rooted in women's experience. The field of feminist epistemology has elaborated ways of knowing that are rooted in the experience and "standpoint" of women.

While there are now many approaches that treat science and scientific knowledge as cultural endeavors, linked to the historically specific culture in which it is produced, these approaches as a whole have been the subject of continuing controversy. In a series of debates known as the science wars, some have objected to efforts to understand the content of science in terms of the culture and social structure of the society in which it is produced. Challenges to the independence of scientific truths from social and cultural conditioning have been regarded as challenges to science as such, and as relativistic (Gross & Levitt 1994).

SEE ALSO: Actor-Network Theory; Feminism and Science, Feminist Epistemology; Knowledge, Sociology of; Mannheim, Karl; Science, Commercialization of; Science across Cultures; Science and Public Participation: The Democratization of Science; Scientific Knowledge, Sociology of; Scientific Revolution; Social Worlds; Technology, Science, and Culture

REFERENCES AND SUGGESTED READINGS

Bacon, F. (2001) *The Advancement of Learning.* Modern Library, New York.

Ben-David, J. (1971) *The Scientist's Role in Society: A Comparative Study.* Prentice-Hall, Englewood Cliffs, NJ.

Bloor, D. (1991) *Knowledge and Social Imagery.* University of Chicago Press, Chicago.

Gross, P. R. & Levitt, N. (1994) *Higher Superstition: The Academic Left and its Quarrels with Science.* Johns Hopkins University Press, Baltimore.

Keller, E. F. (1985) *Reflections on Gender and Science.* Yale University Press, New Haven.

Knorr-Cetina, K. D. (1981) *The Manufacture of Knowledge: An Essay on the Constructivist and Contextual Nature of Science.* Pergamon, New York.

Latour, B. & Woolgar, S. (1979) *Laboratory Life: The Construction of Scientific Facts.* Sage, Beverly Hills, CA.

Lynch, M. (1985) *Art and Artifact in Laboratory Science: A Study of Shop Work in a Research Laboratory.* Routledge, London.

Merton, R. K. (1973) *The Sociology of Science: Theoretical and Empirical Investigations.* University of Chicago Press, Chicago.

Shapin, S. (1979) *On the Margins of Science: The Social Construction of Rejected Knowledge.* Sociological Review Monograph 27. Blackwell, Oxford, pp. 139–78.

science across cultures

Amanda Rees

Science is often thought of as a western invention, a way of thinking about the world that originated in Europe during the "Scientific Revolution," and which proved to be such an effective means of manipulating nature that its techniques and practices were readily adopted by the rest of the world, once other societies had had the chance to consider science in action. However, this version of events depends on the assumption that science and technology are objective, culturally neutral, ahistorical, apolitical, and asocial elements in society. The reality, however, is rather more complicated. Rather than being a neutral aspect of relationships between different cultures, science has had an active role to play in intercultural engagement, both historically and at the present day. Rather than being the sole product of European ingenuity, science emerged out of the relationships that existed between Europe and the rest of the world; instead of simply being communicated to other societies as a more effective toolset for controlling the natural world, science was a key element in the processes whereby Europeans were able to dominate and to control other societies, both historically and at the present day.

There were at least two crucial historical contributions made by other societies to the European Scientific Revolution. The first was that made by Islamic scholars and natural philosophers. When the Roman Empire split into two halves in the third century CE, many if not most of the books and writings of the ancient Greek philosophers were lost to the western part of the empire, and remained so until the beginning of the European Renaissance. However, they were not lost to the eastern half, where they made crucial contributions to the self-consciously Islamic society that grew up there after the death of Mohammed. Islamic scholars translated Greek natural philosophy into Arabic, creating a language of science for Islam, and developing cultures of Islamic natural philosophy, medicine, and mathematics that built on and expanded the knowledge acquired from the original Greek texts. When the works of Aristotle, Euclid, Ptolemy, and others were rediscovered by Europeans, they were written not in Greek but in Arabic. The versions of Greek philosophy that were available to the scholars of the Renaissance were those that had been created by Islamic philosophers.

The second major contribution came several hundred years later, at the beginning of the nineteenth century. Science in Europe was in the early stages of professionalization, and increasingly, expeditions of scientific discovery were being sent around the world. They brought back specimens of plant, animal, and human life, measurements of temperature, height, and pressure, maps and histories – but rarely credited the local observers and informants from whence they had obtained these specimens and data. For example, Michael Bravo's work on the "geographical gift" is based on the observation that huge areas of the globe were being mapped by a relatively small number of observers, and shows how many such maps were in fact drawn by local people at the behest of the "explorer." Crucially, these voyages were not just voyages of scientific discovery, but were also closely tied to empire. They were conducted by the same men – colonial officials, military officers, naval captains, missionaries, and commercial speculators – who were at the same time building empires. Expeditions were used to claim sovereignty and to assess resources, and the voyages of ships such as *The Beagle* around the world were determined as much, if not more, by geopolitical and national issues as by purely scientific questions.

Sciences such as anthropology, medicine, geology, and natural history were deeply implicated in the imperial project. To survey the land and to record the distribution of plants and animals ultimately meant to assess an area's natural resources with regard to future exploitation. The creation of the discipline of anthropology was inseparable from empire building, since anthropologists actively sought to link their work in with that done by nascent colonial administrators – learning more about how the societies of the colonized worked would improve the ability of the colonizers to govern them. The discipline of tropical medicine was invented to deal with the illnesses white people fell prey to in hot countries, and the offering and occasionally the withholding of medical aid and equipment became a critical element in both the practice and rhetoric of empire. As such, in the postcolonial period, disciplines such as anthropology have had to seriously reconsider their place and role in public life.

However, the postcolonial period has also seen a reconsideration of the impact that science, medicine, and technology had on the colonized cultures. The work of the subaltern studies program (the work of Ranajit Guha and others) in relation to the history of the British in India has continuously demanded the recognition of the existence of a series of fundamentally different ways of perceiving the world, and this has been taken a step further by other postcolonial writers such as Homi Bhabha and Gyan Prakash. Prakash in particular has studied the use of science in colonial India, and has shown that the role of "science" as part of the civilizing mission of the British in India was not used in precisely the way the British administrators expected. Western science was explicitly used to educate sections of the Indian population, to make them more "western" in their outlook, through the establishment of museums, the deployment of periodic exhibitions, and so on. However, when Prakash examined the responses of the audience, it was possible to demonstrate that what was appropriated by these various Indian groups was no longer quite "science," and no longer quite "western," but had become much more ambivalent and chimeric in nature.

Currently, there are few extensive sociological studies of what could be called "postcolonial science," or science carried out in the developing world or by scientists from the developing world in the latter half of the twentieth century. More are desperately needed.

SEE ALSO: Decolonization; Empire; Eurocentrism; Islam; Science and Culture; Scientific Racism; Scientific Revolution; Technology, Science, and Culture

REFERENCES AND SUGGESTED READINGS

Adas, M. (1990) *Machines as the Measure of Man: Science, Technology, and Ideologies of Western Dominance.* Cornell University Press, Ithaca, NY.

Bhabha, H. (1985) Signs Taken For Wonders: Questions of Ambivalence and Authority Under a Tree Outside Delhi, 1817. *Critical Inquiry* 12: 144–65.

Bravo, M. (1996) Ethnological Encounters. In: Jardine, N. et al. (Eds.), *Cultures of Natural History*. Cambridge University Press, Cambridge, pp. 338–57.

Browne, J. (1995) *Charles Darwin: Voyaging*. Princeton University Press, Princeton.

Lindberg, D. (1992) *The Beginnings of Western Science: The European Scientific Tradition in Philosophical, Religious, and Institutional Context, 600 BC to AD 1450.* University of Chicago Press, Chicago.

Palladino, P. & Worboys, M. (1993) Science and Imperialism. *Isis* 84: 91–102.

Prakash, G. (1992) Science Gone Native in Colonial India. *Representations* 40: 153–78.

science, ethnographic studies of

Wenda K. Bauchspies

Ethnographies of science have their origins in the interdisciplinary field of science and technology studies (STS) that emerged out of the Civil Rights Movement, feminism, and environmentalism of the 1960s. STS research illustrates that science and technology are a human achievement, composed of actors, social systems, and social processes. Or, in other words, science and technology are social constructions created in a sociocultural framework with social institutions, actors, and networks, social practices, material culture, and worldviews. STS scholars use ethnographies of science to contextualize science, to study the culture of science, to provide alternative perspectives of science, and to help science and its publics to design new research questions, programs, and policies.

The 1970s saw the entrance of laboratory studies into the STS repertoire for analyzing the "institutional circumstances of scientific work," technical content, and the production of scientific knowledge (Knorr Cetina 1995: 140). In the laboratory, STS scholars studied "unfinished knowledge" or the process of knowledge creation. These early laboratory studies were done by Bruno Latour and Steve Woolgar (1979), Karen Knorr Cetina (1981), Michael Lynch (1985), and Michael Zenzen and Sal Restivo (1982). They represented diverse methodological approaches from actor-network theory to ethnomethodology and constructivism and showed the products of science to be cultural entities. Scientific knowledge was not simply "discovered" but was co-created by the scientific practitioners and reconfigured within scientific practice. Ultimately, laboratory studies were able to explain how scientific knowledge production occurred in terms of social factors, and thus began the process of demystifying science.

The primary methodological tool of these early laboratory studies was fieldwork-based participant observation, and David Hess (1997: 134) has named them the "first wave of ethnographic studies in STS." This first generation of science ethnographers (mainly Europeans) focused primarily on the social processes that created objective, pure, neutral, descriptive science and the politics within the scientific community. Their work paved the way for the second wave of science ethnographers, who used social constructivism as a given to detail the cultural and political influences shaping knowledge and, thus, allowing the ethnographers and their work to contribute to and intervene in the dialogue of knowledge production (Hess 2001).

Sharon Traweek's (1988) ethnographic and comparative study of a US high energy physics lab and a Japanese high energy physics lab symbolizes the shift from laboratory studies to a more complete ethnographic description of science that included actors, spaces, artifacts, descriptions of scientific practice, and the ethnographer's reflections. More recent ethnographies of science (done primarily by American researchers) have followed in this genre while also addressing the roles of science and technology in the everyday/night world of not only scientists but also users, recipients, policy-makers, activists, administrators, educators, and ethnographers. Recent STS ethnographic studies are moving beyond simply situating the ethnographer in the study and are seriously questioning how their theorizing might be applied or intervene in the process (Downey & Dumit 1997).

Medical anthropologist Rayna Rapp (1999) focused on the "geneticization of lives" through genetic counseling and technology that illustrated how the contemporary US reproductive process is embedded in language, religion, ethnicity, class, gender, sexuality, age, and education. Her ethnography was structured not by chronology or ecology but by the technology as it moved through lived lives. She documented the ripples of genetic technology and the response and resolution of its passing. This form of ethnography highlighted the social spaces of reproductive technologies and the multiple, diverse, and varied perspectives that need to be considered within the culture of genetic science. These types of "findings" echo the roots of STS in 1960s social movements and contribute to the discussion and role of researcher and/or activist.

Another ethnographer of science, Joe Dumit (2004), focused on the virtual community of PET scans in US culture to create an "ethnography of images." He "followed" the images from their inception in experimental design to "everyday notions of personhood." Dumit's work is a thick description of the images evolving in a crisscrossed space inhabited by actors from popular, forensic, activist, and neuroscience culture. It is a culture/artifact in creation, still being defined, that maps out gaps in expertise, knowledge, and consequences. Ethnographies of science are more than a description of a culture. They are an active contribution to the culture that the informants read, use, critique, and participate in. Laboratory studies and ethnographies of science have matured quickly into a dynamic tool that ethnographers are using to document culture and formulate applicable theory.

SEE ALSO: Anthropology, Cultural and Social: Early History; Civil Rights Movement; Culture; Environmental Movements; Ethnography; Ethnomethodology; Feminism; Science; Science and Culture; Science across Cultures; Technology, Science, and Culture

REFERENCES AND SUGGESTED READINGS

Allen, B. (2003) *Uneasy Alchemy: Citizens and Experts in Louisiana's Chemical Corridor Disputes.* MIT Press, Cambridge, MA.

Collin, H. & Pinch, T. (1982) *Frames of Meaning.* Routledge, London.

Downey, G. & Dumit, J. (Eds.) (1997) *Cyborgs and Citadels.* School of American Research, Sante Fe, NM.

Dumit, J. (2004) *Picturing Personhood: Brain Scans and Biomedical Identity.* Princeton University Press, Princeton.
Hess, D. (1997) *Science Studies: An Advanced Introduction.* New York University Press, New York.
Hess, D. (2001) Ethnography and the Development of Science and Technology Studies. In: Atkinson, P., Coffey, A., Delamont, S., Lofland, L., & Lofland, J. (Eds.), *Sage Handbook of Ethnography.* Sage, London, pp. 234–345.
Knorr Cetina, K. (1981) *The Manufacture of Knowledge: An Essay on the Constructivist and Contextual Nature of Science.* Pergamon, Oxford.
Knorr Cetina, K. (1995) Laboratory Studies: The Cultural Approach to the Study of Science. In: Jasanoff, S., Markle, G. E., Petersen, J. C., & Pinch, T. (Eds.), *Handbook of Science and Technology Studies.* Sage, Thousand Oaks, CA, pp. 140–66.
Latour, B. & Woolgar, S. (1979) *Laboratory Life: The Social Construction of Scientific Facts.* Sage, Beverly Hills, CA.
Lynch, M. (1985) *Art and Artifact in Laboratory Science: A Study of Shop Work and Shop Talk in a Research Laboratory.* Routledge & Kegan Paul, London.
Rapp, R. (1999) *Testing Women, Testing the Fetus: The Social Impact of Amniocentesis in America.* Routledge, New York.
Traweek, S. (1988) *Beamtimes and Lifetimes: The World of High Energy Physicists.* Harvard University Press, Cambridge, MA.
Zenzen, M. & Restivo, S. (1982) The Mysterious Morphology of Immiscible Liquids: A Study of Scientific Practice. *Social Science Information* 21(3): 447–73.

science and the measurement of risk

Claire Haggett

The definition and measurement of risks is controversial and much in debate, with risk assessments made by scientists often differing from those of the lay public. Scientific measurements are based on logic and rationality. They tend to ignore or invalidate lay understandings of risk, not taking into account social, experiential, or perceptual influences. However, sociological work has highlighted that responses to risk are governed by a huge number of interrelated factors and have to be considered as part of the social context from which they arise. Lay people also have their own knowledge and expertise to draw upon when making assessments of the immanency and impact of any risk. It is not necessarily the case, therefore, that the public is being "irrational" in its decision-making, but that it uses a different rationality to that of scientists. These differences can lead to conflicts over risks, and resistance from the public to the measurements, and subsequent recommendations, imposed upon them by scientific research.

Risk assessments carried out by scientists are based on technical rationality. Risks are determined by experts, founded on evidence and logic, and described in terms of statistical probabilities. Results are depicted as objective, universal, and value free. They are designed to improve decision-making, and are presented as a means for human advancement. The focus is on identifying risks and people's responses to them in order to build prescriptive models for their avoidance. Such prescriptions often note a divergence between the public fear of a risk and the actual incidence of the danger; the controversy over genetically modified foods is often cited as an example of where the risk does not warrant the public alarm caused by it. Indeed, scientific rationality about risks is intended to counter any public *ir*rationality. The public is often considered to be unable to decide accurately and realistically about the existence and magnitude of the risks that it faces. It is deemed to use non-scientific factors and base its judgments on emotions or misinformation. Scientific assessments may characterize the public as ignorantly or willfully disregarding the neutral, objectively derived facts, and there is often a focus therefore on how to overcome this ignorance – or how to act in spite of it. Reassurances may be given about the "real facts" of a risk, and attempts made to educate the public about its true likelihood. This is based on a view that educating people will win their support, and that if they knew the facts, they would behave accordingly – the "public deficit" model, whereby problems arise because people misunderstand or are unable to grasp the facts being presented to them. Any continued public concern is then often dismissed as hysteria or hype.

While scientific risk assessments are designed to make people appreciate the irrationality of their position, what they overlook is that people may simply be drawing on another form of rationality; one that is not any more or less irrational, but just different from that employed by scientists. This "sociocultural rationality" is based on experience, social values, and the social context in which an individual lives. Assessment of the impacts and implications of a risk are shaped by the circumstances in which that risk is anticipated. Moreover, rather than being ignorant of the methods and results of risk assessment, lay people may draw on their own expertise, definitions, and meanings, and use these to reflect upon the validity and credibility of the technical information they are given.

Debates and assessments of risk are rooted in the context from which they arise. It is not possible to separate the likelihood and impacts of any particular risk from the broader social situation and the everyday social reality in which they are experienced. For example, researchers examining the effects of pollution from petrochemical factories in the northeast of the UK found that people tolerated the discharge from the smoke stacks because the factories were an intrinsic part of the local community. They were the main source of employment and had been for several previous generations. The factories were central to the identity of the area, and had been the reason for the economic boom and prestige accorded to it. The impacts of the pollution were known about, accommodated for, and were adopted into patterns of life (see Phillimore & Moffatt 1999). The scientific risk assessments of the distribution and effects of the pollution did not reflect anything of the social context in which the risks of the emissions were perceived.

As well as the influence of the wider social context, people may also bring their own knowledge and experience to bear in assessing risks. The hierarchical scientific "top-down" model of informing the public about the facts does not incorporate any notion of a two-way relationship between people and scientists, or any negotiation between them. Sociological work, however, highlights the potential validity of a public response to a risk. Williams and Popay (1994) describe the situation in the town of Camelford in Cornwall, UK, where toxic substances were accidentally tipped into the local water reservoir. Residents were concerned about both the short- and long-term risks to their health, but a committee of government scientists convened to look into the issue stated that chronic symptoms were not associated with the toxic dumping. However, in the light of continuing ill health, local residents continued to campaign for recognition of their claims, in what was to become a long-running and contentious battle. At the heart of this dispute is the notion that the shared experiences that formed local knowledge could not be invalidated by reference to standards of objectivity derived from abstract scientific knowledge.

Considering local experience also highlights problems with the presumed universality of scientific assessments of risk. Technical information in any communications about risk is simplified in order for people to be able to understand it and to reassure them. While risk assessment and prediction may incorporate a great deal of uncertainty, this is rarely discussed in any public communications. However, understating any uncertainty can antagonize rather than reassure, and damage credibility when such standardization may not fit with normal experience.The invalidity of idealized and universal versions of "laboratory science" is highlighted when contrasted with "real-world" experience and expertise. For example, Wynne (1989) documents differences between scientists' and farmers' knowledges in the aftermath of the Chernobyl accident. Concerns about the spread of radiation led to controversial restrictions being placed on farming practices and the movement and sale of livestock in the UK. However, the abstract knowledge applied by scientists in determining the levels of radiation and subsequent restrictions did not take account of local variations in the distribution of radiation, ignored local farming realities, and neglected the local knowledge and expert judgments of farmers. For the farmers, the supposedly universal scientific knowledge was out of touch with the practical reality and thus of no validity. It ignored factors that were obvious to them but invisible to outsiders, and made no attempt to accommodate (or even communicate with) their understandings and knowledge of the situation.

What universal risk assessments also overlook is that the nature of a risk affects the response to it. Sociological research has documented increased public concern over risks perceived as unfamiliar, unfair, invisible, or involuntary. This is not necessarily "irrational," but rather highlights the contingent nature of risk assessment that technical analyses ignore. For example, people may accept risks many times greater if they are voluntarily assumed rather than forced upon them. Research has found that when people willingly engage in "risky behavior," they report greater knowledge, less fear, and more personal control over the risks. Examples include engaging in extreme sports, or taking recreational drugs. The imposition of a risk, as well as the perceived degree of risk and likelihood of danger, is an important factor, and people are therefore less likely to accept a risk imposed upon them, with consequences they have no control over. The outcry over safety on the railways is an example of this. Risk assessments based on rationality outline the statistical likelihood of being involved in a train crash or car accident, and the latter is much higher. But traveling by train means handing over the control and responsibility for the journey, and powerless passengers thus demand to be kept safe and free from risks.

Finally, differences in the definitions of risks relate to issues of trust in experts and scientific decision-making. As well as any divergence between public and expert understanding of risks, the knowledge that the public receive from those experts is increasingly being met with skepticism. Accordingly therefore, individuals faced with a risk consider not only the probability of harm but also the credibility of whoever generates the information. The controversies over nuclear power, waste incinerators, and even renewable energy are all examples of this. Assurances from scientists and engineers that the noise from a windfarm will not disturb people living nearby, however authoritative and objective they seem, will be disregarded if the information is presented on behalf of the developer, or if it does not take into account the particular contingencies of the local area. Increasingly, scientific risk assessments are discounted and discredited by people who use their own knowledge and experience to determine the risks they face.

The disjuncture between scientists and lay assessment of risk has therefore led to increased public resistance of both the procedures and results of expert measurement. Indeed, as discussed above, the notion of the division between local and scientific knowledge can be seen as part of a trend challenging scientific work more generally. Public resistance of technical assessment arises because people's experiences, meanings, and knowledges are not expressed in this definition; and are often ignored, ridiculed, and contradicted. When the control of the basis for which assessments about risk can be made is claimed by scientific experts, there may be little similarity between perceptions of risk embedded in lived experience and those based on ideals of rationality and logic. In the light of risk, divisions are opened up between lay and scientific knowledge and those who have access to and expertise of these seemingly opposing epistemologies. Scientific definitions tend to exclude those without access to the technical knowledge needed to understand them, and preclude any negotiation between experts and the public. They are intended to educate and inform, not empower, and are imposed upon a context in which they may be seen to have little validity. What sociology has done is to highlight the differing rationalities that scientists and lay people use in their risk assessments, and shown how conflicts arise because of these. Work in the tradition of the sociology of scientific knowledge (SSK) demonstrates that the "public deficit" model of understanding has little validity, and serves to problematize the public rather than the operation of science. Instead, a more symmetrical view of different knowledge and expertise is required.

SEE ALSO: Risk, Risk Society, Risk Behavior, and Social Problems; Science and the Precautionary Principle; Scientific Knowledge, Sociology of; Scientific Literacy and Public Understandings of Science

REFERENCES AND SUGGESTED READINGS

Green, J. (1997) *Risk and Misfortune: The Social Construction of Accidents*. UCL Press, London.

Irwin, A. (1995) *Citizen Science: A Study of People, Expertise, and Sustainable Development*. Routledge, London.

Leach, M., Scoones, I., & Wynne, B. (Eds.) (2005) *Science and Citizens: Globalization and the Challenge of Engagement.* Zed Books, London.
Lupton, D. (Ed.) (1999) *Risk and Sociocultural Theory: New Directions and Perspectives.* Cambridge University Press, Cambridge.
Phillimore, P. & Moffatt, S. (1999) "If We Have Wrong Perceptions of Our Area, We Cannot Be Surprised If Others Do As Well": Representing Risk in Teesside's Environmental Politics. *Journal of Risk Research* 7(2): 171–84.
Williams, G. & Popay, J. (1994). Lay Knowledge and the Privilege of Experience. In: Gabe, J., Kelleher, D., & Williams, G. (Eds.), *Challenging Medicine.* Routledge, London.
Wynne, B. (1989) Sheep Farming After Chernobyl: A Case Study in Community Scientific Information. *Environment* 31: 10–15.

science/non-science and boundary work

Yuri Jack Gómez Morales

The problem of demarcation – how to identify the unique and essential characteristics of science that distinguish it from other intellectual activities – has been addressed both as an analytical matter mainly by philosophers and epistemologists, and as a practical matter by sociologists and historians.

The philosophical quest for demarcating science has advanced along different avenues. It has been claimed that science is recognizable by its results, by its methods, and more often by the way in which statements claimed to be scientific are evaluated. Early in the twentieth century a philosophical school of thought known as logical positivism (the Vienna Circle) advanced an answer for demarcating science: demarcating science from religion and metaphysics was mainly a matter of semantics. Only statements about empirical observations are meaningful. Verification was then espoused as a safe criterion to decide whether or not one is dealing with a scientific statement. However, although any generalization can be tested by verification, it guarantees little, since the status of such generalizations is always uncertain, in that any following observation may counter it.

Correcting verificationism, Popper's falsificationism starts by noticing that meaningfulness may not necessarily serve to demarcate science since a theory might well be meaningful without being scientific. By contrast, if the analysis starts by asserting under which conditions a theory can prove to be false (falsificationism), this serves better the quest for demarcating falsifiable scientific theories from unscientific (non-falsifiable) ones. Popper argued that scientific knowledge cannot be *proven* to be true; all that science can do is *disprove* theories. And to do so, criteria of refutation have to be laid down beforehand. Falsificationism is then an effort at producing instances which may counter a generalization. The failure to verify such instances, the failure to falsify a theory, generalization, or statement, gives credence to them as scientific. Alternatively, the failure to assess under which conditions the theory could be proved false is a clear sign of its unscientific nature.

But much that would be considered meaningful and useful in science is not necessarily falsifiable. Non-falsifiable statements have a role in scientific theories themselves, as in the case of cosmology, for example. If the acceptance or failure of scientific theories relied simply on falsification, no theory would ever survive long enough to be fruitful, as all theories contain anomalies. Besides, falsificationism does not provide a way to distinguish meaningful generalizations from meaningless ones. And more importantly, since falsificationism is based on factual propositions serving as instances to counter scientific claims, it implies a controversial observational theory. This last statement is the departure point of Lakatos's reassessment of falsificationism. The difficulties inherent in Popper's theory led Lakatos to propose a more subtle theory of falsification. His view, which he calls "sophisticated falsification" to distinguish it from Popper's, can be summarized thus: no experiment, experimental report, observational statement, or well-corroborated low-level falsifying hypothesis alone can lead to falsification. There is no falsification before the emergence of a better theory. Thus, Lakatos argued that no factual proposition can ever be proved by experiment; propositions can only be derived from other propositions, they cannot be derived from facts. Therefore, if factual propositions are unprovable then they are fallible, and if they are fallible, clashes between theories and propositions are not falsifications but merely inconsistencies. Evaluation on Lakatos's view should be practiced, then, over a series of theories "in the long run" rather than one at a time. Both falsification and verification and the idea of a scientific method are useful demarcation criteria, but only within the temporal confines of an established scientific *paradigm*. This is a familiar line of argument associated with Kuhn, who went further than Lakatos in pointing out that sophisticated falsification sidesteps the fact that numerous preliminary decisions are involved in Lakatos's criteria. In order to decide whether a theory is indeed a better theory than another, scientists must, for example, decide which statement to make "unfalsifiable by fiat" and which not. Or dealing with a probabilistic theory, they must decide on a probability threshold below which statistical evidence will be held "inconsistent" with that theory; they have to decide what is going to be called "facts," "new facts," and so on.

Both Kuhn and Feyerabend's contributions to the problem of demarcation push it forward by opening up its subjective and sociohistorical dimension. Both argued that the sorts of decisions scientists take are made in the light of shared ideological commitments within a given paradigm. The questions of truth and falsity and correct or incorrect understanding are not uniquely empirical (as the analytical approach held) and many meaningful questions surrounding the problem cannot be settled this way.

Despite the fact that at the analytical level there is no full agreement on what it is that distinguishes science from other kinds of intellectual activities, at the practical level there are many examples of temporary and localized agreements about such a distinction, achieved on a daily basis in scientific practice. From academic curricula in schools and colleges to the design of public or private organizations for the funding and management of scientific research, from ideas of science and scientific practice disseminated throughout the news and media-entertainment industries to the process of peer evaluation in specialized journals, the existence of tacit agreements on what is science accounts for practical decisions that must be taken in these various contexts: defining curricula content for a discipline, allocating resources for research, announcing a new discovery, keeping the record of science, and even to tell someone a science fiction story involves a degree of tacit agreement on what science looks like. These practical dimensions of demarcation in science are what the notion boundary work attempts to describe. Boundary work is about an *ideological* style found in scientists' attempts to create a public image for science by contrasting it favorably to other intellectual or technical activities in order to advance their interests or resolve their inner strains (Gieryn 1983).

The capacity to create convincing distinctions between science and exemplars of non-sciences or pseudo-sciences serves a variety of goals pursued by scientists for the advancement of their professional careers: acquisition of intellectual authority and career opportunities as much as the denial of these resources to others (supposedly pseudo or non-scientists), and the protection of the autonomy of scientific research from external interference.

From a boundary-work standpoint, the authority of science is a result of its successful claim to autonomy, its expansion into areas previously claimed by others, and its successful rejection of other claimants to cognitive authority. Thus, boundary work comprises at least three kinds of strategies: expansion, expulsion, and the protection of autonomy. The work of expulsion operates when scientists seek to marginalize competing claims, to distinguish between orthodox and fringe, and to keep out specific social practices (e.g., magic, alchemy, witchcraft). Expansion occurs when scientists seek to extend their claim over areas previously claimed by others (e.g., religion, folk knowledge, craft expertise). Autonomy protection occurs when scientists seek to minimize interference in their domain by politicians or managers. On these grounds, cognitive authority turns out as the result, rather than the source, of successful boundary work and the novelty that this point of view brings to the fore is the extension of this argument from particular claims to scientific knowledge to the claims-making surrounding the institution of science itself.

Because of the considerable material opportunities and professional advantages at stake, demarcating science is not merely an academic matter. Epistemologists and philosophers of science draw demarcations between types of knowledge without mentioning that these demarcations mean borderlines between people. They construct hierarchies in the realm of knowledge without making explicit the claims of domination which can be based on them. They separate "true reality" from the merely phenomenal world of sensation and fantasy as if these differentiations were given by truth itself and not expressions of a social struggle about what the decisive facts are.

Boundary work has wider applications since expansion, monopolization, and protection of autonomy are generic features of professionalization. Thus, it is not surprising that the notion is useful for describing ideological demarcations of disciplines, specialties, or theoretical orientations within science as well. Content analysis of these ideologies suggests that science is not one single thing. Characteristics attributed to science vary widely depending upon the specific intellectual or professional activity designated as non-science and the particular goals of the boundary work. The rich argumentative repertoire detected in scientific ideologies often results in inconsistency. In the public domain science is at once presented as theoretical and empirical, pure and applied, objective and subjective, exact and estimative, democratic and elitist, limitless and limited. These inconsistencies can be explained, however, when considering that scientists build boundaries according to the kind of obstacles they find in their pursuit of authority and resources. In their quest scientists may find themselves competing with each other and needing to erect boundaries that ground identical aims on different bases. By the same token, variability may result from a simultaneous pursuit of separate professional goals, each requiring a boundary to be built in a different way.

Boundary work, based as it is on relatively unstructured observation of relatively unstructured ideological activities, has been considered insufficient. Further scholarly work on this topic has focused attention on crucial and more structured activities performed by boundary workers. This is how boundary work – a notion initially formulated to explain how scientists maintain the boundaries of their community against threats to its cognitive authority – has found useful policy-relevant applications. One example is studying the strategic demarcation between political and scientific tasks in the advisory relationship between scientists and regulatory agencies. In this context, derivative notions such as boundary objects, boundary organizations, and even co-production have been advanced. Boundary objects stand between different social worlds and they can be used by individuals within each world for specific purposes without losing their own identity as members of a specific community of practice. In some cases entire organizations can serve as boundary objects, as did many of the public interest organizations created by scientists in the mid-twentieth century to facilitate political goals while protecting scientific ones (Guston 1999, 2001). Yet boundary organizations are also involved in co-production, that is, the simultaneous production of knowledge and social order. Boundary organizations co-produce society as they facilitate collaboration between scientists and nonscientists, and they create the combined scientific and social order through the generation of boundary objects (Jasanoff 1996; Bowker & Star 1999).

SEE ALSO: Expertise, "Scientification," and the Authority of Science; Ideology; Positivism; Stratification: Functional and Conflict Theories; Stratification: Technology and Ideology

REFERENCES AND SUGGESTED READINGS

Bowker, G. & Star, S. (1999) *Sorting Things Out: Classification and Its Consequences.* MIT Press, Cambridge, MA.

Gieryn, T. F. (1983) Boundary-Work and the Demarcation of Science from Non-Science: Strains and Interests in Professional Ideologies of Scientists. *American Sociological Review* 48(6): 781–95.

Gieryn, T. F. (1995) Boundaries of Science. In: Jasanoff, S., Markle, G. E., Petersen, J. C., & Pinch, T. (Eds.), *Handbook of Science and Technology Studies.* Sage, Thousand Oaks, CA, pp. 393–443.

Gieryn, T. F. (1999) *Cultural Boundaries of Science: Credibility on the Line.* University of Chicago Press, Chicago.

Guston, D. H. (1999) Stabilizing the Boundary between US Politics and Science: The Role of the Office of Technology Transfer as a Boundary Organization. *Social Studies of Science* 29(1): 87–111.

Guston, D. H. (2001) Boundary Organizations in Environmental Policy and Science: An Introduction. *Science, Technology, and Human Values* 26(4): 399–408.
Jasanoff, S. (1996) Beyond Epistemology: Relativism and Engagement in the Politics of Science. *Social Studies of Science* 26(2): 393–418.
Kuhn, T. S. (1970) *The Structure of Scientific Revolutions.* University of Chicago Press, Chicago.
Lakatos, I. (1970) The Methodology of Scientific Research Programmes. In: Lakatos, I. & Musgrave, A. (Eds.), *Criticism and the Growth of Knowledge.* Cambridge University Press, Cambridge.
Popper, K. (1959) *The Logic of Scientific Discovery.* Hutchinson, London.

science and the precautionary principle

Saul Halfon

The precautionary principle is a regulatory approach, under conditions of scientific *uncertainty*, requiring that a new chemical or technology be regulated or banned until it is proven safe. This principle was developed in opposition to the dominant regulatory standard, which requires affirmative evidence of harm before regulatory action can be taken. These two approaches designate a central conflict in environmental and food regulation, particularly related to chemical release and use of genetically modified organisms.

Precautionary approaches to regulation have existed for much of the past century. For example, the United States Food and Drug Administration works on a precautionary model for drugs and food additives. Thus, pharmaceutical companies cannot market a drug in the United States until it is explicitly approved following affirmative evidence of safety.

Precaution as an explicit principle of policymaking has more recent origins. It arose out of 1970s German environmental policy, particularly the *Vorsorgeprinzip* (foresight principle). In international regulation it was first codified in the 1984 First International Convention on Protection of the North Sea. Its most important articulation may be found in the Rio Declaration of the 1992 UN Conference on Environment and Development, which states in Principle 15 that the "lack of full scientific certainty" should not prevent environmental protection. Other influential statements on precaution can be found in the 1998 "Wingspread Statement on the Precautionary Principle" and a 2000 "Communication from the Commission of the European Communities on the Precautionary Principle." Several countries have explicitly endorsed the precautionary principle, most notably the European Union in the 1992 Treaty of Maastricht.

While naming an approach to scientific evidence, the precautionary principle is associated with a general orientation toward regulation that is directly counter to the "risk paradigm" or "sound science" approach. It is a crucial feature of what Martin Hajer calls the "ecological modernization" discourse coalition, and Joe Thornton treats it as part of the "ecological paradigm" of regulation, thus supporting a particular orientation toward scientific uncertainty, risk, expertise, proof, regulation, responsibility, public participation, and progress. As such, it is tied up with the politics of modernity and the culture wars: precaution is often favored by environmental, health, and consumer activists and advocates who support greater regulation; risk is often favored by corporations and free trade advocates who prefer minimal regulation.

Most proponents of precaution favor prevention rather than management (control and remediation) of pollution, are skeptical of scientific claims and standards in arenas of extreme complexity, respect democratic input as an important adjunct to technical knowledge, seek to regulate classes of phenomena rather than individual chemicals or products, question the assimilative capacity of the environment, prefer known to unknown risks, and would require proof of safety from the producer of a new product (often called a reversed onus of proof). They also favor Type I errors (false positives for harm) rather than Type II (false negatives).

By contrast, the risk paradigm generally takes a "command and control" approach to regulation, which focuses on defining "acceptable discharge" rates. This paradigm admits a relatively narrow set of quantifiable and measurable risks for consideration; that is, risks to human health and the environment rather than economic, cultural, or community risks. It thus supports expert-driven and technocratic modes of regulation. The refusal to regulate based on uncertain knowledge derives from a *positivist* stance toward science that buttresses their claim that this is the only "sound science" approach to regulation.

Proponents of precaution reject the "sound science"/"anti-science" designation. Neither formulation is inherently more scientific than the other, although they do understand regulatory science differently – as either positivistic or as inherently uncertain. Precautionary approaches also tend to treat science policy as a science/politics hybrid, whereas risk-based approaches appeal to the separation (purification) of science and politics into separate realms.

These paradigms are discursive packages rather than logical constructions, and as such can be reconstructed. Ongoing attempts at harmonizing these approaches seek to recombine various elements in a number of different ways. Some proponents of the precautionary principle fear that it will be coopted as it is thus separated from its historical entailments.

Both risk-based and precautionary approaches have logical extremes, which would make the policy untenable in practice. Positive proof of harm is very rare, and thus an absolutist risk perspective effectively undermines regulation. Critics of risk-based regulation claim that this is currently the case for persistent, bioaccumulative, and synergistic chemicals and those with complex or non-linear modes of action in human and environmental systems. Ecosystem theories and theories of endocrine disruption in particular raise such concerns (the endocrine disruption hypothesis posits that many synthetic chemicals have powerful hormonal effects at extremely low doses). Likewise, positive proof of safety is very difficult, suggesting that no new chemical or genetically modified organism could be approved under precaution. Proponents of strong precaution suggest that most synthetic chemicals have historically proven harmful to human health and the environment, so such an approach is warranted. Critics suggest that this approach is completely untenable and would ultimately stall all innovation, costing many more lives than it would save. Most proponents of precaution reject such extremes, suggesting instead that precaution shifts the calculus of regulation rather than providing a specific legal rule against innovation. Some suggest that precaution should be invoked only when there exists a prima facie case for the danger of a new substance and that priorities for precautionary regulation should be based on the degree of scientific uncertainty in combination with degrees of possible harm.

SEE ALSO: Genetic Engineering as a Social Problem; Global Politics; Knowledge; Positivism; Risk, Risk Society, Risk Behavior, and Social Problems; Science and Culture; Science and the Measurement of Risk; Science, Proof, and Law

REFERENCES AND SUGGESTED READINGS

Goklany, I. (2001) *The Precautionary Principle: A Critical Appraisal of Environmental Risk Assessment.* CATO Institute, Washington, DC.

Hajer, M. A. (1995) *The Politics of Environmental Discourse: Ecological Modernization and the Policy Process.* Clarendon Press, Oxford and New York.

Harremoës, P., Gee, D., Mac Garvin, M., Stirling, A., Keys, J., Wynne, B., & Vaz, S. G. (Eds.) (2002) *The Precautionary Principle in the 20th Century: Late Lessons from Early Warnings.* Earthscan, London.

Levidow, L. (2001) Precautionary Uncertainty: Regulating GM Crops in Europe. *Social Studies of Science* 31: 842–74.

Martuzzi, M. & Tickner, J. A. (Eds.) (2004) *The Precautionary Principle: Protecting Public Health, the Environment, and the Future of Our Children.* World Health Organization Europe, Copenhagen.

Raffensperger, C. & Tickner, J. (Eds.) (1999) *Protecting Public Health and the Environment: Implementing the Precautionary Principle.* Island Press, Washington, DC.

Thornton, J. (2000) *Pandora's Poison: Chlorine, Health, and a New Environmental Strategy.* MIT Press, Cambridge, MA.

science, proof, and law

Stephen K. Sanderson

Science seeks to describe, explain, and predict features of the natural and social worlds. Scientists try to develop theories or explanations of phenomena by means of producing bodies of empirical evidence that play a major role in determining whether theories are accepted, modified, or rejected. In general, scientists seek theories that are logically consistent, empirically testable, well supported by available empirical evidence (and not too severely contradicted by other available evidence), parsimonious or simple, and that continue to be a source of new ideas and lines of research. Scientists also generally seek to produce theories that yield a unified understanding of the phenomena they study. For example, Wilson (1998) talks of *consilience*, and some physical scientists claim they are moving very close to a "theory of everything" (Barrow 2001).

In the early decades of the twentieth century the Vienna Circle of logical positivists insisted that science consisted only of those propositions which could be verified by facts drawn from experience. However, Popper (1959) responded by arguing that theories could never be verified because a scientist can never possess all of the possible facts bearing on a theory. Popper's solution to this problem was that the scientist had to proceed in a sort of reverse manner, by trying to *falsify* rather than verify a theory. In fact, for Popper, whether a theory was falsifiable or not was the line of demarcation between science and nonscience: science consists of falsifiable statements, and theories are retained so long as they survive these falsifying tests.

Popper recognized that a theory could rarely be falsified by a single disconfirming instance. There are degrees of falsification. In this regard, he spoke of the *corroboration* of theories. Theories are corroborated by being submitted to the most, and the most severe, falsifying efforts possible, and by withstanding them. But corroboration is not "truth." It simply means that a theory is provisionally accepted pending further testing. Better theories are those that are logically stronger, that contain greater empirical content, that have greater explanatory and predictive capabilities, and that have been more severely tested. Any newly proposed theory should also be independently testable, have new and testable consequences, and must predict the existence of phenomena thus far unobserved. And, in the end, Popper admits *verification* back in, because he contends that, just as science would stagnate if it fails to produce refutations, it would also stagnate if new theories failed to produce verifications (i.e., supportive evidence).

Popper's philosophical model is not without its problems, yet his notion that no theory can ever really be "proved true" stands, as does his notion that statements that are unfalsifiable are not to be regarded as scientific. For Popper, science was perhaps the only epistemic activity in which errors can be identified and corrected over time (Harris 1979: 27). This is what allows science to progress toward greater *verisimilitude*, or increasingly accurate approximations to the truth.

Lakatos (1970) argued that Popper's falsificationism was highly inconsistent with actual scientific practice and that it was so strict that it would make scientific advance impossible. Literally applied, Popper's falsificationism would bring science to a halt because virtually every scientific theory that has ever been proposed has *anomalies*, or facts that are inconsistent with it. Indeed, Lakatos contended that every theory is born in an "ocean of anomalies," and that scientists often retain theories for decades or even longer even though they know there are many inconsistencies.

However, Lakatos's critique applies largely only to the very early Popper, who was a *naïve falsificationist*. Later, Popper became more nuanced in adopting a far less restrictive, or *sophisticated*, falsificationism in admitting degrees of falsification (or corroboration). Lakatos regarded sophisticated falsificationism as an improvement on naïve falsificationism, but thought it was still limited in the sense of conceiving of scientific testing as simply a comparison between a single theory and a body of evidence. What is needed is a three-way comparison in which one not only compares a theory to evidence, but at the same time judges it *with respect to its main rivals*.

Moreover, Lakatos argued, it is not really theories that scientists test, but series of theories or research programs. Even if individual theories end up being decisively refuted, the research programs of which they are a part can still stand. Lakatos then went on to identify what he called theoretically progressive problem shifts. These are research programs that can explain everything their rivals explain, and at least some additional content. They can make novel predictions not made by their rivals. Lakatos's own philosophical model of science he called the methodology of scientific research programs. Every research program contains a *negative heuristic* or "hard core" of fundamental assumptions or principles, around which scientists build a "protective belt" of auxiliary hypotheses. And it is the auxiliary hypotheses, rather than the hard core, that is subjected to empirical test.

There is also a *positive heuristic*, which consists of suggestions, hints, and insights that help the scientist to modify the protective belt in order to save the irrefutable hard core, and it is this positive heuristic that "saves the scientist from being confused by the ocean of anomalies" (Lakatos 1970: 135). The anomalies are acknowledged but temporarily shoved aside in hopes that they will eventually be shown to be explainable in the basic terms of the research program. Progress in science, for Lakatos, is therefore a matter of theoretically progressive research programs. However, progressive programs seldom last forever. They often become theoretically degenerating research programs, or programs in which too many (or too severe) anomalies accumulate that can no longer be explained away. Such a research program will then give way to one or more rivals that are theoretically progressive.

Following somewhat in the Lakatosian tradition is Laudan (1977), who agrees that science is a matter of evaluating research programs, and also that one can only evaluate them comparatively. However, Laudan points out that scientists do not consider only empirical evidence when evaluating theories. They also use conceptual problems, which may play at least as large a role in scientists' acceptance or rejection of theories as empirical evidence. Moreover, scientists are rational to consider such conceptual problems if they have been a reliable guide to past knowledge. Conceptual problems are problems that arise from either the internal inconsistencies or ambiguities of a theory, or from conflicts between a theory and another theory (or nonscientific doctrine) that is thought to be well founded.

One type of conceptual problem is methodological disputes. For example, Laudan avers that much of the opposition to psychoanalysis and psychological behaviorism turned on methodological concerns, and many of the arguments over quantum mechanics also involved methodological questions. Another type of conceptual problem is worldviews, which are moral, theological, or ideological stances. Examples abound. After Darwin published *Origin of Species* in 1859, biologists fairly rapidly came to accept the reality of evolution, but there was great resistance to the mechanism he proposed to explain how evolution occurred – natural selection. This was because natural selection eliminated the concept of purpose, to which scientists were deeply attached as a worldview. It was only after about 1930 that an empirical foundation was developed that was capable of convincing scientists to abandon their entrenched concept of purpose and accept natural selection. Worldviews play a particularly crucial role in the acceptance or rejection of theories in the social sciences. For example, there has been great resistance to sociobiology, especially among sociologists, because it clashes with the entrenched Durkheimian worldview – "explain social facts only by relating them to other social facts" – and is seen as a threat to the discipline's identity. Sociobiology has also been resisted because it is widely viewed as promoting a conservative view of society, which clashes with sociologists' strong left-leaning political views.

An important difference between Laudan on the one hand and Popper and Lakatos on the other concerns the debate over realism and antirealism. For Popper and Lakatos, who were scientific realists, science is truth-seeking and is progressive in the sense of producing cumulative knowledge. Laudan, however, advocates antirealism, which means that, as Kuhn (1962) famously argued, science only solves puzzles or problems. Laudan emphasizes that in scientific change there is genuine progress (something Kuhn denied), but this change is not cumulative because new theories (or research traditions) cannot explain all of the phenomena explained by their predecessors. There are losses as well as gains when new research programs replace old ones.

In the 1970s there emerged a whole subfield of sociology, the sociology of scientific knowledge (SSK), which has grown and expanded by leaps and bounds. (For citations to the very large literature, see Laudan 1996: 183–209;

Kincaid 1996: 37–43; and several essays in Segerstrale 2000). Although its proponents vary in the degree to which they hold it, the essential premise is that the content of scientific knowledge is influenced much more by social and cultural factors than by canons of scientific rationality. This is one of the legacies of Kuhn. In addition to his argument that science is a problem-solving rather than a truth-seeking activity, Kuhn also contended that scientists operate within paradigms that are regularly overthrown by the advocates of rival paradigms, and that scientific progress only occurs *within* paradigms, not *between* them. Kuhn often spoke as if commitment to a paradigm is more a matter of group psychology or sociology rather than the rational weighing of evidence, and that paradigmatic change is much like a type of Gestalt switch. Many philosophers of science regard Kuhn's views as highly problematic because of what they see as their subjectivism and relativism.

More recently, science has come in for enormous criticism at the hands of postmodernists and other "antiscientists," who regard science as undeserving of its epistemically privileged position and as just one way of knowing among others. This is one of the legacies of the "epistemological anarchism" of Feyerabend (1975), whose views were considerably more radical than Kuhn's. For Feyerabend, all modes of knowledge are essentially on the same plane, whether science or witchcraft, and thus his basic methodological rule was that there should be no methodological rules – "anything goes." The postmodern attack on science has emphasized its alleged "Eurocentrism" and claimed that commitment to science as a superior epistemology is rooted in western cultural values rather than objective criteria (since, for postmodernism, there can be no such criteria). (For excellent summaries and commentaries, see Segerstrale 2000.) Those philosophers and sociologists who see science as a mere social construction seem to be engaged in a completely self-refuting argument, since they do not "think *their own work* is only a social construction with no claim on evidence and truth as traditionally understood" (Kincaid 1996: 41).

Sociology is a very immature science, and most sociologists have an impoverished understanding of real science. For example, the majority of sociologists study only one society (usually their own) and no general theories can be built on the basis of one case. (It would be like trying to build biological science by studying only penguins.) Many sociologists resolve the acrimonious debates among rival theoretical camps by settling for an eclectic position, but eclecticism as it is understood by sociologists is a strategy rarely if ever favored by natural scientists. Eclecticism violates the principle of parsimonious and highly unified explanation – one of the most fundamental of all scientific goals – and it makes the comparative evaluation of theories impossible (Sanderson 1987). Many sociologists who do highly quantitative survey research build unwieldy models that contain a large number of variables, but real science does not work that way. What results is a kind of "multivariate chaos" that is the antithesis of parsimonious explanation.

Sociology today lacks a highly cumulative body of knowledge, and there is very little agreement on key epistemological, methodological, and theoretical questions. Conceptual problems are particularly acute in sociology, especially in the form of political ideology and its role in settling theoretical debates. From the standpoint of the enormous successes of the natural sciences, sociology is an extremely immature discipline in terrible disarray. At the most general theoretical level, the vast majority of sociologists continue to adhere to the standard social science model, which assumes that human behavior is overwhelmingly determined by the social environment. However, this is a massively degenerating research program, for the accumulated anomalies are extreme. Sociologists cling to it for conceptual, not empirical, reasons.

Although the overall picture in sociology and social science more generally is not an impressive one, the social sciences do have some genuine research programs that may be regarded as at least mildly to moderately progressive. In anthropology, there is the cultural materialism of Harris (1979), which is coherent and unified and has made some impressive accomplishments. In psychology, anthropology, and to some extent sociology, there is a very coherent research program that now goes under the name of evolutionary psychology (Barkow et al. 1992; Crawford & Krebs 1998). Thus far it has proven to be a highly progressive research program.

A closely related research program in anthropology is evolutionary ecology (Smith & Winterhalder 1992). And in sociology a good example of a coherent research program is rational choice theory. This program has been attached to the study of early modern and modern states (Kiser et al. 1995), to the study of human sexuality (Posner 1992), and to numerous other substantive areas. There are also dependency and world-system approaches to economic development, which have the merit of being research programs that have been subjected to extensive empirical testing, even though, unfortunately, the anomalies have become severe and in many ways these approaches are now degenerating programs (Sanderson 2005a). There is also the state-centered approach to revolutions (Wickham-Crowley 1992; Goldstone 1991; cf. Sanderson 2005b), which is something like a research program and seems to be a highly progressive one.

So the situation is by no means totally bleak. Natural scientists do not really need to study the history and philosophy of science, and few do. Indeed, scientists are often highly antagonistic toward philosophy of science. The reason natural scientists do not need philosophy of science is that they have a keen sense of what they are doing, and they generally do it extremely well. Social scientists, by contrast, very badly need to study the history and philosophy of science because they need to gain a much better understanding of how real science actually works and try to emulate it.

One major barrier to success in social science is the complexity and relative unpredictability of the phenomena being studied. The other major barrier is conceptual, and mainly ideological. Ideology is an enormous barrier to scientific objectivity, and indeed to the very practice of science at all. Sociologists and other social scientists can do nothing to alter the nature of the phenomena they study, but they are entirely free to embark along the path of objective social science if they choose to recommit themselves to doing so.

It should be clear that proof is not really possible in science, if by proof we mean "establishment with certainty." It has long been noted by philosophers of science of many stripes that theories will always be "underdetermined" by empirical evidence. (This is the famous Duhem-Quine underdetermination thesis, which has often been used by postmodernists and other relativists to attack science. However, such conclusions are complete non sequiturs.) There is only disproof or, lacking that, provisional acceptance. Proof must be restricted to the domains of logic and mathematics. As for laws, these certainly exist in the physical sciences and to some extent in the biological sciences, but they rarely exist in the social sciences. Social scientists still have enough work to do to bring themselves up to minimal scientific standards. The development of widely agreed upon laws of social behavior, organization, and change are far off into the future.

SEE ALSO: Fact, Theory, and Hypothesis: Including the History of the Scientific Fact; Falsification; Induction and Observation in Science; Kuhn, Thomas and Scientific Paradigms; Paradigms; Science and the Precautionary Principle; Science, Social Construction of; Scientific Knowledge, Sociology of

REFERENCES AND SUGGESTED READINGS

Barkow, J. H., Cosmides, L., & Tooby, J. (Eds.) (1992) *The Adapted Mind.* Oxford University Press, New York.

Barrow, J. D. (2001) *Theories of Everything.* Oxford University Press, New York.

Crawford, C. & Krebs, D. L. (Eds.) (1998) *Handbook of Evolutionary Psychology.* Lawrence Erlbaum, Mahwah, NJ.

Feyerabend, P. (1975) *Against Method.* Verso, London.

Goldstone, J. A. (1991) *Revolution and Rebellion in the Early Modern World.* University of California Press, Berkeley.

Harris, M. (1979) *Cultural Materialism.* Random House, New York.

Kincaid, H. (1996) *Philosophical Foundations of the Social Sciences.* Cambridge University Press, New York.

Kiser, E., Drass, K. A., & Brustein, W. (1995) Ruler Autonomy and War in Early Modern Europe. *International Studies Quarterly* 39: 109–38.

Kuhn, T. S. (1962) *The Structure of Scientific Revolutions.* University of Chicago Press, Chicago.

Lakatos, I. (1970) Falsification and the Methodology of Scientific Research Programmes. In: Lakatos, I. & Musgrave, A. (Eds.), *Criticism and the Growth of Knowledge.* Cambridge University Press, Cambridge.

Laudan, L. (1977) *Progress and Its Problems: Towards a Theory of Scientific Growth*. University of California Press, Berkeley.
Laudan, L. (1996) *Beyond Positivism and Relativism*. Westview Press, Boulder.
Popper, K. R. (1959) *The Logic of Scientific Discovery*. Basic Books, New York.
Posner, R. A. (1992) *Sex and Reason*. Harvard University Press, Cambridge, MA.
Sanderson, S. K. (1987) Eclecticism and Its Alternatives. *Current Perspectives in Social Theory* 8: 313–45.
Sanderson, S. K. (2005a) World-Systems Analysis After Thirty Years: Should it Rest in Peace? *International Journal of Comparative Sociology*, 46: 179–213.
Sanderson, S. K. (2005b) *Revolutions*. Paradigm Publishers, Boulder.
Segerstrale, U. (Ed.) (2000) *Beyond the Science Wars*. State University of New York Press, Albany.
Smith, E. A. & Winterhalder, B. (Eds.) (1992) *Evolutionary Ecology and Human Behavior*. Aldine de Gruyter, New York.
Wickham-Crowley, T. (1992) *Guerrillas and Revolution in Latin America*. Princeton University Press, Princeton.
Wilson, E. O. (1998) *Consilience*. Random House, New York.

science and public participation: the democratization of science

John Forrester

Thomas Jefferson, quoted in Fischer's *Citizens, Experts, and the Environment* (2001), said that wherever the people are well informed, they can be trusted with their own government. But, nowadays, who can claim to be well informed enough about science to govern it except the scientists themselves? In 1959, Sir Charles Snow put forward the thesis in the Rede Lecture that there was what amounted to an opposition between literary intellectualism at one end, and proficiency in the physical sciences at the other. Snow dated his realization of this distinction to the 1930s. What we can say for certain is that there was a coming into common understanding that a reasonably well-educated or cultured person could not, now, be expected to be normally able to comprehend both the sciences and the arts. This state of affairs is not by any means all the scientific community's fault, although science is guilty of creating, along with other forms of knowledge and understanding, elites. Elitism fosters disciplinization and subdisciplinization, and has given rise to mistrust and lack of understanding between the members of different disciplines and of science and scientists in general. The term "lay" was commonly used until the 1990s to describe those untutored in science, thus emphasizing the idea of a scientific priesthood or elite. For various reasons not dealt with here, this state of affairs is seen as being iniquitous, and so public participation in science, also known as public engagement in science, is seen as a means whereby that balance can be redressed.

This broad generalization of why science "needs" to be democratized hides several distinct rationales as to why the public should engage with science or vice versa. Before dealing with these rationales, there is one distinction that needs to be introduced: who or what "the public" or "publics" are engaging in or with. In many "western-style" democracies, members of the public are engaging and being engaged in the governance of science, but not in knowledge creation itself. In contrast, in some continental European countries and in a few developing countries, citizen participation in science is seeing citizens more as co-creators of new knowledge alongside traditional experts, new knowledge that is both "reliable" (after Gibbons 1999 – i.e., knowledge that is scientifically correct) and also "socially robust" (i.e., that overcomes the elitism of traditionally generated scientific knowledge). These two major dimensions to public engagement may be distinguished as public engagement *with* science on the one hand, and public engagement *in* science on the other. Stirling (2005) characterizes the first more exactly as "participation in the social appraisal of science and technology," while the other is also about knowledge production, as is illustrated by the title of the book *The New Production of Knowledge* published in 1994 by an international team of scholars including

Michael Gibbons and Peter Scott from the UK, Camille Limoges, Simon Schwartzmann, and Martin Trow from the Americas, and Helga Nowotny from continental Europe.

Since the end of World War II, there has been an almost logarithmic increase in the number of initiatives to open up new spaces for science and the public to interact. In 1985 in the UK, the Bodmer Report (see Miller 2001 for a fuller history) introduced the phrase "the Public Understanding of Science" (PUS) into the English language and also the idea that the public suffered from a deficit of knowledge about science. This thesis – that if only the public knew more about science and how it worked then they would be happier to allow science more funding, more control over science to scientists, and so on – can be seen to fit firmly into the dimension of public engagement with science. In the US during this period, science and scientists were engaged in a much more polarized debate sometimes referred to as the Science Wars (see Rose 1997), where the scientific elite defended itself against all critiques which it characterized as "anti-science." The Sociology of Scientific Knowledge (SSK) often found itself on the receiving end of attacks and rebuttals, particularly for its social constructionist stance. Yet, in the US, the American Association for the Advancement of Science (AAAS) has, over the years, had little more effect in generating public engagement in or with science than has its UK counterpart(s): the Royal Society, the Royal Institution, and the British Association for the Advancement of Science, who jointly formed the Committee on the Public Understanding of Science (CoPUS) after the Bodmer Report. The deficit model informed much of the early work of CoPUS and the AAAS. The deficit model, and projects based upon it, proved powerless to assist in improving science literacy.

SSK really did not engage with PUS as the former's social constructionist thesis suggested that increasing scientific literacy was not going to serve any useful purpose except to science itself. UK SSK practitioners (see Irwin & Wynne 1996 for one collection of their works) were suggesting that science needed to be, at the very least, studied in context. Still using the terminology of elites, they made the argument that "lay knowledge" should be considered alongside expert knowledge as epistemologically different but no less valid. The deficit model was moribund. However, the application of social constructionist ideas needs to be handled carefully, as while the governance and application of science – what Stirling called science's "social appraisal" – is clearly open to public engagement and participation, the inclusion of the public's (and publics') knowledge in the creation of "new knowledge" is still a largely uncharted territory. Nonetheless, we have now moved from PUS to PEST (Public Engagement with Science and Technology), and PEST seems to be able to attract the interest of SSK practitioners and scientists alike. The UK Economic and Social Research Council has its *Science in Society* program, as does the Royal Society, CoPUS is to be reformed and renamed, and the influential House of Lords Select Committee on Science and Technology Third Report (2000) was entitled *Science and Society*. With the change from PUS to PEST, the mood has changed from edification to dialogue. Science is now expected to seek to democratize itself through engagement. The form that this engagement takes is still largely undecided.

In the last decade, many rationales have emerged for encouraging public participation, particularly with environmental policymaking spurs such as global climate change and, in particular, sustainable development (see Forrester 1999). Some have adopted the pragmatic argument that public involvement will assist with the effective implementation of policy; when members of the public are consulted and engaged with, they are more likely to lend their support to (or, at least, not oppose) science-based policy measures. Others have argued that in democratic societies, people simply have a right to a participatory role. Further, the argument has been made that people may have access to knowledge that is unknown to experts; local people may themselves count as experts about their own localities. Such participative initiatives have been further spurred and legitimated by the participatory emphasis within Local Agenda 21. This was important in that it encouraged people to participate in the issues affecting their localities. Stirling (2005) has characterized these three rationales as:

- Normative democratic – in other words, the motive is the engagement. It is simply people's democratic right to be involved in decision-making in society and in an increasingly technocratic society this involves increased involvement in science policy.
- Instrumental – this rationale is different in that it has a purpose related to an output or outcome. Citizens are engaged in order to change their behavior, or to inform the creation of new knowledge. PUS was clearly instrumental.
- Substantive – this is the most complex in that this rationale almost subsumes the other two, but at its most naïve it can be described that substantive engagement leads to a "better" decision. In can be argued that the move toward PEST sets the scene for substantive engagement to occur.

There will remain times when the public will be engaged "only" in the governance of science; engaged in making decisions about science funding, research priorities, and so on. There will also be times when what is required is engagement in the creation of new knowledge. The major methodological issues with science governance include: redefining the "norms" of science (after Merton's 1973 *The Sociology of Science*), deciding on the funding of science, the transparency of decision-making within the governance of science and science research, and also the application of scientific knowledge (see Ziman 1996). Thus, this level of engagement concentrates upon science itself, its outworkings in the policy sphere. The major methodological concepts or issues involved in public engagement in the creation of [new] knowledge are to do with the nature of that knowledge itself – what the concept's authors call "mode-2 knowledge production" (Nowotny et al. 2001) – and where and how the conditions necessary for the growth of a "socially distributed expertise" (ibid.) may be fostered.

As science becomes increasingly answerable to a range of publics including both funders and users, sociology has begun to suggest that "new spaces" are needed to fulfill a new contractual arrangement between science and its primary constituency, society. Policymakers (see House of Lords *Science and Society* referred to above) warn against creating new institutions to provide these spaces, instead emphasizing the need for trust and transparency in existing institutions. The focus, however, is on the need for transparency and trust; science still needs to reestablish relations of trust between science practitioners and members of different publics. One area where this is particularly critical is where science is deemed to suffer from a lack of certainty. The idea that under certain conditions of uncertainty (to wit, "post-normal" science) there should be extended peer review was one put forward by Silvio Funtowicz and Jerry Ravetz in a series of papers (see Yearley et al. 2001 for a fuller exposition). They sought to develop a theoretical framework for understanding on what grounds and under what conditions the public should be involved. Put simply, they said that where the scientists had no firm evidence on what to base a decision, then the non-scientist's view was just as valid, but they also made the point that where there were high "decision stakes" – in other words, when the outcome of the decision might impact upon a large number of people – then under those conditions the public too should have a voice. This framework was particularly influential in the 1990s. It has fed into the underlying PEST principle that science itself should no longer be controlled by a restricted corps of insiders.

One attempt to produce "mode-2 knowledge" was made by an interdisciplinary team of researchers from the UK (see Yearley et al. 2003) using a form of participatory mapping (see Cinderby & Forrester 2005): the idea was to create a common understanding as a basis to bring together the technological assessment or "evidence-based knowledge" about local air quality with the experience and concerns of local stakeholders and residents. In the City of York (UK), local authority officers were sufficiently impressed with the technique that they supported the running of mapping groups to generate maps of local perceptions of problem areas (of air quality). A political decision was made to use these maps rather than those based on technical assessment alone in the designation of the city's air quality management area. Thus, it can be argued that the "new" knowledge superseded the technical assessment, but there is little evidence for this experience in York being replicated elsewhere in the UK, even in this area of air quality, a "common good" where technical and "lay" understandings are so close. Thus it may be argued that, for the moment, the democratization of science is actually the democratization of the use – and governance – of science with little associated democratization of expertise.

SEE ALSO: Expertise, "Scientification," and the Authority of Science; Peer Review and Quality Control in Science; Realism and Relativism: Truth and Objectivity; Science and the Measurement of Risk; Science and the Precautionary Principle; Science, Social Construction of; Scientific Knowledge, Sociology of; Scientific Literacy and Public Understandings of Science; Social Movements, Participatory Democracy in

REFERENCES AND SUGGESTED READINGS

Cinderby, S. & Forrester, J. (2005) Facilitating the Local Governance of Air Pollution using GIS for Participation. *Applied Geography* 25: 143–58.

Forrester, J. (1999) The Logistics of Public Participation in Environmental Assessment. *International Journal of Environment and Pollution* 11: 316–30.

Gibbons, M. (1999) Science's New Social Contract With Society. *Nature* 402 (Suppl.): C81–4.

Irwin, A. & Wynne, B. (Eds.) (1996) *Misunderstanding Science? The Public Reconstruction of Science and Technology.* Cambridge University Press, Cambridge.

Miller, S. (2001) Public Understanding of Science at the Crossroads. *Public Understanding of Science* 10: 115–20.

Nowotny, H., Scott, P., & Gibbons, M. (2001) *Rethinking Science: Knowledge and the Public in an Age of Uncertainty.* Polity Press, Cambridge.

Rose, H. (1997) Science Wars: My Enemy's Enemy is – Only Perhaps – My Friend. In: Levinson, R. & Thomas, J. (Eds.), *Science Today: Problem or Crisis?* Routledge, London and New York, pp. 51–64.

Stirling, A. (2005) Opening Up or Closing Down? Analysis, Participation, and Power in the Social Appraisal of Science and Technology. In: Leach, M., Scoones, I., & Wynne, B. (Eds.), *Science and Citizens: Globalization and the Challenge of Engagement.* Zed Books, London and New York, pp. 218–31.

Yearley, S., Forrester, J., & Bailey, P. (2001) Participation and Expert Knowledge: A Case Study Analysis of Scientific Models and their Publics. In: Hisschemöller, M., Hoppe, R., Dunn, W. N., & Ravetz, J. R. (Eds.), *Knowledge, Power, and Participation in Environmental Policy Analysis.* Policy Studies Review Annual, Vol. 12. Transaction, New Brunswick and London, pp. 349–70.

Yearley, S., Cinderby, S., Forrester, J., Bailey, P., & Rosen, P. (2003) Participatory Modelling and the Local Governance of the Politics of UK Air Pollution: A Three-City Case Study. *Environmental Values* 12: 247–62.

Ziman, J. (1996) Is Science Losing its Objectivity? *Nature* 382: 751–4.

science and religion

Steve Bruce

It is commonly held that the declining power and popularity of religion that we see in almost all modern industrial societies owes much to the rise of science; science and religion are competitors in a zero-sum game, with the former being vastly more persuasive.

As US sociologist Robert Merton pointed out, many of the pioneering natural scientists in the seventeenth century (e.g., Robert Boyle) were pious men who saw their work as demonstrating the glory of God's creation. Yet science has challenged what were once taken-for-granted elements of theistic belief systems (such as the idea that the earth was the center of creation and that God created the variety of life forms). In 1633 the Catholic Church tried, condemned, and imprisoned Galileo for continuing to promote the Copernican view that the earth moved around the sun after he had been instructed to desist. In the nineteenth century, leaders of the Church of England tried to refute the evolutionary theories of Charles Darwin and his followers. In the contemporary United States, conservative Protestants try to use the courts to force schools to give equal time to "creation science" as an alternative to naturalistic evolution.

This zero-sum game view of the relationship between science and religion is largely misleading as an explanation of change. That many highly educated people whose standard of living depends very directly on natural science can continue to hold traditional supernaturalistic beliefs shows us that there are a number of ways in which the disconfirming effect of science can be deflected. One successful way of responding is to rewrite theistic religious beliefs so that they accommodate new knowledge. In the second half of the nineteenth century, the mainstream Christian churches reconstructed their belief systems: heaven and hell were changed from being external realities to being psychological states. Heaven became a sense of contentment; hell became alienation, loneliness, and so on. Miracles were explained away. For example, events described in the Bible as miraculous (such as Noah's flood or the parting of the Red Sea) were taken to be misunderstandings of natural phenomena. Faith healing was explained not as divine intervention but as the workings of a placebo effect. By such trimming an omnipotent deity was preserved, not as an alternative to the causes of phenomena discovered by scientific explanation but as the author of the complex processes which natural science was discovering.

An alternative to rewriting the faith is to turn science against itself. Those who wish to continue to believe in divine creation, for example, can cite the Popperian view of the logic of scientific discovery to the effect that the findings of science are only ever hypothetical. In natural science properly understood, nothing is ever firmly proved to be the case. The cautious claim that our current state of knowledge is only the best we have at this point in time is, judo-like, used to throw any scientific proposition that threatens religion.

More generally, the idea that scientific discoveries undermined religion requires that believers were aware of the conflict and of the weight of evidence behind the problematic findings. That may not often have been the case. Even in those societies with extensive compulsory schooling, very many people have little or no understanding of physics, chemistry, or medical science. For example, very many consumers of alternative medical therapies are unaware that they are implicitly subscribing to models of causation for which the best science offers no empirical support. It is difficult to see how homeopathy, with its central idea that a chemical agent can be so watered down that no trace of it can be detected and yet retain the ability to stimulate in the body a curative response, can be sustained within conventional notions of causation. Yet some trained medical scientists use homeopathy and many patients seem satisfied that such cures are legitimately "scientific."

What this suggests is that while the battle between specific findings of natural scientific and religious ideas engaged the experts on each side, it probably played little part in the long-term decline of religion. Too many people are simply unaware of the ideological clashes or were insulated by the sorts of rhetorical strategies listed above. To explain secularization, we must identify the social changes associated with industrialization that weakened the ability of ideological communities to reproduce themselves; the rise of individual freedom and the increase in social and cultural diversity are much more powerful agents of change than any particular naturalistic idea.

But science does threaten religion in two rather subtle ways: it alters our images of the world and our images of ourselves. Religions assume that there is a supernatural realm: a world beyond the material. Although most modern scientists are careful not to stray beyond their competence and hence do not directly challenge such beliefs, the general assumption of the scientific community (and of the wider culture informed by it) is that the material world is to be understood in its own terms and that those terms are wide enough to encompass most of what interests us. For example, natural disasters are just that; they are not divine interventions. Personality defects are the result of biological or psychological, rather than spiritual, problems.

Science has also given us unprecedented technological power, which has two sorts of effects on religion. Firstly, the occasions for resort to religion have been much reduced. In pre-industrial societies, appeal to God or the gods often provided the only response to uncertainty and risk. Without accurate weather forecasting and self-righting boats, the best a fishing community could do to ensure the safe return of its crews was to pray and to placate a possibly wrathful God. When effective solutions to problems are devised, it is possible to continue in the old ways – to suppose that the chemical that will kill worms in sheep only works if we pray before we administer the dose – but it soon becomes apparent that the worm dose works as well for the ungodly as for the godly. In 1349, when the Black Death ravaged England, the national church instituted weeks of special prayers and fasting. When AIDS (at first dubbed the "gay plague") appeared in Britain in the early 1980s, the Church of England's response was to call for the government to invest more money in scientific research. And the second response was more successful than the first: systematic research provided first the explanation for AIDS, and then the technology that allowed HIV-positive people to live relatively normal lives. The rise of effective technologies reduces God from being omnipotent to being the much lesser "God of the gaps." Gradually, the number and range of occasions on which people resort to religious activities to solve problems are reduced and the authority of the churches is correspondingly reduced. Religious authorities can no longer claim to validate all knowledge and are left with the much reduced role of safeguarding religious doctrine and trying to maintain control over sociomoral issues.

Technology has also produced a fundamental change in human self-images. It is characteristic of most religions that they present humankind as tiny and powerless in the face of divine providence. Like the tormented Job of the Old Testament, people are expected to put up with whatever God or the gods inflict on them and hope that their obedience will eventually be rewarded, in some future life if not in this one. Although there is an obvious dark side to technology, it has made us considerably more powerful than we have ever been before. Instead of having to work within the natural world, we can hope to dominate it. A people that can extract oil from the depths of the North Sea and use it to vastly increase the comfort and lengths of our lives is a people of power and significance. Right or wrong, and for good or ill, we differ from our ancestors of the pre-industrial world in being able to imagine ourselves masters of our fate.

SEE ALSO: Diversity; Individualism; Industrialization; Religion; Science; Science and Culture; Secularization; Technology, Science, and Culture

REFERENCES AND SUGGESTED READINGS

Bruce, S. (2004) *God is Dead: Secularization in the West*. Blackwell, Oxford.

Carlson, R. F. (2000) *Science and Christianity: Four Views*. InterVarsity Press, Downers Grove, IL.

Cox, H. (1968) The Christian in a World of Technology. In: Barbour, I. G. (Ed.), *Science and Religion: New Perspectives on the Dialogue*. SCM Press, London, pp. 21–80.

Merton, R. K. (1970) *Science, Technology, and Society in the 17th Century*. Fettig, New York.

Polkinghorne, J. (2003) *Belief in God in an Age of Science*. Yale University Press, New Haven.

science, social construction of

Lena Eriksson

In its simplest form, the claim that science is socially constructed means that there is no direct link between nature and our ideas about nature – the products of science are not themselves natural. This claim can be taken to mean different things and a distinction is often made between strong and weak interpretations of social constructivism. The stronger claim would not recognize an independent reality or materiality outside of our perceptions of it, or at least dismiss it as of no relevance as we cannot access it. This stance is, however, not a very common one. A weaker social constructivism tends to leave ontological queries to one side and instead focus on epistemological matters – how we gain knowledge about the world. What we count as knowledge is dependent on, and shaped by, the contexts in which it is created. Knowledge is thus made by people drawing on available cultural material, not preexisting facts in a world outside of human action, waiting to be uncovered.

The philosopher Ian Hacking has discussed and criticized different uses of the concept social construction. Hacking (1999) takes apart and analyzes the many and varying meanings of social construction. According to Hacking, the concept is routinely used in a way that makes it devoid of meaning. "The phrase has become code. If you use it favorably, you deem yourself rather radical. If you trash the phrase, you declare that you are rational, reasonable, and respectable" (p. vii). Furthermore, the concept often comes with an inbuilt value judgment that implies that things should ideally be constructed differently.

When teasing out different meanings that different authors have given to social construction, Hacking found three main types: contingency, nominalism, and external reasons for stability (Sismondo 2004). The first kind of social constructivism essentially comes to mean that things could have been different – there was nothing inevitable about the current state of affairs and it was not determined by the nature of things. The second kind of social constructivism focuses on the politics of categories and points to how classifications are always human impositions rather than natural kinds. The third kind of social constructivism points to how stability and success in scientific theories are due to external, rather than evidential, reasons.

Whereas the idea of science and scientific knowledge as socially constructed can be traced to many a scholar, the very concept of social construction was introduced into mainstream social sciences by Peter L. Berger and Thomas Luckmann in their influential book *The Social Construction of Reality. A Treatise in the Sociology of Knowledge* (1966). In it, the authors combine ideas from Durkheim and Weber with perspectives from George Herbert Mead, to form a theory of social action. This theory would not only deal with plurality of knowledge and reality – for example what counts as knowledge in Borneo may make little sense in Bath and vice versa – but also study the ways in which realities are taken as known in human society. How is it that a concept such as gender is taken to be "natural" and "real" in every culture, while at the same time it is perceived and performed very differently in different cultures? Knowledge about the society in which we live is "a realization in the double sense of the word, in the sense of apprehending objectivated social reality, and in the sense of ongoingly producing this reality." An objectivated social reality is a reality that is not "private" to the person who produced it, but accessed and shared by others. As humans we are continuously creating and recreating reality, and the role of the sociologist is to analyze the process of how reality is constructed, that is, how knowledge becomes institutionally established as real.

One way of understanding science as socially constructed is to point to obvious and "external" social factors, such as funding structures or political influences. These affect the way in which science develops; business interests can determine which projects are pursued, policy decisions can effectively close down entire avenues of research, and so on. The way in which research is institutionally organized is another much-cited example of "external" social shaping of science – for example how heavy bureaucracy and strict disciplinary boundaries render the pursuit of trans-disciplinary science difficult. Another variety of this brand of social constructivism is the argument that only scientific knowledge deemed to be "relevant" or interesting will be pursued. Social theorists such as Helen Longino and Evelyn Fox-Keller have pointed to how male dominance in society in general, and in the scientific profession in particular, has resulted in certain kinds of scientific knowledge. The definition of scientific problems and framing of hypotheses come with an inbuilt gender bias. Male contraception is an under-researched area because reproductive responsibilities are firmly placed with women in our society and it is thus assumed that it is the female body that is to be manipulated. Such social values are also reflected in the very methods that scientists will use – most human trials of medicines are performed on young men between 18 and 20 years of age. The generic "human" is thus a young man, whereas elderly women are the more likely consumers of the medicines that are being trialled.

Theorists such as Sandra Harding have argued that certain social positions – such as gender, race, or class – will render particular epistemological perspectives. A science conducted and shaped by black women would not contain the same knowledge as a science created by white men. What we call the collective body of knowledge in our society is really the knowledge of a dominant group – in this case men. This is not only due to "female" questions falling outside the framework of what is perceived to be "real science," but because our entire view of knowledge is a (male) ideological construct. A Cartesian dualism such as body/mind is a construction built on the male experience of nature and culture as separate entities, as men tend to be free to engage in intellectual activity without having to take responsibility for their own or others' bodies. The precondition for this male focus on matters intellectual is that women take care of the shopping, cooking, childrearing, laundry, cleaning, and other tasks that subsequently are not included in men's abstract conceptualizations of reality.

Other prominent feminist thinkers, notably Donna Haraway, instead view (scientific) knowledge as fragmented and physically anchored (but not necessarily the epistemological perspective of a particular social group). A knowing subject's perspective can always be located to a specific field – there is no objective "view from nowhere." The arguments above differ both in their conceptualizations of the subject and of society, but have in common that they see scientific knowledge as dependent on the social frameworks in which they are produced. Science is not a neutral activity, but instead reflects institutional values.

Scientists tend to insist that their *way* of arriving at knowledge makes their claims more true and more valuable than other groups' knowledge claims (who arrived at their conclusions by different means and on different grounds). They argue that while it may be the case that certain types of knowledge – such as ideas about morality – are socially constructed, scientific knowledge should be exempt from such a mode of analysis. Scientific knowledge has a special authority and status because of the way in which we arrive at such knowledge. The "scientific method" – rigorous and systematic examination, testing, and replication – thus guarantees the veracity of scientific claims. "Truthfulness" is taken to mean that the claim in question is a direct representation of a reality that exists outside of, and independent from, our perceptions of it. A social constructivist view of science instead holds that scientific knowledge is as "social" as other types of knowledge.

A social constructivist perspective of science common in the field of science studies emphasizes the social influence at the very core of technical judgments. Scientific theories, it is argued, are always underdetermined by empirical data – there are a potentially infinite number of hypotheses that could serve to explain the same set of data. Despite this, scientists manage to "gel" around a limited number of possible explanations and eventually agree on which one they consider to be true. This process of "truthmaking" is a social activity where the meaning of data is continuously being negotiated and renegotiated.

Sociologists of science have shown that scientific work in practice is rather more messy than in theory (Knorr-Cetina 1981; Collins 1985; Fujimura 1988; Pickering 1992) and that data always require interpretation, that machines are continuously calibrated to generate information that "makes sense" (i.e., fits into a given frame of meaning), and that tests and models build on the assumption that the circumstances correspond precisely to "real-world" circumstances. Furthermore, experiments routinely go wrong and scientists spend a substantial amount of their time attempting to discipline wayward material and tweak variables until they work (Knorr-Cetina 1981; Latour & Woolgar 1986). The success of an experiment is determined by its outcome and thus measured against a host of prior assumptions about what "nature" looks like and whether the result at hand corresponds with that nature. If the result is deemed to fit into that framework it will eventually become a fact and taken to be not only a good model of nature, but part of nature itself.

Social constructivists of all extractions also tend to argue that the success of science in claiming to be the highest form of knowing in part rests on its ability to appear as though it lacks both temporal and spatial location. Harry Collins uses the metaphor of a ship in a bottle – once in place, science, like the ship, appears to have a timeless quality, as though it has always been there and always will be. The processes by which science and scientific knowledge are produced tend to disappear from later narratives when scientific "discoveries" or "facts" are presented. A scientific fact is like a ship in a bottle; it is near-impossible to conceive of how the ship was ever outside the bottle, because the bottleneck is far too narrow for the ship to have been pressed through it. At one time it was, however, a mere pile of sticks outside the bottle (Collins 1985: preface). The mistake we make is to assume that the ship has always been a ship, and, in the case of science, that the fact has always been a fact.

Another common source of scientific authority is the notion of "objectivity." The "human factor" – that is, the scientist(s) who produced the knowledge – is made invisible, as are the circumstances under which the work was conducted. Porter (1992, 1995) has suggested that an inherently social relationship such as "trust" has taken the shape of objectivity by means of the apparent removal of individual, and therefore subjective, assessments. Porter (1995) argues that objectivity has nothing to do with truth and nature, but that it is instead the effort to exclude subjectivity – the "struggle against judgment." As scientific communities are growing increasingly larger and span several continents, trust has to be achieved at a distance, without personal contact (Luhman 1979; Giddens 1989; Porter 1995). Trust relations, previously negotiated in direct interaction or via a personal contact, have been institutionalized – the checkpoints are no longer embodied in scientists but rather located in seemingly impersonal sets of procedures. One of the most successful examples of this is quantification, an almost ubiquitous feature in today's natural sciences.

The interesting question to pursue is then – to speak with Berger and Luckmann – how knowledge becomes reality. Other theorists prefer not to speak of reality in such relativist terms, but still seek to study the genesis and development of facts. The task of the social scientist is to unpack so-called black boxes (i.e., unproblematic givens that we no longer question) and analyze the processes that went before this fact, or set of facts, became taken-for-granted knowledge. In order to study how knowledge claims come to be established as facts, when they were once merely one of many competing theories, analysts need to go "upstream" and examine a time when these claims were more contentious (Latour 1987; Sismondo 2004). Latour and Woolgar (1986) show how an initially "nonsensical" statement gradually becomes a reasonable claim, to then be labeled "false," only to retrieve its air of probability, to finally take on the status of a fact. This is done through a series of operations that aim to mobilize and "hook up" with other facts, scientists, and artifacts (Latour 1987).

So why is science a social construction, rather than just a construction? Woolgar has criticized the inherent asymmetry in the so-called interest model, where scientific knowledge is explained by reference to social interests held by individual stakeholders or groups, but the social interests themselves are taken as "real" and stable entities. Latour (2005) purports not to be a social constructivist, but "certainly a full-blooded constructivist." The first edition of Latour and Woolgar's seminal work *Laboratory Life* had as its subtitle "the social construction of scientific facts," which in the second edition was changed to merely "the construction of scientific facts." According to Latour, an ideal subtitle would have read "the practical construction of scientific facts." He has sought to clarify this position by arguing for a "constructivist realism." The notion of construction must, according to Latour, be reconfigured altogether if science in action is to be understood. The trouble with the social constructivist view is that it builds on a false dualism – objects are taken to reside in nature, whereas subjects dwell only in society. Latour's alternative actor-network theory (ANT) is a materialist theory which puts "social" and "natural" on an equal footing – studying scientists' practices should reconfigure what we traditionally think of as "social" just as much as it challenges our traditional views of "science" or "nature." Latour does not want to talk about nature in the way it is commonly understood, but equally he does not want to talk of society. "Society" has been ruined by sociologists and social constructivists, as they have made sure that it has been purged of what Latour calls not objects, but "nonhumans." If the social constructivist is to be believed, says Latour, only social relations exist in society. Furthermore, as nature is not awarded a reality status in its own right, but is simply a series of social inscriptions, the entire project becomes tautological. Latour thus disputes what he calls a dualist paradigm and seeks to avoid a subject–object distinction altogether. As "society" has become tainted, he prefers instead the notion of "collective." This collective is extended to include nonhumans as well as humans. Latour's society is constructed, but not socially constructed.

SEE ALSO: Actor-Network Theory; Classification; Constructionism; Feminism and Science, Feminist Epistemology; Nature; Science across Cultures; Science/Non-Science and Boundary Work; Science, Proof, and Law; Scientific Knowledge, Sociology of; Strong Objectivity; Strong Program; Women in Science

REFERENCES AND SUGGESTED READINGS

Collins, H. (1985) *Changing Order: Replication and Induction in Scientific Practice.* Sage, Beverly Hills.

Fox-Keller, E. & Longino, H. (Eds.) (1996) *Feminism and Science.* Oxford University Press, Oxford.

Fujimura, J. H. (1988) The Molecular Biological Bandwagon in Cancer Research: Where Social Worlds Meet. *Social Problems* 35: 261–83.

Giddens, A. (1989) *The Consequences of Modernity.* Stanford University Press, Stanford.

Hacking, I. (1999) *The Social Construction of What?* Harvard University Press, Cambridge, MA.

Haraway, D. (1991) *Simians, Cyborgs, and Women: The Reinvention of Nature.* Routledge, New York.

Harding, S. (1991) *Whose Science? Whose Knowledge?* Cornell University Press, Ithaca, NY.

Knorr-Cetina, K. (1981) *The Manufacture of Knowledge.* Pergamon Press, Oxford.

Latour, B. (1987) *Science in Action.* Harvard University Press, Cambridge, MA.

Latour, B. (1999) *Pandora's Hope: Essays on the Reality of Science Studies.* Harvard University Press, Cambridge, MA.

Latour, B. (2005) Bruno Latour. Online. www.ensmp.fr/~latour/faq-en.html.

Latour, B. & Woolgar, S. (1986) *Laboratory Life.* Princeton University Press, Princeton.

Luhman, N. (1979) *Trust and Power: Two Works.* John Wiley, Chichester.

Pickering, A. (Ed.) (1992) *Science as Practice and Culture.* University of Chicago Press, Chicago.

Porter, T. M. (1992) Quantification and the Accounting Ideal in Science. *Social Studies of Science* 22: 633–52.

Porter, T. M. (1995) *Trust in Numbers: The Pursuit of Objectivity in Science and Public Life.* Princeton University Press, Princeton.

Sismondo, S. (2004) *An Introduction to Science and Technology Studies.* Blackwell, Oxford.

scientific knowledge, sociology of

Lena Eriksson

The sociology of scientific knowledge (SSK) is a field of sociology that started to take form in the early 1970s. Sociologists, historians, and philosophers who shared a common interest in studying the social underpinnings of science took as a joint focus the very *content* of scientific knowledge. Previously, a division of labor had existed between philosophy and sociology. Philosophers' role was to analyze and define norms of science, discussing and drawing up demarcation criteria between science and non-science. Sociologists were to study the structure of scientific institutions and provide explanations when science went wrong. Thus, the only type of knowledge qualifying for sociological attention was knowledge perceived to be somehow faulty. SSK, however, approached all scientific knowledge claims – regardless of whether they were held to be true or false – as material for sociological investigation (Bloor 1991 [1976]).

The intellectual roots of SSK are many and varied. Definite influences are philosophers and sociologists such as Weber, Durkheim, and Marx with their ideas about social construction, Wittgenstein's argument about the extension of rules, and Mannheim's writings about ideas as socially located. Later scholars, such as Robert Merton and Thomas Kuhn, are also recognized as predecessors to a field that started to take a more definite form with the publication of the Strong Program in the mid-1970s. The Strong Program was a programmatic statement from a transdisciplinary group of academics based at the University of Edinburgh, the so-called Edinburgh School. It proposed that scientific knowledge should not be treated as a special case of knowledge, but instead be analyzed and explained in terms of its social origin and causes. A sociological account of the emergence of scientific knowledge should be causal, impartial, symmetrical, and reflexive.

Around the same time, a similar approach to the study of scientific knowledge was being developed elsewhere in Britain. EPOR, the Empirical Program of Relativism, formed the basis for the Bath School and was led by Harry Collins. As the name suggests, EPOR proposed that scientific knowledge production should be studied empirically and that a relativist approach should be taken to the object of study. It was, however, emphasized that the relativist stance should be deployed as a methodological tool and not necessarily reflect an ontological position. Sociological studies of science should demonstrate the "interpretive flexibility" of knowledge claims, describe the institutional and network-based mechanisms that would achieve "closure," and, finally, connect such closure mechanisms to wider social and political structures.

One assumption underlying the SSK approach is summarized in the Duhem-Quine hypothesis, which states that a theory always is underdetermined by data. No one theory can ever singularly explain a specific set of data; there are hypothetically an infinite number of theories that could be supported by the same data set. Therefore, a theory can never be tested on its own, and with reference to nature, e.g., the data themselves. Instead there tends to be a whole weave of interconnected assumptions being tried. The pertinent question for the sociology of scientific knowledge is that if theories are underdetermined by data – that is, if "truth" cannot be determined by reference to nature – how is it that scientists still manage to gather around more or less stable theoretical constructs?

One commonly used model in SSK has been to analyze different positions in a given debate in terms of what wider interests they represent. Interests are invoked to explain how closure and consensus can be achieved in science despite the inherent potential for innumerable developments.

Interest explanations are often macrosocial and "interests" are, for example, the interests of the professional middle class in attaining or retaining moral and intellectual legitimacy for power and influence (Shapin 1975; Barnes & MacKenzie 1979), interests linked to investments in certain kinds of skills, models, or technologies (Fujimura 1988), or the interests of a professional group to claim or to maintain the cognitive authority over an issue or area (Gieryn & Figert 1986).

Stability can also be explained on a more microsocial level, as the result of negotiations between different scientists who achieve local agreement (Knorr-Cetina 1981). Such a microsocial approach represented a new trend in SSK, often known under the label of "laboratory studies." In early SSK studies there had been a focus on scientific controversies. Typically, such analyses would encompass two or more competing "sides" of scientists arguing over a given theory or result. One of the perceived methodological advantages of such an approach was that in times of contentious science, "normal" rules and practices in scientific everyday life tend to be questioned and are thereby made visible to the analyst. The proponents of laboratory studies, conversely, wanted to study such "normal" scientific practice and the everyday production of knowledge.

In 1979, Bruno Latour and Steve Woolgar published a landmark book called *Laboratory Life*, an ethnographic study of the Salk laboratory in San Diego. The authors took an anthropological approach to their objects of study and chose to "make the familiar strange," thereby not taking anything for granted – so, for example, one of the drawings at the beginning of the book describes in detail the air conditioning system in the laboratory. Two years later, Karin Knorr-Cetina published another important ethnographic study in which she described how successful laboratory work required a vast amount of "tinkering." Like her French colleagues, Knorr-Cetina noted the "messiness" of science in practice and how much of scientists' time is spent making difficult objects behave properly so as to get a desired or acceptable outcome. Laboratory studies dispelled the popular belief that scientists go into the laboratory with a hypothesis to test, set up the experiment, test it, and then accept whichever result they get as the answer to their query. Instead, only certain kinds of outcomes will count as a "result" – most anomalies will fall under the category of experimental failings and only result in the scientist calibrating his or her equipment, or changing the parameters of the experiment.

During the 1980s, a new perspective gained ground among social scientists who studied science and technology. Actor-network theory (ANT), developed by Michel Callon and Bruno Latour in Paris, and John Law in Britain, proposed that successful scientific work was a result of successful networks. ANT made no difference between science and technology, but instead used the term "technoscience." To build a large, strong, and successful network, a given actor needs to enroll allies and translate their interests so that they aim toward the same, or a compatible, goal. In that respect, ANT networks and the activities of actors within them are similar to what one would traditionally think of as politicking. However, ANT networks include not only human actors but also so-called actants – non-human objects or phenomena. Actants do not differ from their human counterparts in important ways – they, too, have interests and agency. Actants can be proteins, scallops, doorstops, or referendums, and anything in between.

ANT thus took issue with the traditional SSK way of explaining the emergence and shape of natural science knowledge. Actor-network theorists wanted to extend the concept of symmetry so as to include nature, a generalized or so-called supersymmetry. There is, it was argued, an inherent asymmetry in the SSK approach because of its insistence on only allowing social explanations, thus imputing that the social world is more "real" than the natural world. Scientific knowledge is explained by reference to social interests, but the social interests themselves are taken as "real" and stable entities.

ANT also took a radically different approach to "interests." With an actor-network approach, interests are regarded as both cause and consequence. These co-produced interests are both a resource that can be used when enrolling actors and a result of that enrollment activity. If one actor manages to translate the interests of others and thereby successfully align them, this transform-and-enroll strategy will increase the actor's possibilities of creating and defining reality. This creates a self-perpetuating movement, as the abilities to define and translate are co-produced. An actor who successfully translates will gain ever more interpretive power. In Michel Callon's famous study of the fishermen in St. Brieuc Bay, the question posed by the marine biologists – "How do scallops anchor?" – served to simultaneously translate the interests of the fishermen, the scientists, and the scallops, making it a question of survival for the scallops, of future livelihoods for the fishermen, and the pivotal question that needed to be answered – the obligatory passage point – in the scientists' field of research (Callon 1986).

SSK critics of actor-network theory have pointed to how agency appears to be unevenly distributed among actors and actants, in two different ways. Firstly, it appears that the initiative to network building always has to come from human actors. Secondly, it is the privilege of the analyst to decide which non-human object will enjoy the role of "actant" – in Callon's St. Brieuc Bay study, only the scallops are assumed to have agency. The ships, test tubes, etc. are treated as "normal" objects.

Other critics have highlighted a focus on scientific "heroes" in ANT studies, a tendency to take rationality to be unproblematic and disconnected from cultural understandings of "rational," and a failure to account for cultures or practices in their analyses. ANT was thus not unreservedly accepted into the realm of SSK, but provoked a long-running debate on matters ontological, methodological, and epistemological – perhaps best summarized in the so-called "chicken debate" between the Paris School, championed by Michel Callon and Bruno Latour, and the Bath School, represented by Harry Collins and Steve Yearley. Points of contention were, in particular, the role and status of actants and, thus, the role and status of "nature" versus "the social."

Some 20 years after the emergence of the Strong Program, the field of SSK had grown in so many disparate directions that it no longer had its firm 1970s identity as one distinct perspective. Many other approaches, such as discourse analysis and symbolic interactionism, had gathered their own followings and developed discrete methodological tool kits and theoretical frameworks. In the present day, SSK has taken its place as one of many perspectives in the larger field of science studies.

SEE ALSO: Actor-Network Theory; Durkheim, Émile; Knowledge, Sociology of; Kuhn, Thomas and Scientific Paradigms; Laboratory Studies and the World of the Scientific Lab; Marx, Karl; Merton, Robert K.; Science/Non-Science and Boundary Work; Science, Social Construction of; Scientific Literacy and Public Understandings of Science; Strong Program

REFERENCES AND SUGGESTED READINGS

Barnes, B. & MacKenzie, D. (1979) On the Role of Interests in Scientific Change. In: Wallis, R. (Ed.), *On the Margins of Science: The Social Construction of Rejected Knowledge*. University of Keele Press, Keele, pp. 49–66.

Bloor, D. (1991 [1976]) *Knowledge and Social Imagery*. University of Chicago Press, Chicago.

Callon, M. (1986) Some Elements of a Sociology of Translation: Domestication of the Scallops and the Fishermen of St. Brieuc Bay. In: Law, J. (Ed.), *Power, Action, and Belief.* Routledge & Kegan Paul, London.
Collins, H. M. (1981) Stages in the Empirical Programme of Relativism. *Social Studies of Science* 11: 3–10.
Fujimura, J. H. (1988) The Molecular Biological Bandwagon in Cancer Research: Where Social Worlds Meet. *Social Problems* 35: 261–83.
Gieryn, T. F. & Figert, A. (1986) Scientists Protect their Cognitive Authority: The Status Degradation Ceremony of Sir Cyril Burt. In: Böhme, G. & Stehr, N. (Eds.), *The Knowledge Society: The Growing Impact of Scientific Knowledge on Social Relations.* Reidel, Dordrecht.
Knorr-Cetina, K. (1981) *The Manufacture of Knowledge.* Pergamon, Oxford.
Kuhn, T. (1970 [1962]) *The Structure of Scientific Revolutions.* University of Chicago Press, Chicago.
Latour, B. & Woolgar, S. (1986 [1979]) *Laboratory Life: The Construction of Scientific Facts.* Princeton University Press, Princeton.
Merton, R. K. (1973) *The Sociology of Science: Theoretical and Empirical Investigations.* University of Chicago Press, Chicago.
Shapin, S. (1975) Phrenological Knowledge and the Social Structure of Early Nineteenth-Century Edinburgh. *Annals of Science* 32: 219–43.
Wittgenstein, L. (1958) *Philosophical Investigations.* Blackwell, Oxford.

scientific literacy and public understandings of science

Conor M. W. Douglas

Scientific literacy, and more so the public understanding of science, have recently become areas of study in their own right within the sociology of science and science and technology studies (STS). This emergence is partly due to the increased focus on science as an inherently social activity, but more specifically it is due to the mounting challenges that the scientific community has faced in dealing with this fact. Science is not only a social activity in that it is governed by a set of norms and values (as Robert Merton's classic work in the 1950s posited, with the identification of the CUDOS norms of communism, universality, disinterestedness, and organized skepticism), but it is also a social activity in the respect that it plays an instrumental role in the construction of everyday life.

Science is perhaps one of the most demarcated and professionalized human activities because it argues to have a different evidential basis for its knowledge claims. This evidential basis is largely the product of the scientific method that collects bits of information from the observation of a phenomenon in the form of induction, then operates in the deductive fashion by the creation of hypotheses to explain the phenomenon, the conducting of experiments in attempts to confirm and/or falsify the said hypotheses, and the building of a theory based on the results of experiments. Without elementary training and education in the fundamental aspects of science, the operations and products of the scientific community can become almost unintelligible to the outsider. This convolution is partly due to the increasing complexity of new specializations emergent within disciplines, coupled with the transformation of theories and the evolving nature of understanding. As a result, there is often a break, or chasm, between what the scientific community claims it is doing and what "the public" – those who find themselves outside of the scientific community – understand of the processes and products of science. Attempts at comprehending and explaining this break have become the work of sociologists, and other related fields of social science, who are interested in the public understanding of science (PUS).

Early quantitative surveys in the PUS found that there is "a tendency for better-informed respondents to have a more positive general attitude towards science and scientists" (Durant et al. 1989). It was consequently argued that any public opposition to science and technology policies, decisions, and/or advancements was largely due to the fact that the public did not understand the arguments and reasoning behind the science in question. This view of the public understanding of science came to be known (largely by its critics) as the "deficit model" (Wynne 1991; Ziman 1991). Proponents of this deficit model of PUS feel that if the public were simply better informed about science, then they would generally be more supportive of it. Glossing the work of Alan Gross, Sturgis and Allum (2004) put it like this: "in this formulation, it is the public that are assumed to be 'deficient' while science is 'sufficient' ... lacking a proper understanding of the relevant facts, people fall back on mystical belief and irrational fears of the unknown."

Much focus in PUS has therefore been paid to one of the central problematics within the communication of information from scientists to the public: the role of the media. Based on the assumption that all information is mediated by the source from which it emanates, many of the investigators have taken up the media as a sight of examination and queried the effects that it may have on the public understanding of science. Some have argued that the media are responsible for misconstruing the message of the science and perpetuating misconceptions, while others have sought to explain the use of expert scientific testimony within the media.

Other central concerns in the PUS are the notion of "the public" as well as the notion of "science." Different people experience different aspects of science in very different ways, and thus studies that have made reference to "the public" as a homogeneous group, or ones which have tried to comprehend levels of understanding in "science" in general, have largely worked to cloud the picture of PUS. Consequently, much of the work carried out in the late twentieth and early twenty-first centuries has focused on national contexts and case studies.

After considerable work done on the PUS in the West, more recent investigations have sought to open up the area of study to other countries and cultures that have traditionally been located outside of the dominant discourse. Such work includes a focus on PUS in ex-Soviet countries, the contextualization of differences in PUS within European peripheral states, and international comparisons between PUS in oriental and western countries.

Not only have the more recent works been increasingly contextualized to specific national perspectives, but also much of the work done in PUS is case specific. Such investigations do not concentrate on the public understanding of science in general, but rather the public's understanding of a particular scientific advancement. Examples include cases from around the world (e.g., East Asia, Oceania, Europe, and ex-Soviet countries) and cut across technoscientific specializations (e.g., medical gene technology, genetically modified foods, nuclear sciences, and xenotransplantation). Traditional sociological categories such as gender, political affiliation, and socioeconomic status have also been areas of concentration within the PUS in an attempt to further contextualize "the public" within the PUS.

While the work carried out in the PUS is vast and diverse, some take for granted the assumption of the deficit model and continue to operate on the belief that a more informed public will necessarily lead to an increasing amount of support for scientific endeavors. Debate and controversy remain around this assumption of the deficit model, and contestation is not new to PUS, as it is an area of investigation that has altered and changed throughout the years.

In the early post-war years in the US and the UK, the scientific community took very little interest in engaging the public with its processes, content, and (social) structure. Conversely, the popularization of science was high on the agenda for various social groups and institutions who worked in and around scientific areas, but as Lewenstein (1992) argues, this did not mean critical engagement with science as, "the term 'public understanding of science' became equated with 'public appreciation of the benefits that science provides to society.'" This era of science policy in 1940s and 1950s America is what Sarewitz (1996) has called the "myth of infinite benefit." Sarewitz's historical treatment shows how this myth posited that increasing state funding for scientific research would lead directly to increased public good and thus public support. Heavy state involvement in the promotion of science for the public good was championed by the likes of Vannevar Bush – the chief research adviser to President Roosevelt and one of the central figures in mobilizing science for use to the state and military, particularly during and after World War II. During this period new universities and research institutions were established, and existing ones witnessed an eruption in state funding for scientific activities. Dreams of flying cars and homes operated on nuclear energy filled the imaginations of the uncritical public until the 1960s.

In the US some attempts to gauge the concepts of scientific literacy (SL) and to distinguish them from PUS began around 1979 when social scientists working in these areas were commissioned to overhaul the *Science Indicators*. The goal of these social scientists was to

> significantly expanded the scope of the surveys and begin to focus more attention on attitudes, knowledge measures, and expected participation measures for specific issues and controversies, such as nuclear power. Measures of policy preferences were expanded beyond spending preferences to specific regulatory areas. New measures concerning the individual's sources of scientific and technical information were added, allowing the formation of scales reflecting adult participation in informal science education activities. (Miller 1992)

In constructing this self-professed "first measure of scientific literacy," Miller also created a construct to divide "the public" into subgroups:

> individuals who report a high level of interest in science and technology policy issues and a sense of being very well informed about those issues (called the attentive public ...), those individuals who report a high level of interest in science and technology policy issues but who do not classify themselves as being very well informed about those issues (called the interested public), and those individuals who report that they are not very interested in science and technology policy issues (called the residual public). (Miller 1992)

In Britain, initiatives were taken up around the same time in an attempt to gauge the public's relationship with science. In 1985 the Bodmer report was published by the Royal Society, which called into question the degree of public support for science. As a response to the Bodmer report a body was established called the Committee for Public Understanding of Science (or COPUS) that was jointly founded by the Royal Society, the British Association, and the Royal Institution.

In both the US and the UK these reports, surveys, and indicators produced results that suggested that while there might be interest in science, knowledge about process and content was seriously lacking. In other words, findings suggested that the public was largely scientifically illiterate, which acted as the basis for the deficit model.

Predictably, the deficit model led to a major backlash from some of those within the constructivist school of STS and the social sciences more broadly who were interested in the PUS. The constructivists argued that it was shortsighted to assume that the public simply lacked an understanding of science, and it was rather that the public experienced science within their own specific social contexts and consequently sometimes chose to question the authority or validity of scientific claims (Wynne 1991). The debate boiled with such fervor and the research and interest in the area grew with such intensity that the journal *Public Understanding of Science* was created in 1992, dedicated solely to its namesake.

Constructivists and those supporters of the deficit model converge and diverge at interesting points within the PUS. For instance, both sides seem to agree that PUS entails an understanding of some of the formal content of science, the methods and processes of science, alongside a crucial third factor that differs for each party. For those of the deficit school this third factor is the "awareness of the impact of science and technology on individuals and society" (Miller 1992), whereas for constructivists like Wynne this third factor is the understanding of the "forms of institutional embedding, patronage and organizational control" of science (Wynne 1992). This third differing factor is paramount because in the constructivists' understanding the authority of science can legitimately be called into question.

According to constructivists like Wynne and Steven Yearley, scientific knowledge and expert claims are "always mediated by knowledge of the institutional arrangements under which expertise is authorized. Claims of expert knowledge are always contestable, depending on what one knows of the relevant institution" (Sturgis & Allum 2004, discussing Yearley). Consequently, the "scientific" advice of daily intake of "the four basic food groups" provided by the scientists from the American Food and Drug Association can be mediated by the knowledge that this institution has had a close working relationship with the National Dairy Council, and that years before the four basic food groups existed there were indeed twelve basic food groups in which dairy played a much smaller role (Haughton et al. 1987).

Constructivists assert that if a problem exists in the communication of science's content, processes, and structure, then the responsibility for the problem of PUS must swing both ways. This argument represents a flat rejection of the claim of the deficit model that the blame for the problem of PUS rests solely on the shoulders of the public (or even the media for that matter), and instead asserts that responsibility for the PUS must also be located within the scientific community.

Comprehending how the public integrates its knowledge about the "existing political culture of science and its social relations" (Wynne 1992) should not be taken for granted when analysts are attempting to gauge the public's understanding of science. Constructivists argue that it is not ignorance that leads the public to contest scientific claims and to be hesitant with support for the scientific community; rather, in some situations, scientific claims appear inconsistent, irrational, and/or contradictory to preexisting knowledge. Some of the constructivists' reasons as to why a member of the public might choose to contest scientific knowledge are "when the reasoning behind the information is not made plain (often because of concerns about 'alarming' the public)"; "when it contradicts local experience (reassurance about safety when incidents have previously occurred)"; "when it is conveyed in unreasonable categorical terms (e.g., concerning the precise course of the envisaged emergency)"; and "when it seems to deny accepted social norms" (Wynne 1991).

For better or for worse, scientific literacy (SL) only enjoys a marginally more conceptual clarity than the PUS, which is perhaps counter-intuitively due to its relatively lesser degree of treatment in the literature. Like most conceptual categories, including PUS, SL is a fluid and dynamic area of study, which "has changed somewhat over the years, moving from the ability to read and comprehend science-related articles to its present emphasis on understanding and applying scientific principles to everyday life" (Burns et al. 2003). Evidently, not only has the topic of SL changed over time, but it also has had to be broadened through time. As a consequence, nailing down a single contemporary definition for SL is also problematic. In accord with this position, academics such as B. S. P. Shen and later J. D. Miller (who has been immersed in this area in one way or another for nearly three decades) have been forced to contextualize the concept of SL. For Shen (1975), SL was more clearly understood once broken into three subcategories: practical scientific literacy, civic scientific literacy, and cultural scientific literacy. Practical scientific literacy, he conceptualized, is the application of scientific concepts, skills, and ideas for the resolution of everyday and concrete problems. In this case practical scientific literacy might mean understanding the chemistry of how to balance the acidity/PH level in your garden, or pregnant parents being able to understand statistical significance and the concept of inheritance when the doctor explains an inheritable disease. Cultural scientific literacy, on the other hand, is the recognition of science as a major human achievement, and thus might entail a respectful understanding of the complexity of physical laws of gravity and engineering that landed humans on the moon.

Miller has taken pains to elaborate on the third of Shen's subcategories of scientific literacy: civic scientific literacy. Those who would be considered to exhibit civic scientific literacy would, for instance, be able to engage critically with the science content of a daily newspaper. This critical engagement would be done for constructive purposes so that the individual could more readily be involved in the processes by which science emerges within a democratic society. A good example of civic scientific literacy might be those people who constructively and open-mindedly participated in the public debate over the integration of genetically modified foods in the UK in 2003. For Miller, civic scientific literacy involved not only the content dimension (i.e., being able to read and understand the science section of the newspaper or magazine), but also having an understanding of the process of scientific inquiry (i.e., construction of theory, hypothesis testing, and the experimental method), as well as some degree of understanding of the impact of science and technology on individuals and society (e.g., carbon emissions from automobiles get trapped within our atmosphere and lead to a greenhouse effect that warms our planet).

At the turn of the millennium the British House of Lords, a body firmly rooted outside of academic discourses, rather vaguely defined the public understanding of science as "the shorthand term for all forms of outreach (in the UK) by the scientific community, or others on their behalf (e.g., science writers, museums, event organizers), to the public at large aimed at improving understanding" (Burns et al. 2003: 187). In the vast expanses of literature on the topic of PUS within academic discourses there exists no single clear-cut definition. As one of the central commentators on the topic stated: "PUS is an ill-defined area involving several different disciplinary perspectives" (Wynne 1995), including sociology, political science, science and technology studies, communication studies, and psychology, to name a few. SL does not present any clearer picture, as similar qualities have been used in its and PUS's definitions, which include understanding science content, understanding methods of inquiry (or process), and understanding science as a social enterprise. Clearly, there is still much conceptual confusion around and between these terms. With that in mind, contestations over formless terms such as "the public" and "science," and constructivist debate about the authority of science, have opened up the discourse within the PUS and moved it away from the rather vague definition offered by the British House of Lords. As science and technology continue to grow in terms of their pervasiveness in all aspects of society, PUS will surely continue to be a site of important academic discussion.

SEE ALSO: Media; Public Opinion; Science and Culture; Science and Public Participation: The Democratization of Science; Science/Non-Science and Boundary Work

REFERENCES AND SUGGESTED READINGS

Burns, T. W. et al. (2003) Science Communication: A Contemporary Definition. *Public Understanding of Science* 12(2): 183–202.

Durant, J. et al. (1989) The Public Understanding of Science. *Nature* 340 (July 6): 11–14.

Haughton, B. et al. (1987) A Historical Study on the Underlying Assumptions for United States Food Guides from 1917 through the Basic Four Food Group Guide. *Journal of Nutritional Education and Behaviour* 19(4): 169–76.

Lewenstein, B. (1992) The Meaning of "Public Understanding of Science" in the United States after World War II. *Public Understanding of Science* 1(1): 45–68.

Miller, J. D. (1992) Toward a Scientific Understanding of the Public Understanding of Science and Technology. *Public Understanding of Science* 1(1): 23–6.

Miller, J. D. (1998) The Measurement of Civic Scientific Literacy. *Public Understanding of Science* 7(3): 203–23.

Sarewitz, D. (1996) *Frontiers of Illusion: Science, Technology, and the Politics of Progress.* Temple University Press, Philadelphia.

Shen, B. S. P. (1975) Scientific Literacy and the Public Understanding of Science. In: Day, S. (Ed.), *Communication of Scientific Information.* Karager, Basel, pp. 44–52.

Sturgis, P. & Allum, N. (2004) Science in Society: Re-Evaluating the Deficit Model of Public Attitudes. *Public Understanding of Science* 13(1): 55–74.

Wynne, B. (1991) Knowledge in Context. *Science, Technology and Human Values* 16(1): 111–21.

Wynne, B. (1992) Public Understanding of Science Research: New Horizons or Hall of Mirrors? *Public Understanding of Science* 1(1): 37–43.

Wynne, B. (1995) Public Understanding of Science. In: Jasanoff, S. et al. (Eds.), *Handbook of Science and Technology Studies.* Sage, Newbury Park, CA, pp. 361–88.

Ziman, J. (1991) Public Understanding of Science. *Science, Technology and Human Values* 1(1): 99–105.

scientific models and simulations

Mikaela Sundberg

The term model is used in multiple ways in science and there are several different kinds of models. The most basic scientific models are material and conceptual analogues. They are copies that stand in for more opaque systems. Cloud chambers and cell cultures are examples of material models, whereas conceptual models are more abstract analogies that seek to render theories more comprehensible. Mathematical models are typically applications, approximations, or specifications of theories and principles that cannot be applied in their original form.

Computer simulations tend to be more obvious analogues than models, aptly characterized as virtual copies of systems. Simulations employ a generative mechanism to imitate the dynamic behavior of the underlying process that the simulations aim to represent. Simulation is an ambiguous term, but in all cases of scientific simulations they are based on some form of model. However, simulation models can be divided into two overall types, both of which tend to be used for representations of complex dynamics. The first type is based on mathematical models, which aim to represent established theoretical statements or physical laws. Simulations in physically based sciences usually exemplify this type of simulation. The second type of simulation model is based on simpler models, which consist of a few assumptions about leading mechanisms. This is generally the case in simulations of social phenomena using so-called agent-based models.

Although models and simulations are increasingly used in science, studies of them remain rare compared to the extensive studies of experiments that have taken place in the sociology of science since the 1970s. Models and simulations that represent the application of theoretical knowledge have also received less attention in the philosophy of science, where the traditional line of inquiry has mostly been in the theoretical domains.

From the perspective of the philosophy of science, models and simulations tend to be discussed in relation to theories. In the classic contribution *Models and Analogies in Science* (1966), Mary Hesse sees models as heuristically essential to the development and extension of theories, and also essential to the explanatory power of theories. However, the epistemological characteristics of models and simulations are less clear than those of theories. Models do not have the same epistemic tradition as theorizing and do not have transparent object domains. This is perhaps most significant in the case of simulations and it has thus been argued that simulation has its own epistemology (Winsberg 1999). In constructing simulation models, theoretical structures are transformed into specific knowledge of systems and further into computational models that are implemented in a computer in the form of an algorithm. This is what makes simulations produce data sets. Because simulation modeling produces these types of results, a standard for deciding whether the results are reliable is required. For this reason, results of simulations are often compared to observations. In this respect modeling and simulations share similar relations to experimentation as does theory. However, models and simulations are often seen in more pragmatic terms and therefore evaluated in relation to the purpose of modeling. This approach differs clearly from the epistemological view on theories, where theories are judged according to their being true or false.

A different way to approach modeling, not limited to epistemic questions such as the truth of models and how they should be verified, is to consider the instrumentality and autonomy of models. As partly dependent on theories and experiment, and partly independent, models can serve as bridges between theory and the world. This is suggested by Mary Morgan and Margaret Morrison in their influential book *Models as Mediators* (1999), where models are conceptualized as autonomous mediators. However, to only see models and simulations in the space between theories and the world assumes that theory and the world are stable entities, at the same time as it directs the attention toward a philosophical focus on what a model essentially is. From a sociological perspective, it is more appropriate to address the character of models in relation to the role that models and simulations play in scientific practice.

The characterization of the role of models and simulation models has often been based on the idea of models and simulation models as tools or objects for knowledge. The use of models and simulations as tools is most evident in applied science, where models are used to predict the development of various dynamic processes. Thus, in those cases where empirical data exist, the correspondence of outcomes with data becomes an important indicator of the performance of the model or simulation.

Because of their character as analogues, models and simulations can also themselves be studied the same way as natural systems are studied in empirical research. By acting as objects of knowledge in their own right, simulation models are explored to answer questions about how and why certain processes develop. In this situation, both the inner theoretical structure of the model and how well its results correspond to data are important to the evaluation of the performance of the simulation model itself.

Some models and simulation models are constructed and used for only one of the abovementioned purposes. However, in principle, a particular simulation model can serve multiple purposes, depending on its role in practice and which questions it is being asked to address. Consequently, some models and simulations may serve as tools like technical artifacts or objects of knowledge depending on the setting where they are used.

Another line of research focuses on what people who model and simulate do, and how they work. While simulations can be described as both experimenting and theorizing depending on what aspects researchers talk about, the use of simulations as "virtual laboratories" in fact makes working with models very similar to experimenting (Dowling 1999). Models tend to integrate a broad range of ingredients such as, for example, metaphors, theoretical notions, and mathematical concepts and, not least from this point of view, the construction of models requires much experience and hard work (cf. Boumans 1999). In simulation modeling, questions related to the role of researchers are fundamental because the construction of simulation models and the interpretation of simulation results primarily depend on the researchers, their research areas, and their experience (Becker et al. 2005). In short, the role of human agency needs to be taken into account in developing the sociological understanding of how models and simulation models are constructed and used.

What appears as a particularly useful and important way to approach the practice of modeling and simulation is to acknowledge the materiality of modeling and simulations. Models are objects that have their own construction and ways of functioning that constrain interpretation and use (Knuuttila & Voutilainen 2003). What makes the materiality of simulation modeling even more evident is the transformation of a theoretical model into a computer program, and this intertwining is indeed a fundamental aspect to attend to in understanding simulation modeling practice (cf. Sundberg 2005).

However, further exploration is needed in terms of how the practices of modeling and simulating can be conceived of in different ways rather than only in relation to theorizing and/or experimenting. In addition, an important question for future research concerns whether the concepts, metaphors, and methodologies developed on the basis of studies of experiments and experimental work can be successfully applied to and used in studies of modeling and simulations. For example, the participant observation approach, which has been the basis of many so-called laboratory studies, is more difficult when studying modelers. Compared to the traditional work in a "wet laboratory," it is more difficult for an observer to follow activities like writing equations or programming computers. To conclude, there is a growing but limited interest in, and knowledge of, the practices involved in modeling and simulations, but a more rigorous sociological approach remains to be developed.

SEE ALSO: Epistemology; Experiment; Practice; Scientific Knowledge, Sociology of; Science; Simulation and Virtuality; Theory

REFERENCES AND SUGGESTED READINGS

Becker, J., Niehaves, B., & Klose, K. (2005) A Framework for Epistemological Perspectives on Simulation. *Journal of Artificial Societies and Social Simulation* 8(4). Online. jasss.soc.surrey.ac.uk/8/4/1.html.

Boumans, M. (1999) Built-in-Justification. In: Morgan, M. S. & Morrison, M. (Eds.), *Models as Mediators: Perspectives on Natural and Social Science*. Cambridge University Press, Cambridge.

Dowling, D. (1999) Experimenting on Theories. *Science in Context* 12(2): 261–73.

Knuuttila, T. & Voutilainen, A. (2003) A Parser as an Epistemic Artifact: A Material View on Models. *Philosophy of Science* 70: 1484–95.

Lenhard, J., Küppers, G., & Shinn, T. (Eds.) (2006) *Simulation: Pragmatic Constructions of Reality. Sociology of Sciences Yearbook*. Springer, New York.

Sundberg, M. (2005) *Making Meteorology: Social Relations and Scientific Practice*. Acta Universitatis Stockholmiensis. Stockholm Studies in Sociology, N.S. 25. Almqvist & Wiksell, Stockholm.

Winsberg, E. (1999) Sanctioning Models: The Epistemology of Simulations. *Science in Context* 12(2): 275–92.

Zeigler, B. (1976) *Theory of Modeling and Simulation*. Krieger, Malabar.

scientific networks and invisible colleges

J. I. (Hans) Bakker

The notion that scientists and other scholars constitute a kind of community of scholars has frequently been asserted and discussed (Godfrey-Smith 2003). The "invisible college" of natural philosophers is a seventeenth-century idea (Price 1963). The phrasing is reminiscent of Adam Smith's later "invisible hand," except that the scientists are real persons and it is only the "colleges" that are sometimes invisible. It stems from Robert Boyle's allusion to the importance to the founding of the Royal Society of Freemasons. An early driving force behind the society was Sir Robert Moray, a Mason who was not himself a natural philosopher (Lomas 2002). Jonathan Swift satirizes the Royal Society as "Laputa" in *Gulliver's Travels* (Toulmin 1961), but the general consensus is that frequent communication among specialists is one of the hallmarks of modern science. A "scientometrics" approach makes it clear that the exponential growth in scientific fields and discoveries has resulted in various kinds of networks, including "networks of scientific papers" (Price 1986). It was only gradually over the course of the seventeenth century that the brief scientific paper replaced the book and Newton might well not have written his *Principia Mathematica* had there not been controversy about his papers on optics; "afterward he did not relish publication until it could take the [then] proper form of a finished book, treating the subject from beginning to end and meeting all conceivable objections and side arguments" (Price 1963: 64).

Of course, there have also been very visible ties among natural philosophers and scientists. Merton's (1968) study of the origins of science stresses the close personal relationships among many of the members of the Royal Society in England. Whether they were aesthetically inclined Puritans or perhaps more hedonistic in their outlook (Feuer 1963), they were in any case part of the same collectivity. Other scientists across Europe corresponded with the Royal Society. When scholars sympathetic to logical positivism met at Harvard in 1939 they articulated a concept of science as members of an illustrious community, but they were also individuals (Wilson 1999). Recent interest in network theory has prompted the idea of a scientific network.

The sociological study of science by early pioneers like Price (1963) and Merton (1968) has given way to science and technology in society (STS), a subdisciplinary field devoted to empirical research on the actual way in which research is carried out (Godfrey-Smith 2003). Latour and Woolgar (1979) have studied the social construction of empirical findings in lab work. Sociological study of Nobel Prize winners in science indicates that those who study with Nobel Prize winners are themselves the most likely recipients of the Nobel Prize, presumably because they have first-hand information about the cutting-edge topics and techniques.

In hermeneutics the idea of a "hermeneutic circle" or "spiral" in science (Føllesdal 1994) is associated with "interaction between agents" and close ties among theorists and empirical researchers. In semiotics the notion of an interpretive community or network has been postulated as an aspect of Peirce's (1998) more abstract notion of a recursive "interpretant." Collins (1998) has stressed the general importance of networks. His theory holds that there is a "law of small numbers" and that the half a dozen or so major "philosophers" in any particular time and place are very likely to know one another. Each thinker searches for a niche. Full comprehension of the theory requires an understanding of the network of ties that cross over several generations.

Scientific networks are not just limited to physical or natural sciences. In classical and contemporary mathematics, statistics, arts, humanities, and social sciences the importance of such affiliations is sometimes made transparent through commemorative volumes. The *Festschrift* for Herbert Simon (Augier & March 2004) is a good example. The list of contributors reads like a "who's who" of noteworthy thinkers on topics like bounded rationality (Arrow 2004) and "Hawkins-Simon conditions" (Samuelson 2004). The history of economics is replete with cross-fertilization within scientific networks, including the German Historical School that influenced Max Weber (Pearson 2002).

The analysis of science from the standpoint of its internal organizational structure in terms of networks of affiliation and communication has not gone unchallenged. Steinmetz (2005) points out that emphasizing the idea of the scientific community as a kind of cultural system can lead to a failure to notice outside influences and forces. Moreover, the "communal" qualities of a network are not always a matter of egalitarian values; they often involve gate keeping and personality conflicts (Abbott 1999). There is a sense in which all those who can participate in a "culture" larger than that of a gathering and hunting community are part of a largely invisible network (Robbins 2005). At the same time, the existence of invisible colleges (of at most 100 or so members) also brings problems of cooperation within and among such communities (Price 1986). The question of "incommensurability" among invisible colleges holding different paradigmatic positions, even within recognized subdisciplinary fields, continues to interest a broad interdisciplinary group of scholars (Kuhn 2000). Once scientific theories have become widely accepted by members of a network they are then no longer as directly linked to a specific subset of all scientists and become the common property of "science" in general, often influencing individuals and groups who are working on quite different sets of empirical problems.

SEE ALSO: Big Science and Collective Research; Culture; Hermeneutics; Networks; Science and Culture; Science across Cultures; Signs

REFERENCES AND SUGGESTED READINGS

Abbott, A. (1999) *Department and Discipline.* University of Chicago Press, Chicago.

Arrow, K. J. (2004) Is Bounded Rationality Unboundedly Rational? Some Ruminations. In: Augier, M. & March, J. G. (Eds.), *Models of a Man: Essays in Memory of Herbert A. Simon.* MIT Press, Cambridge, MA, pp. 47–55.

Augier, M. & March, J. G. (Eds.) (2004) *Models of a Man: Essays in Memory of Herbert A. Simon.* MIT Press, Cambridge, MA.

Collins, R. (1998) *The Sociology of Philosophies.* Harvard University Press, Cambridge, MA.

Feuer, L. S. (1963) *The Scientific Intellectual: Psychological and Sociological Origins of Modern Science.* Basic Books, New York.

Føllesdal, D. (1994) Hermeneutics and the Hypothetico-Deductive Method. In: Martin, M. & McIntyre, L. C. (Eds.), *Readings in the Philosophy of Social Science.* MIT Press, Cambridge, MA, pp. 233–45.

Godfrey-Smith, P. (2003) *Theory and Reality: An Introduction to the Philosophy of Science.* University of Chicago Press, Chicago.

Kuhn, T. (2000) *The Road Since Structure: Philosophical Essays, 1970–1993.* Ed. J. Conant & J. Haugeland. University of Chicago Press, Chicago.

Latour, B. & Woolgar, S. (1979) *Laboratory Life.* Sage, London.

Lomas, R. (2002) *The Invisible College: The Royal Society, Freemasonry and the Birth of Modern Science.* Headline, London.

Merton, R. K. (1968 [1936]) Puritanism, Pietism and Science. In: *Social Theory and Social Structure.* Free Press, New York, pp. 628–60.

Merton, R. K. & Garfield, E. (1986) Foreword. In: Price, D. J. de Solla, *Little Science, Big Science . . . and Beyond.* Columbia University Press, New York, pp. vii–xiv.

Oddie, G. (1989) Partial Interpretation, Meaning Variance, and Incommensurability. In: Gavraglu, K. et al. (Eds.), *Imre Lakatos and Theories of Scientific Change.* Kluwer, Dordrecht, pp. 305–22.

Pearson, H. (2002) The German Historical School of Economics: What It Was Not, and What It Was. In: Nau, H. H. & Schefold, B. (Eds.), *The Historicity of Economics.* Springer, Berlin, pp. 23–43.

Peirce, C. S. (1998) *Charles S. Peirce: The Essential Writings.* Prometheus Books, Amherst, NY.

Price, D. J. de Solla (1963) *Little Science, Big Science.* Columbia University Press, New York.

Price, D. J. de Solla (1986) *Little Science, Big Science . . . and Beyond.* Columbia University Press, New York.

Robbins, R. H. (2005) *Global Problems and the Culture of Capitalism.* Pearson, Boston.

Samuelson, P. A. (2004) The Hawkins and Simon Story Revisited. In: Augier, M. & March, J. G. (Eds.), *Models of a Man: Essays in Memory of Herbert A. Simon.* MIT Press, Cambridge, MA, pp. 153–67.

Steinmetz, G. (2005) Sociology: Scientific Authority and the Transition to Post Fordism. In: Steinmetz, G. (Ed.), *The Politics of Method in the Human Sciences: Positivism and Its Epistemological Others.* Duke University Press, Durham, NC.

Toulmin, S. (1961) Seventeenth Century Science and the Arts. In: Rhys, H. H. (Ed.), *Seventeenth Century Science and the Arts.* Princeton University Press, Princeton, pp. 3–28.

Wilson, E. O. (1999) *Consilience: The Unity of Knowledge.* Alfred A. Knopf, New York.

scientific norms/counternorms

Stephen Turner

The classic sociological formulation of the "norms of science" was given by Robert K. Merton, in an article originally published as "A Note on Science and Democracy" (1942) and reprinted as "Science and Democratic Social Structure" in his *Social Theory and Social Structure* (1968 [1949, 1957]) and as "The Normative Structure of Science" in *The Sociology of Science* (1973). The formulation is sometimes known by its initials, CUDOS, which stands for the four norms: communism, universalism, disinterestedness, and organized skepticism. Merton's representation of the normative character of science has proved to be one of the most enduring of all sociological analyses. It has been discussed at length by both critics, who proposed the concept of counternorms, and sympathizers, and in the late 1960s and early 1970s became emblematic of the "Mertonian" approach to the social study of science. Nor has it remained static. "Replication" is sometimes called the fifth norm. John Ziman suggested that "originality" be added as a norm, and in many recent explanations of the acronym CUDOS the O is used for originality.

THE ORIGINS OF THE NORMS

Merton wrote two papers on the norms of science, both concerned with a political problem: the autonomy of science. The first was "Science and the Social Order" (1938, in Merton 1973). This paper was presented during a period of intense political activity, a response to the political crisis over Nazi science, and in particular to the publication in the journal *Nature* of a translation of an article by J. Stark, originally published in Germany in a Nazi journal, that attacked "Jewish" science. This translation caused a large outcry at a time when scientists in Britain and the United States were largely supportive of peace in Europe, but recognized the threat of Nazism and were coming to recognize the threat that science in Germany would be forced to conform to Nazi ideology. At the time of Merton's first publication on this topic, there was a movement among scientists to respond to the Nazi threat to science politically. A series of resolutions and petitions was circulated, and scientists became politically active in defense of the autonomy of science, that is, the freedom of science from political control and direction (Kuznick 1987). The norms repeat ideas expressed in the petitions. The original title of the paper in which the CUDOS model appears, "Notes on Science and Democracy," written during the war, reflected Merton's anxiety over conflicts that might arise between science and religion that might be given political expression in democracies.

Merton's paper was preceded in the sociological tradition by another deeply influential work, a speech by Max Weber entitled "Science as a Vocation." Weber asks a question on behalf of the students who were the audience for his speech: how does one know that one has a calling for science? The answer is given in terms of the personal qualities that enable one to properly fulfill the role of the scientist (or scholar). Much of the essay is devoted to explaining the limitations of science, and that science cannot provide a worldview. Weber does not give a simple list of personal qualities but speaks of "the plain duty of intellectual integrity" (1946 [1921]: 155, cf. 146, 156), denounces the idea of "personality" in science (p. 137), and says that "the primary task of a useful teacher is to teach his students to recognize 'inconvenient facts'" (p. 147). Weber's comments may be compared to the list of virtues in the first of Merton's papers, "Science and the Social Order." Here, Merton's list of the special virtues of scientists was "intellectual honesty, integrity, organized skepticism, disinterestedness, impersonality" (1973: 259).

Merton's point about these virtues, however, was that they formed an "ethos." This fact was relevant to the autonomy of science. Merton characterized "a liberal society" as one in which "integration derives primarily from the body of cultural norms toward which human activity is oriented" in contrast to a dictatorial structure, where integration is produced through formal organization and centralized social control (1973: 265). Science, because it was governed by an ethos, was already akin to "a liberal society" and thus in effect already autonomous or self-governed. The notion of ethos reappears in the more famous 1942 paper, but the list of virtues changes and the emphasis shifts to the norms of science understood primarily as external constraints, or, as Merton puts it, an "affectively toned complex of values and norms that is held to be binding on the man of science" (1973: 268–9), which the scientist is at least partly socialized into.

THE FOUR NORMS

The list of norms begins with universalism, which Merton explains in terms of "the canon that truth-claims, whatever their sources, are to be subjected to preestablished impersonal criteria" (1973: 270). Acceptance of claims is not to be based on personal or social attributes of the claim-maker, such as race, as the Nazis were encouraged to do by Stark (1938). Universalism is thus rooted in the impersonal character of science. Universalism is potentially a source of conflict with the larger society, particularly when the ethnocentrism of the larger society comes into conflict with science. But there are also cases in which the norm is breached by scientists, for example in wartime, when nationalism leads scientists to denounce the science of other nations for patriotic reasons, as occurred in World War I. Universalism also means that science should be open to talent, whatever the ethnic or status properties of the talented are. In this respect the values of science are similar to, and supported by, the values of democracy.

The second is communism. Merton says that the "substantive findings of science are a product of social collaboration and are assigned to the community. They constitute a common heritage in which the equity of the individual producer is severely limited" (1973: 273). The "property rights" of the scientist to his ideas are limited to that of recognition and esteem. Scientists compete for recognition and are consequently greatly concerned with priority claims about discoveries, a concern which reflects the importance of originality in science. But "the products of competition are communized" (1973: 274). Merton's evidence for this norm includes the mild disapproval given to scientists who fail to communicate their discoveries, and by the fact that scientists acknowledge "standing on the shoulders of giants."

It is sometimes claimed that this norm has nothing to do with communism in the political sense, but this is not true. Merton was influenced by J. D. Bernal, a British scientist and communist who wrote an important book on the social character of science, in which he said that science was already a kind of communism, because scientists "have learned consciously to subordinate themselves to a common purpose without losing the individuality of their achievements," that "each one knows that his work depends on that of his predecessors and colleagues, and that it can only reach its fruition through the work of his successors," and because scientists understand the necessity of collaboration which they accept without the blind following of leaders (1939: 415–16). Bernal, like many of his contemporaries on the left, wrote about the "frustration of science," the idea that capitalism was an obstacle to the application of science to human welfare. Merton alludes to these writings with the comment that the "communism of the scientific ethos is incompatible with the definition of technology as 'private property' in a capitalistic economy" (1973: 275), and notes that one response to the conflict by scientists has been to advocate socialism. His discussion of this and other conflicts produced by this norm points in the direction of his later discussions of the conflicting feelings or ambivalence which norms produce.

"Disinterestedness" is a feature of the professions in general that was important to Talcott Parsons, who related it to the dealings of professionals and clients. Merton observes that scientists do not have "clients" in this way, but do have the problem of fraud and the problem of pseudosciences. Merton observes that fraud is rare in science, and explains this, in a remarkable passage, by saying that "the activities of scientists are subject to rigorous policing, to a degree perhaps unparalleled in any other field of activity" as a result of the public and testable character of science (1973: 276). Socialized sentiment combines with this "rigorous policing" to make this norm especially stable.

Organized skepticism requires the "temporary suspension of judgment and the detached scrutiny of beliefs in terms of empirical and logical criteria" (1973: 277). This is a source of potential friction with religion, and occurs especially when science extends into new topics previously covered by other institutions.

THE COUNTERNORMS AND THE CRITICS

The literature on the norms expanded in the 1950s, with various clarifications and additions, many of which related to the central fact of the passionate, personal commitment of scientists, one of the features of Weber's discussion of science that Merton had omitted. It loomed larger as a result of such influential works as Michael Polanyi's *Personal Knowledge* (1958). Bernard Barber (1952) had suggested that "emotional neutrality" was a separate norm and an important brake on the passions. But Merton and Barber moved away from this image of science. Merton noted that priority disputes were an example of the affective involvement of scientists with their own ideas, and Barber observed that the problem of resistance of scientists to discovery was intrinsic to science. This new view fit better with a functionalist account of science in which both the norms and the passions they contained were functional for science. But it also fit with Merton's developing sense that norms typically involved conflicting feelings or "ambivalence."

The idea that the norms had counternorms was developed by Ian Mitroff, whose study of elite moon scientists showed that tenacity in support of one's own idea was an accepted part of science and a condition for its progress. On the basis of this research, Mitroff proposed counternorms for each norm. The counternorm to organized skepticism, for example, was "organized dogmatism," which he formulated in this way: "The scientist must believe in his own findings with utter conviction while doubting those of others with all his worth" (Mitroff 1974: 592). Michael Mulkay expanded on this discussion, and turned it in a radically different direction. He argued that there were no strongly institutionalized norms of the Mertonian sort in science, and treated the Mertonian norms as an "ideology," asking what purposes this ideology served, suggesting that we understand science "not just as a community with special professional concerns and with normative components appropriate to these concerns, but also as an interest group with a domineering elite and a justificatory ideology" (1976: 654).

This line of argument drove the discussion toward the question of whether the norms were applicable to the new situation of science, which was understood to be more commercialized and "private." The norms came to appear to some critics as the idealization of a previous form of science that systematically distorted the present understanding of science. New models of transdisciplinary research with specific practical goals also seemed to fit poorly with the norms, which now could be seen to relate primarily to competition for prestige in a disciplinary setting.

SEE ALSO: Ambivalence; Communism; Merton, Robert K.; Nobel Prizes and the Scientific Elite; Norms; Science and Culture; Science and Public Participation: The Democratization of Science; Science and Religion

REFERENCES AND SUGGESTED READINGS

Barber, B. (1952) *Science and the Social Order.* Free Press, Glencoe, IL.

Bernal, J. D. (1939) *The Social Function of Science.* MIT Press, Cambridge, MA.

Kuznick, P. J. (1987) *Beyond the Laboratory.* University of Chicago Press, Chicago.

Merton, R. K. (1942) A Note on Science and Democracy. *Journal of Legal and Political Sociology* 1: 15–26.

Merton, R. K. (1968 [1949, 1957]) *Social Theory and Social Structure.* Free Press, New York.

Merton, R. K. (1973) *The Sociology of Science.* University of Chicago Press, Chicago.

Mitroff, I. (1974) Norms and Counternorms in a Select Group of Apollo Moon Scientists: A Case Study of the Ambivalence of Scientists. *American Sociological Review* 39: 579–95.

Mulkay, M. J. (1976) Norms and Ideology in Science. *Social Science Information* 15(4/5): 637–56.

Polanyi, M. (1958) *Personal Knowledge: Towards a Post-Critical Philosophy.* University of Chicago Press, Chicago.

Stark, J. (1938) The Pragmatic and the Dogmatic Spirit in Physics. *Nature* 141 (April 30): 770–1.

Weber, M. (1946 [1921]) Science as a Vocation. In: *From Max Weber: Essays in Sociology.* Trans.

H. H. Gerth & C. W. Mills. Oxford University Press, New York, pp. 129–56.
Ziman, J. (2000) *Real Science: What It Is and What It Means*. Cambridge University Press, Cambridge.

scientific productivity

Sooho Lee

Scientific productivity refers to the productivity of scientists in their research performance. In other words, the term concerns how much output scientists produce within a certain time period, or compared to the inputs that are utilized for the research. The major outputs from research are publications, patents, inventions, and product developments. However, especially in research institutions, productivity more directly refers to publication or publishing productivity since most research results are reported as forms of publication. Therefore, being "more or less productive" simply indicates that a scientist produces more or fewer publications than do others. Scholarly journal articles, books, conference papers, and monographs are included in publication counts. Among the publication forms, peer-reviewed journal articles are most frequently used as a productivity measure.

Three different methods are used for counting publications: normal count (also called *standard* count), fractional count (also called *adjusted* count), and first-author count (also called *straight* count). In normal count, each of the co-authors is given full credit for the multi-authored publications regardless of how much each contributed to the publications. This counting method is most often used due to the convenience of data collection. However, inflating the number of publications is a major disadvantage. In contrast, in a fractional count, each publication is counted as one divided by the number of co-authors. The main purpose of using fractional count is to remove an overestimation of normal count and estimate the individual contribution to a publication. But the process of fractional counting is very tedious since all the co-authors are not always identified. First-author count is another way to remove the inflated credit by normal count and to determine the individual's major contribution to publications. This method only recognizes publications in which the individual has contributed as the main author.

While publication counts deal with the quantity of research performance, citation counts, on the other hand, address the quality of publications. It is often said that the more qualified the publication, the greater the number of citations. However, citation count is less frequently used for measuring productivity because it is not a direct output but shows the impact or influence of publications.

Since scientific productivity is of interest not only to academics but also for public policy in more recent times, what determines scientific productivity has been extensively studied in many disciplines. The literature identifies many determinants including psychological characteristics, demographic characteristics, environmental characteristics, cumulative advantages, and reinforcement. Psychological characteristics indicate that motivation, inner compulsion, capacity to work hard, cognitive and perceptual style, and work habits all affect the productivity of scientists significantly. It is almost always true that productive scientists have strong motivation and orientation for research.

Among the demographic characteristics, age is an important predictor for productivity. Early studies found that a productivity peak occurs in scientists' late thirties and early forties and thereafter declines steadily. By contrast, some recent studies identify another productivity peak around age 50. Although there are many different life cycle models of productivity, they should be interpreted appropriately in the context of a specific discipline. For example, the productivity cycle in physics is different from that in sociology. In most cases, scientists become less productive as they age, especially after 50. It is also often pointed out that the age effect is attributed to age and not to the possibility that older scientists have different attributes, values, or access to resources than younger members. Like age, gender is also an important variable affecting productivity difference. Early studies commonly pointed out that women tend to have somewhat lower publication rates than men. But more recent studies do not agree with this proposition, rather believing that sex differences in publication productivity are negligible, with the exception of women with young children. In a similar vein, one recent study found that sex differences in the number of publications increase during the first decade of the career, but are reversed later in the career.

Environmental and organizational factors also play a significant role in determining scientific productivity. For example, prestigious institutions tend to have more research resources and many "star" scientists in more specific research fields. The advantages are likely to help their scientists to collaborate more easily with experts inside the organization and also to attract more joint research and research grants from outsiders. Especially when research projects require more expensive equipment and infrastructure (not only physical but also human capital), the institutional capacity and external supports significantly affect research performance.

Cumulative advantage and reinforcement theories explain the difference of scientific productivity among scientists by using a concept of "feedback" processes. They propose that prior exceptional performance is conducive to later performance. The ideas are largely based on Merton's so-called "Matthew effect" in science: once scientists receive recognition from their colleagues, they accrue additional advantages as they progress through their careers. The advantages typically begin with doctoral training in a prestigious department. The training, in turn, leads to a position in a major research university amply supplied with adequate resources for research. The initial appointment has a major impact on later productivity, and in turn, the prestige of second department and subsequent productivity. Cumulative advantage deals with resources and prestige of institutions, whereas reinforcement addresses the feedback one receives from successful publication of works, works being cited, and formal and informal praise from colleagues. Reinforcement theory typically explains that when scientists publish, the recognition they receive for the contribution stimulates further publication.

Although publication productivity measures scientists' research performance efficiently, it still loses many aspects of scientists' research performance. In particular, the outputs of teaching and mentoring as important research activities are often neglected in measuring scientific productivity. So a better measurement needs to be developed to include broader aspects of scientific activity.

SEE ALSO: Matthew Effect; Peer Review and Quality Control in Science; Science; Scientific Networks and the Invisible Colleges

REFERENCES AND SUGGESTED READINGS

Creswell, J. (1985) *Faculty Research Performance: Lessons from the Sciences and the Social Sciences.* ASHE, Washington, DC.

Fox, M. (1983) Publication Productivity Among Scientists: A Critical Review. *Social Studies of Science* 2: 285–305.

Gaston, J. (1978) *The Reward System in British and American Science.* Wiley, New York.

Lee, S. & Bozeman, B. (2005) The Impact of Research Collaboration on Scientific Productivity. *Social Studies of Science* 35: 673–702.

Levin, S. & Stephan, P. (1991) Research Productivity over the Life Cycle: Evidence for Academic Scientists. *American Economic Review* 81(1): 114–32.

Long, S. (1992) Measure of Sex Differences in Scientific Productivity. *Social Forces* 71(1): 159–78.

Merton, R. K. (1973) *The Sociology of Science: Theoretical and Empirical Investigations.* University of Chicago Press, Chicago.

Pelz, D. & Andrews, F. (1966) *Scientists in Organizations: Productive Climate for Research and Development.* Wiley, New York.

scientific racism

Jessica Blatt

Science has a long and fraught history of entanglement with the social myth of biological race. The modern sciences of biology and physical anthropology were founded on the conviction that racial difference was real, fundamental, and key to understanding the proper relationships between human groups. Advances in these very sciences, however, have shown that race is in no way an objective, natural category. While there are certainly biological differences among human populations, these differences are both relatively trivial and impossible to map onto conventional racial divides. Genetic research, similarly, has yielded no statistically significant patterns of variation by race (Marks 2002). However, this is not a simple story of scientific progress, in which bad ideas are systematically displaced by better ones. The rise and (incomplete) retreat of scientific racism is an eminently political story.

In general terms, scientific racism is characterized by two central fallacies: a classificatory fallacy (race formalism) and a fallacy of reductionism and determinism in which complex phenomena such as intelligence or the capacity for self-restraint are reified and explained as resulting straightforwardly from apparently simple causes, such as genes. Race formalism is the idea that humanity can be subdivided into groups that form "real," objective, natural units, sharing significant biological, and usually cultural and behavioral, characteristics. Originating in the rage for classification in Enlightenment science and philosophy, this idea reached a peak of scientific respectability in the decades around the turn of the twentieth century.

In *Systema Naturae* (1740), Carolus Linneaus, the father of zoological classification, proposed four subdivisions of humankind: Americanus, Europaeus, Asiaticus, and Afer, or African. In a 1795 revision of his seminal work *On the Natural Variety of Mankind,* the German naturalist Johann Friedrich Blumenbach elaborated on this scheme, identifying five "races," the first and most perfect being, in his coinage, "Caucasian." Along with his invention of the Caucasian race, Blumenbach is remembered for introducing an explicit hierarchy into the Linnaean scheme. Nevertheless, Blumenbach recognized clearly that boundaries between races are artificial, and in fact his classification reflected the widely shared Enlightenment belief in the essential unity of humankind, with any variations explained in environmental terms.

As debates over slavery heightened during the nineteenth century, however, this view of humanity's natural history was rejected by many who argued that human races were in fact unrelated, hierarchically ranked species. Known as polygenesis or "multiple creations," this theory reached its height of popularity around the time of the American Civil War. Polygenetic theories spurred the collection of reams of physical data, particularly relating to skull size and form, meant to define race differences. (This data and its uses have been effectively critiqued by Gould 1996.)

After the publication of Charles Darwin's *Origin of Species* (1859), polygenesis was largely displaced in scientific discourse by notions of races as groups sharing a common origin but occupying distinct rungs of an evolutionary ladder (though many scientists persisted in labeling these groups as separate species). The late decades of the nineteenth century saw intense interest both in using evolutionary frameworks to understand social reality and in racial classification specifically. (This was particularly so in the United States following the abandonment of Reconstruction-era attempts to establish civic equality for freed slaves.) These trends were most prominently expressed in attempts to explain social hierarchy in terms of relative evolutionary fitness (social Darwinism, associated with Herbert Spencer), to measure and quantify racial difference (ethnology), and to reconstruct the evolutionary history of Europeans through study of living groups of "savages" (an enterprise known as the "comparative method").

Efforts to systematize racial classification, however, proved elusive. The 1911 *Report of the Dillingham Commission on Immigration to the US Senate* illustrates this difficulty. The report's "Dictionary of Races or Peoples" (even the title is indecisive) follows a racial classification recognizing 5 races, 6 "stocks," and 64 "peoples." At the same time, it acknowledges five distinct, competing schemes, proposing as few as 3 and as many as 29 races. However, the difficulty of imposing racial boundaries on human diversity, while it frustrated many biologists and physical anthropologists, did not by itself lead many to abandon the attempt. This required the confluence of external, political events with the efforts of scientific activists.

Throughout the nineteenth century, the physical characteristics of race were generally seen to be associated with behavioral characteristics as well, almost universally in ways that favored Europeans over other races, with "Negroes" or "Africans" at the bottom. The dissemination, just after the turn of the twentieth century, of Gregor Mendel's theories of heredity lent support to the idea that these behavioral traits were fixed, hereditary, and determined by what eventually came to be called "genes." These reductionist and determinist notions fueled the American eugenics movement, which defended the regime of racial segregation and advocated (with considerable success) anti-miscegenation laws, immigration restriction, and compulsory sterilization of the "unfit," all in the name of racial purity and "betterment." They were also linked to a series of attempts to quantify (and map the racial distribution of) human potential, as with the development of IQ and other mental tests. The emerging discipline of industrial relations also used racial classifications, attempting to determine which groups were best suited to particular kinds of work. To be sure, such ideas were not confined to the United States. Arguments about the biologically determined inferiority of non-white groups figured in justifications of European colonialism broadly and helped to legitimize the regime of segregation that would come to be known as apartheid in South Africa, for instance.

Eugenics would see its most complete and horrific expression in Germany, where "race hygiene," as the movement was known there, helped to justify the Holocaust. Nonetheless, American scientific racism was particularly virulent and influential. (The first compulsory sterilization law promulgated by the Nazi regime was in fact copied from a model drafted by American eugenist Harry Laughlin.)

Widespread revulsion provoked by revelations of Nazi atrocities helped fuel an international reaction against scientific racism in the post-World War II era. The United Nations Education, Scientific, and Cultural Organization (UNESCO) issued a series of "statements on race" signed by leading social and natural scientists beginning in 1950 (Montagu 1972). These statements, while not entirely unambiguous, were generally understood as a collective statement by the scientific community declaring racial doctrines to be harmful ideology without basis in natural science. They were the long-delayed fruit of lobbying efforts by activist, anti-racist scientists, led to a significant degree by anthropologist Franz Boas, to combat scientific racism (Barkan 1992). These efforts largely discredited scientific racism within the mainstream science and larger academic communities. More broadly, over the ensuing decades the US civil rights revolution and decolonization in Asia and Africa worked to delegitimize popular racism to an extent, decreasing the appeal of scientific racism in and outside the academy.

Nevertheless, scientific racism is far from gone. Even in the immediate aftermath of the first UNESCO statements, white supremacists continued to try to turn racialist theories to political advantage, for example in a series of lawsuits aimed at overturning *Brown* v. *Board of Education* (1954), the landmark Supreme Court decision outlawing racial segregation in American schools. More recently, a number of attempts to explain racial stratification in biological terms have surfaced since the 1980s, probably the best known of which is Richard Herrnstein and Charles Murray's *The Bell Curve* (1994). While widely criticized and largely discredited within mainstream science, scientific racism continues to tap into widespread folk ideas about racial difference and hierarchy.

SEE ALSO: Apartheid and Nelson Mandela; *Bell Curve, The* (Herrstein and Murray); Eugenics; Holocaust; Immigration; Industrial Relations; Race; Race (Racism); Racial Hierarchy; Racist Movements; Spencer, Herbert; Stratification, Race/Ethnicity and

REFERENCES AND SUGGESTED READINGS

Barkan, E. (1992) *The Retreat of Scientific Racism: Changing Conceptions of Race in Britain and the United States Between the World Wars.* Cambridge University Press, Cambridge.

Degler, C. N. (1991) *In Search of Human Nature: The Decline and Revival of Darwinism in American Social Thought.* Oxford University Press, New York.

Gould, S. J. (1996) *The Mismeasure of Man*, revd. edn. W. W. Norton, New York.

Marks, J. (2002) *What It Means to Be 98% Chimpanzee: Apes, People, and Their Genes.* University of California Press, Berkeley.

Montagu, A. (1972) *Statements on Race.* Oxford University Press, New York.

Stepan, N. (1982) *The Idea of Race in Science.* Archon Books, Hamden, CT.

Stocking, G. (1968) *Race, Culture, and Evolution: Essays in the History of Anthropology.* Free Press, New York.

Tucker, W. (1994) *The Science and Politics of Racial Research.* University of Illinois Press, Urbana.

scientific revolution

J. I. (Hans) Bakker

To summarize the scientific revolution in one phrase: it was the time when a new way of studying the natural, physical world became widely accepted by a small "community of scholars," although not necessarily by nonscientists. But the specific status of that "new way" is hotly disputed and the precise historical steps involved in that development are extremely complex. Standard histories are those by Dampier (1966) and Cohen (2001). Cohen stresses the stages involved from initial creative insight to dissemination (orally or in letters, later on in print) and then widespread acceptance. For example, Descartes' theory of inertia of 1633 was held back when the Inquisition condemned Galileo's theological interpretations and Descartes decided it was not a good time to publish. In the seventeenth century there was a significant qualitative transformation in the approach to the study of natural philosophy and that major change is now often called the "scientific revolution," but it is clear that small-scale "revolutions" took place before and have happened since. It was at that time that the transition from undifferentiated "astronomy/astrology" and "alchemy/chemistry" first really got under way. Moreover, great advances were made in mathematics. The story of the rise of modern science begins even earlier, however, with the Arab contacts with Greek science, and modern science eventually led to Enlightenment philosophy (Hellemans & Bunch 1988: 58–188). Different natural philosophies changed at different rates and in different ways. For example, empirical and theoretical progress in astronomy and physics was different from progress in other physical sciences like chemistry (Goodman & Russell 1991: 387–414). However, it was between circa 1500 and 1800 that the distinction between true science and proto-science or pseudo-science (Shermer 2001: 22–65) became somewhat clearer. Many thinkers have seen the essence of the intellectual revolution as a leap beyond the tradition inherited from Aristotelianism and rationalism. But the notion that simple inductive empiricism, often identified with Francis Bacon's New "Organon" (*Novum organum*) of 1620, is the basis of the scientific method has been rejected. It should be remembered that the introduction of Aristotle's *Organon* concerning "categories" and "interpretation," and his physics, astronomy, and biology transferred into Roman Catholic theology by Thomas Aquinas, was considered a radical step and indeed did open a window to the study of the actual order of nature and the universe (Funkenstein 1986). The idea of the importance of nuances of general theoretical assumptions concerning ontology and epistemology has been widely shared ever since the early 1960s, when Kuhn's (1970) history of paradigmatic changes in physical science became widely accepted. Indeed, the social sciences now also regularly use Kuhn's general theory of an oscillation between "normal science" and "paradigmatic revolutions." The link between Kuhn's theories and earlier views concerning a dialectic of reason – views primarily associated with Hegel's critique of Cartesian dualism (Russon 1991) – should be noted. However, the seventeenth-century paradigmatic revolution associated with Descartes, Galileo, Copernicus, Kepler, von Helmont, and many others was extremely important, since it laid the foundation for what was considered to be true science for the next four centuries. Newton's laws of gravitational attraction, motion, and force (i.e., inverse square law) in the *Principia Mathematica* (1687 manuscript) led to British Newtonianism, which was widely exported throughout Europe (e.g., the Low Countries), but Cartesianism in France was a rival for many years (Russell 1991). In the eighteenth century botany and zoology became more systematic with the use of binomial nomenclature, although Linnaeus's theories of nature and of society were deeply flawed (Koerner 1999). It was only at the beginning of the twentieth century that a series of new ideas constituting a general change in worldviews made a radical shift in scientific thinking possible. Einstein's theory of relativity did not reject Newtonian mechanics, but did make it clear that Newton's assumptions about space and time were too limited and that a true explanation of gravity required postulating "space-time." Similarly, discoveries in mathematics and statistics, particularly the invention of non-Euclidean geometry, revolutionized science in the twentieth century in somewhat the same way they had in earlier times (Newman 1956). The same can be said for Boolean and Fregean mathematical and symbolic logic (Bartley in Dodgson 1986: 3–42). Comte (1957) wrote that scientific thinking moves only gradually, but inevitably, from the study of distant objects, such as stars, to that which is closest to human life – society itself. His positivism had a profound impact on logical positivism and the quest for "consilience," a unified general science of all of the natural world (Wilson 1998). In English the distinction between science and social science is more rigid than in many other languages. In German the term *Wissenschaft* encompasses not only physical and natural sciences, but also social sciences and other disciplines such as history and jurisprudence.

SEE ALSO: Comte, Auguste; Hegel, G. W. F.; Kuhn, Thomas and Scientific Paradigms; Science

REFERENCES AND SUGGESTED READINGS

Aristotle (1941) *Organon*. In: Mc Keon, R. (Ed.), *The Basic Works of Aristotle*. Random House, New York, pp. 1–212.

Cohen, I. B. (2001) *Revolution in Science*. Belknap/ Harvard University Press, Cambridge, MA.

Comte, A. (1957) *A General View of Positivism*. Trans. J. H. Bridges. Robert Speller & Sons, New York.

Dampier, W. C. (1966 [1929]) *A History of Science*, 4th edn. Cambridge University Press, Cambridge.

Dodgson, C. L. (1986 [1896]) *Lewis Carroll's Symbolic Logic*. Ed. W. W. Bartley, III. Clarkson N. Potter Publishers, New York.

Funkenstein, A. (1986) *Theology and the Scientific Imagination: From the Middle Ages to the Seventeenth Century*. Princeton University Press, Princeton.

Goodman, D. & Russell, C. A. (Eds.) (1991) *The Rise of Scientific Europe: 1500–1800*. Hodder & Stoughton, London.

Hellemans, A. & Bunch, B. (1988) *The Timetables of Science*. Simon & Schuster, New York.

Koerner, L. (1999) *Linnaeus: Nature and Nation*. Harvard University Press, Cambridge, MA.

Kuhn, T. (1970) *The Structure of Scientific Revolutions*, 2nd edn. University of Chicago Press, Chicago.

Newman, J. R. (Ed.) (1956) *The World of Mathematics*, 4 vols. Simon & Schuster, New York.

Russell, C. A. (1991) The Reception of Newtonianism in Europe. In: Goodman, D. & Russell, C. A. (Eds.), *The Rise of Scientific Europe: 1500–1800*. Hodder & Stoughton, London, pp. 253–78.

Shermer, M. (2001) *The Borderlands of Science*. Oxford University Press, Oxford.

Wilson, E. O. (1998) *Consilience*. Random House, New York.

Wilson, F. (1999) *The Logic and Methodology of Science in Early Modern Thought*. University of Toronto Press, Toronto.

scientology

Peter B. Anderson

Scientology, or officially the "Church of Scientology," was founded by adherents of Lafayette Ron Hubbard (1911–86) in 1954, but the movement behind Scientology dates back to Hubbard's publication of the book *Dianetics: The Modern Science of Mental Health* in 1950. Dianetics was a therapeutic system which Hubbard claimed could cure psychosomatic illness. Dianetics can be described as an attack on what Hubbard considered to be the materialistic position of psychiatry. Hubbard stressed that he wanted to overcome the unspiritual therapeutic strategies he saw in psychiatry and to deliver the techniques for everyone to reach mental wholesomeness. In his anthropology, man is basically good and strives for survival of various collectives termed "dynamics," in Dianetics from the individual level to that of humanity, and in Scientology he added further levels up to the "urge towards existence as infinity," termed the "God Dynamic."

Dianetics assumes that a person receives and stores impressions, the so-called "engrams," painful memories from this or earlier lives, leading an individual to irrational acts. The aim of Dianetics was that man should reach the state of "clear" – completely rational. The Dianetics therapy is based on "auditing," which involves an auditor who listens to the statements of the "pre-clear," as the person in an auditing session is termed. Besides the principles underlining the early steps of the auditing, the contents up towards and above clear are not known to outsiders, as it is considered dangerous knowledge for people who have not acquired it through proper auditing.

After a number of conflicts – including conflicts with the established psychiatric and psychological therapeutic system – economic crisis, and the fact that he lost the copyright to his own book, Hubbard formed a new organization and the first Church of Scientology was founded in 1954. From an organizational point of view the Church of Scientology appears to be in contrast to Dianetics. Dianetics was loosely organized, public, and impossible to manage for Hubbard, whereas the Church of Scientology is hierarchic, with control systems making sure that all employees act in accordance with the wishes of the organization. This has been reshuffled and strengthened a number of times. The Sea Organization (Sea Org) was founded as an elite group of Scientologists committing themselves up to a billion years in 1967. In 1981 the religious activities were collected in the Church of Scientology International and since 1982 the religious activities have been overseen by the Religious Technology Center, which holds all the trade and service marks of Hubbard's work since his death.

The organizational development has been identified as one of the rare transformations from a so-called cult to a sect. The cult consists of open-minded seekers in a cultic milieu, whereas the sect claims to have a unique way of salvation which the adherents have to follow (Wallis 1977).

In its belief system, influences from theosophy, Eastern religions, and interplanetary activity can be seen, and Scientology emphasizes that members may sustain other religious memberships as well. As a consequence it is difficult to determine the exact number of Scientologists. In many countries Scientology does not keep central membership files, and beyond an active core many Scientologists have little or no contact with the church, even if they consider themselves Scientologists. World-based estimates vary from about 1 million to the official figure of 8 million in 2004.

Hubbard's utilitarian ethics led him to investigate a number of social phenomena and based on his findings there are now separate organizations for the improvement of education (Association for Better Living and Education (ABLE) and Applied Scholastics) and drug habilitation (Narconon). Other organizations include the Way to Happiness Foundation, and the Citizens Commission for Human Rights (CCHR). Apart from general human rights activities, the CCHR continues Hubbard's fight with the psychiatric system, where it tries to document abuses in medication and links to Nazi medicine.

Whereas social activities have been kept within the general frame of Scientology, there have recently been attempts to disseminate techniques to improve the situation of individuals beyond the lines of Scientology. This is a reaction to the events following the attack on the Twin Towers in New York in 2001. Scientology considers the "War against Terror" dangerous for humanity, and thinks that it has set the world on a course towards destruction. The attempt to disseminate techniques to improve individuals has been accompanied by a general recruitment campaign, to "clear the world."

Scientology's widespread activities have been difficult to fit into classificatory frameworks of health science, psychiatry, religion, and social activities in general. Scientology insists that auditing is a primary religious activity, and has faced problems being recognized as a full fledged religious body in countries (e.g., Great Britain) where religious activities are deemed to be collective. Many countries have allowed Scientology to register as a religious body due to the general religious content of the system (e.g., in the USA, Australia, Sweden, Germany). In some places the related social activities are considered religious, and in others charitable, independent of whether Scientology is recognized as a religious body in the country or not.

SEE ALSO: Charisma; Cults: Social Psychological Aspects; New Religious Movements; Religion, Sociology of; Sect

REFERENCES AND SUGGESTED READINGS

Frenschkowski, M. (1999) L. Ron Hubbard and Scientology: An Annotated Bibliographical Survey of Primary and Selected Secondary Literature. *Marburg Journal of Religion* 4(1): July.

Melton, J. G. (2000) *The Church of Scientology*, Signature Books, Lexington, KY.

Wallis, R. (1977) *The Road to Total Freedom: A Sociological Analysis of Scientology.* Columbia University Press, New York.

Whitehead, H. (1987) *Renunciation and Reformulation: A Study of Conversion in an American Sect.* Cornell University Press, Ithaca, NY.
Willms, G. (2005) *Scientology. Kulturbeobachtungen jenseits der Devianz.* Verlag, Bielefeld.
Wilson, B. R. (1990) Scientology: A Secularized Religion. In: *The Social Dimensions of Sectarianism: Sects and New Religious Movements in Contemporary Society.* Oxford University Press, Oxford, pp. 267–88.

scientometrics

Yuri Jack Gómez Morales

Scientometrics is a methodological discipline and an administrative practice. In the first case, its major concern has been the identification of patterns of communication among scientists supporting theoretical models of cognitive and institutional development of science. In the second case, its concern is the identification of patterns in science and technology activities conceived as an input/output productive system. In both cases the identification of patterns is quantitative oriented and the interpretation of data has relied heavily on economic and sociological models and in recent times, on informational models, too.

SCIENTOMETRICS AS AN ADMINISTRATIVE PRACTICE

The integration of science and technology into national account systems became a necessity when the activity reached financial prominence after World War II. Science and technology activities constitute so large an enterprise that nowadays they employ hundreds of thousands of scientists and engineers all over the world, requiring significant proportions of GNP. Thus, countries have felt the need to render these activities accountable for scientists themselves, the general public, the state, and for those engaged in the administration, funding, and execution of science and technology activities.

The official history of scientometrics as an administrative practice often signals J. D. Bernal's *The Social Function of Science* (1939) as its inaugural work. Bernal's contribution set the quantitative study of scientific literature and personnel and the utilization of mathematical models as the foundations of objective examination and deliberation on science policy and management. Yet, as the developmental age that followed the war took off, scientometrics also began to be considered among the developmental sciences (Anderson & Buck 1980).

Due to its potential for empowering actors in controlling science and technology activities by scientific means, scientometrics developed greatly, in contrast with earlier and more encompassing proposals such as the *Science of Science* program proposed by Price (1964), which gradually went into decline. If this program once comprised the "history, philosophy, sociology, psychology, economics, political science, and operations research (etc.) of science, technology, medicine (etc.)," the development of scientometrics has been more decidedly oriented towards the making of metrics for the measurement of relevant social variables that would make possible the study of science and technology activities from the plethora of theoretical perspectives just mentioned.

Through quantification, scientometrics is at first glance prone to and easily integrated into economics, and through it to developmental policies for science and technology. Indeed, at different times economists have seen science, technology, or both (depending on the underlying model) as the missing factor or the key element explaining economic growth and sociocultural development. In a broader sense, scientometrics as an administrative practice involves the construction and use of a wide range of measurements and models employed in prospective studies (i.e., the assessment of future trends in science and technology within plausible socioeconomic scenarios, in technical change studies, demographic studies on human resources for science and technology, technology choice, science and technology planning, and more recently, knowledge management within commercial and private organizations) (Tisdell 1981).

SCIENTOMETRICS AS A METHODOLOGICAL DISCIPLINE

As a methodological discipline scientometrics is conceived in a more restrictive sense limited to the study of scientific communication processes (Borgman 1990) and more often than not to the identification of quantitative patterns found in scientific literature. Despite the fact that there is no real agreement about this reduction of scientometrics to bibliometrics, nor about the identity between scientometrics and *informetrics* (*Scientometrics* 1994), from this bibliometric viewpoint scientometrics has been more often associated with the sociological understanding of science, both as a social system and as a socio-technical network.

As regards the literature there is a clear set of contributions starting from the 1960s that might be grouped as belonging to scientometrics as a methodological discipline. One of the most significant is *Little Science, Big Science* published in 1963 by the physicist and historian of science Dereck de Solla Price. The significance of this contribution is that it brought together previously published isolated results into an all-encompassing model for the quantitative study of science based on its formal communication patterns. The three main problems this model addresses are the growth, structure, and consumption of scientific literature.

The logistic model of scientific growth states that if any sufficiently large segment of science is measured in any reasonable way, this measurement will show that at any time in history, science's rate of growth is proportional to its size, whatever the index chosen for measurement. In the first mathematical approach, the empirical law of growth (as Price named it) can be represented by an exponential function with a doubling period of about 10 to 15 years, depending on how stringent are the criteria used for defining the chosen index. It is evident that such sustained growth, starting in the sixteenth century, cannot continue indefinitely. Eventually, exponential growth will reach some limit, when the process must slacken and stop or, as a result of substantial contextual changes, science will undergo a redefinition so that further growth can be achieved. Price's exciting conclusions about the future of science once it reaches saturation were not subject to further investigation or monitoring.

As to the structure of scientific production, the model resumed investigations undertook as early as 1874 by Galton's inquiries into social elites developed in his *Hereditary Genius* (1984) and Lotka's empirical work on *The Frequency Distribution of Scientific Productivity* (1926). Having defined science in terms of the time-series of scientific papers obeying a particularly fast pattern of growth, a further characterization of this growth can be made by showing that a relatively small and stable core of authors is responsible for a large fraction of scientific papers, and that the bulk of the population contributing the rest flows through rapidly.

Finally, the model integrates studies concerned with the consumption of scientific literature. Although Price was aware of its importance, it was the technical and conceptual contributions of Eugene Garfield (1955) that made possible the development of empirical research on this parameter. He introduced *citation indexing*, a method that revolutionized the way in which published knowledge (previously arranged by subject matter) was organized, using the relationships between documents established by authors themselves when referencing other papers. Garfield implemented this new form of bibliographical control using 1960s state-of-the-art technology (computing) in order to process massive bibliographic data. Thus, by contrast to previous quantitative studies of the literature (including Price's) that were developed from the production side of the communication process using traditional bibliographic control, Garfield's development, which focused on the consumption side of the communication process, yielded an entirely new arena for bibliometrics whose results were consistent with Price's previous conclusions regarding the structure of scientific literature.

Scientometrics as a methodological discipline has developed many more important concepts and techniques, such as invisible colleges, the citation cycle, the Price Index, the co-citation analysis, and the impact factor. However, the three notions of logistic growth, distribution of productivity, and citation of scientific literature constitute the heart of bibliometrics and have been the departure point of scientometrics as an administrative practice, as any input/output analysis of science and technology takes into consideration bibliometrics as part of its battery of indicators.

Most interesting, however, are the interpretations and uses sociologists have made of bibliometrics. The very idea of bibliometrics as a specialty research method for the sociology of science is due to Merton and it was put into practice by his pupils when empirical investigations of the *normative structure of science* took off by the mid-1960s. At its outset the empirical program of the sociology of science focused on the problem of *stratification* within the social system of science (i.e., how to explain the social standing and value assigned to individuals within the community and the mechanism of social mobility within this community). Functionalists focused on the formal communication system of science – the scientific journals – as a privileged field for studying stratification, in as much as this system embodied, via peer reviewing, the complex of values and technical norms practiced by the scientific community when evaluating the originality, significance, and ultimately the quality of a contribution. Social standing within the community is then a result of rewards and other *cumulative advantages* conferred to a scientist on the basis of the significance of his or her contribution to the advancement of science and the fulfilment of the code of practice in achieving it. From this point of view, the basic reward a scientist may receive for his or her contribution is a citation to it. So it was that citation started to be considered as an indicator of scientific quality which, together with data on the productivity and growth of scientific literature, reveals a clear correlation between consumption, productivity, and social standing within the community. Moreover, soon after the introduction of the Science Citation Index, the range of applications of bibliometric data for the study of science was rapidly enhanced to include the history of scientific discoveries, cognitive maps of research fronts, and differentiated patterns of development among the sciences (natural and applied) and between these sciences and the humanities.

There is another bibliometric strand associated with actor-network theory (Callon et al. 1986). According to this view, publishing scientific results is part of a more comprehensive strategy scientists use in the social making of scientific facts. Indeed, publication is an important part of the strategy, for it is by that means that the socio-technical network required for supporting a knowledge claim is constructed. Thus, if scientists' performance is guided by interests rather than values, the methodological question was to develop means for following those interests and their textual translations as they are performed in the scientific paper via referencing. The starting point of qualitative scientometrics is the indexicality of words-like-problems used by scientists in their texts. Actor-network theorists focused on the way in which an author indexes a bibliographic reference within a line of argument that a paper develops. For analytical purposes, then, an article may be reduced to a network of powerful words that can be represented as a simple graph linking all of them. Each point on the graph represents a word, while a line indicates that the words linked in this way co-occur in the article. The graph that summarizes an article can be read, like the original article, as a structured network of claimed equivalences. Such claimed equivalences between heterogeneous elements represent an authors's strategy of translation. Thus, an author's socio-technical network can be described to an extent through the equivalences and linkages between problems-like-words and through the measurement of the number of times such an equivalence appears in the total body of literature in which it might occur. The co-word approach allows successful translations to be traced and distinguished. This visualization makes possible a departure from the network of textual translations to the network of socio-technical problems, interests, and actors.

SEE ALSO: Actor-Network Theory; Citations and Scientific Indexing; Matthew Effect; Scientific Norms/Counternorms; Scientific Productivity

REFERENCES AND SUGGESTED READINGS

Anderson, M. B. & Buck, P. (1980) Scientific Development: The Development of Science, Science and Development, and the Science of Development. *Social Studies of Science* 10: 215–30.

Borgman, C. (Ed.) (1990) *Scholarly Communication and Bibliometrics*. Sage, Newbury Park, CA.
Callon, M., Law, J., Rip, A., Latour, B., Bastide, F., Bauin, S., & Turner, W. A. (1986) *Mapping the Dynamics of Science and Technology: Sociology of Science in the Real World*. Macmillan, Basingstoke.
Elkana, Y., Lederberg, J., Merton, R. K., Thackray, A., & Zuckerman, H. A. (1978) *Toward a Metric of Science: The Advent of Science Indicators*. John Wiley, New York.
Garfield, E. (1955) Citation Index for Science. *Science* 122: 108–111.
Geisler, E. (2000) *The Metrics of Science and Technology*. Quorum Books, Westport.
Gilbert, N. G. (1978) Measuring the Growth of Science. *Scientometrics* 1(1): 9–34.
Leydesdorf, L. (1999) *Universities and the Global Knowledge Economy: A Triple Helix of University-Industry-Government Relations*. Cassell, London.
Price, D. J. D. S. (1964) The Science of Science. In: Goldsmith, M. & Mackay, A. (Eds.), *The Science of Science: Society in the Technological Age*. Souvenir Press, London, pp. 195–208.
Scientometrics (1994) Special Issue. *Scientometrics* 30 (2–3).
Tisdell, C. A. (1981) *Science and Technology Policy: Prorities of Governments*. Chapman & Hall, London.
Van Raan, A. F. J. (1988) *Handbook of Quantitative Studies of Science and Technology*. North-Holland, Amsterdam.

scripting theories

David Knapp Whittier

To articulate a sociological approach to human sexuality, William Simon and John Gagnon drew upon Kenneth Burke's dramatism and view that it is inappropriate and inaccurate to apply physical models to social phenomena. The "sexual script" concept (Gagnon & Simon 1973) summarizes their approach and their fullest articulation is known as "sexual scripting theory" (Simon & Gagnon 1986). The theory stresses three major areas of social life as significant for the production of sexuality: (1) cultural scenarios for sexuality, (2) interpersonal sexual scripting, and (3) intrapsychic sexual scripting. "Cultural scenarios" refers to definitions of and instructions for sex which can be found in social institutions and cultural materials. "Interpersonal scripting" refers to the social arrangement of actual sexual interactions. "Intrapsychic scripting" refers to the activity and content of the mind, like sexual thoughts, fantasies, beliefs, and emotions. Sexual scripting analysis is the examination of the separate roles and interrelationships of these three areas of social life as they help produce sexuality.

Sexual scripting theory was built up out of the application of sociological ideas to sexuality. Gagnon and Simon's book, *Sexual Conduct: The Social Sources of Human Sexuality*, was revised and reissued in 2005. It is an important and prescient conceptualization predating Foucault's postmodernist position on sexuality and presaging queer theory approaches. Perhaps its greatest impact has been its conceptual-theoretic contribution to the field – although it is rarely acknowledged. Even more rarely have empirical studies explicitly used sexual scripting theory.

When the theory has explicitly guided research the analyses have tended to emphasize one level only, most frequently that of cultural scenarios. For example, Laumann et al. (1994) correlate sociocultural contexts with sexual behaviors. Analyses which only match cultural scenarios with behaviors do not relate the mechanisms by which individuals acquire, and social life helps to create, sexuality. The attention to culture, interaction, and mind in sexual scripting theory is similar to that found in symbolic interactionism (Longmore 1998). However, there exists little work proclaiming guidance by both symbolic interactionism and sexual scripting theory. Only a couple of studies of interpersonal sexual interaction claim sexual scripting theory parentage (e.g., Escoffier 2003). Similarly, all but a few social psychological studies (e.g., Whittier & Melendez 2004) of sexuality embrace sexual scripting theory. Carr's (1999) cognitive sociology contribution notably implicates interrelationships of sexual scripting levels.

Sexual scripting theory also engages broad sociohistorial analysis and theorization of the self in pointing to a relationship between sexuality and modernity in helping to bring about individuation. Simultaneous specification of sexual change and forms at all three sexual scripting levels may require an extremely wide range of data and substantial cross-disciplinary abilities. The ambitiousness of this theory may deter use and even result in misunderstandings of it. Sexual scripting theory sincerely asks for depictions of the emergence of sociosexual facts like sexual intercourse and titillation. It is a bold framework for specifying how, in time and place, social life forms sexuality.

SEE ALSO: Constructionism; Self; Social Psychology; Symbolic Interaction

REFERENCES AND SUGGESTED READINGS

Carr, C. L. (1999) Cognitive Scripting and Sexual Identification: Essentialism, Anarchism, and Constructionism. *Symbolic Interaction* 22(1): 1–24.

Escoffier, J. (2003) Gay-for-Pay: Straight Men and the Making of Gay Pornography. *Qualitative Sociology* 26(4): 531–55.

Gagnon, J. H. & Simon, W. (1973) *Sexual Conduct: The Social Sources of Human Sexuality.* Aldine, Chicago.

Gagnon, J. H. & Simon, W. (2005) *Sexual Conduct: The Social Sources of Human Sexuality*, rev. edn. Transaction, Piscataway, NJ.

Laumann, E. O., Gagnon, J. H., Michael, R. T., & Michaels, S. (1994) *The Social Organization of Sexuality.* University of Chicago Press, Chicago.

Longmore, M. (1998) Symbolic Interactionism in the Study of Sexuality. *Journal of Sex Research* 35: 44–57.

Simon, W. & Gagnon, J. (1986) Sexual Scripts: Permanence and Change. *Archives of Sexual Behavior* 15: 97–120.

Whittier, D. K. & Melendez, R. (2004) Intersubjectivity in the Intrapsychic Sexual Scripting of Gay Men. *Culture, Health, and Sexuality* 6(2): 131–43.

second demographic transition

Ron J. Lesthaeghe

The first or "classic" demographic transition refers to the historical declines in mortality and fertility, as witnessed from the eighteenth century onward in several European populations, and continuing at present in most developing countries. The end point of the first demographic transition (FDT) was supposed to be an older stationary and stable population corresponding with replacement fertility (i.e., just over two children on average), zero population growth, and life expectancies higher than 70 years. As there would be an ultimate balance between deaths and births, there would be no "demographic" need for sustained immigration. Moreover, households in all parts of the world would converge toward the nuclear and conjugal types, composed of married couples and their offspring.

The second demographic transition (SDT), on the other hand, sees no such equilibrium as the end point. Rather, new developments bring sustained sub-replacement fertility, a multitude of living arrangements other than marriage, the disconnection between marriage and procreation, and no stationary population. Instead, populations would face declining sizes if not complemented by new migrants (i.e., "replacement migration"), and they will also be much older than envisaged by the FDT as a result of lower fertility and additional gains in longevity. Migration streams will not be capable of stemming aging, but only stabilize population sizes. Nonetheless, the outcome is still the further growth of "multicultural societies." On the whole, the SDT brings new social challenges, including those associated with further aging, integration of immigrants and other cultures, less stability of households, and high levels of poverty or exclusion among certain household types (e.g., single persons of all ages, lone mothers).

HISTORY OF THE CONCEPT

The idea of a distinct phase stems directly from Philippe Ariès's analysis of the history of childhood and his paper on two successive motivations for low fertility (Ariès 1980). In his view, during the FDT, the decline in fertility was "unleashed by an enormous sentimental and financial investment in the child." Ariès refers to this as the "Child-king era," and the fertility transition was carried by an altruistic investment in child quality. This motivation is no longer the dominant one. Within the SDT, the motivation for parenthood is adult self-realization, and the choice for just one particular lifestyle in competition with several others. The altruistic element focusing on offspring has weakened and the adult dyadic relationship has gained prominence instead.

The second element that sparked the SDT theory was the conviction that the cyclical fertility theory as formulated by Richard Easterlin would no longer hold and that sub-replacement fertility was to become a structural, long-term feature in western populations. In Easterlin's theory, small cohorts would have better employment opportunities and hence earlier marriage and higher fertility, whereas large cohorts would have worse economic life chances and display the opposite demographic responses. The cyclical reinforcement then stems from large cohorts of parents giving birth to small cohorts of children and vice versa. The SDT does not expect cyclical effects that would be strong enough to determine the fertility trend. Rather, it advances that other effects, both economic and cultural, have an overriding capacity in conditioning these trends.

The third element that conditioned the SDT theory is the major role given to the ideational factor and to the dynamics of cultural shift. The SDT theory fully recognizes the effects of macro-level structural changes and of micro-level economic calculus. As such it is not at odds with the core arguments of neoclassic economic reasoning. However, the SDT view does not consider these explanations as sufficient but merely as non-redundant. By the same token, the cultural factors involved are non-redundant elements and not sufficient ones. The SDT is therefore an "overarching" theory that spans both economic and sociological reasoning. And it does not do so by taking value orientations as endogenous or by considering culture as a form of addiction, but by treating ideational changes as exogenous influences that add stability to trends over and beyond economic fluctuations. The SDT furthermore links cultural shifts to dynamic processes of cohort succession, and to a recursive model of values-based selection and individual values reorientation as a function of paths followed during the life course.

Fourth, a major stepping stone of the SDT theory has also been Abraham Maslow's theory of changing needs. As populations become more wealthy and more educated, attention shifts away from needs associated with survival, security, and solidarity. Instead, greater weight is attached to individual self-realization, recognition, grassroots democracy, and expressive work and education values. The SDT theory is therefore closely related to Ron Inglehart's concept of "postmaterialism" and its growing importance in political development. The direct consequence of this is that SDT also predicts that the typical demographic outcomes (sustained sub-replacement fertility, growth of alternative living arrangements) are likely to emerge in non-western societies that equally develop in the direction of capitalist economies, with multilevel democratic institutions, and greater accentuation of Maslowian "higher order needs."

FIRST DEMOGRAPHIC TRANSITION–SECOND DEMOGRAPHIC TRANSITION CONTRASTS

Having pointed out the intellectual origins of SDT, more attention can be given to the FDT–SDT contrast. Originally, SDT was viewed as the mere continuation of FDT, but such a "single transition" view obscures major differences of both a demographic and a social nature. The major contrasts have therefore been listed in Table 1.

Opposite Nuptiality Trends

The FDT transition in the West is characterized by the gradual weakening of the old Malthusian "preventive check" located in late and non-universal marriage. Ages at first marriage are lowered and proportions marrying increased during the FDT. Furthermore, the areas where cohabitation and out of wedlock fertility had survived until the twentieth century, join the mainstream characterized by low illegitimacy and low incidence of unmarried partnerships. The earliest age at marriage is reached in the 1960s. Thereafter, all trends are reversed and rapidly so: ages at first marriage increase, more single persons start living alone or start to cohabit prior to marriage, long-term cohabitation replaces marriage, and ultimately fertility outside marriage becomes much more frequent.

Table 1 Overview of demographic and societal characteristics respectively related to the FDT and SDT (Western Europe)

FDT	*SDT*
A. Marriage	
• Rise in proportions marrying, declining age at first marriage	• Fall in proportions married, rise in age at first marriage
• Low or reduced cohabitation	• Rise in cohabitation (pre- and postmarital)
• Low divorce	• Rise in divorce, earlier divorce
• High remarriage	• Decline of remarriage following both divorce and widowhood
B. Fertility	
• Decline in marital fertility via reductions at older ages, lowering mean ages at first parenthood	• Further decline in fertility via postponement, increasing mean age at first parenthood, structural subreplacement fertility
• Deficient contraception, parity failures	• Efficient contraception (exceptions in specific social groups)
• Declining illegitimate fertility	• Rising extra-marital fertility, parenthood within cohabitation
• Low definitive childlessness among married couples	• Rising definitive childlessness in unions
C. Societal background	
• Preoccupations with basic material needs: income, work conditions, housing, health, schooling, social security. Solidarity prime value	• Rise of "higher order" needs: individual autonomy, self-actualization, expressive work and socialization values, grassroots democracy, recognition. Tolerance prime value
• Rising memberships of political, civic, and community-oriented networks. Strengthening of social cohesion	• Disengagement from civic and community-oriented networks, social capital shifts to expressive and affective types. Weakening of social cohesion
• Strong normative regulation by state and churches. First secularization wave, political and social "pillarization"	• Retreat of the state, second secularization wave, sexual revolution, refusal of authority, political "depillarization"
• Segregated gender roles, familistic policies, embourgeoisement	• Rising symmetry in gender roles, female economic autonomy
• Ordered life course transitions, prudent marriage and dominance of one single family model	• Flexible life course organization, multiple lifestyles, open future

A similar turnaround also takes place with respect to remarriage. During FDT, divorce (or widowhood) is often followed by remarriage, and even by continued childbearing. During SDT, post-marital relationships are channelled into cohabitation or living apart together (LAT)-relationships rather than remarriage. In parts of Central and in Eastern Europe, where the historical Malthusian late marriage pattern did not exist, SDT is equally characterized by a new trend toward later marriage and more cohabitation after 1990. Also, out of wedlock fertility now follows the western trend. Moreover, such features are now also emerging in the western part of Southern Europe (Italy, Malta, Spain, and especially Portugal).

Opposite Timing of Fertility

During FDT, fertility became increasingly confined to marriage, contraception mostly affected fertility at the older ages (stopping) and higher marriage durations, mean ages at parenthood declined, but childlessness among married couples remained low. There are examples of below replacement fertility during FDT, but these correspond to exceptional periods of deep economic crisis or war.

SDT starts in the 1960s with a multifaceted revolution. First, there was the contraceptive revolution with the introduction of hormonal contraception and far more efficient IUDs. Second, there was the sexual revolution, with declining ages at first sexual intercourse. Third, there was the gender revolution that questioned the sole breadwinner household model and the gender division of labor that accompanied it. These three "revolutions" fit within the framework of an overall rejection of authority, the assertion of individual freedom of choice (autonomy), and an overhaul of the normative structure. The overall outcome of this with respect to fertility is postponement: mean ages at first parenthood rise again, opportunities for childbearing are lost due to higher divorce, the share of childless women increases, and higher parity births (4 +) become rare. The net result is structural and long-term below replacement fertility.

Social Contrasts

With the exception of the very early fertility decline in France and a few other small European regions, much of FDT was an integral part of a development phase during which economic growth fostered material aspirations and improvements in material living conditions. The preoccupations of the 1860–1960 era were mainly concerned with increasing household real incomes, improving working and housing conditions, raising standards of health, improving human capital through mass education, and providing a safety net for all via the gradual construction of a social security system. In Europe, these goals were shared and promoted by all major democratic political parties, their organizations, and by churches as well. In this endeavor solidarity was a central concept. All such political or religious "pillars" had their views on the desirable evolution of the family. For the religious organizations, these views were based on the holiness of matrimony in the first place, but their defense of the closely knit conjugal family also stemmed from fears that urbanization and industrialization would lead to immorality and atheism. The secular pillars, such as socialist or liberal parties, equally saw the family as the cornerstone of society. Both moral and material uplifting would be served best by a sharp gender-based division within the family: husbands assume their roles as devoted breadwinners and women as guardians of all quality related issues (order and neatness, health, education, etc.). In other words, all religious and political factions – including the communist one – contributed to the "embourgeoisement" of the family.

SDT, on the other hand, is founded on the rise of the higher order needs. Once the basic material preoccupations are satisfied, further income growth and educational expansion jointly lead to the articulation of more existential and expressive needs. These are centered on a triad: *self-actualization* in formulating goals, *individual autonomy* in choosing means, and claiming *recognition* for their realization. These issues emerge in a variety of domains, and this is why the SDT is related to such a broad array of indicators of ideational or cultural shift (Lesthaeghe and Surkyn 2004a). SDT occurs in tandem with the growth of "postmaterialism" (Inglehart 1990) and political or religious "depillarization" (Lesthaeghe & Moors 1995), the disengagement from civic, professional, or community-oriented associations, a critical stand vis-à-vis all forms of authority, the stress on expressive values in socialization and in work, and, of course, a quest for far more egalitarian gender relations. Also at the individual level, the choices for new types of households (premarital single living, cohabitation, and parenthood within cohabitation) are all linked to such individualistic and non-conformist value orientations in a great variety of spheres. Furthermore, these associations between household types and value orientations not only hold for Northern and Western Europe but, by now, equally for Southern, Central and Eastern Europe.

CRITICISMS

Several criticisms have been launched against the SDT view. First, some argue there is no "second" demographic transition, but just the continuation of a single one. Second, some suggest that SDT is typical only of Northwestern Europe. Third, SDT does not envisage a "new equilibrium" at the end, unlike the original FDT. In addition to these objections, others dislike the strong "cultural" interpretation. A reply to these criticisms argues that SDT correctly predicted the trends in Central, Eastern, and Southern Europe, and that all correlations at the micro-level between household type and value orientations emerge there as well.

SEE ALSO: Cohabitation; Demographic Transition Theory; Secularization; Values

REFERENCES AND RECOMMENDED READINGS

Ariès, P. (1980) Two Successive Motivations for the Declining Birth Rate in the West. *Population and Development Review* 6(4): 645–50.

Inglehart, R. (1990) *Culture Shift in Advanced Industrial Society*. Princeton University Press, Princeton, p. 484.

Lesthaeghe, R. & Moors, G. (1995) Living Arrangements, Socioeconomic Position and Values Among Young Adults: A Pattern Description for Belgium, France, the Netherlands and West Germany, 1990. In: van den Brekel, H. & Deven, F. (Eds.), *Population and Family in the Low Countries 1994*, Kluwer Academic Publishers, Dordrecht, pp. 1–56. Also in: Coleman, D. (Ed.) (1996) *Europe's Population in the 1990s*. Oxford University Press, Oxford, pp. 163–221.

Lesthaeghe, R. & Surkyn, J. (1988) Cultural Dynamics and Economic Theories of Fertility Change. *Population and Development Review* nr. 1.

Lesthaeghe, R. & Surkyn, J. (2002) New Forms of Household Formation in Central and Eastern Europe: Are They Related to Newly Emerging Value Orientations? *Economic Survey of Europe*, UN Economic Commission for Europe, Geneva, ch. 6, 1: 197–216.

Lesthaeghe, R. & Surkyn, J. (2004a) Value Orientations and the Second Demographic Transition (SDT) in Northern, Western and Southern Europe: An Update. *Demographic Research*, Max Planck Institute for Demographic Research, Rostock, April 17, Special Collection 3, nr 3: 45–86.

Lesthaeghe, R. & Surkyn, J. (2004b) When History Moves On: Foundations and Diffusion of a Second Demographic Transition. Seminar on the Ideational Perspectives on International Family Change, Center for Population Studies and Institute for Social Research, University of Michigan, Ann Arbor, June 2–5.

Lesthaeghe, R. & van de Kaa, D. J. (1986) Twee demografische transities? (Two demographic transitions?). In: R. Lesthaeghe & D. van de Kaa (Eds.), *Bevolking – Groei en Krimp*, Mens en Maatschappij, Van Loghum Slaterus, Deventer, pp. 9–24.

van de Kaa, D. J. (2003) Second Demographic Transition. In: Demeny, P. and McNicoll, G. (Eds.), *Encyclopedia of Population*, Vol. 2. Macmillan Reference, Thomson-Gale, New York, 2003, pp. 872–5.

secondary data analysis

Russell K. Schutt

Secondary data analysis is the method of using preexisting data in a different way or to answer a different research question than that intended by those who collected the data. The work of the secondary data analyst begins where the survey, experiment, or qualitative method that generates the data ends. The most common sources of data used in secondary analyses are social science surveys and data collected by government agencies, often with survey research methods, but it is also possible to reanalyze data that have been collected in experimental studies or with qualitative methods. Even reanalysis by researchers of data that they collected previously qualifies as secondary analysis if it is for a new purpose or in response to a methodological critique.

Secondary data analysis has been an important social science methodology since the earliest days of social research – Karl Marx reviewed government statistics in the Reading Room of the British Library; Émile Durkheim analyzed government records for his study of suicide rates. However, it is only with the advent of modern computers and, even more importantly, the Internet that secondary data analysis has become the most popular and accessible social research method. Literally thousands of large-scale data sets are now available for the secondary data analyst, often with no more effort than the few commands required to download the data set; a number of important data sets can even be analyzed directly on the Web by users who lack their own statistical software.

There are many sources of data for secondary analysis within the United States and internationally. The most traditional source is data compiled by governmental units. The decennial population census by the US Bureau of the

Census is the single most important governmental data source, but many other data sets are collected by the Census and by other government agencies, including the US Census Bureau's Current Population Survey and its Survey of Manufactures or the Bureau of Labor Statistics' Consumer Expenditure Survey. These government data sets typically are quantitative; in fact, the term "statistics" – state-istics – is derived from this type of data.

There are many other readily available sources: administrative data from hospitals, employers, and other institutions; records of transactions or other business conducted in government offices; both cross-sectional and longitudinal social surveys conducted under many different auspices, ranging from university-based researchers to international organizations like the Organization for Economic Development (OECD) (Hakim 1982: 6).

In the United States, the University of Michigan's Inter-University Consortium for Political and Social Research (ICPSR) archives the most extensive collection of social science data sets outside of the federal government: more than 9,000 data sets from 130 countries, particularly from government units, social survey projects, and international organizations are made available online to individuals at more than 500 colleges and universities around the world that have joined ICPSR.

Far fewer qualitative data sets are available for secondary analysis, but the number is growing rapidly. The Human Relations Area Files at Yale University, established in 1949, currently contain over 800,000 pages of information on more than 365 different groups (HRAF 2005). More recently, multistudy qualitative archive projects have been developed by the Murray Research Center at Harvard's Radcliffe Institute for Advanced Study, and by the Economic and Social Data Service of the Universities of Sussex and Manchester in England, although these data sets are not available for direct public access. However, the ICPSR archives now include close to 100 data sets that have a qualitative component and the University of Southern Maine's Center for the Study of Lives makes life interview data available for reanalysis.

There are fundamental differences between a secondary and a primary analysis of social science data and there are unique challenges faced by the secondary data analyst. What is most distinctive about the method of secondary data analysis is that it does not allow the progression from formulating a research question to designing specific methods that are best suited to answer that question. The secondary data analyst also cannot test and refine the methods to be used on the basis of preliminary feedback from the population or processes to be studied. Nor is it possible for the secondary data analyst to engage in the iterative process of making observations, developing concepts, making more observations, and refining the concepts that is the hallmark of much qualitative methodology.

These limitations of secondary data analysis mean that it may not be possible for a researcher to focus on the specific research question of original interest nor to use the most appropriate sampling or measurement approach for studying it. Secondary data analysis inevitably involves a tradeoff between the ease with which the research process can be initiated and the specific hypotheses that can be tested and methods that can be used. If the primary study was not designed to measure adequately a concept that is critical to the secondary analyst's hypothesis, the study may have to be abandoned until a more adequate source of data can be found. Alternatively, hypotheses or even the research question itself may be modified in order to match the analytic possibilities presented by the available data (Riedel 2000: 53).

Data quality is always a concern with secondary data, even when the data are collected by an official government agency. Government actions result at least in part from political processes that may not have as their first priority the design or maintenance of high-quality data for social scientific analysis. For example, political opposition over the British Census's approach to recording ethnic origin led to changes in the 1991 Census that rendered its results inconsistent with prior years and that demonstrated the "tenuous relationship between enumeration [census] categories and possible social realities" (Fenton 1996: 155).

The basis for concern is much greater in research across national boundaries, because different data collection systems and definitions of key variables may have been used (Glover 1996). Census counts can be distorted by incorrect answers to census questions as well as by inadequate coverage of the entire population (Rives & Serow 1988: 32–5).

Reanalyzing qualitative data collected by someone else also requires setting aside the interpretive research principle of letting the researcher's evolving understanding of a setting shape the focus of data collection efforts (Heaton 2004: 30–1). Instead, the secondary analyst of qualitative data must seek opportunities for testing new conceptualizations with the data already on hand as well as, when possible, by carrying on a dialogue with original researchers.

These problems can be lessened by seeking conscientiously to review data features and quality before deciding to develop an analysis of secondary data (Stewart & Kamins 1993: 17–31; Riedel 2000: 55–69) and then developing analysis plans that maximize the value of the available data. Replicating key analyses with alternative indicators of key concepts, testing for the stability of relationships across theoretically meaningful subsets of the data, and examining findings of comparable studies conducted with other data sets can each strengthen confidence in the findings of a secondary analysis.

In an environment in which so many important social science data sets are instantly available for reanalysis, the method of secondary data analysis should permit increasingly rapid refinement of social science knowledge, as new hypotheses can be tested and methodological disputes clarified, if not resolved, quickly. Both the necessary technology and the supportive ideologies required for this rapid refinement have spread throughout the world. Social science researchers now have the opportunity to take advantage of this methodology as well as the responsibility to carefully and publicly delineate and acknowledge the limitations of the method.

SEE ALSO: Demographic Data: Censuses, Registers, Surveys; Descriptive Statistics; Social Change and Causal Analysis; Survey Research

REFERENCES AND SUGGESTED READINGS

Fenton, S. (1996) Counting Ethnicity: Social Groups and Official Categories. In: Levitas, R. & Guy, W. (Eds.), *Interpreting Official Statistcs*. Routledge, New York, pp. 143–65.

Glover, J. (1996) Epistemological and Methodological Considerations in Secondary Analysis. In: Hantrais, L. & Mangen, S. (Eds.), *Cross-National Research Methods in the Social Sciences*. Pinter, New York, pp. 28–38.

Hakim, C. (1982) *Secondary Analysis in Social Research: A Guide to Data Sources and Methods with Examples*. George Allen & Unwin, London.

Hantrais, L. & Mangen, S. (1996) Method and Management of Cross-National Social Research. In: Hantrais, L. & Mangen, S. (Eds.), *Cross-National Research Methods in the Social Sciences*. Pinter, New York, pp. 1–12.

Heaton, J. (2004) *Reworking Qualitative Data*. Sage, Thousand Oaks, CA.

HRAF (2005) eHRAF Collection of Ethnography: Web. Yale University. Online. www.yale.edu/hraf/collections_body_ethnoweb.htm. Accessed July 3, 2005.

Riedel, M. (2000) *Research Strategies for Secondary Data: A Perspective for Criminology and Criminal Justice*. Sage, Thousand Oaks, CA.

Rives, N. W., Jr. & Serow, W. J. (1988) *Introduction to Applied Demography: Data Sources and Estimation Techniques*. Sage University Paper Series on Quantitative Applications in the Social Sciences, Series No. 07-039. Sage, Thousand Oaks, CA.

Stewart, D. W. & Kamins, M. A. (1993) *Secondary Research: Information Sources and Methods*, 2nd edn. Sage, Thousand Oaks, CA.

secondary groups

Patrick J. W. McGinty

A secondary group is a unique form of social group that tends to be formally organized or highly structured and based on predominantly impersonal or role-based instrumental (task oriented) interactions that are of a nonpermanent nature. Examples of secondary groups include the impersonal relationship between salesclerk and customer in a department store; large lecture courses at popular universities; and complex organizations such as the American Sociological Association.

Despite its centrality in the sociological perspective and its being an omnipresent theme as well as an ongoing interest of sociologists in a variety of forms, the concept of a secondary group is rather poorly conceptualized. This problematic status of the concept and its usage within the discipline is further conditioned by a unique confluence of understandings regarding the concept. First, it is deemed of central significance to the discipline, but is generally relegated to little more than a concept that students in "Introduction to Sociology" courses need only memorize and be able to identify. Second, the concept is widely understood in practice, and where it appears in the sociological literature it is consistently applied with little variation in meaning or definition. At the same time, however, the development and usage of the concept as a central concern in sociological research has declined significantly over time. Third, as a result, where the concept of secondary group is discussed in the contemporary sociological literature it is generally defined or treated only in relation to one or more sociological concepts – the most common referent concepts being community, social organization, and primary group.

This relational and yet dualistic conceptual definition and operationalization of secondary groups has its origins in the history of sociology and classical sociological theory. This is particularly evident in the historically and theoretically contextualized understanding of the relationship between community and society. It is common for the work of both Émile Durkheim and Georg Simmel (which sought to explicate the relationship between social groups and the organization of society) to be referenced in this context. However, it is the work of Charles Horton Cooley (1909) and Ferdinand Tönnies (1963) that continues to drive the historically and theoretically relational understanding of the concept.

In *Social Organization* (1909) Cooley provides in great detail the forms, functions, and attributes of the social units he called "primary groups." However, what Cooley did not do was develop a term for those social units which were not primary groups. Thus, the conventionally accepted set of attributes and characteristics of secondary groups were simply extrapolated from Cooley's understanding of primary groups. Or in other words, knowing what primary groups are, secondary groups by corollary must be anything or everything that primary groups are not. Accordingly, it follows that for over a century sociologists have defined the concept of secondary group simply in relation to the associated (and similarly limited) conceptualization of primary group. To Cooley's credit, both his explicit definition of primary groups and the associated implicit definition of secondary groups have withstood the test of time. Ironically, Cooley's intent in *Social Organization* was to develop a processual and non-dichotomous understanding of the relationship between community and social organization, the conceptualization of primary groups being only one aspect of the larger argument.

In addition, Ferdinand Tönnies's (1963) work regarding the dualistic conception of *Gemeinschaft* and *Gesellschaft* also sought to explain the relationship between community and social organization. Accordingly, Tönnies's explanations and assumptions regarding the forms, attributes, and characteristics of *Gesellschaften* – including but not limited to short-term and impersonal relationships – have become closely associated with the conventional definition of secondary groups.

Despite the contemporary limitations regarding the conceptualization of secondary groups, there are a couple of theoretical developments that stand to alter significantly the manner in which secondary groups are conceptualized and defined. The more dramatic of the two developments is founded on a relational understanding of human interaction. Lyn H. Lofland (1989) reviews an extensive literature which shows how the emergent and informal but role-based "unpersonal" relationship blurs the boundaries between forms of interactions generally shown as typical of both primary and secondary groups. However, in a more recent iteration, Lofland (1998) proposes an end to the unreflective use of the concept of secondary groups. Although suggesting that the ideal typical understanding of secondary groups does have its benefits, Lofland instead posits the need for a more dynamic set of concepts that can better capture the variety of forms of human relationships. Among the concepts Lofland proposes are the "fleeting relationship" (Davis 1959), "routinized relationships," "quasi-primary relationships" (Stone 1954), and "intimate-secondary relationships." The continued development of these and similar insights stands to clarify as well as further our collective comparative understanding of social groups and their organization and processes.

Second, although still overwhelmingly understood in terms of the ideal typical conceptualizations similar to those now used, other practitioners are calling for the replacement of the concept of secondary groups with that of the seemingly more explanatory concept of "complex groups." Such a change in conceptual label seeks to shift explanatory focus of the concept from its current gaze – which highlights concerns such as the role and/or function of the social group – to that of the size, scope, and forms of relationships within the group and the associated forms of intergroup and intragroup relations. The underlying logic associated with this proposal is based on analyses of interaction networks. While it is the issue of complexity that drives this proposal for changing the conceptual label, it should be noted that such a change in conceptualization could provide greater theoretical synchronicity by narrowing the conceptual gap between our conventional understanding of secondary groups and micro/macro linkages, particularly with regard to one of the concepts' more widely accepted expressions: the complex organization (for the treatment of similar concerns in terms of weak and strong ties, see Granovetter 1973, 1983).

While the complex organization is one form of secondary group, it is the bureaucratically organized form of complex organization that is commonly held up as the classic epitome of the secondary group – being a large, impersonal organization based on a network of complex status relationships which maintains a set of instrumental goals and processes, and in which the length of individual associations varies. The expression of the bureaucratic organization as an ideal typical example of a secondary group should serve to heighten our awareness of the importance of the study of secondary groups. This same expression should then, by corollary, serve to heighten our sensitivity to the study of the variety of forms of human interaction and relations in contemporary social life. This is the case not only because of the increasing significance of secondary groups to our general social welfare, but also because of their implicit relationship to the ever increasing growth and development of rationalized forms of organizing (Ritzer 2004), as well as expressions of individualism and unbridled self-interest in human social life (for related but differing perspectives on the result of said forms of organizing, see also de Tocqueville 1966; Michels 1966).

SEE ALSO: Community; Cooley, Charles Horton; Primary Groups; Role; Tönnies, Ferdinand; Weak Ties (Strength of)

REFERENCES AND SUGGESTED READINGS

Cooley, C. H. (1909) *Social Organization: A Study of the Larger Mind.* Scribner, New York.

Davis, F. (1959) The Cabdriver and His Fare: Facets of a Fleeting Relationship. *American Journal of Sociology* 65(2): 158–65.

Granovetter, M. S. (1973) The Strength of Weak Ties. *American Journal of Sociology* 78(6): 1360–80.

Granovetter, M. S. (1983) The Strength of Weak Ties: A Network Theory Revisited. In: *Sociological Theory* Vol. 1. Jossey-Bass, San Francisco, pp. 201–33.

Jones, L. C. (1997) Both Friend and Stranger: How Crisis Volunteers Build and Manage Unpersonal Relationships with Clients. In: *Social Perspectives on Emotion* Vol. 4. JAI Press, Greenwich, CT, pp. 125–48.

Lofland, L. H. (1989) Social Life in the Public Realm: A Review Essay. *Journal of Contemporary Ethnography* 17(4): 453–82.

Lofland, L. H. (1998) *The Public Realm.* Aldine de Gruyter, New York.

Michels, R. (1966 [1911]) *Political Parties.* Free Press, New York.

Ritzer, G. (2004) *The McDonaldization of Society: Revised New Century Edition.* Pine Forge Press, Thousand Oaks, CA.

Simmel, G. (1955) *Conflict and the Web of Group Affiliation.* Free Press, Glencoe, Il.

Stone, G. (1954) City Shoppers and Urban Identification: Observations on the Social Psychology of City Life. *American Journal of Sociology* 60(1): 36–45.

Tocqueville, A. de (1966 [1835]) *Democracy in America.* Ed. J. P. Mayer & M. Lerner. Harper & Row, New York.

Tönnies, F. (1963 [1887]) *Community and Society.* Harper & Row, New York.

secrecy

Laurence Moss

George Orwell's celebrated novel, *Nineteen Eighty-Four*, presents a haunting and horrific account of how the thought police in a totalitarian world can monitor the private thoughts and uproot the deepest emotional sentiments held by individuals. Keeping secrets has become a capital offense. The "Party" has reduced the sphere of individual autonomy and privacy to practically nothing at all. According to Orwell, in this dystopia it became "intolerable [to the Party] that an erroneous thought should exist anywhere in the world, however secret and powerless it may be" and "in the eyes of the Party there was no distinction between the thought and the deed" (Orwell 2003 [1949]: 250, 263). Either one resulted in immediate arrest and eventual execution.

Orwell's prose frightens us because private thoughts and personal secrets are profoundly important to our sense of personhood and to the expression and development of human personality. A world without the possibility of personal secrets is a world that is intolerable.

SOCIOLOGY AND ECONOMICS

Orwell's world is not our world. Most people possess secrets about themselves that they intentionally prefer to keep to themselves and share with only a few. According to Miller, most of us fake things about our roles, our dispositions, emotions, our commitments, and even our entire identity. We intentionally persuade others about things that are simply not true (Miller 2003; see also Goffman 1963). The origins of these insights date back to the canonical writings in modern sociology and especially to the work of Georg Simmel (Ritzer 2000: 282–6).

According to Donald Levine, the nineteenth-century sociologist Simmel was one of the earliest to advance the view that "sociology should describe the ideal types of forms of social interaction abstracted from their contents" (1971: lii). Simmel's search for the *forms of human interaction* and how they help illuminate the most interesting real-life examples of people at work and at play has earned him a reputation as one of the most insightful of the German sociologists at the start of the twentieth century.

In 1906, Simmel's "The Sociology of Secrecy and of Secret Societies" appeared in the *American Journal of Sociology* in which the phenomenon of the intentional misrepresentation of information by one individual or a group of individuals gives rise to the rituals and customs of the "secret society," such as the legendary Carbonari in Italy and the multitude of religious sects that spring up to practice a faith that the powerful state tries to stamp out. According to Simmel, "the secret society emerges everywhere as correlate of despotism and of police powers. This is true, not alone in political relations, but in the same way within the church, the school, and the family" (1906: 472). Simmel's idea that one strategy for coping with the demands and pressures of modern society involves camouflaging oneself with lies and falsehoods has spawned an enormously fertile field of analysis within modern sociology (cf. Goffman 1963; Bergmann 1993 [1987]).

Simmel pioneered several novel forms of analysis in the study of secrecy that still have influence today. For example, when an individual lies to another, that other person is not only deceived but also has a "misconception about the true intention of the person who [has told] the lie" (Simmel 1906: 445). These misconceptions are much less threatening to the persistence of the group in simple societies then they are in modern credit-economies where the entire civilized structure is based on thousands of presuppositions about individuals and their intentions. A modern credit-based economy in which money and its electronic forms permit myriad secret transactions right under the nose but out of the sight of the governing authorities has turned out to be an important and still unappreciated form of modern social life. The twenty-first-century terrorists finance their nefarious deeds by transferring funds from one currency area to the next and, as a result, the current "war on terror" is fought not only on the ground but also in the abstract financial world of electronic transfers and banking.

In modern business, "white-collar crime" and the enormous magnitude of selected corporate crimes have become central to popular media reporting. At the heart of many of these criminal enterprises is the notion of "secrecy" and the intentional presentation of false and misleading information, both to the victims and to many others. And so we can read Simmel as warning more about the potency of secrecy and dissimulation in modern complex financial network societies than in less developed and perhaps more primitive societies.

There is a geometry of social relations that we find in Simmel (Ritzer 2000: 268). As early as the seventeenth century, Thomas Hobbes recognized that groups of individuals who assemble for their defense against a threatening enemy need large numbers to succeed, but large numbers of individuals are prone to quarreling and intrigues as one individual faces off against another, revealing the antagonistic side of human nature. Certainly, after the danger of invasion has passed, their cohesion is apt to splinter and large numbers end up bickering, quarreling, and worse. Collective action would not succeed unless there were a strong central kingly power to keep the individual egos in check (Hobbes 1928 [1650]: 78–9). The idea that small groups of agents are capable of some forms of social action of which large groups are not resurfaced in Simmel's writings more than two and half centuries later.

Simmel discussed the differences between the dyad and the triad and emphasized, as Hobbes had done, the importance of the "impact of numbers of people on the quality of interaction" (cf. Ritzer 2000: 268). With two individuals there is not much of a group structure to appreciate and study, but add merely a third individual and the structure and form of the interaction undergo fundamental change. For one thing, a genuine social structure finally comes into existence. Emergent structures are certainly present in the case with secrecy and secret dealings.

According to Simmel, in small groups it is difficult to keep and maintain secrets. Just about everyone is too close and there are repeated temptations to "slip" and tell all. In large groups, secrets can more easily emerge and be maintained. In large secret societies, a secret is shared by all members of the group but there is the constant tension "caused by the fact that the secret can be uncovered, or revealed, and thus the entire basis for the existence of the secret society can be eliminated" (Ritzer 2000: 283). The contrast between secret-keeping in small and large groups and the social structures that emerge somewhat spontaneously to improve the likelihood of success in secret-keeping are grist for the mill of the sociologist. In his 1906 article, Simmel broke new ground when he carefully outlined the methods secret societies use to conceal their size and their leadership through the use of decentralized methods of information and control.

THE COSTS OF MAINTAINING SECRETS

It is a well-established principle in the social sciences, and especially in economics, that the costs and difficulties of keeping *certain types of secrets* increase exponentially with the number of individuals sharing the secret. This is the large group problem that fascinated Simmel, but in economics seemingly opposite conclusions emerge.

Many business conspiracies to secretly set prices or restrict output, and in that way monopolize markets, fall apart of their own accord. This unraveling is quicker the larger the number of businesses trying to coordinate their business strategies. In the study of industrial organization and especially the study of cartels, it is often found that conspiracies to "fix" prices or rig contract competitions are often unraveled by dissenting members of the conspiracies who complain that their production quotas are unfair (i.e., "too low"). Former conspirators try to gain a private advantage for themselves by going their own way by only pretending to be a member of the cartel.

A different sort of problem may arise when one individual knows that one or more other individuals knows something important but may lie about it to the first individual. Some experts claim that this situation establishes the fundamental condition for secrecy itself. According to Ritzer, "secrecy is defined as the condition in which one person has the intention of hiding something while the other is seeking to reveal that which is being hidden" (Ritzer 2000: 282). Indeed, the holders of the non-public information know that the others with whom they deal know that they know something they do not. In this way, a complicated strategic problem of move and countermove begins. The subfield of economics known as "game theory" has gone a considerable distance investigating these forms of social interaction and the actual geometries involved.

For example, a physician knows whether his or her patient is mildly ill rather than seriously ill. Still, that doctor may prescribe additional expensive tests expecting the "kick-back and special considerations" that may come his way from enriched colleagues who get paid to perform those unnecessary tests. This physician has a conflict of interest. He has been hired to diagnose and to heal. Instead, he lies and steals.

When the patient worries that he or she may be defrauded by the strategic use of "asymmetric information" by an unscrupulous expert, we have the conditions under which market structures evolve to permit the authentication of information and the creation of "good reputation." The professions are often governed by emergent structures of "professional ethics and responsibility" that help dampen rapacious individual behavior that make up secrecy and lying to enhance fees and revenues. This was the claim of American sociologist Talcott Parsons in numerous writings (Parsons 1937). Modern sociologists often criticize economists for not considering the regulative role norms play compared with raw self-interest.

When a number of persons share a secret, and keep that secret in absolute silence, we have another social phenomenon of special interest. Sociologist Eviatar Zerubavel summarizes what is known about silence and denial. His thesis follows the insights of Sigmund Freud and Carl Jung in psychology (Bok 1982: 8). Many jointly held secrets grow more difficult to keep over time. It is like an elephant in the room that the co-conspirators ignore, but as a result the elephant keeps growing larger and larger until the secret can be bottled up no longer. The co-conspirators suffer together in icy silence until all hell breaks loose and the elephant has shattered the conspiracy of silence. This phenomenon wreaks havoc on individual conscience and personality.

During the Nazi war against the Jews, there were homeowners living in close proximity to the death camps but no one discussed or even mentioned what everyone knew was going on over there right in front of their eyes. A "social norm" emerged that limited what perceptions were permissible and what had to be ignored (Zerubavel 2006: 23). Other examples include child abuse in a family that is covered up by a shared secret held among family members.

LAW AND ECONOMICS

The common law defines a trade secret as any sort of formula or procedure that gives one seller a competitive advantage over another. For economists, a valuable trade secret means that one seller can score more profits than his or her rivals. Furthermore, it may allow that seller to price the product above its marginal cost of production, and that form of pricing results in "allocative inefficiency" in the sense that resources are not being allowed to move to what the market prices indicate are the most valued uses.

But allocative efficiency is not all that is important to economic welfare. The evidence suggests that regions are richer or poorer according to how much investment is taking place. While some of that investment is replacing worn-out equipment and updating skills, other investment is part of entrepreneurialism and the creation of new products and services. That means a capitalist economy is constantly changing what is produced, how it is produced, and when it comes to the market in sometimes novel and unexpected ways. If the prospect of discovering a formula or recipe that will result in financial success is what motivates discovery and innovation, then a different type of efficiency argument can be made and has been made for "trade secrecy." We speak of *dynamic efficiency* and identify this type of efficiency with the revolutionary and unexpected changes in the ways we work and live with one another. Many entrepreneurs and their backers try to maintain secrets so that they can generate "first mover" advantages before a large number of competitors get wind of the innovation and start to imitate and reduce the value of the secret.

In some specific cases, a trade secret might qualify for a patent award. The patent gives the owner the exclusive right to use his or her invention for a limited period of time. But not all information that is valuable in a market system is eligible for patent protection. Certain secrets such as marketing methods, pricing formulae, customer lists, and knowledge about supply chains unknown to competitors constitute valuable information that cannot be patented because it does not come within the "subject matter" of the patent system as set down by the legislature. In these instances, patenting is not an option at all. Keeping secrets is the only business option.

PROFESSIONAL MAGICIANS

It is a myth that magicians cherish their secrets and zealously guard them from prying eyes and public disclosure. Magicians are theatrical entertainers with their own associations and journals and increasingly receive academic attention and stature. If magicians were ever part of secret societies with Simmel-like rituals of admission and inclusion, that is certainly no longer the case. Magicians are often erudite, scholarly, and instructive and they share their novel art in books, films, and seminars.

During the Vaudeville period in the history of the American theater, many magicians actually *patented* their major illusions. Since a patent requires that all the secrets that are necessary to the use and replication of the invention be disclosed, it is puzzling that magicians would actually patent their magicians' secrets. Of course, magicians did this not because they wanted to "keep the secret." Instead, they wanted to monopolize the presentation of a magic illusion and have the legal right to prevent other magicians from replicating that illusion (Steinmeyer 2003: 73–113).

CONCLUSION

Secrecy is an intentional act that gives rise to many interesting social phenomena. It is consistent with individual autonomy and dynamic entrepreneurial capitalism. It is an area of sociology brought to our attention by the pioneering work of Georg Simmel and is today capable of spawning many areas of research and insightful analysis.

SEE ALSO: Goffman, Erving; Magic; Public and Private; Simmel, Georg; Sociometry

REFERENCES AND SUGGESTED READINGS

Bergmann, J. R. (1993 [1987]) *Discreet Indiscretions: The Social Organization of Gossip*. Aldine de Gruyter, New York.

Bok, S. (1982) *Secrets: On the Ethics of Concealment and Revelation*. Pantheon Books, New York.

Ellis, T. (2006) Viewpoint: Can You Keep a Secret? *Magic: The Magazine for Magicians* 15 (January): 26–7.

Goffman, E. (1963) *Behavior in Public Places*. Free Press, New York.

Hobbes, T. (1928 [1650]) *The Elements of Law Natural and Politic*. Ed. F. Tönnies. Cambridge University Press, Cambridge.

Levine, D. (1971) Introduction. In: Simmel, G., *On Individuality and Social Forms: Selected Writings*. University of Chicago Press, Chicago, pp. ix–lxv.

Miller, W. I. (2003) *Faking It*. Cambridge University Press, Cambridge.

Moss, L. (1991) The Chicago Intellectual Property Rights Tradition and the Reconciliation of Coase and Hayek. *Eastern Economic Journal* 17 (April/June): 145–56.

Orwell, G. (2003 [1949]) *Nineteen Eighty-Four*. Harcourt Brace, New York.

Parsons, T. (1937) *The Structure of Social Action*. McGraw-Hill, New York.

Ritzer, G. (2000) *Classical Sociological Theory*, 3rd edn. McGraw-Hill, New York.

Simmel, G. (1906) The Sociology of Secrecy and of Secret Societies. *American Journal of Sociology* 11: 441–98.

Steinmeyer, J. (2003) *Hiding the Elephant: How Magicians Invented the Impossible*. Carroll & Graf, New York.

Zerubavel, E. (2006) *The Elephant in the Room: Silence and Denial in Everyday Life*. Oxford University Press, Oxford.

sect

William H. Swatos, Jr.

Although the term sect has played a role in both political sociology and the study of social movements at the hands of many Marxians as well as such early sociologists as LeBon, Sighele, Park, and Simmel, its primary continuing application has been among sociologists of religion in the context of church-sect theory. The dominance of this use has led to its virtual abandonment in other sociological subfields. In this context, a sect may be defined as a voluntary religious association whose members enter it as a result of a personal decision to join, which decision is then subject to confirmation by the existing members of the association. It contrasts with a church, whose members are said to be "born" into it, either by nationality or ongoing familial commitment.

In its many permutations and combinations as an explanation of religious organization and religiosity, church-sect theory may be the most important middle-range theory that the sociology of religion has to offer. It is also the case that, though termed church-sect theory, a more accurate phrasing for actual usage of the construct would be sect-church theory, since the preponderance of research and debate has been directed toward the sect type and changes that do or do not occur in religious organizations from sectarian origins into other sociological types.

Although the terms church and sect have a long heritage in the writings of church historians, credit for their first attachment to sociological concepts belongs to Max Weber. Their popularization among scholars of religion in the modern sense, however, was through ethicist H. Richard Niebuhr's adaptation of the work of Weber's sometime associate Ernst Troeltsch, himself a historical ethicist. To understand much of the debate and confusion in contemporary sociological usage, it is necessary to review how the concepts fit into Weber's sociology of religion and how the Troeltsch–Niebuhr synthesis introduced corruptions into that use that impaired their analytical power.

WEBERIAN SOCIOLOGY AND TROELTSCHIAN ETHICS

Weber's sociology is united by the overarching thematic element of the processes of the rationalization of action. Weber was attempting to answer the question of why the universal-historical rationalization-disenchantment process had come to fruition most completely in the Anglo-American "spirit" of capitalism. As part of this project Weber wanted to employ an analytical method that would allow him to maintain his commitment to the principle that sociology was a scientific discipline while dealing with historical data, wherein heretofore empathic *verstehende Soziologie* had failed to achieve conclusions that could in any way be compared to the accuracy of the experimental method. Weber's answer was the comparative method using the tool of the ideal-type: a hypothetically concrete reality, a mental construct based upon relevant empirical components, formed and explicitly delineated by the researcher to facilitate precise comparisons on specific points of interest. The conceptualizations of "church" and "sect," like an inch in the measurement of length, serve to enable two or more religious organizations to be compared to each other. Church-sect theory in Weber's usage was not a standard *to* which religious organizations were compared but *by* which they were compared. The critical differentiating variable for Weber was "mode of membership" – whether the normal method of membership recruitment of the organization was by "birth" (church) or "decision" (sect).

In the transition from Weber to Troeltsch's *The Social Teachings of the Christian Churches* (1912), the church-sect typology underwent significant alterations. Troeltsch was not a social scientist but a theologian attempting to relate types of religious experiences with the varieties of social teachings to which they might be correlated. In doing so, he parted company with Weber's work in two critical ways. First, he shifted the emphasis of the type from social-organizational to behavioral. Second, he stressed the notion of "accommodation" or "compromise" as differentiating between the different religious styles. The first departure is most clearly seen in Troeltsch's positing of *three* types of religious behavior: churchly, sectarian, and mystical. The third of these is now generally dropped from consideration by church-sect theorists – in Weber's work it occurs in a separate bipolar typology of behavioral orientation, namely that of asceticism-mysticism. Nevertheless, the presence of the mystical type within Troeltsch's formulation suggests that he was actually using the terms in a conceptually different operation from that to which church-sect is usually put in organizational analysis. The "dichotomy" of church-sect that has been attributed to Troeltsch must be understood within both his three-way scheme and the instrumental context of Weberian ideal-typical method. Troeltsch shared with Weber primarily method, partially content, and peripherally project. Weber and Troeltsch were working on different, although related, questions. Troeltsch understood Weber's concept of the ideal-type, capitalized on what Weber termed its "transient" nature, and hence reformulated the concepts of church, sect, and mysticism to work for his own purposes.

Subsequent church-sect debates have largely been the result of an overemphasis upon the Weber–Troeltsch association that assumes that because the two men were colleagues (and even lived in the same building for a number of years) and Troeltsch used Weber's method and to some extent his content, the *intention* of Troeltsch's work was the same as Weber's, which it was not. What Troeltsch himself calls a "sociological formulation" of a theological question has been misidentified with Weber's attempt to solve a sociological problem. The difference between the two projects is clear in the critical distinguishing elements that form the focus for each one's work. Whereas Weber uses mode of membership, Troeltsch adopts accommodation or compromise. While mode of membership can be ascertained relatively directly, accommodation has a more mediated character: what is and is not accommodation is more perspectival. A theological rather than organizational – hence sociological – focus comes to frame the theory.

The basis for the shift in usage and concomitant confusion lies in the way in which the sect construct was introduced to the English-speaking audience, with the corresponding void created in German scholarship as a result of the two world wars. The first major English-language publication to use the types was the work of another sociologically inclined theological ethicist, Yale professor H. Richard Niebhur's *The Social Sources of Denominationalism* (1929). Although at times possessed by a rather naïve evolutionism and narrow perspective, Niebhur's work contributed a significant element that was lacking in earlier treatments. He used church and sect as poles of a continuum, rather than simply as discrete categories. Niebuhr did not merely classify groups in relation to their relative sect-likeness or church-likeness, but analyzed the dynamic process of religious history as groups moved along this continuum. This approach found its down side, however, in that taken by itself it tended toward the reification of the types and the hypothetical continuum that he posited. It thus contained powerful seeds for church-sect theory to grow into an evaluative device, quite outside the "value-free" comparative sociological frame of reference in which it was conceived. Sect-to-church modeling not only turned the word order around, it also turned church-sect theory from an analytical device to a quasi-ethical evaluation. This disjuncture was compounded by the fact that Troeltsch's *Social Teachings* was translated in 1931, providing a kind of "classic" legitimation for Niebuhr's approach, whereas Weber's methodological work was not available in translation until 1949. Many of the subsequent difficulties that have attended church-sect theory can be traced to the strange movements of this framework and its methodological base across the Atlantic.

ELABORATION, REACTION, AND REVISION

Subsequent elaborations of church-sect theory have been clearly dependent upon the work of Troeltsch via Niebuhr. The original church-sect dichotomy became generally interpreted as a continuum having a multicriteria basis for its analyses.

Howard Becker was the first American trained as a sociologist to use and extend church-sect theory. Attempting to facilitate increased specificity, Becker delineated two types within each of the original two types, resulting in a cult-sect-denomination-ecclesia model. In thus developing the typology, Becker abandoned the ideal-type method for that of "abstract collectivities," ideal realities rather than constructs. J. Milton Yinger in his *Religion and the Struggle for Power* (1946) increased the limitations for specific points along the continuum, extending Becker's four types to six: cult, sect, established sect, class church/denomination, ecclesia, and universal church – the latter most clearly evidencing the increasingly theological focus of the usage.

Yinger subsequently went further in his specification, however, by subtyping sects in terms of their relationship to the social order – whether they were accepting, avoiding, or aggressive. This development began a wave of interest in the sect type within church-sect theorizing, with numerous writers offering contributions on the best way of treating this possibility, the most lasting of which is Bryan Wilson's "An Analysis of Sect Development" (1959). The results of this strategy were, on the one hand, to shift the focus of church-sect theory away from *both* comparative and evaluative analyses toward a classificatory system of the bases and outcomes of religious organizational development in the wake of social systemic variables; and on the other hand, it invited a focus on religious movements that were relatively marginal to mainstream society, hence prepared the way for the emergence of the subfield within the sociology of religion known as New Religious Movements (NRMs) beginning in the 1970s.

An exception to this general tendency to focus on societally marginal religious organizations (first "sects," later "cults") was the publication in the *British Journal of Sociology* of a seminal essay by David Martin in 1962 simply titled "The Denomination." Although it did little to stem the tide of interest in marginal groups at the time, Martin's article would bear fruit in various ways in new typological formulations that appeared in the late 1970s. The action sociology models of both Roy Wallis and William H. Swatos, Jr., as well as the rational choice models of Rodney Stark and his colleagues, emphasize the importance of denominational religiosity as the typological alternative to sectarianism (and cultic forms).

On the heels of these developments also came criticism of the framework. A number of critics denounced the orientation as meaningless or, at best, woefully inadequate to systematic investigation of the empirical world. Church-sect theorizing has been criticized as ambiguous and vague, lacking precise definitions, unsuited to tests for validity and reliability, merely descriptive rather than explanatory, less informative than other possible approaches, historically and geographically restricted, and unrelated to the rest of sociological theory. Despite all of these criticisms, however, the theoretical framework into which church-sect has evolved has allowed a tremendous amount of data to be organized and reported.

In response to these criticisms, a number of scholars made revisions within the church-sect framework, making it a more viable theoretical orientation for the sociological study of religion. Yinger, Wallis, Swatos, Paul Gustafson, and Roland Robertson, for example, have each suggested the value of an explicit visual scheme for modeling and analyses. Wilson, whose work on sects spanned over 40 years, came increasingly to accept a Weberian approach and was among the first to attempt to take aspects of sect analysis outside the orbit of Western religions and societies in his *Magic and the Millennium* (1973). Stark and colleagues have reached back into earlier empirical work by Glock and Stark to use pieces of church-sect theorizing in their "rational choice" modeling, demonstrating that it is possible to tie the framework to large data sets.

NEO-WEBERIAN ANALYSES

Particularly significant to the process of rethinking church-sect theory was the work of Benton Johnson. As early as 1957, Johnson critiqued the Troeltschian approach to church-sect. In subsequent work, he returned to Weber – not directly to Weber's discussion of church-sect, but to his distinction between emissary and exemplary prophets. From this perspective, Johnson focuses upon the single universal variable property of a group's relationship to the social environment in which it exists. "Church" is employed as the polar type of *acceptance* of the social environment, whereas "sect" is the polar type of its *rejection*. Wilson thereafter also embraced "response to the world" as the principal basis for classification of sects in an ideal-typical (rather than taxonomic) way. Johnson contends that the sociologist should strive toward the discovery of universal properties at a high level of generality that vary in such ways that typologies might be constructed. He sees "acceptance/rejection of the social environment" as a single variable around which empirical church-sect distinctions may be grouped and asserts that this typological approach is superior to one that simply adds "types" as historical circumstances alter. These are in fact not types at all, in the Weberian sense, but categories. Johnson's work has significantly affected such differing streams as Swatos's situationalism and the rational choice modeling of Stark and his colleagues.

Although Johnson's distinction possesses enormous advantages in terms of conceptual parsimony, its lack of integration of the historical differences in the various sociocultural systems in which religious organizations function produces potential difficulties in macrosociological analyses. Whereas the microsociologically based rational choice model focuses primarily on the effects of the organizational experience of the decision-maker and only secondarily on the organization-system component, a more culturally oriented analysis would note that different system contexts produce different styles of organizational response that cannot be entirely comprehended by a single universal variable component. Thus, Swatos cross-cuts Johnson's acceptance–rejection dichotomy with the sociocultural system polarity of monopolism–pluralism. Following on the work of David Little, Swatos contends that the nature of the sociocultural system shapes the patterns of acceptance and rejection that become expressed in specific religious organizational forms and rationales. In related work, following leads from Martin and Wallis, Swatos has criticized the use of "cult" in Stark's church-sect modeling; Swatos argues that from the Weberian point of view out of which church-sect theorizing sprang, "cult" is properly contrasted to "order" as polar organizational manifestations of the mysticism–asceticism typology, rather than incorporated into church-sect theory. Cults in turn have charismatic leaders, while orders have virtuosos. Patricia Wittberg's analysis of the dramatic decline of Roman Catholic religious orders in the western societies during the second half of the twentieth century, *The Rise and Fall of Catholic Religious Orders* (1994), particularly illustrates the appropriate use of the order/virtuoso combination and then deploys it within an explanatory structure that suggests the sociosystemic characteristics that lead not only to that decline but also to the corresponding rise of charismatic types of religious experiences and organizations.

Building on these foundations, Michael York's study of New Age and neopagan movements, *The Emerging Network* (1995), demonstrates the continued value of church-sect typologizing as a conceptual tool within a larger analytical framework through which these phenomena may also be studied profitably. The concept of *network* which York introduces in his work has been further elaborated by Hizuru Miki in a church-sect schema as a polar type to *organization*. These advances facilitate both cross-cultural comparisons and the analysis of both new religious movements and quasi-religions, some of which have heretofore been treated under the now ideologically loaded concept of cult. Thus, church-sect theorizing continues to be a part of ongoing sociological scholarship, well beyond its initial foundations, but also more closely linked in analytical style to those foundations than it was in the period from the 1930s to the 1970s.

SEE ALSO: Asceticism; Denomination; Ideal Type; Jehovah's Witnesses; Networks; Religion, Sociology of; Scientology; Weber, Max

REFERENCES AND SUGGESTED READINGS

Berger, P. (1954) The Sociological Study of Sectarianism. *Social Research* 21: 467–85.

Glock, C. & Stark, R. (1965) *Religion and Society in Tension*. Rand-McNally, Chicago.

Gustafson, P. (1973) Exegesis on the Gospel According to St. Max. *Sociological Analysis* 34: 12–25.

Johnson, B. (1963) On Church and Sect. *American Sociological Review* 28: 539–49.

Johnson, B. (1971) Church and Sect Revisited. *Journal for the Scientific Study of Religion* 10: 124–37.

Miki, H. (1999) Towards a New Paradigm of Religious Organizations. *International Journal of Japanese Sociology* 8: 141–59.

O'Toole, R. (1976) Underground Traditions in the Study of Sectarianism: Non-Religious Uses of the Concept "Sect." *Journal for the Scientific Study of Religion* 15: 145–56.

Robertson, R. (1970) *The Sociological Interpretation of Religion*. Schocken, New York.

Stark, R. & Bainbridge, W. (1979) Of Churches, Sects, and Cults: Preliminary Concepts for a Theory of Religious Movements. *Journal for the Scientific Study of Religion* 18: 117–31.

Swatos, W. (1979) *Into Denominationalism: The Anglican Metamorphosis*. Society for the Scientific Study of Religion, Storrs, CT.

Swatos, W. (1981) Church-Sect and Cult: Bringing Mysticism Back In. *Sociological Analysis* 42: 17–26.

Wallis, R. (1975) Scientology: Therapeutic Cult to Religious Sect. *Sociology* 9: 89–100.
Weber, M. (1949) *Max Weber on the Methodology of the Social Sciences.* Free Press, Glencoe, IL.
Weber, M. (2002) *The Protestant Ethic and the "Spirit" of Capitalism and Other Writings.* Penguin, New York.
Yinger, J. (1970) *The Scientific Study of Religion.* Macmillan, New York.

secularization

Karel Dobbelaere

Secularization is a term used by sociologists to refer to a process by which the overarching and transcendent religious system of old is reduced in modern functionally differentiated societies to a subsystem alongside other subsystems, losing in this process its overarching claims over these other subsystems. This is the original meaning, but this process has consequences for the organizational and individual levels, which suggests that secularization needs to be analyzed on the societal (macro), the organizational (meso), and the individual (micro) levels.

The concept was introduced by Longueville in the negotiations that led to the Peace of Westphalia in 1648 when he used the term *séculariser* to describe the change in statute of certain ecclesiastical territories that were being added to Brandenburg as compensation for its territorial losses. The emergence of the term is linked to the notion *secularis* that had already been in use for centuries, not only to distinguish the secular from the sacred, but also especially to indicate the former's subordination to and dependence on the latter. However, the connotation associated with the term secularization has reversed this relationship: it expresses the advancing "emancipation" of the secular from the sacred. For the religious, however, it means rather the "confinement" of the religious to the religious sphere. The concept has a long history (which will not be analyzed here), and many authors have emphasized that it has always retained the ambiguous and consequently controversial meaning that it had from the start.

If the founding fathers rarely used the term, concepts and views related to theories of secularization were nonetheless canvassed, e.g., generalization and differentiation (Durkheim), and Weber (1920) used the term to typify the way in which, in the United States, membership in distinguished clubs and fraternal societies replaced membership of sects in guaranteeing moral rectitude and creditworthiness. Later generations of sociologists continued to employ the term, but attached different meanings to it (Shiner 1967). Not until the late 1960s and 1970s were several theories of secularization developed, most prominently by Berger (1967), Luckmann (1967), Wilson (1976), and Martin (1978). These theories subsequently led to discussions concerning their reliability and validity (e.g., Hammond 1985). In similar vein, others have suggested an alternative, i.e., rational choice theory (Young 1997), to explain the religious situation in the US, which they considered to be radically different from that of Europe, where secularization theory emerged. Finally, Tschannen and Dobbelaere have systematically analyzed the existing theories, since some discussions failed to scrutinize the ideas, levels of analysis, and arguments of those being criticized. Tschannen (1992) has suggested treating secularization theories as a paradigm and has described different "exemplars," or shared examples, typical of the paradigm. Dobbelaere (2002 [1981]) has stressed the need to differentiate the different levels of analysis one from another, suggesting convergences and divergences between existing theories. To describe the core of secularization theory, the different exemplars will be discussed here according to the levels of analysis.

THE MACRO LEVEL: SOCIETAL SECULARIZATION

Modern societies are primarily differentiated along functional lines that overlay the prior forms of segmentary and social class differentiation, and have developed different subsystems (e.g., economy, polity, science, family, and education). These subsystems are similar in the sense that society has equal need of them all, but dissimilar since each performs its own particular function (production and distribution of goods and services; taking binding decisions; production of valid knowledge; procreation and mutual support; and teaching). Their functional autonomy depends of course on their communication with other functional systems and the environment. To guarantee these functions and to communicate with their environment, organizations (enterprises; political parties; research centers and academies; families; schools and universities) have been established (the meso level). Each of these organizations functions on the basis of its own medium (money; power; truth; love; information and know-how) and according to the values of its subsystem and its specific norms.

Regarding religion, these organizations affirm their autonomy and reject religiously prescribed rules, i.e., the *autonomization* of the subsystems – e.g., the emancipation of education from ecclesiastical authority; the separation of church and state; the rejection of church prescriptions about birth control, abortion, and euthanasia; the decline of religious content in literature and arts; and the development of science as an autonomous secular perspective. Consequently, the religious influence is increasingly confined to the religious subsystem itself. Thus, the sociological explanation of societal secularization starts with the process of functional differentiation and the autonomization of the so-called secular subsystems; as a consequence, religion becomes a subsystem alongside other subsystems, losing in this process its overarching claims over those other subsystems. On the global level, one could of course point to countries that are not secularized because "church and state" are not functionally differentiated – Iran, for example. But as Pace (1998) has pointed out, this is not typical of all Muslim countries; there are many where politics progressively asserts itself to form an independent sphere of action, which is the start of the secularization of these countries. In fact, societal secularization is only the particularization of the general process of functional differentiation in the religious subsystem and is a purely descriptive concept.

Berger and Luckmann stressed a consequence of the process of functional differentiation and the autonomization of the secular spheres, to wit, the *privatization of religion.* According to Luckmann (1967), the validity of religious norms became restricted to its proper sphere, i.e., that of private life. Berger (1967) stressed the functionality of this for the maintenance of the highly rationalized order of modern economic and political institutions, the so-called *public sphere*. This dichotomy, private/public, carries with it at least two shortcomings. First of all, it suggests that secularization was limited to the so-called public sphere, which is incorrect: family life has also been secularized. This became very clear in the reactions of lay Catholics who objected to the rules enunciated in the papal encyclical *Humanae Vitae* (1968). Married couples rejected the claim of the church to define the goals of the family and to dictate the acceptable means by which these goals might be achieved. In other words, they defended the functional differentiation of family and religion. Secondly, it is the adoption in sociological discourse of ideological concepts used by liberals and socialists in the nineteenth century to legitimize functional differentiation and the autonomization of so-called secular institutions: "religion is a private matter."

It is clear that the private/public dichotomy is not a structural aspect of society. It is not a societal subsystem with institutionalized roles (professional versus public), as, for example, is the case in the economy (producers versus consumers), the educational system (teachers versus students), the polity (politicians versus voters), and the judicial system (magistrates and lawyers versus clients). It is, rather, a legitimizing conceptualization of the secular world, an ideological pair used in conflicts between opponents. For example, to defend their political, religious, or family options against possible sanctions and eventual dismissal by the management of Christian organizations, e.g., schools or hospitals, employees used this dichotomy if they failed to behave according to ecclesiastical rules in matters of family life, politics, or religion. They defended their private options, their private life, in what the managers of ecclesiastical organizations called the public sphere, since, according to the managers, these private options were publicly known. The outcome of such conflicts in court was that managers had to accept employees' right to privacy. Of course, sociologists should study the use of this dichotomy in social discourse and conflicts, to analyze its strategic application by groups wanting to promote or to retard the secularization of the social system. The private/public dichotomy is not a sociological conceptualization. In sociological discourse, this ideological pair might better be replaced by Habermas's (1982) conceptual dichotomy: system versus life world, used in a purely descriptive sense.

HOW ARE FUNCTIONALLY DIFFERENTIATED SOCIETIES INTEGRATED?

Pluralization, or the segmentary differentiation of the subsystem religion, was only possible, according to Parsons (1967), once the Christian ethic was institutionalized in the so-called secular world: in other words, once the Christian ethic became *generalized*. Consequently, pluralization may not be considered an indicator of secularization – quite the contrary. However, the relationship is not unidirectional, since a growing pluralization may augment the necessity of generalization. Indeed, together with Bellah (1967), Parsons stressed the need for a civil religion which, to legitimize the system, overarches conventional religions. Martin (1978) suggests that when religion adapts to every status group through every variety of pullulating sectarianism, then there is a need to preserve the unity of the nation by a national myth which represents a common denominator of all faiths: one nation under God. Indeed, civil religion generalizes the different notions of God present in the various denominations: the God of the Jews, Catholics, Unitarians, Calvinists, and so forth. National myths sacralize their prophets, martyrs, and historical places: they have their ritualistic expressions and may also use biblical archetypes (Bellah 1967). Such myths and legitimations are not always religious: civil religion is one possibility; there are also secular myths, such as the French myth based on *laïcité*, which legitimizes the French state, its schools and laws. One may also consider the need for secular laws overarching divergent, religiously inspired mores in religiously divided states.

How might the emergence of such a myth – religious or secular – be explained? Fenn (1978) has suggested that this is possible only when a society conceives of itself as a "nation," as "really real" – typical examples are the US, Japan, and France. On the other hand, the myth is rather seen as a cultural "fiction" to the extent that a society views itself as an arena for conflicting and cooperative activities of various classes, groups, corporation, and organizations. What explains the emergence of a "religious" rather than a "secular" myth, or vice versa, and what accounts for the secularization of a religious myth? For example, the "religious" civil religion of France, "la fille aînée de l'Église," was progressively secularized after the French Revolution and anchored in *laïcité*. Another issue for inquiry is how and to what extent in certain countries a conventional religion may function as a civil religion in a religiously pluralistic society, and at what price, e.g., Anglicanism in England, Lutheranism in the Scandinavian countries, and Calvinism in the Netherlands. What degree of pluralism is congruent with a church fulfilling the role of civil religion?

Not all sociologists suggest that modern societies are integrated by common values, a point long since made by Durkheim. In a functionally differentiated society, the grip of the total societal system on the subsystems has changed, argues Luhmann (1977). A subsystem belongs to a societal system not because it is guided in its structural choices by requirements, values, and norms that apply to *all* subsystems. Integration is mediated by the fact that all subsystems are an inner-societal environment for one another, they have to mutually accept one another's functions – which does not preclude "performances," i.e., that a given subsystem intervenes in another subsystem if this subsystem is unable to solve some of its problems, as long as the intervening subsystem applies the values and norms of the subsystem in which it is intervening. Secondly, they have to prevent their own operations from producing insoluble problems in other subsystems, hence church leaders should not intervene in political elections by giving guidance to their flock about how to vote, since this would diminish the degree of functional differentiation. If such interventions are still acceptable in some countries, which was the case up to the 1980s in the Republic of Ireland and in Belgium until the 1950s, this would indicate a limitation of the differentiation of church and polity, and ipso facto a lesser degree of secularization. However, the system cannot prevent private individuals from failing to differentiate some functions and, for example, voting according to their religious beliefs or choosing a school for their children appropriate to their religious views. A structural equivalent is, therefore, according to Luhmann (1977), built into the system to prevent the dedifferentiation of the system: the "Privatisierung des Entscheidens" (the individualization of decisions), which may cancel out some individual combinations by other combinations owing to the law of great numbers. This means that our societies function according to the principle of the *individualization* of decisions and actions, which implies that this principle is a *structural* component of modern societies. Publicity campaigns by industrial firms and political parties point to the individualization of decisions.

THE MESO LEVEL: ORGANIZATIONAL SECULARIZATION

The autonomization of the so-called secular subsystems allowed the development of *functional rationality* within organizations. The economy lost its religious ethos (Weber). Goals and means were evaluated on a cost-efficiency basis. This typical attitude implying observation, evaluation, calculation, and planning – which is based on a belief that the world is indeed calculable, controllable, and predictable – is not limited to the economic system. The political system was also rationalized, leaving little room for traditional and charismatic authority, as modern states developed their rational administration. Since these economic and political organizations needed ever greater numbers of people trained in science and rational techniques, the educational curriculum had to change. A scientific approach to the world and the teaching of technical knowledge increasingly replaced a religious-literary formation. The development of scientifically based techniques also had its impact on the life world: domestic tasks became increasingly mechanized and computerized. Even the most intimate human behavior, sexuality, became governed by it. This is also the case with the so-called *natural* method of birth control proposed by the Catholic Church. It is based on the basal temperature of the woman registered when waking, which has to be plotted on a chart. On the basis of the temperature curve, the fertile and infertile periods can be calculated. Thus, it was on the basis of observation, calculation, and evaluation that sexual intercourse could be planned to prevent pregnancy. Another example in the field of sexuality was the Masters and Johnson research to "enhance" sexual pleasure. It was based on experimentation with couples and involved observation, calculation, and evaluation, by which means the researchers sought to produce guidelines to ensure and augment sexual pleasure: sexuality became a technique that could be improved by better performances according to the published "technical rules." The consequences of such developments were the *disenchantment* of the world and the *societalization* of the subsystems.

First, the disenchantment of the world. The growing propensity to consider the natural, material, social, and psychological world and the human body as calculable and human-made, the result of controlled planning (e.g., in vitro fertilization and plastic surgery), engendered not only new roles but also new, basically rational and critical attitudes and a new cognition. Theses were replaced by hypotheses, the Bible by the encyclopedia, revelation by knowledge. According to Acquaviva (1979), this new cognition has been objectified in a new language that changed the image of reality, thus eliminating "pre-logical," including religious, concepts. The mass media, using this new language, have radicalized this development and made it a social phenomenon. This suggests a possible impact of these changes on the micro level, i.e., the consciousness of the individual. Having internalized this new language, which produced a certain vision of the world, people may to some extent have lost the vision of a sacred reality. For example, when artificial insemination is discussed on television, technical interventions produce life and the issue is debated in a secular, technical language, reducing life's sacredness.

Second, it is in the systemic relations that societalization occurs, and these relationships became secondary: formal, segmented, utilitarian. By contrast, in the life world – family, friends, and social networks – primary relations are still the binding force, they are personal, total, sympathetic, trustful, and considerate. The trend toward societalization or *Vergesellschaftung* is very clear in the distribution sector: neighborhood stores are increasingly replaced by large department stores, where interactions between customers and employees are limited to short, informative questions and exchanges of money for goods. Economic production developed large-scale economic organizations in which Taylorism, which is based on the specialization of tasks and the elimination of unnecessary movement, was extensively applied. This innovation led to the development of the assembly line. The organized world is based on impersonal role relationships, the coordination of skills, and essentially formal and contractual patterns of behavior, in which personal virtue, as distinguished from role obligations, is of small consequence (Wilson 1982). In such systems, control is no longer based on morals and religion but has become impersonal, a matter of routine techniques and unknown officials – legal, technical, mechanized, computerized, and electronic – for example, speed control by unmanned cameras and video control in department stores. Thus religion has lost one of its important latent functions: as long as control was interpersonal, it was founded on religiously based mores and substantive values. In Wilson's view, there is another argument to explain why secularization is a concomitant of societalization: since religion offers redemption, which is personal, total, an indivisible ultimate that is not susceptible to rational techniques or cost-efficiency criteria, it has to be offered in a "community" (Wilson 1976), and the *Vergesellschaftung* has destroyed communal life.

RELIGION ON THE MESO LEVEL

How did the organizations within the religious subsystem react to the secularization of the subsystems? The scientific approach to the world and the teaching of technical knowledge that replaced a religious-literary formation in the schools distressed, for example, the leaders of the Seventh-Day Adventist Church, who stimulated the expansion of their own religiously oriented educational network. In the Christian world, especially in the Catholic world, the secularization of state schools, culture, and social life gave rise to the process of pillarization at the end of the nineteenth century. This was a deliberate attempt by the church to recover as much as possible of what was lost by secularization. It emerged in a context in which a separation was progressively being made – not only in principle but also structurally – between religion and other functional spheres, and to the extent that non-Christians became a "fact," i.e., acquired real power to implement their secular views. The procedure for such recovery was the establishment of a multiplicity of organizations in which Catholics, *casu quo* Protestants, could be insulated from the secular environment – e.g., schools and universities, hospitals, old people's homes, youth and adult movements, cultural associations, sports clubs, mass media, trade unions, health insurance funds, and political parties. Pillarization was a defensive reaction and a typical process of segmented differentiation.

The emergence of new religious movements (NRMs) is related to the process of globalization and intercontinental mobility, and to the secularization that undermined the credibility of the "Christian collective consciousness." Pluralism had undermined its "objectivity," and the slowly perceived lack of impact of Christian religions on the societal level, expressed in the loss of its representatives' status and power, allowed exotic religions to improve their position on the religious market. Some NRMs, such as the Unification Church, the Family, and ISCON, wanted to resacralize the world and its institutions by bringing God back into the different groups operating in different subsystems such as the family, the economy, and even the polity. Wallis (1984) has called these "world-rejecting new religions." However, the vast majority are of another type, "world affirming." They offer their members esoteric means for attaining immediate and automatic assertiveness, heightened spirituality, recovery, success, and a clear mind, e.g., Mahikari provides an "omitama" or amulet; transcendental meditation (TM) a personal mantra for meditation; Scientology auditing with an e-meter; human potential movements offer therapies, encounter groups, or alternative health and spiritual centers.

Luckmann (1990) suggested that in many NRMs, the level of transcendence was lowered and has become "*this worldly*" or *mundane*. The historical religions, to the contrary, are examples of "great transcendences," referring to something other than everyday reality, notwithstanding the fact that they were also involved in mundane or "this-worldly" affairs. However, the reference was always transcendental, e.g., the incantations for healing, for success in examinations or work, or for "*une âme sœur.*" Most world-affirming NRMs appear to reach *only* the level of "intermediate transcendences." They bridge time and space and promote intersubjective communication, but remain at the immanent level of everyday reality. Consequently, some, like TM, claim to be spiritual rather than religious movements. Whether we call NRMs spiritual or religious is not important, what matters is that we register a change: the ultimate has become "this-worldly." If one were to employ a substantive definition of religion, referring to transcendent beliefs and practices, to the supernatural, many NRMs would not be considered as religions. Even when we use a functional definition of religion, we may come to the same conclusion. Luhmann (1977) stated that the problem of simultaneity of indefiniteness and certainty is the typical function of religion. Indeed, most of these world-affirming new religions are not concerned with the problems of *simultaneity* of transcendence and immanence since they focus only on the immanent, on everyday life, on the secular. They have adapted to the secular world.

These mundane orientations of religion are not new. Berger (1967) and Luckmann (1967) have suggested that the higher church attendance in America compared to Europe might be explained by the mundane orientation of religion in America. Luckmann called it internal secularization, a radical inner change in American church religion: the secular ideas of the American Dream pervade church religion today. In asserting that American churches were themselves becoming highly secularized, these authors sought to reconcile empirical findings at the individual level, i.e., church attendance, which appeared to conflict with secularization theories, by pointing out changes at the organizational level, i.e., within the churches. The point of interest for our argument is that the idea of organizational secularization is not new: the concept of internal secularization was its predecessor.

SECULARIZATION AND LAICIZATION

The processes of societal and organizational secularization may be the consequence of a latent and/or a manifest process. In Belgium, pillarization was a reaction against a manifest policy, starting in the second part of the nineteenth century, by the radical liberal faction and, later, supported by the socialists to subvert the Catholic Church's control in matters of education, culture, and charity. This *manifest* process of secularization is called *laicization.* France is a very good example of the laicization of schools, and the 2005 law prohibiting ostentatious religious signs in state schools underlines this. Marx, Lenin, and the Marxist parties also propounded a deliberate policy of laicization of the state. According to Marx, the state that presupposes religion is not yet a real and genuine state, and even in his first articles in the *Rheinische Zeitung* he upheld the autonomy of politics. This position was later affirmed by Lenin and implemented in the USSR with the January 1918 decree on the separation of church from state and school from church. Other examples of the "logic of laicization," most typical of Catholic European societies, may be found in Champion (1993). In Belgium and the Netherlands, recent governments have laicized laws on life and death by legalizing abortion and depenalizing euthanasia, and they have extended marriage to homosexual couples, changing, according to a religious view, a so-called God-given law. These examples also clearly indicate that secularization is not a mechanical, evolutionary process but a consequence of divergent definitions, the outcome of which is dependent upon the balance of power. Such manifest conflicts do not occur only on the national level but may be situated on the city level and linked to so-called secular issues such as homelessness and black neighborhood development, as pointed out in a study by Demerath and Williams (1992).

However, secularization may also be the result of a *latent* process. The secularization of the medical subsystem was a consequence of the development of medical science and professionalization: medical rationality reduced the place of religion. Even in Catholic hospitals, the organizational structure is based on medical specialisms and the development of administrative rationality, which marginalized religion and, in the second half of the twentieth century, confined it to a small optional service – the chaplaincy. In Catholic schools, the professionalization of teachers stressed the scientific approach of the so-called profane branches and reduced religion to a specific class, taught by a special teacher: it became one class among others. These are examples of a latent process of secularization: the secularization of Catholic hospitals and schools was the manifest purpose neither of medical doctors nor of teachers.

It is not only professionals who may secularize the world, as is evident from a study undertaken by Voyé (1998) on Christmas decorations in a Walloon village in Belgium. Isambert (1982) underscored the slide from the scriptural and liturgical basis of the nativity, which is oriented toward the incarnation and redemption, toward the Christ child. Indeed, the Christ child is placed at the center of familial Christmas celebrations and also in the decorations displayed by the city authorities. In this Walloon village, however, the decorations evoke a further sliding away: signboards several meters square, erected on lawns in front of houses and illuminated at night, represented Walt Disney cartoon characters. Here, Christmas is not only child-oriented but, as Voyé rightfully underscores, with the Disney characters we are no longer in the realms of history but in a fairytale, peopled with fictive beings. These decorations convey implicitly the idea that Christmas is a marvelous fairytale, far removed from the original incarnation–redemption idea that the religious message of Christmas carries. By putting up these decorations, people latently secularize the Christian message.

THE MICRO LEVEL: INDIVIDUAL SECULARIZATION AND COMPARTMENTALIZATION

Luhmann's contention that the social structure is secularized but not the individual is controversial. Most sociologists will not challenge the first part, although some will question the second part. Berger, Davie, Martin, and Stark point out the religious fever in the United States, which is contested by other sociologists (e.g., Demerath 2001), and in the world, and they reject the universal pattern of individual secularization, while accepting that Europe is to a large extent secularized on the micro level. For this reason they call Europe the exception, although Davie (2002) relativizes this by highlighting the persistence of religious beliefs and "religious sensitivity," and by referring to what she calls "vicarious religion": people drawing on religious capital at crucial times in their individual or collective lives, e.g., for the celebration of rites of passage. Her interpretation is based on data from the European Values Study referring, among other indicators, to belief in God. However, it may be remarked that the content of belief in God has greatly changed: the number of people believing in a "personal God" is shrinking and is replaced by a growing number of agnostics and persons believing in "a spirit or life force." Although sociological research in Belgium shows that a certain percentage of the unchurched still pray and define themselves as religious, a more detailed analysis reveals that, among those who have been at least two generations unchurched, fewer people define themselves as religious and fewer maintain a private practice than among the first-generation unchurched. Does this not suggest that it is difficult to remain religious the longer one is severed from a religious congregation?

Recent qualitative research in Belgium has also revealed that for those unchurched persons and marginal church members who still ask for a religious rite of passage, the meaning of these rites has changed: it expresses for them more of a cultural and family tradition than a religious one. Hiernaux and Voyé led a study of Catholics in French-speaking Belgium who intended to have a religious burial. The study revealed important changes. When Latin was used in ritual and hymns, the priest had the central role and used standardized formulae, which he knew and understood, creating a distance between daily life and the afterlife. Formerly, the ritual was centered on the life to come and the mystery surrounding it, whereas now the ritual centered upon the deceased: his life, loves, friendships, and accomplishments: the texts read and the songs and music played were chosen by the family with reference to the deceased. If religious texts and hymns were used, they were chosen to express the qualities of the deceased and not because they refer to God. Quite often God was not brought in except in the rare sacramental words pronounced by the priest (Voyé 1998). Studying the motivations of the unchurched and marginal church members who had their children baptized, it was found that both the cultural tradition of the country and familial tradition were important elements in the motivation. By being baptized, the children would later be socialized in the basic values of their culture during the catechism preceding their first and solemn communion, and this was considered by parents to be important in giving their children a "good start." The evaluation of religious changes at the individual level as secularization is in fact based on a substantive definition of religion in reference to institutionalized religion. Researchers who question individual secularization use terms like religious sensitivity, spirituality, religious metamorphoses, or the changing contours of religious matters (for a discussion see Beckford 2003). On the micro level, secularization is here defined as declining religiosity and a change in motivation in the use of religious rites: from a traditional religious reference to a secularly motivated use.

How is such a decline in religiosity to be explained? There are no comparative studies between countries that allow us to link the mean degree of individual secularization to the level of societal secularization in these countries (Dobbelaere 2002 [1981]). Several other factors also play a role, including individualization as a *structural* component of modern societies, and migration and the mass media, which bring individuals in contact with other religions and undermine the taken-for-granted certainties of their own religion. Studies in the western world have highlighted religious bricolage resulting from individuals shopping on the religious market, as on other markets, and building their own meaning system (Dobbelaere et al. 2003). Pace (1998) has pointed out that in Muslim countries the conflict between country and city – the latter having created new social classes with different attitudes to religious traditions and a greater willingness to accept new choices and values – and emigration, which has affected the religion not only of emigrants but also of those who stay behind, as they compare themselves with their emigrated children, relatives, or friends, have had an impact on individual secularization.

However, on the micro level, secularization could also be defined as "*secularization of mind*" or *compartmentalization*: to what extent do people *think* in terms of separation of the religious subsystem and the juridical, educational, economic, family, scientific, medical, and political subsystems? In other words, do they think along the same lines as the secularized society is structured, i.e., that religion should *not* inform the so-called profane subsystems, that these are autonomous and that any interference of religion in these subsystems should be eradicated and disallowed? In a study in Western and Central European countries, researchers were able to measure the degree of compartmentalization and to establish that the unchurched and members of the Protestant and Catholic churches with the lowest degree of church commitment think most in terms of compartmentalization (Billiet et al. 2003).

If researchers want to study the effect of societal secularization on individual secularization and on compartmentalization, then there should be international surveys that allow the measurement of these concepts in countries with different levels of societal secularization. Researchers should first establish the degree of societal secularization using a comprehensive *secularization index*. This will allow them to distinguish between countries according to their degree of societal secularization. Then they should be able to build an *individual secularization index* and a comprehensive *compartmentalization index*. Studying the association between societal secularization and compartmentalization, and between compartmentalization and individual secularization – defined as level of church commitment – should allow researchers to study the impact of societal changes on individual thinking and behavior.

In the United States an alternative theory to secularization, which was not considered applicable in the US context, was developed: rational choice theory (RCT). Are both theories mutually exclusive? RCT holds that a religious pluralistic situation may promote church commitment. This theory makes three important points (Young 1997). It postulates a *latent religiosity* on the demand side, which should become manifest by *active competition* between religious firms on the supply side. However, this is only possible in a *pluralistic religious situation* where religious firms compete for customers, and to the extent that the supply side is not limited by state regulations, suppressing or subsidizing religions. Stated thus, RCT only works in states that are secularized on the societal level. State and religion should be deregulated to allow competition between religious firms; in the opposite case religious firms are "lazy," since there is no need for competition. Consequently, there is no opposition between secularization theory and RCT: both theories are complementary. Sociologists of religion should combine both theoretical approaches and integrate them (Dobbelaere 2002 [1981]).

SEE ALSO: Civil Religion; Globalization, Religion and; Humanism; Laicism; New Religious Movements; Rational Choice Theories; Religion; Religion, Sociology of; Sacred, Eclipse of the; Sacred/Profane; Structural Functional Theory

REFERENCES AND SUGGESTED READINGS

Acquaviva, S. S. (1979) *The Decline of the Sacred in Industrial Society*. Blackwell, Oxford.

Beckford, J. A. (2003) *Social Theory and Religion*. Cambridge University Press, Cambridge.

Bellah, R. N. (1967) Civil Religion in America. *Daedalus* 96: 1–21.

Berger, P. L. (1967) *The Sacred Canopy: Elements of a Sociological Theory of Religion*. Doubleday, Garden City, NY.

Billiet, J. et al. (2003) Church Commitment and Some Consequences in Western and Central Europe. In: Piedmont, R. L. & Moberg, D. O. (Eds.), *Research in the Social Scientific Study of Religion*, Vol. 14. Brill, Leiden, pp. 129–59.

Champion, F. (1993) Les rapports Église–État dans les pays européens de tradition protestante et de tradition catholique: Essai d'analyse. *Social Compass* 40: 589–609.

Davie, G. (2002) *Europe, the Exceptional Case: Parameters of Faith in the Modern World*. Darton, Longman, & Todd, London.

Demerath, III, N. J. (2001) *Crossing the Gods: World Religions and Worldly Politics*. Rutgers University Press, New Brunswick, NJ.

Demerath, III, N. J. & Williams, R. H. (1992) Secularization in a Community Context: Tensions of Religion and Politics in a New England City. *Journal for the Scientific Study of Religion* 31: 189–206.

Dobbelaere, K. (2002 [1981]) *Secularization: An Analysis at Three Levels*. PIE-Peter Lang, Brussels.

Dobbelaere, K., Tomasi, L., & Voyé, L. (2003) Religious Syncretism. In: Piedmont, R. L. & Moberg, D. O. (Eds.), *Research in the Social Scientific Study of Religion*, Vol. 13. Brill, Leiden, pp. 221–43.

Fenn, R. K. (1978) *Toward a Theory of Secularization*. Society for the Scientific Study of Religion, Storrs, CT.

Habermas, J. (1982) *Theorie des kommunikativen Handelns*. Vol. 2: *Zür Kritik der funktionalistischen Vernunft*. Suhrkamp, Frankfurt.

Hammond, P. E. (Ed.) (1985) *The Sacred in a Secular Age*. University of California Press, Berkeley.

Isambert, F.-A. (1982) *Le Sens du sacré: Fête et religion populaire*. Éditions de Minuit, Paris.

Luckmann, T. (1967) *The Invisible Religion: The Problem of Religion in Modern Society*. Macmillan, New York.

Luckmann, T. (1990) Shrinking Transcendance, Expanding Religion. *Sociological Analysis* 51: 127–38.

Luhmann, N. (1977) *Funktion der Religion*. Suhrkamp, Frankfurt.

Martin, D. A. (1978) *A General Theory of Secularization*. Blackwell, Oxford.

Pace, E. (1998) The Helmet and the Turban: Secularization in Islam. In: Laermans, R., Wilson, B., & Billiet, J. (Eds.), *Secularization and Social Integration*. Leuven University Press, Leuven, pp. 165–75.

Parsons, T. (1967) Christianity and Modern Industrial Society. In: Tiryakian, E. A. (Ed.), *Sociologi-* ociological Theory: Values and Sociocultural Change. Harper & Row, New York, pp. 33–70.

Shiner, L. (1967) The Concept of Secularization in Empirical Research. *Journal for the Scientific Study of Religion* 6: 207–20.

Tschannen, O. (1992) *Les Théories de la sécularisation*. Librairie Droz, Geneva.

Voyé, L. (1998) Death and Christmas Revisited. In: Laermans, R., Wilson, B., & Billiet, J. (Eds.), *Secularization and Social Integration*. Leuven University Press, Leuven, pp. 287–305.

Wallis, R. (1984) *The Elementary Forms of the New Religious Life*. Routledge & Kegan Paul, London.

Weber, M. (1920) Die protestantischen Sekten und der Geist des Kapitalismus. In: Weber, M., *Gesammelte Aufsätze zur Religionssoziologie I*. J. C. B. Mohr (Paul Siebeck), Tübingen, pp. 207–36.

Wilson, B. R. (1976) *Contemporary Transformations of Religion*. Oxford University Press, Oxford.

Wilson, B. R. (1982) *Religion in Sociological Perspective*. Oxford University Press, Oxford.

Young, L. A. (Ed.) (1997) *Rational Choice Theory and Religion: Summary and Assessment*. Routledge, New York.

segregation

Kristina Wolff

In 1906, W. E. B. Du Bois wrote that the "problem of the twentieth century is the problem of the Color Line" (Du Bois 1995: 42). This statement has come to represent the perpetual effects of racism in US society. It also is often used as a precursor to discussing the social phenomenon of segregation. While segregation in US society largely focuses on issues of race and ethnicity, it is more complex than this. Segregation is both the formal and informal separation of one group from another. Often this division is based on markers of difference, where race, ethnicity, gender, social class, sexual orientation, or religion is used as the foundation for justifying a split between groups and populations. The repercussions of these separations are vast, creating and supporting structural inequality within societies.

The most common form of segregation is de facto, which consists of divisions between groups of people in specific areas of their social lives such as in the workplace, housing, and schools. Historically, this often occurred as the result of immigration; people tend to move to where they know other people or where there is a population similar to them. The effects of this are visible today as many cities have neighborhoods that have large concentrations of people of the same ethnicity and/or religion. This type of segregation is shaped by a host of systemic influences such as nationwide discriminatory hiring policies and unfair practices in the banking, insurance, and real estate industries. Historically, these institutions practiced redlining, which determines what neighborhoods are not eligible for mortgages, loans, or other services due to their deteriorating conditions. Often these decisions were influenced by the religious, racial, ethnic, or gender characteristics of residents.

Segregation may also be de jure or required by law. Often these regulations determine access to public services and accommodations, housing, education, employment, and property ownership. Limits are placed on individuals' rights to inheritance, ability to adopt children, or "who" they may marry. Examples of this practice include "male-only" jobs, the creation of the Jewish ghettos in Nazi Germany, the separation of Catholics and Protestants in Northern Ireland, miscegenation laws as well as barriers to same-sex marriage in the United States. These formalized practices provide the foundation for de facto segregation. While some nations have eliminated de jure segregation, isolation and discrimination continue on informal levels.

Sociologists have focused on a variety of reasons why de facto segregation continues to exist in society. Conscious self-segregation, such as residential segregation where groups of immigrants or lesbians and gays choose to live in the same geographical location, can foster a spirit of community while maintaining common cultural practices. However, residential segregation is heavily influenced by race/ethnicity and/or economic class. Early research, such as the work by Glazer and Moynihan, sought to understand the relationship of inequality with what they identified as ethnically organized neighborhoods in New York City (Glazer & Moynihan 1963). They concluded that as each group became more assimilated into US society, the less likely they were to face issues related to inequality. A limit to this research is Glazer and Moynihan's treatment of people who are labeled "black" as an ethnic rather than racial group. The effects of race and racism play out differently than ethnicity in US society.

Scholarship by Wilson and by Massey and Denton represents two major debates surrounding segregation in US society. They have demonstrated that racism and classism, often perpetuated by segregation, are structural barriers to success (Massey & Denton 1993; Wilson 1987, 1991). Wilson recognizes the relationships of race and class in maintaining poverty, particularly in urban ghettos. His overarching conclusion is that due to structural economic issues such as loss of job opportunities, the flight of the middle class out of inner-city neighborhoods, geographical location, and inadequate social policy reinforce segregation. Massey and Denton complement and challenge Wilson's conclusions. While recognizing that economic opportunities and physical location contribute to the inability of the urban underclass, particularly impoverished black communities, to rise out of poverty, they demonstrate that residential segregation is based on racial segregation. Inequality will continue as long as racism exists, creating barriers to adequate education, employment, and other services people need to have thriving communities.

Current research has shown that while society has become more integrated on some levels, inequality due to practices of segregation remains a significant factor in the areas of work, education, and health. Racial and ethnic groups, particularly blacks and Latinos/Chicanos, continue to have low high school and college graduation rates. Proportionally, they make up a larger percentage of people residing at the bottom of the economic ladder and black Americans have consistently higher mortality rates (Collins & Williams 1999; Charles 2003). This is heavily influenced by lack of access to adequate health care. Studies have also shown that residential segregation is increasing rather than decreasing.

Glazer and Moynihan's vision of integration based on assimilating into US society has not materialized due to a variety of factors including the strength of "isms," particularly racism, sexism, and heterosexism in society. Combined with classism and increasing economic disparity, social isolation is on the rise. While more whites are facing economic hardship, studies have shown that they continue to live in better neighborhoods than blacks who are at the same economic level. Research has shown that integration of neighborhoods, on race, ethnic, and economic class levels, significantly reduces crime and violence, improves academic performance and economic opportunities, and reduces bias and discriminatory practices.

SEE ALSO: Assimilation; Class, Status, and Power; Color Line; Culture of Poverty; Du Bois, W. E. B.; Homophobia and Heterosexism; Migration, Ethnic Conflicts, and Racism; Race; Race (Racism); Redlining; Residential Segregation; School Segregation, Desegregation; Sexism

REFERENCES AND SUGGESTED READINGS

Charles, C. (2003) The Dynamics of Racial Residential Segregation. *Annual Review of Sociology* 29: 167.

Collins, C. & Williams, D. (1999) Segregation and Mortality: The Deadly Effects of Racism? *Sociological Forum* 14(3): 495.

Cox, O. (1948) *Caste, Class, and Race.* Modern Reader, New York.

Delgado, R. (1995) *Critical Race Theory: The Cutting Edge.* Temple University Press, Philadelphia.

Du Bois, W. E. B. (1995) The Color Line Belts the World. In: Lewis, D. (Ed.), *W. E. B. Du Bois: A Reader.* Henry Holt, New York, pp. 42–3.

Glasgow, D. (1980) *The Black Underclass: Poverty, Unemployment, and the Entrapment of Ghetto Youth.* Vintage, New York.

Glazer, N. & Moynihan, D. (1963) *Beyond the Melting Pot: The Negroes, Puerto Ricans, Jews, Italians, and Irish of New York City.* MIT Press, Cambridge, MA.

Jargowsky, P. (1985) *Poverty and Place: Ghettos, Barrios, and the American City.* Russell Sage Foundation, New York.

Massey, D. & Denton, N. (1993) *American Apartheid: Segregation and the Making of the Underclass.* Harvard University Press, Cambridge, MA.

Myrdal, G. (1944) *An American Dilemma.* McGraw-Hill, New York.

Wilson, W. J. (1987) *The Truly Disadvantaged: The Inner City, the Underclass, and Public Policy.* University of Chicago Press, Chicago.

Wilson, W. J. (1991) Another Look at *The Truly Disadvantaged. Political Science Quarterly* 106(4): 639.

seikatsu/seikatsusha

Wolfgang Seifert

Seikatsu and *seikatsusha* are expressions in colloquial Japanese as well as technical terms in the discipline of sociology. As the meaning of the words differs widely, depending on their usage, a translation into any western language is difficult, although a very basic translation of *seikatsu* would be "everyday life" and *seikatsusha* a person who pursues it. To understand the use of these terms in Japanese sociological research, one must know their historical background and intellectual context.

Seikatsu originates in classical Chinese texts and in ancient times had the meaning of "life/to live" or "existence/to exist." In modern times the word is most frequently used in the sense of "livelihood" or "everyday life," in contrast to biological and physical aspects of life or its philosophical interpretations. Finally, the word *seikatsu* serves in an accentuated and positive sense as the fundamental category of an integrative science, developed in Japan and called *seikatsugaku* ("lifology").

Surprisingly, most Japanese encyclopedias and dictionaries of social sciences do not include the term *seikatsusha*, although its use is widespread nowadays. *Seikatsusha* also defies precise translation into a western language. Therefore, a whole range of meanings has to be kept in mind, reaching from "consumer" on the one hand to "a man, who actively organizes his own life" on the other hand. One of the rare definitions, coined in the 1970s after the first oil crisis, maintains: "*Seikatsusha* is used in the sense of an existence within which one is independent as an individual, freed from being a mere *company man*, not biased by rigid ideas of gender-specific divisions of labor. A man who is concerned about global environmental problems as well as recycling, and being committed to local affairs and voluntary work" (Hamashima et al. 1997). In the early 1990s, *seikatsusha* became a fashionable word in politics and the media, but was often used without its critical implications. For instance, when the Japanese government announced its "Five-Year Plan for Making Japan a Leading Nation with Regard to the Quality of Life" in 1992, it used *seikatsusha* almost synonymously with "consumer."

In addition, many words combined with *seikatsu* are used as specialist terms in sociology: *seikatsu jikan* = time use, *seikatsu kikai* = life chances (Dahrendorf), *seikatsu taido* = *Lebensführung* (Weber), *seikatsu no shitsu* = quality of life, *seikatsu sekai* = lifeworld/*Lebenswelt* (Husserl, Schütz, Habermas).

MAJOR DIMENSIONS OF *SEIKATSU* AND *SEIKATSUSHA*

In Japanese economic science the term *seikatsu* traditionally is related to consumption (*shôhi*); the consumer (*shôhisha* or *seikatsusha*) is seen in opposition to the producer. To cover theoretically and empirically the economic tasks and functions of everyday life, the subdiscipline of home economics (*kaseigaku, katei keizaigaku*) was developed. Furthermore, the attempt to establish domestic science (*seikatsu kagaku*) is worth mentioning. Its subject is everyday life, basically covering all aspects of food, clothing, and housing. This interdisciplinary approach also includes sciences such as physics, chemistry, and biology.

Even before 1945 some scholars tried to separate the area of everyday life and material conditions of living from economics in order to establish it as a subject of sociological research. Kon Wajirô and sociologists who picked up his ideas rejected the understanding of *seikatsu* prevalent at the time (i.e., that everyday life was to be seen in relation to production). According to Kon, *seikatsu* is not limited to the reproduction of working power, but means the active shaping of one's conditions of life. The new interpretation of *seikatsu* led to a complete reversal of the emphasis put on life (*seikatsu*) and labor (*rôdô*) in research. The research object of the new interpretation was how people actively shaped their living conditions, such as food, clothing, and housing. Therefore, individual sources such as life histories and life documents are of prime importance for this kind of research.

Partly connected to this ethnographic approach and partly independent of it, the sociological concept of "life structure" (*seikatsu kôzô*) aims at specifically and systematically covering all spheres of the *seikatsusha*. While this concept is not yet fully established, what has to be done in research has been unanimously identified as follows: (1) research on life activities in relation to its material aspects; (2) grasping the outer shape of everyday life and its temporal and spatial structure; (3) including everyday social relations. When the Institute of Journalism and Communication Studies of Tokyo University started researching political consciousness and life consciousness (*seikatsu ishiki*) as early as 1959, the latter term covered (1) the interests in everyday life and the conditions supporting them; (2) lifestyle; and (3) consumers' consciousness. A second school in Japanese sociology that emerged around 1980 refers to the term "world of everyday life," as Schütz developed it following Husserl in his phenemenological sociology. Habermas's theorem of the *Lebenswelt* his *Theorie des kommunikativen Handelns* (Theory of Communicative Action, 1981) and its critical dimension of the "colonization of the lifeworld" were also employed.

From the early 1990s, political science started to analyze women's power in politics, partly based on Consumer Club Coops (*Seikatsu kurabu seikyô*). This new social movement and its political influence at regional levels are widely viewed as a symptom of a more mature stage of civil society in Japan.

Coping with everyday life demands a kind of pragmatist philosophy that is barely researched in academia. Intellectuals centering around the journal *Shisô no kagaku* after World War II realized the importance and potential of the "philosophy" of ordinary people, and tried to explore the thought and imagination of the common man.

INTELLECTUAL AND SOCIAL CONTEXT

Contemporary sociological research on *seikatsu* was stimulated by the three discourses on *Lebenskultur* (*seikatsu bunka*), consumer society (*shôhi shakai*), and new social movements (*shin shakai undô*).

In 1926 dramatist Kurata Hyakuzô used *seikatsusha* for the first time as an independent expression for man struggling for truth and peace of mind. In 1940 this religious coloring of *seikatsusha* was criticized by philosopher Miki Kiyoshi. Miki pointed out that the "cultural life," which had become gradually accepted in Japan after the opening of the country in 1853, was in fact western consumer culture. Miki instead advocated a "culture created by humans" – "life culture" (*seikatsu bunka*). This "ordinary culture" was rooted in the "language, food, social contacts, and customs" of Japan (i.e., in "our ancient traditions"). With this, Miki connected the idea of an "individual actively shaping his everyday life" (*seikatsusha*). Since then, Japanese intellectuals have been able to write on "low" culture or offer practical advice on coping with everyday life. Even before 1945, the architectural historian and sociologist influenced by ethnology, Kon Wajirô, began to record the everyday culture of his compatriots. According to Kon, *seikatsu* covers the four sectors of work, recreation, entertainment, and education, and therefore includes the whole of life activities. Kon related to an earlier criticism by welfare economist Kagoyama Takashi on the restriction of those in work to their function as wage-earning producers. In contrast, labor and social economist Ôkôchi Kazuo used the term *seikatsu* as the sector of reproduction of working power. He analyzed the connection between productivity and poverty, as well as reasons for fluctuations in living expenses.

Kon, on the other hand, focused on the concrete shape of everyday life and its changes in food, clothing, and housing. After 1945 he opposed the so-called "modernist" theories which viewed the democratization of Japan as solely related to politics and law. He saw the range of possibilities offered by democracy in the organization of everyday life (*seikatsu no shikata*) and did not oppose the Japanese traditional lifestyle (*kurashikata*), but positively stressed its simplicity, plainness, and reason, and advocated integrating it into the changing environment of everyday life. The Japan Society for Lifology (*Nihon seikatsu gakkai*), founded in 1972, refers to Kon's concept of *seikatsujin*. Influenced by American pragmatism, after 1945 philosophers such as Kuno Osamu and Tsurumi Shunsuke felt compelled to study the "philosophy of ordinary people." In 1959 the journal *Shisô no kagaku* pointed out the importance of "nameless *seikatsusha*" (*mumei no seikatsusha*) for society. Such ideas later were integrated into the objectives of consumer cooperatives.

The discourse on the consumer society evolved in times of rapid economic growth and was started by Ôkuma Nobuyuki. As an economist, Ôkuma enhanced the appreciation of the term *seikatsusha* as early as 1940. According to him, economic sciences attributed all activities of preserving human life to the two sectors of production and consumption, while mainly focusing on matters of production. Consequently, the existence of human beings, as well, was subsumed merely under these two categories. Thus, we lost sight of our own "life activity" (*seikatsu*). Ôkuma's criticism of economic sciences was based on a new definition of *seikatsu* and *seikatsusha*: *seikatsusha* was not used as a synonym, but as a counterpart of consumer (*shôhisha*). As skepticism towards industrialism, mass production, and consumption emerged in the 1960s and 1970s, some scholars once again took up Ôkuma's concept of *seikatsu*.

In the 1960s and 1970s, political and social movements of a new type used the expression *seikatsusha* in a positive sense, as well, and caused sociology and political science to broaden to some extent their analytical approach to society. The Citizens' Alliance for Peace in Vietnam (*Beheiren*) – active since 1965 – was based on a loose union of individuals, neither affiliated to political parties nor any other political organizations. Its participants considered themselves to be citizens (*shimin*) and "ordinary people" living in their personal circumstances (*seikatsu*), claiming a sphere of decision-making which was autonomous from government and state. On the other hand, the new consumers' movements emerging from 1965 onwards tried to distance themselves from the previous consumers' cooperatives that had a large membership in Japan. They named themselves *Seikatsu kurabu seikyô* (literally, livelihood cooperatives; the translation "Consumers' Club Coops" slightly misses the meaning). These coops openly tried to gain political influence, to some extent succeeding in local and regional elections. In view of the globally widening gap between the rich and the poor they aimed ideologically at altering their lifestyle and organized the communal purchase of healthy food. To these, three goals were added: first, developing from a consumer (*shôhisha*) to an individual which actively shaped its everyday life (*seikatsusha*); second, establishing a political power independent from parties by freeing oneself from the conception of being an abstract national citizen (*kokumin*) by not electing representatives (*daihyôsha*) but deputies (*dairinin*); and third, connecting the "consumer" to the "productively shaping" being. Starting from this point, the political scientist Takabatake Michitoshi developed his idea of *seikatsusha-citizen*. Thus, new perspectives for civil society in Japan were emphasized.

CURRENT DEVELOPMENTS

Today, research on the material circumstances (culture) of life (*seikatsu*) of the Japanese is multifaceted. Research on marketing and consumption examines the selling potential of certain products or services, as well as the behavior of the consumer. Numerous surveys are conducted on time budget and leisure behavior. On the other hand, education to conduct responsible consumption and to strengthen the consumer's independence is attempted. Economic studies starting from the consumer's point of view are numerous.

Recently, works on the relation between social welfare and poverty that argue in favor of social politics based on economic reasoning have gained importance. The reason for this is that social cleavages have become more apparent and the problem of different life standards (*seikatsu suijun*) of different strata of society is being discussed again. New approaches to the relation of social security systems and *seikatsusha* are taken, and the relation between health and *seikatsusha* as wage earners is still being examined. Sociological works often relate to the concept of lifeworld, while many studies belong to the ethnographically influenced school of Kon. In political science and in sociology, the discourse on the perspectives for civil society in Japan is continuing. However, there seems to be a marked disillusionment with the potential of consumer goods associations, in particular the Consumers Club Coops, to change society in general (Hartmann 2003).

SEE ALSO: Civil Society; Consumer Movements; Everyday Life; Lifeworld

REFERENCES AND SUGGESTED READINGS

Amano, M. (1996) *"Seikatsusha" to wa dare ka* (Who is the *seikatsusha*?). Chkô shinsho, Tokyo.

Chbachi, M. (1951) *Katei seikatsu no kôzô* (Structure of Home Life). Ygakusha, Tokyo.

Hamashima, A., Takeuchi, I., & Ishikawa, A. (Ed.) (1997) *Shakaigaku shôjiten, shinpan* (Compact Dictionary of Sociology, new edition). Yhikaku, Tokyo.

Hartmann, P. (2003) *Konsumgenossenschaften in Japan: Alternative oder Spiegelbild der Gesellschaft?* (Consumer's Cooperatives in Japan: Alternative or Mirror Image of Society?), Iudicium, Munich.

Kagoyama, T. (1943) *Kokumin seikatsu no kôzô* (The Structure of People's Living).

Kawaguchi, K. & Ôsawa, M. (Eds.) (2004) *Shimin ga tsukuru kurashi no sêfuti netto* (A Social Security Net Organized by Citizens). Nihon Hyôronsha, Tokyo.

Kon, Wajirô (1972 [1947]) Seikatsu no kôzô (The Structure of Life). In: *Kon Wajirô sh*, Vol. 6. Domesu sha, Tokyo, pp. 93–104.

Maclachlan, P. L. (2002) *Consumer Politics in Postwar Japan: The Institutional Boundaries of Citizen Activism.* Columbia University Press, New York.
Nakagiri, S. (1993) *Nichijô seikatsu shakaigaku* (Sociology of Everyday Life), Kôbundô, Tokyo.
Nihon seikatsu gakkai (Ed.) (1999) *Seikatsugaku jiten* (Encyclopedia of Lifology). TBS Buritanika, Tokyo.
Ôkuma, N. (1974–5) *Seimei saiseisan no riron* (Theory of Reproduction of Life). Tokyo.
Satô, Y. (1996) *Josei to kyôdô kumiai* (Women and Consumers' Cooperatives). Bunshindô, Tokyo.
Takabatake, M. (1993) *Seikatsusha no seijigaku* (The Political Science of *seikatsusha*). San'ichi shobô, Tokyo.

seken

Tomoko Kurihara

The Japanese script for *seken* combines the two Chinese characters meaning "world" (pronounced as either *yo* or *se*) with "space-between" (pronounced as either *aida*, *ma*, *kan*, or *ken*). The core features of the concept are as follows. *Seken* refers to the appearance of the total network of social relations that surround an individual. It conveys the corresponding cultural norms and values that function to regulate social behavior, and hints at how such relations and behavior are maintained. *Seken* is thought to be a concept native to Japan that has existed since the seventh century. It corresponds roughly to *shakai*, the translated word for "society," derived from the West, which came into circulation in the Meiji period (1898–1920) as western concepts, ideals, and values became popularized by politicians and intellectuals. "The public" is at times used as *seken*'s English equivalent. However, the two terms are by no means synonymous; a conceptual lacuna exists between "the public," with its universalistic connotations, and *seken*, which, by comparison, when referring to one of its meanings – network – points rather more specifically to a social context or *aidagara*. Hamaguchi (1985) discerns how interrelations that constitute *aidagara* include encounters which are functional as well as unintentional and non-transactional. Thus *seken* can be described as the sum of interrelations as a result of the accumulation of subnetworks of *aidagara*.

A diagrammatic depiction of *seken* clearly embodies the two core features given above. The model represents the interrelations between individuals as a stratified concentric structure: the individual in the center, the people known to the individual (or friends, work colleagues, neighbors) in the adjacent ring, and people in society that the individual does not know (or strangers) in the outermost ring. *Seken* points to the body of people who fall in the mid-region between the two. This model also accounts for the *breadth* of relations which surrounds the individual in everyday life; this mirrors a macro-level reality that extensive networks sustain many aspects of Japanese social and economic life.

Seken is a relational term with a spatial reference, and the relation between the self and *seken* is ambiguous and precarious because the boundaries of the term are flexible, relatively arbitrary, and dependent on context. This situationally determined feature of *seken* poses three practical implications for its use. First, there is no singular or set way of identifying who – friends or strangers – fits these positions at any one time. For example, a particular individual, say, x-san, might include another individual, y-san, among the *seken* category on one occasion, but depending on how x-san feels toward y-san the following day, y-san might no longer be considered *seken*. Second, the term *seken* does not necessarily correspond to a particular individual; it can also be applied, as in most cases, to refer to a group of individuals who are neither close nor other. In this way, *seken* is highly sensitive to the shifting positions of individuals within social interaction, and in *seken*, therefore, positioning is interchangeable and inconsistent. Third, the substance of *seken* can differ, dependent on sex, age, social origin, occupation, level of education, region, and marital status. The *seken* referent is therefore constituted either by the relations between these properties, each of which has its specific value, or by a single pertinent one.

Seken is a relational concept which entails a comparison between self and social norms and ideals in the context of daily practice. *Seken*'s presence regulates the thought and hence behavior of individuals which brings them in alignment with society's standards. Japanese people on the whole take seriously the implications of deviating from *seken*'s standards and they continually and minutely adjust the inconsistency arising between self and *seken*. The term *seken* is in frequent daily usage in contemporary Japan, where it can be experienced by the individual as an omnipresent force, constantly serving to judge and regulate behavior in a collectivist society. This sense is conveyed well by anthropologist Takie Sugiyama Lebra: "In parallel to the 'face'-focused self, the *seken*-other is equipped with its own 'eyes,' 'ears,' and 'mouth,' watching, hearing and gossiping about the self. This body metaphor contributes to the sense of immediacy and inescapability of the *seken*'s presence" (Lebra 1992: 107).

As *seken* expresses a type of obligation and conformity to the group, it can be related to the dyadic concept of *tatemae* and *honne*, which mean, respectively, rules that are natural or proper, that have formed on the basis of group consensus, and, in spite of a display of conformity to the group, the individual's true intentions (see Doi 1986). *Tatemae* is also an essential technique in the presentation of the self. It is acquired by individuals through the learning and judging of social codes, thereby used to survive in society by reducing the potential for conflict. In this sense of technique *tatemae* differs from *seken*, which refers either to people or to a controlling force. Furthermore, insofar as *seken* indicates social norms which induce the conformity of individuals, the concept can be related to the western sociological and psychoanalytical notions of habitus, social fact/collective conscience, and the superego.

It is not entirely clear, even in practice, how the notion of *seken* operates: it is equally relevant to understand that the individual is somehow regulated by *seken* as much as the individual can regulate his or her own behavior in accordance to *seken*'s standards. *Seken*, insofar as it can be construed as a disciplining force, can be interpreted as functioning similarly to the sociological concept of habitus (see Kurihara 2006). The concept of habitus is a "structuring structure" that shapes the practice of people at the level of the unconscious through a process of implicit pedagogy (Bourdieu 1977, 1990). Habitus is an internalized concept. The operation of habitus and *seken* is similar in the way socially appropriate norms of conduct become internalized by individuals whereby their practice becomes shaped implicitly. Yet the difference between habitus and *seken* is that individuals are conscious of the presence and pressures of *seken* to a relatively greater extent than Pierre Bourdieu claims about habitus: *seken* seems to have a greater force of control. Furthermore, the boundary of the term habitus seems more stable than *seken*.

The concept of *seken* is often defined as being unique to Japanese society, but similar accounts of forces of control that regulate the body exist cross-culturally. As discussed, it appears to fit descriptions of habitus, a French sociological concept, applied both to its provenance (Bourdieu 1984) and to Kabyle society (Bourdieu 1977, 1990). Marcel Mauss (1979 [1935]), who originally described habitus as an encultured bodily way of behaving, indeed intended the concept to apply cross-culturally, and his examples of habitus were developed based around his observations of French and American society. Parallel examples of forces operating like *seken* are also found in ancient democratic Athenian society and in Victorian England. For example, Allen (2000) writes that the practice of naming and shaming, gossip, and the close scrutiny of others functioned in ancient Athens to keep people in their place. In the absence of any official punitive system possessing concrete techniques of control, order in Athenian society was produced by such discourses concerning punishment and the substance of the law. Discourse about order tended to have the desired ordering effect whereby such discourses functioned to perform an endless maintenance of distinctions, values, and meaning in society. In these examples, public opinion sanctions behavior.

Ultimately, *seken* refers to the relation between the individual and society. As *seken* regulates the behavior of individuals in relation to norms, an understanding of the way *seken* functions can be compared to the functioning of group norms and ideals outlined in Émile Durkheim's deterministic model of society, in his concept of social fact. To be precise, the relation between individual action and society is the object of theorization. For Durkheim, social facts, which consist of ways of thinking and behaving, are coercive forces that penetrate the individual without the individual perceiving that they do. The social fact becomes part of the individual's thought and behavior in a way that transforms the individual by somehow tying him/her to the group by providing norms and ideals. By believing in the externality of social facts, Durkheim treated norms as properties of collectivities, which functioned to constrain. Combined with his view that social facts are moral phenomena, he explained how adherence to moral ideals incites action. By connecting the three spheres of morals, norms, and action, Durkheimean sociology offered an explanation for how sanctions/constraints regulate individuals' behavior.

At the level of an individual's psychic structure and processes, the psychoanalytic work of Sigmund Freud provides a comparable explanation of how *seken* regulates an individual's behavior. According to Freud's model, the repository of social norms within individuals called the superego functions by holding the individual's desires within the bounds set by society. The superego includes two subsystems: an ego-ideal and conscience. The ego-ideal is the child's conception of what his parents will approve; conscience is the child's conception of what his parents will condemn as morally bad. Both are assimilated by the child from examples and teachings provided by his parents. The ego-ideal is learned through rewards; conscience is learned through punishments. Freud's explanation of how these social restraints become internalized to form the superego contain a European, middle-class bias; however, it is possible to infer from this how the internal psychic process might work in adults when they are faced with social norms to which they should conform. In the case of *seken*, the role of the parents in Freud's model would pass on to the social body as a whole.

The theoretical proximity between *seken* and western sociological and psychological concepts – habitus, social fact, superego – would appear to illustrate the extent of commonality in the human condition. It is also clear that the concepts are by no means commensurate with one another due to inevitable cultural specificities rising from the regional scale of observation and conditions of analysis. Our understanding of *seken* and similar phenomena would profit from a body of future research which applies in-depth ethnographic methods to explore more comprehensively how *seken* works and impacts on individual daily lives in all spheres of social life.

SEE ALSO: Collective Consciousness; Durkheim, Émile; Freud, Sigmund; Habitus/Field; Self; Social Fact; *Tatemae/Honne*

REFERENCES AND SUGGESTED READINGS

Allen, D. (2000) *The World of Prometheus: The Politics of Punishing in Democratic Athens.* Princeton University Press, Princeton.

Bachnik, J. M. & Quinn, J. (Eds.) (1994) *Situated Meaning: Inside and Outside in Japanese Self, Society, and Language.* Princeton University Press, Princeton.

Bourdieu, P. (1977) *Outline of a Theory of Practice.* Trans. R. Nice. Cambridge University Press, Cambridge.

Bourdieu, P. (1984) *Distinction: A Social Critique of the Judgment of Taste.* Trans. R. Nice. Routledge, London.

Bourdieu, P. (1990) *The Logic of Practice.* Trans. R. Nice. Polity Press, Cambridge.

Doi, T. (1986) *The Anatomy of Society: The Individual versus Society.* Trans. M. A. Harbison. Kodansha International, Tokyo.

Freud, S. (1991) The Ego and the Id. In: *The Essentials of Psycho-analysis: The Definitive Collection of Sigmund Freud's Writing.* Penguin, London, pp. 439–83.

Hamaguchi, E. (1985) A Contextual Model of the Japanese: Toward a Methodological Innovation in Japan Studies. Trans. S. Kumon & M. R. Creighton. *Journal of Japanese Studies* 11(2): 289–321.

Hendry, J. (1995 [1987]) *Understanding Japanese Society,* 2nd edn. Routledge, London.

Kurihara, T. (2006) *Japanese Corporate Transition in Time and Space.* Palgrave Macmillan, New York.

Lebra, T. S. (1992) Self in Japanese Culture. In: Rosenberger, N. (Ed.), *Japanese Sense of Self.* Cambridge University Press, Cambridge, pp. 105–20.

Mauss, M. (1979 [1935]) The Notion of Body Techniques. In: *Sociology and Psychology: Essays by Marcel Mauss.* Trans. B. Brewster. Routledge & Kegan Paul, London, pp. 95–123.

Mita, M., Kurihara, A., & Tanaka, Y. (Eds.) (1988) *Encyclopaedia of Sociology* (*shakaigaku jiten*), s.v. "*seken.*" Kobundo, Tokyo, p. 544.
Rosenberger, N. (Ed.) (1992) *Japanese Sense of Self.* Cambridge University Press, Cambridge.

self

Kathy Charmaz

The concept of self is simultaneously social and subjective; the self exists in social life. Common definitions of the self, however, accentuate its subjective side: all those qualities, attributes, values, feelings, and moral sentiments that a person assumes to be his or her own. The social sources of self make subjectivity possible because the person's experience of feelings, images, and interpretations emerges and takes on meaning through social interaction.

The concept of self lacks a coherent history; however, its intellectual antecedents appear throughout the history of philosophical and theological reflections about essential qualities comprising human nature and consciousness. A concept of self emerged in Renaissance European philosophy as transcending social and corporeal existence. As industrialization progressed, conceptions of the self became embedded in social life, rather than separate from it. The industrial age recast social relationships in new forms that vitiated prior assumptions. The classical theorists placed the self in society but did not explicitly theorize it. Marx theorized an inherently social conception of self without adopting a language of self. An implicitly theorized but explicitly social conception of self also emerged in Émile Durkheim's contrasting analyses of transformations wrought by the emerging industrial order.

A fundamental shift in the concept of self occurred when the early pragmatists resituated the self in ordinary experience. The pragmatists cut remaining ties to transcendental values and wove a *theoretical concept* of self from its social fabric. William James (1890) initiated a tradition of theorizing the self that has continued relevance today. He differentiated the "I," the self as subjective knower, from the "me," the object of consciousness. James's concept of the "empirical self" developed in practical existence. For James, the number of a person's selves equaled the number of individuals who knew him or her. James contended that the self relied on its realization through experience and, moreover, brought communication into the forefront of theorizing the self. James viewed the self as inseparable from communication of its experience.

Charles Horton Cooley (1902) also emphasized communication and meanings of personal pronouns observed in everyday life. Building on James's empirical self, Cooley's concept of the "social self" brought the self into interaction. Cooley observed how children learn to distinguish between self and other, me and you, mine and yours. Moreover, Cooley brought sentiments and reflections into theorizing the self. In his concept of the "looking-glass self," Cooley gave a central position to introspection and imagination: we first imagine how we appear to others; then, we imagine their judgment of our appearance, followed by "some sort of self-feeling, such as pride or shame." Later textbook authors sometimes misunderstood Cooley's point here despite his emphasis that the judgment eliciting this self-feeling is an "imputed sentiment," not a mechanical reflection.

George Herbert Mead (1929) criticized Cooley's introspective method as asocial and solipsistic; Mead believed that Cooley's view of self relied too heavily on biological explanations and gave too little attention to its fundamentally social nature. The criticisms of Cooley's concept of self that began with Mead continue to the present. Nonetheless, Cooley made sentiments central to the self and spawned a nascent sociology of emotions. Relationships between the self and emotions remain evident in Erving Goffman's (1956) analysis of embarrassment and mortification, Arlie Hochschild's (1983) portrayal of feeling rules and emotion management, Norman Denzin's (1987) analysis of the alcoholic self as living in a dis-ease of emotions and time, and Thomas Scheff's (1990) argument that pride and shame are basic human emotions.

In the major statement of sociological theorizing of the self, George Herbert Mead (1934) advanced the most explicit theory of a socially structured reflexive self. Mead's social self is cognitive and embedded in communication. It arises within and remains a part of interactional processes. For Mead, the self is both social process and social object. It is contingent upon "minded activity" that emanates from social existence. As we participate in social life, we learn to envision our group's activities and to anticipate possible future actions – our own as well as other people's. To accomplish this minded activity, we learn symbols, understand meanings, and converse with ourselves. Therefore, Mead and his intellectual descendants, Herbert Blumer and Anselm Strauss, argue that language plays a pivotal role in the development of self. Language gives us tools to view ourselves as objects for scrutiny. Through using language we invoke terms to make nuanced distinctions about ourselves as well as our worlds. We can envision, evaluate, and act toward ourselves as objects like we treat any other object. Furthermore, we mediate our responses during interaction because we can imagine the view of the other person.

Mead (1934) adopted James's terms, the "I" and the "me," to portray the self. The "I" is the creative part of the self that initiates action. It is spontaneous, immediate; the self enters the act without deliberation. The socialized "me" then monitors and directs the act because it assesses the "I" through a conversation with and about self. This conversation takes into account the internalized views and values of the group. Thus, the self is a social structure; it differs according to the social situation. Mead said that the situation calls forth a response from the self. More accurately, a situation calls forth *a* self because people's varied situations lead to possessing different selves.

Mead wrested the concept of self from behaviorism. His concept of a social self counters portrayals of people as stimulus-response creatures or as beings determined by social, cultural, or economic forces. Mead's self develops in active response to what occurs around it. This response may consist of internalization, adaptation, innovation, or resistance. Much of social life is routine; however, when we reflect on new or problematic situations, we can choose how to respond, rather than react, to them. In short, Mead's concepts of mind and self mean that we have agency: we can choose and control our actions.

Symbolic interactionist social psychology made the Meadian concept of self a cornerstone of its perspective. As a result, symbolic interactionists kept the idea of an agentic self alive throughout mid-century structural-functionalist disciplinary dominance. The functionalist perspective ignored the self in favor of a static concept of roles and disregarded the interactive and interpretive features of socialization. More recently, theorizing about agency has brought interactionist conceptions of an acting, interpreting self into the mainstream of the discipline, although its pragmatist antecedents often go unrecognized (Maines 2001).

Throughout the later part of the twentieth century, Blumer's (1969) Meadian view of the self and Goffman's (1959) dramaturgical self sparked a vibrant dialogue about the self among symbolic interactionists and some structural social psychologists. Dramaturgical analysts view the self as constructed in action in response to concrete situations and settings in which people find themselves. Action, not individual reflection, becomes the distinguishing feature of self. Thus, dramaturgical analysts assume that what people do reveals more about their selves than what they say.

Erving Goffman (1959) observes that whenever we are in the real or imaginary presence of others, our behavior has social meaning and a promissory character. Subsequently, our actions express ourselves and give an impression of self to others, whether favorable or not. Goffman argues that people intend to bring about a certain impression of self. How we approach other people derives from the nature of the shared situation. Yet they realize that we try to make favorable impressions on others. Thus, our audience looks for cues we give off as well as what we say. Despite intentions and staged performances, social actors give off unwitting messages about self.

The dramaturgical perspective brings the occasion and its structure into theorizing the self. If the interaction order of the occasion produces selves, can the self be a unique personal possession of its holder? Might it not be a mask to cover a role? Learning the interaction order of an occasion requires only a minimal model of the actor – and self – who could behave sensibly in it.

The empirical study of the self has gained momentum over the past fifty years. Manford H. Kuhn's (1960) Twenty Statements Test

(TST) advanced the empirical study of the self by asking people to state how they see themselves. A major strength of the TST is that research participants give their own definitions of self without the researcher's preconceptions or suggestions imposed on them. A weakness is that the TST treats the self as stable attributes and does not take situations and processes into account.

The identity theorists have advanced connections between quantitative empirical studies and theoretical conceptions of the self. In Stryker's (1980; Stryker & Burke 2000) statement of the structural approach to identity theory, he asks how social structure affects the self and how the self affects social behavior. For identity theorists, the self is constituted by an organized set of identities (Burke 1980; Serpe 1987). Serpe's (1987) study of college freshmen supports the major premise of stability of self in identity theory and makes the significance of choice explicit. Serpe finds that identity change is expected in those identities in which choice is structurally possible. Burke (1980) not only emphasizes the relational aspect of identities, but also points out that their salience takes hierarchical form and that potential identities can motivate individuals. Burke calls for quantitative testing to measure the theoretical properties of identity, which he and Franzoi (1988) aim to do in their study of experiential situations. They used an innovative sampling method of signaling research participants with a timer to respond to a questionnaire about their direct experience, including their identities and roles. Burke and Franzoi found that how participants viewed their immediate situations shaped how they viewed themselves and, in turn, their behavior depended on how they viewed themselves.

Late twentieth-century sociologists restored the self to its central place in theorizing. When using the term "self," however, they sometimes blur distinctions by reifying a single, static notion of self, rather than theorizing the multiplicity of selves and their processural nature. Following Mead, Viktor Gecas (1982) answers this problem. He distinguishes between the self as process from the self as stable structure, the self-concept. Selves are built on processes; the stability of self-concept is built on consistent processes; meanings about self last. Interaction processes constitute human existence. Thus the self is continually in process. Yet human beings often display remarkable consistency of self over time. If the self is continually in process, why are selves not more mutable? People learn ways to define themselves. They take some things as mirroring their "real" selves, but do not claim their other enacted behaviors as reflecting them. Ralph Turner's (1976) notion of the self-concept indicates why. Turner defines the self-concept as an *organized* set of definitions of self, sentiments, values, and judgments, through which a person describes himself or herself. Enduring self-concepts typically develop when people receive consistent responses from others. The self-concept has boundaries, whether firm and impenetrable, or flaccid and permeable. Once a person's self has congealed into a self-concept, it becomes more or less enduring.

The narrative turn of recent decades locates the self in stories people tell about themselves and how they tell them. The self becomes accomplished through active processes of self-construction that entail rhetorical skills and occur within social contexts. Bjorklund (1998) shows how cultural discourse about the self speaks through autobiographies. Authors of autobiographies invoke historically and culturally situated vocabularies of the self to make sense of their lives and to present them to readers as moral performances.

Narrative analysts take literary forms as a point of departure and ask how people adopt and improvise on these forms. Thus their interests include plots, narrative coherence and logic, narrative sequence, composition of the story, and its specific content. Conversational analysts account for the production of self in the structure of ordinary conversations, but note that certain situations invite a self-story and others require entitlement, negotiation, or cooperation for a story to ensue at all. They attend to the linguistic and interactional practices which make selves discernible in conversations. Both approaches foster placing primary focus on the texts in which discourse and conversation occur. Paradoxically then, these analysts may garner stories of the self produced under special conditions such as the research interview rather than those developed in everyday practices.

Most sociologists agree on the centrality of the self for understanding human existence, but views of its relative coherence and methods of studying it remain contested. The postmodern self is tenuous, mobile, provisional, and fragmented. The self stands on shifting ground and thus shifts and becomes inconsistent, fragmented. Thus, contemporary life strips the self of its once coherent core and weakens the attachments on which this core was based. Despite its fragmented incoherence, these depictions of a postmodern self rely on a conception of society and cannot be divorced from it. Moreover, Gubrium and Holstein (1991; Holstein & Gubrium 1999) argue that if we reframe postmodern discourse and examine it empirically in everyday interpretive practices, then researchers can retrieve the concept of self for traditional sociological theory and research.

The concept of self in its many forms and varied emphases has inspired research that spans numerous substantive fields, such as occupations and professions, health and illness, aging, emotions, deviant behavior, race and ethnicity, and gender, as well as social psychology. These literatures contribute to an emphasis on development and change throughout the life course. Themes of reconstruction, development, and sometimes transformation of the adult self pervade studies of life changes, whether through experiencing losses or gains. Through these studies, sociologists have challenged assumptions of an asocial, reductionist, and static self. In sum, the self, and its attendant concepts, self-image, self-concept, and identity provide sharp tools to understand how, why, and when people develop, change, or retain a stable self throughout their lives.

SEE ALSO: Agency (and Intention); Cooley, Charles Horton; Dramaturgy; Goffman, Erving; Identity Control Theory; Identity: Social Psychological Aspects; Identity Theory; Looking-Glass Self; Mead, George Herbert; Narrative; Rosenberg, Morris; Self-Concept; Self-Esteem, Theories of; Symbolic Interaction

REFERENCES AND SUGGESTED READINGS

Bjorklund, D. (1998) *Interpreting the Self: Two Hundred Years of American Autobiography*. University of Chicago Press, Chicago.

Blumer, H. (1969) *Symbolic Interactionism*. Prentice-Hall, Englewood Cliffs, NJ.

Burke, P. J. (1980) The Self: Measurement Implications from a Symbolic Interactionist Perspective. *Social Psychology Quarterly* 43: 18–29.

Burke, P. J. & Franzoi, S. J. (1988) Studying Situations and Identities Using Experiential Sampling Methodology. *American Sociological Review* 53: 559–68.

Cooley, C. H. (1902) *Human Nature and Conduct*. Scribner's, New York.

Denzin, N. K. (1987) *The Alcoholic Self*. Sage, Newbury Park, CA.

Gecas, V. (1982) The Self-Concept. *Annual Review of Sociology* 8: 1–33.

Goffman, E. (1956) Embarrassment and Social Organization. *American Journal of Sociology* 62: 264–74.

Goffman, E. (1959) *The Presentation of Self in Everyday Life*. Doubleday, Garden City, NY.

Gubrium, J. F. & Holstein, J. A. (1991) Grounding the Postmodern Self. *Sociological Quarterly* 35: 685–703.

Hochschild, A. R. (1983) *The Managed Heart: Commercialization of Human Feeling*. University of California Press, Berkeley.

Holstein, J. S. & Gubrium, J. (1999) *The Self We Live By*. Oxford University Press, New York.

James, W. (1890) *Principles of Psychology*. Henry Holt, New York.

Kuhn, M. H. (1960) Self-attitudes by Age, Sex, and Professional Training. *Sociological Quarterly* 1: 39–55.

Maines, D. R. (2001) *The Faultline of Consciousness*. Aldine, Hawthorne, NY.

Mead, G. H. (1929) Cooley's Contribution to American Social Thought. *American Journal of Sociology* 35: 693–706.

Mead, G. H. (1934) *Mind, Self and Society*. University of Chicago Press, Chicago.

Scheff, T. J. (1990) *Microsociology: Discourse, Emotion, and Social Structure*. University of Chicago Press, Chicago.

Serpe, R. T. (1987) Stability and Change in Self: A Structural Symbolic Interactionist Explanation. *Social Psychology Quarterly* 50: 44–55.

Strauss, A. L. (1959) *Mirrors and Masks*. Sociology Press, Mill Valley, CA.

Stryker, S. (1980) *Symbolic Interactionism: A Social Structural Version*. Benjamin Cummings, Menlo Park, CA.

Stryker, S. & Burke, P. J. (2000) The Past, Present, and Future of an Identity Theory. *Social Psychology Quarterly* 63: 284–97.

Turner, R. (1976) The Real Self: From Institution to Impulse. *American Journal of Sociology* 81: 989–1016.

self-concept

Scott Schieman

Sociological interest in the self-concept, rooted in the early writings of Cooley and Mead, has evolved into a multifaceted quest to describe the connections between social contexts and personal functioning. In his classic work, *Conceiving the Self* (1979), Rosenberg defines the self-concept as all of the thoughts and feelings that individuals maintain about the self as an object. Gecas and Burke (1995) have expanded on the definition: the self-concept "is composed of various identities, attitudes, beliefs, values, motives, and experiences, along with their evaluative and affective components (e.g., self-efficacy, self-esteem), in terms of which individuals define themselves" (p. 42). These processes involve reflexivity and self-awareness; that is, a level of consciousness or awareness about one's self that emerges from the distinctly human capacity to be an object and a subject to one's self.

A substantial core of the content of the self-concept involves identities – the meanings that individuals attach to the self. Identities embody the answer to the question: "Who am I?" Often, but not always, identities are connected to the major institutionalized social roles of society such as "spouse," "parent," "worker," "student," "church member, "Muslim," and so on. In many respects, identity is the most "public" feature of the self-concept because it typically describes one's place or membership in structural arrangements and social organization. At a social event, for example, individuals will ask each other about their work, their interests, their neighborhoods, and other pieces of information that typically peel back the layers of their identities. However, there may be a cost to the public nature of identities. Goffman illustrated the "spoiled identity" as socially undesirable or stigmatized aspects of the self-concept. Spoiled identities contain discredited elements of the self-concept that the individual is encouraged to conceal or "manage." Failure to do so often exacts social costs. Collectively, these ideas underscore the highly *social* nature of the self-concept: other people have substantial influence on the form, content, consequences, and revelation of the self-concept.

Some of the most widely known research on the self-concept has focused on its evaluative and affective components, especially self-esteem and self-efficacy. Self-esteem is "the evaluation which the individual makes and customarily maintains with regard to himself or herself: it expresses an attitude of approval or disapproval toward oneself" (Rosenberg 1965: 5). Survey researchers have sought to measure self-esteem with responses to statements that include: "I feel that I have a number of good qualities," "I feel that I'm a person of worth at least equal to others," "I am able to do things as well as most other people," "I take a positive attitude toward myself," and so on. By contrast, self-efficacy – also referred to as the sense of mastery or personal control – involves the extent to which one feels in control of events and outcomes in everyday life. Measures of the sense of mastery ask about agreement or disagreement with statements like: "I have little control over the things that happen to me," "There is really no way I can solve some of the problems I have," "What happens to me in the future mostly depends on me," "I can do just about anything I really set my mind to," and so on. Sociologists are interested in mastery and self-esteem for several reasons: because they are socially distributed, because their absence may erode well-being, and because of their potential as psychosocial resources that help people avoid or manage stressors. That is, what groups have higher or lower levels of self-esteem than others? How does a low sense of mastery influence psychological well-being? And, do people who possess more favorable self-evaluations have a different capacity to cope with the presence and consequences of stressful adversity?

The complexity of processes involving self-dynamics has also provided researchers with terrain for theoretical and empirical developments about the self-concept. For example, actors are often motivated to protect the self-concept from external threats. In broader terms, an array of socialization forces and social-structural arrangements shape the formation and content of the self-concept; thus, it is a *social product.* In terms of self-concept formation, the notion of personal or self-investment evokes the ideas of identity salience and the centrality of achieved statuses, such as education, for the emergence of positive self-evaluations. Analyses of the structural determinants of personal qualities, especially with respect to achieved statuses and dimensions of social stratification, have a long tradition in sociology, from Marx's broad portrait of estranged labor to more specific occupational sources of alienation and powerlessness. Marx asserted that, although individuals may strive for self-fulfillment, the physical quality and organization of many work environments can thwart self-enhancement and lead to personal misery. Thus, Marx provides some of the earliest pieces of evidence about "structural social psychology" because he traced linkages among objective social-economic conditions and the subjective, inner lives of individuals. Since then, sociologists of mental health and others have followed his efforts by documenting and describing the role of the self-concept in the connections between structural strains and psychological distress. For example, a typical sequence of hypotheses about the distressing effects of poor work conditions is as follows: (1) poor work conditions elevate unfavorable self-evaluations; (2) unfavorable self-evaluations increase the risk for undesirable mental health outcomes; and (3) unfavorable self-evaluations explain why poor work conditions increase the risk for undesirable mental health outcomes.

Building off the early sociological traditions of Marx, Cooley, and Mead, social stratification theory and research has sought to identify in detail the links between features of social structure (e.g., education, income, occupation, and work conditions) and self-concepts. For example, individuals in higher-status jobs with more authority and autonomy and more creative, stimulating, and challenging tasks tend to experience higher levels of self-esteem and sense of mastery. Autonomous and non-routine work, especially in higher-status positions, reflects arrangements that contain greater chances for mobility and achievement. Such arrangements often include responsibility for vital operations that can shape the course and success of the organization. Individuals whose work has such qualities may feel more devoted to their jobs as a source of identity and feel a greater sense of confidence, causal importance, and relevance. It may also enhance another evaluative aspect of the self-concept: the sense of mattering. Individuals who feel a sense of mattering believe that their actions are acknowledged and relevant in the lives of other people. It is easy to understand the importance of mattering as a socially determined self-evaluation by reflecting on the dreadful notion that one does not matter to anyone or anything. Here, there are roots to other classical notions about the powerful effects of social integration versus social isolation – and their ultimate implications for the self-concept.

In sum, the self-concept reflects a multidimensional and complex set of processes that contain numerous overlapping parts. Sociological social psychology has sought to document and describe the ways that social contexts influence and are influenced by the self-concept. Numerous domains of study of the self-concept provide fertile grounds for advances in knowledge, including: the structure and organization of self-conceptions; the internal dynamics of self-concepts; the relationship between social structure and self-conception; and the ways that self-concepts influence the effects of social stressors on health and emotional well-being. Long ago, Cooley and Mead laid the conceptual and theoretical groundwork for the sociological study of the self-concept. More recently, Rosenberg (1992) asserted that "although the individual's view of himself may be internal, what he sees and feels when he thinks of himself is largely the product of social life" (p. 593). One of the main quests for sociological analyses of the self-concept, then, continues to involve the documentation and description of the ways that fundamental sociological variables – especially those that designate one's location in the social structure – impress upon the self-concept across the life course. While this "social product" side of analysis is critical, it is important to underscore the "social force" role of the self-concept; that is, the ways that the self-concept impresses upon social structures and arrangements.

SEE ALSO: Cooley, Charles Horton; Identity: The Management of Meaning; Identity: Social Psychological Aspects; Identity Theory; Mead, George Herbert; Rosenberg, Morris; Self; Stress, Stress Theories

REFERENCES AND SUGGESTED READINGS

Cooley, C. H. (1964 [1902]) *Human Nature and the Social Order.* Schocken, New York.

Gecas, V. (1982) The Self-Concept. *Annual Review of Sociology* 8: 1–33.

Gecas, V. & Burke, P. J. (1995) Self and Identity. In: Cook, K., Fine, G. A., & House, J. S. (Eds.), *Sociological Perspectives on Social Psychology.* Allyn & Bacon, Boston, pp. 41–67.

Goffman, E. (1963) *Stigma: Notes on the Management of Spoiled Identity.* Simon & Schuster, New York.

McLeod, J. D. & Lively, K. J. (2003) Social Structure and Personality. In: Delamater, J. (Ed.), *Handbook of Social Psychology.* Kluwer Academic/Plenum, New York, pp. 77–102.

Pearlin, L. I. & Schooler, C. (1978) The Structure of Coping. *Journal of Health and Social Behavior* 19: 2–21.

Pearlin, L. I., Menaghan, E. G., Lieberman, M. A., & Mullan, J. T. (1981) The Stress Process. *Journal of Health and Social Behavior* 22: 337–56.

Rosenberg, M. (1965) *Society and the Adolescent Self-Image.* Princeton University Press, Princeton.

Rosenberg, M. (1979) *Conceiving the Self.* Basic Books, New York.

Rosenberg, M. (1992) The Self-Concept: Social Product and Social Force. In: Rosenberg, M. & Turner, R. H. (Eds.), *Social Psychology: Sociological Perspectives.* Transaction, New Brunswick, NJ, pp. 593–624.

Rosenberg, M. & McCullough, B. C. (1981) Mattering: Inferred Significance and Mental Health among Adolescents. *Research in Community and Mental Health* 2: 163–82.

Rosenberg, M. & Pearlin, L. I. (1978) Social Class and Self-Esteem among Children and Adults. *American Journal of Sociology* 84: 53–78.

Ross, C. E. & Sastry, J. (1999) The Sense of Personal Control: Social-Structural Causes and Emotional Consequences. In: Aneshensel, C. S. & Phelan, J. C. (Eds.), *Handbook of the Sociology of Mental Health.* Kluwer, New York, pp. 369–94.

Schwalbe, M. L. (1985) Autonomy in Work and Self-Esteem. *Sociological Quarterly* 26: 519–35.

Seeman, M. (1967) On the Personal Consequences of Alienation in Work. *American Sociological Review* 32: 273–85.

Spenner, K. I. (1988) Social Stratification, Work, and Personality. *Annual Review of Sociology* 14: 69–97.

Stryker, S. (1980) *Symbolic Interactionism.* Benjamin/Cummings, Menlo Park, CA.

Turner, R. J. & Lloyd, D. A. (1999) The Stress Process and the Social Distribution of Depression. *Journal of Health and Social Behavior* 40: 374–404.

Turner, R. J. & Roszell, P. (1994) Psychosocial Resources and the Stress Process. In: Avison, W. R. & Gotlib, I. H. (Eds.), *Stress and Mental Health: Contemporary Issues and Prospects for the Future.* Plenum, New York, pp. 179–210.

self-control theory

Michael R. Gottfredson

Self-control is a concept used by sociologists to explain differences among people in the frequency of engaging in a wide variety of acts that cause harm to others (Gottfredson & Hirschi 1990). It is defined as the tendency to avoid acts whose long-term costs exceed their momentary advantages. The costs include penalties from institutions such as schools and the criminal justice system, the loss of affection from family and friends, loss of jobs and advancements in employment, and bodily injury and physical pain. Individuals with relatively high levels of self-control tend to have low rates of crime, delinquency, and substance abuse because these behaviors entail potential long-term costs. They tend to have relatively high rates of school and employment success and lasting interpersonal relationships.

In criminology, the concept of self-control derives from the branch of sociological theories known as control theories. These theories are distinguished by the assumption that people are rational actors, seeking pleasure and avoiding pain. Basic human needs and desires are seen as fairly uniformly distributed among people (even if access to the means to satisfy these needs and desires is far from uniformly distributed). They include the desire for affection from others, material goods, and pleasurable physical and psychological experiences. In general, people pursue these wants in everyday life; controls are established by social groups (including parents, communities, and states) to channel the pursuit of these wants in ways that cause the least harm to others. Because these controls are exerted or not in the social environment, and because individuals experience different environments related to these controls, the extent to which individuals are "free to deviate" varies. When these controls need always be present in the environment to be effective, they are often referred to as external or social controls. When the process of socialization during the early years of life establishes concern about others and the long-term costs of behaviors, the form of control is referred to as self-control.

The concept of self-control was created to account for the fact that many delinquencies, crimes, and other problem behaviors seem to "go together" and therefore must have something in common. Behavioral research has consistently found that those who engage in high levels of delinquency, crime, and other social problems do not tend to specialize in the acts they commit. Interpersonal violence, stealing, drug use, accidents, and school misbehavior are commonly found in association. The acts associated with these problems all provide some immediate benefit for the actor (money, pleasure, the end of a troubling dispute), as do many other behaviors. But each also carries with it the possibility of harmful consequences to actor or to others. What is problematic for control theorists is not the idea that such acts may provide benefits to the actor, but rather that some people can disregard these benefits most of the time. Thus, self-control theory is sometimes called a "restraint" theory or a theory that focuses on why people do not engage in crime and delinquency rather than why they do (Hirschi 1969). Self-control theory does not focus on crime as defined by the legal system. Rather, self-control theorists have argued that sociologists should create their own dependent variable for theories about crime and delinquency, drawn from empirical studies of what harmful behaviors seem to cluster together, regardless of the legal definitions present at any one time or legal system.

Self-control theory is influenced by the observation that differences among people in the tendency to disregard long-term costs appear to be established in childhood and, once established, tend to persist throughout life. Criminologists have long observed that the single best predictor of delinquency or crime is the prior history of delinquency or crime.

Self-control theory begins with the assumption that human nature includes the general tendency to pursue satisfaction of individual needs and desires. Left unregulated, the pursuit of these needs and desires causes inevitable conflict with others and, because of that, potentially harmful consequences to the actor. As a result, those who care about the child seek to train the child to restrict the pursuit of self-interest by attending to the needs and wants of others. For self-control theory, this process is what socialization entails. As the child develops, caregivers (parents, other relatives, friends and neighbors, and schools) sanction behavior harmful to others and harmful to the child. Children are taught to pay attention to the longer-term consequences of their action. When a caring adult is present in the developing child's environment, and takes an active role in socialization, high levels of self-control are established and appear to become a fairly stable characteristic of the individual over the life course. But sometimes such early caregiving is not present in the child's environment because an adult who cares about the long-term interests of the child is not around or because the caregiver who is around lacks the skills necessary to create self-control in the child. Furthermore, there are differences among groups and even nations in the level and duration of this socialization process. These differences are thought by control theory to produce the differences in levels of crime, violence, and other problem behaviors among individuals and communities and in different time periods.

Differences in self-control are not the only cause of delinquency and crime according to this theory, but they consistently play an important role. Another feature of self-control theory is a focus on the concept of opportunity as an additional cause of crime. Self-control theory was influenced by developments in opportunity or routine activity theories which themselves focused attention on situational elements of crime as it typically occurs (Hindelang et al. 1978). This perspective studies the common features of delinquencies and crimes that occur, such as the times, places, and circumstances of crime, and attempts to infer how and why people interact with these features. These studies have suggested that crimes, delinquencies, and other problem behaviors do have many things in common. They seem to be overwhelmingly opportunistic events, in the sense that they are not typically planned much in advance, but seem to happen as opportunities "present themselves." Most often the delinquencies or crimes do not result in much gain for the offender – a little cash or stolen property, momentary excitement or fun, a temporary high, or a physical end to an argument. They tend to take place in the absence of "capable guardians" (Cohen & Felson 1979).

Self-control theory assumes that differences among people in self-control are also associated with the distribution of people in settings that vary in the opportunities for crime and delinquency. Thus, being among adolescent males in unsupervised settings, especially at night and in the presence of readily available drugs or alcohol, enhances opportunity for delinquency and is also a function of low self-control. Similarly, persistence in school is a characteristic of those with higher levels of self-control and also with reduced opportunities for delinquency. Throughout the life course, self-control influences friend and family associations, employment patterns, and many other life experiences (essentially the opportunities for crime), which in turn are related to levels of crime and related behaviors.

Researchers have found self-control theory to be a fruitful object of study. The theory has been applied to a wide variety of topics, ranging from white-collar crime to genocide, and from motor vehicle accidents to victimization. Other research has focused on using the theory to help explain patterns in crime and delinquency, such as gender differences, peer effects, and between-country variation in crime (for examples, see Britt & Gottfredson 2003; Hirschi & Gottfredson 1994). Most studies have found the measured level of self-control to usefully predict the problem behavior under study. Internal to the theory, attention has focused on the proper measurement of self-control, with some scholars finding attitudinal measures suitable and others preferring behavioral indicators.

Critics of self-control theory have argued that the theory is merely a tautology, that it invokes an overly simplistic view of human nature, and that it is best regarded only as one form of social learning theory. Considerable debate has centered on the assumption that, once established in early childhood, differences among people in self-control are stable. Some theorists argue instead that there are important life experiences that can elevate the level of self-control in adulthood, such as marriage. A persistent, but still very active, research dispute centers on the influence of peers on delinquency. Self-control theory would predict that the correlation between the delinquency of an individual and the delinquency of his or her friends is due to the selection of friends and associates that is heavily influenced by self-control and its determinants, whereas other perspectives argue that delinquent peers themselves cause delinquency to increase by supporting alternative norms or beliefs about the acceptability of delinquent conduct (for an excellent review of these issues, see Warr 2002).

The socialization idea in self-control theory is itself subject to controversy and alternative explanations. That is, the view that people begin life similarly situated with respect to the imperative to seek self-interest, and differ as adolescents largely as a consequence of differential socialization in childhood, is actively debated. Some argue that there are heritable predispositions that effect both variation in motivation for crime and amenability to socialization. Self-control theory takes the position that the benefits of delinquencies and crimes are obvious and ubiquitous such that no special motivation or learning is required to explain why individuals may engage in them. Furthermore, the socialization required for self-control is relatively easily achieved and is so effective that individual predispositions are likely to have minor effects in the generation of delinquency and crime. This debate will very likely shape future research and be increasingly active as techniques to establish predisposition and the studies necessary to examine the sources of self-control are undertaken.

Self-control theory has strong implications for public policies about delinquency and crime. Because the important causes of crime are thought to originate in early childhood, there is considerable promise in programs that focus resources for childcare among high-risk populations. A body of research has been created showing that such programs do indeed have important effects in reducing the level of delinquency and other problem behaviors and improving the life chances of children who otherwise would not benefit from self-control (Greenwood 2002). On the other hand, the theory predicts that efforts to control crime by targeting adolescents or adults by policing and incarceration will be ineffective, since they inevitably come too late in the developmental process. As control theory predicts, the evidence appears to support the notion that variation in the practices of the criminal justice system has only negligible effects on individual criminal tendencies and on the crime rate overall (Gottfredson & Hirschi 2003).

SEE ALSO: Crime, Life Course Theory of; Crime, Social Control Theory of; Criminology; Juvenile Delinquency; Social Learning Theory

REFERENCES AND SUGGESTED READINGS

Britt, C. & Gottfredson, M. (2003) *Control Theories of Crime and Delinquency*. Advances in Criminological Research, Vol. 12. Transaction, New Brunswick, NJ.

Cohen, L. & Felson, M. (1979) Social Change and Crime Rate Trends: A Routine Activities Approach. *American Sociological Review* 44: 588–608.

Gottfredson, M. & Hirschi, T. (1990) *A General Theory of Crime*. Stanford University Press, Stanford.

Gottfredson, M. & Hirschi, T. (2003) Self-Control and Opportunity. In: Britt, C. & Gottfredson, M. (Eds.), *Control Theories of Crime and Delinquency*. Transaction, New Brunswick, NJ, pp. 5–20.

Greenwood, P. (2002) Juvenile Crime and Juvenile Justice. In: Wilson, J. & Petersilia, J. (Eds.), *Crime*. ICS Press, Oakland, CA.

Hindelang, M., Gottfredson, M., & Garofalo, J. (1978) *Victims of Personal Crime: An Empirical Foundation for a Theory of Personal Victimization*. Ballinger, Cambridge.

Hirschi, T. (1969) *Causes of Delinquency*. University of California Press, Berkeley.

Hirschi, T. & Gottfredson, M. (Eds.) (1994) *The Generality of Deviance*. Transaction, New Brunswick, NJ.

Warr, M. (2002). *Companions in Crime: The Social Aspects of Criminal Conduct*. Cambridge University Press, Cambridge.

self-determination

Daniele Conversi

Self-determination is a principle in international law that a people ought to be able to determine its own future and political status free from external interference. It hence embodies the right for all peoples to decide their own political, economic, and cultural development.

The principle was first implemented on European soil following the post-World War I collapse of the dynastic Central European empires (Russian, Austro-Hungarian, and Ottoman). It was zealously fostered by the president of the United States, Woodrow Wilson (1856–1924), thus becoming the cornerstone for the entire post-World War I order heralding the beginning of the "American century." Accordingly, the boundaries of newly formed states had to be made congruent with "existing" ethnonational divisions. In order to achieve this goal, each self-determined unit had ideally to be conceived as an internally homogeneous entity. On the other hand, wherever possible, oppressed minorities should be granted the same right. Although the original idea was to establish a more stable world order, the effect was just the opposite, to increase European disorder, since all newly created entities included numerous minorities in their midst. The resulting convulsions became propitious for the consolidation of the United States as the hegemonic power at the global level.

Some of the new states, like Yugoslavia and Czechoslovakia (both established in 1918), lacked clear majorities. Subsequently, incipient fascist movements began to use this principle to exploit the presence of "stranded" minorities in what had suddenly become "foreign lands." German, Italian, and Hungarian irredentists wished to apply the very Wilsonian principle of self-determination to their "unredeemed" kin minorities on strict nationality lines. They strove to reunite entire ethnic diasporas within their respective *Heimaten*.

Among other things, Woodrow Wilson's 14 Points mandated that "the peoples of Austria-Hungary ... should be accorded the freest opportunity of autonomous development," while the "nationalities ... under Turkish rule should be assured an undoubted security of life and an absolutely unmolested opportunity of autonomous development." All these changes threatened to undo the tattered fabric of European and Ottoman pluri-ethnic and multireligious societies, indeed, that is what they achieved.

Given the later rise of aggressive nationalism, particularly irredentism and Nazi-fascism, the failure of this project was global in terms of international security, human rights, and the maintenance of peace. Like all attempts at "reordering the world" characteristic of totalitarian ideologies, it entailed tragic human costs, even though these had been largely unanticipated. However, while the Ottoman and Austro-Hungarian empires were being dissolved, Russia could save part of its territorial integrity by adopting the political praxis of Marxism-Leninism. The Constitution of the Soviet Union formally recognized the right to self-determination of its constituent Republics. This was a move initially envisioned by V. I. Lenin to capture the support of regional elites and hence assure the continuation of the "empire," although with a different name. Lenin had theorized about the need to use self-determination as an avenue to integrate the empire's nationalities into the new socialist order (Connor 1994 [1967]). But this legal principle was never fully put into practice due to the extremely centralized character of Soviet party politics.

After World War II, decolonization unleashed a second wave of self-determination claims, spreading the doctrine further. When the UN Charter was ratified in 1951, the signatories included a clause on the right of peoples to self-determination. Accordingly, all former colonies, that is, those which were already on the map prior to 1939, should be allowed to achieve sovereignty within their existing boundaries. Indeed, the doctrine of *uti possidetis* (from late Latin, "as you now possess") mandated that the states emerging from decolonization had to inherit the colonial administrative borders that existed at the time of independence. This term originally referred to a militaristic principle of international law allowing a belligerent to retain the captured territory it occupied at the termination of hostilities. In its decolonization form, the doctrine of *uti possidetis* was first applied in Latin America in the 1820s when the Spanish empire began to crumble.

Imperial powers, emerging elites, and "realist" politicians wished to restrict the concept to existing colonial possessions and fiercely opposed its application to entire nationalities. In this way, fully fledged UN member governments could uphold the principle of "non-interference" in their internal affairs together with a strenuous defense of their state's territorial integrity. Their main rationale was provided by the supposed threat emanating from secessionist movements and epitomized by the ill-fated partition between India and Pakistan in 1947. But the major obstacle to a wider implementation of the principle was the Cold War's freeze on all conflicts beyond the logic of mutually opposed blocs. The unchallenged dogma was then that self-determination should never apply to ethnic groups or stateless nations. This consensus was only broken by the secession of Bangladesh (1971), when India succeeded in attracting the support of the international community. On the other hand, the Federation of Malaysia willingly allowed Singapore to secede in 1965. The right to self-determination is solemnly upheld by the United Nations Declaration on Human Rights (1970), the International Covenant on Economic, Social, and Cultural Rights (1966), and the International Covenant on Civil and Political Rights (1976).

A third wave of self-determination spread by the end of the Cold War, with German unification (1990), the breakup of former socialist "federations" (1990–3), and, finally, the independence of Eritrea (1993) and East Timor (1999). More recently, the concept has been used throughout the world by indigenous peoples, stateless nations, minorities, and sovereign states alike, but in a looser and more flexible way.

The principle of self-determination is rooted in British liberal thought, particularly in John Stuart Mill's idea of representative government (Connor 1994 [1967]). Mill notoriously argued that in a country which consists of several nationalities, free institutions of a representative government are "next to impossible" (Mill 1977 [1861]: 361). In this way, the door was left open for the advent of modern-day ethnic intolerance. The western liberal principle of "one nation, one state" deeply influenced Eastern European political thought during the period of state building, just at a moment when German ethnicism and French Jacobinism were providing the inspiring models for national mobilization. Both liberals and Marxists had failed to deal with the issue of ethnic dissent because the European nation-state provided the unique empirical referent for their political theories.

The principle indicates the aspiration of a group (the "*self*") to freely "determine" its own political structure. But in order for the "self" to be "determined," someone must first determine who the "self" is – or establish who are the people to be "determined." The exercise of this right presupposes a previous process of "boundary definition" and "group recognition" (Conversi 1997). As Ivor Jennings (1956: 56) pointed out: "On the surface, it seemed reasonable: let the people decide. It was in fact ridiculous because the people cannot decide until somebody decides who are the people." This is referred to as the concept's paradoxical *indeterminacy* (Moore 1998). The principle remained often impossible to implement and, when attempted, it frequently led to further chaos and conflict.

The concept of self-determination is often placed in opposition to that of *territorial integrity*, with which it is thought to be incompatible. However, self-determination does not necessarily imply political separation, sovereignty, or secession. Many movements for national liberation, regional autonomy, and indigenous rights refer to self-determination as a broad umbrella term which allows for a vast array of possibilities based on the recognition of collective rights. Calls for self-determination can often be settled relatively easily with concessions of regional autonomy and/or cultural rights. Secession would work as a practical tool with high moral value if it could provide an avenue for ethnic or religious minorities to escape their persecution by dominant elites. However, the achievement of statehood through political separation does not always result in an improvement in either economic or human rights. Less drastic tools, short of independence, are available and can be implemented to address calls for self-determination.

Contrary to self-determination, *secession* is considered a capital sin in international politics. It is sternly resisted by states and governments worldwide for obvious reasons. In the US its prejudicial connotation also derives from the negative myth of the Civil War, when 11 Southern states attempted to secede by forming the "Confederate States of America" (1861–5). This myth still reverberates in US foreign policy's general hostility to secession. The initial refusal to recognize the independence of Slovenia and Croatia as they came under attack from the Yugoslav army (1991–2) and George Bush's condemnation of Ukraine's secessionist drive in 1990 stem both from *realpolitik* and from this anti-secessionist legacy. However, this attitude was tempered by the US support for the independence of Estonia, Latvia, and Lithuania, which had been illegally annexed by the Soviet Union in 1943 as a consequence of the secret Hitler–Stalin Pact (Ribbentrop–Molotov Pact, August 23, 1939).

The right to self-determination of peoples remains a cardinal principle in international law. On the one hand, denying this principle would flagrantly violate the companion principle of democracy – a contradiction disregarded in the early 1990s when the West failed to couple the two concepts as Yugoslavia disintegrated. On the other hand, the capacity of every people to take advantage of this concept is minimized by the unprecedented invasiveness of sweeping "external" forces, such as global law, consumerism, Americanization, and ecological disaster. The unbridled power of multinational companies often exceeds that of supposedly "sovereign" states. In an increasingly interdependent world, where megacorporations command greater resources than many single countries, the concept of self-determination might become irrelevant for human development unless it can contain the most destructive aspects of globalization.

SEE ALSO: Boundaries (Racial/Ethnic); Decolonization; Diaspora; Indigenous Movements; Mill, John Stuart; Nation-State and Nationalism; Nationalism

REFERENCES AND SUGGESTED READINGS

Cobban, A. (1969) *The Nation-State and National Self-Determination*, 2nd rev. edn. Collins, London.

Connor, W. (1994 [1967]) Self Determination: The New Phase. In: *Ethnonationalism: The Quest for Understanding*. Princeton University Press, Princeton.
Conversi, D. (1997) Reassessing Theories of Nationalism: Nationalism as Boundary Maintenance and Creation. In: Agnew, J. (Ed.), *Political Geography: A Reader*. Edward Arnold, New York, pp. 325–36.
Hannum, H. (1990) *Autonomy, Sovereignty, and Self-Determination: The Accommodation of Conflicting Rights*. University of Pennsylvania Press, Philadelphia.
Higgins, R. (1994) Self Determination. In: *Problems and Process: International Law and How We Use It*. Oxford University Press, New York, ch. 7.
Jennings, I. (1956) *The Approach to Self-Government*. Cambridge University Press, Cambridge.
Lenin, V. I. (1995 [1914]) *The Right of Nations to Self-Determination*. Pathfinder, London.
Mill, J. S. (1977 [1861]) Of Nationality as Connected with Representative Government. Chapter 16 of *Considerations in Representative Government*. In: Robson, J. M. (Ed.), *Essays on Politics and Society*, Vol. 19 of the *Collected Works of John Stuart Mill*. University of Toronto Press, Toronto, pp. 359–66.
Moore, M. (1998) *National Self-Determination and Secession*. Oxford University Press, New York.
Neuberger, B. (1995) National Self-Determination: Dilemmas of a Concept. *Nations and Nationalism* 1(3): 297–325.
Simpson, G. (2000) The Diffusion of Sovereignty: Self-Determinations in the Post-Colonial Age. In: McCorquodale, R. (Ed.), *Self-Determination in International Law*. Ashgate/Dartmouth, Aldershot.
Wilson, W. (1918) *Self-Determination and the Rights of Small Nations*. Candle Press, Dublin.

self-esteem, theories of

Timothy J. Owens

Self-esteem refers to the overall positive or negative attitude an individual takes toward himself or herself. Understanding self-esteem also requires awareness of related terms, especially *self* and *self-concept*, along with an appreciation of their similarities and differences. Figure 1 illustrates how self, self-concept, and self-esteem are causally related, and the outcomes typically associated with self-esteem. Although hierarchical in terms of abstractness and general causality, lower order concepts and outcomes can also influence higher order ones. (Note that *identity* and *ideal self* are listed to acknowledge that self-concept is composed of more than self-esteem, but the former, and related concepts, are beyond the scope of this entry.)

Self may be defined sociologically as an organized and interactive system of thoughts, feelings, identities, and motives that (1) is born of self-reflexivity and language, (2) people attribute to themselves, and (3) characterizes specific human beings. Psychologists tend to conceptualize the self as a set of cognitive representations indicating a person's personality traits, organized by linkages, across representations created by personal experience or biography. It is sometimes extended to include things besides trait attributes, such as social roles and even identities. In this case, the self is a cognitive structure incorporating such elements as intelligent, persistent, excitable, and truthful, or middle class, Jewish, female, and Canadian.

Self-concept is how we imagine and perceive our self. It is inextricably tied to the "I–me" dialectic expounded by James and Mead. Self-concept may be defined as the totality of an individual's thoughts and feelings about a particular object – his or her self. It includes cognition and emotion, since it is both an object of perception and reflection and an emotional response to those perceptions. As a product of its own objectification, self-concept entails a particular person (i.e., subject, "knower," or

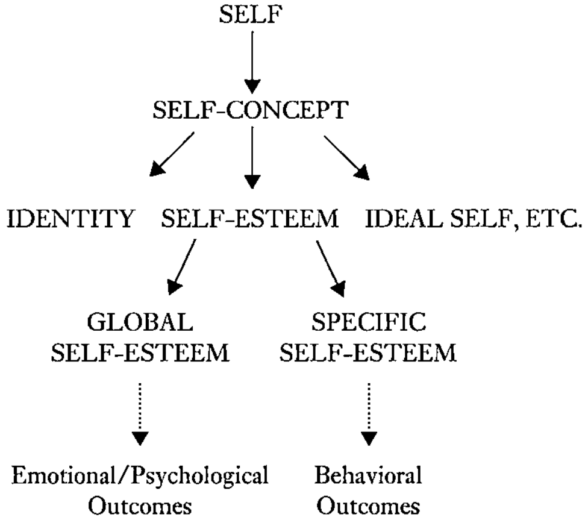

Figure 1 Outcomes associated with self-esteem.

"I") figuratively standing outside himself or herself, and perceiving and reacting to the self as an object of consideration (i.e., object, the "known," or "me"). Accepting that the self may be both subject and object serves as the rationale for conducting studies of the self-concept, and consequently self-esteem.

Historically, theologians and philosophers were the first to delve into the nature of the self, that presumably quintessential characteristic of the human animal. Over the millennia, scholars have been acutely interested in such questions as: Who am *I*? What does *my* life mean? Am *I* a good person? Am *I* loved? Can *I* love? And what makes me, *me* and you, *you*? All of these questions imply a self, and self-concept.

While philosophers and theologians still grapple with these questions, the bulk of contemporary research on the self is done by sociologists and psychologists. The key to the social science research perspective on the self is human reflexivity. This entails not only being able to view oneself as others might (self-as-object), but also labeling, categorizing, evaluating, and manipulating one's self (self-as-subject). Reflexivity hinges on language, whether emanating from a broader culture's written or non-written language (e.g., Arabic and Ojibwe, respectively) or a subculture's argot (e.g., military idiom). In short, the reflexive self allows people to view themselves from a putatively external point of view, just as others do. Additionally, since the self can reflect back on itself, it is an integral part of many features we associate with being human: the ability to plan, worry about personal problems, ruminate about past actions, lament present circumstances, or envy others.

There are many theories of self-esteem development in sociology. Most are embedded in symbolic interaction (especially labeling theory) and Festinger's theory of social comparisons. James presented the earliest social scientific formulation of self-esteem. He regarded self-esteem as a balancing act between an individual's perceptions of his or her success in some realm of life (e.g., sports) versus one's pretensions (i.e., aspirations) of success (e.g., wanting to be the top seeded tennis player in college sports). James used the equation Self-esteem = Success/Pretensions as illustration. Changing the numerator or denominator can increase or decrease self-esteem. When aspirations substantially outweigh perceived success, for example, the imbalance drives self-esteem down.

Contemporary research on self-esteem has been codified into four basic principles of self-concept formation: reflected appraisals, social comparisons, self-attributions, and psychological centrality. The principle of reflected appraisals is central to the symbolic interactionist's insistence that the self is a social product derived from the attitudes that others have toward one's self and that one eventually comes to see himself or herself as others do, à la Cooley's idea of the looking-glass self and Mead's notion of role-taking, both products of symbolic interaction. The contemporary literature recognizes three basic kinds of reflected appraisals or feedback. *Perceived selves* are the most important aspect of reflected appraisals for the self. Here, ego speculates on how he or she *believes* specific alters perceive him or her. One's *perception*, whether accurate or not, is the vital element. *Direct reflections* are the actual and direct responses that alter has toward ego, regardless of how subjectively ego perceives and thus assesses them. The *generalized other* is ego's composite sense of what others think of him or her.

Through social comparisons, people judge and evaluate themselves in comparison to particular individuals, groups, or social categories. The main function of this process, according to much contemporary research, is to test reality, especially when knowledge about oneself is ambiguous or uncertain. Two aspects of social comparisons are worth noting: criteria bases (i.e., superior/inferior, better/worse) and normative bases (i.e., deviance/conformity, same/different). Self-attributions, the most intrinsically psychological of the four principles, hold that individuals draw conclusions about themselves (e.g., funny, popular, attractive, bookish) by observing their own behaviors, the outcomes they produce, and then making some kind of inference about themselves. Finally, psychological centrality, perhaps the most understudied of the four principles, holds that the self is an interrelated system of hierarchically organized components, with some identities and attributes being more important or more central to the self than others. Since psychological centrality is the weight or importance individuals assign to their various personal attributes, identities, and abilities, it serves to protect self-esteem by pushing potentially damaging self-attributes and identities to the periphery of the self system, while holding enhancing attributes closer to the center.

Theories of self-esteem as a *motive* hold that individuals desire to protect and if possible enhance their self-concept. The motives of self-esteem and self-consistency are crucial in this regard. The self-esteem motive goads individuals to think well of themselves. Many self-theorists from James to the present regard this motive as universally dominant in the human motivational system. The self-consistency motive asserts that people struggle to validate their self-concepts, even when they are negative. To do otherwise requires revising one's self-concept, a daunting task (Lecky 1951).

Self-esteem is both a social product and a social force. As a social product, the social origins of the self-concept and self-esteem are investigated. It is taken axiomatically that the self arises out of society. Self-esteem theory helps explain how this occurs. As a social force, self-esteem serves as an important sociometer by which a population's general health and well-being may be gauged. Self-esteem has thus been linked to a variety of positive and negative outcomes, such as mental health and well-being, prosocial behavior, participation in social movements, and deviant and risky behavior.

Self-esteem may be usefully divided into two broad categories: specific self-esteem and global self-esteem. Each tends to be associated with different outcomes (see Fig. 1). Specific self-esteem is tied to a person's roles, identities, activities, contexts, or attributes (e.g., academic, physical, social, moral, family). It is multifaceted and hierarchical, depending upon the importance one places on particular attributes. Global self-esteem refers to overall characterizations of one's self as good or bad, worthy or worthless, acceptable or unacceptable, moral or immoral, likeable or dislikeable, and so on. It is imperative to recognize that global self-esteem is a general portrayal of one's state or trait with respect to the self, without reference to an individual's particular roles, identities, or social contexts. A parallel viewpoint sees global self-esteem as an amalgamation of one's many specific self-esteems. Specific self-esteem tends to predict behavioral outcomes (e.g., school grades) better than global self-esteem, whereas global self-esteem tends to be more predictive of emotional and psychological outcomes (e.g., depression).

Attaining or maintaining high self-esteem and avoiding low self-esteem are perennial interests of social scientists and the lay public alike. People with high self-esteem (HSE) possess self-respect and feelings of worthiness. Aside from extremely arrogant HSE people, most possess other positive attributes such as humility and a willingness to acknowledge, though not dwell on, their personal faults and shortcomings. In contrast, people with very low self-esteem (LSE) lack self-respect and see only their faults, weaknesses, and unworthiness, coupled with a belief that they are seriously deficient people. In reality, very low LSE is fairly rare, probably no more than 15 percent of the population and perhaps much less. Most people have medium to high self-esteem. Still, LSE is an important social problem. To have LSE is to live a life of misery. However painful and discomforting LSE may be, it is not a mental illness. Rather, it is a form of psychological distress characterized by such unpleasant subjective states as depressive affect, anxiety, general dissatisfaction with life, resentment, enmity, and suspicion.

Cognitively, self-esteem theory and research shows that LSE people, in contrast to HSE people, tend to be more cynical, negative toward institutions, to harbor disapproving attitudes toward other persons and groups, and to be harshly critical of themselves. With these emotional and cognitive orientations, a LSE person's general approach to life is frequently twofold: avoid risk and a "moat" or defensive mentality. LSE people feel more threatened by others and believe personal failure or a misstep is right around the corner. Trying to avoid risk pushes LSE people into protective styles of life (in contrast to acquisitive styles) focusing on avoiding damage to one's feeling of self-worth, regardless of how meager that may be. LSE people see their chief risks as interpersonal, thus making a moat mentality appealing. This allegorical barrier entails restricting interaction with others, marginalizing oneself in groups, being reticent about expressing one's thoughts and feelings about other people, actively concealing one's ideas and feelings, and putting up fronts or pretenses.

Investigating the origins of and consequences for high and low self-esteem continues to be vigorously researched. To date, the vast majority of research and theorizing on self-esteem has been focused on children and adolescence. More research is needed on adult self-esteem, especially as it relates to change and stability over the life course and the wide variety of adult roles and social contexts which influence and are influenced by self-esteem. Specifying the link between macro structures and processes (i.e., social stratification, organizations and networks, and collective behavior) and self-esteem awaits further sociological analysis. Accepting the truism that self and society are twin-born also indicates the need for additional research on the reciprocal effects of self-esteem and a variety of social problems.

SEE ALSO: Culture; James, William; Language; Looking-Glass Self; Rosenberg, Morris; Self; Social Psychology; Socialization; Symbolic Interaction

REFERENCES AND SUGGESTED READINGS

Cooley, C. H. (1902) *Human Nature and the Social Order*. Charles Scribner's Sons, New York.

Gecas, V. (1982) The Self-Concept. *Annual Review of Sociology* 8: 1–33.

James, W. (1890) *The Principles of Psychology*. Henry Holt, New York.

Lecky, P. (1951) *Self-Consistency: A Theory of Personality*, 2nd edn., edited and interpreted by F. C. Thorne. Island Press, New York.

Mead, G. H. (1934) *Mind, Self, and Society from the Standpoint of a Social Behaviorist*. University of Chicago Press, Chicago.

Owens, T. J. (2003) Self and Identity. In: Delamater, J. D. (Ed.), *Handbook of Social Psychology*. Kluwer Academic/Plenum Publishers, New York, pp. 205–32.

Owens, T. J., Stryker, S., & Goodman, N. (Eds.) (2001) *Extending Self-Esteem Theory and Research: Sociological and Psychological Currents*. Cambridge University Press, New York.

Rosenberg, M. (1979) *Conceiving the Self*. Basic Books, New York.

Rosenberg, M. (1981) The Self-Concept: Social Product and Social Force. In: Rosenberg, M. & Turner, R. H. (Eds.), *Social Psychology: Sociological Perspectives*. Basic Books, New York, pp. 593–624.

Rosenberg, M., Schooler, C., Schoenbach, C., & Rosenberg, F. (1995) Global Self-Esteem and Specific Self-Esteem: Different Concepts, Different Outcomes. *American Sociological Review* 60: 141–56.

self-fulfilling expectations

Alison J. Bianchi

A self-fulfilling expectation (or as it is often referred to, a self-fulfilling prophecy) is a person's anticipation about how a situation will end that prompts the person to behave in ways that cause the anticipated ending to come true. Individuals often have a sense that a situation's outcome is a foregone conclusion, even if the outcome is not necessarily inevitable. A person with this sense may be compelled to act in ways that encourage the presumed conclusion to happen in actuality. Hence, what the individual expects to occur often does occur because the individual has had a hand in producing the event. Thus, the self does indeed fulfill the promise of the expectation.

Consider, for instance, a professor in an engineering college who has very stereotypical views about the performance of males and females in his classes. He (wrongly) believes that men always perform better than women because they possess the genetic predisposition to be naturally better at mathematics. During this professor's classes, he tends to call on male students more than females; he non-consciously grades males' exams more gently than females; and he spends more time with male students during office hours than with his female students. Due to these very biased behaviors, the male students get more academic attention and help while taking this professor's classes. Not surprisingly, the male students do tend to perform better than the female students in his courses. The professor expects them to perform better, and has had a hand in producing this outcome, despite his feelings that this is just the natural order of things!

Robert K. Merton first posited the concept of the self-fulfilling expectation in 1948. He based this concept on the "Thomas theorem," named for W. I. Thomas. A summary of the Thomas theorem was: if an individual defines a situation as real, then it is real in its consequences. Merton reasoned that rather than relying completely on the objective elements presented by circumstances, persons often construct their own meanings about a situation, and then respond to these subjective understandings. Actors' definitions of the situation also included notions about its outcome. Hence, if subjectively constructed expectations were part of actors' understandings of the situation, then they would play a role in how actors behaved. The actors' behavior would also influence the situation's objective outcome.

An interesting facet of self-fulfilling expectations is that actors who experience them seldom consciously recognize their part in causing outcomes to occur. Instead, actors view situational conclusions as inevitable, and non-consciously take steps to produce the inevitability. Another interesting facet of this phenomenon is the reaction of other persons to an actor's self-fulfilling expectations. An actor's expectation of another person's behavior tends to educe that behavior from the other person, even if the expectation was erroneous. Thus, the other person's behaviors that are elicited by an actor's expectation will be interpreted as confirmation of the actor's definition of the situation and its concomitant outcome. The self-fulfilling expectation is realized, yet again, as the focal actor's speculation about the other person's reaction to him or her comes true.

Merton believed that persons often had false definitions of the situation, and these false understandings evoked behavior that made the false conception come true. The classic example Merton used, for which he is often quoted, is the run on a bank. If rumors are spread that a bank is suffering from financial difficulties and will collapse, then those with savings in the bank may try to withdraw their money en masse, causing the bank to collapse in fact. Note how the original rumors about the bank's fragile pecuniary state may have been false; nonetheless, the resulting behavior of the bank customers fulfills the predictions of the gossip concerning the bank's financial health.

Sociologists have since disputed Merton's original conception of self-fulfilling expectations. They have noted that an individual's anticipation of how a situation would end could not be truly false if it could in fact happen. Sociologists have theorized that the impetus behind the behavior that realizes the predicted outcome could be any understanding of the situation that the individual feels is real, and could indeed become real, despite others' judgments of the anticipation as true or false.

Another aspect of Merton's discussion about self-fulfilling expectations is their functionality for maintaining social inequalities through cultural beliefs. He asserts that cultural beliefs about who is and who should be the "haves" and "have-nots" in a society must be shared and perpetuated to maintain social disparities. Members of a society who internalize these beliefs about the social order may behave as if they were true. Thus, Merton argued, the purpose of cultural beliefs regarding unequal distributions of power, status, or other valued social markers is to prod societal members into experiencing self-fulfilling expectations.

Consider, again, the example of the biased engineering professor. How did he learn that women are not expected to do well in math-oriented classes? He learned this from cultural stereotypes that women are not as adept at mathematics as men are. By internalizing these beliefs, the professor came to feel that women were less competent than men in the subject of engineering, and then he behaved as if women were, in fact, incompetent. If women then do perform less well in the professor's class, and this outcome is reproduced by many other biased professors, women may not obtain good jobs in this field, and probably will not rise to positions of influence in it; or, women may not get jobs in engineering at all. Thus, the disparity of power between men and women in engineering would be maintained by the mechanism of internalized cultural beliefs, and perpetuated by the poor performance of females experiencing the results of professors' self-fulfilling expectations based on those beliefs. Note, too, that men in this discipline also experience the bias of professors' self-fulfilling expectations, except the cultural beliefs about them are positive: professors may believe that men are good in math, and as a result the male students may receive more attention from these professors and do very well in college and in the field. Merton would have argued that it is no accident that men receive higher grades in engineering classes. The explanation for the phenomenon involves a cultural stereotype stimulating self-fulfilling expectations.

Sociologists who have pondered the problems presented by self-fulfilling expectations include methodologists who specialize in causal modeling. One of the predicaments they face is the reaction of the population under study to their causal model. Researchers may formulate a cause-and-effect relation between variables measuring some aspect within a group. The research participants for whom this relation is hypothesized to hold may suspect, or even learn about, the posited relation. They may then take this relation into consideration when they act. As a result, the posited relation may be rendered false, since the group members may change the outcome of the situation. In other words, predictions of causal relations could themselves turn out to be a part of the interconnected social conditions that result in future outcomes. If these predictions factor into group members' subjective meanings of the situational outcome, and the group members disagree with the predictions, then these disagreements become beliefs about the situation, and could become self-fulfilling expectations.

To provide an example of this dilemma, suppose citizens of a town are having a political race to elect the next mayor. Candidate A, a very handsome man, is running against candidate B, a very unattractive man. A sociologist studying the election suggests that gender is related to predicting the outcome in the race because females are more likely to vote for an attractive man than an unattractive one. The sociologist forecasts that candidate A will win the election. This forecast is based on her causal model that gender is related to voting behavior. The sociologist then publishes this supposition in the local newspaper. After reading about this, the women in the town become quite offended, feeling that the sociologist has portrayed them as focusing on shallow concerns about the candidates rather than the candidates' opinions about the issues. To prove that they are not superficial, the town's females overwhelmingly vote for candidate B, and the sociologist's causal relation is rendered false. The disagreement about the supposed portrayal of women by the sociologist becomes a belief about how the town's women should vote, and they in fact vote in this manner.

Another problem that self-fulfilling expectations present for causal modeling has to do with the temporal ordering of causal and outcome variables. One of three necessary conditions for claiming causation between a cause and an effect is that the cause must occur prior to the effect. For example, a researcher might posit that students' effort during the semester is one of the causes for getting a good grade at the end of the semester. This causal claim, that "effort is related to grades," would be acceptable as long as the sociologist made it clear that she was measuring effort during the course and prior to the assignment of grades at the end of the semester. In the case of a self-fulfilling expectation, however, it is difficult to claim that the cause of the outcome clearly occurs prior to the outcome. The nature of a self-fulfilling expectation is that an actor anticipates the outcome (or effect), behaves in a way to produce the outcome (the cause), and then the outcome is produced. In this chain of events, the anticipated effect becomes the real effect, with the cause being the mediating behavior. Without the anticipation of the effect, the real effect would not happen. And, in fact, the anticipated effect actually leads to the cause. Some would consider this phenomenon a violation of the temporal order condition required to claim causation. Therefore, when a self-fulfilling expectation is modeled as a causal relation, researchers suggest that the person conceiving the model must declare it to be a weak causal claim.

In current sociological social psychological theories, self-fulfilling expectations are rarely studied explicitly. An exception is a research program on the relation between expectations and attraction. More often, self-fulfilling expectations are assumed to be operating as part of the process being explained. Two examples of this type of theory are status characteristics theory, a branch of expectation states theory, and stereotype threat theory. Both theories explain how cultural stereotypes affect performance, and use the concept of self-fulfilling expectations to describe the group- and individual-level processes they examine.

In conclusion, despite this concept's recent relative neglect, it still has a great deal of potential to explain social behavior; there is much to gain, both theoretically and empirically, by incorporating the concept more rigorously into studies that attempt to tease out "processes" of interaction. Subjects ranging from interpersonal dynamics (e.g., couples' communications) to the persistence of discriminatory evaluations could benefit from using the concept, as its theoretical versatility has yet to be fully realized.

SEE ALSO: Expectation States Theory; Merton, Robert K.; Self-Fulfilling Prophecy; Social Psychology; Stereotyping and Stereotypes

REFERENCES AND SUGGESTED READINGS

Henshel, R. L. (1982) The Boundary of the Self-Fulfilling Prophecy and the Dilemma of Social Prediction. *British Journal of Sociology* 33: 511–28.

Jones, E. E. (1986) Interpreting Interpersonal Behavior: The Effects of Expectancies. *Science* 234: 41–6.

Klein, O. & Snyder, M. (2003) Stereotypes and Behavioral Confirmation: From Interpersonal to Intergroup Perspectives. In: Zanna, M. P. (Ed.), *Advances in Experimental Social Psychology*, Vol. 35. Academic Press, San Diego, pp. 153–234.

Krishna, D. (1971) "The Self-Fulfilling Prophecy" and the Nature of Society. *American Sociological Review* 36: 1104–7.

Merton, R. K. (1948) The Self-Fulfilling Prophecy. *Antioch Review* 8: 193–210.

Ridgeway, C. L. (1991) The Social Construction of Status Value: Gender and Other Nominal Characteristics. *Social Forces* 70(2): 267–86.

Steele, C. M. (1997) A Threat in the Air: How Stereotypes Shape Intellectual Identity and Performance. *American Psychologist* 52(6): 613–29.

Webster, M., Jr. & Foschi, M. (1988) Overview of Status Generalization. In: Webster, M., Jr. & Foschi, M. (Eds.), *Status Generalization: New Theory and Research*. Stanford University Press, Stanford, pp. 1–20.

Wilkins, W. E. (1976) The Concept of a Self-Fulfilling Prophecy. *Sociology of Education* 49: 175–83.

self-fulfilling prophecy

Takako Nomi

The self-fulfilling prophecy is the process by which one's expectations of other persons or groups lead those persons or groups to behave in ways that confirm those expectations. An influential and controversial idea in education, the concept of the self-fulfilling prophecy is used to illuminate the ways that teacher expectations influence students' behavioral and achievement outcomes. The self-fulfilling prophecy predicts that positive teacher expectations lead to positive student outcomes, while negative expectations lead to negative student outcomes.

The term "self-fulfilling prophecy" was coined in 1948 by Robert K. Merton, who drew upon W. I. Thomas's well-known dictum: "if men define situations as real, they are real in their consequences" (see an excellent review by Wineberg 1987). The Thomas theorem suggests that the meanings of human actions are not inherent merely in their actions. Rather, people attribute meanings to those actions, and the meanings have consequences for future actions. Merton (1948) illustrated the concept with the example that a groundless rumor of a bank's insolvency could cause bankruptcy when enough customers believe in the rumor and rush to withdraw their deposits. The idea is simple: a false prediction could become true if it is widely believed to be true. Certainly, the self-fulfilling prophecy is a unique social concept that has no application in the physical world. A false prediction about a hurricane does not bring gusty winds and torrential rain. However, the prediction of human actions may have a powerful effect on their outcomes.

At the micro level, the self-fulfilling prophecy has theoretical roots in social phenomenology. The notion of the social construction of reality implies that reality is produced through social interactions among actors, who use symbols to interpret one another and assign meanings to perceptions and experiences. From this perspective, the self-fulfilling prophecy is understood as reciprocal processes whereby cultural beliefs and human consciousness create and recreate social life.

At the macro level, self-fulfilling prophecies serve the function of maintaining the existing social order and social relationships. Patterns of self-fulfilling prophecies mirror structural arrangements in society as well as social beliefs that represent those structural arrangements. For example, social relationships between dominant and minority groups are defined and redefined through self-fulfilling prophecies. Expectations for minority groups' behaviors are defined according to their social status, and the interpretation of their behaviors by dominant groups justifies what is being defined.

The self-fulfilling prophecy is also known as the Pygmalion effect after the publication in 1968 of *Pygmalion in the Classroom* by Richard Rosenthal, an educational psychologist at Harvard University, and Lenore Jacobson, an elementary school principal in South San Francisco. In 1964 they initiated an experiment in a low-income elementary school where they created different teacher expectations and examined how such expectations influenced students' academic progress. At the beginning of the school year, an IQ test was administered and teachers were given false information about students' IQ scores. At the end of the school year, the IQ score gains were compared between students in experimental groups and those in control groups. Rosenthal and Jacobson found that students who were falsely identified as "spurters" – those who were predicted to "show an academic spurt" (Rosenthal & Jacobson 1968: 66) – made significantly greater gains in IQ scores than did those who were not so identified. Thus *Pygmalion* established a positive relationship between teacher expectations and students' intelligence, confirming the existence of the educational self-fulfilling prophecy.

Soon after the publication of *Pygmalion*, Ray Rist (1970) began in 1967 to collect sociological data to test the self-fulfilling prophecy in a ghetto school. By examining student–teacher interactions in an all-black elementary school, Rist was able to answer questions about the mechanisms through which the self-fulfilling prophecy in the classroom was manifested. One of the most striking findings in this study was that the teacher formed expectations during the first days of kindergarten. The teacher then assigned her students to three ability groups based on students' socioeconomic backgrounds, rather than their academic ability, and treated each ability group differently. She gave more freedom and encouragements to students in the highest ability group, but gave more criticisms and restrictions to students in the lowest ability group. Students in the highest ability group could get physically closer to the teacher than could students in the lowest ability group. Eventually, students in the highest ability group received more instruction and showed better performance than did students in the lowest ability group.

Based on such observation, Rist (1970) described the self-fulfilling prophecy in the classroom as a process of several steps. First, a teacher forms expectations about students' potential to achieve based on non-academic factors. Then the teacher acts on these expectations and applies differential treatments. When the teacher's treatment is consistent, and if students do not resist, students will internalize and respond to the teacher in a way that confirms his/her expectations. Students' differential responses reinforce the teacher's differential treatment. The vicious cycle is then complete. Teacher expectations become "true" because the teacher acts as though they are true.

Both *Pygmalion* and Rist's ethnographic study sparked controversies during the years after their publication, as researchers searched for evidence to support or refute the prophecy. By the late 1980s, there were about 400 experiments and meta-analyses on the self-fulfilling prophecy in education. Critics have raised important issues about the validity of the tests and the lack of significant results beyond the second grade in the Pygmalion study, the lack of representativeness of Rist's study sample, and the leap from the classroom to the broader society in Rist's conclusions (Wineberg 1987). More importantly, many researchers failed to replicate the effect of self-fulfilling prophecy. Such failure did not stop other researchers, policymakers, and the mass media from hailing these two major studies as providing a model for social science research and for teacher training. Educational self-fulfilling prophecy even played a role in the courts' decisions over equity issues in education, including testing, desegregation, busing, and ability tracking (Wineburg 1987). More recently, the concept of the self-fulfilling prophecy was applied to settings other than classrooms. These include work organizations, judicial settings, substance uses, delinquency, and health care, to name a few.

In the field of sociology of education, researchers have applied the concept to critique functionalist assumptions on the role of schools in social stratification. They challenged the earlier view that education is a meritocratic vehicle for social mobility and began to see schools as institutions responsible for reproducing existing social inequalities. Since the publication in 1969 of James Coleman's report on the *Equality of Educational Opportunity*, which revealed greater achievement inequalities within schools than inequalities between schools, a focus has been placed on in-school processes to understand how educational inequalities are created and reinforced. An area of research where educational self-fulfilling prophecies are actively applied is in school organization. Sociologists have turned their attentions to ability grouping and tracking in K-12 schooling to examine if and how students' race and socioeconomic status affect student assignment to different ability groups or tracks, and how teacher expectations impact instructional practices in different ability groups or tracks, which, in turn, shape student learning. Students in different ability groups or tracks may be exposed to different hidden curricula and opportunities to learn, which mediate the relationship between teacher expectations and students' achievement outcomes. Another area of research related to the educational self-fulfilling prophecy is the study of racial and gender stereotypes. This research seeks to better understand race and gender disparities in students' educational outcomes in post-secondary levels. Most sociological findings support the notion of the educational self-fulfilling prophecy in the US, as well as in other countries, including England, New Zealand, Australia, and South Korea, among others (Tauber 1997).

Today we have more information about the mediating mechanisms of the Pygmalion effect. A four-factor theory (Rosenthal 1974) explains how teachers convey expectations to students in classrooms. These four factors are climate, feedback, input, and output. Climate refers to the tendency for the teacher to create a warm socio-emotional climate, communicated both verbally and non-verbally (e.g., smiling, nodding, and eye-contacting), for high expectancy students but not for low expectancy students. Feedback refers to the tendency for the teacher to give more positive feedback to high expectancy students than to low expectancy students for the correctness or incorrectness of their responses. Input is the tendency for the teacher to teach more and harder curricula to higher expectancy students than to lower expectancy students. Finally, output is the tendency for the teacher to encourage greater responsiveness from high expectancy students but not from low expectancy students. Teacher expectations are translated to student behavior in a two-stage process. First, differential teacher expectations lead to differential teacher behavior. The teacher is likely to create a warmer climate, give more positive feedback, and display greater inputs and outputs for high expectancy students than for low expectancy students. Second, differential teacher behavior leads to differential student outcomes. Warm climate, positive feedback, and greater inputs and outputs lead to more positive student outcomes.

Not only is the study of the self-fulfilling prophecy a good example of cross-fertilization of academic disciplines, e.g., psychology and sociology, it is also a good example of how quantitative and qualitative methods are integrated. Rosenthal and Jacobson, as well as many other researchers, used experimental designs, whereas Rist applied ethnographic methods in his study. Rist's ethnography helps to advance the self-fulfilling prophecy by illuminating the mechanism through which teacher expectations shaped learning opportunities. Both qualitative and quantitative studies have received methodological criticisms, however. Ethnographic studies were often based on observations in a small number of classrooms or schools and thus were criticized for non-transferability of research results to other settings. Early replications of Rosenthal and Jacobson's experimental study also failed to confirm the findings of the Pygmalion effect. While these experimental studies also received methodological criticisms, such criticisms led researchers to investigate *why* these studies failed to observe the teacher expectancy effects. Later studies, using teacher interviews, revealed that the teacher did not believe the false information about students given by the experimenter when he/she already knew about the student. Meta-analyses also supported the hypothesis that the timing of "expectancy induction" was critical for the formation of teacher expectation in experimental studies (Raudenbush 1984).

In the past 35 years, our knowledge about the self-fulfilling prophecy has greatly increased. That said, more work is needed to recognize the positive force as well as the negative implication of the prophecy for education policies.

In the US, schoolteachers today are trained to avoid talking about problem students for fear of creating a self-fulfilling prophecy. Similarly, school counselors' professional ethics emphasize the need to keep important student information confidential. This division of labor between teachers and school counselors leads to organizational secrecy, preventing school personnel from detecting and building a case regarding a troubled student. Outside of the US, we know relatively little about the self-fulfilling prophecy and how it varies across countries. Cross-national comparisons may illuminate how cultural beliefs about student ability influence the ways in which teachers form expectations, organize instruction, and adopt certain pedagogical practices. These factors may, in turn, affect the processes by which schools alter achievement inequalities. The investigation of such questions offers many directions for future fruitful research.

SEE ALSO: Coleman, James; Educational Inequality; Expectations and Aspirations; Hidden Curriculum; Merton, Robert K.; Self-Fulfilling Expectations; Stereotyping and Stereotypes; Tracking

REFERENCES AND SUGGESTED READINGS

Harris, M. J. & Rosenthal, R. (1985) The Mediation of Interpersonal Expectancy Effects: 31 Meta-Analyses. *Psychological Bulletin* 97: 363–86.

Merton, R. K. (1948) The Self-Fulfilling Prophecy. *Antioch Review*: 193–210.

Merton, R. K. (1986) *Social Theory and Social Structure.* Free Press, Glencoe, IL.

Raudenbush, S. (1984) Magnitude of Teacher Expectancy Effects on Pupil IQ as a Function of the Credibility of Expectancy Induction: A Synthesis of Findings from 18 Experiments. *Journal of Educational Psychology* 76: 85–97.

Rist, R. (1970) Student Social Class and Teacher Expectations: The Self-Fulfilling Prophecy in Ghetto Education. *Harvard Educational Review* 40: 411–51.

Rosenthal, R. (1974) *On the Social Psychology of the Self-Fulfilling Prophecy: Further Evidence for Pygmalion Effects and their Mediating Mechanisms.* MSS Modular, New York.

Rosenthal, R. & Jacobson, L. (1968) *Pygmalion in the Classroom.* Holt, Rinehart, & Winston, New York.

Tauber, R. T. (1997) *Self-Fulfilling Prophecy: A Practical Guide to its Use in Education.* Praeger, Westport, CT.

Wineberg, S. S. (1987) The Self-Fulfillment of the Self-Fulfilling Prophecy. *Educational Researcher* 16: 28–44.

semi-domestication

Hiroyuki Torigoe and Yukiko Kada

The notion of semi-domestication originated to refer to a kind of plant that is in between wild plants and domesticated crops and has been extended to refer to a particular mode of interaction between humans and animals. Botanists and archeologists have been very interested in semi-cultivated plants for their potential to reveal origins. Anthropologists, in contrast, have begun to accumulate field data that show the usefulness of such plants to local communities. For example, research in a village in the foothills of the Himalayas has analyzed the use of a particular kind of grass root called *Namitoa* which grows in semi-cultivated areas. Although there are wild roots growing in the same area, these semi-domesticated roots grow larger in size and produce more seed roots. According to the anthropologist, the semi-cultivated roots are "gathered" rather than "harvested," but in contrast to the cultivated roots that are planted in prepared fields, these semi-domesticated roots do not grow as well under human control. It is also well known that in various regions of Asia, numerous semi-cultivated plants are relied upon in times of pending famine.

Thus, in contrast to botanists and archeologists, anthropologists do not consider semi-cultivated plants to be in a "developmental" process from wild to domesticated plants, but instead regard them as having their own specific cultural roles and meanings; they are good as they are (Matsui 1989). Among the positive meanings of semi-cultivated plants is the fact that they require less work than fully domesticated plants. Although human societies cannot survive on semi-cultivated plants alone, they add variety to the diet and are useful in times of scarcity.

These anthropological findings led Japanese environmental sociologists to explore the idea of semi-domestication for clues to developing environmental policy. They have interpreted the phenomenon as evidence of the interaction between nature and humans. In Japan and other regions of Asia with high population densities, people often live in close proximity to mountains, rivers, and the sea. In such areas, attempting to preserve pristine "wilderness areas," untouched by humans, as an ideal of environmental policy is unrealistic. This leads to accepting the fact that extracting numerous resources from forests, rivers, and the sea toward people's basic subsistence is a prerequisite to conserving nature while making environmental policies effective and realistic.

Japanese environmental sociologists identified one of the motivations for utilizing semi-domesticated plants without any substantial changes as nature conservation. Environmental sociologists have focused on two aspects of semi-domesticated plant usage. One is ownership. For example, when someone plants bamboo, the ownership is clear and widely acknowledged in the community; but the bamboo will multiply each year without anyone's care. Under these circumstances, researchers are interested in who has ownership rights to either use or dispose of the bamboo. Another question concerns ownership of lands or spaces where such plants grow. Semi-cultivated plants often grow on riversides, in glades or vacant lots where ownership is ambiguous. Normally, however, there are hidden and shared community rules concerning these areas. By revealing these community rules, which are often closely related to the people's involvement in nature and space, analysis of the ownership of semi-cultivated plants is meaningful for developing environmental policies appropriate to each local community.

Extending from this research, a new field of study is emerging that considers the interactions between animals and humans from the perspective of semi-domestication. Monkeys, wild boars, and deer, for example, live in close proximity to or in the community, and they are certainly influenced by humans; but people do not appear to have any intentions of fully domesticating these animals (and that may be impossible). Humans eat wild boar and deer, and may derive other benefits from monkeys (some types of which are also eaten), but these animals might also inflict damage on crops. Studies that attempt to analyze these "give and take" interactions are being conducted by environmental sociologists and have something in common with the concept of life environmentalism developed in Japanese environmental sociology. This is a different approach to conventional ones that consider such animals simply as pests that can ruin crops as well as the natural environmental approach that attempts to minimize contact with these animals as much as possible in the interests of protecting nature.

SEE ALSO: Ecological View of History; Ethnography; Knowledge; Life Environmentalism; Lifeworld; Nature; Plural Society; Tradition; Values; Yanagita, Kunio

REFERENCES AND SUGGESTED READINGS

Furukawa, A. (2001) Environmental Planning of Nature and Culture. In: Torigoe, H. (Ed.), *Natural Environment and Environmental Culture.* Yuuhikaku, Tokyo (in Japanese).

Matsui, T. (1989) *Semi-Domestication.* Kaimeisha, Tokyo (in Japanese).

Miyauchi, T. (2001) Life Tactics of Residents and Commons. In: Inoue, M. & Miyauchi, T. (Eds.), *Sociology of Commons.* Sinyousha, Tokyo (in Japanese).

Tsuchiya, K. & Yamamoto, N. (2000) Eating the Toxic Potatoes: Utilization of Semi-Domesticated Plants. In: Yamamoto, N. & Inamura, T. (Eds.), *Environmental Monograph of the Himalayas.* Yasaka Shobou, Tokyo (in Japanese).

semiotics

E. Valentine Daniel

From the perspective of one who surveys the ever-shifting and ever-expanding field of modern semiotics/semeiotic, the long shadows of two dominant thinkers span the landscape: Charles Peirce and Ferdinand de Saussure. The history of the identification and use of signs as appropriate to certain culturally specified domains of knowledge and practice is, however, far richer and deeper. Such a history has been traced to divination and medicine in ancient Mesopotamia, extending to philosophy as well as in Greek antiquity, and by the first century BCE to aesthetics and semantics in India (*Nyaya Sutra*). St. Augustine was the first thinker, however, to identify the sign (*signum*), in *De Doctrina Christiana* (ca. 397–426), as a universal that functions in any and all contexts where significance (including information and meaning) of any sort is communicated from one living being to another. That is, he proposed a point of view that enabled us to see things exclusively in terms of their signs' signifying function. By defining the sign, however, as "a thing, which, over and above the impression it makes on the senses, causes something else to come into thought as a consequence," he made sense-perception into a necessary component of the sign. In its application, he chose to narrow the sign's compass even further, to sacramental theology. Both choices served to limit the full analytic power of the sign right through the Latin period and well into the Renaissance.

Augustine's definition excluded ideas from being signs because they were unavailable to sense-perception. This unwarranted limitation troubled several post-Augustinian Latin "semeioticians." Given the awesome power of tradition, even the most independent thinkers tried to accommodate Augustine by proposing several dichotomous sign-types in which at least one half would represent continuity with tradition and only the other half, change. Fonseka, for instance, suggests distinctions such as formal vs. instrumental, conventional (social) vs. natural, internal vs. external, and mind-dependent vs. mind-independent signs. In the end he too is forced by tradition to concede that the first in each pair was not a sign as such, for to do otherwise would have gone against customary usage of the term, traceable not just to Augustine but to the Aristotelian dichotomies of substance and accident, *semeion* and *symbolon*, nature and culture. The Portuguese Dominican philosopher John of Poinsot (1632) was the first to critique and systematize what Augustine had thematized, by removing the sense-perception requirement from the sign's definition, thereby clearing the ground for a truly general semeiotic that included words and ideas in its perspective. The message of Poinsot's magnum opus was drowned in the Cartesian heralding of epistemological and solipsistic conundra that would keep modern philosophy preoccupied for another 300 years and more.

Some 58 years later, at the very end of his purported anti-Cartesian *Essay Concerning Human Understanding* (1690), in which he made his case for empiricism, John Locke part hoped for, part prophesied, and part proposed a new field of inquiry called *semiotic*. In this "doctrine of signs" that he characterized as "aptly enough also, logic," we were invited to "consider the nature of signs, the mind makes use of for the understanding of things, or conveying knowledge to others." His *Essay* bequeathed us two ironies. Locke was totally unaware that an Iberian philosopher-monk had already done his bidding the very year that he, Locke, was born. This was the first irony. Apart from giving it the name *semiotic*, he was also the first, in the non-Latin world, to set the sign free from the tether of sense-perception by which Augustine's definition had bound the sign. "For since the things, the mind contemplates are none of them, besides itself, present to the understanding," he argued, "'tis necessary that something else, as a sign or representation of the thing it considers, should be present to it." These he called *ideas*. Ideas were not directly available to the senses and needed "articulate sounds" to convey them to others, fit to be understood. Ideas and signs of ideas – words – could be "seen as the great instruments of knowledge" in which lay "the seeds of an overthrow" of his own purported anti-Cartesian labor contained in the rest of the *Essay*. This was the second irony.

TWO TRADITIONS?

Locke's proposal lay idle from the seventeenth century until the American logician-philosopher-mathematician Charles Sanders Peirce picked up its charge in his writings from 1866 onward, in which he plumbed its depths and spanned its breadth to extents unimagined by Locke. Nevertheless, following Locke and in keeping with what he considered the "ethics of terminology," Peirce named his effort *semeiotic* (in keeping with its Greek origin, *semeion* for "sign," and emphatically preserving the diphthong "ei" of *semeion* in its pronunciation) and at times *semiotic*. Peirce's writings on *semeiotic* are conspicuously and not so conspicuously distributed among the totality of his life's work, an ever-evolving architectonic philosophical system, which fills almost 100,000 (mostly unpublished) manuscript pages. A shift in philosophical fashions in the years following his death, the disarray in which his papers were found more than a decade later, the decision by the editors of his *Collected Papers* to publish his already published papers rather than select from among the unpublished versions of the same (which Peirce himself had considered better for not having had to be trimmed to suit various editors' tastes), his not having had an academic position or students to disseminate his ideas, and his pithy style of writing had collectively conspired to put his work relatively out of reach of the average scholar and impenetrable to a novice, until quite recently.

Independently of both Peirce and Locke, the Swiss linguist Ferdinand de Saussure had determined to study the "life of signs in social life" and named his "new" science *semiology*. His ideas survived thanks to his students' lecture notes, published posthumously in 1916 as *Cours de linguistic generale*. In contrast to Peirce's writings, *Cours* had caught the attention of several leading linguists and "signophiles" of the twentieth century. As for nomenclature, in addition to *semiology*, *semeiotic*, and *semiotic* there were also available *significs*, *signology*, and *semiotics*. But the struggle for recognition was between *semiology* and *semiotics*, and *semiotics* won, as it were, the popular choice. Apart from their deliberated extension of their inquiries into extra-linguistic sign systems and their choice of label to describe their work, most *semioticians* were *semiologist* by another name and the *Cours* remains their foundational text. Of the rest, *semeiotic* and *semiotic* were to become associated with those whose research followed, more or less, Peircean lines. Nevertheless, there is considerable cross-over in choice of label, and, more rarely, mixing up of theoretical orientations. Many Peirceans use *semiotics* and non-Peirceans *semiotic* (though more as an adjective than a noun) in their writings. *Semeiotic* is never used by Saussurians; and Peirceans who use this form do so in order to mark the difference of their own approach to the sign in contradistinction to the Saussurians.

SAUSSURE AND SEMIOTICS

The rock upon which Saussure chose to build his *semiology* was *langue*. *Langue* is the linguistic system, which is but one component of *langage* (language or the language faculty). To get to and isolate *langue*, one strips away one half of each of two hierarchically ordered pairs that constitute language itself. The first half of language to go is diachrony (i.e., the history of a language) of the synchrony–diachrony dyad. The synchronic dimension of language – the structure of language at any given moment in time – consists of two aspects, *parole* (speech) and *langue*. Of these two, the one to be stripped away as irrelevant to the analysis of structural linguistics is *parole*: the idiosyncratic, contingent, pragmatic functions of language. *Langue* is an analytic construct, an abstraction from language as a means of explaining the regularities and typical patterns of a language that are normally hidden from the consciousness of individual speakers in a community that uses that language; it is not an ontological reality. And it is in *langue* that one locates the dynamo of not only the linguistic system, but also the generator of wider, non-linguistic sign-systems or *semiotics*, the sign. Structuralism, the earliest and the most ambitious extension of semiology into non-linguistic systems of signs, goes even further by exploiting the dichotomy concealed within *langue* itself: paradigm and syntagm (also called the selective and combinatorial axes, respectively.) Lévi-Straussian structuralists go on to disregard the syntagmatic dimension of *langue*, saving the paradigmatic dimension as the basis of structural analysis.

A linguistic sign, as defined by Saussure, is one and the same two-sided phenomenon, a relationship that links an acoustic image and a concept, or a signifier and a signified. The link is not between a thing and its name, but between a concept and a sound pattern. The concept–sound pattern relationship is internal to language, internal to the mind, and is independent of external reality. Thus, the linguistic sign does not "stand for" an external world but construes it: a tree that is signified by the word "tree" is not an actual tree, but the concept "tree." Nor does a signifier "stand for" the signified but rather construes it. The signifier and the signified are "functives" that are co-present or co-occurrent albeit on different strata, the first more abstract than the second. In their respective strata they "exist" in a context of other signifiers and signifieds, respectively. Each is held together with and held apart from the other signifieds and signifiers in their respective strata by similarities and differences, which is what makes them part of a system or structure. Which signifier pairs with which signified is a matter of convention, arbitrary from an empirical point of view. How then is the external world brought into a relationship with the internal structure? The semiologically structured internal relationship of the signifier–signified analogically structures, organizes, and orients sign-users to the flux of percepts they receive from the external world. This is a totally nominalistic view of both language and world.

There are many reasons why the semiological model of the sign – dyadic, non-material, confined to a hermetically sealed system called language – came to assume paradigmatic power over semiotics generally. The foremost reason is structural and its reasoning unfolds more or less in the following manner. Only human beings have culture. Not all the features that constitute culture are, however, uniquely human. But language is uniquely human. What makes human language unique is *langue*. The linguistic sign is the defining element of *langue*. The defining feature of the linguistic sign is its binary structure, in which the elements of the dyad are held together by a relationship that is arbitrary or conventional (as opposed to natural). From this it is hypothesized that even though the uniquely human institution called culture is not identical to language, since its only assuredly human feature is language, the elementary form of culture must be structured along the lines of the elementary form of language, the linguistic or semiological sign.

The popularity of Saussurian *semiology* is made transparent by its inspiration of so many *semioticians* and schools of *semiotics*: Roman Jakobson of the Prague school of linguistics, Yuri Lotman of the Tartu-Moscow school of semiotics and culture, the A. J. Greimas and lexicology, Louis Hjelmslev of the Danish school of glossematics, and Roland Barthes the literary critic, who is best known for teaching us how to read literary and sociocultural texts semiologically. Some scholars see the Saussurian quest for the elementary structure of language as paralleling Durkheim's quest for the elementary form of the religious life. There is no doubt, however, that Lévi-Strauss (who introduced French structuralism into anthropology) self-consciously patterned his quest for the elementary structure of kinship along Saussurian lines that converged with Durkheim's quest for the elementary forms of the religious life. Indeed, the most successful application of the extension of the linguistic sign beyond linguistics was in French structuralism, which made its appearance around 1929, maturing into its most powerful and best-known form in the anthropological writings of Lévi-Strauss in the post-war years. His pioneering application of Saussurian structuralism, read through Jakobson and N. S. Troubetzkoy's phonology, to the study of kinship, mythology, and food had a profound effect on sociocultural anthropology. Structuralism spawned structuralist novelists like Alain Robbe-Grillet. It provided new ways of rereading sociological classics such as the writings of Weber, Simmel, and Marx. Structural Marxism came into being mainly through the writings of Althuser in social theory and Sahlins in anthropology. Structuralism's popularity spread to literary study and criticism and peaked in the late 1960s before it was gradually overshadowed by poststructuralism. The impress of the Saussurian sign, however, persists indelibly in both poststructuralism and postmodernism, not to mention the semiotic/semiotics of Kristeva and the post-Freudian psychoanalysis of Lacan.

Among those who came to Saussure via Lévi-Strauss, the most prominent was the philosopher Merleau-Ponty, who believed that in structuralism he had found the way of resolving the subject–object impasse. The fact that even Saussure's critics continue to base their own research on essentially Saussurian epistemology and assumptions is a further testimony to the compacted power of Saussure's general theory of (even if mostly linguistic) signs. The Russian Marxist critic V. N. Volishinov, and those like Derrida, Eco or Jacobson, who consider Peirce to have had a deeper and keener understanding of *semiosy* than Saussure, in the final analysis, despite their disclaimers, also remain Saussurians.

PEIRCE AND SEMEIOTIC

Robert Marty found 76 definitions of the sign in Peirce's published and unpublished writings; Alfred Lang found 12 more or its equivalents. Peirce defined and adjusted the definition of the sign to a range of contexts, a short list of which includes mathematics, logic, philosophy, pendulum experiments, chemistry, psychology, language, history, realism–nominalism debates, scholasticism, metaphysics, theories of mind, and discussions of truth. He bent his definitions for the benefit of his interlocutors and correspondents' comprehension. In his correspondences he discussed signs with his lifelong friend William James, with the like-minded correspondent and exponent of *significs* Lady Welby, and with uncomprehending editors who wanted him to pitch his definitions to a general readership. He often obliged them with what he called "sops to Cerebrus," describing those Cartesians who were cognitively incapacitated by their mind-body dualism. For Peirce had a pan-semeiotic view of the sign. The sign easily transgressed such dichotomies as mind-body, nature-culture, human-animal, and matter-spirit. The cosmos, for him, was perfused with signs. He considered thought as semeiotically active signs. He held that thought-signs existed in crystals as much as they did in the brain; he considered the view of the mind being confined to the brain as far too nominalistic.

Many are the differences between Saussure and Peirce's concepts of the sign. One could begin with the fact that Saussure's is a dyadic sign, which originates in linguistics. The semeiosic sign is based on logic, and logic as semeiotic is a normative or formal science, in contrast to empirical sciences such as linguistics that Peirce classified as special sciences. As a formal science, semeiotic is concerned with the necessary conditions for what makes something a sign as such, with what bases one may determine its truth, and with the conditions that are required for the communication and growth of signs.

From the very start, Peirce determined that the sign was irreducibly triadic. The proof for the sign's triadicity he derived from logic, mathematics, and phenomenology. With a certain amount of familiarity with a number of his scattered definitions of the *semeiosic* sign one could gradually build up one's understanding of it, by additions and refinements, until one comes nearer to grasping the sign in all its complexity that Peirce intended for us to grasp. After appreciating the fact that the sign is triadic, the first step would be to know that the first correlate of the triad is the *sign* (at times called the *representamen*), the second correlate is the *object*, and the third the *interpretant.* So the *semeiosic Sign* (upper case) is constituted by an irreducible triadic correlation in which a *sign* (lower case) stands for an *object* to an *interpretant.* The *sign* mediates the object and interpretant by representing the object to the interpretant; the object mediates the sign and the interpretant by grounding the sign; the interpretant mediates the sign and object by interpreting or translating the sign. Remove any one of the three correlates and the *Sign* as such will not be an actual *Sign*, but a mere potential sign.

It should be noted, however, that the *sign* represents the *object* to the *interpretant* only in "some respect or capacity" – not in every respect and capacity. The sign is not arbitrary and open. Peirce speaks of *signs* themselves having or not having the "fitness to represent" a given object. Such a fitness to represent a given object may be amply present, sparsely present, or not present at all in a sign, making it respectively quite appropriate, less appropriate, or inappropriate to represent the object in question. In other words, signs have built-in limits to what they can and cannot represent or are likely or not likely to represent. What is being introduced here is the notion of a certain measure of motivation or tendency constitutive of the sign to represent something. Saussure denies such motivation, with a very few exceptions, to signs.

As for the *object*, Peirce tells us that it may be a:

> single known existing thing or a thing believed formerly to have existed or expected to exist, or a collection of such things, or a known quality or relation or fact, which single object may be a collection, or a whole of parts, of it may have some other mode of being, such as an act permitted whose being does not prevent its negation from being equally permitted, or something of a general nature desired, required, or invariably found under certain general circumstances.

This is a wide understanding of an object indeed. The *semeiotic object* is of two types: *immediate* and *dynamic*. The *immediate object* is the *object* represented to us in the *sign* itself. The sentence "It is snowing downtown" will bring before my mind the idea that the word "snowing" represents. That idea or image is an *immediate object*. When one opens the window and sees cars coming from downtown with snow on them, then one sees the dynamic counterpart of the immediate object. The dynamic object is not necessarily a "real" or existing object. A "possible" one daydreams about can be the dynamic object that exerts an inner force in you that makes you seek for the possible. The same holds true for an idea. Insofar as it draws one towards it, it is *dynamic*. So an existent like a falling bookcase can be the *dynamic* counterpart of the warning that your friend shouts out ("Watch out! The bookcase!"), which would be the *immediate object*.

The *interpretant* is not the same as an *interpreter*, though an interpreter may be a species of interpretant. Peirce defines the *interpretant* as the "proper significate effect" of the sign on a third. At one point Peirce says that "a sign is not a sign unless it is translated into another sign in which it is more fully developed." In this case the translation or the meaning is the interpretant; it is the sign's "significate effect."

What is the motivating force of a sign based on? It is what Peirce calls the *ground*. The *ground* is the basis on which the sign "picks up" an object to represent. There are three common *grounds*. First, a *sign* may represent an *object* by virtue of the property or quality it shares with the object, or its similarity up to identity with the object. Such a *sign* is called an *icon*, provided there is an *interpretant* to interpret or be significantly affected by the representation of the object as such. When an icon is identical to an object, information is concealed rather than conveyed. Such is the case in protective coloration in nature where, for example, the color of a chameleon that is identical to that of its background is iconic; and so is the impeccable con-artist. And as long as there is no interpretant to "read" the icon, it remains a potential sign. Second, when a *sign* represents an *object* on the grounds of its regular contiguity with the *object*, the sign is an *index* – again, assuming the existence of an *interpretant*. Thus, the gathering darkness over the landscape indexes the setting of the sun to "something or somebody in some respect or capacity." Thus, to both human and beast, it would indicate the end of the day and the beginning of night. To an informed human being (a human being who is predisposed to interpret it one way rather than another) it could also signify the beginning of a solar eclipse, an omen, a god, an ancestor's presence. Whereas to most animals – inferring from their fixed response – it would appear that it indicates, as always, the day's end. Third, when a sign and object are related to each other by convention, the sign is a symbol – once more the existence of an interpretant is assumed. The cultural interpretation of an eclipse is such a symbol and so are most words. But some words, such as demonstratives (that! there! they! etc.), also known as *deictics* (from the Greek: to point), serve as indexes. Deictic indexes poke holes, as it were, through the symbolic cocoon or the hermetically sealed view of Language or linguistic signs as a world unto itself, attributed to Saussure, and touch the external, extralingual world or reality. For a "there!" to make sense, that has to be a there there. There are also iconic symbols such as metaphors and symbolic icons such as onomatopoeia. In fact, Peirce cautions us that, neither in nature nor in culture are there pure symbols, pure indexes, or pure icons. Every sign is a blend of all three, with one or more type being accentuated to the *interpretant*.

Despite his numerous attempts to fix the sign in a definition, Peirce's fundamental conception of semeiotic was that of "signing" activity or *semiosy* rather than the sign per se.. This is evident in the following definition: "The *sign* is anything which determines something else (its *interpretant*) to refer to an object to which itself refers (its *object*) in the same way, the interpretant becoming a *sign* in turn, and so on *ad infinitum*." The sign so defined brings out the open and dynamic nature of sign activity or semiosy. Semiosy is the very life of the sign. When semiosy ceases, the sign either dies or goes into hibernation until an interpretant sign predisposed to receiving its representation of the object arrives. Thus, a potsherd from an antique goblet would "hibernate" until a knowledgeable archeologist finds it and is able to represent it as a sign of an antique goblet to his student. She would, as the next interpretant sign along the chain of revivified semeiosis who is fit to receive (by training) the representation, translate and communicate the object to yet another interpretant sign (her own students, say) as her professor's representation of the potsherd as representing the original goblet, which will then be represented to ... *ad infinitum*.

The very structure of the semeiotic sign establishes it as fundamentally dialogic. If we were to anthropomorphize the three correlates of the Sign-triad, *sign*, *object*, and *interpretant*, we could imagine a Mr. (S)ign's representation of Mrs. (O)bject to Mr. (I)interpretant as being "determined by" – that is, constrained or delimited by – Mrs. (O)bject. And Mr. S "determines" Mr. (I) to represent Mrs. (O) "in the same way as" and "stand in the same relation to" Mrs. (O) as he, (Mr. (S)), himself had represented and stood in relation to Mrs. (O).

First, it is very unlikely that the Mrs. (O) that Mr. (S) represented to Mr. (I) is the Mrs. (O) as such, but rather, Mr. (S)'s Mrs. (O). In other words, no S(ign) is a *tabula rasa* upon which an O(bject) can impress or reproduce itself perfectly. Every S(ign) contains its own prior semeiotic genealogy and its attendant prejudices, and therefore the O(bject) represented will be the (S)ign's O(bject). For semeiosis to continue, Mr. (I) has a dual role to play: (1) he receives Mr. (S)'s Mrs. (O) in his role as Mr. I and (2) he represents what he has received, and in receiving inevitably modified, to Mr. I^a in his new role as Mr. S^a. It is equally unlikely that the Mrs. (O) whom Mr. (I) in his role as S^a will represent in his turn to another Interpretant, Mr. I^a, will be identical either to the Mrs. (O) prior to Mr. (S)'s representation of her or to the Mrs. (O) as represented to him by Mr. (S). That is, every "interpretant is an equivalent (not identical) or a more developed sign of the object" than the preceding sign. In other words, a subsequent interpretant-sign need not necessarily be less revealing of the "original" object than an earlier sign of the same object. Rather, by having a greater interpretive fitness, and a more conducive interpretive context, be a more developed interpretant sign, providing us with greater knowledge of the said object than the earlier representation.

At the most abstract level there are three types of *interpretants*: the *immediate*, the *dynamic*, and the *final*. Peirce describes the *immediate interpretant* as "the immediate pertinent possible effect in its unanalyzed primitive entirety." A *dynamic interpretant* is the actual manifestation of a significant effect. And a *final interpretant* is the teleological growth of a sign that ends in an interrelated system of signs. The three *interpretants* that correspond in human experience to these abstract interpretants are the *emotional*, the *energetic*, and the *logical interpretants*. The feeling of *deja vous* would be an example of an *emotional interpretant*; the bodily reaction of one at whom the command "halt!" is barked out by a soldier after the declaration of a curfew would be an example of an *energetic interpretant*; and the habitualized mode of conditional reasoning such as "if the light turns red I will not cross the road" would be a *logical interpretant*. The *dynamic interpretant* does not possess meaning, it is a brute reaction; neither does an *emotional interpretant* that remains at the level of a mere feeling, before being put into words. A logical interpretant is meaningful. The path a river takes is a *final interpretant*: a habit carved into the earth. There are many other triadic sets of sign types and other triadic phenomena that one is likely to encounter in Peirce's writings. They are generated by the logic of Peirce's phenomenological categories of Firstness, Secondness, and Thirdness. In Peirce's semeiotic there are no impermeable or unmovable boundaries between internal and external, cultural and natural, mind and body, organic and inorganic that signs cannot cross and connect. Ecology is as amenable to semeiotic analysis as economics, music, or literature would be.

In semiology and semiotics there linger questions that have been at best inadequately answered and at worst not answered at all. How does the sound-pattern/concept relationship take form in the mind of an individual or in the understanding of a speech community in the first place? How is the sign in one mind communicated in the first instance to another in the absence of the a priori of a shared language? Is incommensurability the only answer? How does the hermetically sealed internal linguistic sign precisely engage with the non-linguistic external world and make such an engagement warrantable and workable? Can we assign a truth-value to any such engagement or is it all relative? How does a sign that is objectified in such an ideational abstraction have a bearing on concrete social intercourse (Voloshinov)? How does a synchronic structure theoretically accommodate both habit and change? (This question was most effectively posed by Bourdieu.) And finally, how does one account for the comparatively rapid and successful dissemination of semiology/semiotics in analyses of other domains of sociocultural life and how did it come to figure so much more prominently in so many disciplines than has semeiotic?

Other than the early discovery of Saussure's thoughts, the compactness and brilliant simplicity of his theory, the sparseness of his writings, the modesty of his aims, and the *Cours*'s accessibility have facilitated its dispersal. Its inherent Cartesianism is hidebound with the Cartesian categories that are ubiquitous in the modern West and make his ideas easily assimilable. This is also why even self-professed anti-Cartesian warriors that one encounters in deconstruction, postmodernism, and poststructuralism are shot through with Cartesian thinking. Justifiably or not, both admirers and detractors of Saussurian semiology and semiotics are convinced that they understand Saussure well enough and therefore are ready and able to raise jugular-snipping questions.

Most questions that are justified in semiotics are either anticipated and answered or become irrelevant in semeiotic. Peirce's semeiotic is non-dualist, incorrigibly diachronic, and inherently trans-disciplinary. The semiological sign which is constrained only by convention can by convention be made free and available for redeployment in hemeneutic play. This is not so with the semeiotic sign, whose accountability to place, time, and purpose is far more exacting. For those wishing to understand Peirce, his voluminous writings and the state of disarray that his papers are in, however, create forbidding hurdles to scale. His project was anything but modest, and any topic that might engage the reader is spread out widely over time and contexts. His ideas grew and changed, and not always for the better. He aimed to connect the three large areas of his philosophy – realism, semeiotic, and pragmatism – with debatable success. This forces anyone who wishes to explore only one area into exploring all of them, which is not a task for the hasty or the weak-willed. For these and similar reasons, Peirce scholars find themselves raising questions in one place only to find them already anticipated and answered elsewhere in his writings. Questions are posed but not from a place of confidence of having full control over his ideas; they are raised only for the sake of working through his texts for the answers, and sooner or later they do find them. Perusers of semeiotic tend to conclude prematurely that semiotics and semeiotic cover the same area of inquiry and then revert to the friendlier semiotics. Some make selective use of Peirce's ideas, as do Derrida and Deleuze, or stop short of accepting his semeiotic along with his realism, as does Eco, or are discouraged by the apparent anachronistic language and style of the author. Attempts to borrow from semeiotic into semiotic piecemeal either do not work or dangle like a graft that does not take. The conflation of semiotics and semeiotic is not helpful. As for whether the two approaches to the sign can be combined at all, the decision is split. French philosopher Gerard Deledalle denies such a possibility and discourages the search for one; but Joseph Liszka, an American philosopher, says that it is possible, arguing that Saussure's concept of value is the equivalent of Peirce's *logical interpretant*, thereby completing the incomplete *signifier–signified* dyad. But then, Peirce's sign and object are not the same at any level as the signifier and the signified. Despite these difficulties, much of Peirce's semeiotic has begun to make inroads into a range of fields and has even managed to introduce both complexity as well as simplifications into semiotics as well.

Peircean ideas entered sociology indirectly through Dewey, who was Peirce's student for a brief while, during which time he was introduced to Peircean pragmatism and logic, and would later modify these to suit his theoretical needs. The symbolic interactionism of George Herbert Mead had many semeiotic elements in it. C. Wright Mills was Mead's student and wrote in his dissertation a chapter each on James, Peirce, and Dewey. Charles Morris, another of Mead's students, and also part of the Chicago School's logical positivists, was the one who brought Peirce to center-stage in his debate with

Dewey about the status of the "interpretant." Morris, it is widely believed, misrepresented Peirce's realist semeiotic by transforming it into a behaviorist theory of signs. More recently, Habermas and Apel have drawn heavily from Peirce for their own theories of pragmatism and communication. But, on the whole, relative to its sister discipline anthropology, sociology has been untouched by either semiotics or semeiotic, even though the writings of Bourdieu seem to have independently discovered some of Peirce's seminal ideas, such as habitus.

SEE ALSO: Barthes, Roland; Cultural Studies; Culture; Derrida, Jacques; Durkheim, Émile; Habitus/Field; James, William; Language; *Langue* and *Parole*; Logocentrism; Mead, George Herbert; Mills, C. Wright; Pragmatism; Saussure, Ferdinand de; Sign; Structuralism

REFERENCES AND SUGGESTED READINGS

Deeley, J. (1982) *Introducing Semiotic: Its History and Doctrine*. Indiana University Press, Bloomington.

Deledalle, G. (1964) *Charles Peirce's Philosophy of Signs: Essays in Comparative Semiotics*. Indiana University Press, Bloomington.

Hodge, R. & Kress, G. (1988) *Social Semiotics*. Cornell University Press, Ithaca, NY.

Lévi-Strauss, C. (1968) *The Savage Mind*. University of Chicago Press, Chicago.

Liszka, J. J. (1996) *A General Introduction to the Semeiotic of Charles Sanders Peirce*. Indiana University Press, Bloomington.

Locke, J. (1996 [1690]) *An Essay Concerning Human Understanding*. Ed. K. P. Winkler. Hacket Publishing, Indianapolis.

Manetti, G. (1993) *Theories of the Sign in Classical Antiquity*. Trans. C. Richardson. Indiana University Press, Bloomington.

Peirce, C. S. (1931–5) *Collected Papers*, Vols. 1–6. Ed. C. Hartshorne & P. Weiss. Harvard University Press, Cambridge, MA.

Peirce, C. S. (1958) *Collected Papers*, Vols. 7–8. Ed. A. Burks. Harvard University Press, Cambridge, MA.

Peirce, C. S. (1980–96) *The Writings of Charles S. Peirce: A Chronological Edition*, Vols. 1–5. Indiana University Press, Bloomington.

Saussure, F. de. (1966) *Course in General Linguistics*. Trans. W. Baskin. McGraw Hill, New York.

Thibault, P. J. (1997) *Re-Reading Saussure: The Dynamics of Signs in Social Life*. Routledge, London.

separatism

Rutledge M. Dennis

The concept of separatism refers to the idea that racial, ethnic, cultural, religious, political, and linguistic differences, when accompanied by a legacy of oppression, exclusion, persecution, and discrimination, are justifications for groups to terminate their political and legal ties to other groups. Generally, the ultimate aim of the termination is the establishment or reestablishment of control over a specific territory in order to establish or reestablish sovereign control. The separatist claim is accompanied by intense feelings of rage, anger, hurt, and humiliation which often fuel the flames of revolts and revolutions. Above all, the claims of separatists are premised on a desire to erect an impenetrable social distance and barrier between themselves and the people, state, or territory against which they have grievances. We may distinguish between two general types of separatism: external separatism and internal separatism.

External separatism is rooted in the historical expansionism of nation-states. As nation-states expand and become imperial powers, they annex large areas which include diverse people, religions, and cultures. This process is seen in a review of ancient empires (Roman, Holy Roman), and the more recent empires (Ottoman, Russian, Austrian, Spanish, Portuguese, French, and British) from which contemporary nation-states emerged in Europe, Asia, Africa, and the Middle East.

Empires are created when strong political, economic, and military powers wage war, and/or threaten, surrounding or distant political units. The resulting conquest often ends in the annexation of defeated nations, states, and societies, which then extends the political and military boundaries of the conquering power. This annexation process will include, against their will, numerous culturally, ethnically, and racially diverse groups. The imperial or colonial power is an external, distant, and occupying force because the gravitation of power lies not in the land or people occupied, but in the "mother country" or the political and economic center of the imperial power. The external separatist impulse, therefore, is the conquered people's quest to reconnect or to sustain a loyalty to the myths and symbols of their past, real or imagined, and to validate a claim for their pre-conquest independence. Even if they lacked complete independence prior to their colonial conquest, they now wish to assert such an independence. This desire for freedom and independence is even more overwhelming if a large number of the conquered people are old enough to have had the legacy of their way of life embedded in their social consciousness. For these reasons, the separatist desire is one of escaping foreign and external domination and to rebuff rule by the "other." In external separatism the separatist is engaged in a battle to separate and disconnect the interlocking external web of control, within which the imperial and colonial powers have engulfed a distant population. Though time (the 1920s as opposed to the 1950s and 1960s) and situational variables (world wars and regional wars) would be intervening factors in any discussion of the various empires and colonial countries mentioned earlier, the establishment of independent nations which greatly accelerated from the 1960s to the present era speaks volumes for the reasons this could not have been true in the period before 1960: prior to the 1960s many currently independent nations were integrated, partially or totally, within existing empires and colonial powers.

Internal separatism is the separatist impulse within groups occupying the same land mass, though they may occupy a special and recognizable region of the nation-state or society where their relationship to the land is deeply rooted in their legends, myths, and history. In internal separatism, relations between the divergent groups traditionally alternate between harmony and conflict. The aspirations leading to a claim for internal separatism stem from the fact that the groups have different languages and cultural or religious backgrounds. More crucial to the separatist impulse, however, is the feeling, among the less dominant or smaller group, that it is the object of domination, discrimination, suppression, oppression, and persecution. Unlike the countries or areas of the world which successfully waged a war or negotiated their freedom, internal separatists are often less successful and many political entities are currently engaged in a struggle to assert their freedom from a federation or nation-state of which they are currently a part. There is often an ebb and flow in this internal separatist conflict and it may involve ultimately a case for total or partial separation from an existing nation-state. Among this group one finds Kashmir, the Kurdish section of Iraq, Tibet, the Basque provinces, Kosovo in the greatly reduced Yugoslavia, the southern part of Sudan, Spanish Sahara, and the off-and-on position of Québec. We might also mention, though they differ from the others just mentioned, Wales and Scotland in Great Britain, in which there are periodic cries for independence, though very few will view this as a possibility. Finally, there are provinces and groups which opted for total or complete separation from countries within which they were the smaller and less dominant groups. In this category one finds Slovenia, Croatia, Bosnia Herzegovina, Serbia, and Macedonia, which separated from Yugoslavia. Estonia, Latvia, Lithuania, and Moldavia separated from the Soviet Union. There are also the countries which chose to become separate republics after the collapse of the Soviet Union. Then there was the peaceful separation of the Czechs and the Slovaks from Czechoslovakia, Eritrea's peaceful separation from Ethiopia, then the two countries' almost three-year war to adjust their border boundaries, and the more recent independence of East Timor from Indonesia after a brief war.

In the United States the main separatist impulse was generated over the issue of slavery: the Southern desire to maintain and even extend slavery, and the Northern desire to limit and abolish the practice. Among African Americans the major separatist desire was created and sustained by Marcus Garvey from 1916 to the 1920s. Garvey's separatism entailed a version of Black Nationalism in which black Americans would emigrate to Africa. Though Garvey created a government-in-exile, with duly appointed cabinet members, a highly developed infrastructure, and purchased five ships to aid in the emigration, in the end he failed, and his movement died long before he did in England. Later, in the 1920s and 1930s, communists and socialists asserted that blacks in the South constituted a "nation within a nation" as an oppressed people. However, given the class position advocated by both groups, and given the fact that blacks themselves did not rally behind that cause, separatism, which many blacks would have viewed as another form of segregation, was not considered a viable solution. In the 1950s and 1960s, the Nation of Islam sought to resurrect Garveyism, but instead of emigration their separatism called for the creation of a black nation within the seven Southern states with large black populations. There was no support among the black population for such a venture, especially as the massive Civil Rights Movement was slowly evolving at the time.

The separatist impulse presents an enormous challenge to nation-states, especially democratic nation-states, with diverse racial, ethnic, religious, and linguistic populations. The greatest challenge is that of creating the social and cultural institutions and organizations which will provide opportunities for groups to participate in the body politic and freely engage in cross-racial, ethnic, cultural, and religious relationships in neighborhoods and communities, at work, in religious institutions, and in educational institutions. A test for democratic nations entails their ability to mix and blend and to incorporate divergent people and cultures. If this is possible, democratic and free societies would move toward constructing a new core culture. Lacking this, the separatist impulse will continue to loom large over the twenty-first century just as it did over the twentieth.

SEE ALSO: Accommodation; Colonialism (Neocolonialism); Ethnic Cleansing; Indigenous Movements; Melting Pot; Nation-State; Nationalism; Plural Society; Racial Hierarchy

REFERENCES AND SUGGESTED READINGS

Bell, W. & Freeman, W. (1974) *Ethnicity and Nation-Building*. Sage, Beverly Hills.

Cruse, H. (1968) *Rebellion or Revolution*. Morrow, New York.

Dennis, R. M. (1994) *Race and Ethnic Relations*, Vol. 7. JAI Press, Greenwich, CT.

Esman, M. (1994) *Ethnic Politics*. Cornell University Press, Ithaca.

Stone, J. & Dennis, R. M. (Eds.) (2003) *Race and Ethnicity: Comparative and Theoretical Approaches*. Blackwell, Malden, MA.

sex-based wage gap and comparable worth

Juanita M. Firestone

An extensive body of empirical literature has addressed the issue of sex-based wage differentials in the United States. The fact that this gap persists over time means that a large body of literature exists on the topic. Most recent research suggests that while the gap may vary based on a variety of factors including type of job, years of experience, economic sector, etc., sex-based wage differences remain. Comparable worth is a process that is supposed to address the sex-based wage gap by objectively comparing dissimilar jobs in order to determine relative worth to the objectives of a particular organization. The process involves a complex system of fine-tuning an entire compensation structure. The information required to engage in comparable worth is considerable: jobs must be ranked according to the worth to the employer. This implies measuring the value of each job and calculating degrees of difference between the values of different jobs. Thus, if two jobs require equivalent levels of skill, education, responsibility, etc., the two should also have equivalent salaries.

Within this research tradition much attention has been paid to the impact of the sex composition of an occupation on the wages of men and women. Findings consistently report that lower hourly wages are associated with those occupations having a larger proportion of women. Many researchers contend that this difference in wages is based on discrimination rather than the actual contribution of the jobs to the goals and objectives of the organization. Comparable worth has been discussed as one means of addressing this problem, and narrowing, if not eliminating, wage disparity based on sex.

COMPARABLE WORTH AS A SOLUTION TO THE SEX-BASED WAGE GAP

The phenomenon of sex-based wage differentials is a fundamental and persistent social problem in the US and in countries around the world. Common approaches to studying the problem are rooted in both sociological and economic research. Sociological explanations include socialization processes that dichotomize men's and women's roles and reward men for instrumental activities focused on accruing wealth, power, and status, and reward women for relational activities focused on providing love and care within family contexts. Economic explanations include human capital differences, rational choice, and organizational or bureaucratic theories of labor pattern formation. These efforts are further distinguished by their specialized focus on any of the following areas: the effects of job market competition, the systematic segregation of minorities and women into low-paying jobs, the devaluation of female dominated professions, and within-occupation wage discrimination. Depending on the focus of the explanation, the recommendations to solve the problem also differ widely. One such recommendation, which was more popular in the past, was a focus on comparable worth.

REASONS FOR THE SEX-BASED WAGE GAP

Many economists argue that differences in wages are due to the fact that individuals may come to their job with greatly different talents/ ability levels (human capital). These individuals typically oppose comparable worth because they contend that in a free labor market, fair wages will follow efficiency. Thus, differences in wages are attributed to the differences in human capital, which impact the efficiency with which an individual contributes to the organization's goals and objectives. Any differences in human capital obtained by men and women are then attributed to their individual choices, which are presumed to be free from constraints.

In any case, focusing exclusively on the economic analysis of the sex-based wage gap disregards the historical and social context that could produce differences in choices by men and women. It seems clear that women's primary responsibility for housework and childcare affects the types of jobs many women prefer, since flexibility in terms of hours and turnover (entry/exit/re-entry opportunities) can help women combine job and family responsibilities. Most agree that those occupations that are female-typed are more flexible in terms of hours and turnover. What is unclear is whether the flexibility associated with female-typed jobs emerges because employers prefer to hire women in these jobs, or whether these jobs become female-typed because of sex stereotyping. For example, women (and men) could be "guided" into certain jobs by social expectations about what is appropriate work. The processes used to guide women into female-typed jobs might include implicit signals that women don't belong in men's jobs or explicit harassment or intimidation. In any event, as individuals we may have choices, but those choices do not occur in a vacuum, but occur within the complex social context in which we live.

CURRENT STATE OF RESEARCH

Among research focusing on wage differentials between men and women, most suggest that occupations with a larger proportion of women have lower hourly wages than those with a larger proportion of men. For example, studies that use data from the US Census-detailed occupational categories as units of analysis have found that controlling for occupational characteristics (work demands, education level, supervisory capacity, etc.), occupations with a larger percentage of females have lower average hourly earnings. In other words, even with extensive controls for the amount of human capital an individual brings to the job included in the model, both men and women earn less if they work in a female-dominated occupation.

Firm or organization specific studies also confirm that even after controlling for unique job skills, female jobs pay less. A few studies have documented that as the proportion of women increases over time in an occupation, the wages for men and women decrease, and that as the proportion of men increases, the wages for men and women increase. Results of this type of research have been unable to ascertain whether the change in the sex composition of the occupation impacted wages, or whether a change in wages altered the sex composition. Regardless, the data support the claims that (1) on average, women earn less than men, (2) men and women are segregated into different occupations, and (3) female-typed occupations (sometimes referred to as pink-collar jobs) earn lower wages.

On the one hand, there is support for the idea that men and women still have different types/levels of human capital. For example, men are more likely to have engineering and science degrees, and women are more likely to have degrees in elementary education and social work. On the other hand, evidence suggests that human capital and/or individual preferences cannot account for occupational segregation and the sex-based wage gap. In fact, at the individual level we are likely to find enormous amounts of overlap in the abilities and preferences of men and women. It is also clear that the majority of female-typed occupations reinforce stereotypical female traits such as nurturance and cooperation, suggesting that socialization processes impact occupational choices.

ARGUMENTS FOR AND AGAINST COMPARABLE WORTH

Opponents of comparable worth argue that implementing policies which focus on equalizing women's wages would be engaging in reverse discrimination against men. They further contend that it is an environment free from comparable worth that would allow women and men to choose jobs based on extrinsic factors such as pay and promotion and intrinsic factors such as challenge, variety, and compatibility with co-workers. However, if women's wages were raised to a level where there would be no evidence of discrimination then the process would not discriminate against men.

In addition, opponents worry about the negative impact of holding over-compensated wages (which are typically male dominated) frozen until pay equity adjustments and other increases (cost of living, etc.) create sex equity in wages. The argument is that comparable worth can be accomplished in theory, but is unlikely to work in practical applications. Proponents argue that comparable worth provides fairness in the job market by removing any residual discrimination, and that both men and women will benefit because neither men nor women would be guided into choosing jobs based on social stereotypes about what is acceptable. Finally, individuals would earn wages commensurate with the effort and value of their work, rather than the proportion of men and women who hold the job or the flexibility associated with a specific job.

CONCLUSION

The supply of labor is more than an economic process – it is also the result of sex-based socialization. It seems unlikely that a vibrant and strong economy can exist if the labor market continues to undermine the productive contribution that women are capable of making. The issue is how to overcome the unfair and degrading practices of occupational segregation in which female-typed jobs earn less primarily because the workers are women. Comparable worth is only one of several policies, which have been discussed as means to this goal. Since wage equity between men and women has not yet been attained, perhaps researchers should reinvestigate old ideas with new eyes and updated tools.

SEE ALSO: Gender Bias; Gendered Enterprise; Inequality/Stratification, Gender; Occupational Segregation; Stratification, Gender and; Stratification and Inequality, Theories of

REFERENCES AND SUGGESTED READINGS

Acker, J. (1989) *Doing Comparable Worth: Gender, Class and Pay Equity.* Temple University Press, Philadelphia.

Anker, R. (1997) Theories of Occupational Segregation by Sex: An Overview. *International Labour Review* 136(3): 315–39.

Becker, G. (1985) Human Capital, Effort and the Sexual Division of Labor. *Journal of Labor Economics* 533(1): S32–S58.

England, P. (1992) *Comparable Worth: Theories and Evidence.* Aldine de Gruyter, Hawthorne, NY.

Pincus, L. and Shaw, B. (1998) Comparable Worth: An Economic and Ethical Analysis. *Journal of Business Ethics* 17(5): 455–70.

sex and crime

Ruth Triplett

Sex is one of the strongest correlates of crime. Researchers using a variety of ways of measuring crime find that females are less likely to be involved in crime than males. Beyond the amount of crime, there is evidence that though there is some similarity in the types of crimes males and females commit, sex is related to the nature of offending as well. Despite the strength of the relationship of sex to crime, criminologists have historically ignored it, with a result that criminology's ability to explain this relationship is limited.

SEX AND THE EXTENT OF CRIME

Females are less likely to be involved in crime than males. Looking at data from the Uniform Crime Reports, clear evidence of this difference is readily seen. In 2000, for example, only 20 percent of all those arrested in the US were female. The rate of arrests for all crimes in 2000 was 9,752 out of 100,000 for males and 2,366 out of 100,000 for females.

The greater involvement in crime by males is consistent across time. Arrest data demonstrate that females offend at a rate across time that is consistently lower than that of males. This can be seen by a comparison of the percent of those arrested and the arrest rate for 2000 given above to that for 1965. The UCRs shows that in 1965, females accounted for 10 percent of all arrests and offended at a rate of 942 per 100,000. This is in comparison to males who, in 1965, accounted for 90 percent of all arrests and offended at a rate of 8,612 per 100,000.

Despite the consistent difference over time by sex, there is evidence that, in recent years, the involvement of females in crime is on the increase. In a careful analysis of arrest data from 1965 to 2000, Steffensmeier and Schwartz (2004) report that females moved from accounting for 10 percent of total arrests to 20 percent. At first glance these statistics might indicate the rise of a new "breed" of female offenders, but Steffensmeier and Schwartz's analysis reveals that this is not the truth. First, much of the increase in arrests for females overall was in minor property crimes, in particular larceny theft and fraud. Second, there are a number of crimes for which the female percent of arrests went down. For example, females accounted for 17 percent of all arrests for homicide in 1965 and 11 percent in 2000. Third, there has been a rise in the share of arrests for some violent crimes for females. As Steffensmeier and Schwartz point out, the percent of arrests for aggravated assault and misdemeanor assault for females has risen. Between 1965 and 2000 the percent of female arrests for aggravated assault rose from 13 to 18 percent and for misdemeanor assault the percent rose from 9 to 20. The increase in some types of violent crime for females has raised the alarm among some. However, there is evidence that much of the increase in arrests for females for some violent crimes is caused more by a change in societal tolerance for these crimes than a real change in the behavior of females.

SEX AND THE NATURE OF CRIME

The relationship of sex to crime is found not only in the extent of offending but also in the nature of offending. Arrest data from the UCRs shows the difference is greatest in the violent and serious property crimes. For example, in 2000, females comprised only 11 percent of all those arrested in the US for homicide and 18 percent of those arrested for felony assault, while they accounted for 10 percent of all robbery arrests and 13 percent of all arrests for burglary. Females come closer to males in percent of arrests for minor property crimes, however. In 2000, females accounted for 33 percent of all larceny theft arrests and 48 percent of all arrests for embezzlement. The only crime for which females accounted for a greater percentage of arrests than males in 2000 was prostitution.

The difference in the nature of offending by sex is seen best in the difference between arrests for youths. Evidence suggests that the types of crime in which girls are involved are quite different from those of boys. Many of these differences parallel those between males and females overall: girls, like females overall, are much less likely to be involved in violent crimes. Arguably, the most significant feature of female involvement in juvenile crime, however, comes in the arrest rates for status offenses.

Status offenses are behaviors which are illegal for youths, but not for adults. They include such behaviors as running away from home, skipping school, violating curfews, the use of alcohol or tobacco, and incorrigibility. Since the development of the juvenile court, status offenses have been an important part of girls' offending. Further, if we compare the nature of the offenses of female delinquents with those of males, it is clear that girls are considerably more likely to be arrested for status offenses. In 2000, for example, 21 percent of the arrests of females were for status offenses, while only 10 percent of the arrests of boys were in those categories. Girls comprised more than half of the arrests for running away from home (58 percent) – one of only two offenses recorded by the FBI for which females are more than half of the arrests (the other being prostitution).

Running away from home was, in fact, the third most likely offense for which girls were taken into custody in 2000 (larceny was the most common and "other offenses" were second). The top three offense categories for boys were "other offenses," larceny, and drug abuse violations – running away ranks tenth in the arrest categories of boys in 2000. This difference in arrest rates for status offenses is striking because self-report data suggests that boys and girls commit these offenses at similar rates. This strongly suggests that girls are more likely than boys to be arrested for behavior such as running away from home and incorrigibility.

There is also evidence that when they are arrested for status offenses, girls are likely to be dealt with more harshly than boys by the juvenile justice system. In spite of the fact that the 1974 Juvenile Justice and Delinquency Prevention Act specifically recommended the deinstitutionalization of status offenders, a significant number of girls continue to be sentenced to public or private juvenile institutions for these acts. In 1997, for example, 23 percent of all girls in residential placement within the justice system had a status offense as their most serious violation. Only 4 percent of boys in residential placement were there for status offenses. In 1997, almost half of the girls placed in private institutions were charged with status offenses, compared with 11 percent of privately placed boys. Overall, girls are a small minority of the juveniles in the US who are in residential placement (about 14 percent in 1997); however, they are quite close to a majority of youths who are incarcerated for status offenses. Clearly, the nature of the offenses that bring girls to a residential placement is different from that for boys. Girls are more likely to be institutionalized for a minor offense.

SEX AND CRIMINOLOGICAL THEORY

Despite its strength, historically, criminology has paid little attention to the relationship between sex and crime, spending much of its efforts focused on the criminality of males. In the 1960s, feminist criminologists began to develop a critique of mainstream criminology that focused on this neglect. They argue that, in the past, females have been neglected in theory and research, and that when they are present they are viewed in a stereotyped manner. The result is that criminology has been, and continues to be, unable to explain why it is that males offend at such higher rates than females.

SEE ALSO: Crime; Crime, Biosocial Theories of; Feminist Criminology; Juvenile Delinquency; Masculinities, Crime and Measuring Crime

REFERENCES AND SUGGESTED READINGS

Adler, F. (1975) *Sisters in Crime*. McGraw Hill, New York.

Canter, R. (1982) Differences in Self-Reported Delinquency. *Criminology* 20: 373–93.

Daly, K. & Chesney-Lind, M. (1988) Feminism and Criminology. *Justice Quarterly* 5: 497–538.

Klein, D. (1995) The Etiology of Female Crime: A Review of the Literature. In: B. R. Price & N. J. Sokoloff (Eds.), *The Criminal Justice System and Women*, 2nd edn. McGraw-Hill, New York, pp. 30–53.

Naffine, N. (1996) *Feminism and Criminology*. Temple University Press, Philadelphia.

Steffensmeier, D. & Schwartz, J. (2004) Trends in Female Criminality: Is Crime Still a Man's World? In: Raffel Price, B. & Sokoloff, N. (Eds.), *The Criminal Justice System and Women*, 3rd edn. McGraw-Hill, Oxford, pp. 95–111.

US Department of Justice (1960–2000) *Uniform Crime Reports*. US Government Printing Office, Washington, DC.

sex education

Debbie Epstein

The term sex education covers a multitude of approaches, meanings, and pedagogical strategies.

It is highly contextual, with localized cultures and understandings making significant differences both to the purposes and practices involved. It is also often highly politicized.

Sex education in both the UK and US has its origins in what Frank Mort (1987), among others, has termed the "medico-moral" discourses of the second half of the nineteenth century. However, as Pilcher (2005: 154) points out, the inclusion of sex education in the British school curriculum was controversial, since children were seen as simultaneously innocent and easily corruptible (a theme that has persisted into the twenty-first century). Pilcher describes how serious concerns about the prevalence and spread of syphilis and gonorrhea, especially during World War I, propelled sex education into the school curriculum. The UK government subsequently began to provide funding for the National Council for Combating Venereal Disease (later the British Schools Hygiene Council) to carry out sex education in schools and also encouraged the introduction of lessons about sex hygiene and reproduction in biology lessons. This direct funding was withdrawn and discretional funding for sex education devolved to local education authorities in the late 1920s. Often, they chose not to provide such instruction, particularly after the Chief Medical Officer to the Board of Education questioned "whether direct class instruction in this subject is either advisable or practicable" (Board of Education 1930: 48).

World War II brought new moral panics about "dangerous ignorance" and the likelihood that sexual knowledge might be acquired in "ways which are likely to distort or degrade" (BoardofEducation 1943: 4). The 1950s marked a change in beginning to debate what the content of sex education should be rather than whether it should be taught at all. As Pilcher (2005: 160) points out, in the relatively short period between 1939 and 1956 sex had moved from a position of conspicuous absence in the health education curriculum to being rated as "the single most immediate problem" within it.

In the settler colonies (Australia, Canada, South Africa, and New Zealand), the development of sex education followed similar lines to those of the UK. Although little attention was paid to the formal education (let alone sex education) of indigenous people in these or other colonies, there was a concern within the Colonial Office to prevent both "excessive breeding" by "natives" and "miscegenation."

Similarly, in the United States, social purity activists in the nineteenth century called for women to teach their children about sex and argued for the introduction of sex education in schools in order to combat venereal disease in the early twentieth century. The actual introduction of sex or sex hygiene lessons into schools varied from state to state, depending to some extent on the relative strength of vice crusaders and social purity activists. While both these activist groups had the regulation of sexuality at the core of their campaigns (D'Emilio & Freedman 1988), they had very different approaches to this. Vice campaigners opposed sex education, believing that it would encourage "corruption" amongst the young. Social purity activists, in contrast, believed that the regulation of sexuality could best be achieved by the expansion of sex education (Irvine 2002).

Sex education curricula, practices, and theorizations in western Anglophone countries, as they have developed in the last years of the twentieth and first decade of the twenty-first centuries, may be broadly divided into three categories:

- those taking, as their starting point, the promotion of sexual abstinence;
- those which, while not specifically promoting abstinence, nevertheless focus mainly on sexual reproduction and danger;
- more emergent approaches which are rooted in the sociological, psychological, and historical study of sexuality more generally.

The promotion of sexual abstinence ("abstinence-only") education is particularly strong in the US. The view underlying these approaches is that sex education is directly responsible for increases in sexual activity, the growth of sexually transmitted diseases, and an increasing number of unwanted teenage pregnancies. "Abstinence-only" education avoids discussion of sex, sexual relationships, or contraception, focusing instead on the idea that sexual intercourse should be delayed until after marriage and, in some programs, getting young people to pledge that they will remain virgins until they marry. Strictly speaking, therefore, "abstinence-only" education is not a form of sex and relationships education at all (Sex Education Forum 2004). However "abstinence-only" education has a long tradition and has been promoted in at least some US states for at least two decades. Despite this, there is no evidence that "abstinence-only" education has the desired effects. Indeed, a number of researchers argue that it places young people at risk through their ignorance and the fact that if they expect to remain virgins, they are unlikely to be prepared to use contraception if and when they decide to become sexually active (Bearman & Bruckner 2001; Swann et al. 2003).

Despite the promotion of "abstinence-only" education in the US, the dominant approach to sex education in most Anglophone countries is much more embedded in the teaching of sexual reproduction (e.g., in biology lessons) and the transmission of messages about danger and disease. Such approaches have been extensively described and critiqued by major theorists of sexuality and education. Michelle Fine (1988) was one of the first writers from a sociological perspective who engaged critically with sex education. Fine identified a number of discourses of sexuality in sex education lessons: "sexuality as violence," "sexuality as victimization," and "sexuality as individual morality" were the most common. She also identified a "discourse of desire," which she found to be present only as a "whisper" – or even missing completely from sex education. Fine argues strongly that a language of desire is critical in allowing young women in particular to explore sexuality. She concludes that: "the absence of a discourse of desire, combined with the lack of analysis of the language of victimization, may actually retard the development of sexual subjectivity and responsibility in students" (Fine 1988: 49).

Research on sex education in the US (Trudell 1993), the UK (Thomson 1994; Measor et al. 2000), and Australia (Harrison & Hillier 1999) has shown that the mainstream approach to sex education in these (and other) places continues to focus mainly on sexual danger, moral imperatives, and sexual reproduction. With this fairly narrow focus this could be regarded as "sex education" in the strict sense. In this context, young people may be taught about the biology of sexual reproduction, the importance of, as the UK government stresses, "marriage for family life, stable and loving relationships" (DfEE 2000, 5: para. 9), and the dangers of pregnancy and sexually transmitted diseases. As Fine (1988) showed, this approach excludes discussion of pleasure or desire.

Peter Redman (1994) has suggested that we should differentiate between "sex education" and "sexuality education," and proposed the development of the latter to supplant the former. Epstein et al. (2003) define sexuality as encompassing the "sexual cultures and sexual meanings [that] are constructed through a range of discursive practices across social institutions including schools" (p. 3), and argue that sexuality education in schools should be part of the humanities and social sciences curriculum rather than, as currently, included in biology and/or personal, social, and health education (in the UK), life skills education (in South Africa), or taught as a separate subject. They propose that young people should study the history and sociology of sexualities at different times and in different places, enabling them to question their own assumptions around, for example, heterosexuality, race and sexuality, and the stability of legitimated sexual forms.

Because sex education must be understood contextually, attention must also be paid to what happens in poor to middle-income countries, especially those with severe problems due to the high prevalence of HIV/AIDS. There have been two primary approaches in these contexts. The first, as promoted particularly by supra- and international organizations such as the World Bank and the OECD, sees education for women generally, and sex education in particular, as a means of limiting population growth in poor countries. This approach has been described as analogous to a "silver bullet" (Jeffery & Jeffery 1998; Jeffery & Basu 1996), which will act as a kind of contraceptive for women in these countries. Thus sex education in "developing" countries is often seen very instrumentally and, with its emphasis on biology and danger, is similar to the mainstream approach outlined above (see Pattman & Chege 2003).

Second, with the advent of the HIV/AIDS pandemic, there has been a further urgency added to the need for sex education and changing behavior in countries particularly affected by the virus. One of the key problems identified by those who are researching sex and HIV/AIDS education in the context of the pandemic is that the burden of prevention of the spread of HIV/AIDS has, to a large extent, been placed on women. One of the key points made by such researchers is that any sex, sexuality, or HIV/AIDS education programs need to pay much greater attention to promoting gender equality if they are to have any chance of success (see, e.g., Abdool Karim et al. 2002; Unterhalter et al. 2002; Campbell 2003; Morrell 2003).

SEE ALSO: Childhood Sexuality; Education; Gender, Education and; HIV/AIDS and Population; Sex and Gender; Sexuality Research: History

REFERENCES AND SUGGESTED READINGS

Abdool Karim, Q., Epstein, D., Moletsane, R., Morrell, R., & Unterhalter, E. (2002) The School Setting: Opportunities for Integrating Gender Equality and HIV Risk Reduction Interventions. In: What Kind of Difference Can We Make: Education, Youth and the HIV/AIDS Pandemic. *Agenda* 53 (Special issue): 11–21.

Bearman, P. & Bruckner, H. (2001) Promising the Future: Virginity Pledges and First Intercourse. *American Journal of Sociology* 106(4): 859–912.

Board of Education (1930) *The Health of the Schoolchild.* His Majesty's Stationery Office, London.

Board of Education (1943) *Sex Education in Schools and Youth Organizations.* His Majesty's Stationery Office, London.

Campbell, C. (2003) *Letting Them Die: Why HIV/AIDS Intervention Programmes Fail.* Indiana University Press, Bloomington.

D' Emilio, J. & Freedman, E. (1988) *Intimate Matters: A History of Sexuality in America.* Harper & Row, New York.

DfEE (2000) *Sex and Relationship Education Guidance.* Department for Education and Employment, London.

Epstein, D., O'Flynn, S., & Telford, D. (2003) *Silenced Sexualities in Schools and Universities.* Trentham Books, Stoke on Trent.

Fine, M. (1988) Sexuality, Schooling, and Adolescent Females: The Missing Discourse of Desire. *Harvard Educational Review* 58(1): 29–53.

Harrison, L. & Hillier, L. (1999) What Should Be the "Subject" of Sex Education? *Discourse: Studies in the Cultural Politics of Education* 20(2): 279–88.

Irvine, J. (2002) *Talk About Sex: The Battles Over Sex Education in the United States.* University of California Press, Berkeley and Los Angeles.

Jeffery, P. & Jeffery, R. (1998) Silver Bullet or Passing Fancy? Girls' Schooling and Population Policy. In: Jackson, C. & Pearson, R. (Eds.), *Feminist Visions of Development: Gender Analysis and Policy.* Routledge, London and New York.

Jeffery, R. & Basu, A. (Eds.) (1996) *Girls' Schooling, Women's Autonomy, and Fertility Change in South Asia.* Sage, New Delhi and Newbury Park, CA.

Measor, L., Tiffin, C., & Miller, K. (2000) *Young People's Views on Sex Education: Education, Attitudes and Behaviour.* RoutledgeFalmer, London.

Morrell, R. (2003) Silence, Sexuality, and HIV/AIDS in South African Schools. *Australian Educational Researcher* 30(1): 41–62.

Mort, F. (1987) *Dangerous Sexualities : Medico-Moral Politics in England since 1830.* Routledge & Kegan Paul, London.

Pattman, R. & Chege, F. (2003) "Dear diary I saw an angel, she looked like heaven on earth": Sex Talk and Sex Education. *African Journal of AIDS Research* 2(2): 103–12.

Pilcher, J. (2005) School Sex Education: Policy and Practice in England 1870 to 2000. *Sex Education: Sexuality, Society, and Learning* 5(2): 153–70.

Redman, P. (1994) Shifting Ground: Rethinking Sexuality Education. In: Epstein, D. (Ed.), *Challenging Lesbian and Gay Inequalities in Education.* Open University Press, Buckingham.

Sex Education Forum (2004) *"Abstinence-Only" Education.* Sex Education Forum, London.

Swann, C., Bowe, K., McCormick, G., & Kosmin, M. (2003) *Teenage Pregnancy and Parenthood: A Review of Reviews.* Health Development Agency, NHS, London.

Thomson, R. (1994) Moral Rhetoric and Public Health Pragmatism: The Recent Politics of Sex Education. *Feminist Review* 48: 40–60.

Trudell, B. (1993) *Doing Sex Education: Gender Politics and Schooling.* Routledge, London.

Unterhalter, E., Morrell, R., Moletsane, R., & Epstein, D. (2002) Instituting Gender Equality in Schools: Working in an HIV/AIDS Environment. *Perspectives in Education* 20(2): 37–53.

sex and gender

Barbara Ryan

Often confused or used as if the terms were the same, sex and gender are in actuality different designations of human behavior based on physical capabilities and social expectations.

Sex is related to the biological distinctions between males and females primarily found in relation to the reproductive functions of their bodies. Biological sex is usually stated as if there are two, and only two, distinct bodies: male and female. But, in fact, there are gradations between male and female accounting for at least five sexes (Fausto-Sterling 1999). In the past called hermaphrodites, and today intersexual, these are people with a mixture of male and female genitalia. In addition, there are those who feel they are encased in a body of the wrong sex, some of whom take hormones and eventually undergo surgery to become transsexuals. Another classification is transgender, which is often used in the same way as the word transsexual, but also indicates people who cross the barrier of gender without physical change.

Sex is not a clear-cut matter of chromosomes, hormones, and genitalia that produce females and males. All humans have hormones, such as estrogen and testosterone, but they are found in varying and changing levels (Fausto-Sterling 1999; Kimmel 2004). Men as well as women have breasts. Some men have bigger breasts than some women and some men get breast cancer. Women have facial hair. Indeed, some women have more facial hair than some men.

Gender is a social definition of how to be or the ways of "being" considered appropriate for one's sex category. Because gender can be enacted in an infinite variety of ways, and indeed is, we know that gender is a social construction and, therefore, learned behavior.

Other terms closely related and often confused with sex/gender are sexual orientation and sexuality. Sexual orientation is descriptive of who you desire to have sexual relations with; that is, who is the object of your desire. Same-sex desires indicate homosexuality; opposite-sex desires indicate heterosexuality; sexual desire for both men and women indicates bisexuality (Ryan & DeMarco 2003).

Depending upon where and when you live, these classifications can affect your life in multiple ways. Thus, there is a long history, as well as ongoing processes, of differential treatment based upon one's sex, gender, and sexual orientation. What this leads to is privileged groups, those having access to the goods of society and those who are prohibited from such things. The casual dismissal of people who are different from the powerful and dominant group carries with it a superior/inferior connotation that permeates every aspect of social life and, beyond that, can also lead to internalized oppression.

Most people live their lives with unquestioned assumptions about men and women based on an overemphasis of the role of biology in shaping human behavior (Rosenblum & Tavris 2000). This tendency is called biological reductionism (or essentialism) and is often justified as the work of nature or God. Although it is doubtful that Freud believed the differences between men and women were reducible to naturalistic thinking, the term he coined – "anatomy is destiny" – has been used as a justification for keeping women out of work deemed unfeminine (and typically higher paying) or to expect men to display masculine behavior at all times. Defining human-designed categories as the result of biology or "intelligent design" is meant to remove that categorization from debate and, even further, to deny questioning of the concepts at all.

The fact is, the effects of social interaction on human behavior far override biological differences (Kimmel 2004). It is a western tendency, particularly American, to embrace a binary and biologically based perspective rather than one focusing on social forces as an understanding of how we think, talk, and otherwise behave and that this early determination is unchanging – that it is fixed for life. It is a belief that has been reinforced and promoted through the mass media, law, religion, and other social institutions.

For some time now, scholars, researchers, and activists have challenged perceived differences among people, such as race and gender. Research has shown a profound social influence on sex, gender, and sexuality (Connell 2000; Fenstermaker and West 2002; Glenn 1999; Seidman 2003). This new emphasis is a social constructionist perspective rooted in the understanding that reality is created in everyday interactions (Berger & Luckmann 1966). From a social construction perspective, differences among people emerge through interaction and the social processes of institutions such as religion, politics, economic positioning, and work relations.

Babies do not develop on their own into adult human beings. Socialization is the process by which we learn the ways of society and our place in the social world. It is how we become "human." Society is around and within us. We learn from others how we are expected to live in our culture, our subcultures, and in accordance with our gender. That is, we are taught to have attitudes and behaviors based on our designation of male or female. Gendered messages are everywhere and constant, beginning with the family.

Family interactions are pivotal in the construction and the maintenance of gender ideologies and roles. As children grow, their agents of socialization broaden. They go to school and learn new ways of defining gender distinctiveness. They also begin interacting with peer groups that have an influence on their sense of self. This peer influence increases as the child progresses towards adolescence when the peer group becomes more powerful than family expectations.

A powerful influence on how gender is socially constructed comes from the mass media, particularly television. Gender socialization does not end with childhood; it continues throughout our life. Traditional stereotypes of men and women are perpetuated because women are still cast as younger, supportive counterparts to men, and older women are still the most underrepresented group (Gahahl et al. 2003). Likewise, movies provide scripts for how to live our lives while "doing gender." From the time of the earliest films, they have shown us the stereotypical gender roles we are meant to play on the stage of life.

Sex and gender are related yet distinctive terms, both heavily imbued with definitions, restrictions, privileges, and misconceptions based on the ways they have been socially constructed in different societies around the world. Sex, the biological component, is often used as a justification to privilege men over women. Gender, which has the widest and deepest applications, is often treated as if it were a biological condition rather than a social categorization that can and is used for placement in stratification systems.

SEE ALSO: Doing Gender; Intersexuality; Sexism; Sexuality; Socialization; Socialization, Gender; Stratification, Gender and; Transgender, Transvestism, and Transsexualism

REFERENCES AND SUGGESTED READINGS

Berger, P. L. & Luckmann, T. (1966) *The Social Construction of Reality*. Doubleday, New York.

Connell, R. W. (2000) *The Men and the Boys*. University of California Press, Berkeley.

Fausto-Sterling, A. (1999) The Five Sexes: Why Female and Male Are Not Enough. *The Sciences* (March/April): 20–4.

Fenstermaker, S. & West, C. (Eds.) (2002) *Doing Gender, Doing Difference*. Routledge, New York.

Gahahl, D., Prinsen, T., & Netzley, S. B. (2003) A Content Analysis of Prime Time Commercials: A Contextual Framework of Gender Representation. *Sex Roles: A Journal of Research* 49: 545–62.

Glenn, E. N. (1999) The Social Construction and Institutionalization of Gender and Race: An Integrative Framework. In: Ferree, M., Lorber, J., & Hess, B. (Eds.), *Revisioning Gender*. Sage, Thousand Oaks, CA.

Kimmel, M. S. (2004) *The Gendered Society*. Oxford University Press, New York.

Rosenblum, K. E. & Travis, T.-M. C. (2000) *The Meaning of Difference*. McGraw Hill, New York.

Ryan, B. & DeMarco, J. (2003) Sexual Orientation: An International Perspective. In: Scales, T. L. (Ed.), *The International Encyclopedia of Marriage and the Family*, 2nd edn, Vols. 1–4. Macmillan Reference, New York, pp. 1491–9.

Seidman, S. (2003) *The Social Construction of Sexuality*. W. W. Norton, New York.

sex panics

Benjamin Shepard

The concept of a sex panic builds on the idea of moral panic – a term first coined within British sociology and Stuart Hall's cultural studies. Sex panics are a distinct form of moral panic. The term moral panic builds on themes from American sociology of deviance, theories of collective behavior, social problems, French structuralist theory, and Frankfurt School social theory. Moral panics about youth have been assessed as studies of subcultures, while other inquiries have adopted social and psychological perspectives borrowed from disaster studies. As theorists grappled with the meanings of the AIDS epidemic and public policies aimed at alleviating social problems, conceptions of moral panics overlapped with debates about "the underclass." A frequent theoretical approach to studying representations of moral panics about sexuality is to analyze "discourses" that regulate sexuality and demarcate hierarchies of what is and is not normal and moral, worthy and unworthy. Thus, panics have been analyzed from a range of different perspectives. In *Moral Panics*, a reader on moral panic as a "key idea" for sociological inquiry, Thompson (1998: 72) counsels: "It may be a sensible tactic to adopt insights from each of these in an eclectic manner or to combine them where appropriate, depending on the particular type of moral panic being studied."

The first reference to the term moral panic was by sociologist Stanley Cohen in 1972. His point was that to the extent that cultural institutions draw parameters around deviance, they create moral panics. The process can be described through an escalating cycle. The cycle begins as a distinct group – perhaps a youth gang, gay men, or teenagers on welfare – engages in distinct acts, such as having sex in public or being on public assistance. These acts are viewed as a threat to traditional values and society at large. Once the threat is identified, it is presented in a highly charged, black and white manner in the media (Cohen 2002). This reduces the understanding of the complexity of the group or circumstances (Bourdieu 1998). From here, "right-thinking" moral entrepreneurs such as state officials, police, social workers, bishops, psychologists, and other licensed experts establish diagnoses which pathologize and punish. These solutions tend to assert social control over activities and groups.

For Cohen, the moral panic scapegoat becomes a "folk devil" onto whom cultural anxieties are projected. Cohen focuses on the symbolic controls, the mythologies, and the labels at play as folk devils inspire widespread reaction. Thus, studies of panic consider the highly charged symbolic functions generating collective behavior, the stereotypes which from time to time inspire profound widespread hysteria.

Weeks (1985) suggests that the mechanics of these moral panics are quite familiar. They start with a threat from a youthful event or gathering. Those involved are stereotyped as demons; discourse about the threat escalates; this leads to a simplified view of the problem and a draconian policy solution; anxiety wanes while the victims, the "folk devils," are left to withstand often-brutal legal penalties.

At its core, the concept of moral panic considers the role of political demonology: the labeling of opponents as threats to moral and social order. These are the folk devils Cohen describes. Stereotyping often has the effect of establishing power of one group over another group of people, in favor of a status quo. For this reason, people generally do not like to be categorized, labeled, or attributed with certain common characteristics. The process of being labeled limits freedom of movement and self-determination. Labeling is used to scapegoat – blame – and therefore control other people (Fisk 1993).

This process only escalates in the case of sexual panic. Historian Allan Bérubé suggests that the term sex panic refers to a moral crusade which results in "crackdowns on sexual outsiders" (Gaywave 1997). Duggan (1995) notes that such panics, red scares, and even witch hunts can be witnessed throughout countless chapters of US history. They are generally advanced by vocal interest groups with animosity toward cultural difference. In their most dangerous expression, these panics have been championed by crusaders hoping to establish one distinct brand of orthodoxy on the majority. These panics tend to deflect public discourse away from social problems involving race, sex, or poverty, which if addressed might shift social arrangements. Thus, panics can be understood as distractions.

For this reason activists have consistently sought to challenge these structures. By the mid-1980s, queer activists recognized that panic over the AIDS crisis impeded an effective response. From 1987 through the 1990s the AIDS Coalition to Unleash Power (ACT UP) enjoyed great success in its struggle against a panic over the AIDS epidemic. Much of the winning strategy involved the use of colorful, theatric, playful, inventive, and aesthetic interventions which changed hearts and minds. Art critic and former ACT UP member Douglas Crimp suggests ACT UP's work helped transform public discourse about the epidemic away from blame and hysteria toward a recognition that AIDS was a public health issue which required an assertive government response (Takemoto 2003). Yet, panic was never far away.

In the summer of 1997 an ad hoc group of activists and scholars declared: *J'accuse*. They suggested that the policies of New York Mayor Rudy Giuliani's Quality of Life crusade fit a distinctively American political schema. The group noted this was not the first time government has advanced repressive policies around sexuality in the name of the larger public good. The group noted that since the ante bellum days of labor unrest and Anthony Comstock's social purity crusade (Gilfoyle 1992; Beisel 1997; Wagner 1997), attacks on sexuality have emerged within a distinct, recurrent pattern: morals are invoked; folk devils are found in gay people, prostitutes, and other sexual outsiders who function as scapegoats; and finally, a fantastical notion of social purity, which few live up to, is presented as a social norm. "Historians have come to call this pattern a 'sex panic,'" the group noted. Thus, they borrowed the term as the name for their group in order to highlight their view that with the mid-1990s effort to clean up New York City they were witnessing yet another sex panic (Crimp et al. 1997).

With that, SexPanic! was born. SexPanic! led the struggle against Guiliani's war on public sexual culture taking place under the auspices of his Quality of Life Crusade. Their work included a struggle against panic in private spaces where communities of sexual outsiders converge; it compared Guiliani's struggles with those of anti-vice crusader Anthony Comstock. The group utilized a politics of play and pleasure to challenge structures of panic. These struggles can be understood as part of a lineage of protest against prohibition dating back to the days of the Temperance Movement (Wagner 1997).

The concept is useful in that it helps explain collective behavior – including periods of "hysteria," "red scares," and "prohibition." Yet Cohen (2002) is frank to acknowledge that just because something is stirred by irrational behavior does not necessarily mean it is a panic. Future research on the topic must work to make sense of these elements of collective behavior, which create panic. Hence, it must do more than name and acknowledge that panics exist. It must identify and highlight best-practice approaches to combat periods of panic.

SEE ALSO: AIDS, Sociology of; Moral Panics; Queer Theory; Safer Sex; Sexualities and Culture Wars

REFERENCES AND SUGGESTED READINGS

Beisel, N. (1997) *Imperiled Innocents: Anthony Comstock and Family Reproduction in America.* Princeton University Press, Princeton.

Bourdieu, P. (1998) *On Television.* New Press, New York.

Cohen, S. (2002 [1972]) *Folk Devils and Moral Panics: The Creation of the the Mods and Rockers.* Routledge, New York.

Crimp, D., Pelligrini, A., Pendleton, E., & Warner, M. (1997) This is SexPanic! In: *SexPanic!* Sheep Meets Sheep Collective, New York.

Duggan, L. (1995) Sex Panics. In: Duggan, L. & Hunter, N. (Eds.), *Sex Wars: Sexual Dissent and Political Culture.* Routledge, New York.

Fisk, B. (1993) Controlling Other People: The Impact of Power on Stereotyping. *American Psychologist* 621–8.

Gaywave (1997) Sex-Lib Activists Confront "Sex-Panic." *Gaywave* (December 2).

Gilfoyle, T. (1992) *City of Eros: New York City, Prostitution, and the Commercialization of Sex, 1790–1920.* W. W. Norton, New York.

Takemoto, T. (2003) The Melancholia of AIDS: Interview with Douglas Crimp. *Art Journal* (Winter).

Thompson, K. (1998) *Moral Panics.* Routledge, New York.

Wagner, D. (1997) *The New Temperance: The American Obsession with Sin and Vice.* Westview Press, Boulder.

Weeks, J. (1985) *Sexuality and Its Discontents: Meanings, Myths, and Modern Sexualities.* Routledge, New York.

sex tourism

Susan L. Wortmann

Sex tourism is a multibillion dollar global industry wherein individuals (sex tourists) from industrialized, developed nations travel abroad with the distinct purpose of purchasing a variety of sexually associated services. Destinations vary, but most sex tourists seek the services of individuals from developing nations. Sex tourists' travel and consumption, facilitated by technology and an unequal and increasingly interconnected world system, have raised the profitability of this industry to a historically unprecedented level. Blending global race, ethnicity, class, gender, and age inequalities with capitalist consumption, sex tourism creates and perpetuates a range of problems for sex workers and host countries. A growing body of interdisciplinary studies reveals a complex blend of exploitation and agency involved in sex tourism, the links between local and global, the need for inclusive and further study of homosexual, transgendered and bisexual, as well as heterosexual sex tourism, and the importance of understanding rather than stereotyping workers and experiences.

Worldwide, tourism itself is a major business. According to Williams (2002), 83 countries list tourism as one of their top five export categories. Economically vulnerable developing countries with exploitable resources often welcome the revenue that tourism brings. Indeed, because it can be a country's largest revenue source, there is also a tendency to uncritically associate all types of tourism with economic advancement. International organizations such as the World Bank and the International Money Fund (IMF) have provided loans for tourism as a mechanism to end poverty in developing nations. Many scholars question the impact of these loans, however, illustrating that because of devalued currencies, immigration, urbanization, and gendered labor markets, tourism is, especially for women of developing nations, a likely entry to service and sex work.

Fun, sun, adventure, and consumption of an affordable exotic Other are internationally associated with sex tourism's allure. This appeal is a commodity manufactured and maintained by technologies of developed countries. For example, foreign consumers have ready access to information and services from afar: through the Internet, chat rooms, e-diaries, blogs, Internet promotional videos, and guidebooks. Readily accessible is advice on how to arrange a sex tour, how to bargain with submissive sex workers, best sites, and best workers. Some Internet sites allow tourists to arrange and customize complete packaged sex tours online. Importantly, sex tourists' destination countries have little control over how their citizens are represented. For example, a number of sex trade brochures and magazines are produced in Europe. Additionally, cyberspace sites often feature stereotypical "sexy, willing, and submissive natives," and charter services advertise "exotic scenery" counterpoised against nearly naked bodies. Entire populations, in effect, become sexually commodified.

Air travel facilitates access to a number of developing countries with warm climates. While popular destinations include Thailand, the Philippines, the Dominican Republic, Costa Rica, and Brazil, sex tourism is not limited to locations in Southeast Asia and South America. Specific cities and regions are often associated with sex tourism, e.g., Holland's Amsterdam, Kenya's coast along the Indian Ocean, Cuba's Havana, and Thailand's Patpong region. While some locations have established cultural patterns of prostitution (for instance, brothels are traditional in Thailand), the influx of tourists looking specifically for sex-associated services, along with developing nations' poverty and lack of jobs, have increased the local sex economy to a historic high. In some cases, this increase can be directly traced to deliberate intervention by governments and financial organizations. For instance, the sex trade in Thailand grew substantially during and after the Vietnam War when the governments of the US and Thailand negotiated a contract for American soldiers to be sent there for rest and relaxation (R&R). Both governments were thereby indirectly responsible for an increase in brothels.

While gay, lesbian, bisexual, transgendered, and heterosexual individuals engage in sex tourism as buyers and sellers, statistics and studies of the demography, psychology, experience, and motivations of tourists and workers are limited. Most, for example, explore the sex tourism of heterosexual middle/upper-class males from industrialized nations such as Japan, Germany, or the US who seek young, submissive women for sex and companionship. The most commonly researched sex worker is a poor, young woman of color who has often migrated from a rural to an urban setting or to another country to support herself and/or her family. Accounts suggest that she may have found the sex trade much more lucrative than factory and domestic-related trades, she may have found it the only job available, or she may have been tricked or forced into sex work. Buyer and seller fantasy, according to many narratives, is an important industrial feature. Ethnographies reveal that, in addition to sex, some heterosexual male tourists seek submissive companionship, while some heterosexual women sex tourists seek romance or racialized exotic Others. Homosexual, bisexual, transgendered, and heterosexual sex workers alike appear to fantasize that their clients will offer more than money. For example, in overtly patriarchal countries, female sex workers may seek men who can provide them with more egalitarian gender relations, extended relationships, a visa that allows them to travel abroad, or even marriage. Gay sex workers appear to be motivated by gifts, money, promise of travel, and migration. Sexual identities are not necessarily stable among buyers and sellers – several accounts note that some male sex workers who service primarily men continue to have women as intimate partners, and that male tourists who are married to women purchase services from male and transgendered sex workers.

Sex tourism is credited with both the creation and intensification of micro and macro social problems including, but not limited to, violence against individuals (workers and tourists); disease and morbidity; child prostitution; and social/environmental destruction. Sex workers often suffer abuse and exploitation from clients, including refusal to wear condoms, physical or emotional violence, and failure to pay. They are likely to experience harassment by club operators and law enforcement. In most countries the sex trade is illegal and sex workers are unlikely to be legally protected. AIDS and sexually transmitted diseases (STDs) are prevalent and can impact buyer, seller, or future and present sex partners and children. Paradoxically, the threat of AIDS is reported to appeal to some sex tourists who regard it as adventure and high-risk sport. Child prostitution, reported in many areas, has attracted international attention. International actions, such as passing legislation to make those who engage children as prostitutes liable abroad and in their own countries, may deflect attention and resources from adult workers and may make them scapegoats for the sex trade. Furthermore, all types of tourism strain developing countries' environments, increase demands for natural resources, and produce additional pollution and waste.

Feminist scholars such as Enloe (1989) were instrumental in bringing academic attention to sex tourism. Interdisciplinary engagement has revealed a complex portrait of a range of issues that problematize earlier understandings of sex tourism as solely exploitative, that seek to broaden the focus to all types of workers and tourists, and that point to the importance of academics understanding their own positionality and tendency to "other" sex workers and tourists. Some challenge traditional definitions of sex tourism itself. For instance Ryan (2000) defines sex tourism merely as "sexual intercourse while away from home." Research emphases differ; some explore sex tourism on the macro level of global economic, social, and historical factors, while others emphasize the importance of inequalities of race, ethnicity, class, and gender separately, or together, and how these impact workers and tourists. Still others emphasize micro levels of interaction by stressing that the sex trade involves negotiation, agency, and opportunity for buyer and seller. Each of these conceptualizations impacts research emphases, findings, the resultant local and international policies, and, ultimately, the lives of individuals engaged in the global phenomenon of sex tourism.

SEE ALSO: Child Labor; Consumption, Tourism and; Gender, Consumption and; Globalization, Sexuality and; Imperialism; Prostitution; Sexual Markets, Commodification, and Consumption; Traffic in Women

REFERENCES AND SUGGESTED READINGS

Aggelton, P. (Ed.) (1999) *Men Who Sell Sex: International Perspectives on Male Prostitution and HIV/AIDS*. Temple University Press, Philadelphia.

Belk, R., Ostergaard, P., & Groves, R. (1998) Sexual Consumption in the Time of AIDS: A Study of Prostitute Patronage in Thailand. *Journal of Public Policy and Marketing* 17(12): 197–214.

Ehrenreich, B. & Hochschild, A. (Eds.) (2003) *Global Woman: Nannies, Maids, and Sex Workers in the New Economy*. Henry Holt, New York.

Enloe, C. (1989) *Bananas, Beaches, and Bases: Making Feminist Sense of International Politics.* University of California Press, Los Angeles.
Jeffreys, S. (2003) Sex Tourism: Do Women Do It Too? *Leisure Studies* 22: 223–38.
Kempadoo, K. (Ed.) (1999) *Sun, Sex, and Gold Tourism and Sex Work in the Caribbean.* Rowman & Littlefield, Lanham, MD.
Kibicho, W. (2005) Tourism and the Sex Trade in Kenya's Coastal Region. *Journal of Sustainable Tourism* 13(3): 256–80.
Odzer, C. (1994) *Patpong Sisters: An American Woman's View of the Bangkok Sex Work.* Arcade, New York.
Ryan, C. (2000) Sex Tourism. In: Clift, S. & Carter, S. (Eds.), *Tourism and Sex Culture, Commerce and Coercion.* Continuum International, New York.
Tate, B. (2004) *The Hedonist: World Red Light District Vacation Guide Professional.* Bachelor Publishing, LLC.
Williams, M. (2002) Tourism Liberalization, Gender and the GATS. *Economic Literacy Series: General Agreement on Trade in Services* 5: 1–12.
Wonders, N. A. & Michalowski, R. (2001) Bodies, Borders, and Sex Tourism in a Globalized World: A Tale of Two Cities – Amsterdam and Havana. *Social Problems* 48(4): 545–71.

sexism

Amy Lind

Sexism is discrimination on the basis of sex and/or gender. It occurs at various levels, from the individual to the institutional, and involves practices that promote gender-based prejudice and stereotyping of social roles. Most commonly, sexism refers to inequalities that exist among men and women, particularly where women are treated as unequal or inferior to men. Like other forms of discrimination, sexism can occur through blatant or covert actions, including outright displays of hatred or disdain for an individual or group; the privileging of one gender over another; or tokenism, where, for example, a woman is hired only because she is a woman, rather than because of her skills and experience. How sexism plays out varies according to the social location of the individual or group involved, particularly in regard to racial, ethnic, class, sexual, and/or religious background.

Beginning in the 1960s, sexism became a commonly used term by participants in second wave feminist movements in the US, Britain, Canada, and Europe and elsewhere. In the US, the National Organization for Women (NOW, co-founded by Betty Friedan) fought for an Equal Rights Amendment (ERA) which, had it passed, would have provided full equality to men and women under the law. Affirmative action policies (a type of positive discrimination) also became an important strategy for reversing historical gender inequalities. In Britain, Europe, and other regions, legislation was proposed to end gender discrimination in the workplace, educational system, and political system. In the 1990s and 2000s many developing countries began to propose affirmative action policies to reverse gender discrimination as well (IWRAW 2005).

Beginning in the 1960s, US feminists organized widely against sex segregation in the labor market and workplace and introduced notions of unequal pay and comparable worth to address the unequal value assigned to "feminine" vs. "masculine" types of employment in US society (England 1992). Several studies address the gender wage gap in earnings among men and women; some break these figures down according to race/ethnicity (Jacobsen 1998). Comparable worth advocates have argued that increasing women's wages is not enough; rather, it is also necessary to rethink how certain types of jobs or employment sectors are viewed as "feminine" and therefore as inherently less economically worthy than those jobs viewed as "masculine." For example, physicians, astronauts, and attorneys tend to be paid more than nurses, teachers, and secretaries (Lindsey 1997: 76). Men who provide administrative assistance are "office managers" whereas women are "secretaries."

In relation to this, sociologists have also addressed how sexism is inherent in language: in the structure of language and in everyday communication. They have pointed out how male pronouns are used to define all of humanity, as in the phrases, "all men are created equal," "we need the right man for the job," and "we live in a manmade society." Just as "man" is assumed to refer to both men and women, "he" is assumed to refer to "she." Similarly, many titles and occupations are biased toward men, as in "businessmen," "newsmen," or "mailmen," despite the fact that women work in these professions (Lindsey 1997). Advocates of gender equality have worked to create more gender-neutral language and one may now hear references to "business people," "news reporters," and "mail carriers." Scholars have also pointed out how, in everyday communication, informal exchanges, gossip, or jokes may reproduce stereotypical gender roles and identities. Verbal sexual harassment at work or on the street is one example of this.

Sexism has been challenged in the courts in many countries, as in the case of the US with the passage of the 1972 Educational Amendment to the Civil Rights Act. Typically referred to as Title IX, this legislation mandated that schools, colleges, and universities that received public funds must provide equality in funding for male and female students at all levels. This allowed female students equal opportunity in their academic pursuits and athletic activities for the first time in history. Gender-based affirmative action policies, based on the racial model proposed originally by civil rights leaders, were introduced in the early 1970s, particularly in the areas of employment and education to ensure that women "enjoyed the same opportunities for promotions, salary increases, career advancement, school admissions, scholarships, and financial aid" as men (Brunner 2005). An example of positive discrimination, these policies were seen as temporary and remedial rather than permanent. During the 1990s, critics challenged the constitutionality of gender-based and race-based affirmative action policies in the courts, arguing that they were a form of reverse discrimination. Defenders contend that such policies are necessary in societies where gender (and racial) inequality is institutionalized and ongoing. Discrimination against women, sometimes referred to as sexual discrimination in legal discourse, is now illegal in many countries, although these laws are difficult to uphold. The United Nations Convention on the Elimination of All Forms of Discrimination against Women (CEDAW), adopted in 1979 by the UN General Assembly, urged governments around the world to adopt legislation that promotes gender equality. As of 2005, 90 percent (180 member countries) have ratified the Convention.

The definition of sexism has changed over time, reflecting contemporary sociological debates on sex vs. gender and nature vs. nurture. During the early stage of second wave feminism, sexism was typically defined as unequal treatment on the basis of sex. Later social theorists emphasized gender, rather than sex, as the appropriate level of analysis, since, they argued, discrimination is based on cultural, rather than biological, difference (Lorber 1994). Some went even further to argue that how a given society defines sex difference in human anatomy is also a product of culture and not a predetermined, natural given.

To the extent that sexism is based on the assumption that there are essential differences between men and women (be they biologically or culturally based), then it is an *essentialist* notion. Postmodern scholars have emphasized how individuals of both dominant and marginalized groups reproduce sexism, pointing out, for example, that women themselves reinforce structures of domination by engaging in sexist jokes and competing unfairly with other women. While the nature–nurture debates continue, many feminist scholars would continue to agree that the social context, rather than any assumed biological difference between men and women, is crucial to understanding how and why women are viewed as the "weaker sex" and therefore subject to sexism.

Critics have argued that sex/gender difference does not imply sex/gender discrimination per se, and that by blaming men, feminists are promoting reverse sexism. Other critics argue that sexism alone is not enough to understand gender-based discrimination, particularly for non-European, non-white women; rather, one needs to assess gender inequality in conjunction with, for example, racial, ethnic, sexual, or class inequality (Collins 1998). Most feminist scholars would agree that the most pervasive type of sexism is that which continues to exist in people's belief systems and cultural attitudes – beliefs and attitudes which cannot be changed immediately through legislation.

SEE ALSO: Discrimination; Feminist Activism in Latin America; Gender Bias; Gender Ideology and Gender Role Ideology; Gender

Oppression; Sex-Based Wage Gap and Comparable Worth; Sex and Gender

REFERENCES AND SUGGESTED READINGS

Brunner, B. (2005) Bakke and Beyond: A History and Timeline of Affirmative Action. Online. www.infoplease.com/spot/affirmative1.html.

Collins, P. H. (1998) *Fighting Words: Black Women and the Search for Justice.* University of Minnesota Press, Minneapolis.

de Beauvoir, S. (1980 [1952]) *The Second Sex.* Random House/Alfred Knopf, New York.

England, P. (1992) *Comparable Worth: Theories and Evidence.* Aldine de Gruyter, New York.

Friedan, B. (2001 [1963]) *The Feminine Mystique.* W. W. Norton, New York.

International Women's Rights Action Watch (IWRAW) (2005 [1997]) Achieving the Rights Result: Affirmative Action and Article 4 of the Women's Convention. IWRAW Consultation Report. Online. www.iwraw.igc.org/cr/1997.html.

Jacobsen, J. P. (1998) *The Economics of Gender.* Blackwell, Oxford.

Lindsey, L. L. (1997) *Gender Roles: A Sociological Perspective*, 4th edn. Prentice-Hall, Englewood Cliffs, NJ.

Lorber, J. (1994) *Paradoxes of Gender.* Yale University Press, New Haven.

National Organization for Women (NOW) (1984 [1968]) NOW Bill of Rights. In: Jaggar, A. & Rothenberg, P. S. (Eds.), *Feminist Frameworks*, 2nd edn. McGraw-Hill, New York.

sexual citizenship

David T. Evans

All sociological analyses of human sexualities contain implications of differential social exclusion, and social movements such as Gay Liberation, feminism, and Queer activism fight for sexual "rights" employing the rhetoric of equality. However, only in the last decade have such issues been explicitly theorized and researched under the rubric of sexual citizenship, focusing on the political, legal, and economic construction of sexualities through the institutionalized principles and processes of heteronormative liberal democratic citizenship, though precisely how has remained open to considerable disagreement.

In earlier micro and middle-range sociological accounts, hegemonic heterosexism was invariably acknowledged, but as an implicit ideological, rather than explicitly structural, dominant presence. Discussion and analysis of the patterned discriminatory consequences of hegemonic heterosexism on aspects of mundane citizenship, such as taxation, life insurance, health care provision, home ownership, inheritance rights, conditions of employment, use of "public" and "private" spaces, etc., were thereby absent. Given the institutionalization of the family as the natural "dominant regime of (heterosexual) truth" (Mort 1980), these omissions were unsurprising and unrecognized. As one result, the early sociology of sexuality commenced its critiques of naturalist explanations by responding to the latter's focus on discrete forms of "deviance" requiring explanation, as heteronormative forms did not. During the 1980s the impact of postmodernist and "queer" perspectives further discouraged macro-analysis of sexualities deemed to be increasingly fragmented, fluid, and unstable. However, during the same decade, citizenship in general excited new social scientific interest. The conceptual and interpretive origins and disagreements in sociological accounts of sexual citizenship derive from these differences in academic and political provenance, at the heart of which reside contested accounts of late modernity and citizenship in general.

Citizenship has had a sustained presence in British sociology due to the lasting influence of Marshall's (1950) classic account of civil, political, and social rights, the development of the modern British welfare state as part of post-World War II regeneration and, since the 1950s, the growing impact of conditions of "disorganized" capitalism: fragmentation of economic interest groups with greater industrial flexibility in economies increasingly consumption driven; breakdown of neo-corporatist state regulation; growing contradictions between state and capital; growth of new, seemingly fragmented and discrete, social movements, and active citizens as reflexive consumers. "Capital, culture, technology and politics merely came together to roam beyond the regulatory power of the national state" (Urry 2000), which of necessity retreated from moralist to causalist principles. Rather than appraising sexual behaviors as "immoral" and interfering in the private lives of citizens "to seek to enhance any particular pattern of behavior," the law became primarily concerned with proven deleterious effects on "victims," the preservation of "public order and decency," protection of the citizen from "public" offense and injury (Wolfenden 1957), and the restriction of tolerated sexual deviance to "private" spaces. This reformulation of regulatory principles inevitably impinged on those of citizenship. While justifications for partial or complete citizenship exclusion are to be found in classic accounts such as Marshall's (1950) specification that social rights include "all ... rights which accrue from the fundamental right to share to the full in the social heritage and to the life of a civilized being according to the standards prevailing in the society," their implicit heteronormative (dis) qualifications remained largely unrecognized and unaddressed until post-Wolfenden legal reformulations began to have a concrete impact.

Under these new social conditions of disorganized capitalism, the citizenship space in civil society opened up between criminality (sexual murder, rape, pedophilia, etc.) and heteronormativity became occupied by conditionally "legal" but relatively differentiated "immoral" and thus partial sexual citizens, with their own specific rights and duties, which in turn underpinned the development of associated niche markets of leisure and lifestyle consumption. Inevitably, traditional forms of governance were strained by the structural disjunction between growing amoral market pressures on such "private" urban sexual spaces and "moral" state authority, leading to heightened pressure on key normative distinctions such as "morality," "legality," "public," and "private." By the 1980s this underlying disjunction resulted in a political hiatus in which New Right free-market liberalism encouraged the expansion and expression of "private" sexual lifestyles, amid strident reaffirmations of family values in the face of AIDS, child sex abuse, and other moral panics.

Liberal democratic citizenship had apparently reached a breaking point, but the crisis was "resolved" in Britain by the Citizen's Charter (HMSO 1991), which gave due regard to citizens' "privacy," "dignity," and diverse "cultural beliefs," still exemplified by such references to "citizens, especially as parents." The citizenship balance shifted from welfare rights and the relationship between individual, community, and state, to rights of informed choice by autonomous individuals as consumers. Rather than citizenship being conditional on conformity to "standards prevailing in the society," it became "that set of practices (juridical, political, economic, and cultural) which define a person as a competent member of society, and which as a consequence shape the flow of resources to persons and social groups" (Turner 1993a), competence being defined as responsible self-regulation. Liberal democratic citizenship was thus revitalized as an "inclusive" status regardless of class, ethnic, gender, and sexual difference, in which competent "legal" but "immoral" minorities regulated themselves into forms of "privacy," but still leaving the "ideal citizen" as a married, white, male, heterosexual property owner.

Only during the early 1990s did mainstream academic discourses begin to acknowledge this economization and sexualization of citizenship, hesitantly noting, for example, that some citizenship tensions "appear to be centered around ... the struggle for homosexual rights" (Turner 1993a). Homosexual and lesbian citizenship has dominated subsequent sexual citizenship concerns, though other forms of citizenship tension, conflict, and even chaos have emerged concerning the citizenship status of, for instance, sex workers and their clients, users of pornography, transsexuals, children, claimants for access to reproductive technologies, surrogacy and adoption, sex tourists, and unmarried heterosexual partners.

The sociology of sexual citizenship emerged out of the political and intellectual hiatus of this period. It did so through two perspectives which, despite common and complementary elements, differ markedly in their basic conceptualizations. Both agree that citizenship rights are not "natural" and inalienable," but forged out of social activities built into notions of community and identity. Their disagreements hinge on the always vexed relationship between dominant power structures and actor sovereignty, disputes over the extent to which dominant political and economic forms have become increasingly compromised, and the state's adaptive capacity to sustain fundamental heterosexist patriarchal principles and practices of citizenship despite ostensibly making "liberal" concessions, by enforcing differential forms of unequal and partial sexual citizenship.

Though not always using the term, Plummer (1992, 2003), Giddens (1992), and Weeks (1998) explore alternative "pure" and "intimate" forms of sexual citizenship, outside the civil, political, and social dimensions of convention. In contrast, Evans (1993) concentrates on a materialist exploration of the inherent heterosexism of conventional citizenship, and on the increasingly overt sociosexual consequences of late modern reformulations, and these analytical distinctions are reflected in their different political prognoses.

Plummer (1992) hailed the emergence of the "culture of sexual citizenship" out of the 1980s "uncertainty over politics": the rise and decline of the New Right, failure of socialism, the rise of new utopian social movements, etc. He asked: "where does the lesbian and gay politics which flourishes in the latter part of the twentieth century in the Western world sit in all this end of century change?" The tone is of optimism and empowerment of diverse sexual citizens beyond traditional formal citizenship control, enabling "a radical, pluralistic, democratic, contingent, participatory politics of human life choices and difference ... in the making" (Plummer 2003). While older sexual minorities discoursed in terms of civil, political, and social rights, this new regime is distinguished by the emergence of a fourth citizenship dimension: intimate citizenship, manifest through new communities of discourse, sexual stories and identities, diverse alternative rights and responsibilities, pleasures, bodies, visibility, and relationships. "Such stories play a prominent role in understanding the workings of the political and moral life of late modern societies ... and carry potential for the radical transformation of the social order" (Plummer 2003). This new "culture of sexual citizenship" is dependent on new cultural intermediaries (mass media, advertising, Internet technologies, markets for "symbolic goods," etc.), which facilitate "imagining," "vocalizing," and "invention" of identities and cultures of shared problems. Similarly, Giddens (1992) refers to the emergence of "pure relationships," sexual relationships based on equal vulnerability, mutual trust and respect, "relationships of social and economic equality." For Weeks (1998), the "sexual citizen" "could be anyone ... (who) exists or ... wants to come into being – because of the new primacy given to sexual subjectivity in the contemporary world.

In contrast to this culturalist emphasis, Evans (1993), drawing on similar symptoms of 1980s political crisis, concentrates on the crisis management of the late modern state to maintain its "moral" authority through reformulations of heteronormative citizenship to incorporate and depoliticize "competent" sexual and other "partial" citizens, through the extension of single-issue "rights" (fetishized as "equal"), while using examples of sexual "incompetence" to reaffirm dominant heterosexist values. Given "disorganized" conditions, it is acknowledged that periodic crises in governance enable the emergence of intimate alternative claims on citizenship, but these in turn are defused through further citizenship readjustments. Thus, while for Plummer (1992) "'rights' campaigns around 'being gay' and 'lesbian' have had some remarkable payoffs in the western world ... (in which) being gay and lesbian ... has become a positive experience bringing no more problems than any other way of living and loving," for Evans such claims demonstrate how effectively bourgeois citizenship adapts and incorporates, as evidenced by the extent to which sexual political movements "now talk in the language of citizenship – rather than of liberation as in an earlier generation" (Richardson 2000). Thus, new forms of sexual citizenship, behind the rhetorical facade of "liberty" and "equality," provide the means whereby the state fragments, neutralizes, and distracts sexual dissidence to sustain and protect its own "moral authority" and the greater capitalist and heteronormative good.

Disagreements at the heart of both versions extend to a range of key structural and political elements. While sexual communities exist as central to the emergence and sustenance of intimate citizenship, for structuralists they are fetishized "communities," riven by internal divisions of class, ethnicity, age, and gender, etc. Numerous studies of the differential impact of HIV and AIDS on "the gay community" reveal deep inequalities between such constituencies and access to sexual health care, information, and treatment. Uncritical references to "the gay community" thus in effect sustain the gay political dominance of white middle-class males. Furthermore, "gay" media, advertising, and consumption of "symbolic goods" reflect not empowered intimate citizenship, but effective consumer exploitation and self-regulatory cultural and structural ghettoization.

Despite these fundamental disagreements, ultimately these two approaches do provide complementary perspectives on the macro-dynamic structuration of sexualities in late modernity, facilitating detailed comparative research and analysis, not only in sociology but in such cognate disciplines as political theory, geography, and social policy. The strengths of the paradigm are many: hitherto discrete sexualities are grounded in the same material conditions of disorganized capitalism; all aspects of conventionally desexualized citizenship rights and duties are revealed as heteronormatively discriminating between sexually differentiated populations; and perhaps most important of all, hegemonic heteronormativity itself, so often left as an all-powerful but nebulous organizing principle, is revealed in all its concrete complexity, inconsistency, and duplicity.

Inevitably, areas of tension, uneven development, and omission remain. Culturalist perspectives can underemphasize or even ignore the importance of materialist influences on the construction of sexualities. Structuralism can be too reductionist and (given its primary focus on formal citizenship principles and processes) can give less attention to sexual constituencies ignored by the latter. Corrective responses have been forthcoming, however, with, for example, an expansive literature on distinctive forms of lesbian citizenship ranging from the gendered general (because all citizenship formulations ignore structural processes of gendered power) to the politically specific: "Why should we attempt to further rights within a system whose very operation depends on logic that defines lesbians as 'deviant outsiders' in order to confirm the 'normality' of heterosexuality?" (Jackson 1996–7).

Reference here to "further rights" highlights the need for sexual citizenship studies to resist fragmentation into specific "equal rights" such as "same-sex marriage" and thus lose sight of the wider citizenship context. Same-sex marriage may initially be a dissident challenge, but it is the first step of incorporation into citizenship compliance with heteronormative standards of "husband"/"wife" gendered roles, "monogamy," economic interdependence, and, however achieved, "parenthood," which leaves the "dominant regime of truth" intact. Similarly, advocations of "queering" the state from within – in education, adoption, fostering, and health care, etc. – are effectively neutralized by institutional practice. Meanwhile, with the institutionalization of rights through the United Nations charter and the European Court of Human Rights, attention now moves to "transnational" arenas of sexual citizenship, in which, however, current evidence suggests, the "right to family life" still takes precedence over all others.

SEE ALSO: Capitalism; Citizenship; Gay and Lesbian Movement; Queer Theory; Sexual Identities

REFERENCES AND SUGGESTED READINGS

Evans, D. T. (1993) *Sexual Citizenship: The Material Construction of Sexualities.* Routledge, London.

Giddens, A. (1992) *The Transformation of Intimacy: Sexuality, Love and Eroticism in Modern Societies.* Polity Press, Cambridge.

HMSO (1991) *Citizen's Charter: Raising the Standard.* Cmnd. 1599, July. HMSO, London.

Jackson, S. (1996–7) Taking Liberties. *Trouble and Strife* 34: 36–43.

Marshall, T. H. (1950) *Citizenship and Social Class, and other Essays.* Cambridge University Press, Cambridge.

Mort, F. (1980) Sexuality, Regulation and Contestation. In: Gay Left, Collective (Ed.), *Homosexuality, Power and Politics.* Allison & Busby, London.

Plummer, K. (1992) Speaking Its Name: Inventing a Lesbian and Gay Studies. In: Plummer, K. (Ed.), *Modern Homosexualities.* Routledge, London.

Plummer, K. (2003) Intimate Citizenship and the Culture of Sexual Story Telling. In: Weeks, J., Holland, J., & Waites, S. (Eds.), *Sexualities and Society.* Polity Press, Cambridge.

Richardson, D. (2000) Claiming Citizenship? Sexuality, Citizenship and Lesbian/Feminist Theory. *Sexualities* 3(2): 255–72.

Turner, B. S. (1993a) Contemporary Problems in the Theory of Citizenship. In: Turner, B. S. (Ed.),

Citizenship and Social Theory. Sage, London, pp. 1–19.
Turner, B. S. (1993b) Outline of a Theory of Human Rights. *Sociology* 27(3): 489–512.
Urry, J. (2000) Mobile Sociology. *British Journal of Sociology* 51: 185–203.
Weeks, J. (1998) The Sexual Citizen. *Theory, Culture and Society* 15(3–4): 35–52.
Wolfenden Report (1957) The Report of the Committee on Homosexual Offences and Prostitution. Cmnd. 247. HMSO, London.

sexual cultures in Africa

Suzanne Leclerc-Madlala

Sexual cultures throughout the world comprise the socially and culturally created experience of human sexuality, including shared norms, values, beliefs, attitudes, and knowledges that shape and give meaning to behaviors related to sex. In Africa, a continent that is exceedingly diverse, patterns of sexual culture can be expected to exhibit considerable variation. In terms of religion, language, culture, topography, climate, economy, and governance, Africa presents a rich tapestry of distinctive ways of life. While Islamic cultures predominate in the semi-tropical and desert regions north of the Sahara, extending southwards along both the east and west coasts, Christianity pervades in much of the forest and savannah regions south of the Sahara. Life in most all African societies today resonates with an infusion of traditions derived from these major religions plus more indigenous aspects of culture such as animism and matrilineal descent (western and central Africa), or ancestor honoring and patrilineal descent (eastern and southern Africa). The large cattle-keeping pastoral societies of the east and south such as the Masai, Buganda, Shona, and Zulu present a stark contrast to the much smaller agricultural and foraging societies that inhabit the central rainforest belt. Africa is also home to the San people (often termed Bushmen), one of the world's longest surviving hunter-gathering groups. Perhaps what is most common to all these societies is their rapid integration into national cash economies and global networks of trade and industry. Modern scholarship on African sexual cultures gives recognition to the great diversity of Africa and seeks to accurately reflect this diversity through empirically grounded studies of people's experiences of sexuality.

As a specific area of academic inquiry, the study of African sexual cultures is fairly recent. In many of the early writings by western explorers, missionaries, colonial administrators, and academics, descriptions of particular aspects of sexual culture were most often alluded to with reference to marriage and kinship (e.g., Radcliffe-Brown & Forde 1950). Thus, a major point of departure for modern scholars is the previous silencing of African subjectivity during the colonial encounter followed by the employment of tropes of excess, unrestrained carnality, irrationality, and violence when describing African sexuality. In addition to perpetuating negative stereotypes, much of the previous literature did little to portray the variegated nature of the African continent and its people. Thus, while studies by McClintock (1995), Stoler (2002), and Nagel (2003) have contributed much to our understanding of the intersections between African sexual cultures and the historic experience of oppression, erstwhile representations of a "hypersexed" African and persistent ignorance of the continent's diversity continue to dog the study of this important topic.

NEW DIMENSIONS

How are sex and sexuality played out, performed, constituted, interrogated, and reconfigured in the context of a modernizing Africa? How have the legacies of colonialism, Christianity, Islam, and apartheid as well as the ongoing effects of poverty, civil war, and racism contributed to the construction of sexual cultures and the norms that guide sexual relations? What is the impact of globalization on sexual identities and people's ideas and behaviors related to sex? These are amongst the most significant questions guiding contemporary studies of African sexual cultures. A major approach to the topic involves the application of modern theoretical frameworks such as gender and "queer" theory to issues that have long been of interest to scholars of African culture more generally, for example bridewealth, wife-inheritance, polygamy, and customary systems of power and authority. Of recent significance is a collection of works dedicated to exploring sexuality in the context of Africa edited by Signe Arnfred (2004) entitled *Rethinking African Sexualities.* Various contributors to this volume explore a range of contemporary sexualities and the multiple ways in which they are being addressed. Included is work by Haram that examines the meanings that women attach to "survival sex," which involves having children with several men and maintaining sexual relationships with them as a way to meet their own and their children's material needs. Using the term "polyandrous motherhood" (as theorized by Guyer in the mid-1990s), Haram raises a perennial question of the applicability and universality of western-derived notions such as prostitution.

Of particular theoretical importance to the study of African sexual cultures are two opposing arguments. Firstly, that traditional African arrangements of sexuality and gender have allowed for a far richer diversity than is suggested by western terms of sexual identity; and secondly, that traditional African morality did not allow for sexualities beyond heterosexualism. Lending support to the first argument are scholars such as Amadiume (1987), Teunis (1996), Murray and Roscoe (1998), and more recently Tamale (2003) and Wieringa (2005). Teunis's description of the *gordjiguene* of Senegal, literally translated as man-woman, reveals a long acceptance of "feminine" men who have sex with other men and today are referred to as homosexual. For the *gordjiguene* the label of homosexual is too limited and misleading. Theirs is a way of life that betrays a certain institutionalized bisexuality with the concurrent maintenance of heterosexual identity. Blackwood and Wieringa (1999) have reported similar examples of flexible sexualities from across the continent. Others, such as Zimbabwean President Robert Mugabe, continue to argue that homosexuality and anything other than peno-vaginal intercourse are the imported practices of western decadence and inherently "un-African." Yet, ongoing research consistently suggests otherwise. What appears to be a long history of cultural tolerance for multifarious and unfixed sexualities is currently at odds in many African states with conservative public discourses and "denialism" about alternative sexualities. According to Reddy (2004), this discordant situation encourages homophobia and the silencing of local voices on matters of sex. While modern constitutional laws in many African countries provide for freedom of expression and protection from sexual discrimination, present-day same-sex relationships are often denounced and not uncommonly subject to acts of violence. Political sensitivities around issues related to sex are doubtless a factor in both the paucity of African scholars writing about sexual cultures and a result of that same paucity. Increased participation by African scholars in the study of and reporting on the continent's sexual cultures should help to obviate some of the prevailing inconsistencies, stereotypes, and sexual prejudices that currently exist.

AIDS AND DEMOCRACY

The entrenchment of the HIV/AIDS pandemic and the consolidation of democratic systems across the continent over the past few decades have given a certain urgency to the topic of sexual cultures and have informed the nature of much recent research. Work by Schoeph (1991), Ankomah (1992), Caldwell et al. (1992), McGrath et al. (1993), and Orubuloye et al. (1993) amongst others defined a subfield of African studies in gender and AIDS during the early phases of the pandemic. Analyzing how hegemonic sexual cultures tend to lend support for various forms of sexual discrimination, or how such cultures (especially those where marriage customarily entails a large bridewealth) tend to subordinate women and contribute to their vulnerability to HIV infection, emerged as crucial areas of study in the 1990s. Ongoing debates around practices such as female circumcision which persists in many African Islamic societies continue to point up the tensions between tradition and modern democratic notions of gender and sexual rights (Shell-Duncan & Hemlund 2000). A recent collection of work edited by Ouzgane and Morrell entitled *African Masculinities* (2005) highlights the need for more research on social constructions of manliness and the role these play in the production of sexual cultures. A contribution here by Silberschmidt demonstrates how shrinking employment opportunities for East African men in the past two decades, accelerated by structural adjustment programs, have eroded men's ability to be breadwinners and contributed to increased violence toward women and multipartnered casual sex. These behaviors in turn have had, and continue to have, a direct bearing on the consistently high rates of HIV/AIDS in that part of the world. Morgan and Wieringa's (2005) work on female same-sex practices addresses the issue of applying universal norms of freedom, human rights, and sexual identity to societies with very different social and cultural structures from those which produced dominant constructs such as "gay" or "lesbian." These authors consider the institutionalized practice of women marriages amongst groups where the continuity of the patrilineage and royal statuses are of prime concern. In these societies (reported to be customary in some 40 African societies), women paid bridewealth for another woman who was expected to bear children as heirs to the bloodline of the female-husband. While various scholars have suggested different sociological reasons for women marriages in Africa (e.g., Herskovits 1937; Amadiume 1987), it is only recently that scholars such as Morgan and Wieringa (2005) have attempted to discern elements of sexual attraction or other qualities that would invoke a western understanding of lesbianism.

GLOBALIZATION

According to Altman (2001), a leading scholar on the impact of globalization on sexual cultures, many non-western societies including those in Africa can expect to see the rapid emergence of new "hybridities," that is, where old forms of acting out sexuality increasingly coexist with new imported identities. Amongst younger, better-educated, and more urbanized African women, there is an emerging lesbian identity with links to global movements and networks. In societies long familiar with customs such as women marriage, a major dimension of current research involves discerning the extent, if any, new globalized forms of sexuality are rooted or shaped by past local practices.

The sexual cultures of all human societies are based on complex norms, values, and moral codes. Traditionally in many African societies, notions of respect, restraint, and avoidance were key notions related to sexual behavior. As African societies have become more modernized and increasingly subjected to the forces of globalization with greater exposure to foreign media, traditional ways of regulating sexuality have declined while new forms of sexual behavior and norms have arisen. In South Africa for example, the practice of older age-mates instructing youth on how to avoid pregnancies through the use of non-penetrative "thigh sex" known as *ukumetsha* amongst the Xhosa and *ukusoma* amongst the Zulu virtually disappeared by the 1950s with increasing Christianization and rapid urbanization (Delius & Glaser 2002). Scholars have argued that contemporary patterns of sexual culture in Africa that often include multipartnered casual sex, high levels of sexual violence, teenage pregnancy, and HIV/AIDS are not so much a result of traditional permissiveness as a result of the breakdown of traditional norms and regulations surrounding sex (e.g., Standing & Kisekka 1989; Ahlberg 1994). Reflecting on the rapid pace of change in the developing world, Altman (2001) reminds us that for many people sexual desire coexists with a "desire for modernity," that is, a desire to be part of the affluence and freedom associated with images of the rich world. With reference to Africa, Leclerc-Madlala (2003) suggests that one way to understand contemporary practices of "transactional sex" or sex-for-gifts exchanges is as an "updated" version of "survival sex," with the new pressures of consumerism having replaced the former pressures of survival in communities with growing wealth and growing wealth disparities.

As the study of African sexual cultures expands, there is an increasing awareness of the need for more sensitive, ethically sound, and accurate methodologies for collecting data on one of the most private and complex of all human behaviors. The future direction of study on this topic will be shaped by efforts to develop these methodologies along with theories that more accurately explain the linkages between sexual behaviors and the economic, material, social, cultural, and political forces that are active in the environment. With increasing intellectual input by African scholars, it is likely that there will emerge more Afrocentric perspectives to challenge not only dominant discourses and current interpretations of sexual desire and performance, but also the structural conditions that play a role in promoting sexual practices that have dire consequences in the context of AIDS. In many ways we are just beginning to gain knowledge on the vast array of sexual cultures and subcultures in Africa; those that once existed, those that currently exist, and those that are still in the making.

SEE ALSO: AIDS, Sociology of; Apartheid and Nelson Mandela; Essentialism and Constructionism; Female Genital Mutilation; Globalization, Sexuality and; Islamic Sexual Culture; Kinship; Postmodern Sexualities; Prostitution; Religions, African; Same-Sex Marriage/Civic Unions; Sexual Practices; Transgender, Transvestism, and Transsexualism

REFERENCES AND SUGGESTED READINGS

Ahlberg, B. (1994) Is There a Distinct African Sexuality? A Critical Response to Caldwell et al. *Africa* 64(2): 220–42.

Altman, D. (2001) *Global Sex*. University of Chicago Press, Chicago.

Amadiume, I. (1987) *Male Daughters, Female-Husbands, Gender, and Sex in an African Society*. Zed Books, London.

Ankomah, A. (1992) Premarital Sexual Relationships in Ghana in the Era of AIDS. *Health Policy and Planning* 7(2): 135–43.

Blackwood, E. & Wieringa, S. (Eds.) (1999) *Female Desires: Same-Sex Relations and Transgender Practices Across Cultures*. Columbia University Press, New York, pp. 1–39.

Caldwell, J., Caldwell, P., & Orubuloye, I. (1992) The Family and Sexual Networking in Sub-Saharan Africa: Historic Regional Differences and Present-Day Implications. *Population Studies* 46: 385–410.

Delius, P. & Glaser, C. (2002) Sexual Socialization in Historical Perspective. *African Studies* 61: 22–47.

Guyer, J. (1996) Traditions of Invention in Equatorial Africa. *African Studies Review* 39(3): 1–28.

Heald, S. (1995) The Power of Sex: Reflections on the Caldwells' "African Sexuality" Thesis. *Africa* 65(4): 489–505.

Herskovits, M. J. (1937) A Note on Woman Marriage in Dahomey. *Africa* 10(3): 335–41.

Leclerc-Madlala, S. (2003) Transactional Sex and the Pursuit of Modernity. *Social Dynamics* 29(2): 213–33.

McClintock, A. (1995) *Imperial Leather: Race, Gender, and Sexuality in the Colonial Conquest*. Routledge, New York.

McGrath, J., Rwabukwali, C., Schmann, D., Pearson, J., Nakayiwa, S., Namande, B., Nakyobel, R., & Mukassa, R. (1993) The Cultural Context of Sexual Risk Behaviour Among Urban Women of Kampala. *Social Science and Medicine* 36(4): 429–39.

Morgan, R. & Wieringa, S. (Eds.) (2005) *Tommy Boys, Lesbian Men, and Ancestral Wives*. Jacana, Johannesburg.

Murray, S. & Roscoe, W. (Eds.) (1998) *Boy-Wives and Female Husbands: Studies of African Homosexualities*. St. Martin's Press, New York.

Nagel, J. (2003) *Race, Ethnicity, and Sexuality: Intimate Intersections, Forbidden Frontiers*. Oxford University Press, New York.

Orubuloye, I., Caldwell, P., & Caldwell, P. (1993) African Women's Control Over Their Sexuality in an Era of AIDS. *Social Science and Medicine* 37(7): 859–71.

Radcliffe-Browne, A. & Forde, D. (1950) *African Systems of Kinship and Marriage*. Oxford University Press, Oxford.

Reddy, V. (2004) Sexuality in Africa: Some Trends, Transgressions, and Tirades. *Agenda* 62: 3–11.

Schoeph, B. (1991) Sex, Gender, and Society in Zaire. In: Dyson, T. (Ed.), *Sexual Behavior and Networking: Anthropological and Socio-Cultural Studies on the Transmission of HIV*. International Union for the Scientific Study of Population. Liège, Belgium.

Shell-Duncan, B. & Hemlund, Y. (2000) *Female "Circumcision" in Africa: Culture, Controversy, and Change*. Lynn Reiner, Boulder, CO.

Standing, H. & Kisekka, M. (1989) *Sexual Behaviour in Sub-Saharan Africa: A Review and Annotated Bibliography*. School of African and Asian Studies, University of Sussex.

Stoler, A. (2002) *Carnal Knowledge and Imperial Power: Race and the Intimate in Colonial Rule*. University of California Press, Berkeley.

Tamale, S. (2003) "Out of the Closet": Unveiling Sexuality Discourses in Uganda. *Feminist Africa* 2: 38–51.

Teunis, N. (1996) Homosexuality in Dakar: Is the Bed the Heart of a Sexual Subculture? *Journal of Gay, Lesbian, and Bisexual Identities* 1(2): 153–69.

Wieringa, S. (2005) Women Marriages and Other Same-Sex Practices: Historical Reflections on African Women's Same-Sex Relations. In: Morgan, R. & Wieringa, S. (Eds.), *Tommy Boys, Lesbian Men, and Ancestral Wives*. Jacana, Johannesburg, pp. 281–308.

sexual cultures in Asia

Travis S. K. Kong

Sexual cultures in Asia refer to the ways of sexual life – the shared beliefs, values, meanings, and practices – that are common to members of Asian societies.

The sexual cultures of a society refer to its sexual belief systems, usually stemming from folktales, myths, and religions, which provide a framework for what we should think and how we should feel and behave in terms of sexuality. These sexual belief systems in turn give impetus to the forming of a hierarchy of sexual value systems that define what is sexually right or wrong, normal or pathological, honorable or shameful. Sexual belief and value systems, governed by sexual norms and manifested in customs and laws, are shared meanings and practices that are common to different segments of a society and historical periods. Different sexual cultures exist within a society and change over time.

Sexual cultures in Asia refer to many different and somewhat conflicting sexual value systems, as Asia is not a unified entity but a collective term that refers to many countries with divergent and even contradictory social, cultural, economic, and political values and systems.

Studies on sexuality are relatively a new area in sociology. Studies of Asian sexuality have been limited as sociologists have focused overwhelmingly on Anglo-European countries. As anthropologists have the tradition of studying "other" cultures (with the earliest studies having been based mainly on travel reports from missionaries, traders, and seamen), anthropological texts and ethnographic materials provide some discussion of non-western sexuality. Early key scholars such as Bronislaw Malinowski, Ruth Benedict, and Margaret Mead touched upon the issues of gender and sexuality.

With the affirmation of gender and sexuality studies by feminists and gay and lesbian scholars, the rise of postcolonialism, and the growing force of Asian (diasporic) academics, studies on non-western sexual cultures, including Asia, are now being taken seriously (e.g., Herdt 1997; Jackson & Cook 1999; Altman 2001; Ruth 2002). The scholars who carried out these studies tend to charge former scholars with being Eurocentric, pointing to the fact that they exoticized/erotized the "other" and overemphasized such "differences" between Asian and European cultures as sexual "excess," "promiscuity," largely ritualized or visible homosexuality and transgenderism, and so forth. They also point out that the sex/gender system in Asia seems to be different from the systems found in Anglo-European countries, in that terms such as male/female, man/woman, or masculine/feminine are not easily distinguished in Asia and are believed to be a modern invention, heavily influenced by western biological and medical discourses. Thus, studies of gender, sex, and sexuality in Asia tend to show a picture that does not necessarily reflect Anglo-European knowledge.

Recent studies on modern sexual cultures in Asia, as part of studies on Asian cultures and modernity, usually focus on various factors such as colonial histories (if any), traditions and religions, the growing affluence of most Asian countries, and the (de)colonialization strategies of the states, which play crucial roles in shaping ideas about gender, sex, and sexuality and which liberate or regulate possible forms of sexual expression (e.g., on dating, romance, premarital sex, virginity, abortion, divorce, birth control, homosexuality, pornography, prostitution) under the whole process of globalization and decolonization. They also focus on how the emergence of new sexual identities, cultures, and communities simultaneously shapes and reshapes the social life of a particular country or even the global processes of change. Common features of Asian sexual cultures seem to be an interplay or coexistence of indigenous sexual traditions with postmodern western aestheticism, rhetoric, and outlooks.

CHANGES IN MARRIAGE, LOVE, AND SEXUALITY

It is argued that traditional Asian sexual cultures were largely governed by patriarchic structures (rituals, religions, family) that legitimized the power of men (e.g., polygamy or a lineage structure organized around fathers and sons in China, South Korea, Japan) and marginalized women in various ways such as female infanticide (China, India), footbinding (China), chastity (wife burning, *Sati*, in India; chastity shrines in China), reproduction, birth control, and so forth. This discourse of dominance seems to have been less prevalent in Southeast Asia (where women tended to attain a higher status) and has been challenged by other studies that emphasize the subversive power of females (e.g., chastity – abstaining from (re)marriage could be read as female control of sexuality, independence, or hidden lesbianism) (e.g., Ong & Peletz 1995; Manderson & Jolly 1997).

The modern capitalist era has witnessed a profound transformation in the spheres of sexuality and intimacy in Asia, whereby traditional sexual values and practices coexist with modern sexual thoughts of individualism and libertarianism.

The monogamous marriage that is based on personal choice, love, and fulfillment has gradually become the norm, overtaking the traditional arranged marriage which was based on social and economic considerations, although arranged marriages are still practiced in South Asian countries such as India, Pakistan, Bangladesh, and Sri Lanka. There is an increasing variety of traditional extended family patterns such as non-marital cohabitation, voluntary childlessness, never-married singlehood, stepfamilies, and single parenthood, which in turn might lead to problems in caring for the young, the old, and the sick.

Although the traditional gender split in which men are regarded as breadwinners and women as housewives is still maintained in poor countries or in poor/rural regions of a country (e.g., China, India), it has also been challenged as women have become better educated and have come to participate in the job market, especially in developed countries (e.g., Hong Kong, Singapore, Taiwan). Economic achievements and individualistic libertarian ideas have given women a large degree of freedom to create their sexual spaces. Sexual relations between men and women have shifted, and egalitarianism between the sexes seems to have emerged with regard to initiating sex, demanding sexual satisfaction including orgasms, and in patterns of marital, extramarital, and post-marital sex.

The state still has strong control over issues involving sexuality (e.g., the one-child policy in China), but there has been a liberalization in attitudes toward such issues as birth control, abortion, divorce, premarital sex, cohabitation, and homosexuality. Sex and love are increasingly commercialized or commodified. Commercial establishments that facilitate sexual or intimate liaisons (e.g., bars and clubs, massage parlors, saunas, sex shops, dating services, prostitution, etc.) are abundant, which legitimates sex as a domain of pleasure in contrast with the family as the confined site for intimacy.

HOMOSEXUALITY

The dominant discourse describing modern Asian homosexuality tends to assume that most countries in Asia had a longstanding tradition of tolerating men who had desired other men (lesbianism has always been underrepresented). The stories of *yu tao* (the peach remainder) and *tuan-hsiu* (the cut sleeve) were two famous euphemisms among the literati for male homosexuality (*nanse*, *nangfeng*) in Chinese history, dating back to as early as the Zhou period (1122?–256 BCE) (Hinsch 1990). Likewise, Buddhist monasteries and samurai societies (*Shudo*, a young samuri who is befriended by an older man) were believed to be centers for homosexual activities (*nanshoku*) in ancient Japan from the medieval period to the end of the nineteenth century (Leupp 1995).

Social or religious systems of thought such as Confucianism, Taoism, Buddhism, and Hinduism, which are prevalent in most Asian countries, are not concerned with the gender of sexual activity or the object of sexual desire, and thus do not strongly condemn homosexuality in the way that Abrahamic religions (e.g., Christianity) do. As a result, traditional Asian literature does not generally refer to same-gender desire as an innate essence (indicating an identity) but rather as an action, tendency, or preference. Correspondingly, a man who engaged in homosexual acts did not cause much trouble so long as he conformed to or did not challenge the patriarchal family (lineage) structure (e.g., by getting married and bearing children). Homosociality, or same-sex friendships, were largely condoned.

Civic religions and customs tend to encourage sexual and gender ambivalence. In some countries, the presence of a "third gender" is evident. For example, a *hijra* (in India) is a person who is born biologically male or born with ambiguous genitalia but identifies himself as belonging to a "third sex," "neither man nor woman," although he usually picks up a female gender identity. Or in Thailand, a male-to-female transgendered person is called a *katheoy* (or lady boy). Likewise, *bakla* and *bantut* are terms referring to a transgendered person in the Philippines, with the corresponding terms being *banci* in Java and *waria* in Indonesia. The case of Asian homosexuality thus provides a new understanding of the debate over essentialism/constructionism that raged throughout the 1980s in the West.

This relatively tolerated homosexual tradition seemed to come to an end with the advent of modernity and colonialism. For example, homosexual activities in Hong Kong and India were tolerated prior to British colonization but then became a criminal act after the introduction of British laws and legal codes. While male homosexual acts were decriminalized in Hong Kong in 1991, India still has penal laws against homosexual acts.

The present situation regarding homosexuality in Asia seems to be a mixture of state intervention (which can be reflected through penal sanctions against anal sex), large visible and commercial gay scenes (bars, clubs, saunas, etc.), annual gay pride walks or festivals (e.g., South Korea, Bangkok, Manila, Tokyo, Taipei, Phnom Penh, Nepal), and the rise of gay and lesbian organizations.

Countries that have laws penalizing homosexuality include India, Bangladesh, Pakistan, Sri Lanka, Nepal, Malaysia, and Singapore, while countries such as China, Taiwan, Hong Kong, Japan (some cities), South Korea, Thailand, Indonesia, and Cambodia have decriminalized homosexual acts. The legal status of homosexuality does not necessarily refer to a fair or positive attitude from the government. For example, although male homosexuality is not illegal in China, gay men and lesbians are easily arrested (and charged with hooliganism) and gay bars and clubs are frequently raided.

Studies tend to suggest that national political and cultural characteristics play a crucial role in the creation of modern gay and lesbian identities and in the development of national lesbian and gay movements (Adam et al. 1999). Although many modern Asian countries refer to homosexuals as gays and lesbians, each country seems to have its own terms of reference. The creation of a new sexual self is not necessarily a repetition of the gay and lesbian liberation movement in the West. Non-politicized identities and non-political social interactions seem to be dominant in Asian countries. It seems that gay identities have been reconciled within a family-oriented culture and that gay rights have been subsumed under the notion of social harmony. Coming out is not a common way of asserting one's gayness, and desires do not seem to be framed in terms of political interests. There has been a division between personal identity and community politics (e.g., Jackson 1995, on Thailand; Kong 2002, on Hong Kong; McLelland 2000, on Japan).

Moreover, the scale and activities of gay and lesbian organizations depend very much on their economic resources and the political situation in a specific country. Some of these organizations have been quite shortlived. Although gay and lesbian groups in Asia tend to be more inward-looking and to focus on the building of identity, some (e.g., Hong Kong, Taiwan) take on a more visible and confrontational approach to fighting against discrimination and for human rights (e.g., same-sex marriages).

Popular culture has, on the one hand, created a discourse about homosexuality that presents a biased or one-dimensional image of gay men and lesbians (e.g., gay men as sissy fashion queens and lesbians as tough women). On the other hand, it has led to the making of many movies (e.g., *Wedding Banquet*, 1992; *Happy Together*, 1997; *Iron Ladies*, 2001; *Arisan!*, 2003) that directly address the issue of homosexual love, which can be seen from the various lesbian and gay film festivals that are held in Asia (e.g., Hong Kong, Thailand, Tokyo, the Philippines).

Recent studies have not just examined the dynamics between straight and gay communities, but have also discussed the diversity within the gay and lesbian communities, in which differences and marginalization can occur along the lines of gender, class, race, age, and body (Kong 2004), and the Internet as a new way for gay men and lesbians (especially young people and those who live in a homophobic Asian society) to identify one another through sexuality, language, and values (Berry et al. 2003).

THE SEX TRADE

The sex industry is an important economic sector in most countries of Asia. It not only provides sexual services to local people, but also attracts foreign tourists from western and nearby countries.

Sex work can broadly refer to any exchange of sex for money, with or without sexual contact, from striptease shows, live performances, peep shows, telephone sex, sex shops, pornography, and prostitution. Sex work in Asia takes many different forms, ranging from the "standard" forms such as street prostitution, brothels, saunas, and massage parlors to bars and nightclubs. Particular forms can also be found in certain countries. For example, in Taiwan betel nut beauties refer to young girls who dress in fancy clothes, sit in a glass booth, and sell betel nuts to lorry and truck drivers. Live shows in Thailand refer to women injecting objects in their vaginas. And in South Korea, Filipino women work in military bases.

In Asia, the legal status of prostitution varies from one country to another. For example, prostitution is illegal in Vietnam, Indonesia, Japan, and Korea, but not in Hong Kong, Macao, and Singapore (only legal in designated red light areas). However, the legality of prostitution does not necessarily mean that sex workers in those countries receive better treatment. For example, although prostitution is illegal in Japan, female sex workers are rarely prosecuted, while in Hong Kong, prostitution is legal but sex workers are usually arrested for committing other crimes (e.g., soliciting in a public place for "immoral" purposes). There are many loopholes in the law as well as different interpretations of the law which usually discriminate against workers rather than clients or other parties. The punishments for sex workers usually range from being put in jail (e.g., Indonesia), being forced to join labor camps (e.g., China), simply being punished by having to stand up for hours (e.g., Macao), being deported back to one's place of origin if the worker is a foreigner, and/or being fined (Zi Teng & AMRC 2001).

Women who engage in prostitution should be seen not as a unified entity but as a highly stratified group of women whose life experiences vary greatly accordingly to their income, the amount of control and autonomy they have over their work, their impact on the community, and so on. These women differ in age, education, marital status, race, and ethnicity.

The overwhelming reason why women enter prostitution seems to be economic, i.e., they simply need money for their own survival, for their parents and/or their own families, to help their siblings to pay tuition fees, to pay debts that may have been incurred by misfortunes in the family or by a husband addicted to drugs or gambling, and so forth. However, studies also show that some of these women also use prostitution as a way to escape from their families, from unhappy marriages, abusive husbands, and to gain sexual pleasure, economic freedom, and independence. Moreover, there are many women who are forced to engage in prostitution (e.g., women who have been trafficked or under-age girls who are beaten up, raped, and locked up by pimps and/or owners of brothels), but there are also women who choose to work in prostitution (e.g., Wang 2002; Ho 2003). This reflects the feminist debate on prostitution, which centers around the issue of the sexual victim (e.g., Catharine MacKinnon, Andrea Dworkin) versus the sexual agent (e.g., Annie Sprinkle, Pat Califia) with the focal point being choice, consent, and autonomy (see Chapkis 1997).

Child prostitution and the trafficking of children and/or women have received a great deal of attention from academics as well as policymakers. Mobility is a salient feature of the sex industry in Asia which can occur internally (from rural areas to big cities) or externally (to other countries). The sex industry in most Asian countries is a mixture of local and transient migrant workers, forming a "circuit of desire." Although sex workers suffer from many forms of legal discrimination and societal prejudice, a large-scale, visible, and confrontational labor movement is rare. A notable example is when the Taiwanese government decided to abolish licensed sex workers in 1997, and sex workers and supporters protested for days.

Male prostitution is understudied in both Anglo-European and Asian countries (Aggleton 1999). Male prostitution also takes many different forms such as hustling in public places, working in bars and clubs and in massage parlors, and providing escort services. Male prostitution complicates the debate on prostitution:

male prostitution (serving women) challenges that it is the woman – as a customer – who holds economic power and pays for her own pleasure. Male prostitution (serving men) poses a greater challenge as it recognizes the inequalities among members of the same gender, reinforces the logic of desire and consumption, and upsets the egalitarian ideal of the gay liberation movement (Kong 2005).

HIV/AIDS

HIV/AIDS has spread in Asia in diverse ways. It seems to be most extensive in Cambodia, Myanmar, Thailand, and parts of India, while there has been a sharp increase in China, Indonesia, Nepal, and Vietnam; although Bangladesh, Laos, and the Philippines have reported some of the lowest HIV rates in the world. As Asia comprises nearly 60 percent of the world's population, the epidemic in Asia has huge implications for the globe (www.unaids.org).

In contrast to Africa, where the major route of transmission is through casual heterosexual relationships, the key risk populations in Asia include drug users who inject drugs, men who have sex with men, sex workers and their clients, and the immediate sexual partners of these three populations. In Asia, the HIV epidemic has tended to be multiple and interrelated in nature. For example, drug users might make use of commercial sex services or even sell sex, sex workers may use drugs, and men who have sex with men may also visit female sex workers.

Tackling HIV/AIDS seems to be an urgent issue for most governments, but the problem is difficult to combat as it is not just a medical disease but a social problem involving issues of social stigma, morality, and control. Although ignorance or lack of knowledge might be a significant reason for HIV infection especially in poor countries, sexual cultures and values seem to be far more important in influencing safer-sex practices than the transmission of information or even the availability of condoms.

For example, drug users who inject drugs play an important role in the spread of the virus in many countries (e.g., China, Vietnam, and Malaysia). However, in certain parts of China, drug users have been known to deliberately inject infected blood into themselves in order to avoid being admitted to reeducation centers for drug users. Men who have sex with men (MSM) are a largely ignored group in certain countries (e.g., India, China) that do not officially recognize the existence of such people. Most sex workers might be serious about using condoms with their clients but are ambivalent about using them with their non-paid affective partners, with whom they might not be in a monogamous relationship. Unprotected penetrative sex in the context of an affective relationship has a significant symbolic meaning for sex workers.

SEE ALSO: AIDS, Sociology of; Coming Out/Closets; Drag Queens and Drag Kings; Essentialism and Constructionism; Globalization, Sexuality and; Homosexuality; Postmodern Sexualities; Prostitution; Safer Sex; Same-Sex Marriage/Civic Unions; Sexual Identities; Sex Tourism; Sexual Identities; Sexual Practices; Transgender, Transvestism and Transsexualism

REFERENCES AND SUGGESTED READINGS

Adam, B. D., Duyvendak, J. W., & Krouwel, A. (Eds.) (1999) *The Global Emergence of Gay and Lesbian Politics: National Imprints of a Worldwide Movement.* Temple University Press, Philadelphia.

Aggleton, P. (Ed.) (1999) *Men Who Sell Sex: International Perspectives on Male Prostitution and AIDS.* UCL Press, London.

Altman, D. (2001) *Global Sex.* University of Chicago Press, Chicago.

Berry, C., Martin, F., & Yue, A. (Eds.) (2003) *Mobile Cultures: New Media in Queer Asia.* Duke University Press, Durham, NC.

Chapkis, W. (1997) *Live Sex Acts: Women Performing Erotic Labor.* Routledge, New York.

Herdt, G. (1997) *Same Sex, Different Cultures: Exploring Gay and Lesbian Lives.* Westview Press, Boulder, CO.

Hinsch, B. (1990) *Passions of the Cut Sleeve: The Male Homosexual Tradition in China.* University of California Press, Berkeley.

Ho, J. (Ed.) (2003) *Sex Work Studies.* Center for the Studies of Sexualities, National Central University, Taiwan (in Chinese).

Jackson, P. A. (1995) *Dear Uncle Go: Male Homosexuality in Thailand.* Bua Luang Books, California.

Jackson, P. A. & Cook, N. M. (Eds.) (1999) *Genders and Sexualities in Modern Thailand.* Silkworm, Chiang Mai.
Kong, T. S. K. (2002) The Seduction of the Golden Boy: The Body Politics of Hong Kong Gay Men. *Body and Society* 8(1): 29–48.
Kong, T. S. K. (2004) Queer at Your Own Risk: Marginality, Community, and the Body Politics of Hong Kong Gay Men. *Sexualities* 7(1): 5–30.
Kong, T. S. K. (2005) *The Hidden Voice: The Sexual Politics of Chinese Male Sex Workers.* Center for Social Policy Studies, Hong Kong Polytechnic University, Hong Kong.
Leupp, G. P. (1995) *Male Colors: The Construction of Homosexuality in Tokugawa Japan.* University of California Press, Berkeley.
McLelland, M. J. (2000) *Male Homosexuality in Modern Japan: Cultural Myths and Social Realities.* Curzon, Surrey.
Manderson, L. & Jolly, M. (Eds.) (1997) *Sites of Desire/Economies of Pleasure: Sexualities in Asia and the Pacific.* University of Chicago Press, Chicago.
Ong, A. & Peletz, M. G. (Eds.) (1995) *Bewitching Women, Pious Men: Gender and Body Politics in Southeast Asia.* University of California Press, Berkeley.
Ruth, V. (2002) *Queering India: Same-Sex Love and Eroticism in Indian Culture and Society.* Routledge, New York.
Wang, Huan et al. (2002) *Asian Sex Workers' Stories.* Zi Teng and Stepforward Multimedia, Hong Kong (in Chinese).
ZiTeng & AMRC (Eds.) (2001) *Building an Effective Network in the Service of Migrant Sex Workers in East and South East Asia.* Asia Monitor Resource Center, Hong Kong.

sexual cultures in Latin America

Salvador Vidal-Ortiz

A definition of "sexual cultures in Latin America" necessarily rests on a series of assumptions that need to be unpacked, thereby offering productive ways of thinking about what "sexual cultures in Latin America" means – and how to empirically engage with them in related research. First, the notion of "Latin America" is based on the disparate unification of many countries (from the rest of the Americas) through a perceived cultural homogeneity that ignores language variability, rival historical relations, economic and political differences, and national distinctions (including nationalistic discourses of difference between many of these countries). As well, Latin Americanist and ethnographic scholars debate what fits within the notion of "Latin America," since there are often a variety of linguistic, geographic, and political reasons given in such scholarship to exclude or include nations or regions, as exemplified by the challenges in placing or excluding countries like Puerto Rico, Brazil, Spain, the English-speaking Caribbean, and even the Southern cone.

The second assumption is that using "Latin American" negates the relationship between Latin Americans in Latin America, Latin Americans in the US, and US Latinos, and it inherently erases racialization processes for those that migrate to the US. Third, like any other definitions containing the word "culture," it presupposes anthropological colonization strategies that situate such culture in oppositional frameworks. And last, the framing of "sexual cultures" in Latin America (often meaning "not here") presupposes a distinction between some of the theoretical frameworks through which social scientists understand culture and regions all over the world, which is often using the US as a referent. Views of gender and sexuality systems that are not US or western-based tend to be labeled as premodern (Decena 2004), without in turn exploring how in US or western contexts alternative ways of looking at the gender/sexuality relationship are taking place within these borders, whether by Latinos or *United Staters* alike. Linked to this last assumption is a bias: framing sexual cultures, like any other framing of cultural elements, has the potential to foreground a culturalist argument that hides political economic relations between countries and regions in other parts of the world facing similar relations to that of "Latin American" countries – a key example is the Pacific Islands and their relationship to US militarization and colonialism to countries like Puerto Rico (Vidal-Ortiz 2004). As well, it ignores how the US is as much a Latin American region as any other country, given the demographics of US society.

These assumptions notwithstanding, the available social science literature today does provide several crucial issues inherent in this scholarship's currency. Issues like how sex, gender, and sexuality are conceptualized in "Latin America," HIV/AIDS (Carrillo 2002), sex tourism (Cantú 2002), the impact of Latin Americans' migration to the US (and the migration back and forth between rural and urban contexts in Latin American countries, and between those countries and the US) (Decena 2004; Peña 2005), ideas about bisexuality in Latin American culture (Cantú 1999), and heterosexual sexuality research discussions (González-López 2005) are important and central to such scholarship. For reasons of space, the discussion here focuses only on the sex/gender system implicit in Latin American studies (including masculinity and sexuality studies), sex tourism, and finally migration and sexuality.

SEX/GENDER AND POWER

Most of the "sexual cultures" scholarship in Latin American societies engages the relationship between sex(uality) and gender, namely, the assumption that links gendered expectations to that of oppositional sexual acts and identifications (Almaguer 1993; Guzmán 2006). Almaguer (1993) argued that unlike western countries, where sexuality and gender are distinct aspects of the "self" enacted through different vectors, in Mexico, and by extension Mexican families and in other Latin American countries, the distinction of gender and sexuality has been notoriously marked by an understanding of the (male) actors' positioning in sexual activity. Succinctly, a heterosexual man is still considered such in the event of having sex with another man, if he is the *activo*, relegating the homosexual stigma to the penetrated, or *pasivo* person (see also Lancaster 1992; Carrier 1995; Murray 1995). It has been this system, linked as it is to the inequalities faced by women, that many scholars have discussed as *machismo* in Latin American societies. Further sociological and anthropological writings have expanded and contested Almaguer's work, stating how this is simplifying Anglo sexualities, noting how sexual identity and sexual behavior do not have to be congruent (Cantú 2002), that this typology ignores the mutual influence of migration (Carrier 1995), and that indeed partial sexual identities emerge out of this *activo/pasivo* notion, and are "part and parcel of the culture itself" (Guzmán 1997: 217), and not merely an incision or segment of political movements.

Specific anthropological research has tackled the question of how sexuality and gender apply to other countries, regions, or different configurations of culture, such as *travestis* in Brazil (Kulick 1998). Kulick notes that research before his looked at homosexual roles in Latin America, and such research has perceived a relationship to sexuality and gender, but, he qualifies, has mistakenly conflated sex and gender, thus not theorizing those links to cultural understandings of the interplay of sexuality, gender, and sex. As Guzmán (1997) and Kulick (1998) have both argued (in the US and in Brazil), the "man/non-man" categorization of sexuality and gender offers us possibilities to reconceptualize the relationship between sexuality and gender, sexual desire, and notions of sexual actors in gendered terms. (Using this "man/non-man" categorization helps understand the relationship of homosexual men and all women into what may be understood as "sexual minorities.") Research by these two scholars has suggested that the "man/non-man" categorization through terms such as *mayate*, *bugarrón*, *loca*, or *travestí* offer possibilities to reconceptualize the relationship between sexuality and gender.

In addition, as Guzmán (2006) has recently suggested, racial difference might be interpreted in the US as different sexual identificatory practices among "Latin American" "sexual minorities." Notions of "Latin American" identities are often used as a foundation to "racially" distinguish between North Americans and "Latin Americans." (Even though "Latinos" are ethnicized in US society, these frameworks create a difference in racialized terms [Urciuoli 1996], as will be seen in the sex tourism section.) As recently discussed by Lancaster (2005), this difference of *homology* (fusing the sexual activity of men with men into a homosexual identity, supposedly common in US society) and *heterology* (a consideration not only of the sexual actors, but also of the acts themselves and how those are read in gendered ways, credited to Latin Americans) is then discussed as "sexual culture." While these differences are "intriguing" anthropologically speaking, if we are not careful, we are only one step away from claiming them as oppositional to those of US culture, reifying the meaning of culture altogether.

Taking this literature in general, comparisons between Latin America and the US indicate that these sexualities and sexual cultures are more complex than previously argued. As well, the relationship between sex and gender as theorized until now greatly misses women, and lesbians in particular (for a recent, refreshing exception offering a great history of lesbian organizing in Latin America, refer to Mogrovejo 2005), and, to a lesser extent, transgender, transsexual, and *travestí* Latin Americans in Latin America or the US.

SEX TOURISM

Sexual tourism feeds into this US/Latin American opposition often posed by social scientists. Countries like Cuba, Puerto Rico, Mexico, Panama, Colombia, the Dominican Republic, and Brazil are considered sex tourist destinations by foreigners (Perlongher 1999; La Fountain-Stokes 2002; Hill 2004). This sex tourism exists in great part due to local economic needs and individual obligations to one's family. Herein the issue of seeking, for instance, gay male tourists by non-self-identified gay men is recurrent in the literature. (While there is limitation to migrate outside of these Latin American countries, Parker 1999 and Agustín 2003 have discussed the migration of Latin American sex workers to Europe.)

Because of notions of hypersexualized "Latin American" women and men, many of these destinations flourish in terms of their local supply of sex workers. And because many of these countries have a hybrid racial classification (and offer various African, Asian, and indigenous phenotypical readings of race), often a sexualized racialization takes place where those tourists have an idea of racial difference that is highly eroticized. Add to that mix the reading of heterosexually identified men who have sex with men and there is a significant system of sexual-racial difference that feeds in those oppositions – both by the tourists and by the locals. Another significant element is the international debt in which many of these countries are involved, and the often lower socioeconomic and educational status of sex workers, forcing a serious class distinction to exist between a European or US tourist whose money will be exchanged and the cost of a sex worker that will be a fraction of the type of escort and sex work services in many US cities (see Perlongher 1999; Hill 2004).

SEXUAL MIGRATION AND SEXUAL IDENTITY

In social scientific literature, terms like *sexual migration* (see, e.g., Carrillo 2004) help us to understand the seemingly strong pool of "sexual minorities" that come to the US for support and a space that presumably is missing in their Latin American country of origin. This notion of sexual migration, however, begins in the US. "Canonical" works on "gay and lesbian" migration have argued for the formation of such enclaves as a departure from an oppressive home to a more open space where communities have formed (D'Emilio 1983; Rubin 1993 [1984]). An assumed rupture from one's family of origin was the basis for massive migratory patterns that created "gay cities" all over the US. Rubin's and D'Emilio's work has been critiqued for its inability to address the supposedly "better" place – the urban center (Cantú 1999; Decena 2004; Guzmán 2006). This sexual migration has also been discussed internationally – in this particular case, Latin America – where it depends on linearly articulated ideas of oppression of "gays" that migrate from rural to urban places, and it uses the notion of a Latin American tight familial control as its axis. Decena, for instance, in his work on Dominican homosexual men and migration, brings out the capitalist tendencies of such scholarship in opposing a "gay" identity and lack of familial ties when he states that: "the sexually liberated capital is exciting and attractive because it allows one to break away from the bonds of patriarchal family relations" (2004: 4). Cantú's work is also helpful: he signaled that a similar "urban" migration to that of gays and lesbians of European descent was taking place, by homosexual Mexican men – in his research, from Mexico to metropolitan areas in Southern California. Cantú troubles the relationship between political economy and culturalist arguments by asking: "If the literature on the social construction of a Western gay identity is correct in linking sexual identities to capitalist development, then why should our understanding of sexual identities in the 'developing world' give primacy to culture and divorce it from political economy?" (2002: 141). His answer is that among US scholars, and specifically in the anthropological literature cited by Almaguer, "culture became the mechanism that reified difference and reproduced the imagined distance of 'the others' in academic discourse itself." Additional answers to these questions are also being currently produced by a number of academic scholars.

Other terms have furthered this notion of migration caused by sexual oppression; in particular, the concept of the *sexile* (coined by Guzmán 1997) serves us well in recognizing the trajectory of "sexual minorities" who have left their countries of origin *because of* their sexuality and/or atypical gendered behavior. "Sexual migration" and "sexile" both indicate an interplay between culture, sexual agency, identity, and transnational flows, but say little about the economic and social characteristics of life in Latin American society, or the reasons for seeking to move to the US (or Europe for that matter – see, e.g., Pichardo Galán 2003). Even though it may seem logical to think that most migration by "sexual minorities" from Latin America involves travel to the US because of their sexual identity, no evidence can support this as a central reason for migrating. Instead, economic factors continue to be a leading reason for the migration of "sexual minorities" (see, e.g., Cantú 1999). To complicate matters somewhat, whereas in US social movements and identity politics the lesbian, gay, bisexual, and transgender (LGBT) acronym is representative of different, if related, "sexual minorities," scholars and lay folk outside such a community (and outside the US) might simply locate all within the same category: *gay*. Whatever "gay" means, it often means "non-man," where man is understood as heterosexual and with a particular (hegemonic) masculinity. We see an increasing exportation of human rights based on neatly defined categories in the advocacy for political asylum for gay-, lesbian-, bisexual-, and transgender-identified people (refer to the work by Cantú 2005; Miller 2005; Randazzo 2005), partly in order to sustain a dichotomy that establishes the US as a more developed and accepting society.

CONCLUSION

Unfortunately, sexuality research tends to focus on Mexico, and then attempts are made to generalize such findings to the rest of Latin America. In addition, the abundant research on gender/sexuality and race conducted in Brazil focusing on *travestis* (Kulick 1998) and sex/gender and masculinities (Parker 1999) is often utilized to compare Latino US-based populations to Latin American ones. This is, we have been told, because in the "American" imaginary, "Latin Americans" are simply just like each other. But perhaps that perception actually covers another one: some groups under that "Latino" or "Latin American" umbrella are much more exotic, or those sexualities are labeled much more based on gender constructs in premodern societies, or inadvertently converted into sexual machines, in some places than others. Thus this sexualized racialization is selective in terms of how gendered it is: some may see people from countries such as Brazil as ultra masculine and heterosexually identified, and simultaneously see men from Mexico as smaller and more feminized. Sexual desire may follow the racialization at hand. In this sense, "Latin American" itself is a construct that does no justice to the sexual variability within those countries – nor to the consumption of those sexual actors in "Latin America." Instead of oppositional cultural arrangements where "Latin American" is simply read culturally – not in terms of racialization – a newer analysis may hold a conversation with such scientific frameworks and force them to acknowledge alternative analyses besides binary systems.

SEE ALSO: Culture; Feminist Activism in Latin America; Globalization, Sexuality and; Hegemonic Masculinity; Sex and Gender; Sex Tourism; Sexual Identities; Sexual Practices; Transgender, Transvestism, and Transsexualism

REFERENCES AND SUGGESTED READINGS

Agustín, L. M. (2003) La industria del sexo, migrantes en Europa, y prostitución. In: Guasch, O. & Viñuales, O. (Eds.), *Sexualidades: Diversidad y Control Social.* Edicions Bellaterra, Barcelona, pp. 259–75.

Almaguer, T. (1993) Chicano Men: A Cartography of Homosexual Identity and Behavior. In: Abelove, H., Barale, M. A., & Halperin, D. M. (Eds.), *The Lesbian and Gay Studies Reader.* Routledge, New York, pp. 255–73.

Cantú, L. (2005) Well Founded Fear: Political Asylum and the Boundaries of Sexual Identity in the US–Mexico Borderlands. In: Luibhéid, E. & Cantú, L., Jr. (Eds.), *Queer Migrations: Sexuality, US Citizenship, and Border Crossings.* University of Minnesota Press, Minneapolis, pp. 61–74.

Cantú, L., Jr. (1999) Border Crossings: Mexican Men and the Sexuality of Migration. Unpublished dissertation, Department of Social Relations, University of California, Irvine.

Cantú, L., Jr. (2002) *De Ambiente*: Queer Tourism and the Shifting Boundaries of Mexican Male Sexualities. *GLQ* 8: 139–66.

Carrier, J. (1995) *De Los Otros: Intimacy and Homosexuality Among Mexican Men.* Columbia University Press, New York.

Carrillo, H. (2002) *The Night is Young: Sexuality in Mexico in the Time of AIDS.* University of Chicago Press, Chicago.

Carrillo, H. (2004) Sexual Migration, Cross-Cultural Sexual Encounters, and Sexual Health. *Sexuality Research and Social Policy* 1(3): 58–70.

D'Emilio, J. (1983) *Sexual Politics, Sexual Communities: The Making of a Modern Minority.* University of Chicago Press, Chicago.

Decena, C. U. (2004) Queering the Heights: Dominican Transnational Identities and Male Homosexuality in New York City. Unpublished dissertation, American Studies, New York University.

González-López, G. (2005) *Erotic Journeys: Mexican Immigrants and their Sexual Lives.* University of California Press, Berkeley.

Guzmán, M. (1997) "Pa' la escuelita con mucho cuida'o y por la orillita": A Journey through the Contested Terrains of the Nation and Sexual Orientation. In: Negrón-Muntaner, F. & Grosfoguel, R. (Eds.), *Puerto Rican Jam: Rethinking Colonialism and Nationalism.* University of Minnesota Press, Minneapolis, pp. 210–29.

Guzmán, M. (2006) *Gay Hegemony/Latino Homosexualities.* Routledge, New York.

Hill, R. (2004) *El cuerpo como empresa: Los sexiservidores.* Grupo Editorial Lumen, Buenos Aires.

Kulick, D. (1998) *Travesti: Sex, Gender, and Culture Among Brazilian Transgendered Prostitutes.* University of Chicago Press, Chicago.

La Fountain-Stokes, L. (2002) De Un Pájaro Las Dos Alas: Travel Notes of a Queer Puerto Rican in Havana. *GLQ* 8(1–2): 7–33.

Lancaster, R. (1992) *Life is Hard: Machismo, Danger, and the Intimacy of Power in Nicaragua.* University of California Press, Berkeley.

Lancaster, R. (2005) Tolerance and Intolerance in Sexual Cultures in Latin America. In: Epps, B., Valens, K., & Johnson González, B. (Eds.), *Passing Lines: Sexuality and Immigration.* Harvard University Press, Cambridge, MA, pp. 255–74.

Miller, A. (2005) Gay Enough: Some Tensions in Seeking the Grant of Asylum and Protecting Global Sexual Diversity. In: Epps, B., Valens, K., & Johnson González, B. (Eds.), *Passing Lines: Sexuality and Immigration.* Harvard University Press, Cambridge, MA, pp. 137–77.

Mogrovejo, N. (2005) Immigration, Self-Exile, and Sexual Dissidence. In: Epps, B., Valens, K., & Johnson González, B. (Eds.), *Passing Lines: Sexuality and Immigration.* Harvard University Press, Cambridge, MA, pp. 411–24.

Murray, S. O. (1995) *Latin American Male Homosexualities.* University of New Mexico Press, Albuquerque.

Parker, R. (1999) *Beneath the Equator: Cultures of Desire, Male Homosexuality, and Emerging Gay Communities in Brazil.* Routledge, New York.

Peña, S. (2005) Visibility and Silence: Mariel and Cuban American Gay Male Experience and Representation. In: Luibhéid, E. & Cantú, L., Jr. (Eds.), *Queer Migrations: Sexuality, US Citizenship, and Border Crossings.* University of Minnesota Press, Minneapolis, pp. 125–45.

Perlongher, N. (1999) *El Negocio del Deseo: La prostitución masculina en San Pablo.* Editorial Paidós, Buenos Aires.

Pichardo Galán, J. I. (2003) Migraciones y Opción Sexual. In: Guasch, O. & Viñuales, O. (Eds.), *Sexualidades: Diversidad y Control Social.* Edicions Bellaterra, Barcelona, pp. 277–97.

Randazzo, T. (2005) Social and Legal Barriers: Sexual Orientation and Asylum in the United States. In: Luibhéid, E. & Cantú, L., Jr. (Eds.), *Queer Migrations: Sexuality, US Citizenship, and Border Crossings.* University of Minnesota Press, Minneapolis, pp. 30–60.

Rubin, G. (1993 [1984]) Thinking Sex: Notes for a Radical Theory of the Politics of Sexuality. In: Vance, C. (Ed.), *Pleasure and Danger: Exploring Female Sexuality.* Routledge, New York, pp. 267–319.

Urciuoli, B. (1996) *Exposing Prejudice: Puerto Rican Experiences of Language, Race, and Class.* Westview Press, Boulder, CO.
Vidal-Ortiz, S. (2004) On Being a White Person of Color: Using Autoethnography to Understand Puerto Ricans' Racialization. *Qualitative Sociology* 27(2): 179–203.

sexual cultures in Russia

Dan Healey

Russia's hybrid condition, combining European and Asian geography, cultures, and histories, makes it a complex national tradition to study, and sexuality in Russia reflects that complexity. At the same time, the country's often violent historical experience and its significant divergence from the familiar currents of European religious, cultural, and intellectual life have marked Russian approaches to sexuality.

The leading religion of the Great Russian ethnic majority is the Russian Orthodox faith, and this church's conception of sexuality was inherited from Byzantium during Christianization in the tenth century. Orthodoxy distinguished itself from western Christianity by an extremely ascetic view of human sexuality, denying the sanctity of sexual intercourse even between married partners, and hailing celibate marriage as the purest form of conjugal life. Proclaimed frequently, but seldom adhered to, the wholesale rejection of (or call to sublimation of) sexuality is an enduring feature of Russian intellectual life, characteristic of thinkers as diverse as Leo Tolstoy and Vladimir Lenin. If sexuality was to be suppressed for the benefit of the soul in the opinion of generations of Orthodox confessors and sermon-writers, by the nineteenth century radicals and socialists believed the energy diverted from sexuality could be channeled into political action.

Until Stalin's first Five-Year Plan (declared fulfilled in four years, 1928–32), about 80 percent of Russian society consisted of peasants. Peasant sexual culture had both Christian and pre-Christian elements, a reflection of the weak influence of Orthodoxy in a vast and poor country. Thus the Orthodox wedding ceremony and all its rituals formed a key stage in the lives of virtually all peasants, yet the courtship rituals that led up to it encouraged sexual intimacy with prospective partners and even with the wider peer group. Information about sex might be suppressed in formal public speech, especially religious discourse, but peasants shared jokes, songs, and limericks (*chastushki*) that gave the genitals ribald personalities and celebrated the comedy and pathos of human sexuality. Obscene, sex-themed speech in elaborate and linguistically productive formulations (a sublanguage of Russian known as *mat*) offered young men the opportunity to entertain peers and compete for attention while establishing their masculine credentials. Crude prints (*lubki*) and chap-books recording sexual images and stories were in circulation by the early nineteenth century, Russia's peasant version of the beginnings of a modern pornography.

Scholarly study of Russian sexuality began in the second half of the nineteenth century with medical, legal, and ethnographic works. Inquiry focused on peasant customs and legal concepts regarding marriage and the family, on the medicolegal understanding of sexual crime, and on the medical policing of legalized prostitution. Gynecologists defining sexual maturity conducted massive surveys of the onset of first menstruation in various ethnic groups. Doctors investigated and deplored the early marriage patterns of the "primitive" peoples of Imperial Russia's south and eastern periphery, an internal Orient.

Nihilists and socialists developed a stringent critique of Russian middle-class mores, supposedly derivative of Western European bourgeois capitalist values. An alternative tradition of "fictional marriage" (to liberate intelligentsia women from oppressive parents), of "free love" (unchained from property and religion), and a demanding cult of sublimation for the good of the coming revolution grew up. Jealousy in personal relations was seen as petty-bourgeois selfishness. These values were projected by gentry and middle-class intellectuals on to a romanticized "politically conscious" proletariat. Liberals absorbed much of this alternative tradition and added to it with a focus on the emancipation of women from legal and professional restraints, and campaigns to end regulated prostitution.

Most public discussion about sexuality, until the 1905 Revolution brought an end to censorship, took place in the form of literary fiction. Tolstoy's story of adultery and murder, "Kreutzer Sonata" (1891), set the pattern: a tale initially banned by the censor circulated in educated society and aroused passionate debate about the nature of sexuality inside and beyond marriage. After 1905 an explosion of discourse about sexualities erupted. Sexological terminology acquired extensive purchase on public consciousness, and not only in the urban, educated population, as cheap novels and newspapers proliferated and a commercial leisure culture used sensational sexual themes to sell publications. Soviet commentators later viewed the era from 1905 to 1917 as a "decadent" period when quickening capitalism animated a deplorably sexualized bourgeois public culture. It was a moment when new voices emerged: Mikhail A. Kuzmin's *Wings* (1906) celebrated a young man's acceptance of his homosexuality in an unapologetically optimistic key that was unique in European literature, and Lidiia Zinov'eva-Annibal's *Thirty-Three Monsters* (1907) explicitly portrayed lesbian love, albeit with less optimism and more French-inspired "decadent" gloom. Mikhail Artsybashev's bleak novel of ideas, *Sanin* (1907), depicted a generation disillusioned by the failed revolution and turning instead to predatory sexuality. Russia's emerging cinema explored sexual themes with enthusiasm, especially in the films of Evgenii Bauer. The year 1905 also accelerated the development of scholarly sexology in Russia, with surveys of student sexual behavior (especially that of Moscow medical expert M. A. Chlenov, published in 1909), psychiatric theorizing about the origins of perversion, and a deepening commitment to sexual "enlightenment" among educators in military and civilian life.

Between 1914 and 1921, war, revolution, and civil war brought death, famine, and violence that disrupted family ties, sent 2 million "bourgeois" Russians into emigration, and established the world's first anti-capitalist state, Soviet Russia (later united with republics on the old imperial periphery as the Union of Soviet Socialist Republics, 1922). Revolutionary Bolshevik (communist) legislation secularizing marriage and greatly relaxing divorce (1918, 1926), legalizing abortion on demand (1920), and decriminalizing sodomy (1922, 1926) seemed to fulfill the radical dream of love unchained from constraints of religion, property, and petty-bourgeois prejudice. A People's Commissariat (ministry) of Health was inaugurated, with Bolshevik physician Nikolai Semashko at its head. As the key state patron of medical research, he encouraged the development of a socialist sexology under the revealing rubric of "social hygiene." Sexological knowledge would serve the building of socialism by offering scientific solutions to humanity's most perplexing difficulties. Such nostrums were hailed internationally by reformers like Germany's Magnus Hirschfeld; communist parties in Europe and elsewhere paraded their sex radicalism as a component of the march to social revolution. Official prescriptions at home, however, favored a profoundly rationalist program of sublimation, deferral, and sexual enlightenment that owed much to the pre-revolutionary radical credo putting politics before the personal.

Nevertheless, during the mixed-economy era of the New Economic Policy (1921–8), Semashko was by no means the sole manager of sexual discourse. Private doctors published sex advice pamphlets, hot-headed Communist Party youth and women's leaders debated the meaning of sexual revolution avidly, psychiatrists and criminologists explored some of Soviet society's sexual underworlds, and literature and cinema continued to probe the "accursed questions" of sexual life in a revolutionary setting. The Bolsheviks' chief exponent of radical sexual revolution, Aleksandra Kollontai, published theoretical and literary portraits of the new sexual freedom and its positive and negative consequences. Non-party novelists succeeded in publishing gritty fiction about the sex problem that aroused consternation in the conservative ruling elite. "Free love" became a tag that acquired a negative, "petty-bourgeois" political value, often tied to oppositionist inclinations more generally. Leader of the Communist Party Vladimir Lenin branded the so-called "glass of water theory" (the notion that under socialism sexual desire would be slaked as easily and naturally as thirst) "antisocial" and "un-Marxist." Sexual atrocities later in the 1920s aroused revulsion at the persistent street-level attitude that women who refused sexual favors were indulging in "petty-bourgeois" prejudices; the rape of a young student by a gang of "conscious" workers and young communists in Leningrad in 1926 was Russia's first modern sex scandal. In the face of the negative consequences of sexual revolution, communists, the inheritors of Russia's nineteenth-century radical ethos, continued to preach restraint for the good of the cause and a scientific approach to all sexual activity, while calling for increasingly stern punishment for irresponsible sexual behavior.

The roots of a Stalinist approach to sexual questions thus predated Joseph Stalin's consolidation of power (1929) and the launch of the first Five-Year Plans. The 1930s saw the end of any remaining state sponsorship for sexual radicalism. Official attempts to articulate a sexual value system emphasizing stability of heterosexual family relations and parental responsibility for offspring gathered pace during the decade. Male–male sexual relations were recriminalized in 1934, apparently in response to secret police observation of male prostitution and fears that the "caste-like nature" of homosexual circles would facilitate espionage. The Party made conservative, patriarchal pronouncements about the psychology of married life, a topic previously evaded as unworthy of ideologists' attention. As war approached, the regime worried about the birthrate and banned abortion in 1936, while divorce was simultaneously made much less accessible. Birth control devices were removed from sale by a secret decree. Literature and cinema, now under the ideological control of "socialist realism," promoted fecundity and made a striking attempt to revive feminine makeup and hairstyles, fashion and allure, all previously marked as "degenerate" and "capitalist" but now revalued as appropriate for a prosperous socialist way of life. Science was starved of funds to investigate what ought to come naturally in a well-organized socialist society; thus sexological studies came to a virtual standstill, not to be revived until Stalin's death in 1953.

The Great Patriotic War (1941–5) resulted in the loss of 27 million Soviet lives, and an enduring gender imbalance, with 10 percent more women than men in the population well into the 1960s. After the war as soldiers returned from the front, sexually transmitted disease was a major concern. The abortion ban was proving difficult to enforce as restive doctors argued behind closed doors against having to denounce women who tried to terminate their own pregnancies. Measures to increase the birthrate included a "bachelor tax" on less prolific couples and unmarried persons of fertile age. Censorship made sexual topics even more taboo than they had been in the 1930s. Pent-up expectations for reform, the pressures of reconstruction and famine (1946–7), and worker migration in search of better working conditions regardless of the state penalties fueled a volatile social context. Stalin's successors legalized abortion on demand in 1955 and opened public debate on the "sexual question" (marriage, women's roles at home and at work, morality, sex education). Ruler Nikita Khrushchev's housing reforms gave the majority of urban households a flat with its own front door, an innovation that increased privacy and created intimate settings for the development of both officially approved domestic heterosexual monogamy and less orthodox arrangements.

Research on sexuality in the late Soviet era was characterized by a plumbing-and-mechanics functionality that evaded questions of psychology, tabooed pleasure as a goal in itself, and confined the study of sex to branches of gynecology, urology, and endocrinology. The discipline of "sexual pathology" (*seksopatologiia*) acquired independent status by promising medical fixes for technical problems (frigidity, infertility, impotence). As Igor Kon explains, there was no need for a Soviet sexology since mature socialism provided the material conditions in which nature was free to assert an unproblematic heterosexual normality; only the abnormal, the deviant, and the perverse needed scientific attention. Medical or sociological interest in "normal" sexuality was regarded in academic circles as prurient and unsound. Much of the Soviet-trained medical and academic establishment retains this view, and even today sex counselors in the Russian Federation call themselves "*seksopatologi*," i.e., sexual pathologists.

Despite this rather bleak picture, less orthodox approaches to sexuality appeared in the "era of stagnation" (1965–85) associated with the rule of Leonid Brezhnev. Freudian psychology made a limited revival after half a century of official suppression. Some jurists called for the decriminalization of sodomy, citing examples from the socialist satellite regimes. Neuroendocrinologist Aron Belkin, the father of the Soviet sex change operation, began working on transsexual patients in his Moscow clinic. He also began "correcting" the sex of intersex patients, who often journeyed from the far corners of the Soviet Union seeking help. His work was greatly influenced by developments not only in socialist countries but also in the US and other capitalist states. Attention to the diverse international sources of sexological knowledge was also evident in the sexual pathology textbooks of G. S. Vasilchenko (1977, 1983). During Mikhail Gorbachev's reforming tenure (1985–91) and the collapse of communist rule, even more liberal approaches to the study of sexuality emerged. The leader of this tendency was and remains Igor Kon, a member of the Russian Academy of Sciences, whose training was not as a "*seksopatolog*" but in philosophy and sociology. Kon's work has promoted ideas that remain very much at odds with the medical mainstream: Scandinavian-style sex education, an acceptance of teenage sexuality as normal and healthy (a view denied by vociferous Russian experts in a host of disciplines), a relaxed attitude toward same-sex relations, and a view of human sexuality predicated on the individual's rights rather than on the demands of the nation-state.

Beyond medicine, Russian sexuality studies have developed impressively in history, sociology, and other humanistic disciplines long suppressed or distorted by Marxist–Leninist ideology. The Boris Yeltsin Russian presidency (1991–9) saw the establishment of new liberal universities and the adaptation of some older ones to liberal humanist scholarly traditions. The opening of previously sequestered library and archival collections resulted in a wave of new publications of documents, reprints of pre-revolutionary monographs, and new studies of tabooed topics like pornography and swearing. Natalia Pushkareva's (1999) work on medieval Russian sexual culture, A. L. Toporkov's (1995, 1996) document collections of Russian erotic folklore and essay collection on pornography (with M. Levitt 1991) demonstrate how historians of sexuality are freer to explore the topic and to collaborate with foreign Russianists as well. There has been a mini-boom in gay and lesbian historical studies, of varying quality; the most influential single work is an anecdotal guide to the gay history of St. Petersburg by a curator under the pseudonym Konstantin K. Rotikov (1998). Prostitution under tsar and commissar has found its historians.

Sociological explorations of contemporary sexualities are well advanced, and apply methodologies previously impossible for Soviet academic researchers, such as interviews about intimate relations, and discourse analysis of sexual memoirs and of the mass media. A noteworthy trend has been the rapid translation of canonical feminist and queer texts into Russian and their reflection, adaptation, and rejection in the work of a generation of younger scholars. Two monographs on hazing culture and sexuality in the Russian army (2002, 2003) show that even this conservative national institution cannot resist scrutiny of its sexual secrets; in fact, these studies hint at a return to a pre-revolutionary tendency for the tsarist army to license the new sexological discourses of the late nineteenth century to resolve problems of cadet education. Recent collections of essays from the European University of St. Petersburg (2001, 2002) demonstrate the range of work typical of post-Soviet sociology with its exploration of the Soviet legacy of "official and unofficial norms" of sexual culture, of youth sexuality, of sexuality among disabled people, of women's alienation from their bodies and from pleasure, and of methodological dilemmas associated with the study of sexuality. The most ambitious critical work shows a healthy skepticism for models received from canonical western texts and a questioning of the ways in which they might be applied to Russia's specific historical and social experience. While politically a conservative nationalism remains on the ascendant and the sexual liberalization associated with Igor Kon and the Yeltsin years is in the shade, academic studies of sexuality are likely to prosper if only because a large cohort of energetic scholars now work in this field in Russia's universities.

SEE ALSO: Globalization, Sexuality and; Hirschfeld, Magnus; Intersexuality; Marx, Karl; Revolutions; Sexual Identities; Sexual Politics; Sexuality and the Law; Sexuality Research: History; Transgender, Transvestism, and Transsexualism

REFERENCES AND SUGGESTED READINGS

Bannikov, K. L. (2002) *Antropologiia ekstremal'nykh grupp: Dominantnye otnosheniia sredi voennosluzhashchikh srochnoi sluzhby Rossiiskoi Armii.* RAN Institute of Ethnology and Anthropology, Moscow.

Engelstein, L. (1992) *The Keys to Happiness: Sex and the Search for Modernity in Fin-de-Siècle Russia.* Cornell University Press, Ithaca, NY.

Healey, D. (2001) *Homosexual Desire in Revolutionary Russia: The Regulation of Sexual and Gender Dissent.* University of Chicago Press, Chicago.

Kashchenko, E. A. (2003) *Seksual'naia kul'tura voenno-sluzhashchikh.* Editorial URSS, Moscow.

Kharkhordin, O. (Ed.) (2001) *Mishel' Fuko i Rossiia: Sbornik statei.* European University of St. Petersburg, St. Petersburg.

Kon, I. S. (1988) *Vvedenie k seksologiiu.* Meditsina, Moscow.

Kon, I. S. (1995) *The Sexual Revolution in Russia.* Free Press, New York.

Lebina, N. B. & Shkarovskii, M. B. (1994) *Prostitutsiia v Peterburge.* Progress-Akademiia, Moscow.

Levin, E. (1989) *Sex and Society in the World of the Orthodox Slavs, 900–1700.* Cornell University Press, Ithaca, NY.

Levitt, M. & Toporkov, A. (Eds.) (1991) *Eros i pornografiia v russkoi kul'ture/Eros and Pornography in Russian Culture.* Ladomir, Moscow.

Naiman, E. (1997) *Sex in Public: The Incarnation of Early Soviet Ideology.* Princeton University Press, Princeton.

Pershai, A. (2002) Kolonizatsiia naoborot: gendernaia lingvistika v byvshem SSSR. *Gendernye issledovaniia* (7–8).

Pushkareva, N. L. (Ed.) (1999) *"A se grekhi zlye, smertnye...": Liubov', erotika i seksual'naia etika v doindustrial'noi Rossii (X-pervaia polovina XIX v.).* Ladomir, Moscow.

Rotikov, K. K. (1998) *Drugoi Peterburg.* Liga Plius, St. Petersburg.

Toporkov, A. L. (Ed.) (1995) *Russkii eroticheskii fol'klor.* Ladomir, Moscow.

Toporkov, A. L. (Ed.) (1996) *Seks i erotika v russkoi traditsionnoi kul'ture.* Ladomir, Moscow.

Vasilchenko, G. S. (1977) *Obshchaia seksopatologiia. Rukovodstvo dlia vrachei.* Meditsina, Moscow.

Vasilchenko, G. S. (1983) *Chastnaia seksopatologiia. Rukovodstvo dlia vrachei.* Meditsina, Moscow.

Zdravomyslova, E. & Temkina, A. (Eds.) (2002) *V poiskakh seksual'nosti.* Dmitrii Bulanin, St. Petersburg.

Zvereva, G. (2001) "Chuzhoe, svoe, drugoe...": feministskie i gendernye kontsepty v intellektual'noi kul'ture postsovetskoi Rossii. *Adam i Eva. Almanakh gendernoi teorii* 2: 238–78.

sexual cultures in Scandinavia

Jan Löfström

Scandinavia as a social and cultural entity comprises the Nordic countries – Denmark, Sweden, Norway, Iceland, and Finland – plus the autonomous territories of Greenland and the Faroe Islands, which belong to Denmark, and the Aland Islands, which are part of Finland. The social and cultural distinctions of the countries notwithstanding, it is often justified to consider them in aggregate. For example, in terms of prevailing values and ideals the Nordic societies are more secularized and less traditional than most other western societies, and values pertaining to "self-expression" (tolerance, post-materialist values, etc.) are also relatively speaking very prominent in Nordic societies (Inglehart & Baker 2000). This has a bearing on various issues of sexual life and sexual norms.

The Nordic countries have often been regarded as in the global vanguard in endorsing and promoting gender equality and progressive sexual politics. There are good grounds for this view, though it is clear also that in the Nordic countries a lot of work still remains to be done on these issues. They have also been seen as paradigmatic welfare states, where the public power (state, municipality) provides extensive public social security schemes plus education and health care services to the citizens on a universalist basis. The liberalist critique argues that the Nordic-style welfare state has intruded too much into citizens' private lives, but the counter-argument has been that the interventions of public power can be conducive to the sociopsychological well-being of individual citizens, including the delicate area of sexuality.

One of the outcomes of the Nordic welfare state ideology has been women's improved access to social and economic independence. This, naturally, also impinges on the form that sexual cultures have in these societies. From a global perspective the women in Scandinavia have been well-represented in politics, higher education, and full-time paid labor. The reasons for this are varied and include for example the cultural notions of gender that have accomodated the idea of female active subjectivity. These notions are a legacy of a rural cultural mode that survived in Finland and in Norway for example well into the twentieth century. Women's large-scale participation in paid labor entails a degree of economic independence from male breadwinners, be they husbands or kinsmen; thus it is likely to support also female sexual subjectivity. Moreover, welfare state policies such as provision of extensive child daycare and parental leave have also often aimed to help women be better able to combine motherhood and career. This applies to single mothers in particular, whose poverty rate has been low in global comparison, largely because of a supportive social policy which indicates an absence of social stigma for single mothers.

Like single motherhood, cohabitation, abortion, and divorce generally lack any social stigma in contemporary Nordic societies. Premarital sex is not an issue and a clear majority of people choose to live in a marriage-like arrangement before they marry – if they marry at all. Living as a single has become all the more common in the last 10–15 years, and also in these cases it is mostly taken for granted that the single (if not a senior citizen) has long-term or casual intimate relations. The divorce rate is fairly high, but divorce is often followed by a new marriage or cohabitation and it does not usually entail public opprobrium or other social costs. Some may deplore this as a "decline of the family," but in fact family-like formations clearly still have a strong appeal – it is only that they have become highly varied (e.g., registered partnerships). This can be seen as a vindication of the late-modern pure relationships that Anthony Giddens outlined in *The Transformations of Intimacy* (1992): the norm of unbreakable marital ties has faded, in Scandinavia perhaps more than elsewhere in the West. The safety nets provided by the welfare state have probably made it more feasible for individuals (women in particular) to discontinue unsatisfying relationships and to consider, for example, cohabiting or single parenting as real options in life. It is also worth emphasizing that – the reality of frequent divorces and "serial monogamy" notwithstanding – the ideal of lifelong relationships *has* endured in younger generations, and marital fidelity may now rank somewhat higher than a few decades ago as an ideal.

In the Nordic welfare state ideology there has often been at least an implicit equation between individual citizens' sexual health and national well-being. The memorandum that a state committee prepared on "questions of sexuality" in Sweden in 1936 put it very clearly: in modern society sexuality would serve not only as a spring of personal pleasure, but would also propel the progress of society generally. The memorandum embodies the kind of ideal of social engineering that Sweden has often been considered to exemplify, but which has also existed in the other Nordic welfare state regimes – the ideal of a society designed according to rationalist-scientific principles for the good of all citizens. The aspiration to benign social engineering has been visible, for example, in family planning and in sexual education.

One of the key texts in shaping the policy of family planning in Scandinavia (and also more widely) is the 1934 *Kris i befolkningsfrgan* (Crisis in the Population Issue) by the Swedish social scientists Alva and Gunnar Myrdal. In the long run this positive interest in issues of procreation and sexuality has generated arrangements like the provision of public marital advice services and sex education in schools. Indeed, institutionalized sex education has been one of the hallmarks of Nordic sexual politics, compulsory sex education being often part of the school curriculum. Here as well the aim has been to promote the social-sexual health of individuals and society in tandem, recognizing that children mature sexually at an earlier age than before. Against the argument that extensive sex education is an invitation to early sexual experimentation, the Nordic experience rather suggests that professional sex education, including information on contraception, is conducive to adolescent sexual health and well-being (e.g., there are comparatively low rates of teenage pregnancy and abortion). There are, however, distinctions between the Nordic countries that modify this picture and would need to be explained in more detail; for example, in Norway, the rate of teenage abortions has been much higher than elsewhere in Scandinavia.

Issues of contraception, sex education, and adolescent sexuality and abortion have thus been of little concern in Nordic societies in the last few decades. Likewise, both attitudes and legislation regarding the sexual content of films and other cultural products are very liberal. Pornography is easily available to (adult) consumers, the major exception being child pornography, which is banned by law. This overall sexual permissiveness notwithstanding, there has been discussion on the potential problems of pornography and prostitution from the perspective of gender equality, most notably in Sweden where there is in fact a law (since 1999) against sex purchase (i.e., buying sexual services). The rationale is that prostitution might be best curtailed by way of reducing demand for it. The efficacy of the law can not yet be assessed.

The status of sexual minorities, most notably homosexuals, is often considered to be one of the hallmarks of Nordic sexual liberalism. In fact, homosexual relations were decriminalized in some European states in the nineteenth century, whereas the first Nordic countries to take that step were Denmark–Iceland (1930) and Sweden (1944), whereas Finland (1971) and Norway (1972) followed much later. In the last 20–30 years, however, Nordic societies have been at the forefront of expanding institutional rights for gays and lesbians, for example in legislating against discrimination on sexual grounds and in introducing registered partnership laws ("gay marriages"). The laws on registered partnership conferred on lesbian and gay couples a legal status similar to that of married and cohabiting heterosexual couples, with the exception of not being allowed to adopt children. Parental rights remained a differential line between "first class" and "second class" citizens when heterosexual and non-heterosexual lifestyles in other respects were set on equal terms in civil law. However, this difference has partly disappeared in more recent legislation (e.g., in Sweden since 2003). The registered partnership laws seem to show that the "modern homosexual" has lost most symbolic power as the paradigmatic social misfit, yet it would be an overstatement to say that gays and lesbians – and transsexuals – are always treated on an equal basis in everyday encounters. One can argue that the early introduction of partnership laws in the Nordic countries was an offspring of the welfare state doctrine of social equality, rather than any "gay-friendly" sentiments as such. It is noteworthy that some gay and lesbian critics have regarded the partnership laws as a token gesture that opens up the empty institution of marriage to homosexuals and allows them to be as ordinary as straight people, whereas the heterosexual patterns of lifestyle and intimate relations have become similar to what used to be the modern homosexual form of existence, as sociologist Henning Bech has called it.

The Nordic countries have been ethnically, linguistically, and religiously homogeneous societies until recently; it was in the 1960s that Denmark and Sweden began to receive greater numbers of non-European immigrants, and in Norway and Finland similar developments have taken place even more recently. The ensuing cultural diversity has also entailed an increasing variety of sexual cultures in society, and on some occasions the cultural distinctions have resulted in frictions. The pattern of gender relations and male and female social roles in Scandinavian societies may often look bewildering not only to non-çbut also to western observers, and the norms and practices of family arrangements and sex relations in the migrant groups sometimes stand in stark contrast to those prevailing in Nordic cultures. Such differences are present in any multicultural society of course, but what is perhaps characteristic of Nordic societies is that historically there is a powerful thrust toward cultural assimilation that does not easily allow much space to subcultural communities and cultural enclaves. Whether we speak of migrants or lesbians and gays, it is also a demographic fact that Scandinavian societies are small in population. Consequently, any "subgroups" within society are also small; hence, the preconditions for discrete sexual (sub)cultures are limited from the outset.

SEE ALSO: Globalization, Sexuality and; Same-Sex Marriage/Civil Unions; Sexual Citizenship; Sexual Identities; Sexual Politics; Sexual Practices

REFERENCES AND SUGGESTED READINGS

Bech, H. (1997) *When Men Meet: Homosexuality and Modernity*. Polity Press, Cambridge.

Francoeur, R. & Noonan, R. (Eds.) (2004) *Complete International Encyclopedia of Sexuality.* Continuum, New York.
Haavio-Mannila, E. & Kontula, O. (2003) *Sexual Trends in the Baltic Sea Area.* Population Research Institute, Helsinki.
Haavio-Mannila, E., Kontula, O., & Rotkirch, A. (2002) *Sexual Lifestyles in the Twentieth Century: A Research Study.* Palgrave, Houndmills.
Inglehart, R. & Baker, W. (2000) Modernization, Cultural Change, and the Persistence of Traditional Values. *American Sociological Review* 65 (February): 19–51.
Löfström, J. (Ed.) (1998) *Scandinavian Homosexualities: Essays on Gay and Lesbian Studies.* Harrington Park Press, Binghamton.
Mnsson, S.-A. (1993) *Cultural Conflict and the Swedish Sexual Myth: The Male Immigrants' Encounter with Swedish Sexual and Cohabitation Culture.* Greenwood Publishers, Westport.

sexual deviance

Richard Tewksbury

Sexual deviance, and what is defined as sexually deviant, is culturally and historically specific. This concept refers to behaviors that involve individuals seeking erotic gratification through means that are considered odd, different, or unacceptable to either most or influential persons in one's community. As with most forms of deviance, sexual deviance is something that is defined differently by persons of different backgrounds, beliefs, morals, and locations. However, sexual deviance is also an idea about which most persons hold very strong views, and react in stigmatizing and ostracizing ways.

Sexual deviance is a term that refers to behavior that has a sexual aspect to it and is considered a violation of either general societal norms or the expectations and/or limits of behavior for specific cultural settings. Defining some sexually oriented behavior as deviant means that the action meets at least one (or a combination) of four criteria: (1) degree of consent, (2) the nature of the persons/objects involved in the action, (3) the actual action and body parts involved, or (4) the setting in which the behavior is performed. Generally speaking, sexual behavior that is not fully consensual by all persons involved is considered deviant. Rape and exhibitionism (where the persons to whom sexual images are presented are unwilling recipients) are obvious examples of sexual deviance defined by degree of consent. Sexual behavior with children, animals, or "odd" objects (vegetables, firearms, kitchen appliances, etc.) would be considered deviant by most people because such persons and objects are not generally considered sexual. When we speak of sexual deviance based on the action or body parts involved as the defining elements we could think of individuals who receive sexual gratification from violence, setting fires, wearing opposite-gender clothing, or even for some people, masturbation. This category would also include sexual acts that include body parts not typically considered sexual, such as individuals' feet, ears, or noses. Finally, some settings, such as a courtroom, church, or an open field in a public park would be thought of by most people as inappropriate for sexual activities. Therefore, sexual acts performed in these locations (regardless of how "normal" the acts may be) would be considered deviant, simply because of where they were performed.

It is important to keep in mind that sexual deviance, as with all types of deviance, is not usually something that is inherently "wrong." Instead, sexual deviance is so determined by one of two approaches, both based on social conditions. The easier to see of these two approaches is the idea of statistical definitions. This means that sexual behaviors in which only a minority of persons engages would be considered deviant. In this view, behaviors in which a majority of persons participate would be normative, and those actions that only a "few" people do would be "different" (i.e., deviant). A more purely sociological approach to defining sexual deviance is to focus on the ways that society members react and respond to particular acts. In this approach, when others learn of an individual's sexual activities with farm animals and react by showing their distaste for the act and stigmatization of the persons involved, we know that sex with farm animals is considered deviant.

Sexual deviance includes behaviors that are deemed to be violations of all degrees of social norms. Some sexually deviant behavior is a violation of only regular social expectations/norms. This would include premarital sex, sexual activities performed on one's desk at work, or perhaps the exchange of money for sexual acts. Other forms of sexual deviance would be considered violations of social mores; a more is a strong social norm that is usually considered to carry with it a moral aspect. Examples of sexual deviance that violate morally infused, strong social norms would be sexual activities between a supervisor and an employee when the employee is told their job may depend on their "consent," homosexual activities, and the exchange of sexual behavior for illegal drugs. Taboos are our strongest form of social norms and indicate activities that are so extreme that people may have a hard time even imagining that such actions ever occur. Sexual deviance that is a violation of social taboos might include sex with children, sex in a church, or sexually sadistic acts where individuals are forced to endure humiliation, extreme pain, or serious injury/death.

What this clearly points to is the fact that it can be difficult at times to define what is and is not sexual deviance. Individuals have different moral standards based on different cultures and subcultures that may vary in their views of acceptable and unacceptable sexual behaviors, and whether one has/does participate in certain activities will also influence their views and definitions. From the examples given above, it is easy to see that while we may refer to the exchange of sexual acts for money or drugs as deviant, clearly a significant number of persons do such actions. And many such persons do not necessarily see their actions as "deviant." Others with strong moral and religious beliefs might say sexual activities between same-sex persons are wrong (and therefore deviant). However, many other persons (both those who do and do not engage in same-sex sexual activities) do not hold moral or religious objections to such actions. Similarly, some people may believe that it is wrong to engage in sexual acts with persons to whom they are not legally married, while others may in fact believe that it is acceptable, important, or even imperative to become sexually experienced and skilled prior to marrying. This example can be clearly seen in the beliefs and practices of many tribal societies where individuals are expected to enter into marriage with a high level of sexual skill/experience. Other cultures, obviously, do not condone such approaches.

And, finally, it is also important to recognize that definitions (and responses to) sexual deviance may change and vary over time. Consider, for example, the widespread changes in definitions of sexual deviance in the last fifty years. In the mid-twentieth century issues such as premarital sex, homosexuality, oral-genital contact, and even masturbation were considered extremely deviant, and rarely spoken of. Today, television shows, popular magazines, the Internet, and many persons' everyday conversations are filled with graphic, humorous, and clearly endorsing references to such previously "deviant" forms of sexual behavior. Or some acts that at one point in time may have been considered normative and expected may evolve to being seen as deviant. A good example here is the idea of marital rape. For most of known history, at least in western societies, wives were not viewed as having the right or ability to say no to sexual advances/requests from their husbands. A man who desired to have sex with his wife could, and often did, force her to do sexual acts. However, as an outgrowth of the feminist movement in the mid-to-late twentieth century, such actions have come to be viewed as wrong, and in many jurisdictions even illegal. Historical shifts occur in both directions, moving some acts out of the category of deviance and shifting others toward a designation as deviant.

Research documenting and explaining sexual deviance is something that is not overly abundant. Most of the research related to sexual deviance has come from the psychological or psychiatric perspectives. This body of research takes for granted that the behaviors and actors being studied are deviant, and seeks to identify both a cause/motivator for the behavior, and ways to intervene and either control or eliminate the behavior. In part, this can be explained by the fact that psychologists and psychiatrists tend to conduct their research with individuals who are either in therapy/treatment seeking to change their behaviors or who have been compelled to participate in therapy/treatment (often as a result of legal processing). Sociological research on sexual deviance is available, but is not as numerous or readily available as that coming from psychologists and psychiatrists. Sociologists, with a focus on understanding the experiences, supporting social structures, and both contributing factors and experienced consequences of sexual deviance, tend to conduct their research with participants in sexual deviance in the free world, often in the environments where the sexual deviance is performed. Sociologists are less inclined than many psychologists and psychiatrists to study sexual deviance because the qualitative nature of such work takes the researcher to places they may not wish to frequent. As a result, many sociologists – even those who specialize in the study of deviant behavior – choose not to do research on sexual deviance.

Speaking in a sociological sense, we can think of sexual deviance as constituting three main varieties of deviance: normal, sociological, and pathological. These designations, like those discussed above, are also fluid and can introduce controversy over where a particular type of behavior may best fit. However, as analytic tools, thinking of sexual deviance as normal, sociological, or pathological can help to better understand if/how, when, where, by whom, and even why certain aspects of sexual behavior are defined as deviant and others are not.

Normal sexual deviance is sexual behavior that is relatively common, although not something that is widely discussed, acknowledged, or admitted. In fact, according to statistical ways of defining deviance, many acts that would be considered normal sexual deviance would not be deviant – a majority of society members may in fact engage in some normal sexual deviance behaviors. Some types of normal sexual deviance may be viewed as positive by many/some people – such as abstinence – yet also be widely considered deviant. These tend to be behaviors that are individually based and do not have any type of supportive social structure or organization associated with them. This is a key factor distinguishing normal sexual deviance from that which is sociologically defined.

Sociological sexual deviance includes behaviors that violate some type of social norms, but is associated with some variety of social group, structure, or organization that endorses, practices, encourages (at least for members), and therefore sustains activities. Pornography, prostitution, and swinging are examples of sociological sexual deviance. Each has recognizable groups and organizations (or corporations) that promote and keep the activity going. Sustaining the activity may mean active recruitment/marketing for new participants and social support for encouraging individuals already involved to remain involved.

Pathological forms of sexual deviance are those that come to mind most quickly and easily, and that would be likely to most easily produce widespread agreement about the deviance of the acts. Pathological sexual deviance is illegal in nature (usually) and is associated with imposing harm on others. The participants of this type of deviance are seen as psychologically challenged. Examples of pathological forms of sexual deviance include sexual violence, pedophilia, and incest.

Clearly, definitions of sexual deviance vary, and may include a wide range of behaviors. Sexual behavior is largely unknown, but when it is known and deemed deviant many forms of sexual deviance are likely to cause an individual to retreat into hiding. However, when "outed," these individuals are likely to be stigmatized. Obviously, as a social construct, definitions of sexual deviance are powerful and important forces in the structure and process of social settings and groups.

SEE ALSO: Deviance; Pedophilia; Sadomasochism; Sexual Practices; Sexual Violence and Rape; Stigma

REFERENCES AND SUGGESTED READINGS

De Yong, M. (1989) The World According to NAMBLA: Accounting for Deviance. *Journal of Sociology and Social Welfare* 16, (1): 111–26.

Gagnon, J. & Simon, W. (1967) *Sexual Deviance.* Harper & Row, New York.

Hensley, C. & Tewksbury, R. (2003) *Sexual Deviance.* Lynne Rienner Publishers, Boulder.

Humphreys, L. (1970) *Tearoom Trade.* Aldine, Chicago.

Weinberg, T. S. (1995) *S&M: Studies in Dominance and Submission.* Prometheus Books, Amherst, NY.